AF449196
"TREASURE OF SIERRA MADRE"
starring HUMPHREY BOGART and WALTER HUSTON
TIM HOLT · BRUCE BENNETT · Directed by JOHN HUSTON
Produced by HENRY BLANKE
KEY VIDEO

THE VIDEO TAPE & DISC GUIDE TO HOME ENTERTAINMENT™
Fifth Edition
is an original publication of
The National Video Clearinghouse, Inc.
100 Lafayette Drive
Syosset, NY 11791

Printed in the United States of America
ISBN: 0-935478-25-6
Library of Congress: 83-62240

Cover design Donna Weber
Illustration Steve Gordon

Equipment courtesy of Newmark & Lewis

THE VIDEO TAPE AND DISC GUIDE TO

HOME ENTERTAINMENT

5TH EDITION

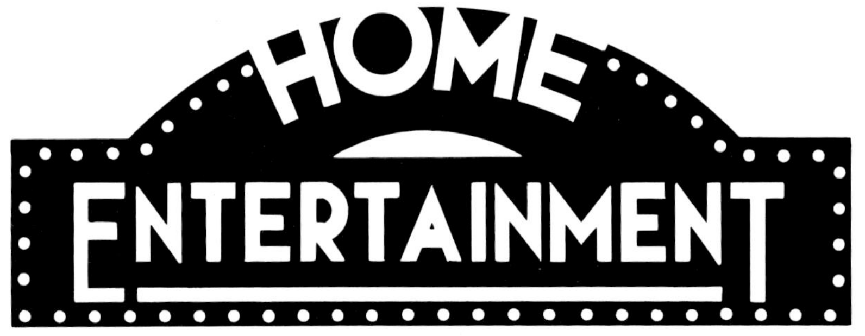

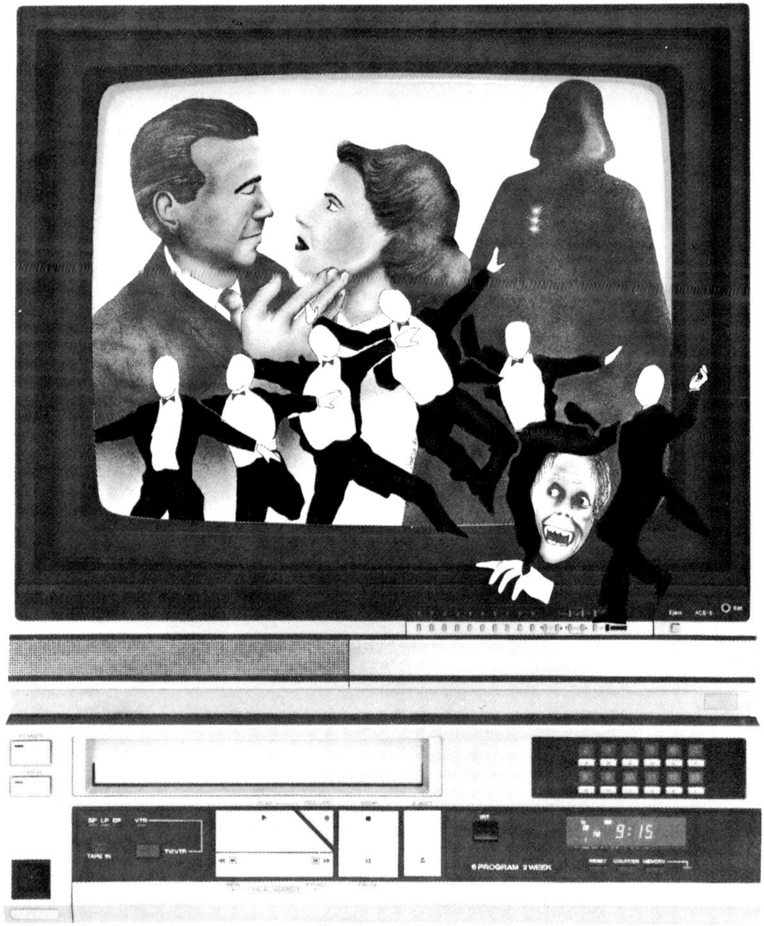

Acknowledgments

This guide is an original work compiled by the staff of The National Video Clearinghouse, Inc. Acknowledged for their hard work and dedication to this project are Geroge Hatch, Chairman of the Board; Harvey Seslowsky, President; Robert M. Reed, Vice President; Susan Brady Svitlik, Editor; Patricia A. Quilliam, Director of Information and Data Services; Arnold Menis, Director of Marketing; Maxine Crystal, Director of Advertising Sales; and their respective staffs: David J. Weiner, Manager of Data Services; Mary S. Bean, Editorial Coordinator; Lisa A. Jones, Vickie Pinksy, Jeffrey M. Kerwin, and Christine LaMarca, Editorial Assistants; Steve Gordon and Donna Weber, Art; Barbara Levine, Assistant Sales Manager; Loretta Duncan, Advertising Coordinator; Denise Mattiace, Marketing Support; Meg Plastino, Editorial Secretary.

Caught In The Act **Styx** Live

MR. ROBOTO, ROCKIN' THE PARADISE, BLUE COLLAR MAN (*Long Nights*),
SNOWBLIND, TOO MUCH TIME ON MY HANDS, DON'T LET IT END,
HEAVY METAL POISONING, COLD WAR, BEST OF TIMES, COME SAIL AWAY,
RENEGADE, HAVEN'T WE BEEN HERE BEFORE?,
DON'T LET IT END (*Reprise*).

© 1984 A&M Records, Inc. All Rights Reserved.

Distributed by RCA/COLUMBIA PICTURES HOME VIDEO
2901 West Alameda Avenue   Burbank, California 91505

RCA
Columbia Pictures
HOME VIDEO

Beta
hi-fi
STEREO
MONO-COMPATIBLE

VHS
STEREO
DOLBY SYSTEM
MONO COMPATIBLE

Angel and the Badman 0107

Dakota 0830

Dark Command 0881

The Fighting Kentuckian 1306

Flame of Barbary Coast 1325

Flying Tigers 1345

In Old California 1977

Lady for a Night 2233

Lady from Louisiana 2248

Rio Grande 3457

Three Faces West 4189

Wheel of Fortune 4501

Classic Films! Classic Entertainment!

We are pleased to present our videocassette library of classic motion pictures. Our extensive list of titles includes something for everyone—classic features, holiday films, cult classics, children's films and theatrical cartoons.
We hope you will make NTA Home Entertainment your source for time-honored film favorites.

DRAMA

ARCH OF TRIUMPH 0144
Ingrid Bergman   Charles Boyer 1948 B/W

BATTLE OF NERETVA 0219
Yul Brynner   Curt Jurgens 1970 COLOR

BODY AND SOUL 0354
John Garfield   Lili Palmer 1947 B/W

CHAMPION 0617
Kirk Douglas   Arthur Kennedy 1949 B/W
Academy Award Winner / Best Film Editing

A DOUBLE LIFE 1092
Ronald Colman 1948 B/W

HIGH NOON 1800
Gary Cooper   Grace Kelly 1952 B/W

INDISCREET 1967
Cary Grant   Ingrid Bergman 1958 COLOR

JOHNNY GUITAR 2126
Joan Crawford   Sterling Hayden 1953 COLOR

LA DOLCE VITA 2212
Marcello Mastroianni   Anita Ekberg 1961 B/W
(Two-cassette package)

LONG DAY'S JOURNEY INTO NIGHT 2433
Katherine Hepburn   Jason Robards 1962 B/W
(Two-cassette package)

MACBETH 2514
Orson Wells   Jeanette Nolan 1948 B/W

THE MEN 2710
Marlon Brando   Teresa Wright 1950 B/W

PARANOIA 3143
Carroll Baker   Lou Castel 1969 COLOR

THE PAWNBROKER 3162
Rod Steiger   Brock Peters 1965 B/W

THE RED PONY 3406
Myrna Loy   Robert Mitchum 1949 COLOR

SHARK! 3981
Burt Reynolds   Barry Sullivan 1968 COLOR

SUBTERFUGE 3636
Joan Collins   Gene Barry 1968 COLOR

MUSICALS

COPACABANA 0742
Groucho Marx   Carmen Miranda 1947 B/W

THE FABULOUS DORSEYS 1236
Tommy and Jimmy Dorsey 1947 B/W

YOUNG AT HEART 4706
Doris Day   Frank Sinatra 1954 COLOR

SCI-FI/HORROR

DORIAN GRAY 1091
Helmut Berger   Herbert Lom 1971 COLOR

INVASION OF THE BODY SNATCHERS
2018 Kevin McCarthy   Dana Winter 1956 B/W

THAT COLD DAY IN THE PARK 4102
Sandy Dennis   Michael Burns 1969 COLOR

FAVORITES

THE BELLS OF ST. MARY'S 0252
Bing Crosby   Ingrid Bergman 1945 B/W
Academy Award / Best Sound Recording

A CURRIER & IVES CHRISTMAS 0771
A unique "Video Christmas Album" COLOR

CYRANO DE BERGERAC 0822
Jose Ferrer 1950 B/W
Academy Award / Best Actor

GOOD SAM 1578
Gary Cooper   Ann Sheridan 1948 B/W

HIGH SCHOOL CONFIDENTIAL 1808
Russ Tamblyn   Mamie Van Doren 1958 B/W

IT'S A WONDERFUL LIFE 2060
James Stewart   Donna Reed 1947 B/W
Winner of 4 Academy Awards

MAGIC TOWN 2556
James Stewart   Jane Wyman 1947 B/W

MIRACLE OF THE BELLS 2766
Fred MacMurray   Frank Sinatra 1948 B/W

ONE TOUCH OF VENUS 3060
Ava Gardner   Robert Walker 1950 B/W

PENNY SERENADE 3173
Cary Grant   Irene Dunn 1941 B/W

THE QUIET MAN 3363
John Wayne   Maureen O'Hara 1952 COLOR

COMEDY

FATHER GOOSE 1285
Cary Grant   Leslie Caron 1964 COLOR

THE FLYING DEUCES 1349
Laurel and Hardy 1939 B/W

THE GRASS IS GREENER 1586
Cary Grant   Doris Day 1962 COLOR

LOVE HAPPY 2467
The Marx Bros.   Raymond Burr 1950 B/W

THE MAGIC CHRISTIAN 2548
Peter Sellers   Ringo Starr 1970 COLOR

OPERATION PETTICOAT 3082
Cary Grant   Tony Curtis 1959 COLOR

THAT TOUCH OF MINK 4115
Cary Grant   Deborah Kerr 1961 COLOR

VIVA MAX 4421
Peter Ustinov   Jonathan Winters 1969 COLOR

JOHN WAYNE CLASSICS

ANGEL AND THE BADMAN 0107
John Wayne   Gail Russell 1947 B/W

DAKOTA 0830
John Wayne   Walter Brennan 1945 B/W

DARK COMMAND 0881
John Wayne   Claire Trevor 1940 B/W

THE FIGHTING KENTUCKIAN 1306
John Wayne   Vera Ralston 1949 B/W

THE FIGHTING SEABEES 1307
John Wayne   Susan Hayward 1947 B/W

FLAME OF BARBARY COAST 1325
John Wayne   Ann Dvorak 1945 B/W

FLYING TIGERS 1345
John Wayne   John Carroll 1942 B/W

IN OLD CALIFORNIA 1977
John Wayne   Binnie Barnes 1942 B/W

LADY FOR A NIGHT 2233
John Wayne   Joan Blondell 1942 B/W

LADY FROM LOUISIANA 2248
John Wayne   Ona Munson 1942 B/W

THE QUIET MAN 3363
John Wayne   Maureen O'Hara 1952 COLOR

RIO GRANDE 3457
John Wayne   Maureen O'Hara 1950 B/W

SANDS OF IWO JIMA 3556
John Wayne   Forrest Tucker 1949 B/W

THREE FACES WEST 4189
John Wayne   Gail Russell 1940 B/W

WAKE OF THE RED WITCH 4429
John Wayne   Francis Dee 1948 B/W

WHEEL OF FORTUNE 4501
John Wayne   Francis Dee 1942 B/W

WAR OF THE WILDCATS 4447
John Wayne   Martha Scott 1943 B/W

CARTOONS

THE BEST OF BETTY BOOP VOL. 1 7045
12 Cartoons in full color

THE BEST OF BETTY BOOP VOL. 2 7046
More Max Fleischer color favorites

THE BEST OF LITTLE LULU 7052
A special full-color cartoon collection

BETTY BOOP CLASSICS 7060
A 1-hour classic program in color

CARTOON CARNIVAL VOL. 1 7090
Featuring Little Lulu COLOR

CARTOON CARNIVAL VOL. 2 7091
Featuring Casper COLOR

GULLIVER'S TRAVELS 1650
Max Fleischer's classic 1939 COLOR

HOPPITY GOES TO TOWN 1866
Full-length feature 1941 COLOR

SING ALONG WITH LITTLE LULU 7735
Full color "sing-along" program

HOME ENTERTAINMENT

12636 Beatrice Street   P.O. Box 66930   Los Angeles, CA 90066-0930   (213) 306-4040

Table of Contents

Preface	**X**
Closed Captioned Index	**XII**
Use Guide	**XVI**
Key	**XXI**
New Releases	**XXII**
Videodisc Index	**XXV**
Program Listings	**1**
Subject Category Index	**637**
Cast Index	**711**
Program Sources Index	**751**
Photo Credits	**760**

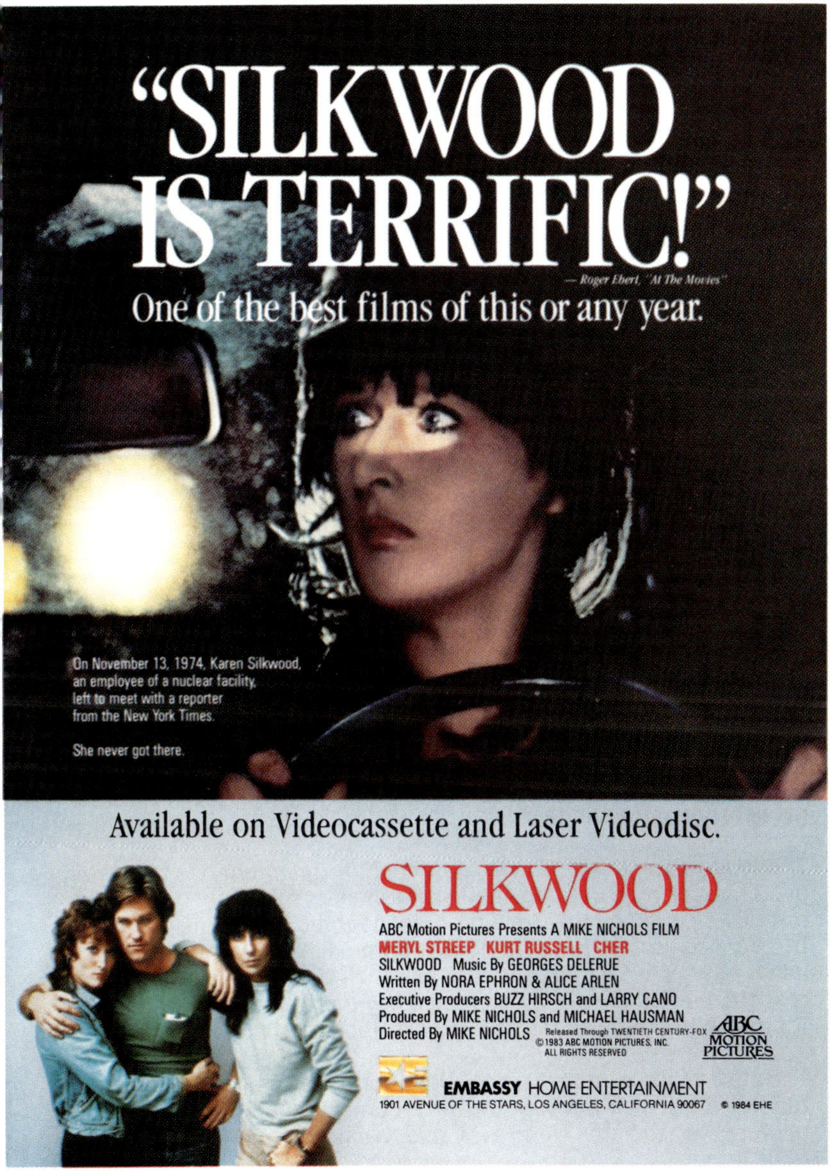
"SILKWOOD IS TERRIFIC!"
— Roger Ebert, "At The Movies"
One of the best films of this or any year.
On November 13, 1974, Karen Silkwood, an employee of a nuclear facility, left to meet with a reporter from the New York Times.
She never got there.
Available on Videocassette and Laser Videodisc.
SILKWOOD
ABC Motion Pictures Presents A MIKE NICHOLS FILM
MERYL STREEP KURT RUSSELL CHER
SILKWOOD Music By GEORGES DELERUE
Written By NORA EPHRON & ALICE ARLEN
Executive Producers BUZZ HIRSCH and LARRY CANO
Produced By MIKE NICHOLS and MICHAEL HAUSMAN
Directed By MIKE NICHOLS
Released Through TWENTIETH CENTURY-FOX
©1983 ABC MOTION PICTURES, INC.
ALL RIGHTS RESERVED
ABC MOTION PICTURES
EMBASSY HOME ENTERTAINMENT
1901 AVENUE OF THE STARS, LOS ANGELES, CALIFORNIA 90067
© 1984 EHE

Preface

The Video Tape & Disc Guide to Home Entertainment, Fifth Edition is designed to provide home viewers with information on more than 7,000 video programs available to them. Most people know that they can obtain recent blockbuster movies, film classics, concerts and music videos, but home video is much more. There are programs on sports, health and physical fitness; instructional programs on everything from learning a foreign language to how to train your dog; and even historical documentaries and current events programs. Most of these will be available from your local video retailer (if he doesn't have them in stock, he may be able to special order them). Some of the programs included in this *Guide* may be available directly from the source(s) listed through mail order.

Special features included in this edition are the Closed Captioned Index, Cast Index, and Videodisc Index. The Closed Captioned Index is a complete listing of all videocassettes and discs which are closed captioned for the hearing impaired. The Cast Index is designed to help you locate the video performances of more than 275 of your favorite stars and directors. The Videodisc Index is a guide to programs available on both the laser optical (LV) and capacitance electronic disc (CED) formats. A special addition to the guide consists of 24 pages of photographs from more than 50 classic and contemporary movies, concerts and television shows on video.

The Video Tape & Disc Guide to Home Entertainment has been compiled from printed catalogs and supplementary lists and from information supplied by the video program sources. No wholesaler or distributor has paid to have its video programs listed, nor does the publisher pay them for information about their titles. The publisher is not responsible for any program changes, withdrawals, or additions, or for the listing of any unauthorized distribution of any title.

The staff of the National Video Clearinghouse has sought to provide the home video viewer with the most comprehensive, up-to-date, useful guide to home video available. We hope you feel that we have done so.

Closed Captioned Index

Following is an alphabetical list of home video programs currently available with closed captions. Distributors of the programs and the formats in which closed captioning is available are listed next to the title. Captioning of all programs is provided by The National Captioning Institute, Falls Church, Virginia.

All the Right Moves (CBS/Fox Video: B, V, LV, CED)
Beany & Cecil Volume 4 (RCA/Columbia Pictures Home Video: B, V)
Beauty and the Beast (CBS/Fox Video: B, V, LV, CED)
The Best of 60 Minutes (CBS/Fox Video: B, V)
The Big Chill (RCA/Columbia Pictures Home Video: B, V, CED)
The Boy Who Left Home to Find Out About the Shivers (CBS/Fox Video: B, V, LV, CED)
Brian's Song (RCA/Columbia Pictures Home Video: B, V, CED)
The Buddy System (Key Video: B, V)
The Care Bears Battle the Freeze Machine (Family Home Entertainment: B, V)
CBS/Fox Guide to Complete Dog Care (CBS/Fox Video: B, V, CED)
Champions (Embassy Home Entertainment: B, V)
Chapter Two (RCA/Columbia Pictures Home Video: B, V)
The China Syndrome (RCA/Columbia Pictures Home Video: B, V)
Close Encounters of the Third Kind: The Special Edition (RCA/Columbia Pictures Home Video: B, V)
D.C. Cab (MCA Home Video: B, V)
The Dead Zone (Paramount Home Video: B, V, LV, CED)
Dot and the Bunny (CBS/Fox Video: B, V, CED)
The Dresser (RCA/Columbia Pictures Home Video: B, V, CED)
Easy Money (Vestron Video: B, V)
Educating Rita (RCA/Columbia Pictures Home Video: B, V, LV, CED)
The Eyes of Laura Mars (RCA/Columbia Pictures Home Video: B, V, LV)
Faerie Tale Theatre (CBS/Fox Video: B, V, LV, CED)
Fail Safe (RCA/Columbia Pictures Home Video: B, V)
The Fantastic Adventures of Unico (RCA/Columbia Pictures Home Video: B, V)
Flashdance (Paramount Home Video: B, V, LV, CED)
The Golden Voyages of Sinbad (RCA/Columbia Pictures Home Video: B, V)
Goldilocks (CBS/Fox Video: B, V, LV, CED)
The Greatest Story Ever Told (CBS/Fox Video: B, V)

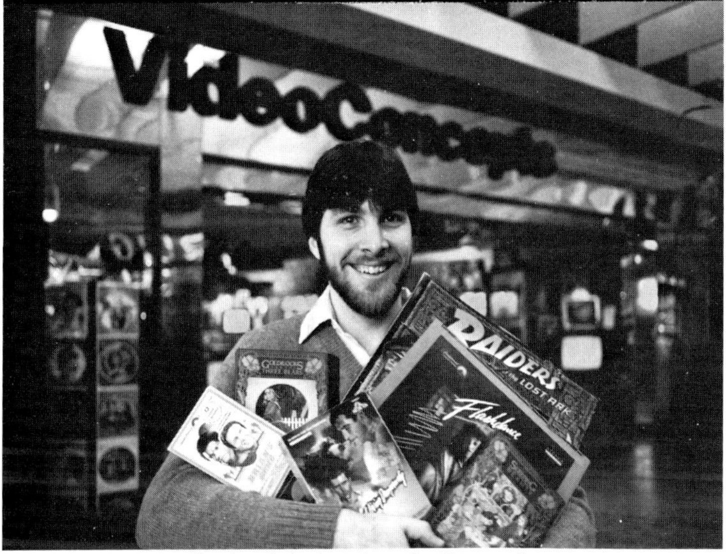

Closed Captioning, There's No Better Sound In Sight!

Closed captioning has put sound on the screen for *D.C. Cab, Easy Money, The Empire Strikes Back, Flashdance, Jane Fonda's Workout Challenge, Sudden Impact* and other home video movies.

These titles are only a few of the many closed-captioned movies that are a part of your home video inventory.

Look for NCI's registered service mark, ®, to identify cassettes and discs closed captioned by the National Captioning Institute.

®

This registered service mark identifies cassettes and discs closed-captioned by NCI. Captions are only visible with a decoder.

National Captioning Institute
5203 Leesburg Pike • Falls Church, VA 22041
(703) 998-2400

For more information on closed-captioned video-cassettes/discs and the decoder necessary to see captions, contact Jane Edmondson at the National Captioning Institute.

NCI Closed Captioning . . . There's no better sound in sight.

Green Ice (Key Video: B, V)
Hanky Panky (RCA/Columbia Pictures Home Video: B, V, CED)
Hansel and Gretel (CBS/Fox Video : B, V, LV, CED)
Hard to Hold (MCA Home Video: B, V, LV)
He-Man and the Masters of the Universe, Volume 7 (RCA/Columbia
  Pictures Home Video: B, V)
Heart Like a Wheel (CBS/Fox Video: B, V)
Hercules (MGM/UA Home Video: B, V, LV)
The Horse Soldiers (CBS/Fox Video: B, V)
Jack and the Beanstalk (CBS/Fox Video: B, V, LV, CED)
Jane Fonda's Workout Challenge (Karl Home Video: B, V)
The Last Waltz (CBS/Fox Video: B, V)
Little Big Man (Key Video: B, V)
Little Red Riding Hood (CBS/Fox Video: B, V, LV, CED)
A Man for All Seasons (RCA/Columbia Pictures Home Video: B, V)
The Man Who Would Be King (CBS/Fox Video: B, V)
Mr. Mom (Vestron Video: B, V)
Mysterious Island (RCA/Columbia Pictures Home Video: B, V)
A Night in Heaven (Key Video: B, V)
The Nightingale (CBS/Fox Video: B, V, LV, CED)
On the Waterfront (RCA/Columbia Pictures Home Video: B, V)
Pink Floyd's David Gilmour (CBS/Fox Video: B, V)
Pinocchio (CBS/Fox Video: B, V, LV, CED)
The Princess and the Pea (CBS/Fox Video: B, V, LV, CED)
Raiders of the Lost Ark (Paramount Home Video: B, V, LV, CED)
Rapunzel (CBS/Fox Video: B, V, LV, CED)
The Right Stuff (Warner Home Video: B, V)
Romancing the Stone (CBS/Fox Video: B, V, CED)
Romantic Comedy (CBS/Fox Video: B, V)
Rumpelstiltskin (CBS/Fox Video: B, V, LV, CED)
Sacred Ground (CBS/Fox Video: B, V)
Sleeping Beauty (CBS/Fox Video: B, V, LV, CED)
Sounder (Paramount Home Video: B, V, LV, CED)
Staying Alive (Paramount Home Video: B, V, LV, CED)
Stripes (RCA/Columbia Pictures Home Video: B, V)
Sudden Impact (Warner Home Video: B, V)
The Tale of the Frog Prince (CBS/Fox Video: B, V, LV, CED)
Tank (MCA Home Video: B, V, LV, CED)
Terms of Endearment (Paramount Home Video: B, V, LV, CED)
Testament (Paramount Home Video: B, V, LV, CED)
The Three Stooges Volume V (RCA/Columbia Pictures Home
  Video: B, V)
The Three Stooges Volume IX (RCA/Columbia Pictures Home
  Video: B, V)
Thumbelina (CBS/Fox Video: B, V, LV, CED)
Thumbelina (RCA/Columbia Pictures Home Video: B, V)
Trading Places (Paramount Home Video: B, V, LV, CED)
Two of a Kind (CBS/Fox Video: B, V, LV, CED)

Uncommon Valor (Paramount Home Video: B, V, LV, CED)
Unfaithfully Yours (1984) (CBS/Fox Video: B, V, LV)
War Games (CBS/Fox Video: B, V)
Where's Poppa (Key Video: B, V)
Willie Nelson and Family in Concert (CBS/Fox Video: B, V)
Wombling Free (RCA/Columbia Pictures Home Video: B, V)
The Year of Living Dangerously (MGM/UA Home Video: B, V, LV, CED)

SHARE HER SECRET OF ETERNAL YOUTH

Let **Billie Lange** (39-24-34½) from North Palm Beach, Florida, a university instructor, show you how to lose inches where desired, reduce stress and build up energy through enjoyable routines in water and on land. Her new and revised version of "In Pool" exercises is the only one of its kind!

SLIM & TRIM YOGA WITH BILLIE
IN AND OUT OF POOL[©] VHS, Beta & 3/4"

A unique video experience for people who care about their general health.

Please make out your check or money order for the total amount, payable to Billie Lange, P.O. Box 386, Cullman, Alabama, 35056, (205) 734-2993.

Please specify: *Price Includes shipping.
In Pool   ____ @$27.50* VHS ____ BETA ____
Out of Pool   ____ @$27.50* VHS ____ BETA ____

Use Guide

The Video Tape & Disc Guide to Home Entertainment, Fifth Edition is divided into six major sections: (1) Videodisc Index; (2) Closed Captioned Index; (3) Program Listings; (4) Subject Category Index; (5) Cast Index; and (6) Video Program Sources Index. A description of each section is given below.

VIDEODISC INDEX

The Videodisc Index is a compilation of all programs available on LV and CED videodisc formats at the time of publication. Titles are listed alphabetically under the Laser Optical Videodisc and Capacitance Electronic Disc headings. For complete information on each title, see entries in the Program Listings.

CLOSED CAPTIONED INDEX

The Closed Captioned Index is a listing of cassettes and discs which are closed captioned. Full information on each title can be found in the Program Listings.

PROGRAM LISTINGS

The main body of this book consists of more than 7,000 program listings. Each entry may contain up to 19 different pieces of information, most of which is supplied by the distributor, or "video program source." NVC utilizes standard film and video reference materials to obtain pertinent information when not supplied by the distributor. Full explanations of the information included are given below; consult the Key for illustrated examples.

ALPHABETIZATION

Each program is listed alphabetically. "A," "an" and "the" and their foreign counterparts are not considered in alphabetization.

RELEASE DATE

"Release date" is defined as the year in which the film or program was initially made available for public viewing. The known release date will be listed as 1982, for example; when the decade is known or determined, but not the precise year, the information will be listed as 198?, indicating the decade of the 1980s. When neither the decade nor the year can be determined, the listing will indicate this by the annotation, 19??.

SUBJECT CATEGORY

Each title has been assigned a specific subject heading, i.e. "Comedy," "Music video," etc. This descriptive category will identify the contents of the program. In some entries, a second category has also been assigned.

ACCESSION NUMBER

Each title is assigned an accession number. The number is simply an identifying code for the publisher and has no other meaning.

RUNNING TIMES

The running time of a program is listed as "88 mins." When edited or different versions of a program are available, they are listed separately with the appropriate running times. The running times of interactive videodisc programs will be listed as "? mins." (An interactive program has no specific running time because the length and pace of the program experience are controlled by the viewer.) In a series entry, the running time given is the average running time of each program in the series. (See sub-heading "Series: Number of Programs.")

COLOR AND BLACK AND WHITE

Each title listing indicates whether the program is available in color (C) or black and white (B/W).

FORMAT AVAILABILITY

Each entry includes the video formats available for that particular program. The most common home video formats are Beta and VHS, although others are listed, when available. Laser optical videodisc (LV) and capacitance electronic disc (CED) availabilities are also included. The format codes are as follows:

	CODE	FORMAT
Videotape:	CV	1/4" compact videocassette
	B	Beta
	V	VHS
	EJ	1/2" open reel (EIAJ)
	3/4U	3/4" U-matic cassette
	1C	1" broadcast type "C"
	Q	2" quadraplex open reel
Videodisc:	LV	Laser optical videodisc
	CED	Capacitance electronic disc
Other:	FO	Formats other than those listed for the program are available from the distributor by special arrangement.

TELEVISION STANDARDS

All programs listed in this *Guide* are available on the U.S. television standard (NTSC).

ANCILLARY MATERIALS

Brochures, study guides, and other printed and audio materials are occasionally available from the distributor to aid in the use of the program. This is noted by the phrase "AM Available."

AUDIENCE RATING

For theatrical films, the standard Motion Picture Association of America ratings are listed according to the MPAA Classification and Rating Program. MPAA ratings, preceded by "MPAA," are coded as follows:

G: GENERAL AUDIENCES. All ages admitted.
PG: PARENTAL GUIDANCE SUGGESTED. Some material may not be suitable for children.
R: RESTRICTED. Under 17 requires accompanying parent or adult guardian.
X: NO ONE UNDER 17 ADMITTED. (Age limit may vary in certain areas.)

No self-imposed ratings are listed. The ratings are the last available from the distributor and MPAA.

FOREIGN LANGUAGE

Virtually all titles found in this publication are available in English. Some foreign films have retained their original foreign language soundtrack; other English-language films have been dubbed into foreign languages. The availability of a foreign language version is indicated according to the following codes:

EL	English	JA	Japanese
AF	Afrikaans	LA	Latin
AB	Arabic	LI	Lithuanian
BE	Belgian	NE	Nepalese
CH	Chinese	NO	Norwegian
CZ	Czech	PO	Polish
DA	Danish	PR	Portuguese
DU	Dutch	RU	Russian
EG	Egyptian	SE	Serbo-Croatian
FI	Finnish	SP	Spanish
FL	Flemish	SA	Swahili
FR	French	SW	Swedish
GE	German	TH	Thai
GR	Greek	TU	Turkish
HE	Hebrew	WE	Welsh
IT	Italian		

When EL is not given along with a foreign language code, the program is not available in English.

SILENT/DUBBED/SUBTITLES

Silent films or those with dubbing or different language soundtracks are noted in the program descriptions. Similarly, a program with sub-titles is so indicated at the end of the program description.

ORIGINAL PRODUCER

The original producer (studio, company, and/or individual person) is listed in each entry. When the actual producer cannot be determined, but the country of origin (other than the U.S.) is known, that information will be listed instead.

VIDEO PROGRAM SOURCES

The video program source, also known as the wholesaler or distributor, appears to the right of the original producer in the listing. More than one source will be listed when the program is legitimately available from more than one wholesaler. This normally occurs when the program is in the public domain, or when it is available from one source on cassette and from another on disc. When multiple sources are listed, the format and acquisition availabilities apply to the first source. Most of the alternate sources will make the program available in Beta and VHS formats; special notations for those companies offering videodisc formats will be found in the Video Program Sources Index at the back of this book.

Most of the sources listed are major national wholesalers. The reader may be referred by the wholesaler to a local retailer or club for sales or rental fulfillment. (No local retailer or club is normally listed unless it is the sole source of the program.) Some sources will fulfill mail-order requests.

SUBJECT CATEGORY INDEX

Each title in *The Video Tape & Disc Guide to Home Entertainment* has been assigned a subject category. A complete list of all subjects and titles within them appears after the Program Listings. When a program is assigned two different subjects, that title is indexed under both. This index is designed to help the reader quickly locate programs in his area of interest, be it drama, gardening, football or any of 200 other subjects.

CAST INDEX

We have compiled videographies of selected performers and directors. This cast listing is by no means complete, since it would be impossible to list every performer in every movie available on video; however, more than 275 entertainers have been included.

VIDEO PROGRAM SOURCES INDEX

The full corporate name, address and telephone number(s) for each video program source whose entries appear in *The Video Tape & Disc Guide to Home Entertainment* are listed alphabetically in the Video Program Sources Index at the back of this book. Contact the individual program sources for further information about their titles.

ACQUISITION AVAILABILITY

Video programs may be acquired in several ways. The following codes are used to indicate the means by which the consumer may obtain the program from the listed sources or its assignee:

R	Rent (user may rent or lease the program)
L	Loan (user may borrow the program for a fee)
P	Purchase (user may purchase the program)
D	Duplication (user may supply the distributor with a blank tape for program duplication for a fee)
S	Subscription (user may obtain the program as part of a membership at an annual fee or through a club)
T	Trade-in (user may exchange a purchased program for a credit on another program)
FL	Free Loan (user may borrow the program for a postage or handling charge)
DL	Duplication License (user may purchase a license to duplicate)
OA	Off-Air Record (user may obtain permission to record the program off-air)

The information supplied in this coding is obtained from the video program source.

PROGRAMS FOR THE HEARING IMPAIRED

When a program has been captioned or signed for the hearing impaired, the entry includes the notation "Open Captioned," "Closed Captioned," or "Signed" below the accession number.

CAST/STARS/HOSTS/GUESTS

The major stars or other members of the cast of dramatic television programs or movies are listed. In some instances, the director is listed as well. For instructional, talk show and documentary programs, the host, narrator or instructor is given, when known.

SERIES: NUMBER OF PROGRAMS

The number of programs in a generic series is listed as "11 pgms." The individual titles of each program within the series are listed in the sequence in which they are given by the distributor. When the distributor will make programs available either as a series or individually, the individual programs may also be listed in the main text.

PROGRAM DESCRIPTION

The narrative program descriptions are designed to briefly identify the major plot, subject, or theme of the program.

AWARDS

The major awards and the year of the award are listed in each entry. Unless there is an obvious abbreviation for well-known awards, the awards are spelled out. Nominations are normally not listed.

KEY

T his sample entry will assist the reader in interpreting the individual Program Listings. For complete explanation of each code, please see the USE GUIDE.

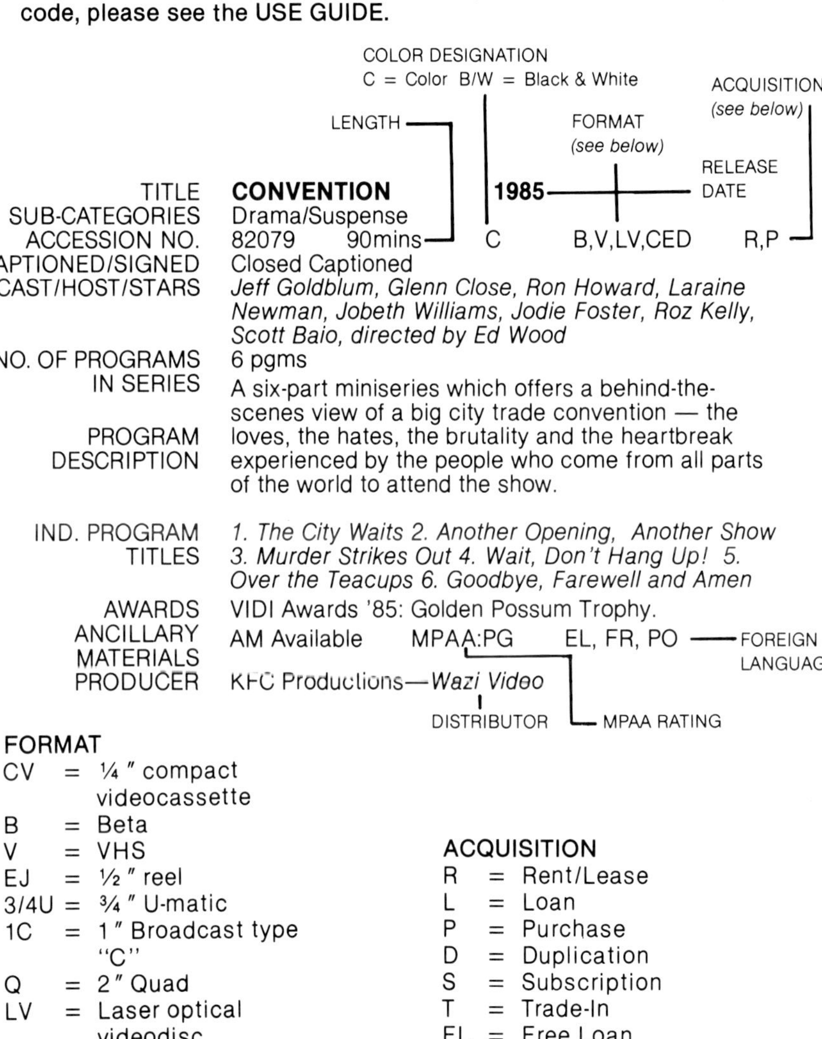

FORMAT

CV	=	¼ " compact videocassette
B	=	Beta
V	=	VHS
EJ	=	½ " reel
3/4U	=	¾ " U-matic
1C	=	1" Broadcast type "C"
Q	=	2" Quad
LV	=	Laser optical videodisc
CED	=	Capacitance electronic disc
FO	=	Other than listed

ACQUISITION

R	=	Rent/Lease
L	=	Loan
P	=	Purchase
D	=	Duplication
S	=	Subscription
T	=	Trade-In
FL	=	Free Loan
FD	=	Free Duplication
DL	=	Duplication License
OA	=	Off-Air Record

New Releases

As we go to press, several companies listed in this *Guide* have announced the release of new programs. All titles listed below are available in Beta and VHS videocassette *only* unless otherwise noted. A notation for closed captioned titles *(cc)* also appears, where applicable.

CBS/FOX VIDEO
Beauty and the Beast *(B, V, LV, CED)*
The Nightingale *(B, V, LV, CED)*
Playboy Playmate Workout *(B, V, LV, CED)*
Playmate Review #2 *(B, V, CED)*
The Princess and the Pea *(B, V, LV, CED)*
Snow White and the Seven Dwarfs *(B, V, LV, CED)*
That Championship Feeling
Thumbelina *(B, V, LV, CED)*
Yentl *(B, V, CED)*

CHILDREN'S VIDEO LIBRARY
The Little Prince

CONTINENTAL VIDEO
Battle Force
City of the Walking Dead
The Executioner Part II

Fighting Mad
Heartland Reggae
In Our Hands
Kool Street Videos
1984 Summer Olympics Highlights
A Woman in Flames

EMBASSY HOME ENTERTAINMENT
Alpine Ski School
The Berenstain Bears' Meet Big Paw
B.C. The First Thanksgiving
The Chain Reaction
The Christmas Raccoons
Groovie Goolies Volume I
The Little Brown Burro
Mary Hartman, Mary Hartman, Volume I
The New Misadventures of Ichabod Crane
Piranha II, The Spawning
Pride & Passion

The Raccoons and the Lost Star
Sabrina Vols. IV-VI
This Is Spinal Tap
Wok Before You Run

FAMILY HOME ENTERTAINMENT
Cantinflas, Volume II: Galaxies and Games
Inspector Gadget, Volume II
Paddy Beaver

GLENN VIDEO VISTAS
The Cat and the Canary
Faust
Great Directors: Early Efforts
The Great K & A Train Robbery
Hollywood Historama
A Mormon Maid

KEY VIDEO
Along Came Jones
Black Fury
Dark Passage
Footlight Parade
The Fountainhead

Golddiggers of 1933
Juarez
The Left Hand of God
The Letter
The Life of Emile
    Zola
Northern Pursuit
Passage to
    Marseilles
The Private Lives of
    Elizabeth and
    Essex
The Sea Hawk
They Died with Their
    Boots On
Watch on the Rhine

KULTUR
Godunov: The World
    to Dance In
The Ultimate Swan
    Lake *(Dolby stereo)*

MCA HOME VIDEO
Bride of Frankenstein
Firestarter
Max Maven's
    Mindgames *(cc)*
Streets of Fire

**MEDIA HOME
ENTERTAINMENT**
Blade Master
Christiane F.
Gold Raiders
Haunts
The Kingfisher Caper
The 2000 Year Old
    Man

**MONTEREY HOME
VIDEO**
The Grim Reaper
Hells Angels on
    Wheels
One Away
Queen of Diamonds

MPI HOME VIDEO
The Battle of China
Hitler's Henchmen

Kennedys Don't Cry
Trilogy of Terror

MUSIC MEDIA
The Band Reunion
The Style Council
    Far East & Far Out
Yoko Ono Then and
    Now

**PACIFIC ARTS
VIDEO RECORDS**
Franken & Davis at
    Stockton State
Musicourt
The Things We Did
    Last Summer

PRISM
The Forest
The Legend of
    Valentino
No Place to Hide
Spider-Man Volume 2
Survival Zone

**RCA/COLUMBIA
PICTURES HOME
VIDEO**
Caught in the Act
The Dresser *(B, V,
    CED) (cc)*
The Fantastic
    Adventures of
    Unico *(cc)*
The Loves of a
    Blonde *(Beta
    Hi-Fi)*
On the Waterfront
    (cc)
Run Stranger, Run
    (Beta Hi-Fi)
The Stranger and the
    Gunfighter
The Wild Swans
Wilma *(Beta Hi-*Fi)
Ziggy Stardust and
    the Spiders from
    Mars

RKO HOMEVIDEO
The Brighton
    Strangler

Call Out the Marines
The Clay Pigeon
The Devil Thumbs a
    Ride
Every Girl Should Be
    Married
Fred Astaire: Change
    Partners and
    Dance
Fred Astaire: Putting
    on His Top Hat
Having a Wonderful
    Time
Hunt the Man Down
Hurry, Charlie, Hurry
The Lady Eve
Lady Scarface
The Mad Miss
    Manton
Mysterious
    Desperado
Pop Always Pays
Rider from Tucson
Riders of the Range
Split Second
Storm Over Wyoming
The Threat

**SONY CORP OF
AMERICA**
Freddie Hubbard
Mel Torme Special
Rubber Rodeo
San Francisco Blues
    Festival

**SYBERVISION
SYSTEMS**
SyberVision Bowling
    with Marshall
    Holman and
    Johnny Petraglia
SyberVision
    Racquetball with
    Dave Peck
SyberVision Golf
    with Patty
    Sheehan

**THORN EMI HOME
VIDEO**
Archie, Cassette #3

The Best of the
Benny Hill Show,
Volume 4
Danger Mouse
Cassette #1
Death Driver
Fake Out
Fat Albert and the
Cosby Kids
Cassette #3
Girls Night Out
The Last Fight
Raquel: Total
Beauty and Fitness
Steel Fisted Dragon

**TRANS WORLD
ENTERTAINMENT**
The Accident
Crazed Duel of the
Seven Tigers
The Intruder
Within
Return of the
Dinosaurs

UNICORN VIDEO
The Cavalier
The Demons
Gemini Affair
Golden Sun
Take Down
To Race the Wind

USA HOME VIDEO
The Adventures of
Topper
Death Valley Days
A Long Way Home

A Matter of Life and
Death
Showbiz Ballyhoo
Torn Between Two
Lovers
The Word

VCL HOME VIDEO
California Girls
Computer Wizard
Nazareth—Live!
Prisoners of the Lost
Universe

VESTRON VIDEO
Beat Street
Breaking with the
Mighty Poppalots
Broadway Danny
Rose *(B, V, LV,
CED)*
Dracula
Frankenstein
House by the
Cemetery
Invasion of the Flesh
Hunters
The Kid from Left
Field
Killpoint
Slapstick of Another
Kind *(B, V, LV)*
Tricks or Treats
Up the Creek

VIDAMERICA
Caesar and Cleopatra
Doctor at Large
Doctor at Sea
Doctor in Distress
Leather Boys

Make Mine Mink
Mango Tree
Squizzy Taylor
VidAmerica Classic
III Pack

**WALT DISNEY HOME
VIDEO**
Disney's Halloween
Treat
Pogo for President—
"I Go Pogo"
Stories and Fables,
Volume 7
Stories and Fables,
Volume 8
The Twelve Tasks of
Asterix

**WARNER HOME
VIDEO**
Greystoke: The
Legend of Tarzan,
Lord of the Apes
(B, V, LV/stereo)
(cc)
House of Wax
Hurray for Betty
Boop
It Lives Again
It's Alive
Master of the World

**WORLDVISION
HOME VIDEO**
The Gathering
Hillbilly Bears
Precious Pupp
Shazzan

The National Video Clearinghouse, Inc.
100 Lafayette Dr., Syosset, NY 11791
Dept. HE4

Want to be kept up-to-date?

For information on the latest publications from National Video Clearinghouse, Inc., just fill out and send in the coupon below (please print):

Name____

Address____

City____

State ________________________ Zip _______________________

We welcome your comments on The Video Tape & Disc Guide to Home Entertainment, Fifth Edition:

____

____

____

____

Videodisc Index

This index is divided into two sections: Capacitance Electronic Discs (CED) and Laser Optical Discs (LV). An alphabetical listing of titles available in both disc formats follows. Please refer to the alphabetical program listings in the main text of this *Guide* to find the disc source.

ABC—Mantrap
Absence of Malice
The Absent Minded
  Professor
The Adventures of
  Robin Hood
Aerobicise: The
  Beautiful Workout
Aerobicise: The
  Beginning Workout
Africa Screams
The African Queen
After the Fox
Agency
Air Force
Airplane!
Airplane II: The
  Sequel
Airport
The Alamo
Alice Doesn't Live
  Here Anymore
Alice in Wonderland
Alice's Restaurant
Alien
All That Jazz
All the Marbles
All the President's
  Men
All the Right Moves
Alone in the Dark
Altered States
The Amateur

The Amazing
  Spiderman
The American
  Alcoholic/
  Reading, Writing
  and Reefer
American Gigolo
American Graffiti
American Hot Wax
An American in Paris
An American
  Werewolf in
  London
The Amityville Horror
Amityville II: The
  Possession
Amityville 3-D
And God Created
  Woman
. . . And Justice for
  All
Angel of H.E.A.T.
Angel on My
  Shoulder (1980)
Angels with Dirty
  Faces
Animal Crackers
Animal House
Annie
Annie Hall
Any Which Way You
  Can
Apache

The Apartment
Apocalypse Now
The Apple Dumpling
  Gang
Armed Forces
  Workout
Arsenic and Old
  Lace
Arthur
Ashford and
  Simpson
Asia in Asia
Atlantic City
Author! Author!
The Autobiography
  of Miss Jane
  Pittman
Avalanche
Back Roads
Bad Boys
The Bad News Bears
The Bad News Bears
  in Breaking
  Training
Baffled
The Baltimore Bullet
Bananas
Bandolero
Barbarella
Barbarosa
Barefoot Contessa
Barefoot in the Park
Baseball: Fun and

Games
Baseball's Hall of
    Fame
Battle Beyond the
    Stars
Battlestar Galactica
The Beach Girls
Beach Party
Beany & Cecil,
    Volumes 1 & 2
The Bears and I
The Beast Within
The Beastmaster
Being There
Bells Are Ringing
Ben Hur
Benji
Best Friends
The Best Little
    Whorehouse in
    Texas
The Best of Popeye
The Best of 60
    Minutes
The Best of
    Terrytoons
Betrayal
The Betsy
The Bette Midler
    Show
Big Bad Mama
Big Blue Marble
The Big Chill
The Big Fights,
    Volumes 1–3
Big Jake
The Big Red One
The Big Sleep
The Billion Dollar
    Hobo
Billy Jack
Billy Joel: Live from
    Long Island
Birdman of Alcatraz
The Birds
The Black Hole
The Black Marble
Black Orpheus
The Black Stallion
The Black Stallion
    Returns
Black Sunday
Blade Runner

Blame It on Rio
Blazing Saddles
Blondie: Eat to the
    Beat
Bloody Mama
Blow Out
Blue Hawaii
The Blue Lagoon
Blue Thunder
Blues Alive
The Blues Brothers
The Boat
Bob Welch & Friends
Bobby Jo and the
    Outlaw
Body and Soul
Body Heat
Bolero
Bonnie and Clyde
The Boogey Man
Born Free
Born Losers
Boxcar Bertha
The Boy Who Left
    Home to Find Out
    About the Shivers
The Boys from Brazil
The Boys in the
    Band
The Boys of Summer
Brainstorm
Brannigan
Breaker Morant
Breakfast at
    Tiffany's
Breakheart Pass
Breaking Away
Breakout
Breathless
Brian's Song
The Bridge on the
    River Kwai
A Bridge Too Far
Brigadoon
Brimstone and
    Treacle
Broadway Danny
    Rose
Bronco Billy
Brubaker
Buddy Buddy
The Bugs Bunny/
    Road Runner Movie

Bullitt
Bullwinkle & Rocky &
    Friends, Vol. I
Bus Stop
Butch Cassidy and
    the Sundance Kid
Butterfly
Cabaret
Caddyshack
La Cage aux Folles
La Cage aux Folles
    II
California Suite
Caligula
Candid Candid
    Camera
The Candidate
Candleshoe
Cannery Row
The Cannonball Run
Capricorn One
Captain Blood
Carbon Copy
Caring for Your
    Newborn
Carlin at Carnegie
Carnal Knowledge
Carny
Carole King: One to
    One
Carrie
Cartoon Classics
    Limited Gold
    Edition: Daisy
Cartoon Classics
    Limited Gold
    Edition: Disney's
    Best: The
    Fabulous '50s
Cartoon Classics
    Limited Gold
    Edition: Donald
Cartoon Classics
    Limited Gold
    Edition: Mickey
Cartoon Classics
    Limited Gold
    Edition: Minnie
Cartoon Classics
    Limited Gold
    Edition: Pluto
Cartoon Classics
    Limited Gold

Edition: Silly
Symphonies
Cartoon Classics
Volume 1: Chip 'n'
Dale Featuring
Donald Duck
Cartoon Classics
Volume 2: Pluto
Cartoon Classics
Volume 3: Disney's
Scary Tales
Cartoon Classics
Volume 4: Sport
Goofy
Casablanca
Cat Ballou
Cat on a Hot Tin
Roof
Cat People
Catch-22
Caveman
CBS/Fox Guide to
Complete Dog
Care
The Challenge
The Champ
A Change of
Seasons
The Changeling
The Charge of the
Light Brigade
Chariots of Fire
A Charlie Brown
Festival I–IV
The Charlie Daniels
Band: The
Saratoga Concert
Charlotte's Web
Charly
Chatterbox
Cheech & Chong's
Nice Dreams
Children of the Corn
The China Syndrome
Chinatown
Chitty Chitty Bang
Bang
The Christine McVie
Concert
Chu Chu and the
Philly Flash
The Cincinnati Kid
Cinderella

Citizen Kane
City Lights
Clarence Darrow
Clash of the Titans
Class of 1984
Class Reunion
Cleopatra
A Clockwork Orange
Close Encounters of
the Third Kind (The
Special Edition)
Coal Miner's
Daughter
Cold River
The Collector
College Football
Classics, Vol. I
Coma
Comancheros
Comedy Tonight
Coming Home
The Compleat
Beatles
Complete Tennis
from the Pros,
Vol. 1:
Strokes and
Technique
Conan the Barbarian
The Count of Monte
Cristo
The Country Girl
Cousin, Cousine
Crackers
Crazy Mama
Creepshow
Crosby, Stills &
Nash:
Daylight Again
Cross Creek
Cruising
Cujo
Cutter's Way
Daffy Duck's Movie:
Fantastic Island
Damien—Omen II
The Dark Crystal
Dark Victory
The Day After
A Day at the Races
The Day of the
Dolphin
Days of Heaven

D.C. Cab
Dead and Buried
The Dead Zone
Deadly Blessing
Deadly Force
Deal of the Century
Death Hunt
Death on the Nile
Death Wish
Death Wish II
The Deep
The Deer Hunter
Defiance
The Defiant Ones
Deliverance
The Desert of the
Tartars
Dial "M" for Murder
Diamonds Are
Forever
Diana Ross in
Concert
The Diary of Anne
Frank
Dillinger
Diner
The Dirty Dozen
Dirty Harry
Disney Cartoon
Parade, Volumes
1–5
Diva
Divine Madness
Dr. Detroit
Doctor Doolittle
Dr. No
The Dr. Seuss Video
Festival
Dr. Strangelove
Dr. Zhivago
Dog Day Afternoon
The Dogs of War
A Doll's House
Dolly in London
The Domino Principle
Don Kirshner's Rock
Concert, Vol. 1
Don't Look Now
The Doobie Brothers
Live
Dot and Santa Claus
Dot and the Bunny
Dot and the

Kangaroo
Double Exposure
Dracula *(1931)*
Dragonslayer
Dressed to Kill *(1980)*
The Dresser
Duck Soup
Dumbo
Dunderklumpen
Duran Duran
Earth, Wind and Fire
    in Concert
The Earthling
East of Eden
Easy Money
Easy Rider
Eddie and the
    Cruisers
Eddie Macon's Run
Educating Rita
El Cid
El Dorado
The Electric
    Horseman
Electric Light
    Orchestra Live at
    Wembly
The Elephant Man
Elephant Parts
Elmer Gantry
Elton John: Visions
Elvis—Aloha from
    Hawaii
Elvis—His 1968
    Comeback Special
Elvis on Tour
Emanuelle in America
Emanuelle in
    Bangkok
Emily
The Emperor's New
    Clothes
The End
Endangered Species
Endless Love
The Endless Summer
The Enforcer
Enter the Dragon
Enter the Ninja
The Entity
Eroticise
Escape from Alcatraz
Escape from New York

Escape to Athena
Escape to Witch
    Mountain
Eubie!
Eurythmics—Sweet
    Dreams (The Video
    Album)
An Evening with
    Robin Williams
An Evening with
    the Royal Ballet
Every Which Way But
    Loose
Everything You
    Always Wanted to
    Know About
    Sex . . .
Evil Under the Sun
Evilspeak
Excalibur
The Exorcist
Exposed
The Exterminator
An Eye for an Eye
The Eyes of Laura
    Mars
Eyewitness
Faerie Tale Theatre
Fairy Tale Classics
Falling in Love Again
Fame
Family Entertainment
    Playhouse, Vol. 2
Fanny and Alexander
Fantastic Voyage
Farewell, My Lovely
Fast Times at
    Ridgemont High
Fear No Evil
Fiddler on the Roof
The Final Conflict
The Final Countdown
Final Exam
Firebird 2015 AD
Firefox
The Firesign Theatre
    Presents Nick
    Danger in The
    Case of the
    Missing Yolk
The First Barry
    Manilow Special
First Blood

F.I.S.T.
A Fistful of Dollars
Five Mile Creek,
    Volume 1
Flaming Star
Flash Gordon
Flashdance
Fleetwood Mac
Fleetwood Mac in
    Concert—Mirage
    Tour 1982
The Flying Deuces
The Fog
Foolin' Around
Footloose
For a Few Dollars
    More
For Your Eyes Only
Forbidden Planet
Forced Vengeance
Foreplay
The Formula
Fort Apache, The
    Bronx
48 Hrs.
42nd Street
Foul Play
Four Friends
The Four Musketeers
The Four Seasons
Fraggle Songs,
    Volume 1
Frances
Frankenstein *(1931)*
The French
    Connection
The French
    Lieutenant's
    Woman
Friday the 13th
Friday the 13th,
    Part II
Frogs
From Russia with
    Love
The Fugitive: The
    Final Episode
Fun in Acapulco
Funny Girl
A Funny Thing
    Happened on the
    Way to the Forum
Futureworld

Fuzz
Game of Death
Gandhi
Gas Pump Girls
The Gauntlet
Gentleman Jim
Get Crazy
The Getting of
    Wisdom
G.I. Blues
Gigi
Gilda
Gimme Shelter
Girl Groups: The
    Story of a Sound
Giselle
Go Tell the Spartans
The Godfather
The Godfather, Part II
Godzilla
Going Berserk
Gold Diggers of 1933
The Golden Seal
Goldfinger
Goldilocks
Good Guys Wear
    Black
The Good, the Bad
    and the Ugly
Goodbye, Columbus
The Goodbye Girl
Grace Jones: One
    Man Show
The Graduate
The Grateful Dead in
    Concert
Grease
Grease II
The Great Caruso
Great Cities: London,
    Rome, Dublin,
    Athens
The Great Dictator
The Great Escape
Great Figures in
    History: John F.
    Kennedy
The Great Gatsby
The Great
    Locomotive Chase
Great Movie Stunts
    and The Making of
    Raiders of the Lost

Ark
The Great Muppet
    Caper
The Great Santini
The Great Scout and
    Cathouse Thursday
The Great Space
    Coaster Supershow
The Great Train
    Robbery
The Greatest
    Adventure
Greatest Fights of
    the 70's
The Greatest Show
    on Earth
The Green Berets
Grover Washington,
    Jr. in Concert
Gulliver's Travels
A Gumby Adventure
Gunfight at the OK
    Corral
The Guns of
    Navarone
Gus
Guys and Dolls
Hair
Halloween II
Halloween III: The
    Season of the
    Witch
Hamlet
Hang 'Em High
Hanky Panky
Hansel & Gretel
Hansel and Gretel
The Happy Hooker
The Happy Hooker
    Goes to
    Washington
Hard Country
A Hard Day's Night
The Harder They
    Come
Harold and Maude
Harper Valley PTA
Harry Chapin: The
    Final Concert
Hawaii
He Knows You're
    Alone
He-Man and the

Masters of the
    Universe
Heart Like a Wheel
Heartaches
Heaven Can Wait
Heaven's Gate
Heidi
Hello, Dolly!
Henry V
Herbie Hancock and
    the Rockit Band
Herbie Rides Again
Hercules
Hercules Unchained
Here It Is, Burlesque
The Heritage of the
    Bible
High Anxiety
The High Country
High Noon
High Road to China
High Sierra
History of the World:
    Part I
The Hobbit
Holocaust
Hooper
Hopscotch
Horowitz in London
The Horse Soldiers
The Hospital
Hospital Massacre
The Hound of the
    Baskervilles
The House on
    Sorority Row
How to Beat the High
    Cost of Living
The Howling
Huckleberry Finn
Hud
The Hunchback of
    Notre Dame (1939)
The Hunger
I Am a Fugitive from
    a Chain Gang
I Love You
I Ought to Be in
    Pictures
I Spit on Your Grave
I, the Jury
If You Could See
    What I Hear

Improper Channels
The In-Laws
In Praise of Older
  Women
In the Heat of the
  Night
The Incubus
Inherit the Wind
Inn of the Sixth
  Happiness
Intermezzo
Invasion of the Body
  Snatchers
Invitation to a
  Gunfighter
Invitation to the
  Dance
Irma La Douce
The Island of Dr.
  Moreau
It Came from
  Hollywood
It's a Mad, Mad,
  Mad, Mad World
Jack and the
  Beanstalk
Jailhouse Rock
James Taylor in
  Concert
Jane Fonda's
  Workout
Jane Fonda's
  Workout for
  Pregnancy, Birth &
  Recovery
Jason and the
  Argonauts
Jaws
Jaws II
Jaws III
Jazz in America
The Jazz Singer
  (1927)
The Jazz Singer
  (1980)
Jeremiah Johnson
The Jerk
Jesus of Nazareth
Jethro Tull—
  Slipstream
Jezebel
Jinxed
Joan of Arc

Joe
John Curry's Ice
  Dancing
Juggernaut
Julia
Julia Child—The
  French Chef, Vol. 1
Junior Bonner
The Keep
Kelly's Heroes
Kenny Loggins Alive
The Kentuckian
Key Largo
Kidnapped
The Kids Are Alright
The Kids from Fame
Killer Force
King Creole
King Kong *(1933)*
King of Comedy
King of Hearts
Kipperbang
Kiss Me Goodbye
Klute
Kotch
Kramer vs. Kramer
Krull
Lady Chatterley's
  Lover
Lady Sings the Blues
The Last American
  Virgin
The Last Chase
Last Tango in Paris
The Last Unicorn
The Last Valley
The Last Waltz
The Last Word
Laura
Lawrence of Arabia
LCA Presents Family
  Entertainment
  Playhouse
The Legend of the
  Lone Ranger
Lenny
Let It Be
Let's Spend the
  Night Together
Liar's Moon
Linda Ronstadt with
  Nelson Riddle &
  His Orchestra

"What's New"
The Lion in Winter
Little Caesar
Little House on the
  Prairie
The Little Mermaid
Little Red Riding
  Hood
Little River Band
  Live Exposure
Little Women
Live and Let Die
Live Infidelity: REO
  Speedwagon in
  Concert
Logan's Run
Lolita
Lone Wolf McQuade
The Lonely Guy
The Lonely Lady
The Longest Day
The Longest Yard
Lookin' to Get Out
Looking for Mr.
  Goodbar
The Looney, Looney,
  Looney Bugs
  Bunny Movie
The Lord of the
  Rings
Losin' It
Love and Death
Love at First Bite
The Love Bug
Love Is a Many-
  Splendored Thing
Love Me Tender
Love Story
Lovers and Liars
Mad Max
Mad Monster Party
Magic
The Magic Pony
The Magnificent
  Seven
Magnum Force
Mahogany
The Main Event
Making Love
Making Michael
  Jackson's Thriller
The Making of Star
  Wars . . .

X X X

The Maltese Falcon
A Man Called Horse
A Man for All
   Seasons
Man from Snowy
   River
Man of La Mancha
Man on the Moon
The Man Who Loved
   Women
The Man Who Shot
   Liberty Valance
The Man Who Would
   Be King
The Man with the
   Golden Gun
The Man with Two
   Brains
Mandingo
The Many Adventures
   of Winnie the Pooh
Marathon Man
Marty
Mary Poppins
The Mary Tyler Moore
   Show, Vol. 1
M*A*S*H
M*A*S*H: Goodbye,
   Farewell and Amen
Matilda
A Matter of Time
Mausoleum
Max Dugan Returns
Meatballs
Meet Me in St. Louis
Meet Mr. Washington/
   Meet Mr. Lincoln
Meet Your Animal
   Friends
Megaforce
Metalstorm
Mick Fleetwood—
   The Visitor
Midnight Cowboy
Midnight Express
Mighty Mouse in The
   Great Space Chase
Mildred Pierce
The Miracle of Lake
   Placid
The Mirror Crack'd
The Misfits
Miss Peach of the

Kelly School
Missing
The Missouri Breaks
Mr. Magoo Cartoons
Mr. Magoo in
   Sherwood Forest
Mr. Mom
Mister Roberts
Mister Rogers Goes
   to School
Mister Rogers:
   Helping Children
   Understand
Moby Dick
Modern Problems
Modern Times
Mommie Dearest
Monique
Monsignor
Monty Python and
   the Holy Grail
Monty Python Live at
   the Hollywood
   Bowl
Monty Python's Life
   of Brian
Monty Python's The
   Meaning of Life
The Moon Is Blue
Moonraker
Movie Movie
The Muppet Movie
Murder by Death
Murder by Decree
Murder on the Orient
   Express
The MUSE Concert:
   No Nukes
The Music of Melissa
   Manchester
My Dinner with Andre
My Fair Lady
My Favorite Year
My Little Chickadee
My Tutor
MysteryDisc #1:
   Murder, Anyone?
MysteryDisc #2:
   Many Roads to
   Murder
Nashville
Nate and Hayes
National Geographic

Presents: Great
   Whales/Sharks
National Geographic
   Society: The
   Incredible Machine/
   Mysteries of the
   Mind
National Lampoon's
   Vacation
Neighbors
Neil Diamond: Love
   at the Greek
Network
Never Say Never
   Again
The New Media
   Bible: The
   Story of Joseph
The New Video
   Aerobics
New York, New York
The New York
   Yankees' Miracle
   Year: 1978
NFL '81 Official
   Season Yearbook
Night Games
Night of the Living
   Dead
The Night Porter
Night Shift
Nighthawks
The Nine Lives of
   Fritz the Cat
9 to 5
Norma Rae
The Norseman
North by Northwest
North Dallas Forty
Nothing Personal
Notorious
Now and Forever
Now, Voyager
The Nutcracker
The Nutty Professor
Octopussy
The Odd Couple
An Officer and a
   Gentleman
Oh! Calcutta!
Oh, God!
Oklahoma!
Old Boyfriends

Old Yeller
Olivia in Concert
Olivia—Physical
The Omen
On a Clear Day You
  Can See Forever
On Golden Pond
On Her Majesty's
  Secret Service
On the Beach
On the Town
One Flew Over the
  Cuckoo's Nest
One from the Heart
The Onion Field
Ordinary People
The Oscar
The Other Side of
  Nashville
Our Town
Outland
The Outsiders
The Owl and the
  Pussycat
The Paper Chase
Paper Moon
Papillon
Paradise
Parasite
The Parent Trap
Paternity
Paths of Glory
Patton
Paul Simon in
  Concert
Pavarotti in London
Pennies from Heaven
Peter Allen and the
  Rockettes
Peter-No-Tail
The Petrified Forest
Phantasm
The Phantom
  Tollbooth
Piaf
The Pied Piper of
  Hamelin
Pink Floyd at
  Pompeii
The Pink Panther
The Pink Panther
  Strikes Again
Pinocchio

Pippin
The Pirate
The Pirate Movie
The Pirates of
  Penzance
The Pit and the
  Pendulum
A Place in the Sun
Planet of the Apes
Play It Again, Sam
Playboy Playmate's
  Workout
Playboy Video,
  Volumes 1–5
Playmate Review
Poco
Pollyanna
Poltergeist
Popeye
Porky's
The Poseidon
  Adventure
The Postman Always
  Rings Twice
Pretty Baby
The Pride and the
  Passion
The Pride of the
  Yankees
The Prince and the
  Pauper
The Prince Charming
  Revue
Prince of the City
Private Benjamin
The Private Eyes
Private Lessons
Private Popsicle
Private School
The Producers
Psycho
Psycho II
Public Enemy
Pumping Iron
Purple Taxi
Puss 'N' Boots
Quadrophenia
Queen—Greatest
  Flix
Quest for Fire
Quick Dog Training
  with Barbara
  Woodhouse

The Quiet Man
Race for Your Life,
  Charlie Brown
Raggedy Ann and
  Andy: A Musical
  Adventure
Raging Bull
Ragtime
Raiders of the Lost
  Ark
Raise the Titanic
Rapunzel
The Raven
RCA's All-Star
  Country Music Fair
Rear Window
Rebel Without a
  Cause
The Red Balloon
Red River
The Red Shoes
Redd Foxx—Video in
  a Plain Brown
  Wrapper
Reds
Reefer Madness
The Return of a Man
  Called Horse
The Return of the
  Pink Panther
The Return of the
  Streetfighter
Return to Boggy
  Creek
Return to Macon
  County
Revenge of the Ninja
Revenge of the Pink
  Panther
Rich and Famous
Richard Pryor: Here
  and Now
Richard Pryor Live
  in Concert
Richard Pryor Live
  on the Sunset Strip
Ring of Bright Water
Rio Bravo
Rio Lobo
Risky Business
Road Games
The Road Warrior
The Roaring Twenties

Rockshow
Rocky
Rocky II
Rocky III
Rod Stewart Live at the L.A. Forum
Rod Stewart: Tonight He's Yours
Rodan
Rollerball
Rolling Thunder
Roman Holiday
Romancing the Stone
Romeo and Juliet
The Rose
Rosemary's Baby
Royal Wedding (with Fred Astaire)
The Ruling Class
Rumble Fish
Rumpelstiltskin
Run Silent, Run Deep
Running Brave
Rush Exit . . . Stage Left
The Russians Are Coming, the Russians Are Coming
Rust Never Sleeps
Sacred Ground
The Sacred Music of Duke Ellington
The Sailor Who Fell from Grace with the Sea
Sands of Iwo Jima
Saturday Night Fever
Saturday Night Live, Vol. 1
Saturday Night Live, Vol. 2
Savannah Smiles
Sayonara
Scandalous
Scanners
Scarface (1982)
Scholastic Productions: As We Grow
The Sea Wolves
Search and Destroy
The Searchers

The Secret of NIMH
The Secret Policeman's Other Ball
The Seduction
Seems Like Old Times
Semi-Tough
Seniors
Separate Tables
Separate Ways
Sergeant York
Serpico
Seven Brides for Seven Brothers
Seven Days in May
The Seven Year Itch
Sex on the Run
Shadows and Light
Shaft
The Shaggy Dog
Shane
Sharky's Machine
Sheena Easton—Live at the Palace, Hollywood
The Shining
Shogun
Shoot the Moon
The Shootist
A Shot in the Dark
The Shout
The Showdown: Sugar Ray Leonard vs. Thomas Hearns
The Silent Partner
Silent Rage
Silkwood
Silver Streak
Simon & Garfunkel: The Concert in Central Park
A Simple Story
Sinbad and the Eye of the Tiger
Singin' in the Rain
Six Pack
Six Weeks
The Slap
Slave of the Cannibal Gods
Sleeping Beauty
Slumber Party '57

A Small Town in Texas
Smokey and the Bandit
Smokey and the Bandit II
Smokey and the Bandit Part 3
The Smurfs and the Magic Flute
The Snow Queen
S.O.B.
The Soldier
Soldier Blue
The Solid Gold Five Day Workout
Some Kind of Hero
Some Like It Hot
Something Wicked This Way Comes
The Sons of Katie Elder
Sophie's Choice
The Sound of Music
Sounder
South Pacific
Southern Comfort
Soylent Green
Spacehunter: Adventures in the Forbidden Zone
Spellbound
Spinal Tap
The Spiral Staircase
Splash
Split Image
Spring Break
The Spy Who Loved Me
Squirm
Stagecoach
Stalag 17
Star Chamber
Star 80
A Star Is Born (1954)
A Star Is Born (1976)
Star Trek I–VI
Star Trek—The Motion Picture
Star Wars
Stardust Memories
Stars on 45
Start to Finish—The

Grand Prix!
Starting Over
Staying Alive
Stevie
Stevie Nicks in
  Concert
Still of the Night
The Sting
Sting II
Stir Crazy
The Story of O
A Stranger Is
  Watching
Strangers on a Train
Straw Dogs
The Street Fighter
A Streetcar Named
  Desire
Stripes
Stroker Ace
The Stunt Man
Sudden Impact
Summer Lovers
Summer of '42
Sunset Boulevard
The Sunshine Boys
Super Bowl XIV:
  Steelers vs. Rams
Super Bowl XV:
  Raiders vs. Eagles
Superman—The
  Movie
Superman II
Superman III
Survival Anglia's
  World of Wildlife,
  Vol. I
Survival Anglia's
  World of Wildlife,
  Vol. II
The Survivors
The Swap
Swept Away
Swing Time
Swiss Family
  Robinson
Sybil
Table for Five
Take the Money and
  Run
Take This Job and
  Shove It
The Taking of Pelham

One Two Three
The Tale of the Frog
  Prince
Tales from
  Muppetland
Tales from
  Muppetland II
The Tales of
  Hoffmann
The Taming of the
  Shrew
Tank
Taps
Tarzan, the Ape Man
  (1981)
Tattoo
Taxi Driver
The Telephone Book
The Tempest
"10"
The Ten
  Commandments
Tender Mercies
Tentacles
Terms of Endearment
The Terry Fox Story
Terrytoons, Vol. 1
  Featuring Mighty
  Mouse
Tess
Testament
Tex
The Texas Chainsaw
  Massacre
That Championship
  Season
That's Entertainment
There's No Business
  Like Show
  Business
They All Laughed
They Call Me Mister
  Tibbs!
They Call Me Trinity
They Drive by Night
They Shoot Horses,
  Don't They?
Thief
The Thing (1951)
The Thing (1982)
Things Are Tough All
  Over
The Third Man

The 39 Steps (1935)
A Thousand Clowns
Three Days of the
  Condor
The Three Little Pigs
The Three Stooges
  Videodisc, Vol. 1
Three Tales of Love
  & Friendship
Thunderball
Thunderbirds Are Go
Thunderbolt and
  Lightfoot
Ticket to Heaven
Till Marriage Do Us
  Part
Time Bandits
The Time Machine
Timerider
To Be or Not to Be
To Forget Venice
To Russia . . . with
  Elton
Tom and Jerry 1–3
Tom Jones
Tom Sawyer
Tommy
A Tony Bennett
  Songbook
Tootsie
Topkapi
Tora! Tora! Tora!
Totally Go-Gos
The Towering Inferno
The Toy
Trading Places
The Trail of the
  Pink Panther
Trapeze
La Traviata
Treasure
Treasure Island
Treasure of the Four
  Crowns
The Treasure of the
  Sierra Madre
Tribute
Trinity Is Still My
  Name
Tron
Truck Stop Women
True Confessions
True Grit

Tubby the Tuba
The Tubes Video
Tulips
The Turning Point
Tut: The Boy King/
 The Louvre
12 Angry Men
20,000 Leagues Under
 the Sea
Twilight Zone—The
 Movie
Two of a Kind
2001: A Space
 Odyssey
Uncommon Valor
The Undersea World
 of Jacques
 Cousteau, Vol. 1
An Unmarried
 Woman
Up in Smoke
Urban Cowboy
Used Cars
Utopia
Valley Girl
Venom
Vera Cruz
The Verdict
Vertigo
Vice Squad
Victor/Victoria
Victory
Victory at Sea
Village of the
 Damned
Visiting Hours
Viva Las Vegas
The Wacky World of
 Mother Goose
War Games
The War of the
 Worlds
Warlords of the 21st
 Century
The Washington
 Affair
Wasn't That a Time!
Watership Down
The Way We Were
A Week at the Races
Weekend Pass
West Side Story
Westworld

What's New
 Pussycat?
What's Up, Doc?
What's Up Tiger
 Lily?
Where's Poppa?
White Heat
White Lightning
The Who Rocks
 America—1982
 American Tour
Wholly Moses!
Who's Afraid of
 Opera? Vols. 1-3
Whose Life Is It
 Anyway?
Wifemistress
The Wild Bunch
The Wild Geese
Wild in the Country
Wimbledon Tennis:
 1979-1980
Wimbledon 1981/
 Wimbledon: A
 Century of
 Greatness
Winter Kills
Witches' Brew
Without a Trace
Witness for the
 Prosecution
The Wizard of Oz
Women in Love
Woodstock
Woody Woodpecker
 and Friends,
 Volume I
The World According
 to Garp
World Series 1980
X-Tro
Yankee Doodle
 Dandy
The Year of Living
 Dangerously
Yes, Giorgio
Yoga Moves with
 Alan Finger
Yor, the Hunter from
 the Future
You Only Live Twice
Young Doctors in
 Love

Young Frankenstein
Z
Zapped!
Zelig
Zero to Sixty
Ziegfeld Follies
Zombie
Zorro, the Gay Blade

LASER OPTICAL DISCS

Abba
Abba in Concert
Absence of Malice
The Absent-Minded
 Professor
The Adventures of
 Robin Hood
The Adventures of
 the Wilderness
 Family
Aerobicise: The
 Beautiful Workout
Aerobicise: The
 Beginning Workout
Aerobicise: The
 Ultimate Workout
The African Queen
Aida
Airplane!
Airplane II: The
 Sequel
Alice in Wonderland
Alien
All That Jazz
Altered States
America Live in
 Central Park
American Gigolo
American Graffiti
An American in Paris
An American
 Werewolf in
 London
The Amityville Horror
Amityville II: The
 Possession
And God Created
 Woman
Angel of H.E.A.T.
Animal House

X X X V

Anne Byrd's Cookery
Annie
Annie Hall
Any Which Way You
   Can
Apocalypse Now
April Wine
Armed Forces
   Workout
Arthur
Ashford & Simpson
Atlantic City
Autumn Sonata
The Bad News Bears
Badlands
The Ballad of
   Gregorio Cortez
Bang the Drum
   Slowly
Barbarella
Barefoot in the Park
Barry Manilow Live
   at the Greek
Basic Karate and
   Self Defense
Battlestar Galactica
The Beach Girls
Belly Dancing—You
   Can Do It!
Bernadette Peters in
   Concert
Best Friends
The Best Little
   Whorehouse in
   Texas
The Bette Midler
   Show
Between the Lines
Billy Joel: Live from
   Long Island
Billy Squier Live in
   the Dark
The Black Hole
The Black Stallion
Blade Runner
Blame It on Rio
Blazing Saddles
Blow Out
Blue Hawaii
The Blue Lagoon
The Blues Brothers
Bob Marley & the
   Wailers

Body Heat
La Bohème
Bolero
Bon Voyage, Charlie
   Brown
Bonnie and Clyde
The Border
The Boy Who Left
   Home to Find Out
   About the Shivers
The Boys from Brazil
Breaker Morant
Breakfast at Tiffany's
Breathless
The Bridge on the
   River Kwai
Brigadoon
Broadway Danny
   Rose
Buck Rogers in the
   25th Century
Bugsy Malone
Bustin' Loose
Butch Cassidy and
   the Sundance Kid
Butterfly
Caddyshack
La Cage Aux Folles
Caledonian Dreams
California Suite
Caligula
Camelot
The Cannonball Run
Capricorn One
Carbon Copy
Carlin at Carnegie
Carnal Knowledge
Carrie
Cartoon Classics
   Volume 1: Chip 'n'
   Dale with Donald
   Duck
Cartoon Classics
   Volume 2: Pluto
Cartoon Classics
   Volume 3: Disney's
   Scary Tales
Cartoon Classics
   Volume 4: Sport
   Goofy
Cartoon Classics
   Volume 5: Disney's
   Best of 1931–1948

Casablanca
Cat on a Hot Tin
   Roof
Cat People (1982)
Catch-22
The Champ
Champions
The Changeling
Chapter Two
Chariots of Fire
The Charlie Daniels
   Band: The
   Saratoga Concert
Charlotte's Web
Charly
Cheech & Chong's
   Next Movie
Cheech & Chong's
   Nice Dreams
Cher: A Celebration
   at Caesar's
Chick Corea/Gary
   Burton Live in
   Tokyo
Children of the Corn
The China Syndrome
Chinatown
Cinderella
Clash of the Titans
Class
Class of 1984
Claude Bolling:
   Concerto for
   Classic Guitar and
   Jazz Piano
A Clockwork Orange
Close Encounters of
   the Third Kind (The
   Special Edition)
Coal Miner's
   Daughter
Coast to Coast
Coma
Come Back to the 5
   and Dime Jimmy
   Dean, Jimmy Dean
Coming Home
The Compleat
   Beatles
Conan the Barbarian
Continental Divide
The Conversation
Cool Hand Luke

Crackers
The Creative Camera
Crosby, Stills &
    Nash: Daylight
    Again
Cujo
Daffy Duck's Movie:
    Fantastic Island
Dave Mason Live at
    Perkins Palace
Davy Crockett and
    the River Pirates
The Day After
A Day at the Races
Days of Heaven
D.C. Cab
Dead Men Don't
    Wear Plaid
The Dead Zone
Deal of the Century
Death Hunt
Death Watch
Death Wish
Death Wish II
The Deer Hunter
Deliverance
Developing Your
    Financial Strategy
Diamonds Are
    Forever
The Dirt Band Tonite
Dirty Harry
Dr. No
Doctor Zhivago
Dolly in London
Don't Look Now
Donovan's Reef
Downhill Racer
Dracula (1979)
Dragonslayer
Dressed to Kill (1981)
Dumbo
Dunderklumpen
Dvorak's Slavic
    Dance
Earth, Wind and Fire
    in Concert
Easy Money
Easy Rider
Eddie and the
    Cruisers
Eddie Macon's Run
Educating Rita

El Cid
The Electric
    Horseman
The Elephant Man
Elephant Parts
Elton John: Visions
Emmanuelle, the
    Joys of a Woman
The Emperor's New
    Clothes
Endless Love
The Endless Summer
Enigma
Enter the Dragon
Ernie Kovacs:
    Television's
    Original Genius
Eroticise
Escape from Alcatraz
Escape from New
    York
Escape to Witch
    Mountain
Eurythmics—Sweet
    Dreams (The Video
    Album)
The Eve
An Evening with Ray
    Charles
The Exorcist
The Eyes of Laura
    Mars
Faerie Tale Theatre
Falstaff
Fame
The Fan
Fanny and Alexander
Fast Times at
    Ridgemont High
Fiddler on the Roof
La Fille Mal Gardee
Finian's Rainbow
Firefox
The First Barry
    Manilow Special
First Monday in
    October
The First National
    Kidisc
Five Mile Creek,
    Volume 1
Flash Gordon
Flashdance

Fleetwood Mac
The Fog
Football Follies/
    Sensational 60's
Footloose
For Your Eyes Only
Forbidden Planet
Force 10 from
    Navarone
Fort Apache, The
    Bronx
48 Hrs.
Foul Play
The Four Seasons
Fraggle Songs,
    Volume One
The French
    Connection
The French
    Lieutenant's
    Woman
Friday the 13th
Friday the 13th, Part
    2
Friday the 13th, Part
    3
The Frog Prince
From Russia with
    Love
From the New World
Fun and Games
A Funny Thing
    Happened on the
    Way to the Forum
Galaxina
Gallipoli
The Gambler
Gardening at Home
Gas Pump Girls
Get Crazy
Ghost Story
Gloria
Go Tell the Spartans
The Godfather
The Godfather, Part II
Godzilla
Goin' South
Going Berserk
A Golden Decade of
    College Football
The Golden Seal
Goldfinger
Goldilocks and the

Three Bears
Good Guys Wear
  Black
The Good, the Bad
  and the Ugly
Goodbye, Columbus
The Goodbye Girl
Gorky Park
Grace Jones: One
  Man Show
The Graduate
Grateful Dead/Dead
  Ahead
Grease
Grease 2
The Great Gatsby
Great Movie Stunts
  and The Making of
  Raiders of the
  Lost Ark
The Great Muppet
  Caper
The Great Train
  Robbery
The Greatest
  Adventure
The Greatest Show
  on Earth
Greystoke: The
  Legend of Tarzan,
  Lord of the Apes
Grover Washington,
  Jr. in Concert
Gunfight at the OK
  Corral
The Guns of
  Navarone
Halloween
Halloween II
Hansel and Gretel
Happy Birthday to
  Me
The Happy Hooker
The Happy Hooker
  Goes Hollywood
The Happy Hooker
  Goes to
  Washington
A Hard Day's Night
Hard to Hold
Harold and Maude
Hatari!
Heartaches

Hearts and Minds
Heaven Can Wait
Hello, Dolly!
Hercules
Here It Is, Burlesque
Hey, Cinderella!
High Road to China
The History Disquiz
History of the World,
  Part I
H.M.S. Pinafore
Hocus Pocus, It's
  Magic
Homework
Honeysuckle Rose
Horowitz in London
House Calls
House on Sorority
  Row
How to Watch Pro
  Football
The Howling
Hud
The Hunter
Hussy
I Spit on Your Grave
Iceman
If You Could See
  What I Hear
I'm Dancing as Fast
  as I Can
Improper Channels
In Praise of Older
  Women
The Incredible
  Shrinking Woman
The Incubus
Islands in the Stream
It Came from
  Hollywood
It's My Turn
Itzhak Perlman
Jack and the
  Beanstalk
James Taylor in
  Concert
Jaws
Jaws III
The Jazz Singer
  (1980)
Jazzercise
Jeremiah Johnson
The Jerk

Jesus Christ
  Superstar
Jim Fixx on Running
Joe
Joy of Family
The Joy of
  Relaxation
The Jungle Book
Kanako
Kenny Loggins Alive
Kentucky Fried Movie
The King and I
King Kong (1977)
Klute
The Knack—Live at
  Carnegie Hall
Kramer vs. Kramer
Lady on the Bus
Lady Sings the Blues
Lassiter
Last of the Red Hot
  Lovers
Last Tango in Paris
The Lenny Bruce
  Performance Film
Let It Be
Let's Bowl
Let's Spend the
  Night Together
Linda Ronstadt with
  Nelson Riddle and
  His Orchestra—
  "What's New"
The Lion in Winter
Lipstick
Little Darlings
The Little Mermaid
The Little Prince
Little Red Riding
  Hood
Little River Band
  Live Exposure
Live and Let Die
Live Infidelity: REO
  Speedwagon in
  Concert
Liza Minnelli in
  Concert
Lone Wolf McQuade
The Lonely Guy
The Lonely Lady
The Longest Yard
Looking for Mr. Goodbar

The Lords of
  Discipline
Loretta
Love at First Bite
The Love Bug
Love Story
Loverboy
Loving Couples
Ma Vlast (My
  Fatherland)
Mad Max
Magic
The Magic Pony
The Magician
Mahogany
Making Michael
  Jackson's Thriller
The Making of Star
  Wars/S.P.F.X.—
  The Empire Strikes
  Back
Mame
The Man Who Shot
  Liberty Valance
The Man with Two
  Brains
Mandingo
Manhattan Transfer
  in Concert
Manon Lescaut
The Many Adventures
  of Winnie the Pooh
Marathon Man
Mary Poppins
M*A*S*H
M*A*S*H: Goodbye,
  Farewell and Amen
The Master Cooking
  Course
Maze Featuring
  Frankie Beverly
Maze Mania
Meatballs
Meet Your Animal
  Friends
Mel Torme and Della
  Reese in Concert
Melvin and Howard
Metalstorm
Mickey Mouse and
  Donald Duck
  Cartoon
  Collections,

Volume 1-3
Midnight Express
Mildred Pierce
Missing
Mission Galactica:
  The Cylon Attack
Mr. Magoo in
  Sherwood Forest
Mr. Magoo's
  Christmas Carol
Mr. Mom
Mommie Dearest
Monty Python and
  the Holy Grail
Mony Python's The
  Meaning of Life
The Moon Is Blue
Moonlighting
The Muppet Movie
The Muppet
  Musicians of
  Bremen
Murder on the Orient
  Express
The Music of Melissa
  Manchester
My Bloody Valentine
My Tutor
MysteryDisc #1:
  Murder, Anyone?
MysteryDisc #2:
  Many Roads to
  Murder
Nashville
Nate and Hayes
National Gallery: Art
  Awareness
  Collection
The National Gallery
  of Art
National Lampoon's
  Class Reunion
National Lampoon's
  Vacation
Neighbors
Neil Diamond: Love
  at the Greek
Neil Sedaka in
  Concert
Network
Never Cry Wolf
Never Say Never
  Again

New Look
NFL SymFunny/
  Legends of the
  Fall
Night Games
The Night Porter
Night Shift
Nighthawks
9 to 5
1941
North Dallas Forty
Notorious
The Nutcracker
Octopussy
The Odd Couple
An Officer and a
  Gentleman
Old Yeller
Olivia
Olivia in Concert
Olivia—Physical
The Omen
On a Clear Day You
  Can See Forever
On Golden Pond
The One and Only
  Genuine Original
  Family Band
One Night Stand—A
  Keyboard Event
The Onion Field
Orca
Ordinary People
Oriental Dreams
The Other Side of
  Nashville
Outland
Paint Your Wagon
Paper Moon
The Parent Trap
Party Games—For
  Adults Only
Passion of Love
Paternity
Patton
Paul Simon in
  Concert
Pavarotti In London
Performance
Peter Allen and the
  Rockettes
Peter Grimes
Pete's Dragon

Phantasm
Picture Music
The Pied Piper of
    Hamelin
The Pink Panther
The Pink Panther
    Strikes Again
Pinocchio
Pippin
The Pirates of
    Penzance
The Pit and the
    Pendulum
A Place in the Sun
Play It Again, Sam
Play Misty for Me
Playboy Video,
    Volumes 1–4
Playmate Review
Pollyanna
Popeye
Porky's
Pretty Baby
The Pride of the
    Yankees
Prince of the City
Private Benjamin
The Private Eyes
Private Lessons
Private School
Prom Night
Psycho
Psycho II
Puss 'N' Boots
Queen—Greatest Flix
Quest for Fire
Race for Your Life,
    Charlie Brown
Raggedy Man
Raging Bull
Ragtime
Raiders of the Lost
    Ark
Rainbow Goblins
    Story
Raise the Titanic
Rapunzel
The Raven
Rear Window
Rebel Without a
    Cause
Redd Foxx—Video in
    a Plain Brown

Wrapper
Reds
The Return of
    Martin Guerre
The Return of the
    Pink Panther
Revenge of the
    Pink Panther
The Right Stuff
Risky Business
The Road Warrior
Rock Adventure
Rockshow
Rocky
Rocky II
Rocky III
Rod Stewart: Tonight
    He's Yours
Rodan
Romeo and Juliet
The Rose
Rosemary's Baby
Rostropovich
Rough Cut
Rumble Fish
Rumpelstiltskin
Running Brave
Rush Exit . . . Stage
    Left
The Sailor Who Fell
    from Grace with
    the Sea
Samson and Delilah
Samson et Dalila
Saturday Night Fever
Saturn 3
Savannah Smiles
Save the Tiger
Scandalous
Scarface *(1982)*
The Searchers
The Seduction of Joe
    Tynan
Seems Like Old
    Times
Semi–Tough
The Sender
Sgt. Pepper's Lonely
    Hearts Club Band
Serial
Serpico
Seven Days in May
Sex on the Run

Shadows and Light
The Shaggy Dog
Shane
Shogun
Shogun Assassin
The Shootist
The Silent Partner
Silkwood
Simon & Garfunkel:
    The Concert in
    Central Park
Sinbad and the Eye
    of the Tiger
Slap Shot
Slapstick of Another
    Kind
Sleeping Beauty
Slumber Party '57
Smokey and the
    Bandit
Smokey and the
    Bandit II
Smokey and the
    Bandit Part 3
The Smurfs and the
    Magic Flute
The Snow Queen
The Solid Gold Five
    Day Workout
Some Kind of Hero
Some Like It Hot
Something Wicked
    This Way Comes
Somewhere in Time
Son of Football
    Follies/Big Game
    America
Sophie's Choice
The Sound of Music
Sounder
Splash
Stalag 17
Star 80
A Star Is Born *(1954)*
Star Trek—The
    Motion Picture
Star Trek II: The
    Wrath of Khan
Star Wars
Stars on 45
Starting Over
Staying Alive
Steel

Stevie Nicks in
Concert
The Sting
The Sting II
Stir Crazy
Strange Invaders
Straw Dogs
Student Bodies
Sudden Impact
Summer Lovers
Super Memories of
the Super Bowls
Super 70's
Superman—The
Movie
Superman II
Superman III
Swamp Thing
Swan Lake
Swing Shift
Swiss Family
Robinson
The Sword and the
Sorcerer
Takanaka World
Take the Money and
Run
The Tale of the Frog
Prince
Tales of Hoffmann
Tank
Tarzan, the Ape Man
(1981)
"10"
The Ten
Commandments
Terms of Endearment
Tess
Testament
Tex
The Texas Chainsaw
Massacre
That's Entertainment
There's a Meetin'
Here Tonight
They All Laughed
They Call Me Bruce
They Shoot Horses,
Don't They?
The Thing (1981)
35mm Photography
Thomas Dolby

Three Days of the
Condor
The Three Little Pigs
Till Marriage Do Us
Part
Time Bandits
To Catch a Thief
Tom & Jerry
Cartoon Festival,
Vol. 1
Tom Jones
Tommy
Tora! Tora! Tora!
The Touch of Love:
Massage
Trading Places
La Traviata
Treasure
Treasure Island
Tribute
Tron
True Confessions
True Grit
The Tubes Video
The Twilight Zone—
The Movie
Twisted Sister's Stay
Hungry
2001: A Space
Odyssey
Uncommon Valor
Under Fire
Unfaithfully Yours
Up in Smoke
Urban Cowboy
Valley Girl
The Verdict
Vertigo
Vice Squad
Videodrome
Vincent Van Gogh: A
Portrait in Two
Parts
War Games
The War of the
Worlds
The Warriors
Weekend Pass
We're All Devo
West Side Story
What's Up Tiger
Lily?

When a Stranger
Calls
When Worlds Collide
White Music
Wholly Moses!
The Wild Bunch
The Wiz
The Wizard of Oz
Woody Woodpecker
and Friends
The World of Martial
Arts
Xanadu
Yankee Doodle
Dandy
The Year of Living
Dangerously
Yellowbeard
Yoga Moves with
Alan Finger
Young Doctors in
Love
Young Frankenstein
Yum-Yum Girls
Zapped!
Zelig

A

A Mi Las Mujeres Ni Fu, Ni   1980
Comedy
64499   90 mins   C   B, V   P
This musical comedy features the well-known
Spanish and Latin American singer Peret.
English title: "I Don't Care for Women."
SP
Jose Antonio Cascales Guijarro — *Media
Home Entertainment*

A Nous La Liberte   1931
Satire
06212   87 mins   B/W   B, V   P
*Raymond Cordy, Henri Marchand, directed by
Rene Clair*
A tramp becomes a wealthy and powerful leader
in this satire that provided the inspiration for
Chaplin's "Modern Times." French dialogue
with English subtitles.
FR
France — *Budget Video; Sheik Video;
Discount Video Tapes; Western Film & Video
Inc*

Abandon Ship   194?
World War II
53652   30 mins   B/W   B, V, 3/4U   P
A training film which contains footage of actual
sinkings, carriers, and transports, and explains
various ways to escape from sinking ships.
US Navy — *International Historic Films*

Abba   1980
Music-Performance
48539   60 mins   C   LV   P
Abba
Popular Swedish rock band gives a visual
concert performance which includes their hits
"Waterloo" and "Dancin' Queen."
Unknown — *MCA Home Video*

Abba   1983
Music-Performance
66008   60 mins   C   B, V   P
The internationally-famous group performs
"Knowing Me, Knowing You," "Take a Chance
on Me," "The Name of the Game," "Dancing
Queen" and other hits.
Polar Music International — *Monterey Home
Video*

Abba in Concert   1979
Music-Performance
64832   ? mins   C   LV   P
This concert combines sequences from an
American tour and London's Wembley Arena in
1979. Features songs such as "I Have a
Dream," "Gimme! Gimme! Gimme!," "Summer
Night," and "Dancing Queen." In stereo.

Curt Edman — *Pioneer Video Imports*

Abbott and Costello Cartoon Carnival # 1   1966
Cartoons
59932   60 mins   C   B, V   P
Animated
Animated Abbott and Costello involved in a
series of comic mishaps. Cartoons include:
"Cherokee Choo Choo," "Pinocchio's Double
Trouble," "Son of Kong," "Teenie Weenie
Genie," "Indestructible Space Suit," "Bouncing
Rubber Man," "Germ Squirm," "Marauding
Mummy," and "Wizardland."
Hanna Barbera — *VCI Home Video*

Abbott and Costello in Hollywood   1945
Comedy
58292   83 mins   B/W   B, V   P
*Bud Abbott, Lou Costello, Frances Rafferty,
Warner Anderson, Lucille Ball*
Bud and Lou appear as a barber and porter of a
high class tonsorial parlor in Hollywood.
MGM — *MGM/UA Home Video*

Abbott and Costello Meet Captain Kidd   1952
Comedy
00384   70 mins   C   B, V   P
Abbott and Costello, Charles Laughton
With Captain Kidd on their trail, Abbott and
Costello follow up on a treasure map.
Warner Brothers — *VCI Home Video*

Abbott and Costello Meet Dr. Jekyll and Mr. Hyde   1952
Comedy/Horror
65204   77 mins   B/W   B, V   P
*Bud Abbott, Lou Costello, Boris Karloff, Helen
Westcott*
Abbott and Costello take on evil Dr. Jekyll, who
has transformed himself into Mr. Hyde, and is
terrorizing London.
Universal — *MCA Home Video*

Abbott and Costello Meet Frankenstein   1948
Comedy
47680   83 mins   B/W   B, V   P
*Bud Abbott, Lou Costello, Lon Chaney Jr., Bela
Lugosi*
Chick and Wilbur, two unsuspecting baggage
clerks, deliver a crate containing the last
remains of Dracula and Frankstein's monster.
Universal — *MCA Home Video*

ABC—Mantrap   1983
Music-Performance
65461   ? mins   C   B, V   P

A music video that follows "Mantrap" on a path that leads from obscurity to international stardom. Includes many of their top hits: "Look of Love," "All of My Heart," and "Poison Arrow." In stereo VHS and Beta Hi-Fi.
Michael Hamlyn — *RCA/Columbia Pictures Home Video; RCA VideoDiscs*

Abduction 1975
Drama
65373   100 mins   C   B, V   P
Leif Erickson, Dorothy Malone, Judith-Marie Berigan
"Abduction" is the explicit and straight-forward account of Patricia Prescott's transformation from distraught captive to knowing participant. Based on the novel by Harrison James.
MPAA:R
Kent E Carroll — *Media Home Entertainment*

Abductors, The 1971
Adventure
63084   90 mins   C   B, V   P
Ginger
Sexy Ginger infiltrates a ring of kidnappers by offering her body as bait.
Abductors Productions — *Monterey Home Video*

Abdulla the Great 1956
Adventure
57344   89 mins   C   B, V, FO   P
Gregory Ratoff, Kay Kendall, Sydney Chaplin
A dissolute Middle-East monarch falls for a model, who spurns him for an army officer critical of the King.
Gregory Ratoff — *Video Yesteryear*

Abe Lincoln: Freedom Fighter 198?
Drama/Biographical
65723   53 mins   C   B, V   P
Allen Williams, Andrew Prine, Brock Peters
A turning point in the young life of Abe Lincoln, the 16th President of the United States, is re-created in this moving historical drama.
James L Conway — *VCI Home Video*

Abe Lincoln in Illinois 1939
Drama
00260   110 mins   B/W   B, V, 3/4U   P
Raymond Massey, Gene Lockhart, Ruth Gordon
Massey portrays a very human backwoods lawyer involved with his two loves—Ann Rutledge and Mary Todd.
RKO; Max Gordon — *Nostalgia Merchant*

Abilene Town 1946
Western
08601   90 mins   B/W   B, V, 3/4U   P
Randolph Scott, Ann Dvorak, Lloyd Bridges, Rhonda Fleming, Edgar Buchanan

Kansas town becomes the scene of conflict between cattlemen and homesteaders, following the Civil War.
United Artists; Jack Broder — *Penguin Video; Cable Films; Video Connection; Sheik Video; Budget Video; Discount Video Tapes*

Aboard the Santa Fe Chief 196?
Trains
68909   11 mins   C   B, V   P
This program takes you aboard the famous train.
J. Allen Hawkins — *Interurban Films*

Abominable Dr. Phibes, The 1971
Horror
64897   90 mins   C   B, V   P
Vincent Price
An evil genius decides that the surgical team that let his wife die shall each perish by a different biblical plague.
American International Pictures — *Vestron Video*

Abraham Lincoln 1930
Drama
11218   93 mins   B/W   B, V   P, T
Walter Huston, Una Merkel, Henry B. Walthall, directed by D. W. Griffith
D.W. Griffith's first talking movie takes Lincoln from his birth through his assassination. This restored version includes the original slavery sequences which were thought lost. Musical score included.
United Artists — *Blackhawk Films; Video Yesteryear; Sheik Video; Cable Films; Budget Video; Discount Video Tapes; Classic Video Cinema Collector's Club*

Abraham's Sacrifice 1979
Drama/Bible
55016   49 mins   C   B, V   P
Gene Barry, Andrew Duggan, Beverly Garland, Ross Martin, Lainie Kazan, Ed Ames, narrated by Victor Jory
The story of Abraham and his son Isaac. Part of the "Greatest Heroes of the Bible" series.
Sunn Classics — *Vanguard Video*

Absence of Malice 1981
Drama
59602   116 mins   C   B, V, LV   P
Paul Newman, Sally Field, Melinda Dillon, Bob Balaban, directed by Sydney Pollack
A private citizen suddenly reads that he is the subject of a criminal investigation when an investigative reporter writes a story that was purposely leaked. A drama about the responsibility of the press.
MPAA:PG

Columbia — *RCA/Columbia Pictures Home Video; RCA VideoDiscs*

Absent-Minded Professor, The   1961
Comedy
55567   97 mins   B/W   B, V, LV   R, P
Fred MacMurray, Keenan Wynn, Tommy Kirk, Ed Wynn, Leon Ames, Nancy Olson, directed by Robert Stevenson
A professor accidentally invents a substance known as flubber which causes cars to fly and people to leap great heights. The invention, however, leads to complications of all kinds.
Walt Disney — *Walt Disney Home Video; RCA VideoDiscs*

Abuelo Made in Spain   1969
Comedy
47724   89 mins   C   B, V   P
Paco Martinez Soria
"Grandfather Made in Spain" is the story of a very funny grandfather who travels to the big city for the first time to be with his children. In Spanish.
SP
Independent — *Telecine Spanish Video*

Accident   1967
Drama
63340   100 mins   C   B, V   R, P
Dirk Bogarde, Michael York, Stanley Baker, Jacqueline Sassard
A tangled web of guilt, remorse, humor and thwarted sexuality is unravelled against the background of the English countryside in this story of an Oxford love triangle.
Royal Avenue Chelsea Productions Ltd — *THORN EMI Home Video*

Accupressure for Common Ailments   1982
Therapeutic cults
47352   23 mins   C   B, V   P
Dr. Michael Smith and Kerry Weinstein demonstrate accupressure techniques that can relieve common ailments such as headaches.
American Home Video Library — *American Home Video Library*

Ace Drummond   1936
Drama/Serials
01773   250 mins   B/W   B, V   P
John King, Jean Rogers, Noah Beery
Complete 13-chapter serial about a murdering organization trying to stop several countries from forming a world wide clipper ship air service. Thirteen untitled episodes.
Unknown — *Budget Video; Video Connection; Penguin Video; Discount Video Tapes*

Acid Rain: The Choice Is Ours   1982
Ecology and environment
60510   20 mins   C   B, V, 3/4U,   P
                   Q
A study of the environmental killer: acid rain. Acid precipitation, attributed to increased fossil fuel consumption in industrial regions of Europe and North America, is examined for its negative effects on life.
Friends of the Boundary Water Wilderness — *TV Sports Scene*

Acompaname (Accompany Me)   197?
Musical/Romance
73583   30 mins   C   B, V   P
Enrique Guzman, Rocio Dural
This film is a musical love story about a rich Mexican student who goes to Spain and falls in love with a Spanish girl.
KNBC — *Aztec Cinevideo*

Across the Great Divide   1976
Adventure
63382   102 mins   C   B, V   P
Robert Logan, George "Buck" Flower, Heather Rattray
Two orphans must cross the rugged snow-covered Rocky Mountains in 1876 in order to claim their inheritance—a 400-acre plot of land in Salem, Oregon.
MPAA:G
Pacific International Enterprises — *Media Home Entertainment*

Act, The   1982
Comedy
73033   90 mins   C   B, V   P
Jill St. John, Eddie Albert
This is a satire about political double dealing.
MPAA:R
Film Ventures — *Vestron Video*

Acting Out   1982
Drama
59656   86 mins   C   B, V, CED   R, P
Cinema verite is applied to the new eroticism in this film which gives real people the ultimate opportunity to act out their most personal fantasy.
MPAA:R
Carl Gurevich — *Wonderlust Video*

Acupressure Massage (Shiatsu)   1980
Massage
47334   50 mins   C   B, V, 3/4U   P
Shiatsu, a Japanese healing and rejuvenating massage, is demonstrated and explained.
Vision Productions — *Vision Productions*

Adam Had Four Sons   1941
Drama
76023   81 mins   B/W   B, V   P
*Ingrid Bergman, Warner Baxter, Susan
Hayward, Fay Wray, and Robert Shaw*
An intense drama of love, jealousy, and hatred;
a governess to a man'sfour sons sees them
growing up.
*Robert Sherwood — RCA/Columbia Pictures
Home Video*

Adam's Rib   1949
Comedy
44647   101 mins   B/W   B, V   P
*Katherine Hepburn, Spencer Tracy, Tom Ewell,
Judy Holliday, directed by George Cukor*
A husband and wife lawyer team clash when the
wife defends a woman on trial for shooting her
spouse. The other half of the team (the
husband) is the prosecutor.
MGM — MGM/UA Home Video

Admiral Byrd: To the   1954
Ends of the Earth
Biographical/Explorers
44257   15 mins   B/W   B, V   P
A look at America's great explorer-scientist
Admiral Richard E. Byrd. Byrd was the first
human to reach the North Pole by airplane.
Classic newsreel footage.
Fox Movietone News — Two Star Films

Admiral Nimitz: 1954
Freedom's Admiral
Biographical/History-US
44252   15 mins   B/W   B, V   P
An account of America's victory at sea in the
Pacific under the direction of Chester Nimitz.
Nimitz is noted as the conqueror of the
Japanese Navy—Midway, Guadalcanal, Makin
Island, Tarawa, Saipan, and the Philippine Sea.
Classic newsreel footage.
Fox Movietone News — Two Star Films

Admiral Rosendahl: The   1954
Sky Giant
Biographical/Aeronautics
44256   15 mins   B/W   B, V   P
The story of Rear Admiral Charles E.
Rosendahl, who was the navigation officer of
the dirigible Shenandoah, which broke in half.
He also commanded the Los Angeles and flew
the maiden voyage of Graf Zeppelin. Classic
newsreel footage.
Fox Movietone News — Two Star Films

Admiral Was a Lady, The   1950
Comedy
59138   87 mins   B/W   B, V   R, P
*Edmund O'Brien, Wanda Hendrix, directed by
Sidney Salkow*

Four ex-GI's try to get by without going to work.
Wanda Hendrix plays an ex-Wave who is
pursued by the entire zany quartet.
United Artists — VCII

Adomas Nori Buti   1959
Zmogumi (Adam Wants
to Be a Man)
Drama
52357   90 mins   B/W   B, V, 3/4U   P
Directed by V. Zhalakyavichus
This Soviet Lithuanian feature film is presented
in its original form, with dialogue in Lithuanian. A
young worker scrapes together with money for a
ticket to Buenos Aires, but the money is stolen
by the manager of the travel office.
LI
Unknown — International Historic Films

Adventure 1: Trailers on   1984
Tape
Movie and TV trailers/Adventure
66480   61 mins   C   B, V   P
Nearly 40 trailers for adventure movies are
compiled on this tape, including "Rebel Without
a Cause," "Lost Horizon," "Torn Curtain,"
"From Russia With Love," "Wild in the Street,"
"The Wild One" and "Sunset Boulevard." Some
black and white segments.
Universal et al — San Francisco Rush Video

Adventure Called   1982
Menudo, An
Musical
69540   90 mins   C   B, V   P
*Xavier, Miguel, Johnny, Ricky and Charlie (the
members of Menudo) sing 14 songs in this story
of their misadventures, which begin with a flight
in a balloon. In Spanish.*
SP
*Embassy Communications — Embassy Home
Entertainment*

Adventures in Life   197?
Ethics
51997   25 mins   C   B, V, 3/4U,   P
                                    Q
Hosted by George Otis 51   pgms
A series of 51 programs with a Christian format
dealing with problems and issues common to
everyday life.
TV Sports Scene — TV Sports Scene

Adventures of Black   1972
Beauty Vol. I, The
Adventure/Cartoons
75891   60 mins   C   B, V   P
Animated
This program is the first volume containing "The
Fugitive" and "Pit Pony" from the animated
story of Black Beauty.

LWI Productions; Tablot Television — *Sony Corporation of America*

Adventures of Black Beauty Vol. 2, The 1972
Adventure/Cartoons
75893   60 mins   C   B, V   P
Animated
This program is the second volume containing "A Member of the Family" from the animated story of Black Beauty.
LWI Productions; Tablot Television — *Sony Corporation of America*

Adventures of Black Beauty Vol. 3, The 1972
Adventure/Cartoons
75894   60 mins   C   B, V   P
Animated
This program is the third volume containing "Mission of Mercy" and "Out of the Night" from the animated story of Black Beauty.
LWI Productions; Tablot Television — *Sony Corporation of America*

Adventures of Buster the Bear, The 1978
Cartoons
53142   52 mins   C   B, V   P
Animated
Joe the Otter doesn't want to share the fish in the stream with Buster, until Grandfather Bullfrog shows him that sharing makes life fun.
EL, SP
Ziv Intl — *Family Home Entertainment*

Adventures of Captain Future Volume 1, The 1980
Science fiction/Cartoons
53159   54 mins   C   B, V   P
Animated
Captain Future and his crew use a time machine to go back a million years into the past to save a planet. They encounter strange prehistoric creatures.
EL, SP
Ziv Intl — *Family Home Entertainment*

Adventures of Captain Future Volume 2, The 1980
Science fiction/Cartoons
53160   54 mins   C   B, V   P
Animated
Captain Future and his crew save an entire planet from destruction by solving the problem of finding a safe energy source.
EL, SP
Ziv Intl — *Family Home Entertainment*

Adventures of Captain Marvel 1941
Adventure/Serials
07334   240 mins   B/W   B, V, 3/4U   P
Tom Tyler, Frank Coghlan Jr., Louise Currie
A serial about the adventures of Captain Marvel in his fight against crime. In twelve episodes.
Republic — *Video Connection*

Adventures of Curley and His Gang, The 1947
Comedy
66112   54 mins   C   B, V   P
Larry Olsen
The children's favorite teacher is replaced.
Hal Roach — *Unicorn Video*

Adventures of Ellery Queen, The 1951
Mystery/Crime-Drama
47487   25 mins   B/W   B, V, FO   P
Richard Hart, Sono Osato, Kurt Katch
The first television portrayal of Ellery Queen featured Richard Hart as the famed detective. In this episode, Ellery solves the murder of a carnival acrobat.
Dumont — *Video Yesteryear*

Adventures of Felix the Cat, The 1960
Cartoons
65482   56 mins   C   B, V   P
Animated
In this episode of light-hearted episodes, Felix is joined by a whole array of amazing characters—the devious and evil Professor, the absent-minded Poindexter, and the Strongman Rock Bottom.
Joseph Oriolo — *Media Home Entertainment*

Adventures of Frontier Fremont, The 1975
Adventure
35366   95 mins   C   B, V   P
Dan Haggerty, Denver Pyle
A rough and tumble story of a man who makes the wilderness his home and the animals his friends.
Sunn Classic — *VCI Home Video*

Adventures of Gallant Bess, The 1948
Western
45016   73 mins   C   B, V   P
Cameron Mitchell, Audrey Long, Fuzzy Knight
A young rodeo performer trains a wild horse to become a rodeo horse, but an unscrupulous rodeo owner fixes it so the cowboy is injured and loses his horse.
Eagle Lion — *Sheik Video*

Adventures of Grizzly Adams at Beaver Dam, The
1987?

Adventure
65759 60 mins C B, V P
Dan Haggerty
Fearing that a dam will flood his valley, Grizzly tries desperately to convince a misplaced family of beavers to build their dam elsewhere.
Charles E Sellier Jr — *VCI Home Video*

Adventures of Huckleberry Finn, The
1939

Adventure
52744 89 mins B/W B, V P
Mickey Rooney, Lynne Carver, Rex Ingram, William Frawley
Mark Twain's immortal classic about a boy who runs away down the Mississippi on a raft, accompanied by a runaway slave, is the basis of this film.
MGM — *MGM/UA Home Video; VidAmerica*

Adventures of Huckleberry Finn, The
1978

Adventure
75616 97 mins C B, V, CED P
Forrest Tucker, Larry Storch
The classic adventure by Mark Twain of a Missouri boy and a runaway slave.
Sunn Classic Productions — *Children's Video Library*

Adventures of Little Lulu and Tubby Volume 1, The
1978

Cartoons
53135 50 mins C B, V P
Animated
In "Good Luck Guard," Lulu tries to join Tubby's club for boys. In "The Endurance Test," Lulu gets back at Tubby when they go on an all-day hike, without any food for Tubby.
EL, SP
Ziv Intl — *Family Home Entertainment*

Adventures of Little Lulu and Tubby Volume 2, The
1978

Cartoons
53136 50 mins C B, V P
Animated
In "Save the Prisoners," Lulu helps Tubby escape from the dreaded Westside gang. In "Little Fireman," Lulu fools all the boys and becomes the first one on the block to ride in a real fire truck.
EL, SP
Ziv Intl — *Family Home Entertainment*

Adventures of Mighty Mouse-Volumes IV & V, The
194?

Cartoons
29125 60 mins C B, V P
Animated
Paul Terry's Mighty Mouse character is featured in two cartoon collections, both available individually. Volume IV runs 90 minutes.
EL, SP
Viacom International — *CBS/Fox Video*

Adventures of Ozzie and Harriet, The
1966

Comedy
38994 57 mins C B, V, FO P
Ozzie, Harriet, David and Ricky Nelson
2 pgms
Two episodes from the long-running television series: "Wally the Author" and "The Sheik of Araby." Commercials are included; they are in black and white.
ABC — *Video Yesteryear*

Adventures of Ozzie and Harriet, The
1964

Comedy/Television
57346 55 mins C B, V, FO P
Ozzie, Harriet, David and Ricky Nelson
Two complete episodes of the long-running situation comedy: "Ricky's Horse," where Ricky finds himself the proud owner of a horse after a financial "discussion" between Ozzie and Harriet, and "Ozzie the Babysitter," where Ozzie's in big trouble after damaging a slot car set belonging to the nine-year-old he's babysitting. Black and white commercials included.
ABC — *Video Yesteryear; Discount Video Tapes*

Adventures of Ozzie and Harriet I, The
195?

Comedy
45022 120 mins B/W B, V, 3/4U P
Ozzie, Harriet, David and Ricky Nelson
Four of the classic shows from 1953, 1955, 1958, and 1964, complete with commercials.
ABC — *Shokus Video*

Adventures of Ozzie and Harriet, The
1956

Comedy
72526 60 mins B/W B, V, 3/4U P
Ozzie, Harriet, David and Ricky Nelson
"A Day in Bed" and "Art Studies," two Ozzie and Harriet television shows from 1956 are offered on this tape which also features a young Mary Tyler Moore selling Hotpoint refrigerators.
ABC — *International Historic Films*

(For Explanation of codes, see USE GUIDE and KEY)

Adventures of Ozzie and Harriet V   1955
Comedy
76013   120 mins   B/W   B, V, 3/4U   P
Four fun filled episodes of the adventures of
Ozzie and Harriet.
ABC — *Shokus Video*

Adventures of Ozzie and Harriet II, The   1980
Comedy
54041   120 mins   B/W   B, V, 3/4U   P
Ozzie, Harriet, David and Ricky Nelson
Four more episodes from the classic TV series
starring America's favorite family. Featured are
shows from 1953—Ozzie has a problem when
he orders two new chairs; 1955—fishing trip for
Ozzie and Thorny turns into disaster;
1957—Ozzie's craving for tutti-fruity ice cream
gets totally out of hand; 1964—Rick's fraternity
must hide their sexy housemother from the
dean. All shows contain original commercials.
ABC — *Shokus Video*

Adventures of Ozzie and Harriet III, The   195?
Comedy
58831   120 mins   B/W   B, V, 3/4U   P
Ozzie, Harriet, David and Ricky Nelson
Four episodes of the classic series: In "The
Party" (1953), Dave and Ricky are miffed
because their friend didn't invite them to his
party; in "A Matter of Inches" (1954), Ozzie
promises Dave $50 as soon as Dave passes
him in height; in "The Road Race" (1957), Ozzie
bets Ricky that an old car can withstand more
than a souped-up hot rod; and, in "Little
Handprints in the Sidewalk" (1961), a cement
slab causes problems for Ozzie.
ABC — *Shokus Video*

Adventures of Ozzie and Harriet IV, The   196?
Comedy
62688   120 mins   B/W   B, V, 3/4U   P
Ozzie, Harriet, David and Ricky Nelson
Four episodes from this popular TV series:
"David's Birthday" (1953), "Ball of Tinfoil"
(1955), "David Becomes a Football Coach"
(1958) and " An Honor for Oz" (1966). The final
show is in color. Original commercials included.
ABC — *Shokus Video*

Adventures of Red Ryder   1940
Adventure/Serials
33957   240 mins   B/W   B, V, 3/4U   P
Don "Red" Barry, Noah Beery Sr.
The thrills of the rugged West are presented in
this twelve-episode series.
Republic — *Video Connection*

Adventures of Reddy the Fox, The   1978
Cartoons
53143   52 mins   C   B, V   P
Animated
While Granny Fox is away, Reddy the Fox gets
into all kinds of trouble, until, much to his relief,
Granny returns to set everything right.
EL, SP
Ziv Intl — *Family Home Entertainment*

Adventures of Rex and Rinty   1935
Adventure/Serials
12530   156 mins   B/W   B, V   P
*Kane Richmond, Harry Woods, Rin Tin Tin, Jr.,
directed by Ford Beebe, B. Reeves Fason*
An adventure serial in twelve chapters, each
thirteen minutes.
Universal — *Video Connection*

Adventures of Robin Hood, The   1938
Adventure
58832   102 mins   C   B, V, LV   P
*Errol Flynn, Basil Rathbone, Claude Rains,
Olivia de Havilland, Alan Hale*
Errol Flynn stars as the rebel outlaw who outwits
Sir Guy of Gisbourne and Prince John and
saves the throne for the absent King Richard.
Academy Awards '38: Interior Decoration; Film
Editing; Original Score (Erich Wolfgang
Korngold).   EL, SP
United Artists — *CBS/Fox Video; RCA
VideoDiscs*

Adventures of Robin Hood—The Inquisitor   1956
Adventure
51428   30 mins   B/W   B, V   P
*Richard Greene, Alexander Gauge, Archie
Duncan, Patricia Driscoll, Donald Pleasance*
Based on the legendary outlaw of Sherwood
Forrest and his Merry Men, who attempt to
usurp Prince John and restore the Saxon throne
to Richard the Lionhearted. An episode from the
1950's TV serial.
CBS — *Video Connection*

Adventures of Sherlock Holmes' Smarter Brother, The   1978
Comedy
29126   91 mins   C   B, V   P
*Gene Wilder, Madeline Kahn, Marty Feldman,
Dom DeLuise*
The unknown brother of the famous Sherlock
Holmes takes on some of his brother's more
disposable excess cases and makes some
hilarious moves.
MPAA:PG
20th Century Fox — *CBS/Fox Video*

Adventures of Sinbad the Sailor, The   1975
Cartoons/Adventure
53138   87 mins   C   B, V   P
Animated
Sinbad receives a map to a treasure island where fabulous stores of jewels are hidden, and, in his search, falls in love with the King's daughter.
Ziv Intl — *Family Home Entertainment*

Adventures of Sir Lancelot—Sheppard's War   1957
Adventure
51429   30 mins   B/W   B, V   P
William Russell, Jane Hylton, Cyril Smith, Ronald Leigh-Hunt
An episode from the 1950's TV series about the exploits of Sir Lancelot du Lac, a Knight of King Arthur's Round Table.
NBC — *Video Connection*

Adventures of Superman, The   194?
Cartoons
53799   55 mins   C   B, V, FO   P
Animated
Seven cartoons from 1942 and 1943 are included in this package: "Underground World," "Terror on the Midway," "Volcano," "Destruction Inc.," "Secret Agent," "Billion Dollar Limited," and "Showdown." Some black and white.
Paramount; Max Fleischer — *Video Yesteryear*

Adventures of Tartu, The   1943
Adventure
29753   103 mins   C   B, V   P
Robert Donat, Valerie Hobson, Glynis Johns
A British secret agent, sent to blow up Nazi poison gas factory in Czechoslavakia, poses as a Romanian.
MGM — *Budget Video; Video Connection*

Adventures of Tarzan, The   1921
Adventure/Serials
11390   153 mins   B/W   B, V, FO   P
Elmo Lincoln
The screen's first Tarzan in an exciting jungle thriller. Silent.
Artclass — *Video Yesteryear; Classic Video Cinema Collector's Club*

Adventures of the Flying Cadets   1944
War-Drama
54163   169 mins   B/W   B, V   P
Johnny Downs, Regis Toomey
An early war adventure serial in thirteen complete chapters.

Universal — *Video Connection*

Adventures of the Wilderness Family, The   1976
Adventure
47749   100 mins   C   B, V, LV   P
Robert F. Logan, Susan Damente Shaw
The story of a modern-day pioneer family who becomes bored with the troubles of city life and head for life in the wilderness.
MPAA:G
Arthur R Dubs — *Media Home Entertainment*

Adventures of Tom Sawyer, The   1938
Adventure
52736   77 mins   C   B, V, CED   P
Tommy Kelly, Jackie Moran, Ann Gillis, Walter Brennan, May Robson, Victor Jory
Mark Twain's classic about a Missouri boy whose adventures range from tricking the neighborhood into whitewashing the fence for him to running away on a raft to become a pirate.
United Artists; David O. Selznick — *CBS/Fox Video*

Adventures of Ultraman, The   1981
Cartoons/Adventure
58541   90 mins   C   B, V   P
Animated
The adventures of Ultraman, a futuristic hero from a distant plant.
EL, SP
Tsuburaya Productions — *Family Home Entertainment*

Aerobic Dancing   1982
Physical fitness
63167   56 mins   C   B, V   P
Jacki Sorensen
Aerobic dancing, a blend of dancing and jogging, is demonstrated on this workout tape by its creator, Jacki Sorensen. She performs a complete exercise session at three activity levels: walking, jogging and running. VHS is in stereo, with music on one track and instructions on the other.
Feeling Fine Productions; Jacki Sorensen's Aerobic Dancing Inc — *MCA Home Video*

Aerobic Dancing   1984
Physical fitness/Dance
72972   30 mins   C   B, V   P
This video cassette shows you the physical aspects of aerobic dancing along with how to lessen your chances of hurting yourself while exercising.
Star Merchants — *Increase Video*

Aerobic Dancing—Encore 1983
Physical fitness/Dance
65205   57 mins   C   B, V   P
Jacki Sorensen
A blending of dancing and jogging into a complete workout. The program is choreographed to strengthen the heart and lungs while firming up the entire body.
Priscilla Ulene — *MCA Home Video*

Aerobic Self-Defense 1984
Physical fitness/Martial arts
72890   60 mins   C   B, V   P
A "How to" program that combines aerobics and the martial arts.
NTA — *NTA Home Entertainment*

Aerobicise: The Beautiful Workout 1981
Physical fitness
58875   113 mins   C   B, V, LV   R, P
Aerobic dancing to original music, produced by Ron Harris, fashion photographer. An erotic exercise program.
Ron Harris — *Paramount Home Video; RCA VideoDiscs*

Aerobicise: The Beginning Workout 1982
Physical fitness
63427   96 mins   C   B, V, LV   R, P
This is a basic, simple exercise regimen for the uninitiated aerobiciser.
Ron Harris — *Paramount Home Video; RCA VideoDiscs*

Aerobicise: The Ultimate Workout 1983
Physical fitness
66032   100 mins   C   B, V, LV   R, P
The last installment of Paramount's Aerobicise trilogy is the most advanced, designed for those in excellent shape. In stereo.
Ron Harris — *Paramount Home Video*

Aerobics 1980
Physical fitness
44286   24 mins   C   V   P
This program suggests the proper attire, speed, and techniques for healthy jogging. Another exercise, the exciting aerobics, is demonstrated. This system is choreographed to provide not only bodily exercise but to develop muscular grace that carries through in one's everyday movements.
American Home Video Library — *American Home Video Library*

Aesop and His Friends 1982
Fairy tales/Cartoons
58577   50 mins   C   B, V   P
A collection of Aesop's most beloved fables: "The Fox and the Crow," "The Lion and the Mouse," "The Grasshopper and the Ant," "The City Mouse and the Country Mouse," plus "The Snowman's Dilemma" and "The Owl and the Pussycat" as told by Cyril Ritchard. Others included as well.
McGraw Hill — *Mastervision*

Affair 1975
Drama
76641   81 mins   C   B, V   P
Lucretia Love, Paola Senatore, Mauro Parenti
A determined wife tries to win back the love of her husband who is having affairs with her best friend as well as his secretary.
Italy — *Trans World Entertainment*

Affairs of Annabel 1938
Comedy
29491   68 mins   B/W   B, V   P, T
Lucille Ball, Jack Oakie, Ruth Donnelly
The first of the popular series of Annabel pictures Lucy made in the late 30's. This appealing adolescent is zoomed to movie stardom by her press agent's stunts. A behind-the-scenes satire on Hollywood, stars, and agents.
RKO, Lou Lusty Republic — *Blackhawk Films; RKO HomeVideo*

Africa, Blood and Guts 1967
Documentary
64996   83 mins   C   B, V   P
Directed by Gualtiero Jacopetti
A documentary that captures the racial, ethnic, political and social upheavals that rocked Africa during the 1960's. Also known as "Africa Addio."
Rizzoli Film — *VIDCREST*

Africa Screams 1949
Comedy
00386   79 mins   B/W   B, V   P
Abbott and Costello
Abbott and Costello go on an African safari in possession of a secret map. Then the trouble begins.
United Artists — *Electric Video; Budget Video; Sheik Video; Media Home Entertainment; VCII; King of Video; Video Connection; Video Yesteryear; Discount Video Tapes; Nostalgia Merchant; Vestron Video (disc only); Classic Video Cinema Collector's Club*

Africa Speaks 1930
Africa/Documentary
48733   50 mins   B/W   B, V, 3/4U   P

(For Explanation of codes, see USE GUIDE and KEY)

Scenes from a pygmy village, lion attacks, a Ubange tribe, and millions of locusts highlight this documentary feature of Africa.
Unknown — *Penguin Video*

African Horse Sickness　　1960
Veterinary medicine
69648　　28 mins　　C　　B, V　　　　P
This program discusses the causes, symptoms and treatment of African Horse Sickness.
US Government — *Mercedes Maharis Productions*

African Queen, The　　1951
Adventure
08471　　105 mins　　C　　B, V, LV　　　P
Humphrey Bogart, Katharine Hepburn, Robert Morley, Theodore Bikel, directed by John Huston
In the Congo during World War I, a spinster persuades a dissolute captain to try to destroy a German gunboat.
Academy Awards '51: Best Actor (Bogart). EL, SP
United Artists; Horizon Romulus
Prod — *CBS/Fox Video; RCA VideoDiscs*

After Mein Kampf　　1942
World War II/Propaganda
52321　40 mins　B/W　　B, V, FO　　　P
British propaganda film which blends German cartoons and contemporary footage to illustrate the rise of Hitler and the Third Reich.
British — *International Historic Films*

After Mein Kampf (The Story of Adolf Hitler)　　1940
Documentary/World War II
69575　43 mins　B/W　　B, V, FO　　　P
This combination of newsreel footage and recreations presents the life story of Hitler, made by the British as a propaganda move during the early months of World War II.
British Lion — *Video Yesteryear*

After the Fox　　1966
Comedy
72894　103 mins　C　　B, V　　　　P
Peter Sellers, Victor Mature
A con artist disguises himself as a film director in order to steal gold from Rome.
Delegate Productions — *CBS/Fox Video*

Afternoon Delight　　1978
Video
08570　30 mins　C　B, V, 3/4U　　　P
A continuous picture of tropical island beauty as seen from a high, offshore point to create a relaxed background.
Nebulae Prods — *Nebulae Productions*

Against the Odds　　1982
Motorcycles
66251　65 mins　C　B, V　　　　P
The story of Jarno Saarinen, a brilliant Finish road racer tragically killed.
CH Wood — *Motor Cycle Video*

Agatha　　1979
Mystery
47391　98 mins　C　B, V　　　R, P
Dustin Hoffman, Vanessa Redgrave, Timothy Dalton, Helen Morse, Tony Britton, Timothy West, Celia Gregory
Agatha Christie mysteriously disappears when faced with a failing marriage. Numerous people turn out to search the British countryside for some sign of her.
MPAA:PG
Warner Bros — *Warner Home Video*

Agency　　1981
Drama
62778　94 mins　C　B, V, CED　　　P
Robert Mitchum, Lee Majors, Valerie Perrine
An advertising agency attempts to manipulate public behavior and opinion through the use of subliminal advertising.
MPAA:R
Jensen Farley Pictures — *Vestron Video*

Ahi Madre (Oh Mother)　　197?
Comedy
73581　30 mins　C　B, V　　　　P
Enrique Cuenca, Eduardo Manzana Cristina Blum, Marco Antonio Muniz
This film is about a Mexican mother who gets into all kinds of scrapes and misunderstandings.
KNBC — *Aztec Cinevideo*

Aida　　1981
Opera
59878　210 mins　C　LV　　　　P
Verdi's tragic opera performed live at the Arena Di Verona. In stereo.
Covent Garden Video — *Pioneer Artists*

Air Force　　1943
War-Drama
65064　124 mins　B/W　CED　　　P
John Garfield, Gig Young, Arthur Kennedy, directed by Howard Hawks
This film about the early days of World War II follows the exploits of the crew of a Flying Fortress bomber as they see action at Pearl Harbor, Manila and the Coral Sea.
Warner Bros — *RCA VideoDiscs*

Air Force Story, The　　1941
Armed Forces-US/Documentary
53646　38 mins　B/W　B, V, 3/4U　　　P
A vintage documentary showing the development of the U.S. Air Forces from its

inception in 1930 through the attack on Pearl Harbor.
US Air Force — *International Historic Films*

Air Force Story: The Beginning, The　　194?
Armed Forces-US
68895　30 mins　B/W　B, V　　　P
This program covers the first uses of the air for military use.
US Air Force — *Interurban Films*

Air Pattern Pacific　　194?
Armed Forces-US
68893　60 mins　B/W　B, V　　　P
Narrated by Ronald Reagan
The story of the U.S. 13th Army Air Force in the Second World War.
Office of War Information — *Interurban Films*

Air Supply Live in Hawaii　　1982
Music-Performance
76024　60 mins　C　B, V　　　P
This concert features Air Supply's biggest hits, including "Lost in Love," "The One That You Love" and "Event the Nights Are Better."
Danny O'Donovan — *RCA/Columbia Pictures Home Video*

Airborne　　1962
War-Drama
29679　80 mins　B/W　B, V　　　P
Bobby Diamond, Carolyn Bird
Portrays the trials and tribulations of three recruits during their transformation into American paratroopers. Filmed at Fort Bragg, North Carolina.
Gillman Film Distributors — *Sheik Video*

Airborne, The　　1979
Aeronautics
35529　60 mins　C　B, V, 3/4U, Q　　　P
The sport of air racing and performing is displayed by some of the greatest aviators in North America: Art Scholl, with his stunning aerobatic maneuvers; The Snowbirds, a graceful, Canadian jet demonstration team; and Darryl Greenmayer, the fastest private aviator on earth.
Harry Subers — *TV Sports Scene*

Aircraft Recognition　　1942
Aeronautics
73027　21 mins　B/W　B, V　　　P
This program covers the identification of United States and British aircraft circa 1942.
Unknown — *Interurban Films*

Airplane!　　1980
Comedy
54667　88 mins　C　B, V, LV　　R, P
Kareem Abdul-Jabbar, Lloyd Bridges, Peter Graves, Ethel Merman, Robert Hays, Jimmie Walker, directed by Jim Abrahams
A comical twist to disaster films. First the passengers on a flight to Chicago are poisoned by their fish dinners. Then the plane must be landed by a shell-shocked veteran who has a drinking problem.
MPAA:PG
Paramount, Howard W Koch — *Paramount Home Video; RCA VideoDiscs*

Airplane II: The Sequel　　1982
Comedy
64505　84 mins　C　B, V, LV　　R, P
Robert Hays, Julie Hagerty, Lloyd Bridges, Raymond Burr, Peter Graves, William Shatner
There's a mad bomber aboard the first lunar shuttle in this loony sequel to "Airplane," which spoofs the familiar cliches of disaster movies.
MPAA:PG
Paramount — *Paramount Home Video; RCA VideoDiscs*

Airport　　1970
Drama
53395　137 mins　C　B, V　　　P
Dean Martin, Burt Lancaster, Jean Seberg, Jacqueline Bisset, George Kennedy, Helen Hayes, Van Heflin, Maureen Stapleton
The first of the "Airport" movies is based on Arthur Hailey's novel about a snow storm, a mired plane, and an aircraft in dire distress after a bomb explodes on it.
Academy Award '70: Best Supporting Actress (Hayes). MPAA:G
Universal; Ross Hunter — *MCA Home Video; RCA VideoDiscs*

Al Ponerse el Sol　　197?
Romance
49746　90 mins　C　B, V　　　P
Serena Hercan
The plot revolves around the relationships between women auditioning for a Madrid stage show, and the men who will choose them.
SP
Independent — *Media Home Entertainment*

Aladdin and the Wonderful Lamp　　1982
Cartoons/Adventure
59668　65 mins　C　B, V　　　P
Animated
Aladdin must use his magical lamp to defeat the wicked wizard and own the most valuable treasures in the land.
Toei Company — *Media Home Entertainment*

Alamo, The   1960
Western
31660   161 mins   C   B, V, CED   P
*John Wayne, Richard Widmark, Laurence
Harvey, Frankie Avalon, directed by John Ford*
An historical account of the men who came to
the aid of Texas in its fight for freedom against
the Mexican army.
Academy Awards '60: Best Sound Recording.
EL, SP
United Artists — *CBS/Fox Video*

Alaska Wilderness   1978
Adventure, The
Adventure
66295   90 mins   C   B, V   P
The tale of a family struggling for survival in the
Arctic wilderness.
Ron Wilton; Bunny Dana — *Paragon Video
Productions*

Albino   197?
Mystery/Drama
53943   85 mins   C   B, V   P
*Christopher Lee, Trevor Howard, Sibyle
Danning, Horst Frank*
An albino, played by Horst Frank, stalks the
street in search of his female victim.
MPAA:R
Jurgen Goslar — *Media Home Entertainment*

Aldrich Family, The   1950
Comedy
42973   27 mins   B/W   B, V, FO   P
*Jackie Kelk, House Jameson, Lois Wilson,
Robert Casey*
Upset because he hasn't received an invitation
to a costume party, Henry decides to go as the
rear end of a horse.
NBC — *Video Yesteryear*

Alexander Nevsky   1938
Drama
08701   107 mins   B/W   B, V, 3/4U   P
*Nikolai Cherkasson, N.P. Okholopkov, Al
Abrikossov, directed by Sergei Eisenstein*
A story of the invasion of Russia in 1241 by the
Teutonic Knights, "Alexander Nevsky" emerges
as more than a film spectacle. Dubbed in
English.
Russian — *Penguin Video; International
Historic Films; Discount Video Tapes; Sheik
Video; Video Yesteryear; Budget Video;
Western Film & Video Inc; Classic Video
Cinema Collector's Club*

Alfred E. Smith: The   1954
Happy Warrior
Biographical/Politics and government-US
44267   15 mins   B/W   B, V   P
A look at Alfred E. Smith, the governor of New
York who was known as the man in the brown
derby. Classic newsreel footage.

Fox Movietone News — *Two Star Films*

Algiers   1938
Drama
01786   96 mins   B/W   B, V   P
*Charles Boyer, Hedy Lamarr, Sigrid Gurie, Gene
Lockhart, directed by John Cromwell*
Spoiled rich girl falls under romantic spell of
Pepe Le Moko, the Casbah's most notorious
citizen.
U A; Walter Wanger — *Budget Video; Movie
Buff Video; Cable Films; VCII; Video
Connection; Video Yesteryear; Western Film &
Video Inc; Discount Video Tapes*

Ali: Skill, Brains and Guts   1975
Boxing
07874   90 mins   C   B, V   P
Muhammad Ali
From teenage Golden Glove to Heavyweight
champion, Ali tells his own story with highlights
of over twenty-five fights.
Big Fights Inc — *VidAmerica*

Alice Adams   1935
Drama
45103   99 mins   B/W   B, V   P, T
Katharine Hepburn, Fred MacMurray
Girl from small, midwestern town falls in love
with a man from the upper level of society and
tries to fit in.
Pandro S Berman — *Blackhawk Films;
Nostalgia Merchant*

Alice Cooper and Friends   1978
Music-Performance
12044   50 mins   C   B, V   P
Alice Cooper, The Tubes, Nazareth, Sha-Na-Na
A rock extravaganza, taped at the Anaheim
Stadium in California in the summer of 1978,
featuring the exotic stylings of Alice Cooper.
Drew Cummings — *Media Home
Entertainment*

Alice Cooper: Welcome   1975
to My Nightmare
Music
65134   66 mins   C   B, V   R, P
Alice Cooper, Vincent Price
An elaborate video version of the "Welcome to
My Nightmare" record album, featuring such
ghoulish tunes as "Department of Youth,"
"Ballad of Dwight Frye" and "Cold Ethyl."
Alive Enterprises — *Warner Home Video*

Alice Doesn't Live Here   1975
Anymore
Drama/Comedy
52706   113 mins   C   B, V   R, P
*Ellen Burstyn, Kris Kristofferson, Diane Ladd,
Jodi Foster, Harvey Keitel, directed by Martin
Scorcese*

A young woman's husband dies suddenly, leaving her to care for their eleven-year-old son. She heads toward Monterey, California, where she was once a singer, but gets delayed in Phoenix where she falls for a rancher.
MPAA:PG
Warner Bros; David Suskind; Audrey Maas — *Warner Home Video; RCA VideoDiscs*

Alice Goodbody 1976
Comedy
66288　83 mins　C　B, V　P
Sharon Kelly, Daniel Kauffman, Keith McConnell
A sex spoof of a lonely girl's misadventures in Hollywood.
MPAA:R
Tom Scheuer — *Media Home Entertainment*

Alice in Wonderland 1977
Satire
55212　76 mins　C　B, V　P
Kristine DeBell
Adult version of the classic tale starring Playboy cover girl Kristine DeBell.
MPAA:R　EL, SP
General National Enterprises — *Media Home Entertainment*

Alice in Wonderland 1951
Fantasy/Cartoons
53794　75 mins　C　CED　P
Animated
Disney's version of Lewis Carroll's fable about a girl who falls into a hole and ends up in Wonderland with the Mad Hatter, the Cheshire Cat, and the Queen of Hearts.
Walt Disney — *RCA VideoDiscs*

Alice in Wonderland 1982
Musical/Fantasy
63841　81 mins　C　B, V　P
Annie Enneking, Solvieg Olsen, Wendy Lehr, Jason McLean, Gary Briggle, Elizabeth Fink
All of Lewis Carroll's beloved characters come alive in this musical adaptation of his classic tale, performed by the Children's Theatre Company and School. VHS in stereo.
Television Theater Company — *MCA Home Video*

Alice Sweet Alice 1976
Suspense
29498　112 mins　C　B, V　P
Brooke Shields, Linda Miller, Paula Sheppard
A spine-chilling story of macabre murders: who and why is this masked person butchering their victims?
Allied Artists — *King of Video; Sound Video Unlimited; Budget Video*

Alice's Adventures in Wonderland 1972
Comedy
03697　96 mins　C　B, V　P
Peter Sellers, Dudley Moore, Fiona Fullerton
An updated film version of the delightful novel by Lewis Carroll.
Rainbow Adventure Films; Joseph Shaftel — *VCI Home Video*

Alice's Adventures in Wonderland 1973
Fantasy
69614　100 mins　C　B, V　P
Peter Sellers, Sir Ralph Richardson, Dudley Moore, Michael Horndern, Spike Mulligan
This adaptation of Lewis Carroll's classic tale features an all-star cast.
Josef Shaftel — *Children's Video Library*

Alice's Restaurant 1969
Comedy/Drama
65333　111 mins　C　B, V, CED　P
Arlo Guthrie
A young folk singer has difficulties with the police, the draft board and a Massachusetts community of flower children.
MPAA:R
United Artists — *CBS/Fox Video*

Alien 1979
Science fiction
44930　116 mins　C　B, V, LV, CED　P
Tom Skerritt, Sigourney Weaver, Veronica Cartwright
Seven astronauts on a routine mission encounter an awesome galactic horror.
MPAA:R
20th Century Fox — *CBS/Fox Video*

Alien Contamination 1981
Horror/Science fiction
59995　90 mins　C　B, V　P
Ian McCulloch
The tale of two astronauts who return to Earth from an expedition on Mars carrying some deadly bacterial eggs.
MPAA:R
Independent — *Paragon Video Productions*

Alien Factor, The 1978
Science fiction
69803　82 mins　C　B, V　P
John Leifert, Tom Griffiths, Mary Mertens
A spaceship crashes in the countryside, and a small town is jolted out of its sleepy state by havoc wreaked by a host of grotesque extraterrestrial monsters.
MPAA:PG
Don Dohler — *VCI Home Video*

Aliens from Spaceship Earth   1977
Science fiction
33805   107 mins   C   B, V   R, P
Donovan, Lynda Day George
Are strange, celestial forces invading our universe? If they are, is man prepared to defend his planet against threatening aliens of unknown strength?
International TF Productions — *Video Gems*

Alison's Birthday   1983
Horror
70048   99 mins   C   B, V   P
A teenage girl learns that some of her family and friends are Satan worshipers at a terrifying birthday party.
David Hannay — *VidAmerica*

All About Eve   1950
Drama
29127   138 mins   B/W   B, V   P
Bette Davis, Anne Baxter, Gary Merrill, Celeste Holme, George Sanders, Marilyn Monroe, directed by Joseph L. Mankiewicz
An aspiring young actress ingratiates herself with a prominent group of theatre people, but passion to perform and jealousy consume her as she viciously betrays her colleagues in her struggle for success.
Academy Awards '50: Best Picture; Best Supporting Actor (Sanders); Best Direction (Mankiewicz); Best Screenplay (Mankiewicz).
20th Century Fox — *CBS/Fox Video*

All About Houseplants   1980
Plants
47322   60 mins   C   B, V, 3/4U   P
This program discusses how to choose, care for, and propagate houseplants, followed by an examination of 38 varieties of houseplants.
Vision Productions — *Vision Productions*

All in a Night's Work   1961
Mystery
16136   94 mins   C   B, V   P
Dean Martin, Shirley MacLaine, Cliff Robertson
The founder of a one-man publishing empire is found dead with a smile on his face.
EL, SP
Paramount; Hal Wallis Prod — *CBS/Fox Video*

All Mine to Give   1956
Drama
10400   102 mins   C   B, V   P
Glynis Johns, Cameron Mitchell
Saga of a family of eight who braved frontier hardships, epidemics, and death in the Wisconsin wilderness a century ago.
RKO — *VCI Home Video*

All Night Long   1981
Comedy
59682   100 mins   C   B, V   P
Gene Hackman, Barbra Streisand, Dianne Ladd, Dennis Quaid
A man who is passed over for a promotion begins his comic liberation and joins the drifters, weirdos and thieves of the night at his new job.
MPAA:R
Universal — *MCA Home Video*

All Quiet on the Western Front   1979
Drama
55528   150 mins   C   B, V   P
Richard Thomas, Ernest Borgnine, Donald Pleasance, Patricia Neal
A sensitive German youth plunges excitedly into World War I and discovers its terror and degradation. Based on the novel by Erich Maria Remarque.
Norman Rosemont Prods; Marble Arch Prods — *CBS/Fox Video*

All Quiet on the Western Front   1930
Drama
55556   103 mins   B/W   B, V   P
Lew Ayres, Louis Wolheim, John Wray
A dramatization of Erich Maria Remarque's novel about a young German soldier facing the horrors of World War I.
Universal — *MCA Home Video*

All Screwed Up   1974
Film-Avant-garde
37406   104 mins   C   B, V   P
Luigi Diberti, Lina Polito, directed by Lina Wertmuller
The story of a group of young immigrants in Milan—where everything is in its place—but nothing is in order.
New Line Cinema — *CBS/Fox Video*

All-Star Batting Tips   1975
Baseball
33844   28 mins   C   B, V   P
Tony Kubek, Mickey Mantle, Stan Musial, Pete Rose, Willie Mays, Harmon Killebrew
Tony Kubek moderates an All-Star panel as they discuss their philosophies on hitting and teach the six essential steps necessary to become a better hitter.
Major League Baseball — *Major League Baseball Productions*

All Star Cartoon Parade   19??
Cartoons
66470   54 mins   C   B, V   P
Animated
A collection of popular vintage cartoons, starring such favorites as Little Lulu, Casper the

Friendly Ghost, Betty Boop and Raggedy Ann and Andy.
Famous Studios — *NTA Home Entertainment*

All-Star Catching and Base Stealing Tips   1975
Baseball
35533   28 mins   C   B, V   P
Johnny Bench, Thurman Munson, Carlton Fisk, Steve Yeager, Del Crandall
The fine points of catching and the art of stealing bases are the featured topics on this program. Game-action footage of today's stars is presented in an easy-to-understand manner.
Major League Baseball — *Major League Baseball Productions*

All-Star Game, 1967   1967
Baseball
49550   30 mins   C   B, V   P
Tony Perez' 15th inning home run off Catfish Hunter gives the National League a 2-1 victory in the longest All-Star game ever played. Young Mets' pitcher Tom Seaver gets credit for the victory.
Winik Films — *Major League Baseball Productions*

All-Star Game, 1970: What Makes an All-Star   1970
Baseball
45030   30 mins   C   B, V   P
The National League wins its eighth straight midsummer classic, 5-4, in 12 innings. Pete Rose barrels into American League catcher Ray Fosse at home plate to score the winning run on Jim Hickman's single.
W and W Prods — *Major League Baseball Productions*

All-Star Game, 1971: Home Run Heroes   1971
Baseball
33843   26 mins   C   B, V   P
Some or the great home run sluggers of the past are paid tribute, including Babe Ruth, Hank Greenberg, Mel Ott, and Mickey Mantle. The game itself produces six home runs, one of them a mammoth blast by Oakland's Reggie Jackson, and the American League goes on to a 6-4 victory.
W and W Productions — *Major League Baseball Productions*

All-Star Game, 1972: Years of Tradition, Night of Pride   1972
Baseball
33841   26 mins   C   B, V   P
Highlights from the first All-Star Game in 1933 to the present ones are shown prior to the National League's 10-inning, 4-3 victory at Atlanta

Stadium. Hank Aaron thrills the home-team crowd with a dramatic home run.
W and W Prods — *Major League Baseball Productions*

All-Star Game, 1973: A New Generation of Stars   1973
Baseball
33840   26 mins   C   B, V   P
The great Willie Mays plays in his last All-Star Game, while the up-and-coming stars such as Bobby Bonds and Johnny Bench lead the National League to victory.
W and W Productions — *Major League Baseball Productions*

All-Star Game, 1974: Mid-Summer Magic   1974
Baseball
33839   26 mins   C   B, V   P
Write-in candidate Steve Garvey leads the National League to its third straight victory at Pittsburgh's Three Rivers Stadium. A sequence of ironic dream game performances by All-Stars throughout the years is included.
W and W Productions — *Major League Baseball Productions*

All-Star Game, 1975: All-Star Fever   1975
Baseball
33838   28 mins   C   B, V   P
National League home runs by Steve Garvey and Jimmy Wynn give them an early lead. Carl Yastrzemski's homer ties the game for the American leaguers. The Nationals score three times in the ninth inning with Bill Madlock's single the key hit in a 6-3 victory at County Stadium in Milwaukee.
Major League Baseball — *Major League Baseball Productions*

All-Star Game, 1976: Champions of Pride   1976
Baseball
33837   28 mins   C   B, V   P
The National League celebrates its 100th anniversary with another victory over the American League. Unusual viewpoints are featured, including Randy Jones' sinkerball, the many motions of Luis Tiant, the aggressive play of Pete Rose and Mickey Rivers, and the zany antics of Tigers' pitcher, "The Bird," Mark Fidrych.
Major League Baseball — *Major League Baseball Productions*

All-Star Game, 1977: The Man Behind the Mask   1977
Baseball
33836   29 mins   C   B, V   P

This program highlights the game and the individual stars of the National League's 7-5 victory over the American League, while featuring the work of home plate umpire Bill Kunkel, from his pre-game preparation to the final out.
Major League Baseball — *Major League Baseball Productions*

All-Star Game, 1978: 1978
What Makes an All-Star
Baseball
33835   26 mins   C   B, V   P
Los Angeles Dodger first baseman Steve Garvey collects two hits, two RBI's, and the game's MVP award as the National League defeats the American League 7-3 in San Diego. "Mr. Cub," Ernie Banks, comments from the stands along with the youngsters who won the "Pitch, Hit, and Run" competition.
Major League Baseball — *Major League Baseball Productions*

All-Star Game, 1979: 1979
Inches and Jinxes
Baseball
45029   30 mins   C   B, V   P
The National League is victorious again. A 7-6 win in Seattle's Kingdome is highlighted by Lee Mazzili's home run and Dave Parker's throw to home plate to nail Brian Downing, a potentially important run for the American League. Ron Guidry walks Mazzili to force in the winning run.
Major League Baseball — *Major League Baseball Productions*

All-Star Game, 1980: 1980
Heroes to Remember
Baseball
49549   30 mins   C   B, V   P
Cubs' relief pitcher Bruce Sutter wins the game's MVP award, as he nails down yet another victory for the National League in the Midsummer's Classic.
Major League Baseball — *Major League Baseball Productions*

All-Star Game, 1981 1981
Baseball
59376   30 mins   C   B, V   P
In the first baseball game played since the great strike, Gary Carter of the Expos captures the MVP award by crashing two home runs in leading the National League to still another victory over the American League, at Cleveland's Municipal Stadium.
Major League Baseball Prods — *Major League Baseball Productions*

All-Star Game, 1982 1982
Baseball
64658   30 mins   C   B, V   P
American and National League All-Star Players

The National League wins again. Cincinnati Reds' shortstop Dave Concepcion homers and is named MVP of this All-Star Game at Montreal. Montreal's own Steve Rogers is the winning pitcher, and Boston's Dennis Eckersley takes the 4-1 loss for manager Billy Martin's American League squad. Detroit catcher Lance Parrish stars in defeat, throwing out three NL runners attempting to steal bases.
Major League Baseball — *Major League Baseball Productions*

All-Star Pitching Tips 1975
Baseball
33845   28 mins   C   B, V   P
Whitey Ford, Tom Seaver, Claude Osteen, Bert Blyleven, Catfish Hunter, Mike Marshall, Nolan Ryan
The basics of pitching are explained by host and Hall of Famer Whitey Ford, along with helpful hints from many major league pitching stars.
Major League Baseball — *Major League Baseball Productions*

All That Jazz 1979
Musical-Drama
48515   120 mins   C   B, V, LV,   P
CED
Roy Scheider, Jessica Lange, directed by Bob Fosse
A show business personality is so obsessed by his career that it takes a heart attack to bring him down to earth. Along the way, the tensions, sweat, and tears that go into the making of a Broadway show are exposed.
MPAA:R
Twentieth Century Fox — *CBS/Fox Video*

All the Best from Russia 1977
Dance/Variety
58564   58 mins   C   B, V   P
An inside look at the Russian Winter Arts Festival which includes performances by the Bolshoi Ballet, the Don Cossack dancers and the American Folk Ensemble.
Canadian — *Mastervision*

All the Marbles 1981
Comedy
59365   113 mins   C   B, V, CED   R
Peter Falk, Burt Young
A manager of two beautiful lady wrestlers has dreams of going to the top.
MPAA:R
MGM — *MGM/UA Home Video*

All the President's Men 1976
Drama
38939   135 mins   C   B, V   R, P
Robert Redford, Dustin Hoffman, Jason Robards, directed by Alan J. Pakula
The investigation into the Watergate break-in by Washington Post reporters Bob Woodward and

Carl Bernstein is dramatized in this powerful film.
MPAA:PG
Warner Bros — *Warner Home Video; RCA VideoDiscs*

All the Right Moves 1983
Drama
Closed Captioned
65752 90 mins C B, V, CED P
Tom Cruise, Lea Thompson, Craig T. Nelson
A young man attempts to move up in the world and out of the dying mill town where he grew up.
MPAA:R
20th Century Fox — *CBS/Fox Video*

All You Need Is Cash 1978
Comedy/Music
65335 70 mins C B, V P
Eric Idle, Neil Innes, Rikki Fataar, Dan Ackroyd, Gilda Radner, John Belushi, George Harrison, directed by Eric Idle
"The Rutles" star in this parody of The Beatles' legend, from the early days of the "Pre-Fab Four" in Liverpool to their worldwide success.
Lorne Michaels — *Pacific Arts Video*

Allegheny Uprising 1939
Western
10074 81 mins B/W B, V P, T
John Wayne, Claire Trevor, George Sanders, Brian Donlevy, Chill Wills
Set in 1759, man clashes with military commander in order to stop sale of firearms to Indians.
RKO — *Blackhawk Films; Nostalgia Merchant*

Alley Cat 1984
Martial arts
73042 82 mins C B, V P
Karin Mani
A woman fights back against a street gang that attacked her.
MPAA:R
Film Ventures — *Vestron Video*

Alone in the Dark 1982
Horror
65063 92 mins C CED P
Jack Palance, Donald Pleasance, Martin Landau
The inmates of an insane asylum escape during a power blackout and terrorize an isolated family.
MPAA:R
New Line Cinema — *RCA VideoDiscs*

Alone in the Dark 1982
Horror
68262 92 mins C B, V P
Jack Palance, Donald Pleasance, Martin Landau

Three patients from a mental hospital decide that they must kill their doctor. They get this chance when there is a city-wide blackout.
MPAA:R
Robert Shaye; New Line Cinema — *RCA/Columbia Pictures Home Video*

Along the Sundown Trail 1942
Western
15443 59 mins B/W B, V P
Bill 'Stage' Boyd, directed by Peter Stewart
Cowboy G-men round up the villains in this Western.
Producers Releasing Corp — *Video Connection*

Alpha Incident, The 1977
Drama/Science fiction
65366 86 mins C B, V P
Ralph Meeker, Stafford Morgan, John Goff, Carol Irene Newell
A frightening doomsday drama about an alien organism with the potential to destroy all living things.
MPAA:PG
Bill Rebane — *Media Home Entertainment*

Alphabet City 1984
Drama
73659 85 mins C B, V R, P
Vincent Spano, Michael Winslow, Kate Vernon, directed by Amos Poe
A drug king pin who runs New York's Lower East Side must burn down his mother's apartment building for the insurance money. The music is composed and performed by Nile Rodgers of Chic.
MPAA:R
Andrew Braunsberg — *Atlantic Video*

Alpine Ski School, The 1983
Sports-Winter
65259 76 mins C B, V P
This program is a five-part series of lessons for skiers of all abilities. Each lesson has two sections, instruction and demonstration.
Lauron Productions Ltd; Special Projects International — *Caravatt Home Entertainment*

Altered States 1980
Science fiction/Drama
58215 103 mins C B, V, LV R, P
William Hurt, Blair Brown, directed by Ken Russell
A research scientist experimenting with altered states of consciousness discovers horrors in the secret landscapes of the mind. Based on the novel by Paddy Chayefsky.
MPAA:R
Warner Bros — *Warner Home Video; RCA VideoDiscs*

Alternative Energy Sources 1984
Energy
72971   30 mins   C   B, V   P
All the different forms of power including geothermal, tidal, and wave energies are explained on this video cassette.
Star Merchants — *Increase Video*

Alvarez Kelly 1966
Western
44786   116 mins   C   B, V   P
William Holden, Richard Widmark, Janice Rule
Holden and Widmark employ some two-fisted action amidst the Civil War setting.
Sol C Siegel — *RCA/Columbia Pictures Home Video*

Always a New Beginning 1973
Children
19401   90 mins   C   B, V, 3/4U,   P
                                Q
How children all over the world relate to their environment with tradition and culture. The program was filmed in 25 different countries.
School Bell Award '74
John Goodell — *TV Sports Scene*

Always for Pleasure 1978
Parades and festivals/Music
60458   58 mins   C   B, V, 3/4U   P
Professor Longhair, The Wild Tchoupitoulas, Art Ryder's Electric Street Band, The Olympia Brass Band, Kid Thomas Valentine
An insider's look at Mardi Gras and the myriad musical traditions the annual celebration supports in New Orleans.
AM Available
Les Blank — *Flower Films*

Am I Normal? 1979
Adolescence/Sexuality
63878   24 mins   C   B, V   P
Focusing on three fictional characters, this program presents the facts about male sexual development, while raising important questions about masculinity, identity and peer pressure.
Copperfield Films — *MGM/UA Home Video*

Amante, La 1971
Drama
47718   90 mins   C   B, V   P
Sarita Montiel, Patrick Bauchau
In "The Lover", passionate love in the jet set leads to a game to conquer a lovely woman. In Spanish.
SP
Independent — *Telecine Spanish Video*

Amante Para Dos 1981
Drama
47858   95 mins   C   B, V   P
Alberto Olmedo, Tato Bores, Maria Casan
Mauricio is a serious man and loves his wife, but his weakness is Monica, his lover. Alberto, another married man, is also Monica's lover, until both men decide that she is dangerous. In Spanish.
SP
Nicolas Carreras; Luis Repetto — *Media Home Entertainment*

Amarcord 1974
Comedy
54798   124 mins   C   B, V   R, P
Magall Noel, Bruno Zanin, Pupella Maggio, Armando Brancia, directed by Federico Fellini
The life of a small Italian coastal town in the 1930's is recalled by a director with a superstar's access to the resources of the Italian film industry.
Academy Awards '74: Best Foreign Film.
MPAA:R
Warner Bros, New World Pictures — *Warner Home Video*

Amateur, The 1982
Adventure
62776   112 mins   C   B, V, CED   P
John Savage, Christopher Plummer, Marthe Keller, Arthur Hill
A computer technologist dives into a plot of international intrigue when he investigates the death of his girlfriend, murdered by terrorists.
MPAA:R
20th Century Fox — *CBS/Fox Video*

Amazing Apes, The 1977
Animals/Documentary
29128   93 mins   C   B, V   R, P
This feature reveals never-before-known facts about these fascinating primates through absorbing highlights such as monkey worship, life-style of snow monkeys in Japan, and studies of gorillas and chimps in the wild.
Bill Burrud Productions — *Walt Disney Home Video*

Amazing Dobermans, The 1976
Adventure
47818   96 mins   C   B, V, 3/4U   P
Fred Astaire, Barbara Eden, James Franciscus
The owner of five trained dogs assists an undercover agent in foiling a small-time criminal's gambling and extortion racket.
MPAA:G
Golden Films — *Nostalgia Merchant*

Amazing Howard Hughes, The 1977
Biographical/Drama
63341   119 mins   C   B, V   R, P

Tommy Lee Jones, Ed Flanders, James Hampton, Tovah Feldshuh, Lee Purcell
This film reveals the full story of the legendary millionaire's life and career, from daring test pilot to inventor to Hollywood film producer to death as a paranoiac in isolation.
Roger Gimbel Productions; EMI Television Programmes — *THORN EMI Home Video*

Amazing Spider-Man, The   1982
Cartoons/Adventure
59038   100 mins   C   B, V   P
A collection of Spider-Man's most exciting adventures.
Marvel Comics Group — *MCA Home Video*

Amazing Spider-Man, The   1977
Adventure
59334   94 mins   C   B, V, CED   P
Nicholas Hammond, David White
Spider-Man's unique powers are put to the test when he comes to the rescue of the government by preventing an evil scientist from blackmailing the government.
Charles Fries Prods — *CBS/Fox Video*

Amazing World of Psychic Phenomena, The   1977
Occult sciences
45039   91 mins   C   B, V   P
Hosted and narrated by Raymond Burr
A look at the mysteries of parapsychology.
Sunn Classic — *VidAmerica*

Ambrose Bierce: The Man and the Snake/The Return   1978
Literature-American/Mystery
58733   60 mins   C   B, V   P
A pair of stories by American author Ambrose Bierce.
Independent — *Mastervision*

America at the Movies   1976
Film-History/Documentary
44776   116 mins   C   B, V   P
John Wayne, Orson Welles, Peter Sellers, James Dean, Gene Hackman, Burt Lancaster, Julie Harris, Deborah Kerr, Al Pacino, Robert De Niro
Scenes from over eighty of the finest American motion pictures tell the story of American movies and give a portrait of America as it has been seen on screen for half a century. Scenes from "The Birth of a Nation," "Citizen Kane," "Dr. Strangelove," "East of Eden," "The French Connection," and "From Here to Eternity," are among the many included. Some black and white scenes.
American Film Institute — *RCA/Columbia Pictures Home Video*

America Between the Great Wars   1978
History-US/Documentary
10153   60 mins   B/W   B, V   P, T
Covers celebrations and tragedies from the roaring twenties. Includes the century of Progress Exposition in Chicago, the Prohibition era, Hindenburg disaster, and off-screen activities of Charlie Chaplin.
Blackhawk — *Blackhawk Films*

America Live in Central Park   1981
Music-Performance
59876   53 mins   C   LV   P
Conceptual sequences combine with stirring performances as the folk-rock group America offers this concert of hits including "Tin Man," "Ventura Highway," "Horse with No Name." In stereo.
Peter Clifton — *Pioneer Artists*

America/The Fall of Babylon   1924
Film-History
50636   56 mins   B/W   B, V   P, T
Neil Hamilton, Lionel Barrymore, Constance Tallmadge, Elmer Clifton, Alfred Paget
A double feature containing abridged versions of these two motion pictures. In "America", a Boston patriot and the daughter of an aristocratic Virginia Tory fall in love during the Revolutionary War. "The Fall of Babylon" is one of the stories in D.W. Griffith's "Intolerance." Silent.
D W Griffith — *Blackhawk Films*

American Alcoholic, The/Reading, Writing and Reefer   1981
Drug abuse/Alcoholism
52609   102 mins   C   CED   P
Two important contemporary issues—alcoholism and marijuana abuse—are explored in two enlightening documentaries.
NBC — *RCA VideoDiscs*

American Challenge   1983
Motorcycles
66253   65 mins   C   B, V   P
The 1982 Belgian GP where American Freddie Spencer gave Honda their first GP win in 15 years is shown.
CH Wood — *Motor Cycle Video*

American Empire   1942
Western
10921   82 mins   B/W   B, V   P
Preston Foster, Richard Dix, Frances Gifford, Leo Carrillo, directed by William McGann

Partners building cattle empire in Texas have trouble between themselves with Mexican rustlers.
United Artists; Harry Sherman Prods — *Discount Video Tapes; Video Yesteryear; Penguin Video; Cable Films*

American Empire　　1942
Western
72052　82 mins　B/W　　B, V　　　　P
Richard Dix, Preston Foster
Mexican rustlers cause trouble for two men trying to establish a cattle empire in Texas.
United Artists; Harry Sherman Productions — *Independent United Distributors*

American Friend　　1982
Drama
72178　127 mins　C　　B, V　　　　P
Dennis Hopper, Bruce Ganz
Reverence is paid to Hitchcock and Fuller in this gripping thriller.
Wim Wenders — *Pacific Arts Video*

American Gigolo　　1979
Drama
48507　117 mins　C　B, V, LV　　R, P
Richard Gere, Lauren Hutton
A professional lover becomes involved with the wife of a California state senator, then is framed for murder.
MPAA:R
Jerry Bruckheimer — *Paramount Home Video; RCA VideoDiscs*

American Graffiti　　1973
Comedy
11565　112 mins　C　B, V, LV　　　P
Richard Dreyfuss, Ronny Howard, Cindy Williams, Mackenzie Phillips, Wolfman Jack, directed by George Lucas
A look at one hectic night in the life of a group of high school friends just before they go off to college, jobs, or the army.
MPAA:PG
Universal; Francis Ford Coppola — *MCA Home Video; RCA VideoDiscs*

American History:　　1982
America Grows Up (1850-1900's)
History-US
58572　50 mins　C　　B, V　　　　P
America's growth from a nation of farms and villages to one of the leading industrial nations of the world from 1850 to 1900 is discussed.
McGraw Hill — *Mastervision*

American History:　　1982
Americans Courageous (1600-Today)
History-US
58566　50 mins　C　　B, V　　　　P
Two films featuring tales of courage: "The Gloucesterman," a filmed celebration of the townsfolk of the historic Massachusetts village who go down to the sea in ships, and "Not for Ourselves Alone," a 200 year history of America's Armed Forces.
WGBH Boston — *Mastervision*

American History:　　1982
Colonial America (1500's-1600's)
History-US
58567　50 mins　C　　B, V　　　　P
A look at the days when France, Spain, and England were fighting for the riches of the New World.
McGraw Hill — *Mastervision*

American History:　　1982
Gathering Strength (1840-1914)
History-US
58571　50 mins　C　　B, V　　　　P
The differences between the old immigrants from northern Europe and the new wave of settlers from the counties of eastern and southern Europe are discussed.
McGraw Hill — *Mastervision*

American History:　　1982
Opening the West (1860-1900)
History-US
58570　50 mins　C　　B, V　　　　P
Lincoln's efforts to reunite the nation after the bloody fratricide of the Civil War and begin the epic westward expansion are discussed.
McGraw Hill — *Mastervision*

American History: Roots of Democracy (1700's)　　1982
History-US
58568　50 mins　C　　B, V　　　　P
This program portrays the relationship between foreign trade and domestic activity which led to the rebellion against English restraints and the American Revolution.
McGraw Hill — *Mastervision*

American History: The Game of Monopoly (1870-1914)　　1982
History-US
58573　50 mins　C　　B, V　　　　P
This program examines the rise to wealth and power of the industrial titans under the

leadership of such men as Morgan, Carnegie, Rockefeller, and Vanderbilt.
McGraw Hill — *Mastervision*

American History: Two Great Crusades (1930-1945)　　1982
History-US/World War II
58575　50 mins　C　B, V　　　P
The New Deal and the Second World War are the focus of this look at the U.S.'s two modern crises.
McGraw Hill — *Mastervision*

American History: War Between the States (1800's)　　1982
History-US
58569　50 mins　C　B, V　　　P
This program analyzes the institution of slavery and shows how it came to divide our country.
McGraw Hill — *Mastervision*

American History: Warring and Roaring (1914-1929)　　1982
History-US/World War I
58574　50 mins　C　B, V　　　P
This program examines the U.S. involvement in World War I and the spirited 1920's, which ended with the stock market crash of '29.
McGraw Hill — *Mastervision*

American Hot Wax　　1978
Comedy
64781　91 mins　C　CED　　　P
Chuck Berry, Jerry Lee Lewis, Tim McIntire, Laraine Newman
1950's rock 'n' roll is revived in this tribute to pioneering disk jockey Alan Freed.
MPAA:R
Paramount — *RCA VideoDiscs*

American in Paris, An　　1951
Musical
39092　113 mins　C　B, V, LV, CED　　　P
Gene Kelly, Leslie Caron, Oscar Levant, directed by Vincente Minnelli
Gene Kelly plays an ex-G.I. artist living in Paris, who is torn between his love for a dancer, Leslie Caron, and his artistic mentor, Nina Foch. George Gershwin score includes a 15-minute ballet based on "An American in Paris." Winner of seven Academy Awards, including Best Picture.
Academy Awards '51: Best Picture; Best Story and Screenplay; Best Musical Scoring.
MGM — *MGM/UA Home Video*

American Navy in Vietnam, The　　1967
Vietnam War/Armed Forces-US
53699　29 mins　C　B, V, 3/4U　　　P
A public relations film emphasizing aircraft carrier operations, bombing strikes, and naval bombardments.
Unknown — *International Historic Films*

American Nightmare　　1983
Drama
64231　85 mins　C　B, V　　　P
Lawrence Day, Lora Stanley, Lenore Zann
A young man searches for his missing sister against a background of pornography, drug peddling and prostitution in the slums of a city.
Independent — *Media Home Entertainment*

American Nitro　　1979
Automobiles-Racing
47626　75 mins　C　B, V　　　P
Don Prudhomme, Tom McEwen, T.V. Tommy Ivo
A funny look at the grins and the gashes, the cars and the crashes, the smiles and the smashes that make drag racing one of America's most exciting sports.
MPAA:PG
Jim Kimberlin; Tim Geideman — *Paragon Video Productions*

American Ski Scene with Billy Kidd, The　　1974
Sports-Winter
33734　30 mins　C　B, V, 3/4U, Q　　　P
Billy Kidd, Claudine Longet, Clint Eastwood, Spider Sabich, Hank Kashiwa 13 pgms
Former Olympic skier Billy Kidd hosts a series of programs featuring a tour of America's most glamorous ski areas, professionals in action on the slopes, and visits with celebrities who enjoy ski life.
1.Steamboat 2.Handicapped Skiing: Winter Park, Colorado 3.New Hampshire 4.Snowbird, Utah 5.Montana 6.Aspen, Colorado 7.Stowe, Vermont 8.Park City, Utah 9.Mount Snow, Vermont 10.Jackson Hole, Wyoming; Beech Mt., North Carolina 11.Jay Peak 12.Taos, New Mexico 13.California Group
TV Sports Scene — *TV Sports Scene*

American Steam　　1981
Trains
55657　30 mins　C　B, V　　　P
This tape of steam locomotive action includes the giant No. 5, an ex-logging Heisler; the Midado No. 45 of the California Western Railway, affectionately referred to as "the skunk"; an ex-Canadian Consolidation No. 17; an ex-NKP Berkshire No. 765; and the Mikado No. 4501, the venerable workhorse of the Southern Railway.

De Luz Video — *De Luz Video*

American Steam Vol. 2 1981
Trains
59170   30 mins   C   B, V   P
A look at various steam locomotives, from old No. 346, to two of the largest on the Union Pacific's roster, No. 8444 and No. 3985. Also includes the D. and R. G. W.'s narrow gauge "Durango and Silverton," and the world famous "Cumbres and Toltec."
De Luz Video — *De Luz Video*

American Werewolf in 1981
London, An
Horror
58629   95 mins   C   B, V, LV   P
Joe Belcher, Griffin Dunne, David Schofield, Brian Glover, Jenny Agutter, Frank Oz, directed by John Landis
Special effects highlight this telling of the werewolf story, as two young Americans backpacking in northern England are attacked by a werewolf.
MPAA:R
Universal; George Folsey Jr — *MCA Home Video; RCA VideoDiscs*

Americana 1983
Drama
65603   90 mins   C   B, V   P
David Carradine, Barbara Hershey
The gripping drama captures the pain and determination of a Vietnam veteran struggling to rebuild his life.
MPAA:PG
David Carradine — *Vestron Video*

Americano, The/Variety 192?
Adventure
10119   54 mins   B/W   B, V   P, T
Douglas Fairbanks, directed by John Emerson
"The Americano" (1917) features Douglas Fairbanks, Sr. saving a revolt-ridden Caribbean country. "Variety" portrays the Flying Artinellis, a trapeze act hampered by jealous love. Both films are abridged.
Fine Arts Triangle; Unknown — *Blackhawk Films*

America's Cup 197?
1977/Heavy Weather
Slalom/Big Boats
Boating
33770   52 mins   C   B, V, 3/4U   P
"America's Cup 1977," "Heavy Weather Slalom," and "Big Boats" comprise this program about competitive and recreational sailing.
Unknown — *Sports World Cinema*

America's Team: The 1982
Dallas Cowboys 1975-79
Football
63164   120 mins   C   B, V, FO   P
Dallas Cowboys
A compilation of individual Dallas Cowboys team highlight films from the second half of the 1970's.
NFL Films — *NFL Films Video*

Amin: The Rise and Fall 1982
Drama/Biographical
69677   101 mins   C   B, V   R, P
This is a dramatization of Idi Amin's 8-year reign of terror in Uganda, which resulted in the deaths of a half million people and the near ruin of a nation.
Sharad Patel — *THORN EMI Home Video*

Amityville Horror, The 1979
Horror
53505   117 mins   C   B, V   R, P
James Brolin, Margot Kidder, Rod Steiger, Don Stroud, Murray Hamilton
The tale of the Lutz family and their supernatural experiences in their Long Island home, once the scene of a mass murder.
MPAA:R
American International Pictures — *Warner Home Video; RCA VideoDiscs; Vestron Video (disc only)*

Amityville 3D 1983
Horror
65473   98 mins   C   B, V, CED   P
Tony Roberts, Tess Harper
The infamous Amityville house is once again the centerpiece of terror.
MPAA:R
Stephen F Kesten — *Vestron Video*

Amityville II: The 1982
Possession
Horror
60438   110 mins   C   B, V, LV,   P
                              CED
Burt Young, Andrew Prine, Moses Gunn, Rutanya Alda
This prequel to "The Amityville Horror" tells the story of how the house became possessed by demonic forces.
MPAA:R
Dino DeLaurentiis — *Embassy Home Entertainment*

Amorous Adventures of 1978
Don Quixote & Sancho
Panza, The
Comedy
69019   103 mins   C   B, V   P
Corey John Fischer, Hy Pyke
Cervantes' classic becomes a hilariously erotic live action musical comedy.

MPAA:R
Raphael Nussbaum — *Imperial Video Corp*

Amos n' Andy   1952
Comedy
72953 120 mins B/W   B, V   P
Four classic episodes brought together on one
video cassette of this classic sitcom series.
CBS — *Budget Video*

Amos 'n' Andy Show, The   195?
Comedy
53052 105 mins B/W   B, V, 3/4U   P
*Alvin Childress, Spencer Williams, Tim Moore,
Ernestine Wade*
Four classic episodes from the comedy series:
"The Rare Coin" (1951), the pilot episode,
dealing with Andy's possession of a nickel worth
$250; "The Kingfish Gets Drafted" (1952), in
which a mix-up at the draft board results in the
Kingfish being summoned to serve his country;
"The Broken Clock" (1953), involving Andy and
the Kingfish trying to exchange a defective
clock; "The Invisible Glass" (1953), in which the
Kingfish learns that a stock certificate he sold to
Andy for $10 is now worth $500.
CBS — *Shokus Video*

**Amos 'n' Andy Show II,
The**   195?
Comedy
53051 100 mins B/W   B, V, 3/4U   P
*Alvin Childress, Spencer Williams, Tim Moore,
Ernestine Wade*
Four classic episodes of the comedy series:
"The Fur Coat" (1952), in which the Kingfish
sells Sapphire's coat to Andy in order to buy her
a new dress; "Cousin Effie's Will" (1952), in
which, in order to claim an inheritance, the
Kingfish adopts a son—Andy; "The Kingfish
Pawns a Gun" (1953), in which the Kingfish tries
to hock a gun he finds, and is mistaken for a
hold-up man; "Andy Buys a House" (1953), in
which the Kingfish, in order to save his new real
estate job, must sell a house that stands on
property designated for a new highway.
CBS — *Shokus Video*

**Amos 'n' Andy Show III,
The**   1952
Comedy
58830 100 mins B/W   B, V, 3/4U   P
*Alvin Childress, Spencer Williams, Tim Moore,
Ernestine Wade*
Four episodes of the classic series: "The
Diner," in which Kingfish buys a diner; "The
Counterfeiters in the Basement," in which Andy
and the Kingfish rent a room to some "printers;"
"Kingfish Has a Baby," in which Sapphire visits
the obstetrician; and "The Boarder," in which
Sapphire takes in a tenant whose singing drives
Kingfish crazy.
CBS — *Shokus Video*

**Amos 'n' Andy Show IV,
The**   1953
Comedy
59314 100 mins B/W   B, V, 3/4U   P
*Alvin Childress, Spencer Williams, Tim Moore,
Ernestine Wade*
Four more episodes from the classic series:
"The Chinchilla Business," features Kingfish
swindling Andy out of $50.00; in "Andy the
Godfather," Andy plays matchmaker; "The
Uranium Mine," features Kingfish selling Andy
some swampland; "Father by Proxy," involves a
case of mistaken identity.
CBS — *Shokus Video*

**Amos 'n' Andy Show V,
The**   1952
Comedy
62689 100 mins B/W   B, V, 3/4U   P
*Alvin Childress, Tim Moore, Spencer Williams,
Ernestine Wade*
Four more episodes from the 1951-52 TV
season: "Call Leheigh 4-9900," "The
Convention," "Andy Needs Eyeglasses" and
"The Happy Stevenses."
CBS — *Shokus Video*

**Amos 'n' Andy Show VI,
The**   1953
Comedy
63781 100 mins B/W   B, V, 3/4U   P
*Alvin Childress, Spencer Williams, Tim Moore,
Ernestine Wade*
Four episodes of this early situation comedy
from 1952-53: "Relatives," "Second
Honeymoon," "Sapphire Disappears" and
"Kingfish's Last Friend."
CBS — *Shokus Video*

**Amos "n" Andy Show VII,
The**   1952
Comedy
76014 100 mins B/W   B, V, 3/4U   P
Four classic episodes from the Amos "n" Andy
series.
CBS — *Shokus Video*

**Amos 'n' Andy—Vol 1
thru 23**   195?
Comedy
66245 55 mins B/W   B, V   R, P
Alvin Childress, Spencer Williams, Tim Moore
18 pgms
Each of the 23 individual cassettes contains two
episodes from the classic TV series.
CBS — *Video City Productions*

Amour, L'   1981
Sexuality
53785   60 mins   C B, V, 3/4U,   R, P
                                    FO

An erotic, humorous program which shows you what you should and shouldn't do to maximize your pleasure and that of your partner.
Cine Video Films — *Star Video Productions*

Amsterdam Connection　　　　1977?
Martial arts/Adventure
47705　　90 mins　　C　　B, V　　　　P
Chen Shing, Jason Pai Piu, Kid Sherrif
A film company acts as a cover for prostitution and drug smuggling, with the girls acting as international couriers.
KK Wong — *Master Arts Video*

Amsterdam Kill, The　　　　1978
Adventure
64574　　93 mins　　C　　B, V　　　　P
Robert Mitchum, Richard Egan, Keye Luke, Leslie Nielsen, Bradford Dillman
An ex-agent of the U.S. Drug Enforcement Agency is hired to hunt down the kingpin of a narcotics syndicate.
MPAA:R
Columbia — *RCA/Columbia Pictures Home Video*

Amy　　　　1981
Drama
53795　　100 mins　　C　　B, V　　　　R, P
Jenny Agutter, Barry Newman, Kathleen Nolan, Margaret O'Brien, Nanette Fabray, Chris Robinson, Lou Fant, directed by Vincent McEveety
Set in the early 1900's, the story follows the experiences of a woman after she leaves her well-to-do husband to teach at a school for the deaf and blind.
MPAA:G
Walt Disney Productions — *Walt Disney Home Video*

Anarchy, U.S.A.　　　　1966
Propaganda
69574　　78 mins　　B/W　　B, V, FO　　P
A blatantly propagandistic film which offers the premise that the Civil Rights Movement in America is part of a worldwide scheme organized by Soviet Communists to enslave mankind.
Independent — *Video Yesteryear*

And God Created Woman　　　　1957
Drama
58894　　93 mins　　C　　B, V, LV,　　P
　　　　　　　　　　　　CED
Brigitte Bardot, Curt Jurgens, Jean-Louis Trintignant, Christian Marquand
An eighteen-year-old is given a home by a local family with three handsome young sons.
Raoul J Levy — *Vestron Video*

...And Justice for All　　　　1979
Drama
52750　　120 mins　　C　　B, V　　　　P
Al Pacino, Jack Warden, John Forsythe, Lee Strasberg, directed by Norman Jewison
A young lawyer battles not only one-on-one injustice in the courts, but the whole system as well.
MPAA:R
Norman Jewison; Patrick Palmer — *RCA/Columbia Pictures Home Video; RCA VideoDiscs*

And Now for Something Completely Different　　　　1972
Comedy
47782　　89 mins　　C　　B, V　　　　P
John Cleese, Michael Palin, Eric Idle, Graham Chapman, Terry Gilliam, Terry Jones
A compilation of skits from BBC-TV's "Monty Python's Flying Circus" featuring Monty Python's own weird, hilarious brand of humor.
Patricia Casey — *RCA/Columbia Pictures Home Video*

And Now the Screaming Starts　　　　1973
Horror
54913　　87 mins　　C　　B, V, 3/4U　　P
Peter Cushing, Herbert Lom, Patrick Magee, Ian Ogilvy, Stephanie Beacham, Geoffrey Whitehead, Guy Rolfe, directed by Roy Ward Baker
The young bride-to-be of the lord of a British manor house is greeted by bloody faces at the window, a severed hand, and five corpses.
MPAA:R
Cinerama Releasing — *Nostalgia Merchant*

And Then There Were None　　　　1945
Mystery
11602　　97 mins　　B/W　　B, V　　　　P
Louis Hayward, Barry Fitzgerald, Walter Huston
Based on Agatha Christie's play about ten people invited to an island who are murdered one by one.
20th Century Fox — *VCI Home Video*

Anderson Tapes, The　　　　1971
Suspense
21279　　98 mins　　C　　B, V　　　　P
Sean Connery, Dyan Cannon, Martin Balsam, directed by Sidney Lumet
The story of an epic million-dollar robbery of a luxury apartment house. Based on the novel by Lawrence Sanders.
MPAA:PG
Columbia — *RCA/Columbia Pictures Home Video*

Android   1982
Science fiction
76019   80 mins   C   B, V   P
Klaus Kinski, Don Opper, Brie Howard
A classic saga of men versus machines
combining science fiction, suspense and cloned
romance.
MPAA:PG
Mary Ann Fisher — *Media Home
Entertainment*

Andromeda Strain, The   1971
Science fiction
58213   131 mins   C   B, V   P
*Arthur Hill, David Wayne, James Olson, Kate
Reid, Paula Kelly, directed by Robert Wise*
A satellite falls back to earth carrying a deadly
bacteria which must be identified in time to save
the population from extermination.
MPAA:G
Universal; Robert Wise — *MCA Home Video*

Andy Warhol's Dracula   1975
Horror
56928   106 mins   C   B, V   R, P
*Joe Dallesandro, Udo Kier, Arno Juergling,
directed by Paul Morrissey*
Sex and camp humor, as well as a large dose of
blood, highlight this tale of the gardener who
beds the young ladies and finally does Dracula
in.
MPAA:R
Bryanston Pictures — *Video Gems*

**Andy Warhol's
Frankenstein**   1975
Horror
56929   95 mins   C   B, V   R, P
*Joe Dallesandro, Monique Van Vooren, Udo
Kier, directed by Paul Morrissey*
One of the most outrageous versions of
Frankenstein, featuring plenty of gore and sex.
MPAA:R
Bryanston Pictures — *Video Gems*

**Andy's Gang—Ramar of
the Jungle**   195?
Adventure
17247   60 mins   B/W   B, V   P
Jon Hall
An episode from the television series "Andy's
Gang" starring Andy Devine and featuring the
serial "Ramar of the Jungle."
NBC — *Video Connection*

Angel   1975
Cartoons/Adventure
56747   48 mins   C   B, V   P
Animated
An animated adventure laced with fantasy,
magic, and music which tells the story of an
independent girl and her travel companions, a
lovable dog and a talking cat. Available in
English and Spanish versions.
EL, SP
ZIV International — *Media Home
Entertainment*

Angel   1984
Drama
65744   94 mins   C   B, V   R, P
*Donna Wilkes, Cliff Gorman, Susan Tyrell, Dick
Shawn*
A 15-year old honor student attends an
expensive Los Angeles private school during
the daytime and by night becomes Angel, a
streetwise prostitute making a living amid the
slime and sleaze of Hollywood Boulevard.
MPAA:R
Roy Watts; Donald P Borchers — *THORN EMI
Home Video*

Angel and the Badman   1947
Western
00282   100 mins   B/W   B, V, 3/4U   P
John Wayne, Gail Russell, Irene Rich
Notorious badman is humanized by the love of a
young Quaker girl.
Republic — *Nostalgia Merchant; Sheik Video;
Discount Video Tapes; Video Dimensions;
Ampro Video Productions; Cable Films; VCII;
Penguin Video; NTA Home Entertainment;
Video Connection; Video Yesteryear; Budget
Video; Cinema Concepts; Western Film & Video
Inc; Media Home Entertainment*

Angel of H.E.A.T.   1982
Adventure
62862   90 mins   C   B, V, LV,   P
                                  CED
Marilyn Chambers
A female super-agent is on a mission to save
the world from total destruction.
MPAA:R
Myrl A. Schreibman; Hal Kant — *Vestron Video*

Angel on My Shoulder   1946
Fantasy
08862   101 mins   B/W   B, V, 3/4U   P
*Paul Muni, Claude Rains, Anne Baxter, Onslow
Stevens*
A murdered convict returns to earth as a
respected judge.
United Artists — *Penguin Video; Budget Video;
Sheik Video; Cable Films; VCII; Video
Connection; Discount Video Tapes; Classic
Video Cinema Collector's Club*

Angel on My Shoulder   1980
Fantasy
64982   96 mins   C   B, V, CED   P
*Peter Strauss, Richard Kiley, Barbara Hershey,
Janis Paige*
In this remake of the 1946 classic, a small-time
hood wrongfully executed for murder comes

back as an incorruptible district attorney, with a little help from the devil.
Mace Neufeld Productions — *Embassy Home Entertainment*

Angela 1977
Drama
65430 91 mins C B, V P
Sophia Loren, Steve Railsback, John Huston
An extraordinary love story which transpires between a mother and son who after a twenty-three year separation meet again, unaware that they are related.
20th Century Fox — *Embassy Home Entertainment*

Angelo My Love 1983
Drama
66350 91 mins C B, V P
Robert Duvall wrote this compassionate tale of New York's gypsy community, following the adventures of 12-year-old Angelo Evans, the streetwise son of a fortune teller.
MPAA:R
Cinecom International — *RCA/Columbia Pictures Home Video*

Angels Die Hard 1974
Drama
35364 86 mins C B, V P
William Smith
Trouble follows an outlaw's entrance into a small town. Motorcycle gang action, extremely violent.
Charles Beach Dickerson — *Budget Video*

Angels with Dirty Faces 1938
Drama
66076 97 mins B/W B, V, CED P
James Cagney, Pat O'Brien, Humphrey Bogart, Ann Sheridan, George Bancroft, Dead End Kids
A classic in which two young hoodlums grow up-one to the priesthood and one to prison. The priest then tries to keep a group of young toughs from idolizing the famed gangster and following in his footsteps.
Warner Bros — *CBS/Fox Video*

Animal Crackers 1930
Comedy
14018 98 mins B/W B, V P
Marx Brothers, Lillian Roth, Margaret Dumont, directed by Victor Neerman
One of the funniest Marx Brothers films, "Animal Crackers" is a screen classic. Complete with the Harry Ruby music score—including Groucho's "Hooray for Captain Spaulding."
Paramount — *MCA Home Video; RCA VideoDiscs*

Animal Farm 1955
Satire
53287 73 mins C B, V, FO P
Animated, directed by John Halas and Joy Batchelor
An animated version of George Orwell's classic political satire about a barnyard full of animals who parallel the growth of totalitarian dictatorships.
Louis de Rochemont; Halas and Batchelor — *Video Yesteryear; Sheik Video; Video Connection; Budget Video; Cable Films; Western Film & Video Inc; Discount Video Tapes*

Animal House 1978
Comedy
11567 109 mins C B, V, LV P
John Belushi, Tim Matheson, John Verna, Donald Sutherland, Thomas Hulce, directed by John Landis
Every college tradition from fraternity rush week to the homecoming pageant, is irreverently and relentlessly mocked in this wild comedy.
MPAA:R
Universal; Matty Simmons; Ivan Reitman — *MCA Home Video; RCA VideoDiscs*

Animal Quiz # 1 1984
Animals
65638 60 mins C B, V R, P
This series is an invitation to children and their parents to test their animal expertise. This volume features "Looney Gooney," a look at the comical aerodynamics of the Gooney bird of Midway Island; the dragon-like lizards of Indonesia in "Komodo Dragons"; and the San Diego Zoo's collection of animal infants in "Zoo Babies."
Walt Disney — *Walt Disney Home Video*

Animal Quiz # 2 1984
Animals
65639 60 mins C B, V R, P
This volume takes viewers to the arid state of Chihuahua, Mexico, for a glimpse of the "Mexican Grizzly", an oasis-like watering hole in Africa for "Kenya's Spring of Life"; and the frigid, desolate realm of the Emperor penguin in "Adventure Antarctica."
Walt Disney — *Walt Disney Home Video*

Animal Quiz # 3 1984
Animals
65640 60 mins C B, V R, P
The third volume provides insights to "The Strange Creatures of the Galapagos," and traces the training and breeding of racehorses in "Thoroughbred" and the monkeyshines performed by "The Apes of Gibraltar."
Walt Disney — *Walt Disney Home Video*

Animal Quiz #4   1984
Animals
72799   84 mins   C   B, V   P
Viewers are shown the creatures of the Sonoran desert, visit the famed Masai warriors of Africa and participate in a Pacific shark watch.
Walt Disney Productions — *Walt Disney Home Video*

Animal Quiz #5   1984
Animals
72800   84 mins   C   B, V   P
Viewers witness unique structures built by animals, visit the Mexican desert where jaguars roam and observe the crocodile population of the Nile.
Walt Disney Productions — *Walt Disney Home Video*

Animal Quiz #6   1984
Animals
72801   84 mins   C   B, V   P
The big cats of South Africa are filmed in their habitat, as are Japan's snow monkeys.
Walt Disney Productions — *Walt Disney Home Video*

Animals Are Beautiful People   1974
Wildlife/Documentary
58216   92 mins   C   B, V   R, P
Narrated by Paddy O'Byrne, directed by Jamie Uys
A profile of the African wilderness that captures the unique mood of the animal community.
MPAA:G
Mimosa Films — *Warner Home Video*

Animalympics   1980
Cartoons
47378   78 mins   C   B, V   R, P
Voices of Gilda Radner, Billy Crystal, Harry Shearer, Michael Fremer
In this animated feature, animals from all over the world gather for the first Animal Olympics—and the fur really flies.
Lisberger Studios Film — *Warner Home Video*

Animation in the 1930's   193?
Cartoons
11288   57 mins   B/W   B, V, FO   P
Animated
A collection of nine cartoons from the studios of Warner Brothers and Max Fleischer, including "Crosby, Columbo and Vallee," "Three's a Crowd," "Hollywood Capers," "Songs You Like to Sing—Margie," "Grampy's Indoor Outing," "Betty in Blunderland," "Let's Sing with Popeye," "Happy You and Me," and "Sinkin' in the Bathtub."
Warner Bros; Max Fleischer — *Video Yesteryear*

Animation Wonderland   1975
Cartoons
58587   75 mins   C   B, V   R, P
Animated
A collection of delightful animated shorts for children.
Peabody Award: Best Children's Entertainment.
MPAA:G
John Wilson — *Video Gems*

Anna Karenina   1974
Dance
74490   81 mins   C   B, V   P
Maya Pilsetskaya, Alexander Godunov
This is a ballet based on Leo Tolstoy's famous novel.
Sovexportfilm USSR — *Video Arts International*

Anna to the Infinite Power   1984
Drama
65466   ? mins   C   B, V   P
Dina Merrill, Martha Byrne, Mark Patton
Based on the book of the same name, this powerful drama follows a young girl who desperately seeks to unravel the mystery of her life. In Beta Hi-Fi.
Bruce Graham; Blue Marble Company Films — *RCA/Columbia Pictures Home Video*

Anne Byrd's Cookery   1981
Cookery
59912   100 mins   C   LV   P
Anne Byrd teaches us how to make quiches, omelettes, crepes, and various Chinese dishes.
AM Available
Inedco Productions — *INEDCO Productions*

Annie   1982
Musical
63437   130 mins   C   B, V, LV   P
Aileen Quinn, Carol Burnett, Albert Finney, Bernadette Peters, Ann Reinking, Tim Curry, directed by John Huston
Based on the hit Broadway musical, this is the story of America's favorite orphan, a plucky, red-haired girl who dreams of a life outside her dingy orphanage.
MPAA:PG
Columbia; Ray Stark — *RCA/Columbia Pictures Home Video; RCA VideoDiscs*

Annie Hall   1977
Comedy
13322   94 mins   C   B, V, LV   P
Woody Allen, Diane Keaton, Paul Simon, Carol Kane, directed by Woody Allen
Autobiographical love story with incisive Allenisms on romance, relationships, fame, and other topics.

Academy Awards '77: Best Picture; Best
Actress (Keaton); Best Direction (Allen); Best
Screenplay (Allen, Brickman). MPAA:PG
United Artists; Jack Rollins; Charles H
Joffe — *CBS/Fox Video; RCA VideoDiscs*

Annie Oakley   1935
Drama
66335   90 mins   B/W   B, V, 3/4U   P
*Barbara Stanwyck, Preston Foster, Melvyn
Douglas, directed by George Stevens*
A biographical drama based on the life and
legend of sharpshooter Annie Oakley and her
on-off relationship with Wild Bill Hickok.
RKO — *Nostalgia Merchant*

Any Family   19??
Family/Animals
69636   18 mins   C   B, V   P
A northern California family of third generation
gypsies raises every type of horse and tours the
country with a mini big top circus and Royal
Horse Fair.
Jay Miracle — *Mercedes Maharis Productions*

Any Which Way You Can   1980
Comedy
58217   116 mins   C   B, V, LV   R, P
Clint Eastwood, Sondra Locke, Ruth Gordon
This sequel to "Every Which Way But Loose"
finds brawler Philo Beddoe and Clyde the
orangutan facing a big bout with big bucks at
stake.
MPAA:PG
Warner Bros — *Warner Home Video; RCA
VideoDiscs*

Anybody Can Catch Fish   197?
Fishing
33742   30 mins   C   B, V, 3/4U,   P
                              Q
Characteristics and habits of northern pike and
walleyes are seen through the fishing adventure
of an old expert and young novice companion.
TV Sports Scene — *TV Sports Scene*

Apache   1954
Western
55583   91 mins   C   CED   P
Burt Lancaster, John Mc Intire, Jean Peters
The chronicle of a bitter battle between the
Indians and the U.S. cavalry in the struggle for
the west.
EL, SP
United Artists — *CBS/Fox Video*

Apache Rose   1947
Western
44149   54 mins   B/W   B, V   P
*Roy Rogers, Dale Evans, Olin Howard, George
Meeker*

Gambling boat owner plots to gain control of oil
found on Vegas Ranch.
Republic — *Video Connection*

Apartment, The   1960
Comedy-Drama
58948   125 mins   B/W   CED   P
*Jack Lemmon, Shirley MacLaine, Fred
MacMurray, Ray Walston, Edie Adams, directed
by Billy Wilder*
A lonely, ambitious clerk rents out his apartment
to philandering executives and finds that one of
them is after his own girl.
Academy Awards '60: Best Picture; Best
Director; Best Screenplay (Wilder, I.A.L.
Diamond).
United Artists — *RCA VideoDiscs*

Ape Man, The   1943
Horror
10372   70 mins   B/W   B, V, 3/4U   R, P
Wallace Ford, Bela Lugosi
A scientist turns himself into a murderous ape.
Prime TV — *Cable Films; Sheik Video; Video
Connection; Discount Video Tapes*

Aphrodite   1983
Drama
65360   89 mins   C   B, V   P
Valerie Kaprisky
A steamy drama based on Pierre Louy's
masterpiece of erotic literature.
Adolphe Viezzi — *Vestron Video*

Apocalypse Now   1979
Drama
58493   139 mins   C   B, V, LV   R, P
*Marlon Brando, Martin Sheen, Robert Duvall,
Fredric Forrest, Sam Bottoms, Dennis Hopper,
directed by Francis Ford Coppola*
Coppola's epic set during the Vietnam War,
concerning one officer's trip through the jungle
to locate and eliminate a megalomaniac officer
whose methods have become "unsound."
Academy Awards '79: Best Cinematography;
Best Sound. MPAA:R
United Artists; Francis Ford
Coppola — *Paramount Home Video; RCA
VideoDiscs*

Apple, The   1980
Musical
59996   90 mins   C   B, V   P
*Catherine Mary Stewart, Alan Love, Grace
Kennedy*
A futuristic musical celebrating New York, life
and youth.
MPAA:PG
Independent — *Paragon Video Productions*

Apple Dumpling Gang, The — 1975
Comedy
44299   100 mins   C   B, V   R, P
Bill Bixby, Susan Clark, Don Knotts, Tim Conway, David Wayne, Slim Pickens, Harry Morgan
Three frisky kids strike it rich and trigger the wildest bank robbery in the gold-mad West.
MPAA:G
Walt Disney — *Walt Disney Home Video; RCA VideoDiscs*

Apple Dumpling Gang Rides Again, The — 1979
Comedy/Western
55570   88 mins   C   B, V   R, P
Tim Conway, Don Knotts, Tim Matheson, Kenneth Mars, Harry Morgan, Jack Elam, directed by Vincent McEveety
Two lovable hombres terrorize the West in their bungling attempt to go straight.
Walt Disney — *Walt Disney Home Video*

Apprenticeship of Duddy Kravitz, The — 1974
Comedy-Drama
59859   121 mins   C   B, V   R, P
Richard Dreyfuss, Randy Quaid, Denholm Elliot, Jack Warden, Micheline Lanctot, Joe Silver, directed by Ted Kotcheff
A young Jewish man in Montreal circa 1948 is driven by an insatiable need to be a "somebody."
MPAA:PG
Paramount — *Paramount Home Video*

April Wine — 1981
Music-Performance
58467   67 mins   C   B, V   R, P
The hard-rock group, April Wine, performs hits from their Capitol LP's.
EMI Music — *THORN EMI Home Video; Pioneer Artists*

Aqua Follies — 1981
Natural resources
51999   25 mins   C   B, V, 3/4U, Q   P
The physical nature and characteristics of water are described. How this resource is being wasted and what man can do to protect it are discussed.
TV Sports Scene — *TV Sports Scene*

Arabian, Palomino and Saddlebred — 19??
Animals
69649   77 mins   C   B, V   P
Four separate programs about different breeds of horses comprise this tape. "The Proud Breed" is about Arabians; "The Color of Gold" covers Palomino history; and "Showtime for Saddlebreds" and "A Horse of History" look at Saddlebreds.
Intl Arabian Horse Assoc; Palomino Horse Breeders of America; American Saddlebred Horse Assoc — *Mercedes Maharis Productions*

Arch of Triumph — 1948
Drama
64537   120 mins   B/W   B, V   P
Ingrid Bergman, Charles Boyer, Charles Laughton, directed by Lewis Milestone
An Austrian refugee searches for the Gestapo agent who tortured him and killed his friends.
United Artists; Enterprise — *NTA Home Entertainment*

Archie — 1978
Cartoons
69624   60 mins   C   B, V   R, P
Animated
Three separate cartoons feature the escapades of Archie, Jughead, Veronica, Betty, Reggie, Mr. Weatherbee and the rest of the gang from Riverdale High.
Filmation — *THORN EMI Home Video*

Archie, Volume 2 — 1978
Cartoons
65745   23 mins   C   B, V   R, P
Animated
Archie and the "Gang" carry on with their hilarious pranks, while Mr. Weatherbee loses his glasses and thinks Hot Dog is the Commodore of a ship.
Filmation — *THORN EMI Home Video*

Arctic Canoe Race, The — 1984
Boating
69913   28 mins   C   B, V   P
This program documents a 1,000 mile canoe and kayak paddling marathon through Finland.
Chrisfilm and Video — *Gravity Sports Films*

Are You in the House Alone? — 1978
Suspense
65664   100 mins   C   B, V   P
Blythe Danner, Kathleen Beller, Tony Bill, Scott Colomby
A high school coed becomes the target of a terror campaign.
Charles Fries — *Worldvision Home Video*

Argentinisima I — 1972
Music
47860   115 mins   C   B, V   P
Inspired by the verses of famed singers like Mercedes Sosa and Atahualpa Yupanqui, various singers and groups relate the tales of

the different regions and music from past and present Argentina. In Spanish.
SP
Luis Repetto — *Media Home Entertainment*

Arizona Bound   1941
Western
15411   57 mins   B/W   B, V   P
Buck Jones, Tim McCoy
Action and gun-play in Arizona.
Monogram — *Video Connection; Discount Video Tapes*

Arizona Days   1937
Western
08791   56 mins   B/W   B, V   P
Tex Ritter, Eleanor Stewart
Cowboys join a minstrel group and rescue the show when a group of toughs try to break it up.
Grand National — *VCI Home Video; Penguin Video; Video Connection; Video Yesteryear; Discount Video Tapes*

Arizona Raiders   1965
Western
11603   88 mins   C   B, V   P
Audie Murphy, Buster Crabbe
Arizona rangers hunt down killers who have been terrorizing the territory.
Columbia; Grant Whytock — *VCI Home Video; Video Connection; Penguin Video*

Arizona Stagecoach   1942
Western
08796   59 mins   B/W   B, V, 3/4U   P
Ray Corrigan, John King, Max Terhune
Innocent man is accused of murder; "Range Busters" step in and find the real murderer.
Monogram — *Penguin Video; Video Connection*

Arizona Terror   1931
Western
11604   64 mins   B/W   B, V   P
Ken Maynard
Fear and vengeance plague Arizona settlers.
Tiffany — *Video Connection*

Armed Forces Workout   1984
Physical fitness
72536   75 mins   C   B, V, CED   P
A U.S. Marine Corps drill instructor instructs a program of daily exercises designed to strengthen one's body and attitude toward working-out.
K Tel International Inc — *Vestron Video*

A.R.M.S. Concert, The   1983
Music-Performance
76642   60 mins   C   B, V   P
Jeff Beck, Eric Clapton, Bill Wyman

An ensemble of rock-n-roll stars from Eric Clapton to Bill Wyman perform in this live benefit concert.
Glyn Johns — *Music Media*

Army on Wheels   1938
Armed Forces-US
72482   27 mins   B/W   B, V, 3/4U   P
The various military uses of trucks on peacetime activities at American military bases are shown in this period documentary.
Dodge Motor Company and the US War Department — *International Historic Films*

Arnold Schwarzenegger: 1982
Mr. Olympia (The Comeback)
Sports-Minor/Physical fitness
59566   50 mins   C   B, V   P
Hosted by Arnold Schwarzenegger
A filmed record of the seventh annual body-building contest for the World Title, comprised of former Mr. Universe winners.
Aspac Prods — *Mastervision*

Around the World in 80   1956
Days
Adventure
65322   178 mins   C   B, V   P
David Niven, Shirley MacLaine, Frank Sinatra, Marlene Dietrich, Robert Newton, Cantinflas
An unflappable Victorian Era Englishman wagers that he can circumnavigate the earth in four-score days, which sends him on a spectacular journey. In VHS stereo and Beta Hi-fi.
MPAA:G
Michael Todd — *Warner Home Video*

Arsenal   1929
Film-History/Propaganda
52341   70 mins   B/W   B, V, 3/4U   P
Semyon Svashenko, directed by Alexander Dovzhenko
Classic Russian silent film; English subtitles. A propagandist drama about strikes affecting the Russian home front during World War I.
USSR;VUFKU — *International Historic Films; Sheik Video; Classic Video Cinema Collector's Club*

Arsenic and Old Lace   1944
Comedy/Mystery
64459   158 mins   B/W   B, V   P
Cary Grant, Josephine Hull, Jean Adair, Raymond Massey, Jack Carson, John Ridgely, James Gleason, Peter Lorre, directed by Frank Capra
Grant plays Mortimer Brester, an easygoing drama critic, who discovers that his gentle maiden aunts derive pleasure from poisoning gentlemencallers and burying them in the cellar.

     (For Explanation of codes, see USE GUIDE and KEY)

Warner Bros — *CBS/Fox Video; RCA VideoDiscs*

Art of High-Impact Kicking, The   1982
Martial arts
64016   69 mins   C   B, V   P
Master Hwang Jang Lee demonstrates fundamental techniques involved in using the feet as weaponry.
Ng See Yuen; Roy Horan — *World Video Enterprises*

Art of the Baltic States   1975
Arts
72497   30 mins   C   B, V, 3/4U   P
A collection of folk art, music, theater and dances of Estonia, Latvia and Lithuania. English subtitles.
Foreign — *International Historic Films*

Arthur   1981
Comedy
58218   97 mins   C   B, V, LV   R, P
Dudley Moore, Liza Minnelli, John Gielgud, Geraldine Fitzgerald, directed by Steve Gordon
A billionaire stands to lose everything unless he gives up the woman he loves. Music by Burt Bacharach.
MPAA:PG
Orion Pictures — *Warner Home Video; RCA VideoDiscs*

Arthur Godfrey Show, The   1955
Variety
12848   29 mins   B/W   B, V, FO   P
Arthur Godfrey, Tony Martin, Jack E. Leonard, Carmel DeQuinn
Godfrey's ukelele solo in "Ain't She Sweet" and Jack E. Leonard's rock version of "Sittin' on Top of the World" highlight this program.
CBS — *Video Yesteryear*

Artur Rubinstein   1981
Music-Performance
57252   78 mins   B/W   B, V   P
Artur Rubinstein, Gregor Piatigorsky, Jascha Heifetz
Rare footage never before seen showcases this great violinist in his home and in the recording studio. Rubinstein is featured in two solo spots and in a trio with cellist Gregor Piatigorsky and violinist Jascha Heifetz.
Kultur — *Kultur*

As You Like It   1936
Comedy
11393   96 mins   B/W   B, V, FO   P
Elisabeth Bergner, Laurence Olivier, Henry Ainley
A Duke's banished daughter poses as a man in this Shakespearian comedy.
Inter Allied — *Video Yesteryear; Blackhawk Films; Sheik Video; Ampro Video Productions; Cable Films; Video Connection; Budget Video; Western Film & Video Inc; Discount Video Tapes; Classic Video Cinema Collector's Club*

Ashford and Simpson   1982
Music-Performance
63351   75 mins   C   B, V   R, P
Nick Ashford, Valerie Simpson
This well-known duo perform their greatest hits live in concert, including "Ain't No Mountain High Enough," "Ain't Nothing Like the Real Thing" and "Let's Go Get Stoned."
EMI Music — *THORN EMI Home Video; Pioneer Artists; RCA VideoDiscs*

Ashford and Simpson   1984
Music-Performance
75912   21 mins   C   B, V   P
This program presents the popular 60's group Ashford and Simpson performing their best songs.
Capital Records Inc — *Sony Corporation of America*

Asi No Hay Cama Que Aguante   1980
Comedy
47856   95 mins   C   B, V   P
Chico Novarro, Patricia Dal
Horacio and Claudio pretend to have money to win the friendship of Marcela and Silvana, who appear to be wealthy. In Spanish.
SP
Nicolas Carreras; Luis Repetto — *Media Home Entertainment*

Asia in Asia   1983
Music-Performance
72217   60 mins   C   B, V   P
Fusion rock group Asia plays a concert at Budokan, Japan.
Independent — *Vestron Video*

Ask Video Dave, Vol. I   1983
Video
66157   120 mins   C   B, V   P
A look inside your VCR (VHS) showing trouble spots and electronic features.
Video Kit Manufacturing Company — *The Video Kit Manufacturing Company*

Assassin, The   1979
Martial arts
64906   86 mins   C   B, V   P
Sonny Chiba
An athletic karate fighter poses as an underworld figure and infiltrates the largest gang in Japan where he is hired as a hit man.

Toei Company — *CBS/Fox Video*

Assassin of Youth　　1935
Drama/Exploitation
08890　70 mins　B/W　B, V, 3/4U　　P
A girl is introduced to marijuana and soon becomes involved in "the thrills of wild parties," and the horrors of the "killer weed."
Unknown — *Penguin Video; Western Film & Video Inc*

Assault　　1970
Drama
59827　89 mins　C　B, V　　P
Suzy Kendall, Lesley-Anne Down, Frank Finlay
Violent sex murders in a girl's school have the police baffled. The school's pretty art teacher offers to act as bait in order to catch the murderer.
George H Brown — *Embassy Home Entertainment*

Assault on Agathon　　197?
Adventure
59349　95 mins　C　B, V　　R, P
Nina Van Pallandt, Marianne Faithful
An "executed" W.W. II guerila leader returns to lead a revolution.
MPAA:PG
Heritage Enterprises — *Video Gems*

Assault on Precinct 13　　1979
Horror
42910　91 mins　C　B, V　　P
This movie from the producers of "Halloween" takes a frightening look at the destruction of law and order.
EL, SP
Irwin Yablans — *Media Home Entertainment*

Assignment Skybolt　　1984
Adventure/Suspense
72339　99 mins　C　B, V　　P
A James Bond-inspired spy film.
MPAA:R
Film Producers — *Best Film & Video Corporation*

Assorted U.S.
Government War Films
Program No. 1　　1943
World War II/Propaganda
53675　30 mins　B/W　B, V, 3/4U　　P
Includes "Japs Over China," "Pacific Step Up," "Strictly for Eskimos," "Aussies and Yanks in New Guinea," "Mountain Fighting in Italy," "Target Germany," and "Attack at the Marshalls."
Unknown — *International Historic Films*

Assorted U.S.
Government War Films
Program No. 2　　1944
World War II/Propaganda
53676　32 mins　B/W　B, V, 3/4U　　P
Includes "Private Snafu," "What Makes a Battle," "How Good Is a Gun," "The Earthmovers."
Unknown — *International Historic Films*

Astro Zombies, The　　1970
Horror
05526　83 mins　C　B, V　　P
John Carradine, Wendell Corey
Human transplants go berserk and threaten the safety of a city.
MPAA:PG
Ram Ltd — *Wizard Video*

Asylum　　1972
Horror
54912　100 mins　C　B, V, 3/4U　　P
Peter Cushing, Herbert Lom, Britt Ekland, Barbara Parkins, Patrick Magee, Barry Morse, directed by Roy Ward Baker
A search of an eerie insane asylum for its former director, now a raving maniac, leads a young psychiatrist on a tour of terror. His interviews with inmates reveal their case histories in flashback—all weird, horrible, or murderous.
MPAA:PG
Cinerama Releasing — *Nostalgia Merchant*

At Gunpoint　　1955
Drama
65687　81 mins　C　B, V　　P
Fred MacMurray, Dorothy Malone
A store owner becomes the town hero when, by accident, he shoots and kills a bank robber.
Allied Artists — *NTA Home Entertainment*

At Sword's Point　　1952
Adventure
00295　81 mins　C　B, V, 3/4U　　P
Cornel Wilde, Maureen O'Hara
Adventure tale based on "The Three Musketeers."
RKO — *Nostalgia Merchant*

At the Circus　　1939
Comedy
59360　87 mins　B/W　B, V　　P
The Marx Brothers, Margaret Dumont, Kenny Baker, Florence Rice, Eve Arden, Nat Pendleton, Fritz Feld
The Marx Brothers, as circus performers, cause their usual comic insanity. Groucho sings, "Lydia the Tattooed Lady."
MGM — *MGM/UA Home Video*

At the Earth's Core 1976
Science fiction
65135 90 mins C B, V R, P
Doug McClure, Peter Cushing, Caroline Munro
A Victorian scientist invents a giant burrowing machine, which he and his crew use to dig deeply into the Earth. To their surprise, they discover a lost world of subhuman creatures and prehistoric monsters.
MPAA:PG
American International — *Warner Home Video*

At War with the Army 1950
Comedy
39009 93 mins B/W B, V P
Dean Martin, Jerry Lewis, Polly Bergen
Martin and Lewis' first starring appearance, as soldiers getting mixed up in all kinds of wild situations at their army base.
Paramount — *Electric Video; Sheik Video; Cable Films; Video Connection; Video Yesteryear*

Atalante, L' 1934
Film-Avant-garde
06225 82 mins B/W B, V P
Dita Parlo, Jean Daste, Michel Simon, directed by Jean Vigo
A bride on her honeymoon becomes bored and starts flirting with other men. French with English subtitles.
FR
J L Nounez; Gaumont — *Budget Video; Sheik Video; Video Yesteryear; Penguin Video; Western Film & Video Inc; Discount Video Tapes*

Atlantic City 1981
Drama
53930 104 mins C B, V, LV R, P
Burt Lancaster, Susan Sarandon, Kate Reid, Michel Piccoli, Hollis Mc Laren, directed by Louis Malle
A smalltime, aging mafia hood falls in love with a clam bar waitress, and they share the spoils of a big score against the backdrop of a changing Atlantic City.
MPAA:R
Dennis Heroux; Cine Neighbor; Selta Films — *Paramount Home Video; RCA VideoDiscs*

Atoll K 1951
Comedy
05436 82 mins B/W B, V, 3/4U P, T
Stan Laurel, Oliver Hardy, Suzy Delair
Laurel and Hardy inherit an island and turn it into a Utopia, but their peace is disturbed when uranium is discovered.
Exploitation Films; Franco-London Films — *Penguin Video; Video Yesteryear; Discount Video Tapes; Sheik Video; Vestron Video (disc only)*

Atom Age Vampire 1961
Horror
65198 71 mins B/W B, V P
Alberto Lupo, Susanne Loret, Sergio Fantoni
A mad scientist falls in love with a woman who has been disfigured in an auto crash. To remove her scars, he treats her with a formula derived from the glands of freshly killed women. English dubbed.
Lion Film; Topaz Film Corp — *Video Yesteryear*

Atom Ant 196?
Cartoons
47686 53 mins C B, V P
Animated
Eight episodes in which the ant with atomic strength battles Ferocious Flea and Karate Ant.
Hanna Barbera — *Worldvision Home Video*

Atomic Cafe, The 1982
Documentary/Satire
64210 92 mins C B, V R, P
A chillingly humorous compilation of newsreels and government films of the 1940's and 1950's that show America's preoccupation with the A-Bomb. Some sequences are in black and white.
Archives Project Inc — *THORN EMI Home Video*

Ator the Fighting Eagle 1983
Adventure/Fantasy
69392 98 mins C B, V R, P
Miles O'Keeffe
According to legend, Ator, son of Thorn, must put an end to the tragic Dynasty of the Spiders.
MPAA:PG
Comworld Pictures — *THORN EMI Home Video*

Atrocities of the Orient 1959
Drama
48736 70 mins B/W B, V, 3/4U P
Shocking scenes of the Japanese invasion of the Philippines all the way through to the final liberation of the Filipinos.
Unknown — *Penguin Video*

Attack Force Z 1984
Adventure
74107 84 mins C B, V P
Mel Gibson, John Philip Law, John Waters
An elite volunteer corps, Force Z, is given the dangerous mission of finding a defected Japanese government official who was lost in a plane crash somewhere in the South Pacific.
Lee Robinson — *VCL Home Video*

Attack of the Killer Tomatoes 1977
Comedy
42912 87 mins C B, V P

In this low-budget spoof, tomatoes suddenly turn savage and begin attacking people. Many familiar cliches of the science fiction genre are parodied and a few musical numbers are included.
MPAA:PG EL, SP
Four Square Productions — *Media Home Entertainment*

Attack of the Robots   1966
Comedy
66133   88 mins   B/W   B, V, FO   P
Eddie Constantine, Fernando Rey
A spy spoof about individuals being turned into robots.
American Intl Pictures — *Video Yesteryear*

Attack!—The Battle of New Britain   1944
World War II
53654   45 mins   B/W   B, V, 3/4U   P
Frank Capra supervised production on this film, which provides a record of the attacks on Arawa and Cape Gouster on New Britain.
Unknown — *International Historic Films*

Audience with Mel Brooks, An   1984
Comedy
75490   60 mins   C   B, V   P
Mell Brooks, Anne Bancroft
Mel Brooks puts on a number of sketches, sings and tells jokes in this live comedy concert appearance.
Prism — *Prism*

Auditions   1973
Comedy
60436   82 mins   C   B, V   P
Real, bizarre, erotic and outrageously funny auditions for X-rated stardom.
MPAA:R
Charles Band Productions — *Wizard Video*

Audrey Rose   1977
Horror
72464   113 mins   C   B, V   P
Marsha Mason, Anthony Hopkins, John Beck
The parents of a young girl are traumatized when a man tells them his dead daughter lives on inside her.
MPAA:PG
United Artists — *MGM/UA Home Video*

Auntie Mame   1958
Comedy
47620   161 mins   C   B, V   R, P
Rosalind Russell, Patrick Knowles, Roger Smith, Peggy Cass
A young boy is brought up by his only surviving relative—flamboyant and eccentric Auntie Mame. Part of the "A Night at the Movies"

series, this tape simulates a 1958 movie evening, with a Road Runner cartoon, "Hook, Line and Stinker," a newsreel and coming attractions for "No Time for Sergeants" and "Chase a Crooked Shadow."
Warner Bros — *Warner Home Video*

Australia: Pace and A Race of Horses   19??
Animals/Horse racing
69645   33 mins   C   B, V   P
Two programs from Australia are contained on one cassette. "Pace" tell of the cycle that one horse goes through to become a winning trotter. "A Race of Horses" transforms a simple horse race into a visual poem of style and grace.
Film Australia — *Mercedes Maharis Productions*

Austrian Enduro   1983
Motorcycles
66254   62 mins   C   B, V   P
The West's top off-road riders pit their skills against the Eastern Bloc countries in no - holds - barred international competition.
CH Wood — *Motor Cycle Video*

Author! Author!   1982
Comedy
63391   100 mins   C   B, V, CED   P
Al Pacino, Tuesday Weld, Dyan Cannon, Alan King, directed by Arthur Hill
Al Pacino portrays a struggling playwright whose wife leaves him with their son and four children from her previous marriage. Pacino becomes involved with the leading lady of his new Broadway play, but she is more concerned with the social scene than with his children.
MPAA:PG
20th Century Fox — *CBS/Fox Video*

Auto Tuneup   1980
Automobiles
44289   25 mins   C   V   P
This program can save automobile owners money on repairs because it offers tips on preventive maintenance. Step by step procedures that can be done easily at home include spark plugs and points, electrical system check up, and troubleshooting.
American Home Video Library — *American Home Video Library*

Autobiography of Miss Jane Pittman, The   1974
Drama
52333   110 mins   C   CED   P
Cecily Tyson, Odetta, Joseph Tremice
This program, based on the novel by Ernest J. Gaines, tells the story of a courageous black woman whose life spans from the Civil War to the Civil Rights movement in the 1960's.

Tomorrow Entertainment — *RCA VideoDiscs*

Autopsy 1978
Horror
69388   89 mins   C   B, V   P
Mimsi Farmer, Barry Primus, Angela Goodwin
A rash of unexplainable, spontaneous suicides
cause a college student to become emotionally
upset.
MPAA:R
Joseph Brenner — *Cinemagreats*

Autumn Born 1979
Drama
60411   76 mins   C   B, V   P
Dorothy Stratten
A young heiress is abducted by her guardian
and imprisoned while she's taught to obey his
will.
MPAA:R
North American Pictures Ltd — *Monterey
Home Video*

Avalanche 1978
Suspense
65072   91 mins   C   B, V, CED   P
*Rock Hudson, Mia Farrow, Robert Forster, Rick
Moses*
Vacationers at a new winter ski resort are at the
mercy of a monster avalanche which leaves a
path of terror and destruction in its wake.
New World Pictures — *Embassy Home
Entertainment*

Avant Garde and 193?
Experimental Film
Program No. 1
Film-Avant-garde
11290   55 mins   B/W   B, V, FO   P
A collection of five avant-garde films: "Un Chien
Andulou," by Luis Bunuel and Salvadore Dali;
"Rain," by Joris Ivens and Mannus Franken;
"Umberfall," by Erno Marzner; "Hearts of Age,"
directed by and starring Orson Welles; and
"Ballet Mecanique," by Fernand Leger.
Unknown — *Video Yesteryear*

Avant-Garde #2 192?
Film-Avant-garde
58266   42 mins   B/W   B, V, FO   P
Three avant-garde films: "Symphonie
Diagonale" (1921, Germany), by Viking
Eggeling, a Dada-ist; "L'Etoile de Mer" (1928,
France), directed by Man Ray, an early
surrealist; and, "Entr'acte" (1924, France),
directed by Rene Clair, pure cinematic imagery.
Germany; France — *Video Yesteryear*

Avengers, The 196?
Adventure
54135   50 mins   B/W   B, V   P

Diana Rigg, Patrick Macnee
This program contains an episode entitled "Dial
a Deadly Number" from this classic TV series.
Associated British Corp — *Video Dimensions;
Video Yesteryear*

Avenging Conscience, 1914
The
Film-History
11388   78 mins   B/W   B, V, FO   P
*Henry B. Walthall, Blanche Sweet, directed by
D.W. Griffith*
An early eerie horror film, based on tales of
Edgar Allen Poe. D.W. Griffith's first large-scale
feature. Silent.
Biograph — *Video Yesteryear; Sheik Video;
Classic Video Cinema Collector's Club*

Aviation Volume I 19??
Aeronautics
10151   60 mins   B/W   B, V   P, T
Newsreels highlight aviation history from Wright
Brothers through evolution of the helicopter.
Includes de Pinedo's death, the Graf Zeppelin,
Lindberg's trans-Atlantic flight, and Pan
American Clippers.
Unknown — *Blackhawk Films*

Awakening, The 1980
Horror
52717   102 mins   C   B, V   R, P
*Charlton Heston, Susannah York, Stephanie
Zimbalist*
An archeologist discovers the tomb of a
murderous queen, but upon opening the coffin,
the mummy's spirit is transferred to his baby
daughter, born at that instant.
MPAA:R
Orion Pictures — *Warner Home Video*

Ay Jalisco No Te Rajes! 197?
Drama
52792   90 mins   C   B, V   P
Rodolfo De Anda, Angel Garasa, Sonia Infante
General Carvajal forbids Salvador Perez Gomez
to woo his daughter. Salvador kills him and must
flee from the general's sons. One year later he
finds the daughter in a convent, and she
professes her love for him. In Spanish.
SP
Gonzalo Elvira — *Media Home Entertainment*

B

Babe Ruth: The Fence 1954
Buster
Biographical/Baseball
44258   15 mins   B/W   B, V   P

The saga of Babe Ruth, his legendary career, and the monument he left behind—Yankee Stadium. Classic newsreel footage.
Fox Movietone News — *Two Star Films*

Babes in Toyland　1961
Musical
63124　119 mins　C　B, V　R, P
Annette Funicello, Ray Bolger, Tommy Sands, Ed Wynn, Tommy Kirk
A lavish production of Victor Herbert's timeless operetta, with Toyland being menaced by the evil Barnaby and his Bogeymen.
Walt Disney Productions — *Walt Disney Home Video*

Baby, The　1972
Suspense
01648　85 mins　C　B, V　P, T
Anjanette Comer, Ruth Roman, Marianna Hill, directed by Ted Post
Bizarre story of a social worker attempting to free a retarted man-child from over-protection of his mother and sisters. Murder follows.
Scotia Intl Films — *King of Video*

Baby Care　1980
Infants
44280　15 mins　C　V　P
This program, prepared by psychologist Karen Warnick and RN Joyce Foster, is a helpful guide for new mothers with infants eighteen months old and less. It covers baby's physical characteristics, needs, and health. Included in the twenty subjects are care of ears, nose, eyes, genitals, bathing, colic, hearing, sleeping, and nursing.
American Home Video Library — *American Home Video Library*

Baby, the Rain Must Fall　1964
Drama
66351　100 mins　B/W　B, V　P
Steve McQueen, Lee Remick, Don Murray, directed by Robert Mulligan
A rootless drifter, paroled from prison, returns home to his wife and daughter, but his outbursts of violence make the reunion difficult.
Columbia; Alan Pakula — *RCA/Columbia Pictures Home Video*

Babylon Story from "Intolerance," The　1916
Drama
58645　25 mins　C　B, V, FO　P
Constance Talmadge, Alfred Paget, directed by D. W. Griffith
A condensation of the Babylon sequence from Griffith's epic, "Intolerance." The story concerns the simple mountain girl befriended by Belshazzar, King of Babylonia, who tries to warn the city of its impending doom. Silent with music score, tinted color.

D W Griffith — *Video Yesteryear*

Bachelor and the Bobby Soxer, The　1947
Comedy
44814　95 mins　B/W　B, V　P, T
Cary Grant, Myrna Loy, Shirley Temple, Rudy Vallee
A playboy is brought before Judge Myrna for disturbing the peace and sentenced to court her teenage sister.
Academy Awards 1947: Best Original Screenplay (Sidney Sheldon).
Dore Schary — *Blackhawk Films; Nostalgia Merchant*

Bachelor Bait　1934
Comedy
44985　75 mins　B/W　B, V　P, T
Stuart Erwin, Rochelle Hudson, Pert Kelton, Skeets Gallagher
A marriage license clerk who's tired of just handing out licenses opens a matrimonial service for men.
Pandro S Berman — *Blackhawk Films*

Bachelor Mother　1939
Comedy
10037　82 mins　B/W　B, V　P, T
Ginger Rogers, David Niven, Charles Coburn
Single salesgirl causes scandal when she finds abandoned baby.
RKO; B G DeSylva — *Blackhawk Films; Nostalgia Merchant*

Back Among the Best/NFL '83　1984
Football
72940　46 mins　C　B, V, FO　P
San Francisco 49'ers
Highlights from the San Francisco 49'ers 1983 season and "NFL 83."
NFL Films — *NFL Films Video*

Back from Eternity　1956
Drama
11608　97 mins　B/W　B, V　P
Robert Ryan, Rod Steiger
Eleven survivors of a plane crash are stranded in a headhunter region of South America's jungle.
Universal; John Farrow — *VCI Home Video*

Back (Rehabilitation and Injury)　1978
Physical fitness
52760　30 mins　C　B, V　P
Hosted by Ann Dugan
Back strengthening exercises to help overcome weaknesses, relieve pain, and condition muscles and tissue to prevent further stress. Part of the "Rehabilitation and Injury" series.

Health 'N Action — *RCA/Columbia Pictures Home Video*

Back Roads 1981
Comedy-Drama
53939 94 mins C B, V, CED P
Sally Field, Tommy Lee Jones, David Keith, directed by Martin Ritt
A Southern hooker meets a down-on-his-luck boxer and both head out for the better life in California.
MPAA:R
Ronald Sheldo — *CBS/Fox Video*

Back to Bataan 1945
War-Drama
10073 95 mins B/W B, V P, T
John Wayne, Anthony Quinn
Colonel forms guerrilla army to raid Japanese and to help Americans landing on Leyte.
RKO; Robert Fellows — *Blackhawk Films; Nostalgia Merchant*

Back-Packer 197?
Camps and camping
19413 25 mins C B, V, 3/4U, P
  Q
A thorough report on the popular new leisure sport covering supplies, clothing, physical condition, weather, and terrain.
TV Sports Scene — *TV Sports Scene*

Backstage at the Kirov 198?
Dance
72179 80 mins C B, V P
A unique look at the Russian Kirov ballet company mixed with a profile of Leningrad.
Dr Armand Hammer — *Pacific Arts Video*

Backstretch, The 1984
Horse racing
74540 51 mins C B, V P
This tape looks at the behind the scenes workforce involved in maintenance and preparation of a racehorse.
EL, SP
Oak Tree Racing Association — *Mercedes Maharis Productions*

Bad Boys 1983
Drama
69039 123 mins C B, V, CED R, P
Sean Penn
Two young hoodlums who hate each other are sent to a Juvenile Hall together and end up in the same dorm. Backed into a corner by their mutual hatred and the escalating peer pressure, the two are pushed over the brink into a final and shattering fight-to-the-death.
Robert Solo — *THORN EMI Home Video*

Bad Man's River 1972
Western
47627 89 mins C B, V P
Lee Van Cleef, Gina Lollobrigida, James Mason
Mexican revolutionaries, a beautiful woman, and a million dollar double-cross result in western action up and down the border.
MPAA:R
Phillip Yordan Productions — *Paragon Video Productions*

Bad News Bears, The 1976
Comedy
38606 102 mins C B, V, LV R, P
Walter Matthau, Tatum O'Neal, Vic Morrow, Joyce Van Patten, Jackie Earle Haley
Family comedy about a misfit little league team who gets whipped into shape by their sloppy, beer-drinking coach (Walter Matthau).
MPAA:PG
Paramount — *Paramount Home Video; RCA VideoDiscs*

Bad News Bears in 1977
Breaking Training, The
Comedy
10984 97 mins C B, V R, P
William Devane, Clifton James
With a chance to play the Houston Toros for a shot at the Japanese champs, the Bears devise a way to get to Texas to play at the famed Astrodome.
MPAA:PG
Paramount; Leonard Goldberg — *Paramount Home Video; RCA VideoDiscs*

Badlands 1974
Drama
51988 95 mins C B, V, LV R, P
Martin Sheen, Sissy Spacek, Warren Oates
A garbage man from South Dakota falls in love with a 15-year-old girl. He doesn't hesitate to kill anyone who tries to interfere with their romance.
MPAA:PG
Warner Bros — *Warner Home Video*

Badmen of Nevada 1933
Western
11609 57 mins B/W B, V P
Kent Taylor, Gail Patrick
The early days of Nevada before law and order.
Unknown — *Video Connection*

Baer vs. Louis/Louis vs. 193?
Schmeling
Boxing
60056 54 mins B/W B, V P, T
Max Baer, Joe Louis
Joe Louis meets ex-champ Max Baer at Yankee Stadium on September 24, 1935. On June 19, 1936 Joe Louis fights with Max Schmeling at Yankee Stadium.

Unknown — *Blackhawk Films*

Baffled   1972
Suspense/Drama
59341   96 mins   C   CED   P
Leonard Nimoy, Susan Hampshire, Vera Miles
A story of the supernatural, blending drama and
suspense with comic undertones.
ATV — *CBS/Fox Video*

Bakery, The/The Grocery   1921
Clerk
Comedy
63994   55 mins   B/W   B, V   P, T
Larry Semon, Oliver Hardy, Lucille Carlisle,
directed by Larry Semon
A package of shorts featuring crazy comedian
Larry Semon, getting tangled up in mayhem and
molasses. Silent with piano score.
Vitagraph — *Blackhawk Films*

Baking Pastry   1982
Cookery
47357   30 mins   C   V   P
Techniques of baking pastries, from simple
biscuits to complex cakes, are presented.
American Home Video Library — *American*
Home Video Library

Bal, Le   1984
Musical
74207   112 mins   C   B, V   R, P
This movie captures a 50-year span of
contemporary history through the music and
dance of periods from the 1930s through 1983.
French Academy Awards '83: Best Picture; Best
Director (Scola); Best Music Score.
Giorgio Silvagni — *Warner Home Video*

Ballad of a Soldier   1959
Drama
29755   88 mins   B/W   B, V   P
Vladimir Ivashow, Shanna Prokhorenko,
directed by Grigori Chukrai
A Russian soldier accidentally knocks out two
German tanks—on leave as a reward, he
reunites a man and wife and falls in love himself.
Russian — *Budget Video; International Historic*
Films; Sheik Video; Penguin Video; Western
Film & Video Inc; Discount Video Tapes; Video
Dimensions

Ballad of Billie Blue, The   197?
Human relations
50754   90 mins   C   B, V   P
Jason Ledger, Marty Allen, Ray Danton
A top country singer, whose wife betrayed him,
has his heart broken and dreams shattered.
Fortunately, he finds that God's love eases the
pain.
Gateway Films — *Vanguard Video*

Ballad of Gregorio   1983
Cortez, The
Drama
64990   99 mins   C   B, V   P
Edward James Olmos
Based on one of the most famous manhunts in
Texas history, this is the story of a Mexican
cowhand who killed a Texas sheriff in self-
defense and tried to elude the law, all because
of a misunderstanding of the Spanish language.
EL, JA
Moctesuma Esparza Productions — *Embassy*
Home Entertainment

Ballad of the Irish Horse,   1984
The
Animals/Horse racing
74536   48 mins   C   B, V   P
This program looks at the Irish horse and its
performance in a variety of competitions.
Pan International Films — *Mercedes Maharis*
Productions

Ballerina: Karen Kain   1980
Dance
58562   58 mins   C   B, V   P
A profile of the dancer about whom Nureyev has
said "in her the star quality is unmistakable."
Includes scenes from "Carmen," "Romeo and
Juliet," and "Cappelia."
MasterVision — *Mastervision*

Ballerina: Lynn Seymour   1980
Dance
58563   58 mins   C   B, V   P
Rudolph Nureyev
Prima ballerina Lynn Seymour is seen dancing
with some of the world's leading male stars.
Scenes from "Romeo and Juliet" and "The Two
Pigeons" are included.
MasterVision — *Mastervision*

Ballet Class for   1982
Beginners, A
Dance
47366   38 mins   C   B, V   P
Basic ballet movements are taught by renowned
dancer Dave Howard.
American Home Video Library — *American*
Home Video Library

Balloonatic, The/One   192?
Week
Comedy
60051   48 mins   B/W   B, V   P, T
Buster Keaton, Phyllis Haver, Sybil Seely
"The Balloonatic" (1923) features Keaton in
several misadventures. In "One Week" (1920)
Buster and his new bride, Sybil, receive a new
home as a wedding gift—the kind you have to
assemble yourself. Silent.

Buster Keaton Prods; Metro — *Blackhawk Films*

Baltic Tragedy, The   194?
World War II
53379   148 mins   B/W   B, V, 3/4U   P
A documentary look, compiled from newsreels, of how the Baltic nations of Latvia, Lithuania, and Estonia witnessed some of the worst battles of the Second World War. (Two cassettes.) English subtitled.
GE
Germany — *International Historic Films*

Baltimore Bullet, The   1980
Adventure
55533   103 mins   C   B, V, CED   P
James Coburn, Omar Sharif, Bruce Boxleitner, Ronee Blakely, Jack O'Halloran
Two men make their living traveling through the country as pool hustlers, bilking would-be pool sharks. Features ten of the greatest pool players in the world.
MPAA:PG
Avco Embassy; John Brascia — *Embassy Home Entertainment*

Banana Splits & Friends, The   197?
Cartoons
66279   60 mins   C   B, V   P
Four large furry creatures, the Banana Splits, perform their slapstick antics and present cartoons.
Hanna Barbera — *Worldvision Home Video*

Bananas   1971
Comedy
58484   82 mins   C   B, V   P
Woody Allen, Louise Lasser, Carlos Montalban, Howard Cosell, Sylvester Stallone, directed by Woody Allen
A frustrated product tester from New York runs off to South America, where he volunteers his support to the revolutionary force of a shaky Latin-American dictatorship and winds up the leader.
MPAA:PG
United Artists; Rollins Jaffe; Jack Grossberg — *CBS/Fox Video; RCA VideoDiscs*

Bandits, The   1973
Western
47667   83 mins   C   B, V   P
Robert Conrad, Jan Michael Vincent, Roy Jenson
Three cowboys team up with a band of Mexican outlaws to fight a Mexican traitor.
Lone Star Pictures — *Unicorn Video*

Bandits of Orogosolo, The   1961
Drama
59224   100 mins   B/W   B, V, 3/4U   P
Directed by Vitorio Deseta
A shepherd's hut is used as a hideout from the police by a group of bandits.
Titanus — *Penguin Video*

Bandolero   1968
Adventure
65412   106 mins   C   CED   P
James Stewart, Raquel Welch, Dean Martin, George Kennedy, Will Geer, Andrew Prine
In Texas, two fugitive brothers run into trouble with their Mexican counterparts.
20th Century Fox — *CBS/Fox Video*

Band Wagon, The   1953
Musical
59136   112 mins   C   B, V   P
Fred Astaire, Cyd Charisse, Oscar Levant, Nanette Fabray, Jack Buchanan, directed by Vincente Minnelli
A Hollywood song-and-dance man finds trouble when he is persuaded to star in a Broadway musical. Songs by Howard Dietz and Arthur Schwartz include "That's Entertainment," and "Dancing in the Dark."
MGM;Arthur Freed — *MGM/UA Home Video*

Bang the Drum Slowly   1973
Drama
59390   97 mins   C   B, V, LV   R, P
Robert DeNiro, Michael Moriarty, Vincent Gardenia, Phil Foster, Ann Wedgeworth, Heather MacRae, Selma Diamond
The story of a major league catcher who suffers from a fatal illness, and his friendship with a quiet, senstive teammate.
NY Film Critics Awards '73: Best Supporting Actor (DeNiro). MPAA:PG
Paramount — *Paramount Home Video*

Bank Dick, The   1940
Adventure/Comedy
69030   73 mins   B/W   B, V   P
W.C. Fields, Cora Witherspoon, Una Richard Purcell, Jack Norton
A man accidentally trips a bank robber and finds himself a guard. A classic W.C. Fields film.
Universal — *MCA Home Video*

Bank on the Stars   1954
Game show
42980   30 mins   B/W   B, V, FO   P
Bill Cullen
Contestants watch an action scene from a newly released movie and then answer questions based on what they've seen. Scenes on this show are from "Apache," "Johnny Dark," "Mr. Hulot's Holiday," and "The Caine Mutiny."

NBC — *Video Yesteryear*

Barabbas　　　　　　　　　　　1961
Drama
64239　　144 mins　　C　　B, V　　　　P
Anthony Quinn, Silvana Mangano, Arthur Kennedy, Jack Palance
Barabbas, a thief and murderer, is freed by Pontius Pilate in place of Jesus, but he is haunted by this event for the rest of his life.
Columbia; Dino de Laurentiis — *RCA/Columbia Pictures Home Video*

Barbarella　　　　　　　　　　1968
Fantasy
38615　　98 mins　　C　　B, V, LV　　R, P
Jane Fonda, John Phillip Law, David Hemmings, directed by Roger Vadim
Based on the popular French sci-fi comic strip drawn by Jean-Claude Forest, this popular film stars Jane Fonda as a sexually emancipated space woman who vanquishes evil robots and monsters and rewards the many men she meets in her travels.
MPAA:PG
Paramount — *Paramount Home Video; RCA VideoDiscs*

Barbarosa　　　　　　　　　　1982
Western
63398　　90 mins　　C　　B, V, CED　　P
Willie Nelson, Gilbert Roland, Gary Busey
Nelson stars as an aging, legendary outlaw whose Mexican in-laws never succeed in killing. He takes in a naive farmboy and teaches him his survival skills to continue the legend.
MPAA:PG
ITC Entertainment — *CBS/Fox Video*

Barbed Wire Dolls　　　　　　1978
Adventure
69018　　84 mins　　C　　B, V　　　　P
Women convicts are doomed to a fate worse than death, in a prison in a South American jungle.
Unknown — *Imperial Video Corp*

Barber Shop, The　　　　　　1933
Comedy
59401　　21 mins　　B/W　　B, V　　P, T
W.C. Fields, Elise Cavanna, Harry Watson, Dagmar Oakland, Frank Yaconelli
Fields portrays the bumbling, carefree barber Cornelius O'Hare, purveyor of village gossip and solver of problems. Havoc begins when a gangster enters the shop and demands that Cornelius change his appearance.
Paramount — *Blackhawk Films*

Barcelona Kill, The　　　　　197?
Suspense
73147　　86 mins　　C　　B, V　　　　P
Linda Hayden, John Austin, Simon Andrew, Maximo Valverde
When a journalist and her boyfriend get in too deep with the Barcelona mob, their troubles begin.
Michael Klinger Production — *VCL Home Video*

Barefoot Contessa, The　　　1954
Drama
55584　　128 mins　　C　　CED　　　　P
Ava Gardner, Humphrey Bogart, Edmond O'Brien
The story, told in flashback, of a girl's rise to stardom and the loneliness she finds at the top.
Academy Awards '54: Best Supporting Actor (O'Brien).
United Artists — *CBS/Fox Video*

Barefoot in Athens　　　　　1966
Drama
64853　　76 mins　　C　　B, V, 3/4U　　P
Peter Ustinov, Geraldine Page, Anthony Quayle, directed by George Schaefer
This presentation from "George Schaefer's Showcase Theatre" chronicles the last years of the philosopher Socrates who, barefoot and unkempt, an embarrassment to his wife and a dangerous critic to the corrupt Athenian leaders, nevertheless believes that democracy and truth are all-important in his city.
Emmy Award '66: Outstanding Single Performance/Actor (Ustinov).
George Schaefer — *Enter-Tel Inc*

Barefoot in the Park　　　　1967
Comedy
54675　　105 mins　　C　　B, V, LV　　R, P
Robert Redford, Jane Fonda, Charles Boyer, Mildred Natwick, directed by Gene Saks
A newly wedded bride tries to get her husband to loosen up and be as free spirited as she is.
Paramount, Hal Wallis — *Paramount Home Video; RCA VideoDiscs*

Bargain, The　　　　　　　　1915
Western
59212　　50 mins　　B/W　　B, V, 3/4U　　P
William S Hart
Hart's first feature in which he portrays a bandit desperately trying to go straight. Original titles with musical score.
Thomas Ince; NY Motion Picture Corp — *Penguin Video; Classic Video Cinema Collector's Club*

Barney Oldfield's Race for a Life/Super-Hooper-Dyne Lizzies 19??
Comedy-Drama
60057   42 mins   B/W   B, V   P, T
Barney Oldfield, Mack Sennett, Mabel Normand, Ford Sterling, Billy Bevan, Andy Clyde
In the first of two shorts on this tape from 1913, Barney chases a villain who has abducted a lovely girl. In the second film from 1925, radio-controlled Model-T Fords co-star with comic Billy Bevan.
Mack Sennett; Pathe — *Blackhawk Films*

Baron Muenchhausen 19??
Comedy-Drama
65643   120 mins   C   B, V   R, P
Kaethe Kaack, Hermann Speelmanns, Leo Slezak, directed by Josef von Baky
The German film studio UFA celebrated its 25th anniversary with the lavish version of the Baron Muenchhausen legends, starring a cast of top-name German performers of the period. Filmed in Agfacolor and stereophonic sound; available in English subtitled or dubbed versions.
GE
UFA — *Video City Productions*

Barricade 1966
Documentary
72504   13 mins   C   B, V, 3/4U   P
A complete study of the Berlin Wall from its construction to its psychological impact on East Germany. Montage shots tell an emotional history of the famous edifice and those who have attempted to escape over it.
Unknown — *International Historic Films*

Barry Lyndon 1975
Drama
68232   184 mins   C   B, V   R, P
Ryan O'Neal, Marisa Berenson
Ryan O'Neal stars as an Irish scoundrel and gentleman in this film.
MPAA:PG
Warner Brothers — *Warner Home Video*

Barry Manilow Live at the Greek 1982
Music-Performance
72445   75 mins   C   LV   P
Pop star Barry Manilow thrills his audience in this live performance at the Greek Theater.
Marty Pasetta; Barry Manilow — *Pioneer Video Imports*

Baseball: Fun and Games 1980
Baseball
29231   60 mins   C   B, V   P
Features great baseball trivia quizzes and gives you another chance to see the close plays and make the calls.
Major League Baseball Productions — *VidAmerica; RCA VideoDiscs*

Baseball Miracles 197?
Baseball
45084   60 mins   C   B, V, 3/4U   P
Lindsay Nelson, Ralph Kiner, Bob Murphy
A videotape of memorable moments from the New York Mets' 1969 and 1973 seasons: their phenomenal play which won them the World Series in 1969, highlights from their amazing comeback in 1973 which was the most spectacular of all time and established the Mets slogan "You Gotta Believe."
Sports World Cinema — *Sports World Cinema*

Baseball: The Now Career 1975
Baseball
33830   26 mins   C   B, V   P
Chuck Connors, Nolan Ryan, Johnny Bench, Tug McGraw
Television star Chuck Connors, a former ballplayer, helps tell the story of the road to the major leagues, along with several of the game's stars.
Major League Baseball — *Major League Baseball Productions*

Baseball's Hall of Fame 1981
Baseball
51658   60 mins   C   B, V, CED   P
Hosted by Donald Sutherland
The most glorious moments in baseball history are relived through speeches and footage of some of baseball's greatest players, such as oldtimers Babe Ruth, Mel Ott, Ted Williams, and Bob Feller, and newer inductees such as Al Kaline, Mickey Mantle, Duke Snider, and Warren Spahn.
Major League Baseball — *VidAmerica*

Basic Automobile Maintenance 1981
Automobiles
47330   45 mins   C   B, V, 3/4U   P
Demonstrations are provided for the non-mechanic, including changing tires, battery care, checking sparkplugs, changing oil, replacing wiper blades, adjusting a fanbelt, and more.
Vision Productions — *Vision Productions*

Basic Bowling 1980
Sports-Minor
54605   24 mins   C   V   P
A top instructor and member of the Bowling Hall of Fame gives step by step lessons on beginning bowling. Included in this program are choice of equipment, grip, steps, and delivery.
American Home Video Library — *American Home Video Library*

Basic Card Magic 1982
Games/Magic
47407   52 mins   C   B, V   P
Famed magician Derek Dingle instructs the viewer on the basics of card tricks.
Allen Sherman — *American Home Video Library*

Basic Carpentry 1980
Woodwork
54607   28 mins   C   V   P
Nat Babcock
In this program every phase of basic carpentry from hand tools to power tools is covered by master carpenter and woodworker Nat Babcock. Hammering, screwing, sawing, and building are shown in detail.
American Home Video Library — *American Home Video Library*

Basic Crocheting—Needlepoint 1980
Handicraft
54604   27 mins   C   V   P
An expert of these two crafts teaches the proper way to select and use yarn in making articles of clothing. Special techniques for difficult projects are portrayed.
American Home Video Library — *American Home Video Library*

Basic English Grammar by Video 1983
Languages-Instruction
74489   90 mins   C   B, V   P
This tape is designed to teach the basic fundamentals of English grammar.
Mastervision — *Mastervision*

Basic French by Video 1983
Languages-Instruction
74488   90 mins   C   B, V   P
This tape is designed to teach basic conversational French.
Mastervision Inc — *Mastervision*

Basic Golf 1 1980
Golf
54610   30 mins   C   V   P
Beginning golf from A to Z is demonstrated by professionals in this program.
American Home Video Library — *American Home Video Library*

Basic Golf 2 1982
Golf
47354   30 mins   C   V   P
Gene Littler demonstrates advanced golf techniques.
Royal Business Funds — *American Home Video Library*

Basic Home Electric Repairs 1980
Electricity/Home improvement
54601   24 mins   C   V   P
David Keiser
Master electrician David Keiser gives step-by-step demonstrations on how to install or repair light sockets, switches, and light fixtures. Included in this program are hints on trouble shooting overloads and short circuits.
American Home Video Library — *American Home Video Library*

Basic Home Painting 1980
Home improvement
54608   26 mins   C   V   P
In this program a professional painter shows how to prepare interior walls prior to painting, how to select the right tools, and techniques for painting ceilings, walls, and woodwork.
American Home Video Library — *American Home Video Library*

Basic Home Wallpapering 1980
Home improvement
54602   24 mins   C   V   P
David Och
In this program David Och, professional paperhanger, shows how to prepare walls for hanging paper, how to cut around windows and doors, and how to hang the paper on the wall, and the tools needed.
American Home Video Library — *American Home Video Library*

Basic Italian by Video 1983
Languages-Instruction
66205   90 mins   C   B, V   P
A basic, working vocabulary of Italian is taught in this program.
Mastervision — *Mastervision*

Basic Karate and Self-Defense 1981
Martial arts
59913   100 mins   C   LV   P
Instructor Ivan Rogers presents and demonstrates the benefits of practicing karate, proper mental and physical conditioning, and basic techniques.
Inedco Productions — *INEDCO Productions*

Basic Marksmanship—45 Caliber Pistol 1972
Armed Forces-US
72502   14 mins   C   B, V, 3/4U   F
A Marine training film on techniques for using the 45-caliber pistol.
US Marine Corps — *International Historic Films*

Basic Photography   1980
Photography
54603   26 mins   C   V   P
Hank Durell
In this program professional photographer Hank Durell reviews the basic settings of a camera. He then gives tips and shows correct and incorrect picture-taking techniques for both indoors and outdoors.
American Home Video Library — *American Home Video Library*

Basic Pool   1980
Sports-Minor
54611   28 mins   C   V   P
Steve Mizerak
Steve Mizerak, trick-shot artist, demonstrates different shots and the basics of pool.
American Home Video Library — *American Home Video Library*

Basic Pottery   1982
Arts/Handicraft
47359   30 mins   C   V   P
Techniques of making pottery are presented, from preparing the piece to firing it.
American Home Video Library — *American Home Video Library*

Basic Racquetball   1980
Sports-Minor
54606   23 mins   C   V   P
Kevin Cunningham
In this program Kevin Cunningham, instructor, gives the basics of equipment, grip, moves, and strategy for learning the fast-growing new sport, racquetball.
American Home Video Library — *American Home Video Library*

Basic Spanish by Video   1983
Languages-Instruction
66204   90 mins   C   B, V   P
This program is designed to provide the viewer with a working vocabulary of Spanish.
Mastervision — *Mastervision*

Basic Tennis   1980
Tennis
54609   30 mins   C   V   P
Professionals demonstrate all aspects of the beginning basics of tennis.
American Home Video Library — *American Home Video Library*

Basin Street Revue   1955
Music-Performance
08909   ? mins   B/W   B, V, 3/4U   P
Sarah Vaughn, Lionel Hampton, Nipsey Russell, Mantan Moreland, Cab Calloway
A compilation of Soundies. An all-black musical revue.

Snader Telescriptions — *Penguin Video*

Basket Case   1982
Horror
63891   89 mins   C   B, V   P
Kevin Van Hentenryck, Terri Susan Smith, Beverly Bonner
A pair of Siamese twins, one deformed and one normal, set out to avenge their surgical separation.
Edgar Ievins — *Media Home Entertainment*

Basketball with Gail Goodrich   1982
Basketball
60439   30 mins   C   B, V   P
Gail Goodrich
Two pros take the viewer through basic shooting, free throws, jump shots, jumps from the dribble and shots close to the basket. For novice and advanced player alike.
MPAA:G
Unknown — *Embassy Home Entertainment*

Bass Fishing: Top to Bottom   1984
Fishing
66631   60 mins   C   B, V   P
Hosted by Rick Clunn and Gordon Andrews
This program shows the why, how and when of catching largemouth bass. Lures, casting accuracy, landing the fish and the equipment necessary are all studied in detail.
3M; Glen Law — *Leisure Time Products Project/3M*

Bass in Heavy Cover   1981
Fishing
65150   30 mins   C   B, V   P
Homer Circle, Al Lindner, Roland Martin
Experts demonstrate how to catch more fish despite such obstacles as trees, stumps and weeds.
Glen Lau — *Leisure Time Products Project/3M*

Bat, The   1982
Mountaineering
69907   25 mins   C   B, V   P
This is a reconstruction of the first ascent of the Bat, an extreme rock climb on Ben Nevis climbed by Dougal Haston and Robyn Smith in 1959.
Telluride Mountainfilm Festival '82: Grand Prize.
Tony Riley — *Gravity Sports Films*

Battle at Elderbush Gulch, The/The Musketeers of Pig Alley   1914
Drama/Film-History
62871   33 mins   B/W   B, V   P, T
Lillian Gish, Mae Marsh, Harry Carey, directed by D.W. Griffith

Two classic D.W. Griffith two-reelers from 1914 and 1912 respectively are contained on this tape.
Biograph — *Blackhawk Films*

Battle Beneath the Earth   1968
Science fiction
75540   112 mins   C   B, V   P
Kerwin Mathews, Peter Arne
American scientists discover a Chinese plot to invade the U.S. via a series of underground tunnels.
MGM — *MGM/UA Home Video*

Battle Beyond the Stars   1980
Science fiction
66100   103 mins   C   B, V, CED   P
Richard Thomas, Robert Vaughn, George Peppard
A variety of extraordinary aliens set out on an intergalactic mission.
MPAA:PG
Orion Pictures — *Vestron Video*

Battle Cry   1955
War-Drama
47617   170 mins   C   B, V   R, P
Van Heflin, Aldo Ray, Mona Freeman, Tab Hunter, Dorothy Malone, Anne Francis
A group of U.S. Marines train, romance, and enter battle in World War II. Part of the "A Night at the Movies" series, this tape simulates a 1955 movie evening, with a cartoon, "Speedy Gonzales," a newsreel and coming attractions for "Mr. Roberts" and "East of Eden."
Warner Bros — *Warner Home Video*

Battle for the Falklands   1984
Great Britain/Documentary
75925   110 mins   C   B, V   R, P
This program documents the complete account of the dramatic battle for the Falklands.
Thorn — *THORN EMI Home Video*

Battle of Britain, The   1943
World War II/Documentary
50615   55 mins   B/W   B, V   P
Directed by Frank Capra
Britain stands alone in her "finest hour," through a tremendous Nazi air onslaught. Part of the "Why We Fight" series.
US War Department — *Sheik Video; Budget Video; Western Film & Video Inc; Discount Video Tapes*

Battle of China, The   1944
Documentary/World War II
44993   67 mins   B/W   B, V   P
Directed by Frank Capra
A look at the people, culture, and industry of China, and Japan's total commitment to

conquer the country during World War II, through authentic newsreel footage.
US War Department — *Budget Video; Western Film & Video Inc; Discount Video Tapes*

Battle of El Alamein, The   1971
War-Drama
59354   92 mins   C   B, V   R, P
George Hilton, Michael Rennie
The world's mightiest tank armadas, the U.S. vs. Rommel's forces, battle for desert supremacy.
MPAA:G
Heritage Enterprises — *Video Gems*

Battle of Elderbush Gulch, The   1913
Film-History
15497   22 mins   B/W   B, V   P
Lillian Gish
Silent western classic starring the famous American silent movie star, Lillian Gish.
Unknown — *Video Connection; Pyramid Film and Video*

Battle of Midway, The   1942
World War II
50628   18 mins   B/W   B, V   P

Directed by John Ford
A failure as a film attempt, but a courageous act of recording the desperate, important battle. John Ford was injured during the fighting, and two of the three cameras were destroyed. Academy Award '42: Special Documentary.
US Navy — *Interurban Films*

Battle of Neretva   1970
Drama
65459   112 mins   C   B, V   P
Yul Brynner, Curt Jurgens, Orson Welles
Yugoslav partisans are facing German and Italian troops and local Chetniks as they battle for freedom.
American International — *NTA Home Entertainment*

Battle of Russia, The   1944
Documentary/World War II
44994   83 mins   B/W   B, V   P
Directed by Frank Capra
Hitler's forces are victorious in Moscow and Leningrad but are thoroughly defeated at the battle of Stalingrad. Authentic newsreel footage.
US War Department — *Budget Video; Blackhawk Films; Western Film & Video Inc; MPI Home Video*

Battle of San Pietro, The   1944
World War II/Documentary
52318   30 mins   B/W   B, V, 3/4U   P
Directed and narrated by John Huston

John Huston's powerful documentary about the famous battle in Italy's Liri Valley, stressing the number of losses sustained in taking this military objective. The film was suppressed by the U.S. government because it was considered to be too strong for general release.
US Office of War Information — *International Historic Films; Western Film & Video Inc*

Battle of Stalingrad, The   1960
World War II/USSR
52350   90 mins   B/W   B, V, 3/4U   P
A Russian documentary which offers the Soviet view of the grueling battle for Stalingrad which changed the course of the Second World War in the Allies' favor. Narrated in English.
USSR — *International Historic Films*

Battle of the Bulge, The   1965
War-Drama
73012   141 mins   C   B, V   P
Henry Fonda, Robert Shaw, Robert Ryan, Dana Andrews, Pier Angeli
A recreation of the famous offensive by Nazi Panzer troops on the Belgian front during 1944-45, an assault that could have changed the course of World War Two.
Sidney Harmon; Warner Bros — *Warner Home Video*

Battlestar Galactica   1978
Science fiction
14066   125 mins   C   B, V, LV, CED   P
Lorne Greene, Richard Hatch, Dirk Benedict, Ray Milland, directed by Richard A Colla
A spaceship tries a desperate attempt to reach the ancient planet called Earth. Spectacular special effects. A movie made for television.
MPAA:PG
Glen Larson — *MCA Home Video*

Battling Bunyan/Home Stretch The   192?
Comedy/Drama
64306   100 mins   B/W   B, V   P
Wesley Barry, Douglas MacLean, Beatrice Burnham
Two silent features are paired on this tape: a comedy, "Battling Bunyan (1924), and a racetrack melodrama, "The Home Stretch" (1921). Musical scores added.
Thomas Ince — *Classic Video Cinema Collector's Club*

Battling Marshal   1948
Western
15541   52 mins   B/W   B, V   P
Sunset Carson
Fast-moving action western starring Sunset Carson.
Astor — *Video Connection*

Battling Outlaws   194?
Western
15512   ? mins   B/W   B, V   P
Bob Steele
Western featuring the American cowboy Bob Steele.
Unknown — *Video Connection*

Battling with Buffalo Bill   1931
Western/Serials
58634   180 mins   B/W   B, V   P
Tom Tyler, Rex Bell, Franklin Farnum
Twelve episodes of the vintage serial concerning the exploits of the legendary Indian fighter.
Universal — *Video Connection*

Batty World of Baseball, The   1982
Baseball
59381   ? mins   C   B, V   P
A humorous look at the personalities who make the game interesting: managers like John McGraw, Leo Durocher, Casey Stengel, and Billy Martin, and a rarely-seen side of Babe Ruth.
Major League Baseball Prods — *RCA/Columbia Pictures Home Video*

Beach Girls, The   1982
Comedy
64030   91 mins   C   B, V, LV   R, P
Debra Blee, Val Kline, Jeana Tomasina
Three voluptuous coeds intend to re-educate a bookish young man and the owner of a beach house.
MPAA:R
Crown International Pictures — *Paramount Home Video; RCA VideoDiscs*

Beach House   1982
Comedy
66187   89 mins   C   B, V   R, P
Adolescents frolic on the beach, get inebriated and listen to rock 'n' roll.
Unknown — *THORN EMI Home Video*

Beach Party   1963
Comedy/Musical
64892   101 mins   C   CED   P
Frankie Avalon, Annette Funicello, Bob Cummings
A scientist studying the mating habits of teenagers intrudes on a group of surfers, beach bums and motorcyclists.
American International Pictures — *Vestron Video (disc only)*

Beachcomber, The   1939
Drama
12401   88 mins   B/W   B, V   P

Charles Laughton, Elsa Lanchester, Robert Newton, Tyrone Guthrie
Beachcomber falls in love with missionary's prim sister when plague breaks out. Story by W. Somerset Maugham.
Mayfair — *Movie Buff Video; Video Connection; Cable Films; Western Film & Video Inc*

Beany & Cecil, Volume III   196?
Cartoons
76035   60 mins   C   B, V   P
Animated
There's lots of fun and adventure in this third volume of cartoons featuring Beany, Cecil the Sea Sick Sea Serpent, Dishonest John, Captain Huffenpuff, and all their friends.
Bob Clampett — *RCA/Columbia Pictures Home Video*

Beany and Cecil, Volume Four   196?
Cartoons
Closed Captioned
72922   60 mins   C   B, V   P
Animated
More classic cartoon adventures with Beany and Cecil including: "Beany and the Boo Birds," and "The Rat Race for Space."
Bob Clampett — *RCA/Columbia Pictures Home Video*

Beany & Cecil, Volumes 1 & 2   196?
Cartoons
66345   60 mins   C   B, V   P
The lovable characters of the little boy Beany and his loyal companion, Cecil the Sea Sick Sea Serpent are featured in 14 classic cartoons. In Beta Hi-Fi.
Bob Clampett; ABC — *RCA/Columbia Pictures Home Video; RCA VideoDiscs*

Bear Who Slept Through Christmas, The   1983
Christmas
65161   60 mins   C   B, V   P
Animated, voices of Tommy Smothers, Arte Johnson, Barbara Feldon, Kelly Lange
As Christmas approaches, all the bears are getting ready to go to sleep for the winter, except Ted E. Bear, who wants to see just what Christmas is.
Dimenmark International — *Family Home Entertainment*

Bears and I, The   1975
Adventure
56874   88 mins   C   CED   P
Patrick Wayne, Chief Dan George, Andrew Duggan, Michael Ansara
A young war veteran in search of himself heads for the wilderness, befriends a trio of orphaned bears, and helps an Indian tribe in their struggle to retain their rights.
MPAA:G
Walt Disney — *RCA VideoDiscs*

Beast in the Cellar, The   1970
Horror
66514   85 mins   C   B, V   P
Beryl Reid, Flora Robson
Two spinster sisters keep a murderous inhuman beast chained in their cellar, but he escapes to terrorize the peaceful English countryside.
MPAA:R
Wrightwood; Graham Harris — *Paragon Video Productions*

Beast Must Die, The   1975
Horror
55563   93 mins   C   B, V, 3/4U   P
Peter Cushing, Calvin Lockhart
A millionaire sportsman invites a group of men and women connected with bizarre deaths or the eating of human flesh to spend the cycle of a full moon at his isolated lodge.
MPAA:PG
Cinerama Releasing; Max Rosenberg — *Nostalgia Merchant*

Beast of I.R.S. Volume I, The   1984
Music video
72864   40 mins   C   B, V   P
Some of I.R.S. artists' best video clips are featured. The Alarm and the Go-Go's are included.
International Record Syndicate Video — *I.R.S. Video*

Beast Within, The   1982
Horror
64568   98 mins   C   B,-V, CED   P
Ronny Cox, Bibi Besch, Paul Clemens, Don Gordon
A young woman is raped by an unseen creature in a Mississippi swamp. Seventeen years later, her son begins to act strangely, forcing a return to the rape scene. In stereo.
MPAA:R
MGM/UA — *MGM/UA Home Video*

Beastmaster, The   1982
Adventure
68239   119 mins   C   B, V, CED   P
Marc Singer, Tanya Roberts, and Rip Torn
This adventure film is set in a wild and primitive world. The Beastmaster is involved in a life and death struggle with overwhelming forces of evil. In stereo.
MPAA:PG
MGM/UA — *MGM/UA Home Video*

Beat Goes On, The — 1981
Football
51168 23 mins C B, V, FO R, P
Houston Oilers
Coach Bum Phillips predicted 1980 would be the year that his team 'broke down the door' to the Super Bowl. Instead, at season's end, he was shown the door. However, when Oiler stars such as Ken Stabler and Earl Campbell were good, there were few better.
NFL Films — *NFL Films Video*

Beatlemania—The Movie — 1983
Music-Performance
65445 60 mins C B, V P
This program pictorially and musically reflects the tumultuous events of the 60's, featuring 30 of the greatest songs of John Lennon and Paul McCartney. In stereo VHS and Beta Hi-Fi. Not the Beatles, but an incredible simulation.
Edie and Ely Landau — *U.S.A. Home Video*

Beatles—Comedy Featurettes — 1984
Movie and TV trailers/Comedy
66484 57 mins C B, V P
Behind the scenes glimpses of the making of seven comedy films are combined in this package: "The Owl and the Pussycat," "Cold Turkey," "Return of the Pink Panther," "A Hard Day's Night," "Yellow Submarine" and "A Funny Thing Happened..."
Walter Shenson et al — *San Francisco Rush Video*

Beau Revel — 1921
Drama
64310 50 mins B/W B, V P
Lewis Stone
A tale of manners and morals, with Lewis Stone as a recklessly extravagant playboy. Silent with musical score.
Thomas Ince — *Classic Video Cinema Collector's Club*

Beautiful Birds/Tropical Fish/Fireside Moments — 1983
Video
66152 120 mins C B, V, 3/4U P
Three "environmental videos" offering beautiful scenes to relax the viewer.
Environmental Video — *Environmental Video*

Beauty and the Beast — 1946
Fantasy
55128 90 mins B/W B, V P
Josette Day, Jean Marais, directed by Jean Cocteau
Cocteau's rendition of this classic fable about the beautiful girl and the soulful beast.
Films De France Ltd — *Video Dimensions*

Beauty Bible — 1983
Cosmetology
69788 60 mins C B, V P
2 pgms
In clear, easy to follow steps a makeup artist demonstrates the beauty secrets that make movie stars look so good. Two separate "Beauty Bibles" are available: a general one, and one designed specifically for the mature woman.
Anthony DiVona; Celebrity Video — *Gold Stripe Video*

Becket — 1964
Drama
51574 148 mins C B, V P
Richard Burton, Peter O'Toole, John Gielgud
A drama dealing with 12th century friendship between Becket and the King of England, Becket's appointment as Archbishop of Canterbury, and the furor which arises when he takes his position too seriously.
Academy Awards '64: Best Screenplay (Edward Anhalt).
Paramount; Hal Wallis — *MPI Home Video; VCI Home Video*

Bed and Sofa — 1927
Drama
55808 73 mins B/W B, V P
Directed by Abram Room
Adultery, abortion, and women's rights are brought about by a housing shortage which forces a man to move in with a married friend. Silent.
Russia — *Festival Films; International Historic Films; Classic Video Cinema Collector's Club*

Bedazzled — 1968
Comedy
58951 107 mins C B, V P
Dudley Moore, Peter Cook, Eleanor Bron, Michael Bates, Raquel Welch, directed by Stanley Donen
A short-order cook is saved from suicide by a man who offers him seven wishes in exchange for his soul.
EL, SP
20th Century Fox — *CBS/Fox Video*

Bedford Incident, The — 1965
Adventure
44787 102 mins B/W B, V P
Richard Widmark, Sidney Poitier, James MacArthur, Martin Balsam, Wally Cox
The U.S.S. Bedford discovers an unidentified submarine in North Atlantic waters. The Bedford's commander drives his crew to the point of nerve-taut exhaustion when they find themselves the center of a fateful controversy.
James B Harris, Richard Widmark, Columbia — *RCA/Columbia Pictures Home Video*

Bedlam 1945
Horror
00317 79 mins B/W   B, V, 3/4U   P
Boris Karloff, Anna Lee, Richard Fraser
Horror melodrama of a seventeenth century insane asylum and a sane female reformer.
RKO — *Nostalgia Merchant*

Bedtime for Bonzo 1951
Comedy
56872 83 mins B/W   B, V   P
Ronald Reagan, Diana Lynn, Walter Slezak, Jesse White, Bonzo the Chimp, directed by Fred deCordova
A professor adopts a chimp to prove that environment determines a child's future, disproving the Dean's theory that his children-to-be might inherit criminal tendencies because his father was a crook.
Universal — *MCA Home Video*

Bees, The 1978
Drama
53506 93 mins C   B, V   R, P
John Saxon, John Carradine, Angel Tompkins
A strain of bees have ransacked South America and are threatening the rest of the world.
MPAA:PG
New World; Bee One Panorama Films — *Warner Home Video*

Beguiled, The 1970
War-Drama
64797 109 mins C   B, V   P
Clint Eastwood, Geraldine Page, Elizabeth Hartman, directed by Donald Siegel
A wounded Union soldier is taken in by the women at a girl's school in the South. He manages to seduce both a student and a teacher, and jealousy and revenge ensue.
MPAA:R
Universal — *MCA Home Video*

Behind the Scenes of Telstar 1962
Communication/Space exploration
72507 42 mins C B, V, 3/4U   P
The first active telecommunications satellite, Telstar, is shown in all stages of development. The first Presidential press conference to reach Europe via satellite is introduced by President Kennedy.
NASA — *International Historic Films*

Behind Your Radio Dial 1948
Mass media/Documentary
12844 45 mins B/W   B, V, FO   P
An early TV show which gives the viewer an entertaining glimpse of NBC radio and many of its stars.
NBC — *Video Yesteryear*

Behold a Pale Horse 1964
Drama
66015 118 mins B/W   B, V   P
Gregory Peck, Anthony Quinn, Omar Sharif, Mildred Dunnock, directed by Fred Zinneman
A post-Spanish Civil War tale concerning an ideological battle between a guerilla leader and a cruel police captain.
Columbia — *RCA/Columbia Pictures Home Video*

Being, The 1983
Horror
73022 82 mins C   B, V   R, P
Ruth Buzzi, Martin Landau, Jose Ferrer
People in Idaho are terrorized by a freak who became abnormal after radiation was disposed in the local dump.
William Osco — *THORN EMI Home Video*

Being There 1979
Comedy
54838 126 mins C   B, V, CED   P
Peter Sellers, Shirley MacLaine, Melvyn Douglas, directed by Hal Ashby
A feeble-minded gardener whose entire knowledge of life comes from watching television is sent out into the real world when his employer dies. Equipped with his prize possession, his remote control unit, the gardener encounters a series of hilarious events.
Academy Awards '79: Best Supporting Actor (Douglas). MPAA:PG
Lorimar Prods, Andrew Braunsberg Prod — *CBS/Fox Video*

Bela Lugosi Meets a Brooklyn Gorilla 1952
Comedy/Horror
73551 74 mins B/W   B, V   P
Bela Lugosi, Duke Mitchell, Sammy Petrillo
Two men who look like Dean Martin and Jerry Lewis get lost in the jungle where they meet a mad scientist.
Jack Broder Prods — *Admit One Video*

Belafonte Presents Fincho 1975
Africa/Documentary
58580 79 mins C   B, V   P
Hosted by Harry Belafonte, directed by Sarn Zebba
A docudrama shot in Nigeria concerning the problems a jungle village faces when suddenly brought into the 20th Century.
Rohauer Films — *Mastervision*

Bell, Book and Candle 1959
Comedy
35378 103 mins C   B, V   P
James Stewart, Kim Novak, Jack Lemmon, Elsa Lanchester, Ernie Kovacs, Hermione Gingold

A young witch makes up her mind to refrain from using her powers. When an interesting man moves into her building, she forgets her decision and enchants him with a love spell.
Columbia — *RCA/Columbia Pictures Home Video*

Bell Jar, The 1979
Drama
65474   113 mins   C   B, V   P
Marilyn Hasset, Julie Harris, Barbara Barrie, Anne Bancroft
Based on poet Sylvia Plath's acclaimed semi-autobiographical novel, this is the story of a young woman who becomes the victim of mental illness.
MPAA:R
Avco Embassy — *Vestron Video*

Belles of St. Trinian's, The 1953
Comedy
66020   86 mins   B/W   B, V   R, P
Alastair Sim
Alastair Sim is superb in a dual role as the prim headmistress of a private girls school and her slick bookmaker brother.
Lauder Gillist Productions — *THORN EMI Home Video*

Bells, The 1926
Drama
69563   92 mins   B/W   B, V, FO   P
Lionel Barrymore, Boris Karloff
The Burgomeister of an Alsatian village kills a wealthy merchant and steals his money. The murderer experiences pangs of guilt which are accentuated when a traveling mesmerist comes to town who claims to be able to discern a person's darkest secrets. Silent with music score.
Independent — *Video Yesteryear*

Bells Are Ringing 1960
Musical/Comedy
58294   126 mins   C   B, V, CED   P
Judy Holliday, Dean Martin, Fred Clark, Eddie Foy Jr., Jean Stapleton, directed by Vincente Minnelli
A girl who works for a telephone answering service can't help but take an interest in the lives of the clients, especially a playwright with an inferiority complex. Based on Adolph Green and Betty Comden's Broadway musical.
MGM — *MGM/UA Home Video*

Bells of Rosarita 1945
Western
07055   54 mins   B/W   B, V   P
Roy Rogers, Dale Evans, Gabby Hayes
Roy helps to foil a play by crooks to swindle a girl out of the ranch her father left her.

Republic — *Video Connection; Discount Video Tapes; Sheik Video; Cable Films*

Bells of St. Mary's, The 1945
Drama
47989   126 mins   B/W   B, V   P
Bing Crosby, Ingrid Bergman, Henry Travers, directed by Leo McCarey
An easy-going priest finds himself in a subtle battle of wits with the Sister Superior over how the children of St. Mary's school should be raised. Songs include the title tune and "Aren't You Glad You're You?"
Academy Awards '45: Best Sound. NY Film Critics Award '45: Best Female Performance (Bergman).
RKO — *NTA Home Entertainment*

Belly Dance for Fitness and Fun 1984
Physical fitness
65696   28 mins   C   B, V, 3/4U   P
3 pgms
Narrated by Alicia Dhanifu, this program will teach proper posture and hip movements, snake arm-arched bends, Egyptian head slides and costuming, the basic repertoire of the belly dancer.
AM Available
A. Dhanifu Productions — *A M Productions Home Video*

Belly Dancing—You Can Do It! 1982
Dance
47678   ? mins   C   LV   P
Four lovely belly dancers teach the basic moves of this ancient art, from basic belidi to the use of veils and zills. An interactive disc which runs 60 minutes when played through.
Asselin Productions — *Optical Programming Associates*

Bellydancing 1980
Dance
47332   86 mins   C   B, V, 3/4U   P
The art of bellydancing is taught, beginning with limbering exercises and progressing to simple and complex dance movements. The uses of finger cymbals, head movements, veils, and bellydancing costumes are discussed.
Vision Productions — *Vision Productions*

Below the Belt 1980
Drama
63330   92 mins   C   B, V   R, P
Regina Baff, Mildred Burke, John C. Becher
A street-smart woman from New York City becomes part of the blue-collar "circus" of lady wrestling.
MPAA:R

(For Explanation of codes, see USE GUIDE and KEY)

Aberdeen/RLF/Tom-Mi
Productions — *THORN EMI Home Video*

Below the Surface   1920
Drama
64315   75 mins   B/W   B, V   P
Hobart Bosworth, directed by Thomas Ince
A tale of crime and adventure involving a group
of deep sea divers who discover a mystery
beneath the sea. Silent with musical score.
Thomas Ince — *Classic Video Cinema
Collector's Club*

Belstone Fox, The   1973
Adventure
59828   103 mins   C   B, V   P
Eric Porter, Rachel Roberts, Jeremy Kemp
An orphaned fox goes into hiding, and is hunted
by the hound he has befriended and his former
owner.
Julian Wintle — *Embassy Home Entertainment*

Ben Hur   1959
Drama
44648   217 mins   C   B, V, CED   P
*Charlton Heston, Jack Hawkins, Stephen Boyd,
Hugh Griffith, Sam Jaffe, directed by William
Wyler*
Jewish nobleman Ben Hur struggles against
Roman tyranny in first-century Palestine. Winner
of ten Academy Awards.
Academy Awards '59: Best Picture; Best Actor
(Heston); Best Supporting Actor (Griffith); Best
Director (Wyler).
MGM — *MGM/UA Home Video*

Ben Jones: Monarch of   1954
the Turf
Biographical/Horse racing
44238   15 mins   B/W   B, V   P
Through classic newsreel footage this program
explores the career of Ben Jones, trainer of
thoroughbreds. Jones is most noted for being
the head trainer of Calumet Farm, one of
America's best racing stables.
Fox Movietone News — *Two Star Films*

Ben Turpin Rides Again   1923
Comedy
42948   45 mins   B/W   B, V, FO   P
Ben Turpin 3 pgms
Ben Turpin, the cross-eyed wonder, stars in
three shorts by Mack Sennett.
*1. The Daredevil 2. Yukon Jake 3. The Eyes
Have It*
Mack Sennett — *Video Yesteryear*

Beneath the Twelve Mile   1953
Reef
Adventure
75934   102 mins   C   B, V   R, P

*Robert Wagner, Terry Moore, Gilbert Roland,
Peter Graves, directed by Robert Webb*
This movie presents the story of murderous
competition for the rich but dangerous sponge
beds between the divers of Tarpon.
20th Century Fox — *Video Gems*

Benjamin   197?
Sports-Winter
19402   90 mins   C   B, V, 3/4U,   P
                                Q
The most famous and scenic ski areas in the
world are featured, along with the best
international skiers.
TV Sports Scene — *TV Sports Scene*

Benji   1973
Comedy-Drama
49626   87 mins   C   B, V   P
*Benji, Peter Brek, Christopher Connelly, Patsy
Garrett, Deborah Walley, Cynthia Smith,
directed by Joe Camp*
In the loveable pooch's first feature-length
movie, he falls in love with a female named
Tiffany, and saves Paul and Cindy from the
danger of sinister intruders.
MPAA:G
Mulberry Square Prods; Joe Camp — *Vestron
Video; CBS/Fox Video (disc only)*

Benji Takes a Dive at   1982
Marineland/Benji at Work
Animals
72230   60 mins   C   B, V   P
Television's Adam Rich goes to Marineland with
Wonder-dog Benji, and chronicles the canine's
busy work schedule.
Carolyn Camp — *Children's Video Library*

Benji's Very Own   1983
Christmas Story
Fantasy/Christmas
69532   60 mins   C   B, V   P
Benji and his friends go on a magic trip and
meet Kris Kringle and learn how Christmas is
celebrated around the world. Also included:
"The Phenomenon of Benji," a documentary
about Benji's odyssey from the animal shelter to
international stardom.
Mulberry Square Productions — *Children's
Video Library*

Berenstain Bears' Comic   1982
Valentine, The
Cartoons
65418   25 mins   C   B, V   P
Animated
The whole Berenstain Bear family gets in on the
fun when Brother Bear receives a mysterious
Valentine from Miss Honey Bear, a secret
admirer; but can he keep his mind on the
upcoming Valentine's Day Championship
Hockey Game against the Beartown Bullies?

Buzz Potamkin — *Embassy Home Entertainment*

Berenstain Bears' Easter Surprise, The   1981
Cartoons
65437   25 mins   C   B, V   P
Animated
Boss Bunny, who usually controls the seasons, has quit, Poppa Bear's vainglorious effort to construct his own Easter egg machine is a failure; and Brother Bear anxiously awaits his "Extra Special" Easter Surprise.
Buzz Potamkin — *Embassy Home Entertainment*

Berenstein Bears' Play Ball, The   1983
Cartoons
74081   25 mins   C   B, V   P
Animated
In this animated feature, Papa Bear learns a valuable lesson about winning and losing.
Buzz Potamkin — *Embassy Home Entertainment*

Berkshires and Hudsons of the Boston & Albany/Railroading in the Northeast   195?
Trains
62870   30 mins   B/W   B, V   P, T
Railroad buffs will enjoy these scenes of classic steam locomotives from the New Haven, New York Central, Central Vermont, Delaware & Hudson and B & A lines.
J W Deely; E R Blanchard — *Blackhawk Films*

Berlin Alexanderplatz   1980
Drama
66463   020 mins   C   B, V   P
Gunter Lamprecht, Hanna Schygulla, Barbara Sukowa, directed by Rainer Werner Fassbinder
Fassbinder's 15 1/2-hour epic, originally produced for German television, follows the life, death and resurrection of Franz Biberkof, a former transit worker who has just finished a lengthy prison term. With the Berlin of the 1920's as a backdrop, Fassbinder has contrived a melodramatic parable with Biblical overtones.
Teleculture Films; Peter Martheshmeimer — *Vandam Productions*

Berlin Express   1948
War-Drama
00306   86 mins   B/W   B, V, 3/4U   P
Robert Ryan, Merle Oberon, Paul Lukas
Battle of wits between the Allies and Nazi fanatics seeking to keep Germans disunited.
RKO — *Nostalgia Merchant*

Berlin—Symphony of a Great City   1927
Film-Avant-garde/Germany
52362   70 mins   B/W   B, V   P
Directed by Walter Ruttman
An expression of the life of a city from morning to nighttime, set to music with many wildly impressionistic camera angles, montages, etc. An important and influential documentary. Silent with musical score.
Fox Europa; Germany — *Sheik Video; International Historic Films; Western Film & Video Inc*

Bermuda Triangle, The   1979
Documentary/Speculation
29227   94 mins   C   B, V   P
Brad Campbell
One of the world's great mysteries, still unsolved in our time. The facts are that in the last 300 years more than 700 boats and planes and thousands of people have vanished without a trace in the area we call "The Bermuda Triangle."
MPAA:G
Sunn Classic Pictures — *VidAmerica*

Bernadette Peters in Concert   1981
Music-Performance
55561   47 mins   C   LV   P
Bernadette Peters, directed by John Blanchard
This two-sided stereo disc presents Bernadette Peters' live performance, recorded at the 3,000 seat Jubilee Auditorium in Edmonton, Canada.
Doug Holtby; Nicholas Wry — *MCA Home Video*

Bernard Baruch: The Trouble Shooter   1954
Biographical/History-US
44233   15 mins   B/W   B, V   P
Through classical newsreel footage this program presents the career of one of America's foremost statesmen, Bernard Baruch. Baruch is most noted for his atomic energy control plan, presented to the United Nations.
Fox Movietone News — *Two Star Films*

Best Defense, The   1978
Boating
51510   60 mins   C   B, V, 3/4U   P
The story of the 1977 America's Cup defense by Ted Turner and the crew of "Courageous" who successfully defended the Cup for the 23rd time.
Unknown — *Sports World Cinema*

Best Friends 1982
Comedy
66121   108 mins   C   B, V, LV,   R, P
CED
*Goldie Hawn, Burt Reynolds, Jessica Tandy,
Barnard Hughes, Audra Lindley, Keenan Wynn,
Ron Silver, directed by Norman Jewison*
A team of screenwriters decide to marry after
years of living and working together.
MPAA:PG
Warner Bros — *Warner Home Video*

**Best Little Whorehouse
in Texas, The** 1982
Musical/Comedy
63168   111 mins   C   B, V, LV,   P
CED
*Dolly Parton, Burt Reynolds, Dom De Luise,
Charles Durning, Jim Nabors, Lois Nettleton,
directed by Colin Higgins*
Dolly Parton is the buxom owner of The Chicken
Ranch, a house of ill-repute that may be closed
down unless Sheriff Burt Reynolds can think of
a way out. Based on the long-running Broadway
musical.
MPAA:R
Universal — *MCA Home Video*

**Best of Amos 'n Andy
Vol. 1, The** 195?
Comedy
44851   100 mins   B/W   B, V, 3/4U   P
Alvin Childress, Spencer Williams
Four classic television shows are contained in
this volume. They include "Young Girls," "The
Rare Coin," "The Turkey Dinner," and "The
Secretary."
CBS — *Nostalgia Merchant*

Best of Benny Hill, The 1981
Comedy
58457   104 mins   C   B, V   R, P
Benny Hill
Humorous sketches featuring the off-beat
comedy of this British funnyman.
Thames Video — *THORN EMI Home Video*

**Best of Betty Boop,
Volume I, The** 193?
Cartoons
64836   90 mins   C   B, V   P
Animated, voice of Mae Questal
Sweet Betty Boop sashays through eleven of
her classic cartoon adventures in this collection
of original shorts. Mastered from the original
negatives.
Max Fleischer; Paramount — *NTA Home
Entertainment*

**Best of Betty Boop
Volume II** 19??
Cartoons
66471   85 mins   C   B, V   P
Animated
Another collection of original cartoons starring
the "Boop-Oop-a-Doop" girl, assisted by Bimbo
and Koko the Clown. These black-and-white
cartoons have been recolored for this release.
Max Fleischer — *NTA Home Entertainment*

Best of Blondie, The 1981
Music-Performance
58880   60 mins   C   B, V   P
*Deborah Harry, Jimmy Destri, Chris Stein, Nigel
Harrison, Frank Infante, Clem Burke*
Original footage from the group's early days
combines with promotional videos to present
fifteen Blondie hits linked with film shot in New
York locations. Songs include: "Rapture," "The
Tide is High," "Heart of Glass," "Call Me" and
others.
Chrysalis Records — *Chrysalis Visual
Programming; Pacific Arts Video*

**Best of Broadway, "The
Philadelphia Story," The** 1958
Drama
12847   55 mins   B/W   B, V, FO   P
*Dorothy McGuire, John Payne, Richard Carlson,
Herbert Marshall, Mary Astor, Charles
Winninger, Dick Moran*
A superb dramatization of the Philip Barry play.
CBS — *Video Yesteryear*

Best of George Pal, The 1979
Cartoons
54123   75 mins   C   B, V   P
Animated
George Pal's "Puppetoon" series produced
between 1938 and 1943 is highlighted. Black
and white selections include "Sleeping Beauty,"
"Captain Kidding," "Cavalcade of Music," and
"Sky Pirates." In color are "Ship of the Ether,"
"Phillips Broadcast of 1938," "Tubby the Tuba,"
"John Henry," "The Little Broadcast," "Jasper
in a Jam," and "Jasper in the Haunted House."
George Pal — *Video Dimensions*

**Best of Heckle and
Jeckle and Friends, The** 19??
Cartoons
69609   60 mins   C   B, V   P
Animated
This cartoon collection features such
memorable characters as Heckle and Jeckle,
Deputy Dawg, Sad Cat, Possible Possum and
Sidney, the baby elephant.
Terrytoons — *Children's Video Library*

**Best of Heckle and
Jeckle—Volumes IV & V,
The** 194?
Cartoons
29130   90 mins   C   B, V   P
Animated

Terrytoons' characters Heckle and Jeckle are featured in two programs, both available individually.
EL, SP
Viacom International — *CBS/Fox Video*

Best of Little Lulu   19??
Cartoons
65688   60 mins   C   B, V   P
Animated
Mischief-prone Little Lulu returns in this special collection of cartoon adventures.
Paramount — *NTA Home Entertainment*

Best of Marvel Comics, The   1982
Fantasy/Cartoons
62878   112 mins   C   B, V   P
Animated
Five episodes featuring Marvel Comics favorites: Spiderman, Mr. Fantastic, Invisible Girl, Spiderwoman and The Thing. Titles are "The Great Magini," "The Mole Men," "The Menace Magneto," "Calamity on Campus" and "Diamond Dust."
Marvel Comics — *MCA Home Video*

Best of Popeye, The   1983
Cartoons
65109   56 mins   C   B, V, CED   P
Animated
Eight classic Popeye cartoons are included in this compilation.
MGM/UA Home Entertainment Group; Max Fleischer — *MGM/UA Home Video*

Best of Sex and Violence, The   1981
Movie and TV trailers
47756   78 mins   C   B, V   P
Narrated by John Carradine, directed by Ken Dixon
A collection of trailers, or coming attractions, from films which feature blood, sexploitation, soft porn, bizarre comedy, bike flicks, blacksploitation, Kung fu, etc.
S and V Prods; Charles Band — *Wizard Video*

Best of 60 Minutes, The   1984
History-Modern/Television
Closed Captioned
65754   60 mins   C   B, V, CED   P
Mike Wallace, Morley Safer, Harry Reasoner, Ed Bradley, Andy Rooney
Included in this program are 4 of the most gripping segments ever shown on this long running news series.
Don Hewitt; CBS News — *CBS/Fox Video*

Best of Steam I   1979
Trains
55520   60 mins   C   B, V   P

A look at seven currently operating steam engines as they roll through the American countryside: Union Pacific's No. 8444; Sierra Railroad's Nos. 3, 28, and 34; the Rio Grande's two steam engines on the Silverton Route; and the Georgetown Loop R.R. No 44.
De Luz — *De Luz Video*

Best of Steam II   1979
Trains
55521   60 mins   C   B, V   P
A look at seven different live-steam locomotives: the Heisler logging engine No. 2; Southern Railway's No. 722 (2-8-0) and famed ex-Canadian Pacific's "Royal Hudson" No 2839; Sierra R.R.'s ten-wheeler No. 3 and 4-4-0 No. 8; Westside Shay-type engine No. 7; and Union Pacific's No. 8444.
De Luz Video — *De Luz Video*

Best of Terrytoons, The   1983
Cartoons
69530   60 mins   C   B, V, CED   P
Animated
This is a compilation of cartoons featuring Mighty Mouse, Heckle and Jeckle, Deputy Dawg, Gandy Goose, Dinky Duck, Terry Bears and Little Roquefort.
Terrytoons — *Children's Video Library*

Best of the Benny Hill Show, Vol. II, The   1981
Comedy
63346   115 mins   C   B, V   R, P
Benny Hill
Another compilation of humorous sketches from "The Benny Hill Show."
Thames Video — *THORN EMI Home Video*

Best of the Benny Hill Show, Vol. III, The   1983
Comedy
65092   110 mins   C   B, V   R, P
Benny Hill
British funnyman Benny Hill mugs and jokes his way through a new collection of comedy sketches from his popular television series.
Thames Video — *THORN EMI Home Video*

Best of the Big Bands, The   1980
Music
38962   80 mins   B/W   B, V, FO   P
Artie Shaw, Benny Goodman, Gene Krupa, Ray Eberle, Jimmy Dorsey, Harry James, Frank Sinatra, Tommy Dorsey, Count Basie
A compilation of big band film excerpts. Highlights include Harry James and Frank Sinatra performing "Saturday Night (1944), the Benny Goodman Trio with Gene Krupa and Teddy Wilson, and Jimmy Dorsey's Orchestra with Bob Eberly and Helen O'Connell.

United Artists et al — *Video Yesteryear*

Best of the Big Laff-Off, The   1983
Comedy-Performance
65546   60 mins   C   B, V   P
Featuring top comics delivering their most hilarious routines, emphasis is from waistlines to punchlines. It's the best, funniest and fastest-moving segments of "The Big Laff-Off". Premiers Eddie Murphy and Robin Williams.
Chuck Braverman — *Karl Video*

Best of the Kenny Everett Video Show, The   1981
Comedy
59705   104 mins   C   B, V   R, P
Kenny Everett
Great scenes from the popular British late-night TV show combining new wave rock music, outrageous dancing and innovative video special effects.
David Mallett — *THORN EMI Home Video*

Best of the New York Erotic Film Festival Parts I & II   197?
Film
64841   210 mins   C   B, V   P
Two cassette collections of prize-winning and specially selected films presented at the annual New York Erotic Film Festival.
Various — *HarmonyVision*

Best of Warner Brothers (Vol. 1)   194?
Cartoons
58718   55 mins   C   B, V   P
Animated
Classic cartoons from the Warner Brothers archives featuring Porky Pig, Daffy Duck, Bugs Bunny and the gang. Titles include: "Get Rich Quick," "Robinson Crusoe, Jr.," "Porky's Railroad," "Porky's Preview," "I Wanna Be a Sailor," "An Itch in Time," and "Corny Concerto." (Some black and white).
Warner Bros — *Video Dimensions*

Bete Humaine, La   1938
Film-Avant-garde
06223   90 mins   B/W   B, V   P
Jean Gabin, Simone Simon, directed by Jean Renoir
Son of drunkard finds his own abstinence from drink is no escape from self-hate and sadness. French; English subtitles.
FR
France — *Budget Video; Sheik Video; Cable Films; Video Yesteryear; Penguin Video; Discount Video Tapes*

Betrayal   1983
Drama
65490   95 mins   C   B, V, CED   P
Ben Kingsley, Patricia Hodge, Jeremy Irons
An unusual drama, beginning at the end of a seven-year adulterous affair and finally ending at the start of the betrayal of a husband by his wife and his best friend.
MPAA:R
20th Century Fox International Classics — *CBS/Fox Video*

Betsy, The   1978
Drama
65753   125 mins   C   B, V, CED   P
Laurence Olivier, Kathleen Beller, Robert Duvall, Lesley-Anne Down, Tommy Lee Jones, Katherine Ross, Jane Alexander
A story of romance, money, power and mystery centering around the wealthy Hardeman family and their automobile manufacturing business.
MPAA:R
Harold Robbins International Productions — *CBS/Fox Video*

Bette Midler Show, The   1976
Music-Performance
65419   84 mins   C   B, V, LV, CED   P
Bette Midler, accompanied by the Harlettes, jokes, dances and belts out a medley of songs ranging from the Andrew Sisters' "Boogie Woogie Bugle Boy" to "Friends."
Home Box Office — *Embassy Home Entertainment*

Better Team, A   1980
Football
50080   24 mins   C   B, V, FO   R, P
Seattle Seahawks
Highlights of the 1979 Seattle Seahawks' football season.
NFL Films — *NFL Films Video*

Betty Boop #1   193?
Cartoons
47790   57 mins   B/W   B, V, 3/4U   P
Animated
A compilation of seven Betty Boop cartoons: "Betty in Blunderland," "A Hunting We Will Go," "Betty Boop's Rise to Fame," "Candid Candidate," "Crazy Inventions," "Is My Palm Read?" and "More Pep."
Paramount; Max Fleischer — *Western Film & Video Inc*

Betty Boop Cartoon Festival   193?
Cartoons
55339   55 mins   B/W   B, V   P
Animated
Max Fleischer produced and directed these campy, racy cartoons of the 1930's including

such titles as "Baby Be Good," "Betty Boop with Grampy," "Betty Boop with Henry," "Candid Candidate," "Ding Dong Doggie," and "Ker-choo."
Paramount; Max Fleischer — *Budget Video; Discount Video Tapes*

Betty Boop Classics 19??
Cartoons
65689 60 mins C B, V P
Animated
A compilation of Betty Boop and her cartoon pals most fun-filled escapades.
Paramount — *NTA Home Entertainment*

Betty Boop Festival # 1 193?
Cartoons
14435 60 mins B/W B, V P
Animated
An hour of classic Betty Boop cartoons featuring "Is My Palm Red," "Betty's Rise to Fame," "So Does an Automobile," "SOS," "Making Friends," and several others.
Paramount; Max Fleischer — *Video Dimensions*

Betty Boop Festival # 2 193?
Cartoons
57283 55 mins B/W B, V P
Animated
A compilation of classic Betty Boop cartoons, including "Baby Be Good," "A Little Soap and Water," "Kerchoo," "Be Human," "Not Now," "Betty and Jimmy," "Betty in Blunderland," and "Crazy Town."
Paramount; Max Fleischer — *Video Dimensions*

Betty Boop Festival # 3 193?
Cartoons
56614 60 mins B/W B, V P
Animated
Nine cartoons are on this cassette: "Happy You and Merry Me," "No, No, A Thousand Times No," "My Friend the Monkey," "A Song a Day," "Training Pidgeons," "Scared Crows," "Whoop's, I'm a Cowboy," "Musical Mountaineers," and "We Did It."
Paramount; Max Fleischer — *Video Dimensions*

Betty Boop Special Collectors Edition 193?
Cartoons
65740 60 mins B/W B, V P
Animated, directed by Max Fleischer
Betty Boop returns in this collection of vintage cartoons, presented in their original black-and-white form, with appearances by jazz stars Louis Armstrong, Cab Calloway and Don Redman.
Paramount; Max Fleischer — *NTA Home Entertainment*

Between Friends 1983
Drama
72225 105 mins C B, V P
Elizabeth Taylor, Carol Burnett
Two women help each other through the traumatic period following their respective divorces.
Robert Cooper Films — *Vestron Video*

Between Men 1935
Western
08799 59 mins B/W B, V, 3/4U P
John Mack Brown, Beth Marlon
Father kills a man he believes killed his son. Later in life the son meets his father.
Supreme — *Penguin Video; Discount Video Tapes*

Between the Lines 1977
Comedy
59871 101 mins C B, V, CED P
John Heard, Lindsay Crouse, Jeff Goldblum, Jill Eikenberry, Stephen Collins, Lewis J. Stadlen, Michael J. Pollard, Marilu Henner, directed by Joan Micklin Silver
A comic exploration of the rapidly changing world of a group of friends working together on a small alternative newspaper.
MPAA:R
Raphael D Silver; Midwest Film Productions — *Vestron Video*

Beulah Show, The 1952
Comedy
39001 51 mins B/W B, V, FO P
Louise Beavers, Ruby Dandridge, Ernest Whitman, Arthur Q. Bryan 2 pgms
Lovable housemaid Beulah outwits her employers as usual in these episodes from the early 1950's TV series: "Marriage on the Rocks" and "Imagination."
ABC — *Video Yesteryear*

Beyond a Mirage 1977
Middle East
53686 30 mins C B, V, 3/4U P
The Jewish and Arab problems in Palestine are investigated.
Israel — *International Historic Films*

Beyond and Back 1978
Documentary/Speculation
48265 93 mins C B, V P
Narrated by Brad Crandall
The supposed reincarnation experiences of a dozen people are explored in this documentary.
Sunn Classic — *VCI Home Video*

Beyond Bengal 1934
Asia/Documentary
48732 50 mins B/W B, V, 3/4U P

A trip into the Malaysian Peninsula with numerous wild animals and other dangers and excitement highlights this documentary feature.
Joseph Schenk — *Penguin Video*

Beyond Death's Door 1979
Death/Speculation
60350   106 mins   C   B, V   P
Tom Hallick, Howard Platt, Jo Ann Harris, Melinda Naud
A documentary look at people who have seen death but lived to tell about it.
MPAA:PG
Stan Siegel; Sunn Pictures — *VCI Home Video*

Beyond Evil 1980
Horror
65111   98 mins   C   B, V   P
John Saxon, Lynda Day George, Michael Dante, Mario Milano
A newlywed couple moves into an old mansion despite rumors that the house is haunted. The wife becomes possessed by the vengeful spirit of a woman murdered 200 years earlier, and a reign of terror begins.
MPAA:R
David Baughn; Herb Freed — *Media Home Entertainment*

Beyond Reasonable Doubt 1984
Drama/Mystery
65396   117 mins   C   B, V   P
David Hemmings, John Hargreaves
A chilling true life murder mystery which shatters the peaceful quiet of a small New Zealand town and eventually divides a country.
Satori Entertainment
Corporation — *VidAmerica*

Beyond the Door 1975
Horror
47853   97 mins   C   B, V   P
Juliet Mills, Richard Johnson
A San Francisco woman finds herself pregnant with a demonic child.
MPAA:R
Avido Assonnitis — *Media Home Entertainment*

Beyond the Door II 1979
Horror
69303   90 mins   C   B, V   P
John Steiner, Daria Nicolodi, David Colin, Jr., Ivan Rassimov
A family is tormented by supernatural revenge.
MPAA:R
Film Ventures — *Media Home Entertainment*

Beyond the Limit 1983
Drama
65398   103 mins   C   B, V   R, P
Michael Caine, Richard Gere
The story of an intense and darkly ominous love triangle which takes place in the South American coastal city of Corrientes. Based on Graham Greene's novel "The Honorary Consul."
MPAA:R
Norma Heyman — *Paramount Home Video*

Beyond the Valley of the Dolls 1970
Drama
56458   109 mins   C   B, V   P
Edy Williams, Dolly Reed, directed by Russ Meyer
Russ Meyer's story of an all-girl rock combo and their search for Hollywood stardom.
MPAA:X
Twentieth Century Fox — *CBS/Fox Video*

Beyond Tomorrow 1940
Comedy
12402   84 mins   B/W   B, V   P
Richard Carlson, C. Aubrey Smith, Jean Parker, Charles Winninger
Young romance is guided from the spirit world during the Christmas season, as two "ghosts" come back to help young lovers.
RKO — *Budget Video; Discount Video Tapes*

Bible, The 1966
Drama
34287   155 mins   C   B, V   P
Richard Harris, Stephen Boyd, George C. Scott, directed by John Huston
The book of Genesis is dramatized, including the stories of Adam and Eve, Cain and Abel, and Noah and the Flood.
EL, SP
Twentieth Century Fox, Dino DeLaurentiis — *CBS/Fox Video*

Big Bad Mama 1974
Drama
54805   83 mins   C   B, V   R, P
Angie Dickinson, William Shatner, Tom Skerritt, Susan Sennett, Robie Lee, Noble Willingham, directed by Steve Carver
A tough, intelligent, pistol-packing mother moves her two teenage daughters out of poverty-stricken Texas in 1932. They become bank robbers.
MPAA:R
New World Pictures; Roger Corman — *Warner Home Video; RCA VideoDiscs*

Big Bird Cage 1972
Drama
54801   88 mins   C   B, V   R, P

Pam Grier, Sid Haig, Anitra Ford, Candice Roman, Teda Bracci, Carol Speed, Karen McKevic, directed by Jack Hill.
Several females living out prison terms in a rural jail decide to defy their homosexual guards and plan an escape. They are aided by revolutionaries led by a Brooklynese expatriate and his lover. Two of the girls survive the escape massacre.
MPAA:R
New World Pictures — *Warner Home Video*

Big Blue Marble 1981
Adventure
59304   105 mins   C   CED   P
Two segments from the award-winning children's series of the same name: ''My Seventeenth Summer'' (1978), an adventure story that crackles with intrigue and suspense while imparting a lesson in understanding people of different origins; and ''Flying for Fun,'' which examines everything from a frisbee championship to the flight of a sailplane (1981).
EL, JA
Blue Marble Co — *RCA VideoDiscs*

Big Breakdowns—Hollywood Bloopers of the 1930's, The 193?
Outtakes and bloopers
47468   27 mins   B/W   B, V, FO   P
Joan Blondell, Humphrey Bogart, James Cagney, Bette Davis, Errol Flynn, John Garfield, Leslie Howard, Boris Karloff, Dick Powell, Edward G. Robinson
Leftover shots, gag scenes, flubs and goofs from Warner Brothers films of the late 30's, featuring nearly every contract player on the lot.
Warner Bros — *Video Yesteryear*

Big Bus, The 1976
Comedy/Adventure
60217   88 mins   C   B, V   R, P
Joseph Bologna, Stockard Channing, Ned Beatty, Ruth Gordon, Larry Hagman
The wild adventures of the world's first nuclear-powered bus as it makes its maiden voyage from New York to Denver.
MPAA:PG
Fred Freeman; Lawrence J. Cohen — *Paramount Home Video*

Big Cat, The 1949
Western
08611   75 mins   C   B, V, 3/4U   P
Lon McCallister, Peggy Ann Garner, Preston Foster, Forrest Tucker
Mountain valley in Utah is ravaged by a cougar; tense excitement is heightened by hatred between two men over a woman who is dead.
Eagle Lion — *Penguin Video; Discount Video Tapes*

Big Chance, The 1933
Drama
08858   70 mins   B/W   B, V, 3/4U   P
John Darrow, Mickey Rooney, J. Carrol Naish, Hank Mann
Boxer Frankie Moran gains a reputation for victories, but no one is aware that his fights are fixed.
Eagle — *Penguin Video*

Big Chill, The 1983
Comedy-Drama
72930   108 mins   C   B, V   P
Tom Berenger, Glenn Close, Jeff Goldblum, William Hurt, Kevin Kline, Mary Kay Place, Meg Tilly, Jobeth Williams, directed by Lawrence Kasdan
A group of college graduates from the 1960's reunite at the funeral of a friend.
MPAA:R
Michael Shambers — *RCA/Columbia Pictures Home Video*

Big Country Live 1984
Music-Performance
72889   75 mins   C   B, V   P
Big Country
This is a concert taped in Scotland on New Year's Eve 1984. Big Country performs ''Wonderland'' ''Fields of Fire'' and ''In a Big Country.''
Aubrey Powell — *Music Media*

Big Fights, Vol. 1—Muhammad Ali's Greatest Fights, The 1980
Boxing
56878   90 mins   C   CED   P
Thrilling moments from the career of Muhammad Ali, including bouts with Sonny Liston, Archie Moore, Floyd Patterson, Ken Norton, Joe Frazier, and Leon Spinks.
ABC — *RCA VideoDiscs*

Big Fights, Vol. 2—Heavyweight Champions' Greatest Fights, The 1981
Boxing
59017   89 mins   C   CED   P
Muhammad Ali, Jack Johnson, Jack Dempsey, Gene Tunney, Joe Louis, Rocky Marciano, Floyd Patterson
All of the heavyweight greats are seen in this collection of boxing's greatest heavyweight matches. Contains rare early footage. Some black and white footage.
ABC — *RCA VideoDiscs*

Big Fights, Vol. 3—Sugar Ray Robinson's Greatest Fights, The　1982
Boxing
60377　90 mins　C　CED　　P
The career of boxer Sugar Ray Robinson is examined in this program, which highlights his greatest title matches.
ABC — *RCA VideoDiscs*

Big Game America　1968
Football
50086　51 mins　C　B, V, FO　　R, P
Pro football's fascinating first fifty years. Don Meredith wired for sound in his last game as a Cowboy is also included.
NFL Films — *NFL Films Video*

Big Heat, The　1963
Drama
13227　90 mins　B/W　B, V　　P
Glenn Ford, Lee Marvin, Gloria Grahame, Jocelyn Brando, Alexander Scourby, directed by Fritz Lang
A detective's wife is killed in an explosion meant for him, as he pursues his quest to trap a nest of criminals.
Columbia; Robert Arthur — *RCA/Columbia Pictures Home Video*

Big Jake　1971
Drama
65496　90 mins　C　CED　　P
John Wayne, Richard Boone, Maureen O'Hara, Patrick Wayne, Chris Mitchum, Bobby Vinton
An elderly Texas cattleman swings into action when his grandson is kidnapped.
Batjac; Cinema Center — *CBS/Fox Video*

Big Picture—The Fight for Vietnam　196?
Vietnam War
53695　30 mins　B/W　B, V, 3/4U　　P
This program explains various aspects of the army's mission in Vietnam.
Unknown — *International Historic Films*

Big Red　1962
Drama
65637　89 mins　C　B, V　　R, P
Walter Pidgeon, Gilles Payant
Set amid the spectacular beauty of Canada's Quebec Province, an orphan boy protects a dog which later saves him from a mountain lion.
Buena Vista — *Walt Disney Home Video*

Big Red One, The　1980
War-Drama
52742　113 mins　C　B, V, CED　　P
Lee Marvin, Robert Carradine, directed by Sam Fuller
Fuller's semi-autobiographical account of the U.S. Army's famous First Infantry Division in World War II, the "Big Red One." A rifle squad composed of four very young men cut a fiery path of conquest from the landing in North Africa to the liberation of the concentration camp at Falkenau, Czechoslovakia.
MPAA:PG
Lorimar Prods — *CBS/Fox Video*

Big Show　1937
Western
07971　54 mins　B/W　B, V　　P
Gene Autry, Smiley Burnette
A western adventure featuring Gene Autry.
Republic; Gene Autry — *Video Connection; Sheik Video*

Big Sleep, The　1946
Suspense
59303　114 mins　B/W　B, V　　P
Humphrey Bogart, Lauren Bacall, Martha Vickers, Elisha Cook Jr, Dorothy Malone, directed by Howard Hawks
Bogie protrays private eye Philip Marlowe, hired to protect a young woman from her own indiscretions, and falls in love with her older sister.
Warner Bros — *CBS/Fox Video; RCA VideoDiscs*

Big Steal, The　1949
Adventure
33901　72 mins　B/W　B, V　　P
Robert Mitchum, William Bendix, Jane Greer, Ramon Novarro
An Army officer recovers a missing payroll and captures the thieves after a tumultuous chase through Mexico.
RKO — *Nostalgia Merchant*

Big Surprise, The　1956
Game show
42979　30 mins　B/W　B, V, FO　　P
Mike Wallace, Errol Flynn
This $100,000 prize quiz extravaganza was NBC's answer to the "$64,000 Question." Mike Wallace hosts as Errol Flynn wins $30,000 answering questions on ships and the sea.
NBC — *Video Yesteryear*

Big Time, The　1960
Comedy
12839　51 mins　B/W　B, V, FO　　P
George Burns, Jack Benny, Eddie Cantor, George Jessell, Bobby Darin, The Kingston Trio, Jeff Alexander
A live TV variety show featuring well-done comedy, singing, and dancing.
Unknown — *Video Yesteryear*

　(For Explanation of codes, see USE GUIDE and KEY)

Big Trains A—Rolling 1952
Trains
68901   25 mins   C   B, V   P
A classic railroad public relation program on how the railroads serve our nation.
Unknown — *Interurban Films*

Big Trees, The 1952
Drama
66509   89 mins   C   B, V   P
Kirk Douglas, Patrice Wymore, Eve Miller, Alan Hale, Jr, Edgar Buchanan
A ruthless lumberman attempts a takeover of the California Redwood Timberlands that are owned by a group of peaceful homesteaders.
Warner Bros — *Discount Video Tapes; Video Gems*

Bigmouth 1981
Fishing
65152   50 mins   C   B, V   P
Narrated by Rod Sterling
This study of largemouth bass contains complete fishing information. Part of the "Sportsman's Video Collection."
Glen Lau — *Leisure Time Products Project/3M*

Bikini Beach 1964
Musical
65068   100 mins   C   B, V   P
Annette Funicello, Frankie Avalon, Martha Hyer, Harvey Lembeck, Don Rickles, Stevie Wonder
The surfing teenagers at Bikini Beach and a visitor, British recording star The Potato Bug, join forces to keep their beach from being turned into a retirement community. Songs include "Bikini Drag," "Love's a Secret Weapon" and "Because You're You."
Alta Vista Productions; American International — *Embassy Home Entertainment*

Bilitis 1977
Drama
50729   95 mins   C   B, V   P
Patti D'Arbanville, Bernard Giraudeau, Mona Kristensen, directed by David Hamilton
A young girl from a private girls' school is initiated into the pleasures of sex and the unexpected demands of love.
MPAA:R
Topar; Sylvio Tabet; Jacques Nahum — *Media Home Entertainment*

Bill 1981
Drama
73532   97 mins   C   B, V   R, P
Mickey Rooney, Dennis Quaid
The true story of Bill Sackler, a mentally retarded adult who was released from a mental institution after 44 years. Available in Beta Hi-Fi and VHS stereo.
Emmy Awards '82: Best Actor (Mickey Rooney); Best Story.

Alan Landsburg — *U.S.A. Home Video*

Bill and Coo 1947
Fantasy
45023   61 mins   C   B, V   P
An unusual love story with a villian and hero using an all bird cast.
Academy Award '47: Special Award.
Republic, Ken Murray — *Budget Video; Discount Video Tapes; Video Connection; Penguin Video; Classic Video Cinema Collector's Club*

Bill Watrous 1983
Music-Performance
76672   24 mins   C   B, V   P
This program presents the jazz trombonist Bill Watrous performing with his Refuge West Band.
Dig it Recordings — *Sony Corporation of America*

Bill Wyman 1983
Music-Performance
64930   11 mins   C   B, V   P
Bill Wyman of the Rolling Stones performs three songs solo on this Video 45: "Si Si (Je Suis Un Rock Star)," "A New Fashion" and "Come Back Suzanne."
Ripple Records — *Sony Corporation of America*

Billion Dollar Hobo, The 1978
Comedy
58707   96 mins   C   B, V, CED   P
Tim Conway, Will Geer, Eric Weston, Sydney Lassick
Tim Conway stars as a poor, unsuspecting heir of a multimillion dollar fortune, who must duplicate his benefactor's experience as a hobo during the Depression in order to collect his inheritance.
MPAA:G
Samuel Goldwyn Home Entertainment — *CBS/Fox Video*

Billy Boy 1979
Adventure
66083   94 mins   C   B, V   P
Duane Bobick, Kim Braden
A young boxer fights his way to the top.
MPAA:R
Falcon American — *Best Film & Video Corporation*

Billy Connolly—Bites Yer Bum 1981
Comedy-Performance
66039   105 mins   C   B, V   P
A live recording of the Scottish Funnyman, capturing his earthy humor in stories and songs.

Chrysalis Group Ltd — *Chrysalis Visual Programming*

Billy Jack   1971
Drama
52705   112 mins   C   B, V   R, P
Tom Laughlin, Delores Taylor, Clark Howat
A half-breed ex-Green Beret stands between a redneck town and a Freedom School for runaways located on an Arizona Indian Reservation.
MPAA:PG
Warner Bros; National Student Film Corp — *Warner Home Video; RCA VideoDiscs*

Billy Joel: Live from Long   1983
Island
Music-Performance
65413   80 mins   C   B, V, LV,   P
                                      CED
A recording of Billy Joel's dynamic New Year's Eve performance at Nassau Coliseum. Classic tunes showcased include "Piano Man," "Allentown," "You May Be Right," and "Still Rock and Roll to Me." In VHS stereo and Beta Hi-Fi.
CBS Fox — *CBS/Fox Video*

Billy Liar   1963
Comedy-Drama
66188   94 mins   B/W   B, V   R, P
Tom Courtenay, Julie Christie
A young Englishman dreams of escaping from his working class family and dead-end job.
Continental — *THORN EMI Home Video*

Billy Squier   1982
Music-Performance
63350   60 mins   C   B, V   R, P
Billy Squier
Billy Squier performs some of his best songs live in concert, including "In the Dark," "Rich Kids" and "My Kinda Lover."
EMI Music — *THORN EMI Home Video; Pioneer Artists*

Billy the Kid in Texas   1940
Western
54164   52 mins   B/W   B, V   P
Bob Steele
The famed outlaw takes on trouble and makes sure the Texans never forget that he has been there.
Producers Releasing Corp — *Video Connection*

Billy the Kid Returns   1938
Western
07187   60 mins   B/W   B, V   P
Roy Rogers
Roy is mistaken for the legendary outlaw, Billy the Kid.

Republic — *Budget Video; Video Connection; Video Dimensions; Cable Films; Discount Video Tapes*

Billy the Kid Versus   1966
Dracula
Horror/Western
69568   73 mins   C   B, V, FO   P
John Carradine, Chuck Courtney
Dracula travels to the Old West, anxious to "put the bite" on a pretty lady ranchowner. Her fiance, the legendary outlaw Billy the Kid, steps in to save his girl from becoming a vampire herself.
Avco Embassy — *Video Yesteryear*

Bing Crosby Festival   193?
Musical
01604   60 mins   B/W   B, V   P
Bing Crosby
Features three of Bing's musical short subjects. Includes "Billboard Girl," "Blue of the Night," "I Surrender Dear."
Mack Sennett — *Budget Video; Discount Video Tapes*

Bing Crosby Show, The   1963
Variety
38990   57 mins   B/W   B, V, FO   P
Bing Crosby, Bob Hope, Edie Adams, the Pete Fountain Quintet, the Smothers Brothers
A Bing Crosby special, with music from Bing and Pete Fountain's group, and comedy sketches by Bing and Bob and the Smothers Brothers. Commercials included.
NBC — *Video Yesteryear*

Bingo Long Traveling All-   1976
Stars & Motor Kings, The
Comedy
64796   111 mins   C   B, V   P
Billy Dee Williams, James Earl Jones, Richard Pryor, directed by John Badham
Set during the Depression of 1939, this film follows the comedic adventures of a lively group of black ball players who have defected from the old Negro National League. The All-Stars travel the country challenging local white teams.
MPAA:PG
Universal — *MCA Home Video*

Bird of Paradise   1932
Romance
51611   80 mins   B/W   B, V   P
Joel McCrea, Dolores Del Rio, Lon Chaney Jr.
An exotic South Seas romance in which an adventurer falls in love with a native girl.
RKO — *Budget Video; Cable Films; Video Connection; Discount Video Tapes; Movie Buff Video; Classic Video Cinema Collector's Club*

Bird with the Crystal Plumage, The — 1970
Mystery
51575   98 mins   C   B, V   P
Tony Musante, Susy Kendall, Eva Renzi
An alleged murderer is cleared when the woman believed to be his next victim is revealed to be a psychopathic murderer.
MPAA:PG
UMC; Salvatore Argento — *VCI Home Video*

Birdman & Galaxy Trio — 197?
Cartoons
66280   60 mins   C   B, V   P
Animated
Birdman, a former secret agent, is bestowed with powerful wings.
Hanna Barbera — *Worldvision Home Video*

Birdman of Alcatraz, The — 1961
Drama
59342   148 mins   B/W   CED   P
Burt Lancaster, Karl Malden, Thelma Ritter, Edmond O'Brien, Neville Brand, Telly Savalas, directed by John Frankenheimer
An imprisoned murderer makes a name for himself as an ornithologist.
United Artists — *RCA VideoDiscs*

Birds, The — 1963
Horror
45001   120 mins   C   B, V   P
Rod Taylor, Tippi Hedren, Jessica Tandy, directed by Alfred Hitchcock
A small shore town north of San Francisco is attacked by thousands of birds of varying shapes, sizes, and colors.
Universal — *MCA Home Video; RCA VideoDiscs*

Birgitt Haas Must Be Killed — 1983
Suspense
66508   105 mins   C   B, V   P
Philippe Noiret, Jean Rochefort, Lisa Kreuzer
A secret agent plots to murder a German female terrorist make it appear that her boyfriend was the killer.
Aida Bure; George Bure; Laurent Heynemann — *Program Hunters*

Birth of a Foal: Red Wing and Rain Drop, The — 1983
Animals
69634   20 mins   C   B, V   P
Earl Tobler, D.V.M., induces birth in a 17-year-old Appaloosa, Red Wing, and discusses this controversial procedure. The foal, Rain Drop, makes his debut and takes his first steps.
Mercedes Maharis — *Mercedes Maharis Productions*

Birth of a Legend, The — 1984
Theater
76011   25 mins   B/W   B, V   P, T
Mary Pickford, Douglas Fairbanks Sr.
A documentary showing the on and off antics of Miss Pickford and Mr. Fairbanks when they reigned as the King and Queen of the movies in 1926.
Matty Kemp; Mary Pickford Company — *Blackhawk Films*

Birth of a Nation, The — 1915
Film-History/War-Drama
47465   175 mins   B/W   B, V, FO   P
Lillian Gish, Henry B. Walthall, Mae Marsh, directed by D. W. Griffith
The Civil War-era classic by D. W. Griffith, presented here from the most complete print of the film known to exist.
Epoch — *Video Yesteryear*

Birth of a Nation — 1915
Film-History
57204   158 mins   B/W   B, V   P, T
Lillian Gish, Henry B. Walthall, Mae Marsh, Wallace Reid, directed by D.W. Griffith
A special tinted and musically scored print of D.W. Griffith's milestone classic recalling the Civil War and Reconstruction.
Epoch — *Blackhawk Films; Glenn Video Vistas; Discount Video Tapes; Cinema Concepts; Classic Video Cinema Collector's Club*

Birth of a Nation, The — 1915
Film-History
08635   124 mins   C   B, V, 3/4U   P
Lillian Gish, Henry B. Walthall, Mae Marsh, Miriam Cooper, Wallace Reid, directed by D.W. Griffith
D. W. Griffith's dramatization of the events leading up to the Civil War. Based on "The Clansman," by Thomas Dixon.
Epoch — *Penguin Video; VCII; Sheik Video; International Historic Films; Cable Films; Video Connection; Budget Video; Western Film & Video Inc*

Bitch, The — 1978
Drama
63337   90 mins   C   B, V   R, P
Joan Collins
This continuation of "The Stud" tells of the erotic adventures of a beautiful divorcee playing sex games for high stakes on the international playgrounds of high society.
MPAA:R
Brent Walker Film Productions — *THORN EMI Home Video*

Bite the Bullet — 1975
Western
76025   131 mins   C   B, V   P

Gene Hackman, James Coburn, Candice Bergen, Jan-Michael Vincent
This exciting action-adventure featuring an all-star cast tells of a grueling 700-mile horse race in the rugged west of the early 1900's.
MPAA:PG
Richard Brooks — *RCA/Columbia Pictures Home Video*

Bittersweet   1933
Musical-Drama
13635   80 mins   B/W   B, V, 3/4U   P
Anna Neagle, Fernand Graavey, Esme Percy
An elderly woman presents the story of her bittersweet romance with a musician through flashbacks. Based on Noel Coward's semi-tragic operetta.
British — *Penguin Video*

Bizarre Bizarre   1939
Comedy
07249   90 mins   B/W   B, V   P
Louis Jouvet, Michel Simon, Francoise Rosay
A revue of comedy-farce sketches that include slapstick, burlesque, black humor and comedy of the absurd. French dialogue with English subtitles.
FR
French — *Budget Video; Festival Films*

Black and Tan/St. Louis Blues   1929
Musical
60048   36 mins   B/W   B, V   P, T
Duke Ellington and his Cotton Club Orchestra, Fredi Washington, Bessie Smith, the Hall Johnson Choir
Two early jazz two-reelers are combined on this tape: "Black and Tan" is the first film appearance of Duke Ellington's Orchestra, featuring Cootie Williams and Johnny Hodges. "St. Louis Blues" is the only surviving film made by legendary blues singer Bessie Smith. She is backed by the Hall Johnson Choir, members of the Fletcher Henderson band directed by James P. Johnson and dancer Jimmy Mordecai.
RKO; Dudley Murphy — *Blackhawk Films*

Black Beauty   1978
Cartoons
47687   49 mins   C   B, V   P
Animated
The tale of a sweet-tempered horse sold into the slavery of a harsh master.
Hanna Barbera — *Worldvision Home Video*

Black Beauty/Courage of Black Beauty   19??
Adventure
59151   145 mins   C   B, V, 3/4U   P
Mona Freeman, Johnny Crawford
Two feature-length films based on Anna Sewell's novel about the love of a child for a black stallion comprise this cassette. "Black Beauty" was first released in 1946; "Courage of Black Beauty" in 1957.
20th Century Fox — *Nostalgia Merchant*

Black Belt   1973
Martial arts
63862   92 mins   C   B, V   P
Two masters of Kung Fu clash when both attempt to steal a shipment of gold bullion.
MPAA:R
United International Pictures — *Budget Video*

Black Belt Karate I   1982
Martial arts
59571   60 mins   C   B, V   P
Hosted by Jay T. Will
An introduction to the basic philosophy and moves of this Oriental self-defense system.
Professional Karate Assn — *Mastervision*

Black Belt Karate II   1982
Martial arts
59572   60 mins   C   B, V   P
Hosted by Jay T. Will
Jay T. Will takes the aficionado up the ladder and sets the athletic stage for the student's next upward move to karate expertise.
Professional Karate Assn — *Mastervision*

Black Belt Karate III   1981
Martial arts
59573   60 mins   C   B, V   P
Hosted by Jay T. Will
This program takes the practitioner into the rarefied atmosphere of the highest karate plane.
Professional Karate Assn — *Mastervision*

Black Bird, The   1975
Comedy
62814   98 mins   C   B, V   P
George Segal, Stephane Audran, Lionel Stander, Lee Patrick
In this satiric "sequel" to "The Maltese Falcon," detective Sam Spade, Jr. searches for the mysterious black falcon statuette that caused his father such trouble.
MPAA:PG
Columbia — *RCA/Columbia Pictures Home Video*

Black Cat, The/The Raven   193?
Horror
63842   126 mins   B/W   B, V   P
Boris Karloff, Bela Lugosi, Jacqueline Wells, John Carradine, Irene Ware, Lester Matthews
Both parts of this double feature star Boris Karloff and Bela Lugosi in leading roles. "The Black Cat" (1934, 65 minutes) features an architect who preserves the corpses of young girls and a doctor who plays chess in an attempt

to keep a new bride from becoming a sacrifice to Satan. In "The Raven" (1935, 61 minutes), an insane plastic surgeon who is obsessed by the works of Edgar Allan Poe creates an elaborate torture chamber.
Universal — *MCA Home Video*

Black Coin, The   1936
Adventure
08620   80 mins   B/W   B, V, 3/4U   P
Ralph Graves, Ruth Mix, directed by Elmer Clifton
A condensation of the "Black Coin" movie serial.
Stage and Screen — *Penguin Video*

Black Dragon, The   1974
Martial arts
63405   93 mins   C   B, V   P
Ron Van Clief, Jason Rai Pow, Jorge Estraga, Nancy Veronica
A young farm boy moves to the city and teams up with an undercover narcotics agent to infiltrate and destroy the underworld syndicate.
MPAA:R
Serafim Karalexis; Yeo Ban Yee — *Sun Video*

Black Dragons   1949
War-Drama
08758   62 mins   B/W   B, V, 3/4U   P
Bela Lugosi, Joan Barclay, George Pembroke, Clayton Moore
A war drama involving sabotage by the Japanese.
Monogram — *Penguin Video; Video Connection; Cable Films*

Black Dragon's Revenge, The   1975
Martial arts
63406   90 mins   C   B, V   P
Ron Van Clief, Charles Bonet, Jason Pai Pow
The Black Dragon arrives in Hong Kong to investigate the death of a great Kung fu master.
MPAA:R
Serafim Karalexis — *Sun Video*

Black Emanuelle   1976
Drama
60584   121 mins   C   B, V   P
Karin Schubert, Angelo Infanti, Don Powell
Emanuelle travels to Africa on an assignment, but work turns to play as she becomes a willing partner.
Independent — *CBS/Fox Video*

Black Hole, The   1979
Science fiction
44297   97 mins   C   B, V, LV   R, P
Maximilian Schell, Anthony Perkins, Ernest Borgnine, Yvette Mimieux
This is your basic mad scientist movie, with Maximilian Schell as a man determined to acquire the secrets of the universe by plunging into a black hole. In preparation for his journey he has manufactured an army of robots to assist him such as his body guard robot, Maximilian.
MPAA:G
Walt Disney — *Walt Disney Home Video; RCA VideoDiscs*

Black Jack   1952
Drama
66363   112 mins   B/W   B, V   P
George Sanders, Agnes Moorehead, Herbert Marshall, Patricia Roc, directed by Julien Duvivier
A Riviera socialite pretends to be an undercover agent, but she is actually a dope smuggler. Also known as "Captain Black Jack."
United Artists; Walter Gould — *Movie Buff Video*

Black Lash   1952
Western
08804   55 mins   B/W   B, V, 3/4U   P
Lash La Rue, Fuzzy St. John, Peggy Stewart, Ray Bennett, Kermit Maynard
Lash and Fuzzy, on a secret mission, have a gang of outlaws believing they are exmarshals.
Western Adventure Prod Inc; Ron Somond — *Penguin Video*

Black Like Me   1964
Drama
45049   110 mins   B/W   B, V   P
Roscoe Lee Browne, James Whitmore, Clifton James, Dan Priest
This movie is based on the true story of a white writer who chemically changes the color of his skin and travels through the South experiencing the humiliation and terror of the black man.
Continental, Alan Enterprises — *VCI Home Video*

Black Magic   1949
Adventure
45148   105 mins   B/W   B, V, 3/4U   P
Orson Welles, Akim Tamiroff, Nancy Guild
Cogliostro the magician becomes involved in a plot to supply a double for Marie Antoinette.
Edward Small; United Artists — *Nostalgia Merchant*

Black Marble, The   1979
Crime-Drama
56454   110 mins   C   B, V, CED   P
Paula Prentiss, Harry Dean Stanton, Robert Foxworth
A beautiful policewoman is paired with a policeman who drinks too much, is divorced, and is ready to retire. Surrounded by urban craziness and corruptness, they eventually fall in love. Based on the Joseph Wambaugh novel.

MPAA:PG
Avco Embassy, Frank Capra Jr — *Embassy Home Entertainment*

Black Market Rustlers   1943
Western
54165   60 mins   B/W   B, V   P
Ray Corrigan
The Range Busters are at it again. This time they break up a cattle rustling syndicate.
Monogram — *Video Connection*

Black Music Video   194?
Special
Music-Performance
59222   90 mins   B/W   B, V, 3/4U   P
A compilation of black music shorts from the 30's and 40's including "Harlem Hotshots" (1940's), "Caledonia" (early 40's), "Variety Time," and "Jivin' in Bebop." Featured performers include Ethel Waters, Louis Armstrong, Duke Ellington, Fats Waller, Lena Horne.
W D Alexander et al — *Penguin Video*

Black Narcissus   1947
Drama
50914   101 mins   C   B, V,   P
Deborah Kerr, Jean Simmons, Flora Robson, Sabu, David Farrar
A group of Anglican nuns attempting to found a hospital and school in the Himalayas confront native distrust and their own human frailties.
Universal — *VidAmerica*

Black Orpheus   1959
Drama
52741   98 mins   C   B, V, CED   P
Breno Mello, Marpessa Dawn, Lourdes De Oliveira, directed by Marcel Camus
The legend of Orpheus and Eurydice unfolds against the colorful background of the carnival in Rio de Janeiro. In the black section of the city, Orpheus is a street-car conductor and Eurydice a country girl fleeing from a man sworn to kill her. Dubbed in English.
Cannes Film Festival '59: Grand Prize Winner; Academy Awards '59: Best Foreign Language Film.
France; Brazil; Lopert Pictures — *CBS/Fox Video*

Black Panthers: Huey   1953
Newton/Black Panther
Newsreel
Minorities
72503   53 mins   B/W   B, V, 3/4U   P
A film focusing on the "Free Huey Newton" rally in California; a separate video features an interview with Newton from Alameda County Jail, plus the Panther 10-point plan presented by Bobby Seale.

Black Panthers — *International Historic Films*

Black Pirate, The   1926
Adventure
47460   122 mins   B/W   B, V, FO   P
Douglas Fairbanks, Donald Crisp, Billie Dove
A shipwrecked mariner vows revenge on the pirates who destroyed his father's ship. Quintessential Fairbanks, this film features astounding athletic feats and exciting swordplay. Originally filmed in Technicolor, this print is in black and white. Silent film with music score.
Elton Corp; Douglas Fairbanks — *Video Yesteryear; Discount Video Tapes; Classic Video Cinema Collector's Club*

Black Planet, The   1983
Cartoons
65707   78 mins   C   B, V   P
Animated
The distant planet of Terre Verte is rapidly running out of energy. To keep the remaining fuel, warhawks Senator Calhoun and General McNab think their part of the Planet should blow up the other part. Will the whole planet be destroyed?
Paul Williams — *Embassy Home Entertainment*

Black Sabbath Live   1984
Music-Performance
76645   60 mins   C   B, V   P
Heavy metal superstar, Ozzy Osbourne, as a member of Black Sabbath, performs such hits as "War Pigs," "Never Say Die" and "Paranoid."
VCL — *VCL Home Video*

Black Stallion Returns,   1983
The
Adventure/Drama
69375   103 mins   C   B, V, LV,   P
                     CED
Kelly Reno, Teri Garr
This sequel to "The Black Stallion" follows the adventures of young Alec as he travels to North Africa to search for his beautiful horse, which was stolen by an Arab chieftain.
MPAA:PG
Zoetrope — *CBS/Fox Video; RCA VideoDiscs*

Black Stallion, The   1979
Adventure
47058   120 mins   C   B, V, LV   P
Kelly Reno, Mickey Rooney, Teri Garr, Clarence Muse, directed by Carroll Ballard
A young boy and a wild Arabian Stallion are the only survivors of a shipwreck, and they develop a deep affection for each other. Music by Carmine Coppola.
MPAA:PG

       (For Explanation of codes, see USE GUIDE and KEY)

United Artists, Francis Coppola — *CBS/Fox Video; RCA VideoDiscs*

Black Sunday   1977
Drama
64451   143 mins   C   B, V   R, P
Robert Shaw, Bruce Dern, Marthe Keller, Fritz Weaver, Steven Keats
An Arab terrorist group plots to kidnap the Goodyear blimp and load it with explosives with the intent for it to explode over a Miami Super Bowl game to assassinate the U.S. president and to kill all the fans.
MPAA:R
Paramount — *Paramount Home Video; RCA VideoDiscs*

Black Sunday: Highlights of Super Bowl XVII   1984
Football
72934   46 mins   C   B, V, FO   P
Highlights from SuperBowl XVIII include playoffs for each of the nine teams that qualified; also included in the program is "NFL 83" a summary of the NFL 1983 Season.
NFL Films — *NFL Films Video*

Black Widow, The   1947
Adventure/Serials
07340   164 mins   B/W   B, V, 3/4U   P
Bruce Edwards, Carol Forman, Anthony Warde
A fortune-teller plots to steal scientific secrets and take over the world. Serial in thirteen episodes.
Republic — *Video Connection*

Blackbeard's Ghost   1967
Comedy
59810   107 mins   C   B, V   R, P
Peter Ustinov, Dean Jones, Suzanne Pleshette, Elsa Lanchester, Richard Deacon
The famed 18th-century pirate's spirit returns to play havoc in a modern-day college town.
Walt Disney Productions — *Walt Disney Home Video*

Blackenstein   1974
Horror
03562   87 mins   C   B, V   P
A doctor restores a man's arms and legs, but a jealous assistant causes the man to turn into a monster who starts attacking people.
MPAA:R
Prestige Pictures Releasing Corp — *Media Home Entertainment*

Blackjack   1982
Gambling
62740   50 mins   C   B, V   P
Strategies and ways to win blackjack are covered in this instructional cassette.

Casino Gaming Instruction — *Marketvisions*

Blackmail   1929
Mystery
01742   86 mins   B/W   B, V   P
Anny Ondra, John Longdon, Sara Allgood, Charles Paton, directed by Alfred Hitchcock
Britain's first sound film and an early visualization of some typical Hitchcockian themes. The story follows the police investigation of a murder, and a detective's attempts to keep his girlfriend from being involved.
British Intl; Wardour — *Budget Video; Sheik Video; Ampro Video Productions; Cable Films; Western Film & Video Inc; Discount Video Tapes; Classic Video Cinema Collector's Club*

Blacksmith, The/Cops   1922
Comedy
60052   38 mins   B/W   B, V   P, T
Buster Keaton, Virginia Fox
"The Blacksmith" is a burlesque of Longfellow's famous poem "The Village Blacksmith." In "Cops" Buster tries a new business venture to win his girl's hand. Chaos ensues. Silent.
Comique Film Company — *Blackhawk Films*

Blacksmith, The/The Balloonatic   192?
Comedy
56909   57 mins   B/W   B, V, FO   P
Buster Keaton, Virginia Fox, Phyllis Haver
Two Buster Keaton shorts: "The Blacksmith (1922) features Buster as the local blacksmith's apprentice who suddenly finds himself in charge. "The Balloonatic" (1923) presents Buster trapped in a runaway hot air balloon. Both films include music score.
First National — *Video Yesteryear*

Blackstar   1981
Cartoons/Adventure
66006   60 mins   C   B, V   P
Animated
Blackstar fights the forces of evil in three animated adventures.
Filmation — *Family Home Entertainment*

Blackstar Volume III   1981
Cartoons
73368   60 mins   C   B, V   P
Animated
John Blackstar and his friends take on the evil overlord in three adventures: "The Mermaid of Serpent Sea," "Lightning City of the Clouds" and "The Airwhales of Anchar."
Filmation Associates — *Family Home Entertainment*

(For Explanation of codes, see USE GUIDE and KEY)

Blackstar, Volume 2 1981
Cartoons/Adventure
69805   60 mins   C   B, V   P
Animated
John Blackstar and his friends on the planet
Sagar continue their never-ending battle against
the cruel and ruthless Overlord in three
animated adventures.
Filmation — Family Home Entertainment

Blade 1972
Crime-Drama
59351   79 mins   C   B, V   R, P
Steve Landesburg, John Schuck, Kathryn
Walker
An honest cop challenges a dirty cover-up in
killer-stalked New York.
MPAA:PG
Heritage Enterprises — Video Gems

Blade Runner 1982
Science fiction
60437   122 mins   C   B, V, LV,   P
                            CED
Harrison Ford, Rutger Hauer, Sean Young, M.
Emmet Walsh, Joanna Cassidy, Leo Gorcey Jr.
A hard-boiled ex-cop (known as Blade Runner)
is forced out of retirement for an extremely
dangerous mission. He must track down and kill
a group of genetically manufactured beings
impersonating humans.
MPAA:R
Ladd Co; Sir Run Run Shaw; Warner
Bros — Embassy Home Entertainment

Blake of Scotland Yard 1936
Drama/Serials
10931   70 mins   B/W   B, V   P
Ralph Byrd, Lloyd Hughes; directed by Robert
Hill
Feature film version of this exciting serial, with
Blake up again a villain who has constructed a
murderous death ray.
Victory — Discount Video Tapes; Penguin
Video; Video Connection; Video Yesteryear

Blame It on Rio 1984
Comedy
72908   90 mins   C   B, V   P
Michael Caine, Joseph Bologna, Demi Moore,
Michelle Johnson
A middle-aged man has a fling with his best
friend's daughter while on a vacation in Rio de
Janeiro.
MPAA:R
Sherwood Productions — Vestron Video

Blaxploitation Cartoons 194?
Cartoons
66189   46 mins   C   B, V, 3/4U   P
Animated
A collection of seldom seen racist cartoons
including Amos 'n' Andy, Jungle Jitters, Scrub

Me Mama, Little Black Sambo. Some black and
white sequences.
Warner Bros et al — Penguin Video

Blazing Saddles 1974
Comedy
38945   90 mins   C   B, V, LV   R, P
Cleavon Little, Harvey Korman, Madeleine
Kahn, Gene Wilder, Mel Brooks, directed by Mel
Brooks
A wild, wacky spoof by Mel Brooks of every
cliche in the western film genre, telling the story
of a black sheriff who is sent to clean up a
frontier town, with unpredictable results.
MPAA:R
Warner Bros — Warner Home Video; RCA
VideoDiscs

Blind Fist of Bruce 197?
Martial arts/Adventure
47696   92 mins   C   B, V   P
Bruce Li
A rich, idle young man learns the techniques of
Kung Fu from a former warrior.
Luk Suie Yee — Master Arts Video

Blind Husbands 1919
Drama
11391   98 mins   B/W   B, V, FO   P
Erich von Stroheim, directed by Erich von
Stroheim
An Austrian officer is attracted to the pretty wife
of a dull surgeon. This film was considered
shocking at the time of its release.
Universal — Video Yesteryear; Sheik Video;
Classic Video Cinema Collector's Club

Blind Man's Bluff 1968
Horror
63403   100 mins   C   B, V   P
Boris Karloff, Jean-Pierre Aumont, Viveca
Lindfors
A blind artist uses the skeletons of murder
victims as armatures for his sculptures. Also
known as "Cauldron of Blood."
Robert Weinbach; Edward
Mann — VIDCREST

Blind Rage 1983
Martial arts
73363   81 mins   C   B, V   P
Fred Williamson
When the United States Government transports
fifteen million dollars to Manilla, five blind Kung
fu masters want a piece of the action.
MPAA:R
MGM; Cannon Films — MGM/UA Home Video

Blob, The 1958
Science fiction
52611   83 mins   C   B, V   R, P

Steve McQueen, Aneta Corseaut, Olin Howlin, Earl Rowe
McQueen's first starring role in this science fiction thriller about a small town's fight against a slimy invader from space.
Paramount; Jack Harris — *Video Gems*

Blockheads 1938
Comedy
33909 55 mins B/W B, V, 3/4U P
Stan Laurel, Oliver Hardy, Billie Gilbert, Patricia Ellis, James Finlayson
Stan is a famous WWI soldier who stays on the battleground for eighteen years after the war had ended, since nobody told him it was over. Old friend Ollie finds him later at an old soldiers' home, and brings him to his house to live.
Hal Roach, MGM — *Nostalgia Merchant; Blackhawk Films*

Blockheads 1938
Comedy
63984 75 mins B/W B, V P, T
Stan Laurel, Oliver Hardy, Billy Gilbert, Patricia Ellis, Jimmy Finlayson
Twenty years after the end of World War I, soldier Stan is found, still in his foxhole, and brought back to America, where he moves in with old pal Ollie. This tape also includes a 1934 Charley Chase short, "I'll Take Vanilla."
Hal Roach; MGM — *Blackhawk Films*

Blondie—Eat to the Beat 1980
Music-Performance
54690 60 mins C B, V R, P
Blondie
This program features the multi-million seller platinum album, "Eat to the Beat," taped on location and in a studio. The program contains twelve songs, including the hit singles "Dreaming" and "The Hardest Part."
Warner Bros — *Warner Home Video; RCA VideoDiscs*

Blondie Live 1983
Music video
75015 55 mins C B, V P
This tape features the group Blondie's last concert. Among the tunes performed are "Heart of Glass," "Call Me" and "Rapture."
MCA Home Video — *MCA Home Video*

Blood and Sand 1922
Drama/Romance
58613 80 mins B/W B, V, 3/4U R, P
Rudolph Valentino, Nita Naldi, Lila Lee, Walter Long
Classic film based on Vincente Blasco Ibanez's novel about the tragic rise and fall of a matador, and the women in his life. (Silent).
Paramount — *Cable Films; Sheik Video; Video Connection; Blackhawk Films; Western Film &*

Video Inc; Classic Video Cinema Collector's Club

Blood and Sand/Son of the Sheik 1926
Film-History
50637 56 mins B/W B, V P, T
Rudolph Valentino, Lila Lee, Vilma Banky
A double feature containing two abridged versions of these motion pictures. In "Blood and Sand," an idolized matador meets another woman just before his wedding. In "Son of the Sheik," a man believes he has been betrayed by a dancing girl, and he abucts her to seek revenge. Silent.
Famous Players Lasky Corp; United Artists — *Blackhawk Films*

Blood Beach 1981
Horror
59047 92 mins C B, V P
David Huffman, Marianna Hill, John Saxon, Burt Young
A group of teenagers is devoured by menacing sand which keeps people from getting to the water.
MPAA:R
Shaw Beckerman Productions — *Media Home Entertainment*

Blood Feud 1979
Drama
65004 112 mins C B, V P
Sophia Loren, Marcello Mastroianni, Giancarlo Giannini, directed by Lina Wertmuller
Set in Italy preceding Europe's entry into WWII, a young widow is in mourning over the brutal murder of her husband by the Sicilian Mafia. A rivalry between two men in her life ensues.
ITC Entertainment — *CBS/Fox Video*

Blood Legacy 1973
Horror
58549 77 mins C B, V R, P
John Carradine, John Russel, Faith Domergue
Four heirs must survive a night in a lonely country estate. Also titled "Legacy of Blood."
MPAA:R
ASW Films Inc — *Video Gems*

Blood of a Poet 1930
Film-Avant-garde
08688 55 mins B/W B, V P
Jean Cocteau, directed by Jean Cocteau
A realistic documentary composed of unreal happenings. Built around the central character of a poet who "lives what he creates'. French with English subtitles.
FR
France — *Budget Video; Video Yesteryear; Sheik Video; Discount Video Tapes; Classic Video Cinema Collector's Club*

Blood of Dracula's Castle   1969
Horror
60347   84 mins   C   B, V   P
John Carradine, Paula Raymond, Alex D'Arcy
Young lovers move into an inherited castle, only
to find it occupied by immovable vampires.
Al Adamson — *VCI Home Video*

Blood on Satan's Claw   1971
Horror
72206   90 mins   C   B, V   P
Patrick Wymark, Linda Hayden
Townspeople in an English village circa 1670
find the essence of Satan taking over their
children.
Cannon Releasing — *Paragon Video
Productions*

Blood on the Moon   1948
Western
00288   88 mins   B/W   B, V, 3/4U   P
*Robert Mitchum, Robert Preston, Walter
Brennan*
Well-acted film about a cowboy's involvement in
a friend's underhanded schemes who mends
his ways to aid a girl.
United Artists — *Nostalgia Merchant*

Blood on the Sun   1945
Suspense
01794   98 mins   B/W   B, V   P
*James Cagney, Sylvia Sydney, Robert
Armstrong, directed by Frank Lloyd*
Politics, violence, and intrigue are combined in
this story of Japan's plans for Pearl Harbor and
world conquest.
United Artists — *Budget Video; Sheik Video;
Video Yesteryear; Discount Video Tapes*

Blood on the Sun   1975
Martial arts/Adventure
59070   81 mins   C   B, V   R, P
Martial arts action highlights this tale of
adventure.
Dandrea Releasing Corp — *Video Gems*

**Blood Spattered Bride,
The**   1980
Horror
75532   82 mins   C   B, V   P
A honeymoon in a deserted mansion is
interrupted by slashes of razor sharp knives.
Unknown — *Gorgon Video*

Bloodbrothers   1978
Drama
52702   116 mins   C   B, V   R, P
*Richard Gere, Paul Sorvino, Tony LoBianco,
Marilu Henner, directed by Richard Mulligan*
An Italian New York family battle with each
other in this story of emotional problems, and a

son who wants to break out of his family
existence.
MPAA:R
Warner Bros; Stephen Friedman — *Warner
Home Video*

Bloodrage   1979
Suspense
66081   86 mins   C   B, V   P
*Ian Scott, Lawrence Tierney, Judith-Marie
Bergan*
A vigilante stalks a psychotic killer through New
York City.
MPAA:R
Picture Company of America — *Best Film &
Video Corporation*

Bloodsucking Freaks   1975
Horror/Comedy
65380   89 mins   C   B, V   P
This outrageous comedic bloodbath has
developed a tremendous cult following, second
only to the "Rocky Horror Picture Show."
MPAA:R
Joel Reed — *Vestron Video*

Bloody Brood, The   1959
Drama
66364   80 mins   B/W   B, V   P
Peter Falk, Barbara Lord, Jack Betts
A young man, searching for his brother's
murderer, encounters a group of beatniks who
kill for thrills.
Key Films — *Movie Buff Video*

Bloody Fight, The   197?
Martial arts/Adventure
47704   89 mins   C   B, V   P
Alan Tang, Yu In Yin, Tan Chin
Two young people learn the cost of courage and
the high price of justice when they avenge a
murderer.
Chiang Chung Pin — *Master Arts Video*

Bloody Fist   197?
Martial arts/Adventure
47700   90 mins   C   B, V   P
An exciting story set in China with outstanding
martial arts scenes.
Independent — *Master Arts Video*

Bloody Mama   1970
Drama
64896   90 mins   C   B, V, CED   P
*Shelley Winters, Robert DeNiro, Don Stroud,
Pat Hingle, Bruce Dern, Diane Varsi*
The story of the infamous Barker Gang, led by
the bloodthirsty and sex-crazed Ma Barker.
MPAA:R
American International Pictures — *Vestron
Video*

Bloopers #1 19??
Outtakes and bloopers
47793 58 mins B/W B, V, 3/4U P
A compilation of bloopers from classic Warner
Brothers films of 1936 and 1937, followed by
outtakes from CBS television programs and
"Laugh-In."
Warner Bros; CBS — *Western Film & Video Inc*

**Bloopers from Star Trek
and Laugh-In** 1966
Outtakes and bloopers
43022 26 mins C B, V, FO P
*William Shatner, Leonard Nimoy, Bill Cosby,
Milton Berle, Jonathan Winters, Orson Welles,
Dick Martin, Dan Rowan*
Some well-known faces are seen and heard
cracking up in this compilation of hilarious
goofs, flubbed lines, and kidding around in the
NBC studios.
NBC — *Video Yesteryear*

Blow Out 1981
Suspense
51992 107 mins C B, V R, P
*John Travolta, Nancy Allen, John Lithgow,
Dennis Franz, directed by Brian De Palma*
When a prominent senator is killed in a car
crash, a sound effects engineer becomes
involved in political intrigue when he tries to
expose a conspiracy with the evidence he has
gathered.
MPAA:R
Filmways Pictures — *Warner Home Video;
RCA VideoDiscs; Vestron Video (disc only)*

Blow-Up 1966
Drama
54101 110 mins C B, V P
*David Hemmings, Vanessa Redgrave, Sarah
Miles, directed by Michelangelo Antonioni*
A young London photographer takes some
pictures of a couple in the park. After blowing
the pictures up he discovers what looks like a
murder involving the couple.
Carlo Ponti — *MGM/UA Home Video*

Blue Angel, The 1930
Film-Avant-garde
08676 93 mins B/W B, V, 3/4U P
*Marlene Dietrich, Emil Jannings, directed by
Josef von Sternberg*
A film classic about how a cheap chanteuse
morally destroys a professor who loves her.
German with English subtitles.
GE
Paramount, Korda; German — *Penguin Video;
VCII; Video Connection; Discount Video Tapes;
Video Dimensions; Sheik Video; Cable Films;
Budget Video; Western Film & Video Inc;
Classic Video Cinema Collector's Club*

Blue Angels 1967
Drama
45021 30 mins B/W B, V P
A program from the TV series about the pilots of
the Blue Angel, a team of four precision US
naval jets.
CBS — *Sheik Video*

Blue Blazes Rawden 1918
Western
48721 50 mins B/W B, V, 3/4U P
William S. Hart, Jack Hoxie
A lumberjack, forced to kill a man in a duel, tries
to make up for it by helping the man's family.
Silent.
Unknown — *Penguin Video*

Blue Box, The 1983
Fantasy/Literature
66214 28 mins C B, V R, P
Animated
Three stories for children - "Alexander and the
Car with a Missing Headlight," "The Owl and the
Pussycat," "Moon Man" - are combined on one
cassette.
AM Available
Weston Woods — *CC Studios*

Blue Canadian Rockies 1952
Western
60050 58 mins B/W B, V P, T
Gene Autry, Pat Buttram
Gene's employer sends him to Canada to
discourage his daughter from marrying a fortune
hunter. The daughter has turned the place into a
dude ranch and wild game preserve. When
Gene arrives, he encounters some mysterious
killings.
BLA — *Blackhawk Films*

Blue Collar 1978
Drama
47412 114 mins C B, V P
*Richard Pryor, Harvey Keitel, Yaphet Kotto,
directed by Paul Schrader*
An auto assembly line worker, tired of the
poverty of his life, hatches a plan to rob his own
union.
MPAA:R
Universal — *MCA Home Video*

Blue Country 1978
Comedy
76026 104 mins C B, V P
Brigitte Fossey, Jacques Serres
A joyful romantic comedy about a pair of free
souls who leave their stagnant lives behind to
seek out a more idyllic existence. This movie is
subtitled in English.
MPAA:PG FR
Alain Poire — *RCA/Columbia Pictures Home
Video*

Blue Fire Lady   1978
Drama
65289   96 mins   C   B, V   P
Cathryn Harrison, Mark Holden, Peter Cummins
This is the heartwarming story of a young girl
and her obsession for horses.
*Antony I Ginnane — Media Home
Entertainment*

Blue Hawaii   1962
Musical
08385   101 mins   C   B, V, LV   P
*Elvis Presley, Angela Lansbury, Joan Blackman,
Roland Winters*
Soldier, returning to Hawaiian home, takes job
with tourist agency against parents' wishes.
EL, SP
Paramount; Hal Wallis — *CBS/Fox Video;
RCA VideoDiscs*

Blue Lagoon, The   1980
Drama
58434   105 mins   C   B, V   P
*Brooke Shields, Christopher Atkins, Leo
McKern, William Daniels, directed by Randal
Kleiser*
Two beautiful teenagers marooned on a desert
isle discover love without the restraints of
society.
MPAA:R
Columbia; Randal Kleiser — *RCA/Columbia
Pictures Home Video; RCA VideoDiscs*

Blue Max, The   1966
Drama
29133   155 mins   C   B, V   P
*George Peppard, James Mason, Ursula
Andress*
During World War II a young German, fresh out
of aviation training school, competes for the
coveted "Blue Max" flying award with other
members of a squadron of seasoned flyers of
the aristocratic set. Based on a novel by Jack D.
Hunter.
EL, SP
20th Century Fox — *CBS/Fox Video*

Blue Skies Again   1983
Comedy
69312   91 mins   C   B, V   R, P
*Robyn Barto, Harry Hamlin, Mimi Rogers,
Kenneth McMillan, Dana Elcar*
A spunky young woman determined to play
major league baseball locks horns with the
chauvinistic owner and the gruff manager of her
favorite team. In Beta Hi-Fi and stereo VHS.
MPAA:PG
Lantana Productions — *Warner Home Video*

Blue Sky, Blue Sea   1978
Video
08568   30 mins   C   B, V, 3/4U   P
A continuous picture of a glimmering ocean
meeting bright blue sky at center screen to
create a relaxed background.
Nebulae Prods — Nebulae Productions

Blue Steel   1934
Western
08827   55 mins   B/W   B, V, 3/4U   P
John Wayne
Typical John Wayne excitement as he rides into
danger and violence.
Monogram — *Penguin Video; Video
Connection; Video Dimensions; Sheik Video;
Discount Video Tapes; Cable Films; Nostalgia
Merchant*

Blue Sunshine   1977
Horror
72909   94 mins   C   B, V   P
A certain brand of L.S.D. called Blue Sunshine
starts to make its victims go insane.
MPAA:R
Excel Video — *Vestron Video*

Blue Thunder   1983
Adventure
65314   110 mins   C   B, V   P
*Roy Scheider, Daniel Stern, Malcolm McDowell,
Candy Clark, Warren Oates*
Roy Scheider is the police helicopter pilot who is
chosen to test an experimental high-tech
chopper that can see through walls, record a
whisper and level a city block. In VHS stereo
and Beta Hi-Fi.
MPAA:R
Gordon Carroll — *RCA/Columbia Pictures
Home Video; RCA VideoDiscs*

Bluebeard   1944
Drama
01651   73 mins   B/W   B, V   P
*John Carradine, Jean Parker, Nils Asther,
directed by Edgar G. Ulmer*
Tormented painter with apsychopathic urge to
strangle his models is seen in this film.
PRC — *Budget Video; Cable Films; Discount
Video Tapes; Classic Video Cinema Collector's
Club*

Bluebeard   1972
Drama
65446   128 mins   C   B, V   P
*Raquel Welch, Richard Burton, Joey
Heatherton, Virna Lisi, Sybil Danning*
An American dancer, married to an Australian
aristocrat, discovers the frozen bodies of seven
women in his refrigerated vault, and fights for
her survival.
MPAA:R
Alexander Salkind — *U.S.A. Home Video*

Blues Accordin' to Lightnin' Hopkins, The — 1967
Music
60467   31 mins   C   B, V, 3/4U   P
In his own words and music, bluesman Lightnin' Hopkins reveals his inspiration for the blues. A companion piece to the film "The Sun's Gonna Shine."
Les Blank — *Flower Films*

Blues Alive — 1983
Music-Performance
64780   91 mins   C   CED   P
Albert King, Junior Wells and Buddy Guy join John Mayall in a concert celebration of their blues roots. Also appearing are ex-Rolling Stone Mick Taylor and Fleetwood Mac's John McVie.
Monarch Entertainment — *RCA VideoDiscs*

Blues Alive — 1984
Music video
72925   60 mins   C   B, V   P
John Mayall, Etta James, Albert King
John Mayall and his Blues Breakers featuring Mick Taylor jam with blues greats such as Albert King and Etta James.
RCA Video Productions — *RCA/Columbia Pictures Home Video*

Blues Brothers, The — 1980
Musical/Comedy
48608   133 mins   C   B, V, LV   P
John Belushi, Dan Akrayd, James Brown, Cab Calloway, Ray Charles, Carrie Fisher, directed by John Landis
As an excuse to run rampant on the city of Chicago, Jake and Elwood Blues attempt to raise $5,000 for their childhood parish by putting their old band back together.
MPAA:R
Universal, Robert K Weiss — *MCA Home Video; RCA VideoDiscs*

Blues 1 — 1983
Music-Performance
65224   58 mins   C   B, V   P
Linda Hopkins, B.B.King, Leatta Galloway, Ernie Andrews, Eddie "Cleanhead" Vinson, Vi Reed, "Pee Wee" Crayton
Brock Peters is the host of this historic journey to "the roots" of the Blues. In Beta Hi-Fi and VHS stereo.
Skylark Savoy Productions Ltd — *Video Gems*

Blume in Love — 1973
Comedy/Drama
58219   115 mins   C   B, V   R, P
George Segal, Susan Anspach, Kris Kristofferson, Shelley Winters, Marsha Mason, directed by Paul Mazursky
An ironic comedy/drama about a man now hopelessly in love with his ex-wife who divorced him for cheating on her while they were married.

MPAA:R
Warner Bros — *Warner Home Video*

Boarding School — 1983
Comedy
72222   100 mins   C   B, V   P
Nastassia Kinski
A group of restless young women hatch a plan to turn their spare time into money.
MPAA:R
Atlantic Releasing — *Vestron Video*

Boardinghouse — 1983
Horror
66512   90 mins   C   B, V   P
Hank Adly, Kalassu, Alexandra Day
Residents of a boardinghouse discover sinister doings in the basement.
MPAA:R
Blustarr Films — *Paragon Video Productions*

Boat, The — 1982
War-Drama
63432   150 mins   C   B, V   P
Jurgen Prochnow, Herbert Gronemeyer
"The Boat" (original title: "Das Boot") is a World War II drama about a German submarine and its crew on patrol in the North Atlantic and their fight for survival. Stereo soundtrack, dubbed in English.
MPAA:PG
Gunter Rohrback; Bavaria Atelier — *RCA/Columbia Pictures Home Video; RCA VideoDiscs*

Boating and Boat Safety — 1982
Boating
47355   30 mins   C   V   P
This program presents a discussion of proper boating techniques and safety procedures to be followed when in and around boats.
American Home Video Library — *American Home Video Library*

Boatniks, The — 1970
Comedy
65635   99 mins   C   B, V   R, P
Robert Morse, Stefanie Powers, Phil Silvers, Norman Fell, Wally Cox, Don Ameche
An accident-prone Coast Guard ensign finds himself in charge of the "Times Square" of waterways: Newport Harbor. Adding to his already "titanic" problems is a gang of ocean-going jewel thieves who won't give up the ship!
Ron Miller — *Walt Disney Home Video*

Bob & Carol & Ted & Alice — 1969
Comedy
47435   104 mins   C   B, V   P
Natalie Wood, Robert Culp, Dyan Cannon, Elliot Gould, directed by Paul Mazursky

Two California couples, influenced by a group sensitivity session, decide to loosen their sexual inhibitions and try wife-swapping
MPAA:R
Columbia — *RCA/Columbia Pictures Home Video*

Bob & Ray, Jane, Laraine & Gilda   1983
Comedy
66284   75 mins   C   B, V   P
Bob & Ray, Jane Curtin, Laraine Newman, Gilda Radner, Willie Nelson, Leon Russell
The whimsical world of Bob & Ray is transferred to video.
Jean Doumanian; Lorne Michaels — *Pacific Arts Video*

Bob Hope Chevy Show   1956
Variety
22234   52 mins   B/W   B, V, FO   P
Bob Hope, Lucille Ball, Desi Arnaz, James Cagney
The first program of this series from the 1956 season, featuring comedy, music and a takeoff on "I Love Lucy."
NBC — *Video Yesteryear; Roll Your Own Video*

Bob Hope Chevy Show I, The   1957
Comedy/Variety
64827   120 mins   B/W   B, V, 3/4U   P
Bob Hope, Joan Davis, Julie London, Perry Como, Rosemary Clooney, Lana Turner, Wally Cox
Two complete programs that were originally telecast on November 11, 1956 and March 10, 1957. Bob and his guest do spoofs of "Playhouse 90" and the Elvis Presley craze; Julie London, Perry Como and Rosemary Clooney sing their current hits. All original commercials are included.
NBC — *Shokus Video*

Bob Hope Chevy Show II, The   1957
Comedy/Variety
64828   120 mins   B/W   B, V, 3/4U   P
Bob Hope, Eddie Fisher, Betty Grable, Harry James, Rowen and Martin, Frank Sinatra, Natalie Wood, Janis Paige
Bob Hope and a stellar array of guest stars present songs and comedy routines in these two complete programs, originally telecast on January 25, 1957 and April 5, 1957. All original commercials are included.
NBC — *Shokus Video*

Bob Le Flambeur   1981
Drama
65464   ? mins   B/W   B, V   P
Roger Duchesne, Isabel Corey, Daniel Cauchy

The story of a compulsive gambler who decides to take a final fling by robbing the casino at Deauville. Subtitled in English. In stereo VHS and Beta Hi-Fi.
FR
Jean Pierre Melville — *RCA/Columbia Pictures Home Video*

Bob Marley and the Wailers Live from the Santa Barbara Bowl   1980
Music-Performance
59880   59 mins   C   LV   P
Reggae king Bob Marley, accompanied by a 12-piece band performs his hits in this stereo presentation filmed during his last complete U.S. tour in the Fall of 1979. Songs include "I Shot the Sheriff," "Jamming," and "Africa Unite." Also includes a personal interview.
Avalon Attractions — *Pioneer Artists*

Bob Welch and Friends   1982
Music-Performance
47805   81 mins   C   CED   P
This stereo concert features the one-time member of Fleetwood Mac, joined by members of Fleetwood Mac, drummer Carmine Appice, and Ann Wilson of Heart. Songs include "Gold Dust Woman," "Rattlesnake Shake," and "Sentimental Lady."
RCA — *RCA VideoDiscs*

Bobby Darin and Friends   1961
Variety
56932   52 mins   B/W   B, V, FO   P
Bobby Darin, Bob Hope, Joanie Summers
Bobby sings several of his hits, followed by Hope's monologue which centers around the Kennedy Inauguration, finally joined by Joanie for a soft shoe—"Won't You Come Home Bill Bailey."
Unknown — *Video Yesteryear*

Bobby Deerfield   1977
Drama
58220   123 mins   C   B, V   R, P
Al Pacino, Marthe Keller, Anny Duperey, Romolo Valli, directed by Sydney Pollack
A cold-blooded Grand Prix driver comes face to face with death each time he races, but finally learns the meaning of life when he falls in love with a critically ill woman.
MPAA:PG
Columbia Pictures; Warner Bros — *Warner Home Video*

Bobby Jo and the Outlaw   1976
Drama/Adventure
64895   89 mins   C   B, V, CED   P
Lynda Carter, Marjoe Gortner
A woman who wants to be a country singer and a man who emulates Billy the Kid are fugitives from the law.

MPAA:R
American International Pictures; Mark L.
Lester — *Vestron Video*

Bobby Jones: Old Man Par   1954
Biographical/Golf
44263   15 mins   B/W   B, V   P
The story of Bobby Jones' rise to golfing
immortality. Classic newsreel footage.
Fox Movietone News — *Two Star Films*

Bobby Vinton   1984
Music-Performance
75285   60 mins   C   B, V   P
This tape features singer Bobby Vinton
performing some greatest hits at the Sands
Hotel in Las Vegas. In Beta Hi-Fi stereo and
VHS Dolby stereo.
RKO Home Video — *RKO HomeVideo*

Bobo, The   1967
Comedy
58221   105 mins   C   B, V   R, P
*Peter Sellers, Britt Ekland, Rossano Brazzi,
Adolfo Celi*
A third-rate matador has three days to woo and
win a legendary beauty.
Gina Productions; Warner Bros — *Warner
Home Video*

Body and Soul   1947
Drama
47991   104 mins   B/W   B, V   P
*John Garfield, Lilli Palmer, Hazel Brooks, Anne
Revere, William Conrad, Canada Lee, directed
by Robert Rossen*
A young boxer fights his way unscrupulously to
the top.
United Artists — *NTA Home Entertainment*

Body and Soul   1981
Drama
68240   109 mins   C   B, V, CED   P
*Leon Isaac Kennedy, Jayne Kennedy, Peter
Lawford, Muhammad Ali*
A hard hitting film about a boxer who loses his
perspective in the world of fame, fast cars and
women.
MPAA:R
Cannon Films — *MGM/UA Home Video*

Body Beautiful   1983
Physical fitness
69791   60 mins   C   B, V   P
8 pgms
Eight programs, each available separately, are
designed to keep your body beautiful through a
variety of interesting methods.
1.Body Beautiful: Women's Basic Bodybuilding
2.Body Beautiful: Women's Advanced
Bodybuilding 3.Body Beautiful: Men's Basic
Bodybuilding 4.Body Beautiful: Men's Advanced
Weight Training 5.Body Beautiful The Exercise
Way 6.Body Beautiful The Dancercise Way
7.Body Beautiful The Yoga Way 8.Body
Beautiful The Belly Dance Way
Celebrity Video; Anthony DiVona — *Gold
Stripe Video*

Body Heat   1981
Suspense/Drama
51993   113 mins   C   B, V, LV   R, P
*William Hurt, Kathleen Turner, Richard Crenna,
Ted Danson*
Two people involved in a steamy love affair plot
to kill the woman's husband in this atmospheric
melodrama.
MPAA:R
Ladd Company — *Warner Home Video; RCA
VideoDiscs*

Body Snatcher, The   1945
Horror
00315   77 mins   B/W   B, V, 3/4U   P
Boris Karloff, Bela Lugosi
Based on R.L. Stevenson's novel about a grave
robber who supplies corpses to research
scientists.
RKO — *Nostalgia Merchant*

Bodyguard, The   197?
Adventure/Martial arts
59045   89 mins   C   B, V   P
Sonny Chiba, Aaron Banks, Bill Louie, Judy Lee
The "yellow mafia" and New York's big crime
families face off in this martial arts
extravaganza.
MPAA:R
Terry Levene — *Media Home Entertainment*

Boheme, La   1982
Opera
60575   116 mins   C   LV   P
*The Royal Opera, Ileana Cortrubas, Neil Shicoff,
Marilyn Zschau, Thomas Allen, Gwynne Howell*
Puccini's opera about the lives and loves of four
19th century Parisian Bohemians performed at
the Covent Garden Opera House on February
16, 1982. Includes libretto. In stereo.
Covent Garden — *Pioneer Artists*

Bohemian Girl, The   1936
Musical/Comedy
47139   74 mins   B/W   B, V, 3/4U   P
*Stan Laurel, Oliver Hardy, Mae Busch, Darla
Hood, Jacqueline Wells, Thelma Todd, Jimmy
Finlayson*
The last of Laurel and Hardy's comic operettas
finds them as guardians of a young orphan,
whom no one realizes is actually a kidnapped
princess.
Hal Roach; MGM — *Nostalgia Merchant*

Boiling Point · 1932
Western
14206   67 mins   B/W   B, V   P
Hoot Gibson
Lawman proves once again that justice always triumphs.
Allied Artists — *VCI Home Video; Discount Video Tapes; Video Connection*

Bold Caballero, The · 1936
Adventure
56599   69 mins   B/W   B, V   P
Robert Livingston, Heather Angel
Rebel chieftain Zorro overthrows oppressive Spanish rule in the days of early California.
Republic — *Video Dimensions; Video Connection; Nostalgia Merchant*

Bolero · 1982
Drama
63970   173 mins   C   B, V, CED   P
James Caan, Geraldine Chaplin, Robert Hossein, Nicole Garcia, Jacques Villeret, directed by Claude Lelouch
Beginning in 1936, this international epic traces the lives of four families across three continents and five decades, highlighting the music and dance that is central to their lives.
Films 13; TF1 Films — *Vestron Video*

Bolo · 197?
Martial arts/Adventure
47698   90 mins   C   B, V   P
Yang Sze
The authorities pardon two tough prison inmates, setting the scene for revenge.
Star Film Company — *Master Arts Video*

Bolshoi Ballet · 1967
Dance
57255   90 mins   C   B, V   P
Raissa Struhkova, Maya Samokhvalova, Vladimir Vasiliev, Ekaterina Maximova, Natalie Bessmertnova, The Bolshoi Ballet and Bolshoi Symphony
The world-famous dancers of the Bolshoi Ballet are featured in excerpts from eight works, including Ravel's "Bolers" and "La Valse," Prokofiev's "Stone Flower," music by Paganini and Rachmaninoff and "Bolshoi Ballet '67."
Kultur — *Kultur*

Bombers Over North Africa · 1941
Armed Forces-US
74482   22 mins   C   B, V   P
This tape looks at the role of the 321st Bomb Group of Northwest African Strategic Air Force during the Tunisia Campaign.
US Office of War Information — *Interurban Films*

Bon Voyage, Charlie Brown · 1980
Comedy/Cartoons
48508   76 mins   C   B, V, LV   R, P
Animated
The comic strip group from "Peanuts" become exchange students in Europe, led by Charlie Brown, Linus, Peppermint Patty, Marcie, and the irrepressible beagle, Snoopy.
MPAA:G
Lee Mendelson, Bill Melendez — *Paramount Home Video*

Bonnie and Clyde · 1967
Drama
44588   105 mins   C   B, V, LV   R, P
Warren Beatty, Faye Dunaway, Michael J. Pollard, Gene Hackman, Estelle Parsons, directed by Arthur Penn
The story of the two infamous bank robbers, Clyde Barrow and Bonnie Parker, who spent their days adrift in the Southwest during the depression era.
Academy Awards '67: Best Supporting Actress (Parsons).
Warner Bros — *Warner Home Video; RCA VideoDiscs*

Bonnie's Kids · 1975
Drama
76658   107 mins   C   B, V   P
Tiffany Bolling, Robin Mattson, Scott Brady, Alex Rocco
A story about two sisters who become involved in murder, sex and stolen money.
MPAA:R
General Film Corp — *Monterey Home Video*

Boogey Man, The · 1980
Horror
52864   86 mins   C   B, V   P
John Carradine, Suzanna Love, Ron James
A horrifying story of a brother and sister and the power of a broken mirror. The sister views the reflection of her brother murdering their mother's lover in a hallway mirror. The memory haunts the sister twenty years later.
MPAA:R EL, SP
Jerry Gross Organization — *Wizard Video; Vestron Video (disc only)*

Boogeyman II · 1983
Horror
64866   90 mins   C   B, V   R, P
Suzanna Love, Shannah Hal, Ulli Lommel, Sholto von Douglas, directed by Bruce Starr
A woman is haunted by a childhood memory whereby she witnessed a murder in the reflection of her mirror.
Ulli Lommel; David DuBay — *VCII*

Boots and Saddles 1937
Western
11383   54 mins   B/W   B, V, FO   P
Gene Autry, Judith Allen, Smiley Burnette
A young English lord wants to sell the ranch he
has inherited but Gene Autry is determined to
make him a real Westerner.
Republic — *Video Yesteryear; Blackhawk
Films; Video Connection; Budget Video;
Discount Video Tapes; Nostalgia Merchant*

Border, The 1982
Drama
59681   107 mins   C   B, V, LV   P
*Jack Nicholson, Harvey Keitel, Valerie Perrine,
Warren Oates, directed by Tony Richardson*
A border guard faces corruption and violence
within his department and tests his own sense
of decency when the infant of a poor Mexican
girl is kidnapped.
MPAA:R
Universal — *MCA Home Video*

Border Romance 1930
Western
38982   58 mins   B/W   B, V, FO   P
Don Terry, Armide, Marjorie Kane
Three Americans have their horses stolen by
bandits while riding through Mexico. Trouble
with the Rurales follows in this early sound
western.
Tiffany — *Video Yesteryear*

Borderline 1980
Drama
65005   106 mins   C   B, V   P
*Charles Bronson, A. Wilford Brimley, Bruno
Kirby, Benito Morales, Ed Harris*
This contemporary human action drama depicts
the plight of illegal Mexican aliens.
MPAA:PG
ITC Entertainment — *CBS/Fox Video*

Born Free 1966
Adventure
21280   95 mins   C   B, V   P
Virginia McKenna, Bill Travers
A game warden in Kenya and his wife raise
three orphan lion cubs. When the last cub is old
enough they try to return her to the wild.
Academy Awards '66: Best Song.
Columbia — *RCA/Columbia Pictures Home
Video; RCA VideoDiscs*

Born Innocent 1974
Drama
66584   92 mins   C   B, V   P
*Linda Blair, Joanna Miles, Kim Hunter, Richard
Jaeckel*
A 14-year-old girl suffers rape and brutality after
being sent to a juvenile detention home for a
minor offense.

Tomorrow Entertainment; NBC — *Program
Hunters*

Born Losers 1967
Drama
66098   103 mins   C   B, V, CED   P
Tom Laughlin
The original "Billy Jack" film in which the Indian
martial arts expert takes on a group of
incorrigible bikers.
American International Pictures — *Vestron
Video*

Born to Kill 1947
Mystery
57127   92 mins   B/W   B, V   P
Lawrence Tierney, Claire Trevor, Walter Slezak
A ruthless killer marries a girl for her money.
RKO — *King of Video*

Born Yesterday 1950
Comedy
21281   103 mins   B/W   B, V   P
*Judy Holliday, Broderick Crawford, William
Holden, directed by George Cukor*
A wealthy racketeer hires a writer to instruct his
girl friend in etiquette. Based on the Broadway
play.
Academy Awards '51: Best Actress (Holliday).
Columbia — *RCA/Columbia Pictures Home
Video*

Borneo 1937
Documentary/Africa
65197   76 mins   B/W   B, V   P
*Martin Johnson, Osa Johnson, narrated by
Lowell Thomas and Lew Lehr*
Explorer and naturalist Martin Johnson
investigates the many unusual sights and
inhabitants of Borneo in this pioneering
documentary.
Osa Johnson; 20th Century Fox — *Video
Yesteryear*

Boss' Son, The 1979
Drama
72223   97 mins   C   B, V   P
Rita Moreno, James Darren
A coming of age tale, as a young man tries to
implement his dreams in the real world.
Boss Son Productions — *Vestron Video*

Boston and Maine—Its 195?
Fitchburg Division and
Hoosac Tunnel in Steam
Days
Trains
64825   11 mins   B/W   B, V   P, T
This vintage film shows steam locomotive
activity on many parts of the B&M Fitchburg
Division, which stretches west from Boston to
Troy and Mechanicsville, N.Y.

(For Explanation of codes, see USE GUIDE and KEY)

J W Dealey; E R Blanchard — *Blackhawk Films*

Boston Strangler, The   1968
Suspense
08437   116 mins   C   B, V   P
Tony Curtis, Henry Fonda, George Kennedy, Murray Hamilton, Sally Kellerman, directed by Richard Fleisher
Based on Gerold Frank's factual book about the killer who terrorized Boston for about a year and a half.
SP
20th Century Fox — *CBS/Fox Video*

Bottoms Up '81   1981
Variety
55547   75 mins   C   B, V   R, P
A screen recreation of this long-running comedy revue, combining slapstick, satire, beautiful showgirls, and lavish musical numbers. Taped on location at Harrah's Lake Tahoe.
Breck Wall Prods — *Paramount Home Video*

Boum, La   1983
Comedy
65699   90 mins   C   B, V   P
Sophie Marceau, Claude Brasseur, Brigitte Fossey
A teenager adjusting to the changes brought about by a move to a new home is compounded by her parents, who are having marital problems.
Alain Poire — *RCA/Columbia Pictures Home Video*

Bourgeois Gentilhomme, Le   1958
Comedy
59371   97 mins   C   B, V, FO   P
Translated "The Would-Be Gentleman." A comedy-ballet in five acts in prose, performed by the Comedie Francais. Subtitled in English.
FR
France — *Video Yesteryear*

Bowery at Midnight   1942
Mystery
73542   60 mins   B/W   B, V   P
Bela Lugosi
A college professor becomes a killer at night, turning criminalsinto zombies who commit crimes for the professor's benefit.
Monogram — *Admit One Video*

Bowery Blitzkrieg   1941
Comedy
49176   61 mins   B/W   B, V, 3/4U   P
Leo Gorcey, Huntz Hall, Bobby Jordan
Muggs enters a Golden Gloves boxing tournament while another member of the Eastside Kids is being led into a life of crime.

Monogram — *Penguin Video*

Boxcar Bertha   1972
Drama
66096   89 mins   C   B, V, CED   P
Barbara Hershey, David Carradine, directed by Martin Scorcese
Scorcese's vivid portrayal of the South during the 1930's Depression.
MPAA:R
American International Pictures — *Vestron Video*

Boxcar Willie in Concert   1983
Music-Performance
73566   60 mins   C   B, V   P
Boxcar Willie performs his story songs of freight-hopping and hoboing in this concert tape at the Hammersmith Odeon in 1983.
Videoform — *Prism*

Boxing's Greatest Champions   1980
Boxing
29230   59 mins   B/W   B, V   P
Hosted by Curt Gowdy, Barney Ross, Rocky Marciano, Archie Moore, Sugar Ray Robinson, Joe Louis
Presented are "the greatest" in each division, as selected by the Boxing Writers Association. Match your boxing knowledge against the Boxing Writers.
Big Fights Inc — *VidAmerica*

Boy and His Dog, A   1976
Science fiction
42909   87 mins   C   B, V   P
Don Johnson, Susanne Benton, Jason Robards
This is a movie adaptation of Harlan Ellison's novella about a misogynistic society in the post World War IV civilizaton of 2024.
EL, SP
Alvy Moore — *Media Home Entertainment*

Boy of Two Worlds   1970
Adventure
59358   103 mins   C   B, V   R, P
Jimmy Sternman
Because he is of a lineage foreign to his late father's town, a boy is exiled to the life of a junior Robinson Crusoe.
MPAA:G
GG Communications — *Video Gems*

Boy Who Left Home to Find Out About the Shivers, The   1981
Fairy tales
73145   60 mins   C   B, V, CED   P
Peter MacNicol, Christopher Lee, Vincent Price, directed by Graeme Clifford

From "Faerie Tale Theatre" comes the story of a young man, played by Peter MacNicol, who had no fear.
Shelley Duvall — *CBS/Fox Video*

Boy with the Green Hair, The 1948
Drama
59061 82 mins C B, V P
Pat O'Brien, Robert Ryan, Barbara Hale, Dean Stockwell, directed by Joseph Losey
When he hears that his parents were killed in an air raid, a boy's hair turns green.
RKO — *King of Video*

Boys from Brazil, The 1978
Drama
44935 123 mins C B, V, LV P
Gregory Peck, James Mason, Sir Laurence Olivier
Incredible plot of human cloning when children formed from Hitler's likeness are used to implement a neo-Nazi takeover.
MPAA:R
20th Century Fox — *CBS/Fox Video; RCA VideoDiscs*

Boys from Brooklyn, The 1952
Comedy
53432 60 mins B/W B, V, FO P
Bela Lugosi, Duke Mitchell, Sammy Petrillo
Two comedians that bear a striking resemblance to Dean Martin and Jerry Lewis get mixed up with a mad scientist and crazed gorillas in Africa.
Jack Broder — *Video Yesteryear; Discount Video Tapes*

Boys in Company C, The 1977
War-Drama
47786 125 mins C B, V P
Stan Shaw, Andrew Stevens, James Canning, Michael Lembeck, Craig Wasson
A frank, hard-hitting drama about five young men involved in the Vietnam War.
MPAA:R
Andre Morgan — *RCA/Columbia Pictures Home Video*

Boys in the Band, The 1970
Drama
54102 120 mins C B, V, CED P
Frederick Combs, Cliff Gorman, Lawrence Luckinbill, Kenneth Nelson, Leonard Frey, directed by William Friedkin
Mart Crowley adapts his own award-winning play concerning the lives of a group of homosexuals. While playing a parlor game where each is to call out the one he loves, they learn a lot about themselves and their way of life.
MPAA:R

National General, Cinema Center Films — *CBS/Fox Video*

Boys of Summer, The 1983
Baseball
66002 90 mins C B, V, CED P
Duke Snider, Roy Campanella, Carl Erskine, Preacher Roe
Based on Roger Kahn's best-selling book, this program tells the story of the 1947-57 Brooklyn Dodgers.
Video Corporation of America; Thorn EMI Video Programming — *VidAmerica*

Bozo the Clown Volume I 196?
Cartoons
47659 59 mins C B, V P
Animated
Animated adventures of Bozo the clown.
EL, SP
Larry Harmon — *Unicorn Video*

Bozo the Clown Volume 2 196?
Cartoons
47660 59 mins C B, V P
Animated
The further animated adventures of Bozo the clown
EL, SP
Larry Harmon — *Unicorn Video*

Bozo the Clown Volume 3 196?
Cartoons
47661 59 mins C B, V P
Animated
Bozo the clown stars in the these animated tales.
EL, SP
Larry Harmon — *Unicorn Video*

Bozo the Clown Volume 4 196?
Cartoons
47662 59 mins C B, V P
Animated
More fun with animated Bozo the Clown.
EL, SP
Larry Harmon — *Unicorn Video*

Brady's Escape 1984
War-Drama
75670 90 mins C B, V P
An American World War II pilot is shot down in the Hungarian countryside and befriended by Hungarian Csikos (cowboys).
Satori Entertainment Corp — *VidAmerica*

Brain From Planet Arous, The 1957
Science fiction
73546 70 mins B/W B, V P
Robert Fuller, John Agar

An evil brain from the Planet Arous possesses a scientist's body intending to conquer the world.
Howco Films — *Admit One Video*

Brain Machine — 1983
Science fiction
72201   90 mins   C   B, V   P
A device that probes thoughts menaces a woman scientist.
Unknown — *Paragon Video Productions*

Brain That Wouldn't Die, The — 1963
Science fiction/Horror
65136   70 mins   B/W   B, V   R, P
Herb Evers, Virginia Leith, Adele Lamont
A brilliant surgeon keeps the decapitated head of his fiancee alive after an auto accident while he searches for a suitable body to transplant the head onto.
American International — *Warner Home Video*

Brainwaves — 1982
Science fiction
66042   83 mins   C   B, V   P
Suzanna Love, Tony Curtis, Kier Dullea
A young woman is treated by a noted neuroscientist with a mysterious form of treatment, "the Clavins Process."
MPAA:R
Ulli Lommel — *Embassy Home Entertainment*

Brainstorm — 1983
Science fiction
66456   106 mins   C   B, V, CED   P
Natalie Wood, Christopher Walken, Cliff Robertson, Louise Fletcher, directed by Douglas Trumbull
A scientist invents a device that can record dreams and allow other people to experience them. Stereo VHS and CED.
MPAA:PG
MGM UA Entertainment Co — *MGM/UA Home Video*

Brainwash — 1984
Drama
76020   98 mins   C   B, V   P
Yvette Mimieux, Christopher Allport, John Considine
Yvette Mimieux stars in a shocking and dramatic commentary on the capitalistic system, and the lengths to which people will go to acquire wealth and power.
MPAA:R
Gary L Mehlman — *Media Home Entertainment*

Brand of the Devil — 1944
Western
08850   62 mins   B/W   B, V, 3/4U   P
Dave O'Brien, Kermit Maynard

Texas Rangers clear the range of a gang of rustlers.
Producers Releasing Corp — *Penguin Video*

Brandy Sheriff — 1978
Western
51105   90 mins   C   B, V   P
Alex Nicol, Maria Contrera, Antonio Casas
A former outlaw tries to make up for the time he lost in prison. In Spanish.
SP
Spanish — *Budget Video*

Braniac, The — 1961
Horror
51101   75 mins   B/W   B, V   P
Abel Salazar, Ariadne Welter, Mauricio Garces, Rosa Maria Gallardo
A sorcerer sentenced for black magic returns to strike dark deeds upon the descendants of those who judged him. He turns himself into a hideous monster, feeding on his victims' brains and blood.
Mexican — *Budget Video*

Brannigan — 1975
Suspense/Crime-Drama
58829   111 mins   C   CED   P
John Wayne, John Vernon, Mel Ferrer, Daniel Pilon, James Booth, Richard Attenborough
The Duke travels across the Atlantic to arrest a racketeer who has fled the States rather than face a grand jury indictment.
MPAA:PG
United Artists — *CBS/Fox Video*

Breach of Promise — 1941
Comedy-Drama
66365   70 mins   B/W   B, V   P
Clive Brook, Judy Campbell, C.V. France
A girl snares the man she wants by serving him with a breach of promise suit.
British Mercury; MGM — *Movie Buff Video*

Breaker, Breaker! — 1977
Drama/Martial arts
63371   86 mins   C   B, V   P
Chuck Norris, George Murdock
A convoy of angry truck drivers launch an assault on the corrupt and sadistic locals of a small Texas town.
MPAA:R
American International — *Embassy Home Entertainment*

Breaker Morant — 1980
Drama
58496   107 mins   C   B, V   P
Edward Woodward, Jack Thompson, John Waters, Bryan Brown, directed by Bruce Beresford

    (For Explanation of codes, see USE GUIDE and KEY)

In 1901 South Africa, three Australian soldiers are put on trial for avenging the murder of a comrade.
MPAA:PG
Matt Carroll; South Australian Film Corp — *RCA/Columbia Pictures Home Video; Embassy Home Entertainment (disc only)*

Breakfast at Tiffany's 1961
Comedy
38587 114 mins C B, V, LV R, P
Audrey Hepburn, George Peppard, Patricia Neal, directed by Blake Edwards
Truman Capote's story of an eccentric New York City playgirl and her shaky romance with a young writer. Music by Henry Mancini. Academy Awards '61: Best Song ("Moon River").
Paramount — *Paramount Home Video; RCA VideoDiscs*

Breakfast in Hollywood 1946
Comedy
11224 93 mins B/W B, V, FO P
Tom Breneman, Bonita Granville, Eddie Ryan, Beulah Bondi, Billie Burke, Zasu Pitts, Hedda Hopper, Spike Jones and His Slickers
A movie about the popular morning radio show of the 1940's hosted by Tom Breneman—a coast-to-coast coffee klatch.
United Artists — *Video Yesteryear; Movie Buff Video*

Breakheart Pass 1976
Western
64936 92 mins C CED P
Charles Bronson, Ben Johnson, Richard Crenna, Jill Ireland, Charles Durning, Archie Moore
A governor, his female companion, a band of cavalrymen and a mysterious man travel on a train through the mountains of Idaho in 1870. The mystery man turns out to be a murderer.
MPAA:PG
United Artists — *CBS/Fox Video*

Breaking Away 1979
Comedy
37410 100 mins C B, V, CED P
Dennis Christopher, Dennis Quaid, Daniel Stern, Jackie Earle Haley
A comedy about a high school graduate's addiction to bicycle racing whose dreams are tested against the realities of a crucial race. Shot on location at Indiana University. Academy Awards '79: Best Original Screenplay.
MPAA:PG
20th Century Fox — *CBS/Fox Video*

Breaking Glass 1980
Musical
54674 104 mins C B, V R, P
Hazel O'Connor, Phil Daniels, Jon Fich, Jonathan Pryce, directed by Brian Gibson
A "New Wave" musical that gives an insight into the punk record business and at the same time tells of the rags-to-riches life of a punk rock star.
Paramount — *Paramount Home Video*

Breaking the Ice 1938
Musical
42954 79 mins B/W B, V, FO P
Bobby Breen, Charles Ruggles, Dolores Costello, Billy Gilbert
An improbable mixture of Mennonites and a big city ice skating show. Musical numbers abound with backing by Victor Young and his Orchestra.
RKO; Sol Lesser — *Video Yesteryear*

Breakout 1975
Drama
21282 96 mins C B, V P
Charles Bronson, Jill Ireland, Robert Duvall, John Huston
The wife of a man imprisoned in Mexico hires a Texas bush pilot to help her husband escape.
MPAA:PG
Columbia — *RCA/Columbia Pictures Home Video; RCA VideoDiscs*

Breakthrough 1979
War-Drama
65666 96 mins C B, V P
Richard Burton, Robert Mitchum, Rod Steiger, Michael Parks, Curt Jurgens
German and American officers join forces to assassinate Hitler.
Wolf C Hartwig; Hubert Lukowski — *Worldvision Home Video*

Breathless 1959
Drama
55801 89 mins B/W B, V P
Jean-Paul Belmondo, Jean Seberg, directed by Jean-Luc Godard
Godard's first feature catapulted him to the vanguard of the French new-wave with this story of a carefree crook who has an affair with an American, with tragic results. English subtitled.
FR
Films Around the World — *Movie Buff Video; Festival Films*

Breathless 1983
Drama
65340 105 mins C B, V, LV P
Richard Gere, Valerie Kaprisky
Richard Gere is a car thief turned cop killer, who has a torrid love affair with a French student studying in Los Angeles as the police slowly close in. This is a remake of Jean-Luc Godard's 1960 classic.
MPAA:R

Jean Luc Godard — *Vestron Video; RCA VideoDiscs*

Breeding by Artificial Insemination
1983
Veterinary medicine
69661 30 mins C B, V P
This program discusses how to breed horses by using the technique of artificial insemination.
Mercedes Maharis — *Mercedes Maharis Productions*

Brian's Song
1971
Drama
Closed Captioned
44788 73 mins C B, V P
James Caan, Billy Dee Williams, Jack Warden, Shelley Fabares, Judy Pace
The story of the unique relationship between Gale Sayers, the Chicago Bears' star running back, and his teammate Brian Piccolo. The friendship between the Bears' first interracial roommates ended suddenly when Brian Piccolo lost his life to cancer.
MPAA:G
Paul Junger Witt, CPT — *RCA/Columbia Pictures Home Video; RCA VideoDiscs*

Bride and the Beast, The
1958
Drama
47309 78 mins B/W B, V P
Charlotte Austin, Lance Fuller, William Justine
While on an African safari honeymoon, a big game hunter's new bride is carried off by a gorilla.
Allied Artists — *Weiss Global Enterprises*

Bride of the Beast
1932
Africa/Documentary
48734 50 mins B/W B, V, 3/4U P
Osa Johnson, Martin Johnson
A husband-and-wife-made documentary shot on location in Africa.
Unknown — *Penguin Video*

Bride of the Monster
1956
Horror
57347 70 mins B/W B, V, FO P
Bela Lugosi, Tor Johnson, Loretta King, Tony McCoy
Lugosi stars as a mad doctor trying to create a race of giants.
Banner Prods; Edward Wood Jr — *Video Yesteryear; Budget Video; Classic Video Cinema Collector's Club*

Bridge Lessons from Shelly de Satnick
1981
Games
53784 60 mins C B, V, 3/4U, FO R, P

Seven lessons with Shelley de Satnick, who has taught bridge all over the world with Gorin and is a top tournament player.
Star Video Prods — *Star Video Productions*

Bridge on the River Kwai, The
1957
Drama
13232 161 mins C B, V, LV P
William Holden, Alec Guinness, Sessue Hayakawa, James Donald, directed by David Lean
A British Colonel is forced to labor in building a bridge for the enemy during World War II, and Holden is assigned to destroy it.
Academy Awards '57: Best Picture; Best Actor (Guinness); Best Director (Lean).
Columbia; Sam Spiegel — *RCA/Columbia Pictures Home Video; RCA VideoDiscs*

Bridge Too Far, A
1977
War-Drama
47144 175 mins C B, V, CED P
James Caan, Michael Caine, Sean Connery, Elliot Gould, Gene Hackman, Laurence Olivier, Ryan O'Neal, Robert Redford, Liv Ullmann, Dirk Bogarde, directed by Richard Attenborough
A meticulous recreation of one of the most disastrous battles of World War II, the Allied defeat at Arnhem in 1944. Misinformation, adverse conditions, and overconfidence combined to prevent the Allies from capturing six bridges that connected Holland to the German border.
MPAA:PG
United Artists; Joseph E. Levine — *CBS/Fox Video*

Brigadoon
1954
Musical
53349 108 mins C B, V, LV, CED P
Gene Kelly, Van Johnson, Cyd Charisse, directed by Vincente Minnelli
The story of a magical, 18th century Scottish village which awakens once every 100 years, highlighted by Lerner and Loewe's score. Songs include: "Heather on the Hill," "Almost Like Being in Love," "I'll Go Home with Bonnie Jean," "Wedding Dance."
MGM; Arthur Freed — *MGM/UA Home Video*

Brimstone and Treacle
1982
Drama
68243 85 mins C B, V, CED P
Joan Plowright, Denholm Elliot, Suzanna Hamilton
A mysterious man charms his way into the lives of a middle-aged couple whose pretty daughter has been paralyzed since a car accident. In stereo.
MPAA:R
Namara Films — *MGM/UA Home Video*

 (For Explanation of codes, see USE GUIDE and KEY)

Brink of Life 1957
Drama
65201 82 mins B/W   B, V   P
*Eva Dahlbeck, Ingrid Thulin, Bibi Andersson,
Max Von Sydow, directed by Ingmar Bergman*
Three pregnant women in a hospital maternity
ward await their respective births with mixed
feelings. Swedish dialogue with English subtitles
SW
Svenskfilmindustri — *Video Yesteryear*

Britannia Hospital 1982
Comedy
69625 111 mins C   B, V   R, P
*Malcolm McDowell, Leonard Rossiter, Graham
Crowden, Jean Plowright*
This is a portrait of a hospital at its most chaotic:
the staff threatens to strike, demonstrators
surround the hospital, a nosey BBC reporter
pursues an anxious professor, and the eagerly-
anticipated royal visit degenerates into a total
shambles.
MPAA:R
Independent — *THORN·EMI Home Video*

Broadway Highlights 1936
Nightclub
56911 40 mins B/W   B, V, FO   P
*Narrated by Ted Husing, Milton Berle, George
Jessel, Babe Ruth, Jack Dempsey, Ed Wynn,
Fannie Brice, Burns and Allen, Jimmy Durante,
Ed Sullivan*
Four different tours through the nightlife of New
York City in the 1930's, with visits to restaurants,
nightclubs, and theaters.
Unknown — *Video Yesteryear; Discount Video
Tapes*

Broadway to Cheyenne 1932
Western
08849 62 mins B/W   B, V, 3/4U   P
Rex Bell, Gabby Hayes
East gets a sample of the West as two
"cowpokes" come to Broadway for a visit.
Monogram — *Penguin Video*

Broken Blossoms 1919
Drama/Film-History
55813 102 mins B/W   B, V   P
*Lillian Gish, Richard Barthelmess, Donald Crisp,
directed by D. W. Griffith*
One of Griffith's most widely acclaimed films,
photographed by Billy Bitzer, about a young
Chinaman in London's squalid Limehouse
district hoping to spread the peaceful philosphy
of his Eastern religion. He befriends a pitiful
street waif who is mistreated by her brutal
father, resulting in tragedy. Silent.
United Artists; D W Griffith — *Budget Video;
Sheik Video; Festival Films; Western Film &
Video Inc; Classic Video Cinema Collector's
Club*

Broken Strings 1940
Drama
11225 50 mins B/W   B, V, FO   P
*Clarence Muse, Sybil Lewis, William
Washington, Stymie Beard*
An all-black feature in which a concert violinist
must come to terms with himself after an auto
accident limits the use of his left hand.
International Roadshows — *Video Yesteryear;
Video Connection; Discount Video Tapes*

Bronco Billy 1980
Comedy
58222 118 mins C   B, V   R, P
*Clint Eastwood, Sondra Locke, directed by Clint
Eastwood*
A Wild West Show entrepreneur leads his
ragged troupe from one improbable adventure
to the next.
MPAA:PG
Warner Bros — *Warner Home Video; RCA
VideoDiscs*

Bronson Lee, Champion 1978
Adventure/Martial arts
66127 81 mins C   B, V   R, P
Kung-fu and karate highlight this action
adventure.
MPAA:PG
Unknown — *Warner Home Video*

Bronson's Revenge 1979
Drama
63407 90 mins C   B, V   P
Robert Hundar, Roy Hill, Emma Cohen
Two frontier soldiers face constant danger as
they attempt to transport death row prisoners, a
large quantity of gold and a stranded woman
across the Rocky Mountains territory.
MPAA:R
Serafin Garcia — *Sun Video*

**Bronze Buckaroo/Harlem
Rides the Range** 1939
Western
51946 120 mins B/W   B, V   P
*Herb Jeffries, Lucious Brooks, Artie Young,
Spencer Williams*
This double feature presents two examples of
the black film industry of the 1930's. All the
western elements, along with some comedy are
represented.
Independent — *Budget Video*

Brood, The 1979
Drama/Horror
65420 92 mins C   B, V   P
A man, whose wife is in a mental hospital
seemingly unable to get better, finds himself
somehow involved in a series of murders, but
neither the doctors nor the police will help him.
MPAA:R

New World — *Embassy Home Entertainment*

Brother, Can You Spare a Dime? 1975
History-US/Documentary
35381   103 mins   C   B, V   P
A compilation of documentary film footage from the 1930's—Hollywood in its heyday, Dillinger vs. the G-men, bread liners, and other memorabilia.
Sandy Lieberson, David Puttnam — *VCI Home Video*

Brother Sun, Sister Moon 1973
Drama
60329   122 mins   C   B, V   R, P
Graham Faulkner, Judi Bowker, Alec Guinness, Leigh Lawson, Kenneth Cranham, Lee Montague, Valentina Cortese
The life of Francis of Assisi. Musical score by Donovan.
MPAA:PG
Paramount — *Paramount Home Video*

Brothers of the West 1937
Western
54166   56 mins   B/W   B, V   P
Tom Tyler
A cowboy saves his brothers from being lynched by proving the guilt of the real outlaws.
Unknown — *Video Connection*

Brubaker 1980
Drama
56900   131 mins   C   B, V, CED   P
Robert Redford, Jane Alexander
Drama about a reform warden who risks his life to replace brutality and corruption with humanity and integrity in a state prison farm.
MPAA:R
Twentieth Century Fox, Ron Silverman — *CBS/Fox Video*

Bruce & Shao Lin Kung Fu with Fierce Boxer 1982
Martial arts/Adventure
72343   90 mins   C   B, V   P
Bruce Lee
Bruce Lee goes up against a skilled boxer in this action-packed martial arts film.
MPAA:R
Telepictures Corporation — *Best Film & Video Corporation*

Bruce Lee Fights Back from the Grave 1976
Martial arts
63892   97 mins   C   B, V   P
Bruce Lee, Deborah Chaplin, Anthony Bronson
Bruce Lee returns from the grave to fight the Black Angel of Death and to wreak vengeance

---

on the evil ones who brought about his untimely demise.
MPAA:R
Bert Lenzi — *Media Home Entertainment*

Bruce Le's Greatest Revenge 1980
Adventure/Martial arts
56922   94 mins   C   B, V   R, P
Kung-fu action and martial arts fighting highlight this film, in which a martial arts student gets involved in a clash between Chinese and a discriminatory European Club.
MPAA:R
Fourseas Film Company — *Video Gems*

Bruce Li in New Guinea 1980
Adventure/Martial arts
56924   98 mins   C   B, V   R, P
Bruce Li
The tribe of a remote island worships the legendary Snake Pearl. Two masters of Kung-fu visit the isle and discover they must defend the daughter of the murdered chief against a cruel wizard.
MPAA:PG
Fourseas Film Company — *Video Gems*

Bruce the Super Hero with Eighteen Weapons of Kung Fu 1981
Martial arts/Adventure
72344   90 mins   C   B, V   P
Bruce Lee
The late Bruce Lee masters eighteen of Kung Fu's deadliest weapons.
MPAA:R
Telepictures Corporation — *Best Film & Video Corporation*

Bruce vs. Bill 197?
Martial arts/Adventure
66082   90 mins   C   B, V   P
Two kung fu experts battle for a cache of money in a hidden box.
MPAA:R
Golden Light Film Company — *Best Film & Video Corporation*

Brute Man, The 1946
Drama
73539   62 mins   B/W   B, V   P
Rondo Hattan, Tom Neal, Jane Adams
After a young man is disfigured by his school mates, he goes out on a trail of revenge later in life.
PRC — *Admit One Video*

Buck and the Preacher 1972
Comedy-Drama/Western
64576   102 mins   C   B, V   P

Sidney Poitier, Harry Belafonte, Ruby Dee, Cameron Mitchell, Denny Miller, directed by Sidney Poitier
A trail guide and a conman join forces to help a wagon train of former slaves who are seeking to homestead out West.
MPAA:PG
Columbia — *RCA/Columbia Pictures Home Video*

Buck Privates   1941
Comedy
69031   84 mins   B/W   B, V   P
Bud Abbott, Lou Costello, Lee Norman, Alan Curtis, The Andrews Sisters
Abbott and Costello star as two dim-witted tie salesmen, running from the law, who become buck privates during World War II.
Universal — *MCA Home Video*

Buck Rogers Conquers   1939
the Universe
Science fiction
29134   91 mins   B/W   B, V   P
Buster Crabbe, Constance Moore, Jackie Moran
The story of Buck Rogers, written by Phil Nolan in 1928, was the first science fiction story done in the modern super-hero space idiom. Many of the "inventions" seen in this movie have actually come into existence—spaceships, ray guns (lasers), anti-gravity belts—as a testament to Nolan's almost psychic farsightedness.
Viacom International — *CBS/Fox Video*

Buck Rogers in the 25th   1979
Century
Science fiction
48628   90 mins   C   B, V, LV   P
Gil Gerard, Pamela Hensley, Erin Gray, Henry Silva
An American astronaut, preserved in space for 500 years, is brought back to life by a passing Draconian flagship. Outer space adventures begin when he is accused of being a spy from Earth. Based on the classic movie serial.
MPAA:PG
Universal — *MCA Home Video*

Buck Rogers: Planet   1938
Outlaws
Science fiction
08630   70 mins   B/W   B, V, 3/4U   P
Buster Crabbe, Constance Moore, Jackie Moran
Drama of the world as it might exist in the 25th century. Compiled from the "Buck Rogers" serial.
Universal — *Penguin Video; Video Yesteryear*

Buckskin Frontier   1943
Western
72053   75 mins   B/W   B, V   P
Richard Dix, Jane Wyatt, Lee J. Cobb

This story is built around Western railroad construction and cattle empires in the 1860's.
United Artists — *Independent United Distributors*

Buddy Buddy   1981
Comedy
59845   96 mins   C   B, V, CED   P
Jack Lemmon, Walter Matthau, directed by Billy Wilder
A professional hitman's well-ordered arrangement to knock off a state's witness keeps being interrupted by the suicide attempts of a man in the next hotel room.
MPAA:R
MGM — *MGM/UA Home Video*

Buddy Hackett: Live and   1984
Uncensored
Comedy-Performance
66610   72 mins   C   B, V   P
Buddy Hackett
Comedian Buddy Hackett lets loose in a no-holds-barred recording of his nightclub show.
USA — *U.S.A. Home Video*

Buddy System, The   1983
Drama
Closed Captioned
76042   110 mins   C   B, V   P
Richard Dreyfuss, Susan Sarandon, Jean Stapleton
A tale of contemporary love and the modern myths that outline the boundaries between lovers and friends.
MPAA:PG
Alain Chammas — *Key Video*

Buffalo Bill and the   1976
Indians
Western
76044   135 mins   C   B, V   P
Paul Newman, Geraldine Chaplin, Joel Grey, Will Sampson
A story about the rough-and-tumble days of Wild Bill Hickok's traveling Wild West Show.
MPAA:PG
David Susskind — *Key Video*

Buffalo Stampede   1933
Western
08610   60 mins   B/W   B, V, 3/4U   P
Randolph Scott, Buster Crabbe, Harry Carey, Noah Beery, Raymond Hatton
The plot deals with the rounding up of buffalo to sell for meat.
Paramount — *Penguin Video; Video Connection*

Bug   1975
Horror/Science fiction
60215   100 mins   C   B, V   R, P

Bradford Dillman, Joanna Miles
The city of Riverside is threatened with destruction after a massive earth tremor unleashes a super-race of mega-cockroaches.
MPAA:PG
William Castle — *Paramount Home Video*

Bugs Bunny/Road Runner Movie, The　　　　1979
Comedy/Cartoons
38948　　90 mins　　C　　B, V　　R, P
Animated
A compilation of classic Warner Brothers cartoons, starring Bugs Bunny, Daffy Duck, Elmer Fudd, the Road Runner, Wile E. Coyote, Porky Pig, and Pepe Le Pew, including some all-new animated sequences.
MPAA:G
Warner Bros — *Warner Home Video; RCA VideoDiscs*

Bugs Bunny's 3rd Movie: 1,001 Rabbit Tales　　　　1982
Cartoons
60560　　74 mins　　C　　B, V　　R, P
Animated, voices by Mel Blanc
A compilation of old and new classic cartoons featuring Bugs, Daffy, Sylvester, Porky, Elmer, Tweety, Speedy Gonzalez and Yosemite Sam.
MPAA:G
Warner Bros — *Warner Home Video*

Bugsy Malone　　　　1976
Musical
58709　　94 mins　　C　　B, V, LV　　R, P
Jodie Foster, Scott Baio, directed by Alan Parker
An all-children's cast highlights this spoof of '30's gangster movies. Songs by Paul Williams.
MPAA:G
Paramount; Alan Marshall — *Paramount Home Video*

Buick-Berle Show, The　　　　1954
Comedy
58722　　60 mins　　B/W　　B, V　　P
Milton Berle, John Raitt, Nancy Walker, Fred Clark, Arnold Stang
"Mr. Television" donates six new cars to a charity raffle—and then wonders how to win them back.
NBC — *Video Dimensions*

Building Blocks of Life, The　　　　1982
Biology/Science
59561　　61 mins　　C　　B, V　　P
A no-nonsense look at the basic unit of life, the cell, of which 60 trillion are required to constitute the human body.
McGraw Hill — *Mastervision*

Bulldog Courage　　　　1935
Western
08818　　66 mins　　B/W　　B, V　　P, T
Tim McCoy, Lois January
Young man is out to avenge his father's murder.
Puritan — *Penguin Video; Video Connection; Discount Video Tapes*

Bulldog Drummond Comes Back　　　　1937
Mystery
10936　　67 mins　　B/W　　B, V　　P
John Howard, John Barrymore, Louise Campbell, Reginald Denny, Sir Guy Standing
Drummond, aided by Colonel Nielson, rescues his fiancee from the hands of desperate kidnappers.
Paramount — *Discount Video Tapes; Cable Films; Penguin Video; Classic Video Cinema Collector's Club*

Bulldog Drummond Double Feature　　　　193?
Mystery
57759　　119 mins　　B/W　　B, V　　P
John Howard
Two Bulldog Drummond films: "Bulldog Drummond's Bride" (1939), wherein Drummond decides to marry, but not until after bomb explosions, a bank robbery, and a rooftop chase; and "Bulldog Drummond Comes Back" (1937), in which Drummond is on the trail of a clever criminal who is looking to get at him by kidnapping his fiancee.
Paramount — *Budget Video*

Bulldog Drummond Escapes　　　　1937
Mystery
08764　　67 mins　　B/W　　B, V, 3/4U　　P
Ray Milland, Heather Angel, Reginald Denny, Sir Guy Standing
Drummond, aided by his side-kick and valet, rescues a beautiful girl from spies. He then falls in love with her.
Paramount — *Penguin Video; Video Yesteryear*

Bullitt　　　　1968
Drama
44589　　105 mins　　C　　B, V　　R, P
Steve McQueen, Robert Vaughn, Jacqueline Bisset, Don Gordon, Robert Duvall, directed by Peter Yates
A detective lieutenant has an assignment to keep a star witness out of danger for 48 hours. He senses that something is fishy about the setup and before the night is out has a murder on his hands. Based on the novel "Mute Witness" by Robert L. Pike.
MPAA:PG
Warner Bros — *Warner Home Video; RCA VideoDiscs*

Bullpen 1974
Baseball
33834   22 mins   C   B, V   P
Joe Page, Jim Konstanty, Roy Face, Hoyt Wilhelm, Ron Perranoski, Tug McGraw
This program about baseball's relief pitchers goes behind the scenes into the relievers' home away from home, the bullpen. Some of the best "firemen" of the past and present are seen in action. Some black and white sequences.
W and W Productions — *Major League Baseball Productions*

Bullwinkle & Rocky and Friends, Volume I 1960
Cartoons
64709   95 mins   C   CED   P
Animated
A collection of cartoon segments featuring all the "Rocky and His Friends" characters, including Rocket J. Squirrel, Bullwinkle Moose, Boris Badenov, Natasha, Dudley Doright, Mr. Peabody and Sherman.
Filmtel; Jay Ward — *RCA VideoDiscs*

Bundle of Joy 1956
Comedy
11643   98 mins   C   B, V   P
Debbie Reynolds, Eddie Fisher
Salesgirl, who saves an infant from falling off the steps of a foundling home, is mistaken for the child's mother.
Universal; Edmund Grainger — *VCI Home Video*

Burmese Harp, The 1956
War-Drama
49557 116 mins B/W   B, V   P
Directed by Kon Ichikawa
A distraught Japanese soldier buries unknown war casualties in the Burmese jungle. The movie examines the trauma of war guilt. Japanese and Burmese dialogue with English subtitles.
JA
Nikkatsu — *Sheik Video*

Burn! 1970
Drama
76045   113 mins   C   B, V   P
Marlon Brando, Evarist Marquez, Renato Salvatori
An Italian-made saga about the rise of a people from slavery to freedom.
United Artists — *Key Video*

Burn 'Em Up Barnes 1934
Adventure/Serials
08871   ? mins   B/W   B, V, 3/4U   P
Frankie Darro, Lola Lane, Jack Mulhall
Twelve episodes each depicting the adventures of "Burn'Em Up Barnes," a racer, and his buddy, Bobbie.

Mascot — *Penguin Video; Video Connection*

Burning, The 1982
Horror
59694   90 mins   C   B, V   R, P
Brian Matthews, Leah Ayres
A story of macabre revenge set in the dark woods of a seemingly innocent summer camp.
MPAA:R
Harvey Weinstein — *THORN EMI Home Video*

Bury Me an Angel 1975
Drama
35363   90 mins   C   B, V   P
Directed by Barbara Peeters
An action-drama filled with extreme violence.
Paul Nobert — *Budget Video*

Bus Is Coming, The 1972
Drama/Romance
66242   95 mins   C   B, V   R, P
A love story entwined with the problems of blacks in a small town.
William Thompson Productions — *Video City Productions*

Bus Stop 1956
Comedy
08460   96 mins   C   B, V, CED   P
Marilyn Monroe, Arthur O'Connell, Hope Lange, Don Murray, Hans Conried, directed by Joshua Logan
A motley collection of travelers arrive at some truths about themselves while snowbound at an Arizona bus stop. Based on William Inge's play.
20th Century Fox — *CBS/Fox Video*

Bushido Blade, The 1980
Adventure/Suspense
59697   92 mins   C   B, V   R, P
Richard Boone, James Earl Jones, Frank Converse
An action-packed samurai thriller of adventure and betrayal set in medieval Japan.
Arthur Rankin Jr — *THORN EMI Home Video*

Buster Keaton: Four Short Films 192?
Comedy
64247 70 mins B/W   B, V   P
Buster Keaton
Four of Keaton's most innovative two-reelers from 1920-23 are combined on this tape: "One Week," "The Blacksmith," "Cops" and "The Balloonatic." Silent with musical score.
Joseph M Schenck — *Classic Video Cinema Collector's Club*

Buster Keaton Rides Again/The Railrodder — 1965

Comedy/Documentary
65229   81 mins   C   B, V, FO   P
Buster Keaton
"The Railrodder" is a silent comedy short that returns Buster Keaton to the type of slapstick he made famous in his legendary 20's films. "Buster Keaton Rides Again" (in black-and-white) is a documentary-style look at Keaton filmed during the making of "The Railrodder." Besides scenes of Keaton at work, there is also a capsule rundown of his career.
National Film Board of Canada — *Video Yesteryear*

Buster Keaton: The Great Stone Face — 1968

Documentary/Comedy
17236   60 mins   B/W   B, V   P
Narrated by Henry Morgan
This program from the Rohauer Collection contains footage of Buster Keaton in "Fatty at Coney Island," "Cops," "Ballonatics," "Day Dreams," and "The General."
Funnyman Inc — *Mastervision*

Bustin' Loose — 1981

Comedy
58211   94 mins   C   B, V, LV   P
Richard Pryor, Cicely Tyson, Robert Christian, George Coe, Bill Quinn, directed by Oz Scott
A fast-talking con man reluctantly shepherds a busload of misplaced kids and their keeper cross-country.
MPAA:R
Universal; Richard Pryor; Michael Glick — *MCA Home Video*

Butch Cassidy and the Sundance Kid — 1969

Adventure
09093   110 mins   C   B, V, LV   P
Paul Newman, Robert Redford, Katharine Ross
A couple of legendary outlaws at the turn of the century take it on the lam with a beautiful, willing ex-school teacher.
Academy Awards '69: Best Song (Raindrops Keep Falling on My Head).   MPAA:PG EL, SP
20th Century Fox — *CBS/Fox Video*

Butler's Dilemma, The — 1943

Comedy
63620   75 mins   B/W   B, V, FO   P
Richard Hearne, Francis Sullivan, Hermione Gingold, Ian Fleming
A jewel thief and a playboy both claim the identity of a butler who never existed, with humorous results.
British National — *Video Yesteryear*

Butterflies Are Free — 1972

Comedy-Drama
13234   109 mins   C   B, V   P
Goldie Hawn, Edward Albert, Eileen Heckart, Michael Glaser, directed by Milton Katselas
An actress helps a blind man gain independence from his over protective mother.
Academy Awards '72: Best Supporting Actress (Heckart).   MPAA:PG
Columbia; MJ Frankovich — *RCA/Columbia Pictures Home Video*

Butterfly — 1982

Drama
59658   105 mins   C   B, V, LV, CED   P
Pia Zadora, Stacy Keach, Orson Welles, Edward Albert, James Franciscus, Lois Nettleton, Stuart Whitman
James M. Cain's novel about an amoral young woman who uses her beauty and sensual appetite to manipulate the men in her life, including her father. Set in Nevada of the 1930's, father and daughter are drawn into a daring and forbidden love affair by their lust and desperation.
Golden Globe Awards '82: Newcomer of the Year (Zadora).   MPAA:R
Analysis Films — *Vestron Video*

Butterfly Affair, The — 1971

Drama
66529   75 mins   C   B, V   P
Claudia Cardinale, Henri Charriere, Stanley Baker
A beautiful singer, involved in a scheme to smuggle two million dollars worth of gems, plots to doublecross her partners in crime.
MPAA:PG
Cannon Films — *Paragon Video Productions*

By Design — 1982

Comedy
63329   90 mins   C   B, V   R, P
Patty Duke Astin, Sara Botsford
Two women who live together want to have a baby, so they embark on a search for the perfect stud.
MPAA:R
Atlantic Releasing Corp; Beryl Fox and Werner Aellen — *THORN EMI Home Video*

Bye, Bye, Birdie — 1963

Musical
21283   112 mins   C   B, V   P
Dick Van Dyke, Janet Leigh, Ann-Margret, Paul Lynde, Bobby Rydell, Trudi Ames, directed by George Sidney
The film version of the Broadway musical in which a rock and roll idol is drafted. Songs include "Put on a Happy Face."
Columbia — *RCA/Columbia Pictures Home Video*

Bye Bye Brazil   1979
Drama
53507   100 mins   C   B, V   R, P
*Jose Wilker, Betty Faria, Fabio Junior, directed
by Carlos Diegues*
A changing Brazil is seen through the eyes of
four wandering minstrels, gypsy actors exploring
the exotic and picturesque north.
Lucy Barreto; Brazil — *Warner Home Video*

C

Cabaret   1972
Musical-Drama
55207   119 mins   C   B, V, CED   P
*Liza Minnelli, Joel Grey, Michael York, directed
by Bob Fosse*
In early 1930's Berlin, singer Sally Bowles
shares her English lover with a homosexual
German baron. Songs include "Money, Money,
Money," "Wilkommen," and "Mein Herr."
Academy Awards '72: Best Actress (Minnelli);
Best Supporting Actor (Grey); Best Director
(Fosse); Best Cinematography; Best Editing.
MPAA:PG
ABC Pictures; Allied Artists — *CBS/Fox Video*

Cabinet of Dr. Caligari   1919
Film-Avant-garde
06215   52 mins   B/W   B, V   P
*Conrad Veidt, Werner Krauss, directed by
Robert Wiene*
Silent classic in surrealistic style about a
somnambulist under spell of mad doctor. New
sound track and music.
Decla Bioscop — *Budget Video; International
Historic Films; Discount Video Tapes; Video
Yesteryear; Sheik Video; Penguin Video;
Western Film & Video Inc; Classic Video
Cinema Collector's Club*

Cabo Blanco   1981
Drama
66599   87 mins   C   B, V   P
*Charles Bronson, Jason Robards, Dominque
Sanda*
A remake of "Casablanca," set in a South
American village in the years just after World
War II.
MPAA:R
Paul Joseph; Lance Hool — *Media Home
Entertainment*

Cactus Flower   1969
Comedy
59604   103 mins   C   B, V   P
*Walter Matthau, Goldie Hawn, Ingrid Bergman,
directed by Gene Saks*

A middle-aged bachelor dentist gets involved
with a kookie mistress and his prim and proper
receptionist.
Academy Awards '69: Best Supporting Actress
(Hawn).   MPAA:PG
Columbia — *RCA/Columbia Pictures Home
Video*

Caddie   1981
Drama
63338   107 mins   C   B, V   R, P
Helen Morse, Jack Thompson
This is the story of a woman who leaves her
unfaithful husband to face hardship and
romance on her own in 1930's Australia.
Anthony Buckley Productions — *THORN EMI
Home Video*

Caddyshack   1980
Comedy
54808   99 mins   C   B, V, LV   R, P
*Chevy Chase, Rodney Dangerfield, Ted Knight,
Michael O'Keefe, Bill Murray, directed by Harold
Ramis*
This comic spoof takes place at Bushwood
Country Club, where a young caddy is bucking
to win the club's college scholarship. Within this
context we meet an obnoxious club president, a
playboy who is too laid back to keep his score, a
vulgar, loud, extremely rich, but hated man, and
a gopher-hunting groundskeeper.
MPAA:R
Warner Bros — *Warner Home Video; RCA
VideoDiscs*

Caesar's Hour   1956
Comedy/Variety
52460   52 mins   B/W   B, V, FO   P
*Sid Caesar, Carl Reiner, Howard Morris,
Nanette Fabray*
This episode of Sid Caesar's famous series is
the last show of the 1956 season. Nanette
Fabray plays Sid Caesar's long-suffering wife in
one of several featured sketches.
NBC — *Video Yesteryear*

Caesar's Hour   1954
Television/Comedy
63624   59 mins   B/W   B, V, FO   P
Sid Caesar, Howard Morris, Carl Reiner
First telecast on October 25, 1954, this is the
fourth show of the comedy-variety series.
Slapstick sketches, dance, and a circus act are
featured, and original commercials for Speidel,
Glenn Miller Records, and others are included.
NBC — *Video Yesteryear*

Cafe Express   1983
Comedy-Drama
66519   90 mins   C   B, V   P
*Nino Manfredi, Gigi Reder, Adolfo Celi, Vettorio
Mezzogiorno*

A con artist stays one step ahead of the law as he raises money to help his ailing son.
Franco Cristaldi; Nicola Carraro — *Paragon Video Productions*

Cage aux Folles, La   1979
Comedy
55585   91 mins   C   B, V, LV   P
Ugo Tognazzi, Michel Serrault
A situation comedy about a club in St. Tropez notorious for putting on a drag show featuring men dressed as women, focusing on the manager of the club and the club's headliner who share an apartment.
MPAA:R
United Artists — *CBS/Fox Video; RCA VideoDiscs*

Cage Aux Folles II, La   1980
Comedy
58844   100 mins   C   B, V, CED   P
Ugo Tognazzi, Michel Serrault, Marcel Bozzuffi, Michel Galabru, directed by Edouard Molinaro
The sequel to the highly successful "La Cage aux Folles." Albin sets out to prove to his companion that he still has sex appeal.
United Artists; Da Ma Produzione — *CBS/Fox Video*

Caged Women   1984
Drama
73038   97 mins   C   B, V   P
An undercover journalist enters a women's prison.
MPAA:R
Motion Picture Marketing — *Vestron Video*

Cahill: United States Marshal   1973
Western
74208   103 mins   C   B, V   R, P
John Wayne, Gary Grimes, George Kennedy
The "Duke" stars as a marshal who comes to the aid of his sons who are mixed up with a gang of outlaws.
MPAA:PG
Michael Wayne; Batjac Productions — *Warner Home Video*

Cake Decorating   1980
Cookery
47321   60 mins   C   B, V, 3/4U   P
This program provides a complete course in cake decorating: preparing the cake; making and coloring icing; writing and drawing with icing; and creating complete pictures.
Vision Productions — *Vision Productions*

Cal-Poly University's 17th Annual Horsemanship Seminar   1983
Sports-Minor
69665   30 mins   C   B, V   P
This program presents a seminar entitled "The Common Sense Approach to Handling Horses."
Mercedes Maharis — *Mercedes Maharis Productions*

Cal-Poly University's 17th Annual Horsemanship Seminar   1983
Sports-Minor
69660   30 mins   C   B, V   P
This program presents a seminar entitled "The English Pleasure Horse from beginning to Champion."
Mercedes Maharis — *Mercedes Maharis Productions*

Cal-Poly University's 17th Annual Horsemanship Seminar   1983
Sports-Minor
69670   30 mins   C   B, V   P
This program presents a seminar entitled "The Logical Application of Dressage Principles."
Mercedes Maharis — *Mercedes Maharis Productions*

Caledonian Dreams   1982
Photography/Music
60577   46 mins   C   LV   P
Directed by Shoji Otake
This sequel to "Oriental Dreams" follows the intimate escapades of three beautiful women as they explore the exotic lifestyle of the South Seas. Music by Norio Maeda and Windbreakers. Stereo.
Japanese — *Pioneer Video Imports*

California Gold Rush   1946
Western
08893   60 mins   B/W   B, V   P
'Wild Bill' Elliott, Bobby Blake
Red Ryder is forced to impersonate Idaho Kid, harmonica-playing Killer, for valuable stagecoach line.
Republic — *Sheik Video*

California Gold Rush   1981
Adventure
65760   100 mins   C   B, V   P
Robert Hays, John Dehner, Ken Curtis
In 1849, a young aspiring writer in search of adventure arrives in Sutter's Fort and takes on a job at the local sawmill. When gold is found, Sutter's Fort is soon overrun with fortune hunters whose greed, violence and corruption threaten to tear apart the peaceful community.

James L Conway — *VCI Home Video*

California in '49   1925
Western
58502   50 mins   B/W   B, V, 3/4U   P
Neva Gerber, Charles Brinly, Ruth Royce, Clark Coffey, Ed Cobb
The beginning of the power struggles that were to come into play on the political outcome of California are chronicled in this film. Slight nitrate decomposition showing.
Unknown — *Penguin Video*

California Suite   1978
Comedy
47023   103 mins   C   B, V, LV   P
Alan Alda, Michael Caine, Bill Cosby, Jane Fonda, Walter Matthau, Richard Pryor, Maggie Smith
This Neil Simon comedy has four different story lines, all set in the Beverly Hills Hotel.
Academy Award '78: Best Supporting Actress (Smith).   MPAA:PG
Columbia; Ray Stark — *RCA/Columbia Pictures Home Video; RCA VideoDiscs*

California's Nude Beaches   1982
Sports-Water
47822   62 mins   C   B, V   P
Activities on several California nude beaches are presented in documentary fashion. The program features nude body painting, recreational activities, and hang-gliding (also available in 120-minute version).
Thomas Page — *Thomas Page*

Caligula   1980
Drama
65475   143 mins   C   B, V   P
Malcolm McDowell, Sir John Gielgud, Peter O'Toole
Impeccably faithful to the historical events of Caligula's Rome, this program also captures in detail the decadence and debauchery that marked his reign. Explicit sex and violence.
Bob Guccione; Franco Rossellini — *Vestron Video*

Caligula   1980
Drama
65476   105 mins   C   B, V, LV, CED   P
Malcolm McDowell, Sir John Gielgud, Peter O'Toole
A slightly edited version, with some of the sexually explicit scenes toned down.
MPAA:R
Bob Guccione; Franco Rossellini — *Vestron Video*

Call of the Canyon   1942
Western
44987   71 mins   B/W   B, V   P, T
Gene Autry, Smiley Burnette
A crooked agent for a local meat packer won't pay a fair price, so Gene goes off to talk to the head man to set him straight.
Republic — *Blackhawk Films; Video Connection*

Call of the Wild   1972
Adventure
47389   105 mins   C   B, V   R, P
Charlton Heston, Michele Mercier, George Eastman
Jack London's famous story about a man whose survival depends upon his knowledge of the Alaskan wilderness comes to life in this film version.
MPAA:PG
Intercontinental Releasing Corp — *Warner Home Video*

Camelot   1967
Musical
58223   150 mins   C   B, V, LV   R, P
Richard Harris, Vanessa Redgrave, Daivd Hemmings, directed by Joshua Logan
The long-running Broadway musical about King Arthur, Guinevere, and Lancelot. Score by Lerner and Loewe includes "If Ever I Would Leave You," "How to Handle a Woman" and "Camelot."
Warner Bros — *Warner Home Video*

Camouflage   194?
World War II
11227   20 mins   C   B, V, FO   P
Animated
A training film by the Walt Disney studios for the Armed Forces, in which Yehudi the Chameleon teaches camouflage to young Air Corps fliers. Contains some condemning attitudes towards Japan.
Walt Disney Productions — *Video Yesteryear*

Camp Classics #1   195?
Film-History
48859   80 mins   B/W   B, V, 3/4U   P
Five corny classics spanning four decades make up this collection: "Mystery of the Leaping Fish" with Douglas Fairbanks "Foreign Press Awards," "Musical Beauty Shop," "Edsel Commercial," and "Nixon's Checkers Speech."
Unknown — *Western Film & Video Inc*

Can I Do It...Till I Need Glasses?   1980
Comedy
56740   72 mins   C   B, V   P
Robin Williams, Roger Behr, Debra Klose, Moose Carlson, Walter Olkewicz

This suggestive comedy features outrageous, risque humor, and stars TV's "Mork," Robin Williams.
Mike Callie — *Media Home Entertainment*

Can She Bake a Cherry Pie? 1983
Comedy-Drama
72448   118 mins   C   B, V   P
Karen Black, Michael Emil, Michael Margotta, Frances Fisher, Martin Frydberg
This critically acclaimed film concerns the doubts involved when two people contemplate getting married. The official U.S. selection at the 1983 Cannes Festival.
International Rainbow Pictures; Jagfilm Productions — *Monterey Home Video*

Canadian Capers... Cartoons Volume I 19??
Cartoons/Christmas
65231   61 mins   C   B, V, FO   P
Animated
A collection of innovative animated shorts produced by the National Film Board of Canada. Titles include: "The Great Toy Robbery," "The Animal Movie," "The Story of Christmas," "The Energy Carol," "The Bear's Christmas," "Carrousel" and "TV Sale."
National Film Board of Canada — *Video Yesteryear*

Canadian Capers... Cartoons Volume II 19??
Cartoons
65232   58 mins   C   B, V, FO   P
Animated
A second collection of thought-provoking cartoons from the National Film Board of Canada, including "Spinnolio," "Doodle Film," "Hot Stuff," "The Cruise," "The Specialists" and "No Apple for Johnny."
National Film Board of Canada — *Video Yesteryear*

Cancion de Juventud (The Song of Youth) 197?
Musical
73585   30 mins   C   B, V   P
A group of girls from a Catholic boarding school on Mexico's coastline go out and raise money for charity.
KNBC — *Aztec Cinevideo*

Candid Candid Camera 1983
Comedy
66106   55 mins   C   B, V, CED   P
Allen Funt
A compilation of funny, sexy escapades compiled especially for home video.
Allen Funt — *Vestron Video*

Candidate, The 1972
Satire
44590   105 mins   C   B, V   R, P
Robert Redford, Peter Boyle, Don Porter, Allen Garfield, Karen Carlson, Melvyn Douglas, directed by Michael Ritchie
A true to life look at politics and political campaigning. A young, idealistic lawyer is talked into trying for the Senate seat and learns the truth about running for office.
Academy Awards '72: Best Story and Screenplay (Larner).   MPAA:PG
Warner Bros — *Warner Home Video; RCA VideoDiscs*

Candleshoe 1977
Adventure/Comedy
56875   101 mins   C   CED   P
Jodie Foster, David Niven, Helen Hayes
A street-wise tomboy poses as a long-lost granddaughter to help a villain steal a fortune on the estate, Candleshoe.
MPAA:G
Ron Miller, Walt Disney — *RCA VideoDiscs*

Candy-Candy 1981
Cartoons
53157   60 mins   C   B, V   P
Animated
This animated program for children is designed in soap opera fashion.
Ziv Intl — *Family Home Entertainment*

Canned Heat Boogie Assault 1983
Music-Performance
65212   60 mins   C   B, V   P
America's premier boogie band comes to life in their very first rock video. In Beta Hi-Fi and stereo VHS.
Full Circle Productions — *Monterey Home Video*

Cannery Row 1982
Comedy-Drama
59846   120 mins   C   B, V, CED   P
Nick Nolte, Debra Winger, directed by David S. Ward
Steinbeck's tale of down-and-outers who struggle to survive in a seedy part of town is brought to life in this screen adaptation.
MPAA:PG
MGM — *MGM/UA Home Video*

Cannon Ball, The/The Eyes Have It 192?
Comedy
58599   41 mins   B/W   B, V   P, T
Chester Conklin, Keystone Cops, Ben Turpin, Georgia O'Dell, Helen Gilmore, Jack Lipson
Chester Conklin stars in "The Cannon Ball" (1915), as an explosives expert in the Boom Powder Factory. "The Eyes Have It" (1928),

stars Ben Turpin involved in another misunderstanding with wifey and mother-in-law. Silent.
Mack Sennett — *Blackhawk Films*

Cannonball 1976
Adventure
51989   93 mins   C   B, V   R, P
David Carradine, Bill McKinney, Veronica Hamel, Gerrit Graham, Robert Carradine
A variety of ruthless and determined people compete for the $100,000 grand prize in an illicit cross-country auto race.
MPAA:PG
New World Pictures — *Warner Home Video*

Cannonball Run, The 1981
Comedy
58895   95 mins   C   B, V, LV, CED   P
Burt Reynolds, Farrah Fawcett, Roger Moore, Dom DeLuise, Dean Martin, Sammy Davis Jr, Jack Elam, Adrienne Barbeau, Peter Fonda
Reynolds and sidekick Dom DeLuise disguise themselves as paramedics in order to foil the cops while they compete in the cross-country Cannonball race.
MPAA:PG
20th Century Fox — *Vestron Video*

Can't Stop the Music 1980
Musical
58456   120 mins   C   B, V   R, P
Valerie Perrine, Bruce Jenner, Steve Guttenberg, Paul Sand, The Village People, directed by Nancy Walker
A retired model invites friends from Greenwich Village to a party to help the career of her roommate, an aspiring disco composer.
MPAA:PG
Allan Carr; Associated Film Distributors — *THORN EMI Home Video*

Cantinflas 1984
Cartoons
74077   60 mins   C   B, V   P
Animated
The delightful cartoon character Cantinflas takes you on a trip through history to meet King Tut, Daniel Boone, Madame Curie and many other famous people.
Diamexsa — *Family Home Entertainment*

Cantonen Iron Kung Fu 197?
Martial arts/Adventure
47706   90 mins   C   B, V   P
Liang Jia Ren
The ten tigers of Quon Tung perfect martial arts skills known as Cantonen Iron Kung Fu.
Jing Kno Jung — *Master Arts Video*

Capricorn One 1978
Science fiction
45059   123 mins   C   B, V, LV, CED   P
Elliot Gould, James Brolin, Brenda Vaccaro
The whole world is watching America's first manned space flight to Mars. But before the countdown ends, three astronauts are plunged into a battle for survival in an incredible cover-up conspiracy.
MPAA:R
Warner Brothers — *CBS/Fox Video*

Captain America 1944
Adventure/Serials
07336   240 mins   B/W   B, V, 3/4U   P
Dick Purcell, Adrian Booth, Lionel Atwill
Captain America battles a mad scientist in this fifteen-episode serial.
Republic — *Video Connection*

Captain Apache 1972
Western
12028   95 mins   C   B, V   P
Lee Van Cleef, Carroll Baker, Stuart Whitman
An Apache is assigned by Union intelligence to investigate an Indian commissioner's murder.
Philip Yordan; Official Films — *King of Video*

Captain Blood 1935
Adventure
60427   99 mins   B/W   B, V, CED   P
Errol Flynn, Olivia DeHavilland, Basil Rathbone, J. Carrol Naish, Guy Kibbee, Lionel Atwill
An exciting adaptation of the Sabatini adventure story of a pirate and his swashbuckling exploits.
Warner Bros — *CBS/Fox Video; RCA VideoDiscs*

Captain Caution 1940
Adventure
64373   84 mins   B/W   B, V, 3/4U   P
Victor Mature, Louise Platt, Bruce Cabot, Alan Ladd
During the War of 1812, a young girl takes over her late father's ship and does battle with the British.
Hal Roach — *Nostalgia Merchant*

Captain Future in Space 197?
Cartoons/Science fiction
56748   54 mins   C   B, V   P
Animated
The outer-space adventures of Captain Future and his crew aboard the spaceship Comet, fighting evil and making the universe safe for mankind. Available in English and Spanish versions.
EL, SP
ZIV International — *Media Home Entertainment*

Captain Harlock   1980
Science fiction/Cartoons
53158   60 mins   C   B, V   P
Animated
Captain Harlock, the space pirate, is left alone
to protect Earth from invasion by an evil alien
planet.
Ziv Intl — *Family Home Entertainment*

Captain Harlock   1981
Cartoons/Adventure
69811   60 mins   C   B, V   P
Animated
The stardate is 2977, and Earth is in grave
danger of being attacked by a mysterious alien
force. Only one man—the famous freedom
fighter, Captain Harlock—can save the planet
from total destruction.
Ziv International — *Family Home
Entertainment*

Captain Kidd   1945
Adventure
01795   83 mins   B/W   B, V   P
*Charles Laughton, John Carradine, Randolph
Scott, directed by Lew Landers*
Adventures of Captain Kidd and his treasure
search on high seas.
UA; Sol Lesser — *Budget Video; Discount
Video Tapes; Cable Films*

Captain Kronos: Vampire   1974
Hunter
Horror/Science fiction
60216   91 mins   C   B, V   R, P
Horst Janson, John Carson, Caroline Munro
Captain Kronos sets out to capture a vampire
before more beautiful young girls fall prey to his
curse.
MPAA:R
Albert Fennell — *Paramount Home Video*

Captains Courageous   1937
Drama
53407   116 mins   B/W   B, V   P
*Spencer Tracy, Lionel Barrymore, Freddie
Bartholemew, Mickey Rooney, Melvyn Douglas,
Charley Grapewin, John Carradine*
A spoiled rich boy falls off a cruise liner and lives
for a while among fisher folk who teach him
about life. Based on the Rudyard Kipling novel.
Academy Award '37: Best Actor (Tracy).
MGM; Louis D Lighton — *MGM/UA Home
Video*

Captain's Paradise, The   1954
Comedy
66019   89 mins   B/W   B, V   R, P
Alec Guinness, Yvonne de Carlo
The amiable Captain of the Golden Fleece
marries two women.
London Films — *THORN EMI Home Video*

Car Wash   1976
Comedy
53392   97 mins   C   B, V   P
*Franklyn Ajaye, Sully Boyar, Richard Brestoff,
George Carlin, Richard Pryor, Ivan Dixon,
Antonio Fargas*
A day in the lives of the people involved in a car
wash operation including the pot-smoking
owner's son and a cab driver looking for a
missing passenger.
MPAA:PG
Universal; Art Linson and Gary
Stromberg — *MCA Home Video*

Carbon Copy   1981
Comedy
59333   92 mins   C   B, V, LV,   P
                          CED
*George Segal, Susan St. James, Jack Warden,
Paul Winfield, Dick Martin, Vicky Dawson, Tom
Poston, directed by Michael Schultz*
A business executive faces the arrival of his
heretofore unknown son who happens to be
black.
MPAA:PG
Carter De Haven; Stanley Shapiro — *Embassy
Home Entertainment*

Care Bears Battle the   1984
Freeze Machine, The
Fantasy
Closed Captioned
66615   60 mins   C   B, V   P
Animated
The Care Bears' adventure with the Freeze
Machine leads off this tape wich also includes
two read-a-long Care Bears stories, "The Witch
Down the Street" and "Sweet Dreams for
Sally."
CPG Products Corp — *Family Home
Entertainment*

Care Bears in the Land   1983
Without Feeling, The
Cartoons
69809   60 mins   C   B, V   P
Animated
The Care Bears attempt to save a little boy
named Kevin from the icy spell of Professor
Coldheart and turn the Land Without Feeling
into a land of friendship and love.
CPG Products Corp — *Family Home
Entertainment*

Career Possibilities: 1984
Computer Programming
Electronic data processing/Occupations
72966   28 mins   C   B, V   P
This program examines all the aspects of
computer programming: the fields where
programmers are needed, a programmer's
responsibilities and a look into the future of
computer programming.

Star Merchants — *Increase Video*

Carefree 1938
Musical
00272   83 mins   B/W   B, V, 3/4U   P
Fred Astaire, Ginger Rogers
Dizzy radio singer falls for her psychiatrist in this classic musical with an Irving Berlin score.
RKO; Pandro S Berman — *Nostalgia Merchant*

Caring for Your Newborn 1980
with Dr. Benjamin Spock
Infants
44953   111 mins   C   B, V   P
In this program Dr. Benjamin Spock gives advice and guidance on baby care. He demonstrates with clear visual presentations everything from bathing the baby to treating early disorders and discomforts.
Gregory Jackson — *VidAmerica; RCA VideoDiscs*

Carlin at Carnegie 1983
Comedy-Performance
65216   60 mins   C   B, V, CED   P
It's George Carlin at his funniest, with his classic routine of the "Seven Words You Can Never Say on Television."
Brenda Carlin — *Vestron Video*

Carmen 1973
Dance
69836   73 mins   C   B, V   P
Maya Plisetskaya, Nikol Fadeyechev
A compilation of Maya Plisetskaya's most famous roles. The centerpiece is of Carmen and also included are scenes from Raymonda, Prelude, and Dying Swan.
Sovexportfilm USSR — *Video Arts International*

Carnal Knowledge 1971
Drama
08369   96 mins   C   B, V, LV, CED   P
Jack Nicholson, Candice Bergen, Art Garfunkel, Ann-Margret, Rita Moreno, directed by Mike Nichols
This adult satire takes a look at two young men from their college days in the 1940's and follows them into the seventies, exploring the way they treat their women.
MPAA:R   EL, JA
Avco Embassy; Mike Nichols Production — *Embassy Home Entertainment; RCA VideoDiscs*

Carnival Lady 1933
Mystery
57989   66 mins   B/W   B, V   P
Boots Mallory, A. Vincent
Romance, thrills, and death under the Big Top.

Goldsmith Prods — *Video Connection*

Carnival Rock 1957
Musical-Drama
73544   80 mins   B/W   B, V   P
Directed by Roger Carman
This early rock movie was one of Roger Corman's earliest and features music by Bob Luman?David Houston and the Blockbusters
Howco Films — *Admit One Video*

Carnival Story 1954
Drama
75933   94 mins   C   B, V   R, P
Anne Baxter, Steve Cochran, Lye Bettger, George Nader
The story of a German girl who joins an American-owned carnival in Germany.
RKO — *Video Gems*

Carnivores, The 1983
Documentary/Animals
63668   90 mins   C   B, V   R, P
The flesh-eaters of the animal kingdom—bears, lions, tigers, and others—and their survival instincts are the focus of this nature documentary.
Bill Burrud Productions — *Walt Disney Home Video*

Carny 1980
Drama
56755   102 mins   C   B, V, CED   P
Gary Busey, Robbie Robertson, Jodie Foster, directed by Robert Kaylor
A carnival "bozo" and the carnival "patchman" both fall in love with a young runaway in this drama set in a traveling carnival.
MPAA:R
Robbie Robertson, Lorimar, Jonathan Taplin — *CBS/Fox Video*

Carol Burnett Show: 1977
Bloopers and Outtakes,
The
Comedy/Outtakes and bloopers
47489   92 mins   B/W   B, V, FO   P
Carol Burnett, Dick Van Dyke, Tim Conway, Steve Lawrence, Eydie Gorme, Harvey Korman, Don Crichton
A collection of flubs, missed lines, malfunctioning props and other goofs from "The Carol Burnett Show," featuring the whole cast cracking up over their mistakes.
CBS — *Video Yesteryear*

Carola de Dia, Carola de 1971
Noche
Drama
47720   90 mins   C   B, V   P
Marisol, Tony Isbert

In "Carola by Day...Carola at Night," a beautiful young heiress is forced to flee her country and accept a job at a night club. In Spanish.
SP
Independent — *Telecine Spanish Video*

Carole King: One to One   1983
Music-Performance
64333   60 mins   C   B, V, CED   P
Grammy Award-winning songwriter and performer Carole King provides an intimate look at her career amidst a live performance. Includes such songs as "Tapestry," "You've Got a Friend," "Jazzman" and "I Feel the Earth Move."
Free Flow Production — *MGM/UA Home Video*

Carriage Restoration;   1979
Coaching in America
Transportation
69637   59 mins   C   B, V   P
Two programs are contained on one cassette. "Carriage Restoration: A to Z" details every procedure and product necessary to restore a carriage. "Coachaing in America" looks at elegant vehicles drawn by prancing horses through the streets of Williamsburg, Virginia and Newport, Rhode Island.
Mercedes Maharis — *Mercedes Maharis Productions*

Carrie   1976
Horror
55590   98 mins   C   B, V, LV, CED   P
Sissy Spacek, Piper Laurie, John Travolta, William Katt, Amy Irving, directed by Brian de Palma
A withdrawn teenager lives in a ramshackle house with her religious fanatic mother. On the night of the senior prom, Carrie gets revenge on all who have hurt her, through her special powers. Based on the novel by Stephen King.
MPAA:R
United Artists — *CBS/Fox Video; RCA VideoDiscs*

Carrier Action off Korea   1954
Armed Forces-US/Korean War
72486   14 mins   B/W   B, V, 3/4U   P
The US Navy's aircraft carriers used during the Korean War are profiled. Superior aircraft footage.
US Navy — *International Historic Films*

Carrott Gets Rowdie   1984
Comedy-Performance
66358   60 mins   C   B, V   P
Popular English comedian Jasper Carrott comments upon the differences between British and American people in this concert taped in Tampa Bay, Florida.

Pacific Arts — *Pacific Arts Video*

Carry On Behind   1975
Comedy
59829   95 mins   C   B, V   P
Kenneth Williams, Elke Sommer, Joan Sims
The "Carry On" crew head for an archeological dig and find themselves sharing the site with a holiday caravan.
Peter Rogers — *Embassy Home Entertainment*

Carry On Cleo   1965
Satire/Comedy
66026   91 mins   C   B, V   R, P
Sidney James, Amanda Barrie, Kenneth Williams, Kenneth Connor, Jim Dale, Charles Hawtrey, Joan Sims
A saucy spoof of Shakespeare's "Antony and Cleopatra" in the inimitable "Carry On" style.
Governor Films — *THORN EMI Home Video*

Carry On Nurse   1958
Comedy
43012   86 mins   B/W   B, V, FO   P
Shirley Eaton, Kenneth Connor
The men's ward in a British hospital declares war on their nurses and the rest of the hospital. English slapstick. The first of the "Carry On" series.
Governor Films; British — *Video Yesteryear*

Carson City Kid   1940
Western
14375   54 mins   B/W   B, V   P
Roy Rogers, Dale Evans
Roy sings and fights his way to justice and love.
Republic — *Video Connection; Nostalgia Merchant*

Carson's Cellar   1954
Comedy
14449   30 mins   B/W   B, V   P
Johnny Carson, Jack Bailey
A program in Johnny Carson's first TV series, seen in the Los Angeles area. Among other things, he prepares a Thanksgiving turkey—his own way.
KNXT Los Angeles — *Video Dimensions*

Carson's Cellar/The Jack   1953
Paar Show
Comedy
72516   90 mins   B/W   B, V, 3/4U   P
An early Johnny Carson show from KNXT-TV in Los Angeles is coupled with the first Jack Parr show aired.
CBS — *International Historic Films*

Cartoon Carnival # 1　　193?
Cartoons
53805　51 mins　C　B, V　　P
Animated
This package includes "Song of the Birds" (Max Fleischer), "Jerky Turkey" (MGM), "The Talking Magpies" (Terrytoons), "Jasper in the Haunted House" (George Pal), "It's a Hap Hap Happy Day" (Max Fleischer), "Boy Meets Dog" (Walter Lantz), and "The Friendly Ghost" (Harvey Cartoons).
Max Fleischer et al — *Budget Video*

Cartoon Carnival # 2　　193?
Cartoons
63852　55 mins　C　B, V　　P
Animated
A compilation of 8 classic cartoons: "Pincushion Man," "Mary's Little Lamb" and "Jack Frost," all by Ub Iwerks; Max Fleisher's "Cobweb Hotel"; "Farm Frolics," a Merrie Melodies cartoon; Porky Pig in "Timid Toreador"; "Pantry Panic," starring Woody Woodpecker; and a Looney Tunes cartoon, "Hollywood Capers."
Ub Iwerks et al — *Budget Video*

Cartoon Carnival Volume I　　194?
Cartoons
64837　90 mins　C　B, V　　P
Animated
A collection of ten original Max Fleischer cartoons, featuring Little Lulu and others, plus two "Bouncing Ball" sing-alongs. Mastered from the original negatives.
Max Fleischer; Paramount — *NTA Home Entertainment*

Cartoon Carnival Volume II　　194?
Cartoons
64838　90 mins　C　B, V　　P
Animated
Another package of ten Max Fleischer cartoons, featuring Casper and several "Bouncing Ball" sing-alongs. Mastered from the original negatives.
Max Fleischer; Paramount — *NTA Home Entertainment*

Cartoon Classics Limited Gold Edition: Daisy　　1984
Cartoons
66590　50 mins　C　B, V, CED　　P
Animated
Donald Duck's girlfriend, Daisy is featured in seven cartoons including her most famous appearance, "Donald's Dilemma" (1947).
Walt Disney — *Walt Disney Home Video*

Cartoon Classics Limited Gold Edition: Disney's Best: The Fabulous 50's　　1984
Cartoons
66591　50 mins　C　B, V, CED　　P
Animated
Several of Disney's most innovative cartoons from the 1950's are combined on this tape, including "Toot, Whistle, Plunk and Boom" (1953), "Noah's Ark" (1959) and "Pigs Is Pigs" (1954).
Academy Awards '53: Best Cartoon Short Subject ("Toot, Whistle, Plunk and Boom").
Walt Disney; Buena Vista — *Walt Disney Home Video*

Cartoon Classics Limited Gold Edition: Donald　　1984
Cartoons
66592　50 mins　C　B, V, CED　　P
Animated
Donald Duck romps through seven cartoon adventures, including a brush with Hollywood stardom in "The Autograph Hound" (1939).
Walt Disney — *Walt Disney Home Video*

Cartoon Classics Limited Gold Edition: Mickey　　1984
Cartoons
66593　50 mins　C　B, V, CED　　P
Animated
The famous Mouse is featured in seven of his greatest adventures, including the first Mickey Mouse cartoon, "Steamboat Willie," made in 1928.
Walt Disney — *Walt Disney Home Video*

Cartoon Classics Limited Gold Edition: Minnie　　1984
Cartoons
66594　50 mins　C　B, V, CED　　P
Animated
Mickey Mouse's faithful girlfriend Minnie is spotlighted in this compilation, including three cartoons which co-star Figaro the cat and Cleo the goldfish, who had made their first appearance in "Pinocchio."
Walt Disney — *Walt Disney Home Video*

Cartoon Classics Limited Gold Edition: Pluto　　1984
Cartoons
66595　50 mins　C　B, V, CED　　P
Animated
Pluto the Pup gets into trouble with his mischievous antics in this collection of his cartoon adventures.
Walt Disney — *Walt Disney Home Video*

Cartoon Classics Limited Gold Edition: Silly Symphonies   1984
Cartoons
66596   50 mins   C   B, V, CED   P
Animated
Seven of Disney's most popular "Silly Symphony" cartoons are combined on this tape.
Walt Disney — *Walt Disney Home Video*

Cartoon Classics of the 1930's   193?
Cartoons
03591   58 mins   C   B, V   P
Animated
Eight cartoon classics of the 1930's including "Felix the Cat," "Daffy and the Dinosaur," and "Bold King Cole."
Ub Iwerks; Warner Bros; Fleischer — *Media Home Entertainment*

Cartoon Classics Volume One: Chip 'n' Dale Featuring Donald Duck   194?
Cartoons
66055   45 mins   C   B, V, LV, CED   R, P
Animated
Six cartoon shorts: "Chip 'n' Dale," "Three for Breakfast," "Winter Storage," "Up a Tree," "Out on a Limb," "Out of Scale," and "Corn Chips."
Walt Disney Productions — *Walt Disney Home Video*

Cartoon Classics Volume Two: Pluto   194?
Cartoons
66056   45 mins   C   B, V, LV, CED   R, P
Animated
Six Pluto shorts: "Pluto's Fledgling," "The Pointer," "Private Pluto," "The Legend of Coyote Rock," "Bone Trouble," "Camp Dog," and "In Dutch."
Walt Disney Productions — *Walt Disney Home Video*

Cartoon Classics Volume Three: Disney's Scary Tales   194?
Cartoons
66177   55 mins   C   B, V, LV, CED   R, P
Animated
Seven "chilling" Disney cartoon treasures including "The Haunted House," "Pluto's Judgement Day," and "The Skeleton Dance," the first of the Silly Symphonies (1929).
Walt Disney Productions — *Walt Disney Home Video*

Cartoon Classics Volume Four: Sport Goofy   194?
Cartoons
66178   50 mins   C   B, V, LV, CED   R, P
Animated
Goofy comically demonstrates how to play tennis, gymnastics, baseball and hockey.
Walt Disney Productions — *Walt Disney Home Video*

Cartoon Classics Volume 5: Disney's Best of 1931-1948   19??
Cartoons
69319   48 mins   C   B, V, LV   R, P
Animated
This collection of six animated short subjects that won or were nominated for Academy Awards from 1931 to 1948 includes "The Ugly Duckling" (1939); "Mickey's Orphans" (black and white; 1931); "Flowers and Trees" (1932); "Truant Officer Donald" (1941); "The Country Cousin" (1936); and "Mickey and the Seal" (1948).
Academy Awards: Cartoon Short Subject Winner '39 ("The Ugly Duckling"); Cartoon Short Subject Winner '31-'32 ("Flowers and Trees"); Cartoon Short Subject Winner '36 ("The Country Cousin").
Walt Disney — *Walt Disney Home Video*

Cartoon Classics Volume 7: More of Disney's Best: 1932-1946   19??
Cartoons
66314   50 mins   C   B, V   R, P
Animated
An assortment of six classic shorts, all of which were Oscar nominees or winners, including "The Three Little Pigs" (1933), "The Brave Little Tailor" (1938) and "The Old Mill" (1937), which was the first cartoon to use Disney's multiplane camera.
Academy Awards '33 and '37: Best Cartoon.
Walt Disney Productions — *Walt Disney Home Video*

Cartoon Classics Volume 8: Sport Goofy's Vacation   1983
Cartoons
66315   41 mins   C   B, V   R, P
Animated
Goofy takes a break from his athletic endeavors to relax on a variety of disastrous vacations.
Walt Disney Productions — *Walt Disney Home Video*

Cartoon Classics Volume 9: Donald Duck's First 50 Years   1983
Cartoons
66316   45 mins   C   B, V   R, P

Animated
Half a century of great Donald Duck cartoons are featured, starting with Donald's first appearance in the 1934 short, "The Wise Little Hen." Other cartoons highlight his first meeting with Daisy Duck and the introduction of his nephews, Huey, Dewey and Louie.
Walt Disney Productions — *Walt Disney Home Video*

Cartoon Classics Volume 10: Mickey's Crazy Careers   1983
Cartoons
66317   46 mins   C   B, V   R, P
Animated
Mickey Mouse shows off some of the unusual occupations he has tried through the years in this collection of vintage cartoons which includes "Clock Cleaners," "Magician Mickey" and "The Mail Pilot." Several are in black-and-white.
Walt Disney Productions — *Walt Disney Home Video*

Cartoon Collection I   194?
Cartoons
33686   115 mins   C   B, V, 3/4U   P
Bugs Bunny, Daffy Duck, Betty Boop, Popeye, Donald Duck, Casper the Friendly Ghost
A collection of sixteen classic cartoons from the thirties, forties and fifties. Included are Bugs Bunny in, "All This and Rabbit Stew," Daffy Duck in, "Scrap Happy Daffy," Popeye in "Eugene the Jeep," and "Poop Deck Pappy," and Betty Boop in "Minnie the Moocher." Some in black and white.
Warner Bros; Max Fleischer; Walt Disney — *Shokus Video*

Cartoon Collection II: Warner Brothers Cartoons   194?
Cartoons
33687   115 mins   C   B, V, 3/4U   P
Animated
A collection of sixteen favorite Warner Brothers cartoons from the forties and fifties including Bugs Bunny in "Fresh Hare," and "Falling Hare," Daffy Duck in "The Daffy Commando," and Daffy's Southern Exposure," and Porky Pig in "Notes to You," and "Porky's Midnight Matinee."
Warner Bros — *Shokus Video*

Cartoon Collection III: Vintage Warner Bros. Cartoons   194?
Cartoons
66458   115 mins   B/W   B, V, 3/4U   P
Animated
Another package of 16 Warner Bros. cartoons from the 1930's and 40's, featuring Bugs Bunny,

Daffy Duck and Porky Pig. Titles include "Coal Black and de Sebben Dwarfs," "Calling Dr. Porky," "Tom Turkey and Daffy" and "Daffy Doc."
Warner Bros — *Shokus Video*

Cartoon Collection IV: Early Animation   193?
Cartoons
76012   110 mins   B/W   B, V, 3/4U   P
Animated
Sixteen golden classics from the depression era, all in their original fully-animated form in glorious black and white.
Max Fleischer et al — *Shokus Video*

Cartoon Magic   19??
Cartoons
65223   55 mins   C   B, V   P
Animated
This first package of vintage cartoons from the MGM vaults contains eight popular favorites: "The Captain and the Kids" (1938), "Blue Danube" (1939), "The Unwelcome Guest" (1945), "Screwball Squirrel" (1944), "The Lonesome Stranger" (1940), "The Captain's Christmas" (1938), "Barney Bear" (1939) and "King-Sized Canary" (1947).
MGM — *MGM/UA Home Video*

Cartoon Parade No. 1   194?
Cartoons
07345   120 mins   C   B, V, 3/4U   P
Animated
A collection of cartoons starring Bugs Bunny, Daffy Duck, Porky Pig, Popeye, Superman, and more.
Warner Bros — *Nostalgia Merchant*

Cartoon Parade No. 2   194?
Cartoons
44857   117 mins   C   B, V, 3/4U   P
Animated
Laugh with some of your favorite cartoon characters. Included are Bugs Bunny in "Wabbit Who Came to Supper," Popeye in "Popeye Meets Ali Baba," Superman in "Terror on the Midway," Little Lulu in "Bored of Education," and many more.
Warner Bros — *Nostalgia Merchant*

Cartoon Parade No. 3   194?
Cartoons
44858   110 mins   C   B, V, 3/4U   P
Animated
A collection of cartoon classics including "Falling Hare" with Bugs Bunny, "Cheese Burglar" staring Herman and Katnip, "Somewhere in Dreamland," "Robin Hood Makes Good," and others.
Warner Bros — *Nostalgia Merchant*

Cartoon Parade No. 4　　　194?
Cartoons
47141　120 mins　C　B, V, 3/4U　　　P
Another collection of popular cartoons from the
30's and 40's, featuring Max Fleischer's
Bouncing Ball, Little Lulu, Superman, Bugs
Bunny, and Porky Pig. Some cartoons are in
black and white.
Warner Bros et al — *Nostalgia Merchant*

Cartoon Supershow #1　　　194?
Cartoons
28922　33 mins　C　B, V　　　P
Animated
A collection of cartoons starring Bugs Bunny,
Porky Pig, Elmer Fudd, and Sylvester the Cat.
The titles on this tape are "Sunshine Makers,"
"Back Alley Oproar," "Jack Frost," and "Corny
Concerto."
Warner Bros et al — *Sheik Video*

Cas du Dr. Laurent, Le　　　1957
Drama
69562　88 mins　B/W　B, V, FO　　　P
Jean Gabin
A country doctor in a small French town tries to
introduce methods of natural childbirth to the
native women, but meets opposition from the
superstitious townspeople.
France — *Video Yesteryear*

Casa Flora　　　197?
Comedy
52795　106 mins　C　B, V　　　P
*Maximo Valverde, Antonio Garisa, Rafael
Alonso*
When the funeral of an important bullfighter is
held in a small Andalusian town, the president of
the Bullfighting Club decides to use every
lodging possible, including those in a hotel of
questionable reputation. In Spanish.
SP
Moviola Films — *Media Home Entertainment*

Casablanca　　　1943
Drama
13316　102 mins　B/W　B, V, LV　　　P
*Humphrey Bogart, Ingrid Bergman, directed by
Michael Curtiz*
Classic story of an American expatriot who
involves himself in romance and espionage in
North Africa during World War II.
Academy Awards '43: Best Picture; Best
Screenplay; Best Direction (Curtiz).　EL, SP
Warner Bros; Hal Wallis — *CBS/Fox Video;
RCA VideoDiscs*

Case of Libel, A　　　1983
Drama
73531　90 mins　C　B, V　　　P
Daniel J. Travanti, Edward Asner
This movie documents the true story of lawyer
Louis Nizer's account of the libel suit Quentin

Reynolds brought against Westbrook Pegler.
Available in Beta hi-fi and VHS stereo.
Showtime — *U.S.A. Home Video*

Case of the Mukkinese　　　1956
Battle Horn, The
Mystery
08719　? mins　B/W　B, V, 3/4U　　　P
Peter Sellers, Spike Mulligan
The plot is based around the theft of a rare
instrument from a museum.
Unknown — *Penguin Video*

Casey's Shadow　　　1978
Comedy-Drama
63443　116 mins　C　B, V　　　P
*Walter Matthau, Alexis Smith, Robert Webber,
Murray Hamilton*
The eight-year-old son of an impoverished
horse trainer raises a quarter horse and enters it
in the world's richest horse race.
MPAA:PG
Columbia; Ray Stark — *RCA/Columbia
Pictures Home Video*

Casino Gambling　　　1983
Gambling
65644　50 mins　C　B, V　　　R, P
Jerry Reed has challenged Binion's Horseshoe
Casino in Las Vegas to 44 consecutive days of
playing their dice table. Jerry explains the most
effective ways known to combat the adverse
odds encountered when casino gaming.
Jerry Reed — *Video City Productions*

Casper and the Angels　　　1979
Cartoons
47688　55 mins　C　B, V　　　P
Animated
Five episodes in which the world's friendliest
ghost teams up with the Angels—Mini and
Maxi—the first policewomen in outer space.
Hanna Barbera — *Worldvision Home Video*

Casper and the Angels II　　　1979
Cartoons
69292　55 mins　C　B, V　　　P
Animated
Five more exciting adventures of Casper the
friendly ghost, Mini, and Maxi.
Hanna-Barbera — *Worldvision Home Video*

Cass Scenic Railroad　　　1980
1980 Special
Trains
46923　101 mins　C　B, V　　　P
Shay locomotives Number 4 and 5 are double-
headed and coupled to the front of today's train,
ready to pull the cars up unbelievably steep
grades, through two switchbacks, and between
Cheat and Back Mountains in Bald Knob.

JMJ Prods — *JMJ Productions*

Castaway Cowboy, The　　　1974
Adventure
72792　　91 mins　　C　　B, V　　　　P
James Garner, Robert Culp
A shanghaied cowboy becomes partners with a widow when she turns her Hawaiian potato farm into a cattle ranch.
Walt Disney Productions — *Walt Disney Home Video*

Cat and Mouse　　　1978
Mystery
39015　　107 mins　　C　　B, V　　　P
Michele Morgan, Serge Reggiani, Jean-Pierre Aumont, directed by Claude Lelouch
A very unorthodox police inspector is assigned to investigate a millionaire's mysterious death. Who done it? French dialogue with English subtitles.
MPAA:PG　FR
Quartet Films — *RCA/Columbia Pictures Home Video*

Cat and the Canary, The　　　1978
Mystery
58959　　96 mins　　C　　B, V　　　P
Carol Lynley, Olivia Hussey, Daniel Masey, Honor Blackman, Wilfred Hyde White
A stormy night, a gloomy mansion, and a mysterious will combine to create an atmosphere for murder.
Grenadier Films Ltd — *RCA/Columbia Pictures Home Video*

Cat and the Canary, The　　　1927
Mystery
57348　　99 mins　　B/W　　B, V, FO　　P
Laura La Plante, Creighton Hale, Tully Marshall, Gertrude Astor
One of the great silent ghost stories, about the ghost of a madman that wanders nightly through the corridors of an old house.
Universal — *Video Yesteryear; Sheik Video; Budget Video; Classic Video Cinema Collector's Club*

Cat Ballou　　　1965
Western
13237　　96 mins　　C　　B, V　　　P
Jane Fonda, Lee Marvin, Michael Callan, Dwayne Hickman, Nat King Cole, Stubby Kaye
School teacher and cattle rustler stage a train robbery.
Academy Awards '65: Best Actor (Marvin).
Columbia; Harold Hecht — *RCA/Columbia Pictures Home Video; RCA VideoDiscs*

Cat from Outer Space, The　　　1978
Comedy
69317　　103 mins　　C　　B, V　　　R, P
Ken Berry, Sandy Duncan, Harry Morgan, Roddy McDowall, McLean Stevenson
An extraterrestrial cat named Jake crashlands his spaceship on Earth and leads a group of people on endless escapades.
MPAA:G
Buena Vista; Walt Disney Prods — *Walt Disney Home Video*

Cat in the Cage　　　19??
Drama
66506　　85 mins　　C　　B, V　　　P
Sybil Danning, Colleen Camp
Members of a wealthy family plot to murder each other in order to claim an inheritance.
SAZ Film Company — *Program Hunters*

Cat on a Hot Tin Roof　　　1958
Drama
53409　　108 mins　　C　　B, V, LV,　　P
　　　　　　　　　　　　　　CED
Paul Newman, Burl Ives, Elizabeth Taylor, Jack Carson, directed by Richard Brooks
Tennessee Williams' play about deception destroying a patriarchal Southern family.
MGM; Lawrence Weingarten — *MGM/UA Home Video*

Cat People　　　1942
Horror
00311　　73 mins　　B/W　　B, V, 3/4U　　P
Simone Simon, Kent Smith, Tom Conway
Young bride believes she's the victim of a curse that can change her into a deadly panther.
RKO — *Nostalgia Merchant; King of Video*

Cat People　　　1982
Horror
47679　　118 mins　　C　　B, V, LV,　　P
　　　　　　　　　　　　　　CED
Nastassia Kinski, Malcolm McDowell, John Heard, Annette O'Toole, directed by Paul Schrader
A beautiful young woman learns that she has inherited a feline characteristic, making a relationship with a man impossible.
MPAA:R
Universal — *MCA Home Video*

Cat Women of the Moon　　　1953
Science fiction
33479　　65 mins　　B/W　　B, V　　　P
Sonny Tufts, Marie Windsor, Victor Jory
Scientists land on the moon and encounter an Amazon-like force of female chauvinists.
Astor Pictures — *Mossman Williams Productions; Nostalgia Merchant*

Catch-22   1970
Satire
38930   121 mins   C   B, V, LV   R, P
Alan Arkin, Martin Balsam, Art Garfunkel, Jon Voight, directed by Mike Nichols
An adaptation of Joseph Heller's black comedy about a group of fliers in the Mediterranean during World War II; biting anti-war satire.
MPAA:R
Paramount — *Paramount Home Video; RCA VideoDiscs*

Catherine and Co.   1976
Comedy
55259   91 mins   C   B, V   P
A lonely, penniless girl arrives in Paris and "opens shop" on the streets of Paris. As business booms, she takes a cue from the big corporations and sells stock in herself.
MPAA:R
Warner Bros — *VidAmerica*

Catherine The Great   1934
Drama
08694   93 mins   B/W   B, V, 3/4U   P
Douglas Fairbanks, Jr., Elisabeth Bergner, Flora Robson, directed Paul Czinner
Historical costume drama based on the life of Catherine of Russia. Her rise to power as Empress of Russia.
UA — *Penguin Video; VCII; Sheik Video; Cable Films; Video Yesteryear; Budget Video; Discount Video Tapes; Classic Video Cinema Collector's Club*

Catholics   1973
Drama
65438   86 mins   C   B, V   P
Martin Sheen, Trevor Howard
A sensitive exploration of contemporary mores and changing attitudes within the Roman Catholic church. Based on Brian Moore's short novel.
Glazier Productions — *U.S.A. Home Video*

Cats' Cradle   1983
Physical fitness
69792   30 mins   C   B, V   P
12 pgms
Catlyn Day candidly discusses intimate beauty secrets and demonstrates a step by step program to develop and maintain a beautiful body. Programs are available individually.
1.Cat's Cradle "Cat's Meow" (Basic Body Toning) 2.Cat Skills (Exercise/Beauty Tips) 3.Classic Cat (Exercise/Ballet Movements) 4.Catlin Around (Waistline) 5.Top Cat (Bustline) 6.Hep Cat (Jazzercise/Aerobics) 7.Persian Cat (Eastern Beauty Secrets/Belly Dance) 8.Cat's Pajamas (Exercise/Meditation) 9.Skin the Cat (Sauna) 10.Cat Lover (Specialty Exercises) 11.Cat Tail (Derriere) 12.Cat O'Nine Tales (Nine Important Exercises)

Anthony DiVona; Gold Stripe Video — *Gold Stripe Video*

Cattle Queen of Montana   1954
Western
52578   88 mins   C   B, V   P
Ronald Reagan, Barbara Stanwyck, directed by Allan Dwan
Reagan stars as an undercover federal agent investigating livestock rustlings and Indian uprisings.
RKO — *Weiss Global Enterprises*

Cavalcade of Stars   1951
Variety
11270   55 mins   B/W   B, V, FO   P
Jackie Gleason, Art Carney, Georgia Gibbs, The June Taylor Dancers, Arthur Lee Simpson
"The Great One" clowns and sings with support from Carney in comedy sketches. Simpson sings, "Back in Donegal," and Gibbs performs "I Can't Give You Anything But Love," in this comedy-variety hour.
DuMont — *Video Yesteryear*

Cavalcade of the West   1927
Western
08844   60 mins   B/W   B, V, 3/4U   P
Hoot Gibson
Action-packed western with Hoot Gibson.
Diversion — *Penguin Video; Video Connection*

Cavaleur, Le (Practice Makes Perfect)   198?
Comedy
76036   90 mins   C   B, V   P
jean Rochfort
A light hearted comedy about a philandering concert pianist features Jean Rochfort with Nicole Aarcia, Annie Girardot, Lila Kedrova and Catherine Leprince as some of the women in his life.
EL, FR
Georges Dancigers; Alexandre Mnouchkine — *RCA/Columbia Pictures Home Video*

Caveman   1981
Comedy
58823   92 mins   C   B, V, CED   P
Ringo Starr, Barbara Bach, John Matuszak, Dennis Quaid, Jack Gilford, Shelley Long
A group of cavemen banished from different tribes band together to form a tribe called "The Misfits."
MPAA:PG
United Artists; Lawrence Turman; David Foster — *CBS/Fox Video*

    (For Explanation of codes, see USE GUIDE and KEY)

**CBS/Fox Guide to
Complete Dog Care, The**   1983
Pets
65411   60 mins   C   B, V, CED   P
A guide to home pet care from feeding to
grooming.
CBS Fox — *CBS/Fox Video*

**CBS/FOX Guide to Home
Videography, The**   1983
Video
65007   45 mins   C   B, V   P
This original home video production follows the
adventures of a fictitious character who owns a
new video camera. Five easy to follow
segments include camera movement, framing
and composition, lighting and sound planning
and production and advanced techniques.
CBS/FOX Video — *CBS/Fox Video*

Celebration, A   1981
Music-Performance
65213   60 mins   C   B, V   P
*Glen Campbell, Kris Kristofferson, Tanya
Tucker, Roger Miller*
A star-studded tribute in memory of a musical
legend—Dorsey Burnett. Available in Beta Hi-fi
and stereo VHS.
DID Productions — *Monterey Home Video*

Centerfold   1980
Photography
57453   60 mins   C   B, V   P
The side of the centerfold model we never
see—in the dressing room preparing for a
shooting session. Model Martha Thomsen talks
candidly about her conflicts with men, how she
felt posing nude for the first time, and her years
growing up "plain."
At Home Video — *VidAmerica*

Centerfold Girls, The   197?
Suspense
59043   93 mins   C   B, V   P
Andrew Prine, Tiffany Bolling
A deranged man is determined to kill the
voluptuous young women who have posed nude
for a centerfold.
MPAA:R
Charles Stroud — *Media Home Entertainment*

**Century of Progress
Exposition, The/New
York World's Fair 1939-40**   193?
Documentary
60055   19 mins   B/W   B, V   P, T
Fox Movietone newsreels of Chicago's Century
of Progress Exposition of 1933-34 and the most
impressive exhibits of the New York World's Fair
of 1939-1940 are combined on this tape.

Blackhawk Movietone
Compilation — *Blackhawk Films*

Ceramics and Pottery   1980
Handicraft
47328   115 mins   C   B, V, 3/4U   P
A professional potter teaches this
comprehensive in three sections: Ceramics,
Pottery, and Glazing. Simple to complex
techniques in all three sections are
demonstrated.
Vision Productions — *Vision Productions*

Cesar   1933
Comedy
06231   117 mins   B/W   B, V   P
*Raimu, Pierre Fresnay, directed by Marcel
Pagnol*
Third part in Pagnol's trilogy depicting lives,
loves, joys, and sorrows of the people of
Provence, France. French film, English subtitles.
FR
France — *Budget Video*

Chained for Life   1951
Drama/Exploitation
55816   81 mins   B/W   B, V   P
Daisy Hilton, Violet Hilton
Daisy and Violet Hilton, the real life siamese
twins, star in this old-fashioned "freak" show.
When a gigolo deserts one twin on their
wedding night, the other twin shoots him dead.
The twins go on trial and the judge asks the
viewer to hand down the verdict.
Unknown — *Festival Films; Admit One Video*

Chained Heat   1983
Drama
65341   97 mins   C   B, V   P
Linda Blair, Stella Stevens, Sybil Danning
A startling and explicit saga exposing the vicious
reality of life for women behind bars.
MPAA:R
Billy Fine — *Vestron Video*

Challenge, The   1938
Drama/Adventure
57349   77 mins   B/W   B, V, FO   P
Luis Trenker, Robert Douglas
This classic mountaineering film features
incredible avalanche scenes, as it follow the
courageous party of explorers who conquered
the Matterhorn.
England — *Video Yesteryear; Movie Buff
Video*

Challenge, The   1982
Adventure
60425   108 mins   C   B, V, CED   P
Scott Glenn, Toshiro Mifune

A contemporary action spectacle which combines modern swordplay with the mysticism and fantasy of ancient Samurai legends.
MPAA:R
CBS Theatrical Production — *CBS/Fox Video*

Challenge to Be Free   1974
Adventure
63379   90 mins   C   B, V   P
Mike Mazurki, Jimmy Kane
This is the legend of a man named Trapper, who struggles across 1,000 miles of frozen wilderness while being pursued by 12 men and 100 dogs.
MPAA:G
Pacific International Enterprises — *Media Home Entertainment*

Challenger Special, The   1982
Trains
68890   60 mins   C   B, V   P
This program watches the Union Pacific's Challenger #3985 make her debut solo excursion run from Salt Lake City to Provo, Utah.
De Luz Video — *De Luz Video*

Chamber of Horrors   1940
Horror
72949   80 mins   B/W   B, V   P
Leslie Banks, Lilli Palmer
A family is brought together at an English castle to claim a fortune left by an aristocrat. But there's one catch—there are seven keys that could open the vault with the fortune.
Monogram — *VCI Home Video*

Champ, The   1979
Drama
44650   121 mins   C   B, V, LV,   P
                                        CED
Jon Voight, Faye Dunaway, Ricky Schroder, Jack Warden, directed by Franco Zeffirelli
An ex-fighter with a weakness for gambling and drinking is forced to return to the ring in an attempt to keep the custody of his son. A remake of the 1931 classic.
MPAA:PG
MGM — *MGM/UA Home Video*

Champagne for Caesar   1950
Comedy
65156   90 mins   B/W   B, V   P
Ronald Colman, Celeste Holm, Vincent Price, Art Linkletter, directed by Richard Whorf
A self-proclaimed genius on every subject goes on a TV quiz show and proceeds to win everything in sight. The program's sponsor, in desperation, hires a femme fatale to distract the contestant before the final program.
Universal — *VCI Home Video*

Champion   1949
Drama
64542   99 mins   B/W   B, V   P
Kirk Douglas, Arthur Kennedy, Marilyn Maxwell, Ruth Roman
An ambitious prizefighter alienates the people who helped him on the way to the top.
United Artists — *NTA Home Entertainment*

Champions, The   1983
Drama
Closed Captioned
64987   90 mins   C   B, V   P
John Hurt, Ben Johnson, Edward Woodward
This is the story of two championsa courageous, cancer-stricken British jockey and the horse he rode to victory in the Grand National, who came back from a severe, near-fatal injury.
Unknown — *Embassy Home Entertainment*

Champions   1984
Drama
72877   113 mins   C   B, V, LV   P
John Hurt
The true story of Bob Champion, who overcame cancer to win England's Grand National, a top horse racing event.
Peter Shaw — *Embassy Home Entertainment*

Champions of the AFC East   1982
Football
47711   23 mins   C   B, V, FO   P
Team highlights of the 1981 Miami Dolphins, who won the AFC Eastern Division with a strong defense.
NFL Films — *NFL Films Video*

Chance   1978
Western
66088   85 mins   C   B, V   P
Chris Clarke, Bruce Fischer, Nila Northsun
In 1880's New Mexico, a renegade Englishman known as "The White Apache" teams up with his real Apache blood brother.
MPAA:R
Appaloosa Ltd — *Best Film & Video Corporation*

Chandu on the Magic Island   1940
Mystery/Adventure
53357   67 mins   B/W   B, V, FO   P
Bela Lugosi, Maria Alba, Clark Kimball Young
Chandu the Magician takes his powers of the occult to the mysterious lost island of Lemuri to battle the evil cult of Ubasti.
United Artists; Sol Lesser — *Video Yesteryear; Sheik Video*

Chanel Solitaire   1981
Drama
72906   124 mins   C   B, V   P
Karen Black, Marie-France Pisier, Rutger Hauer
The biography of Gabrielle "Coco" Chanel, as portrayed by Marie-France Pisier, follows her career as a fabulous dress designer.
MPAA:R
George Kaczender — *Media Home Entertainment*

Change of Habit   1969
Drama/Comedy
55555   93 mins   C   B, V   P
Elvis Presley, Mary Tyler Moore, Barbara McNair
Three novitiates undertake to learn about the world before becoming full-fledged nuns. While working at a ghetto clinic a young doctor forms a strong, affectionate relationship with one of them.
MPAA:G
Universal; Joe Connelly — *MCA Home Video*

Change of Seasons, A   1980
Romance/Comedy
55456   102 mins   C   B, V, CED   P
Shirley MacLaine, Bo Derek, Anthony Hopkins, Michael Brandon, Mary Beth Hurt
A sophisticated comedy that looks at contemporary relationships and values. The wife of a college professor learns of her husband's affair with a seductive student and decides to have a fling with a younger man. The situation reaches absurdity when the couples decide to vacation together.
MPAA:R
Twentieth Century Fox — *CBS/Fox Video*

Changeling, The   1980
Horror
44918   114 mins   C   B, V, LV, CED   P
George C. Scott, Trish Van Devere, John Russell
A music teacher moves into an old house and discovers that a young boy's ghostly spirit is her housemate.
MPAA:R
Associated Film Distribution — *Vestron Video*

Chapayev   1934
Drama/Film-History
52347   101 mins   B/W   B, V, 3/4U   P
Boris Babochkin, Leonid Kmit, directed by Sergei and Gregory Vasiliev
A striking propagandist drama, which deals with the exploits of a Red Army commander during the 1919 battles. English subtitles.
RU
USSR; Lenfilm — *International Historic Films*

Chaplin: A Character Is Born/Keaton: The Great Stone Face   197?
Comedy/Film-History
64842   90 mins   C   B, V   P
Narrated by Keenan Wynn and Red Buttons
Wynn narrates "A Character Is Born," with scenes from "Little Champ," "The Pawnshop," "The Rink" and "The Immigrant." Buttons presents "The Great Stone Face" featuring scenes from "Cops," "The Playhouse" "The Boat" and "The General."
SL Film Productions — *HarmonyVision*

Chaplin at Essanay #1   1915
Comedy
64345   75 mins   B/W   B, V   P
Charlie Chaplin, Edna Purviance, Ben Turpin
A group of Chaplin shorts produced during his stay at the Essanay studios.
Essanay — *Classic Video Cinema Collector's Club*

Chaplin at Essanay #2   1916
Comedy
64346   75 mins   B/W   B, V   P
Charlie Chaplin, Edna Purviance
Five more shorts by Chaplin from the later period at Essanay. Silent with music score.
Essanay — *Classic Video Cinema Collector's Club*

Chaplin at Keystone #1   1914
Comedy
64343   75 mins   B/W   B, V   P
Charlie Chaplin, Mabel Normand
Beginning with his first film, "Making a Living," this tape contains several of Chaplin's earliest shorts. Silent with music score.
Keystone — *Classic Video Cinema Collector's Club*

Chaplin at Keystone #2   1914
Comedy
64344   75 mins   B/W   B, V   P
Charlie Chaplin, Mabel Normand
More one - and two - reelers from Chaplin's earliest days at the Keystone Studios. Silent with music score.
Keystone — *Classic Video Cinema Collector's Club*

Chaplin Cavalcade   1916
Comedy
58727   60 mins   B/W   B, V   P
Charlie Chaplin
Three Chaplin shorts: "The Cure" (1917), in which Charlie visits the mineral springs where a cure is administered; "The Pawn Shop" (1916), in which Charlie plays a handyman in a pawn shop; and, "The Rink" (1916), with Charlie as a waiter who crashes a skating party. Silent with music tracks.

Mutual — *Sheik Video*

Chaplin Mutuals # 1 1916
Comedy
64347 75 mins B/W B, V P
Charlie Chaplin
Chaplin's first four Mutual shorts are contained on this tape: "The Floorwalker," "The Fireman," "The Vagabond" and "One A.M." Silent with music score.
Mutual — *Classic Video Cinema Collector's Club*

Chaplin Mutuals # 2 1916
Comedy
64348 75 mins B/W B, V P
Charlie Chaplin
This tape includes four of Chaplin's middle-period Mutual shorts: "The Count," "The Pawnshop," "Behind the Screen" and "The Rink." Silent with music score.
Mutual — *Classic Video Cinema Collector's Club*

Chaplin Mutuals # 3 1917
Comedy
64349 75 mins B/W B, V P
Charlie Chaplin
Chaplin's last four Mutual comedies are included on this tape: "Easy Street," "The Cure," "The Immigrant" and "The Adventure." Silent with music score.
Mutual — *Classic Video Cinema Collector's Club*

Chaplin Mutuals, Volume I 1917
Comedy
10076 60 mins B/W B, V P, T
Charlie Chaplin, Edna Purviance, John Rand, Eric Campbell, James T. Kelley
Package includes Chaplin's "The Immigrant," "The Count," and Easy Street." Silent.
Mutual — *Blackhawk Films*

Chaplin Mutuals, Volume II 1917
Comedy
10080 60 mins B/W B, V P, T
Charlie Chaplin, Edna Purviance, Eric Campbell, Albert Austin, Henry Bergman, John Rand
Package includes Chaplins "The Pawnshop" (1916), "The Adventurer" (1917), and "One A.M." (1916).
Mutual — *Blackhawk Films*

Chaplin Mutuals, Volume III 1916
Comedy
10084 60 mins B/W B, V P, T
Charlie Chaplin, Edna Purviance, Eric Campbell, Albert Austin

Package includes Chaplin's "The Cure" (1916), "The Floorwalker" (1916), and "The Vagabond."
Mutual — *Blackhawk Films*

Chaplin Mutuals, Volume IV 1916
Comedy
10088 60 mins B/W B, V P, T
Charlie Chaplin, Edna Purviance, Eric Campbell, Lloyd Bacon, Albert Austin, James T. Kelly
Package includes Chaplin's, "Behind the Screen," "The Fireman" (1916), and "The Rink" (1916).
Mutual — *Blackhawk Films*

Chaplin Revue, The 1958
Comedy
08395 119 mins B/W B, V P
Charlie Chaplin
The "Revue," put together by Chaplin in 1958, consists of three of his best shorts: "A Dog's Life" (1918), "Shoulder Arms" (1918), and "The Pilgrim" (1922).
rbc Films — *CBS/Fox Video*

Chapter Two 1979
Romance
Closed Captioned
44789 120 mins C B, V, LV P
James Caan, Marsha Mason, Valerie Harper, Joseph Bologna
A shy mystery writer and widower wins the heart of a young divorcee. The memory of his deceased wife nearly ruins their new marriage.
MPAA:PG
Ray Stark — *RCA/Columbia Pictures Home Video*

Charade 1963
Mystery/Comedy
58212 113 mins C B, V P
Cary Grant, Audrey Hepburn, Walter Matthau, James Coburn, George Kennedy, directed by Stanley Donen
After her husband is murdered, a young wife finds herself on the run from crooks and double agents who want 250,000 dollars her husband stole during World War II. Filmed on location in Paris. Music by Henry Mancini.
Film Daily Poll 10 Best Pictures of the Year '63.
Universal; Stanley Donen — *MCA Home Video*

Charge of the Light Brigade, The 1936
Drama
64783 115 mins B/W B, V, CED P
Olivia De Havilland, Errol Flynn, David Niven, Nigel Bruce, directed by Michael Curtiz
An army officer deliberately starts the Balaclava charge to even an old score with Surat Khan, who's on the other side.

Warner; Hal B. Wallis; Sam
Bischoff — *CBS/Fox Video; RCA VideoDiscs*

Charge of the Model T's   1979
Comedy
69553   94 mins   C   B, V   P
*Louis Nye, John David Carson, Herb Edelman,
Carol Bagdasarian, Arte Johnson*
Set during World War I, this comedy is about a
German spy who tries to infiltrate the U.S. army.
MPAA:G
Jim McCullough — *Embassy Home
Entertainment*

Chariots of Fire   1981
Drama
47788   123 mins   C   B, V, LV   R, P
*Ben Cross, Ian Charleson, Nigel Havers, Nick
Farrell, John Gielgud, Alice Krige, Nigel
Davenport, Ian Holm, Patrick Magee, Cheryl
Campbell, Lindsay Anderson*
Motivation and the will to win are poignantly and
dramatically portrayed in this story of two British
track athletes striving to win major events at the
1924 Paris Olympics.
Academy Awards '81: Best Picture.   MPAA:PG
Enigma Productions; David Puttnam — *Warner
Home Video; RCA VideoDiscs*

Chariots of the Gods   1973
Documentary/Speculation
14643   98 mins   C   B, V   P
Directed by Dr. Harold Reinl
The possibility of extraterrestrial visitors
inhabiting Earth many years ago is examined.
MPAA:G
Sun International Productions — *VCI Home
Video*

Charley Chase Festival   192?
(Vol. 1)
Comedy
60352   70 mins   B/W   B, V   P
Charley Chase
Six classic Charley Chase comedies: "At First
Sight" (1923), "Fighting Fluid" (1924), "Young
Oldfield" (1924), "Ten Minute Egg" (1924),
"Stolen Goods" (1924), and "Long Fliv the
King" (1926).
Pathe; Hal Roach — *Video Dimensions*

Charley Varrick   1973
Drama
68257   111 mins   C   B, V   P
Walter Matthau, Joe Don Baker, Felicia Farr
A crop dusting pilot robs a bank only to find that
the bank belongs to the Mafia.
MPAA:PG
Universal — *MCA Home Video*

Charlie and the Talking   1979
Buzzard
Adventure
75629   70 mins   C   B, V   P
Charlie and his dog uncover a secret plot to
destroy the biggest business in town.
Unknown — *Trans World Entertainment*

Charlie Brown Festival, A   1981
Cartoons
56889   120 mins   C   CED   P
Animated
Four complete stores featuring Charlie Brown,
trying to cope with Peppermint Patty, a losing
baseball team, the Junior Olympics, and his love
for the little red-haired girl.
United Features Syndicate — *RCA VideoDiscs*

Charlie Brown Festival   1981
Vol. II, A
Cartoons
59019   102 mins   C   CED   P
Four animated adventures featuring the
Peanuts gang: "Be My Valentine, Charlie
Brown," "It's the Easter Beagle, Charlie
Brown," "He's Your Dog, Charlie Brown," and,
"Life is a Circus, Charlie Brown."
United Features Syndicate — *RCA VideoDiscs*

Charlie Brown Festival   1982
Vol. III, A
Cartoons
47803   102 mins   C   CED   P
Animated
The Peanuts Gang are featured in this
compilation containing "It Was a Short Summer
Charlie Brown" (1969); "It's the Great Pumpkin
Charlie Brown" (1966); "You're Not Elected
Charlie Brown" (1972); and "A Charlie Brown
Thanksgiving" (1973).
United Features Syndicate — *RCA VideoDiscs*

Charlie Brown Festival   1983
Vol. IV, A
Cartoons
64327   102 mins   C   CED   P
Animated
Snoopy is a super detective, Lucy is after
Schroeder and Charlie Brown is facing a player
walk-out in this collection of Peanuts favorites.
United Features Syndicate — *RCA VideoDiscs*

Charlie Brown's All Stars   1966
Cartoons
75610   30 mins   C   B, V   P
Animated
The team is ready to give up after losing 999
games when Charlie Brown gets an offer to
have the team sponsored in a real league.
Lee Mendelson Bill Melendez
Productions — *Snoopy's Home Video Library*

Charlie Chan and the Curse of the Dragon Queen — 1981
Satire/Comedy
66060   97 mins   C   B, V   P
Peter Ustinov, Lee Grant, Angie Dickinson, Richard Hatch, Brian Kieth, Roddy McDowall.
The famed Oriental sleuth confronts his old enemy the Dragon Queen, and reveals the true identity of a killer.
MPAA:PG
American Cinema — *Media Home Entertainment*

Charlie Chaplin Carnival — 1916
Comedy
08711   80 mins B/W   B, V, 3/4U   P
This features: "The Vagabond," "The Fireman," "The Count," and "Behind the Screen." Sound effects and music added. Silent.
Mutual — *Penguin Video; Budget Video*

Charlie Chaplin Cavalcade — 1916
Comedy
08712   81 mins B/W   B, V, 3/4U   P
Features Chaplin's: "One A.M.," "Pawnshop," "Floorwalker," and "The Rink."
Mutual — *Penguin Video; Budget Video*

Charlie Chaplin Festival, The — 1917
Comedy
08674   115 mins   B, V, 3/4U   P
Charlie Chaplin, Edna Purviance, Henry Bergmna, Eric Campbell, directed by Charlie Chaplin
Features four Chaplin shorts: "The Immigrant," "The Adventurer," "The Cure," and "Easy Street."
Mutual — *Penguin Video; Budget Video*

Charlie Chaplin: The Funniest Man in the World — 1981
Documentary/Comedy
58561   93 mins B/W   B, V   P
Charlie Chaplin, Fatty Arbuckle, Mabel Normand, Ben Turpin, Stan Laurel, narrated by Douglas Fairbanks Jr.
A profile of Chaplin, from his youth in England through his vaudeville days in America to his triumph in Hollywood.
Vernon Becker; Mel May — *Mastervision*

Charlie Chaplin's Keystone Comedies — 1914
Comedy
58655   59 mins B/W   B, V, FO   P
Charlie Chaplin, Mabel Normand, Mack Swain
Six one-reelers which Chaplin filmed in 1914, his first movie-making year: "Making a Living," Chaplin's first, in which he plays a villain; "Kid Auto Races," in which Charlie now sports baggy pants, bowler hat and cane; "A Busy Day," featuring Charlie in drag; "Mabel's Married Life;" "Laughing Gas;" and "The New Janitor." Silent with musical score.
Sennett; Keystone — *Video Yesteryear*

Charlie Daniels Band: The Saratoga Concert, The — 1982
Music-Performance
59133   75 mins   C   B, V, LV, CED   P
The Charlie Daniels Band performs live in concert at Saratoga Springs, New York, September 4, 1981. The program also includes two "conceptualized" songs filmed in North Carolina and narrated by Charlie Daniels. Songs include: "In America," "The Devil Went Down to Georgia," "South's Gonna Do It Again."
Richard Namm — *CBS/Fox Video*

Charlotte's Web — 1972
Musical/Cartoons
38607   94 mins   C   B, V, LV   R, P
Animated, voices of Debbie Reynolds, Agnes Moorehead, Paul Lynde, Henry Gibson
E.B. White's famous story of Wilbur the pig and his friendship with Charlotte the spider, transformed into a cartoon musical for the whole family.
MPAA:G
Paramount — *Paramount Home Video; RCA VideoDiscs*

Charm of La Boheme, The — 1936
Musical
08738   80 mins B/W   B, V, 3/4U   P
Jan Kiepura, Martha Eggerth
Features Europe's most popular singing couple. German with English subtitles.
GE
Germany — *Penguin Video*

Chase, The — 1946
Drama
66366   86 mins B/W   B, V   P
Robert Cummings, Michele Morgan, Peter Lorre, Steve Cochran
A World War II veteran finds a wealthy man's wallet on the street. When he returns it, he becomes involved in a web of intrigue.
United Artists — *Movie Buff Video*

Chatterbox — 1976
Comedy
66099   73 mins   C   B, V, CED   P
Candice Rialson
A young starlet has a very conversant anatomy.
Bruce Cohn Curtis — *Vestron Video*

 (For Explanation of codes, see USE GUIDE and KEY)

Chatterer the Squirrel 1983
Cartoons
65655 60 mins C B, V P
Animated
Chatterer the Squirrel learns a much-needed
lesson in humility in "The Big Boast," and in
"Captive Chatterer," the farmer's son tries to
make a house pet out of Chatterer, but a new
home and plenty of food are no substitute for
freedom!
Ziv International — *Family Home
Entertainment*

Cheaper to Keep Her 1980
Comedy-Drama
68222 92 mins C B, V P
*Mac Davis, Tovah Feldshuh, Jack Gilford, Rose
Marie*
Upon leaving his wife, Bill Dekker (Mac Davis)
begins a new job working for a feminist attorney
who has him investigating husbands of clients,
who happen to be in the same predicament that
he is in.
MPAA:R
American Cinema — *Media Home
Entertainment*

Check and Double Check 1930
Comedy
11226 75 mins B/W B, V, FO P
*Freeman Gosden and Charles Correll (Amos 'n'
Andy), Duke Ellington and His Orchestra*
Radio's original Amos 'n' Andy help solve a
lover's triangle in this film version of the popular
radio series. Duke Ellington's band plays "Old
Man Blues" and "Three Little Words."
RKO — *Video Yesteryear; Discount Video
Tapes; Video Connection; Budget Video;
Western Film & Video Inc*

Cheech and Chong's 1980
Next Movie
Comedy
48629 99 mins C B, V, LV P
Cheech Marin, Tommy Chong, Evelyn Guerrero
A pair of messed-up bumblers adventure into a
welfare office, massage parlor, nightclub, and
flying saucer, while always living in fear of the
cops.
MPAA:R
Universal — *MCA Home Video*

Cheech & Chong's Nice 1981
Dreams
Comedy
60344 97 mins C B, V, LV P
*Richard "Cheech" Marin, Tommy Chong,
Evelyn Guerrero, Stacy Keach*
The spaced-out duo are selling their own
"specially mixed" ice cream to make cash and
realize their dreams.
MPAA:R

Columbia — *RCA/Columbia Pictures Home
Video; RCA VideoDiscs*

Cheerleaders, The 1973
Comedy
59081 84 mins C B, V P
The locker room hi-jinks of rival football teams
and a squad of uninhibited cheerleaders mix
and match in this racy comedy.
MPAA:R
Paul Glickler; Richard
Lerner — *HarmonyVision*

Cheerleader's Beach 1977
Party
Comedy
60401 85 mins C B, V P
Four amorous cheerleaders set out to save their
ailing college football team by "huddling" with
the rival team.
MPAA:R
Cannon Releasing; Dennis Murphy; Alex
Golten — *Paragon Video Productions*

Cheers for Miss Bishop 1941
Drama
63622 95 mins B/W B, V, FO P
*Martha Scott, William Gargan, Edmund Gwenn,
Sterling Holloway, Rosemary DeCamp*
This is the story of a young girl who graduates
from a new college and stays on to teach
English for over 50 years.
United Artists — *Video Yesteryear*

Cherry Hill High 1976
Comedy
62783 86 mins C B, V P
*Carrie Olsen, Nina Carson, Lynn Hastings,
Gloria Upson, Stephanie Lawlor*
Five high school coeds decide to have a contest
to see which of them can lose her virginity first.
MPAA:R
Cannon Films — *MCA Home Video*

Cheryl Ladd—Fascinated 1982
Music-Performance
66018 50 mins C B, V R, P
The ex-Angel performs "Just Like Old Times,"
"I Love How You Love Me," "Cold as Ice" and
more.
EMI Music — *THORN EMI Home Video*

Chessie in Florida 1981
Trains
59177 82 mins C B, V P
Ex-Chesapeake and Ohio No. 614, 4-8-4
Greenbriar type steam locomotive is seen
traveling the rails of Florida.
JMJ Prods — *JMJ Productions*

Chesty Anderson U.S. Navy · 1976
Comedy
47672 90 mins C B, V P
Shari Eubank, Dorri Thompson, Rosanne Katon, Marcie Barkin, Scotman Crothers, Frank Campanella, Fred Willard
The comic adventures of a W.A.V.E.S. unit populated by well-endowed ladies.
Unknown — *Unicorn Video*

Chevy Show, The · 1957
Variety
38993 43 mins B/W B, V, FO P
Pat Boone, Shirley MacLaine, Gisele MacKenzie, George Gobel, Jeff Donnell
Pat Boone sings "Love Letters in the Sand" and does a comedy routine with George Gobel. Gisele MacKenzie vocalizes, and Shirley MacLaine is featured in a dance routine in this TV special originally shown on June 7, 1957.
NBC — *Video Yesteryear*

Cheyenne Kid · 1933
Western
58492 40 mins B/W B, V, 3/4U P
Tom Keene, Mary Mason, Roscoe Ates
Tom plays a bronco buster after the bad guys once again.
RKO — *Penguin Video*

Cheyenne Rides Again · 1938
Western
11261 60 mins B/W B, V, FO P
Tom Tyler, Lucille Browne, Jimmy Fox
Cheyenne poses as an outlaw to hunt a gang of rustlers.
Victory — *Video Yesteryear; Video Connection*

Chick Corea/Gary Burton Live in Tokyo · 1981
Music-Performance
64829 58 mins C LV P
The music of pianist/composer Corea and vibraphonist Burton is captured in a live performance. Features Corea compositions such as "La Fiesta," "Senior Mouse" and "Children's Songs." In stereo.
Chick Corea; Gary Burton — *Pioneer Artists*

Chicken Ranch · 1983
Documentary
65381 84 mins C B, V P
This documentary focuses on the women who work at and the men who frequent "The Chicken Ranch," the country's best-known legal brothel.
MPAA:R
Nick Broomfield — *Vestron Video*

Chicken Real · 1967
Documentary/Agriculture
60451 20 mins C B, V, 3/4U P
A documentary about an automated chicken-growing operation with a tongue-in-cheek narration that makes the program both a fascinating report and a commentary.
Les Blank — *Flower Films*

Chien Andalou, Un/The Dove · 1928
Film-Avant-garde
58738 38 mins B/W B, V P
Directed by Luis Bunuel
"Un Chien Andalou," written and directed by Luis Bunuel and Salvador Dali, is comprised of several visual shocks resulting in a film of pure surrealism (silent with music). "The Dove," with Madeleine Kahn, is a parody of Ingmar Bergman's films, complete with dialogue in "pidgeon English."
Luis Bunuel — *Sheik Video*

Chien Andalou, Un · 1928
Film-Avant-garde
06242 20 mins B/W B, V P
Pierre Batcheff, Simone Marevil, Jaime Miravilles, directed by Luis Bunuel
Succession of surreal images. Silent.
Foreign — *Budget Video*

Child Bride · 1939
Drama/Exploitation
48737 60 mins B/W B, V, 3/4U P
An early exploitation feature which shows marriage customs in the Ozarks. True love wins out in the end when the young maiden doesn't marry the lecherous old man.
Unknown — *Penguin Video*

Children, The · 1980
Mystery/Suspense
65609 93 mins C B, V P
A New England town is unprepared after a school bus passes through a mysterious yellow cloud and the children are transformed to terrifying, powerful menaces.
MPAA:R
World Northal — *Vestron Video*

Children of Sanchez · 1979
Drama
76659 103 mins C B, V P
Anthony Quinn, Dolores Del Rio, Katy Jurado, Lupita Ferrer
A story of one man's attempts to provide for his family with very little except faith and love.
MPAA:R
Paul Bartlett Films — *Monterey Home Video*

Children of the Corn — 1984

Horror
74089   93 mins   C   B, V, LV, CED   P
This is another spine-tingling horror epic from that master of horror, Stephen King. This one is set in a small town in Nebraska where the local children worship the corn by making adult sacrifices.
MPAA:R
Donald P. Borchers; Terrence Kirby — *Embassy Home Entertainment*

Children Shouldn't Play with Dead Things — 1969

Horror
11658   85 mins   C   B, V   P
Alan Ormsby, Jane Daly
An acting company goes to an island to shoot a movie only to find strange and ghoulish things there, which the director decides to use in the film.
Gemeni Film; Benjamin Clark Prod — *Gorgon Video*

Children's Easter Collection — 1980

Holidays
55027   31 mins   C   B, V   P
Animated
A collection of two films illustrating the symbolism of Easter to children: "Easter Is" and "The Very First Easter."
Family Films — *Vanguard Video*

Children's Heroes of the Bible—David and Moses — 19??

Cartoons
72944   46 mins   C   B, V   P
The animated history of David and Moses from the Old Testament is brought to life in this family program.
MPAA:G
VCI — *VCI Home Video*

Chimpo's Wild Animal Safari — 1983

Comedy
69016   98 mins   C   B, V   P
Chimpo, ace reporter, reports on the beauty of African wildlife.
Unknown — *Imperial Video Corp*

China Crisis — 1945

World War II/Armed Forces-US
53658   41 mins   B/W   B, V, 3/4U   P
An Air Force film about the 14th Air Force (the "Flying Tigers") fighting the Japanese.
US Air Force — *International Historic Films*

China Syndrome, The — 1979

Drama
Closed Captioned
44784   122 mins   C   B, V, LV   P
Jack Lemmon, Michael Douglas, Jane Fonda
A television news reporter and cameraman try to make public a dangerous incident which they stumbled upon at a nuclear power plant. The integrity of a nuclear engineer makes him a murder target.
MPAA:PG
Michael Douglas — *RCA/Columbia Pictures Home Video; RCA VideoDiscs*

Chinatown — 1974

Mystery
38592   131 mins   C   B, V, LV   R, P
Jack Nicholson, Faye Dunaway, John Huston, Diane Ladd, directed by Roman Polanski
A complex tangled mystery involving Jack Nicholson as a private detective working on a seemingly routine case that mushrooms into more than he bargained for.
Academy Awards '74: Best Original Screenplay (Robert Towne).   MPAA:R
Paramount — *Paramount Home Video; RCA VideoDiscs*

Chinese Connection, The — 1973

Adventure/Martial arts
55831   107 mins   C   B, V   P
Bruce Lee, James Tien, Robert Baker
Revenge is the motive as Lee sets out to catch the men who murdered the revered teacher of his martial arts school.
MPAA:R
National General Pictures — *CBS/Fox Video; Video City Productions; Master Arts Video*

Chinese Connection II — 1984

Martial arts
66490   96 mins   C   B, V   P
Bruce Li
Bruce Li journeys to Shanghai to honor his brother's dying wish—he must re-establish the Ching Wing Wu Martial Arts School. When Bruce finds that the school has been taken over by Miyamoto, a Japanese karate master, a fight to the death ensues.
Trans World Entertainment — *Trans World Entertainment*

Chinese Gods — 1980

Folklore/China
44341   90 mins   C   B, V   R, P
Animated
This program is an animated story of Chinese mythology. It explains the battles and rivalries occurring circa 1000 B.C. in the period of the Shang Dynasty. Cruel King Cheo's troops defeated the troops of the Marquis Hsi-pa in a huge war. After an evil flying serpent tries but fails to kill him, the Marquis, Chiang, wins a

series of battles, and his rival, Cheo, eventually burns himself to death.
MPAA:G
Four Seas Films — *Video Gems*

Chinese Web, The   1978
Adventure
66069   95 mins   C   B, V   P
Nicholas Hammond
A Spider-man adventure in which Spidey becomes entwined in international intrigue.
Danchuk Productions — *CBS/Fox Video*

Chino   1975
Western
47384   97 mins   C   B, V   R, P
Charles Bronson, Jill Ireland, directed by John Sturges
A half-breed horse trainer with an independent streak "adopts" a runaway fifteen-year-old boy.
MPAA:PG
Intercontinental Releasing Corp — *Warner Home Video*

Chisum   1970
Western
51962   111 mins   C   B, V   R, P
John Wayne, Forrest Tucker, Geoffrey Deuel
A cattle baron meets Billy the Kid and together they fight the corrupt town government.
MPAA:G
Warner Bros — *Warner Home Video*

Chitty Chitty Bang Bang   1968
Musical/Fantasy
58483   142 mins   C   B, V, CED   P
Dick Van Dyke, Sally Ann Howes, Lionel Jeffries, directed by Ken Hughes
An eccentric inventor spruces up an old car and, in fantasy, takes his children to a land where the evil rulers have forbidden children.
MPAA:G EL, SP
United Artists; Albert R Broccoli — *CBS/Fox Video*

Chosen, The   1981
Drama
65404   107 mins   C   B, V   P
Rod Steiger, Robby Benson, Barry Miller
This is the story of two young Jewish men whose friendship survives the deep conflicts arising from having been raised in two different worlds. Based on Chaim Potok's acclaimed novel.
MPAA:PG
Edie and Ely Landau — *CBS/Fox Video*

Christine   1984
Suspense
76034   110 mins   C   B, V   P
Keith Gordon, John Stockwell, Alexandra Paul, Robert Prosley, Harry Dean Stanton, directed by John Carpenter
Christine is a sleek red and white 1958 Plymouth Fury that seduces a teenage boy and demands his complete and unquestioned devotion. Anyone who gets in her way becomes a victim of Christine's wrath. Based on the Stephen King novel.
MPAA:R
Richard Kobritz — *RCA/Columbia Pictures Home Video*

Christine McVie Concert, The   1984
Music-Performance
72535   60 mins   C   B, V, CED   P
Concert footage is intermixed with state-of-the-art videos of Fleetwood Mac's Christine McVie, who is enjoying a successful solo venture.
Time Life Multimedia — *Vestron Video*

Christmas Carol, A   1951
Drama
11659   86 mins   B/W   B, V   P
Alastair Sim, Kathleen Harrison
Dickens' classic story of how a miserly old man is brought to change on Christmas Eve.
United Artists; Renown Pictures — *VCI Home Video*

Christmas Collection, The   1980
Religion/Christmas
55028   120 mins   C   B, V   P
A collection of five films: "Glory in the Highest," a drama about the birth of Christ; "God's Christmas Gift," in which a child realizes that God's gift was His Son; "To Each a Gift," a turn-of-the-century story about the true spirit of Christmas; "Teen-Age Christmas," a tale about discovering the meaning of Christmas; and "The Brightest Night," the story of the Magi.
Family Films — *Vanguard Video*

Christmas on Grandfather's Farm   1959
Christmas
00831   14 mins   C   B, V   P, T
An old-fashioned Christmas celebration at Grandma and Grandpa's big farmhouse reveals what the holiday celebration was like in the 1890's.
Coronet Films — *Blackhawk Films*

Christmas Tree, The   1969
Drama
45054   110 mins   C   B, V   P
William Holden, Virna Lisi, Andre Bourvil, Brook Fuller
When the son of an extremely wealthy businessman contracts radiation poisoning and

is given only a few months to live, his father devotes his entire life to the boy's happiness.
MPAA:G
Alan Enterprises — *VCI Home Video*

Christopher Tree 1969
Music
60459   10 mins   C   B, V, 3/4U   P
A lyrical, spontaneous sound concert of "cosmic music". Set up in a primeval forest, Tree's one-man orchestra includes 40 temple gongs, flutes, tympani and wind chimes.
Les Blank — *Flower Films*

Chu Chu and the Philly Flash 1981
Comedy
58824   102 mins   C   B, V, CED   P
Alan Arkin, Carol Burnett, Jack Warden, Danny Aiello, Ruth Buzzi, Lou Jacobi
A has-been baseball player and a lame dance teacher meet while hustling the same corner, he as a hot watch salesman, she as a one-man bond. Soon, a briefcase full of government secrets gets them involved with the feds, the mob, and a motley collection of back-alley bums.
MPAA:PG
United Artists; Lawrence Turman; David Foster — *CBS/Fox Video*

Chuck Berry Live at The Roxy 1982
Music-Performance
73564   60 mins   C   B, V   P
Chuck Berry, Tina Turner
This is a performance of Chuck taped in 1982 where he performs all his hits and duets with Tina Turner.
Jack Malstead; C D Haifly — *Prism*

Chuck's Choice Cuts 1982
Variety
73541   120 mins   C   B, V   P
Chuck the security guard hosts this wild melange of crazy shorts, vintage TV show segments and musical clips.
Admit One — *Admit One Video*

Chud 1984
Science fiction
76648   90 mins   C   B, V   P
John Heard, Daniel Stern, Christopher Curry, Kim Griest
This program is based on a true New York Times story about life in the tunnels and caverns under the city and the exposure of a possible U.S. government plan to store wastes in these underground passages.
Andrew Bonime — *Media Home Entertainment*

Chulas Fronteras 1976
Music/Folklore
60460   58 mins   C   B, V, 3/4U   P
Los Alegres de Teran, Lydia Mendoza, Falco Jimenez
A look at the American music known as Tex-Mex, indigenous to the Texas-Mexican border. The music of the people is seen embodied in their family life and enjoyment of domestic rituals, as well as in their hardships.
Chris Strachwitz — *Flower Films*

Chump at Oxford, A 1940
Comedy
47140   63 mins   B/W   B, V, 3/4U   P
Stan Laurel, Oliver Hardy, James Finlayson, Wilfrid Lucas, Peter Cushing, Charlie Hall
Street cleaners Laurel and Hardy foil a bank robbery and receive an all-expenses-paid education at Oxford as their reward.
Hal Roach — *Nostalgia Merchant; Blackhawk Films*

Chump at Oxford, A 1940
Comedy
63986   83 mins   B/W   B, V   P, T
Stan Laurel, Oliver Hardy, Jimmy Finlayson, Wilfred Lucas, Peter Cushing
As a reward for foiling a bank robbery, Stan and Ollie receive a free education at Oxford University. This tape also includes a Charley Chase short, "The Tabasco Kid," made in 1932.
Hal Roach; MGM — *Blackhawk Films*

Church Collection, The 1980
Christianity
55037   73 mins   C   B, V   P
A collection of four films explaining the church's role in modern times: "Baptism," "Holy Communion," "How to Visit," and "What Can I Do?"
Family Films — *Vanguard Video*

Cincinnati Kid, The 1965
Drama
60591   104 mins   C   B, V, CED   P
Steve McQueen, Edward G. Robinson, Ann-Margret, Tuesday Weld, Karl Malden, Joan Blondell
A young New Orleans gambler is determined to take the expert crown away from an old dapper man known as the King of Stud Poker.
MGM — *MGM/UA Home Video*

Cinderella 1984
Fairy tales
Closed Captioned
73575   60 mins   C   B, V, CED   P
Jennifer Beals, Jean Stapleton, Matthew Broderick, Eve Arden
From the "Faerie Tale Theatre" comes the story of a girl who gets even with her three

stepsisters and ends up going to the ball to meet the man of her dreams.
Gaylord Productions; Platypus Productions — *CBS/Fox Video*

Cinderella Seahawks/NFL '83, The　　1984
Football
72941　46 mins　C　B, V, FO　　P
Seattle Seahawks
Highlights from the 1983 season of the Seattle Seahawks and "NFL 1983."
NFL Films — *NFL Films Video*

Circle of Death　　1936
Western
56610　55 mins　B/W　B, V　P
Monte Montana, Yakima Canutt
A western with a twist—the hero is an Indian.
Unknown — *Video Dimensions*

Circle of Iron　　1978
Adventure
37419　102 mins　C　B, V　P
Jeff Cooper, David Carradine, Roddy McDowall, Eli Wallach, Christopher Lee
Plenty of action and martial arts combat abound in this story of one man's eternal quest for truth.
MPAA:R
New World — *Embassy Home Entertainment*

Circle of Life I　　1980
Identity/Psychology
55038　57 mins　C　B, V　P
Four films in which people explore their deeply human attitudes and ideas about themselves, their relationships, their ideals, and life as it feels in the living: "To Be A Woman," "To Be a Man," "To Be in Love," and "To Be Married."
Billy Budd Films — *Vanguard Video*

Circle of Life II　　1980
Identity/Psychology
55039　66 mins　C　B, V　P
Four films in which people explore their deeply human attitudes about themselves, their relationships, and their lives in general: "To Be a Person," "To Be a Parent," "To Be a Friend," and "To Be Growing Older."
Billy Budd Films — *Vanguard Video*

Circle of Two　　1981
Drama/Romance
79213　90 mins　C　B, V　P
Richard Burton, Tatum O'Neal
A May September romance blossoms between an art teacher and his student.
MPAA:PG
World Northal — *Vestron Video*

Circus World　　1964
Drama
16808　137 mins　C　B, V　P
John Wayne, Rita Hayworth
American circus owner in Europe searches for aerialist he loved 15 years before and whose daughter he has reared.
Paramount; Samuel Bronston — *VCI Home Video*

Citizen Kane　　1941
Drama
00255　120 mins　B/W　B, V, 3/4U　P
Orson Welles, Joseph Cotton, Agnes Moorehead
Citizen Kane is the story of a powerful newspaper publisher, told by those who thought they knew him best.
Academy Awards '41: Best Original Screenplay; N.Y. Film Critics Award '41: Best Motion Picture
RKO — *Nostalgia Merchant; VidAmerica; King of Video; RCA VideoDiscs*

City Lights　　1931
Comedy
08420　81 mins　B/W　B, V　P
Charlie Chaplin, Virginia Cherrill, Harry Myers, Henry Bergman, Jean Harlow, directed by Charlie Chaplin.
The story is of a tramp (Chaplin) who, by a series of lucky accidents, is able to restore the sight of a blind flowergirl.
United Artists — *CBS/Fox Video; RCA VideoDiscs*

City of Gold/Drylanders　　19??
Documentary/Canada
65233　92 mins　B/W　B, V, FO　P
This tape combines two riveting Canadian documentaries: "City of Gold" (1957), which is about the Klondike Gold Rush of the 1890's, and "Drylanders" (1962), the story of a city family's attempt to live on a lonely Sakatchewan farm.
National Film Board of Canada — *Video Yesteryear*

Civilization　　1916
War-Drama/Film-History
64245　68 mins　B/W　B, V　P
Enid Markey, Howard Hickman, J. Barney Sherry, directed by Thomas Ince
During World War I, a general has a vision of Christ on the battlefield and persuades the opposing armies to sign a peace treaty. Thomas Ince's classic pacifist film was released as a warning, prior to the U.S. entry into the war. Silent with musical score.
Triangle; Thomas Ince — *Classic Video Cinema Collector's Club*

Clarence Darrow — 1974
Drama/Biographical
56888   90 mins   C   CED   P
Henry Fonda
Henry Fonda's tour-de-force, one-man show portraying the controversial trial lawyer who defended over one hundred accused murderers, including Leopold and Loeb, and made history in the Scopes Monkey Trial.
Dome Prods — *RCA VideoDiscs*

Clash by Night — 1952
Drama
11661   105 mins   B/W   B, V   P
Barbara Stanwyck, Paul Douglas, Marilyn Monroe
Lonely woman marries fishing boat captain and falls in love with his best friend.
RKO; Jerry Wald; Norman Krasna; Harriet Parsons — *VCI Home Video*

Clash of the Titans — 1981
Adventure
58702   118 mins   C   B, V, LV, CED   P
Laurence Olivier, Maggie Smith, Claire Bloom, Ursula Andress, Burgess Meredith
Special effects highlight this telling of ancient Greek mythology and Nordic legends.
MPAA:PG
MGM — *MGM/UA Home Video*

Class — 1983
Comedy
65361   98 mins   C   B, V, LV   P
Jacqueline Bisset, Rob Lowe, Andrew McCarthy, Cliff Robertson
A rich and funny farce, this is the outrageous story of a young prep school student whose torrid new love turns out to be his roommate's mother.
MPAA:R
Martin Ransohoff — *Vestron Video*

Class of 1984 — 1982
Drama
66092   93 mins   C   B, V, LV, CED   P
Perry King, Roddy McDowall, Timothy Van Patten
An explosive portrait of a school gang on the loose. A confrontation between the humanity of the past and a darkly violent future.
MPAA:R
United Film — *Vestron Video*

Claude Bolling: Concerto for Classic Guitar and Jazz Piano — 1982
Music-Performance
47810   ? mins   C   LV   P
Pianist George Shearing appears with guitarist Angel Romero, drummer Shelly Manne, and bassist Brian Torff in this definitive performance of Bolling's piece. In stereo.
Unknown — *Pioneer Artists*

Clear Track Ahead — 1952
Trains
51433   30 mins   B/W   B, V   P
Steam and diesel trains of the 1940's Pennsylvania Railroad are featured in this program, along with historic flashbacks to the founding of the railroad.
Pennsylvania Railroad — *Interurban Films*

Clearing the Range — 1931
Western
11660   60 mins   B/W   B, V   P
Hoot Gibson
A cringing coward by day becomes a fearless champion by night in this western.
M H Hoffman — *Video Connection*

Cleopatra — 1963
Drama
08431   246 mins   C   B, V, CED   P
Elizabeth Taylor, Richard Burton, Rex Harrison, Pamela Brown, directed by Joseph L. Mankiewicz
After the death of Julius Caesar, Cleopatra, Queen of Egypt, becomes infatuated with Mark Antony. In stereo.
Academy Awards '63: Best Cinematography.
20th Century Fox; Walter Wanger — *CBS/Fox Video*

Cliffhangers, Comebacks, and Character — 1982
Football
47714   23 mins   C   B, V, FO   P
Team highlights of the 1981 San Diego Chargers, who had the most prolific offense in NFL history.
NFL Films — *NFL Films Video*

Clockwork Orange, A — 1971
Science fiction
54118   137 mins   C   B, V, LV   R, P
Malcolm McDowell, Patrick Magee, Adrienne Corri, directed by Stanley Kubrick
The head of a gang of punks is imprisoned for rape. When he is released he finds the world to be even more violent, especially when he is brutally beaten by his old adversaries. Based on the novel by Anthony Burgess.
MPAA:R
Warner Bros, Stanley Kubrick — *Warner Home Video; RCA VideoDiscs*

Clodhopper, The — 1919
Drama
48702   40 mins   B/W   B, V, 3/4U   P
A country bumpkin travels to the big city and makes good. Silent.

Unknown — *Penguin Video*

Nebulae Prods — *Nebulae Productions*

Clones of Bruce Lee, The   1980
Adventure/Martial arts
50731   87 mins   C   B, V   P
*Dragon Lee, Bruce Le, Bruce Lai, Bruce Thai,
directed by Joseph Kong*
A Kung-Fu fan's delight, as gallant warriors from
the Far East battle to reign supreme over the
land of exotic self-defense.
MPAA:R
Newport Releasing — *Media Home
Entertainment*

Close Encounters of the   1980
Third Kind (The Special
Edition)
Science fiction
Closed Captioned
54107   152 mins   C   B, V, LV   P
*Richard Dreyfuss, Teri Garr, Melinda Dillon,
Francois Truffaut, directed by Steven Spielberg*
A middle class American couple, who have had
encounters of the first and second kinds,
sighting UFO's and finding physical evidence of
them, are determined to have the third
encounter—actual contact with the occupants.
In this special edition, which contains about 15
extra minutes, the man does go inside the UFO
and makes contact.
MPAA:PG
Columbia Pictures — *RCA/Columbia Pictures
Home Video; RCA VideoDiscs*

Closely Watched Trains   1966
Drama
72927   89 mins   C   B, V   P
A young man who works in a train station during
World War Two is going through his rites of
passage. This film is subtitled.
CZ
Filmove Studio Barrandov — *RCA/Columbia
Pictures Home Video*

Cloud Dancer   1980
Drama
66630   108 mins   C   B, V   P
*David Carradine, Jennifer O'Neill, Joseph
Bottoms, directed by Barry Brown*
A champion acrobatic trapeze flier selfishly
pursues his career to the exclusion of those who
care about him.
MPAA:PG
Blossom Pictures; Melvin Simon
Productions — *Prism*

Clouds of Peace   1978
Video
08566   30 mins   C   B, V, 3/4U   P
A continuous picture of slow-moving clouds
against a deep blue sky to create a relaxed
background.

Clown, The   1952
Comedy-Drama
58870   91 mins   B/W   B, V   P
*Red Skelton, Jane Greer, Tim Considine, Steve
Forrest*
A derelict ex-comedian, after several attempts
at a comeback, faces his last chance in a make-
or-break situation.
MGM — *MGM/UA Home Video*

Clowns, The   1971
Drama
03560   90 mins   C   B, V   P
Directed by Federico Fellini
Directed by Federico Fellini, this movie
recreates some of the most famous clown acts
in circus history, presents the two major types of
clowns, and suggests that the world is peopled
with clowns.
Universal — *Media Home Entertainment;
Penguin Video; Discount Video Tapes*

Clutching Hand, The   1936
Mystery/Serials
14261   268 mins   B/W   B, V   P
Jack Mulhall, Rex Lease
The Clutching Hand seeks a formula that will
turn metal into gold and detective Craig
Kennedy is out to prevent him from doing so. A
serial in 15 chapters on three cassettes.
Stage and Screen — *Video Dimensions; Video
Connection; Penguin Video*

Coach   1978
Comedy
63893   100 mins   C   B, V   P
*Cathy Lee Crosby, Michael Biehn, Keenan
Wynn, Sidney Wicks*
A female coach is hired to make a losing high
school boys' basketball team into a
championship one.
MPAA:G
Mark Tenser — *Media Home Entertainment*

Coal Miner's Daughter   1980
Drama
45104   125 mins   C   B, V, LV   P
Sissy Spacek, Tommy Lee Jones
The rags-to-riches story of how Loretta Lynn
became "the queen of country music."
Academy Awards '80: Best Actress (Spacek).
MPAA:PG
Universal, Bernard Schwartz — *MCA Home
Video; RCA VideoDiscs*

Coast Patrol, The   1925
Drama
48703   50 mins   B/W   B, V, 3/4U   P
Fay Wray

The shore is jumping with speedboat chases, fights, and fires. Silent.
Bud Barsky Corp — *Penguin Video*

Coast to Coast 1980
Comedy-Drama
54673   95 mins   C   B, V, LV   R, P
Dyan Cannon, Robert Blake, Quinn Redeker, Michael Lerner, Maxine Stuart, Bill Lucking, directed by Joseph Sargent
A woman whose playboy husband is trying to have her judged insane rather than grant her the divorce she wants escapes from an East Coast hospital and hitches a ride with a trucker. The action centers on their cross-country trip, during which they are pursued by a detective (hired by the husband) and a finance company thug who is trying to repossess the trucker's vehicle.
MPAA:PG
Paramount — *Paramount Home Video*

Coaster Adventure of the 1981
John F. Leavitt
Boating/Documentary
73567   91 mins   C   B, V   P
This movie tells the story of a young man who built a 97-foot wooden schooner and became a modern day merchant adventurer.
Jon Craig Cloutier; Atlantic Film Group — *Atlantic Film Group I*

Cobra 289-427 1983
Automobiles
76388   30 mins   C   B, V   P
The 289 and 427 are examined in both street and race forms, with on-tract driving sessions, and an interview with a Cobra restoration expert.
Armour Productions — *Armour Productions*

Cocaine Cowboys 1979
Drama
42913   90 mins   C   B, V   P
Jack Palance
This modern day thriller tells the story of a rock and roll band smuggling cocaine to help their expenses and, in doing so, run afoul of the mob.
MPAA:R
International Harmony Films — *Media Home Entertainment*

Cocaine Fiends 1937
Drama/Exploitation
03854   74 mins   B/W   B, V   P
Lois January, Noel Madison, directed by W.A. Conner
A camp classic from the 1930's warning of the evils of cocaine. A brother and sister are led to the depths of degradation upon trying cocaine; heroin addiction, prostitution, and suicide are the inevitable results.

New Line Cinema — *Media Home Entertainment; Budget Video; Video Dimensions; Discount Video Tapes*

Cockeyed Cavaliers 1934
Comedy
44809   70 mins   B/W   B, V   P, T
Wheeler and Woolsey, Dorothy Lee, Thelma Todd
Wheeler and Woolsey are stockaded for stealing the Duke's horses and carriage. To escape jail they swap clothes with some drunken royalty.
RKO — *Blackhawk Films*

Cockfighter 1974
Drama
74082   84 mins   C   B, V   P
Warren Oates
This is the story of a man so obsessed with cockfighting he loses his money, possessions and lover because of it.
MPAA:R
Roger Corman — *Embassy Home Entertainment*

Coke Time with Eddie 1955
Fisher and The Perry
Como Show
Variety
42981   26 mins   B/W   B, V, FO   P
Eddie Fisher, Perry Como
Here are highlights of two shows from the early evening live TV era before the news conquered all, when prime time TV had 15-minute programs included. Relaxed singing by both Como and Fisher.
NBC, CBS — *Video Yesteryear*

Cold River 1981
Drama
65406   94 mins   C   B, V, CED   P
An experienced Adirondacks guide takes his two children on an extended trip through the Adirondacks. For the children, it's a fantasy vacation until their father succumbs to a heart attack in the chilly mountains. "Cold River" is a journey of survival, and an exploration of human relationships.
MPAA:PG
Fred G Sullivan — *CBS/Fox Video*

Colditz Story, The 1955
War-Drama
63343   93 mins   B/W   B, V   R, P
John Mills, Eric Portman, Lionel Jeffries, Bryan Forbes, Ian Carmichael
Prisoners of war from the Allied countries join together in an attempt to escape from Colditz, a castle-prison deep within the Third Reich, reputed to be escape-proof.

(For Explanation of codes, see USE GUIDE and KEY)

British Lion; Ivan Foxwell — *THORN EMI Home Video*

Colgate Comedy Hour   1954
Variety
11271   54 mins   B/W   B, V, FO   P
Spike Jones and His City Slickers, Nat King Cole, Bobby Van, Paul Gilbert, Senor Wences
Comedy, music, and a dash of sports give an indication of what the general public enjoyed on television during the early 1950's.
NBC — *Video Yesteryear*

Colgate Comedy Hour,   1955
The
Comedy/Variety
47494   29 mins   B/W   B, V, FO   P
Dean Martin, Jerry Lewis, Margaret Dumont
This partial show features several songs and sketches by Dean and Jerry.
NBC — *Video Yesteryear*

Colgate Comedy Hour,   1951
The
Comedy/Variety
47496   60 mins   B/W   B, V, FO   P
Spike Jones and the City Slickers, Gale Robbins, Dave Garroway, Mike Wallace
Spike Jones' first appearance on this series features his band playing many of their hits: "Laura," "Be My Love," "Glow-Worm," "Chloe" and "Cocktails for Two."
NBC — *Video Yesteryear*

Colgate Comedy Hour,   195?
The
Variety
63853   55 mins   B/W   B, V   P
Eddie Cantor, Brian Donlevy, Eddie Fisher, Frank Sinatra, Harold Arlen
Eddie Cantor does a "Maxie the Taxi" sketch, then joins Brian Donlevy for a Western sketch. Eddie Fisher and Frank Sinatra sing, and Harold Arlen plays a medley of his classic songs.
NBC — *Budget Video*

Colgate Comedy Hour: 1954
"Let's Face It," The
Musical
47497   60 mins   B/W   B, V, FO   P
Bert Lahr, Vivian Blaine, Gene Nelson, Betty Furness
A TV adaptation of Cole Porter's 1941 Broadway musical.
NBC — *Video Yesteryear*

Colgate Comedy Hour   1952
(The Eddie Cantor Show)
Variety
42964   60 mins   B/W   B, V, FO   P
Eddie Cantor, Kirk Douglas, Robert Clary

Aired January 20, 1952, this program stars Eddie Cantor singing and in comedy routines such as "Cantor Goes to College" and "The Detective Story," with Eddie playing the lead.
NBC — *Video Yesteryear*

Colgate Comedy Hour   1951
(The Tony Martin Show)
Variety
42963   53 mins   B/W   B, V, FO   P
Tony Martin, Celeste Holm, Fred Allen
This program, aired April 15, 1951 over NBC, features singing and comedy routines including "One Long Pan," a mystery sketch with Fred Allen as the Chinese sleuth.
NBC — *Video Yesteryear*

Colgate Comedy Hour   1955
with Martin and Lewis,
The
Variety
59089   29 mins   B/W   B, V, FO   P
Dean Martin, Jerry Lewis, Margaret Dumont
Dean and Jerry in a classroom sketch, Dean croons "Sweet Kentucky Babe," and Dean teaches Jerry how to meet girls and handle ruffians on the beach.
NBC — *Video Yesteryear*

Collector, The   1965
Drama
13245   119 mins   C   B, V   P
Terence Stamp, Samantha Eggar, Maurice Dallimore, directed by William Wyler
Lonely clerk kidnaps a girl and locks her in the cellar hoping she will fall in love with him. Filmdoms Famous Five '65: Best Actress (Eggar); Outstanding Director (Wyler).
Columbia — *RCA/Columbia Pictures Home Video; RCA VideoDiscs*

Collectors Item: The Left   1960
Fist of David
Mystery
38999   27 mins   B/W   B, V, FO   P
Vincent Price, Peter Lorre
The pilot program for a TV series that was never produced, featuring Price and Lorre as a pair of art dealers who become embroiled in mysterious doings.
CBS — *Video Yesteryear*

College   1927
Comedy
10093   60 mins   B/W   B, V   P, T
Buster Keaton, A. Cornwall, directed by James W. Horne
Keaton graduates valedictorian from high school, tries out for every sport in college, and works as a soda jerk. Musical score by John Muri.

United Artists — *Blackhawk Films; Video Dimensions; Sheik Video; Video Yesteryear; Classic Video Cinema Collector's Club*

Color Adventures of   194?
Superman, The
Cartoons
57350   52 mins   C   B, V, FO   P
Animated
Seven cartoon adventures of the Man of Steel, as animated by the Fleischer Studio; produced between 1941 and 1943. Titles include "Superman," "The Mechanical Monsters," "The Magnetic Telescope," "The Japoteurs," "The Bulleteers," "Jungle Drums," and "The Mummy Strikes."
Max Fleischer — *Video Yesteryear*

Color Cartoon Program A   194?
Cartoons
14269   30 mins   C   B, V   P
Animated
Includes "Corney Concherto," "Fallen Hare," "Sheepish Wolf," and "Daffy and the Dinosaur." Features Bugs Bunny, Porky Pig, and Daffy Duck.
Warner Bros — *Video Connection*

Color Cartoon Program B   194?
Cartoons
14270   30 mins   C   B, V   P
Animated
Includes "All This and Rabbit Stew," "Daffy Commando," "Hollywood Capers," and "Waikiki Rabbit." Features Bugs Bunny and Daffy Duck.
Warner Bros — *Video Connection*

Color Cartoon Program C   194?
Cartoons
14271   30 mins   C   B, V   P
Animated
Includes "Jungle Jitters," "Wacky Rabbit," "Little Black Samboy," and "Two Kittens Tale." Features Bugs Bunny, Sambo, Tiger, Tweety Pie.
Warner Bros — *Video Connection*

Color Cartoon Program D   194?
Cartoons
14272   30 mins   C   B, V   P
Animated
Includes "Fresh Hare," "Hamateur Night," "Fifth Column Mouse," and "The Rabbit Who Came to Supper." Features Bugs Bunny and Elmer Fudd.
Warner Bros — *Video Connection*

Color Cartoon Program I   19??
Cartoons
14273   30 mins   C   B, V   P
Animated
Includes "Dragon Along," "Underworld Whirl," "Broom Gloom," "Pigs in a Panic," and "Puppet Enemy No. 1."
Unknown — *Video Connection*

Color Cartoon Program II   19??
Cartoons
14274   30 mins   C   B, V   P
Animated
Includes "Long Long Camper," "Dinosaur Dilemma," "The Mark of El Zap," "Not So Sweet Sioux," and "Lube A Tuba."
Unknown — *Video Connection*

Color Cartoon Program   19??
III
Cartoons
14275   30 mins   B/W   B, V   P
Animated
Includes "Super Lou," "Stand In, Stand Off," "Elephantsy," "The Cloud Monster," and "Tiny Terror."
Unknown — *Video Connection*

Color Cartoon Program   19??
IV
Cartoons
14276   30 mins   B/W   B, V   P
Animated
Includes "In the Soup," "The Two Musketeers," "Mounty Bounty," "Magic Mix-Up," and "Super Knight."
Unknown — *Video Connection*

Color in the Movies   1980
Film-History/Photography
58516   113 mins   C   B, V, 3/4U   P
A compilation of fourteen short films dating from 1898 to 1934, featuring early attempts to produce color effects. Hand-painted and tinted films, as well as advanced two and three-color Technicolor shorts are included.
Unknown — *Penguin Video*

Color Me Blood Red   1964
Horror
55131   74 mins   C   B, V   P
Don Joseph, Sandi Conder, directed by Herschell G. Lewis
The first of the gore movies, this film is a tale of an artist who finds that the best shade of red for his paintings is provided by human blood. Mutilations and stabbings abound.
Friedman Lewis Prods — *Video Dimensions*

Color Them Tough   1981
Football
51169   23 mins   C   B, V, FO   R, P
New York Jets
1980 never materialized for the Jets the way they, their fans, and the experts had expected. Key injuries, offensive problems, and defensive

---

inconsistency provided the problems. Still, they did manage to score upsets over strong clubs like Houston, Miami, and Atlanta.
NFL Films — *NFL Films Video*

Colorado　　1940
Western
64390　54 mins　B/W　B, V, 3/4U　　P
Roy Rogers, Gabby Hayes
Roy and Gabby bring law and order to the untamed Colorado Territory.
Republic — *Nostalgia Merchant*

Colorado Rails　　197?
Trains
55516　60 mins　C　B, V　　P
A ride on the rails through the Rocky Mountains features the famed "Zephyr" of the D and RGW line, one of the last privately run major passenger trains. A visit to freight yards and a look at the spectacular Silverton of D and RGW close the program.
De Luz Video — *De Luz Video*

Columbia Pictures　　1980
Cartoons Volume I: Mr.
Magoo
Comedy/Cartoons
44848　40 mins　C　B, V　　P
Animated
The famous near-sighted old codger is seen in five of his adventures: "Barefoot Flatfoot," "Bungled Bungalow," "Bwana Magoo," "Destination Magoo," and "Madcap Magoo."
UPA — *RCA/Columbia Pictures Home Video*

Columbia Pictures　　1980
Cartoons Volume II: Mr.
Magoo
Comedy/Cartoons
44849　40 mins　C　B, V　　P
Animated
Mr. Magoo, through the voice of Jim Backus, entertains in his near-sighted fashion in: "Magoo Beats the Heat," "Magoo Breaks Par," "Magoo Goes Overboard," "Magoo Goes West," and "Magoo Saves the Bank."
UPA — *RCA/Columbia Pictures Home Video*

Columbia Pictures　　1980
Cartoons Volume III:
Gerald McBoing-Boing
Cartoons
44850　30 mins　C　B, V　　P
Animated
This is a compilation of four Gerald McBoing-Boing cartoons: "Gerald McBoing-Boing," "Gerald McBoing-Boing on the Planet Moon," "Gerald McBoing-Boing's Symphony," and "How Now Boing-Boing."
UPA — *RCA/Columbia Pictures Home Video*

Columbia Pictures　　1980
Cartoons Volume IV: UPA
Classics
Cartoons
44839　40 mins　C　B, V　　P
Animated
A collection of five favorite cartoons from UPA: "Christopher Crumpet's Playmate," "The Emperor's New Clothes," "The Jay Walker," "The Man on the Flying Trapeze," and "The Tell Tale Heart."
UPA — *RCA/Columbia Pictures Home Video*

Columbia Pictures　　1983
Cartoons Volume V: Mr.
Magoo
Comedy/Cartoons
63444　60 mins　C　B, V　　P
Animated
Eight more misadventures with the near-sighted Mr. Magoo: "Stage Door Magoo," "Magoo's Glorious July 4th," "Sloppy Jalopy," "Magoo's Homecoming," "Trouble Indemnity," "Fuddy Duddy Buddy," "Magoo's Masquerade" and "Magoo Saves the Bank."
UPA — *RCA/Columbia Pictures Home Video*

Columbia Pictures　　19??
Cartoons, Volume VI
Cartoons
66013　60 mins　C　B, V　　P
Animated
Eight classic cartoons: "Pete Hothead," "Unicorn in the Garden," "Family Circus," "Ballet-Oop," "Christopher Crumpet," "Popcorn Story," "The Rise of Duton Lang," and "Four Wheels, No Breaks."
Columbia — *RCA/Columbia Pictures Home Video*

Columbia Pictures　　196?
Cartoons, Volume VII
Comedy
68265　60 mins　C　B, V　　P
Animated, voice of Jim Backus
Eight more amusing adventures of Mr. Magoo.
UPA — *RCA/Columbia Pictures Home Video*

Coma　　1978
Suspense
44641　113 mins　C　B, V, LV,　　P
　　　　　　　　　　CED
Genevieve Bujold, Michael Douglas, Elizabeth Ashley, Rip Torn, Richard Widmark, Lois Chiles, Harry Rhodes, directed by Michael Crichton
A young doctor at Boston hospital finds that patients, one of which is her best friend, suffer irreparable brain damage when supposed minor operations are performed. All these operations take place in the same operating room. Based on the novel by Robin Cook.
MPAA:PG

MGM — *MGM/UA Home Video*

Republic — *Nostalgia Merchant*

Comancheros, The   1961
Western
64903   108 mins   C   B, V, CED   P
John Wayne, Stuart Whitman, Nehemiah Persoff
Wayne, a Texas Ranger, penetrates the ranks of the Comancheros, an outlaw gang supplying guns and liquor to the dreaded Comanches.
20th Century Fox — *CBS/Fox Video*

Combat Bulletin   194?
World War II
48845   115 mins   B/W   B, V, 3/4U   P
A collection of World War II action newsreels produced for G.I. viewing.
Unknown — *Western Film & Video Inc*

Combat Bulletins Nos. 1-   194?
14
World War II
53677   40 mins   B/W   B, V, 3/4U   P
Fourteen compilations of short wartime films such as "Report from Berlin," "Bombing of Manila," and "Meeting in Yalta." Each bulletin available separately with five to ten films included.
Unknown — *International Historic Films*

Come Back   1984
Champions/NFL '83
Football
72936   46 mins   C   B, V, FO   P
Detroit Lions
Highlights from the Detroit Lions' 1983 season and "NFL 83."
NFL Films — *NFL Films Video*

Come Back to the 5 and   1982
Dime Jimmy Dean, Jimmy
Dean
Drama
60559   109 mins   C   B, V, CED   P
Sandy Dennis, Cher, Karen Black, Sudie Bond, directed by Robert Altman
In 1975, the workers and customers of a small town 5 and Dime are celebrating the 20th anniversary of the death of James Dean. A complex look into the past begins when a woman announces that her son is the product of a one-night stand with the late actor twenty years ago.
Cinecom Intl — *Embassy Home Entertainment*

Come On, Cowboys   1937
Western
64419   54 mins   B/W   B, V, 3/4U   P
Bob Livingston, Ray Corrigan
The Three Mesquiteers rescue an old circus friend from certain death.

Come On Tarzan   1932
Western
56608   60 mins   B/W   B, V   P
Ken Maynard
Ken uses wise words to cheer his horse, Tarzan, into action.
World Wide — *Video Dimensions*

Comeback   1983
Drama/Music
65659   105 mins   C   B, V   P
Eric Burdon
This is the story of a disillusioned rock star who gives up his life in the fast lane and tries to go back to his roots... and to himself.
TeleCulture Inc — *MGM/UA Home Video*

Comedy 1: Trailers on   1984
Tape
Movie and TV trailers/Comedy
66479   60 mins   C   B, V   P
Over thirty theatrical trailers for comedy films are compiled on this tape, including "Paper Moon," "Born Yesterday," "Airplane," "Monty Python and the Holy Grail," "The Producers," "Some Like It Hot," "The Errand Boy" and "The Seven Year Itch." Some black-and-white segments.
20th Century Fox et al — *San Francisco Rush Video*

Comedy and Kid Stuff I   1952
Comedy
33688   120 mins   C   B, V, 3/4U   P
A collection of four light-hearted shows from the 50's including single episodes from "The Burns and Allen Show," and "I Married Joan," "Winky Dink," with host Jack Barry, and "Carson's Cellar," starring a twenty-five year old Johnny Carson and the late Jack Bailey.
CBS et al — *Shokus Video*

Comedy and Kid Stuff II   195?
Comedy
33689   120 mins   C   B, V, 3/4U   P
Four episodes from popular TV shows of the 1950's; "The Burns and Allen 1951 Christmas Show," "The Abbott and Costello Show," featuring the "Who's on First" routine and the retired actor's home, "Howdy Doody," and "The Lucy Show." Some black and white.
CBS et al — *Shokus Video*

Comedy Festival #1   193?
Comedy
00430   60 mins   B/W   B, V   P
Collection of three comic films: " Speed in the Gay Nineties," with Andy Clyde; "Disorder in the Court," with Three Stooges; "Hail Brother," with Billy Gilbert.

Columbia et al — *Budget Video*

Comedy Festival #2 193?
Comedy
00434   60 mins   B/W   B, V   P
Collection of Comedy films: "Bashful Romeo,"
with Gil Lamb; "Super Snooper," with Andy
Clyde; "Super Stupid," with Billy Gilbert.
RKO et al — *Budget Video*

Comedy Festival #3 193?
Comedy
00438   60 mins   B/W   B, V   P
Collection of comic films: "Big Flash," with
Harry Langdon; "Half A Hero;" "Pardon My
Papa," with Shirley Temple.
Educational et al — *Budget Video*

Comedy Festival #4 193?
Comedy
00442   60 mins   B/W   B, V   P
A collection of comic films: "His Weak
Moment," "Fainting Lover," "Shopping with the
Wife."
Mack Sennett et al — *Budget Video*

Comedy Special I 19??
Comedy
54167   60 mins   C   B, V   P
W.C. Fields, The Three Stooges
A compilation of RKO shorts including W.C.
Fields and the Three Stooges.
RKO — *Video Connection*

Comedy Special II 19??
Comedy
54168   60 mins   C   B, V   P
Bob Hope, Bing Crosby, Ritz Brothers
A grouping of outtakes from skits by Bob Hope,
Bing Crosby, and the Ritz Brothers.
Unknown — *Video Connection*

Comedy Tonight 1977
Comedy-Performance
59307   76 mins   C   B, V, CED   P
*Hosted by David Steinberg, Andy Kaufman,
Robin Williams, Gallagher, Ed Bluestone,
Richard Libertini, McIntyre Dixon*
Los Angeles' "Improv" club is the scene for this
night of stand-up comedy. Andy Kaufman
performs his infamous Tony Clifton routine.
Robin Williams reveals his X-rated side, and
Gallagher offers his "Sledge-O-Matic" routine.
Home Box Office — *Vestron Video*

Comes a Horseman 1978
Western
58954   119 mins   C   B, V   P
*James Caan, Jane Fonda, Jason Robards,
Richard Farnsworth, Jim Davis, Mark Harmon,
directed by Alan J. Pakula*

A cattle baron, attempting to gobble up all the
land in his territory, must contend with a woman
who has the courage to stand up to him.
MPAA:PG
United Artists — *CBS/Fox Video*

Comic Book Kids, The 1982
Musical/Fantasy
64950   90 mins   C   B, V   R, P
*Joseph Campanella, Mike Darnell, Robyn Finn,
Jim Engelhardt, Fay De Witt*
Two youngsters enjoy visiting their friend's
comic strip studio, since they have the power to
project themselves into the cartoon stories.
MPAA:G
Century Video — *Video Gems*

**Coming Attractions
#1—The Super Stars** 1975
Movie and TV trailers
42953   31 mins   C   B, V, FO   P
This program in partial color is a collection of
movie trailers from 12 all-time hits, starring
some of Hollywood's biggest stars. Titles
include "Presenting Lily Mars" with Judy
Garland, "The Singing Kid" with Al Jolson,
"Funny Lady" with Barbra Strisand, and others
dating back to 1930.
MGM et al — *Video Yesteryear*

Coming Home 1978
Drama
16051   127 mins   C   B, V, LV   P
*Jane Fonda, Jon Voight, Bruce Dern, directed
by Hal Ashby.*
Fonda falls in love with paraplegic Voight while
her husband is overseas. A look at the effect of
the Vietnam War on people.
Academy Awards '78: Best Actor (Voight), Best
Actress (Fonda).   MPAA:R
Jerome Hellman — *CBS/Fox Video; RCA
VideoDiscs*

**Coming Next Week:
Those Great Movie
Trailers** 1984
Movie and TV trailers
73547   120 mins   C   B, V   P
Here are two hours of the movie previews from
the 30's to the 80's covering all film genres.
Some trailers are in black and white.
Admit One — *Admit One Video*

**Coming of Age: The Story
of the Dallas Cowboys
1970-74** 1982
Football
63163   120 mins   C   B, V, FO   P
Dallas Cowboys
A compilation of individual Dallas Cowboys
team highlight films from the first half of the
1970's.

NFL Films — *NFL Films Video*

Coming Out Alive 197?
Drama
75623   73 mins   C   B, V   P
A woman tries to rescue her kidnapped son
from his estranged father who is involved in an
assassination plot.
Export CBC — *Trans World Entertainment*

Coming Soon 1983
Movie and TV trailers
69029   55 mins   C   B, V   P
Narrated by Jamie Lee Curtis
This program features over 50 excerpts from the
"previews of coming attractions" of the most
famous and infamous of the horror films.
Universal — *MCA Home Video*

Commandos 1972
War-Drama
59355   100 mins   C   B, V   R, P
Lee Van Cleef, Jack Kelly
A 48-hour odyssey of courage lays the
groundwork for Rommel's eventual defeat in
Africa.
MPAA:PG
Heritage Enterprises — *Video Gems*

Commitment to 1983
Excellence/NFL '82
Football
66223   45 mins   C   B, V, FO   P
Highlights of the L.A. Raiders' 1982-83 season
plus an overview of the whole NFL season.
NFL Films — *NFL Films Video*

Committee, The 1968
Satire/Comedy
66028   88 mins   C   B, V   P
*Howard Hesseman, Barbara Bosson, Peter
Bonerz, Gary Goodrow, Carl Gottlieb*
A comedy film of the seminal comedy troupe
"The Committee," specialists in short, punchy
satire.
Allen Myerson; Del Jack — *Pacific Arts Video*

Como Dos Gotas de Agua 197?
(Like Two Drops of
Water)
Musical
73586   30 mins   C   B, V   P
*Pili and Mili, Isabel Garces, Luis Davila, Manolo
Moran*
Two twin sisters have all kinds of problems as
they trade places with each other in this musical
comedy.
KNBC — *Aztec Cinevideo*

Competition, The 1980
Drama
58480   125 mins   C   B, V   P
*Richard Dreyfuss, Amy Irving, Lee Remick,
directed by Joel Oliansky*
Two virtuoso pianists meet at an international
competition and fall in love—something their
careers have taught them to avoid.
MPAA:PG
Columbia — *RCA/Columbia Pictures Home
Video*

Competition Corvettes 1983
Automobiles
76389   37 mins   C   B, V   P
Back in time with the Cunningham team at the
1960 LeMans: Vintage racing with both '62 and
'63 restored racers is seen in action footage.
Armour Productions — *Armour Productions*

Compleat Beatles, The 1982
Music
47738   120 mins   C   B, V, LV,   P
                                   CED
*The Beatles, George Martin, Brian Epstein, Billy
Preston, Milt Oken, Bruce Johnston, Roger
McGuinn, Mike McCartney, Mick Jagger*
Music interviews, film clips, animation and live
performances make up this "rockumentary" on
the Beatles. New interviews are featured, as
well as vintage film clips and studio footage. The
first U.S press conference, legendary Hamburg
footage, and an in-depth interview with George
Martin are highlights.
Delilah Films — *MGM/UA Home Video*

Complete Body Massage 1980
Massage
47326   60 mins   C   B, V, 3/4U   P
A complete massage based on traditional
Swedish techniques is explained and
demonstrated in detail.
Vision Productions — *Vision Productions*

Complete Tennis from 1981
the Pros
Tennis
58660   60 mins   C   B, V, 3/4U   P
*Arthur Ashe, Stan Smith, Roscoe Tanner, Brian
Gottfried, Jack Kramer   4   pgms*
A dozen tennis pros contribute their knowledge
and exhibit their skill in these four, 60-minute
lessons.
*1.Basic and Advanced Forehand, Backhand,
Smash and Ground Strokes 2.Basic and
Advanced Serve, Return of Serve, Lob, and
Volley 3.Basic and Advanced Singles and
Doubles Strategy 4.Practice Techniques,
Fitness, Conditioning and Equipment Choice*
Corp for Entertainment and Learning; Players
Enterprises — *Sports World Cinema*

Computability   1984
Electronic data processing
74075   60 mins   C   B, V   P
This program, hosted by Steve Allen and Jayne Meadows, is the complete guide to computer software. It was developed to help viewers understand how their needs might best be served by current computer software.
Karl Home Video — *Karl Video*

Con Artists, The   1980
Crime-Drama
69585   86 mins   C   B, V   P
Anthony Quinn, Adriano Celentano
A con man recently sprung from prison and his protege set up a sting operation in Italy.
Unknown — *VidAmerica*

Conan the Barbarian   1982
Adventure
47848   115 mins   C   B, V, LV,   P
                                                CED
Arnold Schwarzenegger, James Earl Jones, Max von Sydow, directed by John Milius
Conan sets out to avenge the murder of his parents and retrieve the sword bequeathed him by his father.
MPAA:R
Universal — *MCA Home Video*

Concert For Bangladesh, The   1972
Music-Performance
75926   90 mins   C   B, V   R, P
George Harrison, Bob Dylan, Ringo Starr, Billy Preston, Eric Clapton, Ravi Shankar, Kalus Voorman
This program presents the concert held in 1971 for the benefit of the needy.
Thorn — *THORN EMI Home Video*

Concrete Jungle, The   1982
Drama
64242   106 mins   C   B, V   P
Tracy Bregman, Jill St. John, Barbara Luna
After being set up by her boyfriend, a woman is sent to a correctional facility for drug smuggling.
MPAA:R
Columbia; Billy Fine — *RCA/Columbia Pictures Home Video*

Condemned to Live   1935
Mystery
66367   68 mins   B/W   B, V   P
Ralph Morgan, Maxine Doyle, Mischa Auer
Terror and murder enter a small, peaceful town when a mysterious stranger arrives.
Chesterfield — *Movie Buff Video*

Condorman   1981
Comedy
58623   90 mins   C   B, V   R, P
Michael Crawford, Oliver Reed, Barbara Carrera, James Hampton, Jean-Pierre Kalfon, directed by Charles Jarrott
Woody Wilkins, an inventive comic book writer, adopts the identity of his own character, Condorman, in order to help a beautiful Russian spy defect.
MPAA:PG
Walt Disney Productions — *Walt Disney Home Video*

Confessions of a Blue Movie Star   1982
Drama
69021   87 mins   C   B, V   P
The first documentary drama to take the viewer behind the scenes of porno film making.
Unknown — *Imperial Video Corp*

Confessions of a Young American Housewife   1978
Drama
59675   85 mins   C   B, V   P
Jennifer Wells, Rebecca Brooke, Chris Jordan
A recent divorcee moves in with two younger couples and experiences sexual liberation.
MPAA:R
Joe Sarno — *Media Home Entertainment*

Confessions of Tom Harris   197?
Personality/Religion
50756   90 mins   C   B, V   P
Don Murray, Linda Evans, David Brian
The true story of a Hollywood stunt man, a cold and cruel person whose life was changed by an encounter with Christ.
Gateway Films — *Vanguard Video*

Conformist, The   1971
Drama
60330   115 mins   C   B, V   R, P
Jean-Louis Trintignant, Stefania Sandrelli, Dominique Sanda, Pierre Clementi, directed by Bernardo Bertolucci
Repressing his homosexual drives, Marcello Clerici strives for an "acceptable" life as a member of the Italian Fascist Secret Service, and middle-class would-be wife-chaser, until an odd series of events make him a willing murderer.
MPAA:R
Paramount — *Paramount Home Video*

Connie Mack: Mr. Baseball   1954
Biographical/Baseball
44262   15 mins   B/W   B, V   P
An account of the baseball career of Connie Mack, first three-time World Series winner. Classic newsreel footage.
Fox Movietone News — *Two Star Films*

Conqueror, The   1956
Adventure
65120   111 mins   C   B, V   P
John Wayne, Susan Hayward, William Conrad,
Agnes Moorehead, directed by Dick Powell
John Wayne stars as Genghis Khan in this tale
of the warlord's early life and involvement with
the kidnapped daughter of a powerful enemy.
Universal; Howard Hughes; RKO — *MCA*
Home Video

Contempt   1964
Drama
65428   102 mins   C   B, V   P
Brigitte Bardot, Jack Palance, Fritz Lang
A struggling playwright accepts a writing offer
from a crude, manipulative American producer
to please his wife. When the producer is
attracted to the wife, she thinks her husband is
trying to push her into an affair.
Avco Embassy — *Embassy Home*
Entertainment

Continental Divide   1981
Comedy/Romance
59036   103 mins   C   B, V, LV,   P
                                  CED
John Belushi, Blair Brown, Allen Goorwitz,
directed by Michael Apted
A hard-nosed political columnist takes off for the
Colorado Rockies on an "easy
assignment"—interviewing a reclusive
arnithologist he eventually falls in love with.
MPAA:PG
Universal — *MCA Home Video*

Conversation, The   1974
Drama
58494   113 mins   C   B, V, LV   R, P
Gene Hackman, John Cazale, Frederick
Forrest, Cindy Williams, Robert Duvall, directed
by Francis Ford Coppola
A professional eavesdropper's conscience
interferes with his job when he fears that he
might be acting as an accomplice to murder.
MPAA:PG
Paramount; Francis Ford
Coppola — *Paramount Home Video*

Convoy   1978
Adventure
73018   106 mins   C   B, V   R, P
Kris Kristofferson, Ali McGraw, Ernest Borgnine
A trucker is out to form an indestructible truck
convoy to Mexico. The film was inspired by the
song "Convoy" by C. W. Mc Call.
MPAA:R
Robert M Sherman — *THORN EMI Home*
Video

Coogan's Bluff   1968
Drama
47413   100 mins   C   B, V   P
Clint Eastwood, Lee J. Cobb, Tisha Sterling,
Don Stroud, Betty Field
An Arizona deputy sheriff travels to New York in
order to extradite an escaped murderer.
MPAA:PG
Universal — *MCA Home Video*

Cooking a French Meal   1980
Cookery
44278   28 mins   C   V   P
Joan O'Connell, chef and teacher at "La
Cuisine Bonne Femme" gives tips on French
cooking in general. How to use utensils,
deboning, deglazing, and sauteeing are shown.
Included are recipes for cooking French dishes
such as Shrimp Bisque, Chicken Cordon Bleu,
Sautee of Pears.
American Home Video Library — *American*
Home Video Library

Cooking a Japanese Meal   1980
Cookery
54599   29 mins   C   V   P
Joanne Hush, Aiako
In this program Joanne Hush and Aiako prepare
a Japanese meal consisting of ichiban dashi, sui
mono, tempura, sukiyaki, rice, and dessert.
Included are recipes, demonstrations, and the
proper cooking equipment to be used.
American Home Video Library — *American*
Home Video Library

Cooking a Mexican Meal   1980
Cookery
54600   29 mins   C   V   P
Millie Wilson
Millie Wilson, an expert cook of Mexican dishes,
demonstrates how to prepare refried beans,
rice, guacamole, tortilla, and enchillada (with
sauce). Recipes and the proper cooking utensils
to be used are given.
American Home Video Library — *American*
Home Video Library

Cooking an Italian Meal   1980
Cookery
44279   29 mins   C   V   P
Linda McGuire, chef and instructor at the
Green's Farms Cooking school explains the
proper cooking equipment and its use plus
helpful tips on preparing a superb Italian meal.
This beginning guide includes Prosciutto and
melon, Veal Piccata, and Zuccotto, an unusual
dessert.
American Home Video Library — *American*
Home Video Library

Cooking Chinese Food   1980
Cookery
44290   29 mins   C   V   P
Filmed at Joanne Hush's cooking school, this
expert instructional program shows Chinese
cooking techniques, especially use of the

cleaver, wok, proper heat, stirring, and menus.
Viewers will also learn to prepare and serve rice,
barbecued pork ribs, chicken egg drop soup,
and skewered fruit.
American Home Video Library — *American
Home Video Library*

Cool Cats: 25 Years of 1983
Rock 'n' Roll Style
Music/Documentary
66457   90 mins   C   B, V   P
The effect of rock music on contemporary style
and mores is the subject of this "rockumentary"
which features performance clips and interviews
by thirty-four rock trendsetters, including Elvis,
The Beatles, Culture Club, David Bowie and
many others.
Delilah Films; Stephanie Bennett — *MGM/UA
Home Video*

Cool Hand Luke 1967
Drama
58224   126 mins   C   B, V, LV   R, P
*Paul Newman, George Kennedy, J. D. Cannon,
Strother Martin, Jo Van Fleet, directed by Stuart
Rosenberg*
A man sentenced to sweat out a term on a
prison farm refuses to compromise with
authority.
Warner Bros; Jalem Productions — *Warner
Home Video*

Cool World, The 1963
Documentary/Drama
63628   107 mins   B/W   B, V, FO   P
This docudrama, set on the streets of Harlem,
focuses on a 15-year-old black youth whose
one ambition in life is to own a gun and lead his
gang.
Frederick Wiseman — *Video Yesteryear*

Copacabana 1947
Musical/Comedy
64543   91 mins   B/W   B, V   P
*Groucho Marx, Carmen Miranda, Steve
Cochran, Gloria Jean, Andy Russell*
A quick-thinking theatrical agent books a
nightclub singer into two shows at the same
time, which leads to the expected
complications.
United Artists — *NTA Home Entertainment*

Cordell Hull: The Good 1954
Neighbor
Biographical/History-US
44237   15 mins   B/W   B, V   P
The story of the man known as the Father of the
United Nations, Cordell Hull. Hull was appointed
Secretary of State by Franklin Roosevelt and in
1943 wrote the United Nations Declaration. His
efforts were awarded by his winning of the
Nobel Peace Prize. Classic newsreel footage.

Fox Movietone News — *Two Star Films*

Corpse Vanishes, The 1942
Mystery
16158   64 mins   B/W   B, V   P
Bela Lugosi
Scientist experiments with various potions and
turns himself into an ape.
Prime TV — *VidAmerica*

Corrective Shoeing for 19??
Conformational Defects
Animals
69666   59 mins   C   B, V   P
This 33-minute program looks at various
conformational defects that can be corrected by
proper horseshoeing. This tape also contains a
second program, "Trimming and Shoeing the
Normal Horse Foot" (26 minutes).
Colorado State U — *Mercedes Maharis
Productions*

Corrupt 1984
Crime-Drama
72183   99 mins   C   B, V   R, P
Harvey Keitel
A policeman becomes involved in illegal
activities in order to catch a murderer.
MPAA:PG
Elda Ferri — *THORN EMI Home Video*

Corsican Brothers, The 1942
Adventure
55352   111 mins   B/W   B, V, 3/4U   P
*Douglas Fairbanks Jr, Akim Tamiroff, Ruth
Warrick, J. Carrol Naish*
Alexandre Dumas' classic about siamese twins
who, although separated, remain spiritually tied
through various adventures.
Edward Small; United Artists — *Nostalgia
Merchant*

Cosmos: The 1981
Championship Years
1977-1980
Soccer
51086   115 mins   C   B, V   R, P
New York Cosmos
Highlights of the past four seasons of New York
Cosmos soccer, featuring Pele, Giorgio
Chinaglia, Franz Beckenbauer, and
championship moments, are included in this
program.
Cosmos Soccer Club — *Warner Home Video*

Cosmos—War of the 1980
Planets
Science fiction
66255   90 mins   C   B, V   P
Katia Christine, West Buchanan
The ultimate battle for survival is fought in outer
space.

MPAA:PG
Picturmedia — *Paragon Video Productions*

Count of Monte Cristo, The   1912
Film-History
48697   60 mins   B/W   B, V, 3/4U   P
James O'Neill
One of the first full length features made starring
popular stage stars of the day. The first truly
American feature. Silent.
Adolph Zukor, Famous Players
Company — *Penguin Video; Classic Video
Cinema Collector's Club*

Count of Monte Cristo, The   1934
Adventure
55349   114 mins   B/W   B, V, 3/4U   P
*Robert Donat, Elissa Landi, Louis Calhern,
directed by Rowland V. Lee*
Alexandre Dumas' classic about Edmon Dantes
who, after years in prison, escapes and avenges
himself on those who framed him.
Edward Small; Reliance; United
Artists — *Nostalgia Merchant; Blackhawk
Films*

Count of Monte Cristo, The   1975
Drama/Adventure
56892   120 mins   C   B, V   P
*Richard Chamberlain, Kate Nelligan, Donald
Pleasence, Alessio Orano, Tony Curtis, Louis
Jourdan, Trevor Howard*
The Alexandre Dumas classic with the
swashbuckling Edmond Dantes and the
villainous Mondego.
Norman Rosemont Productions,
ITC — *CBS/Fox Video; RCA VideoDiscs*

Count, The/The Adventurer   1917
Comedy
58657   52 mins   B/W   B, V, FO   P
*Charlie Chaplin, Eric Campbell, Edna Purviance,
Frank Coleman, directed by Charlie Chaplin*
Two Chaplin two-reelers: "The Count (The
Phoney Nobleman)" (1916), in which Charlie
impersonates a count at the home of Miss
Moneybags, and "The Adventurer" (1917),
Chaplin's final film for Mutual, in which he plays
an escaped convict with the law relentlessly on
his trail. Silent with musical score.
Mutual — *Video Yesteryear*

Countdown   1968
Science fiction
65356   102 mins   C   B, V   P
*James Caan, Robert Duvall, Michael Murphy,
Ted Knight, Joanna Moore, Barbara Baxley,
Charles Aidman*
Robert Altman directed this thrilling adventure
about the first moon mission and its toll on the
astronauts and their families.
Warner Brothers — *Warner Home Video*

Countdown to World War II   194?
World War II
10154   59 mins   B/W   B, V   P, T
Newsreels cover rise of Hitler and Mussolini.
Unknown — *Blackhawk Films*

Country Gentlemen   1936
Comedy
46347   54 mins   B/W   B, V, FO   P
*Ole Olsen, Chic Johnson, Joyce Compton, Lila
Lee*
Olsen and Johnson play fast-talking conmen
who sell shares in a worthless oil field to a
bunch of World War I veterans.
Republic — *Video Yesteryear; Discount Video
Tapes*

Country Girl, The   1982
Drama
63344   137 mins   C   B, V   R, P
Dick Van Dyke, Faye Dunaway, Ken Howard
An aging, alcoholic actor, desperate for a
comeback, blames his fiercely loving wife for his
downfall.
Group W Productions — *THORN EMI Home
Video*

Country Girl, The   1954
Drama
64506   104 mins   B/W   B, V   R, P
*Bing Crosby, Grace Kelly, William Holden, Gene
Reynolds, directed by George Seaton*
The wife of an alcoholic actor is unfairly blamed
for his sodden condition. Based on the play by
Clifford Odets
Academy Awards '54: Best Actress (Kelly); Best
Screenplay (George Seaton).
Paramount — *Paramount Home Video; RCA
VideoDiscs*

Country Style USA and Community Jamboree   1959
Variety
38996   30 mins   B/W   B, V, FO   P
*Roy Acuff, the Smoky Mountain Boys, Ferlin
Husky, Carl Smith, Patsy Cline* 2 pgms
Two 15-minute syndicated programs produced
in Nashville featuring a number of popular
country performers from the Grand Ole Opry.
Army Recruiting, National Guard
Recruiting — *Video Yesteryear*

Country-Western All-Stars   1956
Music-Performance/Variety
47479   52 mins   B/W   B, V, FO   P

Carl Smith, Jim Reeves, Faron Young, Hank Snow, Minnie Pearl, Tex Ritter, The Sons of the Pioneers
A live country-western variety show broadcast from the Ryman Auditorium in Nashville.
WSM Nashville — *Video Yesteryear*

Countryman   1983
Drama/Adventure
65371   103 mins   C   B, V   P
Countryman, Hiram Keller, Kristina St. Clair
Countryman is no ordinary man. He is a man of the sea, a man of knowledgde, in effortless harmony with everything that lives and breathes.
MPAA:R
Chris Blackwell — *Media Home Entertainment*

Courageous Dr. Christian, The   1940
Drama
47458   66 mins   B/W   B, V, FO   P
Jean Hersholt, Dorothy Lovett, Tom Neal
Dr. Christian is faced with an epidemic of meningitis among the inhabitants of a shanty town.
RKO — *Video Yesteryear; Discount Video Tapes*

Court Jester, The   1956
Comedy
65399   101 mins   C   B, V   R, P
D. Norman Panama, Melvin Frank, Danny Kaye, Glynis Johns, Basil Rathbone, Angela Lansbury
A 12th century court jester in England becomes involved with a desperate band of outlaws who are attempting to overthrow the king.
Paramount — *Paramount Home Video*

Cousin, Cousine   1976
Drama/Comedy
52745   95 mins   C   B, V, CED   P
Marie-Christine Barrault, Marie-France Pisier, Victor Lanoux, Guy Marchand, directed by Jean-Charles Tacchella
Distant cousins who meet at a round of family parties, funerals, and weddings fall in love with each other, but their relationship soon becomes more than platonic.
France; Libra Films — *CBS/Fox Video*

Cousin Smallmouth Bass   197?
Fishing
33745   30 mins   C   B, V, 3/4U, Q   P
A father an son canoeing downriver on a float trip, and a young couple on a fishing honeymoon set the scene for this fine bass fishing program.
TV Sports Scene — *TV Sports Scene*

Cousteau—Diving for Roman Plunder   1978
Oceanography
47392   59 mins   C   B, V   R, P
Jacques Cousteau and the crew of the Calypso embark upon an underwater search for ancient Roman artifacts.
Cousteau Society — *Warner Home Video*

Cousteau—The Nile   1979
Travel/Documentary
47388   116 mins   C   B, V   R, P
Jacques Cousteau
A double-length episode of the "Cousteau Odyssey" series, taking the viewer on a spectacular journey down the Earth's longest river to reveal the fabled past and challenging present of the Nile River.
Cousteau Society — *Warner Home Video*

Covergirl   1983
Drama
65746   98 mins   C   B, V   R, P
Jeff Conaway, Irena Ferris, Cathie Shirriff
Covergirl tells the story of one girl's meteoric rise to become a superstar model. The heartaches and struggles involved in the climb to success are also depicted.
MPAA:R
Claude Heroux — *THORN EMI Home Video*

Cow Town   1950
Western
66307   70 mins   B/W   B, V   P, T
Gene Autry, Gail Davis, Jock Mahoney
A range war results when ranchers begin fencing in their land to prevent cattle rustling.
Columbia — *Blackhawk Films*

Coward, The   1915
Drama
64316   53 mins   B/W   B, V   P
Charles Ray
A Civil War soldier has to live with his cowardice under fire. Silent with musical score.
Triangle Film Corp — *Classic Video Cinema Collector's Club*

Cowboy Millionaire   1935
Western
58511   56 mins   B/W   B, V, 3/4U   P
George O'Brien, Evalyn Bostock, Edgar Kennedy
George and his partner are hired to give tourists a ride from the station to the hotel, and stage a mock hold-up along the way.
Twentieth Century Fox — *Penguin Video*

Cowboy Previews #1   194?
Movie and TV trailers/Western
64416   60 mins   B/W   B, V, 3/4U   P

A collection of theatrical trailers from over thirty-five "B" westerns. Titles include "Riders in the Sky," "King of the Bullwhip," "Utah Wagon Train," "Trail of Robin Hood," "Sioux City Sue" and many others.
Republic et al — *Nostalgia Merchant*

Cowboys, The 1972
Western
74209   128 mins   C   B, V   R, P
John Wayne, Roscoe Lee Browne, Bruce Dern
Wayne stars as a cattle rancher who is forced to hire eleven schoolboys to help him drive his cattle 400 miles to market.
MPAA:PG
Mark Rydell — *Warner Home Video*

Cowboys from Texas 1939
Western
64402   54 mins   B/W   B, V, 3/4U   P
Bob Livingston, Raymond Hatton, Duncan Renaldo, Carole Landis
The Three Mesquiteers bring about a peaceful settlement to a fight between cattlemen and homesteaders.
Republic — *Nostalgia Merchant*

Coyote Trail 1935
Western
14389   60 mins   B/W   B, V, 3/4U   P
Tom Tyler
Western adventure starring the American Cowboy star, Tom Tyler.
Commodore — *Video Connection; Penguin Video*

CPR for Infants and Children 1982
First aid
60511   28 mins   C   B, V, 3/4U, Q   P
How to administer Cardiopulmonary Resuscitation (CPR) to children and infants who may be drowning or choking is the subject of this program.
Executive Producers — *TV Sports Scene*

Crack Shadow Boxers 197?
Martial arts/Adventure
47699   91 mins   C   B, V   P
Ku Feng, Chou Li Lung
Through a series of misadventures, Wu Lung and Chu San battle to protect the inhabitants of a small village from the onslaught of relentless bandits.
United Enterprises Ltd — *Master Arts Video*

Crackers 1984
Comedy
74090   92 mins   C   B, V, LV, CED   P
Donald Sutherland, Jock Warden, Sean Penn

This is the off beat story of two bumbling thieves who round up a gang of equally inept neighbors and go on the wildest crime spree you have ever seen.
MPAA:PG
Universal — *MCA Home Video*

Cracking Up 1983
Comedy
66323   90 mins   C   B, V   P
Jerry Lewis, Herb Edelman, Foster Brooks, Milton Berle, Sammy Davis Jr., directed by Jerry Lewis
Jerry Lewis stars as an accident-prone misfit whose mishaps on the road to recovery create chaos for everyone he meets.
MPAA:PG
Warner Bros — *Warner Home Video*

Cranes Are Flying, The 1957
Drama
53706   91 mins   B/W   B, V, 3/4U   P
Directed by Mikhail Kaltozov
When her lover goes to war, a girl refuses to believe later reports of his death. English subtitled.
RU
USSR; Mosfilm — *International Historic Films*

Craps 1982
Gambling
62741   50 mins   C   B, V   P
Strategies and ways to win craps are covered in this instructional cassette.
Casino Gaming Instruction — *Marketvisions*

Crash of Flight 401, The 1982
Drama
75459   101 mins   C   B, V   P
William Shatner, Adrienne Barbeau, Lloyd Bridges
This jetliner story is based on an incident that occurred during a landing at Miami's airport.
King Features — *U.S.A. Home Video*

Crater Lake Monster, The 1977
Horror
59655   85 mins   C   B, V   P
Richard Cardella, Glenn Roberts, Mark Siegel, Bob Hyman
A meteor crashes into a mountain lake causing it to warm up. The dormant egg of a prehistoric creature lying at the bottom is incubated, and the newborn creature heads for land.
MPAA:PG
William R Stromberg — *VCI Home Video*

Crawling Eye, The 1958
Science fiction/Horror
44349   87 mins   B/W   B, V, 3/4U   P
Forrest Tucker, Laurence Payne, Janet Munro, Jennifer Jayne

(For Explanation of codes, see USE GUIDE and KEY)

Hidden in a radioactive fog, the crawling eye decapitates its victims and returns these humans to Earth to threaten mankind. Includes previews of coming attractions from classic science fiction films.
VCC Films — *Nostalgia Merchant*

Crawling Hand, The   1963
Horror/Science fiction
59348   89 mins   B/W   B, V   R, P
Alan Hale, Rod Lauren
An astronaut's hand takes off without him, on an unearthly spree of stranglings.
Medallion — *Video Gems*

Crazy Mama   1975
Drama
65074   81 mins   C   B, V, CED   P
Cloris Leachman, Stuart Whitman, Ann Southern, Jim Backus
A band of female outlaws turn to crime on the way to Arkansas to repossess the family farm that was sold during the Depression.
MPAA:PG
New World Pictures — *Embassy Home Entertainment*

Creative Camera, The   1982
Photography
63424   60 mins   C   LV   P
This interactive videodisc is a primer of single lens reflex photography offering a practical and detailed introduction to SLR photographic techniques.
Valley Isle Productions; Jac Holzman — *Pioneer Video Imports*

Creature from the   1960
Haunted Sea
Satire
56914   76 mins   B/W   B, V, FO   P
Antony Carbone, Betsy Jones-Moreland
A monster movie satire set in Cuba shortly after the revolution and centering around an elaborate plan to loot the Treasury and put the blame on a strange sea monster.
Roger Corman — *Video Yesteryear*

Creeping Flesh, The   1972
Horror
62808   89 mins   C   B, V   P
Peter Cushing, Christopher Lee, Lorna Heilbron
A scientist decides he can cure evil by injecting his patients with a serum derived from the blood of evil humans. The plan backfires.
MPAA:PG
Columbia — *RCA/Columbia Pictures Home Video*

Creeping Terror   1964
Horror
59653   81 mins   B/W   B, V   P

Vic Savage, Shannon O'Neal, William Thourlby
A spaceship discovered in the Rocky Mountains contains a creeping monster that devours its human victims while computing their metabolism and sending the information to the mother craft somewhere in space.
A J Nelson — *VCI Home Video*

Creepshow   1982
Horror
60561   120 mins   C   B, V, CED   R, P
Hal Holbrook, Adrienne Barbeau, Viveca Lindfors, E.G. Marshall, Stephen King, Leslie Nielsen, Carrie Nye, Fritz Weaver, Ted Danson, directed by George A. Romero
Stephen King's tribute to E.C. Comics, those pulp horror comic books that delight in the grizzly, the grotesque and morbid humor.
MPAA:R
Warner Bros — *Warner Home Video*

Cricket on the Hearth,   1923
The
Drama/Christmas
66353   68 mins   B/W   B, V   P
Paul Gerson, Virginia Brown Faire, Paul Moore, Joan Standing
An adaptation of Charles Dickens' short story about the life of a mail carrier and his bride, who find the symbol of good luck, a cricket on the hearth, when they enter their new home. Silent with organ score.
Paul Gerson Pictures; Selznick Releasing — *Blackhawk Films*

Cries and Whispers   1972
Drama
54802   94 mins   C   B, V   R, P
Harriet Andersson, Ingrid Thulin, Liv Ullman, Kary Sylway, Erland Josephson, directed by Ingmar Bergman
A Bergman production that dramatizes states of mind. It is the story of the lives of three sisters, all in their thirties. The middle sister is dying of cancer and the other two, along with a peasant woman, take care of her.
MPAA:R
New World Pictures — *Warner Home Video*

Crimes of Dr. Mabuse   1933
Suspense
64352   120 mins   B/W   B, V   P
Rudolf Klein-Rogge, Otto Wernicke, Gustav Diesl, directed by Fritz Lang
Dr. Mabuse, the criminal genius, dies in an asylum and his assistant takes over his identity. Also known as "The Testament of Dr. Mabuse."
Nerofilm — *Classic Video Cinema Collector's Club*

Crimson Ghost, The   1946
Adventure/Serials
07338   152 mins   B/W   B, V, 3/4U   P

Charles Quigley, Linda Stirling, I. Stanford Jolley
The Crimson Ghost plots to enslave the world by stealing an atomic weapon. Serial in twelve episodes.
Republic — *Video Connection*

Cristo Del Oceano (Christ 197?
from the Ocean)
Comedy-Drama
73589   30 mins   C   B, V   P
Nino Del Arco, Perla Cristal, Jose Suarez, Pilar Velazquez
An orphan is cared for by a fisherman in a Mexican sea village in this comedy-drama.
KNBC — *Aztec Cinevideo*

Crocheting with Dee 1981
Handicraft
53276   45 mins   C   B, V   P
A beginner's course, emphasizing the basics of crochet (chain stitch, single, double, half-double, and triple crochet) while making a pillow or afghan.
The Darn Yarn Shoppe — *Daya Inc*

Crocodile 1981
Horror
65510   95 mins   C   B, V   R, P
Nat Puvanai, Tany Tim, directed by Herman Cohen
Nature strikes with unbelievable fury, creating the largest and most savage crocodile on earth. No experts can kill this monster animal that is too huge and powerful to trap. Soon the giant crocodile attacks a beach town, killing and devouring dozens of people.
MPAA:R
Dick Randall; Robert Chan — *THORN EMI Home Video*

Crosby, Stills & Nash: 1983
Daylight Again
Music-Performance
64792   108 mins   C   B, V, LV, P
                                         CED
Directed by Tom Trbovich
This video concert taped in November 1982 at the New Universal Amphitheater in Los Angeles represents the group's first tour since 1977. Includes such songs as "Just a Song Before I Go," "Chicago," "Suite: Judy Blue Eyes," and from the recent "Daylight Again" album, "Wasted on the Way." In stereo.
Universal Pay TV; Neal Marshall — *MCA Home Video*

Cross Country 1983
Crime-Drama/Suspense
65421   95 mins   C   B, V   P
Richard Beymer, Nina Axelrod, Michael Ironside
Action revolves around the brutal murder of a call girl with initial suspicion falling on a TV advertising director involved with the woman.

The story twists and turns from the suspect to the investigating detective.
MPAA:R
Pieter Kroonenburg — *Embassy Home Entertainment*

Cross Creek 1983
Adventure/Biographical
69678   120 mins   C   B, V, CED   R, P
Mary Steenburgen, Rip Torn
This film is based on the life of Marjorie Kinnan Rawlings who, after 10 years as a frustrated reporter/writer, moved to the remote and untamed Everglades, where she received the inspiration to write numerous bestsellers.
Universal — *THORN EMI Home Video*

Cross of Iron 1976
War-Drama
47815   120 mins   C   B, V, 3/4U   P
James Coburn, Maximilian Schell, James Mason, David Warner, Senta Berger, directed by Sam Peckinpah
During World War II, two antagonistic German officers clash over personal ideals as well as strategy in combatting the relentless Russian attack.
MPAA:R
ITC Entertainment — *Nostalgia Merchant*

Crossbar 1980
Handicapped
52428   30 mins   C   B, V   P
John Ireland, Brent Carver, Kate Reid
Aaron Kornylo is determined to reach Olympic qualifications in the high jump despite having only one leg. Inspired by a true story, this program dramatically shows how far determination and work can take a person.
AM Available
Canadian Broadcasting — *Trans World Entertainment*

Crossfire 1979
Religion/Adventure
46830   56 mins   C   B, V, 3/4U,   P
                                         Q
A confrontation between a terrorist and Shelley, a Christian, leads them both to struggle with opposing viewpoints. Meanwhile, a bomb is set to go off on the other side of the city.
Quadrus Films — *TV Sports Scene*

Crossfire 1947
Drama
64368   86 mins   B/W   B, V, 3/4U   P
Robert Young, Robert Mitchum, Robert Ryan, Gloria Grahame, Paul Kelly, directed by Edward Dmytryk
A Jewish hotel guest is murdered and three soldiers are suspected of the crime, one of

whom is violently anti-Semitic. The first Hollywood film that explored racial bigotry.
RKO — *Nostalgia Merchant*

Crowded Paradise　　　　　　1956
Drama
66368　94 mins　B/W　　B, V　　　　P
Hume Cronyn, Nancy Kelly, Mario Alcalde, Frank Silvera
A Puerto Rican auto mechanic encounters discrimination when he looks for a job in New York City.
Tudor Pictures — *Movie Buff Video*

Crucible of Horror　　　　　　1969
Suspense
66523　91 mins　C　　B, V　　　　P
Michael Gough, Yvonne Mitchell, Sharon Gurney
Two women plot the murder of an unsuspecting husband, but he turns the tables on them.
Wrightwood — *Paragon Video Productions*

Crucible of Terror　　　　　　1972
Horror
58548　95 mins　C　　B, V　　　R, P
Mike Raven, Mary Maude, James Bolam
A mad sculptor covers beautiful models with hot wax, then imprisons them in a mold of bronze.
Scotia Barber — *Video Gems*

Cruel Sea, The　　　　　　　1953
War-Drama
58459　121 mins　B/W　　B, V　　　R, P
Jack Hawkins, Stanley Baker, Denholm Elliott
The story of a Royal Navy corvette on convoy duty in the Atlantic.
Ealing Studios — *THORN EMI Home Video*

Cruise Missile　　　　　　　1978
Suspense
60415　100 mins　C　　B, V　　　　P
Peter Graves, Curt Jurgens, Michael Dante
A unique task force is on a mission to keep the world from nuclear holocaust.
Noble Production — *Monterey Home Video*

Cruising　　　　　　　　　1980
Drama
56753　102 mins　C　　B, V, CED　　P
Al Pacino, Paul Sorvino, Karen Allen, directed by William Friedkin
A bizarre murder-mystery set in the homosexual nightlife scene of New York's West Village.
Music by Jack Nitzsche.
MPAA:R
Jerry Weintraub, Lorimar — *CBS/Fox Video*

Cry of the Innocent　　　　　1980
Adventure
74108　93 mins　C　　B, V　　　　P

Rod Taylor, Joanna Pettet, Nigel Davenport
An action-packed thriller about a Vietnam veteran who is out to find a group of Irish terrorists that killed his family.
Michael O'Herlihy — *VCL Home Video*

Crystal Gayle in Concert　　　1984
Music-Performance
66495　60 mins　C　　B, V　　　　P
Crystal Gayle
A live concert by country singer Crystal Gayle, taped at Hamilton Place, Canada.
Prism — *Prism*

Cuando Tu No Estas　　　　　197?
Drama
49743　90 mins　C　　B, V　　　　P
Maria Jose Alfonso, Ricardo Lucia, Margaret Peters, Jose Martin
A young man leaves his provincial town, looking for success in the city. He becomes familiar with the works of a female journalist, and she does likewise with his. Finally they meet, and love runs its course. In Spanish.
SP
Independent — *Media Home Entertainment*

Cuatro Budas de Kriminal, Los　　　　　　1972
Suspense
47721　88 mins　C　　B, V　　　　P
Glenn Saxson, Helga Line
In "The Four Buddhas of Kriminal," there is doublecross and murder as Kriminal attempts to get the pieces of a map which are hidden in four statuettes. In Spanish.
SP
Independent — *Telecine Spanish Video*

Cucaracha, La　　　　　　　1934
Musical-Drama
12832　21 mins　C　　B, V, FO　　P
Steffi Duna
A lavish production filled with Mexican songs and dances. The first three-strip, live-action Technicolor film ever made.
Academy Awards '34: Best Comedy Short Subject.
RKO — *Video Yesteryear*

Cuchillo ("Knife")　　　　　1984
Adventure
72960　90 mins　C　　B, V　　　　P
Cuchillo is the weapon of the Apaches which they use to fight the white man in this violent tale of revenge and murder.
SP
Foreign — *Unicorn Video*

Cuckoo Clock That Wouldn't Cuckoo, The   1958
Fairy tales/Cartoons
00666   12 mins   C   B, V   P, T
Animated
An animated fable of a clockmaker who tries to get the cuckoo in the royal cuckoo clock to break his silence.
Coronet Films — *Blackhawk Films*

Cuisine Pratique, La   1981
Cookery
53782   60 mins   C   B, V, 3/4U,   R, P
FO
Twenty delicious recipes that take about 5 minutes to prepare are demonstrated, including salads, Norwegian-style eggs, ham steak Viennese, Irish coffee, and others.
Cine Video Films — *Star Video Productions*

Cujo   1983
Horror
66324   94 mins   C   B, V, LV,   P
CED
Dee Wallace, Daniel Hugh-Kelly, Danny Pintauro, Ed Lauter, Christopher Stone
A rabid dog goes berserk and attacks a mother and her child who are trapped inside a broken-down car. Based on the Stephen King bestseller.
MPAA:R
Warner Bros — *Warner Home Video*

Culture Club: Kiss Across the Ocean   1984
Music-Performance
72188   60 mins   C   B, V   P
America's favorite drag queen, Boy George, leads his pop group Culture Club through a string of hits performed live at the Hammersmith Odeon in London.
Tessa Walls and Richard Branston — *CBS/Fox Video*

Cumbres and Toltec Revisited   1981
Trains
59179   115 mins   C   B, V   P
The Cumbres and Toltec Scenic Railroad, which runs between Chama, New Mexico, and Antonito, Colorado, is seen in action.
JMJ Prods — *JMJ Productions*

Curious George   1982
Cartoons
75892   30 mins   C   B, V   P
3   pgms
This program is a three-volume animated series of adventures of the monkey Curious George.
LWI Productions; Tablot Television — *Sony Corporation of America*

Curley   1947
Comedy
29758   53 mins   C   B, V   P
Larry Olsen, Frances Rafferty, Eilene Janssen, Walter Abel
A part of the Hal Roach Comedy Carnival in which youngsters play pranks on their schoolteacher.
United Artists — *Budget Video*

Curley and His Gang in the Haunted Mansion   1947
Comedy/Mystery
66111   54 mins   C   B, V   P
Larry Olsen
An eccentric scientist gets involved in a haunted mansion mystery.
Hal Roach — *Unicorn Video*

Currier & Ives Christmas, A   1983
Christmas
66309   90 mins   C   B, V   P
A video music Christmas album that sets the classic American art of Currier & Ives and other early lithographers to a continuous background of favorite Christmas music.
NTA — *NTA Home Entertainment*

Curse of the Cat People   1944
Fantasy
44802   70 mins   B/W   B, V, 3/4U   P
Simone Simon, Kent Smith, Jane Randolph, directed by Robert Wise
A young sensitive girl is guided by the vision of her dead mother.
RKO — *Nostalgia Merchant*

Curse of the Crying Woman, The   1961
Horror
51098   74 mins   B/W   B, V   P
Rosita Arenas, Abel Salazar, Rita Macedo, Carlos Lopez Moctezuma
An unknowing descendant of a witch is lured to her aunt's home to perform the act that will revive the monstrous crying woman and renew a reign of evil.
Mexican — *Budget Video*

Curse of the Mummy, The/The Robot vs. the Aztec Mummy   195?
Horror
51953   130 mins   B/W   B, V   P
Ramon Gay, Rosita Arenas, Crox Alvarado, Luis Aceves Cantaneda, directed by Rafael Portillo
A vengeful mummy of an Aztec warrior stalks those who attempt to steal a fabulous treasure. A mad, criminal scientist wants the treasure and uses gangsters and a human robot to get what he wants.

Azteca — *Budget Video*

NFL Films — *NFL Films Video*

Curse of the Pink Panther, The   1983
Comedy
72465   110 mins   C   B, V   P
Ted Wass, David Niven, Robert Wagner,
Herbert Lom, Capucine, Harvey Korman,
directed by Blake Edwards
Ted Wass stars as Clifton Sleigh, an inept New
York City detective, assigned to find the missing
Inspector Clouseau. The plot is complicated by
an assortment of gangsters and aristocrats who
cross paths with the detective.
MPAA:PG
Tital Productions & United Artists
Corporation — *MGM/UA Home Video*

Curtains   1983
Horror
65351   90 mins   C   B, V   P
John Vernon, Samantha Eggar
A director has a clash of wills with a film star that
spells "Curtains" for a group of aspiring
actresses.
MPAA:R
Peter and Richard Simpson — *Vestron Video*

Custer's Last Fight   1912
Film-History
51229   50 mins   B/W   B, V, 3/4U   P
Directed by Francis Ford
A re-enactment of the American West period
when the Sioux and Cheyenne Indian tribes
bitterly opposed the white man. Silent.
Thomas H Ince — *Penguin Video*

Custer's Last Stand   1936
Western
58543   70 mins   B/W   B, V, 3/4U   P
Rex Lease, Nancy Caseell, Ruth Mix
A feature-length version of the Mascot serial
recounting the last days of the famous General.
Mascot — *Penguin Video; Video Connection*

Custodio de Senoras   1979
Suspense
47857   100 mins   C   B, V   P
Augusto Larreta, Carlos Rotundo
Monica is threatened by death by a grudging
boyfriend. George, the detective, becomes
Monica's protector. In Spanish.
SP
Nicolas Carreras; Luis Repetto — *Media Home
Entertainment*

Cut Above, A   1980
Football
45130   24 mins   C   B, V, FO   R, P
Pittsburgh Steelers
Highlights of the 1979 Pittsburgh Steelers World
Championship season

Cut Above/NFL '83, A   1984
Football
72942   46 mins   C   B, V, FO   P
Washington Redskins
Highlights from the Washington Redskins' 1983
season and "NFL 83."
NFL Films — *NFL Films Video*

Cutter's Way   1981
Mystery/Drama
63109   105 mins   C   B, V, CED   P
Jeff Bridges, John Heard, Lisa Eichhorn,
directed by Ivan Passer
Two friends, one an embittered Vietnam
veteran, become involved in a puzzling murder.
Originally titled "Cutter and Bone."
MPAA:R
United Artists — *MGM/UA Home Video*

Cyrano de Bergerac   1950
Drama
39008   112 mins   B/W   B, V   P
Jose Ferrer, Mala Powers, William Prince, Elena
Verdugo, Morris Carnovsky, directed by Michael
Gordon
The classic film version of the story of Cyrano,
the tragic wit renowned for his nose, but longing
of the love of a beautiful lady, Roxanne. Based
on Edmond Rostand's play of 17th century
Paris.
Academy Awards '50: Best Actor (Ferrer)
United Artists, Stanley Kramer — *NTA Home*
Entertainment; Electric Video; Video Yesteryear;
Sheik Video; Cable Films; Video Connection;
Budget Video; Select-a-Tape; Western Film &
Video Inc; Discount Video Tapes; Classic Video
Cinema Collector's Club

D

Daddy Long Legs   1982
Fantasy
72231   60 mins   C   B, V   P
Animated
Jean Webster's story about an orphaned girl
who is sent to school by an anonymous
benefactor is animated for the first time.
Bunker Jenkins — *Children's Video Library*

Daddy's Deadly Darling   1983
Horror
72199   90 mins   C   B, V   P
Katherine Ross
A young woman and an evil old man conspire to
commit a series of senseless murders.
Unknown — *Paragon Video Productions*

Daffy Duck's Movie: Fantastic Island   1983
Comedy/Cartoons
65323   78 mins   C   B, V, LV, CED   P
Animated
A compilation of classic Warner Brothers cartoons, starring Daffy Duck, Speedy Gonzales, Bugs Bunny, Porky Pig, Sylvester, Tweety, Pepe Le Pew, Pirate Sam, Granny, Foghorn Leghorn and the Tasmanian Devil.
MPAA:G
Warner Brothers — *Warner Home Video*

Dagora, the Space Monster   1965
Science fiction/Horror
69570   80 mins   C   B, V, FO   P
Yosuke Natsuki, Yoko Fujiyama
A giant, slimy, pulsating mass from space lands on Earth and begins eating everything in sight. Scientists join together in a massive effort to destroy the creature.
Toho — *Video Yesteryear*

Dain Curse, The   1978
Mystery/Suspense
64972   118 mins   C   B, V   P
James Coburn, Jason Miller, Jean Simmons, Beatrice Straight
In 1928, private eye Hamilton Nash must recover stolen diamonds, solve a millionaire's suicide, avoid being murdered, and end an insane family curse. Based on the novel by Dashiell Hammett.
Martin Poll Productions — *Embassy Home Entertainment*

Dakota   1945
Western
00284   82 mins   B/W   B, V   P
John Wayne, Vera Ralston, Walter Brennan
Brawling saga with Wayne battling land grabbers in Dakota.
Republic — *NTA Home Entertainment*

Dakota Incident   1956
Western
74484   88 mins   C   B, V   P
Dale Robertson, Ward Bond
This is the story of a group of people brought together by a stagecoach ride across the dangerous Cheyenne territory.
Republic — *NTA Home Entertainment*

Dam Busters, The   1955
War-Drama
63353   119 mins   B/W   B, V   R, P
Michael Redgrave, Richard Todd
In 1942 London, a scientist develops a plan to destroy the great Moehne and Eder dams in Germany.

ABPC; Richard Clark — *THORN EMI Home Video*

Damaged Lives   1933
Drama/Exploitation
08900   60 mins   B/W   B, V, 3/4U   P
Diane Sinclair, Lyman Williams, Jason Robards, Marceline Day
Portrays how venereal disease destroys peoples lives.
Weldon — *Penguin Video*

Damien—Omen II   1978
Horror
45106   110 mins   C   B, V, CED   P
William Holden, Lee Grant, Lew Ayres, Robert Foxworth, Sylvia Sidney, directed by Don Taylor
This sequel to "The Omen" is about a young boy, possessed with mysterious demonic powers, who kills those people he comes in contact with.
MPAA:R   EL, SP
20th Century Fox, Harvey Bernard — *CBS/Fox Video*

Damn Yankees   1958
Musical
74202   110 mins   C   B, V   R, P
Gwen Verdon, Ray Walston, Tab Hunter
This musical feature is adapted from the Broadway hit about a baseball fan who makes a pact with the devil.
George Abbott; Stanley Donen — *Warner Home Video*

Damned, The   1969
Drama
58225   150 mins   C   B, V   R, P
Dirk Bogarde, Ingrid Thulin, Helmut Griem, Charlotte Rampling, directed by Luchino Visconti
Visconti's study of a family's disintegration in greed, lust, and the madness of pre-war Germany. English language version.
MPAA:R
Warner Bros — *Warner Home Video*

Damsel in Distress, A   1937
Musical
63992   101 mins   B/W   B, V   P, T
Fred Astaire, Joan Fontaine, George Burns, Gracie Allen, Ray Noble, directed by George Stevens
Fred falls for an upper-class British girl, whose family wants her to have nothing to do with him. George and Ira Gershwin's memorable songs include "A Foggy Day," "Nice Work If You Can Get It," "Stiff Upper Lip" and "Put Me to the Test."
RKO — *Blackhawk Films; Nostalgia Merchant*

(For Explanation of codes, see USE GUIDE and KEY)

Dance and Body Movement for Children — 1980
Dance
47323   55 mins   C   B, V, 3/4U   P
Dance and creative body movement are introduced to children through demonstrations of locomotor and non-locomotor movements, qualities of movement, making shapes, and rhythm games.
Vision Productions — *Vision Productions*

Dance Masters — 1983
Dance
69789   60 mins   C   B, V   P
4   pgms
These four programs look at various styles of dance. Each program is available individually and contains an instructional segment as well as a demonstration by experts of the techniques taught.
1.Dance Masters—Ballroom 2.Dance Masters—Ballet 3.Dance Masters—Frisco Dance 4.Dance Masters—Modern Jazz
Anthony DiVona; Celebrity Video — *Gold Stripe Video*

Danger Ahead! — 1926
Comedy
74478   15 mins   B/W   B, V   P
This tape is a 1926 comedy featuring an exciting train chase.
Monogram — *Interurban Films*

Danger Lights — 1930
Drama
44992   73 mins   B/W   B, V   P, T
Jean Arthur, Loius Wohleim
This movie depicts the railroads and the railroad men's dedication to the tenet of giving the best possible care to each other and their trains.
RKO — *Blackhawk Films; Sheik Video; Interurban Films*

Danger on Wheels — 1939
Drama
66369   61 mins   B/W   B, V   P
Richard Arlen, Andy Devine
A hotshot race car driver faces tragedy on and off the track.
Universal — *Movie Buff Video*

Dangerous Holiday — 1937
Adventure
12811   54 mins   B/W   B, V, FO   P
Hedda Hopper, Franklin Pangborn, Guinn Williams, Jack La Rue
A young violin prodigy would rather be just "one of the boys." He runs away from his greedy relatives but begins to hang out with a gang of kidnappers.
Republic — *Video Yesteryear*

Dangerous Mission — 1954
Mystery
33900   75 mins   B/W   B, V   P
Victor Mature, Piper Laurie, Vincent Price, William Bendix
A New York girl witnesses a gangland murder and flees to the Midwest, pursued by killers and the police.
RKO;Irwin Allen — *Nostalgia Merchant*

Dangerous Playground — 1952
Trains/Safety education
68892   15 mins   C   B, V   P
This program shows how the switching yard of a railroad is a dangerous place for children to play.
Unknown — *Interurban Films*

Dangerous Relations — 1973
Comedy-Drama
19403   90 mins   C   B, V, 3/4U,   P
                                              Q
Brooke Bundy, Eileen Weston, Kenneth Varnum, Sam Bell
The story of an anti-hero, spiced with suspense and comedy.
TV Sports Scene — *TV Sports Scene*

Dangerous Summer, A — 1982
Suspense
73148   100 mins   C   B, V   P
James Mason, Tom Skeritt
James Mason is sent to Australia to investigate a murderous insurance fraud.
McElroy & McElroy Prods — *VCL Home Video*

Danguard Ace — 1982
Cartoons/Science fiction
63119   100 mins   C   B, V   P
Animated
A heroic young fighter pilot seeks the aid of Danguard Ace, mighty robot, to combat the evil forces of Komisar Krel.
Toei Animation; MK Company; Jim Terry Production Services — *Family Home Entertainment*

Daniel — 1983
Drama
66410   130 mins   C   B, V   R, P
Timothy Hutton, Amanda Plummer, Mandy Patinkin, Lindsay Crouse
The children of a couple who were executed for espionage suffer many agonizing trials as they grow to maturity with the constant reminder of their parents' treasonous activities. Based on E.L. Doctorow's "The Book of Daniel."
MPAA:R
Paramount — *Paramount Home Video*

Daniel and 1979
Nebuchadnezzar
Drama/Bible
55020   49 mins   C   B, V   P
*Donny Most, Hans Conreid, David Hendison,
Jerry Houser, Linwood Boomer, Vic Morrow,
narrated by Victor Jory*
The story of the young Hebrew Daniel, who is
imprisoned but set free once he interprets a
dream of the King's. Part of the "Greatest
Heroes of the Bible" series.
Sunn Classics — *Vanguard Video*

Daniel Boone 1936
Adventure
08613   80 mins   B/W   B, V, 3/4U   P
George O'Brien, Heather Angel, John Carradine
Adventure epic of Daniel Boone, who played a
great part in American history.
RKO — *Penguin Video; Video Connection;
Budget Video; Discount Video Tapes*

Daniel Boone 1936
Western
65228   77 mins   B/W   B, V   P
George O'Brien, Heather Angel, John Carradine
Daniel Boone guides a party of settlers from
North Carolina to the fertile valleys of Kentucky,
facing Indians, food shortages and bad weather
along the way.
RKO — *Blackhawk Films*

Daniel in the Lion's Den 1979
Drama/Bible
55019   43 mins   C   B, V   P
*Robert Vaughn, David Birney, Sherry Jackson,
Nehemiah Persoff, Dean Stockwell*
The story of the Hebrew Daniel, caught in a
sinister plot and condemned to the lion's den.
Part of the "Greatest Heroes of the Bible"
series.
Sunn Classics — *Vanguard Video*

Danny Boy 1946
Comedy-Drama
12864   67 mins   B/W   B, V, FO   P
A returning war dog has difficulty adjusting to
normal life. Things get worse for him and his
young master when Danny Boy is assumed to
be dangerous.
PRC — *Video Yesteryear; Sheik Video*

Danspak II 1984
Music-Performance
76667   30 mins   C   B, V   P
Six different New York groups combining night-
life scenes, dance routines, humor and much
more. The groups include: The Jim Carroll Band,
The Lenny Kaye Connection, Strange Party,
Michael Musto and the Must, Go Ohgami, Jason
Harvey.

Co Directions Inc — *Sony Corporation of
America*

Danton 1982
Biographical
72921   136 mins   C   B, V   P
Gerard Depardieu
An historical period film about the leader of the
French Revolution, Georges Danton. This film is
in French with subtitles.
MPAA:PG   FR
Les Films Du Losange Maragret
Menegoz — *RCA/Columbia Pictures Home
Video*

Darby O'Gill and the Little 1959
People
Fantasy
53796   93 mins   C   B, V   R, P
*Albert Sharpe, Janet Munro, Sean Connery,
Estelle Winwood, directed by Robert Stevenson*
Set in Ireland, a roguish old story teller tumbles
into a well and visits the land of leprechauns,
who give him three wishes in order to rearrange
his life.
Walt Disney — *Walt Disney Home Video*

Daredevils of the Red 1938
Circle
Adventure/Serials
33950   195 mins   B/W   B, V, 3/4U   P
Charles Quigley, Herman Brix, Carole Landis
Three young men set out to free a man held
prisoner by an escaped convict. A serial in
twelve chapters.
Republic Pictures — *Video Connection*

Dark, The 1979
Horror
47317   92 mins   C   B, V   P
*William Devane, Cathy Lee Crosby, Richard
Jaeckel, Keenan Wynn, Vivian Blaine*
A supernatural beast commits a string of
gruesome murders.
MPAA:R
Dick Clark; Film Ventures
International — *Media Home Entertainment*

Dark Command 1940
Western
66310   95 mins   B/W   B, V   P
*John Wayne, Walter Pidgeon, Claire Trevor, Roy
Rogers, Marjorie Main*
The story of Quantrell's Raiders, who patrolled
Kansas territory during the Civil War, in search
of wrongdoers.
Republic — *NTA Home Entertainment*

Dark Crystal, The 1982
Fantasy/Adventure
69390   93 mins   C   B, V, CED   R, P
Directed by Jim Henson

Jen and Kira, two of the last surviving Gelflings, attempt to return a crystal shard (discovered with the help of a sorceress) to the castle where the Dark Crystal lies, guarded by the cruel and evil Skeksis.
MPAA:PG
ITC Entertainment; Jim Henson and Gary Kurtz — *THORN EMI Home Video*

Dark Mountain 1944
Adventure
08606   66 mins   B/W   B, V, 3/4U   P
Robert Lowry, Ellen Drew, Regis Toomey, directed by William Berke
Forest ranger's girl marries a crooked businessman.
Paramount — *Penguin Video*

Dark Places 1973
Horror
65426   91 mins   C   B, V   P
Joan Collins, Christopher Lee, Robert Hardy
Masquerading as a hospital administrator, a former mental patient inherits the ruined mansion of a man who had killed his wife and children and died insane. As he lives in the house, the spirit of its former owner seems to overcome him, and the bizarre crime is repeated.
MPAA:PG
Cinerama — *Embassy Home Entertainment*

Dark Star 1974
Science fiction
01657   95 mins   C   B, V   P
Dan O'Bannon, Brian Narelle, directed by John Carpenter
Scientists try to destroy unstable planets and are forced into a fight with aliens whose technology may dominate the human race.
MPAA:G
Bryanston; John Carpenter — *Budget Video; Video Dimensions; Sheik Video*

Dark Star—The Special Edition 1974
Science fiction
66029   91 mins   C   B, V   P
Dan O'Brian, Brian Narelle, directed by John Carpenter
A scoutship is entrusted with clearing a path in space for a Colony's ships.
MPAA:G
John Carpenter; Bryanston Pictures — *VCI Home Video*

Dark Victory 1939
Drama
64707   106 mins   B/W   CED   P
Bette Davis, George Brent, Geraldine Fitzgerald, Humphrey Bogart, Ronald Reagan
Bette Davis portrays a young heiress who discovers she is dying from a brain condition.

She attempts to pack a lifetime into a few months.
Warner Bros — *CBS/Fox Video; RCA VideoDiscs*

Darling 1965
Drama
64991   122 mins   B/W   B, V   P
Julie Christie, Laurence Harvey, Dirk Bogarde
A young model, searching for love in the world of the jet set, leaves her husband and manages to reach the top of European society by marrying a prince. She learns that life at the top can be very empty.
Academy Awards '65: Best Actress (Christie).
Avco-Embassy — *Embassy Home Entertainment*

D'Artagnan 1916
Film-History
48698   50 mins   B/W   B, V, 3/4U   P
The classic "Three Musketeers" novel by Dumas is brought to the screen in a lavish production. Silent.
Thomas H Ince — *Penguin Video*

Daryl Hall & John Oates—Rock 'n Soul Live 1983
Music-Performance
66349   50 mins   C   B, V   P
Taped during their 1983 "H2O" tour, Daryl Hall and John Oates perform a program of hits including "She's Gone," "Family Man" and "Maneater." Stereo VHS and Beta Hi-Fi.
RCA — *RCA/Columbia Pictures Home Video*

Dastardly & Muttley 196?
Cartoons
66274   53 mins   C   B, V   P
Animated
The villainous commanders of the Vulture Squardon will stop at nothing in their diabolical, do-anything flying machines.
Hanna Barbera — *Worldvision Home Video*

Daughter of Horror 1955
Horror
48724   60 mins   B/W   B, V, 3/4U   P
A demented woman with a sordid past tries to escape the seedy sections of Los Angeles.
Unknown — *Penguin Video*

Daughter of the Tong 1939
Mystery
08772   60 mins   B/W   B, V, 3/4U   P
Evelyn Brent, Grant Withers, Dave O'Brien, Richard Loo
An FBI man attempts to stop the mysterious infiltration of "Oriental influences" smuggled into America.
Times — *Penguin Video*

Dave Mason Live at Perkins Palace 1982
Music-Performance
47811   ? mins   C   LV   P
The veteran rock singer/guitarist performs "We Just Disagree," "Every Woman," "Let It Go," "Feelin' Alright," "Take It to the Limit" and other hits. In stereo.
Unknown — *Pioneer Artists*

David and Goliath 1979
Drama/Bible
55013   41 mins   C   B, V   P
Ted Cassidy, Jeff Corey, John Dehner, Roger Kern, Hugh O'Brian
The story of the battle between the young Israelite David and the Philistine giant Goliath. Part of the "Greatest Heroes of the Bible" series.
Sunn Classics — *Vanguard Video*

David Bowie 1983
Music-Performance
75902   14 mins   C   B, V   P
This program presents David Bowie at his best performing "Let's Dance," "China Girl" and "Modern Love."
EMI America Records — *Sony Corporation of America*

David Bowie—Serious Moonlight 1984
Music-Performance
65683   90 mins   C   B, V   P
Drawing from all phases of his career, Bowie performs 19 songs that have made him rock's most enigmatic and commanding performer. Included are "Space Oddity," "Young Americans," "Let's Dance," and "China Girl."
Anthony Eaton — *Music Media*

Davy Crockett and the River Pirates 1956
Adventure
55566   81 mins   C   LV   R, P
Fess Parker, Buddy Ebsen, Jeff York
The King of the Wild Frontier meets up with Mike Fink, the King of the Ohio River, and the two engage in a furious keelboat race, and then unite to track down a group of thieves masquerading as Indians and threatening the peace.
Walt Disney — *Walt Disney Home Video*

Dawn of the Dead 1978
Horror
69627   126 mins   C   B, V   R, P
Directed by George Romero
Flesh-eating zombies run amok in a shopping mall.
MPAA:R

Richard P Rubinstein — *THORN EMI Home Video*

Dawn of the Mummy 1982
Horror
64213   93 mins   C   B, V   R, P
From the depths of a pharaoh's tomb, a mummy awakes to kill the tomb's desecrators—four beautiful American models.
Frank Agarna; Harmony Gold Productions — *THORN EMI Home Video*

Dawn on the Great Divide 1942
Western
11671   57 mins   B/W   B, V   P
Buck Jones, Tim McCoy, Ray Hatton
Western adventure with the Three Mesquiteers as the heroes.
Monogram — *Video Connection; Sheik Video; Cable Films*

Day After, The 1983
Drama/Nuclear warfare
65387   126 mins   C   B, V, LV, CED   P
A powerful drama which graphically depicts the nuclear bombing of a midwestern city and its aftereffects on the survivors.
ABC Circle Films — *Embassy Home Entertainment*

Day at Disneyland, A 1982
Travel
47411   39 mins   C   B, V   P
A colorful souvenir of the attractions at Disneyland. Highlights include a ride down Main Street, a visit to Sleeping Beauty's castle and trips through Adventureland, Frontierland, Fantasyland and Tomorrowland.
Walt Disney Prods — *Walt Disney Home Video*

Day at the Races, A 1937
Comedy
53938   109 mins   B/W   B, V, LV, CED   P
Marx Brothers, Allan Jones, Maureen O'Sullivan
The Marx Brothers help a girl who owns a sanitorium and a race horse.
MGM — *MGM/UA Home Video*

Day for Night 1973
Drama
58226   116 mins   C   B, V   R, P
Jacqueline Bisset, Jean-Pierre Aumont, directed by Francois Truffaut
An affectionate look at the profession of moviemaking—its craft, its character, and the personalities that interact against the performances commanded by the camera. English language version.
Academy Awards '73: Best Foreign Language Film. MPAA:PG

Les Films Du Carrosse — *Warner Home Video*

Day in the Country, A   1938
Drama
02819   36 mins   B/W   B, V   P
Directed by Jean Renoir
The outing of a simple Parisian family is captured against the lovely French countryside and a theme of love. French with English subtitles.
New York Film Critics Award.   FR
Jean Renoir — *Sheik Video*

Day It Came to Earth, The   1977
Science fiction/Adventure
60402   89 mins   C   B, V   P
A meteor crashes into a lake where a corpse of a Mafia murder is buried. A cosmic reaction from radiation instills new life into the decomposed being.
MPAA:PG
Howco International; John Braden — *Paragon Video Productions; Electric Video*

Day of Frustration—Season of Triumph   1984
Football
72938   46 mins   C   B, V, FO   P
Miami Dolphins
Highlights from the Miami Dolphins' 1983 season and "NFL 83."
NFL Films — *NFL Films Video*

Day of the Animals   1977
Horror
47316   97 mins   C   B, V   P
Christopher George, Leslie Nielsen, Lynda Day George, Richard Jaeckel, Michael Ansara, Ruth Roman
Animals begin attacking human beings when the earth's ozone layer is depleted to a critical level.
MPAA:PG
Edward Montoro; Film Ventures International — *Media Home Entertainment*

Day of the Dolphin, The   1973
Adventure
08370   104 mins   C   B, V, CED   P
George C. Scott, Trish Van Devere, Paul Sorvino, Fritz Weaver, directed by Mike Nichols
Research scientist, after successfully working out a means of teaching dolphins to talk, finds his animals kidnapped.
MPAA:PG
Avco Embassy — *Embassy Home Entertainment*

Day of the Dolphins/NFL '82   1983
Football
66220   45 mins   C   B, V, FO   P
Highlights of the 1982-83 season for the Miami Dolphins combined with an overview of the whole NFL season.
NFL Films — *NFL Films Video*

Day of the Jackal, The   1973
Suspense
60590   142 mins   C   B, V   P
Edward Fox, Alan Badel, Tony Britton, Derek Jacobi, Cyril Cusack, Olga Georges-Picot, directed by Fred Zinnemann
Frederick Forsyth's best-selling novel of political intrigue concerning a suave British assassin hired to kill DeGaulle is the basis of this film.
MPAA:PG
Universal — *MCA Home Video*

Day of the Locust   1975
Drama
66035   140 mins   C   B, V   R, P
Donald Sutherland, Karen Black, Burgess Meredith, William Atherton, Geraldine Page, directed by John Schlesinger
Nathaniel West's novel concerning the dark side of 1930's Hollywood is brought to life in this film.
MPAA:R
Paramount; Jerome Hellman — *Paramount Home Video*

Day of the Triffids   1963
Science fiction
01658   94 mins   C   B, V   P
Howard Keel, Janet Scott, Nicole Maurey, directed by Steve Sekely
Giant pea-pods drop to earth and become man-eating plants. A professor finally discovers a way to destroy them.
Allied Artists — *Media Home Entertainment; King of Video; Budget Video*

Day of Wrath   1943
Horror
07365   110 mins   B/W   B, V   P
Directed by Carl Theodor Dreyer
A psychological horror story based on records of witch trials of the early 1600's.
Danish — *Sheik Video; Western Film & Video Inc; Cable Films*

Day on the Silverton, A   1979
Trains
46927   60 mins   C   B, V   P
Colorado's finest scenery is viewed as two D and RGW Class K-28 locomotives run from Durango to Silverton.
JMJ Prods — *JMJ Productions*

Day the Bookies Wept, The   1939
Comedy
29470   50 mins   B/W   B, V   P, T

Betty Grable, Joe Penner, Tom Kennedy,
Richard Lane
A cab driver who loves pigeons is tricked into
buying an old nag who loves alcohol and
entering him in the big race.
RKO, Robert Sisk — *Blackhawk Films*

Day the Earth Caught   **1962**
Fire, The
Science fiction
58461   100 mins B/W   B, V   R, P
Janet Munro, Edward Judd, Leo McKern
World powers unite to save the earth after faulty
nuclear tests.
Val Guest — *THORN EMI Home Video*

Day the Earth Stood Still,   **1951**
The
Science fiction
08433   92 mins B/W   B, V   P
Michael Rennie, Patricia Neal, Hugh Marlowe,
Bobby Gray
An emissary from another planet lands on Earth
on a mission of peace and is brutally shot down
by Washington, D.C. policemen.
EL, SP
20th Century Fox — *CBS/Fox Video*

Day the Loving Stopped,   **1982**
The
Romance
75458   96 mins C   B, V   P
Dennis Weaver, Valerie Harper
A couple goes through a difficult break-up.
King Features — *U.S.A. Home Video*

Day Time Ended, The   **197?**
Science fiction
42916   80 mins C   B, V   P
Chris Mitchum, Jim Davis, Dorothy Malone
A pair of glowing UFO's streaking across the
sky and an alien mechanical device with long
menacing appendages are only two of the
bizarre phenomena in a house that is slipping
into different dimensions.
Wayne Schmidt; Steve Neil; Paul
Gentry — *Media Home Entertainment*

Daydreamer, The   **1966**
Fantasy/Fairy tales
64974   98 mins C   B, V   P
Paul O'Keefe, Ray Bolger, Jack Gilford,
Margaret Hamilton, voices of Tallulah
Bankhead, Boris Karloff, Burl Ives, Terry
Thomas
Young Hans Christian Andersen falls asleep
and dreams some of his most famous fairy
tales"The Little Mermaid," "The Emperor's New
Clothes," and "Thumbelina." Live action is
combined with animation and highlighted with
songs.

Avco-Embassy — *Embassy Home
Entertainment*

Daylighting the Padre   **195?**
Trail
Trains
68897   21 mins B/W   B, V   P
A trip from Los Angeles to San Francisco on a
train.
Unknown — *Interurban Films*

Days of Heaven   **1978**
Drama
38593   95 mins C   B, V, LV   R, P
Richard Gere, Brooke Adams, Sam Shepard,
directed by Terence Malick
Critically acclaimed story of a drifter (Gere) who
becomes involved in the lives of a Texas
sharecropper family. Story and screenplay by
Terence Malick.
MPAA:PG
Paramount — *Paramount Home Video; RCA
VideoDiscs*

Days of Wine and Roses,   **1958**
The
Drama
65014   89 mins B/W   B, V   P
Cliff Robertson, Piper Laurie, directed by John
Frankenheimer
The original "Playhouse 90" television version
of J.P. Miller's story about a young couple
whose social drinking becomes total
dependence.
CBS — *MGM/UA Home Video*

Days of Wine and Roses   **1962**
Drama
63451   134 mins B/W   B, V   R, P
Jack Lemmon, Lee Remick, Charles Bickford,
Jack Klugman, directed by Blake Reynolds
A harrowing tale of an alcoholic advertising man
who gradually drags his wife down with him into
a life of booze. Part of the 'A Night at the
Movies" series, this tape simulates a 1962
movie evening, with a Bugs Bunny cartoon,
"Martian Through Georgia," a newsreel and
coming attractions for "Gypsy" and "Rome
Adventure."
Academy Awards '62: Best Song ("Days of
Wine and Roses").
Warner Bros — *Warner Home Video*

Daytona '83/1   **1983**
Superbike/Supercross
Motorcycles
72848   53 mins C   B, V   P
The Super Bike Race and the Super Cross race
are shown.
C H Wood Production — *Motor Cycle Video*

Daytona '83/2 200 Classic 1983
Motorcycles
72849 78 mins C B, V P
2 pgms
Highlights from the Daytona 200 Classic are
shown.
1.Daytona '83 Superbike/Supercross 2.Daytona
'83: 200 Classic
C H Wood Production — *Motor Cycle Video*

Daytona 500—1971, The 1971
Automobiles-Racing
15237 30 mins C B, V, 3/4U, P
Q
A. J. Foyt, Richard Petty, Buddy Baker
A classic auto race in which the lead changes
more than twenty times, with six cars running
nose to tail at 200 m.p.h.
Custom Films — *TV Sports Scene; Custom
Films/Video*

Dazzledancin 1984
Dance
65611 60 mins C B, V P
The dance spectacle of the 80's gives an inside
look at the raw, acrobatic finesse of the most
energetic breakdancers, spinners, and
poplockers.
Four Star International — *U.S.A. Home Video*

D.C. Cab 1984
Comedy
Closed Captioned
65516 100 mins C B, V, LV, P
CED
*Mr. T., Adam Baldwin, Charlie Barnett, Irene
Cara, Anne De Salvo, Max Gail, Gloria Gifford,
Gary Busey*
A rag-tag Washington D.C. cab company is the
setting for a young man who brings pride and
esteem to a group of society's outcasts. Closed
captioned in VHS and Beta only. In stereo VHS
and Beta Hi-Fi.
MPAA:R
Universal — *MCA Home Video*

Dead and Buried 1981
Horror
64875 95 mins C B, V, CED P
James Farentino
A sheriff is bewildered and bewitched by the
perpetrator of a series of strange murders in his
town.
MPAA:R
Ronald Shusett; Robert Bentruss — *Vestron
Video*

Dead Easy 1984
Mystery/Suspense
76662 92 mins C B, V P
Scott Burgess

A cop and two street characters team-up to run
a scam and, in the process, cross a hoodlum
who turns every one of his allies on them.
Unknown — *VCL Home Video*

**Dead Men Don't Wear
Plaid** 1982
Comedy
62779 91 mins B/W B, V, LV P
*Steve Martin, Rachel Ward, Reni Santoni, Carl
Reiner, directed by Carl Reiner*
A private detective encounters a bizarre
assortment of suspects while trying to find out
the truth about a scientist's death. This black-
and-white film is ingeniously interspliced with
clips from old Warner Brothers films, featuring
Humphrey Bogart, Bette Davis, Alan Ladd, Burt
Lancaster, Ava Gardner, Barbara Stanwyck,
Ray Milland and others.
MPAA:PG
Universal — *MCA Home Video*

Dead of Night 1945
Suspense
47302 102 mins B/W B, V R, P
*Sir Michael Redgrave, Sally Ann Howes, Basil
Radford, Naunton Wayne, Mervyn Johns,
Roland Culver*
This suspense classic, set in a remote country
house, follows a small group of people as they
find their worst nightmares becoming reality.
Universal International — *THORN EMI Home
Video*

Dead or Alive 1944
Western
54169 56 mins B/W B, V P
Tex Ritter, Dave O'Brien
A western adventure complete with songs,
starring Tex Ritter and the Texas Rangers.
Producers Releasing Corp — *Video
Connection*

Dead Zone, The 1983
Suspense
Closed Captioned
65615 103 mins C B, V, LV, R, P
CED
*Christopher Walken, Brooke Adams, Tom
Skerritt, Martin Sheen*
A man gains extraordinary psychic powers
following a near-fatal accident. He is forced to
decide between seeking absolute seclusion in
order to escape his frightening visions, or using
his "gift" to save mankind from impending evil.
MPAA:R
Debra Hill — *Paramount Home Video*

Deadline 1982
Horror
72198 85 mins C B, V P
A horror film screenwriter's life begins to reflect
his gory tales.

Unknown — *Paragon Video Productions*

Deadly and the Beautiful, The   1974
Adventure
59673   82 mins   C   B, V   P
Nancy Kwan, Ross Hagen
Dr. Tsu sends her "deadly but beautiful" task force to kidnap the world's prime male athletes for use in her private business enterprise.
MPAA:PG
Ross Hagen — *Media Home Entertainment*

Deadly Blessing   1981
Horror
60440   104 mins   C   B, V, CED   P
Ernest Borgnine, Maren Jensen, Jeff East, Lisa Hartman, Lois Nettleton
Imminent danger and relentless psychological terror highlight this frightening story of a young woman who marries a member of a bizarre religious sect.
MPAA:R
Polygram — *Embassy Home Entertainment*

Deadly Eyes   1983
Horror
69311   87 mins   C   B, V   R, P
Sam Groom, Sara Botsford, Scatman Crothers
A genetically altered urban colony of super-rats seeks a new source of food—man.
MPAA:R
Golden Harvest — *Warner Home Video*

Deadly Force   1983
Suspense
64970   95 mins   C   B, V, CED   P
Wings Hauser
An ex-cop turned private detective stalks a killer in Los Angeles who has left an "X" carved in the forehead of each of his 17 victims.
MPAA:R
Sandy Howard/Hemdale — *Embassy Home Entertainment*

Deadly Game, The   1982
Drama/Suspense
60441   108 mins   C   B, V   P
George Segal, Robert Morley
A reunion at a remote hotel leads to an ordeal of psychological terror and murderous intrigue.
Unknown — *Embassy Home Entertainment*

Deadly Games   1980
Horror
63082   94 mins   C   B, V   P
Sam Groom, JoAnn Harris, Steve Railsback, Dick Butkus, June Lockhart
A mysterious strangler terrorizes young women seemingly at random.

Great Plains Entertainment Corp — *Monterey Home Video*

Deadly Strangers   1982
Adventure
72212   89 mins   C   B, V   P
Hayley Mills
Two men must go on a murderous rampage to survive.
Unknown — *Paragon Video Productions*

Deadly Strike/Young Hero   197?
Martial arts/Adventure
66085   183 mins   C   B, V   P
Bruce Le
A kung-fu double feature filled with martial arts action.
MPAA:R
Unknown — *Best Film & Video Corporation*

Deadly Thief   1984
Drama
73559   90 mins   C   B, V   P
Rex Harrison, John Saxon, Sylvia Miles
A retired jewel thief comes out of retirement to challenge his protege to steal the world's most precious gem as the prize.
Unknown — *Prism*

Deal of the Century   1983
Comedy
69799   99 mins   C   B, V, LV, CED   R, P
Chevy Chase, Sigourney Weaver, Gregory Hines, directed by William Friedkin
A first-rate hustler and his cohorts sell second-rate weapons to third-world nations, but their latest deal threatens to blow up in their faces—literally. In stereo on all formats.
MPAA:PG
Warner Bros. — *Warner Home Video*

Dean Martin and Jerry Lewis Television Party for Muscular Dystrophy   1951
Variety
45099   105 mins   B/W   B, V   P
Dean Martin, Jerry Lewis
An early television rarity of wild off-the-cuff clowning and fun entertainment, featuring Phil Silvers, Jane Wyman, and Eddie Cantor.
Unknown — *Budget Video*

Dear Detective   1979
Crime-Drama
64998   92 mins   C   B, V   P
Brenda Vaccaro
A woman head of police homicide takes on the most challenging case of her career.
Viacom Enterprises — *U.S.A. Home Video*

(For Explanation of codes, see USE GUIDE and KEY)

Dear Diary 1981
Adolescence/Sexuality
63877   25 mins   C   B, V   P
Focusing on three fictional characters, this
program presents facts about female sexuality
and physical development, and addresses the
issues of self-image, peer pressure, and
pressure to date.
Copperfield Films — *MGM/UA Home Video*

Death Dimension 197?
Adventure
66079   87 mins   C   B, V   P
*Jim Kelly, George Lazenby, Harold "Odd Job"
Sakata, Aldo Ray*
A man must stop a mad scientist who has
developed a sinister bomb.
MPAA:R
Harry Hope — *Best Film & Video Corporation*

Death Duel of Mantis 1984
Martial arts
72958   90 mins   C   B, V   P
A martial arts film featuring Chin Yin Fei.
Foreign — *Unicorn Video*

Death Games 1982
Suspense
72532   78 mins   C   B, V   P
Two young men shooting a documentary about
an influential music promoter ask too many
wrong questions, causing the powers-that-be to
want them out of the picture for good.
Williams and Gardiner — *VidAmerica*

Death Hunt 1981
Adventure
58851   98 mins   C   B, V, LV,   P
                             CED
*Charles Bronson, Lee Marvin, Ed Lauter,
Andrew Stevens, Carl Weathers, Angie
Dickinson*
A man unjustly accused of murder pits his
knowledge of the wilderness against the
superior numbers of his pursuers.
MPAA:R
20th Century Fox — *CBS/Fox Video*

Death in Venice 1971
Drama
58227   127 mins   C   B, V   R, P
*Dirk Bogarde, Mark Burns, Bjorn Andresen,
directed by Luchino Visconti*
Thomas Mann's novel about a man obsessed
by ideal beauty is brought to life in this film.
Cannes Film Festival '71: Grand Prize Winner.
MPAA:PG
Alta Cinematografica — *Warner Home Video*

Death Journey 1976
Adventure
47669   mins   C   B, V   P
Fred Williamson, D'Urville Martin
Fred Williamson portrays Jesse Crowder, a
man-for-hire hired by the New York D.A. to
escort a key witness cross-country.
MPAA:R
Po Boy Productions — *Unicorn Video*

Death Kiss, The 1933
Mystery
08757   75 mins   B/W   B, V   P
Bela Lugosi, David Manners, Adrienne Ames
Eerie doings at a major Hollywood film studio
where a sinister killer does away with his victims
while a cast-of-thousands movie spectacular is
under production.
World Wide; KBS Prod — *Movie Buff Video;
Penguin Video; Cable Films; Discount Video
Tapes*

Death Machines 1976
Suspense/Martial arts
51117   90 mins   C   B, V   P
Ron Marchini, Michael Chong, Joshua Johnson
One man dares to defy three martial arts
experts, trained to carry the deadly plans of
organized crime.
MPAA:R
Crown International — *VCI Home Video*

Death of a Centerfold 1981
Drama
75535   96 mins   C   B, V   P
*Jamie Lee Curtis, Bruce Weitz, Robert Reed,
Mitch Ryan, Bibi Besch*
A drama based on the life of Dorothy Stratten.
Larry Wilcox Productions — *MGM/UA Home
Video*

Death on the Nile 1978
Mystery
58455   135 mins   C   B, V, CED   R, P
*Peter Ustinov, Jane Birkin, Lois Chiles, Bette
Davis, Mia Farrow, David Niven, Olivia Hussey,
Angela Lansbury, Jack Warden, Maggie Smith*
Agatha Christie's fictional detective, Hercule
Poiret, is called upon to discover who killed an
heiress aboard a steamer cruising down the
Nile.
MPAA:PG
EMI; Paramount — *THORN EMI Home Video*

Death Promise 1978
Adventure
66291   90 mins   C   B, V   P
Charles Bonet
A murderous landlord tries to evict his tenants.
MPAA:R
Serafim Karalexis — *Paragon Video
Productions*

Death Race 2000 — 1975
Drama
54800 80 mins C B, V R, P
David Carradine, Simone Griffeth, Sylvester Stallone, directed by Paul Bartel
Five racing car contenders challenge the national champion of a cross country race in which drivers score points by killing pedestrians. Based on the 1956 story by Ib Melchior.
MPAA:R
New World Pictures; Roger Corman — *Warner Home Video*

Death Rage — 1977
Suspense
44913 92 mins C B, V P
Yul Brynner, Martin Balsam
A hitman comes out of retirement to handle the toughest assignment he has ever faced: search for and kill the man who murdered his brother. But he is trapped by a Mafia doublecross, with himself as the real target.
MPAA:R
S. J. International — *VCI Home Video*

Death Rides the Plains — 1944
Western
11269 53 mins B/W B, V, FO P
Bob Livingston, Fuzzy St. John, Nica Doret, Ray Bennet
A man lures prospective buyers to his ranch, kills them, and steals their money.
PRC — *Video Yesteryear*

Death Rides the Range — 1940
Western
15483 57 mins B/W B, V, 3/4U P
Ken Maynard
Action western with a mystery angle.
NTA — *Penguin Video; Discount Video Tapes; Video Connection*

Death Sport — 1978
Adventure
52703 83 mins C B, V R, P
David Carradine, Claudia Jennings, Richard Lynch
A popular game of the future involves gladiators willing to lose their lives against lethal motorcyclists.
MPAA:R
New World; Roger Corman — *Warner Home Video*

Death Stalk — 1974
Adventure
59353 90 mins C B, V R, P
Vince Edwards, Vic Morrow, Anjanette Comer, Robert Webber, Carol Lynley
Two couples' dream holiday turns into a hostage nightmare.
Heritage Enterprises — *Video Gems*

Death Valley — 1981
Drama
59678 90 mins C B, V P
Paul LeMat, Catherine Hicks, Peter Billingsley
A trio sets out to drive through Death Valley, a trip which soon becomes a nightmare of danger and insanity.
MPAA:R
Universal — *MCA Home Video*

Death Watch — 1979
Drama
72881 117 mins C B, V, LV P
Harvey Keitel, Romy Schneider, Max Von Sydow
A television director implants a video camera in a man's brain to film a documentary on a dying woman without her knowledge.
MPAA:R
Planfilms; Selta Films — *Embassy Home Entertainment*

Death Wish — 1974
Drama
38594 93 mins C B, V, LV R, P
Charles Bronson, Vincent Gardenia, William Redfield, Hope Lange, directed by Michael Winner
Charles Bronson turns vigilante after his wife and daughter are violently attacked and raped by a gang of hoodlums. He stalks the streets of New York seeking revenge on other muggers, pimps, and crooks. Music by Herbie Hancock.
MPAA:R
Paramount — *Paramount Home Video; RCA VideoDiscs*

Death Wish II — 1982
Adventure
60337 89 mins C B, V R, P
Charles Bronson, Jill Ireland, Vincent Gardenia, Anthony Franciosa, directed by Michael Winner
Bronson recreates the role of Paul Kersey, an architect who takes the law into his own hands when his family is victimized once again.
MPAA:R
City Films — *Warner Home Video; Vestron Video (disc only)*

Deathdream — 1972
Horror
69794 98 mins C B, V P
John Marley, directed by Bob Clark
A Vietnam vet returns home as a vampire.
John Treat; Peter James — *Gorgon Video*

Deathtrap — 1982
Suspense
60336 116 mins C B, V R, P
Michael Caine, Christopher Reeve, Dyan Cannon, directed by Sidney Lumet
Ira Levin's Broadway smash concerning a creatively blocked playwright of mysteries, his

ailing rich wife and a former student who has written a surefire hit worth killing for.
MPAA:PG
Warner Bros — *Warner Home Video*

Decameron Nights 1953
Drama
75932 87 mins B/W B, V R, P
Louis Jourdan, Joan Fontaine, Binnie Barnes, Joan Collins
A trio of tales about a beautiful young wife of an older man who is pursued by a tempestuous lover.
RKO — *Video Gems*

Declarations of Faith 1980
Religion
55031 75 mins C B, V P
Tom Graham, Norm Evans, Dave Rose, Jeff Seaman, Cal Jones, Russell Nipp
A collection of two films: "In The Son Again," about an entertainer who struggles with fear, doubt, and insecurity as related to his faith, and "All-Star Witness," in which heroes of the sports world discuss their personal relationship with Jesus Christ.
Family Films — *Vanguard Video*

Deep, The 1977
Suspense
21284 123 mins C B, V P
Nick Nolte, Jacqueline Bisset, Robert Shaw
An underwater search for a shipwreck. Based on the novel by Peter Benchley.
Columbia — *RCA/Columbia Pictures Home Video; RCA VideoDiscs*

Deep in the Heart 1984
Drama
73023 99 mins C B, V R, P
Karen Young, Clayton Day
When a young woman gets raped at gunpoint on a second date she takes the law into her own hands. This film is based upon a true story.
MPAA:R
Tony Garrett and David Streit — *THORN EMI Home Video*

Deep Red: Hatchet Murders 1982
Horror/Suspense
63358 100 mins C B, V R, P
David Hemmings, Daria Nicolodi
A composer reads a book on the occult that relates to the brutal murder of his neighbor. He goes to visit the book's author and discovers that she has been horribly murdered as well.
Rizzoli Films — *THORN EMI Home Video*

Deep Six, The 1958
War-Drama
29800 110 mins C B, V P

Alan Ladd, William Bendix, James Whitmore, Keenan Wynn, Efrem Zimbalist Jr., Joey Bishop
A World War II drama that examines the conflict between pacifism and loyalty to country in wartime. A staunch Quaker is called to active duty as a lieutenant in the U.S. Navy. His pacifism puts him into disfavor with shipmates.
Warner Bros — *VCI Home Video*

Deer Hunter, The 1978
Drama
31585 183 mins C B, V, LV P
Robert DeNiro, Christopher Walken, John Savage, Meryl Streep, directed by Michael Cimino
Three buddies from a Pennsylvania steel town go to Viet Nam and learn that war is a human roulette game. The town, their loves, and their lives will never be the same.
Academy Awards '78: Best Picture; Best Director (Cimino). MPAA:R
Universal — *MCA Home Video; RCA VideoDiscs*

Deerslayer, The 1978
Drama
45052 98 mins C B, V P
Steve Forrest, Ned Romero, John Anderson, Joan Prather
Based on the classic novel by James Fenimore Cooper, this movie about the intrepid frontiersman Hawkeye and his Indian companion Chingachgook who set out to rescue a beautiful Indian maiden and must fight bands of hostile Indians and Frenchmen along the way.
Schick Sunn Classic — *VCI Home Video*

Defenders, The 1980
Football
45123 30 mins C B, V, FO R, P
Narrated by John Facenda
A look at how defensive styles, players, and coaches have evolved into today's hard-hitting offensive stoppers.
NFL Films — *NFL Films Video*

Defiance 1979
Drama
64362 101 mins C B, V, CED P
Jan-Michael Vincent, Art Carney, Theresa Saldona
A former merchant seaman moves into a tenement in a bad area of New York City. When a local street gang begins terrorizing the neighborhood, he decides to take a stand.
MPAA:PG
American International — *Vestron Video*

Defiant Ones, The 1958
Drama
65006 97 mins B/W B, V, CED P

Tony Curtis, Sidney Poitier, Theodore Bikel, Cara Williams, directed by Stanley Kramer
This symbolic story about racism revolves around two prisoners in a chain gang in the rural south who escape. Their societal conditioning to distrust and dislike each other dissolves as they face each constant peril together.
United Artists; Stanley Kramer — *CBS/Fox Video*

Degas, Erte and Chagall　　1977
Arts/Painting
58565　60 mins　C　B, V　　P
"Degas in New Orleans" is a dramatization of the pictures painted when he visited this city. "Erte" is a profile of French designer Romain de Tirtoff. The last film features Marc Chagall giving viewers an inside look at his paint-on-glass technique.
Gary L. Goldman; Chuck Olin — *Mastervision*

Del Mero Corazon　　1978
Music/Folklore
60471　28 mins　C　B, V, 3/4U　　P
Leo Garza, Chavela Ortiz, Brown Express, Little Joe, La Familia
A journey to the heart of Chicano culture as reflected in the Tex-Mex Nortena music tradition.
Chris Strachwitz — *Flower Films*

Delinquent Daughters　　1944
Drama
47637　71 mins　B/W　B, V, FO　　P
June Carlson, Fifi Dorsay, Teala Loring
After a high school girl commits suicide, a cop and a reporter try to find out why so many kids are getting into trouble.
PRC Pictures; American Prods Inc — *Video Yesteryear*

Delirium　　1977
Horror
66289　94 mins　C　B, V　　P
Turk Cekovsky, Debi Shanley, Terry Ten Brock
A homicidal maniac kills a lot of women.
Associates Entertainment Intl — *Paragon Video Productions*

Deliverance　　1972
Drama
38943　105 mins　C　B, V, LV　　R, P
Jon Voight, Burt Reynolds, Ned Beatty, John Boorman
A superb action film about four men who go riding down a wild river for a weekend that turns into a disaster. Based on James Dickey's novel.
MPAA:R
Warner Bros — *Warner Home Video; RCA VideoDiscs*

Delta Fox　　1977
Drama
60221　90 mins　C　B, V　　P
Priscilla Barnes
Delta Fox is carrying a million dollars for the mob, but the mob is carrying a grudge, and the chase is on.
Delta Fox Productions — *Independent United Distributors*

Deluge, The　　1979
Drama/Bible
55015　42 mins　C　B, V　　P
Lew Ayres, Robert Emhardt, Ed Lauter, Eve Plumb, Rita Gam
The story of Noah and the Ark. Part of the "Greatest Heroes of the Bible" series.
Sunn Classics — *Vanguard Video*

Delusion　　1984
Drama
72878　93 mins　C　B, V　　P
Joseph Cotten
A young woman comes to a house to nurse an elderly man only to have a fling with his sixteen year old grandson.
MPAA:R
Unknown — *Embassy Home Entertainment*

Demented　　1980
Horror
59662　92 mins　C　B, V　　P
Sally Elyse, Bruce Gilchrist
A beautiful and talented woman is brutally gang-raped by four men but her revenge is sweet and deadly as she entices each to bed and murders them.
MPAA:R
Arthur Jeffreys; Mike Smith — *Media Home Entertainment*

Dementia 13　　1963
Horror
11315　75 mins　B/W　B, V, FO　　P
William Campbell, Luana Anders, Bart Patton, written and directed by Francis Ford Coppola
A woman drives her husband to a heart attack as her family clings strangely to the memory of a sister who drowned years ago.
American Intl; Roger Corman — *Video Yesteryear; Budget Video; Video Dimensions; Cable Films; King of Video; Discount Video Tapes*

Demi-Paradise, The　　1943
Comedy
08682　110 mins　B/W　B, V, 3/4U　　P
Sir Laurence Olivier, Penelope Dudley Ward, Margaret Rutherford, directed by A. A. Smith
Depicts England as seen through the eyes of a foreigner who falls in love.

British — *Penguin Video*

Demon, The　　　　　　　1981
Horror
51120　　94 mins　C　　B, V　　　　P
Cameron Mitchell, Jennifer Holmes
A small town may be doomed to extinction,
courtesy of a monster's thirst for the blood of its
inhabitants.
MPAA:R
Hollard Productions — *VCI Home Video*

Demon, The　　　　　　　1981
Horror
63355　　94 mins　C　. B, V　　　　R, P
Jennifer Holmes, Cameron Mitchell
A demon-like maniac terrorizes the well-to-do
Parker family's country residence.
Gold Key Entertainment — *THORN EMI Home
Video*

Demon Lover, The　　　　　1975
Horror
47665　　87 mins　C　　B, V　　　　P
*A young girl is the victim of psychic attack from
a demonologist.
MPAA:R
Donald G Jackson; Jerry Younkins — *Unicorn
Video*

Demon Rage　　　　　　　1982
Horror
64843　　98 mins　C　　B, V　　　　P
Britt Ekland, Lana Wood, John Carradine
A neglected housewife drifts under the spell of a
phantom lover.
MPAA:R
MPM — *HarmonyVision*

Demon Seed　　　　　　　1977
Science fiction/Horror
73362　　97 mins　C　　B, V　　　　P
Julie Christie, Fritz Weaver
When a scientist and his wife separate so he
can work on his computer, the computer takes
over the house and impregnates the wife.
MPAA:R
MGM — *MGM/UA Home Video*

Demonoid　　　　　　　　1981
Horror
63386　　85 mins　C　　B, V　　　　P
*Samantha Eggar, Stuart Whitman, Roy
Cameron Jenson*
The discovery of an ancient temple of Satan
worship drastically changes the lives of a young
couple when the husband become possessed
by the Demonoid.
MPAA:R
Zach Motion Pictures; Panorama
Films — *Media Home Entertainment*

Demonstrations of　　　　　1939
Ordance Material,
Aberdeen Proving
Ground, Maryland
World War II/Armed Forces-US
72481　　24 mins　B/W　　B, V, 3/4U　　　P
The latest 1939 military hardware is shown in
action: Anti-aircraft guns, machine guns, tanks,
armored vehicles and other weapons.
US Army — *International Historic Films*

Dentist, The　　　　　　　1932
Comedy
59402　　22 mins　B/W　　　B, V　　　P, T
*W.C. Fields, Elise Cavanna, Babe Kane, Bud
Jamison, Zedna Farley*
Fields treats several oddball patients in his
office.
Paramount — *Blackhawk Films; Festival Films*

Derek and Clive Get the　　　1978
Horn
Comedy
59931　　90 mins　C　　B, V　　　　P
Peter Cook, Dudley Moore
England's favorite comedy team in a four-letter
funfest.
Peter Cook — *Pacific Arts Video*

Desde el Abismo　　　　　19??
Drama
66415　　115 mins　C　　B, V　　　　P
Thelma Biral, Alberto Argibay, Olga Zubarry
After the birth of her son, a young mother takes
to drink while in the throes of post-partum
depression.
SP
Spanish — *Media Home Entertainment*

Desert Fox, The　　　　　　1951
War-Drama
08436　　87 mins　B/W　　　B, V　　　P
*James Mason, Sir Cedric Hardwicke, Jessica
Tandy, directed by Henry Hathaway*
Personal and political sides of Field Marshal
Rommel are featured.
EL, SP
20th Century Fox; Nunnaly
Johnson — *CBS/Fox Video*

Desert of the Tartars, The　　1982
Adventure
74083　　140 mins　C　B, V, CED　　　P
This is the story of a young soldier who dreams
of war and discovers that the real battle for him
is with time.
MPAA:PG
Buz Potamkin; Hal Hoffer — *Embassy Home
Entertainment*

　　　(For Explanation of codes, see USE GUIDE and KEY)

Desert Trail 1935
Western
08828 57 mins B/W B, V, 3/4U P
John Wayne
John Wayne stars as a rough-and-tough
cowboy in this action-packed Western
adventure.
Monogram — *Penguin Video; Discount Video
Tapes; Video Dimensions; Cable Films; Video
Connection; Nostalgia Merchant*

Desert Victory 1943
World War II
53391 60 mins B/W B, V, 3/4U P
Authentic footage of Britain's first major victory
against Rommel at El Alamein.
England — *International Historic Films*

Despair 1979
Drama
66128 120 mins C B, V R, P
*Dirk Bogarde, Andrea Ferreal, directed by
Rainer Werner Fassbinder*
A chilling and comic study of a victimized factory
owner's descent into madness, set against the
backdrop of Nazi Germany.
New Line Cinema — *Warner Home Video*

Desperate Target 1980
Adventure
66290 90 mins C B, V P
Chris Mitchum
The story of courageous people fighting against
all odds to survive.
Henry Park — *Paragon Video Productions*

Destination Moon 1950
Science fiction
49899 91 mins C B, V, 3/4U P
*Warner Anderson, Tom Powers, Dick Wesson,
Erin O'Brien Moore*
This story of man's first lunar voyage contains
Chesley Bonstell's astronomical artwork and a
famous Woody Woodpecker cartoon. Includes
previews of coming attractions from classic
science fiction films.
Academy Award '50: Special Effects.
George Pal — *Nostalgia Merchant*

Destination Moonbase 1975
Alpha
Science fiction
64904 93 mins C B, V P
Martin Landau, Barbara Bain
In the 21st century, an explosion has destroyed
half the moon, causing it to break away from the
earth's orbit. The moon is cast far away, but the
311 people manning Alpha, a research station
on the moon, must continue their search for
other life forms in outer space.
ITC Entertainment — *CBS/Fox Video*

Destination Saturn 1939
Science fiction
07368 90 mins B/W B, V, 3/4U R, P
Buster Crabbe, Constance Moore
Buck Rogers awakens from suspended
animation in the twenty-fifth century.
Universal — *Cable Films; Ampro Video
Productions*

Destination 193?
Saturn/Tarzan the
Fearless
Adventure
58904 174 mins B/W B, V P
*Buster Crabbe, Constance Moore, Jacqueline
Wells*
A Buster Crabbe double feature: "Destination
Saturn" (1939), a superior version of the Buck
Rogers serial in which Buck travels to the 25th
Century; "Tarzan the Fearless" (1933), in which
Tarzan helps a young girl find her missing father.
EL, SP
Universal; Principal — *Ampro Video
Productions*

Destiny 1921
Film-Avant-garde
12422 114 mins B/W B, V P
*Lil Dagover, Walter Janssen, Bernhard Goetzke,
directed by Fritz Lang*
Young girl bargains with death for the life of her
lover. Silent with musical score added.
Janus Films; German — *Video Connection;
Sheik Video; Glenn Video Vistas; Classic Video
Cinema Collector's Club*

Detective, The 1968
Mystery
34286 114 mins C B, V P
Frank Sinatra, Lee Remick
A beauiful woman requests the services of a
detective in order to discover her husband's
killer.
SP
Twentieth Century Fox — *CBS/Fox Video*

Detour 1946
Crime-Drama
11672 69 mins B/W B, V P
Tom Neal, Ann Savage
New York piano player hitchhikes west to be
with singer in California. He encounters murder
along the way.
Producers Releasing Corp — *Video
Yesteryear; Western Film & Video Inc; Festival
Films; Classic Video Cinema Collector's Club*

Detour 1981
Football
50649 24 mins C B, V, FO R, P
Seattle Seahawks
When the passing combination of Jim Zorn to
Steve Largent led the young expansion team to

a winning record in 1979, Seahawks fans had high hopes for the 1980 season. Instead, it turned out to be a year coach Jack Patera and his young team would rather forget.
NFL Films — *NFL Films Video*

Deutsche Wochen-Schau, Die (Nazi Newsreel) 194?
World War II/Propaganda
52466 50 mins B/W B, V, FO P
This wartime propaganda film shows the power of the Nazi war machine, and the way that people on the home front helped to produce planes, tanks, and troops that conquered all obstacles in their path. Original German narration, no subtitles.
GE
Germany — *Video Yesteryear*

Developing Your Financial Strategy 1981
Personal finance
59914 100 mins C LV P
Inflation, investment, and estate planning are covered by host Jim Wilson.
Inedco Productions — *INEDCO Productions*

Devi 1961
Drama
48855 96 mins B/W B, V, 3/4U P
Chhabi Biswas, Sharmila Tagore
A farmer persuades his daughter into believing that she is a goddess.
Satyajit Ray Prods — *Western Film & Video Inc; Festival Films*

Devil and Daniel Mouse, The 1978
Fantasy
54692 30 mins C B, V R, P
Animated
A young songstress, Jan Mouse, sells her soul to the Devil in exchange for fame, fortune, and old records. Features John Sebastian's original songs.
Nelvana Prods Ltd — *Warner Home Video*

Devil and Max Devlin, The 1981
Comedy/Fantasy
58624 95 mins C B, V R, P
Elliott Gould, Bill Cosby, Susan Anspach, Adam Rich, Julie Budd, directed by Steven Hilliard Stern
The recently deceased Max Devlin strikes a bargain with the devil—he will be restored to life if he can convince three mortals to sell their souls. Music by Marvin Hamlisch.
MPAA:PG
Walt Disney Productions — *Walt Disney Home Video*

Devil and Miss Jones, The 1941
Comedy
65738 90 mins B/W B, V P
Jean Arthur, Robert Cummings
A rich department store owner poses as an employee in order to learn about impending labor trouble.
RKO — *NTA Home Entertainment*

Devil at 4 O'Clock, The 1961
Drama
65189 126 mins B/W B, V P
Spencer Tracy, Frank Sinatra, Kerwin Mathews, Jean-Pierre Aumont, directed by Mervyn LeRoy
An alcoholic missionary and three convicts work to save a colony of leper children from a South Seas volcano.
Columbia — *RCA/Columbia Pictures Home Video*

Devil Bat, The 1941
Horror
66370 70 mins B/W B, V P
Bela Lugosi, Dave O'Brien, Suzanne Kaaren
A crazed madman trains a swarm of monstrous blood-sucking bats to attack whenever they smell perfume.
Producers Releasing Corp — *Movie Buff Video*

Devil Doll 1964
Horror
75693 80 mins B/W B, V P
Bryant Holiday, William Sylvester
A ventriloquist's dummy contains the soul of a former performer and eyes a new beautiful victim in the crowd.
Galawored Gordon Film — *Gorgon Video*

Devil Girl from Mars 1955
Science fiction
49898 76 mins B/W B, V, 3/4U P
Patricia Laffan, Hazel Court, Hugh McDermott, Adrienne Corri
A female creature from Mars and her very large robot terrorize the English countryside where they land. The robot is capable of causing mass incineration.
Danzigers — *Nostalgia Merchant; Mossman Williams Productions*

Devil Horse 1932
Adventure
49177 156 mins B/W B, V, 3/4U P
Frankie Darro, Harry Carey, Noah Beery
A boy's devotion to a wild horse marked for destruction as a killer leads him into trouble. A serial in twelve, thirteen-minute chapters.
Mascot — *Penguin Video; Video Connection*

Devil Times Five 1982
Horror
47751 87 mins C B, V P

Gene Evans, Sorrel Booke, Shelly Morrison
To take revenge for being incarcerated in a mental hospital, five children methodically murder the adults who befriend them.
MPAA:R
Dylan Jones; Michael Blowitz — *Media Home Entertainment*

Devils, The   1971
Drama
53508   108 mins   C   B, V   R, P
Vanessa Redgrave, Oliver Reed, directed by Ken Russell
In 1631 France, a young priest is accused of commerce with the devil and of sexually abusing a convent. Based on Aldous Huxley's "The Devils of Loudun."
MPAA:X
Warner Bros; Robert H. Solo; Ken Russell — *Warner Home Video*

Devil's Daughter, The   1939
Horror
11229   60 mins   B/W   B, V, FO   P
Nina Mae McKinney, Jack Carter, Ida James, Hamtree Harrington
A sister's hatred and voodoo ceremonies play an important part in this all-black drama.
Unknown — *Video Yesteryear; Sheik Video*

Devil's Eye   1960
Comedy-Drama
65627   90 mins   B/W   B, V   P
Bibi Anderson, Jarl Kulle, directed by Ingmar Bergman
The devil dispatches Don Juan to tempt and seduce a young virgin bride-to-be.
Janus Films — *Embassy Home Entertainment*

Devil's Rain   1975
Horror
35368   85 mins   C   B, V   P
Ernest Borgnine, Ida Lupino, William Shatner, Eddie Albert, Keenan Wynn
This gruesomely horrifying film relates the rituals and practices of devil worship, possession, and satanism.
MPAA:PG
Sandy Howard — *VCI Home Video*

Devil's Undead, The   1975
Suspense
65451   90 mins   C   B, V   P
Christopher Lee, Peter Cushing
When a Scottish orphanage is besieged by a rash of cold blooded murders, the police are summoned to investigate. Their relentless search to determine the truth leads to a climax as shocking as it is terrifying.
MPAA:PG
Charlemagne Inc — *Monterey Home Video*

Devo   1983
Music-Performance
75919   54 mins   C   B, V   P
This program presents a combination of videos from the group Devo.
Devovision — *Sony Corporation of America*

Devo: The Men Who Make the Music   1979
Music-Performance
42905   55 mins   C   B, V   R, P
New Wave rock group Devo perform robot-like interpretations from their first album, "Q—Are We Not Men? A—We Are Devo." Electronic music tinged thematically with de-evolution processes.
Chuck Statler — *Warner Home Video*

Devonsville Terror, The   1983
Horror
64985   97 mins   C   B, V   P
Suzanna Love, Robert Walker, Donald Pleasance
Strange things begin to happen when a new school teacher arrives in Devonsville, a town which has a history of torture, murder and witchcraft. The hysterical townspeople begin a 20th century witch hunt.
Unknown — *Embassy Home Entertainment*

Diabolique   1955
Mystery
06216   107 mins   B/W   B, V   P
Simone Signoret, Vera Clouzot, Paul Meurisse, Charles Vanet, directed by Henri-Georges Clouzot
Mistress of a school master and his wife plot elaborate murder scheme. French film with English subtitles.
FR
Henri Georges Clouzot — *Budget Video; VCII; Discount Video Tapes; Video Dimensions; Sheik Video; Cable Films; Video Connection; Penguin Video; Western Film & Video Inc; Cinema Concepts*

Diagnosis of Forelimb Lameness   19??
Veterinary medicine
69659   35 mins   C   B, V   P
This program suggests remedies for such equine problems as blocked joints, musculo cutaneus, and fractures and lesions related to navicular disease.
Colorado State U — *Mercedes Maharis Productions*

Diagnosis of Hindlimb Lameness   19??
Veterinary medicine
69650   29 mins   C   B, V   P

This program looks at conditions unique to equine hindlimbs, how lameness relates to fractures of the pelvic area, and heart-related lameness.
Colorado State U — *Mercedes Maharis Productions*

Dial "M" for Murder   1954
Suspense
47616   123 mins   C   B, V   R, P
Ray Milland, Grace Kelly, Robert Cummings, John Williams, directed by Alfred Hitchcock
An unfaithful husband plots to murder his wife for her money. Part of the "A Night at the Movies" series, this tape simulates a 1954 movie evening, with a Daffy Duck cartoon, "My Little Duckaroo," a newsreel and coming attractions for "Them" and "A Star Is Born."
Warner Bros — *Warner Home Video; RCA VideoDiscs*

Diamonds Are Forever   1971
Adventure
59302   120 mins   C   B, V, LV,   P
                                   CED
Sean Connery, Jill St. John, Charles Gray
Connery's last outing as James Bond finds him taking a lighter approach to the spy business, highlighted by spectacular stunt work and special effects.
United Artists — *CBS/Fox Video; RCA VideoDiscs*

Diana Ross in Concert   1982
Music-Performance
63439   90 mins   C   B, V   P
Diana Ross
Diana Ross performs her greatest hits live at Caesar's Palace, including "Baby Love," "Ain't No Mountain High Enough," "Love Hangover," and "Reach Out and Touch."
Diana Ross Enterprises — *RCA/Columbia Pictures Home Video; RCA VideoDiscs*

Diary of a Mad Housewife   1970
Comedy-Drama
47414   94 mins   C   B, V   P
Carrie Snodgress, Richard Benjamin, Frank Langella
Despairing of her miserable family life, a housewife has an affair with a writer, only to find him to be more selfish and egotistical than her husband.
MPAA:R
Universal — *MCA Home Video*

Diary of Anne Frank, The   1959
Drama
29140   150 mins   C   B, V, CED   P
Millie Perkins, Joseph Schildkraut, Shelley Winters, Richard Beymer, Gusti Huber, Ed Wynn
In June 1945, a liberated Jewish refugee returns to the hidden third floor of an Amsterdam factory where he finds the diary kept by his younger daughter during their years in hiding from the Nazis.
National Board of Review '59: Best Picture; Academy Awards '59: Best Supporting Actress (Winters).
20th Century Fox — *CBS/Fox Video*

Dias de Ilusion   1980
Suspense
47861   94 mins   C   B, V   P
Andrea Del Boca, Luisina Brando
The fantasy world in which Lucia and her sister live was created for only one reason, and only Lucia's diary has the secret. In Spanish.
SP
Hector Olivera; Luis Repetto — *Media Home Entertainment*

Dick Cavett's Hocus   1979
Pocus, It's Magic
Magic
39079   101 mins   C   B, V, CED   P
Mark Wilson, Harry Blackstone Jr., Slydini, hosted by Dick Cavett
Amateur magician Dick Cavett hosts this tribute to the great magicians, with many of today's master wizards performing their most spectacular tricks and illusions.
MPAA:G
Unknown — *Vestron Video*

Dick Deadeye   1976
Adventure
59326   80 mins   C   B, V   P
Animated
From the operas of Gilbert and Sullivan, based on drawings by Ronald Searle, comes the unlikeliest of heroes, Dick Deadeye. Sporting an I.Q. of zero, Dick is hired to wipe out pirates, thieves, and a sorcerer.
Sandy Cobe; David Baugh — *Family Home Entertainment*

Dick Tracy   1937
Crime-Drama
11689   100 mins   B/W   B, V   P
Ralph Byrd, Smiley Burnett
Dick Tracy faces the fiend, "Spider," and his demented hunchback.
Republic — *VCI Home Video*

Dick Tracy   1937
Crime-Drama/Serials
14618   310 mins   B/W   B, V   P
Ralph Byrd, Smiley Burnett
Serial, based on the comic strip character, in fifteen chapters. The first chapter is thirty minutes and each additional chapter is twenty minutes.

Republic — *VCI Home Video; Video Connection; Video Yesteryear; Discount Video Tapes*

Dick Tracy   1945
Crime-Drama
58658   62 mins   B/W   B, V, FO   P
Morgan Conway, Anne Jeffreys, Mike Mazurki, Jane Greer, Lyle Latell
The first Dick Tracy feature film, in which Splitface is on the loose, a schoolteacher is murdered, the Mayor is threatened, and a nutty professor uses a crystal ball to give Tracy the clue needed to connect the crimes.
RKO — *Video Yesteryear; Sheik Video; Nostalgia Merchant*

Dick Tracy Double   194?
Feature #1
Crime-Drama
45053   122 mins   B/W   B, V   P
Ralph Byrd, Lyle Latelle, Morgan Conway, Anne Jeffreys
This video double feature presents two Dick Tracy adventures. "Dick Tracy Detective," "Dick Tracy's Dilemma", a mystery-adventure package starring Chester Gould's popular comic strip hero.
RKO, Gold Key — *VCI Home Video*

Dick Tracy Double   194?
Feature #2
Mystery/Adventure
45005   127 mins   B/W   B, V   P
Boris Karloff, Ralph Byrd, Morgan Conway, Anne Jeffreys
Chester Gould's famous comic strip character is personified in: "Dick Tracy Meets Gruesome," "Dick Tracy vs. Cueball;" a double feature videocassette featuring Dick Tracy battling two of his arch enemies.
RKO, Gold Key — *VCI Home Video*

Dick Tracy Meets   1947
Gruesome
Crime-Drama
58642   66 mins   B/W   B, V, FO   P
Boris Karloff, Ralph Byrd, Lyle Latell
Gruesome and his partner in crime, Melody, stage a bank robbery using the secret formula of Dr. A. Tomic. Tracy has to solve the robbery before word gets out and people rush to withdraw their savings, destroying civilization as we know it.
RKO — *Video Yesteryear; Video Connection; Western Film & Video Inc; Nostalgia Merchant; Admit One Video*

Dick Tracy Returns   1938
Crime-Drama
11694   100 mins   B/W   B, V   P
Ralph Byrd, Charles Middleton

Public Enemy Paw Stark and his gang set out on a wave of crime that brings them face to face with Dick Tracy.
Republic — *VCI Home Video*

Dick Tracy Returns   1938
Crime-Drama/Serials
14619   310 mins   B/W   B, V   P
Ralph Byrd, Charles Middleton
Serial, based on the comic strip character, in fifteen chapters. The first chapter is thirty minutes and each additional chapter is twenty minutes.
Republic — *VCI Home Video; Video Connection*

Dick Tracy vs. Crime Inc.   1941
Crime-Drama/Serials
14620   310 mins   B/W   B, V   P
Ralph Byrd, Ralph Morgan
Serial, based on the comic strip character, in fifteen chapters. The first chapter is thirty minutes and each additional chapter is twenty minutes.
Republic — *VCI Home Video; Video Connection*

Dick Tracy vs. Crime Inc.   1941
Crime-Drama
07220   100 mins   B/W   B, V   P
Ralph Byrd, Ralph Morgan
Dick Tracy encounters many difficulties when he tries to track down a criminal who can make himself invisible.
Republic — *VCI Home Video*

Dick Tracy's G-Men   1939
Crime-Drama
11692   100 mins   B/W   B, V   P
Ralph Byrd, Jennifer Jones
Tracy and his G-Men must stop international spy, Aarnoff, from stealing America's top secrets.
Republic — *VCI Home Video*

Dick Tracy's G-Men   1939
Crime-Drama/Serials
14621   310 mins   B/W   B, V   P
Ralph Byrd, Irving Pichel
Serial, based on the comic strip character, in fifteen chapters. The first chapter is thirty minutes and each additional chapter is twenty minutes.
Republic — *VCI Home Video; Video Connection*

Die Laughing   1980
Comedy
52716   108 mins   C   B, V   R, P
Robby Benson, Charles Durning, Bud Cort, Elsa Lanchester

A cab driver unwittingly becomes involved in murder, intrigue, and the kidnapping of a monkey that has memorized a scientific formula that can destroy the world.
MPAA:PG
Orion Pictures — *Warner Home Video*

Dillinger 1973
Crime-Drama
64894   106 mins   C   B, V, CED   P
Warren Oates, Michelle Phillips, Richard Dreyfuss, Cloris Leachman
The most colorful period of criminality in America is brought to life in this story of John Dillinger, "Baby Face" Nelson and the notorious "Lady in Red."
MPAA:R
American International Pictures — *Vestron Video*

Dinah Shore Show, The 1963
Variety
12846   59 mins   B/W   B, V, FO   P
Dinah Shore, Steve Allen, Audrey Meadows, Peter Lind Hayes, Mary Healy, Yves Montand
Steve Allen's hilarious man in the street survey highlights this music and comedy show.
NBC — *Video Yesteryear*

Diner 1982
Comedy-Drama
47777   110 mins   C   B, V, CED   P
Steve Guttenberg, Daniel Stern, Mickey Rourke, Kevin Bacon, directed by Barry Levinson
The bittersweet experiences of a group of Baltimore teenagers growing up, circa 1959.
MPAA:R
MGM — *MGM/UA Home Video*

Dinner at the Ritz 1937
Drama
11392   78 mins   B/W   B, V, FO   P
David Niven, Annabella, Paul Lucas
Daughter of a murdered Parisian banker vows to find his killer with help from her fiance.
20th Century Fox — *Video Yesteryear; Cinema Concepts; Cable Films; Sheik Video; Budget Video; Western Film & Video Inc*

Dionne Quintuplets 1978
Biographical/History-Modern
46693   87 mins   C   B, V, FO   P
The true story of five identical girls born in 1934 who were taken from their parents by a court order. This program presents the tragic story of exploitation and publicity that surrounded this family and the hardships they endured as a result.
National Film Board of Canada — *Video Yesteryear*

Dionne Warwick in Concert 1983
Music-Performance
75492   120 mins   C   B, V   P
Dionne Warwick
Dionne Warwick's Chicago 1983 concert includes great hits such as "Alfie," "Walk On By," "Do You Know the Way to San Jose" and "Deja Vu."
MusicAmerica Live — *Prism*

Diplomaniacs 1933
Comedy
65227   62 mins   B/W   B, V   P
Bert Wheeler, Robert Woolsey, Marjorie White, Hugh Herbert
Wheeler and Woolsey, official barbers on an Indian reservation, are sent to the Geneva peace conference to represent the tribe.
RKO — *Blackhawk Films*

Dire Straits 1981
Music-Performance
52709   21 mins   C   B, V   R, P
Dire Straits
The English rock group performs songs from the album "Making Movies" including "Romeo and Juliet," "Tunnel of Love," and "Skateaway."
Mervyn Lloyd — *Warner Home Video*

Dirt Band Tonight, The 1982
Music-Performance
64830   58 mins   C   B, V   P
Filmed at Denver's Rainbow Music Hall, The Dirt Band performs such classics as "Mr. Bojangles," "Rocky Top," "Will the Circle Be Unbroken" and "Make a Little Magic." In stereo.
EMI Music Video — *THORN EMI Home Video; Pioneer Artists*

Dirty Dozen, The 1967
War-Drama
39090   149 mins   C   B, V, CED   P
Lee Marvin, Ernest Borgnine, Charles Bronson, Jim Brown, George Kennedy
A tough Army major is assigned to train and command twelve hardened convicts on the suicidal mission into Nazi Germany in 1944. Academy Awards '67: Best Sound Effects.
MGM — *MGM/UA Home Video*

Dirty Gertie From Harlem U.S.A. 1946
Drama
08889   60 mins   B/W   B, V, 3/4U   P
Gertie LaRue
An all-black cast does a variation on Somerset Maugham's "Rain." Gertie goes to Trinidad to hide out from her jilted boyfriend.
Unknown — *Penguin Video; Sheik Video; Video Yesteryear; Discount Video Tapes*

Dirty Harry — 1971
Drama
38947　103 mins　C　B, V, LV　R, P
Clint Eastwood, directed by Don Siegel
Clint Eastwood is detective Harry Callahan, who is attempting to track down a psychopathic rooftop killer before a kidnapped girl dies.
MPAA:R
Warner Bros — *Warner Home Video; RCA VideoDiscs*

Dirty Mind of Young Sally, The — 1972
Comedy
53147　84 mins　C　B, V　P
Sharon Kelly
Sally's erotic radio program broadcasts from a mobile studio, which must stay one step ahead of the police.
MPAA:R
Valiant Intl Pictures — *Monterey Home Video*

Dirty Tricks — 1981
Comedy
65070　91 mins　C　B, V　P
Elliot Gould, Kate Jackson, Arthur Hill, Rich Little, directed by Arthur Hill
A history professor searches for an incriminating letter that was written by George Washington.
MPAA:PG
Filmplan International — *Embassy Home Entertainment*

Disappearance, The — 1981
Suspense
65607　80 mins　C　B, V　P
Donald Sutherland, David Hemmings, John Hurt, Christopher Plummer
A hired assassin discovers an ironic link between his new target and his missing wife.
MPAA:R
World Northal — *Vestron Video*

Disaster—Adventure Featurettes — 1984
Movie and TV trailers/Adventure
66483　61 mins　C　B, V　P
This group of movie promotion featurettes show behind the scenes activities during the making of "The Towering Inferno," "The Poseidon Adventure," "The Cassandra Crossing," "The Ten Commandments," "The Train" and "The Golden Voyage of Sinbad." Also included is an additional featurette, "Oscar: The First 50 Years."
Paramount et al — *San Francisco Rush Video*

Disciple, The — 1915
Western
64320　44 mins　B/W　B, V　P
William S. Hart, directed by William S. Hart
Cowboy star William S. Hart portrays a "good bad man" in this early western. Silent.
Triangle Film Corp — *Classic Video Cinema Collector's Club*

Disciple, The/Hell's Hinges — 1916
Western
64322　99 mins　B/W　B, V　P
William S. Hart
A double feature tape of two early William S. Hart western films.
Triangle Film Corp — *Classic Video Cinema Collector's Club*

Diseases of the Hoof — 19??
Veterinary medicine
69655　26 mins　C　B, V　P
This program looks at diseases of and damage to the equine hoof.
Colorado State U — *Mercedes Maharis Productions*

Dishonored Lady — 1947
Suspense
66371　85 mins　B/W　B, V　P
Hedy Lamarr, Dennis O'Keefe, William Lundigan, John Loder
A lady art director is accused of murdering her ex-boyfriend and refuses to testify in her own defense.
Mars Films — *Movie Buff Video*

Disney Cartoon Parade, Vol. 1 — 1981
Cartoons
56877　120 mins　C　CED　P
Animated
Mickey Mouse, Goofy, Minnie, Pluto, Donald, Chip 'n Dale, and Peg-leg Pete star in "On Vacation with Mickey Mouse and Friends," and "The Adventures of Chip 'n Dale."
Walt Disney Productions — *RCA VideoDiscs*

Disney Cartoon Parade, Vol. 2 — 1982
Cartoons
59020　88 mins　C　CED　P
Animated
This Disney compilation includes "At Home with Donald Duck" (1956), a festival of classic cartoons featuring Donald, Mickey, Pluto, and Goofy, and "The Coyote's Lament" (1961), featuring Pluto out West.
Walt Disney Productions — *RCA VideoDiscs*

Disney Cartoon Parade, Vol. 3 — 1982
Cartoons
59641　100 mins　C　CED　P
Animated
Some of Disney's most memorable cartoons: "Kids Is Kids" features the zany antics of Donald Duck and his nephews, as Prof. Ludwig

von Drake tries to answer why kids are hard to handle; "Goofy's Salute to Father" follows Goofy's hilarious misadventures from bachelorhood to the altar to bottles and diapers.
Walt Disney Productions — *RCA VideoDiscs*

Disney Cartoon Parade, Vol. 4   1982
Cartoons
60389   85 mins   C   CED   P
Animated
This volume contains "Thru the Mirror," "The Sleepwalker," "Donald's Golf Game," "Pluto and Gopher," "Dragon Around, " "The Whalers," "Society Dog Show," "Pluto's Sweater," "Donald Applecore," "The Little Whirlwind," "Donald's Diary" and "Pluto's Blue Note."
Walt Disney Productions — *RCA VideoDiscs*

Disney Cartoon Parade, Vol. 5   1983
Cartoons
64328   90 mins   C   CED   P
Animated
This collection includes such Disney favorites as "Goofy Over Sports," "Boat Builders," and "Pluto's Quintuplets," plus many others.
Walt Disney Productions — *RCA VideoDiscs*

Disney's American Heroes   1982
Cartoons/Folklore
63190   39 mins   C   B, V   R, P
Animated, the voices of Roy Rogers and the Sons of the Pioneers
Two Disney tall tales of American folk heroes: "Pecos Bill" and "Paul Bunyan."
Walt Disney Productions — *Walt Disney Home Video*

Disney's Storybook Classics   1982
Cartoons
63127   121 mins   C   B, V   R, P
Animated, the voice of Sterling Holloway and the Andrews Sisters
A collection of classic children's fables, featuring: "Little Toot" (1948—excerpted from "Melody Time"), the story of a little harbor tugboat; "Chicken Little" (1943), "The Grasshopper and the Ants" (1943), "The Grasshopper and the Ants" (1934)," The Grasshopper and the Ants" (1934—a Silly Symphony) and "Peter and the Wolf" (1946—excerpted from "Make Mine Music"), a Disneyized version of Prokofiev's famous concert piece.
Walt Disney Productions — *Walt Disney Home Video*

Diva   1982
Suspense/Romance
60394   123 mins   C   B, V, CED   P
Frederic Andrei, Roland Bertin, Richard Bohringer, Gerard Darmon, Jacques Fabbri, Wilhelmenia Wiggins Fernandez, Dominique Pinon
A young mail courier with a passion for opera manages to tape his idol who has avoided the recording studio. At the same time, a prostitute hides a tape recording in his delivery bag which fingers a local drug kingpin. Bizarre chases and plot twists follow.
Galaxie Films; Greenwich Films — *MGM/UA Home Video*

Divide and Conquer   1943
World War II/Documentary
50614   60 mins   B/W   B, V, 3/4U   P
Directed by Frank Capra
Hitler's Nazis invade Belgium, Holland, Denmark, and Norway. They take France, and drive the British into the sea of Dunkirk. Part of the "Why We Fight" series.
US War Department — *Western Film & Video Inc; MPI Home Video*

Divine Madness   1980
Music-Performance
47374   87 mins   C   B, V   R, P
Bette Midler
Bette Midler is captured at her best in a live concert at Pasadena Civic Auditorium.
MPAA:R
The Ladd Company — *Warner Home Video; RCA VideoDiscs*

Divine Nymph, The   1971
Adventure
69035   100 mins   C   B, V   P
This program tells the erotic adventures of Manuela, beautiful and young, who is dangerously pursued by two cousins.
Unknown — *Cinemagreats*

Diving and Fishing at 11,000 Feet   197?
Sports-Water
53639   25 mins   C   B, V, 3/4U, Q   P
Slim Pickens
This program in the "Under Water Deep Sea Diving" series follows a group of divers who join a scientist to explore fishing on top of an 11,000 foot mountain near Pinedale, Wyoming.
Smokey Roberts — *TV Sports Scene*

Dixiana   1930
Comedy
66190   98 mins   B/W   B, V, 3/4U   P
Wheeler and Woolsey, Bebe Daniels, Bill "Bojangles" Robinson

   (For Explanation of codes, see USE GUIDE and KEY)

A circus story set in New Orleans with comedians Wheeler and Woolsey. Some color sequences.
RKO — *Penguin Video*

Dixie Jamboree   1944
Comedy/Musical
57351   69 mins   B/W   B, V, FO   P
Guy Kibbee, Frances Langford, Louise Beavers, Charles Butterworth
A gangster "on the lam" uses an unusual method of escape from St. Louis—the last Mississippi Showboat.
Producers Releasing Corp — *Video Yesteryear; Discount Video Tapes*

Dizzy Gillespie   1965
Music
60461   20 mins   B/W   B, V, 3/4U   P
A look at the music of one of the inventors of "Bebop" Jazz in the 1940's. Gillespie discusses his beginnings and his theories of music.
Les Blank — *Flower Films*

Dizzy Gillespie   1981
Music-Performance
75895   19 mins   C   B, V   P
This program presents a jazz concert by Dizzy Gillespie featuring his compositions "Be Bop" and "Birks' Works."
Jazz America Ltd — *Sony Corporation of America*

Dizzy Gillespie's Dream Band   1981
Music-Performance
75896   16 mins   C   B, V   P
This program presents a concert by Dizzy Gillespie featuring his songs "Groovin' High" and "Hothouse," played by an all star band of Gillespie alumni.
Jazz American Ltd — *Sony Corporation of America*

D.O.A.   1949
Suspense
33495   83 mins   B/W   B, V, FO   P
Edmond O'Brien, Pamela Britton, directed by Rudolph Mate
A man is accidentally given a lethal, slow-acting poison. As his time runs out, he frantically seeks to learn who is responsible and why he was poisoned.
United Artists — *Video Yesteryear; Sheik Video; Cable Films; Western Film & Video Inc; VCI Home Video; Classic Video Cinema Collector's Club*

Dr. Black, Mr. Hyde   1976
Horror
35383   88 mins   C   B, V   P
Rosalind Cash, Stu Gilliam

Horrifying tale of a black man who can't control himself when drinking the special potion.
MPAA:R
Charles Walker, Manfred Bernhard — *VCI Home Video*

Doctor Butcher M.D.   1981
Horror
60403   81 mins   C   B, V   P
Ian McCulloch, Alexandra Cole, Peter O'Neal, Donald O'Brian
A mad doctor's deranged dream of creating "perfect people" by taking parts of one person and interchanging them with another backfires as his creations develop strange side effects.
MPAA:R
Terry Levene; Aquarius Releasing — *Paragon Video Productions; Electric Video*

Dr. Detroit   1983
Comedy
65117   91 mins   C   B, V, LV, CED   P
Dan Aykroyd, Howard Hesseman, Donna Dixon
A meek college professor becomes involved with four beautiful hookers and creates another identity as their flamboyant pimp, Dr. Detroit.
MPAA:R
Universal — *MCA Home Video*

Doctor Doolittle   1967
Musical
08456   144 mins   C   B, V, CED   P
Rex Harrison, Samantha Eggar, Anthony Newley, Richard Attenborough
An adventure about a 19th century English doctor who embarks on linguistic lessons for his animals. Based on Hugh Lofting's stories.
Academy Awards '67: Best Song ("Talk to the Animals"). EL, SP
20th Century Fox; APJAC — *CBS/Fox Video*

Dr. Heckyl and Mr. Hype   1980
Comedy
59997   100 mins   C   B, V   P
Oliver Reed, Jackie Coogan
A naughty, comical version of the Jeckyl and Hyde story.
MPAA:R
Golan Globus Productions — *Paragon Video Productions*

Dr. I. Q.   1953
Game show
42971   30 mins   B/W   B, V, FO   P
George Ansbro, Art Fleming, Bob Shepherd, Jimmy McLain
Early television quiz fun abounds as the good doctor, Jimmy McLain, gives away silver dollars for the correct answers to questions like "Who wrote the quote, "To err is human, to forgive divine?"

ABC — *Video Yesteryear*

Dr. Jekyll and Mr. Hyde 1920
Horror
48293   65 mins   B/W   B, V   P, T
John Barrymore, Nita Naldi, Brandon Hurst
The first American film version of Robert Louis Stevenson's horror tale about a schizophrenic physician. Silent.
Famous Players Lasky Corp — *Blackhawk Films; Festival Films; Western Film & Video Inc; Discount Video Tapes; Classic Video Cinema Collector's Club*

Dr. Kildare's Strange Case 1940
Drama
05478   76 mins   B/W   B, V   P
Lew Ayres, Lionel Barrymore, Loraine Day
Dr. Kildare adminsters daring treatment to a man suffering from a mental disorder of a dangerous nature.
MGM — *Budget Video; Discount Video Tapes*

Dr. Mabuse: The Fatal Passion 1922
Film-History
08707   100 mins   B/W   B, V, 3/4U   P
Randolph Klein-Rogge, directed by Fritz Lang
Depicts Dr. Mabuse as one of the most evil villians in screen history.
Germany — *Penguin Video*

Dr. No 1963
Adventure
58822   111 mins   C   B, V, LV,   P
                                    CED
Sean Connery, Ursula Andress, Joseph Wiseman, Jack Lord
James Bond, investigating murders in Jamaica, discovers a nuclear base established to divert the course of rockets projected from Cape Canaveral.
United Artists; Eon Prods — *CBS/Fox Video; RCA VideoDiscs*

Doctor of Doom 1962
Horror
51947   77 mins   B/W   B, V   P
Lorene Velazquez, Armando Silvestre, Elizabeth Campbell, Roberto Canedo, directed by Rene Cardona
A mad surgeon conducts an insane series of brain transplants, defying law and order. Two lady wrestlers try to stop him.
Unknown — *Budget Video*

Dr. Seuss Video Festival 1970
Cartoons
63116   48 mins   C   B, V, CED   P
Animated

Two of Dr. Seuss' most popular stories are visualized in these cartoon featurettes: "How the Grinch Stole Christmas" (1966) and "Horton Hears a Who" (1970).
MGM — *MGM/UA Home Video*

Dr. Strangelove 1964
Comedy
63962   93 mins   B/W   B, V   P
Peter Sellers, George C. Scott, Sterling Hayden, Keenan Wynn, Slim Pickens, directed by Stanley Kubrick
Peter Sellers plays a triple role in Stanley Kubrick's classic black comedy about a group of war-eager military men and the psychotic genius who is behind a scheme to attack Russia.
Columbia — *RCA/Columbia Pictures Home Video; RCA VideoDiscs*

Dr. Syn 1937
Drama
08765   90 mins   B/W   B, V, 3/4U   P
George Arliss, Margaret Lockwood, John Loder, directed by Roy Neil
The story tells of a seemingly respectible vicar of Dymchurch who is really a former pirate.
Gaumount; British; London Film Production — *Penguin Video; Cable Films; Discount Video Tapes*

Doctor Zhivago 1965
Drama
44642   197 mins   C   B, V, LV,   P
                                    CED
Omar Sharif, Julie Christie, Geraldine Chaplin, Rod Steiger, Alec Guinness, Tom Courtenay, directed by David Lean
An historical account of the lives of the people who lived through the dark days of the Russian Revolution. Based on the Nobel Prize winning novel by Boris Pasternak.
Academy Awards '65: Best Screenplay From Another Medium (Bolt); Best Costume Design, Color (Dalton); Best Cinematography (Young); Best Art Direction, Color (Box and Marsh).
MGM — *MGM/UA Home Video*

Dodge City 1939
Western
68229   104 mins   C   B, V   P
Errol Flynn, Olivia De Havilland
Errol Flynn stars as Wade Hutton, the roving cattleman who becomes the sheriff of Dodge City. His job is to run the ruthless outlaw and his gang out of town.
Warner Bros — *CBS/Fox Video*

Dog Day Afternoon 1975
Comedy-Drama
44591   120 mins   C   B, V   R, P
Al Pacino, John Cazale, Charles Durning, James Broderick, Chris Sarandon, Carol Kane, directed by Sidney Lumet

The true story of a bank robbery that occured on August 22, 1972 in the early morning of a scorching New York summer day. The gunmen turned the robbery into a bizarre event—from the way they handled their hostages, to their demands, to their order for take-out pizza. Academy Awards '75: Best Original Screenplay (Pierson). MPAA:R
Warner Bros — *Warner Home Video; RCA VideoDiscs*

Dog Training with the Grossmans   1981
Pets
55817   30 mins   C   B, V, 3/4U,   R, P
                                      FO
Puppy pre-school plus six lessons in basic obedience taught by Dick and Enid Grossman, famous Beverly Hills dog trainers since 1952.
Star Video Prods — *Star Video Productions*

Dogs of War, The   1981
Adventure/Drama
47147   102 mins   C   B, V, CED   P
Christopher Walken, Tom Berenger, Colin Blakely
A group of professional mercenaries are hired to overthrow the dictator of a new West African nation. Based on the novel by Frederick Forsythe.
MPAA:R
United Artists — *CBS/Fox Video*

Doin What the Crowd Does   1973
Horror
66108   89 mins   C   B, V   P
Robert Walker Jr, Cesar Romero
The tale of the death of Poe's lover Lenore.
MPAA:PG EL, SP
William Herbert — *Unicorn Video*

Dolce Vita, La   1960
Drama
47990   174 mins   B/W   B, V   P
Morcello Mastroianni, Anita Ekberg, Anouk Aimee, directed by Federico Fellini
A journalist mixes in modern Roman high society and is alternately bewitched and sickened by what he sees.
Riama; Pathe Consortium — *NTA Home Entertainment*

Doll Face   1946
Musical
41075   80 mins   B/W   B, V   P
Vivian Blaine, Dennis O'Keefe, Perry Como, Carmen Miranda, Martha Stewart, Reed Madley
This entertaining film includes songs such as "Somebody's Walking in My Dream," "Hubba Hubba," "Here Comes Heaven Again," and "Chico Chico."

20th Century Fox — *Budget Video; Discount Video Tapes; Video Yesteryear*

Doll's House, A   19??
Drama
66455   89 mins   B/W   B, V   P
Julie Harris, Christopher Plummer, Jason Robards, Hume Cronyn, Eileen Heckart, Richard Thomas
An all-star cast is featured in this original television production of Henrik Ibsen's classic play about an independent woman's quest for freedom in ninettenth-century Norway.
Sonny Fox Productions — *MGM/UA Home Video*

Doll's House, A   1973
Drama
66492   98 mins   C   B, V   P
Jane Fonda, Edward Fox, Trevor Howard, David Warner
Jane Fonda plays Nora, a subjugated housewife who breaks free to establish herself as an individual. Based on Henrik Ibsen's classic play.
World Film Services; Tomorrow Entertainment — *Prism*

Doll's House, A   1973
Drama
52389   109 mins   C   CED   P
Jane Fonda, Edward Fox, Trevor Howard
Henrik Ibsen's 1879 play is the basis of this authentic portrayal of nineteenth century society and values.
World Film Services, Tomorrow Entertainment — *RCA VideoDiscs*

Dolly in London   1983
Music-Performance
69623   50 mins   C   B, V   P
Dolly Parton
Dolly Parton is featured in a video concert from London's Dominion Theatre singing such hits as "9 to 5," "Jolene" and "Here You Come Again," among others. In stereo VHS and Beta Hi-Fi.
Stan Harris; Speckled Bird Inc — *RCA/Columbia Pictures Home Video; RCA VideoDiscs*

Dominique Is Dead   1979
Drama
66493   95 mins   C   B, V   P
Cliff Robertson, Jean Simmons, Jenny Agutter, Simon Ward, Ron Moody
A woman is driven to suicide by her greedy husband—now someone is trying to drive him mad.
Sword and Sorcery Productions — *Prism*

Domino Principle, The 1977
Drama/Prisons
46151   97 mins   C   CED   P
Gene Hackman, Candice Bergen, Richard Widmark, Mickey Rooney, Edward Albert, Eli Wallach, directed by Stanley Kramer
Gene Hackman plays a convict plotting to escape from San Quentin prison.
MPAA:G
Stanley Kramer, Avco Embassy — *CBS/Fox Video*

Don Daredevil Rides Again 1951
Serials
64426   180 mins   B/W   B, V, 3/4U   P
Ken Curtis
Don Daredevil flies into danger in this twelve-episode serial.
Republic — *Nostalgia Merchant*

Don Kirshner's Rock Concert, Vol. 1 1981
Music-Performance
52606   77 mins   C   CED   P
Don Kirshner presents seventeen magnetic performances by Motown superstars Billy Preston, The Commodores, Smokey Robinson, and Bonnie Pointer.
Don Kirshner Prods — *RCA VideoDiscs*

Don Q., Son of Zorro 1925
Adventure
47791   111 mins   B/W   B, V, 3/4U   P
Douglas Fairbanks Sr, Mary Astor
Zorro's son takes up his father's fight against evil and injustice. Silent.
United Artists — *Western Film & Video Inc; Blackhawk Films; Classic Video Cinema Collector's Club*

Don Winslow of the Coast Guard 1943
Adventure/Serials
14265   mins   B/W   B, V   P
Don Terry, Elyse Knox
Serial in 13 episodes.
Universal — *Video Connection*

Don Winslow of the Navy 1943
Adventure/Serials
08876   234 mins   B/W   B, V, 3/4U   P
Don Terry, Walter Sands, Ann Nagel
Thirteen episodes centered around the evil Scorpion, who plots to attack the Pacific Coast.
Universal — *Penguin Video; Video Connection; Sheik Video; Video Yesteryear; Discount Video Tapes; Nostalgia Merchant*

Dona Flor and Her Two Husbands 1978
Comedy
53509   106 mins   C   B, V   R, P
Sonia Braga, Jose Wilker, Mauro Mendonca, directed by Bruno Baretto
A woman becomes a widow when her philandering husband finally expires from drink, gambling, and women. She remarries, but her new husband is so boringly proper, she begins fantasizing husband number one's return.
New Yorker Films; Brazil — *Warner Home Video*

Donner Pass—The Road to Survival 1984
Drama
69802   98 mins   C   B, V   P
Robert Fuller, Diane McBain, Andrew Prine, John Anderson, Michael Callan
Stranded in a mountain pass during an unexpected snowstorm in 1846, a group of settlers trying to reach California is faced with two choices: starvation or cannibalism. Based on a true episode in American history.
James Simmons — *VCI Home Video*

Donnington '82 1984
Motorcycles
72850   55 mins   C   B, V   P
The 1982 Grand Prix of Motorcycle racing is highlighted on this program.
C H Wood Production — *Motor Cycle Video*

Donovan's Reef 1963
Comedy/Romance
64023   109 mins   C   B, V, LV   R, P
John Wayne, Lee Marvin, Elizabeth Allen, Dorothy Lamour
Two ex-Navy buddies are enjoying life on a South Pacific island, where they spend most of their time in the local saloon—until the arrival of a straight-laced Boston woman in search of her father.
Paramount — *Paramount Home Video*

Don's Party 1982
Comedy
65730   91 mins   C   B, V   P
John Hargreaves
This off-beat comedy focuses on a party that is not what anyone expected.
Phillip Adams — *VidAmerica*

Don't Answer the Phone 1980
Horror
47854   94 mins   C   B, V   P
James Westmoreland, Flo Gerrish, Ben Frank
A deeply troubled photographer stalks and attacks the patients of a beautiful psychologist talk show hostess.
MPAA:R

Robert Hammer — *Media Home Entertainment*

Don't Change My World 1983
Drama
69536   89 mins   C   B, V   P
Roy Tatum, Ben Jones
To preserve the natural beauty of the north woods, a wildlife photographer must fight a villainous land developer and a reckless poacher.
MPAA:G
George P Macrenaris — *Children's Video Library*

Don't Cry, It's Only Thunder 1981
Drama
69622   108 mins   C   B, V   P
Dennis Christopher, Susan Saint James
A young army medic who works in a mortuary in Saigon becomes involved with a group of Vietnamese orphans and a dedicated army doctor.
MPAA:PG
Sanrio Communications — *RCA/Columbia Pictures Home Video*

Don't Go in the House 1980
Horror
59666   90 mins   C   B, V   P
Dan Grimaldi, Robert Osth, Ruth Dardick
A long dormant psychosis is brought to life by the death of a young man's mother.
MPAA:R
Ellen Hammill — *Media Home Entertainment*

Don't Go in the Woods 1981
Suspense/Horror
65217   88 mins   C   B, V   P
Four young campers are being stalked by a crazed killer.
MPAA:R
James Bryan — *Vestron Video*

Don't Look in the Basement 1973
Horror
11700   95 mins   C   B, V   P
William Bill McGhee, Jesse Lee Fult
Horror rules when the inmates take over the asylum.
MPAA:R
S F Browrigg — *Gorgon Video*

Don't Look Now 1974
Drama
57280   110 mins   C   B, V, LV   R, P
Donald Sutherland, Julie Christie, Hilary Mason, directed by Nicholas Roeg
Psychic terror in a Gothic setting provides the chilling backdrop in this tale of a couple's search for the ghost of their dead child.

MPAA:R
Paramount — *Paramount Home Video; RCA VideoDiscs*

Don't Raise the Bridge, Lower the River 1968
Comedy
21285   99 mins   C   B, V   P
Jerry Lewis, Terry-Thomas
After his wife leaves him, an American with crazy, get-rich-quick schemes turns her ancestral English home into a Chinese discotheque.
Columbia — *RCA/Columbia Pictures Home Video*

Don't Shove/Two Gun Gussie 1919
Comedy
64823   27 mins   B/W   B, V   P, T
Harold Lloyd, Bebe Daniels, Noah Young, Snub Pollard
Two early Harold Lloyd shorts feature the comedian's embryonic comic style as a young fellow impressing his date at a skating rink ("Don't Shove") and a city slicker out West ("Two Gun Gussie"). Silent with piano scores.
Rolin Film; Pathe — *Blackhawk Films*

Doobie Brothers Live, The 1981
Music-Performance
60381   65 mins   C   CED   P
The seminal rock group performs in Santa Barbara, California, for over 20,000 fans. Songs include "Minute by Minute," "Takin It to the Streets," "What a Fool Believes," "Listen to the Music."
Doobro Corp — *RCA VideoDiscs*

Doomed to Die 1940
Mystery
08755   67 mins   B/W   B, V, 3/4U   P
Boris Karloff, Marjorie Reynolds, Grant Withers
Cargo of stolen bonds leads to a tong war and the murder of a shipping millionaire. Part of Mr. Wong series.
Monogram — *Penguin Video; Cable Films; Discount Video Tapes*

Doonesbury Special, A 1978
Cartoons/Satire
69022   30 mins   C   B, V   P
Animated
This animated program features Doonesbury, Zonker, Joanie Caucus, Mike, B.D, Marcus and Jimmy.
Cannes Film Festival: Special Jury Award.
Barry Trudeau; John and Faith Hubley — *Pacific Arts Video*

Door with Seven Locks   1940
Mystery
66372   86 mins   B/W   B, V   P
Leslie Banks, Lilli Palmer, Cathleen Nesbitt
A police inspector uncovers a mad doctor's
conspiracy to steal jewels from a young heiress.
Rialto; Pathe — *Movie Buff Video*

Doors: A Tribute to Jim   1981
Morrison, The
Music-Performance
47387   60 mins   C   B, V   R, P
*Jim Morrison, Ray Manzarek, Bobby Krieger,
John Densmore*
Interviews and live performance footage
capture the power of this famous rock group
and its quixotic leader, Jim Morrison. Songs
performed include "Light My Fire" and "The
End."
Independent — *Warner Home Video*

Doozer Music   1983
Music-Performance
65641   16 mins   C   B, V   R, P
An exclusive collection of tuneful highlights from
Jim Henson's "Fraggle Rock" series. In stereo
VHS and Beta Hi-Fi.
Jim Henson — *MuppetMusic Home Video*

Dorian Gray   1971
Horror
66311   91 mins   C   B, V   p
Richard Todd, Helmut Berger, Herbert Lom
A modern-day version of the famous tale by
Oscar Wilde about an ageless young man
whose portrait reflects the ravages of time.
MPAA:R
Towers of London Productions — *NTA Home
Entertainment*

Dorm That Dripped   1982
Blood, The
Horror
65374   84 mins   C   B, V   P
Laura Lopinski, Stephen Sachs, Pamela Holland
Five college students volunteer to close the
dorm during their Christmas vacation. In a series
of grisly and barbaric incidents, the students
begin to disappear. As the terror mounts, the
remaining students realize that they are up
against a terrifyingly real psychopathic killer.
MPAA:R
Jeffrey Obrow — *Media Home Entertainment*

Dorothy in the Land of Oz   1981
Cartoons/Fantasy
66180   60 mins   C   B, V   P
Animated, narrated by Sid Ceasar
The further adventures of L. Frank Baum's
characters from the "Wizard of Oz."
Muller Rosen Productions — *Family Home
Entertainment*

Dos Chicas de Revista   197?
Drama
49747   90 mins   C   B, V   P
A former film actor now recovering from a
mental breakdown and drug addiction comes
across a book written about him when he was
big-time. He meets the girl who wrote the book
and they enjoy a happy relationship. In Spanish.
SP
Independent — *Media Home Entertainment*

Dos Gallos Y Dos Gallinas   197?
(Two Roosters For Two
Hens)
Musical
73578   30 mins   C   B, V   P
*Miguel Aceves Mejia, Marco Antonio Muniz,
Maria Duval, Rosina Navarro*
This film accents all the beauty of the Mexican
countryside and the music of Mexican singers.
KNBC — *Aztec Cinevideo*

Dot and Santa Claus   1979
Fantasy
65326   73 mins   C   B, V, CED   P
Animated
Dot has lost her kangaroo and through fate,
meets Santa Claus who helps her find him in
Central Park's zoo.
Yoram Gross — *CBS/Fox Video*

Dot and the Bunny   1982
Cartoons
Closed Captioned
65506   79 mins   C   B, V, CED   P
Animated
The adventures of a spunky young red-haired
heroine on her quest for a missing baby
kangaroo named Joey are followed.
Satori — *CBS/Fox Video*

Dot and the Kangaroo   1981
Fantasy
58834   75 mins   C   B, V, CED   P
Animated
Dot, the small daughter of a settler, wanders
into the forest and gets lost. She meets a
friendly kangaroo who takes her on a fabulous
journey.
Satori Prods — *CBS/Fox Video*

Double Agents   1959
War-Drama/Suspense
69567   81 mins   B/W   B, V, FO   P
Marina Vlady, Robert Hossein
Two double agents are sent on a rendezvous to
exchange vital government secrets. Dubbed in
English.
French Italo Productions — *Video Yesteryear*

Double Bunk   1960
Comedy
58524   90 mins   B/W   B, V, 3/4U   P
Ian Carmichael, Janette Scott
Spending their wedding night on a newly acquired houseboat, a newlywed couple discovers that the roof leaks.
British; Fanfare — *Penguin Video*

Double Exposure   1982
Suspense
64876   95 mins   C   B, V, CED   P
Michael Callan, James Stacy, Joanna Pettet
A young photographer has violent nightmares which seem to become the next day's headlines.
Michael Callan; Von Deming; William Byron Hillman — *Vestron Video*

Double Heading on the Sierra   1981
Trains
51439   11 mins   B/W   B, V   P
This adventure in nineteenth-century railroading takes the viewer on the Sierra Railroad with 4-4-0 and 4-6-0 vintage locomotives.
Bruce Frenzinger — *Interurban Films*

Double Life, A   1947
Drama
64536   103 mins   B/W   B, V   P
Ronald Colman, Shelley Winters, Signe Hasso, Edmond O'Brien, directed by George Cukor
A Shakespearean actor becomes obsessed by the role of Othello and begins to duplicate the character's actions.
Academy Awards '47: Best Actor (Colman).
Universal; Garson Kanin — *NTA Home Entertainment*

Double McGuffin, The   1979
Adventure
75615   100 mins   C   B, V   P
Ernest Borgnine, George Kennedy, Elke Sommer
A group of adventurous youngsters try to avert a plot to assassinate a middle eastern ambassador.
Mulberry Square — *Children's Video Library*

Double McGuffin, The   1979
Comedy
49625   100 mins   C   B, V   P
Ernest Borgnine, George Kennedy, Elke Sommer, Ed "Too Tall" Jones, Lisa Whelchel, directed by Joe Camp
A plot of international intrigue is uncovered when a prime minister and her security guard pay a visit to a small Virginia community.
MPAA:PG
Mulberry Square Prods; Joe Camp — *Vestron Video*

Doug Stevens Special Delivery   197?
Musical
10404   120 mins   C   B, V, 3/4U, Q   P
Jackie Mason, Frank Fontaine, Irwin C. Watson, Gail Wynters, the Doug Stevens Singers
Two one-hour programs featuring a musical comedy and dance combination.
TV Sports Scene — *TV Sports Scene*

Doughnuts and Society   1936
Comedy
69558   70 mins   B/W   B, V, FO   P
Louise Fazenda, Maude Eburne, Eddie Nugent, Ann Rutherford, Hedda Hopper, Franklin Pangborn
Two elderly ladies who run a coffee shop suddenly strike it rich and find that life among the bluebloods is not all it's cracked up to be.
Mascot — *Video Yesteryear*

Down Texas Way   1942
Western
15413   57 mins   B/W   B, V   P
Buck Jones, Tim McCoy, Ray Hatton
The Three Mesquiteers head for new adventures in Texas.
Monogram — *Video Connection*

Downhill Racer   1969
Drama
48510   102 mins   C   B, V, LV   R, P
Robert Redford, Camilla Sparv, Gene Hackman
An undisciplined American skier conflicts with his coach and new-found love on his way to becoming an Olympic superstar.
MPAA:PG
Richard Gregson — *Paramount Home Video*

Dracula   1931
Horror
14023   75 mins   B/W   B, V   P
Bela Lugosi, David Manners, directed by Tod Browning
A vampire terrorizes the countryside in its search for human blood. From Bram Stoker's novel, "Horror of Dracula'.
Universal — *MCA Home Video; RCA VideoDiscs*

Dracula   1979
Horror
45046   109 mins   C   B, V, LV   P
Frank Langella, Sir Laurence Olivier
Remake of the classic story of the count who is among the undead and needs human blood for nourishment.
MPAA:R
Universal — *MCA Home Video*

Dracula and Son — 1976
Horror/Satire
62809   88 mins   C   B, V   R, P
Christopher Lee, Bernard Menez, Marie Breillat
A Dracula spoof, in which the Count fathers a son who prefers girls and football to blood.
MPAA:PG
Quartet Films — *RCA/Columbia Pictures Home Video*

Dracula Sucks — 1979
Satire
55217   91 mins   C   B, V   P
Jamie Gillis, Annette Haven, John Holmes
The erotic undertones of the vampire legend are made quite explicit in this version of the Dracula tale.
MPAA:R
MR Productions — *Media Home Entertainment*

Dracula/The Garden of Eden — 1928
Film-History
50638 52 mins B/W   B, V   P, T
Max Schreck, Alexander Granach, Corrine Griffith, Charles Ray, Louise Dressler
The abridged version of the chilling "Nosferatu" is coupled with "The Garden of Eden," in which Tini Le Brun meets her Prince Charming while vacationing with her Baroness friend.
Janus Films; Lewis Milestone — *Blackhawk Films*

Dracula's Dog — 1978
Horror
48474   90 mins   C   B, V   P
Michael Pataki, Reggie Nalder, Jose Ferrer
An explosion unearths the tomb of one of Dracula's servants and his dog. The dog puts other dogs under his spell to help the two vampires search for their new master.
MPAA:R
Crown International — *VCI Home Video*

Dracula's Last Rites — 1979
Horror
60404   86 mins   C   B, V   P
Patricia Lee Hammond, Gerald Fielding, Victor Jorge
A blood-curdling tale of a housewife and mother who fall victim to the vampire.
MPAA:R
Cannon Releasing; Kelly Van Horn — *Paragon Video Productions*

Draft Horse Pulling — 1984
Animals/Parades and festivals
74544   25 mins   C   B, V   P
This program looks at the big horse pull at the Los Angeles County Fair.
Equestrian Video Library — *Mercedes Maharis Productions*

Dragnet — 1954
Adventure
68256   71 mins   C   B, V   P
Jack Webb, Ben Alexander, Richard Boone, Ann Robinson
The Dragnet team tries to solve a mob slaying but has a rough time. Sgt. Joe Friday and Officer Frank Smith figure it out just in time.
Universal — *MCA Home Video*

Dragon Lives Again, The — 198?
Martial arts
64962   90 mins   C   B, V   P
Bruce Leong, Alexander Grand, Jenny
A martial arts adventure that is dedicated to the memory of Bruce Lee.
Dragon Lady Productions — *Unicorn Video*

Dragon Princess — 197?
Martial arts
60229   90 mins   C   B, V   P
Sonny Chiba
The king of karate and his dragon princess confront the blind master of the bloody blades, and the sparks fly.
Independent — *Independent United Distributors*

Dragon Strikes Back, The — 1975
Martial arts
63864   92 mins   C   B, V   P
A Chinese immigrant, a master of Kung Fu, stands up to a gang of white toughs who are brutally terrorizing and killing poor Mexican farmers.
MPAA:R
United International Pictures — *Budget Video*

Dragon the Hero, The — 1981
Martial arts
69278   80 mins   C   B, V   P
John Liu, Dragon Lee, Tino Wong, Philip Ku, Yang Sze
A crippled gangster kills the winners of fights he stages. Two men seek revenge. Mandarin dialogue, English subtitles.
CH
IFD Films & Arts — *Silverline Video*

Dragonslayer — 1981
Fantasy/Adventure
59423   108 mins   C   B, V, LV   R, P
Peter MacNicol, Caitlin Clarke, Ralph Richardson, John Hallam, Albert Salmi
A sorcerer's apprentice suddenly finds himself the only person who can save the kingdom from a horrible, firebreathing dragon.
Academy Awards '81: Best Special Effects.
MPAA:PG
Walt Disney Productions; Paramount; Barwood Robbins Productions — *Paramount Home Video; RCA VideoDiscs*

Drama—Romance: 1984
Trailers on Tape
Movie and TV trailers/Drama
66481   60 mins   C   B, V   P
Forty theatrical trailers for dramatic movies are
included on this tape, with such titles as "The
Godfather," "Lifeguard," "Shampoo," "Pride of
the Yankees," "Boys in the Band," "One Flew
Over the Cuckoo's Nest" and "Fortune and
Men's Eyes." Some black-and-white segments.
Columbia et al — *San Francisco Rush Video*

Dream Called Walt Disney   1981
World, A
Documentary
58628   25 mins   C   B, V   R, P
This souvenir of Orlando, Florida's Walt Disney
World discusses the creation of the magnificent
theme park.
Walt Disney Productions — *Walt Disney Home
Video*

Dream Never Dies, The   1982
Sports-Winter
59175   58 mins   C   B, V, 3/4U   P
This program centers on Ken Read, the
Canadian downhill skier, and his dream of
winning the World Cup.
Unknown — *Sports World Cinema*

Dream Street   1921
Drama
58646   138 mins   B/W   B, V, FO   P
*Carol Dempster, Ralph Graves, Charles Mack,
Tyrone Power Sr., directed by D. W. Griffith*
A morality tale of London's lower depths. Two
brothers, both in love with the same dancing girl,
woo her in their own way. Silent with music
score.
D W Griffith — *Video Yesteryear*

Dreaming Lips   1937
Drama
13646   70 mins   B/W   B, V   P, T
Raymond Massey, Elizabeth Bergner
Orchestra conductor's wife falls in love with her
husband's friend. Tragedy befalls the couple.
United Artists; Max Schach;
British — *Blackhawk Films*

Dreaming Out Loud   1940
Comedy
05455   65 mins   B/W   B, V, 3/4U   P
Lum 'n Abner, Frances Langford, Phil Harris
Popular radio team Lum 'n Abner get involved in
several capers to bring progress to their small
town.
RKO — *Penguin Video; Discount Video Tapes*

Dreams of Desire   1982
Romance
72202   80 mins   C   B, V   P
An engaged couple goes to Hong Kong to enjoy
that city's sensual pleasures.
Unknown — *Paragon Video Productions*

Dreams of Gold   1983
Sports
72180   60 mins   C   B, V   P
Members of the U.S. Olympic team were filmed
during a qualifying competition. A dramatic
musical score accompanies and enhances the
film.
Bruce Goronsky — *Pacific Arts Video*

Dressed to Kill   1946
Mystery
01753   72 mins   B/W   B, V, 3/4U   R, P
*Basil Rathbone, Nigel Bruce, Patricia Morison,
directed by Roy William Neill*
Sherlock Holmes finds a music box holds the
key to plates stolen from the Bank of England.
Universal; Howard Benedict — *Cable Films;
Western Film & Video Inc; Discount Video
Tapes; Budget Video; VCII; Classic Video
Cinema Collector's Club*

Dressed to Kill   1980
Suspense
53510   105 mins   C   B, V   R, P
*Angie Dickinson, Michael Caine, Nancy Allen,
Keith Gordon, Dennis Franz, directed by Brian
De Palma*
A woman is brutally slashed to death and her
son teams up with a prostitute who saw the killer
in order to reveal the identity of the attacker.
MPAA:R
George Litto; Samuel Z Arkoff — *Warner
Home Video; RCA VideoDiscs; Vestron Video
(disc only)*

Dried Flower Arranging   1980
and Silk Flower Making
Handicraft
47331   88 mins   C   B, V, 3/4U   P
How to make decorative arrangements such as
centerpieces and wall pieces from dried flowers
is demonstrated. Making realistic silk flowers is
also shown.
Vision Productions — *Vision Productions*

Drifter, The   1944
Western
28924   64 mins   B/W   B, V   P
Buster Crabbe, Al "Fuzzy" St. John
In this western, Buster Crabbe plays a dual
role—that of a good guy, Billy Carson, as well as
bad guy look-alike, Drifter Davis, a sharpshooter
appearing in a travelling circus. Carson is
blamed for the bank robbery committed by
Davis.
PRC — *Sheik Video*

Driver's Seat, The 1975
Suspense
64971   101 mins   C   B, V   P
Elizabeth Taylor, Ian Bannon, Mona Washbourne
A deranged woman looks for a man to whom she can give herself completely, but when she finds him she demands much more than love.
MPAA:R
Avco Embassy — *Embassy Home Entertainment*

Drowning Pool, The 1975
Mystery
72917   109 mins   C   B, V   P
Paul Newman, Joanne Woodward, Tony Franciosa
Paul Newman returns as detective Lew Harper to solve another case—the murder of a New Orleans businessman.
MPAA:PG
Warner Bros — *Warner Home Video*

Drum Beat 1954
Western
11701   111 mins   C   B, V   P
Alan Ladd, Charles Bronson, Marisa Pavan
Unarmed Indian fighter sets out to negotiate peace treaty with renegade Indian leader.
Warner Bros — *VCI Home Video*

Drum Course for Beginners 1982
Music
47362   60 mins   C   B, V   P
Louis Bellson teaches sight reading, technique, and basic fundamentals of playing the drums.
American Home Video Library — *American Home Video Library*

Drum Taps 1933
Western
58723   55 mins   B/W   B, V   P
Ken Maynard, Dorothy Dix, Junior Coughlin
Ken saves the day for a young girl who is being pushed off her land by a group of speculators.
Worldwide — *Video Dimensions; Video Yesteryear; Video Connection*

Drums of Fu Manchu 1940
Adventure/Serials
14268   ? mins   B/W   B, V   P
Henry Brandon, John English
Serial in 15 chapters.
Republic — *Video Connection*

Dry Wood 1973
Music/Folklore
60462   37 mins   C   B, V, 3/4U   P
"Bois Sec" Ardoin and his sons, Canray Fontenot
A documentary about the life and music of the French-speaking blacks in southwest Louisiana's Cajun country: A companion film to "Hot Pepper."
Les Blank — *Flower Films*

Dubarry 1930
Romance
58520   81 mins   B/W   B, V, 3/4U   P
Norma Talmadge, Conrad Nagel, William Farnum, Hobart Bosworth
The romantic experiences of Madame Dubarry, the alluring French heroine of David Belasco's "DuBarry." Norma Talmadge's last film.
Artcinema — *Penguin Video*

Duchess and the Dirtwater Fox, The 1976
Comedy/Western
09095   105 mins   C   B, V   P
George Segal, Goldie Hawn
A music-hall girl meets a man on the make.
MPAA:PG EL, SP
20th Century Fox — *CBS/Fox Video*

Duck and Goose Hunting 1984
Hunting
74472   60 mins   C   B, V   P
This tape is designed to answer all your questions about water fowling and help you to become a more successful hunter.
OMNI Visuals — *Leisure Time Products Project/3M*

Duck Hunting Time 197?
Hunting
33748   30 mins   C   B, V, 3/4U, Q   P
Duck hunting scenes, expert decoy patterns, and close ups showing the markings of various species are some of the features provided in this duck and goose hunting lesson.
TV Sports Scene — *TV Sports Scene*

Duck Soup 1933
Comedy
44810   72 mins   B/W   B, V   P
The Marx Brothers
Groucho becomes a dictator in a mythical land while Chico and Harpo run a peanut stand.
Paramount — *MCA Home Video; RCA VideoDiscs*

Dude Bandit, The 1932
Western
11702   68 mins   B/W   B, V   P
Hoot Gibson, Gloria Shea
Unscrupulous money-lender tries to gain control of ranch.
Allied Artists — *Video Connection*

Dude Ranger, The 1934
Western
56611 58 mins B/W B, V P
Smiley Burnette, George O'Brien
A Zane Grey story about an easterner who gets caught up in a range war and cattle rustling when he takes possession of some property out west.
Sol Lesser; Atherton Prods — *Video Dimensions*

Duel 1971
Suspense
14069 90 mins C B, V P
Dennis Weaver, Lucille Benson, Eddie Firestone, Cary Loftin, directed by Steven Spielberg
The story of a man's desperate attempt to stay alive. What begins as an ordinary business trip becomes a life and death battle for a man who is followed by a menacing psychopath.
Universal — *MCA Home Video*

Duel of the Iron Fist 1972
Martial arts
63863 98 mins C B, V P
A master of the martial arts must do battle with a brutal gang to save his own group from extinction.
MPAA:R
United International Pictures — *Budget Video*

Duellists, The 1978
Drama
33714 101 mins C B, V R, P
Keith Carradine, Harvey Keitel, Albert Finney, Edward Fox, Christina Raines, Diana Quick, directed by Ridley Scott
A beautifully photographed picture about the long running feud between two French officers during the Napoleonic wars.
MPAA:PG
Paramount — *Paramount Home Video*

Duke Ellington Story, The 1980
Music
38965 90 mins C B, V, FO P
Duke Ellington and his Orchestra
Three film appearances by Duke Ellington make up this program: the 1929 Paramount short "Black and Tan" (in black and white), "Duke Ellington in Concert" (Goodyear, 1962), and "Duke in Concert on the Cote D'Azur" (1965). Songs performed include "Kinda Dukish," "Such Sweet Thunder," "La Plus Belle African," and "Cotton Club Stomp."
Paramount et al — *Video Yesteryear*

Duke Is Tops, The 1938
Musical
51228 80 mins C B, V P
Ralph Cooper, Lena Horne, Basin St. Boys, Rubber Neck Boys, Marie Bryant
In Lena Horne's earliest existing film appearance, she's off to attempt the "big-time," while her boyfriend joins a traveling medicine show.
Unknown — *Movie Buff Video; Penguin Video; Video Connection; Discount Video Tapes*

Dumbo 1941
Cartoons
55564 64 mins C B, V, LV, CED R, P
Animated
The story of an elephant who is ridiculed for his large ears, until he discovers he can fly.
Walt Disney — *Walt Disney Home Video; RCA VideoDiscs*

Duncan's World 1980
Adventure
56919 93 mins C B, V P
Larry Tobias, Billy Tobias, Calvin Brown Jr.
A modern-day Tom Sawyer and his friends suspect all of the neighborhood's bullies for an explosion, and learn something about fear, courage, and friendship.
MPAA:G
Duncans World Productions Inc, Helen Masson Copeland — *Best Film & Video Corporation*

Dunderklumpen 197?
Fantasy
40730 85 mins C B, V R, P
Animated
Dunderklumpen is a little creature from the forest who is only two feet tall and sneaks into Carmilla's room and steals her dolls. From then on magical things keep happening.
MPAA:G EL, SP
21st Century — *Video Gems; Vestron Video (disc only)*

Dunwich Horror, The 1970
Horror
64984 90 mins C B, V P
Sandra Dee, Dean Stockwell, Lloyd Bochner, Ed Begley
The town of Dunwich has a history of weird and evil happenings. When a young man acquires a rare and banned book on the occult, the horror begins again.
American International Pictures — *Embassy Home Entertainment*

Duran Duran 1982
Music-Performance
66027 55 mins C B, V R, P
The hot new-music group performs "Planet Earth," "Rio," "Hungry Like the Wolf," and others.
EMI Music Video — *THORN EMI Home Video; RCA VideoDiscs*

Duran Duran   1983
Music-Performance
75918   10 mins   C   B, V   P
This program presents the popular British band singing their hits "Girls on Film" and "Hungry Like the Wolf."
Tritec Music Limited — *Sony Corporation of America*

Duran Duran: Girls on   1982
Film/Hungry Like the
Wolf
Music/Video
66160   11 mins   C   B, V   P
A hot, sexy music video clip featuring the smash new group from England. In stereo.
Capitol; EMI MusicVideo — *Sony Corporation of America*

Durango and Silverton   1981
Narrow Gauge Railroad
Trains
59180   108 mins   C   B, V   P
The Durango and Silverton Narrow Gauge R.R., formerly the Silverton Branch of the D and RGW Railroad, is seen in action.
JMJ Prods — *JMJ Productions*

Durango Valley Raiders   1938
Western
15511   55 mins   B/W   B, V   P
Bob Steele, directed by Sam Newfield
Sheriff is the leader of the outlaws, and a young cowboy finds out.
Republic — *Video Connection*

Dvorak's Slavic Dance   1981
Music-Performance
60578   72 mins   C   LV   P
Recorded at Dvorak Hall in Prague, Czechoslovakia, this program presents Dvorak's sixteen colorful and rhythmical Slavonian dances. In stereo.
Koichi Takemoto — *Pioneer Video Imports*

D.W. Griffith: An   1975
American Genius
Film-History/Documentary
29495   56 mins   C   B, V   P, T
Narrated by Richard Schickel
A penetrating documentary of a legendary filmmaker, narrated by the renowned film critic Richard Schickel. Excerpted works include early Biographs, "Birth of a Nation," "Way Down East," and "Intolerance."
Unknown — *Blackhawk Films*

D.W. Griffith: The   191?
Completion of the
Apprenticeship
Film-History
64351   75 mins   B/W   B, V   P
Lillian Gish, Mae Marsh, Mary Pickford, Henry B. Walthall, directed by D.W. Griffith
This tape features a number of Griffith's better short films from his final years at the Biograph studios. Silent with music score.
Biograph — *Classic Video Cinema Collector's Club*

D.W. Griffith: The   191?
Invention of Film
Grammar
Film-History
64350   75 mins   B/W   B, V   P
A compilation of early short films written, directed or acted in by D.W. Griffith during his early days at the Biograph studios. Silent with music score.
Biograph — *Classic Video Cinema Collector's Club*

Dybbuk, The   1939
Drama
53725   108 mins   B/W   B, V, 3/4U   P
The original Yiddish-Polish film based on Sholom Anski's classic play about possession and exorcism.
Poland — *International Historic Films*

Dynamite Chicken   1970
Musical
15786   75 mins   C   B, V   P
Joan Baez, Richard Pryor, Lenny Bruce, Jimi Hendrix, Sha-Na-Na
Focuses on the attitudes of American youth in the 70's. Includes performances by Joan Baez, Lenny Bruce, B. B. King, and others.
MPAA:R
EYR — *Monterey Home Video*

Dynamite Pass   1950
Western
64405   61 mins   B/W   B, V, 3/4U   P
Tim Holt, Richard Martin
Disgruntled ranchers attempt to stop the construction of a new road.
RKO — *Nostalgia Merchant*

E

Eagle, The   1925
Drama
08851   72 mins   B/W   B, V, 3/4U   P
Rudolph Valentino, Vilma Banky, Louise Dresser

Romantic adventure story of a Russian Robin Hood.
United Artists — *Penguin Video; Video Yesteryear; Cable Films; Video Connection; Discount Video Tapes; Western Film & Video Inc; Classic Video Cinema Collector's Club*

Eagle Has Landed, The 1977
War-Drama
45062 123 mins C B, V P
Michael Caine, Donald Sutherland, Robert Duvall
German paratroopers stage a dramatic attempt to kidnap Winston Churchill.
MPAA:PG
Columbia — *CBS/Fox Video*

Early Birds, The 1983
Automobiles
76392 40 mins C B, V P
This program presents coverage of the 1955, 1956, and 1957 Thunderbirds.
Armour Productions — *Armour Productions*

Early Church Collection, The 1980
Christianity
55036 102 mins C B, V P
A collection of six short films dramatizing episodes from the New Testament's account of the development of the early Christian church.
Family Films — *Vanguard Video*

Early Days 1981
Comedy/Drama
60585 67 mins C B, V P
Sir Ralph Richardson
A cantankerous, salty, once-powerful politician now awaits death wandering around the garden rambling on about his life.
Independent — *CBS/Fox Video*

Early Elvis 1956
Music-Performance
58653 56 mins B/W B, V, FO P
Ed Sullivan, Charles Laughton, Elvis Presley
Elvis appears on "Stage Show" with the Tommy and Jimmy Dorsey Orchestra, on the "Steve Allen Show" where he also participates in a comedy sketch, and the "Ed Sullivan Show." Ten songs in all.
CBS et al — *Video Yesteryear*

Early Films #1 192?
Film-History
48854 45 mins B/W B, V, 3/4U P
A collection of silent movies from the very early days of the industry, including: "The Great Train Robbery," "1895 Lumiere Films," "Dreams of a Rarebit Fiend," "Trip to the Moon," and "Life of an American Fireman."

Edwin S Porter et al — *Western Film & Video Inc*

Early Frost 1984
Mystery
76647 95 mins C B, V P
Diana McLean, Jon Blake, Janet Kingsbury, David Franklin
A suspenseful whodunit, centering around a simple divorce investigation that leads to the discovery of a corpse.
David Hannay; Geoff Brown — *VCL Home Video*

Early Warner Brothers 1931
Cartoons
57284 55 mins B/W B, V P
Animated
Eight cartoons from the first days of the Merrie Melodies: "Sinking in the Bathtub," "Lady Play Your Mandolin," "One More Time," "Freddie the Freshman," "You Don't Know What You're Doin'," "Red Headed Baby," "I Love a Parade," and "The Shanty Where Santy Lives."
Warner Bros — *Video Dimensions*

Earth 1930
Drama/Film-History
52343 56 mins B/W B, V, 3/4U P
Semyon Svashenko, Stephan Shkurat, directed by Alexander Dovzhenko
Classic Russian silent film with English subtitles. Problems begin in a Ukranian village when a landowner resists handing over his land for a collective farm.
USSR — *International Historic Films; Sheik Video; Blackhawk Films*

Earth, Wind & Fire in Concert 1982
Music-Performance
66094 60 mins C B, V, CED P
The funky R&B band performs "Sing a Song," "Fantasy," and "Shining Star." (Stereo).
Mike Schultz; Gloria Schultz; Maurice White — *Vestron Video*

Earth, Wind and Fire 1983
Music-Performance
72218 60 mins C B, V P
Using spectacular special effects, Earth, Wind and Fire puts on one of their typically engaging shows.
Independent — *Vestron Video*

Earthling, The 1981
Drama
66093 98 mins C B, V, CED P
William Holden, Ricky Schroder
A tale of two people alone in the Australian wilderness, learning survival and caring.
MPAA:PG

Filmways — *Vestron Video*

Earthquake 1974
Drama
53397 129 mins C B, V P
*Charlton Heston, Ava Gardner, George
Kennedy, Lorne Greene, Genevieve Bujold,
Richard Roundtree, Marjoe Gortner, Barry
Sullivan*
The effects of a major earthquake in Los
Angeles on the lives of an engineer and his
spoiled wife, his mistress, his father-in-law and a
suspended policeman make up the central
theme of this drama.
Academy Award '74: Special Achievement for
Visual Effects. MPAA:PG
Universal — *MCA Home Video*

East End Chant 1934
Drama
59209 70 mins B/W B, V, 3/4U P
George Raft, Jean Parker, Anna Mae Wong
George Raft stars as an oriental who gets
involved with a shady lady.
Paramount — *Penguin Video*

East of Borneo 1931
Drama/Romance
53449 75 mins B/W B, V P
Charles Bickford, Rose Hobart
An idyllic tropical romance.
Universal — *Movie Buff Video; Discount Video
Tapes*

East of Eden 1954
Drama
38940 105 mins C B, V R, P
*James Dean, Julie Harris, Richard Davalos,
Raymond Massey, Jo Van Fleet, directed by Elia
Kazan*
John Steinbeck's sprawling novel provides the
basis for this World War I-era retelling of the
Biblical tale of Cain and Abel. James Dean's
first starring role.
Warner Bros — *Warner Home Video; RCA
VideoDiscs*

East of Eden 1980
Drama
65439 240 mins C B, V P
*Jane Seymour, Bruce Boxleitner, Timothy
Bottoms, Lloyd Bridges*
John Steinbeck's sprawling novel of family
passions is wholly captured in this adaptation
from the popular television mini-series. The
1955 movie version only used a third of the
original story.
Viacom International — *U.S.A. Home Video*

East of Elephants Rock 1981
Drama
72879 93 mins C B, V P

John Hurt, Jeremy Kemp, Judi Bowker
In 1948, a young first secretary of the British
Embassy returns from leave in England to a
tense atmosphere in a Colony in Southeast
Asia.
Great Britian — *Embassy Home Entertainment*

East Side Kids, The 1940
Comedy
16159 60 mins B/W B, V, 3/4U P
Leon Ames, Dennis Moore, Joyce Bryant
A hoodlum wants to prevent his brother from
beginning a life of crime.
Prime TV — *Penguin Video*

Easter Bunny Is Coming 1978
to Town, The
Holidays
75618 60 mins C B, V P
Narrated by Fred Astaire
This animated tale is about the Easter Bunny
and Easter traditions.
Rankin Bass Productions — *Children's Video
Library*

Easter Collection, The 1980
Religion/Holidays
55026 50 mins C B, V P
A collection of two films: "Nail," a contemporary
parable of the biblical "upper room," and "Dawn
of Victory," a drama visualizing the events of the
crucifixion and Easter Sunday.
Family Films — *Vanguard Video*

Easy Come, Easy Go 1967
Musical
29768 95 mins C B, V R, P
*Elvis Presley, Dodie Marshall, Pat Priest, Pat
Harrington*
A Navy frogman accidentally locates what he
believes to be a vast sunken treasure, only to
find it filled with copper coins of little value.
Paramount, Hal Wallis — *Paramount Home
Video*

Easy Money 1983
Comedy
Closed Captioned
65385 95 mins C B, V P
Rodney Dangerfield
A basic slob has the chance to inherit millions...
if he can give up smoking, drinking and
gambling! It's an effort that nearly kills him!
MPAA:R
John Nicolella — *Vestron Video; RCA
VideoDiscs*

Easy Rider 1969
Drama
52752 88 mins C B, V, LV P
Peter Fonda, Dennis Hopper, Jack Nicholson

Two young men undertake a motorcycle trip to New Orleans, meeting hippies, rednecks, prostitutes, and drugs along the way.
MPAA:R
Columbia; Pando Co; Raybert
Prods — *RCA/Columbia Pictures Home Video; RCA VideoDiscs*

Easy Street/The Count/Behind the Screen/The Immigrant   1916
Comedy
58905 80 mins B/W   B, V   P
Charlie Chaplin, Edna Purviance, Eric Campbell, Albert Austin
Four Chaplin shorts, in which Charlie starred, wrote and directed, from 1916 to 1917. This tape is also available combined with "The Vagabond," "The Floorwalker," "The Rink" and "The Fireman."
EL, SP
Mutual — *Ampro Video Productions*

Easy Virtue   1927
Mystery
08746 75 mins B/W   B, V   P
Isabel Jean, Ian Hunter, directed by Alfred Hitchcock
Deals with the eventual destruction of a woman's life. Silent.
Sono Art; World Wide — *Festival Films; Video Dimensions; Penguin Video; Discount Video Tapes; Classic Video Cinema Collector's Club*

Eat My Dust   1976
Drama
65388 89 mins C   B, V   P
Ron Howard, Christopher Norris, Warren Kemmerling
The teenage son of a California sheriff steals the best of stock cars from a race track to take the town's heart throb for a joy ride and leads the town on the wildest car chase ever filmed.
MPAA:PG
New World Pictures; Roger Corman Production — *Embassy Home Entertainment*

Eaten Alive   1976
Horror
73558 90 mins C   B, V   P
Neville Brand, Mell Ferrer, Stuart Whitman, directed by Tobe Hooper
A resident of the Southern swamps takes an unsuspecting group of tourists into a crocodile death trap.
Unknown — *Prism*

Eating Raoul   1982
Comedy
69377 87 mins C   B, V   P
Mary Woronov, Paul Bartel

This is the story of a happily married couple who share many interests: good food and wine, entrepreneurial dreams and an aversion to sex.
MPAA:R
Quartet Films — *CBS/Fox Video*

Echoes   1983
Horror
66001 100 mins C   B, V   P
Mercedes McCambridge, Ruth Roman, Gale Sondergaard
A haunting, erotic thriller journeying into mystic phenomena and reincarnation.
Herbeval — *VidAmerica*

Ecstasy   1933
Drama
08887 88 mins B/W   B, V   P
Hedy Lamarr, Jaromir Rogoz, directed by Gustav Machaty
A romantic, erotic story about a young woman married to an older man. This film brought world fame and notoriety to Hedy Lamarr. Original title: Extase.
Universal Elektra Film — *Movie Buff Video; Penguin Video*

Ed Sullivan Show, The   1964
Variety
12850 51 mins B/W   B, V, FO   P
Ed Sullivan, The Moscow State Circus
Ed Sullivan presents "The Moscow State Circus," performing in Minneapolis as part of a cultural exchange program.
Sullivan Prods; Bob Precht — *Video Yesteryear*

Ed Wynn: Double Feature #1   195?
Comedy/Variety
28935 60 mins B/W   B, V   P
Ed Wynn, Celeste Holm, Buddy Ebsen, Hattie McDaniel
Presents two shows from the Ed Wynn TV program of the early fifties, one of the earliest examples of a television "variety/comedy" show. Shown with original Speidel watchband commercials.
CBS — *Sheik Video*

Ed Wynn: Double Feature #2   195?
Comedy/Variety
28936 60 mins B/W   B, V   P
Ed Wynn, Garry Moore, Lita Baron, Ann Sheridan
Presents two shows from the Ed Wynn program of the early fifties, one of the earliest examples of a television "variety/comedy" show. Shown with original Camel cigarette commercials.
CBS — *Sheik Video*

Ed Wynn: Double Feature #3 195?
Comedy/Variety
28937 60 mins B/W B, V P
Ed Wynn, Vera Vague, Gloria Swanson
Presents two shows from the Ed Wynn program of the early fifties, one of the earliest examples of a television "variety/comedy" show. Shown with original Camel cigarette commercials.
CBS — *Sheik Video*

Ed Wynn: Double Feature #4 195?
Comedy/Variety
28938 60 mins B/W B, V P
Ed Wynn, Ella Raines, Richard Arlen, Cass Daley
Presents two shows from the Ed Wynn program of the early fifties, one of the earliest examples of a television "variety/comedy" show. Shown with original Camel cigarette commercials.
CBS — *Sheik Video*

Ed Wynn Show, The 1949
Comedy/Variety
63782 110 mins B/W B, V, 3/4U P
Ed Wynn, guests Mel Torme, Dinah Shore, Virginia O'Brien, Buster Keaton, the Lud Gluskin Orchestra
Three complete kinescopes of Ed Wynn's early variety series, originally telecast October-December 1949. Original Speidel commercials included. Also on this tape is a 20-minute documentary produced by NBC and RCA in color which reviews the history of television and promotes the latest innovation—color TV.
CBS — *Shokus Video*

Ed Wynn Show, The 1949
Variety/Comedy
11274 24 mins B/W B, V, FO P
Ed Wynn, Diana Lynn
A rare piece of entertainment featuring one of television's great clowns in an early example of TV comedy/variety.
CBS — *Video Yesteryear*

Eddie and the Cruisers 1983
Drama
64989 90 mins C B, V, LV, CED P
Tom Berenger, Michael Pare
In the early 1960's, Eddie and the Cruisers had one hit album; years later, a former band member begins a search for the missing tapes of the Cruisers' unreleased second album.
MPAA:PG
Embassy Pictures — *Embassy Home Entertainment*

Eddie Macon's Run 1983
Drama
68252 95 mins C B, V, LV, CED P
Kirk Douglas, John Schneider, Lee Purcell, Leah Ayers
Based on a true story, Eddie Macon has been unjustly jailed in Texas and plans an escape to run to Mexico. He is followed by a tough cop who is determined to catch Eddie so his dignity will not be hurt.
MPAA:PG
Universal — *MCA Home Video*

Eddie Rickenbacker: Ace of Aces 1954
Biographical/History-US
44250 15 mins B/W B, V P
The life of Eddie Rickenbacker, America's ace of aces, who spent twenty-four days adrift on a raft until rescued, is shown through classic newsreel footage.
Fox Movietone News — *Two Star Films*

Edgar Kennedy Slow Burn Festival, The 19??
Comedy
65196 59 mins B/W B, V P
Edgar Kennedy, Florence Lake, Dot Farley, Jack Rice, Vivien Oakland, Tiny Sandford
Popular 30's comedian Edgar Kennedy stars in three shorts from his long-running "Average Man" series: "Poisoned Ivory" (1934), "Edgar Hamlet" (1935) and "A Clean Sweep" (1938).
RKO — *Video Yesteryear*

Edie in Ciao! Manhattan 1972
Drama
65469 90 mins C B, V P
Edie Sedgwick, Baby Jane Holzer, Roger Vadim, Paul America, Viva
The real-life story of Edie Sedgwick, Warhol superstar and international fashion model, whose life in the fast lane led to ruin.
MPAA:R
David Weisman — *Pacific Arts Video*

Edward and Mrs. Simpson 1980
Drama
59700 260 mins C B, V R, P
Edward Fox, Cynthia Harris
The dramatic reconstruction of the years leading to the abdication of King Edward VII, who gave up the British throne in 1936 so that he could marry American divorcee Wallis Simpson.
Emmy Awards '80: Best Drama.
Andrew Brown; Thames Television — *THORN EMI Home Video*

  (For Explanation of codes, see USE GUIDE and KEY)

Eiger Sanction, The 1975
Suspense
59067   125 mins   C   B, V   P
Clint Eastwood, George Kennedy, Vonetta McGee, Jack Cassidy, directed by Clint Eastwood
An art teacher returns to the CIA as an exterminator, and finds himself in a party climbing the Eiger.
MPAA:R
Universal — *MCA Home Video*

8 1/2 1963
Drama
66102   135 mins   B/W   B, V   P
Marcello Mastroianni, directed by Federico Fellini
Fellini's surreal self-portrait, a cinematic classic. Academy Awards '63: Best Foreign Film.
Embassy — *Vestron Video*

Eisenstein 1958
Film-History/Documentary
12805   48 mins   B/W   B, V, FO   P
A well-done biography of Sergei Eisenstein, the famous Russian director. Footage of his early life, first works and masterpieces such as "Potemkin" and "Ivan the Terrible."
Unknown — *Video Yesteryear*

El Cid 1961
Adventure
16809   180 mins   C   B, V   P
Charlton Heston, Sophia Loren
Story of Spain's 11th century Christian hero who freed his country from Moorish invaders.
Allied Artists; Samuel Bronston — *VCI Home Video; Vestron Video (disc only)*

El Diablo Rides 1939
Western
49178   50 mins   B/W   B, V, 3/4U   P
Bob Steele
A fierce feud between cattlemen and sheepmen develops, with touches of comedy in between.
Metropolitain — *Penguin Video; Video Connection*

El Dorado 1967
Western
64509   126 mins   C   B, V   R, P
John Wayne, Robert Mitchum, James Caan, Charlene Holt, Ed Asner, directed by Howard Hawks
A gunfighter rides into the frontier town of El Dorado in order to bring peace between a cattle baron and farmers who are fighting over land rights.
Paramount — *Paramount Home Video; RCA VideoDiscs*

El Paso Stampede 1953
Western
15546   50 mins   B/W   B, V   P
Allan 'Rocky' Lane
Cowboy investigates raids on cattle herds used to feed Americans fighting in Spanish-American War.
Republic — *Video Connection*

Electric Horseman, The 1979
Drama
29734   120 mins   C   B, V, LV   P
Robert Redford, Jane Fonda, John Saxon
A newspaper woman seeking a story discovers the reason behind a rodeo star's kidnapping of a prized horse. In the process she falls in love with the rodeo star.
MPAA:PG
Columbia, Ray Stark — *MCA Home Video; RCA VideoDiscs*

Electric Light Orchestra Live at Wembly 1978
Music-Performance
44936   58 mins   C   B, V, CED   P
The ELO perform some of their greatest hits, including "Roll Over Beethoven," "Do Ya," "Living Thing" and "Evil Woman," live from the arena in Wembley, England.
MGM — *CBS/Fox Video*

Electric Light Voyage 1980
Film-Avant-garde/Video
56741   60 mins   C   B, V   P
Animated
This electronic fantasy featuring computer animation can control and change your moods of elation and tranquility. The animated visuals are in sync with a mesmerizing soundtrack.
Astralvision Productions — *Media Home Entertainment*

Elementary Guitar Practice and Theory Parts 1 and 2 1982
Music
47363   72 mins   C   B, V   P
Basic techniques of playing the guitar and sight reading aretaught by Barney Kessel in this two-part program.
American Home Video Library — *American Home Video Library*

Elephant Man, The 1980
Drama
55537   123 mins   B/W   B, V, LV   R, P
Anthony Hopkins, John Hurt, Anne Bancroft, directed by David Lynch
The tragic, true-life story of John Merrick, a hideously deformed man who went from freak show to the attraction of London society.
MPAA:PG

Paramount; Jonathan Sanger — *Paramount Home Video; RCA VideoDiscs*

Elephant Parts 1981
Music/Comedy
51226　60 mins　C　B, V, CED　　P
A video album by Michael Nesmith, which contains several amusing comedy sketches and original music by Nesmith.
Grammy Awards '81: Video of the Year Award.
Michael Nesmith; Kathryn Nesmith — *Pacific Arts Video; Pioneer Artists*

Elizabeth of Ladymead 1948
Drama
66373　97 mins　C　B, V　　P
Anna Neagle, Hugh Williams, Bernard Lee
Four generations of a British family live through their experiences in the Crimean War, Boer War, World War I and World War II.
Imperadio Pictures — *Movie Buff Video*

Elizabeth the Queen 1968
Drama
64857　76 mins　C　B, V, 3/4U　　P
Judith Anderson, Charlton Heston, directed by George Schaefer
This historical drama recreates the struggle for power by Robert Devereaux, Earl of Essex, whom the aging Queen Elizabeth I both loves and fears, and whose downfall she finally brings about. Part of "George Schaefer's Showcase Theatre."
Emmy Awards '68: Outstanding Dramatic Program.
George Schaefer — *Enter-Tel Inc*

Ella Fitzgerald in Concert 1980
Music
38964　70 mins　B/W　B, V, FO　　P
Ella Fitzgerald, Duke Ellington, Benny Goodman, Jo Stafford, Harry James, Teddy Wilson, Red Norvo
Ella Fitzgerald performs in concert with Duke Ellington in the 1960's, and with Benny Goodman from the "Swing Into Spring" TV specials of 1958-59. Songs include "Street of Dreams," "Lover Man," "Ridin' High," "Satin Doll," and "Summertime." Instrumental performances by Ellington and Goodman are also included.
CBS et al — *Video Yesteryear*

Elmer Gantry 1960
Drama
68225　146 mins　C　B, V, CED　　P
Burt Lancaster, Jean Simmons, Shirley Jones
Burt Lancaster stars as Elmer Gantry, the charismatic preacher who promises eternal salvation, but in return pursues wealth and power.
United Artists — *CBS/Fox Video*

Elton John 1982
Music-Performance
76670　14 mins　C　B, V　　P
This program presents this rock-n-roll Superstar performing his greatest hits.
Sunport Productions Intl Inc — *Sony Corporation of America*

Elton John Live in Central Park 1984
Music-Performance
74109　59 mins　C　B, V　　P
The largest concert audience in the U.S. since Woodstock was the setting for a fabulous free concert in New York's Central Park. Among the songs performed are "Your Song," "Goodbye Yellow Brick Road" and "Benny and the Jets."
Danny O'Donovan — *VCL Home Video*

Elton John: Visions 1982
Music-Performance
47847　45 mins　C　B, V, LV, CED　　P
Elton John performs "Breaking Down Barriers," "Just Like Belgium," "Nobody Wins," "Elton's Song," and other classics.
Al Schoenberger — *Embassy Home Entertainment*

Elusive Corporal, The 1962
Drama
47648　109 mins　B/W　B, V, FO　　P
Jean-Pierre Cassel, Claude Brasseur, O. E. Hasse, directed by Jean Renoir
Set in a P.O.W. camp on the day France surrendered to Germany, the story of the French and Germans, and memories of a France that is no more is told.
France — *Video Yesteryear*

Elvira Madigan 1967
Romance
63339　90 mins　C　B, V　　R, P
Pia Degermark, Thommy Berggren
This film, based on a true incident, chronicles the 19th-century romance between a young officer and a beautiful circus dancer.
MPAA:PG
Atlantic Releasing; Europa Films — *THORN EMI Home Video*

Elvis...Aloha from Hawaii 1973
Music-Performance
38118　60 mins　C　B, V, FO　　P
Elvis Presley
Elvis' 1973 Hawaiian concert appearance.
Unknown — *Video Yesteryear; Sound Video Unlimited; RCA VideoDiscs*

Elvis—His 1968 Comeback Special   1968
Music-Performance
64453   76 mins   C   CED   P
Elvis Presley, the Jordanaires
Elvis is showcased in this famous TV special, which sparked his return to live performances. Featured are a medley of Elvis' 50's hits, plus newer tunes including "Guitar Man," "If I Can Dream" and "Let Yourself Go."
NBC — *RCA VideoDiscs*

Elvis...1968 Comeback Special   1968
Music-Performance
59375   55 mins   B/W   B, V   P
Elvis Presley
The King returned to television with some of the best performances of his career in this 1968 NBC special. Songs include: "Hound Dog," "If I Can Dream," "Love Me Tender," "Are You Lonesome Tonight," "Blue Christmas," "Can't Help Falling in Love," "All Shook Up," and others.
NBC — *Sheik Video; Sound Video Unlimited; Discount Video Tapes*

Elvis on Tour   1972
Music-Performance/Documentary
63110   93 mins   C   B, V, CED   P
Elvis Presley
A revealing glimpse of Elvis Presley, on stage and off, during a whirlwind concert tour.
MGM — *MGM/UA Home Video*

Elvis: The Early Years   1956
Music-Performance
29503   45 mins   B/W   B, V   P
Elvis Presley
The tape contains two of the King's appearances on the Dorsey Brothers and Ed Sullivan Shows. Includes such songs as "Heartbreak Hotel," "Hound Dog," "Don't Be Cruel," and "Love Me Tender."
CBS — *Sheik Video*

Emanuelle Around the World   1980
Drama
72954   92 mins   C   B, V   P
Laura Gemser
The further erotic adventures of that insatiable lady Emanuelle.
Jerry Gross — *Wizard Video*

Emanuelle in America   1976
Drama
58737   95 mins   C   B, V   P
Laura Gemser
Provocative reporter Emanuelle sets out to expose the inner secrets of the Jet Set at play.
MPAA:R
Monarch — *VidAmerica*

Emanuelle in Bangkok   1978
Drama
55258   94 mins   C   B, V, CED   P
Emanuelle's exotic, erotic experiences in the Far East include the royal masseuse, suspense, and the Asian arts of love.
MPAA:R
Monarch Releasing Corp — *VidAmerica*

Emanuelle on Taboo Island   1976
Drama
66292   95 mins   C   B, V   P
Paul Giusti, Laura Gemser, Arthur Kennedy
A marooned young man discovers a beautiful woman on his island.
MPAA:R
Oscar Dimartino Mansi — *Paragon Video Productions*

Emanuelle the Queen   1975
Drama
63419   90 mins   C   B, V   P
Laura Gemser
Seeking revenge, Emanuelle plots the murder of her sadistic husband. The lecherous assassin she hires in turn tries to blackmail her, and she challenges him at his own game of deadly seduction.
Othello Films; Andromeda Films — *VidAmerica*

Embryo   1982
Science fiction
75460   103 mins   C   B, V   P
Rock Hudson, Roddy McDowell, Diane Ladd
A scientist develops a growth hormone that allows embryos to become adults in 4 1/2
MPAA:PG
King Features — *U.S.A. Home Video*

Emergency First Aid   1980
Emergencies/First aid
47324   50 mins   C   B, V, 3/4U   P
This program demonstrates first aid procedures in situations where immediate action is vital. Mouth-to-mouth resuscitation, CPR, and the Heimlich maneuver are among the techniques shown.
AM Available
Vision Productions — *Vision Productions*

Emilienne   1978
Drama
55257   94 mins   C   B, V   P
An artistic young couple toys with the sexual possibilities that exist outside of, and within, a marriage.
MPAA:X
Gades Films International — *VidAmerica*

Emily 1977
Drama
63120   87 mins   C   B, V, CED   P
Koo Stark
Returning from her exclusive Swiss finishing
school, young Emily is ready for erotic
encounters at the hands of her willing
"instructors."
Christopher Neame — *MGM/UA Home Video*

Emmanuelle 1974
Drama
55261   92 mins   C   B, V   P
Sylvia Kristel, Alain Cuny, Marika Green
Filmed in Bangkok, a young, beautiful, and
restless woman is introduced to an uninhibited
world of sensuality where she experiences her
wildest dreams.
MPAA:X
Columbia; Yves Rousset
Rouard — *RCA/Columbia Pictures Home
Video*

Emmanuelle, the Joys of 1976
a Woman
Drama
55512   92 mins   C   B, V, LV   R, P
Sylvia Kristel, Umberto Orsini, Frederic Lagache
The amorous exploits of a sensuous, liberated
couple take them and their erotic companions to
exotic Hong Kong, Bangkok, and Bali.
MPAA:X
Paramount — *Paramount Home Video*

Emmet Otter's Jug-Band 1977
Christmas
Comedy
47349   50 mins   C   B, V   R, P
Emmet Otter and his Ma enter the Frog Town
Hollow talent contest and try to beat out a rock
group called the Riverbottom Nightmares for the
prize money, which will enable them to have a
merry Christmas.
Henson Associates — *Muppet Home Video*

Emmett Kelly Circus, The 1981
Circus
60222   90 mins   C   B, V   P
The wonders and fun of the circus are
highlighted.
Sunrise Entertainment — *Independent United
Distributors*

Emotions of Life, The 1982
Psychology/Alcoholism
59564   63 mins   C   B, V   P
This program examines three of the most
interesting and critical manifestations of the
human psyche: aggression, depression, and
addiction.
McGraw Hill — *Mastervision*

Emperor Jones, The 1933
Drama
12296   72 mins   B/W   B, V   P
Paul Robeson, Dudley Diggs, Frank Wilson
Based on Eugene O'Neill's classic story, this
program portrays the rise and fall of a Pullman
porter to a king of Haiti.
United Artists — *Budget Video; Western Film &
Video Inc; Cable Films;
Classic Video Cinema Collector's Club*

Emperor's New Clothes, 1984
The
Fairy tales
Closed Captioned
73572   60 mins   C   B, V, CED   P
Art Carney, Alan Arkin, Dick Shawn
From "Faerie Tale Theatre" comes the story of
an emperor and the unusual outfit he gets from
his tailor.
Gaylord Productions; Platypus
Productions — *CBS/Fox Video*

Empire of the Dragon 198?
Martial arts
64964   90 mins   C   B, V   P
Chen Tien Tse, Chia Kai, Chang Shan
A rip-roaring martial arts adventure.
Dragon Lady Productions — *Unicorn Video*

Empire on Parade 1983
Trains
74481   55 mins   C   B, V   P
This program traces the history of the Great
Northern Railway.
Wayne Kerslake — *Interurban Films*

Enchanted Island 1958
Drama
72943   94 mins   C   B, V   P
Jane Powell, Dana Andrews
Based upon Herman Melville's "Typee", Dana
Andrews is a whaler who stops on an island to
find provisions and ends up falling in love with a
cannibal princess.
RKO Radio Pictures — *VCI Home Video*

Enchanted Studio, 1907
The/More from the
Enchanted Studio
Film-History
63982   57 mins   B/W   B, V   P, T
A collection of short films produced by Pathe
Freres studios during the early years of this
century. Titles include: "Policeman's Little
Run," "The Dog and His Various Merits," "A
Diabolical Itching," "The Red Spectre," "The
Yawner," "Poor Coat," "Wiffles Wins a Beauty
Prize," "I Fetch the Bread" and "Down in the
Deep." Silent with music score. Some color-
tinted sequences.
Pathe Freres — *Blackhawk Films*

Encounter with Disaster   1979
Disasters
59330   93 mins   C   B, V   P
Using authentic footage from some of the worst
and most frightening events of the century, this
film explores how tragic events unfold—and
how man has prevailed.
MPAA:PG
Charles E Sellier Jr; James Conway — *VCI Home Video*

Encounter with the   1975
Unknown
Adventure
11704   90 mins   C   B, V   P
Narrated by Rod Serling
Relates three fully documented supernatural
events including a death prophesy and a ghost.
Gold Key — *VCI Home Video*

End, The   1978
Comedy
44941   100 mins   C   B, V, CED   P
*Burt Reynolds, Sally Field, Dom DeLuise, Carl
Reiner, Joanne Woodward*
Burt Reynolds plays a young man who finds out
that he is dying from a rare disease. Deciding
not to prolong his suffering, he tries various
tried-and-true methods for committing suicide,
with little success.
MPAA:R
United Artists — *CBS/Fox Video*

End of St. Petersburg,   1927
The
Film-History
49075   75 mins   B/W   B, V   P
Directed by V. I. Pudovkin
A Russian peasant becomes a scab during a
workers' strike in 1914. He is then forced to
enlist in the army prior to the revolution. Silent.
Russian — *Western Film & Video Inc; Sheik
Video*

End of the World   1977
Science fiction
33889   88 mins   C   B, V   P
*Christopher Lee, Sue Lyon, Lew Ayres,
MacDonald Carey*
A coffee machine explodes, sending a man
flying and screaming through a window and into
a neon sign, where he is electrocuted. A
haunted priest witnesses this and retreats to a
convent where he meets his double and heads
for more trouble.
MPAA:PG
Irwin Yablans Company — *Media Home
Entertainment*

Endangered Species   1982
Drama
64570   97 mins   C   B, V, CED   P
*Robert Urich, Jobeth Williams, Paul Dooley,
Hoyt Axton*
A New York cop on vacation in Wyoming
becomes involved in a mysterious series of
cattle killings.
MPAA:R
MGM/UA — *MGM/UA Home Video*

Endless Love   1981
Drama
58495   115 mins   C   B, V, LV   P
*Brooke Shields, Martin Hewitt, Don Murray,
Shirley Knight, Beatrice Straight, Richard Kiley*
Scott Spencer's novel concerning two
teenagers' doomed romance and sexual
obsession.
MPAA:R
Universal; Dyson Lovell — *MCA Home Video;
RCA VideoDiscs*

Endless Night   1972
Mystery
63356   95 mins   C   B, V   R, P
Hayley Mills, Hywel Bennett
This screen adaptation of an Agatha Christie
tale focuses on a young chauffeur who wants to
build a dream house, and his chance meeting
with an heiress.
British Lion — *THORN EMI Home Video*

Endless Summer, The   1966
Documentary/Sports-Water
59928   90 mins   C   B, V, LV,   P
                                CED
Directed by Bruce Brown
Director Bruce Brown follows two young surfers
around the world in their search for the perfect
wave.
Bruce Brown — *Pacific Arts Video*

Enduro International   1984
Motorcycles
72851   60 mins   C   B, V   P
The Enduro International is considered to be the
Olympics of Motorcycling. This race lasts for
over a thousand miles.
C H Wood Production — *Motor Cycle Video*

Enemy of the Law   1945
Western
57985   59 mins   B/W   B, V   P
Tex Ritter, Dave O'Brien
The Texas Rangers battle evil in an old frontier
town.
Producers Releasing Corp — *Video
Connection; Discount Video Tapes*

Enforcer, The   1976
Crime-Drama
58228   97 mins   C   B, V   R, P
*Clint Eastwood, Tyne Daly, Harry Guardino,
Brad Dillman*

Dirty Harry takes on a vicious terrorist group threatening the city of San Francisco.
MPAA:R
Warner Bros — *Warner Home Video; RCA VideoDiscs*

Enigma 1983
Suspense
69545   101 mins   C   B, V   P
Martin Sheen, Brigitte Fossey, Sam Neill
Trapped behind the Iron Curtain, a double agent tries to find the key to five pending murders by locating a Russian coded microprocessor holding information that would unravel the assassination scheme.
MPAA:PG
Filmcrest International Corp — *Embassy Home Entertainment*

Enigma 1983
Drama/Adventure
66043   101 mins   C   B, V, LV, CED   P
Martin Sheen, directed by Jeannot Szwarc
Five assassins from the Soviet's KGB are sent to the West to eliminate five Soviet dissidents.
MPAA:PG
Ben Arbeid; Peter Shaw — *Embassy Home Entertainment*

Ensign Pulver 1964
Comedy
73013   104 mins   C   B, V   P
Robert Walker, Walter Matthau, Burl Ives, directed by Joshua Logan
A continuation of the further adventures of the crew of the U.S.S. Reluctant from "Mister Roberts," which was adapted from the Broadway play.
Joshua Logan; Warner Bros — *Warner Home Video*

Enter the Dragon 1973
Adventure/Martial arts
38946   90 mins   C   B, V, LV   R, P
Bruce Lee, John Saxon, Jim Kelly
Martial arts film starring Bruce Lee, with spectacular fighting sequences featuring karate, judo, tai kwan do, tai chi chuan, and hapkido techniques.
MPAA:R   EL, SP
Warner Bros — *Warner Home Video; RCA VideoDiscs*

Enter the Ninja 1981
Martial arts/Adventure
60593   101 mins   C   B, V, CED   P
Franco Nero, Susan George
The story of the Ninja warrior's lethal, little-known Art of Invisibility.
MPAA:R

Cannon Films Release — *MGM/UA Home Video*

Enter Three Dragons 1981
Martial arts
63408   90 mins   C   B, V   P
Dragon Lee, Bruce Lea, Yang Tsze, Samuel Walls, Chang Li, Bruce Li, Jackie Chin
Kung Fu artistry abounds in this action-adventure film.
MPAA:R
Thomas Tang; Joseph Lai — *Sun Video*

Entertaining Mr. Sloane 1970
Drama
58886   90 mins   C   B, V   R, P
Beryl Reid, Harry Andrews, Peter McEnery, Alan Webb
Playwright Joe Orton's masterpiece of black comedy concerning a handsome criminal who becomes the guest and love interest of a widow and her brother.
Pathe; Canterbury — *THORN EMI Home Video*

Entity, The 1982
Horror
69376   119 mins   C   B, V, CED   P
Barbara Hershey
An unseen entity repeatedly torments a woman both physically and mentally.
MPAA:R
20th Century Fox — *CBS/Fox Video*

Environmental Video 1982
Video
59513   15 mins   C   B, V, 3/4U   P
15   pgms
A collection of nature scenes notable for their beauty. The camera remains stationary, creating a relaxing effect.
1.Rivers 2.Streams 3.Country Roads 4.The Surf 5.Waterfalls 6.Country Barns 7.Hawaii Experience 8.Tropical Fish 9.Fireside Moments 10.Meadows
Environmental Video — *Environmental Video*

Equine Infectious Anemia 19??
Veterinary medicine
69669   14 mins   C   B, V   P
This program looks at the history and current status of EIA and provides suggestions for preventing this incurable virus.
Mercedes Maharis — *Mercedes Maharis Productions*

Equinox 1975
Horror
58555   82 mins   C   B, V   P
Edward Connell, Barbara Hewitt
Two teenagers are menaced by a gigantic mutant ape after discovering a devil-worshipping cult.

MPAA:PG
Tonlyn; Jack Harris — *Wizard Video*

Eraserhead 1977
Film-Avant-garde/Satire
47783 90 mins C B, V P
John Nance, Charlotte Stewart
A cult classic, with special effects that create an eerie, dreamlike world, about a very strange couple and their deformed child.
David Lynch — *RCA/Columbia Pictures Home Video*

Erick Friedman Plays 1982
Fritz Kreisler
Music-Performance
59393 60 mins C B, V P
A recital of music composed by famed violinist Fritz Kreisler and performed by American violinist Erick Friedman and pianist Pavel Ostrosky. Selections include: "Tambourin Chinois," "Caprice Viennois," "The Old Refrain," "Song without Words" and "Schon Rosmarin."
Kultur — *Kultur*

Ernie Kovacs: 198?
Television's Original
Genius
Television/Comedy
66603 86 mins C B, V, LV P
Ernie Kovacs, Edie Adams, Steve Allen, Jack Lemmon, Chevy Chase, hosted by John Barbour
A comedic tribute to one of television's pioneers, humorist Ernie Kovacs. His career is chronicled through clips from his numerous series and specials. Some black-and-white segments.
Simcom — *Vestron Video*

Erotic Three, The 1983
Comedy
72210 90 mins C B, V P
An unusual love triangle is the focus of this film.
Unknown — *Paragon Video Productions*

Eroticise 1983
Physical fitness
64336 60 mins C B, V, CED P
Kitten Natividad
Kitten and her entourage guide the viewer into a sensual exercise workout, designed for adults. In stereo.
Pisanti Productions — *Vestron Video*

Eruption: St. Helens 1980
Explodes
Volcanoes/Documentary
54108 25 mins C B, V P, T
A look at the eruption of Mount St. Helens on May 18, 1980. Station KOIN-TV in Portland,

Oregon shot the blast, showing the volcanic peak being torn away. They almost lost a $70,000 remote broadcast truck while shooting.
KOIN Portland — *Blackhawk Films*

Escape from Alcatraz 1979
Drama
44752 112 mins C B, V, LV R, P
Clint Eastwood, Patrick McGoohan, directed by Don Siegel
A fascinating account of the one and only successful escape from the maximum security prison at Alcatraz by three men who were never heard from again.
MPAA:PG
Paramount, Don Siegel — *Paramount Home Video; RCA VideoDiscs*

Escape from Death Row 1976
Adventure
60405 85 mins C B, V P
Lee Van Cleef, James Lane, Barbara Moore, Alice Belios
A convicted criminal mastermind, sentenced to die, devises a brilliant and daring plan of escape on the eve of his execution.
MPAA:R
Aquarius Releasing — *Paragon Video Productions; Electric Video*

Escape from New York 1981
Science fiction/Adventure
65193 99 mins C B, V, LV P
Kurt Russell, Lee Van Cleef, Isaac Hayes, Adrienne Barbeau, Season Hubley, directed by John Carpenter
In 1997, the island of Manhattan has been turned into a maximum security prison inhabited by millions of felons. When the President's plane crashes there, a convicted criminal is sent in to save him.
MPAA:R EL, JA
Avco Embassy — *Embassy Home Entertainment; RCA VideoDiscs*

Escape to Athena 1979
Adventure
57460 102 mins C CED P
Roger Moore, Telly Savalas, David Niven
A group of losers are in a German POW camp on a Greek island digging up Greek art treasures. When they manage to escape, the rumors abound.
MPAA:PG
Associated Film Distributors — *CBS/Fox Video*

Escape to the Sun 1972
Adventure/Suspense
66633 94 mins C B, V P
Laurence Harvey, Josephine Chaplin, John Ireland, Jack Hawkins

---

(For Explanation of codes, see USE GUIDE and KEY)

A pair of Russian university students plan to flee their homeland so they can be allowed to live and love free from oppression.
MPAA:PG
Transamerican Productions — *Monterey Home Video*

Escape to Witch Mountain   1975
Fantasy
29745   97 mins   C   B, V, LV   R, P
Kim Richards, Ike Eisenmann, Eddie Albert, Ray Milland
Two young orphans with supernatural powers find themselves on the run from a greedy millionaire who wants to exploit their amazing powers for his own gains.
MPAA:G
Walt Disney, Jerome Coutland — *Walt Disney Home Video; RCA VideoDiscs*

Escape 2000   1983
Science fiction
69541   80 mins   C   B, V   P
Steve Railsback, Olivia Hussey, Michael Craig
In a future society where individuality is considered a crime, those who refuse to conform are punished by being hunted down in a jungle.
MPAA:R
Unknown — *Embassy Home Entertainment*

Esposa y Amante   197?
Drama
49744   95 mins   C   B, V   P
Ramiro Oliveros, Ricardo Merino, Victoria Abril, Frika Wallner
While her daughter contemplates suicide, a mother remembers the happy early years of her marriage, followed by the wrongdoings of her husband which caused her to seek comfort in the arms of an old lawyer friend. Her daughter is now suffering for the problems of her marriage. In Spanish.
SP
Independent — *Media Home Entertainment*

Essential Care: First Aid for Horses   1983
Veterinary medicine
69656   25 mins   C   B, V   P
This program teaches basic first aid procedures for horses.
Mercedes Maharis — *Mercedes Maharis Productions*

Eternally Yours   1939
Comedy
00395   95 mins   B/W   B, V   P
David Niven, Loretta Young, Hugh Herbert, Broderick Crawford
Witty magician's career threatens to break up his marriage.

United Artists; Tay Garnett — *Budget Video; Cable Films; Movie Buff Video; Classic Video Cinema Collector's Club*

Etiquette/Entertaining   1980
Etiquette
44281   22 mins   C   V   P
Narrated by Lynn Rogers
This program covers accepted party etiquette and general good manners normally practiced in this country. Lynn Rogers, actress, narrates the various situations while viewers watch the proper procedures performed on screen. Covered are dinner or party invitations, introductions, table and general etiquette.
American Home Video Library — *American Home Video Library*

Eubie!   1982
Musical
59387   100 mins   C   CED   P
Gregory Hines, Maurice Hines, Leslie Dockery, Alaina Reed, Lynnie Godfrey, Mel Johnson Jr., Jeffrey V. Thompson
The popular Broadway musical revue based on the life and songs of Eubie Blake is presented in a video transfer. Some of Eubie's best known songs, performed here by members of the original cast, include "I'm Just Wild About Harry," "Memories of You," "In Honeysuckle Time" and "The Charleston Rag." In stereo.
American Video Productions — *RCA VideoDiscs*

Eubie!   1981
Musical
74203   85 mins   C   B, V   R, P
Gregory Hines, Maurice Hines
This musical feature about the life of composer Eubie Blake is adopted from the Broadway play of the same name and includes almost all the original cast.
Warner Brothers — *Warner Home Video*

European Operations   194?
World War II
53656   25 mins   B/W   B, V, 3/4U   P
A U.S. government film showing the famous Seabees at war.
Unknown — *International Historic Films*

Europeans, The   1979
Drama
56935   90 mins   C   B, V   P
Lee Remick, Lisa Eichorn, directed by James Ivory
Henry James' satirical novel about two fortune-seeking expatriates and their sober American relations.
MPAA:G
Ismail Merchant — *Vestron Video*

Eurythmics—Sweet Dreams (The Video Album)   1983
Music-Performance
66347   50 mins   C   B, V   P
Directed by Derek Burbidge
Eurythmics' David Stewart and Annie Lennox perform their hits "Sweet Dreams (Are Made of This)" and "Love Is a Stranger" plus twelve other songs in a combination of live concert performances and music videos. In stereo VHS and Beta Hi-Fi.
Jon Roseman — *RCA/Columbia Pictures Home Video; RCA VideoDiscs; Pioneer Artists*

Eve, The   1980
Music-Performance
59872   60 mins   C   LV   P
The Inner Galaxy Orchestra, a contemporary ensemble led by Bingo Miki of the Japanese jazz scene, performs "The Eve," an incredible trip through his audiovisual fantasies. In stereo.
Yutaka Shigenobu — *Pioneer Video Imports*

Evel Knievel   1971
Drama/Biographical
75694   90 mins   C   B, V   P
George Hamilton, Bert Freed, Rod Cameron
The life of stuntman Evel Knievel is depicted in this movie, as portrayed by George Hamilton.
MPAA:PG
Fanfare — *MPI Home Video*

Evening with Liza Minnelli, An   1981
Music-Performance
59626   50 mins   C   B, V   P
Liza Minnelli
Liza is seen performing everything from blues to ballads at this concert recorded at the New Orleans Theater of the Performing Arts. Songs include "Cabaret" and "New York, New York."
Artel Home Video — *CBS/Fox Video*

Evening with Quentin Crisp, An   1981
Biographical/Theater
58582   90 mins   C   B, V   P
Introduction by John Hurt
Taped during performances of Crisp's one-man show during his first theatrical tour of the U.S., this program presents the "gospel according to Crisp," and features Crisp fielding questions from the audience.
Hillard Elkins — *Family Home Entertainment*

Evening with Ray Charles, An   1981
Music-Performance
58807   40 mins   C   B, V   P
Ray Charles
The living legend, Ray Charles, performs live at the Jubilee Auditorium in Edmonton, Canada, showcasing his many musical moods. Songs include: "Riding Thumb," "Busted," "Georgia on My Mind," "Oh What a Beautiful Morning," "Some Enchanted Evening," "Hit the Road Jack," "I Can't Stop loving You," "Take These Chains from My Heart," "I Can See Clearly Now," "What'd I Say," and "America the Beautiful."
Allarco Prods Ltd; Optical Programming Associates — *MCA Home Video; Optical Programming Associates*

Evening with Robin Williams, An   1983
Comedy-Performance
64501   92 mins   C   B, V   R, P
Robin Williams
Robin Williams explodes all over the screen in this live nightclub performance taped at the Great American Music Hall in San Francisco.
Don Mischer — *Paramount Home Video; RCA VideoDiscs*

Evening with Sir William Martin, An   1981
Comedy
49676   30 mins   C   B, V   P
Bill Martin, Michael Nesmith
A "Mr. Toad" encounters his senile father, who is later transported to another planet. Then a moose hands him a cigarette which instantly transports him to Antarctica. This program probably has to be seen to be believed.
Pacific Arts Video Records — *Pacific Arts Video*

Evening with Sister Sledge, An   1984
Music-Performance
72194   55 mins   C   B, V   R, P
The four sisters perform their hits on the stage of the Roxy nightclub and do impressions of some popular singers.
Unknown — *VCII*

Evening with the Royal Ballet, An   197?
Dance
56886   100 mins   C   CED   P
Rudolf Nureyev, Margot Fonteyn
Performances of "La Valse," "Les Sylphides," "Le Corsaire," "Aurora's Wedding," and the last act of "The Sleeping Beauty."
RCA — *RCA VideoDiscs*

Evening with Utopia, An   1983
Music-Performance
60587   85 mins   C   B, V   P
Directed by Joshua White

Utopia, the popular rock group and brainchild of Todd Rundgren, in concert. The 21 songs include "Feet Don't Fail Me Now" and others from the LP "Utopia." Stereo.
Neo Utopian Laboratories Ltd — *MCA Home Video*

Everest in Winter　　　1982
Mountaineering
69911　55 mins　C　　B, V　　　　P
This program records the 1980-81 attempt by eight British mountaineers on Everest via the West Ridge in winter.
Chameleon Films — *Gravity Sports Films*

Everest the Hard Way　　　1978
Mountaineering
69909　75 mins　C　　B, V　　　　P
This program tells the story of the first ascent of the Southwest Face of Everest by a British expedition led by Chris Bonnington in 1975.
Chameleon Films — *Gravity Sports Films*

Evergreen　　　1934
Musical
33506　90 mins　B/W　　B, V, FO　　　P
Jessie Matthews, Sonnie Hale, Betty Balfour, Barry Mackey
The daughter of a retired British music hall star is mistaken for her mother and it is thought that she has discovered the secret of eternal youth.
Gaumont British — *Video Yesteryear; Cable Films; Sheik Video; Western Film & Video Inc; Video Dimensions; Classic Video Cinema Collector's Club*

Everly Brothers Reunion Concert　　　1983
Music-Performance
65658　60 mins　C　　B, V　　　　P
After years of bitter separation and crises, the undisputed NO. 1 duo of the golden age of rock 'n' roll join together at London's Royal Albert Hall and perform such megahits as "Bye Bye Love," "Wake Up Little Susie," "All I Have To Do Is Dream," and "Cathy's Clown."
Delilah Films Inc; The Everly Brothers — *MGM/UA Home Video*

Every Man for Himself and God Against All　　　1975
Drama
69621　110 mins　C　　B, V　　　　P
Bruno S., directed by Werner Herzog
This film tells the story of Kaspar Hauser, a young man who mysteriously appears in a small German town, hardly able to speak, write or even function in the world of 1828. In German with English subtitles.
Cannes Film Festival: Grand Special Jury Prize.
Werner Herzog; Almi — *RCA/Columbia Pictures Home Video*

Every Man's Law　　　1935
Western
54170　60 mins　B/W　　B, V　　　　P
Johnny Mack Brown
A cowboy who poses as a hired gunman is almost lynched by ranchers who think he is a murderer.
Supreme — *Video Connection*

Every Which Way But Loose　　　1978
Comedy/Adventure
54119　119 mins　C　　B, V　　　　R, P
Clint Eastwood, Sondra Locke, Geoffrey Lewis, Beverly D'Angelo, Ruth Gordon, directed by James Fargo
A beer guzzling, country music-loving truck driver earns a living as a barroom brawler. He and his orangutan travel to Colorado in pursuit of a woman he loves. Behind him are a motorcycle gang and an L.A. cop. All have been victims of his fists.
MPAA:R
Warner Bros — *Warner Home Video; RCA VideoDiscs*

Everyday with Richard Simmons: Family Fitness　　　1983
Physical fitness
60558　90 mins　C　　B, V　　　　P
This exercise regimen includes a 15-minute warm-up, an hour long exercise session, and emphasis on toning the face, stomach, legs, and thighs.
Karl Video Corp — *Karl Video*

Everything is Rhythm　　　1936
Musical
08736　75 mins　B/W　　B, V, 3/4U　　　P
Harry Roy and his Band
Story of an orchestra leader trying to make the big time.
Eros Films; Assoc British Pathe Ltd — *Penguin Video*

Everything You Always Wanted to Know About Sex But (Were Afraid to Ask)　　　1972
Comedy
44942　88 mins　C　　B, V　　　　P
Woody Allen, John Carradine, Lou Jacobi, Louise Lasser, Anthony Quayle, Lynn Redgrave, Tony Randall, Burt Reynolds, Gene Wilder, directed by Woody Allen
A series of comical sketches involving sex, such as a timid sperm cell, an oversexed court jester, and a giant disembodied breast.
MPAA:R
United Artists — *CBS/Fox Video; RCA VideoDiscs*

Evictors, The 1979
Horror
65218   92 mins   C   B, V   P
Vic Morrow, Michael Parks, Jessica Harper
Three innocent victims are caught up in the
horror surrounding an abandoned farmhouse in
a small Louisiana town.
MPAA:PG
Charles B Pierce — *Vestron Video*

Evil Dead, The 1979
Horror
69674   126 mins   C   B, V   R, P
Five vacationing college students unwittingly
resurrect demons which transform the students
into monsters.
New Line Cinema — *THORN EMI Home Video*

Evil Mind, The 1935
Drama
08760   81 mins   B/W   B, V, 3/4U   P
Claude Rains, Fay Wray, Jane Baxter
Fraudulent mindreader predicts many disasters
that start coming true.
British — *Penguin Video; VCII; Video
Yesteryear; Cable Films; Video Connection*

Evil Under the Sun 1981
Mystery
63332   102 mins   C   B, V, CED   R, P
*Peter Ustinov, Jane Birkin, Maggie Smith, Colin
Blakely, Roddy McDowall, Diana Rigg, Sylvia
Miles, James Mason*
An opulent beach resort is the setting as
Hercules Poirot attempts to unravel a murder
mystery. Based on the Agatha Christie novel.
MPAA:PG
Universal — *THORN EMI Home Video*

Evilspeak 1982
Horror
50620   80 mins   C   B, V, CED   P
*Clint Howard, Don Stark, Lou Gravance, Lauren
Lester*
A bumbling misfit enrolled at a military school is
mistreated by the other cadets. He retaliates
with satanic power.
MPAA:R
Leisure Investments — *CBS/Fox Video*

Evolutionary Spiral 1983
Music-Performance/Video
76668   45 mins   C   B, V   P
A combination of visual imagery and a musical
soundtrack by the group Weather Report.
Earth Sky and Open Sky Productions — *Sony
Corporation of America*

Ex-Mrs. Bradford, The 1936
Mystery/Comedy
44854   80 mins   B/W   B, V, 3/4U   P
*William Powell, Jean Arthur, James Gleason,
Eric Blore, Robert Armstrong, directed by
Stephen Roberts*
Amateur sleuth Dr. Bradford teams up with his
ex-wife Jean Arthur to solve the race track
murders. Sophisticated comedy-mystery.
RKO — *Nostalgia Merchant*

Excalibur 1981
Fantasy
58229   140 mins   C   B, V   R, P
*Nicol Williamson, Nigel Terry, Helen Mirren,
directed by John Boorman*
An elegant version of the King Arthur legend
focusing on the rise of Christian civilization out
of the magic, murder, and chaos of the Dark
Ages.
MPAA:R
Orion Pictures — *Warner Home Video; RCA
VideoDiscs*

Executive Action 1973
Drama
44753   90 mins   C   B, V   R, P
*Burt Lancaster, Robert Ryan, Will Geer, Gilbert
Green, John Anderson, directed by David Miller*
A recreation of the events that led up to the
assassination of JFK. A millionaire pays a
professional spy to organize a secret
conspiracy; their mission—kill President
Kennedy.
MPAA:PG
National General — *Warner Home Video*

Exercise 1983
Physical fitness
60412   60 mins   C   B, V   P
An adults-only erotic exercise program.
Appaloosa Productions — *Monterey Home
Video*

Exercise at Home 1980
Physical fitness
44291   24 mins   C   V   P
This program gives both men and women of all
ages a valuable home exercise program to
improve muscle tone, increase muscular
strength, increase heart efficiency, and increase
endurance. All that is required to improve ones
health and mental contentment is to do 10
exercises for only 14 minutes each day.
American Home Video Library — *American
Home Video Library*

Exercise Now! 1981
Physical fitness
52766   50 mins   C   B, V   P
An intensive, two-part aerobic exercise program
set to popular music and led by professional
exercise instructors, complete with a poster
detailing each exercise.
AM Available

Karl Video — *Karl Video*

Exercises for Travel　1984
Animals/Horse racing
74541　23 mins　C　B, V　　P
This tape reviews some secrets to keeping a
horse relaxed during long trips.
Equestrian Video Library — *Mercedes Maharis
Productions*

Exit the Dragon, Enter the Tiger　1976
Adventure/Martial arts
37361　84 mins　C　B, V　　P
"Exit the Dragon, Enter the Tiger" is a motion
picture about the death of karate specialist
Bruce Lee.
Dimension — *VCI Home Video*

Exodus　1960
Drama
37523　207 mins　C　B, V　　P
*Paul Newman, Eva Marie Saint, Lee J. Cobb,
Sal Mineo, Ralph Richardson, Peter Lawford, Jill
Haworth, John Derek, directed by Otto
Preminger*
Based on the novel by Leon Uris and filmed in
Cyprus and Israel, this is the story of an Israeli
underground leader who leads a group of
Jewish refugees into Israel, and an American
nurse who becomes involved with the
movement.
Academy Award '60: Best Music Score.
United Artists, Otto Preminger — *CBS/Fox
Video*

Exorcist, The　1973
Suspense
38944　120 mins　C　B, V; LV　　R, P
*Ellen Burstyn, Linda Blair, Jason Miller, Max Von
Sydow, directed by William Friedkin*
A harrowing film based on William Peter Blatty's
novel of a young girl who is possessed by a
demon, raising havoc with her family and the
priests who attempt to exorcise her.
MPAA:R　EL, SP
Warner Bros — *Warner Home Video; RCA
VideoDiscs*

Exorcist II: The Heretic　1977
Horror
44804　118 mins　C　B, V　　R, P
*Richard Burton, Linda Blair, Louise Fletcher,
Kitty Winn, James Earl Jones, Ned Beatty*
A sequel to the 1973 hit "The Exorcist." After
four years Blair is still under psychiatric care,
suffering from the effects of being possessed by
the devil.
MPAA:R
Warner Bros — *Warner Home Video*

Expansion of Life, The　1982
Biology/Science
59560　58 mins　C　B, V　　P
This program deals with the fundamentals of
cell division, invertebrates and fish life in the
early seas, amphibians and reptiles, and the
emergence of man.
McGraw Hill — *Mastervision*

Experience Preferred...　1982
But Not Essential
Comedy
75539　77 mins　C　B, V　　P
Produced by David Puttnam
An English schoolgirl gets her first job at a resort
where she learns about life.
MPAA:PG
Samuel Montagu & Co Ltd — *MGM/UA Home
Video*

Experimental Avant-　19??
Garde Video Special
Video/Film-Avant-garde
58517　120 mins　B/W　B, V, 3/4U　　P
A potpourri of avant-garde film: "Ballet
Mechanique," "Breath Death," "Ghosts Before
Breakfast," "L'Etoile de Mer," "Life and Death
of a Hollywood Extra," "An Occurrence at Owl
Creek Bridge," "Regen (Rain)," "Un Chien
Andalou."
Unknown — *Penguin Video*

Experimental Program　19'3
#1
Film-Avant-garde
48852　47 mins　B/W　B, V, 3/4U　　P
A collection of three short French subjects: "Un
Chien Andalou," a surrealistic work by
Salvadore Dali; "Entr'acte," essentially a chase
scene by Rene Clair; and "A Propos de Nice," a
satirical documentary on the millionaire's
paradise of the French Riviera.
French — *Western Film & Video Inc*

Experimental Program　195?
#2
Film-Avant-garde
48853　58 mins　B/W　B, V, 3/4U　　P
A collection of two short stories. "An
Occurrence at Owl Creek Bridge" and "La
Jetee."
Unknown — *Western Film & Video Inc*

Expertos en Pinchazos　1979
Comedy
47855　100 mins　C　B, V　　P
Porcel and Olmedo
Albert and George, experts at giving injections
to women, inject a patient with venom by
mistake. Now they must find her within 48 hours.
In Spanish.
SP

Luis Osvaldo Repetto; Nicolas
Carreras — *Media Home Entertainment*

Exposed 1983
Suspense
66450   100 mins   C   B, V, CED   P
*Nastassia Kinski, Rudolph Nureyev, Harvey
Keitel, directed by James Toback*
A high fashion model falls in with a terrorist
gang, while at the same time, a group of anti-
terrorists want to use her for their purposes.
MPAA:R
United Artists — *MGM/UA Home Video*

Exterminator, The 1980
Suspense
63369   101 mins   C   B, V, CED   P
Christopher George, Samantha Eggar
A man seeks vengeance and becomes the
target of the police, the CIA and the underworld
in this tale of murder and intrigue.
MPAA:R
Avco Embassy; Interstar
Productions — *Embassy Home Entertainment*

Extra Girl, The 1923
Comedy
64243   69 mins   B/W   B, V   P
Mabel Normand, Max Davidson, Ralph Graves
A small town girl wins a beauty contest and a
trip to Hollywood where stardom waits. Silent
with musical score.
Mack Sennett — *Classic Video Cinema
Collector's Club*

Eye for an Eye, An 1981
Adventure
60346   106 mins   C   B, V, CED   P
*Chuck Norris, Christopher Lee, Richard
Roundtree, Matt Clark*
A story of pursuit and revenge with Chuck Norris
as an undercover cop pitted against San
Francisco's underworld and high society.
MPAA:R EL, JA
Avco Embassy — *Embassy Home
Entertainment*

Eye Hears, the Ear Sees, 1970
The
Filmmaking
36349   59 mins   C   B, V, FO   P
Norman McLaren
This introduction to Norman McLaren and his
work shows how he has created many
innovative films which have become classic
examples of film art. McLaren discusses and
demonstrates some of his techniques, and
excerpts from his films are shown.
BBC — *Video Yesteryear*

Eye of the 196?
Dragon/Vietnamese Junk
Navy
Vietnam War
53693   40 mins   C   B, V, 3/4U   P
The story of American naval advisors working
with Vietnamese junk forces. "Eye of the
Dragon" runs 30 minutes, "Vietnamese Junk
Navy" runs 10 minutes, black and white.
Unknown — *International Historic Films*

Eye of the Needle 1981
Suspense
58848   118 mins   C   B, V   P
*Donald Sutherland, Kate Nelligan, directed by
Richard Marquand*
Ken Follett's novel about a German spy posing
as a shipwrecked sailor on a deserted English
island during World War II.
MPAA:R
United Artists — *CBS/Fox Video*

Eyes of a Stranger 1980
Horror
58230   82 mins   C   B, V   R, P
*Lauren Tewes, John Disanti, Jennifer Jason
Leigh, directed by Ken Wiederhorn*
A terrifying maniac stalks his female prey by
watching their every move.
MPAA:R
Georgetown Productions — *Warner Home
Video*

Eyes of Laura Mars 1978
Mystery
Closed Captioned
35377   104 mins   C   B, V   P
Faye Dunaway, Tommy Lee Jones
A photographer (Dunaway) exhibits strange
powers—she can foresee a murder before it
happens. Title song performed by Barbra
Streisand.
MPAA:H
Columbia — *RCA/Columbia Pictures Home
Video; RCA VideoDiscs*

Eyes of Texas 1948
Western
14374   54 mins   B/W   B, V   P
Roy Rogers, Lynne Roberts, Andy Devine
Westerner turns his ranch into a camp for war-
orphaned boys.
Republic — *Video Connection; Sheik Video*

Eyes Right 1926
Comedy-Drama
11387   65 mins   B/W   B, V, FO   P
Francis X. Bushman
An interesting portrayal of life in a military prep
school. (Silent.)
Goodwill — *Video Yesteryear*

Eyewitness 1981
Suspense
47154   102 mins   C   B, V, CED   P
William Hurt, Sigourney Weaver, Christopher Plummer, James Woods, Steven Hill, directed by Peter Yates
The janitor of an office building tells a TV reporter that he knows something about a murder that took place in his building.
MPAA:R
20th Century Fox; Peter Yates — *CBS/Fox Video*

F

Fables of the Green Forest 19??
Cartoons/Adventure
56750   40 mins   C   B, V   P
Animated
Johnny Chuck, Peter Cottontail, Chatter the Squirrel and other memorable Thorton W. Burgess characters come to life in "Whose Footprint Is That?" and "Johnny's Hibernation." Available in English and Spanish versions.
EL, SP
ZIV International — *Media Home Entertainment*

Fabulous Dorseys, The 1947
Musical/Drama
01609   91 mins   B/W   B, V   P
Tommy and Jimmy Dorsey and Orchestras, Janet Blair, Paul Whiteman, Directed by Alfred E. Green
The musical lives of Tommy and Jimmy Dorsey are portrayed in this biographical film. Guest stars include Art Tatum, Charlie Barnet, Ziggy Elman, Bob Eberly and Helen O'Connell.
UA; Charles R Rogers — *Budget Video; NTA Home Entertainment; Video Connection; Video Yesteryear; Discount Video Tapes; Nostalgia Merchant*

Fabulous Fifties, The 19??
History-US/Documentary
10150   mins   B/W   B, V   P, T
Film covers MacArthur's "Old Soldier's Speech," Eisenhower and Nixon, Korea, Stalin's death, hydrogen bomb testing, Suez Canal crisis, the Cold War, and Castro.
Unknown — *Blackhawk Films*

Fabulous Fred Astaire, The 1958
Variety
38119   70 mins   B/W   B, V, FO   P
Fred Astaire, Barrie Chase
Contains Fred Astaire's 1958 Emmy Award winning special, "An Evening With Fred Astaire," plus a "Person-to-Person" interview by Edward R. Murrow with Astaire.
NBC — *Video Yesteryear*

Fabulous Funnies 1978
Cartoons
75493   60 mins   C   B, V   P
The cartoons in this video include Alley Oop, Broomhilda, Nancy and Sluggo and Tumbleweeds.
Unknown — *Prism*

Fabulous Joe, The 1974
Comedy
66113   54 mins   C   B, V   P
Walter Abel
A dog named Joe gets involved in a necklace caper.
Hal Roach — *Unicorn Video*

Face of War, A 1967
Armed Forces-US/Vietnam War
72487   77 mins   B/W   B, V, 3/4U   P
Produced and directed by Eugene S. Jones
A remarkable film made by four men who traveled with the spearhead squad of a leading platoon; the producer-director was wounded twice and his cameraman once, while more than half the company they traveled with for 97 days, the record time for a crew to travel in a spearhead squad, were killed or wounded.
US Government — *International Historic Films*

Faces of Death 1974
Death/Documentary
65154   88 mins   C   B, V   P
Narrated by Dr. Frances B. Gross
A gruesome documentary look at death experiences around the world. Uncensored film footage offers graphic coverage of close-up autopsies, suicides, executions and animal slaughter. Not for the squeamish.
Rosilyn T Scott — *Gorgon Video*

Fade to Black 1980
Horror/Suspense
63894   100 mins   C   B, V   P
Dennis Christopher, Tim Thomerson, Linda Kerridge
A young man obsessed with movies loses his grip on reality and adopts the personalities of cinematic characters to seek revenge on people who have wronged him.
MPAA:R
Irwin Yablans; Sylvio Tabet — *Media Home Entertainment*

Faerie Tale Theatre 1983
Fairy tales
Closed Captioned
69320   60 mins   C   B, V, LV, CED   P

Shelley Duvall, Robin Williams, Elliot Gould, Jeff Bridges, Christopher Reeve, Tatum O'Neal et al
17   pgms
"Faerie Tale Theatre," conceived and produced by Shelley Duvall, is a series of hour-long enactments of classic fairy tales featuring many well-known actors and actresses. All programs are available individually.
1.The Tale of the Frog Prince 2.Jack and the Beanstalk 3.Rapunzel 4. Sleeping Beauty 5.Goldilocks and the Three Bears 6.Little Red Riding Hood 7.Hansel and Gretal 8.Rumpelstiltskin 9.Boy Who Left Home to Find Out About the Shivers 10.Pinocchio 11.The Snow Queen 12.The Three Little Pigs 13.The Emperor's New Clothes 14.The Pied Piper of Hamelin 15.Puss 'N Boots 16.Cinderella 17.The Little Mermaid
Shelley Duvall — *CBS/Fox Video*

Fail Safe 1964
Drama
Closed Captioned
63440   111 mins   B/W   B, V   P
Henry Fonda, Dan O'Herlihy, Walter Matthau, directed by Sidney Lumet
A computer malfunction sets off events that may possibly result in a nuclear war.
Columbia; Max E. Youngstein — *RCA/Columbia Pictures Home Video*

Fairy Tale Classics 1983
Fairy tales
69533   50 mins   C   B, V, CED   P
Animated
This is a compilation of five of the world's best-loved fairy tales: "Cinderella," "The Ugly Duckling," "The Red Shoes," "Ali Baba and the Forty Thieves" and "The Bremen Band."
MPAA:G
Toei Animation Productions — *Children's Video Library*

Fairy Tale Classics: 19??
Volume II
Fairy tales
69612   60 mins   C   B, V   P
Animated
This collection of animated fairy tales includes "The Owl and the Pussycat," "The Three Bears," Aesop's fable of "The Tiger King," "Beanstalk Jack," and more.
Viacom International — *Children's Video Library*

Fairy Tales, Volume Two 1977
Fairy tales/Cartoons
73664   55 mins   C   B, V   P
Animated
Five animated versions of fairy tale classics are available in one program: "Snow White," "The Emperor's New Clothes," "The Twelve

Months," "The Happy Prince" and "The Three Wishes."
Unknown — *Embassy Home Entertainment*

Fairy Tales, Volume I 1977
Cartoons
72868   55 mins   C   B, V   P
Some of the world's best fairy tales come to life, including "Cinderella" and "Beauty and the Beast."
Unkown — *Embassy Home Entertainment*

Fairytales 1979
Satire
55218   83 mins   C   B, V   P
Don Sparks, Prof. Irwin Corey, Brenda Fogarty
An enchanting musical fantasy for adults. In order to save the kingdom, the prince must produce an heir. The problem is that only the girl in the painting of "Princess Beauty" can "interest" the prince—and she must be found.
MPAA:R
Fairytales Distributing Company — *Media Home Entertainment*

Falcon in Mexico, The 1944
Mystery
64381   70 mins   B/W   B, V, 3/4U   P
Tom Conway, Mona Maris, Nestor Paiva
The manhunt for a dangerous killer leads the Falcon to Mexico.
RKO — *Nostalgia Merchant*

Falcon's Brother, The 1942
Mystery
11299   64 mins   B/W   B, V, FO   P
Tom Conway, George Sanders, Keye Luke, Jane Randolph
Enemy agents intent on killing a South American diplomat are the targets of the Falcon's brother.
RKO — *Nostalgia Merchant*

Fall of Berlin, The 1945
World War II
53708   72 mins   B/W   B, V, 3/4U   P
Over forty Byelorussian and 1st Army cameramen contributed footage for this documentary on the fall of Berlin. English commentary.
USSR — *International Historic Films*

Fall of the House of 1960
Usher, The
Horror
53511   85 mins   C   B, V   R, P
Vincent Price, Myrna Fahey, Mark Damon, directed by Roger Corman
The last of the Usher line is buried alive by her brother and returns to wreak vengeance. Also titled "House of Usher." Based on the story by Edgar Allen Poe.

American Intl; Roger Corman — *Warner Home Video*

Fall of the House of Usher, The — 1979
Drama
37362　101 mins　C　B, V　　P
Martin Landau, Robert Hays, Charlene Tilton, Ray Walston
Another version of Edgar Allan Poe's classic tale of a family doomed to destruction through insanity.
MPAA:PG
Sunn Classic — *VCI Home Video; Classic Video Cinema Collector's Club*

Fall of the Roman Empire, The — 1964
Drama
16810　153 mins　C　B, V　　P
Sophia Loren, Alec Guiness
The licentious son of Marcus Aurelius arranges for his father's murder and takes over as emperor.
Paramount; Samuel Bronston — *VCI Home Video*

Fallen Idol — 1949
Drama
03858　92 mins　B/W　B, V　　P
Sir Ralph Richardson, Bobby Henrey, Michele Morgan, directed by Carol Reed
A young boy wrongly believes that a man he idolizes is guilty of murder, so the child tries to influence the police investigation of the crime. Screenplay by Graham Greene from his short story, "The Basement Room."
Selznick; British — *Budget Video; Cable Films; Western Film & Video Inc; Movie Buff Video; Classic Video Cinema Collector's Club*

Falling in Love Again — 1980
Comedy/Romance
64966　103 mins　C　B, V, CED　　P
Elliot Gould, Susannah York
A middle-aged dreamer and his realistic wife travel from Los Angeles to their hometown of New York, where the man is filled with nostalgia for his youth.
MPAA:PG
Steven Paul — *Embassy Home Entertainment*

Falstaff — 1983
Opera
72446　140 mins　C　LV　　P
Shakespeare's Falstaff is brought to life in this operatic version of the rogue's exploits.
BBC Television; Covert Garden Video Productions Ltd — *Pioneer Video Imports*

Fame — 1980
Musical-Drama
56751　133 mins　C　B, V, LV, CED　　P
Irene Cara, Barry Miller, Paul McCrane, Anne Meara, Joanna Merlin, directed by Alan Parker
Eight talented teenagers from New York's High School of Performing Arts struggle to perfect their skills while aspiring to stardom.
Academy Awards '80: Best Song ("Fame"); Best Original Score (Michael Gore).　MPAA:R
MGM — *MGM/UA Home Video*

Fame Is the Spur — 1947
Drama
66374　116 mins　B/W　B, V　　P
Michael Redgrave, Rosamund John, Bernard Miles, directed by Roy Boulting
The story of Hamer Radshaw, British politician and socialist, from his youth to his days as an elder statesman.
Two Cities — *Movie Buff Video*

Family, The — 1973
Crime-Drama
72059　94 mins　C　B, V　　P
Charles Bronson, Jill Ireland, Telly Savalas, directed by Sergio Sollima
As a hit-man who resists joining the mob, Charles Bronson initiates an all-out war on the syndicate and its boss, played by Telly Savalas.
International Corp; Unidis and Fono Roma — *MPI Home Video*

Family Circus Christmas, A — 1979
Cartoons/Christmas
75468　30 mins　C　B, V　　P
Animated
Cartoonist Bil Keane animates the Family Circus at Christmas time.
Cullen Kasden Productions Ltd — *Family Home Entertainment*

Family Circus Easter, A — 1980
Cartoons/Holidays
75470　30 mins　C　B, V　　P
Animated
Cartoonist Bil Keane animates an Easter with the Family Circus.
Cullen Kasden Productions Ltd — *Family Home Entertainment*

Family Entertainment Playhouse, Vol. 2 — 1979
Literature
59644　106 mins　C　CED　　P
A compilation of stories for children: "The Ransom of Red Chief," based on O. Henry's famed short story about a banker's son who is kidnapped by bumbling conmen; "Mr. Gimme," about a boy who wants everything; "Shoeshine Girl," where a young girl finds that a first job is

more than hard work; "Best Horse," about a strong-willed teenager determined to win a horse race.
Robert McDonald — *RCA VideoDiscs*

Family Life 1972
Drama
59382 108 mins C B, V P
Sandy Ratcliff, Bill Dean, Grace Cave, directed by Ken Loach
A portrait of a 19-year-old girl in the midst of an identity crisis (Also titled, "Wednesday's Child).
Cinema Five — *RCA/Columbia Pictures Home Video*

Family Plot 1976
Suspense
11579 120 mins C B, V P
Karen Black, Bruce Dern, Barbara Harris, William Devane, directed by Alfred Hitchcock
Alfred Hitchcock's last film; the search for a missing heir is undertaken by a phony psychic and her private eye boyfriend. Their search ends when they discover that the heir is dead—or is he?
MPAA:PG
Universal — *MCA Home Video*

Famous Photographer Series Volume I, The 1981
Photography
47754 60 mins C B, V P
Photographer of nudes, David Chan, is shown at work.
Sherwood Video — *Sherwood Video Production Company*

Famous Photographer Series Volume II: Robert Farber 1982
Photography
47810 60 mins C B, V P
Top New York fashion/fine art photographer Robert Farber's work has appeared in Vogue, Esquire and Playboy. This program takes the viewer behind the scenes to watch fashion, beauty, and nude shootings as Farber explains the art and business of fashion photography (some black-and-white).
AM Available
Sherwood Video — *Sherwood Video Production Company*

Famous T and A 1982
Variety
59765 70 mins C B, V P
Ursula Andress, Brigitte Bardot, Jacqueline Bisset, Sybil Danning, Claudia Jennings, Nastassia Kinski, Joan Prather, Laurie Walters, Edy Williams
An all-star collection of recognizable personalities who have displayed their celebrity skins for the camera.

Ken Dixon — *Wizard Video*

Fan, The 1981
Suspense
53931 95 mins C B, V, LV R, P
Lauren Bacall, Maureen Stapleton, James Garner, Hector Elizondo, directed by Edward Bianchi
A Broadway star is threatened by a lovestruck fan who feels he has been rejected by his idol.
MPAA:R
Robert Stigwood — *Paramount Home Video*

Fangface 1983
Cartoons
66573 60 mins C B, V P
Animated
The adventures of Fangface, the teenage werewolf, and his crime-fighting friends Biff, Kim and Puggsy are featured on this tape.
Ruby Spears — *Worldvision Home Video*

Fangs of Hate 1925
Drama
59213 40 mins B/W B, V, 3/4U P
William Patton
An early silent classic.
Unknown — *Penguin Video*

Fanny 1932
Comedy
06320 128 mins B/W B, V P
Raimu, Pierre Fresnay, Directed by Marcel Pagnol
Second part of Pagnol's trilogy depicting the lives, loves, joys, and sorrows of the people of Provence, France. French film, English subtitles.
FR
France — *Budget Video; Discount Video Tapes*

Fanny 1961
Drama
63450 150 mins C B, V R, P
Leslie Caron, Maurice Chevalier, Charles Boyer, Horst Buchholz
A young girl is left with child by an adventuresome sailor in the picturesque port of Marseilles. Part of the "A Night at the Movies" series, this tape simulates a 1961 movie evening, with a Tweety Pie cartoon, "The Last Hungry Cat," a newsreel and coming attractions for "Splendor in the Grass" and "The Roman Spring of Mrs. Stone."
Warner Bros — *Warner Home Video*

Fanny and Alexander 1983
Drama
64992 197 mins C B, V, LV, CED P
Ewa Froling, Erland Josephson, Ingmar Bergman

Set in a rural Swedish town in 1907, this film tells the story of one year in the lives of the Ekdahl family, focusing on the young children, Fanny and Alexander. In Swedish with English subtitles.
MPAA:R SW
Cinematograph AB — *Embassy Home Entertainment*

Fanny Hill: Memoirs of a Woman of Pleasure 1964
Drama
66293   105 mins   B/W   B, V   P
Miriam Hopkins, Walter Giller, Alex D'Arcy, Leticia Roman
The sexual exploits of an innocent in bawdy eighteenth century London.
Russ Meyer — *Paragon Video Productions*

Fantastic Animation Festival 1977
Fantasy/Cartoons
05415   91 mins   C   B, V   P
Animated
Fourteen award-winning animated shorts are combined into one feature-length program. Included are 'Closed Mondays,'' "The Last Cartoon Man,'' "French Windows,'' "Moonshadow,'' and "Cosmic Cartoon.''
MPAA:PG
Crest Film Distributors — *Media Home Entertainment*

Fantastic Balloon Voyage, The 198?
Adventure
64949   100 mins   C   B, V   R, P
Hugo Stiglitz, Jeff Cooper
Three men embark on a journey across the equator in a balloon, encountering countless adventures along the way.
MPAA:G
Unknown — *Video Gems*

Fantastic Planet 1973
Science fiction
57352   68 mins   C   B, V, FO   P
Animated, directed by Rene Laloux
Mind-boggling imagery, vivid colors, and music tell the story of the "Revolt of the Oms''—survivors of Earth who are kept as pets. Cannes Film Festival: Grand Prix.
French; Czech — *Video Yesteryear; Sheik Video*

Fantastic Voyage 1966
Science fiction
08425   100 mins   C   B, V   P
Stephen Boyd, Edmond O'Brien, Raquel Welch, Arthur Kennedy, Donald Pleasence, Arthur O'Connell

A famous scientist, rescued from behind the Iron Curtain, is so severely wounded by enemy agents that surgery is impossible.
Academy Awards '66: Best Art Direction.
20th Century Fox; Saul David — *CBS/Fox Video*

Fantasy in Blue 197?
Drama
59547   81 mins   C   B, V   P
The search for the solution to a sexual stalemate results in a couple's strange experimentation.
Frederick Fox — *Media Home Entertainment*

Farewell, My Lovely 1975
Mystery
56456   95 mins   C   CED   P
Robert Mitchum, Charlotte Rampling, Sylvia Miles, John Ireland
A remake of the 1944 Raymond Chandler mystery, "Murder, My Sweet,'' featuring private eye Phillip Marlowe hunting for an ex-convict's lost sweetheart.
MPAA:R
Avco Embassy — *RCA VideoDiscs*

Farewell to Arms, A 1932
Drama
11215   85 mins   B/W   B, V, FO   P
Helen Hayes, Gary Cooper
The original film version of Ernest Hemingway's novel about a tragic love affair between an ambulance driver and a nurse during World War I.
Academy Awards '33: Best Cinematography; Best Sound Recording.
Paramount — *Video Yesteryear; Budget Video; Sheik Video; Ampro Video Productions; Cable Films; Video Connection; Discount Video Tapes; Western Film & Video Inc; Cinema Concepts; Classic Video Cinema Collector's Club*

Farewell to Arms, A /Meet John Doe 194?
Drama
58907   199 mins   B/W   B, V   P
Gary Cooper, Helen Hayes, Adolphe Menjou, Barbara Stanwyck, Walter Brennan, directed by Frank Capra
A Gary Cooper double feature: "A Farewell to Arms'' (1932), Hemingway's classic story of an American ambulance driver and an English nurse who meet on the Italian front in World War I; "Meet John Doe'' (1941), Frank Capra's ode to the common man.
EL, SP
Paramount; Liberty Films — *Ampro Video Productions*

Farewell to Santa Fe Steam   1980
Trains
51438   30 mins   B/W   B, V   P
Directed by J. Allen Hawkins
This program documents the historic last run on the Santa Fe Railroad.
Bruce Frenzinger — *Interurban Films*

Fargo Express   1932
Western
11714   60 mins   B/W   B, V   P
Ken Maynard
Stagecoach hold-up in the Old West.
World Wide — *Video Connection; Discount Video Tapes*

Farmer and the Sportsman, The   1981
Hunting/Ecology and environment
47287   25 mins   C   B, V, 3/4U, Q   P
This program was designed to teach the hunter the need for cooperation between sportsman and farmer. Safe gun handling and soil conservation methods that will insure hunting for future generations are covered.
TV Sports Scene — *TV Sports Scene*

Farmer's Daughter, The   1947
Comedy
64902   97 mins   B/W   B, V   P
Loretta Young, Joseph Cotten, Ethel Barrymore, Charles Bickford, Rhys Williams, Rose Hobart
Young portrays Katrin Holmstrom, a Swedish farm girl who runs for Congress and captures the heart of a congressman along the way. Academy Awards '47: Best Actress (Young).
RKO; David O. Selznick — *CBS/Fox Video*

Fashions (Fashions of 1934)   1933
Musical
58720   78 mins   B/W   B, V   P
Bette Davis, William Powell, Frank McHugh, Hugh Herbert
A classic thirties musical with choreography by Busby Berkeley.
Warner Bros — *Video Dimensions*

Fast and Clean   1980
Boating
69897   36 mins   C   B, V   P
This program follows the U.S. team in its preparation for the World Canoe Slalom Championships (1979) at Jonquiere, Canada.
Nichols Productions — *Gravity Sports Films*

Fast Break   1979
Comedy
64238   107 mins   C   B, V   P
Gabe Kaplan, Harold Sylvester, Randee Heller
A deli clerk who is a compulsive basketball fan talks his way into a college coaching job.
MPAA:PG
Columbia — *RCA/Columbia Pictures Home Video*

Fast Bullets   1944
Western
54171   52 mins   B/W   B, V   P
Tom Tyler, Rex Lease
Tom Tyler tries to prevent a criminal gang from carrying out an injustice in this fast-paced action western.
Reliable — *Video Connection*

Fast Company   1978
Adventure
73540   90 mins   C   B, V   P
William Smith, John Saxon, Claudia Jennings, directed by David Cronenberg
This is the life story of champion race car driver Lonnie Johnson and his women, the money and the sponsors of drag races.
Michael Lebowitz; Peter O'Brian; Courtney Smith — *Admit One Video*

Fast Fists, The   198?
Martial arts
64959   90 mins   C   B, V   P
Jimmy Wang Tu
A martial arts adventure.
Dragon Lady Productions — *Unicorn Video*

Fast Freight   1954
Trains
68908   15 mins   B/W   B, V   P
A documentary which includes all train action with on-location sound in every scene.
Unknown — *Interurban Films*

Fast Times at Ridgemont High   1982
Comedy
63359   92 mins   C   B, V, LV, CED   P
Sean Penn, Jennifer Jason Leigh, Judge Reinhold, Phoebe Cates, Ray Walston
Based on the bestselling book by Cameron Crowe, this is the story of teenagers' struggles with independence, success, sexuality, money, maturity and school.
MPAA:R
Universal — *MCA Home Video*

Fat Albert and the Cosby Kids   1978
Cartoons
69626   60 mins   C   B, V   R, P
Animated, voice of Bill Cosby
In three separate cartoon episodes, Fat Albert and the Cosby Kids learn something important

about life, growing up, and the people around them.
Filmation Studios — *THORN EMI Home Video*

Fat Albert, Volume 2 1982
Cartoons
65747 23 mins C B, V R, P
Animated
This tape consists of two episodes, with Fat Albert teaching the viewer something important about life, the people around them and growing up.
Filmation — *THORN EMI Home Video*

Fatal Games 1984
Suspense
72904 88 mins C B, V P
Young female athletes are mysteriously disappearing at the Falcon Academy of Athletics and a crazed killer is responsible.
Christopher Mankeiwicz — *Media Home Entertainment*

Fatal Glass of Beer, The 1933
Comedy
59403 18 mins B/W B, V P, T
W.C. Fields, Rosemary Theby, George Chandler, Richard Cramer
Field's son returns to his home in the North Woods after serving a jail term.
Paramount — *Blackhawk Films; Festival Films*

Father 1967
Drama
47459 89 mins B/W B, V, FO P
After World War II, a Hungarian youth becomes obsessed with the facts surrounding his father's death at the hands of the enemy. Hungarian dialogue with English subtitles.
Hungarofilm — *Video Yesteryear*

Father Goose 1964
Comedy
64538 116 mins C B, V P
Cary Grant, Leslie Caron, Trevor Howard
During World War II, a plane-spotter stationed on a remote Pacific isle finds himself stuck with a group of French refugee schoolgirls and their teacher.
Universal — *NTA Home Entertainment*

Father Hubbard: The Glacier Priest 1954
Biographical/Scientists
44236 15 mins B/W B, V P
This program explores the finds of explorer-scientist Father Bernard Hubbard. As a geologist he discovered the secrets behind Alaska's great active volcanoes and as a sociologist, the origins and customs of Eskimos. Presented through classic newsreel footage.

Fox Movietone News — *Two Star Films*

Father Sergius 1917
Film-History
52344 84 mins B/W B, V, 3/4U P
Directed by Yakov Protazanov
Classic Russian silent film, subtitled in English.
USSR — *International Historic Films; Classic Video Cinema Collector's Club*

Fatty and Mabel 1916
Comedy
64250 60 mins B/W B, V P
Fatty Arbuckle, Mabel Normand
Fatty and Mabel are featured, together and separately, in this collection of laughable Sennett shorts. Silent with musical score.
Mack Sennett — *Classic Video Cinema Collector's Club*

Fatty and Mabel Adrift/Mabel, Fatty and the Law 1916
Comedy
64824 40 mins C B, V P, T
Fatty Arbuckle, Mabel Normand, Al St. John, Minta Durfee, Teddy the Dog
Fatty and Mabel have problems enjoying their wedded bliss in these two silent shorts, which have a newly recorded orchestral score on the soundtrack.
Triangle Film; Keystone Film — *Blackhawk Films*

Fatty's Tin-Type Tangle/Our Congressman 192?
Comedy
59410 44 mins B/W B, V P, T
Roscoe "Fatty" Arbuckle, Louise Fazenda, Edgar Kennedy, Frank Hayes, The Keystone Cops, Will Rogers, Jimmy Finlayson
In "Fatty's Tin-Type Tangle" (1915), Fatty and Louise are snapped by a traveling tintyper. In "Our congressman" (1924), Will Rogers offers an "expose" of political life.
Mack Sennett; Hal Roach — *Blackhawk Films*

Faust 1926
Film-History
08706 90 mins B/W B, V, 3/4U P
Emil Jannings, Warner Fuetterer, Gosta Ekman, Camilla Horn, directed by F. W. Murnau
Classic film based on the opera.
MGM — *Penguin Video; Classic Video Cinema Collector's Club*

Favorita, La 1952
Music-Performance
12823 80 mins B/W B, V, FO P
Sophia Loren, voices of Palmira Vitali Marini, Gino Sinimberghi, Paolo Silveri, Alfredo Colella

The great Italian opera with Sophia Loren in a supporting role. Narrated in English.
Unknown — *Video Yesteryear*

Favorite Black Exploitation Cartoons 194?
Cartoons/Film-History
66235   60 mins   B/W   B, V   R, P
Animated
Black stereotype cartoons exhibiting the bigotry of the times they were produced.
Warner Bros et al — *Video City Productions*

Favorite Celebrity Cartoons 194?
Comedy/Cartoons
66236   60 mins   B/W   B, V   R, P
Animated
Famous people, events and literature are seen in comic cartoon portrayals.
Warner Bros et al — *Video City Productions*

Favorite Racists Cartoons 194?
Film-History/Cartoons
66234   60 mins   B/W   B, V   R, P
Animated
A compilation of banned racist cartoons.
Warner Bros et al — *Video City Productions*

Fear 1954
Drama
66375   84 mins   B/W   B, V   P
Ingrid Bergman, directed by Roberto Rossellini
A pitiless study of a woman's gradual disintegration from the daily pressures of life.
Roberto Rossellini — *Movie Buff Video*

Fear in the Night 1972
Horror/Suspense
63342   82 mins   C   B, V   R, P
Judy Gesson, Joan Collins, Ralph Bates, Peter Cushing
The young bride of a school master in a boys' prep school becomes convinced that her husband intends to kill her while the school is closed for the holidays.
Hammer Films — *THORN EMI Home Video*

Fear No Evil 1980
Horror
64986   90 mins   C   B, V, CED   P
Stefan Arngrim, Kathleen Rowe McAllen, Elizabeth Hoffman
A teenager who is the human embodiment of the demon Lucifer commits acts of demonic murder and destruction. His powers are challenged by an 18-year-old girl, who is the embodiment of the archangel Gabriel.
MPAA:R

Avco Embassy — *Embassy Home Entertainment*

Feeding Habits of Bass 1981
Fishing
65148   30 mins   C   B, V   P
Glen Lau
This program from the "Sportsman's Video Collection" explains when and why bass strike and feed and how to use this information to catch more bass.
Glen Lau — *Leisure Time Products Project/3M*

Felix's Magic Bag of Tricks 1984
Cartoons
72900   60 mins   C   B, V   P
Animated
The professor is after Felix's Magic Bag of Tricks once again in this collection of cartoon favorites.
Felix the Cat Productions; Joe Oriolo — *Media Home Entertainment*

Female Bunch, The 1973
Adventure
69017   86 mins   C   B, V   P
Russ Tamblyn, Jenifer Bishop, Lon Chaney Jr.
A group of women involved in smuggling narcotics across the border destroy all who oppose them.
MPAA:R
Burbank International — *Imperial Video Corp*

Femmes de Paris 1953
Musical
60345   79 mins   C   B, V   P
Robert Dhery, Collette Brosset, Louis De Funes, The Bluebell Girls
A funny and risque French musical comedy about the comings and goings of the cast of one of those naughty nightclub shows.
Optimax Lux — *Video Dimensions*

Coppelia with Fernando Bujones 1982
Dance
47406   110 mins   C   B, V   P
Fernando Bujones
Mr. Bujones, the featured dancer of Barishnikov's American Ballet Theater, plays Franz, the young lover. Recorded with the Ballets de San Juan.
Kultur — *Kultur*

Ferrari Daytona 1983
Automobiles
76387   30 mins   C   B, V   P
A look at the car in both European and US trim. The Spyder is profiled against the L.A. skyline.
Armour Productions — *Armour Productions*

Ferrari 275GTB, The   1983
Automobiles-Racing
65172   30 mins   C   B, V   P
Narrated by Ron Hughes
1965-1967 models of the Ferrari 275 GTB/2, GTB/4 and GTB/C are seen, most of them totally restored, some in the process of restoration.
Armour Productions — *Armour Productions*

Ferry to Hong Kong   1959
Adventure
59831   103 mins   C   B, V   P
Curt Jurgens, Orson Welles, Sylvia Sims
A world-weary traveler comes aboard the "Fat Annie," a ship skippered by the pompous Captain Hart. The two men clash, until an act of heroism brings them together.
George Maynard — *Embassy Home Entertainment*

Festival of Funnies, A   1980
Football
50089   48 mins   C   B, V, FO   R, P
The lighter side of pro football. Wacky plays and zany players provide fun and entertainment in a new collection of NFL comedy action. Contains "Sym Funny," "The Jar 'Em and Daze 'Em Circus," "Believe It or Else," and other shorts.
NFL Films — *NFL Films Video*

Feud of the West   1935
Western
14656   60 mins   B/W   B, V   P
Hoot Gibson
Old West disagreements settled with guns.
Grand National — *VCI Home Video; Video Connection*

Feud on the Range   1939
Western
08811   55 mins   B/W   B, V, 3/4U   P
Bob Steele
Hard-riding and hard-fighting cowboy settles a range feud and restores peace.
Webb — *Penguin Video*

Fiction Makers, The   1967
Adventure/Suspense
68230   102 mins   C   B, V   P
Roger Moore, Sylvia Sims
Roger Moore stars as Templer, a sophisticated detective who is hired to help Amos Klein. Amos Klein is just an alias for a beautiful novelist who is being threatened by the underworld crime ring.
ATV/ITC — *CBS/Fox Video*

Fiddler on the Roof   1971
Musical
37524   184 mins   C   B, V, LV   P
Topol, Norma Crane, Leonard Frey, Molly Picon, directed by Norman Jewison
This movie, based on the long-running Broadway musical, is the story of a poor Jewish farmer at the turn of the century in a small Ukranian village, his five dowry-less daughters, his lame horse, his wife, and his companionable relationship with God.
Academy Awards '71: Best Cinematography; Best Adaptation and Original Song Score; Best Sound.   MPAA:G
United Artists — *CBS/Fox Video; RCA VideoDiscs*

Fiend Without a Face   19'5
Science fiction
59404   77 mins   B/W   B, V   P, T
Marshall Thompson, Terence Kilburn
A scientist working on materialized thought produces monsters from his own id.
Producers Associates — *Blackhawk Films*

Fiendish Plot of Dr. Fu Manchu, The   1980
Comedy
52718   108 mins   C   B, V   R, P
Peter Sellers, David Tomlinson, Sid Caesar
Peter Sellers' last film concerns Dr. Fu's desperate quest for the necessary ingredients for his secret life-preserving formula.
MPAA:PG
Orion Pictures — *Warner Home Video*

Fiesta   1941
Musical/Comedy
56908   44 mins   C   B, V, FO   P
Anne Ayars, George Negrete, Armida
A girl comes from Mexico City to her father's hacienda where her old boyfriend awaits her return with a proposal of marriage. Full of authentic Mexican dances and music.
Hal Roach — *Video Yesteryear*

Fifth Floor, The   1980
Mystery/Suspense
69304   90 mins   C   B, V   P
Bo Hopkins, Dianne Hull, Patti D'Arbanville, Mel Ferrer
An alleged suicide victim struggles to prove her innocence and maintain her sanity within the walls of an asylum. The only way out is to escape.
MPAA:R
Howard Avedis — *Media Home Entertainment*

---

55 Days at Peking   1963
Drama
16811   150 mins   C   B, V   P
Charlton Heston, Ava Gardner
The Chinese people's resentment against the infiltration of Western ideas erupts into violence against missionaries and foreigners.

                (For Explanation of codes, see USE GUIDE and KEY)

Samuel Bronston — *VCI Home Video*

$50,000 Reward 1925
Western
65226   49 mins   B/W   B, V   P
Ken Maynard, Esther Ralston, Tarzan the Horse
Ken Maynard's first Western finds him being
victimized by an unscrupulous banker who
wants Ken's land deeds for property on which a
new dam is being built.
Davis Distributing — *Blackhawk Films*

50 Years of Baseball 1980
Memories
Baseball
33829   30 mins   B/W   B, V   P
*Babe Ruth, Lou Gehrig, Tris Speaker, Ty Cobb,
Mel Ott, Joe DiMaggio, Warren Spahn, Mickey
Mantle*
A thrilling and nostalgic look at some of the
most outstanding players in baseball history.
Scenes of baseball's most memorable
moments, dating back to the teens and
twenties, are included.
Lou Fonseca — *Major League Baseball
Productions*

Fight for Survival 1977
Martial arts
65327   101 mins   C   B, V   P
Shang Kuan Ling-Feng
A young female aspirant of kung fu must
recover sacred books that were stolen by
disguised kung fu masters.
MPAA:R
Fann Jiann Gong; Lee Lin Lin — *CBS/Fox
Video*

Fight for the Sky 1945
Documentary/World War II
51440   21 mins   B/W   B, V   P
Narrated by Ronald Reagan
An Army Air Force documentary about U.S.
fighter pilots who flew escort missions over
Germany during World War II.
US Air Force — *Interurban Films*

Fight for the Sky, 1945
The/Mission
Accomplished
World War II
53386   32 mins   B/W   B, V, 3/4U   P
Narrated by Ronald Reagan
An Army Air Force documentary about US
fighter pilots who flew escort missions over
Germany during WW II, and the story of the
"Flying Fortress" over Europe.
USA — *International Historic Films*

Fighter, The 1983
Drama
75454   96 mins   C   B, V   P

Gregory Harrison, Glynnis O'Connor
An out of work millworker decides to become an
amateur boxer against his wife's wishes.
King Features — *U.S.A. Home Video*

Fighting Black Kings 1976
Martial arts/Adventure
66129   90 mins   C   B, V   R, P
Martial arts and karate masters appear in this
tale of action.
MPAA:PG
Unknown — *Warner Home Video*

Fighting Caravans 1932
Western
11373   80 mins   B/W   B, V, FO   P
Gary Cooper
Great outdoor adventure based on a story by
Zane Grey.
Paramount — *Video Yesteryear*

Fighting Devil Dogs 1943
Adventure/Serials
33951   195 mins   B/W   B, V, 3/4U   P
Eleanor Stewart, Montague Love, Hugh Sothern
Two Marine lieutenants are assigned the task of
obtaining a deadly secret weapon controlled by
crooks. A serial in twelve chapters.
Republic Pictures — *Video Connection*

Fighting Lady, The 1944
World War II/Ships
53657   57 mins   C   B, V, 3/4U   P
Made at the height of the war, and considered
to be one of the best documentaries of that
time, this film recounts the life of an aircraft
carrier, "The Fighting Lady."
Academy Award '44: Best Documentary; New
York Film Critics Award '44: Special
Documentary Award.
US Navy — *International Historic Films*

Fighting Life 1980
Martial arts/Adventure
60513   90 mins   C   B, V   P
The tale of two brothers who overcome
immense physical and emotional handicaps and
become vital members of society. The two stars
of the film are both physically handicapped.
Unknown — *Master Arts Video*

Fighting Marines, The 1935
Science fiction/Serials
54172   156 mins   B/W   B, V   P
Grant Withers, Ann Rutherford, Adrian Morris
A strange tale of modern science in which
pirates, ruled by a fiend, scheme to annihilate
the world. A serial in twelve chapters.
Mascot — *Video Connection; Video
Dimensions*

Fighting Marines, The   1936
War-Drama
57353   69 mins   B/W   B, V, FO   P
Jason Robards, Grant Withers, Ann Rutherford, Pat O'Malley
The U.S. Marines are trying to establish an airbase on Halfway Island in the Pacific, but are thwarted by the "Tiger Shark," a modern-day pirate. First appeared as a serial.
Mascot — *Video Yesteryear*

Fighting Renegade   1939
Western
54173   60 mins   B/W   B, V   P
Tim McCoy
A battle between desperadoes on the range.
Unity — *Video Connection*

Fighting Seabees, The   1944
War-Drama
59092   100 mins   B/W   B, V   P
John Wayne, Susan Hayward, Dennis O'Keefe
A salute to the Navy's construction corps, with the Duke as a tough foreman fighting the Japanese and Navy regulations.
Republic — *NTA Home Entertainment*

Fighting Trooper, The   1934
Western
56607   57 mins   B/W   B, V   P
Kermit Maynard
In this James Oliver Curwood story, the Mounties bring law to the Northwest.
Ambassador — *Video Dimensions*

Fighting with Kit Carson   1933
Western/Serials
12537   156 mins   B/W   B, V   P
Johnny Mack Brown, Noah Beery, Sr., directed by Armand Schaefer, Colbert Clark
Famous guide and Indian fighter lead bands of settlers westward. Actionpacked. Twelve chapters, 13 minutes each.
Mascot — *Video Connection*

Fille Mal Gardee, La   1981
Dance
59873   210 mins   C   LV   P
Two young lovers must overcome a disapproving mother and differences in class in this performance by the Royal Ballet. In stereo.
Covent Garden Video — *Pioneer Artists*

Film Firsts   1960
Film-History
10155   51 mins   B/W   B, V   P, T
Documentary-style look at early film segments from the "History of the Motion Picture" series. Includes the first attempt at science fiction with Georges Melies' "Trip to the Moon" (1902), and the first cartoon and western.
Killiam — *Blackhawk Films*

Filming the Big Thrills/Filming the Fantastic   193?
Documentary/Disasters
60054   20 mins   B/W   B, V   P, T
"Big Thrills" includes scenes of the 1920's Florida hurricane, 1930's floods of the Mississippi and Ohio rivers, the tragedy of the Hindenburg, and more. "Fantastic" shows giant boys and midget girls, a library of books inside a walnut, a young man wearing a drape of honeybees and more.
20th Century Fox — *Blackhawk Films*

Filming the Impossible   1982
Sports
69916   38 mins   C   B, V   P
The most exciting moments in sports are filmed as they happen, including mountaineering, kayaking, ballooning and skin diving in such locations as Nepal, Patagonia, Switzerland and Albuquerque.
Banff Festival of Mountainfilms '82: Best Mountain Sports film.
Leo Dickinson; HTV Wales — *Gravity Sports Films*

Final Conflict, The   1981
Horror
58846   108 mins   C   B, V, CED   P
Sam Neill, Lisa Harrow, Barnaby Holm, Rossano Brazzi
The third installment in the "Omen" series, concerning Damien, now 32, who has become the head of an international conglomerate.
MPAA:R
20th Century Fox — *CBS/Fox Video*

Final Countdown, The   1980
Drama
64893   92 mins   C   B, V, CED   P
Kirk Douglas, Martin Sheen, Katherine Ross, James Farentino, Charles Durning
A nuclear warship is transported back in time to Pearl Harbor just hours before the fateful bombing that started World War II.
MPAA:PG
Bryna Company; Peter Vincent Douglas — *Vestron Video*

Final Exam   1981
Horror
66050   90 mins   C   B, V, CED   P
Cecile Bagdadi, Joel Rice
A psychotic killer stalks college students during exam week.
MPAA:R
John Chambliss — *Embassy Home Entertainment*

Final Extra, The 1927
Drama
48706   60 mins   B/W   B, V, 3/4U   P
Grant Withers, Marguerite de la Motte
A fearless reporter is out to expose a gun-running ring. Silent.
Gotham Prods — *Penguin Video*

Final Programme, The 1981
Science fiction/Fantasy
63328   85 mins   C   B, V   R, P
Jon Finch, Jenny Runacre, Sterling Hayden, Patrick Magee
In this futuristic story, a man must rescue his sister and the world from their brother who holds a microfilmed plan for global domination, and himself from a bisexual computer programmer who wants to make him father to a new, all-purpose human being.
EMI Films Ltd — *THORN EMI Home Video*

Finian's Rainbow 1968
Musical
74204   141 mins   C   B, V, LV   R, P
Fred Astaire, Petula Clark
This is the story of a leprechaun who is out to resteal a pot of gold taken by an Irishman and his daughter.
MPAA:G
Joseph Landon — *Warner Home Video*

Fiona 1978
Drama
66199   82 mins   C   B, V   P
Fiona Richmond, Victor Spinetti
A ravishing blonde exposes her legendary sexual appetite.
Assay Films Ltd — *U.S.A. Home Video*

Fiorello La Guardia: The Crusader 1954
Biographical/Politics and government-US
44241   15 mins   B/W   B, V   P
In this program, classic newsreel footage shows Fiorello La Guardia when he was Mayor of New York.
Fox Movietone News — *Two Star Films*

Fire and Ice 1983
Adventure/Fantasy
65463   81 mins   C   B, V   P
Animated, directed by Ralph Bakshi
An animated adventure film that culminates in a tense battle between good and evil, surrounded by the mystical elements of the ancient past. In stereo VHS and Beta Hi-Fi.
MPAA:PG
Ralph Bakshi; Frank Frazetta; Producers Sales Organization — *RCA/Columbia Pictures Home Video*

Fire Over England 1937
Drama
11232   81 mins   B/W   B, V, FO   P
Flora Robson, Raymond Massey, Laurence Olivier, Vivien Leigh
Spain and Great Britain engage in war while Queen Elizabeth is torn between duty and personal desire.
United Artists, British — *Video Yesteryear; Budget Video; Sheik Video; Ampro Video Productions; Cable Films; Discount Video Tapes; Western Film & Video Inc*

Fire Over England/As You Like It 1936
Drama/Comedy
58908   176 mins   B/W   B, V   P
Laurence Olivier, Vivien Leigh, Raymond Massey, James Mason, Elizabeth Bergner
A Laurence Olivier double feature: "Fire Over England" (1936), a costume drama set against the era of Queen Elizabeth and the Spanish Inquisition; "As You Like It" (1936), Shakespeare's pastoral comedy which offered Olivier one of his earliest film appearances.
EL, SP
Pendennis; ICF — *Ampro Video Productions*

Firebird 2015 A.D. 1981
Science fiction
65717   97 mins   C   B, V   P
Darren McGavin, Doug McClure
A tongue-in-cheek adventure involving a 21st century society where automobile use is banned because of extreme oil shortage.
MPAA:PG
Glen Ludlow — *Embassy Home Entertainment*

Firebird 2015 A.D. 1981
Adventure
64976   97 mins   C   B, V, CED   P
Darren McGavin, George Touliatos, Doug McClure
This is a futuristic spectacle about two car enthusiasts, and the thrill and conflict involved in driving a vehicle in a world where oil shortages have led to a total ban on the use of automobiles and driving is a capital offense.
Merritt White Ltd — *Embassy Home Entertainment*

Firecracker 1971
Martial arts/Adventure
63086   83 mins   C   B, V   P
Jillian Kessner, Darby Hinton
A female Martial arts expert retaliates against the crooks who murdered her sister.
New World Pictures — *Monterey Home Video*

Firefox 1982
Adventure
62886   136 mins   C   B, V, LV, CED   R, P

Clint Eastwood, directed by Clint Eastwood
A special agent sneaks into the Soviet Union to
steel a top-secret Russian warplane and fly it
out of the country. VHS in stereo.
MPAA:PG
Warner Bros — *Warner Home Video*

Firemen's Ball　　　　　　　　**1968**
Comedy
66014　　73 mins　　C　　B, V　　　　P
Josef Svet, directed by Milos Forman
A comedy about an honorary ball held for a
retiring fire chief. Czech dialogue, subtitled in
English.
CZ
Barrandov Film Studios — *RCA/Columbia
Pictures Home Video*

Firepower　　　　　　　　　　**1979**
Drama/Suspense
69381　　104 mins　　C　　B, V　　　　P
Sophia Loren, James Coburn, O.J. Simpson
A U.S. government agent is sent to the
Caribbean to capture an American
multimillionaire engaged in illegal activities and
bring him to justice.
MPAA:R
Associated Film Distributors — *CBS/Fox
Video*

Fires on the Plain　　　　　　**1959**
Drama
51948　105 mins　B/W　　B, V　　　　P
*Eiji Funakoshi, Osamu Takizawa, Mickey Custis,
Asao Suno, directed by Kon Ichikawa*
A group of men from the Japanese Army
struggle to survive the perils of war in this
disturbing drama. One soldier maintains his
humanity while those around him resort to any
crime. Japanese dialogue, English subtitles.
JA
Japanese — *Budget Video; Festival Films*

Fireside Theatre:　　　　　　**195?**
Sergeant Sullivan
Speaking
Comedy-Drama
66120　24 mins　B/W　　B, V　　　P, T
*William Bendix, Joan Blondell, William Fawcett,
Sarah Selby*
From the TV series "Return Engagement," a
romance blossoms over the telephone between
a youthful widow and a police sergeant.
Procter and Gamble — *Blackhawk Films*

Firesign Theatre Presents　　**1983**
Nick Danger in The Case
of the Missing Yolk, The
Comedy
63389　　60 mins　　C　　B, V, CED　　P
*The Firesign Theatre (Phil Proctor, Phil Austin,
Peter Bergman)*

Firesign characters Nick Danger and Rocky
Rococo are featured in this story of a truly
interactive family who live through their
television set.
VHD Programs; Pacific Arts
Corporation — *Pacific Arts Video*

First Aid　　　　　　　　　　**1980**
First aid
44294　　22 mins　　C　　V　　　　P
This program provides expert knowledge and
techniques in saving lives in emergency
situations before professional medical
assistance arrives. Covered are shock,
drowning, poisons, burns, choking, gunshot
wounds, and bleeding. Included is a detailed
demonstration of cardiopulmonary
resuscitation.
American Home Video Library — *American
Home Video Library*

First Aid: The Video Kit　　**1984**
First aid
Closed Captioned
65755　　95 mins　　C　　B, V　　　　P
This program provides the viewer with "eyes-
on" experience of basic first aid principles that
could make the difference in those crucial
seconds when a crisis strikes.
CBS Fox Video — *CBS/Fox Video*

First Aid Video Book, The　　**1981**
First aid
52768　　40 mins　　C　　B, V　　　　P
Several emergencies, such as choking,
poisoning, and shock are covered, with
instructions on how to handle each emergency
quickly.
Karl Video — *Karl Video*

First Barry Manilow　　　　**1977**
Special, The
Music-Performance
59844　　60 mins　　C　　B, V, LV,　　P
　　　　　　　　　　　　　　CED
Barry Manilow
Manilow's Emmy-winning TV special highlights
his singing and songwriting talents, while
featuring 15 of his most popular hits.
ABC — *MGM/UA Home Video*

First Blood　　　　　　　　**1982**
Drama
64335　　96 mins　　C　　B, V　　　R, P
*Sylvester Stallone, Richard Crenna, Brian
Dennehy, Jack Starrett*
Stallone portrays a former Green Beret survivor
of Vietnam whose nightmares of wartime
horrors are triggered by a wrongful arrest.
MPAA:R
Orion Picture — *THORN EMI Home Video;
RCA VideoDiscs*

　　　　(For Explanation of codes, see USE GUIDE and KEY)

First Christmas, The 1982
Christmas
72215 27 mins C B, V P
Animated
This animated holiday program depicts the birth of Jesus.
Unknown — *Paragon Video Productions*

First Deadly Sin, The 1980
Drama
72918 112 mins C B, V P
Frank Sinatra, Faye Dunaway, David Dukes, Brenda Vaccaro
A police lieutenant tracks down a homicidal killer in spite of family troubles which intrude on his work.
MPAA:R
Filmways; Artanis; Cinema Seven — *Warner Home Video*

First Family 1980
Comedy
58231 100 mins C B, V R, P
Bob Newhart, Madeline Kahn, Gilda Radner, Richard Benjamin, directed by Buck Henry
A biting satire of life in the White House for one President and his family.
MPAA:R
Warner Bros — *Warner Home Video*

First Love 1977
Romance
29765 92 mins C B, V R, P
William Katt, Susan Dey, John Heard, Beverly D'Angelo
A story of an idealistic college student who takes love, and especially making love, more seriously than the rest of his peers, including his girlfriend.
MPAA:R
Paramount — *Paramount Home Video*

First Love 1970
Drama
65158 90 mins C B, V P
John Moulder-Brown, Dominique Sanda, Maximilian Schell, Valentina Cortese, directed by Maximilian Schell
In the days before the 1917 Revolution, a young Russian boy meets and becomes infatuated with an impoverished princess. Years later, after war and strife have swept the country, he seeks her out again.
MPAA:R
Franz Seitz Filmproduktion; UMC Pictures — *VCI Home Video*

First Monday in October 1981
Comedy
58710 99 mins C B, V, LV R, P
Walter Matthau, Jill Clayburgh, Barnard Hughes, James Stephens, directed by Ronald Neame
A comedy concerning the first woman appointed to the Supreme Court and her colleague, a crusty but benign liberal judge.
MPAA:R
Paramount — *Paramount Home Video*

First National Kidisc, The 1981
Variety
57775 ? mins C LV P
Subtitled "1001 Things to Do on a Rainy Day," this one-sided interactive disc may occupy a child's attention up to 40 or 50 hours.
Bruce Seth Green — *Optical Programming Associates*

First Nudie Musical, The 1975
Comedy
12700 93 mins C B, V P
Cindy Williams, Stephan Nathan, Diana Canova, Bruce Kimmel
Producer attempts success by staging a nudie musical in 1930's style.
MPAA:R
Jack Reeves — *Media Home Entertainment; King of Video; Budget Video*

First Spaceship on Venus, The 1964
Science fiction
11717 78 mins C B, V P
Yoko Tani
Eight scientists set out for Venus and find the remains of a civilization far in advance of Earth's.
Crown International — *VCI Home Video*

First Time, The 1982
Comedy
66023 96 mins C B, V R, P
A comedy about a college student who can't quite succeed with women.
Sam Irvin — *THORN EMI Home Video*

Fish Hawk 1979
Adventure
72903 95 mins C B, V P
Will Sampson
When an alcoholic Indian, Fish Hawk, meets a young boy in the forest, and they strike up a friendship.
MPAA:G
Edgar J. Scherick; Stanley Chase — *Media Home Entertainment*

Fishing/Hunting/Snowmobiling 197?
Fishing/Sports-Winter
45086 30 mins C B, V, 3/4U, Q P
10 pgms
This videotape package contains ten half-hour programs on the sports of fishing, hunting, and snowmobiling, with Forrest Tucker competing in

a 500 mile snowmobile race from Winnipeg to St. Paul, Minnesota in one segment. Programs are available individually.
1.Anybody Can Catch Fish 2.Fishing in the Land of Sky Blue Waters 3.A School of Bass 4.Cousin Smallmouth Bass 5.Old Rock Champ of the Chesapeake 6.Texas Hex 7.Duck Hunting Time 8.500 Miles Below Zero 9.Four Days to St. Paul 10.The Freshness of Skiing
TV Sports Scene — *TV Sports Scene*

Fishing in the Land of the Sky Blue Waters   197?
Fishing
33743   30 mins   C   B, V, 3/4U,   P
                                    Q
This program presents scenes of bass, northern muskie, and lake trout fishing in prime Minnesota waters. Tips on catching these types of fish are included.
TV Sports Scene — *TV Sports Scene*

Fishing the Dry Fly   1983
Fishing
65143   60 mins   C   B, V   P
Gary Borger
This program from the "Sportsman's Video Collection" shows the most effective ways to fish all types of dry flies in riffles, pocket water, pools and ponds.
3M — *Leisure Time Products Project/3M*

Fishing the Last Frontier   197?
Fishing
19405   30 mins   C   B, V, 3/4U,   P
                                    Q
All about fishing in the Arctic Circle, a fisherman's paradise with abundant beauty and plenty of fish.
TV Sports Scene — *TV Sports Scene*

Fishing U.S.A.   1969
Fishing
59072   105 mins   C   B, V   R, P
R. Vernon "Gadabout" Gaddis
Outdoor scenes from Maine to California, including bass fighting on the line, are featured in this program about fishing in America.
GG Communications — *Video Gems*

F.I.S.T.   1978
Drama
53451   145 mins   C   B, V, CED   P
Sylvester Stallone, Rod Steiger, Peter Boyle, Melinda Dillon, Tony Lo Bianco, Kevin Conway, Cassie Yates, directed by Norman Jewison
The story of an idealistic labor union organizer who works his way to the top of the union by accepting mob favors which cost him his integrity.
MPAA:R

United Artists; Norman Jewison — *CBS/Fox Video*

Fist   1979
Adventure/Martial arts
59085   84 mins   C   B, V   P
Richard Lawson, Annazette Chase, Dabney Coleman
A street fighter battles his way through the urban jungle seeking personal freedom and revenge.
MPAA:R
Larrabure Kaye — *HarmonyVision*

Fist of Fear—Touch of Death   1980
Adventure
52858   90 mins   C   B, V   P
Bruce Lee, Fred Williamson, Lee Van Cleef
The three greatest martial arts masters star in this kung-fu action adventure film. A compilation of clips from Bruce Lee's films.
MPAA:R
Aquarius Releasing — *Wizard Video*

Fist of Vengeance   197?
Martial arts/Adventure
47703   90 mins   C   B, V   P
Shoji Karada, Lu Pi Chen
The East Asia Society hires a Samurai to kill a young Chinese officer.
Sung Kuang Lung — *Master Arts Video*

Fistful of Dollars, A   1967
Western
58825   96 mins   C   B, V   P
Clint Eastwood, Gian Maria Volonte, Marianne Koch, directed by Sergio Leone
An avenging stranger gets involved in a feud between two powerful families.
United Artists; Harry Colombo; George Papi — *CBS/Fox Video; RCA VideoDiscs*

Fists of Fury   1973
Adventure/Martial arts
55833   102 mins   C   B, V   P
Bruce Lee, Maria Yi
Bruce Lee stars in this violent Kung Fu action adventure in which Lee must defend his honor and break a solemn vow to avoid fighting.
MPAA:R
National General Pictures — *CBS/Fox Video; Video City Productions; Master Arts Video*

Fists of Fury II   1980
Adventure/Martial arts
44340   90 mins   C   B, V   R, P
Bruce Li, Ho Chung Do, Shum Shim Po
This story centers around character Chen Shan (Bruce Li) and his efforts to survive the Organizations' onslaughts to kill him. He escapes their perilous plots only to return to

battle against them after they had killed his mother for her inability to disclose Chen's hiding place. Finally Chen defeats the evil Organization himself.
MPAA:R
Four Seas Films — *Video Gems*

Fitzcarraldo   1982
Drama
66124   150 mins   C   B, V   R, P
Klaus Kinski, Claudia Cardinale, directed by Werner Herzog
The epic story of a charismatic Irishman's impossible quest to build an opera house in the middle of the Amazon jungles.
Cannes Film Festival '82: Best Director.
MPAA:PG
New World Pictures — *Warner Home Video*

Five Days One Summer   1982
Romance
66123   108 mins   C   B, V   R, P
Sean Connery, Betsy Brantley, Lambert Wilson, directed by Fred Zinnemann
The story of a haunting and obsessive love affair between a married Scottish doctor and a younger woman.
MPAA:PG
Ladd Company — *Warner Home Video*

---

500 Miles Below Zero   197?
Sports-Winter
33749   30 mins   C   B, V, 3/4U,   P
                                    Q
Forrest Tucker
Forrest Tucker competes in the International 500-mile Snowmobile Race from Winnipeg, Canada to St. Paul, Minnesota and finds that it takes a different breed of sportsman to endure the many miles of sub-zero weather.
TV Sports Scene — *TV Sports Scene*

Five Mack Sennett Shorts   192?
Comedy
64249   60 mins   B/W   B, V   P
Gloria Swanson, Chester Conklin, The Keystone Kops
A package of some of Mack Sennett's funniest one and two-reelers, featuring slapstick galore. Silent with musical score.
Mack Sennett — *Classic Video Cinema Collector's Club*

Five Mile Creek, Volume 1   1984
Adventure
72787   94 mins   C   B, V   P
The Australian frontier serves as backscape for this story about a group of American and Australian settlers who make an inspiring drive to establish a stage coach line on the route to Australia's gold fields.

Walt Disney Productions — *Walt Disney Home Video*

Five Mile Creek Volume 2   1984
Adventure
72797   111 mins   C   B, V   P
Treacherous busrangers and an aristocratic entourage threaten the pioneer heroes of the Australian frontier.
Walt Disney Productions — *Walt Disney Home Video*

Flak   1943
Aeronautics/World War II
72479   17 mins   B/W   B, V, 3/4U   P
U.S. Air Force training film which contains innovative animation from the Walt Disney studios used to illustrate evasive maneuvers.
USAF — *International Historic Films*

Flaming Frontiers   1938
Western/Serials
08872   300 mins   B/W   B, V, 3/4U   P
Johnny Mack Brown, Eleanor Hanson, Ralph Bowman
A frontier scout matches wits against gold mine thieves. In fifteen episodes.
Universal — *Penguin Video; Video Connection; Video Yesteryear; Budget Video; Discount Video Tapes*

Flaming Star   1960
Drama
64931   92 mins   C   CED   P
Elvis Presley, Dolores del Rio, Barbara Eden, Steve Forrest, John McIntire
Set in 1870's Texas, a mixed Indian and white family is caught in the midst of an Indian uprising. A half-Indian youth must choose which side he is on.
20th Century Fox — *CBS/Fox Video*

Flash and Firecat   1975
Adventure
60223   90 mins   C   B, V   P
Richard Kiel
A beautiful blonde and a crazy thief steal, race and love their way across the country with the police at their heels.
MPAA:PG
Sebastian Films — *Independent United Distributors*

Flash Gordon   1953
Science fiction
58731   30 mins   B/W   B, V   P
Steve Holland, Irene Champlin
Flash fights for peace in outer space in this episode from the classic 1950's television series.
Syndicated — *Sheik Video*

Flash Gordon — 1980
Science fiction
56870　111 mins　C　B, V, LV,　P
　　　　　　　　　　CED
Sam J. Jones, Melody Anderson, Topol, Max von Sydow
Dino DeLaurentiis-produced version of the adventures of Flash Gordon in outer space. This time, Flash and Dale Arden are forced by Dr. Zarkov to accompany him on a mission to far-off Mongo, where Ming the Merciless is threatening the destruction of Earth. Music by Queen.
MPAA:PG
Universal, Dino DeLaurentiis — *MCA Home Video*

Flash Gordon Conquers the Universe — 1940
Science fiction/Serials
08629　240 mins　B/W　B, V　P
Buster Crabbe, Carol Hughes, Charles Middleton, Frank Shannon
Ravaging plague strikes the earth and Flash Gordon undertakes to stop it. A serial in twelve chapters.
Universal — *Video Connection; Cable Films; Video Yesteryear*

Flash Gordon: Mars Attacks the World — 1938
Science fiction
08634　87 mins　B/W　B, V　P
Buster Crabbe, Jean Rogers, Charles Middleton
The earth is plagued by the evil Ming, but Flash Gordon steps in.
Universal — *Sheik Video; Ampro Video Productions; Cable Films*

Flash Gordon: Rocketship — 1936
Science fiction
13694　75 mins　B/W　B, V, FO　P
Buster Crabbe, Charles Middleton
Flash Gordon saves Earth from a planet that almost collides with it.
Universal — *Video Yesteryear; Sheik Video; Ampro Video Productions; Cable Films; Cinema Concepts*

Flashdance — 1983
Musical-Drama
Closed Captioned
65096　96 mins　C　B, V, LV,　R, P
　　　　　　　　　　CED
Jennifer Beals, Michael Nouri, Belinda Bauer, Lilia Skala
A young female welder dreams of becoming a professional ballet dancer, trying out her original dance routines every night at a local bar. Title song sung by Irene Cara. In stereo.
MPAA:R
Paramount — *Paramount Home Video*

Flask of Fields, A — 193?
Comedy
58654　61 mins　B/W　B, V, FO　P
W.C. Fields, Babe Kane, Elsie Cavanna, Bud Jamison, Rosemary Theby
Three classic Fields shorts: "The Golf Specialist" (1930), in which J. Effington Bellweather finds himself teaching a lovely young lady how to play the game; "The Fatal Glass of Beer" (1933); and "The Dentist" (1932), in which Fields tackles a room filled with patients.
RKO; Paramount — *Video Yesteryear*

Flavors of China — 1979
Cookery
38956　119 mins　C　B, V　R, P
Master chef Titus Chan guides the viewer through classic Chinese recipes that can be prepared at home. Chinese cooking utensils are explained, and basic techniques of cooking such as stir frying, steaming, poaching, and deep frying are presented. Contains instructions on such dishes as lemon chicken, beef with oyster sauce, chicken with cashews, sweet and sour pork, and many others.
AM Available
Valley Isle Productions — *Warner Home Video*

Fleetwood Mac, Documentary and Live Concert — 1980
Music-Performance
54687　60 mins　C　B, V　R, P
Fleetwood Mac
Both interviews with members of Fleetwood Mac and footage from their recent tour are featured in this program. Musical selections include "Sarah," "Sisters of the Moon," "Go Your Own Way," "Angel," and "Tusk."
Warner Bros — *Warner Home Video; RCA VideoDiscs; MCA Home Video (disc only)*

Fleetwood Mac in Concert—Mirage Tour 1982 — 1982
Music-Performance
64240　80 mins　C　B, V　P
Filmed during Fleetwood Mac's 1982 tour, this concert tape features such songs as "Rhiannon," "Gypsy," "Go Your Own Way," and "Songbird." In Dolby stereo.
Marty Callner — *RCA/Columbia Pictures Home Video; RCA VideoDiscs*

Flesh and Blood — 1922
Drama
47342　75 mins　B/W　B, V　P
Lon Chaney
An escaped convict seeks revenge on the crooked industrialist who had him falsely imprisoned. Silent.

Unknown — *Glenn Video Vistas; Classic Video Cinema Collector's Club*

Flesh Gordon   1974
Satire
55213   70 mins   C   B, V   P
Jason Willaims, Suzanne Fields
An adult super-spoof of science fiction films. The Earth is thrown into carnal chaos by a mysterious sex ray, and Flesh travels to the planet Porno to save the earth from an evil emperor.
MPAA:X EL, SP
Graffitti Productions Corp — *Media Home Entertainment*

Flight from Vienna   1958
Drama
69566   54 mins   B/W   B, V, FO   P
Theodore Bikel, John Bentley, Donald Gray
A high-ranking Hungarian security officer, disenchanted with communism, stages a daring escape from his country. In Vienna, he asks the British for political asylum, but is sent back to Hungary to help a scientist escape.
E J Fancey — *Video Yesteryear*

Flight of Dragons   19??
Fantasy
69613   98 mins   C   B, V   P
Animated, voices of John Ritter, Victor Buono, James Earl Jones
This animated tale takes place between the Age of Magic and the Age of Science, in a century when dragons ruled the skies.
Rankin Bass — *Children's Video Library*

Flight of the Century   1935
Trains
68904   18 mins   B/W   B, V   P
A journey on what was once America's fastest and prestigious train.
Unknown — *Interurban Films*

Flight That Became a Legend   1970
Aeronautics
70058   25 mins   C   B, V, 3/4U   P
Soviet flyer Chaklov's flight from Moscow via the North Pole and Vancouver to Washington is the subject of this Russian documentary.
USSR — *International Historic Films*

Flight to Mars   1952
Science fiction
44355   72 mins   C   B, V, 3/4U   P
Cameron Mitchell, Marguerite Chapman, Arthur Franz
An expedition crash lands on the red planet and discovers an advanced underground society. Includes previews of coming attractions from classic science fiction films.

Monogram, Walter Mirisch — *Nostalgia Merchant*

Flights and Flyers   193?
Documentary/Biographical
50635   30 mins   B/W   B, V   P, T
Three Fox-Movietone newsreels covering stories about famous flyers such as Will Rogers, Amelia Earhart, Howard Hughes, Eddie Rickenbacker, and Wrong Way Corrigan, to name a few.
Blackhawk; Movietone — *Blackhawk Films*

Flights and Flyers: Amelia Earhart   19??
Documentary/Biographical
50632   11 mins   B/W   B, V   P, T
The flying exploits and heroics of Amelia Earhart are chronicled in this program. The determination of a woman who made both cross-country and trans-Atlantic flights, and vowed to follow her failures with successes, is emphasized.
Blackhawk; Movietone — *Blackhawk Films*

Flirting with Fate   1916
Comedy
49179   40 mins   B/W   B, V, 3/4U, FO   P
Douglas Fairbanks
When his girlfriend rejects him, Fairbanks hires an assassin to kill him. His girl has a change of heart however, and now staying alive becomes a problem. Silent.
Unknown — *Penguin Video; Classic Video Cinema Collector's Club*

Flock of Seagulls, A   1983
Music-Performance
76669   13 mins   C   B, V   P
This program presents the British band performing "Wishing (If I Had a Photograph of You)," "Nightmares" and "I Ran."
Zomba Productions Inc — *Sony Corporation of America*

Flood of Fury   1952
Adventure
10034   25 mins   B/W   B, V   P, T
Kirby Grant
Town is flooded by ravaging rain, escaped prisoners rob bank, and Penny and Clipper are kidnapped. Sky King attempts to help. From the TV series "Sky King."
CBS — *Blackhawk Films*

Florence Chadwick: The Challenge   1954
Biographical/Sports-Water
44265   15 mins   B/W   B, V   P

The story of swimming champion Florence Chadwick, who swam the English Channel in both directions. Classic newsreel footage.
Fox Movietone News — *Two Star Films*

Florida Connection, The　　1974
Adventure
47673　　90 mins　　C　　B, V　　P
An action thriller set in the Florida Swamps with a collection of villains.
Samuel Hyman — *Unicorn Video*

Flower Angel, The　　1980
Cartoons
53664　　46 mins　　C　　B, V　　P
Animated
The Flower Angel and her friends, a white kitty and a lovable brown dog, are searching for the Flower of Seven Colors. In their travels they help a lonely old man and his beautiful daughter find the love they have for each other.
EL, SP
Ziv Intl — *Family Home Entertainment*

Flower Out of Place, A　　1974
Music
05413　　50 mins　　C　　B, V　　P
Concert performances by Johnny Cash, Roy Clark, Linda Ronstadt, and Foster Brooks.
Independent — *Media Home Entertainment*

Flowing Falls　　1978
Video
08561　　30 mins　　C　　B, V, 3/4U　　P
A continuous picture of a lush cove fed by a majestic waterfall to create a relaxed background.
Nebulae Prods — *Nebulae Productions*

Flowing Sea　　1978
Video
08567　　30 mins　　C　　B, V, 3/4U　　P
A continuous picture of a rocky cove of cross-breaking waves rolling over a green coral reef to create a relaxed background.
Nebulae Prods — *Nebulae Productions*

Fly Fishing for Trout　　1983
Fishing
65144　　60 mins　　C　　B, V　　P
Gary Borger
This program teaches both beginners and experts how to take more trout on dries, nymphs and streamers. From the "Sportsman's Video Collection."
3M — *Leisure Time Products Project/3M*

Fly Fishing Secrets I: The　　1984
Dry Fly
Fishing
74468　　90 mins　　C　　B, V　　P
This program features fishing expert Hal Janssen who talks in detail about fly fishing and how to tie a dry fly.
3M — *Leisure Time Products Project/3M*

Fly Fishing Secrets II: The　　1984
Wet Fly and Nymph
Fishing
74469　　90 mins　　C　　B, V　　P
This program features fishing expert Hal Janssen who examines the aspects of trout Fishing and the tricks of tying techniques for wet fly and nymph lores.
3M — *Leisure Time Products Project/3M*

Flying Blind　　1941
Drama
66376　　69 mins　　B/W　　B, V　　P
Richard Arlen, Jean Parker, Marie Wilson
Foreign agents are thwarted in their attempt to steal a vital air defense secret.
Paramount — *Movie Buff Video*

Flying Deuces, The　　1939
Comedy
08577　　70 mins　　B/W　　B, V　　P
Stan Laurel, Oliver Hardy, Jean Parker, Reginald Gardner
Laurel and Hardy join the Foreign Legion.
RKO — *NTA Home Entertainment; Media Home Entertainment; Nostalgia Merchant; VCI Home Video; VCII; Budget Video; Ampro Video Productions; Cable Films; Video Yesteryear; Discount Video Tapes; Sheik Video; Video Connection; Penguin Video; Vestron Video; Classic Video Cinema Collector's Club; Vestron Video (disc only)*

Flying Down To Rio　　1933
Musical
00268　　89 mins　　B/W　　B, V, 3/4U　　P
Fred Astaire, Ginger Rogers
First Astaire-Rogers musical, featuring Vincent Youmans' score, including "The Carioca."
RKO; Merian C Cooper — *Nostalgia Merchant*

Flying Fool, The　　1929
Adventure
56612　　75 mins　　B/W　　B, V　　P
William "Hopalong Cassidy" Boyd, Marie Prevost, directed by Tay Garnett
Hair-raising adventure of a stunt pilot in love with the same woman his brother loves. Until recently, this film was believed to be lost.
Pathe Exchange — *Video Dimensions*

　　(For Explanation of codes, see USE GUIDE and KEY)

Flying Lariats, The   193?
Western
08843   50 mins   B/W   B, V, 3/4U   P
Wally Wales
An action-filled western with Wally Wales.
Unknown — *Penguin Video*

Flying Leathernecks   1951
War-Drama
29343   102 mins   C   B, V, 3/4U   P
John Wayne, Robert Ryan, Janis Carter
A tough squadron leader wins the admiration
and devotion of his fliers. This memorable World
War II film deals with war in human terms.
RKO — *Nostalgia Merchant; VidAmerica*

Fog, The   1978
Horror
56460   91 mins   C   B, V, LV,   P
                 CED
*Hal Holbrook, Adrienne Barbeau, Jamie Lee
Curtis, Janet Leigh, John Houseman, directed
by John Carpenter*
John Carpenter's contemporary tale of
supernatural horror concerns a ghostly fog that
reappears to fulfill a curse.
MPAA:R
Avco Embassy, Debra Hill — *Embassy Home
Entertainment; RCA VideoDiscs*

Fog Island   1945
Suspense
48692   72 mins   B/W   B, V, 3/4U   P
*George Zucco, Lionel Atwill, Terry Morse,
Jerome Cowen*
Murder and terror lurk in the distance after a
greedy inventor and investor, who was framed
for fraud by his business partner, is released
from prison.
Producers Releasing Corp — *Penguin Video;
Sheik Video; Video Connection*

Follow a Star   1960
Comedy
49068   93 mins   B/W   B, V   P
*Norman Wisdom, Jerry Desmonde, June
Laverick*
A cleaning store employee who is taking voice
lessons meets a professional singer. The singer
recognizes the kid's talent, records his voice,
then tries to pass it off as his own.
Zenith — *Sheik Video*

Follow Me, Boys!   1966
Comedy
65636   120 mins   C   B, V   R, P
*Fred MacMurray, Vera Miles, Lillian Gish,
Charles Ruggles, Elliott Reid, Kurt Russell,
Luana Patten, Ken Murray*
After one year too many on the road with a
ramshackle jazz band, a simple man decides to
put down roots and enjoy the quiet life—a life
that is suddenly just a memory when he

volunteers to head a troop of high-spirited
youngsters.
Buena Vista — *Walt Disney Home Video*

Follow Me Down   197?
Sports-Water
53640   25 mins   C   B, V, 3/4U,   P
                 Q
This program in the "Under Water Deep Sea
Diving" series examines scuba diving, from
various locations around the world.
Smokey Roberts — *TV Sports Scene*

Follow That Camel   1967
Comedy
48070   95 mins   C   B, V   P
*Phil Silvers, Kenneth Williams, Anita Harris, Jim
Dale*
A Foreign Legion sergeant who invents acts of
heroism finally gets a chance to really help out a
friend in need.
Peter Rogers Prods — *Sheik Video*

Follow the Fleet   1936
Musical
01611   110 mins   B/W   B, V, 3/4U   P
*Fred Astaire, Ginger Rogers, Randolph Scott,
directed by Mark Sandrich*
Set to Irving Berlin's score, song and dance
man joins Navy with pal and meets two sisters in
need of help. Look for Betty Grable, Lucille Ball,
and Tony Martin in minor roles.
RKO — *Nostalgia Merchant*

Food Processing   1982
Cookery
47350   30 mins   C   V   P
Techniques of preparing food using a food
processor are explained and demonstrated.
American Home Video Library — *American
Home Video Library*

Foolin' Around   1980
Comedy/Romance
64978   101 mins   C   B, V, CED   P
*Gary Busey, Annette O'Toole, Eddie Albert,
Tony Randall, Cloris Leachman*
An innocent Oklahoma farm boy arrives at
college and falls in love with a beautiful heiress.
He will stop at nothing to win her over including
crashing her lavish wedding ceremony.
MPAA:PG
Columbia — *Embassy Home Entertainment*

Foolish Wives   1922
Drama
12428   75 mins   B/W   B, V   P
*Erich von Stroheim, Maude George, Mae Busch,
directed by Erich von Stroheim*
Monte Carlo: Posing as a Russian Count with
two accomplices, a fiendish man takes
advantage of women. Silent with music track.

Universal — *Budget Video; Penguin Video; Sheik Video; Classic Video Cinema Collector's Club*

Foolish Wives   1922
Drama
47821   107 mins   B/W   B, V   P, T
Erich Von Stroheim, Mae Busch, Maud George, Cesare Gravina, directed by Erich Von Stroheim
A reconstruction of Von Stroheim's classic depicting the confused milieu of post-war Europe traced through the actions of a bogus count and his seductive, corrupt ways. This version is as close as possible to the original film.
Universal; Carl Laemmle — *Blackhawk Films*

Football Follies   1980
Football
45125   30 mins   C   B, V, FO   R, P
The original chaos and comedy collection of wild and wacky events that sometimes happen on the one-hundred yard stage.
NFL Films — *NFL Films Video*

Football Follies/Highlights of Super Bowl V   1980
Football
56790   46 mins   C   B, V   P
A collection of hilarious snafus by the great pro football players, plus highlights of the Cowboys and Colts "Blooper Bowl."
NFL Films — *VidAmerica*

Footloose   1984
Musical-Drama
75808   106 mins   C   B, V, LV,   R, P
                               CED
Kevin Bacon, Lori Singer, music by Kenny Loggins
A teenage boy tries to bring rock music to a small, religious town.
MPAA:PG
Paramount — *Paramount Home Video*

For a Few Dollars More   1967
Western
64705   125 mins   C   CED   P
Clint Eastwood, Lee Van Cleef
A band of cutthroats has a sadistic leader who is pursued by two bounty hunters. When the two offer to help the outlaws crack a stolen safe, the vicious leader is shot. Sequel to "A Fistful of Dollars."
MPAA:PG
United Artists — *CBS/Fox Video; RCA VideoDiscs*

For Ladies Only   1981
Drama
65312   94 mins   C   B, V   P

Gregory Harrison, Lee Grant
Gregory Harrison is a struggling, unemployed actor by day and an exotic male stripper by night.
Viacom International — *U.S.A. Home Video*

For Love of Ivy   1968
Comedy/Drama
47148   102 mins   C   B, V   P
Sidney Poitier, Abbey Lincoln, Beau Bridges, Carroll O'Connor, directed by Daniel Mann
When the black maid of a wealthy family decides to quit, the family tries to find a boyfriend for her so she will stay on. Based on a story by Sidney Poitier.
MPAA:PG
Cinerama Releasing; Palomar — *CBS/Fox Video*

For Pete's Sake   1974
Comedy
44833   90 mins   C   B, V   P
Barbra Streisand, Michael Sarrazin, Estelle Parsons, William Redfield, Molly Picon
Topsy-turvy comedy about a woman who goes to great lengths for her husband.
MPAA:PG
Martin Erlichman, Columbia — *RCA/Columbia Pictures Home Video*

For the Love of Benji   1977
Comedy-Drama
49627   85 mins   C   B, V   P
Benji, Patsy Garrett, Cynthia Smith, Allen Finzat, Ed Nelson, directed by Joe Camp
Benji and his companion Tiffany join their human friends for a Greek vacation. But Benji is kidnapped to be used as a messenger for a secret code. He escapes, and the case is on.
MPAA:G
Mulberry Square Prods; Joe Camp — *Vestron Video*

For the Love of Benji   1983
Animals
75614   85 mins   C   B, V   P
Benji battles an international spy ring.
Mulberry Square Productions — *Children's Video Library*

For the Love of It   1980
Comedy
66616   98 mins   C   B, V   P
Deborah Raffin, Jeff Conaway, Don Rickles, Tom Bosley, Henry Gibson, William Christopher
A young couple steal some top-secret Soviet documents and become the target of bumbling FBI agents.
Charles Fries Productions — *U.S.A. Home Video*

For Your Eyes Only 1981
Adventure
58845 127 mins C B, V, LV, P
CED
Roger Moore, Carole Bouquet, Lynn-Holly Johnson
Another James Bond epic, in which 007 is called upon to keep the Soviets from getting hold of the valuable instrument aboard a sunken British spy ship.
MPAA:PG
United Artists — *CBS/Fox Video; MGM/UA Home Video (disc only)*

For Your Love Only 1979
Drama
66256 90 mins C B, V P
Nastassia Kinski, directed by Wolfgang Petersen
Nastassia Kinski stars in this tale of love directed by "Das Boot's" Wolfgang Petersen.
Dieter Menzs Atlas Intl Films GmbH; NDR; Studio Hamburg — *Paragon Video Productions*

Forbidden Planet 1956
Science fiction
55210 98 mins C B, V, LV, P
CED
Walter Pidgeon, Anne Francis, Leslie Nielsen, directed by Fred McLeod Wilcox
In 2200 A.D., a space cruiser visits the planet Altair Four to uncover the fate of a previous mission of space colonists, and discovers a former civilization.
MGM; Nicholas Nayfack — *MGM/UA Home Video*

Forbidden Trail 1933
Western
15436 60 mins B/W B, V P
Buck Jones, Tim McCoy, Raymond Hatton
This adventure set in the old West features the "Roughriders."
Columbia — *Video Connection; Sheik Video*

Forbidden World 1982
Science fiction/Horror
65715 82 mins C B, V P
Jesse Vint, Dawn Dunlap
The lives of a genetic research team become threatened by the very life form they helped to create: a man-eating organism capable of changing its genetic structure as it grows and matures.
MPAA:R
Roger Corman — *Embassy Home Entertainment*

Forbidden Zone 1980
Film-Avant-garde/Science fiction
66600 75 mins B/W B, V P
Herve Villechaize, Susan Tyrrell, The Kipper Kids, Viva

Frenchy Hercules is flung headlong into the sixth dimension. This kingdom is ruled by the midget, King Fausto and inhabited by dancing frogs, bikini-clad tootsies, robot boxers and degraded beings of all kinds. Original music by Oingo Boingo.
MPAA:R
Richard Elfman — *Media Home Entertainment*

Force Beyond, The 197?
Speculation/Occult sciences
47314 85 mins C B, V P
Don Elkins, Peter Byrne, Renee Dahinden
This program provides a look at inexplicable phenomena, including psychic investigation, alien encounters, Bigfoot, and the Bermuda Triangle.
Donn Davidson — *Media Home Entertainment*

Force: Five 1981
Adventure
68223 95 mins C B, V P
Joe Lewis, Pam Huntington, Master Bong Soo Han
The daughter of a very powerful man has been taken to Rhee's Island, a retreat for people involved in the cult. The mission is to get her back and ruin Rhee's Island. Only a force of five agents can do this job.
MPAA:R
American Cinema — *Media Home Entertainment*

Force of One, A 1979
Martial arts/Adventure
66062 91 mins C B, V P
Chuck Norris, Bill Wallace, Jennifer O'Neill
A team of undercover narcotics agents is being eliminated mysteriously.
MPAA:PG
Alan Belkin — *Media Home Entertainment*

Force 10 from Navarone 1978
War-Drama
64301 118 mins C B, V R, P
Robert Shaw, Harrison Ford, Barbara Bach, Edward Fox
During World War II, five desperate Allied soldiers and one beautiful woman plot to blow up a dam and destroy an impregnable bridge.
MPAA:PG
Orion Pictures — *Warner Home Video; Vestron Video (disc only)*

Forced Entry 1980
Suspense
59082 92 mins C B, V P
Tanya Roberts, Ron Max, Nancy Allen
A psychopathic killer rapist becomes obsessed with a beautiful woman.
MPAA:R
Jim Sotos — *HarmonyVision*

Forced Landing 1942
Drama
66377 70 mins B/W B, V P
Richard Arlen, Eva Gabor
A scientist's daughter, who fears her father may have been captured by Nazis, seeks the aid of an American flyer.
Paramount — *Movie Buff Video*

Forced Vengeance 1982
Adventure/Martial arts
60568 103 mins C B, V, CED P
Chuck Norris, Mary Louise Weller
The story of a Vietnam vet pitted against the Underworld of the Far East.
MPAA:R
MGM; SLM Entertainment — *MGM/UA Home Video*

Forces of Life, The 1982
Chemistry/Physics
59562 56 mins C B, V P
This program examines the essential properties which make up our physical universe.
McGraw Hill — *Mastervision*

Ford GT-40 1983
Automobiles-Racing
65170 56 mins C B, V P
Narrated by Ron Hughes
The history of the Ford GT-40 is shown, including early prototype models, racing footage from Le Mans and several cars in the process of restoration.
Armour Productions — *Armour Productions*

Ford Show, The 1960
Variety
47499 30 mins B/W B, V, FO P
Tennessee Ernie Ford, Keenan Wynn
Country humor with Tennessee Ernie Ford, featuring his hound dog, Ring, and Emmy Lou, the pig.
NBC — *Video Yesteryear*

**Ford Star Jubilee:
"Together with Music"** 1955
Music-Performance
47492 79 mins B/W B, V, FO P
Mary Martin, Noel Coward
A memorable television special—originally broadcast on October 22, 1955—teaming two Broadway luminaries. Mary Martin sings songs from "South Pacific," "Leave It to Me" and other shows. Noel Coward sings his "Mad Dogs and Englishmen" and other tunes, ending with a lengthy duet.
CBS — *Video Yesteryear*

Ford Startime 1960
Drama
69577 50 mins B/W B, V, FO P

Audie Murphy, Thelma Ritter
An original television drama, "The Man" is a psychological study of an unbalanced veteran who visits the mother of an old army buddy and proves impossible to get rid of.
NBC — *Video Yesteryear*

**Foreign
Legionnaire—Court
Martial** 1957
Adventure
51430 30 mins B/W B, V P
Buster Crabbe, Cullen Crabbe, Fuzzy Knight
An episode from the TV serial about the adventures of Captain Michael Gallant and his ward, Cuffy Sanders in the French Foreign Legion of North Africa.
NBC — *Video Connection*

Foreplay 1975
Comedy
64879 100 mins C B, V, CED P
Pat Paulsen, Jerry Orbach, Estelle Parsons, Zero Mostel
A trilogy of hilarious comedy segments. Also known as "The President's Women."
Cinema National Corp — *Vestron Video*

Forever Emmanuelle 1982
Drama
69282 89 mins C B, V P
Annie-Belle, Emmanuelle Arsan, Al Cliver
A sensual young woman finds love and the ultimate erotic experience in the wilds of the South Pacific.
MPAA:R
A-Erre Cinematografica — *Vestron Video*

Formula, The 1980
Drama
55206 117 mins C B, V, CED P
Marlon Brando, George C. Scott, directed by John G. Avildsen
Steve Shagan's novel about a hard-nosed Los Angeles policeman who, despite numerous attempts on his life, continues to search for the formula that could end America's dependence on foreign oil forever.
MPAA:R
Steve Shagan — *MGM/UA Home Video*

Fort Apache 1948
Western
00277 125 mins B/W B, V, 3/4U P
John Wayne, Henry Fonda, Shirley Temple
Indian attacks and conflict between men on the Western frontier arise in this film.
RKO; John Ford — *Nostalgia Merchant; King of Video; VidAmerica*

Fort Apache, The Bronx — 1981
Drama
58896   123 mins   C   B, V, LV,   P
CED
*Paul Newman, Ed Asner, Ken Wahl, Danny
Aiello, Rachel Ticotin, Pam Grier, Kathleen
Beller, directed by Daniel Petrie*
A police drama set in the beleaguered South
Bronx of New York City, based on the real-life
experiences of two former New York cops who
served there.
MPAA:R
Time-Life Films — *Vestron Video*

Fortune's Fool — 1921
Comedy
11231   60 mins   B/W   B, V, FO   P
*Emil Jannings, Daguey Servaes, Reinhold
Schunzel, directed by Reinhold Schunzel*
A beef king and profiteer marries a younger
woman and soon discovers the problems that
ambition can cause.
UFA — *Video Yesteryear*

Forty Carats — 1973
Comedy
63964   110 mins   C   B, V   P
*Liv Ullman, Edward Albert, Gene Kelly, Binnie
Barnes, Deborah Raffin*
A middle-aged, divorced woman falls in love
with a young man half her age; in turn, her
young daughter marries a widower who is in his
forties.
MPAA:PG
Columbia Pictures — *RCA/Columbia Pictures
Home Video*

48 Hrs. — 1982
Comedy
66034   100 mins   C   B, V, LV   R, P
Nick Nolte, Eddie Murphy
A convict and a detective make an unlikely team
trying to solve a crime in San Francisco.
MPAA:R
Paramount — *Paramount Home Video; RCA
VideoDiscs*

40mm Twin Anti-Aircraft Gun — 1943
Armed Forces-US
72484   40 mins   B/W   B, V, 3/4U   P
A training film for the army's gun, produced for
soldiers who would be using these guns in the
European Theater of Operations.
US Army — *International Historic Films*

Forty Ninth Parallel, The — 1941
World War II
75673   90 mins   B/W   B, V   P
*Laurence Olivier, Leslie Howard, Eric Portman,
Raymond Massey, Glynis Johns*
Six Nazi servicemen, seeking to reach neutral
American land, are trapped and their U-boat is
sunk by Royal Canadian Air Force bombers.
Rank Film Distributors — *VidAmerica*

42nd Street — 1933
Musical
55582   89 mins   B/W   B, V   P
*Warner Baxter, Ruby Keeler, Bebe Daniels, Dick
Powell, Guy Kibbee, Ginger Rogers, Una
Merkel, directed by Lloyd Bacon*
A Broadway musical producer has troubles
during rehearsal but reaches a successful
opening night. Choreography by Busby
Berkeley. Songs by Harry Warren and Al Dubin
include the title song, "You're Getting to Be a
Habit with Me," "Young and Healthy," and
"Shuffle Off to Buffalo."
Warner Bros — *CBS/Fox Video; RCA
VideoDiscs*

Foul Play — 1978
Comedy
38931   118 mins   C   B, V, LV   R, P
*Goldie Hawn, Chevy Chase, Dudley Moore,
directed by Colin Higgins*
Chevy Chase is a San Francisco detective who
becomes involved with Goldie Hawn and a plot
to kidnap the Pope in this lighthearted comedy
thriller.
MPAA:PG
Paramount — *Paramount Home Video; RCA
VideoDiscs*

Four Days to St. Paul — 197?
Sports-Winter
33750   30 mins   C   B, V, 3/4U,   P
Q
The world's longest and most rugged race, the
Winnipeg to St Paul International Snowmobile
Race, is the cold, grueling, and challenging
subject of this program.
TV Sports Scene — *TV Sports Scene*

Four Feathers, The — 1978
Adventure
47796   95 mins   C   B, V   R, P
*Beau Bridges, Jane Seymour, Simon Ward,
Harry Andrews*
Determined to return the symbols of cowardice-
four feathers-to his friends and fiancee, a man
courageously saves his friends' lives and
regains the love of his lady.
Trident Films Ltd; Norman Rosemont
Productions — *THORN EMI Home Video*

Four for Thrills — 1982
Cartoons/Literature-American
58578   50 mins   C   B, V   P
*Narrated by Herschel Bernardi and Harry
Belafonte*
A quartet of colorful animated, shorts containing
Edgar Allen Poe's classic "Masque of the Red

Death," Harry Belafonte's presentation of the Hand," the immortal, "Casey at the Bat," and Herschel Bernardi's presentation of "The Hangman."
McGraw Hill — *Mastervision*

Four Friends 1981
Comedy-Drama
60338   116 mins   C   B, V   R, P
Craig Wasson, Jodi Thelen, Michael Huddleston, Jim Metzler, Reed Birney, directed by Arthur Penn
Set against the turbulence of the 1960's, a young immigrant comes of age, learning of life and love from his friends.
MPAA:R
Filmways Pictures — *Warner Home Video; Vestron Video (disc only)*

Four Musketeers, The 1973
Comedy/Adventure
60374   107 mins   C   CED   P
Raquel Welch, Richard Chamberlain, Faye Dunaway, Michael York
A bawdy continuation of the "Three Musketeers" based on the classic Dumas novel.
MPAA:R
Ilya Salkind — *RCA VideoDiscs*

Four Musketeers, The 1974
Adventure
66617   103 mins   C   B, V   P
Michael York, Oliver Reed, Raquel Welch, Faye Dunaway, Charlton Heston, directed by Richard Lester
This continuation of "The Three Musketeers" finds Athos, Porthos, Aramis and D'Artagnan continuing their adventures against the evil forces of Cardinal Richelieu.
MPAA:PG
20th Century Fox; Film Trust SA — *U.S.A. Home Video*

Four Rode Out 1969
Western
65209   99 mins   C   B, V   P
Pernell Roberts, Leslie Nielsen
The story of a woman in love with a suspected killer. To save his life, she rides out with his would be captors.
MPAA:R
Sagittarius Productions — *U.S.A. Home Video*

Four Seasons, The 1981
Comedy
58433   107 mins   C   B, V, LV   P
Alan Alda, Carol Burnett, Sandy Dennis, Len Cariou, Jack Weston, Rita Moreno, Bess Armstrong
Three upper-middle-class New York couples share their vacations together, as well as their friendship, their frustrations and their jealousies.
MPAA:PG

Universal; Martin Bregman — *MCA Home Video; RCA VideoDiscs*

Four Seasons, The 1984
Music
66597   45 mins   C   B, V   P
Orchestre National de France, conducted by Lorin Maazel
Vivaldi's famous concert piece is performed with a visual background of travelog scenes of Paris, New York, Moscow and Venice. In stereo.
Curiator Spiritus Company Ltd; Promedifilm; MGM UA — *MGM/UA Home Video*

Fowl Play 1983
Comedy
72205   90 mins   C   B, V   P
Nancy Kwan
An unlikely threesome encounter various hardships and mishaps on their way to the first cock-fighting Olympics.
Unknown — *Paragon Video Productions*

Fraggle Songs, Volume One 1983
Fantasy/Music
65306   52 mins   C   B, V, LV, CED   R, P
The Fraggles, furry little creatures who come in every color of the rainbow, sing and dance their way into your heart. This program is in stereo on all formats.
Henson Associates — *Muppet Home Video*

Fraidy Cat 1974
Cartoons
75498   45 mins   C   B, V   P
This program includes four animated fantasies for children.
Filmation — *Prism*

Frances 1982
Drama
66021   134 mins   C   B, V, CED   R, P
Jessica Lange, Kim Stanley, Sam Shepherd
The tragic story of Frances Farmer, the beautiful and talented screen actress driven to a mental breakdown by a neurotic, domineering mother.
Universal — *THORN EMI Home Video*

Frank Shorter's Run 1984
Running
65690   57 mins   C   B, V   P
America's foremost authority on running, world-class marathoner Frank Shorter gives information and instruction on warm-up racing and tempo running, injury prevention and treatment.
Paul Rost; Bruce Miller — *Media Home Entertainment*

    (For Explanation of codes, see USE GUIDE and KEY)

Franken and Davis Special, The　1984
Comedy-Performance
66359　60 mins　C　B, V　P
Writer-performers Al Franken and Tom Davis, once featured on "Saturday Night Live," star in this live comedy concert taped in New Jersey
Pacific Arts — *Pacific Arts Video*

Frankenstein　1931
Horror
14025　71 mins　B/W　B, V　P
Boris Karloff, Mae Clark, Colin Clive, John Boles
An adaptation of the Mary Shelley novel about Dr. Henry Frankenstein, the scientist who creates a terrifying yet strangely sympathetic monster.
Universal — *MCA Home Video; RCA VideoDiscs*

Frankenstein '80　1980
Horror
75533　88 mins　C　B, V　P
John Richardson, Marisa Travers
Frankenstein is reborn and wants women.
Unknown — *Gorgon Video*

Frankenstein Island　198?
Mystery
75583　97 mins　C　B, V　P
John Carradine, Andrew Duggan, Cameron Mitchell
Four balloonists get pulled down in a storm and end up on Frankenstein island.
MPAA:PG
Unknown — *Monterey Home Video*

Frankie and Johnnie　1936
Musical-Drama
59407　68 mins　B/W　B, V　P, T
Helen Morgan, Chester Morris
Based on the song of the same name, Helen Morgan portrays a nightclub floozie who shoots her unfaithful lover.
Republic — *Blackhawk Films*

Frankie Laine Show with Connie Haines　1955
Variety
12843　50 mins　B/W　B, V, FO　P
Frankie Laine, Connie Haines, the Harry Zimmerman Orchestra
Two TV shows featuring plenty of songs, variety acts, knife throwers, and girl bagpipers.
CBS — *Video Yesteryear*

Frankie Valli: Twentieth Anniversary Concert　1983
Music-Performance
75497　100 mins　C　B, V　P
Frankie Valli
Frankie Valli's Chicago 1982 concert includes great hits such as "Grease," "My Eyes Adored You," "Sherry," "Walk Like a Man" and "Rag Doll."
MusicAmerica Live — *Prism*

Franklin D. Roosevelt, Declaration of War　1941
Presidency-US/World War II
59651　9 mins　B/W　B, V　P, T
Franklin D. Roosevelt
This Fox Movietone newsreel captures FDR's declaration of war following the December 7th bombing of Pearl Harbor.
William Fox — *Blackhawk Films*

Franklin D. Roosevelt: F.D.R.　1954
Biographical/Presidency-US
44249　15 mins　B/W　B, V　P
The story of Franklin D. Roosevelt from the time he was governor of New York until 1933, when he became President of the United States. Classic newsreel footage.
Fox Movietone News — *Two Star Films*

Frantic　1958
Drama
12803　92 mins　B/W　B, V, FO　P
Maurice Ronet, Jeanne Moreau
A former commando commits murder of an employer's wife, making it look like suicide. A teenage prank then frames him for murders he did not commit.
Times Films; Irenee Leriche — *Video Yesteryear; Budget Video; Penguin Video; Discount Video Tapes*

Freakmaker, The　1984
Horror
72862　90 mins　C　B, V　P
Donald Pleasence, Tom Baker
A professor attempts to breed plants and humans in his lab.
Robert Weinbach — *VIDCREST*

Freaky Friday　1977
Comedy/Fantasy
47409　95 mins　C　B, V　R, P
Barbara Harris, Jodie Foster, Patsy Kelly, Dick Van Patten, Ruth Buzzi
A housewife and her teenage daughter inadvertently switch bodies and each then tries to carry on the other's normal routine.
MPAA:G
Walt Disney — *Walt Disney Home Video*

Freddie Hubbard　1981
Music-Performance
76663　59 mins　C　B, V　P

A top rate jazz performance by one of the greatest trumpet players of our time, Freddie Hubbard.
Audio Visual Images — *Sony Corporation of America*

Frederick's of Hollywood Presents...   1983
Clothing and dress
69790   60 mins   C   B, V   P
Hosted by Mr. Frederick   4   pgms
The world famous Frederick's of Hollywood, acknowledged leader in the world of erotic fashions, introduces a full line of videocassettes for people interested in improving their looks and expanding their horizons.
1.The Frederick's of Hollywood Catalogue Comes to Life, Spring 2.The Frederick's of Hollywood Catalogue Comes to Life, Summer 3.The Frederick's of Hollywood Catalogue Comes to Life, Fall 4.The Frederick's of Hollywood Catalogue Comes to Life, Winter
Anthony DiVona; Celebrity Video — *Gold Stripe Video*

Free to Be... You and Me   1983
Identity/Children
69534   45 mins   C   B, V   P
Marlo Thomas, Alan Alda, Harry Belafonte, Mel Brooks, Diana Ross, Rosey Grier
This is a joyful celebration of childhood through song, story and poetry—created to let children feel "free to be who they are and who they want to be."
Marlo Thomas; Carole Hart — *Children's Video Library*

Freedom Force, The   1984
Adventure/Cartoons
66494   60 mins   C   B, V   P
Animated
The Freedom Force takes on the powers of evil and triumphs over the forces of darkness.
Prism — *Prism*

Freedom's Finest Hour   1965
History-US
52915   56 mins   C   B, V, 3/4U   P
Narated by Ronald Reagan and Robert Taylor
A dramatic documentary on the history of the American Revolution and the founding of our nation. Music by Jimmie Rodgers.
CINE Golden Eagle '65; Valley Forge Freedom Foundation '65: Best Documentary, U.S.A.
Alec Thomas; Samuel Thomas — *Thomas Productions*

Freight Yard, The   1946
Trains
68905   19 mins   B/W   B, V   P
A trip into the freight classification yard to explain and demonstrate it's inner workings.

Unknown — *Interurban Films*

French Connection, The   1971
Crime-Drama
08432   102 mins   C   B, V, LV   P
Gene Hackman, Fernando Rey, Roy Scheider, Tony LoBianco, Marcel Bozzuffi
Two N.Y. hard-nosed narcotics detectives stumble onto what turns out to be the biggest narcotics haul to that time.
Academy Awards '71: Best Picture; Best Actor (Hackman); Best Director (William Friedkin).
MPAA:R   EL, SP
20th Century Fox; Philip D'Antoni — *CBS/Fox Video*

French Detective, The   1975
Suspense
63960   90 mins   C   B, V   P
Lino Ventura, Patrick Dewaere, Victor Lanoux
A cunning detective and an ambitious young politician clash in this story of murder and intrigue. Dubbed in English.
Les Films Ariane; Quartet Films — *RCA/Columbia Pictures Home Video*

French Intrigue   1982
Mystery/Suspense
72340   102 mins   C   B, V   P
A suspense film involving international spies working out of France.
MPAA:R
Swab Productions — *Best Film & Video Corporation*

French Lieutenant's Woman, The   1981
Drama
59392   124 mins   C   B, V, LV   P
Meryl Streep, Jeremy Irons, directed by Karel Reisz
John Fowles' best seller which intertwines two love stories, one between two present-day actors and one between the historical characters they portray.
MPAA:R
United Artists — *CBS/Fox Video; MGM/UA Home Video (disc only)*

French Line   1954
Comedy
10030   102 mins   C   B, V   P, T
Jane Russell, Gilbert Roland, Craig Stevens
Millionairess beauty travels incognito while trying to sort out which men are after her money, and which ones aren't.
RKO; Edmund Graiger — *Blackhawk Films*

French Quarter   1978
Drama
47404   101 mins   C   B, V   P

      (For Explanation of codes, see USE GUIDE and KEY)

Bruce Davison, Virginia Mayo, Lindsay Bloom, Alisha Fontaine, Lance Legault, Ann Michelle
A young girl travels to the French Quarter in New Orleans. Desperate for work, she falls victim to an old woman who practices witchcraft and voodoo. The woman's voodoo causes the young girl to "slip" away. She awakens in the year 1900, under the care of prostitutes.
MPAA:R
Crown Intl Pictures; Dennis Kane — *VCI Home Video*

French Woman, The   1979
Drama
55595   97 mins   C   B, V   P
Francois Fabian, Klaus Kinski
A sensuous story of blackmail, murder, and sex involving French cabinet ministers mixing passion and politics.
MPAA:R
Monarch Pictures; Claire Duval — *VidAmerica*

Frenzy   1972
Suspense
11582   116 mins   C   B, V   P
Jon Finch, Barry Foster, Barbara Leigh-Hunt, Anna Massey, Directed by Alfred Hitchcock
A sex criminal known as The Necktie Murderer is terrorizing London, and Alfred Hitchcock has everyone guessing who the culprit is—including Scotland Yard.
MPAA:R
Universal; Alfred Hitchcock — *MCA Home Video*

Freshness of Skiing, The   197?
Sports-Winter
33751   30 mins   C   B, V, 3/4U, Q   P
Two skiers take a fun-filled trip from a Midwest ski resort through the powder of the Rockies and the West Coast. Techniques of several professional skiers are presented in this program.
TV Sports Scene — *TV Sports Scene*

Friday the 13th   1980
Horror
54669   95 mins   C   B, V, LV   R, P
Betsy Palmer, Adrienne King, Harry Crosby, Laurie Bartrarr, Mark Nelsor, directed by Sean S. Cunningham
A New Jersey camp that's been closed for 20 years after a history of "accidental" deaths reopens and the horror begins again. Six would-be counselors arrive to get the place ready. Each are progressively murdered—knifed, speared, and axed.
MPAA:R
Paramount — *Paramount Home Video; RCA VideoDiscs*

Friday the 13th, Part 2   1981
Horror
53932   87 mins   C   B, V, LV   P
Amy Steel, John Furey, Adrienne King, Betsy Palmer, directed by Steve Miner
A group of teen camp counselors are gruesomely executed by yet another unknown assailant.
MPAA:R
Steve Miner — *Paramount Home Video; RCA VideoDiscs*

Friday the 13th, Part 3   1982
Horror
64021   96 mins   C   B, V, LV   R, P
Dana Kimmell, Paul Krata, Richard Brooker
Yet another group of naive counselors at Camp Crystal Lake fall victim to the maniacal Jason.
MPAA:R
Jason Productions — *Paramount Home Video*

Friends and Neighbors/The Great Outdoors   1982
Parades and festivals
64008   60 mins   C   B, V   P
Highlights of the 1981 and 1982 Tournament of Roses Parades in Pasadena are narrated by Grand Marshals James Stewart and Lorne Greene.
Tournament Video Tapes — *Tournament Video Tapes*

Frightmare   1983
Horror
64874   84 mins   C   B, V   P
A great horror star dies, but he refuses to give up his need for adoration and revenge.
MPAA:R
Patrick and Tallie Wright — *Vestron Video*

Frisco Kid, The   1979
Comedy
58232   119 mins   C   B, V   R, P
Gene Wilder, Harrison Ford, directed by Robert Aldrich
An orthodox rabbi from Poland sets out for the wild west.
MPAA:PG
Warner Bros — *Warner Home Video*

Fritz the Cat   1972
Comedy
59850   77 mins   C   B, V   R, P
Animated
Ralph Bakshi's animated tale for adults about a cat's adventures as he gets into group sex, college radicalism and other hazards of life in the 60's.
MPAA:X
Steve Krantz — *Warner Home Video*

Frog Prince, The 1971
Fairy tales
47346   50 mins   C   B, V, LV   R, P
The Muppets
Kermit the Frog narrates the Muppet version of this classic fairy tale. A handsome prince has been turned into a frog by an evil witch's spell, and only the kiss of a beautiful princess can change him back.
RLP Canada/Henson Associates — *Muppet Home Video*

Frogs 1972
Horror
64839   91 mins   C   B, V   R, P
Ray Milland, Sam Elliott, Joan Van Ark, Adam Roarke, Judy Pace, directed by George McCowan
Amphibians and reptiles on a tropical island take revenge against the family of a wildlife-hating recluse.
MPAA:PG
American International Pictures — *Warner Home Video; Vestron Video (disc only)*

Frolics on Ice 1940
Comedy
38976   65 mins   B/W   B, V, FO   P
Roscoe Karns, Lynne Roberts, Irene Dare, Edgar Kennedy
Pleasant comedy-musical about a family man saving to buy the barber shop he works at. Irene Dare is featured in several ice skating production numbers.
Hal Roach — *Video Yesteryear*

From Broadway to Hollywood 193?
Film-History
10157   48 mins   B/W   B, V   P, T
Ed Sullivan, Eddie Cantor, Shirley Temple
Includes highlights from the 30's such as Shirley Temple's "Biggest Little Star of the Thirties" and Lew Lehr's "Cwazy Monkies." Also features Ed Sullivan, Eddie Cantor, Jack Dempsey, and Little Rascals.
Educational et al — *Blackhawk Films*

From China with Death 1973
Martial arts
63859   90 mins   C   B, V   P
After a vicious War Lord wipes out his family, a young man trains under a martial arts master to prepare himself for revenge.
MPAA:R
United International Pictures — *Budget Video*

From Russia with Love 1963
Suspense
53787   118 mins   C   B, V, LV, CED   P
Sean Connery, Robert Shaw, Daniela Bianchi, Lotte Lenya
A Russian spy joins an international crime organization and develops a plan to kill James Bond and steal a coding machine. The second Bond feature.
United Artists; Eon; Harry Saltzman; Albert Broccoli — *CBS/Fox Video; RCA VideoDiscs*

From the Earth to the Moon 1958
Science fiction
11723   100 mins   C   B, V   P
George Sanders, Joseph Cotton
Jules Verne's thriller in which three men and a woman rocket to the moon.
Warner Bros — *VCI Home Video*

From the New World 1982
Music-Performance
47807   ? mins   C   LV   P
Dvorak's "Symphony No. 9 in E minor, Op.95—From the New World" is performed by the Czech Philharmonic Orchestra (stereo).
Unknown — *Pioneer Video Imports*

From Worst to First 1980
Football
45131   24 mins   C   B, V, FO   R, P
Tampa Bay Buccaneers
Highlights of the 1979 Tampa Bay Buccaneers football season.
NFL Films — *NFL Films Video*

Front, The 1976
Drama
58961   95 mins   C   B, V   P
Woody Allen, Zero Mostel, Herschel Bernardi, Michael Murphy, Diana Marcovicci, directed by Martin Ritt
A bookmaker becomes a "front" for blacklisted writers during the communist witch hunts of the 1950's.
MPAA:PG
Columbia — *RCA/Columbia Pictures Home Video*

Front Page, The 1931
Comedy
57760   101 mins   B/W   B, V   P
Adolph Menjou, Pat O'Brien, Edward Everett Horton, directed by Lewis Milestone
The original version of the Hecht-MacArthur play about a battling newspaper reporter and his editor in Chicago.
United Artists — *Budget Video; Discount Video Tapes; Cable Films; Video Connection; Video Yesteryear; Western Film & Video Inc; Classic Video Cinema Collector's Club*

Frontier Justice 1935
Western
14212   56 mins   B/W   B, V   P
Hoot Gibson, Richard Cramer

Sheepherders and cattlemen clash over land rights in thislively western.
Grand National — *Video Connection; Penguin Video*

Frontier Pony Express　　　　　　1939
Western
64389　54 mins　B/W　B, V, 3/4U　　　P
Roy Rogers
Roy and Trigger do their best to help the Pony Express riders who are being attacked by marauding gangs.
Republic — *Nostalgia Merchant*

Frontier Scout　　　　　　　　1938
Western
08847　60 mins　B/W　B, V, 3/4U　　　P
George Houston, Mantan Moreland
An action-packed western.
Grand National — *Penguin Video; Sheik Video*

Frontier Vengeance　　　　　　1940
Western
64420　54 mins　B/W　B, V, 3/4U　　　P
Don "Red" Barry
A stagecoach driver helps a young girl who is being terrorized by crooks.
Republic — *Nostalgia Merchant*

Frontschau, Die (The　　　　　　1941
Front Shows)
World War II/Propaganda
52316　60 mins　B/W　B, V, 3/4U　　　P
These combat documentaries made by the Nazis, never shown to the German public, were meant to be screened for German troops to initiate them to the reality of life and death at the front. "Front Shows" 5/6, 7 and 8 are included. German dialogue with English subtitles.
GE
Germany — *International Historic Films*

Fuerte Perdido (Fort　　　　　　1978
Lost)
Western
51102　90 mins　C　B, V　　　　P
Esther Rojo, German Cobos, Mario Vidal
Settlers battle for their lives against hostile Indians led by Geronimo. In Spanish.
SP
Spanish — *Budget Video*

Fugitive: The Final　　　　　　1967
Episode, The
Drama
53788　103 mins　C　B, V　　　　P
David Janssen, Barry Morse, Bill Raisch, Diane Baker, Joseph Campanella, Michael Constantine
The final episode of the acclaimed series, aired on August 29, 1967, in which Dr. Richard Kimble meets up with the one-armed man who murdered his wife. This episode was the highest rated program up to that time.
Quinn Martin Prods — *Worldvision Home Video; RCA VideoDiscs*

Fugitive, The (The Taking　　　　1915
of Luke McVane)
Western
66134　28 mins　B/W　B, V, FO　　　P
William S. Hart, Enid Markey
An early silent western in which Hart upholds the cowboy code of honor.
Thomas Ince — *Video Yesteryear*

Full Hearts and Empty　　　　　1963
Pockets
Drama
63623　88 mins　B/W　B, V, FO　　　P
Linda Christian, Gino Cervi, Senta Berger
This film follows the happy-go-lucky adventures of a young, handsome, impoverished gentleman on the loose in Rome. Dubbed in English.
Screen Gems — *Video Yesteryear*

Fun and Fancy Free　　　　　　1947
Musical/Comedy
63126　96 mins　C　B, V　　　R, P
Edgar Bergen, Charlie McCarthy, Jiminy Cricket, Mickey Mouse, Donald Duck, Goofy, the voice of Dinah Shore
This part-animated, part-live-action feature is split into two segments: "Bongo," with Dinah Shore narrating the story of a happy-go-lucky circus bear; and "Mickey and the Beanstalk," a "new" version of an old fairy tale.
Walt Disney Productions — *Walt Disney Home Video*

Fun and Games　　　　　　　1982
Games
47677　? mins　C　LV　　　　P
Maureen McGovern, Meadowlark Lemon, Bill Murray
An innovative participative program combining fun and learning in a collection of old and new games from around the world: tongue twisters, yo-yo, frisbees, etc. An interactive disc which runs 60 minutes when played through.
Scholastic Productions — *Optical Programming Associates*

Fun Factory/Clown　　　　　　196?
Princes of Hollywood
Comedy
10110　56 mins　B/W　B, V　　　P, T
Mack Sennett, Charlie Chaplin, Buster Keaton, Charley Chase, Ben Turpin, Stan Laurel
Collection of various slapstick situations including Keystone Cops segments. From the "History of Motion Pictures" series.
Mack Sennett et al — *Blackhawk Films*

(For Explanation of codes, see USE GUIDE and KEY)　　　

Fun in Acapulco   1963
Musical
08382   97 mins   C   B, V   P
*Elvis Presley, Ursula Andress, Elsa Cardenas,
Paul Lukas*
Elvis romances two beauties and acts as a part-
time lifeguard and night club entertainer.
EL, SP
Paramount; Hal Wallis — *CBS/Fox Video;
RCA VideoDiscs*

Fun with Dick and Jane   1977
Comedy
21286   104 mins   C   B, V   P
George Segal, Jane Fonda, Ed McMahon
An upper-middle class couple turn to armed
robbery to support themselves when the
husband is fired from his job.
MPAA:PG
Columbia — *RCA/Columbia Pictures Home
Video*

Fundamentals of Karate   1982
Martial arts/Physical fitness
47301   98 mins   C   B, V   P
This program teaches practical self-defense
techniques and demonstrates that practicing
Karate is an effective daily exercise workout.
Martial Arts Video — *Martial Arts Video*

Fundamentals of Normal   19??
and Corrective
Horseshoeing
Animals
69664   60 mins   B/W   B, V   P
This program (40 mins.) explores many sizes
and styles of horseshoes. This tape also
contains a second program, "Corrective
Shoeing for Navicular Disease and Laminitis"
(color, 20 mins.).
Colorado State U — *Mercedes Maharis
Productions*

Funeral for an Assassin   1977
Adventure
52610   92 mins   C   B, V   R, P
Vic Morrow, Peter Van Dissel
A professional assassin seeks revenge for his
imprisonment by the government of South
Africa, a former client. Planning to kill all of the
country's leading politicians, he masquerades
as a black man, a cover which is designed to
fool the apartheid establishment.
MPAA:PG
Walter Brough; Ivan Hall — *Video Gems*

Funeral Home   1982
Horror
66257   90 mins   C   B, V   P
Lesleh Donaldson, Kay Hawtry
A terrified teen spends her summer vacation at
her grandmother's tourist home, a former
funeral parlor.

William Fruet — *Paragon Video Productions*

Funhouse, The   1981
Horror
47415   96 mins   C   B, V   P
*Elizabeth Berridge, Shawn Carson, Cooper
Huckabee, Largo Woodruff, Sylvia Miles,
directed by Tobe Hooper*
Four teenagers spend the night at a carnival
funhouse and are brutally hacked and maimed
by a crazed father and son.
MPAA:R
Universal — *MCA Home Video*

Funnier Side of Eastern   1974
Canada with Steve
Martin, The
Comedy/Travel
33708   60 mins   C   B, V   P
In his first television special, Steve Martin
"tours" eastern Canada, taking his viewers to
lunch at a fancy French restaurant, to Toronto's
city hall, and to other attractions. The zany
comedian performs magic tricks, plays the
banjo, and juggles.
Bruce Campbell — *Independent United
Distributors*

Funny Farm, The   1982
Comedy
69675   90 mins   C   B, V   R, P
Miles Chapin, Eileen Brennan, Peter Ackroyd
A group of ambitious young comics strive to
make it in the crazy world of comedy at Los
Angeles' famous club, The Funny Farm.
Independent — *THORN EMI Home Video*

Funny Girl   1968
Musical-Drama
64237   151 mins   C   B, V   P
*Barbra Streisand, Omar Sharif, Walter Pidgeon,
Kay Medford, Anne Francis, directed by William
Wyler*
This films follows the early career of Fanny
Brice, her rise to stardom with the Ziegfeld
Follies and her stormy romance with Nick
Arnstein. The classic songs "People" and
"Don't Rain on My Parade" are featured. In
stereo.
Academy Awards '68: Best Actress (Streisand).
MPAA:G
Columbia; Ray Stark — *RCA/Columbia
Pictures Home Video; RCA VideoDiscs*

Funny Guys and Gals of   193?
the Talkies
Comedy
11285   60 mins   B/W   B, V, FO   P
*W.C. Fields, Shirley Temple, Charlotte
Greenwood, Groucho Marx, Marlene Dietrich*
Four short pictures featuring the comedy stars
of the early talking pictures: "The Golf

Specialist," "Pardon My Pups," "Girls Will Be Boys," and "Band Rally Radio Show."
Mack Sennett et al — *Video Yesteryear*

Funny Thing Happened on the Way to the Forum, A   1966
Comedy
47794   99 mins   C   B, V, LV, CED   P
Zero Mostel, Phil Silvers, Jack Gilford, Buster Keaton, directed by Richard Lester
A bawdy Broadway farce set in ancient Rome where a conniving, eager-to-be-free slave sees his way to freedom.
United Artists — *CBS/Fox Video; RCA VideoDiscs*

Funstuff   193?
Comedy
10042   59 mins   B/W   B, V   P, T
Shirley Temple, Harold Lloyd
Shirley Temple and friends struggle for stardom. Harold Lloyd plays "Non-Stop Kid" and Snub Pollard strives to be an artist.
Educational et al — *Blackhawk Films*

Furniture Refinishing   1982
Home improvement
47360   30 mins   C   V   P
This program provides instruction on how to give furniture a professionally refinished look at home.
American Home Video Library — *American Home Video Library*

Fury, The   1978
Horror
56903   117 mins   C   B, V   P
Kirk Douglas, John Cassavetes, Carrie Snodgress, Andrew Stevens, Amy Irving, Charles Durning, directed by Brian dePalma
The head of a government institute for psychic research finds that his own son is wanted by terrorists who wish to use his lethal powers.
MPAA:R
Twentieth Century Fox, Frank Yablans — *CBS/Fox Video*

Fury on Wheels   1971
Adventure
60406   89 mins   C   B, V   P
Judd Hirsch, Tom Ligon, Paul Sorvino, Logan Ramsey, Colin Wilcox
A tale of men who race cars and wreak havoc.
MPAA:PG
Cannon Releasing; Christopher C Dewey — *Paragon Video Productions*

Futureworld   1976
Science fiction
53512   107 mins   C   B, V   R, P
Peter Fonda, Blythe Danner, Arthur Hill, Yul Brenner, Stu Margolin
In the sequel to "Westworld," two reporters junket to the new "Futureworld," where they support a scheme to clone and control world leaders.
MPAA:PG
American Intl Pictures — *Warner Home Video; Vestron Video (disc only)*

Futz   1969
Drama
60224   90 mins   C   B, V   P
John Pakos, Victor Lipari
This story from off-Broadway is of a man who loves his pig and the world who can't understand it.
Commonwealth United — *Independent United Distributors*

Fuzz   1972
Adventure/Comedy-Drama
69383   92 mins   C   B, V, CED   p
Burt Reynolds, Tom Skerritt, Yul Brynner, Raquel Welch
Combining fast action and sharp-edged humor, this film portrays the life of a band of police officers trying to keep the streets of Boston safe.
MPAA:PG
United Artists — *CBS/Fox Video*

Fyre   1978
Drama
55215   90 mins   C   B, V   P
The story of a young beautiful girl who moves from the midwest to Los Angeles unfolds as she becomes a prostitute and encounters many new experiences.
MPAA:R
Fyre Productions — *Media Home Entertainment*

G

Gaiety   1943
Musical
08737   40 mins   B/W   B, V, 3/4U   P
Antonio Moreno, Armida, Anne Ayers
Explores the lighter side of lion hunting.
Hal Roach — *Penguin Video*

Gaiking   1982
Cartoons
64199   100 mins   C   B, V   P
Animated
The mighty flying rubork, Gaiking, becomes earth's strongest and most heroic defense against the cunning Davius.

EL, SP
Toei Animation; Jim Terry Production — *Family Home Entertainment*

Galactica III: Conquest of the Earth　1980
Science fiction
59684　99 mins　C　B, V　　　　P
Lorne Greene, Kent McCord, Barry Van Dyke, Robin Douglas, Robert Reed
In an encounter with Earth, Commander Adama sends Lt. Troy and Lt. Dillon to the U.S. in order to bring the earthlings up to their level of technology.
MPAA:R
Universal — *MCA Home Video*

Galaxina　1981
Science fiction/Comedy
55550　96 mins　C　B, V, LV　　　P
Dorothy Stratten, Avery Schreiber, Stephen Macht
In the 31st century, a beautiful robot woman capable of human feelings is created. A parody of superspace fantasies.
MPAA:R
Crown International; Marilyn Tenser — *MCA Home Video*

Galaxy Express　1980
Fantasy/Cartoons
65709　94 mins　C　B, V　　　　P
Animated, voices by Booker Bradshaw, Corey Burton
A young boy sets out to find immortality by traveling on The Galaxy Express, an ultra-modern 35th century Ospace train that carries its passengers in search of their dreams.
MPAA:PG
Toei — *Embassy Home Entertainment*

Galaxy of Terror　1981
Science fiction/Horror
65719　85 mins　C　B, V　　　　P
Erin Moran, Edward Albert, Ray Walston
The mind's innermost fears become reality when a spaceship rescue mission lands on a dark and barren planet.
MPAA:R
Roger Corman; Marc Siegler — *Embassy Home Entertainment*

Gallipoli　1981
Drama
59203　111 mins　C　B, V, LV　　R, P
Mel Gibson, Mark Lee, directed by Peter Weir
History blends with the destiny of two friends as they become part of a legendary World War I confrontation between Australia and the German Allied Turks.
MPAA:PG

Paramount; Robert Stigwood — *Paramount Home Video*

Galloping Dynamite　1937
Western
56600　58 mins　B/W　B, V　　　P
Kermit Maynard
Early film western based on a James Oliver Curwood story.
Maurice Conn — *Video Dimensions*

Gambler, The　1974
Drama
59425　111 mins　C　B, V, LV　　R, P
James Caan, Lauren Hutton, Paul Sorvino, Burt Young, directed by Karl Reisz
The story of a college professor who is also a compulsive gambler who falls into debt and trouble with the mob.
MPAA:R
Paramount — *Paramount Home Video*

Gambling Terror, The　1937
Western
15446　60 mins　B/W　B, V　　　P
Johnny Mack Brown
Gambler defies racketeers who sell protection to businessmen.
Republic — *Video Connection*

Gambling with Souls　1936
Drama/Exploitation
48738　60 mins　B/W　B, V, 3/4U　　P
A girl is lured into gambling by her best friend. After losing a large sum of money, she tries to earn it back through prostitution.
Unknown — *Penguin Video*

Game of Death　1979
Martial arts/Adventure
59624　100 mins　C　B, V, CED　　P
Bruce Lee, Dean Jagger, Colleen Camp
Bruce Lee's final kung fu thriller about a young martial arts movie star who gets involved with the syndicate.
MPAA:R
Galaxy Films — *CBS/Fox Video*

Game Show Program　195?
Game show
33692　120 mins　B/W　B, V, 3/4U　　P
Exciting quiz shows of the 1950s are seen in their entirety: "Do You Trust Your Wife," with Edgar Bergen and Charlie McCarthy, "You Bet Your Life," with Groucho Marx, "The Price Is Right," with Bill Cullen, and "Play Your Hunch," with Merv Griffin.
CBS et al — *Shokus Video*

Game Show Program II　196?
Game show
33693　120 mins　B/W　B, V, 3/4U　　P

A collection of four game show programs including: "People Are Funny," with Art Linkletter, "Take a Good Look," with Ernie Kovacs, "Concentration," with Hugh Downs, and "I've Got a Secret," starring Steve Allen and a celebrity panel.
CBS et al — *Shokus Video*

Game Show Program III 196?
Game show
33695　120 mins　C　B, V, 3/4U　P
Four favorite game shows of the past twenty years are seen in their entirety: "The Price Is Right," "Truth or Consequences," "The Face Is Familiar," and "PDQ." Some black and white.
NBC et al — *Shokus Video*

Gandhi 1982
Drama
65186　188 mins　C　B, V　P
Ben Kingsley, Candice Bergen, Edward Fox, John Gielgud, John Mills, Martin Sheen, directed by Sir Richard Attenborough
A sprawling biography of Mahatma Gandhi, India's man of peace, which follows his life from his simple beginnings as a lawyer in South Africa through his struggle to free India from colonial rule.
Academy Awards '82: Best Picture; Best Actor (Kingsley); Best Director. MPAA:PG
Columbia — *RCA/Columbia Pictures Home Video; RCA VideoDiscs*

Gang Wars 1984
Martial arts
73017　90 mins　C　B, V　P
There's a riot going on as Puerto Rican, Black, and Chinese gangs fight it out for control of the city.
MPAA:R
Niki Patton and Steve Madoff — *Sun Video*

Gangbusters 1938
Mystery/Serials
07381　253 mins　B/W　B, V, 3/4U　R, P
Kent Taylor, Irene Hervey, Robert Armstrong
Men battle crime in the city. A serial based on the popular radio series of the same name. In thirteen episodes.
Universal — *Cable Films; Video Connection; Video Dimensions; Video Yesteryear*

Gangs, Inc. 1941
Crime-Drama
58515　72 mins　B/W　B, V, 3/4U　P
Alan Ladd, Joan Woodbury, Jack LaRue, Linda Ware, John Archer, Vince Barnett
The story of how a woman with an unhappy past turned to a life of crime. Also known as "Paper Bullets."
Producers Releasing Corp — *Penguin Video; Discount Video Tapes*

Gangster Wars, The 1981
Crime-Drama
47416　121 mins　C　B, V　P
Michael Nouri, Joe Penny
A specially edited-for-video version of the television mini-series, "The Gangster Chronicles." Based on fact, it deals with the growth of organized crime in America from the early days of this century, concentrating on three ghetto kids who grow up to become powerful mobsters.
Universal — *MCA Home Video*

Gangsters 19??
Crime-Drama
65645　90 mins　C　B, V　R, P
A city is ruled by the mob and nothing can stop their bloody grip except "The Special Squad."
Italian — *Video City Productions*

Gangway 1937
Musical
01634　88 mins　B/W　B, V　P
Jessie Matthews, Nat Pendleton, Alastair Sim, directed by Sonnie Hale
A musical-comedy spoof of gangster pictures in which a girl reporter poses as a maid to get a story.
Gaumont British — *Sheik Video*

Gar Wood: The Silver Fox 1954
Biographical/Boating
44242　15 mins　B/W　B, V　P
Through classic newsreel footage, this program shows the career of speedboat racer Gar Wood.
Fox Movietone News — *Two Star Films*

Garden of the Finzi-Continis, The 1971
Drama
37519　90 mins　C　B, V　R, P
Dominique Sanda, Helmut Berger, Lino Capolicchio, Fabio Testi, directed by Vittorio De Sica
The story of an aristocratic Jewish family living under increasing Fascist opporession in pre-World War II Italy.
MPAA:R
Cinema 5 — *RCA/Columbia Pictures Home Video*

Gardening at Home 1983
Gardening
68889　60 mins　C　LV　P
This program provides the fundamentals of gardening for both the beginner and expert gardener.
AM Available
Xerox Publishing — *Xerox Publishing*

Gardening in the City: I 1982
Gardening/Plants
59574   60 mins   C   B, V   P
Members of the world-famous New York
Botanical Gardens' staff offer an illuminating
introduction to plant life.
New York Botanical Gardens — *Mastervision*

Gardening in the City: II 1982
Gardening/Plants
59575   60 mins   C   B, V   P
The scientists of the New York Botanical
Gardens give examples of proper soil and
planting conditions and offer lessons in the use
of fertilizers and correct pruning methods.
New York Botanical Gardens — *Mastervision*

**Garlic Is as Good as Ten
Mothers** 1980
Folklore/Documentary
60469   51 mins   C   B, V, 3/4U   P
A foray into the history, consumption,
cultivation, and culinary and curvative power of
allium sativum, filmed in the kitchens of Chez
Panisse and Flint's Bar-B-que in Berkeley, and
Truckee's paradise for Lovers of the Stinking
Rose, La Vielle Mansion.
Les Blank — *Flower Films*

**Gary Numan—The
Touring Principal '79** 1980
Music-Performance
54689   60 mins   C   B, V   R, P
Gary Numan
This program features Gary Numan, the British
singer/composer, on his 1979 world tour.
Material includes selections from his second
album "The Pleasure Principle" including the hit
single. "Cars."
Warner Bros — *Warner Home Video*

Gas 1981
Comedy
58711   94 mins   C   B, V   R, P
*Donald Sutherland, Susan Anspach, Sterling
Hayden, Peter Aykroyd, Helen Shaver*
A gas shortage hits an average American town.
MPAA:R
Paramount; Claude Heroux — *Paramount
Home Video*

Gas Pump Girls 1982
Comedy
59657   102 mins   C   B, V, LV   R, P
Five lovely ladies manage a gas station and use
their feminine wiles to win the battle against a
shady oil sheik.
MPAA:R
David A Davies — *Wonderlust Video*

Gates of Hell, The 1983
Horror
66258   90 mins   C   B, V   P
*Christopher George, Katherine MacColl, Robert
Sampson*
A town battles the force of evil.
Jerry Zimmerman; Michael
Franzese — *Paragon Video Productions*

Gator 1976
Adventure
63401   116 mins   C   B, V   P
*Burt Reynolds, Jerry Reed, Lauren Hutton,
directed by Burt Reynolds*
This sequel to "White Lightning" follows the
adventures of Gator (Reynolds), who is
recruited to gather evidence to convict a corrupt
political boss.
MPAA:PG
United Artists — *CBS/Fox Video*

Gator Bait 1973
Drama
60220   90 mins   C   B, V   P
Claudia Jennings
The Louisiana swamp is home to Desiree, and
woe be unto any man who threatens her family.
MPAA:R
Sebastian Films — *Independent United
Distributors*

Gauntlet, The 1977
Crime-Drama/Adventure
58233   111 mins   C   B, V   R, P
*Clint Eastwood, Sondra Locke, directed by Clint
Eastwood*
A cop is ordered to Las Vegas to bring back a
key witness for an important trial—but the
witness turns out to be a beautiful prostitute
being hunted by killers.
MPAA:R
Warner Bros — *Warner Home Video; RCA
VideoDiscs*

Gay Divorcee, The 1934
Musical
00269   107 mins   B/W   B, V, 3/4U   P
*Fred Astaire, Ginger Rogers, Edward Everett
Horton, Alice Brady, Erik Rhodes, Betty Grable*
Fred pursues Ginger to an English seaside
resort, where she mistakes him for her hired co-
respondent. Songs include "Night and Day,"
"Don't Let It Bother You" and "Needle in a
Haystack."
Academy Awards '34: Best Song (The
Continental; Con Conrad and Herb Magidson).
RKO; Pandro S Berman — *Nostalgia Merchant*

Gay Ranchero, The 1942
Western
10700   55 mins   B/W   B, V   P
Roy Rogers, Andy Devine

A sheriff hunts for a commercial airways plane that has disappeared.
Republic — *Video Connection; Cable Films*

General, The 1927
Comedy
12429 80 mins B/W B, V P
Buster Keaton, Marion Mack, directed by Buster Keaton, Clyde Bruckman
A Civil War espionage spoof. A Confederate soldier almost wins the war single handedly when he goes behind Northern lines to recover his beloved locomotive. (Silent).
United Artists — *Budget Video; Blackhawk Films; Interurban Films; Video Yesteryear; Video Dimensions; Sheik Video; Cable Films; Western Film & Video Inc; Discount Video Tapes*

General Della Rovere 1960
Adventure
76638 139 mins B/W B, V P
Vittorio De Sica, Hannes Messemer, Sandra Milo
A petty con man fleeces his victims by posing as a Colonel.
Zebra; Gaumont — *Budget Video*

General Doolittle: Wild Blue Yonder 1954
Biographical/History-US
44254 15 mins B/W B, V P
The story of General Dolittle, test pilot and speed racer, is told in this program. Accounts of his bombing mission against Tokyo and the winning of the Congressional Medal of Honor are discussed. Classic newsreel footage.
Fox Movietone News — *Two Star Films*

General Douglas MacArthur: I Shall Return 1954
Biographical/History-US
44255 15 mins B/W B, V P
Classic newsreel footage of Douglas MacArthur from the start of his military career to the finish. As Army Chief of Staff he returned to the Philippines. Later he became Supreme Commander of the Armed Forces in the Pacific and went on to fight in Korea. Truman's abrupt dismissal ended his military career.
Fox Movietone News — *Two Star Films*

General Line, The 1929
Drama/Film-History
52345 90 mins B/W B, V, 3/4U P
Marta Lapkina, directed by Sergei Eisenstein
Classic Russian silent film with English subtitles, about a country women who starts a village co-operative.
USSR; Sovkino — *International Historic Films; Festival Films*

General Marshall: Soldier of Peace 1954
Biographical/History-US
44253 15 mins B/W B, V P
The career of General George Marshall, "Soldier of Peace," is shown in this program. He won the Nobel Prize, proposed the Marshall Plan, was Secretary of State, and was also Secretary of Defense. Classic newsreel footage.
Fox Movietone News — *Two Star Films*

General Montgomery: The Black Beret 1954
Biographical/World War II
44246 15 mins B/W B, V P
Through classic newsreel footage, this program shows General Field Marshal Bernard Montgomery in his 8th Army defeat of Rommel. This defeat was one of the first turning points of the war and led to the conquest of Africa.
Fox Movietone News — *Two Star Films*

General Patton: The Fighting Man 1954
Biographical/World War II
44247 15 mins B/W B, V P
An historical account of the wartime accomplishments of General Patton. He is noted for his battles in North Africa, Sicily, Italy, Normandy, Metz, and Bastogne during the second World War. Classic newsreel footage.
Fox Movietone News — *Two Star Films*

General Pershing: The Iron Commander 1954
Biographical/History-US
44251 15 mins B/W B, V P
The story of the spirit behind the American doughboy, General Pershing, who when Paris was almost at its knees led his soldiers in the defeat of the Germans. Classic newsreel footage.
Fox Movietone News — *Two Star Films*

General, The/Slapstick 1926
Film-History
50639 56 mins B/W B, V P, T
Buster Keaton, Marion Mack, Charlie Murray, Mabel Normand, Fatty Arbuckle, Edgar Kennedy
A double feature composed of abridged versions of the Buster Keaton spoof on Civil War espionage, and a Mack Sennett anthology of slapstick comedy.
United Artists — *Blackhawk Films*

Genesis/Three Sides Live 1982
Music-Performance
63352 90 mins C B, V R, P
Rock supergroup Genesis performs some of their greatest hits live in concert, including "No

Reply at All," "Misunderstanding" and "Behind the Lines."
Rooster Video — *THORN EMI Home Video*

Genevieve 1953
Comedy
59904   86 mins   C   B, V   P
Dianah Sheridan, John Gregson, Kay Kendall, Kenneth More, directed by Henry Cornelius
Two friendly rivals engage in a race on the way back from the Brighton veteran car rally.
Rank — *Embassy Home Entertainment*

Gentle Hand, The 1968
Vietnam War
53692   29 mins   C   B, V, 3/4U   P
This program shows American surgeons giving medical aid and instruction to South Vietnamese citizens in the village of Rach Gia, Vietnam.
Unknown — *International Historic Films*

Gentleman Jim 1942
Drama
53671   104 mins   B/W   CED   P
Errol Flynn, Alan Hale, Alexis Smith, Jack Carson, Ward Bond, William Frawley, directed by Raoul Walsh
The rise to fame of boxer Jim Corbett, during the 1880's when boxing was outlawed.
Warner Bros; Robert Buckner — *RCA VideoDiscs*

Gentlemen of Titpu 1982
Opera
72216   48 mins   C   B, V   P
Animated version of Gilbert and Sullivan's "The Mikado."
Unknown — *Paragon Video Productions*

Gentlemen Prefer Blondes 1953
Comedy
08441   91 mins   C   B, V   P
Marilyn Monroe, Jane Russell, Charles Coburn, Elliot Reid, directed by Howard Hawks
Two showgirls land in police court while seeking rich husbands or diamonds.
20th Century Fox — *CBS/Fox Video*

George Burns and Gracie Allen Show, The 1951
Comedy
38991   30 mins   B/W   B, V, FO   P
George Burns, Gracie Allen, Harry Von Zell, Bea Benaderet, Fred Clark
A live Christmas show from the first year of the popular series. Gracie gives her unique version of "A Christmas Carol." Originally telecast December 23, 1951.
CBS — *Video Yesteryear*

George Burns Show, The 1959
Comedy
58638   30 mins   B/W   B, V, FO   P
George Burns, Harry Von Zell, Larry Keating, Ronnie Burns, Bea Benaderet, Judi Meredith, Lisa Davis, Carol Channing
Carol Channing sues George in this episode, "The Hollywood Television Courtroom." George sings "Please Don't Take Me Home," and Harry steals the show as an announcer forced to drink his sponsors' products. Sponsored by Colgate, Fab and Ajax, with original commercials included.
NBC — *Video Yesteryear*

George Melies, Cinema Magician 1978
Science fiction/Film-History
59405   17 mins   C   B, V   P, T
A look at film pioneer George Melies who originated the use of special effects in cinema. (Some black and white).
Patrick Montgomery — *Blackhawk Films*

George Mikan: Mr. Basketball 1954
Biographical/Basketball
44261   15 mins   B/W   B, V   P
The story of George Mikan, one of basketball's greatest competitors, who set most of the game's scoring records. Classic newsreel footage.
Fox Movietone News — *Two Star Films*

George Schaefer's Showcase Theatre 196?
Drama
64849   76 mins   C   B, V, 3/4U   P
10   pgms
Originally presented on the "Hallmark Hall of Fame" during the 1960's, these ten dramatic films are among the best of director George Schaefer's works. All programs are available individually; full information is provided in the individual listings.
1.The Tempest 2.Give Us Barabbas! 3.Elizabeth the Queen 4.Soldier in Love 5.Lamp at Midnight 6.The Holy Terror 7.Barefoot in Athens 8.A Punt, a Pass and a Prayer 9.Victoria Regina 10.The Invincible Mr. Disraeli
George Schaefer — *Enter-Tel Inc*

George White's Scandals 1945
Musical
13644   95 mins   B/W   B, V   P, T
Joan Davis, Jack Haley, Jane Greer
Musical comedy look at show biz world. Jazz numbers by Gene Krupa and his band.
RKO; George White — *Blackhawk Films*

Geppetto's Music Shop 1982
Fairy tales
64953   90 mins   C   B, V   R, P

Kindly toymaker Geppetto gathers the children of the village in his house to tell them stories, seen in animation, all drawn from the greats of children's literature.
MPAA:G
Century Video — *Video Gems*

German Invasion of Poland — 1939
World War II
53378   60 mins   B/W   B, V, 3/4U   P
This documentary offers the world's first look at Hitler's army at war. English subtitled.
GE
Germany — *International Historic Films*

German Propaganda Video Special — 193?
Propaganda
58544   30 mins   B/W   B, V, 3/4U   P
Four short propaganda films of Nazi Germany: Leni Riefenstahl's "Day of Freedom;" "Munich 1938 Arts Festival;" "Eternal Jew," and "Harvest Festival."
UFA — *Penguin Video*

Germany Awake — 194?
Documentary/Propaganda
58513   90 mins   B/W   B, V, 3/4U   P
A documentary on the German motion picture and its use as a propaganda tool, from "Triumph of the Will" to the fall of the Third Reich.
Germany — *Penguin Video; Discount Video Tapes; International Historic Films*

Germany Celebrates Hitler's Birthday — 1939
Propaganda/Germany
72476   21 mins   B/W   B, V, 3/4U   P
On April 20th, 1939 the Third Reich celebrated Hitler's birthday with an unprecedented display of pomp and military prowess. This Nazi newsreel records the pageantry that engulfed all of Berlin as well as the military procession that filed past Hitler for four hours.
Germany — *International Historic Films*

Gerry Mulligan — 1981
Music-Performance
75897   18 mins   C   B, V   P
This program presents the jazz music of Gerry Mulligan featuring his compositions "K4 Pacific" and "North Atlantic Run."
Jazz America Ltd — *Sony Corporation of America*

Gervaise — 1957
Drama
10909   89 mins   B/W   B, V   P
Maria Schell, Francoise Perier
Woman must support family when husband takes to drink. Eventually she is dragged down to his level. Based on Emile Zola's "L'Assommier." French film, English subtitles. New York Film Critics Award '57: Best Foreign Film of the Year.   FR
French; Continental — *Discount Video Tapes; Festival Films; Western Film & Video Inc*

Get Crazy — 1983
Comedy/Musical
64981   90 mins   C   B, V, LV,   P
                              CED
Malcolm McDowell, Allen Goorwitz, Daniel Stern, Gail Edwards
The owner of the Saturn Theatre is attempting to stage the biggest rock-and-roll concert of all time on New Year's Eve 1983, and everything is going wrong.
Unknown — *Embassy Home Entertainment*

Get Fit, Stay Fit — 1978
Physical fitness
42778   60 mins   C   B, V   P
Ann Dugan
This series of three 20-minute programs is intended for all ages interested in total body conditioning.
Health N Action — *RCA/Columbia Pictures Home Video*

Get Happy — 193?
Comedy
10043   59 mins   B/W   B, V   P, T
Shirley Temple, Weber and Fields, Bessie Smith
Includes Shirley Temple in "Glad Rags to Riches," Weber and Fields in "Beer is Here," and Bessie Smith in "St. Louis Blues." Also a Flip the Frog Cartoon.
Educational et al — *Blackhawk Films*

Get Out Your Handkerchiefs — 1978
Comedy
47372   109 mins   C   B, V   R, P
Gerard Depardieu, Patrick Dewaere, Casole Laure
Two men try to make one woman happy, then lose her to a precocious, 13-year-old boy. Academy Awards '78: Best Foreign Language Film.   MPAA:R
Springmill Productions — *Warner Home Video*

Getaway, The — 1972
Adventure
68233   122 mins   C   B, V   R, P
Steve McQueen, Ali MacGraw
Steve McQueen and Ali MacGraw star as husband and wife bank robbers traveling across Texas to get away from a corrupt politician and the state police.
MPAA:PG
Warner Brothers — *Warner Home Video*

Getting Around   1934
Trains
68917   14 mins   B/W   B, V   P
This program covers all segments of the Detroit
Street Railway System—trolley service, bus
service, power generation track and overhead
maintenance and fleet repair.
Detroit Street Railway System — *Interurban
Films*

Getting It On   1983
Comedy
72226   100 mins   C   B, V   P
A high school student uses his new-found video
equipment for voyeuristic activity.
MPAA:R
Cromworld — *Vestron Video*

Getting Mama Married   195?
Comedy
12599   60 mins   B/W   B, V   P
Amos and Andy
Special double length episode starring Amos
and Andy.
CBS — *Video Connection*

Getting of Wisdom, The   1980
Drama
52743   100 mins   C   CED   P
Susannah Fowle, directed by Bruce Beresford
An adaptation of the classic Australian novel,
about the trials of an extraordinary teenage girl
at an exclusive finishing school in turn of the
century Melbourne, the heroine—Laura
Rambotham—a gifted pianist who struggles to
assert her individuality in the stuffy climate of
Victorian conformity.
Australia; Southern Cross Films — *CBS/Fox
Video*

Getting Wasted   1980
Comedy
59331   98 mins   C   B, V   P
Brian Kerwin, Stephen Furst, Cooper Huckabee
Set in 1969 at a military academy for
troublesome young men, chaos ensues when
the cadets meet the hippies.
MPAA:PG
David Buanno — *VCI Home Video*

Ghidrah the Three   1965
Headed Monster
Science fiction
01668   85 mins   C   B, V   P
*Yosuke Natsuki, Yuriko Hoshi, Rodan and
Mothra, Directed by Inoshiro Honda*
When three-headed monster from outer-space
threatens world, humans appeal to the friendly
Mothra, Rodan, and Godzilla.
Toho Productions — *Budget Video; Video
Connection; VCII; Discount Video Tapes; Video
Yesteryear; Admit One Video*

Ghost Dance   1983
Horror
75624   93 mins   C   B, V   P
A sacred Indian burial ground is violated, with
grim results.
Looseyard Ltd — *Trans World Entertainment*

Ghost Patrol   1936
Western
11728   57 mins   B/W   B, V   P
Tim Mc Coy
G-Men of the West ride hard in this action
western.
Puritan — *Video Connection; VCI Home Video*

Ghost Story   1981
Suspense
47417   110 mins   C   B, V, LV   P
*Fred Astaire, Melvyn Douglas, Douglas
Fairbanks Jr., John Houseman, Patricia Neal*
Four elderly men, members of an informal social
club called the Chowder Society, share a terrible
secret buried deep in their pasts. Based on the
best-selling novel by Peter Straub.
MPAA:R
Universal — *MCA Home Video*

Ghost Town Law   1942
Western
15412   62 mins   B/W   B, V   P
Buck Jones, Tim McCoy, Raymond Hatton
A sheriff's badge brings trouble. The Three
Mesquiteers step into save the day.
Monogram — *Video Connection; Cable Films;
Discount Video Tapes*

Ghosts of Berkeley   1947
Square, The
Comedy
63621   61 mins   B/W   B, V, FO   P
Robert Morley, Felix Aylmer
The ghosts of two retired soldiers of the early
18th century are doomed to haunt their former
home, and only a visit from a reigning monarch
can free them.
NTA Pictures — *Video Yesteryear*

Ghosts on the Loose   1943
Mystery
08759   67 mins   B/W   B, V, 3/4U   P
Bela Lugosi, East Side Kids, Ava Gardner
Mystery-comedy with zany doings.
Monogram — *Discount Video Tapes*

G. I. Blues   1960
Musical
08386   104 mins   C   B, V   P
*Elvis Presley, Juliet Prowse, Robert Ivers,
James Douglas*
Three G. I.'s form a musical combo while
stationed in Germany.
EL, SP

Paramount; Hal Wallis — *CBS/Fox Video;
RCA VideoDiscs*

Giant Step, A   1982
Football
47712   23 mins   C   B, V, FO   P
Team highlights of the 1981 New York Giants
who posted their first appearance in NFL post-
season play in almost 20 years.
NFL Films — *NFL Films Video*

Gideon's Trumpet   1980
Drama
66277   104 mins   C   B, V   P
*Henry Fonda, Jose Ferrer, John Houseman,
Dean Jagger, Sam Jaffe, Fay Wray*
A true story of how one man's fight for justice
changed the course of U.S. legal history.
John Houseman — *Worldvision Home Video*

Gielgud's Chekhov 1   1981
Literature
58557   52 mins   C   B, V   P
Hosted by John Gielgud
Three tales of escape, literal and figurative:
"The Fugitive," "Desire for Sleep," and
"Rothschild's Violin."
MasterVision — *Mastervision*

Gielgud's Chekhov 2   1981
Literature
58558   52 mins   C   B, V   P
A pair of tales dealing with illicit love: "Volodya"
and "The Boarding House."
MasterVision — *Mastervision*

Gielgud's Chekhov 3   1981
Literature
58559   51 mins   C   B, V   P
A pair of works which investigate the inner world
of hopes and dreams: "Revenge" and "The
Wallet."
MasterVision — *Mastervision*

Gift for Heidi, A   1962
Drama
11731   71 mins   C   B, V   P
Sandy Descher, Van Dyke Parks
An allegorical tale of Heidi and the lessons she
learns uponreceiving three carved figures on
her birthday. They represent Faith,Hope and
Charity and bring her three adventures to teach
their meaning.
RKO — *VCI Home Video*

Gift, The (Le Cadeau)   1982
Drama
69040   105 mins   C   B, V   R, P
The story of 55-year-old Gregoire Dufour, who
chooses early retirement with the hope of
somehow changing his dull and boring life.

Unknown to Gregoire, his co-workers have
arranged the ultimate retirement gifta woman.
Michel Zemer — *THORN EMI Home Video*

Gilda   1946
Drama
21287   110 mins   B/W   B, V   P
Rita Hayworth, Glenn Ford, George Macready
A South American gambling casino owner hires
a young American as his trusted aide, unaware
of his wife's love for the man. Hayworth sings
"Put the Blame on Mame."
Columbia — *RCA/Columbia Pictures Home
Video; RCA VideoDiscs*

Gilda Live   1980
Comedy
54120   124 mins   C   B, V   R, P
*Gilda Radner, "Father" Guido Sarducci,
directed by Mike Nichols*
A live taping of Gilda Radner's stage show at
New York's Winter Garden Theater. Gilda
presents many of her "Saturday Night Live"
characters, including dimwitted Lisa Loopner,
loudmouthed Roseanne Roseannadanna and
punk rocker Candy Slice.
MPAA:R
Warner Bros — *Warner Home Video*

Gimme Shelter   1970
Music-Performance
44777   91 mins   C   B, V   P
The Rolling Stones
Something went wrong at the free concert
attended by 300,000 people in Altamont,
California and this "Woodstock West" became
a bitter remembrance in the history of the rock
generation.
Cinema 5 — *RCA/Columbia Pictures Home
Video; RCA VideoDiscs*

Gin Game, The   1984
Comedy-Drama
75286   82 mins   C   B, V   P
Jessica Tandy, Hume Cronyn
This tape features a performance of the
Broadway play about an aging couple who find
romance in an old age home. In Beta Hi-Fi
stereo and VHS Dolby stereo.
RKO Home Video — *RKO HomeVideo*

Ginger   1970
Adventure
63083   90 mins   C   B, V   P
Ginger
Fabulous super-sleuth Ginger faces the sordid
world of prostitution, blackmail and drugs.
Ginger Productions — *Monterey Home Video*

Gino Vannelli   1981
Music-Performance
47375   60 mins   C   B, V   R, P

Gino Vannelli
Gino Vannelli performs his hit songs in concert, including "I Just Wanna Stop," "Living Inside Myself," "Brother to Brother," and others.
Henry Less and Associates — *Warner Home Video*

Girl Groups: The Story of   1983
a Sound
Music/Documentary
64941   90 mins   C   B, V, CED   P
The Supremes, The Ronettes, The Shangri-Las, The Marvelettes, The Shirelles
This documentary on the "girl group" sound of the early 60's features rare footage and interviews with many of the original singers, record producers and songwriters of that period. Among the 25 songs performed are "Please Mr. Postman," "Be My Baby," "Chapel of Love," "Boby Love" and "Stop! In the Name of Love."
Delilah Films — *MGM/UA Home Video*

Girl in Every Port, A   1952
Comedy
29486   86 mins   B/W   B, V   P, T
Groucho Marx, William Bendix, Marie Wilson, Don Defore, Gene Lockhart
Navy buddies acquire two race horses and try to conceal them aboard ship.
RKO — *Blackhawk Films*

Girl Most Likely, The   1957
Comedy
11732   98 mins   C   B, V   P
Jane Powell, Cliff Robertson
Romance-minded girl dreams of marrying wealthy, handsome man. She runs into a problem when she must choose one of three men.
Universal; RKO — *VCI Home Video*

Girlfriends   1978
Drama
58234   87 mins   C   B, V   R, P
Melanie Mayron, Anita Skinner, Eli Wallach, Christopher Guest, Amy Wright, Viveca Lindfors, directed by Claudia Weill
The bittersweet, true-to-life story of a young woman learning to make it on her own.
MPAA:PG
Claudia Weill — *Warner Home Video*

Girls Are for Loving   1973
Adventure
63085   90 mins   C   B, V   P
Ginger
Undercover agent Ginger faces real adventure when she battles it out with her counterpart, a seductive enemy agent.
Loving Productions — *Monterey Home Video*

Girls, Girls, Girls   1962
Musical
08381   106 mins   C   B, V   P
Elvis Presley, Stella Stevens, Laurel Goodwin, Jeremy Slate, Guy Lee
A boy refuses his girlfriend's gift of a boat. He finds he has a rival for her affections and changes his mind.
EL, SP
Paramount; Hal Wallis — *CBS/Fox Video*

Giselle   1979
Dance
55471   77 mins   C   CED   P
Rudolf Nureyev
An international cast highlights this version of Nureyev's greatest success, produced by Stanley Dorfman for television.
Lord Lew Grade; ITC Entertainment; Stanley Dorfman — *RCA VideoDiscs*

Git Along Little Dogies   1937
Western
08789   60 mins   B/W   B, V, 3/4U   P
Gene Autry, Judith Allen, Champion, Smiley Burnette
Gene Autry and banker's daughter at odds.
Republic — *Penguin Video; Video Yesteryear; Discount Video Tapes*

Give a Horse a Home!   19??
Animals
69633   60 mins   C   B, V   P
This program explains how simple it is to qualify for adoption of a wild horse or burro. The cassette also contains two short features about wild horses: "Mustang: Managing a Misfit" and "Dapples and Bays, Pintos and Greys."
Bureau of Land Management — *Mercedes Maharis Productions*

Give 'Em Hell, Harry!   1975
Biographical/Drama
47684   103 mins   C   B, V   P
James Whitmore
James Whitmore's one-man show as Harry S Truman at his feisty best.
Theatro Vision — *Worldvision Home Video*

Give Us Barabbas!   1961
Drama
64858   76 mins   C   B, V, 3/4U   P
James Daly, Kim Hunter, Dennis King, directed by George Schaefer
Part of "George Schaefer's Showcase Theatre," this is the story of what happens to Barabbas, the thief and murderer, who was set free when Pontius Pilate allowed an unruly mob to choose either him or Jesus for crucifixion.
George Schaefer — *Enter-Tel Inc*

Gizmo! 1977
Documentary/Inventions
47385　77 mins　C　B, V　R, P
A hilarious and affectionate tribute to crackpot
inventors everywhere, with footage of dozens of
great and not-so-great machines and other
creations. Some segments in black-and-white.
Howard Smith — *Warner Home Video*

Gladys Knight & the Pips 1978
and Ray Charles in
Concert
Music-Performance
33979　75 mins　C　B, V　P
Gladys Knight, Ray Charles
Backed by the ever-present Pips, Gladys Knight
sings "Imagination,""Midnight Train to
Georgia," and "Heard It Through the
Grapevine." Ray Charles performs several
numbers after making a surprise appearance.
Gladys and Ray finally combine in a magic blend
of inspired song.
HBO — *Vestron Video*

Gladys Knight & The Pips 1982
and Ray Charles
Music-Performance
72219　78 mins　C　B, V　P
The dynamic combination perform some of their
biggest hits including "Imagination" and
"Midnight Train to Georgia."
Independent — *Vestron Video*

Glass House, The 1972
Drama
66586　92 mins　C　B, V　P
Vic Morrow, Clu Gulager, Billy Dee Williams,
Alan Alda
Truman Capote wrote this story about a power
struggle among the inmates of a state prison.
Tomorrow Entertainment — *Program Hunters*

Glen or Glenda 1953
Drama/Exploitation
08680　70 mins　B/W　B, V, 3/4U　P
Bela Lugosi, Lyle Talbot, Donald Woods,
directed by Ed Woods
A documentary advocating transvestism. The
director Ed Woods portrays the haunted figure
of Glen or Glenda.
Unknown — *Penguin Video; Video Yesteryear;*
Video Dimensions; Festival Films; Admit One
Video

Gloria 1980
Drama
52751　123 mins　C　B, V, LV　P
Gena Rowlands, John Adames, Buck Henry,
directed by John Cassavetes
A fast-shooting, independent woman fights off
the mob in order to protect a young boy.
MPAA:PG

Sam Shaw; Columbia — *RCA/Columbia*
Pictures Home Video

Glorifying the American 1929
Girl
Musical
01614　80 mins　B/W　B, V　P
Mary Eaton, Dan Healey, Eddie Cantor, Rudy
Vallee, directed by Millard Webb
Musical romp with Eddie Cantor and other
Ziegfeld stars.
Paramount; Florenz Ziegfeld — *Budget Video;*
Discount Video Tapes; Festival Films

Glory at Sea 1952
War-Drama
66378　100 mins　B/W　B, V　P
Trevor Howard, Richard Attenborough, Sonny
Tufts, James Donald, Joan Rice, Bernard Lee
A tough officer takes command of an old U.S.
destroyer which has been given to England in
the early days of World War II. Original title:
"The Gift Horse."
Molton — *Movie Buff Video*

Glove, The 1978
Adventure
65290　93 mins　C　B, V　P
John Saxon, Rosey Grier, Joan Blondell
An ex-cop turned bounty hunter has his
toughest assignment ever: bring in a 6'5", 250
pound ex-con.
MPAA:R
Julian Roffman — *Media Home Entertainment*

Go Bears! A Look to the 1980
80's
Football
50079　24 mins　C　B, V, FO　R, P
Chicago Bears
Highlights of the 1979 Chicago Bears' football
season.
NFL Films — *NFL Films Video*

Go for It 1976
Sports
59674　90 mins　C　B, V　P
A potpourri of sports action, including surfing,
skiing, hang-gliding, kayaking and mountain
climbing.
MPAA:PG
Paul Rapp; Richard Rosenthal — *Media Home*
Entertainment

Go! Go! Go! World 1964
Documentary
47647　85 mins　C　B, V, FO　P
A "round the world" tour in the tradition of
"Mondo Cane," showing the strange and
bizarre activities of humankind: mud wrestlers, a
Japanese pachinko parlor, Indian snake

charmers and a Chinese baby exchange, among others.
Italy — *Video Yesteryear*

Go Tell the Spartans   1978
War-Drama
45047   114 mins   C   B, V, LV,   P
CED
Burt Lancaster, Craig Wasson
In Viet Nam, 1964, a hard-boiled major is ordered to establish a garrison at Muc Wa with a platoon of burnt-out Americans and Vietnamese mercenaries.
MPAA:R
Spartan; Mar Vista — *Vestron Video*

Go West   1940
Comedy
58293   82 mins   B/W   B, V   ·   P
The Marx Brothers, John Carroll, Diana Lewis
The brothers Marx help in the making and un-making of the Old West.
MGM — *MGM/UA Home Video*

God Has No Grandchildren   197?
Religion
46828   28 mins   C   B, V, 3/4U,   P
Q
Luis Palau, Cliff Richard
This program points a way to rekindling the fires of evangelism by looking at Wales, a country that took its Christianity for granted, with the result of a dying faith.
Quadrus Films — *TV Sports Scene*

God Respects Us When We Work But Loves Us When We Dance   1967
Documentary/Sociology
60464   20 mins   C   B, V, 3/4U   P
An original music score accentuates this filmed panorama of the memorable 1967 Easter Sunday Love-In in Los Angeles. A colorful record of an historic social phenomenon.
Les Blank — *Flower Films*

Godfather 1902-1959—The Complete Epic, The   1981
Drama
58876   368 mins   C   B, V   R, P
Marlon Brando, Al Pacino, Robert Duvall, James Caan, Richard Castellano, Diane Keaton, Robert DeNiro, John Cazale, Lee Strasberg, Talia Shire, directed by Francis Ford Coppola
The complete Godfather saga, Francis Ford Coppola's epic work concerning the lives of a New York crime family. Both original "Godfather" films have been reedited into a chronological framework of the Corleone family

history, with much previously discarded footage restored.
Paramount; Zoetrope — *Paramount Home Video*

Godfather, The   1972
Drama
38595   171 mins   C   B, V, LV   R, P
Marlon Brando, Al Pacino, James Caan, Robert Duvall, Talia Shire, Diane Keaton, directed by Francis Ford Coppola
Based on the novel by Mario Puzo, this is the epic portrayal of the Corleone family's rise to the top of the criminal world.
Academy Awards '72: Best Picture; Best Actor (Brando); Best Screenplay (Puzo and Coppola). MPAA:R
Paramount — *Paramount Home Video; RCA VideoDiscs*

Godfather Part II, The   1974
Drama
38596   200 mins   C   B, V, LV   R, P
Al Pacino, Robert De Niro, Robert Duvall, Talia Shire, Diane Keaton, directed by Francis Ford Coppola
Two generations of the Corleone family, fictional Mafia chieftains, are portrayed in this sequel to the "Godfather." The story of young Don Vito (De Niro) is intercut with the rise of his son, Michael (Pacino) to leadership of the family.
Academy Awards '74: Best Picture; Best Supporting Actor (De Niro); Best Director; Best Screenplay.   MPAA:R
Paramount — *Paramount Home Video; RCA VideoDiscs*

God's Gun   1975
Western
59998   93 mins   C   B, V   P
Richard Boone, Lee Van Cleef, Jack Palance
A former gunfighter is pressed back into service to avenge the senseless killing of a preacher.
MPAA:R
Independent — *Paragon Video Productions; Electric Video*

God's Little Acre   1958
Drama
55318   110 mins   B/W   B, V   P
Robert Ryan, Tina Louise, Michael Landon, Buddy Hackett, Vic Morrow, Jack Lord, Aldo Ray, directed by Anthony Mann
A man convinced that buried treasure is on his farm ruins his land to get at the gold.
Sidney Harmon — *King of Video; VCII*

God's Wonders   1980
Religion/Ecology and environment
55043   130 mins   C   B, V   P
A collection of short nature films which allow children to make some discoveries about God's handiwork.

    (For Explanation of codes, see USE GUIDE and KEY)

Family Films — *Vanguard Video*

Godsend, The   1979
Horror
69286   93 mins   C   B, V   P
*Cyd Hayman, Malcolm Stoddard, Angela
Pleasence, Patrick Barr*
A little girl is adopted, and she turns her new
family's life into a nightmare.
MPAA:R
Cannon Group — *Vestron Video*

Godzilla   1955
Horror
63423   80 mins   B/W   B, V, LV,   P
                     CED
Raymond Burr, Takashi Shimura
The radioactive monster Godzilla attacks Tokyo
and terrifies the world.
Japanese — *Vestron Video*

Godzilla vs. Monster Zero   1970
Science fiction/Horror
64020   93 mins   C   B, V   R, P
Nick Adams
Godzilla, Monster Zero and Rodan are out to
destroy the earth, but a heroic space pilot tries
to stop them.
MPAA:G
Benedict Pictures Corp — *Paramount Home
Video*

Godzilla vs. Mothra   1964
Horror
64508   90 mins   C   B, V   R, P
Akira Takarada, Yuriko Hoshi, Hiroshi Koizumi
Mighty Mothra is called in to save the populace
from Godzilla, who is on a rampage.
Toho Company; American
International — *Paramount Home Video*

**Godzilla vs. the Sea
Monster**   1966
Science fiction
51612   80 mins   C   B, V   P
The famous giant lizard does battle amidst
fantastic special effects.
Toho — *Discount Video Tapes; Budget Video*

Goin' All the Way   1982
Drama
63088   85 mins   C   B, V   P
Deborah Van Rhyn, Dan Waldman
Seventeen-year-old Monica decides that she
has to prove her love to her boyfriend, Artie, by
going all the way.
Four Rivers and Clark Film — *Monterey Home
Video*

Goin' South   1978
Western
38618   109 mins   C   B, V, LV   R, P
*Jack Nicholson, Mary Steenburgen, John
Belushi, directed by Jack Nicholson*
An outlaw is saved from being hanged by a
young woman who agrees to marry and take
charge of him.
MPAA:PG
Paramount — *Paramount Home Video*

Going Ape!   1981
Comedy
53933   88 mins   C   B, V   R, P
*Tony Danza, Jessica Walter, Danny DeVito, Art
Metrano, Rick Hurst*
A young man inherits a bunch of orangutans. If
the apes are treated well, a legacy of $5 million
will follow.
MPAA:PG
Robert L Rosen — *Paramount Home Video*

Going Berserk   1983
Satire
66331   85 mins   C   B, V, LV,   P
                     CED
*John Candy, Joe Flaherty, Eugene Levy, Paul
Dooley, directed by David Steinberg*
The stars of SCTV's television comedy troupe
are featured in this off-the-wall comedy which
lampoons everything from religious cults to kung
fu movies to "Father Knows Best."
MPAA:R
Universal — *MCA Home Video*

Going in Style   1979
Comedy
44760   90 mins   C   B, V   R, P
*George Burns, Art Carney, Lee Strasberg,
directed by Martin Brest.*
Three elderly gentlemen decide to liven up their
lives by pulling a daylight bank stick-up.
MPAA:PG
Warner Bros — *Warner Home Video*

Going My Way   1944
Musical-Drama
53398   126 mins   B/W   B, V   P
*Bing Crosby, Barry Fitzgerald, Rise Stevens,
Frank McHugh, directed by Leo McCarey*
A priest assigned to a down-trodden parish
works to help the neighborhood's people.
Songs include "Going My Way," "Ave Maria,"
"Swinging on a Star," and "The Day After
Forever."
Academy Awards '44: Best Picture; Best Actor
(Crosby); Best Supporting Actor (Fitzgerald);
Best Director (McCarey).
Paramount; Leo McCarey — *MCA Home Video*

Going Places   1974
Drama
63967   117 mins   C   B, V   P

(For Explanation of codes, see USE GUIDE and KEY)   **227**

Gerard Depardieu, Patrick Dewaere, Jeanne Moreau, Miou-Miou, Isabelle Huppert
A pair of amiable, uninhibited bandits roam the French countryside doing as they please. Dubbed in English.
MPAA:R
Almi-Cinema 5 — *RCA/Columbia Pictures Home Video*

Going Steady 1980
Comedy
59999 90 mins C B, V P
A story of teenage love, set to the beat of fifties rock 'n' roll.
MPAA:R
Independent — *Paragon Video Productions*

Gold Coast, The 1978
Video
08563 30 mins C B, V, 3/4U P
A continuous picture of a coastline which blazes brilliantly golden as the sun shines through to create a relaxed background.
Nebulae Prods — *Nebulae Productions*

Gold Diggers of 1933 1933
Musical
64785 96 mins B/W CED P
Joan Blondell, Ruby Keeler, Dick Powell, Ginger Rogers
Showgirls help a songwriter save his show in this Busby Berkeley musical. Includes the number, "We're in the Money."
Warner Bros. — *RCA VideoDiscs*

Gold Rush, The 1925
Comedy
58614 85 mins B/W B, V, 3/4U R, P
Charlie Chaplin, Mack Swain, Tom Murray, Georgia Hale
Chaplin's tale of the Little Tramp's misplaced love in the days of the Klondike.
United Artists — *Cable Films; Video Yesteryear; Discount Video Tapes; Sheik Video; Budget Video; Penguin Video; Western Film & Video Inc; Blackhawk Films; Classic Video Cinema Collector's Club*

Gold Rush, The/Payday 1925
Comedy
48405 92 mins B/W B, V P
Charlie Chaplin, Georgia Hale, Mack Swain
Chaplin drifts along the Arctic tundra, searching for gold and love in "The Gold Rush." In "Payday," he goes out drinking with his buddies.
United Artists — *CBS/Fox Video*

Golden Age of Comedy, The 1958
Comedy
55593 78 mins B/W B, V P

Ben Turpin, Harry Langdon, Will Rogers, Jean Harlow, Carole Lombard, Laurel and Hardy, Keystone Kops
The great comedians of silent cinema are seen in clips from some of their funniest films.
Robert Youngson — *VidAmerica*

Golden Boy 1939
Drama
68261 101 mins B/W B, V P
William Holden, Adolphe Menjou, Barbara Stanwyck, Lee J. Cobb
A young man gives up being a great concert violinist and becomes a prizefighter.
William Perlberg; Columbia — *RCA/Columbia Pictures Home Video*

Golden Exterminator 1980
Martial arts
69279 80 mins C B, V P
Raymond Chan, James Park, Julia Song, Elliot Ku
Conservative members of the TAI gang battle a powerful group of slave traders and murderers. Mandarin dialogue, English subtitles.
CH
IFD Films & Arts — *Silverline Video*

Golden Lady 1979
Adventure
66283 90 mins C B, V P
Christina World, Suzanne Danielle, June Chadwick
A beautiful woman leads her entourage in a deadly game of international intrigue.
UG Prods — *Monterey Home Video*

Golden Moments 1960
Baseball
49554 25 mins B/W B, V P
A collection of memorable moments in baseball history from 1905-1960, recalling a half-century of stars from Home Run Baker to Ted Williams.
Lew Fonseca — *Major League Baseball Productions*

Golden Rendezvous 1977
Suspense
64891 120 mins C B, V P
Richard Harris, David Janssen, John Carradine, Burgess Meredith
A tale of treachery aboard a "gambler's paradise" luxury liner.
Film Trust-Milton Okun Prods; Golden Rendezvous Prods — *Vestron Video*

Golden Seal, The 1983
Drama
65434 94 mins C B, V, LV, CED P
Steve Railsback, Michael Beck, Penelope Milford, Torquil Campbell

This is the tale of a small boy's innocence put in direct conflict with the failed dreams, pride and ordinary greed of adults.
Samuel Goldwyn Jr — *Embassy Home Entertainment*

Golden Voyage of Sinbad, The 1973
Adventure/Fantasy
Closed Captioned
63445   105 mins   C   B, V   P
John Phillip Law, Caroline Munro, Tom Baker
In the mysterious ancient land of Lemuria, Sinbad and his crew encounter a six-armed sword-brandishing statue, a one-eyed centaur and a griffin.
MPAA:G
Columbia; Charles H Schneer and Ray Harryhausen — *RCA/Columbia Pictures Home Video*

Goldengirl 1979
Drama
55579   107 mins   C   B, V   P
Susan Anton, James Coburn, Curt Jurgens, Robert Culp
A mad neo-Nazi doctor tries to produce a superwoman—specially fed, exercised, and emotionally conditioned since childhood to run in the Olympics.
MPAA:PG
Avco Embassy — *Embassy Home Entertainment*

Goldfinger 1964
Adventure
52602   108 mins   C   B, V, LV   P
Sean Connery, Honor Blackman, Gert Frobe, Shirley Eaton
James Bond, Agent 007, attempts to prevent an international gold smuggler from robbing Fort Knox.
United Artists — *CBS/Fox Video; RCA VideoDiscs*

Goldilocks and the Three Bears 1983
Fairy tales
Closed Captioned
69321   60 mins   C   B, V, LV, CED   P
Tatum O'Neal, Alex Karras, Brandis Kemp, Donovan Scott, Hoyt Axton, John Lithgow, Carole King
This entry from "Faerie Tale Theatre" tells the story of Goldilocks, who wanders through the woods and finds the home of three bears.
Shelley Duvall — *CBS/Fox Video*

Golem, The 1920
Film-History
49069   70 mins   B/W   B, V   P
Directed by Paul Wegener
A huge clay figure is given life by a rabbi in hopes of saving the Jews in the ghetto of medieval Prague. Silent.
German — *Sheik Video; International Historic Films; Video Yesteryear; Classic Video Cinema Collector's Club*

Golf 1978
Golf
44925   30 mins   C   B, V   P
Fitness specialist Ann Dugan demonstrates exercises for golfers to help develop suppleness in hips and shoulders and strength in the back, forearm, and wrist. From the "Sports Conditioning" series.
Health N Action — *RCA/Columbia Pictures Home Video*

Golf Lessons from Sam Snead 1982
Golf
59881   60 mins   C   3/4U, FO   R, P
Hosted by Sam Snead
Golf champ Sam Snead demonstrates the proper grip and swing, how to use woods and irons, how to play on the fairway, in the sand trap, and over the water hazard, the fine art of putting and much more.
Star Video Productions — *Star Video Productions*

Golf My Way 1983
Golf
66276   128 mins   C   B, V   P
Jack Nicklaus
Step-by-step instruction on every element of the game, highlighted in super-slow-motion.
JN Productions — *Worldvision Home Video*

Golf My Way with Jack Nicklaus 1984
Golf
66579   120 mins   C   B, V   P
Champion golfer Jack Nicklaus demonstrates step-by-step lessons on every element of golf for beginners or seasoned players. Crucial points are highlighted in super slow motion to highlight every detail
Worldvision — *Worldvision Home Video*

Gondoliers, The 19??
Opera/Comedy
65491   112 mins   C   B, V   P
Keith Michell
A new version of Gilbert and Sullivan's opera. This is an entertaining lampoon against class bigotry.
Parsons and Whittemore Lyddon Ltd — *CBS/Fox Video*

Good Earth, The   1937
Drama
59361   138 mins B/W   B, V   P
Paul Muni, Luise Rainer, Charley Grapewin, Keye Luke, Walter Connolly, directed by Sidney Franklin
Pearl S. Buck's classic recreating the story of greed which ruined the lives of a simple farming couple in China.
Academy Awards '37: Best Actress (Rainer); Best Cinematography (Karl Freund).
MGM — *MGM/UA Home Video*

Good Guys Wear Black   1978
Adventure
31657   96 mins C   B, V, LV,   P
                               CED
Chuck Norris, Anne Archer, James Franciscus
A mild-mannered professor keeps his former life as leader of a Vietnam commando unit under wraps until he discovers that he's number one on the C.I.A. hit list. He decides to use all his commando skills to stay alive and get to the only man who can stop the C.I.A.
MPAA:PG
Mar Vista — *Vestron Video*

Good Old Days   193?
Documentary/Film-History
63850   55 mins B/W   B, V   P
A compilation of 3 nostalgic newsreels featuring footage of Shirley Temple, William S. Hart, early bathing beauties, and San Francisco at the turn of the century. Some color sequences.
Movietone et al — *Budget Video*

Good Sam   1948
Comedy-Drama
69316   78 mins B/W   B, V   P
Gary Cooper, Ann Sheridan, Ray Collins, Edmund Lowe, Joan Lorring, directed by Leo McCarey
An incurable "Good Samaritan" finds himself in one jam after another as he tries too hard to help people.
RKO Radio; Rainbow Pictures — *NTA Home Entertainment*

Good, the Bad and the Ugly, The   1968
Western
58481   161 mins C   B, V, LV,   P
                               CED
Clint Eastwood, Eli Wallach, Lee Van Cleef, directed by Sergio Leone
A drifter, a Mexican outlaw, and a sadist are all out to get a cash box which was stolen and put in an unmarked grave during the Civil War.
United Artists; Alberto Grimaldi — *CBS/Fox Video; RCA VideoDiscs*

Goodbye Columbus   1969
Comedy/Drama
55541   105 mins C   B, V, LV   R, P
Richard Benjamin, Ali McGraw, Jack Klugman, Nan Martin, directed by Larry Pierce
Philip Roth's novel about a young Jewish librarian who has an affair with the spoiled daughter of a nouveau riche family.
MPAA:R
Paramount; Stanley Jaffe — *Paramount Home Video; RCA VideoDiscs*

Goodbye Emmanuelle   1979
Drama
63347   92 mins C   B, V   R, P
Sylvia Kristel
This film follows the further adventures of Emmanuelle in her quest for sexual freedom and the excitement of forbidden pleasures.
MPAA:R
Miramax Films — *THORN EMI Home Video*

Goodbye Girl, The   1977
Comedy
58872   110 mins C   B, V, LV,   P
                               CED
Richard Dreyfuss, Marsha Mason, Quinn Cummings, Barbara Rhoades, Marilyn Sokol, directed by Herbert Ross
Neil Simon's story of an over-the-hill Broadway chorus girl with a precocious nine-year-old daughter who shares her apartment with a young actor.
Academy Awards '77: Best Actor (Dreyfuss).
MPAA:PG
Warner Bros; MGM — *MGM/UA Home Video*

Goodbye Norma Jean   1975
Drama
47797   95 mins C   B, V   R, P
Misty Rowe, Terrence Locke, Patch Mackenzie
A detailed recreation of Marilyn Monroe's early years in Hollywood.
MPAA:R
A Sterling Gold Ltd; Larry Buchanan — *THORN EMI Home Video*

Goodbye People, The   1983
Comedy-Drama
64988   90 mins C   B, V   P
Judd Hirsch, Martin Balsam, Pamela Reed
An elderly man decides to reopen his Coney Island beachfront hot dog stand that folded 22 years earlier. Two people help him realize his impossible dream.
Unknown — *Embassy Home Entertainment*

Goodbye Pork Pie   1981
Adventure
69547   105 mins C   B, V   P
Tony Barry, Kelly Johnson

With the police on their trail, two young men speed on a 1000-mile journey in a small, brand-new, yellow, stolen car.
MPAA:R
Pork Pie Productions — *Embassy Home Entertainment*

Goodyear Jazz Concert with Bobby Hackett
1961
Music-Performance
46341   24 mins   C   B, V, FO   P
Bobby Hackett, Urbie Green, Bob Wilbur, Dave McKenna, Nabil Totah, Morey Feld
A studio performance by Bobby Hackett's Sextet. The musical program consists of "Deed I Do," "Sentimental Blues," "The Saints," "Bill Bailey," "Struttin' with Some Barbecue," and "Swing That Music."
Mike Bryan, Goodyear — *Video Yesteryear*

Goodyear Jazz Concert with Duke Ellington
1962
Music-Performance
42955   27 mins   C   B, V, FO   P
Duke Ellington and the Band start with "Take the A Train" and run through five other all-time Ellington hits.
Goodyear — *Video Yesteryear*

Goodyear Jazz Concert with Eddie Condon
1961
Music-Performance
46342   28 mins   C   B, V, FO   P
Wild Bill Davison, Cutty Cutshall, Peanuts Hucko, Johnny Varo, Joe Williams, Eddie Condon, Buzzy Drootin
A studio concert by Eddie Condon and friends. The songs performed are "Royal Garden Blues," "Blue and Brokenhearted," "Big Ben Blues," "Stealin' Apples," "Little Ben Blues," and "Muskrat Ramble."
Mike Bryan, Goodyear — *Video Yesteryear*

Goodyear Jazz Concert with Louis Armstrong
1961
Music-Performance
46340   27 mins   C   B, V, FO   P
Louis Armstrong, Trummy Young, Joe Darensbourg, Billy Kyle, Billy Cronk, Danny Barcelona, Jewell Brown
A studio performance by Louis Armstrong's All Stars. Tunes include "When It's Sleepy Time Down South," "C'est si Bon," "Someday You'll Be Sorry," "Jerry," "Nobody Knows de Trouble I've Seen," and "When the Saints Go Marching In."
Mike Bryan, Goodyear — *Video Yesteryear*

Goodyear TV Playhouse: "Marty"
1953
Drama
47483   51 mins   B/W   B, V, FO   P
Rod Steiger, Nancy Marchand, Betsy Palmer, Nehemiah Persoff
One of the best-remembered television dramas of all time, later expanded into an Academy Award-winning feature film. Rod Steiger portrays a lonely Bronx butcher who thinks he has finally found the girl for him. Written by Paddy Chayefsky and originally telecast on May 24, 1953. Opening credits and commercials are missing.
NBC — *Video Yesteryear*

Goodyear TV Playhouse: "The Gene Austin Story"
1957
Musical-Drama/Biographical
47484   51 mins   B/W   B, V, FO   P
George Grizzard, Edward Andrews, Jerome Cowan, Phyllis Newman, Gene Austin
A musical biography of 1920's pop singer Gene Austin, featuring the voice of Gene Austin dubbing for George Grizzard. Songs include "My Blue Heaven," "Ramona" and "My Melancholy Baby." Written by Ernest Kinoy.
NBC — *Video Yesteryear*

Goofy Over Sports
194?
Cartoons
58627   46 mins   C   B, V   R, P
Animated
Goofy stars in this compilation of sports cartoons from the Disney archives: "How to Play Football" (1944), "Double Dribble" (1946), "Art of Skiing" (1941), "How to Swim" (1942), "Art of Self Defense" (1941), and, "How to Ride a Horse" (a segment from the 1941 feature, 'The Reluctant Dragon').
Walt Disney Productions — *Walt Disney Home Video*

Goon Movie (Stand Easy), The
1953
Comedy
64919   75 mins   B/W   B, V   P
Peter Sellers, Spike Milligan, Harry Secombe
The cast of "The Goon Show," Britain's popular radio comedy series, perform some of their best routines in this, their only film appearance.
English — *Video Dimensions*

Goona Goona
1932
Documentary/Anthropology
58523   60 mins   B/W   B, V, 3/4U   P
An authentic love story of the island of Bali, featuring music and ceremonial dances.
First Division — *Penguin Video*

Gorgo
1961
Drama
07011   76 mins   C   B, V   P
Bill Travers, William Sylvester, Vincent Winter, Bruce Seton, Christopher Rhodes

Undersea explosion off the coast of Ireland brings to the surface an unusual monster which is captured and brought to London circus.
MGM; King Brothers Prod — *Sheik Video; Cable Films; Video Connection; Video Dimensions*

Gorilla 1956
Adventure/Documentary
47638   79 mins   C   B, V, FO   P
The story of a white hunter and a black native hunter in Africa searching for a killer gorilla.
Swedish — *Video Yesteryear*

Gorilla, The 1939
Comedy
00400   67 mins   B/W   B, V   P
Ritz Brothers, Anita Louise, Patsy Kelly, Lionel Atwill
Ritz Brothers are hired to protect a country gentlemen receiving strange notes.
20th Century-Fox; Darryl F Zanuck — *Budget Video; Discount Video Tapes; Video Connection; Video Yesteryear; Classic Video Cinema Collector's Club*

Gorky Park 1983
Mystery
79214   127 mins   C   B, V, LV   P
William Hurt, Lee Marvin, Joanna Pacula
A detective is sent to investigate a rash of murders wherein the victims' bodies are left in Gorky Park.
MPAA:R
Gene Kirkwood; Howard Koch — *Vestron Video*

Gospel 1982
Music-Performance
65449   92 mins   C   B, V   P
The Mighty Clouds of Joy, Twinkie Clark and the Clark Sisters, Walter Hawkins and the Hawkins Family
A rousing musical theatrical tribute to the leading exponents of Gospel singing. In stereo VHS and Beta Hi-Fi.
Golden Door Productions — *Monterey Home Video*

Gospel According to St. Matthew, The 1964
Drama
55809   136 mins   B/W   B, V   P
Directed by Pier Paolo Pasolini
The life of Christ, as portrayed in a realistic, almost documentary tone. Dubbed in English.
Alfredo Bini — *Festival Films; Sheik Video; Budget Video; Discount Video Tapes*

Gotta Dance, Gotta Sing 1984
Musical/Documentary
75287   53 mins   C   B, V   P

Fred Astaire, Ginger Rogers, Shirley Temple, Carmen Miranda, Betty Grable
This is a compilation of memorable dance routines from great Hollywood films. In Beta Hi-Fi and VHS Dolby stereo.
RKO Home Video — *RKO HomeVideo*

Grace Jones—One Man Show 1982
Music-Performance
63422   60 mins   C   B, V   P
Grace Jones
In a concert recorded live in New York and at London's Drury Lane Theatre, Grace Jones performs such hits as "Warm Leatherette," "Walking in the Rain" and "Feel Up."
Island Pictures — *Vestron Video*

Graduate, The 1967
Comedy-Drama
08365   106 mins   C   B, V, LV,   P
CED
Anne Bancroft, Dustin Hoffman, Katharine Ross, directed by Mike Nichols
A young man graduates with honors, meets and has an affair with one of his parents' friends, and is urged to date her daughter. He falls in love with the daughter.
Academy Awards '67: Best Director (Nichols); Film Daily Poll 10 Best Pictures of Year '67.
Avco Embassy — *Embassy Home Entertainment; RCA VideoDiscs*

Graduation Day 197?
Horror
58960   90 mins   C   B, V   P
Christopher George, Patch McKenzie, E. Danny Murphy
A chiller about the systematic murder of members of a high school track team.
David Baughn; Herb Freed — *RCA/Columbia Pictures Home Video*

Graham Parker 1982
Music-Performance
75922   60 mins   C   B, V   P
This program presents Graham Parker performing some of his greatest hits.
New Music Inc — *Sony Corporation of America*

Grand Canyon Trail 1948
Western
64387   68 mins   B/W   B, V, 3/4U   P
Roy Rogers, Andy Devine, Charles Coleman
A cowboy's best friend invests his money in a wildcat gold mine.
Republic — *Nostalgia Merchant*

Grand Illusion 1937
Film-Avant-garde
11400   111 mins   B/W   B, V   P

Jean Gabin, Erich von Stroheim, Pierre Fresnay, directed by Jean Renoir
A classic anti-World War I presentation, in which French prisoners attempt to escape from their German captor. French with English subtitles.
FR
Continental — *CBS/Fox Video; Video Yesteryear; Sheik Video; Cable Films; Budget Video; Penguin Video; Western Film & Video Inc; Cinema Concepts; Classic Video Cinema Collector's Club*

Grand Theft Auto   1977
Adventure
51990   89 mins   C   B, V   R, P
Ron Howard, Nancy Morgan, Marion Ross, Barry Cahill, Clint Howard
A young couple elope to Las Vegas. The bride's father, totally against the marriage, offers a reward for her return.
MPAA:PG
New World Pictures — *Warner Home Video*

Grandes Amigos (Great   197?
Friends)
Comedy-Drama
73588   30 mins   C   B, V   P
Nino Del Arco
A young boy finds out the meaning of having a true friend in this comedy-drama.
KNBC — *Aztec Cinevideo*

Grandizer   1982
Cartoons/Science fiction
59329   101 mins   C   B, V   P
Animated
A tale of star civilizations, evil invaders and the quest of one man to protect his adopted homeland, the planet Earth.
EL, SP
Toei Animation; Terry Production — *Family Home Entertainment*

Grapes of Wrath, The   1940
Drama
08553   129 mins   B/W   B, V   P
Henry Fonda, Dorris Bowdon, Charley Grapewin, Jane Darwell, John Carradine, directed by John Ford
Epic story of the Okie migration to California during the depression. From John Steinbeck's great novel.
20th Century Fox; Darryl F Zanuck — *CBS/Fox Video*

Grass Is Greener, The   1961
Comedy
65457   105 mins   C   B, V   P
Cary Grant, Deborah Kerr, Jean Simmons, Robert Mitchum
An American millionaire invades part of an impoverished Earl's mansion and falls in love with the lady of the house. The earl is willing to go to any lengths to keep his wife, even a duel with pistols.
Universal — *NTA Home Entertainment*

Grateful Dead — Dead   1980
Ahead, The
Music-Performance
59851   90 mins   C   B, V   R, P
An historic documentary is presented based on a week long marathon of shows given by the Grateful Dead at Radio City Music Hall.
Stanley Sherman Organization; Grateful Dead Productions — *Warner Home Video; Pioneer Artists*

Grateful Dead in Concert,   1977
The
Music-Performance/Documentary
47046   120 mins   C   CED   P
The Grateful Dead, directed by Jerry Garcia and Leon Gast
A concert by this popular rock group, with 20 songs including "Truckin'," "Casey Jones," and "Sugar Magnolia." The songs are interspersed with backstage shots, interviews with fans, and other scenes. Filmed at the Winterland in San Francisco.
Eddie Washington — *RCA VideoDiscs*

Grazuole   1969
Drama
53716   71 mins   B/W   B, V, 3/4U   P
Directed by Arunas Zhebrunas
A nine-year-old girl is mockingly made "Beauty Queen" by her malicious playmates.
Fourth Soviet Film Festival '70: First Prize.   RU
USSR — *International Historic Films*

Grease   1978
Musical
38932   110 mins   C   B, V, LV   R, P
John Travolta, Olivia Newton-John, Stockard Channing, Eve Arden, Sha-Na-Na
Film version of the hit Broadway musical about high school life in the 1950's. Songs include "You're the One That I Love," "We Go Together," and "Summer Nights."
MPAA:PG
Paramount — *Paramount Home Video; RCA VideoDiscs*

Grease 2   1982
Musical
63426   114 mins   C   B, V, LV   R, P
Maxwell Caulfield, Michelle Pfeiffer, Adrian Zmed, Lorna Luft, Didi Conn, Eve Arden, Sid Caesar, Tab Hunter
The saga of the T-Birds, the Pink Ladies and young love at Rydell High continues.
MPAA:PG
Paramount — *Paramount Home Video; RCA VideoDiscs*

Greased Lightning   1977
Drama
53513   96 mins   C   B, V   R, P
Richard Pryor, Pam Grier, Beau Bridges,
Cleavon Little, Vincent Gardenia
The story of the first black auto racing
champion, Wendell Scott, who had to overcome
racial prejudice to achieve his success.
MPAA:PG
Warner Bros — *Warner Home Video*

Greaser's Palace   1972
Comedy/Western
65321   ? mins   C   B, V   P
Albert Henderson, Allan Arbus
Seaweedhead Greaser, owner of the town's
saloon, faces his arch nemesis.
Cyma Rubin — *RCA/Columbia Pictures Home
Video*

Great Adventure, The   1982
Adventure
65691   90 mins   C   B, V   P
Jack Palance, Joan Collins, Fred Romer
In the severe environment of the gold rush days
on the rugged Yukon Territory, a touching tale
unfolds of a young orpham boy and his eternal
bond of friendship with a great northern dog.
MPAA:PG
Unknown — *Media Home Entertainment*

Great Age of Steam, The   195?
Trains
68898   28 mins   C   B, V   P
A documentary which brings to life examples of
every wheel arrangement.
UnKnown — *Interurban Films*

Great Alligator, The   1981
Horror
77531   89 mins   C   B, V   P
Barbara Bach, Mel Ferrer
A tropical resort begins mysteriously losing its
guests to a carnivorous monster.
VIP Productions — *Gorgon Video*

Great American Diet and   1981
Nutrition Test, The
Nutrition
57548   60 mins   C   B, V   P
Hosted by Dr. Frank Field, Betty Furness
Viewers can test their knowledge on food
additives, labeling, nutrition, obesity, vitamins,
and diets.
NBC; Don Luftig — *Karl Video*

Great Banana Pie Caper,   1979
The
Religion
46826   28 mins   C   B, V, 3/4U,   P
                                  Q

Two friends have to deal with bullies, prejudice,
and responsibilities in this children's comedy
with an evangelistic emphasis.
Quadrus Films — *TV Sports Scene*

Great Battle of the Volga   1961
World War II/Documentary
48846   75 mins   B/W   B, V, 3/4U   P
A fierce World War II Russian front
documentary.
Unknown — *Western Film & Video Inc*

Great Bear Scare, The   1984
Cartoons
73369   60 mins   C   B, V   P
Animated
The bears of Bearbank send Ted E. and Patti
Bear to Monster Mountain to find out if Dracula
is going to invade the town on Halloween.
Dimenmark International — *Family Home
Entertainment*

Great British Striptease   1981
Variety
60413   60 mins   C   B, V   P
Sixteen of England's most fetching young
women are featured performing the "Great
British Striptease."
Kent Waldwin — *Monterey Home Video*

Great Caruso, The   1951
Musical
53937   113 mins   C   B, V, CED   P
Mario Lanza, Ann Blyth, Dorothy Kirsten
The story of Caruso's rise to operatic fame, from
his childhood in Naples, Italy, to his collapse on
the stage of the Metropolitan Opera House.
Academy Awards '51: Best Sound Recording;
Film Daily Poll '51: Ten Best Pictures.
MGM — *MGM/UA Home Video*

Great Cities: London,   1980
Rome, Dublin, Athens
Cities and towns/Europe
59640   100 mins   C   CED   P
*Hosted by Anthony Burgess, John Huston,
Melina Mercouri, Jonathan Miller*
The history and beauty of four magnificent cities
is shown through the eyes of four very special
residents of each city.
Learning Corp of America; John McGreevey;
Neilsen Fearns Intl — *RCA VideoDiscs*

Great Dictator, The   1940
Comedy/Satire
04805 128 mins B/W   B, V   P
*Charlie Chaplin, Paulette Goddard, Jack Oakie,
Billy Gilbert, Reginald Gardner, Henry Daniell*
Chaplin's first dialogue film turned to political
satire. His ratings as Adenoid Hynkel brought

the newreels and radio speeches of Hitler into their perspective.
rbc Films — *CBS/Fox Video; RCA VideoDiscs*

Great Escape, The 1963
Drama
44940   170 mins   C   B, V   P
Steve McQueen, James Garner, Richard Attenborough, Charles Bronson, James Coburn
American, British, and Canadian prisoners in a German P.O.W. camp join in a single mass break for freedom. Based on the novel by Paul Brickhill.
United Artists — *CBS/Fox Video; RCA VideoDiscs*

Great Expectations 1983
Drama
Closed Captioned
73045   72 mins   C   B, V   P
Based upon the Dickens classic about a young boy's rise from a humble childhood to find fortune and happiness.
Burbank Films — *Vestron Video*

Great Expectations 1978
Cartoons/Literature-English
75621   72 mins   C   B, V   P
Animated
This animated version of Charles Dickens' classic is about a boy's meeting with an escaped convict.
WBTV Canada — *Children's Video Library*

Great Expectations/The Man with the Funny Hat 1983
Football
66219   45 mins   C   B, V, FO   P
Highlights from the Dallas Cowboys' 1982-83 and a profile of Head Coach Tom Landry.
NFL Films — *NFL Films Video*

Great Figures in History: John F. Kennedy 1980
Presidency-US/Documentary
56757   105 mins   C   B, V, CED   P
John F. Kennedy, hosted by Harry Reasoner
This program traces JFK through his Presidential years and assassination, and includes an interview with Rose Kennedy. Some scenes are in black-and-white.
CBS News — *CBS/Fox Video*

Great Gabbo, The 1929
Drama
08739   82 mins   B/W   B, V   P
Erich von Stroheim, Betty Compson, Don Douglas, Margie Kane, directed by Erich von Stroheim
A ventriloquist who can only express himself through his dummy.

Sono Art; World Wide — *Movie Buff Video; Penguin Video; Sheik Video; Discount Video Tapes; Cable Films; Video Yesteryear*

Great Gatsby, The 1974
Drama
10973   151 mins   C   B, V, LV   R, P
Robert Redford, Mia Farrow, Bruce Dern, Karen Black, Sam Waterston, directed by Jack Clayton
Adaptation of F. Scott Fitzgerald's novel of the idle rich in the 1920's and one man's devotion to a flirtatious waif. Screenplay by Francis Ford Coppola.
Academy Awards '74: Best Song Score, Original or Adaptation; Best Achievement in Costume Design.   MPAA:PG
Paramount; David Merrick — *Paramount Home Video; RCA VideoDiscs*

Great Gundown, The 1984
Drama
75672   90 mins   C   B, V   P
An outlaw in New Mexico leaves his gang to return to his family and becomes a fugitive from both sides.
Satori Entertainment Corp. — *VidAmerica*

Great Gundown, The 1975
Western
35365   98 mins   C   B, V   P
Robert Padilla, Richard Rust, Milila St. Duval
A violent tale set in the Old West. The peace of frontier New Mexico erupts when a half-breed Indian leads a brutal assault on an outlaw stronghold.
Paul Nobert — *Budget Video*

Great Guy 1936
Drama
08747   50 mins   B/W   B, V, 3/4U   P
James Cagney, Mae Clarke, Ed Brophy
Food inspector wipes out graft in his town.
Grand Natl — *Penguin Video; Ampro Video Productions; Cable Films; Video Connection; Discount Video Tapes; Classic Video Cinema Collector's Club*

Great Leaders 197?
Bible
35372   105 mins   C   B, V   P
Ivo Garrani, Fernando Rey, Giorgio Ceridni
The inspiring stories of two Old Testament heroes, Gideon and Samson, are dramatized in this beautifully constructed film.
Sunn Classic — *VCI Home Video*

Great Locomotive Chase, The 1956
Adventure
66054   85 mins   C   B, V   R, P
Fess Parker, Jeffrey Hunter

Based on a curious episode that unfolded during the Civil War, this film tells the tale of Yankee raiders who commandeered a locomotive deep in the heart of Confederate territory.
Walt Disney Productions — *Walt Disney Home Video; RCA VideoDiscs*

A dastardly villain, a noble hero and a spirited suffragette are among the competitors in an uproarious New York-to-Paris auto race circa 1908, complete with pie fights, saloon brawls, and a confrontation with a feisty polar bear.
Warner Bros — *Warner Home Video*

Great McGonagall, The   1975
Comedy
52865   95 mins   C   B, V   P
Peter Sellers, Spike Milligan, Julia Foster, directed by Joseph McGrath
A nineteenth-century weaver imagines himself made poet laureate by Queen Victoria.
MPAA:PG
Tigon Film Distributors; Daritan Prods — *Wizard Video*

Great Moments in   197?
Baseball
Baseball
45031   30 mins   C   B, V   P
Babe Ruth, Lou Gehrig, Willie Mays, Yogi Berra, Joe DiMaggio, Joe Jackson
Highlights of the many stars and happenings that have made baseball the most spectacular sport of the past century.
Major League Baseball — *RCA/Columbia Pictures Home Video*

Great Movie Stunts and   1981
The Making of Raiders of
the Lost Ark
Filmmaking/Adventure
59857   107 mins   C   B, V, LV   R, P
Harrison Ford
Two TV specials: "Movie Stunts" demonstrates how major action sequences were designed and executed, and "Making of Raiders" captures the cast and crew as they tackle the many problems created in filming the spectacular scenes.
Paramount — *Paramount Home Video; RCA VideoDiscs*

Great Muppet Caper, The   1981
Comedy
58826   95 mins   C   B, V, LV   P
Charles Grodin, Diana Rigg, John Cleese, Robert Morley, Peter Ustinov, Jack Warden, directed by Jim Henson
A group of hapless reporters (Kermit, Fozzie Bear, and Gonzo) travel to London to follow up on a major jewel robbery.
MPAA:G
Universal; AFD; David Lazer — *CBS/Fox Video; RCA VideoDiscs*

Great Race, The   1965
Comedy
69797   147 mins   C   B, V   R, P
Jack Lemmon, Tony Curtis, Natalie Wood, Peter Falk, Keenan Wynn, directed by Blake Edwards

---

Great St. Trinian's Train   1966
Robbery, The
Comedy
63348   90 mins   C   B, V   R, P
Frankie Howerd, Reg Varney, Desmond Walter Ellis
The perpetrators of the Great Train Robbery attempt to stash the loot at a remote school attended by a band of avaricious adolescent girls, with hilarious results.
British Lion — *THORN EMI Home Video*

Great Santini, The   1980
Drama
52710   118 mins   C   B, V   R, P
Robert Duvall, Blythe Danner, Michael O'Keefe, Julie Ann Haddock, Lisa Jane Persky
The "Great Santini" is Lt. Col. Bull Meechum, a Marine pilot who treats his family as if they were a company of marines, abusing them in the name of discipline, as they struggle to show him their love.
MPAA:PG
Orion Pictures — *Warner Home Video; RCA VideoDiscs*

Great Scout and   1976
Cathouse Thursday, The
Comedy/Western
64358   96 mins   C   B, V, CED   P
Lee Marvin, Oliver Reed, Robert Culp, Elizabeth Ashley, Kay Lenz
Three gold prospectors strike it rich, but one of them runs off with the money.
MPAA:PG
American International — *Vestron Video*

Great Shikar, The   1976
Adventure
33737   100 mins   C   B, V, 3/4U, Q   P
Narrated by Lowell Thomas
A hunt in Afghanistan with the Klineburger expedition in the high Himalayas. Hunters look for ibex and Marco Polo sheep amidst danger and breathtaking scenery.
World Adventure Enterprises — *TV Sports Scene*

Great Smokey   1976
Roadblock, The
Adventure
65484   84 mins   C   B, V   P
Henry Fonda, Eileen Brennan, Susan Sarandon, John Byner

While in the hospital, a sixty-year-old truck driver's rig is repossessed by the finance company. Deciding that it's time to make one last perfect cross country run, he escapes from the hospital, steals his truck and heads off into the night.
MPAA:PG
Allen R Bodoh — *Media Home Entertainment*

Great Space Coaster Supershow, The 1982
Variety
60395   59 mins   C   B, V, CED   P
A compilation of episodes from the nationally syndicated television program focusing on subjects of relevance to school children facing the complexities of growing up. A cast of teenagers combine with puppets.
Sunbow Productions — *MGM/UA Home Video*

Great Steamers of the Great Lakes 1983
Ships
74473   60 mins   C   B, V   P
This tape looks at the history of Great Lakes shipping.
Bill Warrick — *Interurban Films*

Great Teams/Great Years Volume One 1981
Football
50653   48 mins   C   B, V, FO   R, P
New York Jets, Buffalo Bills
This program highlights the accomplishments of the 1968 New York Jets, who, led by Joe Namath, pulled a stunning Super Bowl upset over the Baltimore Colts; and the 1973 Buffalo Bills, who set the NFL 14 game rushing record. O. J. Simpson's 2003 individual yards broke Jim Brown's record.
NFL Films — *NFL Films Video*

Great Texas Dynamite Chase, The 1976
Comedy
52704   90 mins   C   B, V   R, P
Claudia Jennings, Johnny Crawford, Jocelyn Jones
Two sexy young women drive across Texas with a carload of dynamite. They leave a trail of empty banks with the cops constantly on their trail.
MPAA:R
New World Pictures; David Irving — *Warner Home Video*

Great Waldo Pepper, The 1975
Adventure
11584   107 mins   C   B, V   P
Robert Redford, Susan Sarandon, Margot Kidder, Bo Svenson, directed by George Roy Hill

After the death of several people as a result of a wing-walking routine, a barnstorming pilot is permanently grounded. He finds he can't adjust to an "earth-bound" life and begins flying again under an assumed name.
MPAA:PG
Universal — *MCA Home Video*

Great White Trail, The 1917
Drama
48708   50 mins   B/W   B, V, 3/4U   P
Doris Kenyon, Thomas Holding
A thriller set in the adventurous Yukon in northern Canada. Silent.
Unknown — *Penguin Video*

Greatest Adventure, The 1982
Space exploration/Documentary
59958   54 mins   C   B, V, LV,   P
CED
Narrated by Orson Welles, Alan Shepard, Gene Cernon, John Glenn, Tom Wolfe
An account of America's race for the moon, from the first orbital flight to Neil Armstrong's landing.
Video Associates — *Vestron Video*

Greatest Comeback Ever, The 1978
Baseball
29355   58 mins   C   B, V   P
Narrated by Phil Rizzuto and Bucky Dent
This program features the key moments that made the Yankees' struggle for the championship the greatest comeback ever.
Unknown — *VidAmerica*

Greatest Fights of the 70's 1981
Boxing
58868   116 mins   C   CED   P
Muhammad Ali, Joe Frazier, George Foreman, Roberto Duran
Champions of the ring are seen in some of their most unforgettable confrontations.
Big Fights Inc — *CBS/Fox Video*

Greatest Heroes of the Bible 1979
Religion
44944   95 mins   C   B, V   P
This program contains two Bible stories. First, an enactment of how the Ten Commandments were handed down to us. Second, the story of Sampson, who lost his extraordinary power and then, with a great effort of will and spirit, regained it.
Sunn Classic Pictures — *VidAmerica*

Greatest Legends of Basketball 1978
Basketball
08372   60 mins   C   B, V   P
Jerry West, Oscar Robertson, Elgin Baylor, John Wooden
Enjoy the highlights of the careers of basketball greats.
Viacom International — *CBS/Fox Video*

Greatest Show on Earth, The 1952
Drama
53789   153 mins   C   B, V, LV   R, P
Betty Hutton, Cornel Wilde, James Stewart, Charlton Heston, Dorothy Lamour, directed by Cecil B. DeMille
Big top drama focusing on the lives and loves of circus performers.
Academy Award '52: Best Picture.
Paramount; Cecil B DeMille; Henry Wilcoxon — *Paramount Home Video; RCA VideoDiscs*

Greatest Story Ever Told, The 1956
Drama
Closed Captioned
65505   196 mins   C   B, V   P
Max Von Sydow, Charlton Heston, Sidney Poitier, Claude Rains, Jose Ferrer, Telly Savalas, Angela Lansbury, Dorothy McGuire
Christ's journey from Galilee to Golgotha and the world of saints, sinners and believers that appear along the way are seen in this epic.
United Artists — *CBS/Fox Video*

Greek Street 1951
Musical
08672   51 mins   B/W   B, V, 3/4U   P
Sari Maritzia, Arthur Ahmbling, Martin Lewis, directed by Sinclair Hill
The owner of small cafe in London discovers a poor girl singing in the street for food. He takes her in and spotlights her songs in his cafe.
Unknown — *Penguin Video*

Greek Tycoon, The 1978
Drama
62877   106 mins   C   B, V   P
Anthony Quinn, Jacqueline Bisset, James Franciscus, Raf Vallone, Edward Albert
The widow of an American president marries a billionaire shipping magnate.
MPAA:R
Universal — *MCA Home Video*

Green Archer, The 1940
Mystery
57354   283 mins   B/W   B, V, FO   P
Victor Jory, Iris Meredith
Fifteen episodes of the famed serial, featuring a spooked castle, complete with secret passages and tunnels, trap-doors, mistaken identity, and the mysterious masked figure, the Green Archer.
Columbia — *Video Yesteryear; Video Connection; Discount Video Tapes*

Green Berets, The 1968
War-Drama
38953   135 mins   C   B, V   R, P
John Wayne, David Janssen, Jim Hutton, Aldo Rey, George Takei, Raymond St. Jacques
John Wayne stars as a Special Forces colonel, leading his troops against the enemy in this war drama of the Vietnam conflict.
Warner Bros — *Warner Home Video; RCA VideoDiscs*

Green Box, The 1983
Fantasy/Literature
66216   29 mins   C   B, V   R, P
Animated
Three stories for children - "Changes, Changes," "Curious George Rides a Bike," "Leopold the See - Through Crumbpicker" - are combined on one cassette.
AM Available
Weston Woods — *CC Studios*

Green Eyes 1980
Drama
75461   97 mins   C   B, V   P
Paul Winfield
A Vietnam veteran returns to Saigon and finds the girl who bore his baby.
King Features — *U.S.A. Home Video*

Green Mountain Railroading on the Rutland & When Steam Was King 1952
Trains
66339   20 mins   C   B, V   P, T
These two short films feature scenes of the Bennington and Rutland Railway, Central Vermont's Bellows Falls—Burlington Line and footage of steam-powered trains and locomotives from all over the country. Some sequences in black and white.
Carl Dudley — *Blackhawk Films*

Green Promise, The 1949
Drama
29686   90 mins   B/W   B, V   P
Walter Brennan, Marguerite Chapman, Robert Paige, Natalie Wood
A drama about a well-meaning but domineering farmer and his four motherless children. When they face disaster as a result of the father's obstinacy, the local 4-H Club arrives with power machinery to assist in reclaiming the fields.
RKO — *Sheik Video*

Green Room, The 1978
Drama
58235 90 mins C B, V R, P
Francois Truffaut, Nathalie Baye, Jean Daste, directed by Francois Truffaut
Truffaut's haunting tale of a man who erects a secret shrine to the dead, including his young bride. Based on Henry James, "Altar of the Dead." Subtitled.
MPAA:PG FR
Les Films du Carrosse — *Warner Home Video*

Grendel, Grendel, Grendel 1982
Fantasy
65653 90 mins C B, V P
Animated, voices by Peter Ustinov, Arthur Dignam, Julie McKenna, Keith Michell
An utterly urbane dragon wants to be friends, but for some reason people are just terrified of Grendel. It's true, he bites a head off once in a while, but nobody's perfect! An ingenious retelling of Beowulf.
Satori Entertainment — *Family Home Entertainment*

Grey Fox, The 1983
Drama/Western
65115 92 mins C B, V P
Richard Farnsworth, Jackie Burroughs, Wayne Robson
A gentlemanly old stagecoach robber tries to pick up his life after thirty years in prison. Unable to resist another heist, he hides out in British Columbia where he meets an attractive suffragette.
MPAA:PG
Zoetrope Studios — *Media Home Entertainment*

Grit of the Girl Telegrapher, The/In the Switch Tower 1915
Drama
65769 47 mins B/W B, V P, T
Anna Q. Nilsson, Hal Clements, Walter Edwards, Frank Borzage
A pair of silent railroad dramas, which feature thrilling chase sequences, nefarious schemers and virginal heroines. Silent with piano scores by Jon Mirsalis.
Kalem — *Blackhawk Films*

Grizzly 1976
Horror
59670 92 mins C B, V P
Christopher George, Andrew Prine, Richard Jaeckel
The largest carnivorous ground beast in the world goes on a killing spree. Also titled: "Killer Grizzly."
MPAA:PG

David Sheldon; Harvey Flaxman — *Media Home Entertainment*

Grooming Pets 1980
Pets
44292 25 mins C V P
This program provides the best and easiest techniques for trimming coats and nails and gives helpful instruction on maintaining the viewer's cat or dog's health through proper diet and exercise.
American Home Video Library — *American Home Video Library*

Groove Tube, The 1972
Satire
03563 75 mins C B, V P
Chevy Chase, Richard Belzer
A series of skits that spoof television.
MPAA:R
Ken Shapiro — *Media Home Entertainment*

Groucho/Howdy Doody Show 195?
Comedy
17246 60 mins B/W B, V P.
Groucho Marx, Howdy Doody
Episodes from television shows featuring Groucho Marx and Howdy Doody.
NBC — *Video Connection*

Group Marriage 1983
Comedy
65724 90 mins C B, V P
Claudia Jennings, Zack Taylor, Victoria Vetri
Six young professionals fall into a marriage of communal convenience and rapidly discover the many advantages and drawbacks of their thoroughly modern group marriage.
MPAA:R
Charles S Swartz — *VCI Home Video*

Grover Washington, Jr. in Concert 1982
Music-Performance
59875 53 mins C B, V P
The lush, soulful music of Grover Washington, Jr. is captured in one of his rare public performances along with musicians Eric Gale, Richard Tee, and Steve Gadd. Songs include "Just the Two of Us," "Winelight," and "Come Morning." In stereo.
Bruce Buschel; Gary Delfiner — *Warner Home Video; Pioneer Artists; MGM/UA Home Video (disc only)*

Grover Whalen: Mr. New York 1954
Biographical/History-US
44245 15 mins B/W B, V P
The story of Grover Whalen, New York's official greeter of celebrities, who planned the New

York World's Fair and organized the wartime Civilian Defense Corps. Shown through classic newsreel footage.
Fox Movietone News — *Two Star Films*

Growing Indoor Plants 1980
Gardening/Plants
44288   22 mins   C   V   P
This program of instruction and demonstration includes expert rules on proper watering, light, food, and temperature for a large variety of house plants.
American Home Video Library — *American Home Video Library*

Grudge Fights 197?
Boxing
07877   60 mins   C   B, V   P
The biggest grudge battles in boxing history are highlighted, including Ali-Frazier, Louis-Schmeling, and Dempsey-Tunney.
Big Fights Inc — *VidAmerica*

GSF Hilites, a Visual Catalog 1984
Sports
69898   70 mins   C   B, V   P
This program contains edited highlights from 16 of Gravity Sports Films' adventure films.
Raccoon Productions — *Gravity Sports Films*

Guerrillera de Villa, La (The Warrior of Villa) 197?
Western
73579   30 mins   C   B, V   P
Carmen Sevilla, Julio Aleman, Vicente Parra, Jose Elias Moreno
This film tells the story of the Warrior of Villa who fought for love, happiness and ideals in old Mexico
KNBC — *Aztec Cinevideo*

Guess What We Learned in School 1970
Comedy
47628   85 mins   C   B, V   P
Richard Carballo, Devin Goldenberg, directed by John Avildsen
Parents in a conservative suburban community protest sex education in the schools.
MPAA:R
Cannon Releasing — *Paragon Video Productions*

Guess Who Reunion, The 1983
Music-Performance
65684   118 mins   C   B, V   P
Before a live audience in Toronto, the original Guess Who perform the hits that made them world-wide superstars. Included are performances of "Shakin' All Over," "These Eyes," and "American Woman."

David Wolinsky; Bill Ballard; Dusty Cohl; Michael Cole; Anthony Eaton — *Music Media*

Guest in the House 1944
Suspense
66379   121 mins   B/W   B, V   P
Anne Baxter, Ralph Bellamy, Ruth Warrick, Marie McDonald, Margaret Hamilton
A seemingly friendly young woman is invited to stay with a family and brings hatred and distrust to them.
Hunt Stomberg; United Artists — *Movie Buff Video*

Guide to Making Love, A 1983
Sexuality
65342   57 mins   C   B, V   P
Bryce Britton, Rona Lee Cohen, R.N., M.N.
This program is a guide to sexual awareness; created to help couples fully realize and express their sexuality. It explains how couples can learn to achieve sexual harmony and overcome their inhibitions.
Guide Productions — *Vestron Video*

Guilty Men 194?
World War II
08624   40 mins   B/W   B, V, 3/4U   P
An historical program including shocking accounts of World War II concentration camps. Contains scenes which may be offensive to some.
Unknown — *Penguin Video*

Gulliver's Travels 1939
Fantasy/Cartoons
03588   77 mins   C   B, V, 3/4U   P
Animated
Animated version of Jonathan Swift's classic about the adventures of Gulliver, an English sailor.
Paramount — *Nostalgia Merchant; Media Home Entertainment; NTA Home Entertainment; Video Yesteryear; Sheik Video; Cable Films; King of Video; Penguin Video; VCII; Video Connection; Budget Video; Discount Video Tapes; Western Film & Video Inc; Vestron Video (disc only)*

Gulliver's Travels 1977
Adventure
54558   80 mins   C   B, V   P
Richard Harris, Catherine Schell
In this partially animated adventure the entire land of Liliput has been constructed in miniature. Cartoon and real life mix in a 3-dimensional story of Dr. Lemuel Gulliver and his discovery of the small people in the East Indies.
MPAA:G
EMI — *VCI Home Video*

Gumby Adventure, A   1956
Cartoons
64196   50 mins   C   CED   P
Animated
Travel with Gumby and his pal Pokey as they meet their friends and rivals, the Blockheads.
EL, SP
Clokey Productions — *Family Home Entertainment*

Gumby Adventure Volume 1, A   1956
Cartoons
59324   50 mins   C   B, V   P
Animated
Includes "Witty Witch," "Hot Rod Granny," "In a Fix," "King for a Day," "The Groobee," "Gopher Trouble," "Rain for Roo," "Chicken Feed," and "The Zoops."
EL, SP
Clokey Productions — *Family Home Entertainment*

Gumby Adventure Volume 2, A   1956
Cartoons
59325   50 mins   C   B, V   P
Animated
Includes "The Magic Wand," "Mirrorland," "Robot Rumpus," "Moon Trip," "Trapped on the Moon," "Gumby on the Moon," "The Eggs and Trixie," "Eager Beavers," and "The Magic Show."
EL, SP
Clokey Productions — *Family Home Entertainment*

Gumby Adventure Volume 3, A   1956
Cartoons
64200   60 mins   C   B, V   P
Animated
This volume includes "Baker's Tour," "Gumby Concerto," "The Black Knight," "Toying Around," "The Blockheads," "Gumby Racer," "Toy Crazy," "Sad King Ott's Daughter," and "The Reluctant Gargoyles."
EL, SP
Clokey Productions — *Family Home Entertainment*

Gumby Adventure Volume 4, A   1956
Cartoons
64201   60 mins   C   B, V   P
Animated
This volume includes "The Kachinas," "The Glob," "School for Squares," "Goo for Pokey," "The Golden Iguana," "A Grobee Fight," "Hidden Valley," "Tricky Ball," and "Ricochet Pete."
EL, SP

Clokey Productions — *Family Home Entertainment*

Gumby Adventure Volume 5, A   1956
Cartoons
64202   60 mins   C   B, V   P
Animated
Includes "Gumby Business," "How Not to Trap Lions," "Lion Drive," "Odd Balls," "Toy Fun," "Train Trouble," "Toy Capers," "Even Steven," "The Ferris Wheel Mystery," and "Lion Around."
EL, SP
Clokey Productions — *Family Home Entertainment*

Gumby for President Volume 9   1984
Comedy
73370   60 mins   C   B, V   P
Animated
Gumby, Pokey and his friends are out on the campaign trail with ten new adventures.
Clokey Productions — *Family Home Entertainment*

Gumby Summer, A   1984
Fantasy
72451   30 mins   C   B, V   P
Runaway robots, malicious blockheads and riled Indians give Gumby and Pokey trouble in the fantasy world of clay animation.
Clokey Productions — *Family Home Entertainment*

Gumby's Holiday Special   1956
Holidays
65162   60 mins   C   B, V   P
Animated
Gumby and Pokey celebrate Thanksgiving and Christmas in eight adventures that revolve around the holiday seasons, including "Pilgrims on the Rocks," "Son of Liberty," "Pokey's Price," "The Golden Gosling" and "Pigeon in a Plum Tree."
Clokey Productions — *Family Home Entertainment*

Gumby's Incredible Journey   1956
Fantasy
66181   60 mins   C   B, V   P
Animated
Ten exciting adventures of Gumby and his claymates.
Clokey Productions — *Family Home Entertainment*

Gun in the House, A   1981
Drama
63976   100 mins   C   B, V   R, P

Sally Struthers, David Ackroyd, Joel Bailey
While being attacked in her own home, a woman shoots one of her assailants. The police find no conclusive evidence of attack and arrest the woman for murder.
Channing-Debin-Locke Productions — *VCII*

Gun Ranger   1934
Western
58504   56 mins   B/W   B, V, 3/4U   P
Bob Steele, Eleanor Stewart
Our hero plays a Texas Ranger who becomes fed up with soft judges and shady prosecutors.
Republic — *Penguin Video; Discount Video Tapes*

Gun Riders   1969
Western
58606   98 mins   C   B, V   P, T
Scott Brady, Jim Davis, John Carradine
A gunman must seek out and stop a murderer of innocent people.
Independent Intl — *Blackhawk Films*

Gunfight at the O.K. Corral   1957
Western
38622   122 mins   C   B, V, LV   R, P
Burt Lancaster, Kirk Douglas, Rhonda Fleming, Jo Van Fleet, directed by John Sturges
The story of Wyatt Earp and Doc Holliday who joined forces in Dodge City to rid the town of the criminal Clanton gang is portrayed definitively in this western classic.
Paramount — *Paramount Home Video; RCA VideoDiscs*

Gung Ho   1943
War-Drama
08775   88 mins   B/W   B, V, 3/4U   P
Randolph Scott, Noah Beery Jr., Alan Curtis, Grace McDonald
Marine raiders, in new outfit, train for invasion during World War II.
Universal; Walter Wanger — *Penguin Video; Video Yesteryear; Budget Video; International Historic Films; Sheik Video; Cable Films; VCII; Video Connection; Discount Video Tapes; Cinema Concepts*

Gunga Din   1939
Adventure
00257   117 mins   B/W   B, V, 3/4U   P
Cary Grant, Douglas Fairbanks Jr., Joan Fontaine
Based on Kipling's adventure book, this story features three soldier comrades battling savages.
RKO; George Seaton — *Nostalgia Merchant; VidAmerica; King of Video; Blackhawk Films*

Gunman From Bodie   1941
Western
15435   62 mins   B/W   B, V   P
Tim McCoy, Buck Jones, Ray Hatton
Action western.
Monogram — *Video Connection; Sheik Video*

Gunners and Guns   1934
Western
15547   51 mins   B/W   B, V   P
Black King, Edmund Cobb, Edna Asetin
Vintage western starring Black King.
Beaumont — *Video Connection*

Gunplay   1951
Western
64406   61 mins   B/W   B, V, 3/4U   P
Tim Holt, Joan Dixon, Richard Martin
Two cowboys befriend a boy whose father has been killed and search for the murderer.
RKO — *Nostalgia Merchant*

Guns and Fury   19??
Drama
66507   90 mins   C   B, V   P
Peter Graves, Cameron Mitchell, Michael Ansara, Albert Salmi
Two American oilriggers in the Middle East, circa 1908, are forced to fight off an attack by a vicious Arab sheik and his tribe.
A and Z Company Ltd — *Program Hunters*

Guns in the Dark   1937
Western
15447   60 mins   B/W   B, V   P
Johnny Mack Brown, Claire Rochelle
Cowboy vows never to use a gun again, believing he accidentally killed his best friend.
Republic — *Video Connection*

Guns of August   19??
World War I
53383   110 mins   B/W   B, V, 3/4U   P
Rare footage and expert narration combined in this film version of Barbara Tuchman's novel, tracing WWI from the abdication of Edward VII and Kaiser Wilhelm through its global involvement.
USA — *International Historic Films*

Guns of Fury   1945
Western
14661   60 mins   B/W   B, V   P
Duncan Renaldo
Cisco and Pancho solve the troubles of a small boy in this wild western.
United Artists — *VCI Home Video; Video Connection*

Guns of Navarone, The — 1961

Adventure
13253   159 mins   C   B, V   P
Gregory Peck, David Niven, Anthony Quinn, Stanley Baker, Anthony Quayle, directed by J. Lee Thompson
British Intelligence in the Middle East sends six men to Navarone to destroy guns manned by the Germans.
Filmdom's Famous Five '61: Best Actor (Peck); Best Supporting Actor (Quinn).
Columbia; Carl Foreman — *RCA/Columbia Pictures Home Video; RCA VideoDiscs*

Gus — 1976

Comedy
55568   96 mins   C   CED   R, P
Ed Asner, Don Knotts, Gary Grimes, Tim Conway, Dick Van Patten, Ronnie Schell, Bob Krane, Tom Bosley, directed by Vincent McEveety
A mule with the ability to kick long field goals saves a professional football team from oblivion.
MPAA:G
Walt Disney — *RCA VideoDiscs*

Guyana Tragedy: The Story of Jim Jones — 1980

Drama
63978   240 mins   C   B, V   R, P
Powers Boothe, Ned Beatty, Brenda Vaccaro, LeVar Burton, Colleen Dewhurst, James Earl Jones
This dramatization traces the story of Jim Jones and the People's Temple from its beginnings in 1953 to the November 1978 mass suicide of more than 900 people.
Emmy Awards '80: Best Actor in a Dramatic Special (Boothe).
The Konigsberg Company — *VCII*

Guys and Dolls — 1955

Musical
53663   149 mins   C   B, V, CED   P
Marlon Brando, Jean Simmons, Frank Sinatra, Vivian Blaine, Stubby Kaye, Sheldon Leonard, directed by Joseph L. Mankiewicz
A New York gangster takes a bet that he can romance a Salvation Army lady. Frank Loesser's score includes "Luck Be a Lady," "If I were a Bell," "Sit Down You're Rocking the Boat."
Samuel Goldwyn — *CBS/Fox Video*

Gypsies — 1961

Documentary/Minorities
72509   30 mins   B/W   B, V, 3/4U   P
A documentary tracing the plight of gypsies across rural Poland in "cinema-verite" style. No narration.
Documentary Film Studio of Poland — *International Historic Films*

Gypsy — 1962

Musical
74205   149 mins   C   B, V   R, P
Rosalind Russell, Natalie Wood, Karl Malden
This is the life story of America's most famous striptease queen, Gypsy Rose Lee. Rosalind Russell gives a memorable performance as the infamous Gypsy.
Mervyn Le Roy — *Warner Home Video*

H

Hail — 1972

Satire
76660   85 mins   C   B, V   P
Richard B. Shull, Dick O'Neil, Phil Foster, Joseph Sirola, Dan Resin
A biting satire of what-might-have-been if certain key cabinet members had their way.
MPAA:PG
Fred Levinson Productions — *Monterey Home Video*

Hair — 1979

Musical
37529   118 mins   C   B, V, CED   P
Treat Williams, John Savage, Beverly D'Angelo
Film version of the 1960's Broadway musical about the carefree life of the flower children and the shadow of the Vietnam War that hangs over them.
MPAA:R
United Artists — *CBS/Fox Video; RCA VideoDiscs*

Hal Janssen's Fly Fishing Secrets -- The Dry Fly — 1983

Fishing
65146   45 mins   C   B, V   P
Hal Janssen
This program from the "Sportman's Video Collection" demonstrates how to tie dry flies and how to fish for trout with them.
SV Angling — *Leisure Time Products Project/3M*

Hal Janssen's Fly Fishing Secrets -- The Wet Fly — 1983

Fishing
65145   45 mins   C   B, V   P
Hal Janssen
This program from the "Sportman's Video Collection" demonstrates how to tie stoneflies, caddis, scuds and leeches and how to fish for trout with them.
SV Angling — *Leisure Time Products Project/3M*

Hal Roach Comedy Classics Volume I — 193?
Comedy
59154   80 mins   B/W   B, V, 3/4U   P
Stan Laurel, Oliver Hardy, Harry Langdon, Charley Chase
Films include: "Hoosegow" (1930), with Laurel and Hardy; "The Head Guy" (1930), with Harry Langdon; "High Gear" (1931), with the Boyfriends and "On the wrong Trek" (1936), with Laurel and Hardy and Charley Chase.
Hal Roach — *Nostalgia Merchant*

Half-Shot at Sunrise — 1930
Comedy
56907   78 mins   B/W   B, V, FO   P
Wheeler and Woolsey, Dorothy Lee
Madcap vaudeville comedians play AWOL soldiers loose in 1918 Paris. Continuous one-liners, sight gags, and slapstick nonsense.
RKO — *Video Yesteryear; Cable Films; Discount Video Tapes; Classic Video Cinema Collector's Club*

Hall of Famers — 1960
Baseball
49551   60 mins   B/W   B, V   P
Three twenty-minute segments which highlight the careers of members of baseball's Hall of Fame who were elected before 1960.
Major League Baseball — *Major League Baseball Productions*

Hallelujah, I'm a "Tramp" — 1933
Musical
64246   80 mins   B/W   B, V   P
Al Jolson, Harry Langdon, Madge Evans, Frank Morgan, Chester Conklin, directed by Lewis Milestone
The leader of a group of Central Park bums falls in love with a young lady who is suffering from amnesia. This unusually downbeat Depression-era musical has a score by Richard Rodgers and Lorenz Hart.
Lewis Milestone; UA — *Classic Video Cinema Collector's Club*

Hallmark Theater (Sometimes She's Sunday) — 1952
Drama
42970   26 mins   B/W   B, V, FO   P
Adult fare about a Portuguese-American fisherman whose daughter becomes engaged to a typical American boy.
NBC — *Video Yesteryear*

Halloween — 1978
Horror
42908   85 mins   C   B, V, LV   P
Jamie Lee Curtis, Nancy Loomis, P.J. Soles, directed by John Carpenter
John Carpenter's horror classic has been acclaimed "the most successful independent motion picture of all time." A deranged youth returns to his hometown after fifteen years in an asylum with murderous intent.
MPAA:R   EL, SP
Debra Hill — *Media Home Entertainment*

Halloween II — 1981
Horror
47418   92 mins   C   B, V, LV, CED   P
Jamie Lee Curtis, Donald Pleasance
Picking up precisely where "Halloween" left off, the sequel begins with the escape of vicious killer Shape, who continues to murder and terrorize the community of Haddonfield, Illinois. VHS in stereo.
MPAA:R
Universal — *MCA Home Video*

Halloween III: The Season of the Witch — 1982
Horror
60586   98 mins   C   B, V, CED   P
Tom Atkins, Stacey Nelkin, Dan O'Herlihy, Ralph Strait, directed by Tommy Lee Wallace
A mad warlock threatens to subject 50 million children to a Halloween they'll never forget, in this sequel produced by John Carpenter.
MPAA:R
Universal; John Carpenter — *MCA Home Video*

Hallucination — 1967
Horror
63404   90 mins   C   B, V   P
George Montgomery, Danny Stone
Expatriate acid heads murder an antique dealer under the influence of LSD. In sepia and color. Also known as "Hallucination Generation."
Edward Mann; Robert D. Weinbach — *VIDCREST*

Ham MasterTapes — 1983
Mass media/Communication
65642   120 mins   C   B, V, 3/4U   P
3 pgms
This program provides a comprehensive survey of all a beginner needs to know to prepare for the FCC Amateur Radio license exam. The Ham MasterTapes consist of 26 lessons, illustrated hands-on instruction, graphics, and review questions. On 3 videocassettes.
Larry Horne — *Ham MasterTapes*

Hamlet — 1948
Drama
44362   142 mins   B/W   CED   P
Sir Laurence Olivier, Jean Simmons, Stanley Holloway, Eileen Herlie, directed by Sir Laurence Olivier

Shakespeare's most famous tragedy about a young prince plagued by murder and madness. Academy Awards '48: Best Production; Best Actor (Olivier); Best Art Design, Black and White; Best Costume Design, Black and White.
Universal, J Arthur Rank — *RCA VideoDiscs*

Hammett   1982
Mystery
69023   97 mins   C   B, V   R, P
This mystery thriller plunges real-life writer and detective Dashiell Hammett into the world of his fictional characters.
MPAA:PG
Zoetrope Studios — *Warner Home Video*

Hand, The   1981
Horror
58236   105 mins   C   B, V   R, P
Michael Caine, Andrea Marcovicci, Annie McEnroe
A gifted cartoonist's hand is severed in an accident. Soon a hand is on the loose seeking out victims to satisfy an obsessive revenge.
MPAA:R
Orion Pictures — *Warner Home Video*

Hang 'Em High   1967
Western
62777   114 mins   C   B, V   P
Clint Eastwood, Inger Stevens, Ed Begley, Pat Hingle, James MacArthur
A cowboy is saved from a lynching and vows to hunt down the gang that nearly killed him.
United Artists — *CBS/Fox Video; RCA VideoDiscs*

Hangar 18   1980
Science fiction/Adventure
47685   97 mins   C   B, V   P
Darren McGavin, Robert Vaughn, Garry Collins, Joseph Campanella, James Hampton, Tom Hallick, Pamela Bellwood
A space drama about two astronauts who witness an unexpected disaster in orbit.
MPAA:PG
Sunn Classic; Charles E Sellier Jr — *Worldvision Home Video*

Hanky Panky   1982
Comedy
Closed Captioned
62810   103 mins   C   B, V   P
Gene Wilder, Gilda Radner, Richard Widmark, Kathleen Quinlan, directed by Sidney Poitier
A comic thriller in the Hitchcock vein, in which Gene Wilder and Gilda Radner become involved in a search for top-secret plans.
MPAA:PG
Columbia — *RCA/Columbia Pictures Home Video; RCA VideoDiscs*

Hanna K   1983
Drama
65512   111 mins   C   B, V   P
Jill Clayburgh, Gabriel Byrne, Jean Yanne, Muhamad Bakri, David Clennon, Oded Kotler
The gripping story of divided passions set in the tumultuous state of Israel.
MPAA:R
Universal — *MCA Home Video*

Hanover Street   1979
Drama
63442   109 mins   C   B, V   P
Harrison Ford, Lesley-Anne Down, Christopher Plummer, Alec McCowan
An American bomber pilot and a British nurse fall in love in war-torn Europe, but another man is in love with the nurse as well.
MPAA:PG
Columbia; Paul N Lazarus II — *RCA/Columbia Pictures Home Video*

Hansel and Gretel   1954
Fairy tales
59048   82 mins   C   B, V   P
Voices of Anna Russell, Mildred Dunnock
This famed Grimms fairy tale tells the story of the woodcutter's children who venture into the forest and are caught in the clutches of a wicked old witch. Puppet animation.
EL, SP
Hansel and Gretel Co — *Media Home Entertainment; RCA VideoDiscs*

Hansel and Gretel   1984
Fairy tales
Closed Captioned
73143   60 mins   C   B, V, CED   P
Ricky Schroeder, Joan Collins, Paul Dooley, Bridgette Anderson, James Frawley
From "Faerie Tale Theatre" comes the story of two young children who get more than they bargained for when they eat a gingerbread house.
Shelley Duvall — *CBS/Fox Video*

Happiest Millionaire, The   1967
Musical
65634   144 mins   C   B, V   R, P
Fred MacMurray, Tommy Steele, Greer Garson, Geraldine Page, Lesley Ann Warren, John Davidson
A newly immigrated lad finds a job as butler to a household that features pet alligators in the conservatory and a Bible-and-boxing school in the stables. In stereo VHS and Beta Hi-Fi.
Buena Vista — *Walt Disney Home Video*

Happy Birthday to Me   1981
Horror
58497   108 mins   C   B, V, LV   P
Melissa Sue Anderson, Glenn Ford, directed by J. Lee Thompson

Several elite seniors at an exclusive private school mysteriously disappear—one by one.
MPAA:R
Columbia; John Dunning — *RCA/Columbia Pictures Home Video*

Happy Hooker, The　1975
Comedy
55219　96 mins　C　B, V, LV,　R, P
　　　　　　　　　　CED
Lynn Redgrave, Jean Pierre Aumont
Xaviera Hollander's cheery memoir of her transition from office girl to "working girl" has been brought to the screen with a sprightly air of naughtiness.
MPAA:R
Cannon Releasing — *Wonderlust Video*

Happy Hooker Goes　1980
Hollywood, The
Comedy
52761　86 mins　C　B, V, LV　P
Martine Beswicke
The third film inspired by Xaviera Hollander's memoirs, in which the fun-loving Xaviera comes to Hollywood with the intention of making a movie based on her book, but soon meets up with a series of scheming, would-be producers.
MPAA:R
Golan Globus Productions; Alan Roberts — *MCA Home Video*

Happy Hooker Goes to　1977
Washington, The
Comedy
55220　89 mins　C　B, V, CED　P
Joey Heatherton, George Hamilton
The further adventures of the world's most famous madam find Xaviera Hollander the target of a U.S. Senate investigation.
MPAA:R
Cannon Releasing — *Vestron Video*

Hardcore　1979
Drama
47433　106 mins　C　B, V　P
George C. Scott, Season Hubley, Peter Boyle, directed by Paul Schrader
A midwestern businessman travels to California to find his runaway daughter, who has become a prostitute and pornographic film star.
MPAA:R
Columbia — *RCA/Columbia Pictures Home Video*

Hard Country　1981
Drama
53352　101 mins　C　CED　P
Jan-Michael Vincent, Kim Basinger, Michael Parks, Tanya Tucker
A young woman decides to break away from her boyfriend and her small Texas town, causing him to re-evaluate his life.

MPAA:PG
ITC; Martin Starger — *CBS/Fox Video*

Hard Day's Night, A　1964
Musical
69037　90 mins　B/W　B, V, LV,　P
　　　　　　　　　　CED
John Lennon, Paul McCartney, George Harrison, Ringo Starr
This program depicts, with good-natured honesty and fun, the Beatles' lighthearted message to youth.
Walter Shenson — *MPI Home Video*

Hard Hombre　1931
Western
14662　60 mins　B/W　B, V, 3/4U　P
Hoot Gibson
In this Western adventure Hoot Gibson rides and shoots across the screen.
Hoffman — *Penguin Video; Video Connection*

Hard Times　1975
Drama
64236　92 mins　C　B, V　P
Charles Bronson, James Coburn, Jill Ireland, Strother Martin
A Depression-era drifter becomes a bare knuckle street fighter, and a gambler decides to promote him for big stakes.
MPAA:PG
Columbia — *RCA/Columbia Pictures Home Video*

Hard to Hold　1984
Musical-Drama
72931　93 mins　C　B, V, LV　P
Rick Springfield, Patti Hansen, Janet Eiber
Rockin' Rick's film debut where he falls in love with a children's counselor after an automobile accident. Rick sings "Love Somebody" with music by Peter Gabriel.
MPAA:PG
D Constantine Conte — *MCA Home Video*

Harder They Come, The　1972
Musical-Drama
47048　93 mins　C　B, V　R, P
Jimmy Cliff, Janet Barkley, Carl Bradshaw
A poor Jamaican youth becomes a success with a hit reggae record, but finds his fame is short-lived.
MPAA:R
New World Pictures — *THORN EMI Home Video; RCA VideoDiscs*

Harder They Fall, The　1956
Drama
21288　109 mins　B/W　B, V　P
Humphrey Bogart, Rod Steiger, Jan Sterling

An unemployed reporter promotes a fighter for the syndicate, while doing an expose on the fight racket. Based on Budd Schulberg's novel.
Columbia — *RCA/Columbia Pictures Home Video*

Hardware Wars and Other Film Farces — 1981
Science fiction/Satire
47397   48 mins   C   B, V   R, P
A collection of four award-winning spoofs of big-budget film epics, featuring "Hardware Wars," "Porklips Now," "Bambi Meets Godzilla" and "Closet Cases of the Nerd Kind." Some black-and-white segments.
MPAA:G
Ernie Fosselius et al — *Warner Home Video*

Harlan County, U.S.A. — 1976
Miners and mining/Documentary
44778   103 mins   C   B, V   P
Directed by Barbara Kopple
The emotions of 180 coal mining families are seen up close in this classic documentary about their struggle to win a United Mine Workers contract in Kentucky.
Academy Award '76: Best Documentary.
Cinema 5 — *RCA/Columbia Pictures Home Video*

Harlem Rides the Range — 1939
Western/Musical
66380   60 mins   B/W   B, V   P
Herb Jeffries, Clarens Brooks, Spencer Williams
A singing cowboy foils the attempt by some bad guys to steal the deed to his sweetheart's radium mine. This all-black musical western hybrid stars popular singer Herb Jeffries, known here as "The Bronze Buckaroo."
Sack Amusement Enterprises — *Movie Buff Video*

Harmony Lane — 1935
Musical
48716   70 mins   B/W   B, V, 3/4U   P
Douglas Montgomery, William Frawley, Lloyd Hughes
A musical tale about the great American composer, Stephen Foster.
Mascot — *Penguin Video*

Harmony Trail — 1944
Western
57987   60 mins   B/W   B, V   P
Ken Maynard
Ken Maynard stars in this rip-roaring western adventure.
Astor — *Video Connection*

Harold and Maude — 1971
Comedy
38588   91 mins   C   B, V, LV   R, P
Ruth Gordon, Bud Cort, directed by Hal Ashby
A classic cult film starring an unlikely pair: a rich, jaded 20-year old man and a wacky 80-year-old woman, who go off on a series of wild adventures.
MPAA:PG
Paramount — *Paramount Home Video; RCA VideoDiscs*

Harold Lloyd's Comedy Classics — 1919
Comedy
69554   47 mins   B/W   B, V, FO   P
Harold Lloyd, Snub Pollard, Bebe Daniels
Four early Harold Lloyd shorts from 1916-1919 are combined on this tape: "The Chef," "The Cinema Director," "Two Gun Gussie" and "I'm On My Way." Silent with musical score.
Pathe — *Video Yesteryear*

Harold Lloyd's Short Films — 191?
Comedy
64248   60 mins   B/W   B, V   P
Harold Lloyd, Bebe Daniels, Mildred Davis
Five early Harold Lloyd shorts from his "Lonesome Luke" period, circa 1915-17. Silent with musical score.
Pathe Exchange — *Classic Video Cinema Collector's Club*

Harper — 1966
Mystery
69024   119 mins   C   B, V   R, P
Paul Newman
Paul Newman stars in this action-charged 1966 private-eye mystery.
Warner Bros — *Warner Home Video*

Harper Valley P.T.A. — 1978
Comedy
66095   93 mins   C   B, V, CED   P
Barbara Eden, Nanette Fabray, Louis Nye, Pat Paulsen, Ronny Cox
A tale of what happened when "my momma socked it to the Harper Valley P.T.A."
MPAA:PG
April Fool Productions — *Vestron Video*

Harrad Experiment, The — 1973
Drama
06006   95 mins   C   B, V   P
James Whitmore, Tippi Hedron, Don Johnson
An experiment in co-ed living in New England, Ivy League-type university. Based on Robert H. Rimmer's novel.
MPAA:R
Cinerama; Dennis Stevens and Cinema Arts Prod — *Wizard Video*

Harrad Summer, The — 1974
Drama
59059   103 mins   C   B, V   P
Richard Doran, Victoria Thompson, Laurie Walters, Robert Reiser, Marty Allen, Bill Dana
Four college students decide to find out if their sexual philosophy can withstand the pressures and prejudices of the outside world by spending two weeks of their summer vacation at each other's homes.
Dennis F Stevens — *Wizard Video*

Harry and Son — 1984
Drama
73031   117 mins   C   B, V   P
Paul Newman, Robby Benson, Joanne Woodward, Ellen Barkin
A widowed construction worker faces the problems of raising his son.
MPAA:PG
Orion — *Vestron Video*

Harry and Walter Go to New York — 1976
Comedy
21289   120 mins   C   B, V   P
James Caan, Elliot Gould, Michael Caine, Diane Keaton
Two vaudeville performers are hired by a crooked British entrepreneur for a wild crime scheme.
MPAA:PG
Columbia — *RCA/Columbia Pictures Home Video*

Harry Chapin:The Final Concert — 1981
Music-Performance
58867   89 mins   C   B, V, CED   P
Harry Chapin
Taped live at Hamilton Place in Hamilton, Canada, this concert features the warm, energetic style which earned the singer-songwriter legions of devoted fans. Songs include, "Taxi," "Sequel," and "Cat's in the Cradle."
GRM Productions Inc. — *CBS/Fox Video*

Harry Tracy — 1983
Drama
65343   111 mins   C   B, V   P
Bruce Dern, Gordon Lightfoot, Helen Shaver
This is the tale of the legendary outlaw whose escapades made him both a wanted criminal and an exalted folk hero.
MPAA:PG
Cid and Marty Krofft; Albert Penzer — *Vestron Video*

Hash House Fraud, A/The Sultan's Wife — 191?
Comedy
59406   33 mins   B/W   B, V   P, T
Louise Fazenda, Hugh Fay, Chester Conklin, The Keystone Cops, Gloria Swanson, Bobby Vernon
"A Hash House Fraud" (1915) features a frenetic Keystone chase. "The Sultan's Wife" (1917) concerns a woman who attracts the unwanted attention of a sultan.
Mack Sennett — *Blackhawk Films*

Hatari — 1962
Adventure
64938   158 mins   C   B, V, LV   R, P
John Wayne, Elsa Martinelli, Red Buttons, Hardy Kruger, directed by Howard Hawks
A team of professional big game hunters have an exciting time capturing wild beasts to send to zoos.
Paramount — *Paramount Home Video*

Haunted, The — 1979
Horror
59144   81 mins   C   B, V   R, P
Aldo Ray, Virginia Mayo, Ann Michelle, Jim Negele, directed by Michael De Gaetano
The ancient curse of an Indian woman haunts a present day family by possessing the body of a beautiful girl. Through the girl, a horrible vengeance is carried out.
Michael De Gaetano — *VCII*

Haunted Castle, The (Schloss Vogelod) — 1921
Film-History
51397   56 mins   B/W   B, V, FO   P
Arnold Korff, Lulu Keyser-Korf
The first German mystery film. Silent, with English subtitles.
FW Murnau — *Video Yesteryear*

Haunted Ranch — 1943
Western
38983   56 mins   B/W   B, V, FO   P
The Range Busters (John "Dusty" King, David Sharpe, Max "Alibi" Terhune)
Reno Red has been murdered and a shipment of gold bullion is missing. A gang on the lookout for the gold tries to convince people that Red's ranch is haunted by his ghost.
Monogram — *Video Yesteryear; Discount Video Tapes*

Haunted Strangler, The — 1958
Horror
59661   78 mins   B/W   B, V   P
Boris Karloff, Elizabeth Allan
The story of a social reformer who discovers that he was once a notorious murderer. The realization causes him to become re-transformed into the killer.
John Croydon — *Media Home Entertainment*

Haunting of Julia, The 1981
Horror
59046   96 mins   C   B, V   P
Mia Farrow, Keir Dullea, Tom Conti
Peter Straub wrote this tale of revenge and
remorse set in a London house reverberating
with the guilty apprehension of a woman who
succumbs to the ghost of a long dead child.
MPAA:R
Peter Fetterman — *Media Home
Entertainment*

Have I Got a Story For 1984
You
Puppets
75534   60 mins   C   B, V   P
Shari Lewis
Favorite children's stories are told by Shari
Lewis and her puppets, including the delectable
Lambchop.
MGM UA — *MGM/UA Home Video*

Hawaii 1966
Drama
58827   161 mins   C   B, V, CED   P
*Max von Sydow, Julie Andrews, Richard Harris,
Carroll O'Connor, Gene Hackman, directed by
George Roy Hill*
James Michener's novel about a New England
farm boy who decides in 1820 that the Lord has
commanded him to the island of Hawaii for the
purpose of "Christianizing" the natives. Filmed
on location.
EL, SP
United Artists; Walter Mirisch — *CBS/Fox
Video*

Hawaii Experience 1983
Video
66151   60 mins   C   B, V, 3/4U   P
Beautiful Hawaii scenery is used to lull the
viewer to relaxation.
Environmental Video — *Environmental Video*

Hawk of the Wilderness 1938
Adventure/Serials
07341   195 mins   B/W   B, V, 3/4U   P
Herman Brix, Mala, William Boyle
A man, shipwrecked as an infant and reared on
a remote island by native Indians, battles
modern day pirates. Serial in twelve Episodes.
Republic — *Video Connection*

Hawmps! 1976
Comedy
49624   98 mins   C   B, V   P
*James Hampton, Christopher Connelly, Slim
Pickens, Denver Pyle, directed by Joe Camp*
A Civil War lieutenant trains his men to use
camels. When the soldiers and animals begin to
grow fond of each other, Congress orders the
camels to be set free. The bad news turns into a
happy ending.
MPAA:G
Mulberry Square Prods; Joe Camp — *Vestron
Video*

Hazel's People 1975
Drama
69276   105 mins   C   B, V   P
Geraldine Page, Pat Hingle, Graham Beckel
A bitter and hostile college student attends his
friend's funeral in Mennonite country. He
discovers not only a way of life he never knew
existed, but a personal faith in a living Christ.
MPAA:G
Happy Production Co. — *Vanguard Video*

He Knows You're Alone 1980
Horror
64567   94 mins   C   B, V, CED   P
Don Scardino, Elizabeth Kemp, Tom Rolfing
A psychotic killer terrorizes young girls in his
search for a suitable "bride."
MPAA:R
MGM/UA — *MGM/UA Home Video*

He-Man and the Masters 198?
of the Universe
Science fiction/Cartoons
65011   91 mins   C   B, V   P
Animated
He-Man, who lives on the planet Eternia, battles
the evil force Skeletor and his band of villains.
Based on the Mattel toys.
Filmation — *RCA/Columbia Pictures Home
Video; RCA VideoDiscs*

He-Man and the Masters 1983
of the Universe, Vol. 5
Cartoons/Adventure
66352   50 mins   C   B, V   P
Animated
The He-Man saga continues with two more
episodes featuring the treacherous Skeletor
plotting more evil deeds in his efforts to gain
control of Castle Greyskull.
Filmation — *RCA/Columbia Pictures Home
Video*

He-Man and the Masters 1984
of the Universe, Volume
VI
Adventure
76027   60 mins   C   B, V   P
Animated
Volume VI of this series features He-Man and
Teela once again battling the forces of evil in
two thrilling episodes.
Filmation Presentation — *RCA/Columbia
Pictures Home Video*

He-Man and the Masters of the Universe: The Greatest Adventures of All
1983
Cartoons
65318   60 mins   C   B, V   P
Animated
He-Man and his friends continue their battles against the evil forces of Skeletor.
Lou Scheimer — RCA/Columbia Pictures Home Video

He Walked by Night
1948
Mystery
08598   80 mins   B/W   B, V   P
Richard Basehart, Scott Brady, Roy Roberts, Jack Webb, directed by Alfred M. Werker
Los Angeles homicide investigators track down a cop killer; from the files of the Los Angeles police.
Eagle Lion; Bryan Foy Productions — Movie Buff Video; Penguin Video; Video Yesteryear; Discount Video Tapes

Headless Horseman, The/Will Rogers
1922
Comedy
10108   52 mins   B/W   B, V   P, T
Will Rogers, directed by Edward Venturini
Will Rogers plays Ichabod Crane in Washington Irving's "Legend of Sleepy Hollow." Second half of program follows Roger's career from early vaudeville days to Ziegfeld.
Hodkinson — Blackhawk Films

Health 'n Action Exercise Programs
1978
Physical fitness
47506   30 mins   C   B, V   P
Ann Dugan 12 pgms
This series offers a diverse program of physical conditioning. Series A, "Get Fit Stay Fit," and series B, "Super Exercises," are 60 minutes each. Series C, "Sports Conditioning," consists of four 30-minute segments. Series D, "Rehabilitation and Injury," is comprised of six 30-minute programs.
1.Get Fit Stay Fit 2.Super Exercises 3.Sports Conditioning (Jog/Run, Golf, Tennis/Racquet Sports, Ski) 4.Rehabilitation and Injury (Prenatal, Postnatal, Hysterectomy, Mastectomy, Knee, Back)
Health n Action — RCA/Columbia Pictures Home Video

Hear O Israel
19??
Middle East/Religion
38987   71 mins   C   B, V, FO   P
Three classic short films about the land of Israel and the Jewish faith: "Hear O Israel," "The Changing Land," and "My Holiday in Israel." The first two have dialogue in English, the last is in Hebrew with no subtitles.

Unknown — Video Yesteryear

Hearse, The
1980
Horror
59672   97 mins   C   B, V   P
Trish Van Devere, Joseph Cotten
While fighting to maintain her sanity, a vacationing schoolteacher finds her life threatened by a sinister black hearse.
MPAA:PG
Mark Tenser — Media Home Entertainment

Heart Like a Wheel
1983
Drama
Closed Captioned
65499   113 mins   C   B, V   P
Bonnie Bedelia, Beau Bridges, Bill McKinney, Leo Rossi
The true story of premier drag racer Shirley Muldowney, who had to break not only speed records but sexual barriers as well and contend with the reluctance of racing officials to license her.
MPAA:PG
20th Century Fox — CBS/Fox Video

Heart of Humanity, The
1919
War-Drama
64317   68 mins   B/W   B, V   P
Erich von Stroheim, Dorothy Phillips
Erich von Stroheim plays his usual role of a despicable villain in this World War I - era melodrama. Silent with musical score.
Jewel Productions — Classic Video Cinema Collector's Club

Heart of Texas Ryan, The
1916
Western
48719   50 mins   B/W   B, V, 3/4U   P
Tom Mix
The flamboyant cowboy star fights with kidnappers and wins. Silent.
Unknown — Penguin Video

Heart of the Golden West
1942
Western
14373   54 mins   B/W   B, V, FO   P
Roy Rogers, Sons of the Pioneers
Roy protects ranchers of Cherokee City from unjust shipping charges.
Republic — Video Yesteryear; Video Connection; Cable Films

Heart of the Rio Grande
1942
Western
58604   70 mins   B/W   B, V   P, T
Gene Autry, Smiley Burnette, Fay McKenzie, Edith Fellows, Joseph Stauch Jr
A spoiled young rich girl tries to trick her father into coming to her "rescue" at a western dude ranch.

Republic — *Blackhawk Films; Video Connection*

Heart of the Rockies   1937
Western
15441   54 mins   B/W   B, V   P
Bob Livingston, Ray Corrigan, Max Terhune
Three Mesquiteers stop mountain family's rustling and illegal game trappers.
Republic — *Video Connection; Nostalgia Merchant*

Heartaches   1982
Comedy
64040   90 mins   C   B, V, LV,   P
                          CED
Margot Kidder, Annie Potts, Robert Carradine, Winston Rekert
Two young women, one of them pregnant, decide to chuck everything and run off to Toronto. Once there, they get jobs in a mattress factory and rent an apartment together.
Canadian Film Development Corp — *Vestron Video*

Heartbeat   1946
Romance
16073   101 mins   B/W   B, V   P
Ginger Rogers, Jean-Pierre Aumont, Basil Rathbone
Romance between a lady pickpocket and an overly polished diplomat with a yen for dancing.
RKO — *Movie Buff Video; Videobrary*

Heartbeat   1980
Drama
52714   109 mins   C   B, V   R, P
Nick Nolte, John Heard, Sissy Spacek, Anne Dusenberry, directed by John Byrum
The story of Jack Kerouac (author of "On the Road"), his friend and inspiration Neal Casady, and the woman they shared, Carolyn Casady, based on her memoirs.
MPAA:R
Orion Pictures — *Warner Home Video*

Heartbeeps   1981
Science fiction/Comedy
47419   79 mins   C   B, V   P
Andy Kaufman, Bernadette Peters
In 1995, two domestic robot servants fall in love and run off together.
MPAA:PG
Universal — *MCA Home Video*

Heartbreak Kid, The   1972
Comedy
37412   106 mins   C   B, V   P
Charles Grodin, Cybill Shepard, Eddie Albert, Jeannie Berlin

A glib, romantic dreamer becomes disillusioned with love and his marriage in this comedy by Neil Simon.
MPAA:PG
20th Century Fox — *Media Home Entertainment*

Heartland   1981
Drama
47303   95 mins   C   B, V   R, P
Conchata Ferrell, Rip Torn
Set in 1910, this film chronicles the story of one woman's life on the Wyoming Frontier, the hazards she faces, and her courage and spirit.
MPAA:PG
Michael Hausman; Beth Ferris — *THORN EMI Home Video*

Hearts and Minds   1974
Documentary/Vietnam War
55546   112 mins   C   B, V, LV   R, P
Directed by Peter Davis
Gripping documentary about America's misguided involvement in Vietnam.
Academy Awards '74: Best Documentary (Schneider, Davis). MPAA:R
Touchstone; Bert Schneider; Audjeff — *Paramount Home Video*

Heart's Desire   1937
Musical-Drama
52210   79 mins   B/W   B, V, FO   P
Richard Tauber, Lenora Corbett
Opera great Richard Tauber stars in this tale of an unknown Viennese singer who falls in love with an English girl.
Gaumont British — *Video Yesteryear*

Hearts of Humanity   1932
Drama
58521   68 mins   B/W   B, V, 3/4U   P
Jean Hersholt, Claudia Dell, J. Ferrell Macdonald
The local beat cop in a New York neighborhood acts as the settler of arguments and a good friend to all.
Majestic — *Penguin Video*

Heat   1972
Comedy-Drama
59050   101 mins   C   B, V   P
Joe Dallasandro, Sylvia Miles, Andy Warhol, directed by Paul Morrissey
Andy Warhol's characters meet in Hollywood, in seedy motels and spacious mansions, and reveal themselves in all their desperate loneliness.
MPAA:R
Levitt Pickman — *Media Home Entertainment*

Heat and Dust 1982
Drama
65519   130 mins   C   B, V   P
Julie Christie, Greta Scacchi, Shashi Kapoor,
Christopher Cazenove, Nickolas Grace
A young bride joins her husband at his post in
India and is inexorably drawn to the country and
its Prince of State. Years later her great niece
journeys to modern day India in search of the
truth about her scandalous and mysterious
relative.
MPAA:R
Universal Classic — *MCA Home Video*

Heathcliff and 1983
Marmaduke
Cartoons
66574   60 mins   C   B, V   P
Animated
A program of animated adventures with the
hapless dog Marmaduke matching wits with
Heathcliff, the cat, his constant nemesis.
Ruby Spears — *Worldvision Home Video*

Heatwave 1983
Drama
73021   92 mins   C   B, V   R, P
Judy Davis, Richard Moir
Local residents oppose a multi-million dollar
residential complex in Australia
MPAA:R
Hilary Linstead — *THORN EMI Home Video*

Heaven Can Wait 1978
Fantasy
38933   100 mins   C   B, V, LV   R, P
Warren Beatty, Julie Christie, Charles Grodin,
Dyan Cannon, James Mason, Jack Warden
Remake of 1941's "Here Comes Mr. Jordan,"
about a football player who is mistakenly
summoned to heaven before his time, and
returns to earth in another man's body.
MPAA:PG
Paramount — *Paramount Home Video; RCA*
VideoDiscs

Heavens Above 1963
Comedy
29796   113 mins   B/W   B, V   R, P
Peter Sellers, Cecil Parker, Isabel Jeans, Eric
Sykes, Ian Carmichael
A sharp, biting satire on British clergy life.
Sellers, a quiet, down-to-earth reverend, is
appointed to a parish in a snooty neighborhood.
British Lion — *THORN EMI Home Video*

Heaven's Gate 1980
Western
66449   220 mins   C   B, V, CED   P
Kris Krisofferson, Christopher Walken, Isabelle
Huppert, Jeff Bridges, John Hurt, directed by
Michael Cimino

The original, uncut version of Michael Cimino's
epic story about Wyoming's Johnson County
cattle wars of the 1890's. Beta Hi-Fi and VHS
stereo.
MPAA:R
United Artists — *MGM/UA Home Video*

Heavy Petting 1983
Comedy
64979   90 mins   C   B, V   P
A hilarious compilation of "love scene" footage
from feature films of the silent era to the sixties,
newsreels, news reports, educational films, old
TV shows, and home movies.
Unknown — *Embassy Home Entertainment*

Heavy Traffic 1973
Comedy
59852   76 mins   C   B, V   R, P
Animated
Ralph Bakshi's animated fantasy portrait of the
hard-edged underside of city life, as a young
cartoonist draws the people, the places and the
paranoia of his environment.
MPAA:X
American International — *Warner Home Video*

Heckle y Jeckle 195?
Cartoons
48408   90 mins   C   B, V   P
Animated
The talking magpies get in and out of mischief.
Available in Spanish only.
SP
Terrytoons — *CBS/Fox Video*

Heidi 1937
Drama
22205   88 mins   B/W   B, V   P
Shirley Temple, Jean Hersholt, Helen Westley
Johanna Spyri's classic tale puts Shirley Temple
in the hands of a mean governess and the
loving arms of her Swiss grandfather.
20th Century Fox — *CBS/Fox Video*

Heidi 1968
Drama
29433   100 mins   C   CED   P
Maximilian Schell, Jean Simmons, Michael
Redgrave
Based on Johanna Spyri's classic story of an
orphan girl living with her grandfather in the Alps
who is taken by her aunt to the city to be a
playmate for a family's crippled daughter.
NBC — *RCA VideoDiscs*

Heidi's Song 19??
Cartoons/Musical
69591   90 mins   C   B, V   P
Animated, voices of Lorne Greene, Sammy
Davis Jr, Margery Gray

The classic tale of Heidi and her grandfather is enhanced by 16 original songs, dance sequences, and full animation.
Hanna Barbera — *Worldvision Home Video*

Heifetz and Piatigorsky   1981
Music-Performance
57251   78 mins   B/W   B, V   P
Jascha Heifetz, Gregor Piatigorsky
Three presentations are featured on one cassette. First, Jascha Heifetz, the incomparable violinist and his accompanist, Emanuel Bay, give an impromptu recital at Pomona College. In a varied program, he plays Mendelsohn's "Sweet Remembrance," Brahm's "Sonatensatz," and "Hungarian Dance No. 7," Gluck's "Melodie," Prokofiev's "March" from "Love for Three Oranges," Wieniawsky's "Polonaise," and Dinicu-Heifetz's "Hora Stacatto." The second presentation features the great cellist Gregor Piatigorsky in a brilliant concert including Bach's "Bouree No. 1" and "Bouree No. 2" from "C-Major Suite," Chopin's "Slow Movement from Cello Sonata," Prokofiev's "Masques" from "Romeo and Juliet," Anton Rubinstein's "Romance," Tschaikowsky's "Waltz," and Schubert-Piatigorsky's "Introduction, Theme and Variations." The tape concludes with "The Portrait of an Artist," a look at the home and practice life of Jascha Heifetz. The varied program consists of Vitali's "Chaconne," Bach's "Prelude E-Major," Debussy's "Girl with the Flaxen Hair," Wieniawsky's "Scherzo Tarantella," and Paganini's "24th Caprice."
Kultur — *Kultur*

Helen Keller: Separate Views   1982
Handicapped/Women
58560   91 mins   C   B, V   P
Narrated by Martha Graham and President Eisenhower
A trio of upbeat films dealing with different views of the handicapped, including the "Helen Keller Story" and "One Eyed Men Are Kings," which offers a serio-comic look at blindness.
Academy Awards '74: Best Live Action Short ("Kings").
Mastervision et al — *Mastervision*

Helen Wills: Miss Poker Face   1954
Biographical/Tennis
44231   15 mins   B/W   B, V   P
"Miss Poker Face" is Helen Wills, queen of the tennis courts. At seventeen she was the women's champion of the United States. Classic newsreel footage.
Fox Movietone News — *Two Star Films*

Hell Fire Austin   1932
Western
57986   60 mins   B/W   B, V   P
Ken Maynard
Ken Maynard finds himself mixed up with outlaws in the Old West.
Tiffany — *Video Connection*

Hell Night   1981
Horror
59044   100 mins   C   B, V   P
Linda Blair, Vincent Van Patten, Kevin Brophy
Three young people must spend the night in a mysterious mansion as part of their initiation into Alpha Signa Rho fraternity.
MPAA:R   EL, SP
Compass International Pictures — *Media Home Entertainment*

Hell on Frisco Bay   1955
Drama
11771   93 mins   C   B, V   P
Alan Ladd, Edward G. Robinson, Joanne Dru
Ex-waterfront cop, falsely imprisoned for manslaughter, sets out to clear his name.
Warner Bros — *VCI Home Video*

Hell River   1975
War-Drama
66241   100 mins   C   B, V   R, P
Rod Taylor, Adam West
In 1941 Yugoslavia, Yugoslav partisans and Nazis battle it out at a place called Hell River.
Nobel Productions — *Video City Productions*

Hellcats of the Navy   1957
War-Drama
58956   82 mins   B/W   B, V   P
Ronald Reagan, Nancy Davis (Reagan), Arthur Franz
The true saga of the World War II mission to sever the vital link between mainland Asia and Japan. This was the only film that Ronald and Nancy Reagan appeared in together.
Columbia — *RCA/Columbia Pictures Home Video*

Helldorado   1946
Western
54174   54 mins   B/W   B, V   P
Roy Rogers, directed by William Witney
A lively western starring the singing cowboy, Roy Rogers.
Republic — *Video Connection; Cable Films; Discount Video Tapes*

Hello, Dolly!   1969
Musical
08424   146 mins   C   B, V, LV   P
Barbra Streisand, Walter Matthau, Michael Crawford, Louis Armstrong, directed by Gene Kelly
Widow Dolly Levi, while matchmaking for her friends, sets her mind on a Yankee merchant.

Based on the stage musical adapted from Thornton Wilder's play "Matchmaker".
Academy Awards '69: Best Score of a Musical Picture; Best Art Direction; Best Sound.
MPAA:G EL, SP
20th Century Fox; Ernest Leham — *CBS/Fox Video*

Hells Angels Forever 1983
Adventure
65367   93 mins   C   B, V   P
The Hells Angels, Willie Nelson, Jerry Garcia, Johnny Paycheck, Bo Diddley
"Hells Angels Forever" is a revealing ride into the world of honor, violence, and undying passion for motorcycles on the road.
MPAA:R
Richard Chase; Sandy Alexander; Leon Gast — *Media Home Entertainment*

Hell's Angels '69 1969
Adventure
65483   97 mins   C   B, V   P
Tom Stern, Jeremy Slate, Conny Van Dyke
Two wealthy brothers plot a deadly game by infiltrating the ranks of the Hell's Angels.
MPAA:PG
Tom Stern — *Media Home Entertainment*

Hell's Brigade: The Final Assault 19??
War-Drama
69386   89 mins   C   B, V   P
Jack Palance, John Douglas, Carlos Estrada
A small band of American commandos is ordered on the most dangerous and important mission of World War II.
MPAA:PG
Unknown — *Cinemagreats*

Hell's Hinges 1916
Western
64321   55 mins   B/W   B, V   P
William S. Hart, directed by Thomas Ince
William S. Hart stars in one of his most successful early westerns. Silent.
Triangle Film Corp — *Classic Video Cinema Collector's Club*

Hell's House 1932
Drama
08766   72 mins   B/W   B, V, 3/4U   P
Bette Davis, Pat O'Brien, Junior Dirken, directed by Howard Higgin
Following the death of his mother, a young boy goes to city to live with relatives and becomes involved with a bootlegger.
Bennie F Ziedman Prod — *Penguin Video; VCII; Video Yesteryear*

Hellstrom Chronicle, The 1971
Documentary/Insects
63966   90 mins   C   B, V   P
A powerful documentary about man's impending struggle against insects.
Academy Awards '71: Best Documentary Feature. MPAA:G
Almi-Cinema 5 — *RCA/Columbia Pictures Home Video*

Helltown 1938
Western
12230   60 mins   B/W   B, V   P
John Wayne, directed by Charles Barton
Western film based on Zane Grey's novel.
Paramount — *Discount Video Tapes; Video Connection; Cable Films*

Help Yourself to Better Color TV 197?
Television
44991   30 mins   C   B, V   P, T
Through the use of the indian-head test pattern and the color bar chart you can determine brightness, focus, contrast, tint, and color line-up with the help of this program.
AM Available
Unknown — *Blackhawk Films*

Henry Ford: The Mark of a Man 1954
Biographical/Automobiles
44232   15 mins   B/W   B, V   P
The life of Henry Ford, inventor of the automobile, is told in this program through classic newsreel footage. This is also the story of America growing up on wheels.
Fox Movietone News — *Two Star Films*

Henry Ford's America 1977
Automobiles
21251   57 mins   C   B, V, FO   P
A look at the history of the automobile, the dynastic Ford talent that created it, and the business empire that rules it.
National Film Board of Canada — *Video Yesteryear*

Henry V 1945
Drama
44363   137 mins   C   B, V   P
Laurence Olivier, Robert Newton, Leslie Banks, Leo Genn
The first movie version of Shakepeare's great drama, with brilliant dialogue and color.
J Arthur Rank — *Sheik Video; RCA VideoDiscs*

Her Silent Sacrifice 1917
Drama
59205   25 mins   B/W   B, V, 3/4U   P
Alice Brady

        (For Explanation of codes, see USE GUIDE and KEY)

A young woman is accused of being a witch and is cruelly teased by the villagers.
Select Pictures Corp — *Penguin Video*

Herbie Hancock and the Rockit Band　　1984
Music-Performance
65756　70 mins　C　B, V, CED　　P
Filmed live at the Hammersmith Odeon and Camden Hall in London, England, this program takes the home viewer through a multi-media presentation of break dancing, scratch music, robots and an explosive light show. In VHS Hi-Fi and Beta Hi-Fi.
CBS Records — *CBS/Fox Video*

Herbie Rides Again　　1974
Comedy
59063　88 mins　C　B, V　　R, P
Helen Hayes, Ken Berry, Stephanie Powers, John McIntire, Keenan Wynn, directed by Robert Stevenson
In this "Love Bug" sequel, Herbie comes to the aid of an elderly woman who is trying to stop a ruthless tycoon from raising a skyscraper on her property.
MPAA:G
Walt Disney Productions — *Walt Disney Home Video; RCA VideoDiscs*

Hercules　　1959
Adventure
66268　107 mins　C　B, V, CED　　P
Steve Reeves, directed by Pietro Frandisci
The mythological demigod teams up with Jason and the Argonauts in search of the Golden Fleece.
MPAA:G
Oscar Film Galatea; Warner Bros; Embassy — *Embassy Home Entertainment*

Hercules　　1983
Adventure
Closed Captioned
66446　100 mins　C　B, V　　P
Lou Ferrigno, Sybil Danning, William Berger, Brad Harris, Ingrid Anderson
Legendary muscleman Hercules fights against the evil King Minos for his own survival and the love of Cassiopeia, a rival king's daughter.
MPAA:PG
Cannon Films — *MGM/UA Home Video*

Hercules Goes Bananas　　197?
Comedy
66109　75 mins　C　B, V　　P
Arnold Schwarzenegger
Schwarzenegger plays Hercules in this hilarious comedy.
Arbor Weisberg — *Unicorn Video*

Hercules Unchained　　1959
Adventure
64969　101 mins　C　B, V, CED　　P
Steve Reeves, Sylva Koscina, Primo Carnera
In this sequel to "Hercules," the superhero must use all his strength to save the city of Thebes and the woman he loves from the giant Antaeus.
Lux/Galatea — *Embassy Home Entertainment*

Herculoids, The　　196?
Cartoons/Adventure
66275　60 mins　C　B, V　　P
Animated
Zandor, Tara, Dorno and the towering man of stone, Igoo, encounter adventures on a wild, semi-primitive planet.
Hanna Barbera — *Worldvision Home Video*

Here Comes Mr. Jordan　　1941
Fantasy
21290　94 mins　B/W　B, V　　P
Robert Montgomery, Claude Rains, James Gleason, Evelyn Keyes
A young prizefighter, killed in a plane crash because of a mix-up in heaven, returns to life in the body of a murdered millionaire.
Academy Awards '41: Best Original Story; Best Screenplay.
Columbia — *RCA/Columbia Pictures Home Video*

Here Comes Trouble　　1948
Comedy
66114　54 mins　C　B, V　　P
William Tracy
A newspaperman returns from war to get his old job back.
Fred Guiol — *Unicorn Video*

Here It Is, Burlesque　　1979
Variety
44917　88 mins　C　B, V, CED　　P
Ann Corio, Morey Amsterdam
Male and female striptease, baggy-pants comedians, exotic dancers and classic comedy sketches in this tribute to the living art, burlesque.
HBO; Michael Brandman — *Vestron Video*

Here We Go Again!　　1942
Comedy
64535　76 mins　B/W　B, V　　R, P
Fibber McGee and Molly, Edgar Bergen, Charlie McCarthy, Mortimer Snerd, Ray Noble and his Orchestra
Fibber McGee and Molly are planning their 20th anniversary celebration, but no one wants to come. Based on the popular NBC radio series.
RKO — *Blackhawk Films*

Heritage of the Bible, The   1982
Bible
60380   111 mins   C   CED   P
A recreation of Biblical history: "The Law and
the Prophets" features inspired images of
Raphael, Michelangelo, and others; "The
Inheritance" uses famous archeological sites of
Biblical times to recount stories of the Old
Testament.
NBC Enterprises — *RCA VideoDiscs*

Hero High Volume 1   1981
Cartoons
74084   44 mins   C   B, V   P
Animated
This fun-filled animated feature introduces you
to future superheros and their ill-fated attempts
to master their special powers.
Lou Scheimer; Norm Prescott — *Embassy
Home Entertainment*

**Heroes in the Ming
Dynasty**   1984
Martial arts
72959   90 mins   C   B, V   P
A martial arts period film set in the Ming
Dynasty.
Foreign — *Unicorn Video*

Heroes of the Hills   1938
Western
64422   54 mins   B/W   B, V, 3/4U   P
Bob Livingston, Ray Corrigan, Max Terhune
The Three Mesquiteers back up a plan that
would allow trusted prisoners to work for
neighboring ranchers.
Republic — *Nostalgia Merchant*

Heroes of the West   1932
Western/Serials
54175   ? mins   B/W   B, V   P
Noah Beery Jr.
An early sound action western serial.
RKO — *Video Connection*

Hey Abbott!   1978
Comedy/Film-History
59862   76 mins   B/W   B, V   P
*Bud Abbott, Lou Costello, Phil Silvers, Steve
Allen, Joe Besser, narrated by Milton Berle*
A compilation of A and C routines from their
classic TV series. Sketches include "Who's on
First," "Oyster Stew," "Floogle Street" and
"The Birthday Party."
Ziv International — *VidAmerica*

Hey Cinderella!   1970
Fairy tales/Comedy
47348   58 mins   C   B, V, LV   R, P
The Muppets
The Muppets present their version of the classic
fairy tale, in which Cinderella arrives at the ball

in a coach pulled by a purple beast named
Splurge and driven by Kermit the singing frog.
Henson Associates — *Muppet Home Video*

Hey Good Lookin'   1982
Satire
63121   77 mins   C   B, V   R, P
Animated, directed by Ralph Bakshi
Ralph Bakshi's irreverent look back at growing
up in the 1950's bears the trademark qualities
that distinguish his other adult animated
features, "Fritz the Cat" and "Heavy Traffic."
Warner Bros — *Warner Home Video*

Hi-Di-Ho   1947
Musical
51227   60 mins   B/W   B, V, 3/4U   P
Cab Calloway, Ida James, The Peters Sisters
The great Cab Calloway and his red hot jazz are
featured in this film, which lacks a storyline but
has plenty of music.
Unknown — *Penguin Video; Video Connection*

Hidden Gold   1933
Western
15535   57 mins   B/W   B, V   P
Tom Mix
A western starring Tom Mix, a U.S. Marshal
turned actor.
Universal — *Video Connection*

Hide in Plain Sight   1980
Suspense
53350   96 mins   C   B, V   P
*James Caan, Jill Eikenberry, Robert Viharo,
directed by James Caan*
A distraught blue-collar worker searches for his
children who disappeared when his ex-wife and
her mobster husband were given new identities
by federal agents.
MPAA:PG
Robert Christiansen; Rick Rosenberg;
MGM — *MGM/UA Home Video*

Hideaways, The   1973
Drama
63974   120 mins   C   B, V   R, P
*Ingrid Bergman, Sally Prager, Johnny Doran,
Madeline Kahn*
A 12-year-old girl and her brother run away and
hide in the Metropolitan Museum of Art. The girl
becomes enamored of a piece of sculpture and
sets out to discover its creator. Original title:
"From the Mixed-Up Files of Mrs. Basil E.
Frankweiler."
Cinema 5 — *VCII*

Hideous Sun Demon   1959
Horror
36920   74 mins   B/W   B, V, 3/4U   P
Robert Clarke, Patricia Manning, Nan Peterson

A physicist exposed to radiation must stay out of sunlight or he will turn into a scaly, lizard-like creature. Includes previews of coming attractions from classic science fiction films.
Clark King Entprs, Bob Clark — *Nostalgia Merchant*

High Adventure   197?
Religion
33736   30 mins   C   B, V, 3/4U, Q   P
Debby Boone, Dale Evans, Susan Stafford, Don Sutton, Dean Jones, Roger Staubach, Tom Landry
A series of over 150 programs in which celebrities and other accomplished guests are interviewed about their profession and credits within that profession. Later, these guests provide an insight into their Christian outlook and discuss the role which Christianity plays in their lives.
George Otis — *TV Sports Scene*

High Altitude Ship Recognition   194?
World War II/Armed Forces-US
53650   50 mins   B/W   B, V, 3/4U   P
A classified film made for the U.S. Strategic Air Force in Europe, describing Axis shipping routes, as well as techniques for identifying specific enemy ships.
Unknown — *International Historic Films*

High Anxiety   1977
Comedy
52739   92 mins   C   B, V, CED   P
Mel Brooks, Madeline Kahn, Cloris Leachman, Harvey Korman, Ron Carey, Howard Morris, Dick Van Patten, directed by Mel Brooks
An anxiety-prone psychiatrist arrives at a sanitorium to take up his official duties as the new head, and is immediately caught up in a twisted murder mystery. Brooks' "homage" to Hitchcock.
MPAA:PG
Twentieth Century Fox; Mel Brooks — *CBS/Fox Video*

High Ballin'   1978
Drama/Adventure
69289   100 mins   C   B, V   P
Peter Fonda, Jerry Reed, Helen Shaver
Three angry independents are set to take on the most vicious gang of hijackers ever to run the highways.
MPAA:PG
American International — *Vestron Video*

High Command   1938
Drama
47467   84 mins   B/W   B, V, FO   P
Lionel Atwill, Lucie Mannheim, James Mason

To save his daughter from an ugly scandal, the British general of a Colonial African outpost traps a blackmailer's killer.
Fanfare — *Video Yesteryear; Movie Buff Video*

High Country, The   1981
Drama
62863   101 mins   C   B, V, CED   P
Timothy Bottoms, Linda Purl, George Sims, Jim Lawrence, Bill Berry
Two misfits on the run from society learn mutual trust as they travel through the mountain country of Alberta, Canada.
MPAA:PG
Crown International — *Vestron Video*

High Crime   1973
Crime-Drama
57064   91 mins   C   B, V, 3/4U   P
James Whitmore, Franco Nero, Fernando Rey
A "French Connection"-style suspense story about the heroin trade, featuring high-speed chases and a police commissioner obsessed with capturing the criminals.
Ambassador Releasing — *Nostalgia Merchant*

High Gear   1933
Drama
08912   70 mins   B/W   B, V   P
James Murray, Jackie Searle, Joan Marsh, Eddie Lambert
The story of a race car driver who loses his nerve and winds up as a taxi cab driver.
Goldsmith — *Penguin Video*

High Grass Circus   1976
Circus
21258   57 mins   C   B, V, FO   P
A tour of the Royal Brother Circus, the only tent circus in Canada.
National Film Board of Canada — *Video Yesteryear*

High Ice   1980
Drama
69285   97 mins   C   B, V   P
David Janssen, Tony Musante
A forest ranger and a lieutenant colonel are involved in a clash of wills over a rescue mission high in the snow-capped Washington state peaks.
ESJ Productions — *Vestron Video*

High Noon   1952
Western
00259   85 mins   B/W   B, V   P
Gary Cooper, Grace Kelly, Lloyd Bridges
Newly-married town marshal must choose between love and his duty to an ungrateful town. Academy Awards '52: Best Actor (Cooper); Best Music Scoring (Dimitri Tiomkin); Best Song (High Noon).

United Artists; Stanley Kramer — *NTA Home Entertainment; RCA VideoDiscs*

High Noon, Part II: The Return of Will Kane 1980
Western
72453   100 mins   C   B, V   P
Lee Majors, David Carradine
Will Kane returns to Hadleyville with his wife to find the town controlled by a sadistic marshall. This is a sequel to the 1952 film.
Charles Fries Productions; Ed Montage Prod — *U.S.A. Home Video*

High Plains Drifter 1973
Western
59037   105 mins   C   B, V   P
Clint Eastwood, directed by Clint Eastwood
A stranger is hired to protect a community against the imminent return of three gunmen sent to jail a year before.
MPAA:R
Universal; The Malpaso Co — *MCA Home Video*

High Risk 1976
Adventure
60442   74 mins   C   B, V   P
James Coburn, Lindsay Wagner, James Brolin, Anthony Quinn
Four Americans battle foreign armies, unscrupulous gunrunners and jungle bandits in a harrowing attempt to steal five million dollars.
Unknown — *Embassy Home Entertainment*

High Risk 1976
Adventure
65422   74 mins   C   B, V   P
James Brolin, Anthony Quinn, Lindsay Wagner, James Coburn, Ernest Borgnine
An action-adventure of four Americans who battle foreign armies, unscrupulous gunrunners, and jungle bandits in a harrowing attempt to steal five million dollars from an expatriate American living in the peaceful splendor of his Columbian villa.
MPAA:R
MGM — *Embassy Home Entertainment*

High Road to China 1983
Adventure
66126   107 mins   C   B, V, LV, CED   R, P
Bess Armstrong, Tom Selleck, Jack Weston, Robert Morley
A hard-drinking 1920's air ace is recruited by a young heiress to find her father.
MPAA:PG
City Films — *Warner Home Video*

High School Confidential 1958
Drama
65458   85 mins   B/W   B, V   P
Russ Tamblin, Mamie Van Doren
A tough-talking gang leader comes in contact with a drug ring and its leader. His dealings put him in constant danger.
MGM — *NTA Home Entertainment*

High Sierra 1941
Drama
64706   96 mins   B/W   B, V, CED   P
Humphrey Bogart, Ida Lupino, Arthur Kennedy, Joan Leslie, Cornel Wilde, Alan Curtis, directed by Raoul Walsh
Bogart is Roy "Mad Dog" Earl, an aging gangster who hides out from the police in the High Sierras. Screenplay by John Huston and W.R. Burnett, whose novel this movie is based on.
Warner Bros — *CBS/Fox Video; RCA VideoDiscs*

High Velocity 1976
Adventure
45048   105 mins   C   B, V   P
Ben Gazzara, Paul Winfield
An action-packed adventure of two mercenaries involved in the challenge of a lifetime.
MPAA:PG
Takashi Ohashi — *Media Home Entertainment*

High Voltage 1929
Comedy/Adventure
55345   60 mins   B/W   B, V   P
Carole Lombard, William Boyd, Gwen Moore, Billy Bevan
A fast-moving comedy adventure set in the High Sierras.
Pathe — *Sheik Video*

Higher and Higher 1943
Musical
10049   90 mins   B/W   B, V   P, T
Frank Sinatra, Leon Errol, Michele Morgan, Jack Haley, Victor Borge, Mary McGuire
Bankrupt aristocrat conspires with servants to regain his fortune. Tries to marry his daughter into money.
RKO — *Blackhawk Films*

Hijazo De Mi Vidaza (Son of My Life) 197?
Comedy
73580   30 mins   C   B, V   P
Enrique Cuenca, Eduardo Manzano, Maria Fernanda, Fernando Casanova
This film is about the history of a family as told by a mother to her son.
KNBC — *Aztec Cinevideo*

Hillbillys in a Haunted House   1967
Horror/Musical
59654   88 mins   C   B, V   P
Ferlin Husky, Joi Lansing, Don Bowman, John Carradine, Lon Chaney, Basil Rathbone, directed by Jean Yarbrough
Two country and western singers enroute to the Nashville jamboree encounter a group of foreign spies "haunting" a house.
Bernard Woolner — *VCI Home Video*

Hills Have Eyes, The   1977
Adventure
59080   83 mins   C   B, V   P
Susan Lanier, Robert Houston, Martin Speer, Dee Wallace, Russ Grieve, John Steadman, James Whitworth
A desperate family battles for survival and vengeance against a brutal band of belligerent terrorists.
MPAA:R
Peter Locke — *HarmonyVision*

Hills of Utah, The   1951
Western
65771   70 mins   B/W   B, V   P, T
Gene Autry, Pat Buttram, Denver Pyle
Gene finds himself in the middle of a feud between the local mine operator and a group of cattlemen, while searching for his father's murderer.
Columbia — *Blackhawk Films*

Hindenburg, The   1975
Adventure/Suspense
47850   125 mins   C   B, V   P
George C. Scott, Anne Bancroft, William Atherton, Roy Thinnes, Gig Young, Burgess Meredith, directed by Robert Wise
Intrigue and suspense highlight this fictionalized account of the historic disaster.
MPAA:PG
Universal — *MCA Home Video*

Hips, Hips, Hooray   1934
Comedy/Musical
54113   68 mins   B/W   B, V   P, T
Wheeler and Woolsey, Ruth Etting, Thelma Todd, Dorothy lee
Two supposed "hot shot" salesmen are hired by a cosmetic company to sell flavored lipstick. "Hot shot" salesmen they are not, but funny they are.
RKO — *Blackhawk Films*

Hiroshima, Mon Amour   1959
Film-Avant-garde
06219   88 mins   B/W   B, V   P
Emmanuelle Riva, Elji Okada, Bernard Fresson, directed by Alain Resnais
French actress in Tokyo meets and falls in love with Japanese architect. Both are married. French film with English subtitles.
FR
Argos; Pathe — *Budget Video; Video Dimensions; Sheik Video; Penguin Video; Western Film & Video Inc; Discount Video Tapes*

His Fighting Blood   1935
Western
56606   63 mins   B/W   B, V   P
Kermit Maynard
Northwest Mounties in action. Based on a James Curwood story.
Maurice Conn — *Video Dimensions; Penguin Video*

His Girl Friday   1940
Comedy
08728   92 mins   B/W   B, V   P
Cary Grant, Rosalind Russell, Ralph Bellamy, Gene Lockhart, directed by Howard Hawks
Reporter helps condemned man escape. Based on hit play "Front Page."
Columbia — *Movie Buff Video; Penguin Video; Budget Video; Video Yesteryear; VCII; Cinema Concepts; Discount Video Tapes; Video Dimensions; Sheik Video; Cable Films; Video Connection; Western Film & Video Inc*

His Kind of Woman   1951
Drama
57137   120 mins   B/W   B, V   P
Robert Mitchum, Jane Russell, Vincent Price, Tim Holt, Charles McGraw
A fall guy, being used to bring a racketeer back to the U.S. from Mexico, discovers the plan and tries to halt it.
RKO — *King of Video*

His Royal Slyness/Haunted Spooks   1920
Comedy
56912   52 mins   B/W   B, V, FO   P
Harold Lloyd
Two Harold Lloyd shorts. "His Royal Slyness" (1919) offers Harold impersonating the king of a small kingdom, while in "Haunted Spooks" (1920), Harold gets suckered into living in a haunted mansion. Both films include music score.
Hal Roach — *Video Yesteryear; Blackhawk Films*

Historical Yesterdays   197?
History-US/Documentary
52456   ? mins   B/W   B, V   P
Narrated by Lowell Thomas 4 pgms
Lowell Thomas hosts this series of documentaries about America in the twentieth century. Each program covers the events of one

decade. Programs are available individually and were originally telecast by PBS under the series title, "Lowell Thomas Remembers."
1.The Roaring Twenties 2.The New Deal—The Thirties 3.The War Years—The Forties 4.The Fabulous Fifties
Unknown — *Blackhawk Films*

History Disquiz, The   1983
History-Modern
64547   60 mins   C   LV   P
Hosted by Steve Allen
This challenging game tests players' knowledge of 20th century events. More than 1500 questions are built around 50 film clips from the Hearst Time Capsule Library.
King Features Entertainment — *Optical Programming Associates*

History of Aviation, The   19??
Aeronautics
65646   120 mins   B/W   B, V   R, P
This program gives a glimpse into aviation's past with authentic documentary footage.
Unknown — *Video City Productions*

History of Pro Football, The   1983
Football/Documentary
65015   87 mins   C   B, V, FO   P
Rare footage and interviews with NFL personalities highlight this comprehensive program on the NFL's landmark events and its greatest players.
NFL Films — *NFL Films Video*

History of the World: Part I   1981
Comedy
52699   90 mins   C   B, V, LV   P
Mel Brooks, Dom DeLuise, Madeline Kahn, Harvey Korman, Cloris Leachman, Ron Carey, Howard Morris, Sid Caesar, Jackie Mason
Mel Brooks' wildly satiric vision of human evolution, from the Dawn of Man to the French Revolution.
MPAA:R
Brooksfilms Ltd — *CBS/Fox Video; RCA VideoDiscs*

Hit and Run   1982
Drama
69041   96 mins   C   B, V   R, P
David Marks, a Manhattan cab driver, is haunted by recurring flashbacks of a freak hit-and-run accident in which his wife was struck down on a city street.
Charles Braverman — *THORN EMI Home Video*

Hit Men, The   1973
Crime-Drama
60392   90 mins   C   B, V   P
Henry Silva, Mario Adorf, Woody Strode, Adolfo Celi
Double crosses and gun battles highlight this tale of inner city crime.
Daunia 70 — *VIDCREST*

Hit the Saddle   1937
Western
15439   54 mins   B/W   B, V   P
Bob Livingston, Ray Corrigan, Max Terhune
Three Mesquiteers track down a gang involved in capturing wild horses in protected areas.
Republic — *Video Connection*

Hitchhikers, The   1972
Drama
60225   90 mins   C   B, V   P
Misty Rowe, Norman Klar
A pregnant girl leaves home and finds herself living on a hippie ranch where a male hippie hides out with his family of four females. The scantily clad girls thumb rides from male motorists to rob them.
MPAA:R
Sebastian Films — *Independent United Distributors*

Hitler—February 10th, 1933   1933
Documentary/Germany
72474   32 mins   B/W   B, V, 3/4U   P
An original National Socialist Party film of Hitler's first and most important speech at the Berlin Sports Palace. He had come to power one week before this speech was given. Heard by millions on the radio, the speech gave a volatile audience specific goals of grandeur.
Germany — *International Historic Films*

Hitler: The Last Ten Days   1973
Drama
68249   106 mins   C   B, V   R, P
Based on an eyewitness account, the story of Hitler's last days in an underground bunker gives insight to his madness.
MPAA:PG
World Film Services Ltd; Tomorrow Entertainment — *Paramount Home Video*

Hitler's Children   1943
Drama
00267   83 mins   B/W   B, V, 3/4U   P
Tim Holt, Bonita Granville
Two young people are caught in the horror of Nazi Germany.
RKO — *International Historic Films*

Hitler's Newsreels   194?
World War II/Propaganda
45028   85 mins   B/W   B, V, 3/4U   P
Actual newsreels seen by the German people
during WWII. A prime example of propaganda in
five sections: "The German Invasion of
Russia—June 1941," "The Battle of
Sevastopol—June 1942," "The Battle for the
Rhineland—October 1944," "The Battle of
Kursk—July 1943," and "The Battle for
Germany—March 1945." Printed English
translation is supplied.
AM Available
German — *International Historic Films*

Hitler's Newsreels, Part 2   194?
World War II/Germany
72510   96 mins   B/W   B, V, 3/4U   P
The battle of Stalingrad, dogfights between
German fighters and American bombers over
Germany and the invasion of Normandy are
seen through the German point of view in
original newsreels. Included are profiles of Hitler
and some of his officers as the Nazis faced their
final battles.
International Historic Films — *International
Historic Films*

Hitler's Newsreels, Part 3   1940
World War II/Germany
72511   98 mins   B/W   B, V, 3/4U   P
Five original German newsreels are on this
program, from 1940 the Nazis' most successful
year militarily, looking at the activities of the
German Navy, a Nazi yuletide celebration and
the countenance of German soldiers preparing
the great offenses.
International Historic Films — *International
Historic Films*

H.M.S. Pinafore   1982
Opera
72447   90 mins   C   LV   P
The opera is captured in a live performance.
Judith DePaul — *Pioneer Video Imports*

Hobbit, The   1978
Fantasy
00239   78 mins   C   B, V   P
*Narrated by Orson Bean, John Huston, and
others*
Based on Tolkien's Middle Earth fantasy, this
tale illustrates the Hobbit's battle against the
evil forces of dragons and goblins.
Rankin Bass — *Sony Corporation of America;
RCA VideoDiscs*

Hobson's Choice   1954
Comedy
63321   102 mins B/W   B, V   R, P
*Charles Laughton, John Mills, Brenda de
Banzie, directed by David Leon*

A prosperous businessman in the 1890's tries to
keep his daughter from marrying, but the strong-
willed daughter has other ideas.
British Lion — *THORN EMI Home Video*

Hold 'Em Jail   1932
Comedy
59408   65 mins   B/W   B, V   P, T
Wheeler and Woolsey, Edgar Kennedy
Wheeler and Woolsey get involved in a prison
football game.
RKO — *Blackhawk Films*

Hold That Ghost   1941
Comedy
63360   86 mins   B/W   B, V   P
*Bud Abbott, Lou Costello, Joan Davis, Richard
Carlson, Mischa Auer, the Andrews Sisters, Ted
Lewis and his Band*
Abbott and Costello inherit an abandoned
roadhouse where the illicit loot of its former
owner, a "rubbed out" mobster, is supposedly
hidden.
Universal — *MCA Home Video*

Hold That Woman   1940
Comedy
66191   55 mins   B/W   B, V, 3/4U   P
Eddie Bracken, Frances Gifford
A classic Eddie Bracken comedy.
Producers Releasing Corp — *Penguin Video*

Holiday in Mazatland   197?
Fishing
19406   30 mins   C   B, V, 3/4U,   P
                      Q
A report on fishing off the coast of Mexico for
marlin. The culture and environment of the area
is also featured.
TV Sports Scene — *TV Sports Scene*

Holiday Inn   1942
Musical
53399   101 mins B/W   B, V   P
*Bing Crosby, Fred Astaire, Marjorie Reynolds,
Walter Abel, Virginia Dale*
A song and dance man decides to turn a
Connecticut farm into an inn, open only on
holidays. Songs include: "Happy Holiday," "Be
Careful It's My Heart," and "White Christmas."
Academy Award '42: Best Song ("White
Christmas").
Paramount; Mark Sandrich — *MCA Home
Video*

Hollywood at War   194?
Film-History
03999   60 mins   C   B, V   P
Bob Hope, Donald Duck, Superman, and others
Collection of war time shorts featuring "All Star
Bond Rally," "Spirit of '43," "Stamp Day for
Superman."

Walt Disney et al — *Budget Video*

Hollywood Bloopers   195?
Outtakes and bloopers
14444   40 mins   B/W   B, V   P
Lauren Bacall, Ronald Reagan, James Stewart, Joan Blondell, Barbara Stanwyck, and others
Hilarious outtakes from some of Hollywood's finest movies featuring stars such as Bette Davis, James Cagney, Humphrey Bogart, Rosalind Russell, Errol Flynn, Kirk Douglas, and many more.
Warner Bros et al — *Video Dimensions*

Hollywood Boulevard   1976
Comedy/Filmmaking
64840   93 mins   C   B, V   R, P
Candice Rialson, Mary Woronov, Rita George, Jeffrey Kramer, Dick Miller, Paul Bartel, directed by Joe Dante and Allan Arkush
This behind-the-scenes glimpse of shoestring-budget moviemaking offers comical sex, violence, sight gags, one-liners, comedy bits, and mock-documentary footage. Commander Cody and His Lost Planet Airmen are featured.
MPAA:R
New World Pictures — *Warner Home Video*

Hollywood Goes to War   1954
Documentary/Film-History
58651   41 mins   B/W   B, V, FO   P
Bob Hope, Bing Crosby, Frank Sinatra, Betty Grable, Harpo Marx, Jimmy Durante, Eddie Cantor, Red Skelton, Abbott and Costello, Dinah Shore, Dorothy Lamour, Carmen Miranda
Five shorts produced for the entertainment of G.I.'s overseas or for home front bond drives: "The All-Star Bond Rally" features Bob Hope, Fibber McGee and Molly, Bing Crosby, Harry James and his Orchestra, Sinatra, Grable, Harpo Marx, and the Talking Pin-Ups; "Hollywood Canteen Overseas Special" features Dinah Shore, Eddie Cantor, Jimmy Durante, and Red Skelton; "Mail Call (Strictly G.I.)" is a filmed "Mail Call" radio program with Don Wilson announcing guests Dorothy Lamour, Cass Daley, and Abbott and Costello doing 'Who's on First'; "G.I. Movie Weekly—Sing with the Stars" features Carmen Miranda and her fruit-basket hat, a Portuguese 'follow-the-bouncing-ball' sing-along, Richard Lane, and Mel Blanc's voice; and "Invaders in Greasepaint," the story of 'Four Jills in a Jeep'—the North African USO tour by Martha Raye, Carol Landis, Mitzi Mayfair, and Kay Francis. Also includes newsreel footage of the girls touring, plus their memorable rendition of the wartime classic tune 'Snafu,' which was banned from the airwaves for its racy lyrics.
Office of War Information; Army Pictorial Service; Army-Navy Screen Magazine — *Video Yesteryear*

Hollywood Man   1976
Drama
66282   90 mins   C   B, V   P
William Smith
The story of a Hollywood actor and his crew in a desperate fight against all odds to complete their independent film.
MPAA:R
Olympic Films — *Monterey Home Video*

Hollywood My Hometown   195?
Film-History
33803   60 mins   B/W   B, V   P
Ken Murray
Hollywood host Ken Murray looks at the stars of the glittering movie world.
Unknown — *Video Connection; Discount Video Tapes; Budget Video; Roll Your Own Video*

Hollywood on Parade   1934
Variety
52463   59 mins   B/W   B, V, FO   P
Fredric March, Ginger Rogers, Jean Harlow, Jeanette MacDonald, Maurice Chevalier, Mary Pickford, Jackie Cooper
A collection of several "Hollywood on Parade" shorts produced by Paramount Studios between 1932 and 1934. Nearly every big star of the era is featured singing, dancing, or taking part in bizarre sketches.
Paramount — *Video Yesteryear; Discount Video Tapes*

Hollywood Outtakes and Rare Footage   1983
Outtakes and bloopers/Film-History
66382   85 mins   C   B, V   P
Marilyn Monroe, James Dean, Joan Crawford, Judy Garland, Humphrey Bogart, Ronald Reagan, Bette Davis, Vivien Leigh, Carole Lombard and others
A collection of rare and unusual film clips and excerpts that feature dozens of Hollywood stars in screen tests, promotional shorts, home movies, outtakes, TV appearances and World War II propaganda shorts. Some segments in black and white.
Manhattan Movietime — *Movie Buff Video*

Hollywood Palace   1968
Variety
56906   55 mins   B/W   B, V, FO   P
Victor Borge, Steve Allen, Jayne Meadows, King Family, Dino Desi and Billy, Mitchell Ayres Orchestra, Scots Guards
A program from the popular comedy-variety show, complete with commercials for Playtex, Bayer, Johnson's Wax, Kool, and Tegrin.
ABC — *Video Yesteryear*

Hollywood Palace, The   1967
Variety
12841   52 mins   B/W   B, V, FO   P

      (For Explanation of codes, see USE GUIDE and KEY)

Vicki Carr, The Temptations, Mac Ronee, Jimmy Dean, Van Johnson, hosted by Jimmy Durante
Hollywood TV variety show highlighted by Durante and Johnson in a crazy "song writing team" sketch.
ABC — *Video Yesteryear*

Hollywood Palace Farewell Show, The   1970
Variety
38989   52 mins   B/W   B, V, FO   P
Ella Fitzgerald, Fred Astaire, Ethel Merman, Nat King Cole, Judy Garland, hosted by Bing Crosby
The last program in the series; a retrospective of great moments and performers who appeared on the "Hollywood Palace." Featuring, in addition to those named above, Jimmy Durante, Sammy Davis, Jr., Martha Raye, Herb Alpert, Ray Bolger, Gene Kelly, Bette Davis, Buster Keaton, Gloria Swanson, Imogene Coca, Groucho Marx, George Burns, and others.
ABC — *Video Yesteryear; Video Dimensions*

Hollywood Without Makeup   1965
Film-History
04789   51 mins   C   B, V   P
Home movie footage taken over the years by Ken Murray includes candid shots of over 100 stars of the film world.
Filmaster — *Budget Video; Video Yesteryear; Discount Video Tapes; Video Connection; Roll Your Own Video*

Hollywood's Greatest Trailers   194?
Movie and TV trailers
64418   60 mins   B/W   B, V, 3/4U   P
Theatrical previews from an assortment of classic films, including "Citizen Kane," "Top Hat," "It's a Wonderful Life," "Fort Apache" and many others. Some are in color.
RKO et al — *Nostalgia Merchant*

Holocaust   1978
Drama
60387   475 mins   C   B, V   P
Meryl Streep, James Woods
The war years of 1935 to 1945 are relived in this account of the Nazi atrocities, focusing on the Weiss family, destroyed by the monstrous crimes, and the Dorf family, Germans who thrived under the Nazi regime.
Titus Productions — *Worldvision Home Video; RCA VideoDiscs*

Holocaust: Susan Sontag   1982
World War II/Religion
59557   58 mins   C   B, V   P
Writer Susan Sontag explores the meaning of Hitler's genocide in this retrospective of the Holocaust.

Unknown — *Mastervision*

Holt of the Secret Service   1942
Adventure/Serials
64425   225 mins   B/W   B, V, 3/4U   P
Jack Holt
A secret service agent runs afoul of saboteurs and fifth-columnists in this fifteen-episode serial.
Columbia — *Nostalgia Merchant*

Holy Koran, The   1982
Islam/Middle East
59555   60 mins   C   B, V   P
This program shows why Islam is such a force in the world today. Islam's contributions to world science and culture are examined.
Unknown — *Mastervision*

Holy Land and Holy City   1982
Religion/Christianity
59556   58 mins   C   B, V   P
A look at the Holy Land at Christmas, and an artist's chronicle of the activities of the Holy City, the Vatican in Rome, over the four year period of the Vatican Council during the reign of Pope John XXIII.
Unknown — *Mastervision*

Holy Terror, The   1965
Drama
64854   76 mins   C   B, V, 3/4U   P
Julie Harris, Denholm Elliot, Torin Thatcher, Kate Reid, directed by George Schaefer
The story of Florence Nightingale, who shocked Victorian society by organizing a nursing staff to aid British soldiers in the Crimean War, is told in this presentation from "George Schaefer's Showcase Theatre."
Emmy Award '65: Outstanding Individual Achievement/Art Direction.
George Schaefer — *Enter-Tel Inc*

Hombre   1967
Western
08434   111 mins   C   B, V   P
Paul Newman, Fredric March, Richard Boone, Diane Cilento, Cameron Mitchell, Barbara Rush, Martin Balsam
A white man, raised by Apaches, is forced to a showdown. He has to help save the lives of people he loathes.
EL, SP
20th Century Fox; Martin Ritt; Irving Ravetch — *CBS/Fox Video*

Hombres sin Alma   197?
Drama
63854   90 mins   B/W   B, V   P
Rosa Carmina, directed by Juan Orol
A woman who has been treated callously by men all her life keeps searching for true love. In Spanish.

SP
Mexican — *Budget Video*

Home Bartending　1980
Alcoholic beverages
44277　28 mins　C　V　　　P
This program describes the practical equipment needed for home bartending as well as professional bartender tips on how to mix 22 popular drinks. Each drink is mixed on camera.
American Home Video Library — *American Home Video Library*

Home Exercise for All Ages　1980
Physical fitness
47329　45 mins　C　B, V, 3/4U　　P
This program presents a series of stretching and flexing exercises which, if followed, can improve muscle tone, posture, and health.
Vision Productions — *Vision Productions*

Home Sweet Home　1914
Drama
58644　62 mins　B/W　B, V, FO　　P
Lillian Gish, Dorothy Gish, Henry Walthall, Mae Marsh, Blanche Sweet, Donald Crisp, Robert Haron, directed by D. W. Griffith
Suggested by the life of John Howard Payne, actor, poet, dramatist, critic, and world-wanderer, who wrote the title song amid the bitterness of his sad life. Silent with musical score.
Reliance Majestic Release — *Video Yesteryear*

Homesteaders of Paradise Valley　1947
Western
14353　54 mins　B/W　B, V　　　P
Allan Lane, Bobby Blake
Hume brothers oppose Red Ryder and a group of settlers building a dam in Paradise Valley.
Republic — *Video Connection; Cable Films; Nostalgia Merchant*

Homework　1982
Drama
63843　90 mins　C　B, V, LV　　P
Joan Collins, Michael Morgan, Betty Thomas, Shell Kepler, Wings Hauser
A young man's after-school lessons with a teacher are definitely not part of the curriculum.
MPAA:R
Jensen Farley — *MCA Home Video*

Honda—The Technology　1983
Motorcycles
72853　35 mins　C　B, V　　　P
The production of Honda Motorcycles is demonstrated.

Honda Motor Company — *Motor Cycle Video*

Honey　1981
Drama
65352　89 mins　C　B, V　　　P
Clio Goldsmith, Fernando Rey, Catherine Spaak
An attractive writer pays an unusual visit to the home of a distinguished publisher. Brandishing a pistol, she demands that he read aloud from her manuscript. As he reads, a unique fantasy unfolds, a dreamlike erotic tale.
Toni De Carlo — *Vestron Video*

Honeysuckle Rose　1980
Musical-Drama
54807　119 mins　C　B, V, LV　　R, P
Willie Nelson, Dyan Cannon, Amy Irving, Slim Pickens, Joey Floyd, Charles Levin, Priscilla Pointer, directed by Jerry Schatzberg
A road-touring country-Western singer whose life is a series of one night stands, falls in love with an adoring young guitar player who has just joined his band. This nearly costs him his marriage when his wife, who waits patiently for him at home, decides she's had enough.
MPAA:PG
Warner Bros — *Warner Home Video*

Honky Tonk Freeway　1981
Comedy
47304　107 mins　C　B, V　　　R, P
Teri Garr, Howard Hesseman, Beau Bridges, directed by John Schlesinger
An odd assortment of people become involved in a small town Mayor's scheme to turn a dying hamlet into a tourist wonderland.
MPAA:PG
Universal — *THORN EMI Home Video*

Honkytonk Man　1982
Drama
60562　123 mins　C　B, V　　　R, P
Clint Eastwood, Kyle Eastwood, John McIntire, Alexa Kenin, directed by Clint Eastwood
Set during the Depression, this film spins the tale of a country singer who helps his nephew through the rites of passage.
MPAA:PG
Warner Bros — *Warner Home Video*

Honor Thy Father　1973
Drama
73560　97 mins　C　B, V　　　P
Raf Vallone, Richard Castellano, Brenda Vaccaro, Joe Bologna
The everyday life of a Mafia family as seen through the eyes of Bill Bonanno, the son of mob chieftan Joe Bonanno which was adapted from the book by Gay Talese.
CBS — *Prism*

Hoodoo Ann   1916
Film-History
50633   27 mins   B/W   B, V   P, T
Mae Marsh, Robert Harron
The story of Hoodoo Ann, from her days in the orphanage to her happy marriage. Silent.
Triangle — *Blackhawk Films*

Hooper   1978
Comedy
38950   90 mins   C   B, V   R, P
Burt Reynolds, Jan-Michael Vincent, Robert Klein, directed by Hal Needham
A behind-the-scenes look at the world of movie stuntmen. Burt Reynolds is a top stuntman who becomes involved in a rivalry with an up-and-coming young man out to surpass him.
MPAA:PG
Warner Bros — *Warner Home Video; RCA VideoDiscs*

Hoppity Goes to Town   1941
Cartoons/Fantasy
64544   78 mins   C   B, V   P
Animated
This full-length animated feature from the Max Fleischer studios tells the story of the inhabitants of Bugville, who live in a weed patch in New York City. Songs by Frank Loesser and Hoagy Carmichael. Original title: "Mr. Bug Goes to Town."
Paramount; Max Fleischer — *NTA Home Entertainment; Classic Video Cinema Collector's Club*

Hopscotch   1980
Comedy
55580   107 mins   C   B, V, CED   P
Glenda Jackson, Walter Matthau, Ned Beatty, Sam Waterston
A C.I.A. agent drops out when his overly zealous chief demotes him to a desk job. When he writes a book designed to expose the dirty deeds he leads his boss and KGB pal on a merry chase.
MPAA:R
Avco Embassy — *Embassy Home Entertainment*

Horowitz in London   1982
Music-Performance
60570   116 mins   C   LV   P
In June 1982, Vladimir Horowitz returned to London for the first time in over 30 years for a performance including Chopin, Scarlatti Sonatas, Schumann's "Scenes from Childhood," and Rachmaninoff. In stereo.
John Vernon; Peter Gelb — *Pioneer Artists; RCA VideoDiscs*

Horowitz in London   1982
Music-Performance
75898   116 mins   C   B, V   P
Vladimir Horowitz
This program presents a rare recital by one of the greatest pianists today, playing in London for Prince Charles at a benefit.
Columbia Artists — *Sony Corporation of America*

Horrible Double Feature   192?
Horror
10135   56 mins   B/W   B, V   P, T
John Barrymore, Lon Chaney
Package includes John Barrymore in "Dr. Jekyll and Mr. Hyde" (1920). Also features "Hunchback of Notre Dame." Both films are condensed. From the "History of the Motion Picture" series.
Universal et al — *Blackhawk Films*

Horror Express   1973
Horror
08588   95 mins   C   B, V   P
Christopher Lee, Peter Cushing, Telly Savalas, directed by Gene Martin
A creature from Prehistoric times, which has been removed from its tomb, is transported on the Trans-Siberian railroad. Passengers discover strange things happening.
MPAA:R
Scotia Intl; Bernard Gordon — *Media Home Entertainment; Budget Video; VCII; Sheik Video; King of Video; Video Connection*

Horror Hospital   1973
Horror
48475   91 mins   C   B, V   P
Michael Gough, Robin Askwith, Vanessa Shaw
Patients are turned into zombies by a mad doctor in this hospital where no anesthesia is used. Those who try to escape are taken care of by the doctor's guards.
MPAA:R
Richard Gordon Productions — *VCI Home Video*

Horror Hotel   1963
Horror
23227   75 mins   B/W   B, V, 3/4U   P
Dennis Lotis, Christopher Lee, Betta St. John, Venetia Stevenson
A woman burned as a witch in 1692, makes a pact with the devil for eternal life in exchange for providing him with human sacrifices from the hotel she runs.
Trans Lux; British — *Penguin Video*

Horror of Frankenstein   1970
Satire/Horror
63349   93 mins   C   B, V   R, P
Ralph Bates, Kate O'Mara
This spoof of the standard Frankenstein story features a philandering Baron whose interest in a very weird branch of science creates some

shocking up-to-date innovations in the
conventional plot.
Levitt-Pickman — *THORN EMI Home Video*

Horror Planet   1982
Science fiction/Horror
65718   93 mins   C   B, V   P
Robin Clarke
An alien creature needs a chance to breed
before escaping to spread its horror. When a
group of explorers disturb it, the years of waiting
are over, and the unlucky mother-to-be will
never be the same.
MPAA:R
Richard Gordon; David Speechley — *Embassy
Home Entertainment*

Horror—Sci-Fi: Trailers   1984
on Tape
Movie and TV trailers/Science fiction
66477   60 mins   C   B, V   P
Theatrical trailers for 35 films are included, with
such classic movies represented as: "Psycho,"
"Night of the Living Dead," "Jaws," "The War
of the Worlds," "The Time Machine," "King
Kong," "Freaks" and "The Texas Chainsaw
Massacre." Some black-and-white segments.
Universal et al — *San Francisco Rush Video*

Horse Sense   1953
Animals
74537   23 mins   C   B, V   P
This tape reviews a variety of valuable tips for
trail riders.
US Forest Service — *Mercedes Maharis
Productions*

Horse Soldiers, The   1959
Adventure/Drama
59643   119 mins   C   CED   P
*John Wayne, William Holden, Constance
Towers, directed by John Ford*
Union Army cavalry officers travel deep into
Confederate territory, squaring off against the
southern army, and each other, along the way.
United Artists — *RCA VideoDiscs*

Horse Soldiers, The   1959
Western
72895   119 mins   C   B, V   P
John Wayne, William Holden
An 1863 Union cavalry officer is sent 300 miles
into Confederate territory to destroy a railroad
junction.
United Artists — *CBS/Fox Video*

Horseshoeing   1946
Animals
69667   18 mins   B/W   B, V   P
Techniques of horseshoeing are presented in
this program.

US Government — *Mercedes Maharis
Productions*

Hospice   1979
Medical care
55032   26 mins   C   B, V   P
Narrated by Robert McNeil
A report on a special kind of health care which
emphasizes concern for the whole family.
Billy Budd Films — *Vanguard Video*

Hospital, The   1971
Drama
65497   101 mins   C   CED   P
*George C. Scott, Diana Rigg, Barnard Hughes,
Nancy Marchand, Richard Dysart*
A city hospital is beset by weird mishaps, and it
transpires that a killer is on the loose.
United Artists — *CBS/Fox Video*

Hospital Massacre   1981
Horror
65108   89 mins   C   B, V, CED   P
Barbi Benton, Jon Van Ness
A psychopathic killer who wants to play doctor
with a young woman in the hospital repeatedly
demonstrates his brutal bedside manner.
MPAA:R
Cannon Films — *MGM/UA Home Video*

Hostage Tower, The   1980
Drama
65711   97 mins   C   B, V   P
*Peter Fonda, Maud Adams, Britt Ekland, Billy
Dee Williams*
A group of internatioal crime figures capture a
VIP, hold her hostage in the Eiffel Tower and
demand $30 million in ransom.
MPAA:PG
Burt Nodella — *Embassy Home Entertainment*

Hot Bubblegum   1981
Comedy
47629   94 mins   C   B, V   P
Jonathan Segal, Zachi Noy, Yftach Katzur
Three teenagers discover sex, the beach, rock
'n' roll, sex, drag racing and sex.
MPAA:R
Independent — *Paragon Video Productions*

Hot Pepper   1973
Music/Folklore
60463   54 mins   C   B, V, 3/4U   P
Clifton Chenier
This look at Cajun music focuses on Clifton
Chenier and its sources in the surroundings of
rural and urban Louisiana. The great French
accordionist mixes rock, blues and zydeco
music. A companion film to "Dry Wood."
Les Blank — *Flower Films*

Hot Rock, The 1970
Comedy
08466   97 mins   C   B, V   P
Robert Redford, George Segal, Ron Leibman,
Zero Mostel, Paul Sand, directed by Peter Yates
Four incredible goofs try to steal the world's
hottest diamond.
MPAA:PG SP
20th Century Fox; Hal Landers and Bobby
Roberts — *CBS/Fox Video*

Hot Stuff 1980
Comedy
51570   91 mins   C   B, V   P
Dom Deluise, Jerry Reed, Suzanne Pleshette,
Ossie Davis, directed by Dom Deluise
Officers on a burglary task force decide the best
way to obtain convictions is to go into the
fencing business themselves.
MPAA:PG
Columbia Pictures — *RCA/Columbia Pictures*
Home Video

Hot Summer in Barefoot 1982
County
Comedy
66259   90 mins   C   B, V   P
Sherry Robinson, Tonia Bryan
A State Law Enforcement officer on the search
for illegal moonshiners finds more than he
bargained for.
MPAA:R
W Henry Smith — *Paragon Video Productions*

Hot Summer Night.. With 1984
Donna, A
Music-Performance
76028   60 mins   C   B, V   P
Donna Summer gives an electrifying
performance of her hits at a concert held at
California's Pacific Amphitheater. Songs include
"She Works Hard For the Money," "Bad Girls"
and "Hot Stuff."
Christine Smith — *RCA/Columbia Pictures*
Home Video

Hot T-Shirts 1979
Comedy
47681   86 mins   C   B, V   P
Ray Holland, Stephanie Lawlor, Pauline Rose,
Corinne Alphen
A small town bar owner needs a boost for
business, finding the answer in wet T-shirt
contests.
MPAA:R
Cannon Films — *MCA Home Video*

Hot Times 1974
Drama
65452   80 mins   C   B, V   P
Henry Cory
A high school boy, after striking out with the high
school girls, decides to go to New York and
have the time of his life!
MPAA:R
Extraordinary Films — *Monterey Home Video*

Hot Wire 197?
Comedy
66260   92 mins   C   B, V   P
George Kennedy, Strother Martin
A comedy about the unscrupulous side of the
car repossession racket.
Associates Entertainment Intl — *Paragon*
Video Productions

Hotel New Hampshire, 1984
The
Comedy-Drama
73037   110 mins   C   B, V   P
Jodie Foster, Rob Lowe, Beau Bridges,
Nastassia Kinski
This is an adaptation of John Irving's novel
about a family's adventures in New Hampshire,
Vienna and New York City.
MPAA:R
Orion — *Vestron Video*

Hothead (Coup de Tete) 1978
Comedy
66016   90 mins   C   B, V   P
Patrick Dewaere, directed by Jean-Jacques
Annaud
A talented soccer player's quick temper causes
him to be cut from his team, lose his job and
even be banned from the local bar.
Gaumont SFP — *RCA/Columbia Pictures*
Home Video

Hound of the 1959
Baskervilles, The
Mystery
47146   86 mins   C   B, V, CED   P
Peter Cushing, Christopher Lee, Andre Morell
Sherlock Holmes solves the mystery of a
supernatural hound threatening the life of a
Dartmoor baronet.
EL, SP
United Artists; Hammer — *CBS/Fox Video*

Houndcats, The 1981
Cartoons
75625   43 mins   C   B, V   P
Animated 2 pgms
This program consists of two animated stories,
starring the Houndcats.
1.The Misbehavin' Raven Mission 2.The Double
Dealing Diamond Mission
DePatie Freleng — *Trans World Entertainment*

House Across the Bay, The   1940
Drama
66634   88 mins   B/W   B, V   P
George Raft, Walter Pidgeon, Joan Bennett, Lloyd Nolan
An ex-con discovers that his wife was having an affair during his imprisonment.
Walter Wanger Productions — *Monterey Home Video*

House Calls   1978
Comedy
47420   105 mins   C   B, V, LV   P
Walter Matthau, Glenda Jackson, Art Carney, Richard Benjamin, Candice Azzara
A widowed surgeon turns into a swinging bachelor until he meets a stuffy English divorcee.
MPAA:PG
Universal — *MCA Home Video*

House of Exorcism, The   197?
Horror
69036   100 mins   C   B, V   P
Good and evil come into deadly conflict in this glimpse into the lives of the followers of Satan.
Unknown — *Cinemagreats*

House of Seven Corpses, The   1973
Horror
58546   90 mins   C   B, V   R, P
John Carradine, John Ireland, Faith Domergue
On the site of a lonely country estate, a motion picture company arrives planning to film a make-believe occult thriller.
MPAA:PG
Philip Yordan — *Video Gems; Budget Video; King of Video*

House of Shadows   1983
Horror
63387   90 mins   C   B, V   P
John Gavin, Yvonne DeCarlo
A 20-year-old murder comes back to haunt the victim's friends in this suspenseful tale of mystery and terror.
Intercontinental Releasing — *Media Home Entertainment*

House on Chelouche Street, The   1973
Drama
66135   111 mins   C   B, V, FO   P
A well thought-out story of life in Tel Aviv under the rule of the British, before the creation of the country of Israel.
Israel — *Video Yesteryear*

House on Garibaldi Street, The   1979
Suspense/Crime-Drama
72454   100 mins   C   B, V   P
Topol, Nick Mancuso
This is Isser Harel's account of the capture of Adolph Eichmann.
Charles Fries Production — *U.S.A. Home Video*

House on Sorority Row, The   1983
Horror
64898   90 mins   C   B, V, LV, CED   P
The harrowing story of what happens when seven senior sisters have a last fling and get back at their housemother at the same time.
Artists Releasing Corp — *Vestron Video*

House That Vanished, The   1973
Horror/Mystery
50728   84 mins   C   B, V   P
Andrea Allan, Karl Lanchbury, directed by Joseph Larraz
A mysterious house provides horror, screams, and death for most of those who challenge it.
MPAA:R
Diana Daubeney — *Media Home Entertainment*

How Funny Can Sex Be?   1976
Comedy
66078   97 mins   C   B, V   P
Giancarlo Giannini, Laura Antonelli, Dulio Del Prete
Eight ribald sketches about loveItalian style.
MPAA:R
Howard Mahler Films — *CBS/Fox Video*

How the Animals Discovered Christmas   1956
Christmas/Cartoons
56153   13 mins   C   B, V   P, T
Animated
A delightful tale about the animals of Cozy Valley and how they discover the spirit of Christmas.
AM Available
Coronet Films — *Blackhawk Films*

How the Automobile Works   1984
Automobiles
72965   28 mins   C   B, V   P
A step by step breakdown on the interior workings of a car.
Star Merchants — *Increase Video*

How to Avoid Being Cheated at Cards　1980
Games
53781　60 mins　C　B, V　P
Card expert Buddy Farnan demonstrates ways to avoid being cheated at cards, all the tricks-of-the-trade impossible to detect, unless you know how they are done.
Unknown — *Essex Video*

How to Beat Home Video Games Volume I　1982
Video/Games
63365　60 mins　C　B, V　P
Narrated by Philip M. Wiswell
"Volume I: The best Games" features strategies for high scoring on such Atari VCS games as "Space Invaders," "Asteroids," "Chopper Command" and "Frogger."
Vestron Video — *Vestron Video*

How to Beat Home Video Games Volume II　1982
Video/Games
63366　60 mins　C　B, V　P
Narrated by Philip M. Wiswell
"Volume II: The Hot New Games" features strategies for beating 20 of the newest games for the Atari VCS, including "MegaMania," "Demons to Diamonds," "Pitfall" and "Riddle of the Sphynx."
Vestron Video — *Vestron Video*

How to Beat Home Video Games Volume III　1982
Video/Games
63367　60 mins　C　B, V　P
Narrated by Philip M. Wiswell
"Volume III: Arcade Quality for the Home" previews new arcade quality game systems such as ColecoVision, Vectrex and Atari 5200, and demonstrates how to score high on games for these systems, including "Cosmic Chasm," "Donkey Kong," "Zaxxon" and "Galaxian."
Vestron Video — *Vestron Video*

How to Beat the High Cost of Living　1980
Comedy
64890　105 mins　C　B, V, CED　P
Jessica Lange, Susan St. James, Jane Curtin, Richard Benjamin
Three women execute a crazy, comic shopping mall heist.
MPAA:PG
Filmways — *Vestron Video*

How to Marry a Millionaire　1953
Comedy
08552　96 mins　C　B, V　P
Lauren Bacall, Marilyn Monroe, Betty Grable, William Powell, David Wayne, Cameron Mitchell
Three models pool their money and rent a lavish apartment to wage campaign to trap millionaire husbands.
20th Century Fox; Nunnally Johnson — *CBS/Fox Video*

How to Play Your Best Golf, Volume 1　1983
Golf
65261　90 mins　C　B, V　P
A program of instruction using state-of-the-art video effects to demonstrate shots and techniques.
Carovatt Communications; National Golf Foundation — *Caravatt Home Entertainment*

How to Play Your Best Golf, Volume 2　1983
Golf
65262　90 mins　C　B, V　P
An instructional program featuring "The Scoring Shots," "The Trouble Shots," "Playing the Game," and "Drills."
Carovatt Communications; National Golf Foundation — *Caravatt Home Entertainment*

How to Stuff a Wild Bikini　1965
Comedy
66130　90 mins　C　B, V　R, P
Annette Funicello, Dwayne Hickman, Buster Keaton, Harvey Lembeck, Mickey Rooney
A young man in the Navy asks a local witchdoctor to keep on eye on his girl.
American Intl Pictures — *Warner Home Video*

How to Watch Pro Football　1981
Football
57776　53 mins　C　B, V　P
Tom Landry, Marv Levy, John McKay, Chuck Noll, Sam Rutigliano, Don Shula, Dick Vermeil
A step-by-step guide designed to enhance every fan's enjoyment of the game. Seven top coaches take the viewer through everything from zone defense pass coverage to offensive strategy at the goal line. The two-sided interactive disc offers the same program content utilizing the unique technology of the interactive disc.
Optical Programming Associates — *MCA Home Video; Optical Programming Associates*

How to Win in Blackjack　1981
Games
53780　90 mins　C　B, V　P
Ken Uston, professional blackjack player, demonstrates his "card-counting" method, in which he keeps track of the cards so well that he can determine if the remaining cards will tip the odds in his favor.

Ken Uston — *Essex Video*

Howdy Doody 195?
Comedy
59086   49 mins   B/W   B, V, FO   P
Buffalo Bob Smith
Clarabell and Buffalo Bob show movies of Clarabell's recent trip. Princess Summerfall Winterspring and Zippy the Chimp, Flubadub, Dilly Dally, Inspector John, Mr. Bluster, and others also appear. Two complete shows.
NBC — *Video Yesteryear; Discount Video Tapes*

Howling, The 1981
Horror
59340   91 mins   C   B, V, LV, CED   P
Dee Wallace, Patrick MacNee, Dennis Dugan, Kevin McCarthy
A pretty television reporter takes a rest at a clinic inhabited by loonies, and located near woods inhabited by werewolves.
MPAA:R
Michael Finell;Jack Conrad — *Embassy Home Entertainment; RCA VideoDiscs*

Huberman Festival, The 1984
Music-Performance
65852   45 mins   C   B, V   P
This program is a remarkable concert series for violin and orchestra performed by the Israeli Philharmonic and the world's seven most famous violinists.
Pacific Arts Video Records — *Pacific Arts Video*

Huckleberry Finn 1978
Adventure
29235   97 mins   C   B, V, CED   P
Kurt Ida, Don Manahan, Forrest Tucker
Based on the classic story by Mark Twain of the adventures of a Missouri boy and a runaway slave.
Sunn Classic Pictures — *VidAmerica*

Huckleberry Finn 1975
Adventure
55535   78 mins   C   B, V, CED   P
Ron Howard, Jack Elam, Merle Haggard, Donny Most
Television version of the Mark Twain classic about a boy and a runaway slave who take off together on a raft down the Mississippi.
ABC Pictures International — *CBS/Fox Video*

Hud 1963
Drama
10952   112 mins   B/W   B, V, LV   P
Paul Newman, Melvyn Douglas, Patricia Neal, Brandon DeWilde
Hard-driving, hard-drinking, woman-chasing young man, whose life is a revolt against the principles of his father, is the idol of his teenage nephew.
Academy Awards '63: Best Actress (Neal); Best Supporting Actor (Douglas); Best Cinematography.
Paramount — *Paramount Home Video; RCA VideoDiscs*

Hughes Flying Boat, The 1980
Documentary/Aeronautics
57431   11 mins   C   B, V   P, T
A look at Howard Hughes' legendary aircraft, "The Spruce Goose," hidden from public view for over thirty years, and the mystery hangar on Terminal Island. This program includes live commentary by Hughes from the cockpit during flight.
Bruce Frenzinger — *Blackhawk Films; Interurban Films*

Hughie 1984
Drama
75288   53 mins   C   B, V   P
This is a tape of the Broadway play about a hotel night clerk who develops friendships with the residents that come in during the night. In Beta Hi-Fi and VHS Dolby stereo.
RKO Home Video — *RKO HomeVideo*

Hugo the Hippo 1976
Cartoons
08483   90 mins   C   B, V   P
Animated, voices of Paul Lynde, Burl Ives, Robert Morley, Marie and Jimmy Osmond
A forlorn baby hippo struggles to survive in the human jungle of old Zanzibar.
MPAA:G
20th Century Fox — *CBS/Fox Video*

Hullabaloo 1965
Music-Performance
47480   45 mins   B/W   B, V, FO   P
Gene Pitney, Junior Walker and the All-Stars, Leslie Uggams, hosted by Dean Jones
A March 23, 1965 episode of the popular rock 'n' roll variety show, featuring top hits by the artists of the day.
NBC — *Video Yesteryear*

Hullabaloo 1965
Music-Performance
58263   47 mins   B/W   B, V, FO   P
David McCallum, Beau Brummels, Brenda Lee, Animals, Peter and Gordon, Michael Landon, Paul Revere and Raiders, Byrds, Chad Stewart, Jackie De Shannon
Two programs from the mid-Sixties Teenage rock 'n' roll show complete with mini-skirts. David McCallum appears as Illya Kuryakin,

Chad drops Jeremy, and the Byrds transcend the proceedings with a performance of "The Times They Are A-Changin."
NBC — *Video Yesteryear*

Human Experiments 1979
Horror
53327 82 mins C B, V P
Linda Haynes, Jackie Coogan, Aldo Ray
A psychiatrist in a women's prison conducts a group of experiments in which he destroys the "criminal instinct" in the inmates through brute fear.
MPAA:R
Summer Brown; Gregory Goodell — *VidAmerica*

Human Gorilla, The 1938
Drama
08768 62 mins B/W B, V, 3/4U P
Richard Carlson, Lucille Bremer, Richard Moore
Judge, escaping from the police, seeks a hiding place in an insane asylum.
Eagle Lion — *Penguin Video*

Human Monster, The 1939
Horror
72948 73 mins B/W B, V P
Bela Lugosi
A mad doctor played by Bela Lugosi is using his house as a front for some strange experiments.
Monogram — *VCI Home Video*

Human Monster, The 1940
Mystery
08753 78 mins B/W B, V, 3/4U P
Bela Lugosi, Hugh Williams Greta Gynt
Scotland Yard inspector investigates five drownings.
Pathe; Monogram — *Penguin Video; Sheik Video; Ampro Video Productions; Cable Films; Video Connection; VCI Home Video*

Human Values 1980
Ethics
55033 31 mins C B, V P
A collection of three films spanning the spectrum of human liberty: "Keith," about a mime who takes his performance to the streets, demonstrating the transition from total immobility to freedom at last; "Mimi," a portrait of a young woman with a permanent disability; and "Holy War," a nonromantic look at war narrated by Cliff Robertson.
Billy Budd Films — *Vanguard Video*

Humanoids from the Deep 1980
Horror
54809 81 mins C B, V R, P

A horror tale wherein strange creatures rise from the depths of the ocean and attack mankind.
MPAA:R
New World Pictures — *Warner Home Video*

Humans: Happy Hour, The 1984
Music
65850 40 mins C B, V P
This program represents a pioneering step into the next wave of long-form music video with the Humans' songs fitting into the overall plot.
Pacific Arts Video Records — *Pacific Arts Video*

Humongous 1982
Horror
63374 93 mins C B, V P
Janet Julian, David Wallace, Janet Baldwin
A deranged giant must kill to survive.
MPAA:R
Embassy Pictures — *Embassy Home Entertainment*

Hunchback of Notre Dame, The 1923
Drama
07278 90 mins B/W B, V P, T
Lon Chaney, Patsy Ruth Miller, Norman Kerry, Ernest Torrance
The first film version of Victor Hugo's novel about the tortured hunchback bellringer of Notre Dame Cathedral. Silent.
Universal — *Blackhawk Films; Video Yesteryear; Budget Video; Western Film & Video Inc; Classic Video Cinema Collector's Club*

Hunchback of Notre Dame, The 1939
Drama
00309 117 mins B/W B, V, 3/4U P
Charles Laughton, Maureen O'Hara, Edmund O'Brien
Victor Hugo's classic tale of the tortured hunchback bellringer of Notre Dame.
RKO — *Nostalgia Merchant; VidAmerica; King of Video; Blackhawk Films; Sheik Video; Cable Films; Video Connection; RCA VideoDiscs*

Hunger, The 1983
Horror
65220 100 mins C B, V, CED P
Catherine Deneuve, David Bowie, Susan Sarandon, Cliff de Young, directed by Tony Scott
A 2000-year-old vampire finds that her current lover is aging fast and therefore sets out to find some "new blood" to replace him.
MPAA:R
MGM UA — *MGM/UA Home Video*

Hungry i Reunion   1981
Comedy-Performance/Music-Performance
59930   90 mins   C   B, V   P
*Bill Cosby, Phyllis Diller, Ronnie Schell, Bill
Dana, Mort Sahl, Irwin Corey, Jackie Vernon,
Jonathan Winters, Kingston Trio, Limelighters,
Lenny Bruce*
A reunion of stars who made the "Hungry i" San
Francisco's favorite nightclub of the 50's and
60's. Includes rare footage of Lenny Bruce in
performance.
Tom Cohen — *Pacific Arts Video*

Hunter, The   1980
Drama/Adventure
54671   97 mins   C   B, V, LV   R, P
*Steve McQueen, Eli Wallach, Kathryn Harrold,
LeVar Burton, directed by Buzz Kulik*
An action-drama based on the real life
adventures of Ralph (Papa) Thorson, a modern
day bounty hunter who makes his living by
finding fugitives who have jumped bail.
MPAA:PG
Paramount — *Paramount Home Video*

Hurricane   1979
Drama
63430   119 mins   C   B, V   R, P
*Mia Farrow, Jason Robards, Trevor Howard,
Max Von Sydow*
A hurricane wreaks havoc in a tropical paradise.
Paramount; Dino DeLaurentiis — *Paramount
Home Video*

Hurricane Express   1932
Adventure
08881   70 mins   B/W   B, V, 3/4U   P
John Wayne, Conway Tearle, Shirley Gray
Adapted from the twelve-episode serial. John
Wayne pits his courage against an unknown,
powerful individual out to sabotage a railroad.
Mascot — *Penguin Video; Sheik Video; Ampro
Video Productions; Cable Films; Interurban
Films*

Hurricane Express   1932
Adventure/Serials
58633   223 mins   B/W   B, V   P
John Wayne, Joseph Girard
Twelve episodes of the vintage serial, in which
the Duke pits his courage against an unknown,
powerful individual out to sabotage a railroad.
Mascot — *Video Connection; Video
Yesteryear; Cable Films; Discount Video Tapes*

Hurricane Express/Angel   194?
and the Badman
Adventure/Western
58909   178 mins   B/W   B, V   P
*John Wayne, Shirley Grey, Gail Russell, Harry
Carey, Bruce Cabot*
A "Duke" double feature: "Hurricane Express"
(1932), the feature version of the exciting action
serial; "Angel/and the Bad Man" (1947), in
which the love of a Quaker girl converts a
wounded gunslinger to an honorable life.
EL, SP
Republic — *Ampro Video Productions*

Hussy   1980
Drama
66604   95 mins   C   B, V, LV   P
Helen Mirren, John Shea
An unlikely pair of lovers find themselves
enmeshed within an underworld conspiracy.
MPAA:R
World Northal — *Vestron Video*

Hustle   1975
Mystery
38934   120 mins   C   B, V   R, P
*Burt Reynolds, Catherine Deneuve, directed by
Robert Aldrich*
Burt Reynolds plays a detective investigating a
young girl's supposed suicide who becomes
romantically entangled with a high-priced call
girl.
MPAA:R
Paramount — *Paramount Home Video*

Hustler Squad   1976
War-Drama
64297   98 mins   C   B, V   P
*John Ericson, Karen Ericson, Lynda Sinclaire,
Nory Wright*
A U.S. Army major and a Philippine guerrilla
leader stage a major operation to help rid the
Philippines of Japanese Occupation forces: they
have four combat-trained prostitutes infiltrate a
brothel patronized by top Japanese officers.
MPAA:R
Crown International Pictures — *VCI Home
Video*

Hustling   1975
Drama
65665   96 mins   C   B, V   P
Jill Clayburgh, Lee Remick
A reporter writing a series of articles on
prostitution in New York City takes an incisive
look at their unusual and sometimes brutal
world.
Lillian Gallo — *Worldvision Home Video*

Hymn of the Nations   1944
Music-Performance
11235   25 mins   B/W   B, V, FO   P
*Jan Peerce, Arturo Toscanini and the NBC
Symphony, the Westminster Choir*
This wartime short features a rare filmed
appearance by Arturo Toscanini, conducting
two Verdi works: the overture to "La Forza del
Destino" and "Hymn of the Nations."
Office of War Information — *Video Yesteryear;
Blackhawk Films*

Hypnovision Stop Smoking Video Programming   1983
Smoking
69927   22 mins   C   B, V   P
Through a number of positive subliminal messages, this program helps viewers to be more relaxed in their daily life without cigarettes; learn to take "one day at a time" to reduce anxiety, and substitute new positive behaviors for old, poor habits.
Self Improvement Video — *Self Improvement Video*

Hypnovision Weight Loss Video Programming   1983
Physical fitness
69928   22 mins   C   B, V   P
To help the viewer lose weight, this program uses a number of positive subliminal messages to deeply relax and then permantly change poor eating habits of the overeater.
Self Improvement Video — *Self Improvement Video*

Hysterectomy (Rehabilitation and Injury)   1978
Physical fitness
52757   30 mins   C   B, V   P
Hosted by Ann Dugan
Exercises for women who have had a hysterectomy, including both specific-area and total-body movements to gradually improve muscle tone. Part of the "Rehabilitation and Injury" series.
Health 'N Action — *RCA/Columbia Pictures Home Video*

Hysterical   1983
Comedy
65389   86 mins   C   B, V   P
The Hudson Brothers
This is a comedy about a haunted lighthouse occupied by the vengeful spirit of a spurned woman.
MPAA:PG
Gene Levy — *Embassy Home Entertainment*

I

I Accuse My Parents   1943
Drama/Exploitation
08621   70 mins   B/W   B, V, 3/4U   P
Mary Beth Hughes, Robert Lowell, John Miljan
A startling exposure of the truth behind wayward youths in the '40s.
PRC — *Penguin Video*

I Am a Dancer   1972
Dance/Biographical
58460   90 mins   C   B, V   R, P
Rudolph Nureyev, Margo Fonteyn, Carla Fracci, Lynn Seymour, Deanne Bergsma
Nureyev is seen as a pupil in ballet class, exhibiting the sweat and dedication needed.
Evdoros Demetriou — *THORN EMI Home Video*

I Am a Fugitive from a Chain Gang   1932
Drama
65065   90 mins   B/W   CED   P
Paul Muni, Glenda Farrell, Helen Vinson, Preston Foster, directed by Mervyn LeRoy
An innocent man is convicted and sentenced to a Georgia chain gang, where he is brutalized and degraded. Based on a true story.
Warner Bros — *RCA VideoDiscs*

I Cover the Waterfront   1933
Drama
11234   70 mins   B/W   B, V, FO   P
Claudette Colbert, Ben Lyon, Ernest Torrance, Hobart Cavanaugh
A reporter exposes a fisherman who brings Chinese aliens into the country on his boat, or kills them when authorities are after him.
Edward Small Prods — *Video Yesteryear; Movie Buff Video; Budget Video; Video Connection; Discount Video Tapes; Western Film & Video Inc*

I Crave the Waves   1983
Sports-Water/Documentary
66620   90 mins   C   B, V   P
Bobby Owens, Lynne Boyer, Allen Sarlo, Becky Benson
A lighthearted tour around the world to some of the most exciting surf spots in California, Hawaii, Brazil and South Africa. Twenty of the world's top surfers are seen in action and at play. An additional California skateboarding short, "Four-Wheel-Drive," is also included.
MPAA:PG
Robert Rey Walker — *U.S.A. Home Video*

I Do! I Do!   1984
Musical
69923   116 mins   C   B, V   P
Lee Remick, Hal Linden
This Los Angeles production of the Broadway musical covers 50 years of a marriage, beginning just before the turn of the century. In VHS Dolby stereo and Beta Hi-Fi.
Bonnie Burns — *RKO HomeVideo*

I Dream Too Much   1935
Musical/Opera
52309   90 mins   B/W   B, V   P
Lily Pons, Henry Fonda, Eric Blore, Lucille Ball, Mischa Auer

A musical vehicle for opera star Lily Pons, as a French singer who falls for an American composer.
RKO — *Budget Video*

I Hate Blondes   1983
Comedy
72208   90 mins   C   B, V   P
A ghostwriter and a female jewel thief get entangled.
Unknown — *Paragon Video Productions*

I Heard the Owl Call My Name   1973
Drama
75491   74 mins   C   B, V   P
Tom Courtenay, Dean Jagger
An Anglican priest meets with mystical Indian tribesmen of Northwest America.
Tomorrow Entertainment — *Prism*

I Love You   1982
Satire
60569   104 mins   C   B, V, CED   P
Sonia Braga, Paulo Cesar Pereio, directed by Arnaldo Jabor
A man down on his luck mistakenly assumes a woman he meets is a hooker. She plays along, only to find that they are becoming emotionally involved.
MPAA:R
Atlantic Releasing Corp; Brazil — *MGM/UA Home Video*

I Love You, Alice B. Toklas   1968
Comedy
58237   93 mins   C   B, V   R, P
Peter Sellers, Jo Van Fleet, Leigh Taylor-Young, directed by Hy Averback
A straight, uptight lawyer decides to join the peace and love generation. Screenplay by Paul Mazursky.
Warner Bros — *Warner Home Video*

I Married a Monster from Outer Space   1958
Horror/Science fiction
60213   78 mins   B/W   B, V   R, P
Tom Tryon, Gloria Talbott
The vintage thriller about a race of monster-like aliens from another planet who try to conquer earth.
Gene Fowler Jr — *Paramount Home Video*

I Married Joan   1955
Comedy
58640   50 mins   B/W   B, V, FO   P
Joan Davis, Jim Backus
Two episodes of this vintage sitcom: "Joan's Testimonial Luncheon," in which Joan thinks

the girls in the bridge club don't like her when they plan a surprise luncheon; and "The St. Bernards," in which the Stevens' end up with three unwanted canines.
NBC — *Video Yesteryear*

I Married Joan   1954
Comedy
63783   105 mins   B/W   B, V, 3/4U   P
Joan Davis, Jim Backus, Beverly Wills
Four episodes from the popular TV series, with Joan Davis getting into mischief and mayhem: "Joan Sees Stars," "Joan the Matchmaker," "Joan Throws a Wedding" and "Joan's Surprise for Brad."
NBC — *Shokus Video*

I Married Joan/The Burns and Allen Show   1952
Comedy
72525   60 mins   B/W   B, V, 3/4U   P
Joan Davis, Jim Backus, George Burns, Gracie Allen
Joan Davis and Jim Backus star in an episode of "I Married Joan," wherein Joan's expectations of an acting job she lands are shattered when she learns the specifics of her role. On the same tape, Gracie Allen visits a fortune teller and concludes she must divorce George Burns.
CBS — *International Historic Films*

I Never Promised You a Rose Garden   1977
Drama
58238   90 mins   C   B, V   R, P
Kathleen Quinlan, Bibi Anderson, Sylvia Sidney, Diane Varsi
A disturbed 16-year-old girl spirals down into madness and despair while a hospital psychiatrist struggles to bring her back to life.
MPAA:R
Imorah Productions — *Warner Home Video*

I Ought to Be in Pictures   1982
Comedy
63397   107 mins   C   B, V, CED   P
Walter Matthau, Ann-Margret, Dinah Manoff, Lance Guest
An estranged father and daughter come to terms in this Neil Simon comedy.
MPAA:PG
20th Century Fox — *CBS/Fox Video*

I Remember Mama   1948
Drama
07871   134 mins   B/W   B, V   P, T
Irene Dunne, Barbara Bel Geddes, directed by George Stevens
A Norwegian family's life at the turn of the century is recreated.
RKO — *Blackhawk Films; Nostalgia Merchant*

I Sent a Letter to My Love   1981
Drama
63335   102 mins   C   B, V   R, P
Simone Signoret, Jean Rochefort, Delphine Seyrig
An aging spinster, faced with the lonely prospect of the death of her crippled brother, places a personal ad for a companion in a local newspaper, using a different name. Unknown to her, the brother is the one who answers it.
Atlantic Releasing — *THORN EMI Home Video*

I Spit on Your Grave   1980
Horror
52853   98 mins   C   B, V   P
Camille Keaton, Aaron Tabor, Richard Pace, Anthony Nichols
A woman is ravaged by a group of four men but gets her revenge against them with extreme violence.
MPAA:R
Jerry Gross — *Wizard Video; Vestron Video (disc only)*

I, the Jury   197?
Suspense
66075   100 mins   C   B, V, CED   P
Armand Assante, Barbara Carrera
A remake of the 1953 Mike Hammer mystery as the famed PI investigates the murder of his best friend.
MPAA:R
20th Century Fox — *CBS/Fox Video*

I Walked with a Zombie   1943
Horror
00316   69 mins   B/W   B, V, 3/4U   P
Frances Dee, Tom Conway, James Ellison
Suspense thriller about a nurse's experience with a zombie on a remote tropical isle.
RKO — *Nostalgia Merchant*

I Will Fight No More Forever   1975
Drama
09106   74 mins   C   B, V   R, P
James Whitmore, Ned Romero, Sam Elliott
Recounts the epic story of the legendary Chief Joseph who led the Nez Perce tribe on an historic 1,600-mile trek in 1877.
Stan Margulies — *Video Gems*

Icarus Mania   197?
Sports-Minor/Documentary
45087   60 mins   C   B, V, 3/4U, Q   P
This fascinating documentary is about four types of free flight: hot-air ballooning, soaring, hang-gliding and sky-diving, with a particularly outstanding piece of footage; as the cameraman is filming a skydiving segment his first shoot fails to open, but before using his reserve parachute, he leans back, films his own problem, and then proceeds to land safely.
TV Sports Scene — *TV Sports Scene*

Ice Castles   1979
Drama
44843   110 mins   C   B, V   P
Robby Benson, Lynn-Holly Johnson
A young figure skater's Olympic dreams are dimmed by an accident, but her boyfriend gives her the strength, encouragement, and love necessary to perform a small miracle.
MPAA:PG
John Kemeny — *RCA/Columbia Pictures Home Video*

Ice Pirates, The   1984
Science fiction/Comedy
73364   93 mins   C   B, V   P
Robert Urich, Mary Crosby
A group of pirates steal frozen blocks of ice to fill the needs of a thirsty galaxy.
MPAA:PG
MGM UA Entertainment Co — *MGM/UA Home Video*

Iceman   1984
Drama
73184   101 mins   C   B, V   P
Timothy Hutton, Lindsay Crouse, directed by Fred Schepisi
Timothy Hutton and Lindsay Crouse star as a pair of scientists who find a frozen prehistoric man in a glacier and try to bring him back to life.
MPAA:PG
Patrick Palmer; Norman Jewison — *MCA Home Video*

Idaho   1943
Western
29438   70 mins   B/W   B, V   P
Roy Rogers, Harry J. Shannon, Virginia Grey
A cowboy and a ranger vie for the affections of the daughter of an ex-thief turned philanthropist.
Republic — *Sheik Video; Video Connection*

If...   1969
Drama
64026   111 mins   C   B, V   R, P
Malcolm McDowell, David Wood, Christine Noonan, Richard Warwick
Three unruly seniors at a British boarding school refuse to conform.
MPAA:R
Paramount — *Paramount Home Video*

If I Perish   1977
Religion
55035   75 mins   C   B, V   P
The true story of a young Korean who defied her Japanese persecutors during World War II, spreading her faith behind prison walls.

Family Films — *Vanguard Video*

If You Could See What I Hear　1982
Comedy-Drama
64032　103 mins　C　B, V, LV,　P
　　　　　　　　　　　　CED
Marc Singer, R. H. Thomson, Sarah Torgov, Shari Belafonte Harper
The true-life story of blind singer-musician Tom Sullivan covers his life from college days to marriage. His refusal to acknowledge his limitations led to many incidents, some hilarious, some tragic.
MPAA:PG
Jensen Farley Pictures; Cypress Grove Productions — *Vestron Video*

If You Knew Susie　1948
Musical
29485　90 mins　B/W　B, V　P, T
Eddie Cantor, Joan Davis, Allyn Joslyn, Charles Dingle
Two retired vaudeville actors living in a New England town are not accepted socially, that is until a letter from George Washington establishes them as descendants of a colonial patriot. They travel to Washington to claim $7,000,000,000 from the government.
RKO, Eddie Cantor — *Blackhawk Films*

Igor Sikorsky: Explorer of the Sky　1954
Biographical/Inventions
44266　15 mins　B/W　B, V　P
A look at the life of Igor Sikorsky, the inventor and developer of the helicopter. He also built the world's first four-engine plane. Classic newsreel footage.
Fox Movietone News — *Two Star Films*

Ill Met by Moonlight　1959
War-Drama
62866　104 mins　B/W　B, V　P
Dirk Bogarde, Marius Goring, David Oxley, Cyril Cusack
During the German occupation of Crete, a group of British agents attempt to capture a Nazi general.
Rank; Lopert Films — *Embassy Home Entertainment*

Illinois Steam Freight　1980
Trains
55519　60 mins　C　B, V　P
A thrilling train ride, featuring Consolidation No. 17 rolling out for an active day of steam railroading and making a fast run on the Crab Orchard line.
De Luz — *De Luz Video*

I'm All Right Jack　1959
Comedy
33958　101 mins　B/W　B, V　R, P
Peter Sellers, Ian Carmichael, Terry-Thomas
A shop steward is caught between two sides in a crooked financial scam in this satire on labor-management relations.
British Lion — *THORN EMI Home Video*

I'm Dancing as Fast as I Can　1982
Drama
64027　107 mins　C　B, V, LV　R, P
Jill Clayburgh, Nicol Williamson, Geraldine Page
A successful television producer becomes hopelessly dependent on tranquilizers.
MPAA:R
Paramount — *Paramount Home Video*

I'm on My Way/The Non-Stop Kid　191?
Comedy
59990　30 mins　B/W　B, V　P, T
Harold Lloyd, Snub Pollard, Bebe Daniels
A Harold Lloyd double feature. Two classic shorts: "I'm on My Way" (1919), in which Harold's dreams of an idyllic marriage are shattered, and "The Non-Stop Kid" (1918), in which Harold must contend with a rival for the affection of his beloved. Silent.
Hal Roach — *Blackhawk Films*

Image of Bruce Lee, The　197?
Martial arts/Adventure
53944　88 mins　C　B, V　P
Bruce Li, Chang Wu Lang, Chang Lei, Dana
Martial arts fight scenes prevail in this story about a jeweler who is swindled out of $1 million worth of diamonds.
MPAA:G
Alex Gouw — *Media Home Entertainment*

Immortal Battalion　1944
War-Drama
57355　89 mins　B/W　B, V, FO　P
David Niven, Stanley Holloway, Reginald Tate, Peter Ustinov, directed by Carol Reed
The story of how newly-recruited civilians are molded into a hardened batallion of fighting men.
J Arthur Rank; 20th Century Fox — *Video Yesteryear*

Impact　1949
Drama
58545　83 mins　B/W　B, V, 3/4U　P
Brian Donlevy, Ella Raines, directed by Arthur Lubin
A woman and her lover plan the murder of her rich industrialist husband, but the plan backfires and he survives.

United Artists — *Movie Buff Video; Penguin Video*

Improper Channels 1982
Comedy
63361   91 mins   C   B, V, LV,   P
                              CED
Alan Arkin, Mariette Hartley
A man launches an all-out attack on the world of computers.
MPAA:PG
Alfred Pariser; Maury Ravinsky — *Vestron Video*

In Cold Blood 1967
Drama
13257   133 mins   B/W   B, V   P
Robert Blake, Scott Wilson, John Forsythe, directed by Richard Brooks
Truman Capote's factual novel provided the basis for this hard-hitting film about two misfit ex-cons who murdered a Kansas family in 1959.
Columbia — *RCA/Columbia Pictures Home Video*

In Hot Pursuit 1982
Adventure
66297   90 mins   C   B, V   P
Bob Watson, Don Watson, Debbie Washington
Convicted for drug smuggling, two young men stage a daring escape from a southern prison.
James I West Jr — *Paragon Video Productions*

In-Laws, The 1979
Comedy
38949   103 mins   C   B, V   R, P
Peter Falk, Alan Arkin, directed by Arthur Hiller
A wild comedy with Peter Falk as a CIA agent and Alan Arkin as a dentist who becomes involved in Falk's crazy adventures.
MPAA:PG
Warner Bros — *Warner Home Video; RCA VideoDiscs*

In Love With An Older Woman 1982
Comedy/Romance
72455   100 mins   C   B, V   P
John Ritter, Karen Carlson
This movie shows the social difficulties that arise when a man dates an outgoing woman who is fifteen years his senior.
Poundridge Prods Ltd; Charles Fries Prods — *U.S.A. Home Video*

In Name Only 1939
Drama
10053   102 mins   B/W   B, V   P, T
Carole Lombard, Cary Grant, Kay Francis
Heartless woman marries for wealth and prestige and holds her husband to loveless marriage.

RKO; John Cromwell — *Blackhawk Films; RKO HomeVideo*

In Old Caliente 1939
Western
57980   60 mins   B/W   B, V   P
Roy Rogers
Roy Rogers battles the bad guys in the frontier town of Caliente.
Republic — *Video Connection*

In Old California 1942
Western
66312   89 mins   B/W   B, V   P
John Wayne, Patsy Kelly, Binnie Barnes, Albert Dekker
A young Boston pharmacist searches for success in the California gold rush.
Republic — *NTA Home Entertainment*

In Old Cheyenne 1941
Western
49175   60 mins   B/W   B, V, 3/4U   P
Roy Rogers, Gabby Hayes
Bank holdups, cattle rustling, fist fights, and even car crashes mix with some good ol' guitar plunking in this "modern day" western.
Republic — *Penguin Video; Cable Films*

In Old New Mexico 1945
Western
11264   60 mins   B/W   B, V   P
Duncan Renaldo, Martin Garralaga, Gwen Kenyon, Pedro de Cordoba
The Cisco Kid and Pancho reveal the murderer of an old woman—a mysterious doctor who was after an inheritance.
United Artists — *VCI Home Video; Video Yesteryear*

In Old Santa Fe 1934
Western
11785   60 mins   B/W   B, V   P
Ken Maynard
Action western starring Ken Maynard—veteran of the plains.
Mascot — *Video Connection; Discount Video Tapes; Video Yesteryear; Sheik Video*

In Person: Noel Paul Stookey 1979
Music-Performance/Religion
46829   33 mins   C   B, V, 3/4U,   P
                              Q
Noel Paul Stookey (Paul of "Peter, Paul and Mary") is featured in concert in this program with rich spiritual applications.
Quadrus Films — *TV Sports Scene*

In Praise of Older Women — 1978
Comedy
09096   110 mins   C   B, V, LV,   P
CED
Karen Black, Tom Berenger, Susan Strasberg, Helen Shaver
A Hungarian "boy," 12-years-old, is corrupted by World War II. Based on a novel by Stephen Vizinczey.
Astral Films; Astral Bellevue Pathe and RSL Prod — *Embassy Home Entertainment; RCA VideoDiscs*

In Search of Historic Jesus — 1979
Speculation/Religion
48476   91 mins   C   B, V   P
John Rubenstein, John Anderson, narrated by Brad Crandall
The story attempts to pull together a careful tabulation of data about Jesus Christ, who was hardly known to the historians of his time.
MPAA:PG
Schick Sunn Classic — *VCI Home Video*

In Search of Noah's Ark — 1976
Bible/Documentary
35373   95 mins   C   B, V   P
Narrated by Brad Crandell
This documentary covers research and information gathered during the last 5,000 years concerning the story of Noah and the universal flood.
Sunn Classic — *VCI Home Video*

In Search of the Castaways — 1962
Adventure
66318   98 mins   C   B, V   R, P
Hayley Mills, Maurice Chevalier, George Sanders, Wilfrid Hyde-White
A teenage girl and her younger brother search for their father, a ship's captain who was reportedly lost at sea years earlier. Based on a story by Jules Verne.
Buena Vista — *Walt Disney Home Video*

In the Days of the Thundering Herd — 1914
Western
64323   40 mins   B/W   B, V   P
Tom Mix, Bessie Eyton, directed by Tom Mix
Tom Mix and his horse, Tony, gallop off for high adventure in this early silent western. Musical score added.
Selig Polyscope — *Classic Video Cinema Collector's Club*

In the Heat of the Night — 1967
Drama
37525   109 mins   C   CED   P
Sidney Poitier, Rod Steiger, Warren Oates, Lee Grant, directed by Norman Jewison
A wealthy industrialist in a small Mississippi town is murdered. A black man is accused, but when it is discovered that he is a homicide expert, he is asked to help solve the murder, despite resentment of the part of the town's chief of police.
Academy Awards '67: Best Picture; Best Actor (Steiger); Best Screenplay; Best Film Editing; Best Sound.
United Artists, Walter Mirisch — *CBS/Fox Video; RCA VideoDiscs*

In Which We Serve — 1942
War-Drama
59833   114 mins   B/W   B, V   P
Noel Coward, John Mills, Bernard Miles, directed by Noel Coward
The spirit of the British Navy in World War II is captured in this classic about the sinking of the destroyer HMS Torrin during the Battle of Crete.
Noel Coward — *Embassy Home Entertainment*

Incoming Freshmen — 1979
Comedy
47851   84 mins   C   B, V   P
Ashley Vaughn, Leslie Blalock, Richard Harriman, Jim Overbey
A young innocent girl discovers sex when she enrolls in a liberal co-ed institution.
MPAA:R
Cannon Films — *MCA Home Video*

Incredible Hulk, The — 1977
Adventure/Science fiction
58631   100 mins   C   B, V   P
Bill Bixby, Susan Sullivan, Lou Ferrigno, Jack Colvin
A scientist achieves superhuman strength after he is exposed to a massive dose of gamma rays. The pilot for the television series.
Universal TV — *MCA Home Video*

Incredible Journey, The — 1963
Adventure/Animals
72795   80 mins   C   B, V   P
A labrador retriever, bull terrier and Siamese cat mistake their caretakers intentions when he leaves for a hunting trip, believing he will never return. The three set out on a 250 mile adventure-filled trek across Canada's rugged terrain.
Walt Disney Productions; Buena Vista — *Walt Disney Home Video*

Incredible Master Beggars — 1982
Martial arts
64945   88 mins   C   B, V   R, P
Tan Tao Liang, Ku Feng, Han Kuo Tsai, Li Tang Ming, Li Hai Sheng, Lui I Fan, Pan Yao Kun

Against all odds, the Beggars challenge the Great Iron Master, using "Tam Leg" tactics versus the "Iron Cloth" fighting style.
MPAA:R
L and T Films Corp Ltd — *Video Gems*

Incredible Rocky Mountain Race, The   1977
Adventure/Comedy
65761   97 mins   C   B, V   P
Christopher Connelly, Forrest Tucker, Larry Storch, Mike Mazurki
The townspeople of St. Joseph, fed up with Mark Twain's destructive feud with a neighbor, devise a shrewd scheme to rid the town of the troublemakers.
Robert Stabler — *VCI Home Video*

Incredible Shrinking Woman, The   1981
Comedy
55548   88 mins   C   B, V, LV   P
Lily Tomlin, Charles Grodin, Ned Beatty, Henry Gibson
A model homemaker and perfect mother and wife discovers that she is shrinking due to a unique blood condition that is effected by the chemicals found in her household products.
MPAA:PG
Universal; Hank Moonjean — *MCA Home Video*

Incubus, The   1982
Horror
63969   90 mins   C   B, V, LV, CED   P
John Cassavetes, Kerrie Keane, Helen Hughes, Erin Flannery, John Ireland
A doctor and his teenaged daughter settle in a quiet New England community, only to encounter the incubus, a terrifying, supernatural demon.
MPAA:R
Artists Releasing Corp; Mark Boyman — *Vestron Video*

Independence Day   1983
Drama
68234   110 mins   C   B, V   R, P
Kathleen Quinlan, David Keith
Kathleen Quinlan stars as a small town photographer who falls in love with a racing car enthusiast.
MPAA:R
Warner Brothers — *Warner Home Video*

Indian Cooking   1982
Cookery
47356   30 mins   C   V   P
Recipes for preparing Indian dishes such as curry are demonstrated and explained.

American Home Video Library — *American Home Video Library*

Indiscreet   1931
Comedy
58528   81 mins   B/W   B, V, 3/4U   P
Gloria Swanson, Ben Lyon, Barbara Kent, directed by Leo McCarey
A fashion designer's past catches up with her when her ex-lover starts romancing her sister. Gloria sings "If You Haven't Got Love" and other songs.
United Artists; Artcinema — *Penguin Video; Festival Films; Classic Video Cinema Collector's Club*

Indiscreet   1958
Comedy
66464   100 mins   C   B, V   P
Cary Grant, Ingrid Bergman, Phyllis Calvert, directed by Stanley Donen
An American diplomat in London falls in love with an actress but protects himself by saying he is married.
Grandon; Stanley Donen — *NTA Home Entertainment*

Indiscretion of an American Wife   1954
Romance
65410   63 mins   C   B, V   P
Jennifer Jones, Montgomery Clift
Set almost entirely in Rome's famous Terminal Station, the romance centers arount an ill-fated couple facing a turning point in their lives. They have only hours to decide whether they can have a future together, or whether Jones will go back to the United States and rejoin her husband.
Columbia — *CBS/Fox Video*

Infamous Crimes   1947
Mystery
08770   64 mins   B/W   B, V, 3/4U   P
William Wright, Terry Austin, Leon Belasko, directed by William Beaudine
Philo Vance investigates the murder of a playboy and his singer fiancee.
Producers Releasing Corp — *Penguin Video*

Infierno de los Pobres, El   197?
Drama
63856   98 mins   B/W   B, V   P
Rosa Camina, Jorge Mondragon, directed by Juan Orol
An abandoned woman creates a world of false illusions. In Spanish.
SP
Mexican — *Budget Video*

Informer, The　1935
Drama
00262　91 mins　B/W　B, V, 3/4U　P
Victor McLaglen, directed by John Ford
Tells of a hard-drinking man who informs on a buddy to collect a reward during the Irish Rebellion.
Academy Award '35: Best Actor (McLaglen); N.Y. Film Critics '35: Best Film amd Director.
RKO; John Ford — *Nostalgia Merchant; King of Video*

Inherit the Wind　1960
Drama
64562　127 mins　B/W　B, V, CED　P
Spencer Tracy, Fredric March, Florence Eldridge, Gene Kelly, Dick York, directed by Stanley Kramer
A courtroom drama based on the 1925 Scopes "Monkey Trial," where a schoolteacher was indicted for teaching Darwin's Theory of Evolution to his students.
United Artists; Stanley Kramer — *CBS/Fox Video; RCA VideoDiscs*

Inheritance, The　1947
Suspense
66383　103 mins　B/W　B, V　P
Jean Simmons, Katina Paxinou, Derrick de Marney, Derek Bond
The guardian of a young heiress plots to murder his mistress for her inheritance. Original title: "Uncle Silas."
Two Cities — *Movie Buff Video*

Inheritance, The　1976
Drama
52953　121 mins　C　B, V　P
Anthony Quinn, Fabio Testi, Dominique Sanda
A poor woman who hungers for fortune marries into a wealthy family. After becoming the sole heiress, the family unites against her.
MPAA:R
Titanus; Gianni Hecht Lucari — *VidAmerica*

Inn of the Sixth Happiness, The　1958
Drama
66068　158 mins　C　B, V, CED　P
Ingrid Bergman, Curt Jurgens, Robert Donat
The life of Gladys Aylward, an English servant girl who becomes a missionary in 1930's China, provides the basis of this story.
20th Century Fox — *CBS/Fox Video*

Inner Circle I　1980
Psychology/Identity
55040　59 mins　C　B, V　P
A collection of four short films which enhance awareness about the tough inner struggles people face in life: "To Be Aware of Death," "To Be Alone," "To Be Afraid," and "To Be Continued."
Billy Budd Films — *Vanguard Video*

Inner Circle II　1980
Identity/Identity
55041　63 mins　C　B, V　P
Four films enhance awareness about the inner struggles people face in life: "To Be True to Yourself," "To Be Creative," "To Be the Most You Can Be" and "To Be Assertive."
Billy Budd Films — *Vanguard Video*

Innocent, The　1978
Drama
39077　115 mins　C　B, V, CED　P
Laura Antonelli, Jennifer O'Neill, Giancarlo Giannini, directed by Luchino Visconti
Visconti's last film is the story of a husband who is drawn between the love of his faithful wife and his mistress, in turn-of-the-century Rome. Filmed on location in Italy; English language version.
MPAA:R
Italy — *Vestron Video*

Inside Moves　1980
Drama
55457　113 mins　C　B, V　P
Jon Savage, Diana Scarwid, David Morse, directed by Richard Donner
A look at handicapped citizens trying to make it in everyday life, focusing on the relationship between an insecure, failed suicide and a volatile man who is only a knee operation away from a dreamed-about basketball career.
MPAA:PG
Goodmark Productions — *CBS/Fox Video*

Inside Russia with an American Cameraman　1941
USSR
72515　75 mins　B/W　B, V, 3/4U　P
An overview of Russia before World War II reproduced from original source material. English narration.
Imperial Pictures — *International Historic Films*

Inside the Lines　1930
Drama
66136　73 mins　B/W　B, V, FO　P
Betty Compson, Montagu Love, Mischa Auer, Ralph Forbes
A World War I tale of espionage and counter-espionage.
RKO — *Video Yesteryear*

Inspector Gaget, Volume 1　1984
Cartoons
74079　90 mins　C　B, V　P
Animated, the voice of Don Adams
Comedian Don Adams lends his voice to the impeccable Inspector Gaget who along with his

trusted companions, Penny and Brain, go up against the evil Dr. Claw.
Dic Enterprises — *Family Home Entertainment*

Inspector General, The   1949
Comedy
59663   97 mins   C   B, V   P
Danny Kaye, Walter Slezak, Barbara Bates, Elsa Lanchester
A classic Danny Kaye vehicle of mistaken identities with the master comic portraying a carnival medicine man who is mistaken by the villagers for their feared Inspector General.
Warner Bros — *Media Home Entertainment; Budget Video; Video Yesteryear; Sheik Video; Cable Films; Discount Video Tapes; King of Video; Video Connection*

Intermezzo   1939
Drama/Romance
69385   70 mins   B/W   B, V, CED   P
Ingrid Bergman, Leslie Howard
A married violinist falls in love with his protege, but while on a concert tour of Europe together, his longing for the family he left behind overshadows their happiness.
Selznick — *CBS/Fox Video*

International Crime   1937
Mystery
73550   72 mins   B/W   B, V   P
Rod La Rogue
This film is an adventure of the Radio hero The Shadow as he solves another touch crime.
Grand National — *Admit One Video*

International Velvet   1978
Drama
66452   126 mins   C   B, V   P
Tatum O'Neal, Anthony Hopkins, Christopher Plummer
In this sequel to "National Velvet," a young orphan overcomes all obstacles and becomes an internationally renowned horsewoman.
MPAA:PG
Unknown — *MGM/UA Home Video*

Intimate Moments   1982
Drama
66044   82 mins   C   B, V   P
Alexandra Stewart, Dirke Altevogt
Madame Claude runs an exclusive call-girl operation catering to the upper echelons of power in France, when she discovers that a newspaper is investigating her business.
MPAA:R
Claire Duval — *Embassy Home Entertainment*

Intolerance   1916
Film-History
33548   120 mins   B/W   B, V   P
Lillian Gish, Mae Marsh, Constance Talmadge, Bessie Love, Elmer Clifton, directed by D.W. Griffith
D. W. Griffith's most expansive effort, which contains four separate stories detailing mankind's intolerance through the centuries. Original color-tinted and toned print, with music score.
D W Griffith — *Glenn Video Vistas; Video Yesteryear; Budget Video; Sheik Video; Penguin Video; Blackhawk Films; Discount Video Tapes; Western Film & Video Inc*

Introduction to Casino Gaming   1982
Gambling
62739   50 mins   C   B, V   P
This instructional cassette covers casino rules with an in-depth look at baccarat, blackjack, roulette and craps.
Casino Gaming Instruction — *Marketvisions*

Introduction to Computers   1983
Electronic data processing
72969   20 mins   C   B, V   P
A history of computers and a trip through the main components of a computer are explained on this program.
Star Merchants — *Increase Video*

Introduction to Computers for Children   1984
Electronic data processing
72967   35 mins   C   B, V   P
Complicated phrases and terminology dealing with computers are simplified for children in this program.
Star Merchants — *Increase Video*

Invaders from Mars   1953
Science fiction
37400   78 mins   C   B, V   P
Helena Carter, Arthur Franz, Jimmy Hunt, Leif Erickson, directed by William Cameron Menzies
A twelve-year-old boy witnesses the landing of a strange spacecraft, and he and his father set out to investigate. The father becomes possessed by alien entities who threaten to overtake the entire world. Includes previews of coming attractions from classic science fiction films.
20th Century Fox — *Nostalgia Merchant*

Invasion of the Body Snatchers   1956
Science fiction
55472   80 mins   B/W   B, V   P
Kevin McCarthy, Dana Wynter, Carolyn Jones, King Donovan, directed by Don Siegel
The classic about the invasion of Southern California by seeds of giant plant pods which

---

exude blank human forms that drain the emotional life of people and threaten to destroy the world.
Walter Wanger; Allied Artists — *NTA Home Entertainment; RCA VideoDiscs*

Invasion of the Body Snatchers   1978
Science fiction/Horror
66451   115 mins   C   B, V, CED   P
Donald Sutherland, Brooke Adams, Veronica Cartwright, Leonard Nimoy, Jeff Goldblum, Kevin McCarthy, Don Siegel
A remake of the 1956 sci-fi classic—this time, the "pod people" are infesting San Francisco, with only a small group of people aware of the invasion. Beta Hi-Fi and VHS stereo.
MPAA:PG
United Artists — *MGM/UA Home Video*

Invasion of the Body Stealers   1983
Science fiction
75462   93 mins   C   B, V   P
Beings from another planet are stealing earthlings to revitalize their civilization.
King Features — *U.S.A. Home Video*

Invincible from Hell, The   1981
Martial arts
69280   80 mins   C   B, V   P
Master Lee, Johnny Kin, Robert Ann, Linda Han
Japanese gangsters terrorize a small town near Shanghai until one man gets the townspeople to fight back. Mandarin dialogue, English subtitles.
CH
IFD Films & Arts — *Silverline Video*

Invincible Mr. Disraeli, The   1963
Drama
64850   76 mins   C   B, V, 3/4U   P
Trevor Howard, Greer Garson, Hurd Hatfield, Kate Reid, directed by George Schaefer
This presentation from "George Schaefer's Showcase Theatre" deals with the life and career of Benjamin Disraeli, novelist, philosopher, first Earl of Beaconsfield, statesman, and Prime Minister.
Emmy awards '63: Outstanding Single Performance/Actor (Howard); Outstanding Achievement/Electronic Camera Work.
George Schaefer — *Enter-Tel Inc*

Invincible, The   1980
Adventure/Martial arts
56927   93 mins   C   B, V   R, P
Bruce Li, Chen Sing, Ho Chung Dao
A martial arts student must find and correct another student who has turned bad.
MPAA:R
Fourseas Films — *Video Gems*

Invisible Ghost, The   1941
Horror
05520   70 mins   B/W   B, V, 3/4U   R, P
Bela Lugosi, Polly Ann Young
A man carries out a series of grisly stranglings while under hypnosis by his insane wife.
Monogram — *Movie Buff Video; Sheik Video; Ampro Video Productions; Cable Films; Video Yesteryear; Discount Video Tapes*

Invisible Ghost, The/The Human Monster   194?
Horror
58910   134 mins   B/W   B, V   P
Bela Lugosi, Polly Ann Young, Hugh Williams, Greta Gynt
A Bela Lugosi double feature: "The Invisible Ghost" (1941), in which a man, hypnotized by his insane wife, commits several bloodthirsty murders; "The Human Monster," (1939), based on Edgar Wallace's thriller "The Dark Eyes of London."
NTSC, PAL
Monogram — *Ampro Video Productions*

Invitation au Voyage   1983
Drama
65317   ? mins   C   B, V   P
Laurent Malet, Nina Scott, Aurore Clement, Mario Adorf
This program follows the journey of a twin who refuses to accept the death of his sister, a rock singer. Subtitled in English.
MPAA:R
Claude Nedjar — *RCA/Columbia Pictures Home Video*

Invitation to a Gunfighter   1964
Drama
65498   92 mins   C   CED   P
Yul Brynner, George Segal, Janice Rule, Pat Hingle
A small-town tyrant hires a smooth gunfighter to keep down the farmers he has cheated.
United Artists — *CBS/Fox Video*

Invitation to Paris   1960
Variety/France
58652   51 mins   B/W   B, V, FO   P
Maurice Chevalier, Les Djinns, Patachou, Fernandel, Les Compagnons de La Chanson, Jean Sablon, George Ulmer, Line Renaud
A French musical revue, set in the streets of Paris, which features the girls of the French Can-Can revue.
A Parisian — *Video Yesteryear*

Invitation to the Dance   1957
Musical
60400   93 mins   C   B, V, CED   P
Gene Kelly, Igor Youskevitch, Tomara Toumanova

Three classic dance sequences, "Circus,"
"Ring Around the Rosy" and "Sinbad the
Sailor," based on music by Rimsky-Korsakov.
MGM; Arthur Freed — *MGM/UA Home Video*

**Invitation to the Japan
Cup**   1980
Horse racing
69653   26 mins   C   B, V   P
Highlights of the 1980 Japan Cup are
presented.
Japan Racing Association — *Mercedes
Maharis Productions*

Iphigenia   1979
Drama
60343   100 mins   C   B, V   P
*Irene Papas, Costa Kazakos, Tatiana
Papamoskou*
Based on the classic Greek tragedy by
Euripides, this story concerns the Greek leader,
Agamemnon, and his lovely daughter, Iphigenia.
Almi Cinema 5 Film — *RCA/Columbia Pictures
Home Video*

IRA   1984
Personal finance
69672   60 mins   C   B, V   P
This program explains why an IRA (individual
retirement account) investment is wise at any
age and how it helps the individual build a
financial nest egg for retirement years.
Independent — *Independent United
Distributors*

Irishman, The   1978
Drama
65477   90 mins   C   B, V   P
Bryan Brown
The tale of a proud North Queensland family
and their struggles to stay together.
Anthony Buckley — *Vestron Video*

Irma La Douce   1963
Comedy
58843   146 mins   C   CED   P
*Jack Lemmon, Shirley MacLaine, Herschel
Bernardi, directed by Billy Wilder*
A gendarme pulls a one-man raid on a back-
street Parisian joint and falls in love with one of
the ladies he arrests.
EL, SP
United Artists — *CBS/Fox Video*

Iron Duke, The   1934
Drama/Biographical
47789   88 mins   B/W   B, V, 3/4U   P
George Arliss, Gladys Cooper
An historical account of the life of the Duke of
Wellington.
Gaumont; British — *Western Film & Video Inc*

Iron Horse, The   1924
Western
64324   111 mins   B/W   B, V   P
*George O'Brien, Madge Bellamy, directed by
John Ford*
A workman on the first transcontinental railroad
seeks to avenge his father's murder. Silent with
musical score.
Fox Film Corp — *Classic Video Cinema
Collector's Club*

**Iron Horses at
Promontory**   197?
Trains
68907   10 mins   C   B, V   P
A look at beautiful locomotives.
Unknown — *Interurban Films*

Iron Maiden   1983
Music-Performance
75903   18 mins   C   B, V   P
This program presents the heavy metal group
Iron Maiden performing songs such as "Run to
the Hills," "The Trooper" and "Flight of Icarus."
EMI Records Ltd — *Sony Corporation of
America*

Iron Mask, The   1929
Adventure
08729   87 mins   B/W   B, V, 3/4U   P
*Douglas Fairbanks, Sr., Nigel de Brulier,
Marguerite de la Motte, directed by Allan Dwan*
Based on Alexandre Dumas' "Three
Musketeers" and "The Man in the Iron Mask',
the fearless d'Artagnan rights the wrongs in
France. (Part talkie.)
United Artists — *Penguin Video; Blackhawk
Films; Cable Films; Discount Video Tapes;
Classic Video Cinema Collector's Club*

Isabel's Choice   1981
Drama/Romance
75456   96 mins   C   B, V   P
Jean Stapleton, Richard Kiley, Peter Coyote
A middle-aged executive secretary must choose
between romance and success.
King Features — *U.S.A. Home Video*

**Isla Encantada, La
(Enchanted Island)**   1984
Drama
72962   90 mins   C   B, V   P
The new adventures of Robinson Crusoe and
Man Friday, as they pursue wild beasts and
cannibals and fight off pirates.
Foreign — *Unicorn Video*

Island, The   1961
Drama
53724   96 mins   B/W   B, V, 3/4U   P
Directed by Kaneto Shindo

One of Japan's best directors turns his talents to the existence of a family, the sole inhabitants of a small island. No dialogue.
Japan — *International Historic Films; Video Yesteryear; Penguin Video; Budget Video; Discount Video Tapes*

Island, The 1980
Adventure
48633   113 mins   C   B, V   P
A New York reporter embarks on a Bermuda triangle investigation, only to meet with the murderous descendants of seventeenth-century pirates on a deserted island.
MPAA:R
Universal, Richard D Zanuck, David Brown — *MCA Home Video*

Island, The 1981
Motorcycles
66246   43 mins   C   B, V   P
The story of the 1980 Isle of Man TT Races.
CH Wood — *Motor Cycle Video*

Island at the Top of the World, The 1974
Adventure
63191   89 mins   C   B, V   R, P
David Hartman, Donald Sinden, Jacques Marin, Mako, David Gwillim
A rich Englishman, an American archeologist, a French aeronaut and an Eskimo guide travel to the Arctic in 1908 aboard the airship Hyperion on a rescue mission.
Walt Disney Productions — *Walt Disney Home Video*

Island Highlights 1984
Motorcycles
72854   45 mins   C   B, V   P
Highlights from the 1978 Isle of Man Motorcycle race are shown.
Halamar Video — *Motor Cycle Video*

Island Magic 1981
Sports-Water
52769   72 mins   C   B, V   P
This program, shot on location in Hawaii, takes you through a dramatic tour of all of Hawaii's best surfing spots.
John Hitchcock — *Karl Video*

Island of Adventure 1981
Adventure
72887   85 mins   C   B, V   P
Four children explore an island and find a gang of criminals inhabitating it.
Unknown — *Embassy Home Entertainment*

Island of Dr. Moreau, The 1977
Science fiction
53514   98 mins   C   B, V   R, P
Burt Lancaster, Michael York, Barbara Carrera, Richard Basehart
The story of a scientist who has isolated himself on a Pacific island in order to continue his chromosome research, which has developed to the point where he can transform animals into semi-humans. Based on the H. G. Wells novel.
MPAA:PG
American International Pictures — *Warner Home Video; Vestron Video (disc only)*

Island of Nevawuz, The 1980
Fantasy
65708   50 mins   C   B, V   P
A beautiful island is in trouble when J.B. Trumphorn decides to make lots of money by building factories and refineries on it. Will the Island of Nevawuz end up a polluted mess?
Paul Williams — *Embassy Home Entertainment*

Islands in the Stream 1977
Drama
38609   110 mins   C   B, V   R, P
George C. Scott, David Hemmings, Claire Bloom, Susan Tyrrell
Ernest Hemingway's last novel provides the basis for this story of an American artist living with his sons on the island of Bimini shortly before the outbreak of World War II.
MPAA:PG
Paramount — *Paramount Home Video*

Israel—The Pressure Cooker 197?
Middle East
19418   60 mins   C   B, V, 3/4U, Q   P
Prime Minister Begin, Eli Rubinstein, hosted by George Otis.
A news documentary featuring interviews and discussion between top Israeli officials.
TV Sports Scene — *TV Sports Scene*

It 1927
Drama
54109   71 mins   B/W   B, V   P, T
Clara Bow, Gary Cooper, Antonio Moreno
To have "It" the possessor must have that strange magnetism which attracts both sexes. A female department store worker is out to land the store owner but isn't doing well, until she goes on his yachting trip and with "It" wins her man.
Unknown — *Blackhawk Films*

It Came from Hollywood 1982
Documentary/Science fiction
64502   87 mins   C   B, V, LV   R, P

          (For Explanation of codes, see USE GUIDE and KEY)

Narrated by Dan Aykroyd, Cheech and Chong, John Candy and Gilda Radner
A compilation of scenes from "B" horror and science fiction films of the 1950's, highlighting the funny side of these classic schlocky movies. Some sequences are in black and white. MPAA:PG
Paramount — *Paramount Home Video; RCA VideoDiscs*

It Don't Come Easy: 1978 New York Yankees — 1978
Baseball
33846   45 mins   C   B, V   P
New York Yankees
Highlights of the turbulent but terrific season which saw manager Billy Martin fired and replaced by Bob Lemon is mid-season. The Yankees fell to fourteen games behind the Boston Red Sox in July, only to respond with the most memorable comeback in baseball history. They beat the Red Sox in a one-game playoff, whipped the Kansas City Royals in four games, then quickly dropped two games to the Los Angeles Dodgers in the World Series before sweeping the next four games and capturing their second straight title. Thurman Munson, Reggie Jackson, Bucky Dent and others led the way.
Major League Baseball — *Major League Baseball Productions*

It Happened in New Orleans — 1936
Musical-Drama
11240   86 mins   B/W   B, V, FO   P
Bobby Breen, Mae Robson, Alan Mowbray, Benita Hume
A charming portrayal of levee life in post-Civil War New Orleans.
RKO — *Video Yesteryear; Sheik Video*

It Should Happen to You — 1953
Comedy
65700   87 mins   B/W   B, V   P
Judy Holliday, Jack Lemmon, Peter Lawford
An aspiring model, unable to find steady work, rents a large billboard in New York to attract attention. In Beta Hi-Fi.
Fred Kohlmar — *RCA/Columbia Pictures Home Video*

Italian Finale — 1983
Motorcycles
72855   45 mins   C   B, V   P
The final round of the 1983 Motorcycle World Championship in Imola, Italy is highlighted.
Videovision Broadcast Production — *Motor Cycle Video*

Italian Straw Hat, The — 1927
Romance
48748   72 mins   B/W   B, V   P

Directed by Rene Clair
A Mack Sennett-styled chase farce in which a straw hat must be replaced to save a woman's virtue. Silent with English subtitles and musical score.
French — *Sheik Video; Video Yesteryear*

It's a Big Job — 197?
Trains
68900   22 mins   C   B, V   P
Los Angeles Transit Lines made this film to impress on its operators the meaning of the company's slogan, "Safety—Courtesy—Service."
Los Angeles Transit — *Interurban Films*

It's a Joke Son — 1947
Comedy
08580   60 mins   B/W   B, V, 3/4U   P
June Lockhart, Una Merkel, Kenny Delmar, directed by Ben Stoloff
A comedy featuring more antics of the famous Senator Claghorn—a regular on the Fred Allen radio show.
Producers Releasing Corp — *Penguin Video*

It's a Mad, Mad, Mad, Mad World — 1963
Comedy
47145   192 mins   C   B, V, CED   P
Spencer Tracy, Sid Caesar, Milton Berle, Ethel Merman, Jonathan Winters, Jimmy Durante, Buddy Hackett, Mickey Rooney, Phil Silvers, Dick Shawn, Edie Adams, Dorothy Provine, Buster Keaton?The Three Stooges?Jack Benny?Jerry Lewis?directed by Stanley Kramer
A motley collection of people are overcome with greed and take off in all manner of conveyances after a hidden stash of money. No shtick is overlooked along the way.
United Artists; Stanley Kramer — *CBS/Fox Video; RCA VideoDiscs*

It's a Wonderful Life — 1946
Drama
44796   125 mins   B/W   B, V, 3/4U   P
James Stewart, Donna Reed, Lionel Barrymore, directed by Frank Capra
A sentimental classic about a man who has worked hard all his life, but feels he is a failure and tries to commit suicide. A guardian angel comes to show him his mistake.
Liberty Films; RKO — *Nostalgia Merchant; NTA Home Entertainment; Media Home Entertainment; Select-a-Tape; Sheik Video; Cable Films; VCII; Video Connection; Video Yesteryear; Budget Video; Discount Video Tapes; Western Film & Video Inc; Cinema Concepts*

It's in the Bag — 1945
Comedy
44794   87 mins   B/W   B, V, 3/4U   P

(For Explanation of codes, see USE GUIDE and KEY)

Fred Allen, Jack Benny, William Bendix, Binnie Barnes, Robert Benchley, directed by Richard Wallace
A shiftless flea circus owner sells chairs he has inherited, not knowing that a fortune is hidden in one of them.
United Artists — Nostalgia Merchant

It's Love Again   1936
Musical
66192   83 mins   B/W   B, V, 3/4U   P
Jesse Matthews, Robert Young
A beloved stage couple fight like cats and dogs.
Gaumont — Penguin Video

It's Magic, Charlie Brown!   1981
Cartoons
75609   25 mins   C   B, V   P
Animated
Snoopy as "The Great Houdini" makes Charlie Brown disappear and can't make him reappear.
Lee Mendelson Bill Melendez Productions — Snoopy's Home Video Library

It's My Turn   1980
Comedy-Drama
52749   91 mins   C   B, V, LV   P
Jill Clayburgh, Michael Douglas, Charles Grodin, directed by Claudia Weill
A mathematics professor has her life upset when she falls in love with a retired baseball player, causing her to question her relationship with her live-in boyfriend.
MPAA:R
Rastar; Martin Elfand — RCA/Columbia Pictures Home Video

Itzhak Perlman   1982
Music-Performance
64208   45 mins   C   B, V   R, P
Itzhak Perlman, Carlo Maria Giulini and the Philharmonic Orchestra
Violinist Itzhak Perlman is featured in this performance of Beethoven's Concerto in D for Violin. In stereo.
EMI Music — THORN EMI Home Video; Pioneer Artists

Ivan the Terrible—Part I   1943
Drama
08702   96 mins   B/W   B, V, 3/4U   P
Nikolai Cherkasov, Ludmila Tselikovskaya, Serafina Birman, directed by Sergei Eisenstein
Ivan, Grand Duke of Russia, is crowned as the first Czar of Russia. His struggles to preserve his country are the main concerns of this first half of Eisenstein's masterwork. Russian dialogue with English subtitles.
Russian — Penguin Video; Budget Video; International Historic Films; Sheik Video; Video Yesteryear; Western Film & Video Inc; Discount Video Tapes

Ivan the Terrible—Part II   1946
Drama
08703   84 mins   B/W   B, V, 3/4U   P
Nikolai Cherkassov, Serafima Birman, Piotr Kadochnikev, directed by Sergei Eisenstein
The landed gentry of Russia conspire to dethrone Ivan in the second part of this classic epic. Russian dialogue with English subtitles; contains color sequences.
RU
Russian; Janus Films — Penguin Video; Budget Video; International Historic Films; Sheik Video; Video Yesteryear; Western Film & Video Inc; Discount Video Tapes

Ivanhoe   1953
Adventure
58706   106 mins   C   B, V   P
Robert Taylor, Elizabeth Taylor, Joan Fontaine, George Sanders
Sir Walter Scott's classic novel of chivalric romance and courtly intrigue among the knights of medieval England.
Film Daily Poll '53: Ten Best of Year.
MGM — MGM/UA Home Video

J

J. Geils Band   1984
Music-Performance
75904   16 mins   C   B, V   P
This program presents the J. Geils Band performing their hits "Freeze Frame," "Centerfold," "Love Stinks" and "Angel in Blue."
EMI Records — Sony Corporation of America

Jabberwalk   1979
Comedy
66237   110 mins   C   B, V   R, P
A "Mondo Cane" American-style. A reckless and funny view of the bizarre in U.S. life.
MPAA:R
Intl Talent; Romano Vanderbis — Video City Productions

Jabberwocky   1977
Comedy
63961   104 mins   C   B, V   P
Michael Palin, Max Wall, Deborah Fallender, directed by Terry Gilliam
Chaos prevails in the medieval cartoon kingdom of King Bruno the Questionable, who rules with cruelty, stupidity, lust and dust.
MPAA:PG
Almi-Cinema 5 — RCA/Columbia Pictures Home Video

Jacare   19??
Adventure
29678   72 mins   C   B, V   P
Frank Buck
Presents Frank Buck in the first feature filmed in
the wilds of the Amazon jungles.
Producers Releasing Corp — *Sheik Video*

Jack and the Beanstalk   1952
Comedy
11795   78 mins   C   B, V   P
Bud Abbott, Lou Costello, Buddy Baer
While baby-sitting, Lou falls asleep and dreams
he's Jack in the classic fairy tale.
Warner Bros — *VCI Home Video; Discount
Video Tapes*

Jack and the Beanstalk   1967
Cartoons/Fairy tales
47689   51 mins   C   B, V   P
Gene Kelly
Live action blends with animation in this telling
of the classic story about a boy and his magic
beans. Music by Sammy Cahn and Jimmy Van
Heusen.
Hanna Barbera — *Worldvision Home Video*

Jack and the Beanstalk   1976
Musical/Fairy tales
64578   80 mins   C   B, V   P
*Animated, written and directed by Peter J.
Solmo*
An animated musical version of the familiar
story of Jack, the young boy who climbs a magic
beanstalk up into the clouds, where he meets a
fearsome giant.
Sheridan View Properties
Associates — *RCA/Columbia Pictures Home
Video*

Jack and the Beanstalk   1983
Fairy tales
Closed Captioned
69325   60 mins   C   B, V, LV,   P
                               CED
*Dennis Christopher, Katherine Helmond, Elliot
Gould, Jean Stapleton*
From the "Faerie Tale Theatre," this is the
classic tale of Jack, who sells his family's cow
for 5 magic beans, then climbs the huge
beanstalk that sprouts from them and
encounters an unfriendly giant.
Shelly Duvall — *CBS/Fox Video*

Jack Benny   196?
Variety
59312   110 mins   B/W   B, V, 3/4U   P
*Jack Benny, Bob Hope, George Burns, Bing
Crosby, Walt Disney, Martin and Lewis, Elke
Sommer, The Beach Boys, Rochester, Don
Wilson*
Three complete Benny shows spanning the
period from 1953 to 1965. Sketches include a

spoof of Hope's "Road" movies, and a Mary
Poppins take-off.
CBS; NBC — *Shokus Video*

Jack Benny, II   1953
Comedy
66486   120 mins   B/W   B, V   P
*Jack Benny, Mary Livingston, Rochester, Don
Wilson, Kirk Douglas, Dick Powell, Humphrey
Bogart, Ronald Reagan*
This tape contains three 1953 episodes of "The
Jack Benny Show" plus Jack's dramatic
appearance on "The General Electric Theater."
Original commercials and network I.D.'s
included.
CBS — *Shokus Video*

Jack Benny Program, The   1959
Comedy
58641   30 mins   B/W   B, V, FO   P
Jack Benny, Ernie Kovacs, Don Wilson
Ernie shows Jack his collection of moustaches,
and Jack and Ernie play jailbirds in a prison of
the future as Killer Kovacs and Benny the
Louse. Sponsored by Lucky Strike.
CBS — *Video Yesteryear*

Jack Benny Program, The   1958
Comedy
65337   60 mins   B/W   B, V   P
Jack Benny, Don Wilson, Mel Blanc
Two shows, "The Christmas Show" and "The
Railroad Station," are shown in complete form
with Mr. Benny at his best.
J and M Productions — *MCA Home Video*

Jack Benny Show, The   1951
Comedy
58726   30 mins   B/W   B, V   P
Jack Benny, Bob Hope, Martin and Lewis
Bob Hope ad libs his way through the show, and
Martin and Lewis make a surprise appearance.
CBS — *Sheik Video*

Jack Benny Show, The   1958
Comedy
42976   25 mins   B/W   B, V, FO   P
Jack Benny, Dennis Day, Audrey Meadows
The cast does a parody of the "The
Honeymooners" with Dennis playing Ed Norton
and Jack playing Ralph Kramden (with the help
of a pillow under his shirt).
CBS — *Video Yesteryear*

Jack London Story   1943
Adventure
16074   93 mins   B/W   B, V   P
*Michael O'Shea, Susan Hayward, Virginia Mayo,
Frank Craven*
Biographical treatment of the famous author's
life.

(For Explanation of codes, see USE GUIDE and KEY)   **287**

United Artists; Samuel Bronston — *Movie Buff Video; Videobrary*

Jack Nicklaus Sports Clinic
1977

Golf
37418   18 mins   C   B, V   P
Jack Nicklaus
Golf pro Jack Nicklaus demonstrates proper golf techniques.
Sports Concepts — *CBS/Fox Video*

Jack the Ripper
1980

Drama
65379   82 mins   C   B, V   P
Klaus Kinski
The inimitable Kinski assumes the role of the most heinous criminal of modern history—Jack the Ripper.
MPAA:R
Cine Showcase — *Vestron Video*

Jackson County Jail
1976

Drama
51986   85 mins   C   B, V   R, P
Yvette Mimieux, Tommy Lee Jones, Robert Carradine
While driving cross-country a young woman is robbed, imprisoned, and raped by a deputy, whom she kills. Faced with a murder charge she flees, with the law in hot pursuit.
MPAA:R
New World Pictures — *Warner Home Video*

Jacob: The Man Who Fought with God
197?

Bible
35371   118 mins   C   B, V   P
Jacob's struggle to receive his father's blessing and inheritance rights is depicted, as well as his marriage to Rachel and the return of his brother Esau. From the "Bible" series.
Sunn Classic — *VCI Home Video*

Jacob Two—Two Meets the Hooded Fang
19??

Adventure
69611   90 mins   C   B, V   P
Alex Karras
Based on the children's book by Mordecai Richler, this is the story of a young boy who meets the dreaded Hooded Fang, warden of the prison "from which no brat returns."
MPAA:G
John Flaxman — *Children's Video Library*

Jacob's Challenge
1979

Drama/Bible
55018   50 mins   C   B, V   P
Barry Williams, Stephen Elliott, June Lockhart, Tanya Roberts, Bruce Fairbairn, Peter Fox, narrated by Victor Jory

The story of Jacob's deception, outwitting Esau for their father's blessing. Part of the "Greatest Heroes of the Bible" series.
Sunn Classics — *Vanguard Video*

Jailbait
1954

Drama
73545   80 mins   B/W   B, V   P
Lyle Talbot, Steve Reeves, directed by Ed Wood
This is one of Ed Wood's earlier films, about a group of small time crooks who are always in trouble with the law.
Howco Films — *Admit One Video*

Jailhouse Rock
1957

Musical-Drama
44643   96 mins   B/W   B, V, CED   P
Elvis Presley, Judy Tyler, Vaughn Taylor, Dean Jones, Mickey Shaughnessy, directed by Richard Thorpe
While in jail for manslaughter, a teenager learns to play the guitar. After his release, he slowly develops into a top recording star. Songs include "Jailhouse Rock," "Treat Me Nice," "Baby, I Don't Care" and "Young and Beautiful."
MGM — *MGM/UA Home Video*

Jamaica Inn
1939

Drama
58615   98 mins   B/W   B, V   P
Charles Laughton, Maureen O'Hara, Leslie Banks, Robert Newton, directed by Alfred Hitchcock
In old Cornwall, an orphan girl becomes involved with smugglers.
Paramount — *Movie Buff Video; Cable Films*

James Bond 007—Coming Attractions
197?

Adventure
38977   32 mins   C   B, V, FO   P
Sean Connery, Roger Moore, George Lazenby
A collection of promotional trailers from all ten James Bond films produced between 1962 and 1977, beginning with "Dr. No" and concluding with "The Spy Who Loved Me."
United Artists — *Video Yesteryear*

James Brown Live in Concert
1979

Music-Performance
56745   48 mins   C   B, V   P
James Brown
James Brown and his band perform such hits as "Boogie Wonderland," and "Georgia," and takes the audience through the best of jazz, rock, and blues fusion. Taped before a capacity audience at the Summer Festival in Toronto, Canada.

    (For Explanation of codes, see USE GUIDE and KEY)

Network Talent Intl — *Media Home Entertainment*

James Dean Story, The   1957
Drama/Biographical
65470   57 mins   B/W   B, V   P
An intimate portrait of James Dean presented by Robert Altman. The program includes never before seen outtakes from "East of Eden" and rare footage from the Hollywood premiere of "Giant" and the infamous Highway Public Safety message Dean made for television.
Warner Brothers — *Pacific Arts Video*

James Dean: The First American Teenager   1976
Biographical/Film-History
59861   83 mins   C   B, V   P
James Dean, Elizabeth Taylor, Sammy Davis Jr., Rock Hudson, Sal Mineo, Natalie Wood, Julie Harris, Jack Larson, Nicholas Ray
A look at the life and legend of the charismatic filmstar, with comments by those who knew him best and scenes from his films. (Some black and white footage.)
MPAA:PG
Ziv Intl; Goodtime Enterprises — *VidAmerica*

James Taylor in Concert   1979
Music-Performance
48861   90 mins   C   B, V, LV,   P
                                CED
James Taylor's first video concert features live performances of "Sweet Baby James," "Carolina on My Mind," "Steam Roller," "Whenever I See Your Smiling Face," "Up on the Roof," and "Handy Man."
CBS — *CBS/Fox Video*

Jane Fonda Challenge   1983
Physical fitness
Closed Captioned
65547   90 mins   C   B, V   P
Included in the offering are fast paced warm-up, exercise, balance and stretching sections, plus an exciting 20-minute choreographed aerobic routine that can be performed separately by those with too few hours in a day.
Karl Video; RCA — *Karl Video*

Jane Fonda's Workout   1982
Physical fitness
59073   90 mins   C   B, V   P
Jane Fonda
An exercise program designed for both beginners and intermediate exercise buffs.
Karl Video; RCA — *Karl Video; RCA VideoDiscs*

Jane Fonda's Workout for Pregnancy, Birth and Recovery   1983
Physical fitness/Pregnancy
65116   60 mins   C   B, V   P
Jane Fonda
Jane Fonda supervises a complete fitness program for pregnant women from conception to recovery.
Stuart Karl — *Karl Video; RCA VideoDiscs*

Japanese Connection   1982
Martial arts
64947   96 mins   C   B, V   R, P
Li Chao, Yang Wei, Wu Ming-Tsai
Warring crime chiefs fight furiously with deadly kung-fu action.
Foreign — *Video Gems*

Jason and the Argonauts   1963
Fantasy
44179   104 mins   C   B, V   P
Todd Armstrong, Nancy Kovack, Gary Raymond, Laurence Naismith, Michael Gwynn
Jason, son of King of Thessaly, sails on the Argo to the land of Colchis, where the Golden Fleece is guarded by a seven-headed hydra.
Columbia; Morningside; World Wide Productions — *RCA/Columbia Pictures Home Video; RCA VideoDiscs*

Jaws 3   1983
Suspense
69538   97 mins   C   B, V, LV,   P
                                CED
Dennis Quaid, Bess Armstrong, Louis Gossett Jr.
In a deluxe amusement park, a great white shark escapes from its tank and proceeds to cause terror and chaos.
MPAA:PG
Universal — *MCA Home Video*

Jaws   1975
Suspense
11590   124 mins   C   B, V, LV,   P
                                CED
Roy Scheider, Robert Shaw, Richard Dreyfuss, Lorraine Gary, directed by Steven Speilberg
A 25-foot long Great White Shark attacks and terrorizes residents of a Long Island beach town. Three men set out on a boat to kill it at any cost. Based on the novel by Peter Benchley.
MPAA:PG
Universal, Richard Zanuck — *MCA Home Video; RCA VideoDiscs*

Jaws II   1978
Suspense
11591   116 mins   C   B, V, CED   P
Roy Scheider, Lorraine Gary, Murray Hamilton, directed by Jeannot-Szwarc

---

(For Explanation of codes, see USE GUIDE and KEY)

The sequel to "Jaws". It's been four years since the maneating shark plagued the resort town of Amity. Suddenly a second shark stalks the waters and the terror returns.
MPAA:PG
Universal; Richard Zanuck; David Brown — *MCA Home Video*

Jaws of Death 1976
Adventure
66261   91 mins   C   B, V   P
Richard Jaeckel, Harold Sakata
A "Jaws"-like saga of shark terror.
Cannon Releasing — *Paragon Video Productions; Electric Video*

Jaws of the Dragon 1976
Adventure/Martial arts
51089   96 mins   C   B, V   R, P
James Nam, Johnny Taylor, Kenny Nam
The story of two rival gangs in the Far East.
MPAA:R
Robert Jeffery — *Video Gems*

Jazz and Jive 193?
Music
13645   60 mins   B/W   B, V   P, T
Duke Ellington, Major Bowes, Dewey Brown
Duke Ellington provides early jazz background in "Black and Tan," his first movie. Dance numbers accompany Dewey Brown in "Toot the Trumpet," followed by Major Bowes in "Radio Revels."
Paramount et al — *Blackhawk Films*

Jazz in America 1981
Music-Performance
60443   90 mins   C   B, V   P
Dizzy Gillespie, Max Roach, Gerry Mulligan, Pepper Adams, Candido
An historical tribute to bebop by way of two concerts performed at Lincoln Center by Dizzy Gillespie and his Dream Band.
Gary Keys — *Embassy Home Entertainment; RCA VideoDiscs*

Jazz in America 1981
Music-Performance
65423   60 mins   C   B, V   P
Gerry Mulligan, Billy Hart, Frank Luther, Harold Danko
With continuity and structure, this program shows contemporary jazz in an entertaining manner with "respect" for the music and performances.
Dick Reed; Paul Rosen — *Embassy Home Entertainment*

Jazz Singer, The 1980
Musical-Drama
53934   110 mins   C   B, V, LV   R, P
Neil Diamond, Laurence Olivier, Lucie Arnaz, Catlin Adams, Franklyn Ajaye, directed by Richard Fleischer
Another remake of the 1927 classic about a Jewish boy who rebels against his father and family tradition to become a popular entertainer.
MPAA:PG
Paramount; Jerry Leider — *Paramount Home Video; RCA VideoDiscs*

Jazz Singer, The 1927
Musical-Drama
55581   88 mins   B/W   CED   P
Al Jolson, Mary McAvoy, Warner Oland, William Demarest, directed by Alan Crosland
A Jewish cantor's son breaks with his family to become a singer of popular music. This film is of historical importance as the first successful part-talkie. Jolson's songs include "Toot Toot Tootsie," "Blue Skies," and "My Mammy."
Warner Bros; Vitaphone — *CBS/Fox Video*

Jazzercise 1982
Physical fitness
63166   60 mins   C   B, V   P
Judi Sheppard Missett
Total physical fitness is the goal of this "jazz dance" exercise program, designed for all ages and stages of health. VHS is in stereo, has the music programmed on one track and the instructions on the other. This tape is a completely different production from the disc of the same name.
Jazzercise/Feeling Fine Productions — *MCA Home Video*

Jazzercise 1982
Physical fitness
59132   ? mins   C   LV   P
Judi Sheppard Missett
An exercise program requiring total participation from the viewer, which allows the participant to proceed at his own pace. A one-sided interactive disc.
AM Available
Art Ulene — *Optical Programming Associates*

JD and the Salt Flat Kid 1978
Comedy
74085   90 mins   C   B, V   P
Singer JD tears up the road to Nashville with quick cars, speeding romance and fast times.
MPAA:PG
Jesse Turner; Tommy Amato — *Embassy Home Entertainment*

Jefferson Starship 1984
Music-Performance
76037   60 mins   C   B, V   P
Jefferson Starship delivers both recent hits, as well as some of their classic Jefferson Airplane numbers: "White Rabbit," "Somebody to Love," and "Winds of Change."

Norman Stangl; Ian McDougall — *RCA/Columbia Pictures Home Video*

Jekyll and Hyde...Together Again　1982
Comedy
64503　87 mins　C　B, V　R, P
Mark Blankfield, Bess Armstrong, Krista Errickson
A New Wave comic version of the classic story of Dr. Jekyll and Mr. Hyde, with a serious young surgeon who turns into a drug-crazed punk rocker after sniffing a mysterious powder.
MPAA:R
Paramount — *Paramount Home Video*

Jeremiah Johnson　1972
Drama/Adventure
58239　108 mins　C　B, V, LV　R, P
Robert Redford, Will Geer, directed by Sydney Pollack
The story of a man who turns his back on civilization, circa 1850, and learns a new code of survival in a brutal land of isolated mountains and hostile Indians.
MPAA:PG
Warner Bros; Sanford Productions — *Warner Home Video; RCA VideoDiscs*

Jericho　1937
Adventure
07162　77 mins　B/W　B, V　P
Paul Robeson, Henry Wilcoxon, Wallace Ford, directed by Thornton Freeland
Adventure in Africa as a court-martialed captain pursues a murderous deserter.
Britain — *Budget Video; Discount Video Tapes*

Jerk, The　1979
Comedy
42938　94 mins　C　B, V, LV　P
Steve Martin, Bernadette Peters, Catlin Adams directed by Carl Reiner
A jerk, not a bum, tells his rags-toriches-to-rags story in comedic flashbacks. Martin's ridiculous misadventures pay tribute to Jerry Lewis movies of the late sixties.
MPAA:R
David V Picker and William E McEuen — *MCA Home Video; RCA VideoDiscs*

Jerry Lewis Show, The　1967
Variety
42967　50 mins　C　B, V, FO　P
Jerry Lewis, Sonny and Cher, Baja Marimba Band
Jerry plays a bumbling oaf trying to make the swinging singles scene, while Sonny and Cher sing and the Baja Marimba Band plays.
NBC — *Video Yesteryear*

Jerry Lewis Show, The　1968
Variety
38992　50 mins　B/W　B, V, FO　P
Jerry Lewis, Helen Traubel, Lionel Hampton, Gary and Ronnie Lewis, Joey Faye
A program from Jerry Lewis' variety series, featuring some typical comedy routines from Jerry and musical performances by Gary Lewis, Helen Traubel, and Lionel Hampton.
NBC — *Video Yesteryear*

Jesse James at Bay　1941
Western
14223　54 mins　B/W　B, V　P
Roy Rogers, Gabby Hayes
Exciting saga of the notorious Jesse James and his fight against the railroads.
Republic — *Video Connection; Cable Films; Video Yesteryear; Discount Video Tapes; Nostalgia Merchant*

Jesse Owens Story, The　1984
Drama
75931　200 mins　C　B, V　R, P
Dorian Harewood, Debbi Morgan, George Stanford Brown, Le Var Burton
The moving story of the four-time Olympic Gold medal winner's triumphs and misfortunes.
Harold Gast — *Paramount Home Video*

Jesse Rae　1980
Music-Performance
75917　10 mins　C　B, V　P
This program presents the music of the award winning Scottish video artist Jesse Rae.
Scotland Video — *Sony Corporation of America*

Jesse Rae: Rusha/D.E.S.I.R.E.　1980
Music/Video
66159　13 mins　C　B, V　P
Music combines with video art in these two music concept pieces. In stereo.
Scotland Video — *Sony Corporation of America*

Jessi's Girls　1983
Drama
65450　86 mins　C　B, V　P
Sondra Currie, Regina Carrol, Jennifer Bishop
In retaliation for the murder of her husband, an angry young woman frees three female prisoners, and they embark on a bloody course of revenge. Together, they track down the killers, and one by one, they fight to even the score.
MPAA:R
Manson International — *Monterey Home Video*

(For Explanation of codes, see USE GUIDE and KEY)

Jesus 1979
Drama/Religion
47379   117 mins   C   B, V   R, P
Brian Deacon
The Biblical story of Jesus Christ is dramatized in this family-oriented film, which was made on location in the Holy Land.
MPAA:G
The Genesis Project — *Warner Home Video*

Jesus Christ Superstar 1973
Musical-Drama
11592   108 mins   C   B, V, LV   P
Ted Neeley, Carl Anderson, Yvonne Elliman, directed by Norman Jewison
A rock opera that portrays, in music, the last seven days in the life of Christ.
MPAA:G
Universal; Norman Jewison, Robert Stigwood — *MCA Home Video*

Jesus of Nazareth 1977
Drama/Biographical
48403   371 mins   C   B, V   P
Robert Powell, Anne Bancroft, Ernest Borgnine, Claudia Cardinale, James Mason, Laurence Olivier, Anthony Quinn
An all-star cast portrays the life of Jesus Christ.
ATV Ltd; RAI Productions — *CBS/Fox Video; RCA VideoDiscs*

Jethro Tull—Slipstream 1981
Music-Performance
58881   60 mins   C   B, V   P
Jethro Tull
This legendary English rock'n'roll group presents ten songs in this program conceived for video. Concert footage is combined with animation and special effects. The band members appear in a number of guises, with Ian Anderson adopting such roles as Aqualung and Dracula.
Chrysalis Records — *Chrysalis Visual Programming; RCA VideoDiscs; Pacific Arts Video*

Jezebel 1938
Drama
64456   104 mins   B/W   B, V, CED   P
Bette Davis, George Brent, Henry Fonda, Fay Bainter, directed by William Wyler
A willful Southern belle loses her boyfriend through her selfish and spiteful nature. When he becomes ill, she realizes her cruelty and rushes to nurse him back to health.
Academy Awards '38: Best Actress (Davis); Best Supporting Actress (Bainter).
Warner Bros — *CBS/Fox Video; RCA VideoDiscs*

J.F.K. 1964
Presidency-US/Documentary
69305   60 mins   B/W   B, V   P
Narrated by Cliff Robertson
This documentary chronicles the life and turbulent times of America's most beloved President.
Art Lieberman — *Media Home Entertainment*

Jig Saw 1978
Adventure
65302   97 mins   C   B, V   P
Angie Dickinson, Lino Ventura
A father searches for his "dead" son, repeatedly risking his own life to stop the criminals from completing the deadly task.
Les Films Ariane; Lafferty; Harwood and Partners Ltd — *U.S.A. Home Video*

Jill 1978
Death/Religion
46827   26 mins   C   B, V, 3/4U, Q   P
An evangelistic story of a young Christian girl who has terminal cancer.
Quadrus Films — *TV Sports Scene*

Jim Fixx on Running 1980
Running
55560   60 mins   C   B, V   P
The nation's most prominent authority on running discusses physical and psychological aspects of running, diet, clothes, measuring improvement, and other topics of interest to running enthusiasts.
Lee Bobker — *RCA/Columbia Pictures Home Video; MCA Home Video*

Jimi Hendrix at Rainbow Bridge 1971
Music-Performance
18882   60 mins   C   B, V   P
Jimi Hendrix
The one and only master of the electric guitar is seen in a live concert performance.
Antahkaram Productions — *Independent United Distributors*

Jimi Plays Berkeley 197?
Music-Performance
71292   55 mins   C   B, V   P
"Jimi Hendrix Live" views the musical intensity of this man at the peak of his career. Performances by Hendrix include "Purple Haze," "Hey Joe," and "Wild Thang."
Unknown — *HarmonyVision*

Jimi Plays Berkeley 1973
Music-Performance
72220   55 mins   C   B, V   P
The master guitarist Jimi Hendrix electrifies a Berkeley audience.
Independent — *Vestron Video*

   (For Explanation of codes, see USE GUIDE and KEY)

Jimmy the Kid　　　1982
Comedy
69676　95 mins　C　B, V　R, P
Gary Coleman, Ruth Gordon, Dee Wallace, Paul Le Mat, Don Adams
A young boy becomes the unlikely target for an improbable gang of would-be crooks on a crazy, "fool-proof" crime caper.
Zephyr Films — *THORN EMI Home Video*

Jinxed　　　1982
Comedy
64569　104 mins　C　B, V, CED　P
Bette Midler, Ken Wahl, Rip Torn, directed by Don Siegel
A Las Vegas nightclub singer tries to convince a gullible blackjack dealer to murder her crooked boyfriend, but the plan backfires when the gangster electrocutes himself while taking a shower.
MPAA:R
United Artists — *MGM/UA Home Video*

Jive Junction　　　1943
Musical
69559　62 mins　B/W　B, V, FO　P
Dickie Moore, Tina Thayer, Gerra Young
A group of patriotic teenagers convert a barn into a canteen for servicemen and name it "Jive Junction."
Producers Releasing Corp — *Video Yesteryear*

Jivin' in Bebop　　　1946
Music-Performance
57762　60 mins　B/W　B, V　P
Dizzy Gillespie and His Orchestra, Helen Humes, R Sneed
A compilation of all-black music from the 1940's, featuring singers and dancers of the period known as "jive."
WD Alexander — *Budget Video; Video Yesteryear*

Joan of Arc　　　1948
Drama
58736　100 mins　C　B, V　P
Ingrid Bergman, Jose Ferrer, John Ireland, Leif Ericson, directed by Victor Fleming
The life of Joan of Arc, based on the play by Maxwell Anderson.
Academy Awards '48: Best Cinematography, Color; Best Costume Design.
Sierra Pictures — *VidAmerica; MGM/UA Home Video (disc only)*

Joe　　　1970
Comedy-Drama
59305　107 mins　C　B, V　P
Peter Boyle, Susan Sarandon, Dennis Patrick, directed by John Avildsen
An odd friendship grows between a businessman and a blue-collar worker as they search together for the executive's runaway daughter. Thrust into the midst of the counter-culture, they react with an orgy of violence.
MPAA:R
Cannon; David Gil — *Vestron Video*

Joe Gibbs' Washington Redskins: Two Years to the Title　　　1983
Football
66217　45 mins　C　B, V, FO　P
Team highlight of the 1981-82 and 1982-83 seasons for the Washington Redskins
NFL Films — *NFL Films Video*

Joe Kidd　　　1972
Western
47421　88 mins　C　B, V　P
Clint Eastwood, Robert Duvall, John Saxon, Don Stroud, directed by John Sturges
A land war breaks out in New Mexico between Mexican natives and American land barons.
MPAA:PG
Universal — *MCA Home Video*

Joe Louis Story, The　　　1953
Biographical/Drama
66384　88 mins　B/W　B, V　P
Coley Wallace, Paul Stewart, Hilda Simms
The story of Joe Louis' rise to fame as Boxing's Heavyweight Champion of the world.
United Artists — *Movie Buff Video*

Joe Piscopo　　　1984
Comedy-Performance
73577　60 mins　C　B, V　P
Joe Piscopo, Eddie Murphy
Joe does some of his best impressions from Frank Sinatra to Jerry Lewis and some memorable improvisations from Saturday Night Live in this one hour special.
HBO — *Vestron Video*

Jog/Run　　　1978
Running
44924　30 mins　C　B, V　P
Ann Dugan demonstrates warm-up exercises for joggers to help them stay "loose" and strengthen leg, foot, and ankle muscles used for running. From the "Sports Conditioning" series.
Health N Action — *RCA/Columbia Pictures Home Video*

John Curry's Ice Dancing　　　1980
Dance
47380　75 mins　C　B, V　R, P
John Curry, Peggy Fleming, Jo-Jo Starbuck
This production combines the artistry of classical ballet with championship figure skating. Musical selections choreographed by John Curry, Peter Martins, Twyla Tharp and others.

WCI — *Warner Home Video; RCA VideoDiscs*

John F. Kennedy: Pursuit of Happiness   1956
Politics and government-US/Presidency-US
72505   20 mins   B/W   B, V, 3/4U   P
Senator John F. Kennedy narrates a history of the Democratic Party that begins with the administration of Thomas Jefferson and concludes with Harry Truman's. The film was originally produced for the 1956 Chicago Democratic Convention.
Democratic Party of the United States — *International Historic Films*

John Jay's Wonderful World of Skiing   1982
Sports-Winter
60509   30 mins   C   B, V, 3/4U,   P
Q
13   pgms
This series, filmed on location throughout the world, combines excitement, humor, and the breathtaking beauty of the world's finest snow-skiing experts. Programs are available individually.
1.New England Trails 2.Ski West 3.Ski New Zealand 4.The New States of Skiing 5.Ski High on Skis 6.Japanese Holiday 7.Ski Wild! 8.Japanese Holiday II 9.From Canada to Dixie 10.Australian Adventure 11.Ski Here and There 12.Ski the Alps 13.Search for Powder
John Jay — *TV Sports Scene*

John Lennon: Interview with a Legend   1981
Music/Interview
52671   60 mins   C   B, V   P
John Lennon, Tom Snyder
A television interview with John Lennon, made with Tom Snyder on the "Tomorrow Show," originally aired April 28, 1975. Lennon discusses what it was like to be a Beatle, how he dealt with worldwide popularity, the breakup of the group, and his life in New York during the post-Beatle era.
NBC — *Karl Video*

John McEnroe Story: The Rites of Passage, The   1981
Tennis
51750   90 mins   C   B, V   P
John McEnroe
This program documents the rise to stardom of John McEnroe, the brash youngster from New York, who most tennis experts reluctantly agree is the best tennis player on tour. His 1981 Wimbledon victory over Bjorn Borg is included, as are his classic matches with Jimmy Connors.
Michael Mattei — *Karl Video*

Johnny Angel   1945
Mystery
10064   79 mins   B/W   B, V   P, T
George Raft, Claire Tervor, Signe Hasso, Lowell Gilmore, Hoagy Carmichael
Merchant Marine captain unravels mystery of his father's murder.
RKO — *Blackhawk Films*

Johnny Belinda   1982
Drama
73533   95 mins   C   B, V   P
Rosanna Arquette, Richard Thomas, Dennis Quard, Candy Clark
A VISTA worker teaches a blind girl sign language and opens a whole new world for her. Available in Beta Hi-Fi and VHS stereo.
Dick Berg; Stonehenge Productions — *U.S.A. Home Video*

Johnny Carson   197?
Comedy
33698   60 mins   C   B, V, 3/4U   P
Johnny Carson, Don Rickles, Pearl Bailey, Joey Heatherton, Ed McMahon
Highlights of the fabulous career of "The Tonight Show," starring Johnny Carson. The program shows material not seen in "The Tonight Show" anniversary programs.
NBC — *Shokus Video*

Johnny Got His Gun   1971
Drama
59671   111 mins   C   B, V   P
Timothy Bottoms, Jason Robards, Donald Sutherland, Diane Varsi, Kathy Field
Dalton Trumbo's story of a young war victim who realizes that his arms and legs have been amputated.
MPAA:R
Bruce Campbell — *Media Home Entertainment*

Johnny Guitar   1953
Western
00298   110 mins   C   B, V   P
Joan Crawford, Ernest Borgnine, Sterling Hayden
Tough saloon owner finds her wealth can't buy everything—not even love.
Republic — *NTA Home Entertainment*

Johnny Jupiter   1953
Science fiction
72523   60 mins   B/W   B, V, 3/4U   P
One of the few shows that survived after the closing of the now defunct DuMont TV network, Johnny Jupiter featured puppets as the natives of Jupiter who are zeroed in on an interplanetary television set by a general store clerk.
DuMont — *International Historic Films*

   (For Explanation of codes, see USE GUIDE and KEY)

Johnny Mathis' Twenty-Fifth Anniversary Concert   1983
Music-Performance
72335   90 mins   C   B, V   P
Celebrated singer Johnny Mathis performs his hit songs to mark his 25th year in show business. Guest star Denise Williams joins Mathis.
Music America Live Productions — *Prism*

Johnny Tremain and the Sons of Liberty   1958
Adventure/Drama
66053   85 mins   C   B, V   R, P
Luanna Patten, Richard Beymer
The story of the gallant American patriots who participated in the Boston Tea Party.
Walt Disney Productions — *Walt Disney Home Video*

Johnny Winter Live   1984
Music-Performance
76643   45 mins   C   B, V   P
This program presents the best young, white blues artists of the '60's in a live concert appearance.
Concert Productions International — *Music Media*

Johnny Woodchuck's Adventures   1978
Cartoons
47862   60 mins   C   B, V   P
Animated
Little Johnny Woodchuck is more precocious than his well-behaved brothers. One day, he leaves home and family behind and sets out on an adventure. Available in both English and Spanish versions.
EL, SP
ZIV Intl — *Family Home Entertainment*

Jon Gnagy Learn to Draw I & II   1984
Drawing
72341   60 mins   C   B, V   P
2 pgms
Jon Gnagy's syndicated TV show has been credited with teaching many artists from every age group to draw over the last twenty years. In these videos ten subjects are used to teach the viewer to draw using step-by-step guidance. Each tape comes with a complete drawing kit.
1.Jon Gnagy Learn to Draw I 2.Jon Gnagy Learn to Draw II
AM Available
Bill Einhorn — *Best Film & Video Corporation*

Jonathan Livingston Seagull   1973
Fantasy
63431   114 mins   C   B, V   R, P
James Franciscus, Juliet Mills, Music by Neil Diamond
Based on the bestselling novella by Richard Bach, this film quietly envisions a world of love, understanding, achievement, hope and individuality.
Paramount — *Paramount Home Video*

Jonathan Winters Show, The   1957
Comedy/Variety
47475   29 mins   B/W   B, V, FO   P
Jonathan Winters, Jeri Southern, Betty Johnson, the Eddie Sefranski Orchestra
Two complete 15-minute shows from Jonathan Winters' first network TV series, featuring several impromptu sketches by the host about fishing and General Custer. Original commercials included.
NBC — *Video Yesteryear*

Joni Mitchell: Shadows and Light   1980
Music-Performance
53858   60 mins   C   B, V   P
Joni Mitchell
Singer/songwriter Joni Mitchell performs her unique blend of folk, jazz and rock 'n' roll music.
CFJ Enterprises — *Warner Home Video; Pioneer Artists; RCA VideoDiscs*

Joseph and His Brethren   1960
Drama
15595   103 mins   C   B, V   P
Geoffrey Horne, Robert Morley
A dramatization of the Biblical story of Joseph, whose jealous brothers sell him into slavery.
Colorama — *Vanguard Video*

Joseph and His Brothers   1979
Drama/Bible
55010   55 mins   C   B, V   P
Sam Bottoms, Walter Brooke, Harvey Jason, Bernie Kopell, Barry Nelson, Carol Rossen, Albert Salmi
The story of Joseph, sold into slavery by his jealous brothers. Part of the "Greatest Heroes of the Bible" series.
Sunn Classics — *Vanguard Video*

Joseph Andrews   1977
Drama
10987   98 mins   C   B, V   R, P
Ann-Margret, Peter Firth, Jim Dale, Michael Hordern, Beryl Reid, directed by Tony Richardson
This adaptation of a 1742 Henry Fielding novel chronicles the rise of Joseph Andrews from

servant to personal footman (and fancy) of Lady Booby.
MPAA:R
Paramount; Neil Hartley — *Paramount Home Video*

Josepha 1982
Drama
64909   114 mins   C   B, V   P
Miou-Miou, Claude Brasseur, Bruno Cremer
A husband and wife, both actors, are forced to re-examine their relationship when the wife finds a new love while on a film location. In French with English subtitles.
MPAA:R
Albina Productions-Mondex Films-TFl Films — *RCA/Columbia Pictures Home Video*

Josie and the Pussycats in Outer Space 197?
Cartoons
47690   58 mins   C   B, V   P
Animated
Three episodes of the all-girl rock group launching their music into the far corners of the galaxy.
Hanna Barbera — *Worldvision Home Video*

Jour Se Leve, Le 1939
Drama
08686   85 mins   B/W   B, V, 3/4U   P
Jean Gabin, Jules Berry, Arletty, directed by Marcel Carve
A distorted and maddening love affair causes a tormented man to commit murder. French with English subtitles.
FR
Sigma Prod — *Penguin Video; Budget Video; Sheik Video; Video Yesteryear*

Journey 1977
Adventure
45007   87 mins   C   B, V   P
Genevieve Bujold, John Vernon
A violent story of a girl who is rescued from the Sagueney River and falls in love with her rescuer. Choosing to remain in the remote pioneer community of this "hero," she brings everyone bad luck and misery.
MPAA:PG
First American Films — *VCI Home Video*

Journey Back to Oz 1980
Fantasy/Cartoons
65105   88 mins   C   B, V   P
Animated, voices of Liza Minnelli, Ethel Merman, Danny Thomas, Milton Berle, Mickey Rooney, Mel Blanc, Margaret Hamilton
Dorothy and Toto return to the magical land of Oz just in time to help Scarecrow, Lion and Tin Man fend off an invasion of magic green elephants created by the Wicked Witch Mombi.

Filmation Associates — *MGM/UA Home Video*

Journey Back to Oz 1971
Fantasy
69583   90 mins   C   B, V   P
Animated, voices of Liza Minnelli, Ethel Merman, Milton Berle, Mickey Rooney, Danny Thomas
This animated special features Dorothy and Toto returning to visit their friends in the magical land of Oz.
Filmation — *Family Home Entertainment*

Journey—Frontier and Beyond 1984
Music-Performance
72888   98 mins   C   B, V   P
Journey, narrated by John Facenda
A musical documentary showing Journey on tour and the bandmembers up close. Features their hits "Open Arms" and "Separate Ways."
Steve Sabol — *Music Media*

Journey—Frontiers and Beyond 1983
Music-Performance
76650   98 mins   C   B, V   P
Platinum rock group Journey is profiled on and behind the stage. Includes "Wheel in the Sky," "Stone in Love," "After the Fall" and "Escape."
Music Media — *Music Media*

Journey into Art, A 1982
Drawing
47358   42 mins   C   V   P
Knox Martin presents a complete course on creative drawing.
American Home Video Library — *American Home Video Library*

Journey Into Fear 1942
Suspense
64369   71 mins   B/W   B, V, 3/4U   P
Joseph Cotten, Dolores del Rio, Orson Welles, Agnes Moorehead, directed by Norman Foster and Orson Welles
An American armaments expert is smuggled out of Istanbul with Axis agents close behind who are determined to kill their enemy.
RKO — *Nostalgia Merchant*

Joy of Family 1981
Family
59915   100 mins   C   LV   P
Dr. Denis Waitley discusses love, teaching children responsibility, purpose in life and faith in oneself.
Inedco Productions — *INEDCO Productions*

          (For Explanation of codes, see USE GUIDE and KEY)

Joy of Relaxation, The   1983
Physical fitness
64548   ? mins   C   LV   P
This fully participative program is designed to
help people manage everyday tension. The
exercises are derived from clinically-tested
relaxation techniques such a yoga, breathing,
progressive relaxation, autogenics, visualization
and meditation. Questionnaires are included.
Feeling Fine Productions — *Optical
Programming Associates*

Joy of Stocks: The   1983
Forbes Guide to the
Stock Market, The
Finance
72463   104 mins   C   B, V   P
This introductory video to the stock market is
divided into ten instructional segments.
MGM UA — *MGM/UA Home Video*

Joy Sticks   1983
Comedy
65350   88 mins   C   B, V   P
Joe Don Baker
Something outrageously hilarious, very sexy and
thoroughly entertaining is going on at the local
video arcade!
MPAA:R
Greydon Clark — *Vestron Video*

Joyless Street   1925
Drama
48751   90 mins   B/W   B, V   P
Greta Garbo, directed by G. W. Pabst
A mid-twenties social criticism of Vienna. Silent
with subtitles and musical score.
UFA — *Sheik Video; Festival Films; Classic
Video Cinema Collector's Club*

Jubilee   1978
Musical/Drama
73149   103 mins   C   B, V   P
*Adam Ant, Toyah Willcox, Jenny Runacre, Little
Nell*
Adam Ant stars as a punk who takes over
Buckingham Palace and turns it into a recording
studio. Music by Eno, Adam and the Ants, and
Siouxsie and the Banshees.
Megalovision — *VCL Home Video*

Jubilee U.S.A.   1960
Music-Performance
47649   58 mins   B/W   B, V, FO   P
*Red Foley, Slim Wilson, Harold and Jimmy,
Betty Patterson, Buddy Childre, The
Harmonettes, The Pitch-Hikers, Bill Ring*
Two episodes of this variety/country and
western music show, complete with ABC's
promos for their western series ("Maverick,"
"Colt 45," "The Lawman").
ABC — *Video Yesteryear*

Judex   1964
Drama
06222   103 mins   B/W   B, V   P
*Channing Pollock, Francine Berge, directed by
Georges Franju*
Judex, a cloaked hero-avenger, fights master
criminal gangs. French film with English
subtitles.
FR
France; Italy — *Budget Video; Festival Films;
Penguin Video; Western Film & Video Inc;
Discount Video Tapes*

Judge Priest   1934
Comedy-Drama
08864   80 mins   B/W   B, V, 3/4U   P
Will Rogers
Comedy-drama set in the old South.
Fox Film Corp — *Penguin Video; Budget
Video; Discount Video Tapes; Cable Films;
Western Film & Video Inc; Classic Video
Cinema Collector's Club*

Judgement of Solomon,   1979
The
Drama/Bible
55014   37 mins   C   B, V   P
*John Carradine, Kevin Dobson, Tom Hallick,
Stephen Keats, Carol Lawrence, John Saxon*
The story of Solomon and his judgement
between two women who both claim to be the
mother of the same baby. Part of the "Greatest
Heroes of the Bible" series.
Sunn Classics — *Vanguard Video*

Judgment at Nuremburg   1961
Drama
69380   178 mins   B/W   B, V   P
*Spencer Tracy, Burt Lancaster, Marlene
Dietrich, Richard Widmark, Judy Garland,
Montgomery Clift, Maximilian Schell, directed by
Stanley Kramer*
This film centers on the post-WWII trial of four
Nazi officials accused of war crimes.
Academy Awards '61: Best Actor (Schell); Best
Screenplay.
United Artists; Stanley Kramer — *CBS/Fox
Video*

Judith of Bethulia   1913
Film-History
49076   44 mins   B/W   B, V   P
*Blanche Sweet, Henry B. Walthall, Lillian Gish,
Dorothy Gish, Lionel Barrymore, Mae Marsh,
directed by D.W. Griffith*
A Biblical spectacle which tells the story of a
Jew who kills the general in command of the
besieged Bethulia. Silent.
Biograph — *Sheik Video; Penguin Video*

Judy and Her Guests 1963
Music-Performance
15370   60 mins   B/W   B, V, FO   P
Judy Garland, Phil Silvers, Robert Goulet
Judy and her guests perform "I Happen to Like New York," "Get Happy," "Almost Like Being in Love," and other hits.
CBS — *Video Yesteryear*

Judy Garland Show, The 1964
Music-Performance
57172   55 mins   B/W   B, V   P
Judy Garland, the Bobby Cole Trio, Mort Lindsey Orchestra
Judy Garland is featured in a concert show from her television series, originally broadcast March 22, 1964. Songs include "Sail Away," "Comes Once in a Lifetime," "Joey, Joey," "Poor Butterfly" and "As Long as He Needs Me."
CBS — *King of Video; Electric Video*

Judy Garland Christmas 1963
Show
Variety
57173   50 mins   B/W   B, V   P
Judy Garland, Liza Minnelli, Lorna Luft, Joey Luft, Jack Jones, Mel Torme
A holiday special from Judy Garland's mid-sixties television series, featuring the whole gang joining in on Christmas standards. Songs include "Have Yourself a Merry Little Christmas," "Sleigh Ride," "Winter Wonderland," "The Christmas Song," "What Child Is This," "Over the Rainbow," and others.
CBS — *King of Video*

Judy, Judy, Judy 1949
Music
15371   60 mins   C   B, V, FO   P
Judy Garland
Outakes of the unreleased Garland version of "Annie Get Yor Gun," and footage from a February 1962 concert. (Some segments in black and white.)
MGM et al — *Video Yesteryear*

Juggernaut 1937
Drama/Mystery
46349   64 mins   B/W   B, V, FO   P
Boris Karloff, Mona Goya, Arthur Margetson
A young woman hires a sinister doctor to murder her wealthy husband. The doctor, who happens to be insane, does away with the husband and then goes on a poisoning spree.
British, Grand National — *Video Yesteryear*

Juke Joint 194?
Comedy
53416   60 mins   B/W   B, V   P
Spencer Williams, Judy Williams
"Amos 'n Andy" star Spencer Williams starred in and directed this tale of two men who arrive in Hollywood with only 25 cents between them. Features an all-black cast and musical numbers.
Sack Prods — *Video Connection*

Jules et Jim 1962
Romance
54129   104 mins   B/W   B, V   P
Jeanne Moreau, Oskar Werner, Henri Serre, Marie Dubois, Vanna Urbino, directed by Francois Truffaut
The story of a friendship between two men, one German and the other French, and their twenty-year love for the same woman. Adapted from the novel by Henri-Pierre Roche. English subtitles.
Mar Del Plata Festival '62: Best Director (Truffaut) FR
Janus Films — *Video Dimensions; Sheik Video*

Julia 1977
Drama
44931   118 mins   C   B, V, CED   P
Jane Fonda, Vanessa Redgrave, Jason Robards
Story of a writer who becomes involved in the holocaust of World War II when her friend, Julia, asks her to smuggle money into Berlin.
MPAA:PG
20th Century Fox — *CBS/Fox Video*

Julia 1976
Drama
58552   83 mins   C   B, V   R, P
Sylvia Kristel
"Emmanuelle's" Sylvia Kristel stars as a young woman coming of age in a sophisticated society.
MPAA:R
Cine Media Intl — *Video Gems*

Julia Child—The French 197?
Chef, Vol. I
Cookery
56890   120 mins   C   CED   P
Julia Child
Julia Child prepares four wonderful creations in her entertaining style: roasted chicken, lasagna a la Francaise, strawberry souffle, and mousse au chocolat.
WGBH Boston — *RCA VideoDiscs*

Jungle Book, The 1942
Adventure
29360   105 mins   C   B, V, LV   P
Sabu, Joseph Calleia, Rosemary de Camp, Ralph Byrd
A lavish version of Rudyard Kipling's stories about Mowgli, the boy who was raised by wolves in the jungles of India. Musical score by Miklos Rosza.
United Artists; Alexander Korda — *Movie Buff Video; Budget Video; Penguin Video; Video Connection; VCII; Cinema Concepts; Sheik*

          (For Explanation of codes, see USE GUIDE and KEY)

Video; Cable Films; Video Yesteryear; Discount Video Tapes; Western Film & Video Inc; Nostalgia Merchant; Media Home Entertainment

Jungle Heat   1984
Adventure
75627   93 mins   C   B, V   P
Peter Fonda, Deborah Raffin
Anthropoid mutants feed on living flesh and blood.
MPAA:PG
Unknown — *Trans World Entertainment*

Junior G-Men   1940
Adventure/Serials
08873   237 mins   B/W   B, V, 3/4U   P
Billy Halop, Huntz Hall
The Dead End Kids fight Fifth Columnists who are trying to sabotage America's war effort. Twelve episodes.
Universal — *Penguin Video; Video Connection; Video Yesteryear*

Junior G-Men of the Air   1942
Adventure/Serials
64385   215 mins   B/W   B, V, 3/4U   P
The Dead End Kids
The Dead End Kids become teenage flyboys in this twelve-episode serial adventure.
Universal — *Nostalgia Merchant*

Junkman, The   1982
Adventure
66614   97 mins   C   B, V   P
H. B. Halicki, Christopher Stone, Susan Shaw, Hoyt Axton, Lynda Day George, Freddy Cannon and the Belmonts
A moviemaker whose new film is about to be premiered is being chased by a mysterious killer. The ultimate car chase film, this production used and destroyed over 150 automobiles.
MPAA:R
H B Halicki International — *Trans World Entertainment*

Jupiter Menace, The   1982
Speculation
64211   84 mins   C   B, V   R, P
George Kennedy
An examination of speculative theories dealing with the inevitable end of the world. Kennedy predicts a continuing cycle of unnatural occurrences and disasters which will culminate with the tilting of the earth's axis in the year 2000.
Jupiter Menace Ltd — *THORN EMI Home Video*

Just Before Dawn   1971
Horror
66262   90 mins   C   B, V   P
Chris Lemmon, Deborah Benson, Gregg Henry, George Kennedy
In this tale of struggle for survival, humans resort to their animal instincts.
MPAA:R
David Sheldon — *Paragon Video Productions*

Just Tell Me What You Want   1980
Comedy
52700   112 mins   C   B, V   R, P
Alan King, Ali McGraw, Myrna Loy, Keenan Wynn, Tony Roberts, directed by Sidney Lumet
A wealthy married man's mistress wants to take over the operation of a failing movie studio he has acquired.
MPAA:R
Jay Presson Allan; Sidney Lumet; Warner Bros — *Warner Home Video*

Just Win, Baby/NFL 83   1984
Football
72937   46 mins   C   B, V, FO   P
Los Angeles Raiders
Highlights from Los Angeles Raiders 1983 season and "NFL 83."
NFL Films — *NFL Films Video*

Justice   1955
Crime-Drama
66137   26 mins   B/W   B, V, FO   P
William Prince, Jack Klugman, Biff McGuire, Jack Warden
A crusading attorney tries to keep a waterfront kangaroo court from applying its harsh justice to an admitted killer. A TV crime-drama also titled "Flight from Fear."
NBC — *Video Yesteryear*

Justice Rides Again   193?
Western
57988   55 mins   B/W   B, V   P
Tom Mix
Tom Mix tries to uphold law and order, but he's up against some very tough outlaws.
Universal — *Video Connection*

Justin Morgan Had a Horse   1981
Drama
47410   91 mins   C   B, V   P
Don Murray, Lana Wood, Gary Crosby
The true story of a colonial school teacher in post-Revolutionary War Vermont who developed the Morgan horse, the first and most versatile American breed.
Walt Disney — *Walt Disney Home Video*

K

K2—The Savage Mountain — 1979
Mountaineering
69914   55 mins   C   B, V   P
This program documents the British expedition's attempt on the West Ridge of K2 in 1979. It also includes rare footage of the 1938, 1953 and 1975 American expeditions.
Chameleon Films — *Gravity Sports Films*

Kagemusha — 1980
Adventure
55458   160 mins   C   B, V   P
Directed by Akira Kurosawa
A thief is rescued from the gallows because of his striking resemblance to a warlord in 16th Century Japan, but, unfortunately for him, he is required to pose as the ambitious lord when the lord is fatally wounded. In Japanese with English subtitles.
Cannes Film Festival '80: Co-winner of Grand Prize. MPAA:PG JA
Twentieth Century Fox — *CBS/Fox Video*

Kajagoogoo — 1983
Music-Performance
75905   11 mins   C   B, V   P
This program presents the new band Kajagoogoo performing their songs "Too Shy," "Ooh to Be An" and "Hang on Now."
EMI Records Ltd — *Sony Corporation of America*

Kameradschaft — 1931
Drama/Film-History
52361   80 mins   B/W   B, V, 3/4U   P
Directed by G. W. Pabst
Early sound "message" film; French miners are buried in a shaft explosion and German co-workers struggle to free them. English subtitles. GE
Nerofilm; Germany — *International Historic Films; Festival Films; Classic Video Cinema Collector's Club*

Kamikaze — 1961
World War II
53662   89 mins   B/W   B, V, 3/4U   P
A documentary film about the war in the Pacific, comprised of Allied and Japanese newsreel footage.
Unknown — *International Historic Films*

Kamikaze — 194?
World War II
68894   90 mins   B/W   B, V   P
The Pacific Theater War is covered in this documentary from beginning to end.

Office of War Information — *Interurban Films*

Kamikaze '89 — 1983
Science fiction
66447   106 mins   C   B, V   P
Rainer Werner Fassbinder, Gunther Kaufman, Boy Gobert, directed by Wolf Gremm
German director Fassbinder has the lead acting role in this offbeat story of a police lieutenant in Berlin, circa 1989, who investigates a puzzling series of bombings. Music by Tangerine Dream.
TeleCulture; Trio Film — *MGM/UA Home Video*

Kanako — 19??
Photography
60579   ? mins   C   LV   P
Kanako Higuchi, one of Japan's most famous and adored actresses, is presented by renowned photographer Kishin Shinoyama in this series of nude photographs. Stereo.
Japan — *Pioneer Video Imports*

Kansan, The — 1943
Western
72054   79 mins   B/W   B, V   P
Richard Dix, Victor Jory, Albert Dekker
A tyrant is confronted by a marshall when he tries to take over the state of Kansas.
United Artists — *Independent United Distributors*

Kansas — 1982
Music-Performance
75920   87 mins   C   B, V   P
This program presents a live concert by the rock group Kansas.
Radio & Records Inc; The Carr Company — *Sony Corporation of America*

Karate Killer — 1973
Martial arts
63861   95 mins   C   B, V   P
A Kung Fu master seeks revenge on a brutal and vicious gang.
MPAA:R
United International Pictures — *Budget Video*

Karate Warriors — 197?
Martial arts
60228   90 mins   C   B, V   P
Sonny Chiba
Chiba takes his battle against crime to the streets.
Independent — *Independent United Distributors*

Kardiac Kids...Again — 1981
Football
50650   24 mins   C   B, V, FO   R, P
Cleveland Browns

The 1980 Cleveland Browns football season was full of thrilling, last-minute, come-from-behind victories which propelled the Browns into the playoffs, where they met the Oakland Raiders in subzero weather. Quarterback Brian Sipe was named AFC Player of the Year.
NFL Films — *NFL Films Video*

Kashmiri Run 1969
Adventure
65000 96 mins C B, V P
Pernell Roberts
A group of men race through the Himalayas for the Kashmiri border to avoid capture by Chinese Communists.
Sagittarius Productions — *U.S.A. Home Video*

Kate Bush, Live at Hammersmith 1979
Music-Performance
65089 52 mins C B, V R, P
Kate Bush
Kate Bush displays her wide range of talents as a songwriter, singer, pianist and choreographer in this live concert show taped at London's Hammersmith Theater in May, 1979.
Kate Bush; London Films — *THORN EMI Home Video*

Katy Caterpillar 1983
Cartoons
75612 85 mins C B, V P
Animated
Katy Caterpillar tells storybook tales.
Unknown — *Children's Video Library*

Katyn Forest Massacre 1943
World War II
72477 19 mins B/W B, V, 3/4U P
In April, 1943, the bodies of several thousand Polish officers were discovered by the advancing German army. A Polish emigre group produced this testament using the German film record of an international investigation into the murders. They concluded Stalin ordered the murders, despite Soviet denials. Graphic.
Poland — *International Historic Films*

Kavik the Wolf Dog 1984
Adventure
76653 99 mins C B, V P
Ronny Cox, Linda Sorensen, Andrew Ian McMillian, Chris Wiggins, John Ireland
A heartwarming story of a courageous dog's love and suffering to be with the boy he loves.
Stanly Chase — *Media Home Entertainment*

Keaton Special/Valentino Mystique 192?
Film-History
10159 56 mins B/W B, V P, T
Buster Keaton, Rudolph Valentino
Film shows Buster Keaton in his peak years in excerpts from "College" and "Steamboat Bill Jr." Also recounts career of Rudolph Valentino using newsreels, home movies, and feature excerpts.
United Artists et al — *Blackhawk Films*

Keeneland 1984
Horse racing
74538 22 mins C B, V P
This tape features a look at the great race horse, Keeneland and its world class yearlings.
Mercedes Maharis Productions — *Mercedes Maharis Productions*

Keep, The 1983
Horror
65762 96 mins C B, V, CED R, P
Scott Glenn, Alberta Watson, Jurgen Prochnow, Robert Prosky
At the height of the Nazi onslaught, several German soldiers unleash an unknown power from a medieval stone fortress which begins to overtake them all.
MPAA:R
Gene Kirkwood; Howard W. Koch — *Paramount Home Video*

Keep My Grave Open 1975
Horror
47670 85 mins C B, V P
Camilla Carr, Gene Ross
A bizarre tale of murder, a strange house, and a sexually driven woman.
MPAA:R
S F Brownrigg — *Unicorn Video*

Keep Rollin' 1940
Western
58503 54 mins B/W B, V, 3/4U P
Gene Autry, Smiley Burnett, Duncan Renaldo
A crooked meat packer tries to monopolize the beef and cattle industry, but Gene sings him to justice.
Republic — *Penguin Video*

Keeper, The 1984
Horror
66488 96 mins C B, V P
Christopher Lee, Tell Schreiber
The patients at Underwood Asylum suffer unspeakable horrors while under the care of the Keeper.
Trans World Entertainment — *Trans World Entertainment*

Kellogg Dream, The 19??
Animals/Documentary
69638 27 mins C B, V P
This documentary about the famed Kellogg Ranch in Pomona, California, incorporates rare black-and-white footage from the 1920s footage

---

of the ranch, its famous Arabian stallions and some visiting celebrities.
Joe Burnham — *Mercedes Maharis Productions*

Kelly's Heroes 1970
Suspense
68244   143 mins   C   B, V, CED   P
Clint Eastwood, Donald Sutherland, Telly Savalas, Don Rickles, Carroll O'Connor
A group of men set out to rob a bank and almost win World War II. In stereo.
MPAA:PG
MGM — *MGM/UA Home Video*

Kennel Murder Case 1933
Mystery
01713   73 mins   B/W   B, V   P
William Powell, Mary Astor, Jack LaRue, directed by Michael Curtiz
Debonair detective Philo Vance suspects that a clearcut case of suicide is actually murder.
Warner Bros — *Budget Video; Discount Video Tapes; Nostalgia Merchant; Video Dimensions; Sheik Video; Cable Films; Video Yesteryear; Video Connection*

Kenny Loggins Alive 1981
Music-Performance
59879   60 mins   C   B, V   P
Pop artist Kenny Loggins performs "This Is It," "Angry Eyes," "I Believe in Love," "Celebrate Me Home," and other hits before a hometown crowd in Santa Barbara during the final performance of his 1981 tour. In stereo.
Kenny Loggins Productions — *CBS/Fox Video; Pioneer Artists; RCA VideoDiscs*

Kentuckian, The 1955
Adventure/Western
68228   104 mins   C   B, V, CED   P
Burt Lancaster, Walter Matthau, Diana Lynn, John McIntire, Dianne Foster
Burt Lancaster stars as a rugged frontiersman who leaves with his son to go to Texas. On their journey the two are harassed by fighting mountaineers.
Hecht-Lancaster Productions — *CBS/Fox Video*

Kentucky Blue Streak 1935
Adventure
59373   61 mins   B/W   B, V, FO   P
Eddie Nugent, Junior Coughlin, Patricia Scott, Ben Carter's Colored Octette
A young jockey is framed for murder while riding at an "illegal" racetrack. Later, almost eligible for parole, he escapes from jail to ride "Blue Streak", in the Kentucky Derbys
Puritan Pictures Corp. — *Video Yesteryear*

Kentucky Fried Movie 1977
Comedy
66064   85 mins   C   B, V, LV   P
Bill Bixby, Jerry Zucker, James Abrahams, David Zucker, Donald Sutherland
A zany potpouri of satire about movies, TV, commercials, and contemporary society.
MPAA:R
Robert K. Weiss — *Media Home Entertainment*

Key Largo 1948
Drama
31662   101 mins   B/W   B, V   P
Humphrey Bogart, Lauren Bacall, Claire Trevor, Edward G. Robinson, Lionel Barrymore, directed by John Houston
A gangster melodrama set in Key West, Florida, where a group of hoods take over a hotel, intimidating the proprietor. Based on a play by Maxwell Anderson.
Academy Awards '48: Best Supporting Actress (Claire Trevor).
Warner Bros, Jerry Wald — *CBS/Fox Video; RCA VideoDiscs*

Kid, The and The Idle Class 1921
Comedy
08399   90 mins   B/W   B, V   P
Charlie Chaplin, Jackie Coogan, Edna Purviance, directed by Charlie Chaplin
The Little Tramp adopts a homeless orphan in "The Kid," Chaplin's first feature-length film. This tape also includes "The Idle Class" a rare Chaplin short.
Charlie Chaplin Productions; First National — *CBS/Fox Video*

Kid and the Killers, The 198?
Adventure
75633   90 mins   C   B, V   P
Jon Cypher
A young orphan and a hardened criminal band together to pursue a villain.
MPAA:PG
Unknown — *Independent United Distributors*

Kid Dynamite 1943
Comedy
05428   70 mins   B/W   B, V   P
The East Side Kids
Friction develops between two members of the gang.
Monogram — *Sheik Video*

Kid from Not-So-Big, The 1978
Drama
47381   87 mins   C   B, V   R, P
Jennifer McAllister, Veronica Cartwright, Robert Viharo, Paul Tulley
A family film that tells the story of Jenny, a young girl left to carry on her grandfather's

frontier-town newspaper. When two con men come to town, Jenny sets out to expose them.
Boomming Ltd — *Warner Home Video*

Kid 'n' Hollywood & Polly Tix in Washington   1933
Comedy
64918   20 mins   B/W   B, V   P, T
Shirley Temple
These two "Baby Burlesks" shorts star a cast of toddlers, featuring the most famous moppet of all time, Shirley Temple, in her earliest screen appearances.
Educational Pictures — *Blackhawk Films*

Kid Sister, The   1945
Comedy
47502   56 mins   B/W   B, V, FO   P
Roger Pryor, Judy Clark, Frank Jenks, Constance Worth
A young girl is determined to grab her sister's boyfriend for herself, and enlists the aid of a burglar to do it.
Producers Releasing Corp — *Video Yesteryear*

Kid Vengeance   1975
Adventure/Western
60407   90 mins   C   B, V   P
Leif Garrett, Jim Brown, Lee Van Cleef, John Marley
After witnessing the brutal slaying of his family, a boy carries out a personal vendetta against the outlaws.
MPAA:R
Cannon Releasing; Menahem Golan; Alexander Hacohen — *Paragon Video Productions*

Kid with the Broken Halo, The   1981
Comedy
65441   96 mins   C   B, V   P
Gary Coleman, Robert Guillame
A wisecracking 12-year-old angel is always in and out of trouble and always needs help from his teacher.
Satellite Productions — *U.S.A. Home Video*

Kidnapped   1960
Adventure
56876   94 mins   C   CED   P
Peter Finch, James MacArthur, Peter O'Toole, directed by Robert Stevenson
The Robert Louis Stevenson classic about a boy who sets out to try to collect the inheritance which is rightfully his but is being withheld by his uncle.
Walt Disney — *RCA VideoDiscs*

Kidnapped   1960
Adventure
69318   94 mins   C   B, V   R, P
Peter Finch, James MacArthur, Peter O'Toole

A young boy is sold by his wicked uncle as a slave, and is helped by an outlaw. Based on the Robert Louis Stevenson classic.
Buena Vista — *Walt Disney Home Video*

Kidnapping of the President, The   1980
Drama
72170   100 mins   C   B, V   P
William Shatner, Hal Holbrook
While visiting Canada on a state mission, the President of the United States is abducted by terrorists.
Crown International — *Continental Video*

Kids Are Alright, The   1979
Music-Performance
59130   106 mins   C   B, V   R, P
The Who, Ringo Starr, Keith Richard, Steve Martin, Tom Smothers, Rick Danko
A feature-length compilation of performances and interviews spanning the first fifteen years of the rock group, The Who. Includes rare footage from the "Rolling Stones Rock and Roll Circus" film. Songs include: "My Generation," "I can't Explain," "Young Man's Blues," "Won't Get Fooled Again," "Baba O' Reilly," and excerpts from "Tommy."
MPAA:PG
Tony Klinger; Bill Curbishley — *THORN EMI Home Video; RCA VideoDiscs*

Kid's Auto Race/Mabel's Married Life   191?
Comedy
66119   21 mins   B/W   B, V   P, T
Charlie Chaplin, Mabel Normand, Mack Swain
"Kid's Auto Race" (1914), also known as "Kid Auto Races at Venice," concerns a kiddie-car contest; "Mabel's Married Life" (1915) is about flirtations in the park between married individuals. Piano and organ scores.
Keystone — *Blackhawk Films*

Kids from Fame, The   1983
Music-Performance/Dance
65106   75 mins   C   B, V, CED   P
Debbie Allen, Gene Anthony Ray, Lee Curreri, Erica Gimpel, Lori Singer, Carlo Imperato
The cast of the TV show "Fame" sings and dances in a live sold-out performance at London's Royal Albert Hall. VHS in stereo.
MGM/UA Home Entertainment Group — *MGM/UA Home Video*

Kiel Olympiad   1972
Boating
33768   56 mins   C   B, V, 3/4U   P
This program provides highlights of the 1972 Olympic sailing events.
Unknown — *Sports World Cinema*

Kill and Go Hide 1976
Horror
53149   95 mins   C   B, V   P
A young girl visits her mother's grave nightly to
communicate with and command the ghoul-like
creatures that haunt the surrounding woods.
Valiant Intl Pictures — *Monterey Home Video*

Kill and Kill Again 197?
Martial arts/Drama
47315   100 mins   C   B, V   P
*James Ryan, Anneline Kriel, Stan Schmidt, Bill
Flynn, Norman Robinson, Ken Gampu, John
Ramsbottom*
A martial arts champion attempts to rescue a
kidnapped Nobel Prize-winning chemist who
has developed a high-yield synthetic fuel.
Igo Kantor — *Media Home Entertainment*

Kill Castro 1980
Drama
66635   90 mins   C   B, V   P
Stuart Whitman, Robert Vaughn, Caren Kaye
A Key West boat skipper is forced to carry a CIA
agent to Cuba on a mission to assassinate
Castro.
MPAA:R
No Frills Inc — *Monterey Home Video*

Kill or Be Killed 1980
Martial arts/Adventure
47852   90 mins   C   B, V   P
*James Ryan, Charlotte Michelle, Norman
Combes*
A martial arts champion is lured to a phony
martial arts contest by a madman bent on
revenge.
MPAA:PG
Ben Vlok — *Media Home Entertainment*

Kill Squad 1981
Martial arts/Adventure
59084   85 mins   C   B, V   P
*Jean Claude, Jeff Risk, Jerry Johnson, Bill
Cambra, Cameron Mitchell*
A squad of martial arts masters follow a trail of
violence and bloodshed to a vengeful, deadly
battle of skills.
MPAA:R
Michael Lee — *HarmonyVision*

Kill the Golden Goose 1979
Suspense/Martial arts
54079   91 mins   C   B, V   R, P
*Brad Von Beltz, Ed Parker, Master Bong Soo
Han*
Two martial arts masters work on opposite sides
of a government corruption and corporate
influence peddling case.
MPAA:R
Skytrain Kim Films — *Video Gems*

Killer Bait 1949
Suspense
66385   99 mins   B/W   B, V   P
*Lizabeth Scott, Don Defore, Arthur Kennedy,
Dan Duryea*
A money-obsessed woman gets involved with
gangsters, blackmail and murder.
Universal — *Movie Buff Video*

Killer Bats (Devil Bat) 1942
Horror
11673   70 mins   B/W   B, V, FO   P
Bela Lugosi, Dave O'Brien
Monstrous, blood-sucking bats are trained to kill
at the smell of perfume.
PRC — *Video Yesteryear; Video Connection;
Cable Films; Penguin Video; Ampro Video
Productions*

Killer Bats/White Zombie 194?
Horror
58911   137 mins   B/W   B, V   P
*Bela Lugosi, Dave O'Brien, Madge Bellamy,
Robert Frazier*
A Bela Lugosi double feature: "Killer Bats"
(1940), in which Bela trains an army of
bloodthirsty bats to kill; "White Zombies"
(1932), in which zombies rob graves and take
the bodies to a sugar mill where they work
around the clock for the mad White Zombie.
EL, SP
United Artists — *Ampro Video Productions*

Killer Diller 1948
Musical
66386   70 mins   B/W   B, V   P
*Nat King Cole, Butterfly McQueen, Moms
Mabley*
A all-black musical revue, featuring Nat King
Cole and his Trio.
Albert Sack Productions — *Movie Buff Video*

Killer Force 1975
Adventure
66104   100 mins   C   B, V, CED   P
Telly Savalas, Peter Fonda, Maud Adams
An adventure of international diamond
smuggling.
MPAA:R
American International Pictures — *Vestron
Video*

Killers, The 1964
Drama/Suspense
56873   95 mins   C   B, V   P
*Ronald Reagan, Lee Marvin, Angie Dickinson,
John Cassavetes*
After two hired assassins kill a teacher, they
look into his past and try to find leads to a
$1,000,000 robbery. Based on Ernest
Hemingway's story.
Universal — *MCA Home Video*

   (For Explanation of codes, see USE GUIDE and KEY)

Killing of Angel Street, 1983
The
Drama
65731   100 mins   C   B, V   P
Liz Alexander, John Hargreaves
A courageous young woman unwittingly
becomes the central character in an escalating
nightmare about saving a community from
corrupt politicians and organized crime.
MPAA:PG
Anthony Buckley — *VidAmerica*

Killing of President 1983
Kennedy, The
Documentary/Presidency-US
69584   80 mins   C   B, V   P
This documentary explores all of the conspiracy
theories and the alleged cover-up by the Warren
Commission.
Independent — *VidAmerica*

Killing of President 1983
Kennedy: New
Revelations Twenty
Years Later, The
Documentary
72527   60 mins   C   B, V   P
An in-depth look at new evidence that has
surfaced and suggests President John
Kennedy's assassination was carried out
differently from government accounts.
Mark Hollo — *VidAmerica*

Kim Carnes 1984
Music-Performance
75911   15 mins   C   B, V   P
This program presents a performance by Kim
Carnes singing her songs "Bette Davis Eyes,"
"Invisible Hands," "Voyeur" and others.
EMI America Records — *Sony Corporation of
America*

Kind Hearts and 1949
Coronets
Comedy
36934   101 mins   B/W   B, V   R, P
*Alec Guinness, Dennis Price, Valerie Hobson,
Joan Greenwood, directed by Robert Hamer*
Guinness plays eight different roles in this movie
as the relatives of an ambitious young man who
sets out to bump them off in an effort to attain
the ducal crown, with hilarious results.
J Arthur Rank — *THORN EMI Home Video*

King and I, The 1956
Musical
08427   133 mins   C   B, V, LV   P
*Deborah Kerr, Yul Brynner, Rita Moreno, Martin
Benson*
From the musical play based on the biography
"Anna and the King of Siam" by Margaret
Landon.

Academy Awards '56: Best Actor (Brynner);
Best Scoring Musical.   EL, SP
20th Century Fox — *CBS/Fox Video*

King Arthur & the Knights 1981
of the Round Table Vol. 1
Cartoons
59327   60 mins   C   B, V   P
Animated
The tale of King Arthur is told beginning with his
birth to the mighty sword Excalibur.
EL, SP
ZIV International — *Family Home
Entertainment*

King Arthur & the Knights 1981
of the Round Table Vol. 2
Cartoons
59328   60 mins   C   B, V   P
Animated
The tales of King Arthur continue with the
Knights of the Round Table, Camelot, Lady
Guinevere and his adventures with Sir Lancelot.
EL, SP
ZIV International — *Family Home
Entertainment*

King Arthur, the Young 197?
Warlord
Adventure
59350   90 mins   C   B, V   R, P
Oliver Tobias
The struggle that was the other side of
Camelot—the campaign against the Saxon
hordes.
MPAA:PG
Heritage Enterprises — *Video Gems*

King Boxers, The 1980
Adventure/Martial arts
56925   90 mins   C   B, V   R, P
Yasuka Kurate, Johnny Nainam
Japan's top actor, Yasuka Kurate, stars in this
tale of elephant hunts, warding off Triad Society
gangs, and personal combat. Also stars Johnny
Nainam, Thailand's fists and kicks boxing
champion.
MPAA:R
Fourseas Films — *Video Gems*

King Creole 1958
Musical-Drama
08383   115 mins   B/W   B, V   P
*Elvis Presley, Carolyn Jones, Walter Matthau,
Dean Jagger, Dolores Hart, Vic Morrow*
A teenager with a criminal record becomes a
successful pop singer in New Orleans.
Paramount — *CBS/Fox Video; RCA
VideoDiscs*

King Edward VIII: For Love of a Woman   1954
Biographical/Great Britain
44248   15 mins   B/W   B, V   P
Classic newsreel footage presents one of
history's most famous love stories: that of the
Duke of Windsor, who gave up a kingdom and
all of his power for the woman he loved.
Fox Movietone News — *Two Star Films*

King in New York, A   1957
Satire
08423   105 mins   B/W   B, V   P
*Charlie Chaplin, Dawn Addams, Michael
Chaplin, directed by Charlie Chaplin*
Chaplin plays the deposed king of a European
mini-monarchy who comes to the United States
in hope of making a new life.
Charlie Chaplin Productions — *CBS/Fox Video*

King Kong   1933
Horror
00308   105 mins   B/W   B, V, 3/4U   P
Fay Wray, Bruce Cabot, Robert Armstrong
The original film classic which tells the story of
Kong, a giant ape captured in Africa and brought
to New York as a sideshow attraction. He
escapes from his captors and rampages
through the city, ending up on top of the newly
built Empire State Building.
RKO — *Nostalgia Merchant; VidAmerica; King
of Video; RCA VideoDiscs*

King Kong   1977
Horror
38616   135 mins   C   B, V, LV   R, P
Jeff Bridges, Charles Grodin, Jessica Lange
An updated remake of the 1933 movie classic,
about a giant ape on the loose in New York City,
climbing skyscrapers and generally wreaking
havoc, with the climax taking place atop the
World Trade Center.
MPAA:PG
Paramount — *Paramount Home Video; RCA
VideoDiscs*

King of Comedy, The   1983
Comedy-Drama
68258   101 mins   C   B, V   P
*Robert De Niro, Jerry Lewis, Diahnne Abbott,
Sandra Bernhard*
Lewis portrays a late-night talk show host and
De Niro his greatest fan. De Niro cannot get on
the show so he decides to kidnap Lewis to force
him to put him on.
MPAA:PG
20th Century Fox — *RCA/Columbia Pictures
Home Video; RCA VideoDiscs*

King of Hearts   1966
Satire
53672   101 mins   C   B, V, CED   P
*Alan Bates, Genevieve Bujold, directed by
Philippe de Broca*
In World War I, a Scottish soldier finds a war-
torn town occupied only by lunatics who have
escaped from the asylum and who want to make
him their king.
United Artists; Fildebroc; Montoro — *CBS/Fox
Video*

King of Jazz, The   1930
Musical
68254   93 mins   C   B, V   P
*Paul Whiteman, John Boles, Jeanette Loff, Bing
Crosby and the Rhythm Boys, directed by John
Murray Anderson*
A lavish revue built around the Paul Whiteman
Orchestra with comedy sketches and songs by
the stars on Universal Pictures' talent roster.
Musical numbers include George Gershwin's
"Rhapsody in Blue," "Happy Feet" and "It
Happened in Monterey." Filmed in two-color
Technicolor with a cartoon segment by Walter
Lantz.
Academy Award '30: Best Interior Decoration
Universal — *MCA Home Video*

King of Kong Island   1978
Horror
35370   92 mins   C   B, V   P
Brad Harris, Marc Lawrence
Intent on world domination, a group of mad
scientists implant receptors in the brains of
gorillas on Kong Island, and the monster apes
run amok.
Independent — *VCI Home Video*

King of Kung-Fu   198?
Martial arts
64963   90 mins   C   B, V   P
Bobby Baker, Nam Chun Pan, Lam Chun Chi
A martial arts adventure featuring plenty of
kung-fu kicks.
Dragon Lady Productions — *Unicorn Video*

King of Sports   19??
Horse racing
69632   50 mins   C   B, V   P
Taking the viewer behind the scenes at a
racetrack, this program provides an orientation
to the sport of horse racing by covering
everything from riding styles to racing luck.
Joe Burnham — *Mercedes Maharis
Productions*

King of the Bullwhip   1951
Western
54177   59 mins   B/W   B, V   P
Lash LaRue, Tom Neal, Anne Gwynne
Two undercover U.S. Marshals are sent to Tioga
City to stop the killing and looting of a masked
bandit, whose whip is as dangerous as his gun.

Howco Prods — *Video Connection; Penguin Video; Discount Video Tapes*

King of the Cowboys 1943
Western
07974   54 mins   B/W   B, V   P
Roy Rogers, Smiley Burnette, James Bush
Roy fights a gang of saboteurs and saves a defense installation.
Republic; NTA — *Video Connection*

King of the Gypsies 1978
Drama
29767   112 mins   C   B, V   R, P
Sterling Hayden, Eric Roberts, Susan Sarandon, Brooke Shields
A young man, scornful of his gypsy heritage, runs away from the tribe and tries to make a life of his own. He is summoned home to his grandfather's deathbed, where he is proclaimed the new king of the gypsies, a role he is unwilling to accept.
MPAA:R
Paramount — *Paramount Home Video*

King of the Hill 1974
Baseball
21303   57 mins   C   B, V, FO   P
The career of big league ballplayer Ferguson Jenkins is followed in this program, through his last two seasons with the Chicago Cubs.
National Film Board of Canada — *Video Yesteryear*

King of the Kongo 1929
Adventure/Serials
57356   213 mins B/W   B, V, FO   P
Jacqueline Logan, Boris Karloff, Richard Tucker
A handsome young man is sent by the government to Nuhalla, deep in the jungle, to break up a gang of ivory thieves. A newly-discovered sound-silent serial.
Mascot — *Video Yesteryear*

King of the Mountain 1981
Adventure
60444   92 mins   C   B, V   P
Harry Hamlin, Dennis Hopper, Joseph Bottoms, Deborah Van Valkenburgh, Dan Haggerty
The "Old King" and the "New King" must square off in this tale of daredevil roadracers.
MPAA:PG
Polygram — *Embassy Home Entertainment*

King of the Rocketmen 1949
Adventure/Serials
07335   156 mins B/W   B, V, 3/4U   P
Tris Coffin, Mae Clark, I. Stanford Jolley
Jeff King thwarts an attempt by traitors to steal government scientific secrets. Serial in twelve episodes. Later released as a feature titled "Lost Planet Airmen'.

Republic — *Nostalgia Merchant; Video Connection; NTA Home Entertainment*

King of the Texas Rangers 1941
Adventure/Serials
33954   195 mins B/W   B, V, 3/4U   P
Sammy Baugh, Neil Hamilton
Tom King finds that his father's killers are a group of saboteurs who have destroyed American oil fields. A full-length serial.
Republic — *Video Connection*

King of the Zombies 1941
Horror
51443   67 mins   B/W   B, V, FO   P
Joan Woodbury, Dick Purcell
A scientist creates his own zombies without souls, to be used as the evil tools of a foreign government.
Monogram — *Video Yesteryear*

King, Queen, Knave 1974
Drama
65431   94 mins   C   B, V   P
Gina Lollobrigida, David Niven, John Moulder Brown
A shy, awkward 19-year old boy, keenly aware that his interest in girls is not reciprocated, has to go live with his prosperous uncle and his much younger wife when his parents are killed.
Avco Embassy — *Embassy Home Entertainment*

King Rat 1965
War-Drama
13258   134 mins B/W   B, V   P
George Segal, Tom Courtenay, James Fox, directed by Bryan Forbes
This drama, set in a World War II Japanese prisoner-of-war camp, focuses on the effect of captivity on the English, Australian and American prisoners.
Columbia; James Woolf — *RCA/Columbia Pictures Home Video*

King Solomon's Mines 1937
Adventure
59834   80 mins   B/W   B, V   P
Sir Cedric Hardwicke, Paul Robeson, Roland Young, directed by Robert Stevenson
The search for King Solomon's Mines leads a safari through the treacherous terrain of the desert, fending off sandstorms, Zulus, and a volcanic eruption.
Gaumont — *Embassy Home Entertainment*

Kingdom of the Spiders 1978
Horror
51119   90 mins   C   B, V   P
William Shatner, Tiffany Bolling, Woody Strode

A desert town is invaded by swarms of killer tarantulas, which begin to consume townspeople.
MPAA:PG
Dimension Pictures — *VCI Home Video*

Kings, Queens, Jokers 193?
Comedy
10112   60 mins   B/W   B, V   P, T
Harold Lloyd, Marie Dressler, Polly Moran, Edward G. Robinson, Gary Cooper, Joan Crawford
Package includes a foolish lover and ghosts in "Haunted Spooks," an escaped convict in "Dangerous Females," and a search for lost jewels in "Stolen Jools."
MGM et al — *Blackhawk Films*

Kinks: One for the Road, The 1980
Music-Performance
65478   60 mins   C   B, V   P
A showcase for the Kinks' vast repertoire, including "Victoria," "Lola," "You Really Got Me," and many more. Also included is authentic footage of The Kinks on British and American television shows. In stereo VHS and Beta Hi-Fi.
Independent — *Vestron Video*

Kipperbang 1982
Drama/Romance
65110   85 mins   C   B, V, CED   P
John Albasiny, Abigail Cruttenden, directed by Michael Apted
During the summer of 1948, a 13-year-old boy wishes he could kiss the girl of his dreams, and he finally gets his big break in a school play.
MPAA:PG
David Puttnam; Enigma Television Ltd — *MGM/UA Home Video*

Kipps 1941
Drama
03811   95 mins   B/W   B, V   P
Michael Redgrave, Phyllis Calvert, Michael Wilding, directed by Carol Reed
Based on H. G. Wells' satirical novel, young British spendthrift inherits a fortune and clashes with his love over economy and waste.
20th Century Fox; British — *Budget Video; Cable Films*

Kismet 1955
Musical
47399   113 mins   C   B, V   P
Howard Keel, Ann Blyth, Dolores Gray, Vic Damone, directed by Vincente Minnelli
An Arabian Nights extravaganza about a Baghdad street poet who manages to infiltrate himself into the Wazir's harem. The music was adapted from Borodin by Robert Wright and George Forrest, producing such standards as

"Baubles, Bangles and Beads," "Stranger in Paradise" and "And This Is My Beloved."
MGM — *MGM/UA Home Video*

Kiss Me Goodbye 1982
Comedy/Fantasy
66073   101 mins   C   B, V, CED   P
Sally Field, James Caan, Jeff Bridges, Paul Dooley, Mildred Natwick
A woman must choose between her new fiance or the returned ghost of her late husband.
MPAA:PG
20th Century Fox — *CBS/Fox Video*

Kiss Me, Kill Me 1969
Suspense
66516   91 mins   C   B, V   P
CarrollBaker, George Eastman, Isabelle DeFunes, Ely Gallo
A confused woman is on the run after she may have murdered someone.
MPAA:R
Salvatore Crocella; Giancarlo Lugli — *Paragon Video Productions*

Kiss of the Tarantula 1975
Science fiction/Horror
65454   85 mins   C   B, V   P
Eric Mason
The story of a young girl and her pet spiders as they spin a deadly web of terror.
MPAA:PG
Cinevu Productions — *Monterey Home Video*

Kiss of the Tarantula 1972
Horror
69795   84 mins   C   B, V   P
Eric Mason, Suzanne Ling
A pretty young girl has some very unusual pets—a menacing horde of creeping tarantulas—and some very, very sorry enemies.
Kurt Drady; John Holokan — *Gorgon Video*

Kit Carson 1940
Western
64376   97 mins   B/W   B, V, 3/4U   P
John Hall, Dana Andrews, Ward Bond, Lynn Bari
Frontiersman Kit Carson leads a wagon train to California, fighting off marauding Indians all the way.
Edward Small — *Nostalgia Merchant*

Kitty: A Return to Auschwitz 1981
World War II/Judaism
47564   90 mins   C   B, V   R, P
Kitty Hart spent her teenage years at the Auschwitz concentration camp and survived. Thirty-four years later, she returned to the camp with her grown son to walk over the land and recall the past.

CBC — *THORN EMI Home Video*

Kitty and the Bagman   1983
Comedy
72872   95 mins   C   B, V   P
A comedy about two rival madams who ruled
Australia in the 1920's.
MPAA:R
Anthony Buckley — *Embassy Home
Entertainment*

Kitty Foyle   1940
Drama
07882   107 mins   B/W   B, V   P
Ginger Rogers
From the novel by Christopher Morley, Ms.
Rogers symbolizes the white-collar working girl
whose involvement with a married man presents
her with both romantic and social conflicts.
Academy Awards '40; Best Actress (Rogers).
RKO — *VidAmerica; Nostalgia Merchant;
Blackhawk Films*

Klaipedos Atvadavimas   1923
Documentary
72500   20 mins   B/W   B, V, 3/4U   P
Actual newsreel footage of an inssurectionist
capture of Klaipeda by Lithuanian rebels in
1923.
Foreign — *International Historic Films*

Klute   1971
Drama
54116   114 mins   C   B, V, LV   R, P
*Jane Fonda, Donald Sutherland, Charles Cioffi,
Roy Scheider, directed by Alan J. Pakula*
A small town policeman comes to New York in
search of a missing friend and gets involved
with a would-be actress, call-girl who is trying to
break out of her surroundings.
Academy Awards '71: Best Actress (Fonda).
MPAA:R
Warner Bros — *Warner Home Video; RCA
VideoDiscs*

Knack—Live at Carnegie   1982
Hall, The
Music-Performance
47812   ? mins   C   LV   P
The power pop quartet performs "My Sharona,"
"Good Girls Don't," and other hits at their
March 18, 1979 Carnegie Hall Concert In
stereo.
Unknown — *Pioneer Artists*

Knee (Rehabilitation and   1978
Injury)
Physical fitness
52759   30 mins   C   B, V   P
Hosted by Ann Dugan
Exercises for knee strengthening, relief of pain,
and conditioning muscles and tissue to prevent

further stress. Part of the "Rehabilitation and
Injury" series.
Health 'N Action — *RCA/Columbia Pictures
Home Video*

Knife in the Water   1962
Film-Avant-garde
11399   90 mins   B/W   B, V   P
*Leon Niemczyk, Jolanta Umecka, Zygmunt
Malandowicz, directed by Roman Polanski*
A journalist, his wife and a hitchhiker spend a
day aboard a sailboat in this tension-filled,
psychological drama. English subtitles.
Venice Film Festival: International Film Critics
Award.
Kanawha Films Ltd — *CBS/Fox Video; Video
Yesteryear; Budget Video; Western Film &
Video Inc; Video Dimensions; Sheik Video*

Knightriders   1981
Adventure
66065   145 mins   C   B, V   P
Ed Harris, Gary Lahti, Tom Savini, Amy Ingersoll
The story of a troup of motorcyclists who are
members of a traveling Renaissance Fair.
MPAA:R
Richard Rubinstein — *Media Home
Entertainment*

Knights of the Range   1940
Western
15549   66 mins   B/W   B, V   P
*Russell Hayden, Victor Jory, directed by Lesley
Selander*
Vintage western.
Paramount — *Video Connection; Sheik Video*

Knitting with Dee I   1980
Handicraft
55320   28 mins   C   B, V   P
Instructor Dee Russo conducts an easy-to-
follow lesson for beginners featuring an
introduction and basic stitches to knit a 45-inch
wool scarf.
The Yarn Shop — *Daya Inc*

Knitting with Dee II   1980
Handicraft
55321   70 mins   C   B, V   P
Instructor Dee Russo conducts another easy-to-
understand lesson for beginners featuring
terminology, pattern interpretation, stitch gauge,
and assembly of a wool sweater.
The Yarn Shop — *Daya Inc*

Knock on Any Door   1949
Drama
44840   100 mins   B/W   B, V   P
*Humphrey Bogart, John Derek, George
Macready*

A young hoodlum from the slums is tried for murdering a cop. He is defended by a prominent attorney who has known him from childhood.
Columbia — *RCA/Columbia Pictures Home Video*

Knockout, The/Dough and Dynamite   1914
Comedy
59369   54 mins   B/W   B, V, FO   P
Charlie Chaplin, Roscoe 'Fatty'' Arbuckle, Mabel Normand, Keystone Cops
Two Chaplin shorts: "The Knockout" (1914), in which Charlie referees a big fight; "Dough and Dynamite" (1914), in which a labor dispute at a bake shop leaves Charlie in charge when the regular baker walks out.
Keystone — *Video Yesteryear*

Know Your Enemy—Japan   1945
World War II
50644   63 mins   B/W   B, V, 3/4U   P
One of the last works of Frank Capra's Special Service Unit, intended to familiarize the American soldier with the fighting characteristics of the Japanese.
US War Dept — *International Historic Films*

Know Your Enemy—The Viet Cong   1964
Vietnam War
53701   22 mins   B/W   B, V, 3/4U   P
An Armed Forces informational film.
Unknown — *International Historic Films*

Knute Rockne: The Rock of Notre Dame   1954
Biographical/Football
44259   15 mins   B/W   B, V   P
This program tells of the football career of Knute Rockne, who helped to make Notre Dame's football team the most famous. Classic newsreel footage.
Fox Movietone News — *Two Star Films*

Koko the Clown   193?
Cartoons
54121   55 mins   B/W   B, V   P
Animated
Examples from this silent cartoon series include "The Tantalizing Fly," "Perpetual Motion," "The Clown's Little Brother," "Ouija Board," "Bubbles," "Modeling," "In the Good Old Summertime," and "Koko the Kop."
Max Fleischer — *Video Dimensions*

Kol Nevelu (Before It's Too Late)   1957
Drama
52358   85 mins   B/W   B, V, 3/4U   P

Directed by J. Fogulmanas and V. Zhalakyavichus
A Soviet Lithuanian feature film, presented in its original form, with dialogue in Lithuanian.
LI
Unknown — *International Historic Films*

Kongur   1982
Mountaineering
69902   30 mins   C   B, V   P
This program documents Chris Bonnington's 1981 British climb of Mount Kongur in Chinese Tibet.
Banff Festival of Mountain Films '83: Best Expedition Film.
Jardine Matheson Productions — *Gravity Sports Films*

Kool and the Gang in Concert   1981
Music-Performance
60226   60 mins   C   B, V   P
The group's greatest hits are performed live including "Celebration," "Too Hot," "Ladies Night," and "Jones vs Jones."
Sunrise Entertainment — *Independent United Distributors*

Kovacs on the Corner   1952
Comedy
39003   30 mins   B/W   B, V, FO   P
Ernie Kovacs, Edie Adams, the Dave Appell Trio
A program from Ernie Kovacs' first television series, originating in Philadelphia. Creative video comedy by the first master of the genre, and a song or two from Edie Adams.
NBC — *Video Yesteryear*

Koyaanisqatsi   1983
Film-Avant-garde
65471   87 mins   C   B, V   P
A totally unconventional program that takes an intense look at modern life. Without dialogue or narration, it brings what are traditionally considered background elements—landscapes and cityscapes-up front, producing a unique view of the superstructure and mechanics of our daily lives.
Godfrey Reggio — *Pacific Arts Video*

Kraft Music Hall   1959
Variety
42966   25 mins   B/W   B, V, FO   P
Milton Berle, Yvonne DeCarlo, The Trio Cotters
Aired March 25, 1959, this program offers a monologue by Uncle Miltie, a song by Yvonne DeCarlo, and the acrobatic Trio Cotters tossing a young lady around the stage.
NBC — *Video Yesteryear*

**Kraft Music Hall Presents
"Alan King Stops the
Press"**   1969
Variety
56904   55 mins   B/W   B, V, FO   P
Alan King, Paul Lynde, Barbara Feldon
A comedy-variety show spoofing the newspaper
industry. Paul Lynde interviews star quarterback
Boyd Blowhard, the food editor reviews the
cuisine at the Last Chance Diner, and a look
behind the scenes at the Advice to the Lovelorn
column.
NBC — *Video Yesteryear*

Kraft Music Hall, The   1969
Music/Variety
52459   60 mins   B/W   B, V, FO   P
*Eddy Arnold, the Lettermen, Judy Carne, Tom
Seaver*
A program from this popular TV series hosted by
Eddy Arnold, who sings "You're Just Too Good
to Be True" and "Love Is Blue."
NBC — *Video Yesteryear*

Kraft Television Theater   1951
Drama
47639   60 mins   B/W   B, V, FO   P
*Olive Deering, Mark Roberts, E. G. Marshall,
George Reeves, Ed Herlihy*
"Kelly" by Eric Hatch, the story of an average
Kansas gas pump jockey who remembers the
girl he knew in France during the war, and is
surprised to find her in the U.S.A.
NBC — *Video Yesteryear*

Kramer vs. Kramer   1979
Drama
58498   105 mins   C   B, V, LV   P
*Dustin Hoffman, Meryl Streep, Jane Alexander,
Justin Henry, Howard Duff, directed by Robert
Benton*
A woman abandons her husband and young
son, leaving them to struggle and make a new
life for themselves. Eventually she returns to
fight for custody. Based on the novel by Avery
Corman.
Academy Awards '79: Best Picture; Best Actor
(Hoffman); Best Supporting Actress (Streep);
Best Director (Benton); Best Screenplay
Adaptation (Benton). MPAA:PG
Columbia; Stanley Jaffe — *RCA/Columbia
Pictures Home Video; RCA VideoDiscs*

Kriegsmarine, Die   194?
World War II
53382   45 mins   B/W   B, V, 3/4U   P
Two featurettes of historic interest and
importance—Nazi Germany's own cinematic
tribute to her WWII surface navy. English
subtitled.
GE
Germany — *International Historic Films*

Kriemhilde's Revenge   1924
Drama/Film-History
64304   95 mins   B/W   B, V   P, T
*Paul Richter, Margareta Schoen, directed by
Fritz Lang*
The concluding part of Fritz Lang's massive
version of the Nibelungenlied, which was the
basis of Richard Wagner's Ring operas. Silent
with organ score.
UFA — *Blackhawk Films; Classic Video
Cinema Collector's Club*

Kronos   1957
Science fiction
44356   78 mins   B/W   B, V, 3/4U   P
Jeff Morrow, Barbara Lawrence, John Emery
A giant robot from space drains the Earth of all
its energy resources. Includes preview of
coming attractions from classic science fiction
films.
Lippert; 20th Century Fox — *Nostalgia
Merchant*

Krull   1983
Adventure
65460   ? mins   C   B, V, CED   P
*Ken Marshall, Lysette Anthony, Freddie Jones,
Francesca Annis*
In a fantasy adventure, set in a world peopled by
creatures of myth and magic, a prince embarks
on a quest to find the magical Glaive and then
rescues his young bride. In stereo VHS and
Beta Hi-Fi.
MPAA:PG
Ted Mann; Ron Silverman — *RCA/Columbia
Pictures Home Video*

Kung-Fu Commandos   1980
Martial arts/Adventure
59347   90 mins   C   B, V   R, P
John Lui, Shangkuan Lung
Five masters must face a warlord's army to
rescue a captured agent.
MPAA:R
Unifilm International — *Video Gems*

**Kurt Carlsen: Man
Against the Sea**   1954
Biographical/History-US
44244   15 mins   B/W   B, V   P
The story of Kurt Carlsen, whose heroic battle
with the sea won him worldwide acclaim. Classic
newsreel footage shows how he faught to save
the Flying Enterprise for his American owners.
Fox Movietone News — *Two Star Films*

Kwaidan   1964
Horror/Suspense
65203   161 mins   C   B, V   P
Directed by Masaki Kubayashi
A haunting, stylized quartet of supernatural
stories, each with a suprise ending. Japanese
dialogue with English subtitles.

JA
Bungei Production; Ninjin Club; Toho
Company — *Video Yesteryear*

L

La Sylphide   1971
Dance
58903   81 mins   C   B, V, 3/4U   R, P
*Ghislaine Thesmar, Michael Denard, the Paris
Ballet Opera Company, conducted by Patrick
Flynn, directed and choreographed by Pierre
Lacotte*
The Paris Opera Ballet's faithful adaptation of
"the ballet that changed the course of ballet
history," based on the 1832 production staged
by Taglioni.
Kultur; Paris Ballet Opera Company — *Kultur*

Ladies Night Out   1983
Nightclub
65344   80 mins   C   B, V   P
Peter Adonis Traveling Fantasy Show
"Ladies Night Out" is an all-male burlesque,
featuring the highly acclaimed Peter Adonis
Traveling Fantasy Show. In stereo.
Joanne Sobolewski; John J
Burzichelli — *Vestron Video*

Lady Chatterley's Lover   1981
Drama
60592   107 mins   C   B, V, CED   P
*Sylvia Kristel, Nicholas Clay, Shane Briant,
directed by Just Jaeckin*
D.H. Lawrence's classic novel of an English lady
who has an affair with the gamekeeper of her
husband's estate is the basis of this film.
MPAA:R
Cine-Artist GmbH; London-Cannon Films Ltd
and Producteurs Associes — *MGM/UA Home
Video*

Lady Chatterley's Lover   1959
Literature-English
06224   102 mins   B/W   B, V   P
Danielle Darrieux, Erno Crisa, Leo Genn
Based on D.H. Lawrence's novel, English
woman has affair with game keeper of her
husband's estate. French; English subtitles.
FR
Kingsley Intl; French — *Budget Video; Festival
Films; Penguin Video; Discount Video Tapes*

Lady Cocoa   1975
Drama
72956   93 mins   C   B, V   P
Lola Falana, Mean Joe Greene
A young woman gets released from jail for
twenty-four hours and sets out for Las Vegas to
find the man who framed her.

MPAA:R
Matt Cimber — *Unicorn Video*

Lady for a Night   1942
Drama
66465   88 mins   B/W   B, V   P
John Wayne, Joan Blondell, Ray Middleton
The lady owner of a gambling ship does her
best to break into high society.
Republic — *NTA Home Entertainment*

Lady from Louisiana, The   1942
Drama
66313   84 mins   B/W   B, V   P
*John Wayne, Ona Munson, Dorothy Dandridge,
Ray Middleton*
A lawyer in old New Orleans out to rid the city of
corruption falls in love with the daughter of a
big-time gambler.
Republic — *NTA Home Entertainment*

Lady Ice   1973
Mystery/Drama
66585   93 mins   C   B, V   P
*Donald Sutherland, Jennifer O'Neill, Robert
Duvall, Eric Braeden, directed by Tom Gries*
An insurance investigator, on the trail of jewel
thieves, follows them to Miami Beach and the
Bahamas.
MPAA:PG
National General; Tomorrow
Entertainment — *Program Hunters*

Lady in Red   1979
Drama
66103   90 mins   C   B, V, CED   P
*Pamela Sue Martin, Louise Fletcher, Robert
Conrad*
A story of America in the 30s, and the progress
through the underworld of the woman who was
Dillinger's last lover.
Julie Corman — *Vestron Video*

Lady of Burlesque   1943
Mystery
12446   91 mins   B/W   B, V   P
*Barbara Stanwyck, Michael O'Shea, Janis
Carter, Pinky Lee*
Burlesque dancer is found dead, strangled with
her own G-string. Based on Gypsy Rose Lee's
"The G-String Murders."
United Artists; Stromberg — *Video Connection;
Sheik Video; Cable Films; Video Yesteryear;
Cinema Concepts*

Lady of the House   1978
Drama
75496   100 mins   C   B, V   P
Dyan Cannon, Susan Tyrell
A true story about a madame who rose from
operator of a brothel to become a political force
in San Francisco.

William Kayden Productions — *Prism*

Lady on the Bus　　　　　　　1978
Drama
66605　　102 mins　　C　　B, V, LV　　　　P
Sonia Braga
A sexually frustrated newlywed bride turns to other men for satisfaction.
MPAA:R
Atlantic Releasing — *Vestron Video*

Lady Refuses, The　　　　　　1931
Drama
08673　70 mins　B/W　B, V, 3/4U　　　P
Betty Compson, John Darrow, Margaret Livingston
A three-sided love affair leads to tragedy.
RKO — *Penguin Video; Discount Video Tapes*

Lady Sings the Blues　　　　　1972
Musical
38612　　144 mins　　C　　B, V, LV　　R, P
Diana Ross, Billy Dee Williams, Richard Pryor
Jazz singer Billie Holiday's autobiography becomes a musical drama covering her early career and problems with racism and drug addiction. Songs include "God Bless the Child" and "Lover Man."
MPAA:R
Paramount — *Paramount Home Video; RCA VideoDiscs*

Lady Takes a Chance　　　　　1943
Comedy/Romance
65395　86 mins　B/W　　B, V　　　　P
John Wayne, Jean Arthur
A romantic comedy about a New York working girl with matrimonial ideas and a rope-shy rodeo rider who yearns for the wide open spaces.
RKO — *VidAmerica*

Lady Vanishes, The　　　　　1938
Mystery
01743　99 mins　B/W　　B, V　　　　P
Michael Redgrave, Paul Lukas, Margaret Lockwood, directed by Alfred Hitchcock
When a kindly old lady disappears from a fast-moving train, her young friend finds an imposter in her place.
Gaumont British — *Embassy Home Entertainment; Media Home Entertainment; Budget Video; Video Dimensions; Sheik Video; Cable Films; Video Connection; Discount Video Tapes; Western Film & Video Inc; Cinema Concepts*

Ladykillers, The　　　　　　1955
Comedy
36940　　87 mins　　C　　B, V　　R, P
Alec Guinness, Cecil Parker, Katie Johnson, Herbert Lom, Peter Sellers, directed by Alexander Mackendrick

A gang of bumbling bank robbers is foiled by a little old lady from whom they rent a room. Hilarious antics follow, especially on the part of Guinness, who plays the slightly demented-looking leader of the gang.
British Film Academy '55: Best Screenplay; Best Actress (Johnson).
Continental, J Arthur Rank — *THORN EMI Home Video*

Lamaze Method:　　　　　　　1984
Techniques for Childbirth
Preparation, The
Childbirth
65386　　45 mins　　C　　B, V　　　　P
Patty Duke Astin introduces the 3 basic areas of the method: relaxation, breathing and expulsion techniques. ASPO-certified Lamaze instructor Marilyn Libresco leads an expectant couple through demonstrations.
Embassy Home Entertainment; Al Eicher — *Embassy Home Entertainment*

Lambos, The　　　　　　　　1983
Automobiles
76390　　35 mins　　C　　B, V　　　　P
This program offers coverage of 12 cylinder Lamborghinis, the 350 GT, Miura "S" with a driving impression, Espada, and the wild Countach on the move and next to a P-51 Mustang; comments from owners and Lambo engineer Bob Wallace.
Armour Productions — *Armour Productions*

Lameness of Both Fore　　　　19??
and Hindlimbs
Veterinary medicine
69651　　53 mins　　C　　B, V　　　　P
This program looks at such causes of equine lameness as Wobbler syndrome, compressed spinal cord, cut flexor tendons, fractures and toe cracks.
Colorado State U — *Mercedes Maharis Productions*

Lameness of the　　　　　　19??
Forelimb, Part 1
Veterinary medicine
69639　30 mins　　C　　B, V　　　　P
Dr. O.R. Adams, DVM, provides special case illustrations of forelimb lameness in horses, including bow tendon, septic arthritis, hygroma, and various fractures, among others.
Colorado State U — *Mercedes Maharis Productions*

Lameness of the　　　　　　19??
Forelimb, Part 2
Veterinary medicine
69640　　36 mins　　C　　B, V　　　　P

Dr. Adams discusses lameness occurring below the fetlock joint on the forelimb and describes the treatment of the more common types.
Colorado State U — *Mercedes Maharis Productions*

Lameness of the Forelimb, Part 3 19??
Veterinary medicine
69641   46 mins   C   B, V   P
This program covers equine forelimb lameness between the shoulders in conjunction with prognosis and possible treatment of carpus.
Colorado State U — *Mercedes Maharis Productions*

Lameness of the Forelimb, Part 4 19??
Veterinary medicine
69642   42 mins   C   B, V   P
This program describes treatment techniques for the areas below the carpus down through fractures of the sesamoid bone.
Colorado State U — *Mercedes Maharis Productions*

Lameness of the Forelimb, Part 5 19??
Veterinary medicine
69643   40 mins   C   B, V   P
Dr. O.R. Adams, DVM, discusses equine lameness of the lower forelimb and describes treatments for certain conditions.
Colorado State U — *Mercedes Maharis Productions*

Lameness of the Hindlimb, Part 1 19??
Veterinary medicine
69647   35 mins   C   B, V   P
This program presents diagnosis of wobbler syndrome, hip joint rupture of the round ligament, and other conditions related to equine hindlimb lameness.
Colorado State U — *Mercedes Maharis Productions*

Lameness of the Hindlimb, Part 2 19??
Veterinary medicine
69654   23 mins   C   B, V   P
This program discusses signs of equine hindlimb lameness, hock and below.
Colorado State U — *Mercedes Maharis Productions*

Lameness of the Hindlimb, Part 3 19??
Veterinary medicine
69652   42 mins   C   B, V   P
This program provides a review of the general causes of equine hindlimb lameness, including

thrombus, hip luxation, nerve paralysis, bonitis and others.
Colorado State U — *Mercedes Maharis Productions*

Lamp at Midnight 1966
Drama
64855   76 mins   C   B, V, 3/4U   P
Melvyn Douglas, David Wayne, Michael Hordern, Hurd Harfield, Kim Hunter, directed by George Schaefer
This presentation from "George Schaefer's Showcase Theatre" deals with three critical periods in the life of Italian astronomer Galileo Galilei, from his invention of the telescope, through his appearance at the Holy Office of the Inquisition, to the publication of his "Dialogue on the Two Systems of the World."
George Schaefer — *Enter-Tel Inc*

Land of the Minotaur 1977
Horror
60348   88 mins   C   B, V   P
Donald Pleasance, Peter Cushing, Luan Peters
A small village is the setting for horrifying ritual murders, demons and disappearances of young terrorists.
MPAA:PG
Frixos Constantine — *VCI Home Video*

Land That Time Forgot, The 1975
Science fiction
64889   90 mins   C   B, V   P
Doug McClure, John McEnery, Susan Penhaligon
A WWI veteran, a beautiful woman, and their German enemies are stranded in a land of life outside time. Based on the novel by Edgar Rice Burroughs.
MPAA:PG
American International Pictures — *Vestron Video*

Land Without Bread 1932
Documentary/Spain
59225   27 mins   B/W   B, V, 3/4U   P
A classic documentary showing the poorest region of northern Spain, notable for some stunningly unpleasant scenes.
Luis Bunnel — *Penguin Video*

Land Without Bread 1932
Documentary/Spain
72470   28 mins   B/W   B, V, 3/4U   P
Directed by Luis Bunuel
Surrealist Luis Bunuel takes his camera to the Las Hurdes region of Spain to make a documentary on the extreme poverty existing there. His film captures the usually unseen, and therefore only imaginable, consequences of starvation, sickness and death.

Luis Bunuel — *International Historic Films*

Language in Life 1982
Language arts/Science
59563   50 mins   C   B, V   P
Human communications from a psychological standpoint, based on recent studies in language acquisition, are examined, as well as a survey of the basic units of speech.
McGraw Hill — *Mastervision*

Laramie Kid, The 1935
Western
58512   52 mins   B/W   B, V, 3/4U   P
Tom Tyler, Alberta Vaughn, Snub Pollard
Tom is framed for a bank robbery he didn't commit.
Commodore — *Penguin Video*

Las Vegas Story, The 1952
Drama
57141   88 mins   B/W   B, V   P
Victor Mature, Jane Russell, Vincent Price, Hoagy Carmichael
Gambling, colorful sights, and a murder provide the framework for this fictional, guided-tour of the city.
RKO — *King of Video*

Laserblast 1978
Science fiction
33888   87 mins   C   B, V   P
Kim Milford, Cheryl Smith, Keenan Wynn, Roddy McDowall
A frustrated young man finds a powerful and deadly laser which was left near his home by aliens. Upon learning of its devastating capabilities, his personality changes and he seeks revenge against all who have taken advantage of him.
MPAA:PG
Charles Band — *Media Home Entertainment*

Lash of the Penitentes 1936
Documentary/Exploitation
08902   ? mins   B/W   B, V, 3/4U   P
A Newspaper reporter investigates a strange cult in the American Southwest, who worship pain as a means of repenting their sins.
Unknown — *Penguin Video*

Lassie's Rescue Rangers 1982
Cartoons/Adventure
66005   60 mins   C   B, V   P
Animated
The courageous collie saves the day in two spine-tingling adventures.
Filmation — *Family Home Entertainment*

Lassie's Rescue Rangers, Volume 2 1982
Cartoons/Adventure
69807   60 mins   C   B, V   P
Animated
Three action-packed cartoon adventures feature Lassie as she joins forces with the courageous Rescue Rangers to help protect people and wildlife in the national forests.
Filmation — *Family Home Entertainment*

Lassiter 1984
Drama
72919   100 mins   C   B, V   P
Tom Selleck, Lauren Hutton, Jane Seymour
Tom Selleck plays a jewel thief who is asked to steal diamonds for the FBI.
MPAA:R
Al Ruddy; Warner Bros — *Warner Home Video*

Last American Virgin, The 1982
Comedy
60567   92 mins   C   B, V, CED   P
Lawrence Monoson, Diane Franklin, Steve Antin, Louisa Moritz
Three school buddies must deal with a plethora of problems in their search for girls who are willing. Music by Blondie, The Cars, The Police, The Waitresses, Devo, U2, Human League, Quincy Jones.
MPAA:R
Cannon Films Inc; Golan Globus Productions — *MGM/UA Home Video*

Last Bomb, The 194?
Armed Forces-US
68899   36 mins   C   B, V   P
This program covers the strategic B-29 bombing campaign, that lead to the defeat of Japan.
US Army — *Interurban Films*

Last Challenge of the Dragon, The 1980
Adventure/Martial arts
56926   90 mins   C   B, V   R, P
Bruce Lee
A son brings death to his family by humiliating the underworld martial arts king of the city.
MPAA:R
Goldig Film — *Video Gems*

Last Challenge of the Dragon 198?
Martial arts
64958   90 mins   C   B, V   P
A martial arts adventure.
Dragon Lady Productions — *Unicorn Video*

Last Chase, The 1980
Adventure
47755   106 mins   C   B, V, CED   P

Lee Majors, Burgess Meredith, Chris Makepeace
A famed race car driver becomes a vocal dissenter against the sterile society that has emerged, in this drama set in the near future.
MPAA:PG
Martyn Burke; Fran Rosati — *Vestron Video*

Last Days of Man on Earth   1973

Science fiction
65713   70 mins   C   B, V   P
Jon Finch, Jenny Runacre, Hugh Griffith
In a deteriorating world, a search is on for a piece of microfilm which holds the formula for immortality.
MPAA:R
New World — *Embassy Home Entertainment*

Last Days of Pompeii, The   1935

Adventure
57142   96 mins   B/W   B, V   P
Preston Foster, Basil Rathbone, Louis Calhern
A peace-loving blacksmith strives for wealth by becoming a gladiator.
RKO — *King of Video*

Last Detail, The   1974

Comedy-Drama
59603   104 mins   C   B, V   P
Jack Nicholson, Randy Quaid, Otis Young, directed by Hal Ashby
A hard-boiled career petty officer commissioned to transfer a young sailor from one brig to another attempts to show the prisoner a good time.
MPAA:R
Columbia — *RCA/Columbia Pictures Home Video*

Last Flight of Noah's Ark, The   1980

Adventure/Drama
63192   97 mins   C   B, V   R, P
Elliott Gould, Genevieve Bujold, Ricky Schroder, Vincent Gardenia, Tammy Lauren
This tale of adventure concerns a high-living pilot, a prim missionary and two stowaway orphans who must plot their way off a deserted island following the crash landing of their broken-down plane.
Walt Disney Productions — *Walt Disney Home Video*

Last Frontier, The   1932

Western/Serials
54179   216 mins   B/W   B, V   P
Lon Chaney Jr., Yakima Canutt
This serial of 12 chapters contains shades of spectacular figures in Western history: Custer, Hickok, and others in a background of grazing buffalo, boom towns, and covered wagon trails.

RKO Radio — *Video Connection*

Last Horror Film, The   1982

Horror
65692   87 mins   C   B, V   P
Joe Spinell, Caroline Munro
A beautiful queen of horror films is followed to Cannes by her number one fan who, unbeknownst to her, is slowly murdering members of her entourage in a deluded and vain attempt to capture her attentions.
MPAA:R
David Winters; Judd Hamilton — *Media Home Entertainment*

Last House on Dead End Street   1979

Horror
63409   90 mins   C   B, V   P
Steven Morrison, Dennis Crawford, Lawrence Bornman, Janet Sorley
Evil inhabits the last house on Dead End Street.
MPAA:R
Production Concepts Ltd — *Sun Video*

Last Laugh, The   1924

Drama
08709   77 mins   B/W   B, V, 3/4U   P
Emil Jannings, Maly Delshaft, Max Hiller
An elderly man, who as the doorman of a great hotel was looked upon as a symbol of "upper class," due to his age, is demoted to wash room attendant.
Janus; Germany — *Penguin Video; International Historic Films; Sheik Video; Western Film & Video Inc; Discount Video Tapes; Cable Films*

Last Married Couple in America, The   1980

Comedy
59683   103 mins   C   B, V   P
George Segal, Natalie Wood, Richard Benjamin, Valerie Harper, Dom DeLuise
A couple fight to stay happily married amidst the rampant divorce epidemic engulfing their friends.
MPAA:R
Universal — *MCA Home Video*

Last Mile, The   1932

Crime-Drama
64341   70 mins   B/W   B, V   P
Preston Foster, Howard Phillips, George E. Stone
The staff of a prison prepares for the execution of a celebrated murderer.
World Wide — *Classic Video Cinema Collector's Club*

Last of Sheila, The 1973
Drama/Suspense
51963 118 mins C B, V R, P
Richard Benjamin, James Coburn, James Mason, Dyan Cannon, Joan Hackett, Raquel Welch
The yacht "Sheila" is the setting for a "Whodunit" parlor game to discover which of six people is a murderer.
MPAA:PG
Warner Bros — *Warner Home Video*

Last of the Mohicans 1932
Adventure/Serials
12541 156 mins B/W B, V P
Edwina Booth, Harry Carey, directed by Ford Beebe, B. Reaves Eason
Based on James Fenimore Cooper's novel of the Indian's life and death struggle during the French and Indian War. Twelve chapters, 13 minutes each.
Mascot — *Video Connection; Video Yesteryear; Discount Video Tapes*

Last of the Mohicans 1977
Adventure
57621 97 mins C B, V P
The classic novel by James Fenimore Cooper about the scout Hawkeye and his Mohican companions, Chingachgook and Uncas, comes to life in this film.
Schick Sunn — *VCI Home Video*

Last of the Mohicans, The 1936
Adventure
55351 91 mins B/W B, V, 3/4U P
Randolph Scott, Binnie Barnes, Bruce Cabot
James Fenimore Cooper's classic about the French and Indian War in colonial America.
Edward Small; United Artists — *Nostalgia Merchant; Blackhawk Films; Classic Video Cinema Collector's Club*

Last of the Pony Riders 1953
Western
64533 59 mins B/W B, V R, P
Gene Autry, Smiley Burnette, Kathleen Case
When the telegraph lines linking the East and West Coasts is completed, Gene and the other Pony Express riders find themselves out of a job. This was Autry's final feature film.
Columbia — *Blackhawk Films*

Last of the Red Hot Lovers 1972
Comedy
59424 98 mins C B, V, LV R, P
Alan Arkin, Paula Prentiss, Sally Kellerman, Renee Taylor, directed by Gene Saks
Neil Simon's Broadway hit about a middle-aged man who decides to have a fling and uses his mother's apartment to seduce three very strange women.
MPAA:PG
Paramount — *Paramount Home Video*

Last Outlaw, The 1936
Western
15502 79 mins B/W B, V P
Harry Carey, Hoot Gibson, Henry B. Walthall, directed by Christy Cabanne
The last of the famous badmen of the old West is released from jail and returns home to find that times have changed. The action climaxes in an old-time blazing shoot-out.
RKO — *Video Connection*

Last Tango in Paris 1973
Drama
13323 129 mins C B, V, LV P
Marlon Brando, Maria Schneider, Jean-Pierre Leaud, directed by Bernardo Bertolucci
Brando plays a middle-aged American who meets a French girl. Many revealing moments follow in their frantic, unlikely, and short-lived affair.
MPAA:X
United Artists — *CBS/Fox Video; RCA VideoDiscs*

Last Unicorn, The 1982
Cartoons/Fairy tales
60583 95 mins C B, V, CED P
Animated, voices of Alan Arkin, Jeff Bridges, Tammy Grimes, Angela Lansbury, Mia Farrow, Robert Klein, Christopher Lee, Keenan Wynn
Peter Beagle's popular tale of a beautiful unicorn who goes in search of her lost, mythical "family." Music by Jimmy Webb.
MPAA:G
ITC Entertainment — *CBS/Fox Video*

Last Waltz, The 1978
Music-Performance
73141 117 mins C B, V P
The Band, Bob Dylan, Joni Mitchell, Ringo Starr, Van Morrison, directed by Martin Scorsese
The Band's farewell 1976 concert on Thanksgiving Day was documented by Martin Scorsese and features performances by Bob Dylan, Eric Clapton and many other rock notables.
MPAA:PG
Robbie Robertson; Warner Bros — *CBS/Fox Video*

Last Waltz, The 1978
Music-Performance
52603 117 mins C CED P
The Band, Bob Dylan, Neil Young, Joni Mitchell, Van Morrison, Eric Clapton, Neil Diamond, Emmylon Harris, Muddy Waters, Ronnie Hawkins

Martin Scorcese filmed this rock documentary featuring the farewell performance of The Band, joined by a host of musical guests that they have been associated with over the years. Songs include: "Upon Cripple Creek," "Don't Do It," "The Night They Drove old Dixie Down," "Stage Fright" (The Band), "Helpless" (Young), "Coyote" (Mitchell), "Caravan" (Morrison), "Further On Up the Road" (Clapton), "Who Do You Love" (Hawkins), "Mannish Boy" (Waters), "Evangeline" (Harris), "Baby, Let Me Follow You Down" (Dylan).
MPAA:PG
United Artists — *RCA VideoDiscs*

Last Wave, The　　　　　　　　**1978**
Drama/Suspense
47382　103 mins　C　B, V　R, P
Richard Chamberlain, Olivia Hamnett, Gulpilil, Frederick Parslow, directed by Peter Weir
An Australian attorney takes on a murder case involving an aborigine. He finds himself becoming distracted by apocalyptic visions concerning tidal waves and drownings that seem to foretell the future.
MPAA:PG
Australian; Peter Weir — *Warner Home Video*

Last Word, The　　　　　　　　**1980**
Comedy-Drama
69546　103 mins　C　B, V, CED　P
Richard Harris, Karen Black, Martin Landau, Dennis Christopher
A man fights to protect his home, family and neighbors from a corrupt real estate deal involving shady politicians, angry policemen, and a beautiful television reporter.
MPAA:PG
Richard G Abramson; Michael Varhol — *Embassy Home Entertainment*

Late Liz, The　　　　　　　　**197?**
Women/Identity
50755　90 mins　C　B, V　P
Anne Baxter, Jack Albertson, Steve Forrest, Foster Brooks
The story of a society woman struggling to make her life work as she battles through her alcoholism, a divorce, and a son who disowns her. When she finds the Gospel, she finds a source of new life.
Gateway Films — *Vanguard Video*

Late Show, The　　　　　　　　**1977**
Mystery/Comedy
51964　94 mins　C　B, V　R, P
Art Carney, Lily Tomlin, Bill Macy, Eugene Roche, Joanna Cassidy, John Considine
A veteran private detective finds his world turned upside down when a former colleague arrives to visit nearly dead, and a woman whose cat is missing becomes his sidekick.
MPAA:PG

Warner Bros; Robert Altman — *Warner Home Video*

Laughfest　　　　　　　　**191?**
Comedy
10098　59 mins　B/W　B, V　P, T
Ben Turpin, Barney Oldfield, Mabel Normand, Charlie Chaplin, Snub Pollard
Five classic slapstick shorts are included on this tape: "It's a Gift" (1923), with Snub Pollard, "Barney Oldfield's Race for a Life" (1913), "Kid Auto Races" and "Busy Day" (1914), both with Charlie Chaplin, and "Daredevil" (1923), starring Ben Turpin.
Mack Sennett et al — *Blackhawk Films*

Laura　　　　　　　　**1944**
Mystery/Crime-Drama
56463　85 mins　B/W　B, V　P
Gene Tierney, Clifton Webb, Dana Andrews, Vincent Price, directed by Otto Preminger
A detective assigned to the murder investigation of the late Laura Hunt finds himself falling in love with her painted portrait.
Academy Awards '44: Best Cinematography.
Twentieth Century Fox — *CBS/Fox Video*

Laura　　　　　　　　**1979**
Drama/Romance
65433　95 mins　C　B, V　P
Maud Adams, Dawn Dunlap
A journey through beauty, sensuality and innocence revolving around a 16 year old ballet dancer's first stirrings of sexuality.
MPAA:R
20th Century Fox — *Embassy Home Entertainment*

Laurel and Hardy Comedy Classics Volume I　　　　　　　　**1933**
Comedy
33910　84 mins　B/W　B, V, 3/4U　P
Stan Laurel, Oliver Hardy, Mae Busch, May Wallace, Charlie Hall, Billy Gilbert
A collection of four classic comedy shorts starring Laurel and Hardy: "The Music Box," which won an Academy Award for Best Short Subject, "Country Hospital," "The Live Ghost," and "Twice Twos," all from 1932-33.
Hal Roach, MGM — *Nostalgia Merchant*

Laurel and Hardy Comedy Classics Volume II　　　　　　　　**1930**
Comedy
33911　75 mins　B/W　B, V, 3/4U　P
Stan Laurel, Oliver Hardy, Billy Gilbert, Tiny Sandford, Anita Garvin
A collection of four Laurel and Hardy shorts from 1930 including "Blotto," "Towed in a Hole," "Brats," and "Hog Wild."

Hal Roach, MGM — *Nostalgia Merchant*

Laurel and Hardy   1934
Comedy Classics Volume
III
Comedy
33912 75 mins B/W B, V, 3/4U   P
Stan Laurel, Oliver Hardy, Billy Gilbert, Mae Busch, Tiny Sandford
Laurel and Hardy star in four separate comedy shorts, including "Oliver the 8th," "Busy Bodies," "Their First Mistake," and "Dirty Work," all from 1933-34.
Hal Roach, MGM — *Nostalgia Merchant*

Laurel and Hardy   1932
Comedy Classics Volume
IV
Comedy
33913 75 mins B/W B, V, 3/4U   P
Stan Laurel, Oliver Hardy, Jacqueline Wells, James Finlayson, Thelma Todd
Laurel and Hardy star in four of their comedy shorts from 1931-32. Included are "Another Fine Mess," "Come Clean," "Laughing Gravy," and "Any Old Part."
Hal Roach, MGM — *Nostalgia Merchant*

Laurel and Hardy   1931
Comedy Classics Volume
V
Comedy
33914 84 mins B/W B, V, 3/4U   P
Stan Laurel, Oliver Hardy, Edgar Kennedy, James Finlayson, Blanche Payson
Four classic comedy shorts starring Laurel and Hardy. Included are "Be Big," "The Perfect Day," "Night Owls," and "Help Mates," from 1929-31.
Hal Roach, MGM — *Nostalgia Merchant*

Laurel and Hardy   1935
Comedy Classics Volume
VI
Comedy
33915 75 mins B/W B, V, 3/4U   P
Stan Laurel, Oliver Hardy, Charlie Hall, Billy Gilbert, Ben Turpin, Mae Busch, James Finlayson
Laurel and Hardy comedy shorts are presented in this package: "Our Wife," "The Fixer Uppers," "Them Thar Hills," and "Tit for Tat," from 1932-35.
Hal Roach, MGM — *Nostalgia Merchant*

Laurel and Hardy   193?
Comedy Classics Volume
VII
Comedy
47142 90 mins B/W B, V, 3/4U   P
Stan Laurel, Oliver Hardy, Mae Busch, Daphne Pollard, James Finlayson
Four Laurel and Hardy two-reelers are combined on this tape: "Me and My Pal" (1933), "The Midnight Patrol" (1933), "Thicker than Water" (1935), and the classic "Below Zero" (1930).
Hal Roach; MGM — *Nostalgia Merchant*

Laurel and Hardy   193?
Comedy Classics Volume
VIII
Comedy
59153 90 mins B/W B, V, 3/4U   P
Stan Laurel, Oliver Hardy
This compilation of Laurel and Hardy shorts includes: "Men O' War" (1929), "Scram" (1932), "Laurel and Hardy Murder Case" (1930) and "One Good Turn" (1931).
Hal Roach — *Nostalgia Merchant*

Laurel and Hardy   193?
Comedy Classics Volume
IX
Comedy
60422 100 mins B/W B, V, 3/4U   P
Stan Laurel, Oliver Hardy
Includes the shorts: "Beau Hunks" (1931), "Chickens Come Home" (1931), "Going Bye-Bye" (1934), and "Berth Marks" (1929).
Hal Roach — *Nostalgia Merchant*

Laurel and Hardy Volume   196?
1
Cartoons
47655   59 mins C   B, V   P
Animated
Animated adventures of Laurel and Hardy.
EL, SP
Larry Harmon — *Unicorn Video*

Laurel and Hardy Volume   196?
2
Cartoons
47656   59 mins C   B, V   P
Animated
Animated short cartoons starring Laurel and Hardy.
EL, SP
Larry Harmon — *Unicorn Video*

Laurel and Hardy Volume   196?
3
Cartoons
47657   59 mins C   B, V   P
Animated
More animated adventures of Laurel and Hardy.
EL, SP
Larry Harmon — *Unicorn Video*

Laurel and Hardy Volume 4 196?
Cartoons
47658   59 mins   C   B, V   P
Animated
Animated shorts starring cartoon characters of
Laurel and Hardy.
EL, SP
Larry Harmon — *Unicorn Video*

Lavender Hill Mob, The 1951
Comedy
50942   78 mins   B/W   B, V   R, P
*Alec Guinness, Audrey Hepburn, Stanley
Holloway*
A prim and prissy bank clerk schemes to melt
the bank's gold down and re-mold it into
miniature Eiffel Tower paperweights.
Academy Award '52: Best Story and Screenplay
(T.E.B. Clarke).
Universal; J Arthur Rank — *THORN EMI Home
Video*

Law of the Lash 1947
Western
54180   54 mins   B/W   B, V   P
Lash LaRue, Al "Fuzzy" St. John
Cowboys and rustlers battle it out.
Monogram — *Video Connection; Discount
Video Tapes*

Law of the Saddle 1945
Western
57979   60 mins   B/W   B, V   P
Bob Livingston
The Lone Rider pits himself against a gang of
outlaws.
Producers Releasing Corp — *Video
Connection*

Law of the Wild 1934
Adventure
54181   156 mins   B/W   B, V   P
Rex, Rin Tin Tin Jr., Bob Custer
The search for a magnificent stallion that was
hijacked by race racketeers before a big
sweepstakes race is shown in this 12 chapter
serial.
Mascot — *Video Connection*

Law of the Wolf 1924
Adventure
08751   50 mins   B/W   B, V, 3/4U   P
Rin-Tin-Tin, Dennis Moore
High speed chases, auto wrecks, gunfights, and
fist fights highlight this adventure.
Warners — *Penguin Video*

Law Rides, The 1936
Western
08814   57 mins   B/W   B, V, 3/4U   P
Bob Steele

Rush of gold claims causes an outbreak of
murder and robbery.
Monogram — *Penguin Video; Discount Video
Tapes*

Law West of Tombstone 1938
Western
64415   73 mins   B/W   B, V, 3/4U   P
Tim Holt, Harry Carey, Evelyn Brent
An ex-outlaw moves to a dangerous frontier
town in order to clean things up.
RKO — *Nostalgia Merchant*

Lawless Frontier 1935
Western
58972   53 mins   B/W   B, V, 3/4U   P
John Wayne, Gabby Hayes
In the early West, the Duke fights for law and
order.
Monogram — *Cable Films; Video Connection*

Lawmen 1944
Western
51638   55 mins   B/W   B, V   P
Johnny Mack Brown, Raymond Hatten
Government agents fight to enforce the law in
the badlands.
Monogram — *Discount Video Tapes; Sheik
Video*

Lawrence of Arabia 1962
Drama
68260   221 mins   C   B, V   P
*Peter O'Toole, Omar Sharif, Alec Guinness,
Anthony Quinn*
The true life story of T.E. Lawrence, the English
officer who gained fame in the Middle East
during World War I. In stereo.
MPAA:G
Sam Spiegel; Columbia — *RCA/Columbia
Pictures Home Video; RCA VideoDiscs*

Lawrence Welk Show, The 1957
Television/Music
63625   60 mins   B/W   B, V, FO   P
*Lawrence Welk and his Orchestra, Alice Lon,
The Lennon Sisters, Big Tiny Little Jr.*
Originally telecast in March 1957, this show
features Welk performing a rare accordion solo
and dancing a polka with 10-year-old Peggy
Lennon. Contains original commercials for the
tail-finned 1957 Dodge.
ABC — *Video Yesteryear*

Lazarus Syndrome, The 1979
Drama
65303   90 mins   C   B, V   P
Lou Gossett, Jr
This is a hard-hitting film of a doctor's effort to
expose illicit operating practices of the resident
Chief of surgery.

Viacom Enterprises — *U.S.A. Home Video*

LCA Presents Family Entertainment Playhouse　1197?
Drama/Mystery
56883　120 mins　C　CED　　　　P
Geraldine Fitzgerald
Edgar Allan Poe's "The Gold Bug" pits an adventurous teenager against quicksand, a terrifying storm, and Captain Kidd's curse. "Rodeo Red" stars Geraldine Fitzgerald as a farm woman who teaches a runaway girl about facing her own problems.
Unknown — *RCA VideoDiscs*

Learn to Dance: Disco/Hustle　1980
Dance
44282　25 mins　C　V　　　　P
Paula Fichtencort teaches the beginning and intermediate steps for disco dancing. Each session begins with a repeat exercise of the basic steps, followed by a combination of all variations, providing the viewer with a guide for becoming a fine intermediate disco dancer.
American Home Video Library — *American Home Video Library*

Learn to Dance: Fox Trot/Cha Cha　1980
Dance
44283　24 mins　C　V　　　　P
Paula Fichtencort teaches the beginning and intermediate steps for dancing the fox trot and cha-cha. Using the rote method, she repeats each set of steps with close visual contact so that the viewer can imitate and practice each combination in front of the television set.
American Home Video Library — *American Home Video Library*

Leben von Adolf Hitler, Das (The Life of Adolf Hitler)　1961
Documentary/World War II
47472　101 mins　B/W　B, V, FO　　P
Directed by Paul Rotha
A startling West German documentary feature on the life of Hitler, using much never-before-seen archival footage of Hitler's early life and rise to power. The full twelve-year span of the Third Reich is covered in painstaking detail.
West Germany — *Video Yesteryear*

Legend of Hiawatha, The　1982
Cartoons
72452　35 mins　C　B, V　　　P
Hiawatha must confront a demon who casts a plague on his people. This animated program is based on Henry Wadsworth Longfellow's poem.
Unknown — *Family Home Entertainment*

Legend of Sleepy Hollow, The　1949
Cartoons/Adventure
59808　45 mins　C　B, V　　R, P
Narrated by Bing Crosby
The story of Ichabod Crane and the legendary ride of the headless horseman. Also includes two classic short cartoons, "Lonesome Ghosts" (1932) with Mickey Mouse and "Trick or Treat" (1952) with Donald Duck.
Walt Disney — *Walt Disney Home Video*

Legend of Sleepy Hollow, The　1979
Drama
37363　100 mins　C　B, V　　　P
Washington Irving's classic tale of the Headless Horseman of Sleepy Hollow is brought to life on the screen.
Sunn Classic — *VCI Home Video*

Legend of the Lone Ranger, The　1981
Western
47153　98 mins　C　B, V, CED　　P
Klinton Spilsbury, Michael Horse, Jason Robards
The origin of the fabled Lone Ranger and the story of his first meeting with his Indian companion, Tonto, are brought to life in this new version of the famous legend.
MPAA:PG
Universal; Walter Coblenz — *CBS/Fox Video*

Legend of the Northwest　1978
Adventure
51657　83 mins　C　B, V　　R, P
Denver Pyle
The loyalty of a dog is evidenced in the fierce revenge he has for the drunken hunter who shot and killed his master.
MPAA:G
GG Communications — *Video Gems*

Legend of the Wolfwoman　1977
Horror
48328　84 mins　C　B, V　　　P
Anne Borel, Fred Stafford
The beautiful Daniella assumes the personality of the legendary wolfwoman, leaving a trail of gruesome killings across the countryside.
MPAA:R
Dimension Pictures — *VCI Home Video*

Legend of Valentino, The　1983
Documentary/Biographical
74086　71 mins　B/W　B, V　　　P
This is a biographical documentary of perhaps the world's greatest lover beginning with his

immigration to America and ending at his unexpected, sudden death.
Wolper Productions — *Embassy Home Entertainment*

Legend of Young Robin Hood, The   197?
Drama
50963   60 mins   C   B, V   R, P
The early life of the robber of the rich is depicted in this movie. He learns to use a longbow, and forms his convictions as he and other Saxons struggle at their integration into the Norman culture.
MPAA:G
Michael Christian Productions — *Video Gems*

Legendary Greats   1960
Baseball
49552   30 mins   B/W   B, V   P
Men who left an everlasting mark on the game of baseball are profiled. Included are Hall of Famers Christy Mathewson, Babe Ruth, Ty Cobb, Connie Mack, and nine distinguished others.
Major League Baseball — *Major League Baseball Productions*

Legendary Personalities   193?
Film-History
10156   60 mins   B/W   B, V   P, T
Package offers serious and light side of pre-40's years. Newsreel cameras film celebrities like Haile Selassie, George Bernard Shaw, and Sir Arthur Conan Doyle.
Unknown — *Blackhawk Films*

Legion of Missing Men, The   1937
War-Drama
59372   62 mins   B/W   B, V, FO   P
Ralph Forbes, Ben Alexander, Hala Linda
Professional soldiers of fortune, the French Foreign Legion, fight the evil sheik Ahmed in the Sahara.
Unknown — *Video Yesteryear*

Legion of the Lawless   1940
Western
64412   59 mins   B/W   B, V, 3/4U   P
George O'Brien, Virginia Vale
A group of outlaws band together in order to spread terror and confusion among the populace.
RKO — *Nostalgia Merchant*

Legon   19??
Romance
48739   60 mins   B/W   B, V, 3/4U   P
An all-native cast on the island of Bali plays out a story about a love triangle among two girls and a boy.

Henry de la Talaise — *Penguin Video*

Lena Horne: The Lady and Her Music   1984
Music-Performance
69922   134 mins   C   B, V   P
Lena Horne's definitive Broadway performance of all the music she has been identified with during her career includes "Can't Help Lovin' That Man," "Stormy Weather," and "The Lady Is a Tramp." In VHS Dolby stereo and Beta Hi-Fi.
James Nederlander, Michael Frazier et al — *RKO HomeVideo*

Lenny Bruce   1967
Comedy-Performance
10815   60 mins   B/W   B, V, FO   P
Lenny Bruce
An uncensored San Francisco nightclub performance recording Bruce's off-beat, bewitching, and often unprecedented humor.
Filmmakers — *Video Yesteryear*

Lenny Bruce Performance Film, The   1968
Comedy-Performance
58897   72 mins   B/W   B, V, CED   P
Lenny Bruce
A videotape of one of Lenny Bruce's last nightclub appearances at Basin Street West in San Francisco. Also included is "Thank You Mask Man," a color cartoon parody of the Lone Ranger legend, with Lenny Bruce providing all the character voices.
Columbus Prods — *Vestron Video*

Leonor   1975
Drama
37403   90 mins   C   B, V   P
Liv Ullman
Liv Ullman demonstrates her versatility as an actress in this movie, in which she plays the mistress of the Devil.
France — *CBS/Fox Video*

Leopard in the Snow   1978
Drama
72880   89 mins   C   B, V   P
Keir Dullea, Susan Penhaligon, Kenneth More, Billie Whitelaw
The romance between a race car driver allegedly killed in a crash and a young woman is the premise of this film.
MPAA:PG
Harlequin Productions — *Embassy Home Entertainment*

Leopard Man, The   1943
Horror
00314   66 mins   B/W   B, V, 3/4U   P
Dennis O'Keefe, Margo, Rita Corday

An escaped leopard terrorizes a small town. After a search, the big cat is found dead, but the killings continue.
RKO — *Nostalgia Merchant*

Let 'Em Have It 1935
Crime-Drama
58519   92 mins   B/W   B, V, 3/4U   P
Richard Arlen, Virginia Bruce, Bruce Cabot
Cabot gets out on parole, busts his gang out of prison and terrorizes the eastern seaboard until finally nabbed.
United Artists — *Penguin Video*

Let It Be 1970
Musical
55586   80 mins   C   B, V, LV   P
John Lennon, Paul McCartney, George Harrison, Ringo Starr, Billy Preston, Yoko Ono
A documentary look at a Beatles recording session, giving glimpses of the conflicts which led to the breakup.
United Artists — *CBS/Fox Video; RCA VideoDiscs*

Let the Balloon Go 1976
Drama
64790   92 mins   C   B, V   P
Robert Bettles, Sally Whiteman, Matthew Wilson, Terry McQuillan
Based on the international children's bestseller by Australian author Ivan Southall, the story is set in the year 1917 and centers around the plight of a slightly handicapped boy and his struggle to win respect.
MPAA:G
Film Australia — *MCA Home Video*

Let There Be Light 1945
Documentary
51949   60 mins   B/W   B, V   P
Narrated by Walter Huston, directed by John Huston
This moving documentary of shell-shocked soldiers in an army hospital was shelved by the War Department because of its revealing content.
US War Department — *Budget Video; Festival Films*

Let's Do It Again 1975
Comedy
53515   112 mins   C   B, V   R, P
Sidney Poitier, Bill Cosby, John Amos, Jimmie Walker, Ossie Davis, Denise Nicholas, Calvin Lockhart
An Atlanta milkman and his pal, a factory worker, bilk two big-time gamblers out of a large sum of money in order to build a meeting hall for their fraternal lodge. A sequel to "Uptown Saturday Night."

MPAA:PG
Warner Bros; First Artists Film — *Warner Home Video*

Let's Bowl 1981
Sports-Minor
59916   100 mins   C   LV   P
Bowling professional Dick Weber teaches the basics, how to improve your game, and how to perfect an individual style.
Inedco Productions — *INEDCO Productions*

Let's Break 1984
Dance
72865   60 mins   C   B, V   P
This tape provides a step-by-step instructional guide to break dancing.
Mary Perillo — *Image Magnetic Associates*

Let's Break: A Visual 1984
Guide to Break Dancing
Dance
70074   60 mins   C   B, V   P
An instructional guide to breakdancing featuring New York City dancers showing off basic moves to the original music of Dennis McCarthy and Jim Cox.
Image Magnetic Associates Inc — *Warner Home Video*

Let's Dance with Arthur 1980
Murray
Dance
56943   115 mins   C   B, V   P
This instructional program features dance steps from the world-famous Arthur Murray technique, including basic ballroom etiquette, the waltz, the cha cha, the foxtrot, the samba, the rumba, and two types of disco.
Time-Life Video — *Vestron Video*

Let's Do It 1982
Comedy
72342   110 mins   C   B, V   P
An amusing teenage sex comedy.
Shere Productions — *Best Film & Video Corporation*

Let's Get Tough 1942
Comedy
44798   60 mins   B/W   B, V   P
The East Side Kids, Florence Rice
The East Side Kids get mixed up with a suspected spy ring. They tackle the spies and capture the deadly saboteurs of the Black Dragon Society.
Monogram — *Sheik Video; Penguin Video*

Let's Go Catalina — 1939
Travel
73028   30 mins   B/W   B, V   P
This program takes place at Catalina Island. The Bird Park, a Glass Bottom Boat and the Flying Fish are shown.
Unknown — *Interurban Films*

Let's Jazzercise — 1983
Physical fitness/Dance
65206   57 mins   C   B, V   p
Judi Sheppard Missett
This program includes a warm up aerobic activity and muscle toning and is completed by a cool down routine.
Priscilla Ulene; Judi Sheppard Missett — *MCA Home Video*

Let's Spend the Night Together — 1983
Music-Performance
66040   94 mins   C   B, V, LV, CED   P
Rolling Stones, directed by Hal Ashby
A chronicle of the Stones' 1981 American tour including 25 songs spanning their career. Stereo.
MPAA:PG
Ronald Schwary — *Embassy Home Entertainment*

Letter of Introduction — 1938
Drama
33801   104 mins   B/W   B, V   P
Adolphe Menjou, Edgar Bergen, George Murphy, Eve Arden, Ann Sheridan
Struggling young actress learns that her father is really a well-known screen star and agrees not to reveal the news to the public.
Universal — *Budget Video; Discount Video Tapes*

Letter to Nancy, A — 1963
Religion/Identity
55034   80 mins   C   B, V   P
The daughter of a self-centered and comfortable family starts dating the minister of an inner city church.
Family Films — *Vanguard Video*

Ley del Revolver, La (The Law of the Gun) — 1978
Western
51106   90 mins   C   B, V   P
Michael Rivers, Angel Del Pozo, Lucia Gil Fernandez
An Old West adventure where the law of the gun speaks for and against justice. In Spanish.
SP
Spanish — *Budget Video*

Liana — 1983
Drama
65383   110 mins   C   B, V   P
Acclaimed screenwriter/director John Sayles wrote and directed this story of a woman's romantic involvement with another woman.
MPAA:R
Jeffrey Nelson — *Vestron Video*

Liar's Moon — 1982
Drama
64877   106 mins   C   B, V, CED   P
Matt Dillon
A local boy woos and weds the town's wealthiest young lady, only to be trapped in a family's intrigue.
MPAA:PG
Don P Behrns — *Vestron Video*

Liberace in Las Vegas — 1980
Music-Performance
47377   84 mins   C   B, V   R, P
Liberace, the Jimmy Mullander Orchestra, the Ballet Folklorico de Nacionale de Mexico
A musical extravaganza starring the multitalented Liberace and his special guests. Taped at the Las Vegas Hilton.
VC — *Warner Home Video*

Liberace Show Volumes 1 & 2, The — 195?
Musical/Variety
60423   58 mins   B/W   B, V, 3/4U   P
A camp classic, these two half-hour episodes of "Mr. Showmanship's" TV series feature some of the world's best-loved music.
NBC — *Nostalgia Merchant*

Lietuviskos Dainos Suente — 1955
Music-Performance/Dance
72498   20 mins   C   B, V, 3/4U   P
A color film of the first post-World War II traditional culture festival in Vilnius, Lithania.
Lithuania Film — *International Historic Films*

Lietuvos Dainu Svente (Lithuanian Song Festival) — 1975
Music-Performance
52359   25 mins   C   B, V, 3/4U   P
This lively musical production was originally produced for British television, and is narrated in English.
Unknown — *International Historic Films*

Life and Times of Grizzly Adams, The — 1974
Adventure
13007   93 mins   C   B, V   P
Dan Haggerty, Denver Pyle, Don Shanks

This adventure film for the whole family is based on the rugged life of legendary frontiersman, Grizzly Adams.
MPAA:G
Sunn Classic — *VCI Home Video*

Life and Times of Judge Roy Bean, The   1972
Western
68235   123 mins   C   B, V   R, P
Paul Newman
Paul Newman stars as the famous hanging judge in the West.
MPAA:PG
National General — *Warner Home Video*

Life Is a Circus, Charlie Brown!   1980
Cartoons
75607   30 mins   C   B, V   P
Animated
Snoopy joins the traveling circus to be close to the dog of his dreams, Fifi, a French Poodle performer.
Bill Melendez — *Snoopy's Home Video Library*

Life Is Worth Living   1955
Religion
47481   71 mins   B/W   B, V, FO   P
Bishop Fulton J. Sheen
Three programs from Bishop Sheen's long-running TV series, one of the most popular shows of the 1950's. The Bishop discussed religious matters, family life, read poetry and told jokes in an engagingly informal manner that was loved by audiences.
Dumont — *Video Yesteryear*

Life of Christ I   1980
Bible
55021   120 mins   C   B, V   P
Biblical events from the birth of Christ to the Lord's ascension, as told in the four gospels: Birth of the Savior; Childhood of Jesus; First Disciples; Jesus, Lord of the Sabbath; Jesus teaches Forgiveness; The Transfiguration.
Family Films — *Vanguard Video*

Life of Christ II   1980
Bible
55022   100 mins   C   B, V   P
Biblical events in the life of Christ are depicted: Last Journey to Jerusalem; Thirty Pieces of Silver; The Upper Room; Betrayal in Gethsemane; Jesus Before the High Priest.
Family Films — *Vanguard Video*

Life of Christ III   1980
Bible
55023   100 mins   C   B, V   P
Biblical events from the life of Christ are depicted: Trial Before Pilate; The Crucifixion;

Nicodemus; The Lord is Risen; The Lord's Ascension.
Family Films — *Vanguard Video*

Life of Oharu   1952
Drama
69561   136 mins   B/W   B, V, FO   P
Kinuyo Tanaka, Toshiro Mifune, directed by Kenji Mizoguchi
Oharu, the beautiful daughter of a samurai who serves the Imperial Court, falls in love with a lower class servant. When they are caught together, the slave is executed and Oharu is banished from the kingdom. Japanese dialogue with English subtitles.
Japan — *Video Yesteryear*

Life with Father   1947
Comedy
11305   118 mins   C   B, V, FO   P
William Powell, Irene Dunne, Elizabeth Taylor, Edmund Gwenn, Zasu Pitts
New York City of the 1880's is the delightful setting for this story of a stern but susceptible father and his relationship with his knowing wife and four red-headed sons.
New York Film Critics Award '47: Best Male Performance (Powell).
Warner Bros; Robert Buckner — *Video Yesteryear; Budget Video; Video Connection; Sheik Video; Discount Video Tapes; Cinema Concepts; King of Video*

Light at the Edge of the World, The   1971
Adventure
72905   126 mins   C   B, V   P
Kirk Douglas, Yul Brynner, Samantha Eggar
A lighthouse keeper near Cape Horn is tormented by a band of pirates.
MPAA:PG
Brynafilm; Triumfilm — *Media Home Entertainment*

Light of Faith   1922
Film-History
18588   33 mins   C   B, V   P
Lon Chaney, Hope Hampton, directed by Clarence Brown
A sick young woman is cured when she touches the Holy Grail, which a man stole from her former lover in order to help her. Silent.
Unknown — *Classic Video Cinema Collector's Club*

Lightning Strikes West   1940
Western
15485   57 mins   B/W   B, V   P
Ken Maynard
U.S. Marshal trails an escaped convict, eventually catches him, and brings him in to finish paying his debt to society.

Colony — *Video Connection*

Lightning Warrior   1931
Western/Serials
12542   156 mins B/W   B, V   P
George Brent, Frankie Darro, Rin Tin Tin, Jr.,
directed by Armand Schaefer, Ben Kline
Western suspense about pioneer life and the
unraveling of a baffling mystery. Twelve
chapters, 13 minutes each.
Mascot — *Video Connection*

Lights of Old Santa Fe   1947
Western
51448   60 mins B/W   B, V   P
Roy Rogers
A cowboy rescues a beautiful rodeo owner from
bankruptcy.
Producers Releasing Corp — *Sheik Video*

Like a Mighty River...   1981
Football
50648   24 mins   C   B, V, FO   R, P
Dallas Cowboys
Danny White stepped into Roger Staubach's
role as Cowboy quarterback drawing much
praise. Although the defense was weak at times
during the 1980 season, it toughened when it
had to. The Cowboys, under the guidance of the
ever-present Tom Landry, surged all the way to
the NFC championship game, where they finally
ran out of gas.
NFL Films — *NFL Films Video*

Li'l Abner   1940
Musical
08730   78 mins   C   B, V   P
Cranville Owen, Martha Driscoll, Buster Keaton
Al Capp's famed comic strip comes to life in this
comedy, featuring all of the Dogpatch favorites.
RKO — *Discount Video Tapes; Sheik Video;*
Video Yesteryear

Lili   1953
Musical
66454   81 mins   C   B, V   P
Leslie Caron, Jean-Pierre Aumont, Mel Ferrer,
Kurt Kasznar, Zsa Zsa Gabor
A 16-year-old orphan joins a traveling carnival
and falls in love with a crippled, embittered
puppeteer. Leslie Caron sings the films's song
hit, "Hi-Lili, Hi-Lo."
Academy Awards '53: Best Scoring of a
Dramatic or Comedy Film (Bronislau Kaper).
MGM — *MGM/UA Home Video*

Limelight   1952
Drama
48406   144 mins B/W   B, V   P
Charles Chaplin, Claire Bloom, Buster Keaton,
Nigel Bruce

A nearly washed-up music hall comedian is
stimulated by a young ballerina to a final hour of
glory.
Charles Chaplin — *CBS/Fox Video*

Lincoln Conspiracy, The   1977
Documentary
55596   87 mins   C   B, V   P
This film uncovers startling new evidence, and
concludes that high-level cabinet members
conspired to assassinate President Lincoln.
MPAA:G
Sunn Classics — *VidAmerica*

Linda Ronstadt—Nelson   1984
Riddle "What's New"
Music-Performance
72916   60 mins   C   B, V, LV,   P
                        CED
Linda Ronstadt performs great songs of the
1930s and '40s in concert with Nelson Riddle
and His Orchestra.
Peter Asher — *Vestron Video*

Lion Has Wings, The   1939
World War II/Propaganda
53661   74 mins B/W   B, V, 3/4U   P
Britain's first World War II propaganda film
depicting Nazi conquests and England's
national defense efforts.
Britain — *International Historic Films*

Lion in Winter, The   1968
Drama
08367   134 mins   C   B, V, LV,   P
                        CED
Peter O'Toole, Katharine Hepburn, directed by
Anthony Harvey
Katharine Hepburn portrays Eleanor of
Aquitaine in this historical drama of twelfth-
century English political history.
Academy Awards '68: Best Actress (Hepburn).
Avco Embassy — *Embassy Home*
Entertainment; RCA VideoDiscs

Lion Man   1979
Adventure
66090   91 mins   C   B, V   P
Steve Arkin
A man raised by lions fights to reclaim his
family's throne.
MPAA:R
Filmeks — *Best Film & Video Corporation*

Lion of the Desert   1979
Drama
65447   164 mins   C   B, V   P
Anthony Quinn, Oliver Reed, Irene Papas, Rod
Steiger, Raf Vallone, John Gielgud
This is the story of Omar Mukhtar, the great
Libyan patriot whose twenty year long struggle
to free his people from the yoke of Mussolini's

Italian occupying forces became one of the most heroic sagas of the twentieth century.
MPAA:PG
Falcon International — *U.S.A. Home Video*

Lionel Hampton 1983
Music-Performance
75915　24 mins　C　B, V　P
This program presents the jazz music of Lionel Hampton backed up by a 20-piece band.
digit recordings — *Sony Corporation of America*

Lionel Hampton's One Night Stand 197?
Music-Performance
75632　50 mins　C　B, V　P
Mel Torme, Buddy Rich, B.B. King, Johnny Mercer
This is a jazz music extravaganza, featuring vibraphonist Lionel Hampton's Orchestra with some special guests.
Evart Enterprises — *Independent United Distributors*

Lipstick 1976
Drama
38935　88 mins　C　B, V, LV　R, P
Margaux Hemingway, Anne Bancroft, Perry King, Chris Sarandon, Mariel Hemingway
A fashion model (Margaux Hemingway) seeks revenge on the man who brutally attacked and raped her.
MPAA:R
Paramount — *Paramount Home Video*

Liquid Madness 1983
Boating
69901　30 mins　C　B, V, 3/4U　P
This program contains dramatic big water and hair boating footage including Slaughterhouse on the Roaring Fork, Pine Creek on the Arkansas, and the Crystal River.
Bluegrass Paddling Film Festival '83: Grand Prize.
Paul Sharpe — *Gravity Sports Films*

Liquid Sky 1983
Science fiction
65114　112 mins　C　B, V　P
Anne Carlisle, Paula Sheppard, Bob Brady
An androgynous model living in Manhattan is the primary attraction for a UFO, which lands atop her penthouse in search of the chemical nourishment that her sexual encounters provide.
MPAA:R
Slava Tsukerman — *Media Home Entertainment*

Listen to Your Heart 1983
Drama
76046　90 mins　C　B, V　P
Tim Matheson, Kate Jackson
In a contemporary love story, Tim Matheson and Kate Jackson find the strength of their relationship put to the test when they try to work together as well as love together.
CBS Motion Pictures for Television — *Key Video*

Lisztomania 1975
Fantasy
53516　105 mins　C　B, V　R, P
Roger Daltry, Sara Kestelman, Paul Nicholas, Fiona Lewis, Ringo Starr, directed by Ken Russell
Ken Russell's vision of what it must have been like to be Franz Liszt and Richard Wagner, who are depicted as the first pop stars.
MPAA:R
Warner Bros — *Warner Home Video*

Lithuanian Ethnographic Ensemble, The 1974
Music-Performance
52360　30 mins　C　B, V, 3/4U　P
This group performs authentic Lithuanian folksongs and dances. Narrated in English.
Lithuanian Film Studio — *International Historic Films*

Little Annie Roonie 1925
Drama
10125　60 mins　B/W　B, V　P, T
Mary Pickford, William Haines, Walter James, Gordon Griffith, Vola Vale, directed by William Beaudine
Tomboy policeman's daughter spends her time mothering her father and brother while getting into mischief with street punks. Tragedy ensues. (Silent).
Pickford — *Blackhawk Films*

Little Brown Burro, The 1979
Christmas/Cartoons
17270　23 mins　C　B, V　P
Animated, narrated by Lorne Greene
Forlorn donkey realizes that by doing his best he can make his own kind of contribution.
AM　Available
Learning Corp of America — *Embassy Home Entertainment*

Little Caesar 1930
Crime-Drama
64457　80 mins　B/W　B, V, CED　P
Edward G. Robinson, Douglas Fairbanks, Jr.
A small-time hood rises to become a gangland czar but his downfall is as rapid as his advancement. The role of Rico made Edward G. Robinson a star and also typecast him as a crook for all time.

Warner Bros — *CBS/Fox Video; RCA VideoDiscs*

Little Darlings   1980
Comedy
48511   95 mins   C   B, V, LV   R, P
Tatum O'Neal, Kristy McNichol, directed by Ronald F. Maxwell
A summer camp full of fun, friendship, and rivalries is the setting for a race—between a pair of very opposite teenage girls—to lose their virginity.
MPAA:R
Stephen J. Friedman — *Paramount Home Video*

Little Dory Story   1983
Boating
69899   30 mins   C   B, V   P
Twelve-foot dories take on the Grand Canyon of the Colorado at flood stage.
Raccoon Productions — *Gravity Sports Films*

Little Engine That Could,   1963
The
Literature
00692   10 mins   C   B, V   P, T
Animated
The classic story about a little train engine that struggles to carry a load of children's toys over a mountain.
Coronet Films — *Blackhawk Films*

Little Girl...Big Tease   1975
Drama
60408   86 mins   C   B, V   P
A 16-year-old society girl is kidnapped and exploited by a group which includes her teacher.
MPAA:R
Hostage Company Prod; Cannon Releasing — *Paragon Video Productions*

Little Girl Who Lives   1976
Down the Lane, The
Suspense
65345   90 mins   C   B, V   P
Jodie Foster, Martin Sheen
A 13-year-old girl, when her father dies, is discovered to be keeping her mother's corpse in the cellar, and doesn't stop at more murders to keep her secret.
MPAA:PG
Harold Greenberg; Alfred Pariser — *Vestron Video*

Little House on the   1974
Prairie
Drama
53790   100 mins   C   CED   P
Michael Landon, Karen Grassle, Melissa Gilbert, Melissa Sue Anderson, Lindsay Sidney Greenbush, Victor French
The original pilot movie for the popular TV series, in which Charles Ingalls uproots his young family for the plains of Kansas.
NBC — *RCA VideoDiscs*

Little Humpbacked   1961
Horse, The
Dance
69835   85 mins   C   B, V   P
Maya Plisetskaya, Vladimir Vasiliev
A magical tour through the land of flying horses, dancing fish, and tumbling clowns highlight this Bolshoi Ballet production.
Sovexportfilm USSR — *Video Arts International*

Little Johnny Jones   1980
Musical
68236   92 mins   C   B, V   R, P
George M. Cohan's classic musical in a 1980 revival. Songs include "Yankee Doodle Dandy" and "Give My Regards to Broadway."
Goodspeed Opera House — *Warner Home Video*

Little Kid's Dynamite All-   1982
Star Band, The
Musical
64955   90 mins   C   B, V   R, P
Marty Brill, Jay Stuart, Willie De Jean, Mischa Bond, Bunky Butler
A children's rock group rehearses in a garage that has an antique brass mirror lying against a wall. The mirror has magical properties that allow two wacky musketeers to join the children in their adventures.
MPAA:G
Century Video — *Video Gems*

Little Laura and Big John   1973
Adventure
13010   82 mins   C   B, V   P
Fabian Forte, Karen Black
Follows the true-life exploits of the small-time Ashley Gang in turnof-the-century Florida.
Gold Key — *VCI Home Video*

Little Lord Fauntleroy   1936
Comedy-Drama
12449   102 mins   B/W   B, V   P
Freddie Bartholomew, Mickey Rooney, Delores Costello, C. Aubrey Smith
Movie version of Frances Hodgson Burnett's juvenile story. Brooklyn boy becomes a Lord and is brought up by a doting mother.
Selznick — *Video Connection; Budget Video; Cable Films; Discount Video Tapes; Classic Video Cinema Collector's Club*

Little Lord Fauntleroy 1980
Drama
73534 98 mins C B, V P
Ricky Schroeder, Alec Guinness, directed by Jack Gold
A poor young boy growing up in New York City at the turn of the century suddenly discovers his aristocratic background. Available in Beta Hi-Fi and VHS stereo.
Norman Rosemont Productions — *U.S.A. Home Video*

Little Lulu 194?
Cartoons
56746 48 mins C B, V P
Animated
The popular comic book heroine gets into mischief with her pals, Tubby, Iggie, Wilbur and others. Includes "Little Angel" and "Operation Babysitting." Available in English and Spanish versions.
EL, SP
Paramount; Famous Studios — *Media Home Entertainment*

Little Match Girl, The 1984
Fairy tales/Musical
72882 54 mins C B, V P
A musical version of the Hans Christian Andersen classic.
Unknown — *Embassy Home Entertainment*

Little Men 1940
Drama
08615 86 mins B/W B, V, 3/4U P
Jack Oakie, Jimmy Lydon, Kay Francis, George Bancroft
A modern version of the famous classic juvenile story by Louisa May Alcott.
RKO — *Penguin Video; Video Connection*

Little Mermaid, The 1981
Fantasy
72232 75 mins C B, V P
In this animated version of a Hans Christian Andersen fable a princess of the mermaids yearns to be human.
N W Russo — *Children's Video Library*

Little Mermaid, The 1984
Fairy tales
Closed Captioned
73576 60 mins C B, V, CED P
Pam Dawber, Treat Williams
From "Faerie Tale Theatre" comes the adaptation of the Hans Christian Andersen tale of a little mermaid who makes a big sacrifice to win the prince she loves.
Gaylord Productions; Platypus Productions — *CBS/Fox Video*

Little Mermaid, The 1978
Fairy tales/Cartoons
40728 71 mins C B, V R, P
Animated
An animated version of Hans Christian Andersen's tale about a little mermaid who rescues a prince whose boat has capsized. She immediately falls in love and wishes that she could become a human girl.
21st Century — *Video Gems*

Little Miss Marker 1980
Comedy
60589 112 mins C B, V P
Walter Matthau, Julie Andrews, Tony Curtis, Bob Newhart, Lee Grant, Sara Stimson
The often retold tale of Sorrowful Jones, a grouchy, stingy bookie who accepts a little girl as a security marker for a ten dollar bet.
MPAA:PG
Universal — *MCA Home Video*

Little Night Music, A 1977
Musical/Romance
69544 110 mins C B, V P
Elizabeth Taylor, Diana Rigg, Hermione Gingold, Len Cariou, Lesley Ann Down
Adapted from the Broadway play, this film centers around four ingeniously interwoven, contemporary love stories. Musical score by Stephen Sondheim.
MPAA:PG
New World Pictures — *Embassy Home Entertainment*

Little Orphan Annie 1932
Drama
10041 60 mins B/W B, V P, T
Mitzie Green, Edgar Kennedy, directed by John S. Robertson
Based on the comic strip, Annie is an orphan being cared for by a bum. He follows money making scheme, leaving her alone, but Annie finds newly orphaned boy in her travels.
RKO — *Blackhawk Films*

Little Prince, The 1974
Musical
38608 88 mins C B, V, LV R, P
Richard Kiley, Bob Fosse, Steven Warner, Gene Wilder, directed by Stanley Donen
Based on the story by Antoine de Saint-Exupery, this musical fable tells of a little prince from Asteroid B-612 who comes to visit the earth. Music and lyrics by Lerner and Loewe.
MPAA:G
Paramount — *Paramount Home Video*

Little Princess, The 1939
Drama
05445 91 mins C B, V, 3/4U P
Shirley Temple, Richard Greene, Ian Hunter, Cesar Romero, Arthur Treacher, Anita Louise

The story of a little girl who doesn't believe that her missing Army Officer father is really dead. Daryl Zanuck; 20th Century Fox — *Video Connection; VCII; Program Hunters; Video Yesteryear; Penguin Video; Sheik Video; Cable Films; Budget Video; Discount Video Tapes; Nostalgia Merchant; Media Home Entertainment*

Little Rascals, Book I, The　　　　193?

Comedy
66117　59 mins　B/W　　B, V　　　P, T
Farina Hoskins, Joe Cobb, Stymie Beard, Spanky McFarland, Scotty Beckett, Alfalfa Switzer, Mary Ann Jackson
Three "Our Gang" shorts: "Railroadin'" (1929), in which the gang takes off on a runaway train; "A Lad and a Lamp" (1932), wherein they find an Aladdin's lamp; "Beginner's Luck" (1935), in which Spanky wins a dress for a young actress.
Hal Roach — *Blackhawk Films*

Little Rascals, Book II, The　　　　193?

Comedy
64826　56 mins　B/W　　B, V　　　P, T
Stymie Beard, Wheezer Hutchins, Spanky McFarland, Alfalfa Switzer
A second package of "Our Gang" two-reelers: "Bear Shooters" (1930), in which the Gang goes hunting but runs into some bootleggers; "Forgotten Babies" (1933), has Spanky babysitting for the gang's brothers and sisters; and "Teacher's Beau" (1935), where the gang cooks up a scheme to chase their teacher's fiance away.
Hal Roach — *Blackhawk Films*

Little Rascals, Book III, The　　　　1938

Comedy
64917　54 mins　B/W　　B, V　　　P, T
Wheezer Hutchins, Dorothy De Borba, Stymie Beard, Spanky McFarland, Alfalfa Switzer, Darla Hood
Three more "Our Gang" two reelers are packaged on this tape: "Dogs Is Dogs" (1931), "Anniversary Trouble" (1935) and "Three Men in a Tub" (1938).
Hal Roach — *Blackhawk Films*

Little Rascals, Book IV, The　　　　193?

Comedy
65083　52 mins　B/W　　B, V　　　P, T
Wheezer, Stymie, Spanky, Alfalfa, Darla, Porky, Buckwheat
Another package of Our Gang favorites, including "Helping Grandma" (1931), "Little Papa" (1935) and "Bear Facts" (1938).
Hal Roach — *Blackhawk Films*

Little Rascals, Book V, The　　　　193?

Comedy
65084　49 mins　B/W　　B, V　　　P, T
Breezy Brisbane, Stymie, Spanky, Scotty, Alfalfa, Darla, Porky, Buckwheat
The comic adventures of the Little Rascals continue in this package of three original shorts: "Readin' and Writin'" (1932), "Sprucin' Up" (1935) and "Reunion in Rhythm" (1937).
Hal Roach — *Blackhawk Films*

Little Rascals, Book VI, The　　　　193?

Comedy
65085　48 mins　B/W　　B, V　　　P, T
Stymie, Breezy, Spanky, Fidgets, Alfalfa, Darla, Porky, Buckwheat, Dorothy DeBorba, Billy Gilbert
Three more classic "Our Gang" comedy shorts are packaged on this tape: "Free Eats" (1932), "Arbor Day" (1936) and "Mail and Female" (1937).
Hal Roach — *Blackhawk Films*

Little Rascals, Book VII, The　　　　193?

Comedy
65086　47 mins　B/W　　B, V　　　P, T
Spanky, Breezy, Dickie Moore, Stymie, Scotty, Alfalfa, Darla, Porky, Buckwheat
The "Our Gang" kids serve up another portion of comedy in these three shorts: "Hook and Ladder" (1932), "The Lucky Corner" (1936) and "Feed 'Em and Weep" (1938).
Hal Roach — *Blackhawk Films*

Little Rascals Book VIII, The　　　　19??

Comedy
66305　42 mins　B/W　　B, V　　　P, T
Wheezer, Mary Ann Jackson, Spanky, Alfalfa, Buckwheat, Porky, Darla Hood
More fun and nuttiness with "Our Gang" in three original short comedies, "Bouncing Babies" (1929), "Two Too Young" (1936) and "The Awful Tooth" (1938).
Hal Roach — *Blackhawk Films*

Little Rascals Book IX, The　　　　19??

Comedy
66306　48 mins　B/W　　B, V　　　P, T
Farina, Stymie, Spanky, Alfalfa, Buckwheat, Porky, Darla
The Little Rascals scamper into more mischief in these three original shorts: "Little Daddy" (1931), "Spooky Hooky" (1936) and "Hide and Shriek" (1938).
Hal Roach — *Blackhawk Films*

Little Rascals, Book X, The — 19??

Comedy
66308 41 mins B/W B, V P, T
Jackie Cooper, Mary Ann Jackson, Spanky, Alfalfa, Buckwheat, Porky, Darla, Butch, Woim
The tenth compilation of original "Our Gang" comedies includes "The First Seven Years" (1929), "Bored of Education" (1936) and "Rushin' Ballet" (1937).
Academy Awards '36: Best Short Subject ("Bored of Education").
Hal Roach — *Blackhawk Films*

Little Rascals, Book XI, The — 1938

Comedy
66340 42 mins B/W B, V P, T
Spanky McFarland, Alfalfa Switzer, Darla Hood, Porky, Buckwheat
The Little Rascals go dramatic in these three shorts, all with a "putting-on-a-show" theme: "Pay As You Exit" (1936), "Three Smart Boys" (1937) and "Our Gang Follies of 1938."
Hal Roach — *Blackhawk Films*

Little Rascals, Book XII, The — 1937

Comedy
66341 53 mins B/W B, V P, T
Jackie Cooper, Farina Hoskins, Mary Ann Jackson, Spanky McFarland, Alfalfa Switzer, Darla Hood
The Little Rascals explore a haunted house, take a train ride and play football in these three original shorts: "Moan and Groan, Inc." (1929), "Choo-Choo!" (1932) and "The Pigskin Palooka" (1937).
Hal Roach — *Blackhawk Films*

Little Rascals, Book XIII, The — 1937

Comedy
66442 48 mins B/W B, V P, T
Jackie Cooper, Farina, Wheezer, Chubby, Mary Ann, Spanky, Scotty, Alfalfa, Edgar Kennedy
The Our Gang kids return in three more original shorts: "Shivering Shakespeare" (1930), "The First Round-Up" (1934) and "Fishy Tales" (1937).
Hal Roach — *Blackhawk Films*

Little Rascals, Book XIV, The — 193?

Comedy
65704 52 mins B/W B, V P, T
Wheezer, Mary Ann, Spanky, Porky, Alfalfa, Buckwheat, Darla
This package of shorts leads off with Our Gang's first talkie, "Small Talk" (1929), a three-reeler. The other two entries are "Little Sinner" (1935) and "Hearts Are Thumps" (1937).

Little Rascals, Book XV, The — 193?

Comedy
65770 50 mins B/W B, V P, T
Edgar Kennedy, Tommy "Butch" Bond, Spanky McFarland, Scotty Beckett, Wheezer Hutchins
Those rascally imps return once again in three more original shorts: "When the Wind Blows" (1930), "For Pete's Sake" (1934) and "Glove Taps" (1937).
Hal Roach; MGM — *Blackhawk Films*

Little Rascals, Book XVI, The — 193?

Comedy
65768 50 mins B/W B, V P, T
Jackie Cooper, Chubby Chaney, Spanky McFarland, Alfalfa Switzer, Darla Hood, Wally Albright
More Little Rascals mayhem in these three original shorts: "Love Business" (1931), "Hi-Neighbor!" (1934) and "Came the Brawn" (1938).
Hal Roach; MGM — *Blackhawk Films*

Little Rascals Christmas Special, The — 1979

Christmas
65160 60 mins C B, V P
Animated, voices of Darla Hood, Matthew "Stymie" Beard
Spanky and the Little Rascals attempt to raise enough money to buy a winter coat for Spanky's mom and learn the true meaning of Christmas along the way.
King World Productions — *Family Home Entertainment*

Little Rascals Comedy Classics 1 — 193?

Comedy
65739 50 mins B/W B, V P
Spankie, Stymie, Alfalfa, Buckwheat
The Little Rascals romp again in this collection of original comedy two-reelers.
Hal Roach — *NTA Home Entertainment*

Little Red Riding Hood — 1984

Fairy tales
Closed Captioned
73142 60 mins C B, V, CED P
Mary Steenburgen, Malcolm McDowell, directed by Graeme Clifford
From "Faerie Tale Theatre" comes the retelling of the story about a girl (Mary Steenburgen) off to give her grandmother a picnic basket only to get stopped by a wolf.
Shelley Duvall — *CBS/Fox Video*

Little River Band 1982
Music-Performance
47798   75 mins   C   B, V   R, P
Selections from this Australian rock'n'roll band's
six LP's, such as "It's a Long Way There,"
"Mistress of Mine," and "Just Say That You
Love Me," are featured.
Capitol EMI Music — *THORN EMI Home
Video; RCA VideoDiscs; Pioneer Artists*

Little Romance, A 1979
Drama
38942   105 mins   C   B, V   R, P
*Laurence Olivier, Thelonius Bernard, Diane
Lane, directed by George Roy Hill*
Two lonely, gifted children set out on a charming
adventure that carries them across Europe to
find love in Venice.
MPAA:PG
Orion Pictures — *Warner Home Video*

Little Sex, A 1982
Comedy
47849   94 mins   C   B, V   P
*Tim Matheson, Kate Capshaw, Edward
Herrmann, Wallace Shaw*
A young newlywed finds himself perpetually
tempted by young women.
MPAA:R
Universal — *MCA Home Video*

Little Shop of Horrors 1960
Horror
00408   70 mins   B/W   B, V   P
*Jackie Joseph, Jonathan Haze, Mel Welles,
Jack Nicholson, directedby Roger Corman*
Simple minded boy develops man-eating plant.
Attempting to destroy it, he becomes its victim.
Filmgroup — *Budget Video; Movie Buff Video;
Penguin Video; Sheik Video; Video Connection;
Video Yesteryear; Western Film & Video Inc;
Discount Video Tapes*

Little Tough Guys 1938
Drama
01717   84 mins   B/W   B, V, FO   P
*Helen Parrish, Billy Halop, Leo Georcy, Marjorie
Main*
When father goes to jail, the children must fend
for themselves. Son gets involved in gang
warfare plus reform school.
U I — *Video Yesteryear; Cable Films; Budget
Video; Discount Video Tapes*

Little Women 1933
Drama
58297   107 mins   B/W   B, V   P
*Katharine Hepburn, Joan Bennett, Paul Lukas,
Edna May Oliver, Frances Dee, directed by
George Cukor*
Louisa May Alcott's Civil War story of the four
March sisters, Jo, Beth, Amy, and Meg, who
share their loves, their joys, and their sorrows.

Academy Awards '33: Writing Adaptation (Victor
Heerman, Sarah Y. Mason).
RKO — *MGM/UA Home Video*

Little Women 1983
Cartoons/Literature
69535   60 mins   C   B, V, CED   P
Animated
Louisa May Alcott's classic tale of four loving
sisters who face the joys and hardships of life
together comes to life in this animated program.
Toei Animation Productions — *Children's
Video Library*

Littlest Warrior, The 1975
Cartoons/Adventure
53139   70 mins   C   B, V   P
Animated
Zooshio, the Littlest Warrior, is forced to leave
his beloved forest and experiences many
adventures before he is reunited with his family
forever.
Ziv Intl — *Family Home Entertainment*

Live and Let Die 1973
Adventure
64329   121 mins   C   LV   P
Roger Moore, Jane Seymour, Yaphet Kotto
Agent 007 is out to thwart the villainous Dr.
Kananga, a black mastermind who plans to
control western powers with voodoo and hard
drugs. Title song by Paul McCartney and Wings.
MPAA:PG
United Artists — *CBS/Fox Video; RCA
VideoDiscs*

Live and Let Die 1973
Adventure
65328   121 mins   C   B, V   P
Roger Moore, Jane Seymour, Geoffrey Holder
James Bond, while investigating the murder of 3
agents, runs afoul of a multi-identity enemy
involved in narcotics smuggling.
MPAA:PG
Harry Saltzman; Albert Broccoli — *CBS/Fox
Video*

Live Infidelity: REO 1981
Speedwagon in Concert
Music-Performance
53410   90 mins   C   B, V, LV,   P
                                    CED
A live performance by REO Speedwagon,
featuring selections from their album, "Hi
Infidelity."
MGM; CBS — *CBS/Fox Video*

Live Television 195?
Drama
33696   110 mins   B/W   B, V, 3/4U   P
*Bob Cummings, Martin Balsam, Rip Torn, Ralph
Edwards, Laurel and Hardy*

Two classic examples from the live, pioneer days of television: "Playhouse 90: Bomber's Moon," and "This Is Your Life, Laurel and Hardy."
CBS, NBC — *Shokus Video*

Living Dead, The   1934
Horror
08779   85 mins   B/W   B, V, 3/4U   P
Gerald de Maurier, George Curzon, Belle Chrystall
A Brtiish crime story about a mad doctor. Some science fiction and horror overtones.
Britain — *Penguin Video*

Living Head, The   1963
Adventure
56913   75 mins   B/W   B, V, FO   P
Archeologists discover the ancient sepulcher of the great Aztec warrior, Acatl. Ignoring a curse, they steal his severed head and incur the fury of Xitsliapoli. Dubbed in English.
Mexican — *Video Yesteryear*

Liza in Concert   1981
Music-Performance
52670   60 mins   C   LV   P
Liza Minnelli performs at the Theatre for the Performing Arts in New Orleans, featuring a New York medley: "Lullaby of Broadway," "I Guess the Lord Must Be in New York City," "Forty Second Street," "On Broadway," and "Theme from New York, New York." Also performed are "City Lights," "Arthur in the Afternoon," and "Cabaret."
Artel Home Video — *Pioneer Artists*

Loaded Pistols   1948
Western
14399   80 mins   B/W   B, V   P
Gene Autry, directed by John English
Story set in the old West starring Gene Autry.
Columbia — *Video Connection*

Loading and   19??
Transporting the Horse
and Knots for Restraint
Animals
69662   44 mins   C   B, V   P
Two programs are contained on one cassette. "Loading" demonstrates simple techniques for trailering the horse; "Knots" demonstrates how to tie 11 different knots that can be used to restrain the horse. Some black and white segments.
Colorado State U — *Mercedes Maharis Productions*

Local Hero   1983
Adventure
65324   112 mins   C   B, V   P

Peter Riegert, Denis Lawson, Fulton Mackay, Burt Lancaster
A Texas oil company sends an ace trouble-shooter to buy out a sleepy Scottish fishing village for a refinery and supertanker port, but both the oil men and the citizenry get more than they bargained for.
MPAA:PG
Puttnam — *Warner Home Video*

Loch Ness Monster, The   197?
Documentary
19414   16 mins   C   B, V, 3/4U,   P
                              Q
On location, eye-witness reports of the famous supposed inhabitant of Scotland's Loch Ness. The history of sightings are covered from the early 1500's to the present.
Ted Higgenbotham — *TV Sports Scene*

Lockheed L-1011 Tristar   1971
Aeronautics
52507   42 mins   C   B, V, 3/4U   P
A promotional film for this durable passenger plane, tracing its conception to actual test flights with fascinating assembly footage.
Lockheed — *International Historic Films*

Locomotion of the Horse   1984
Horse racing
74539   19 mins   C   B, V   P
This program is an up-close look at the motion of a thoroughbred as he walks, trots and gallops.
Michigan State University — *Mercedes Maharis Productions*

Lodger, The   1926
Suspense
47469   91 mins   B/W   B, V, FO   P
Ivor Novello, Marie Ault, Arthur Chesney, Malcolm Keen, directed by Alfred Hitchcock
A mysterious lodger is thought to be a rampaging mass murderer of young women. This is the first Hitchcock film to explore themes and ideas that would become trademarks of his work.
Gainsborough — *Video Yesteryear; Video Dimensions; Festival Films; Classic Video Cinema Collector's Club*

Logan's Run   1976
Science fiction
58298   120 mins   C   B, V, CED   P
Michael York, Richard Jordan, Jenny Agutter, Roscoe Lee Browne, Farrah Fawcett-Majors, Peter Ustinov
In the 23rd century, a hedonistic society exists in a huge bubble and takes it for granted that there is no life outside.
MGM — *MGM/UA Home Video*

Lolita 1962
Drama
53941   152 mins   B/W   B, V, CED   P
James Mason, Shelley Winters, Peter Sellers, Sue Lyon, directed by Stanley Kubrick
Vladimir Nabokov's novel about a middle-aged professor's obsession with a teenage nymphet is the basis of this film.
MGM — *MGM/UA Home Video*

Lombardi 1980
Football
50088   48 mins   C   B, V, FO   R, P
A tribute to Vince Lombardi and his legendary Green Bay Packers, 1960's "Team of the Decade."
NFL Films — *NFL Films Video*

Lone Avenger, The 1933
Western
08839   60 mins   B/W   B, V, 3/4U   P
Ken Maynard, Muriel Gordon, James Marcus
The plot centers around a bank panic and two-gun Maynard clears up the trouble.
World Wide — *Penguin Video; Video Connection; Cable Films; Discount Video Tapes*

Lone Bandit, The 1933
Western
15536   57 mins   B/W   B, V   P
Lane Chandler
Vintage western starring Lane Chandler.
Empire — *Video Connection*

Lone Ranger, The 1980
Cartoons/Western
66003   60 mins   C   B, V   P
Animated
Three tales of derring-do from the masked man and his faithful Indian sidekick.
Lone Ranger Television Inc — *Family Home Entertainment*

Lone Ranger, The 1938
Western/Serials
57357   234 mins   B/W   B, V, FO   P
Western serial, extremely rare, about the masked man and his faithful Indian sidekick. From a long-sought print found in Mexico, this program is burdened by a noisy sound track, two completely missing chapters, an abridged episode #15, and containing Spanish subtitles.
Republic — *Video Yesteryear; Video Connection*

Lone Wolf, The 1972
Drama
65436   45 mins   C   B, V   P
A boy learns kindness by befriending an old military dog which villagers think is mad and responsible for killing their sheep. After a brush with death, the boy convinces the villagers of the dog's good qualities and wins the admiration of his friends.
Columbia — *Embassy Home Entertainment*

Lone Wolf McQuade 1983
Western/Martial arts
64899   107 mins   C   B, V, LV   P
Chuck Norris, Leon Isaac Kennedy, David Carradine, Barbara Carrera
Martial arts action abounds in this modern-day Western which pits a Texas Ranger against a band of mercenaries.
Orion Pictures — *Vestron Video; RCA VideoDiscs*

Loneliness of the Long Distance Runner 1962
Drama
48746   103 mins   B/W   B, V   P
Tom Courtenay, Michael Redgrave, Avis Bunnage, James Bolam
A young man is found to be the fastest runner in his reformatory. He trains for the upcoming Sports Day race, and when that day arrives, he strikes a blow for his individuality.
Continental, Tony Richardson — *Sheik Video*

Lonely Boy/Satan's Choice 19??
Music/Documentary
65230   55 mins   B/W   B, V, FO   P
This tape contains two cinema-verite documentaries from the National Film Board of Canada. "Lonely Boy" (1962) follows the early career of pop singer Paul Anka; and "Satan's Choice" (1966) provides an inside look at the members of a motorcycle gang.
National Film Board of Canada — *Video Yesteryear*

Lonely Guy, The 1984
Comedy
74091   91 mins   C   B, V, LV, CED   P
Steve Martin, Charles Grodin, Judith Ivey, Steve Lawrence
This romantic comedy features Steve Martin as a jilted writer who writes a best-selling book about being a lonely guy and finds stardom does have its rewards.
MPAA:R
Universal — *MCA Home Video*

Lonely Hearts 1983
Romance/Comedy
65624   95 mins   C   B, V   P
Wendy Hughes, Norman Kaye
This is a quiet story about a piano tuner, who at 50 finds himself alone after years of caring for his mother, and a sexually insecure spinster, whom he meets through a dating service.
MPAA:R

John B Murray — *Embassy Home Entertainment*

Lonely Lady, The   1983
Drama
66328   92 mins   C   B, V, LV, CED   P
Pia Zadora, Lloyd Bochner, Bibi Besch, Joseph Cali
A young writer comes to Hollywood with dreams of success. She gets involved with the seamy side of moviemaking and is driven to a nervous breakdown.
MPAA:R
Universal — *MCA Home Video*

Lonely Wives   1931
Comedy
58728   86 mins   B/W   B, V   P
Edward Everett Horton, Patsy Ruth Miller, Laura La Planta, Esther Ralston
A lawyer hires an entertainer to serve as his double because of his marital problems.
RKO — *Sheik Video; Video Yesteryear*

Long Ago Tomorrow   1971
Drama
65703   90 mins   C   B, V   P
Malcolm McDowell, Nanette Newman
A paralyzed athlete enters a church-run home rather than return to his family as the object of their pity.
MPAA:PG
Bruce Cohn Curtis — *RCA/Columbia Pictures Home Video*

Long Dark Hall, The   1951
Drama
66387   86 mins   B/W   B, V   P
Rex Harrison, Lilli Palmer, Denis O'Dea
A chorus girl is murdered and her married lover is accused of the crime.
British Lion — *Movie Buff Video*

Long Day's Journey Into Night   1962
Drama
66473   174 mins   B/W   B, V   P
Katharine Hepburn, Ralph Richardson, Jason Robards, Dean Stockwell
Eugene O'Neill's autobiographical drama deals with the life of his family, circa 1912, as his father and brother were forced to come to grips with his mother's drug addiction.
Landau Unger — *NTA Home Entertainment*

Long Good Friday, The   1979
Crime-Drama
63331   109 mins   C   B, V   R, P
Bob Hoskins, Helen Mirren, Dave King, Bryan Marshall, Derek Thompson, Eddie Constantine
Set in London's dockland, this is the story of an underworld king out to beat his rivals at their own game.
Hand Made Films; Barry Hanson — *THORN EMI Home Video*

Long Shot   1981
Drama
73026   100 mins   C   B, V   R, P
Two foosball enthusiasts work their way through local tournaments to make enough money to make it to the World Championships in Tahoe.
Unknown — *THORN EMI Home Video*

Longest Day, The   1962
War-Drama
08443   179 mins   C   B, V   P
Richard Burton, Peter Lawford, Rod Steiger, John Wayne, Edmond O'Brien
The complete story of the D-Day landings at Normandy, as seen through the eyes of American, French, British and German participants.
EL, SP
20th Century Fox; Darryl F. Zanuck — *CBS/Fox Video*

Longest Yard, The   1974
Comedy
38589   121 mins   C   B, V, LV   R, P
Burt Reynolds, Eddie Albert, directed by Robert Aldrich
A one-time pro football quarterback, now a prisoner, organizes his fellow convicts into a football team to play against the prison guards for a special game. Filmed on location at Georgia State Prison.
MPAA:R
Paramount — *Paramount Home Video; RCA VideoDiscs*

Look Back in Anger   1959
Drama
51965   99 mins   B/W   B, V   R, P
Claire Bloom, Richard Burton, Mary Ure
Almost too late, a young man realizes how much he needs and wants his wife.
Warner Bros — *Warner Home Video*

Looker   1981
Science fiction
47368   93 mins   C   B, V   R, P
Albert Finney, James Coburn, Susan Dey, Leigh Taylor-Young
Stunning models are made even more beautiful by a plastic surgeon, but one by one they begin to die.
MPAA:PG
The Ladd Company; Howard Jeffrey — *Warner Home Video*

Lookin' to Get Out   1982
Adventure/Comedy
65503   70 mins   C   B, V, CED   P
Ann-Margret, Jon Voight, Burt Young
An ex-call girl living with her infant son in the owner's penthouse of a swank Las Vegas hotel spots the father of her child, and revenge is the only thing on her mind.
MPAA:R
Lorimar — *CBS/Fox Video*

Looking for Mr. Goodbar   1977
Drama
38597   136 mins   C   B, V, LV   R, P
Diane Keaton, Tuesday Weld, Richard Gere, directed by Richard Brooks
Diane Keaton portrays a young teacher who seeks escape from her claustrophobic existence by frequenting singles bars. Based on Judith Rossner's novel.
MPAA:R
Paramount — *Paramount Home Video; RCA VideoDiscs*

Looking Glass War, The   1969
Horror
65468   108 mins   C   B, V   P
Christopher Jones, Ralph Richardson, Pia Degermark, Anthony Hopkins
A Polish defector is sent behind the Iron Curtain on a final mission. Adapted from John Le Carre's best-selling spy novel. In Beta Hi-Fi.
MPAA:PG
John Box — *RCA/Columbia Pictures Home Video*

Looney Looney Looney Bugs Bunny Movie, The   1981
Cartoons
47394   80 mins   C   B, V   R, P
A feature-length compilation of classic Warner Brothers cartoons tied together with new animation. Cartoon stars featured include Bugs Bunny, Elmer Fudd, Porky Pig, Yosemite Sam, Duffy Duck and Foghorn Leghorn.
Warner Bros — *Warner Home Video; RCA VideoDiscs*

Looney Tunes and Merrie Melodies I   1933
Comedy/Cartoons
38967   56 mins   B/W   B, V, FO   P
Animated
A collection of eight Warner Brothers Vitaphone cartoons dating from 1931-33, most with jazzy musical accompaniments. Titles include "It's Got Me Again," "You Don't Know What You're Doin'," "Moonlight for Two," "Battling Bosko," "Red-Headed Baby," and "Freddy the Freshman."
Warner Bros — *Video Yesteryear*

Looney Tunes and Merrie Melodies II   194?
Comedy/Cartoons
38969   51 mins   B/W   B, V, FO   P
Animated
A second collection of seven Warner-Vitaphone cartoons from 1931-33, 1937, and 1941-43. Porky Pig, Daffy Duck, and Bugs Bunny are featured in the later World War II-oriented titles, "Scrap Happy Daffy" and Porky Pig's Feat." Earlier titles include "One More Time," "Smile, Darnya, Smile," and "Yodeling Yokels."
Warner Bros — *Video Yesteryear*

Looney Tunes and Merrie Melodies #3   194?
Cartoons
59367   60 mins   C   B, V, FO   P
Cartoon classics from Warner Bros: "A Corny Concerto" (1943), with Porky and Bugs; "Foney Fables" (1942), a retelling of old fairy tales; "The Wacky Wabbit" (1942), featuring Bugs and Elmer Fudd; "Have You Got Any Castles" (1938); "Fifth Column Mouse" (1943); "To Duck or Not to Duck" (1943), with Elmer and Daffy; "The Early Worm Gets the Bird" (1940); and "Daffy the Commando (1943), with Daffy Duck.
Warner Bros — *Video Yesteryear*

Looney Tunes Video Show #1, The   195?
Cartoons
62879   49 mins   C   B, V   R, P
Animated
Seven Warner Brothers cartoon classics of the 1940's and 50's: Bugs Bunny and the Tasmanian Devil in "Devil May Hare," Sylvester in "Birds of a Father," "Daffy Duck and Porky Pig in "The Ducksters," the Road Runner and Wile E. Coyote in "Zipping Along," Sylvester and Tweety in "Room and Bird," Elmer Fudd in "Ant Pasted" and Speedy Gonzales in "Mexican Schmoes."
Warner Bros — *Warner Home Video*

Looney Tunes Video Show #2, The   195?
Cartoons
62880   48 mins   C   B, V   R, P
Animated
More Warner Brothers cartoon favorites: Daffy Duck in "Quackodile Tears," Porky Pig in "An Egg Scramble," Sylvester and Speedy Gonzales in "Cats and Bruises," Foghorn Leghorn in "All Fowled Up," Bugs Bunny and Yosemite Sam in "14 Carrot Rabbit," Professor Calvin Q. Calculus in "The Hole Idea" and Pepe Le Pew in "Two Scents Worth."
Warner Bros — *Warner Home Video*

    (For Explanation of codes, see USE GUIDE and KEY)

Looney Tunes Video Show #3, The   195?
Cartoons
62881   38 mins   C   B, V   R, P
Animated
Seven more Warner Brothers cartoon shorts: Daffy Duck and Speedy Gonzales in "The Quacker Tracker," the Wolf and Sheepdog in "Double or Mutton," Claude Cat and Bulldog in "Feline Frameup," Bugs Bunny in "Eight Ball Bunny," Foghorn Leghorn in "A Featured Leghorn," Porky Pig and Sylvester in "Scaredy Cat" and Pepe Le Pew in "Louvre, Come Back to Me."
Warner Bros — *Warner Home Video*

Looney Tunes Video Show #4, The   195?
Cartoons
62882   47 mins   C   B, V   R, P
Animated
Another Warner Brothers cartoon assortment: Sylvester and Tweety in "Ain't She Tweet," Daffy Duck and Speedy Gonzales in "Astroduck," Bugs Bunny in "Backwoods Bunny," Pepe Le Pew in "Heaven Scent," Elmer Fudd in "Pests for Guests," Sylvester in "Lighthouse Mouse" and the Wolf and Sheepdog in "Don't Give Up the Sheep."
Warner Bros — *Warner Home Video*

Looney Tunes Video Show #5, The   195?
Cartoons
62883   51 mins   C   B, V   R, P
Animated
An additional package of Warner Brothers cartoons: Sylvester and Tweety in "Tugboat Granny," Daffy Duck in "Stork Naked," the Road Runner and Wile E. Coyote in "Fastest with the Mostest," Bugs Bunny in "Forward March Hare," Foghorn Leghorn in "Feather Dusted," Daffy Duck and Porky Pig in "China Jones" and Pepe Le Pew in "Odor of the Day."
Warner Bros — *Warner Home Video*

Looney Tunes Video Show #6, The   195?
Cartoons
62884   49 mins   C   B, V   R, P
Animated
More classic Warner Brothers cartoons: Foghorn Leghorn in "Feather Bluster," the Road Runner and Wile E. Coyote in "Lickety Splat," Bugs Bunny in "Bowery Bugs," Daffy Duck and Speedy Gonzales in "Daffy Rents," Porky Pig in "Dough for the Dodo," Sylvester and Elmer Fudd in "Heir Conditioned" and Pepe Le Pew in "Scent of the Matterhorn."
Warner Bros — *Warner Home Video*

Looney Tunes Video Show #7, The   195?
Cartoons
62885   48 mins   C   B, V   R, P
Animated
Seven additional Warner Brothers cartoon classics: Bugs Bunny in "A-Lad-In His Lamp," the Road Runner and Wile E. Coyote in "Beep Beep," Yosemite Sam in "Honey's Money," Foghorn Leghorn in "Weasel Stop," Daffy Duck and Elmer Fudd in "Don't Ax Me," Sylvester and Tweety in "Muzzle Tough" and Foghorn Leghorn in "The Egg-Cited Rooster."
Warner Bros — *Warner Home Video*

Loophole   1983
Adventure
65353   105 mins   C   B, V   P
Albert Finney, Martin Sheen, Susannah York
An out-of-work architect, hard pressed for money, joins forces with an elite team of expert criminals, in a scheme to make off with millions from the most established holding bank's vault.
David Korda; Julian Holloway — *Media Home Entertainment*

Lord Jim   1965
Drama
13261   154 mins   C   B, V   P
Peter O'Toole, James Mason, Curt Jurgens, Eli Wallach, Jack Hawkins, directed by Richard Brooks
A ship officer commits an act of cowardice that results in his dismissal and disgrace.
Columbia; Richard Brooks — *RCA/Columbia Pictures Home Video*

Lord of the Rings   1978
Fantasy
58883   133 mins   C   B, V   R, P
Animated
Ralph Bakshi's animated interpretation of Tolkien's classic tale of the hobbits, wizards, elves, and dwarfs who inhabit Middle Earth.
MPAA:PG
United Artists — *THORN EMI Home Video; RCA VideoDiscs*

Lords of Discipline, The   1983
Drama
66031   103 mins   C   B, V, LV   R, P
David Keith, Robert Prosky, Barbara Babcock, Judge Reinhold
A military academy cadet is given the unenviable task of protecting a black freshman from racist factions at a southern school circa 1964.
MPAA:R
Paramount — *Paramount Home Video*

Loretta   1980
Music-Performance
45105   61 mins   C   B, V, LV   P

Loretta Lynn
The queen of country music, Loretta Lynn, performs some of her best material, including "Coal Miner's Daughter," "Hey Loretta," "You're Looking at the Country," "Out of My Head and Back in Bed," "Wine, Women, and Song," "Naked in the Rain," and "Gospel Medley."
David Skepner — *MCA Home Video*

Losin' It   1982
Comedy
66047   104 mins   C   B, V, CED   P
Tom Curtis, John Stockwell, Shelly Long
A shy young man travels to a Mexican border town to lose his virginity.
MPAA:R
Joel Michaels; Garth Drabinsby — *Embassy Home Entertainment*

Lost and Found   1979
Comedy
63434   104 mins   C   B, V   P
George Segal, Glenda Jackson, Maureen Stapleton, Hollis McLaren, John Cunningham, Paul Sorvino
An American professor of English and an English film production secretary fall in love on a skiing vacation.
MPAA:PG
Columbia; Melvin Frank — *RCA/Columbia Pictures Home Video*

Lost City, The   193?
Adventure
08882   ? mins   B/W   B, V, 3/4U   P
Russell Hayden, Jane Adams, Lionel Atwill
Adventure in an isolated city in the Himalayas.
Krellberg — *Penguin Video; Video Connection*

Lost Honeymoon   1947
Drama
66193   69 mins   B/W   B, V, 3/4U   P
Franchote Tone, Ann Richards
An amnesiac victim discovers he's the father of two children.
Eagle Lion Films — *Penguin Video*

Lost Honor of Katharina Blum, The   1975
Drama
69550   97 mins   C   B, V   P
Angela Winkler, Mario Adorf, Dieter Lasar
Adapted from Heinrich Boll's Nobel Prize-winning novel, this film is about a woman who fights political and social injustice.
MPAA:R
New World Pictures — *Embassy Home Entertainment*

Lost in Space   1965
Science fiction
14446   52 mins   B/W   B, V   P
Guy Williams, June Lockhart, Jonathan Harris, Billy Mumy
The complete pilot episode of the series, in which the Robinson family becomes stranded somewhere in the universe.
Irwin Allen Prod — *Video Dimensions; Video Yesteryear*

Lost Jungle, The   1934
Mystery/Serials
14262   156 mins   B/W   B, V   P
Clyde Beatty, Cecelia Parker
Exciting animal treasure hunt; danger and mystery. Serial in 12 chapters, 13 minutes each.
Mascot — *Video Connection; Penguin Video; Video Dimensions; Video Yesteryear; Discount Video Tapes*

Lost Patrol, The   1934
Adventure
10075   66 mins   B/W   B, V   P, T
Victor McLaglen, Boris Karloff, Wallace Ford, Reginald Denny, Alan Hale
British soldiers lost in desert are shot down one by one by Arab marauders.
RKO — *Blackhawk Films; Nostalgia Merchant*

Lost Squadron   1932
Adventure
57144   79 mins   B/W   B, V   P
Richard Dix, Erich von Stroheim
A look at the dangers stuntmen go through in movie-making.
RKO — *King of Video*

Lost World, The   1925
Drama
08855   62 mins   B/W   B, V, 3/4U   P
Wallace Beery, Louis Stone, Bessie Love, Lloyd Hughes
A zoology professor leads a group on a South American expedition in search of the "lost world."
First National — *Penguin Video; Video Yesteryear; Discount Video Tapes*

Lost Years of Jesus, The   1976
Religion/Speculation
13013   93 mins   C   B, V   P
This production sheds light on the period of Christ's life from ages 13 to 29, a time of which little is known.
Richard Bock Productions — *Vanguard Video*

Lottery Bride, The   1930
Drama
54111   85 mins   B/W   B, V   P, T

    (For Explanation of codes, see USE GUIDE and KEY)

Jeanette MacDonald, Joe E. Brown, Zasu Pitts, John Garrick, Carroll Nye
A young woman enters a dance marathon against the wishes of her boyfriend, to get funds to aid her criminal brother. When the police arrive at the contest in search for the brother, the woman aids in his escape. For this she is put in prison. It is not until a series of misunderstandings are cleared up that her and her boyfriend are reunited.
United Artists — *Blackhawk Films*

Lou Gehrig: King of Diamonds
1954
Biographical/Baseball
44264   15 mins   B/W   B, V   P
An account of the baseball career of Lou Gehrig, "Iron Man" of baseball, including his touching farewell at Yankee Stadium, on July 4th, 1939. Classic newsreel footage.
Fox Movietone News — *Two Star Films*

Louisiana Gal
1937
Western
08805   71 mins   B/W   B, V, 3/4U   P
Rita Hayworth, Tom Keene
Differences of opinion result in the Louisiana Purchase.
Crescent — *Penguin Video*

Love and Anarchy
1973
Drama
63446   108 mins   C   B, V   P
Giancarlo Giannini, Mariangela Melato, directed by Lina Wertmuller
An oppressed peasant vows to assassinate Mussolini after a close friend is murdered. Italian dialogue, English subtitles.
IT
Euro International Films
Technicolor — *RCA/Columbia Pictures Home Video*

Love and Death
1975
Comedy
59336   89 mins   C   B, V   P
Woody Allen, Diane Keaton, Georges Adel, Despo, Frank Adu, directed by Woody Allen
In 1812 Russia, a man condemned reviews the follies of his life. Woody Allen's satire on "War and Peace."
MPAA:PG
United Artists; Jack Rollins; Charles H Joffe — *CBS/Fox Video; RCA VideoDiscs*

Love at First Bite
1979
Comedy
53517   96 mins   C   B, V   R, P
George Hamilton, Susan Saint James, Richard Benjamin, Dick Shawn, Arte Johnson, Sherman Hemsley, Isabel Sanford
Dracula is forced to leave his Transylvanian home as the Rumanian government has designated his castle a training center for young gymnasts. Once in New York, the Count takes in the night life and falls in love with a woman whose boyfriend embarks on a campaign to warn the city of Dracula's presence.
MPAA:PG
American International — *Warner Home Video; RCA VideoDiscs; Vestron Video (disc only)*

Love Bug, The
1968
Comedy
29736   110 mins   C   B, V, LV   R, P
Dean Jones, Michele Lee, Hope Lange, Robert Reed, Bert Convy
A race car driver is followed home by a white Volkswagen which has a mind of its own.
MPAA:G
Walt Disney — *Walt Disney Home Video; RCA VideoDiscs*

Love Butcher, The
1982
Horror
75586   84 mins   C   B, V   P
Erik Stern, Kay Neer, Robin Sherwood
A crippled old gardener kills his female employers with his garden tools and cleans up neatly afterward.
MPAA:R
Desert Production — *Monterey Home Video*

Love Child
1982
Drama
60563   97 mins   C   B, V   R, P
Amy Madigan, Beau Bridges, MacKenzie Phillips, Albert Salmi, directed by Larry Peerce
The story of a young woman in prison who becomes pregnant and fights to have and keep her baby.
MPAA:R
Warner Bros — *Warner Home Video*

Love Goddesses, The
1974
Documentary/Women
65425   87 mins   B/W   B, V   P
Marlene Dietrich, Greta Garbo, Jean Harlow, Gloria Swanson, Mae West, Betty Grable, Rita Hayworth, Elizabeth Taylor, Marilyn Monroe
A sixty-year treatment of woman on the screen reflecting with extraordinary accuracy the customs, manners and mores of the times.
Saul J Turell — *Embassy Home Entertainment*

Love Happy
1950
Comedy
47992   85 mins   B/W   B, V   P
The Marx Brothers, Vera-Ellen, Ilona Massey, Marion Hutton, Raymond Burr, Marilyn Monroe
A group of impoverished actors accidentally gain possession of valuable diamonds.
United Artists — *NTA Home Entertainment*

Love in the City   1953
Drama/Romance
63857   90 mins   B/W   B, V   P
*Directed by Federico Fellini, Michelangelo
Antonioni, Dino Risi et. al.*
This film incorporates five stories of life, love
and tears in Rome. Italian dialogue with English
subtitles and narration.
EL, IT
Italian — *Budget Video; Festival Films*

Love Is a Many-   1955
Splendored Thing
Drama
08465   102 mins   C   CED   P
*William Holden, Jennifer Jones, Torin Thatcher,
Isobel Elsom*
Hong Kong in 1949. True story of a romance
between lovely Eurasian doctor and an
American war correspondent.
Academy Awards '55: Best Song, "Love Is a
Many-Splendored Thing" (Sammy Fain, Paul
Francis Webster).
20th Century Fox; Buddy Adler — *CBS/Fox
Video*

Love Laughs at Andy   1946
Hardy
Comedy
49134   93 mins   B/W   B, V   P
*Sara Haden, Lina Romay, Bonita Granville, Fay
Holden, Lewis Stone, Mickey Rooney*
Andy Hardy, college boy, is in love and in
trouble. Financial and romantic problems come
to a head when Andy is paired with a six-foot tall
blind date.
MGM — *Budget Video; Discount Video Tapes;
VCII; Sound Video Unlimited; Classic Video
Cinema Collector's Club*

Love Me Tender   1956
Musical-Drama
64932   89 mins   B/W   CED   P
*Elvis Presley, Richard Egan, Debra Paget,
Neville Brand, Mildred Dunnock, James Drury,
Barry Coe*
A Civil War-torn family is divided by in-fighting
between two brothers who both seek the
affections of the same women. Presley's first
film.
20th Century Fox — *CBS/Fox Video*

Love of Jeanne Ney, The   1929
Drama
49074   102 mins   B/W   B, V   P
Brigitte Helm, directed by G. W. Pabst
The moral disintegration of post-war European
life is observed in a love story set in Paris during
the Russian Civil War. Silent with English title
cards.
German — *Sheik Video; Classic Video Cinema
Collector's Club*

Love of Three Queens,   1954
The
Drama
59210   100 mins   C   B, V   P
Hedy Lamarr
The loves, on and off stage, of a beautiful
actress in a European traveling theatre group.
Robert Patrick Productions — *Paragon Video
Productions; Penguin Video*

Love on the Run   1978
Drama
58240   90 mins   C   B, V   R, P
*Jean-Pierre Leaud, Marie-France Pisier, Claude
Jade, directed by Francois Truffaut*
The further amorous adventures of Antoine
Doinel, hero of "The 400 Blows," "Stolen
Kisses," and "Bed and Board." This time out,
the women from Doinel's past resurface to
challenge his emotions.
MPAA:PG
Elsenoor Belleggin — *Warner Home Video*

Love Story   1970
Drama
38598   100 mins   C   B, V, LV   R, P
*Ryan O'Neal, Ali McGraw, Ray Milland, directed
by Arthur Hiller*
Ryan O'Neal and Ali McGraw achieved stardom
in this popular adaption of Erich Segal's novel,
with portrayals of a young couple who cross
social barriers to marry.
Academy Awards '70: Best Original Score
(Francis Lai). MPAA:PG
Paramount — *Paramount Home Video; RCA
VideoDiscs*

Love Under the High   197?
Seas
Sports-Water
53641   9 mins   C   B, V, 3/4U,   P
                                   Q
This program in the "Under Water Deep Sea
Diving" series follows the story of a porpoise,
roaming free in the warm ocean waters of the
Bahamas.
Smokey Roberts — *TV Sports Scene*

Love Your Body   1983
Physical fitness
68524   60 mins   C   B, V   P
Jayne Kennedy
Jayne Kennedy presents her own exercise
program which will make you love your body.
Jeff Tuckman Prods; Chicago Teleprods; Jayne
Kennedy Prod — *RCA/Columbia Pictures
Home Video*

Loveless, The   1983
Drama
65693   85 mins   C   B, V   P
Robert Gordon, Willem Dafoe, J. Don Ferguson

          (For Explanation of codes, see USE GUIDE and KEY)

A menacing glance into the exploits of an outcast motorcycle gang. In the 50's, a group of bikers on their way to the Florida Cycle Races stop for lunch in a small-town diner. While repairs are being made on their motorcycles, they decide to take full advantage of their situation.
MPAA:R
G Nunes; A K Ho — *Media Home Entertainment*

Lovers and Liars　　　　**1981**
Comedy/Romance
69548　　93 mins　　C　　B, V, CED　　P
Goldie Hawn, Giancarlo Giannini
A romantic adventure in Rome turns into a series of comic disasters.
MPAA:R
Alberto Grimaldi — *Embassy Home Entertainment*

Lovesick　　　　**1983**
Comedy
66122　　94 mins　　C　　B, V　　R, P
Dudley Moore, Elizabeth McGovern, Alec Guinness, John Huston, directed by Marshall Brickman
A New York psychiatrist falls in love with one of his patients.
MPAA:PG
Ladd Company — *Warner Home Video*

Loving Couples　　　　**1980**
Comedy
57229　　120 mins　　C　　B, V, CED　　P
Shirley MacLaine, James Coburn, Susan Sarandon, Stephen Collins, Sally Kellerman, directed by Jack Smight
Two happily married couples meet each other after an automobile accident and two new couples emerge, only to collide hilariously at a weekend resort.
MPAA:PG
Time-Life Films — *Vestron Video*

Loving You　　　　**1957**
Musical
47373　　92 mins　　C　　B, V　　R, P
Elvis Presley, Wendell Corey, Lizabeth Scott, Dolores Hart
A small town boy with a musical style all his own becomes a big success. Features many early Elvis hits, including "Teddy Bear."
Hal B Wallis — *Warner Home Video*

Lucky Jim　　　　**1958**
Comedy
63327　　91 mins　　B/W　　B, V　　R, P
Ian Carmichael, Terry-Thomas, Hugh Griffith
A junior lecturer in history at a small university tries to get himself in good graces with the head of his department, but is doomed from the start

by doing the wrong things at the worst possible times.
Roy Boulting — *THORN EMI Home Video*

Lucky Luke: Daisy Town　　　　**1983**
Cartoons
66319　　75 mins　　C　　B, V　　R, P
Animated
A full-length animated feature starrring Lucky Luke, the all-American cowboy who saves the little community of Daisy Town from the hot-headed Dalton Brothers gang. A wacky western spoof.
Dargaud Editeur — *Walt Disney Home Video*

Lucky Luke: The Ballad of the Daltons　　　　**1983**
Cartoons
66320　　82 mins　　C　　B, V　　R, P
Animated
Easygoing cowboy hero Lucky Luke gets involved in a wild feud with the bumbling Dalton Brothers gang in this animated feature.
Dargaud Editeur — *Walt Disney Home Video*

Lucky Terror　　　　**1936**
Western
08784　　60 mins　　B/W　　B, V, 3/4U　　P
Hoot Gibson, Kone Andre, Charles King
Western with a style consistent with Hoot Gibson, the star.
Grand Natl — *Penguin Video; Video Connection*

Lucky Texan　　　　**1934**
Western
15490　　61 mins　　B/W　　B, V　　P
John Wayne
"Texas" John Wayne finds himself involved in a range war.
Monogram — *Video Connection; Video Dimensions; Cable Films; Video Yesteryear*

Lum and Abner　　　　**1949**
Television/Comedy
63626　　29 mins　　B/W　　B, V, FO　　P
Chester Lauck, Norris Goff, Andy Devine, Zasu Pitts
This rare kinescope features an episode from the 1949 TV series "Lum and Abner," adapted from the duo's network radio show.
CBS — *Video Yesteryear*

Lumia Lights　　　　**1983**
Video
60516　　60 mins　　C　　B, V　　P
This video turns your TV set into a living painting with flowing colors and everchanging design. In stereo.
Video Naturals — *Video Naturals*

Lumiere Program 19??
Film-History
57337 25 mins C B, V P
Two experimental shorts by early animators, the
Lumiere Brothers, are featured: "Red Spectre"
and "Early Melies." Circa 1892-1920.
Louis Lumiere; Auguste Lumiere — *Budget
Video*

Lunatics and Lovers 1976
Comedy
47795 92 mins C B, V P
Marcello Mastroianni, Lino Toffalo
A bizarre nobleman meets a door-to-door
musician who is in love with an imaginary
woman.
MPAA:PG
Independent — *CBS/Fox Video*

Lunch Wagon 1981
Comedy
59660 88 mins C B, V P
Pamela Bryant, Rosanne Katon
Two co-eds are given a restaurant to manage
during summer vacation and wind up involved in
a hilarious diamond chase and sex romp.
MPAA:R
Mark Bor — *Media Home Entertainment*

Lust for a Vampire 1970
Horror
63322 92 mins C B, V R, P
Ralph Bates, Barbara Jefford, Suzanna Leigh
A deadly vampire preys on pupils and teachers
alike when she enrolls at a British finishing
school.
Hammer Films — *THORN EMI Home Video*

Lusty Men, The 1952
Western
65157 113 mins B/W B, V P
*Robert Mitchum, Susan Hayward, Arthur
Kennedy, directed by Nicholas Ray*
Two rival rodeo champions, both in love with the
same woman, work the rodeo circuit until a
tragic accident occurs.
RKO — *VCI Home Video*

Luv 1967
Comedy
66012 95 mins C B, V P
*Jack Lemmon, Peter Falk, Elaine May, directed
by Clive Donner*
A suicidal man is saved by a friend who takes
him home. The would-be suicide finds new
meaning by falling in love with his friend's wife.
MPAA:PG
Columbia — *RCA/Columbia Pictures Home
Video*

Luv-Ya Blue! 1980
Football
45128 24 mins C B, V, FO R, P
Houston Oilers
Highlights of the 1979 Houston Oilers football
season.
NFL Films — *NFL Films Video*

Lying Lips 194?
Mystery
53417 60 mins B/W B, V P
*Edna May Harris, Carmen Newsome, Earl
Jones, Amanda Randolph, directed by Oscar
Micheaux*
An all-black detective mystery about a young
nightclub singer framed for murder. Her
boyfriend then turns detective to clear her
name.
Oscar Micheaux; Sack Prods — *Video
Connection*

M

M 1930
Film-Avant-garde
06226 95 mins B/W B, V P
*Peter Lorre, Ellen Widmann, Inge Landgut,
Directed by Fritz Lang*
Notorious child killer is hunted by police and the
underworld. German film, English subtitles.
GE
German — *Budget Video; VCII; Video
Connection; Discount Video Tapes; Sheik
Video; Penguin Video; International Historic
Films; Cinema Concepts*

Ma Vlast (My Fatherland) 1982
Music-Performance
47808 ? mins C LV P
The traditional performance of Smetana's "My
Fatherland" which opened the 1981 Prague
Spring International Music Festival performed
by the Czech Philharmonic Orchestra (stereo).
Unknown — *Pioneer Video Imports*

**Macabre Moments from
The Phantom of the
Opera** 1925
Horror
62872 34 mins B/W B, V P, T
Lon Chaney Sr., Norman Kerry, Mary Philbin
An edited version of this classic film, with story
continuity maintained. Silent; includes color
sequence.
Universal — *Blackhawk Films*

Macao 1952
Drama
64374 81 mins B/W B, V, 3/4U P

Robert Mitchum, Jane Russell, William Bendix, Gloria Grahame
A wandering adventurer and a cafe singer cross paths with a wanted criminal in the exotic Far East.
RKO — *Nostalgia Merchant*

MacArthur
1977
War-Drama
58426   144 mins   C   B, V   P
Gregory Peck, Ivan Bonar, Ward Costello, Nicholas Coster, directed by Joseph Sargent
General Douglas MacArthur's life from Corregidor in 1942 to his dismissal a decade later in the midst of the Korean conflict.
MPAA:PG
Universal; Zanuck Brown Prods — *MCA Home Video*

Macbeth
1948
Drama
66474   111 mins   B/W   B, V   P
Orson Welles, Jeanette Nolan, Dan O'Herlihy, Roddy McDowall, Robert Coote, directed by Orson Welles
Shakespeare's classic tragedy is performed in this film with a celebrated lead performance by Orson Welles as the tragic king.
Republic — *NTA Home Entertainment*

Macon County Line
1974
Drama/Adventure
65390   89 mins   C   B, V   P
Alan Vint, Jesse Vint, Cheryl Waters, Geoffrey Lewis, Joan Blackman, Max Baer
A series of deadly mistakes and misfortunes lead to a sudden turn around in the lives of 3 young people when they enter a small Georgia town and find themselves accused of brutally slaying the sheriff's wife.
MPAA:R
American International Pictures — *Embassy Home Entertainment*

Mad About Money
1938
Comedy
66194   74 mins   B/W   B, V, 3/4U   P
Lupe Velez, Harry Langdon
Harry Langdon meets the "Mexican Spitfire." Also known as "He Loved an Actress."
British — *Penguin Video*

Mad Bomber
1972
Suspense
12027   80 mins   C   B, V   P
Vince Edwards, Chuck Connors, Neville Brand
Police search for a mad bomber who has terrorized the city.
Philip Yordan Prod; Official Films — *King of Video*

Mad Max
1980
Adventure
66105   93 mins   C   B, V, LV, CED   P
Mel Gibson
Set on the highways of the post-nuclear future, this film concerns rebel bikers who challenge the police who guard what is left of civilization.
MPAA:R
American International Pictures — *Vestron Video*

Mad Monster
1942
Horror
51447   78 mins   B/W   B, V   P
Johnny Downs, Anne Nagel
A scientist invents a formula that turns men into monsters.
Producers Releasing Corp — *Video Connection*

Mad Monster Party
1968
Comedy
64975   94 mins   C   B, V, CED   P
Animated, voices of Boris Karloff, Ethel Ennis, Phyllis Diller
Dr. Frankenstein is getting older and wants to retire from the responsibilities of being senior monster, so he calls a convention of creepy creatures to decide who should take his placethe Wolfman, Dracula, the Mummy, the Creature, It, the Invisible Man, or Dr. Jekyll and Mr. Hyde.
Avco-Embassy — *Embassy Home Entertainment*

Madame Bovary
1949
Romance/Drama
58871   114 mins   B/W   B, V   P
Jennifer Jones, Van Heflin, Louis Jordan, James Mason, directed by Vincente Minnelli
Gustave Flaubert's classic novel concerning a woman's abandoned pursuit of love and the three men who loved her.
MGM; Pandro S Berman — *MGM/UA Home Video*

Madame Rosa
1978
Drama
59421   105 mins   C   B, V   P
Simone Signoret, Claude Dauphin, directed by Molshe Mizrahi
The evocative portrayal of a survivor of both Nazi concentration camps and a life of prostitution.
Academy Awards '78: Best Foreign Film.
MPAA:PG
Raymond Danon; Roland Girard; Jean Bolvary; Libra Film Prod — *Vestron Video*

Made for Each Other
1939
Drama
08677   100 mins   B/W   B, V, 3/4U   P

(For Explanation of codes, see USE GUIDE and KEY)

Carole Lombard, James Stewart, Charles Coburn, Lucille Watson
A touching drama of young love and its disappointments; interfering mother-inlaw who wants to baby her married son and control the grandchild.
David O Selznick — Movie Buff Video; Penguin Video; Budget Video; VCII; Video Dimensions; Sheik Video; Cable Films; Video Connection; Video Yesteryear; Discount Video Tapes

Madhouse 1984
Horror
72460   90 mins   C   B, V   P
Trish Everly
A woman has bizarre recollections of her twin sister whom she finally meets in a hospital.
unknown — *VCL Home Video*

Madman 1982
Horror
66186   89 mins   C   B, V   R, P
Alexis Dubin, Tony Fish
A cocky young man, mocking a legend about an ax murderer, sets the wheels of terror in motion.
MPAA:R
Jensen Farley — *THORN EMI Home Video*

Magic 1978
Drama
59835   106 mins   C   B, V, LV, CED   P
Anthony Hopkins, Ann-Margret, Burgess Meredith, Ed Lauter, directed by Richard Attenborough
A ventriloquist and his dummy, an all-too-human counterpart, get involved with a beautiful but impressionable woman lost between the world of reality and the irresistible world of illusion.
MPAA:R
Joseph E Levine; Richard P Levine — *Embassy Home Entertainment*

Magic Christian, The 1970
Comedy
47988   88 mins   C   B, V   P
Peter Sellers, Raquel Welch, Ringo Starr, Laurence Harvey, Richard Attenborough
The richest man in the world adopts a vagrant for his son, to prove that any man can be corrupted by money.
MPAA:PG
Grand Film; Commonwealth United — *NTA Home Entertainment*

Magic Garden, The 1960
Comedy
11239   60 mins   B/W   B, V, FO   P
Tommy Ramokgopa, directed by Donald Swanson
A thief loses his stolen money and it is found by honest people who put it to good use while the thief goes mad trying to locate it.

Donald Swanson — *Video Yesteryear; Sheik Video*

Magic Horse, The 1942
Fantasy/Cartoons
72508   56 mins   C   B, V, 3/4U   P
Animated
The first Russian feature cartoon based on a popular folk tale concerning a boy befriending a horse with mystic powers. Dubbed in English.
USSR — *International Historic Films*

Magic Pony, The 1978
Adventure
40733   80 mins   C   B, V   R, P
Voices of Jim Backus and Erin Moran
Ivan and his three brothers are sent to watch the fields and catch the culprit who has been destroying the wheat crop. The Magic Pony starts them on new adventures.
21st Century — *Video Gems; Vestron Video (disc only)*

Magic Pony, The 19??
Fantasy
69610   80 mins   C   B, V   P
Animated, voices of Jim Backus and Erin Moran
With the help of a beautiful flying horse, a young man battles a greedy emperor to become the kind-hearted prince and live happily ever after with a beautiful princess and his Magic Pony.
MPAA:G
Samuel J Phillips — *Children's Video Library*

Magic Show, The 198?
Magic/Comedy
72214   60 mins   C   B, V   P
Shari Lewis, Lambchop
A combination of comedy and illusion as four of the world's best magicians get together and perform.
Unknown — *Paragon Video Productions*

Magic Sword, The 1962
Adventure
38974   80 mins   C   B, V, FO   P
Basil Rathbone, Estelle Winwood
A family-oriented adventure film about a young knight who sets out to rescue a beautiful princess who is being held captive by an evil sorcerer and his dragon.
United Artists — *Video Yesteryear; Sheik Video*

Magic Town 1947
Comedy-Drama
64539   103 mins   B/W   B, V   P
Jane Wyman, James Stewart, Kent Smith, directed by William Wellman
An opinion pollster investigates a small town which exactly reflects the views of the entire nation, making his job a cinch.

RKO — *NTA Home Entertainment*

Magical Mystery Tour   1967
Musical
53945   55 mins   C   B, V   P
The Beatles, Victor Spinetti
On the road with an oddball assortment of people, the Beatles experience a strange assortment of incidents around the English countryside. Originally made for British television. Songs include: "The Fool on the Hill," "Blue Jay Way," "Your Mother Should Know," and the title tune.
Apple Films — *Media Home Entertainment; Western Film & Video Inc*

Magician, The   1959
Comedy-Drama
65626   101 mins   B/W   B, V, LV   P
Max von Sydow, Gunnar Bjornstrand, directed by Ingmar Bergman
A wandering magician arrives in 19th century Stockholm with his troupe where they encounter considerable skepticism.
Janus Films — *Embassy Home Entertainment*

Magician, The   1958
Drama
59649   101 mins   B/W   B, V   P
Max von Sydow, Ingrid Thulin, Gunnar Bjornstrand, Bibi Andersson, Naima Wifstrand, directed by Ingmar Bergman
Max von Sydow portrays Dr. Vogler, a hypnotist and master of legerdemain who uses his powers to create harm. Subtitled in English.
Venice Film Festival '59: Special Juy Prize, Cinema Nuova Prize. SW
A B Svensk Filmindustri; Janus — *Budget Video; Festival Films*

Magnavox Theater (The Three Musketeers)   1950
Drama
42969   53 mins   B/W   B, V, FO   P
John Hubbard, Robert Clarke, Mel Archer, Marjorie Lord
This teleplay which remains true to the novel by Alexandre Dumas, was directed by Budd Boetticher and includes flashing swords and romance.
Hal Roach Jr — *Video Yesteryear*

Magnificent, The   1981
Martial arts
69277   80 mins   C   B, V   P
Chen Sing, Carter Hwang, Casanova Wong, Bruce Lai, Doris Chen
After the 1911 Revolution, supporters of the deposed Ching government plot to overthrow the new government. Mandarin dialogue, English subtitles.
CH

IFD Films & Arts — *Silverline Video*

Magnificent Ambersons, The   1942
Drama
00261   88 mins   B/W   B, V, 3/4U   P
Joseph Cotten, Agnes Moorehead, directed by Orson Welles
A turn-of-the century family clings to its genteel traditions during an era of rapid change. Orson Welles' second directorial effort.
RKO — *Nostalgia Merchant*

Magnificent Kick, The   1980
Adventure/Martial arts
60514   90 mins   C   B, V   P
The story of a master Wong-Fai-Hung, inventor of the "Kick without Shadow," which was practiced by the late Bruce Lee.
Unknown — *Master Arts Video*

Magnificent Matador   1955
Drama/Romance
59139   94 mins   C   B, V   R, P
Anthony Quinn, Maureen O'Hara, Thomas Gomez
The story of a matador who faces death at the horns of the bull to win the love of a woman.
20th Century Fox — *VCII*

Magnificent Seven, The   1960
Western
53791   126 mins   C   B, V, CED   P
Yul Brenner, Steve McQueen, Robert Vaughn, James Coburn, Charles Bronson, Horst Buchholz, Eli Wallach, directed by John Sturges
Mexican villagers hire seven American gunmen to defend them against bandits.
United Artists; Walter Mirisch — *CBS/Fox Video; RCA VideoDiscs*

Magnum Force   1973
Suspense/Crime-Drama
54796   124 mins   C   B, V   R, P
Clint Eastwood, Hal Holbrook, Mitchell Ryan, David Soul, directed by Ted Post
A San Francisco homicide detective investigating a rash of gangster murders discovers that they are the work of a rookie police assassination squad whose members have been frustrated by red tape and civil liberties. A sequel to "Dirty Harry."
MPAA:R
Warner Bros, Robert Daly Prods — *Warner Home Video; RCA VideoDiscs*

Mahalia Jackson and Elizabeth Cotten: Two Remarkable Ladies   1974
Music/Documentary
58581   58 mins   C   B, V   P

A close-up look at a pair of successful black women performers: "Mahalia Jackson," a filmed biography of the legendary singer, and "Freight Train," the courageous story of pioneer folksinger Elizabeth Cotten.
CBS — *Mastervision*

Mahogany 1976
Drama
59202   109 mins   C   B, V, LV   R, P
Diana Ross, Billy Dee Williams, Jean Pierre Aumont
A world-famous high fashion model and designer gets a career boost when she daringly appears in a dress of her own creation at a Roman fashion show.
MPAA:R
Paramount — *Paramount Home Video; RCA VideoDiscs*

Maid in Sweden 1983
Drama
66511   90 mins   C   B, V   P
Kristina Lindberg, Monika Ekman, Kriste Ekman
A naive country girl visits Stockholm for the first time and has some bizarre encounters with men.
Sweden — *Paragon Video Productions*

Main Event, The 1979
Comedy
37426   112 mins   C   B, V   R, P
Barbra Streisand, Ryan O'Neal
A wisecracking young woman obtains the contract of a prize fighter who is about to retire. She becomes his manager and gets him back into the ring.
MPAA:PG
Warner Bros — *Warner Home Video; RCA VideoDiscs*

Mainline U.S.A. 195?
Trains
73029   18 mins   C   B, V   P
This program highlights how railroads from all over the United States are used in industry, agriculture and by the public.
American Railroad Association — *Interurban Films*

Maintenance and Show Grooming 1984
Animals
74535   72 mins   C   B, V   P
This tape features a complete visual text on the basics of daily show horse care.
Mercedes Maharis Productions — *Mercedes Maharis Productions*

Major Dundee 1965
Adventure
76029   124 mins   C   B, V   P
Charlton Heston, Richard Harris, James Coburn, Jim Hutton, directed by Sam Peckinpah
A union army officer with a hundred criminals volunteers from the prison he commands to chase a savage Indian leader through Mexico.
Jerry Bresler — *RCA/Columbia Pictures Home Video*

Make a Million 1935
Comedy
69557   66 mins   B/W   B, V, FO   P
Charles Starrett, Pauline Brooks
An economics professor is fired from his post because of his radical theories about redistributing the country's wealth. To prove his point, he becomes a millionaire by advertising for money.
Monogram Pictures — *Video Yesteryear*

Make a Wish 1937
Drama
08671   80 mins   B/W   B, V, 3/4U   P
Basil Rathbone, Leon Errol, Bobby Breen, Ralph Forbes
A noted composer goes stale in this colorful tale of backstage life. Music by Oscar Strauss.
RKO — *Penguin Video; Sheik Video; Video Yesteryear*

Make Mine Mink 1960
Comedy
55343   100 mins   B/W   B, V   P
Terry Thomas, Billie Whitelaw, Hattie Jacques
A madcap comedy about larceny, with a seasoned cast playing guests at an elegant but slightly run-down mansion. Bored, the group takes up a Robin Hood-like hobby of stealing from the rich and giving to the poor.
Continental — *Sheik Video*

Making Love 1982
Drama
59630   112 mins   C   B, V, CED   P
Kate Jackson, Harry Hamlin, Michael Ontkean, directed by Arthur Hiller
A love story concerning a young married couple whose seemingly-perfect world is shattered by the husband's homosexuality.
MPAA:R
Twentieth Century Fox — *CBS/Fox Video*

Making Michael Jackson's Thriller 1983
Music-Performance
65347   60 mins   C   B, V, LV, CED   P
Michael Jackson
The program is a behind-the-scenes look at how an unprecedented music video was created. The program includes highlights of Jackson's highly acclaimed videos for "Billie Jean" and "Beat It," as well as the 10-minute video for the

title song of the "Thriller" album. In stereo and Beta Hi-Fi.
John Landis — *Vestron Video*

Making of Star Wars, The/S.P.F.X. — The Empire Strikes Back　1980
Filmmaking/Science fiction
08478　100 mins　C　B, V, LV, CED　P
Mark Hamill, Carrie Fisher, Harrison Ford, narrated by William Conrad
Behind-the-scenes look at the special effects of these two popular movies directed by George Lucas. The viewer will see how Luke's automobile is able to cruise above ground, how the droids, C-3PO and R2-D2 move around, and the workings of Yoda.
EL, SP
20th Century Fox; Gary Kurtz — *CBS/Fox Video*

Making of Superman, The　1979
Filmmaking
75466　96 mins　C　B, V　P
Christopher Reeve, Margot Kidder
A behind-the-scenes look at the making of "Superman-The Movie."
Salkind — *Family Home Entertainment*

Making of Superman—The Movie and Superman II, The　1984
Science fiction/Filmmaking
66621　120 mins　C　B, V　P
Christopher Reeve, Margot Kidder, Susannah York
These two hour-long documentaries chronicle the making of the Superman films, showing the construction of sets, special effects work and off-screen moments with the actors.
Dovemead Limited, Film Export; International Film Productions — *U.S.A. Home Video*

Making of Superman II, The　1981
Filmmaking
75467　96 mins　C　B, V　P
Christopher Reeve, Margot Kidder
A behind-the-scenes look at the making of "Superman II."
Salkind — *Family Home Entertainment*

Making Stained Glass　1982
Handicraft
47351　30 mins　C　V　P
Techniques of making stained glass are explained and demonstrated.
American Home Video Library — *American Home Video Library*

Making the Grade　1984
Comedy
73365　105 mins　C　B, V　P
A hoodlum poses as a preppy to settle some debts owed to the mob.
MPAA:PG
Cannon Films — *MGM/UA Home Video*

Malcolm Campbell: Man Against Time　1954
Biographical/Automobiles-Racing
44239　15 mins　B/W　B, V　P
A look at the driving skills of Sir Malcom Campbell, who in 1930 drove his car "Bluebird" 302 m.p.h. Shown through classic newsreel footage.
Fox Movietone News — *Two Star Films*

Malibu Beach　1978
Comedy
48477　93 mins　C　B, V　P
Kim Lankford, James Daughton
The California beach scene is the setting for this movie filled with bikini clad girls, tanned young men, and instant romances.
MPAA:R
Crown International — *VCI Home Video*

Malibu High　1979
Drama
48480　92 mins　C　B, V　P
Jill Lansing, Stuart Taylor
The accidental death of a young prostitute's client leads her to a new series of illegal activities of the "sex and hit" variety.
MPAA:R
Crown International — *VCI Home Video*

Malibu Hot Summer　1981
Drama
59145　89 mins　C　B, V　R, P
Terry Congie, Leslie Brander, Roselyn Royce
Three aspiring young women combine their talents in acting, music and athletics to find their careers as they spend a fun-filled summer in Malibu.
Eric Louzil — *VCII*

Malicious　1974
Drama
44592　98 mins　C　B, V　R, P
Laura Antonelli, Turi Ferro, Alessandro Momo, Tina Aumont, directed by Salvatore Samperi
A housekeeper hired for a widower and his three sons becomes the object of lusty affection of all four men. As Papa makes plans to court and marry her, his fourteen-year-old son plots to have her as a companion on his road to sensual maturity. Dubbed in English.
MPAA:R
Paramount, Silvio Clementelli — *Paramount Home Video*

Malta Story　　　　　　　1953
War-Drama
62867　103 mins　B/W　　B, V　　　P
*Alec Guinness, Jack Hawkins, Anthony Steel,
Flora Robson*
A British World War II flier becomes involved
with the defense of Malta.
UA British; GFD — *Embassy Home
Entertainment*

Maltese Falcon, The　　　　1941
Mystery
13594　101 mins　B/W　　B, V　　　P
*Humphrey Bogart, Mary Astor, Sydney
Greenstreet, Peter Lorre, directed by John
Huston*
After the death of his partner, detective Sam
Spade finds himself enmeshed in the search for
a priceless statuette.
National Board of Review Awards '41: Best
Performances (Bogart and Astor).
Warner Brothers — *CBS/Fox Video; RCA
VideoDiscs*

Mama (I Remember　　　　195?
Mama)
Comedy
59313　55 mins　B/W　　B, V, 3/4U　　　P
Peggy Wood, Dick Van Patten
This family comedy series set in San Francisco
at the turn of the century includes two episodes:
"Mama's Bad Day" (1950), in which Mama feels
she's being taken for granted; and, "Mama's
Nursery School" (1955), in which Mama
becomes a substitute teacher. Includes original
commercials.
CBS — *Shokus Video; Discount Video Tapes;
Roll Your Own Video*

Mama (I Remember　　　　1950
Mama)
Comedy
39002　30 mins　B/W　　B, V, FO　　　P
*Peggy Wood, Judson Laird, Rosemary Rice,
Robin Morgan*
A representative episode from the famous early
TV series, "Madame Zodiac," in which Aunt
Jenny has her fortune told with surprising
results. Original commercials included.
CBS — *Video Yesteryear*

Mama (I Remember　　　　1951
Mama)
Comedy-Drama
47503　29 mins　B/W　　B, V, FO　　　P
*Peggy Wood, Judson Laird, Robin Morgan,
Rosemary Rice, Dick Van Patten, Ruth Gates*
This episode of the popular TV series is titled
"Mama's Bad Day." Family problems become
more than Mama can bear, and she is
conscience-stricken when she wishes she had
never married.
CBS — *Video Yesteryear*

Mama (I Remember　　　　1950
Mama)
Drama
42977　29 mins　B/W　　B, V, FO　　　P
*Peggy Wood, Judson Laire, Dick Van Patten,
Rosemary Rice*
Little Dagmar is entered in a spelling bee and
Papa bets his life insurance money that she'll
win.
CBS — *Video Yesteryear*

Mame　　　　　　　　1974
Musical
74206　131 mins　C　　B, V　　　R, P
Lucille Ball, Beatrice Arthur
This is the story of Auntie Mame, who takes it on
herself to teach a group of eccentrics how to
live life to its fullest.
MPAA:PG
Robert Fryer; James Cresson — *Warner Home
Video*

Man, a Woman, and a　　　1979
Bank, A
Comedy
48404　100 mins　C　　B, V　　　P
*Donald Sutherland, Brooke Adams, Paul
Mazursky*
Two con men plan to rob a bank by posing as
workers during the bank's construction. An
advertising agency woman snaps their picture
for a billboard to show how nice the builders
have been, then becomes romantically involved
with one of the would-be thieves.
MPAA:PG
John B Bennett, Peter Samuelson — *Embassy
Home Entertainment*

Man Against Crime　　　　1956
Volume I
Adventure
47640　60 mins　B/W　　B, V, FO　　　P
Frank Lovejoy
A gunless gumshoe travels the globe in search
of crooks and intrigue. Vintage television.
NBC — *Video Yesteryear*

Man Against Crime　　　　1956
Volume II
Crime-Drama
47650　60 mins　B/W　　B, V, FO　　　P
Frank Lovejoy, Herschel Bernardi
Two episodes of the vintage TV series with
Frank Lovejoy as detective Mike Barnett. In
episode one, Mike is challenged to a duel by a
nasty jai alai player who's been blackmailing his
employer. In episode two, Mike gets involved
with a Parisian narcotics ring.
NBC — *Video Yesteryear*

Man Alone, A　　　　　　1955
Western
74485　96 mins　C　　B, V　　　P

　　　(For Explanation of codes, see USE GUIDE and KEY)

Ray Milland, Raymond Burr
This is the story of a sheriff who defends a man falsely accused of robbing a stagecoach.
Republic — *NTA Home Entertainment*

Man Betrayed, A   1942
Mystery
58529   83 mins   B/W   B, V, 3/4U   P
John Wayne, Frances Dee, Edward Ellis
A country lawyer exposes a girl's father for the crooked politician he is. Also known as "Wheel of Fortune."
Republic — *Penguin Video*

Man Called Horse, A   1970
Adventure
65495   114 mins   C   CED   P
Stanford Howard
An English aristocrat is captured by Indians, lives with them and eventually becomes their leader.
Cinema Center — *CBS/Fox Video*

Man for All Seasons, A   1966
Drama
Closed Captioned
21291   120 mins   C   B, V   P
Paul Scofield, Robert Shaw, Orson Welles, Wendy Hiller, Susannah York, directed by Fred Zinneman
A biographical drama concerning sixteenth century Chancellor of England, Sir Thomas More, and his personal conflict with King Henry VIII.
Academy Awards '66: Best Picture; Best Actor (Scofield); Best Director (Zinneman).
Columbia — *RCA/Columbia Pictures Home Video; RCA VideoDiscs*

Man from Atlantis   1977
Science fiction
66278   00 mins   C   B, V   P
Patrick Duffy
Patrick Duffy stars as the water-breathing alien who emerges from his undersea home—the Lost City of Atlantis.
NBC — *Worldvision Home Video*

Man from Beyond   1922
Adventure/Drama
59219   50 mins   B/W   B, V, 3/4U   P
Harry Houdini, Arthur Maude
Frozen alive, a man returns 100 years later to try and find his lost love. Silent.
Houdini Picture Corp — *Penguin Video; Video Yesteryear*

Man from Button Willow, The   1975
Adventure
37393   79 mins   C   B, V   P

Animated, voices of Dale Robertson, Edgar Buchanan, Barbara Jean Wong, Howard Keel
This classic animated adventure is the story of Justin Eagle, a man who leads a double life. He is a respected rancher and a shrewd secret agent for the government, but in 1869 he suddenly finds himself the guardian of a four-year-old Oriental girl, leading him into a whole new series of adventures.
MPAA:G
David Detiege, AFC — *Paragon Video Productions*

Man From Cheyenne   1942
Western
08607   54 mins   B/W   B, V, 3/4U   P
Roy Rogers, Gale Storm, Gabby Hayes, Sally Payne
Cowboy comes home to find his town under a seige of terror from a lawless gang of cattle rustlers.
Republic — *Penguin Video; Discount Video Tapes*

Man from Clover Grove, The   1978
Comedy
56738   97 mins   C   B, V   P
Ron Masak, Cheryl Miller, Jed Allan, Rose Marie
Hilarity takes over a town when a nutty boy inventor puts the sheriff in a spin.
EL, SP
Drew Cummings — *Media Home Entertainment*

Man from Music Mountain, The   1938
Western
08788   54 mins   B/W   B, V, 3/4U   P
Gene Autry, Smiley Burnette, Carol Hughes, Polly Jenkins
Worthless mining stock is sold in a desert mining town, but Gene and Smiley clear that up.
Republic — *Penguin Video; Budget Video; Video Connection; Discount Video Tapes; Nostalgia Merchant*

Man from Snowy River, The   1982
Adventure
65002   104 mins   C   B, V, CED   P
Kirk Douglas, Tom Burlinson
Stunning cinematography highlights this heroic adventure story set in Australia in the 1880's, as a young man accepts the challenge of taming a herd of wild horses.
MPAA:PG
20th Century Fox — *CBS/Fox Video*

Man from Utah, The   1934
Western
11268   55 mins   B/W   B, V, FO   P
John Wayne, Gabby Hayes

The Duke tangles with the crooked sponsor of some rodeo events who has killed several of the participants.
Monogram — *Video Yesteryear; Video Connection; Penguin Video; Cable Films; Discount Video Tapes*

Man in Grey, The　　　　1945
Romance
76639　116 mins　B/W　　　B, V　　　　P
James Mason, Margaret Lockwood, Stewart Granger, Phyllis Calvert
An intriguing story of a criss-cross love affair among 19th century English royalty.
Gainsborough — *VidAmerica*

Man in the Iron Mask, The　　　1939
Adventure
55350　110 mins　B/W　B, V, 3/4U　　P
Louis Hayward, Alan Hale, Joan Bennett, directed by James Whale
Alexandre Dumas' classic novel provides the basis for this tale about the twin brother of King Louis XIV of France, who was kept prisoner with his face covered by a locked iron mask.
Edward Small; United Artists — *Nostalgia Merchant*

Man in the White Suit, The　　　1951
Comedy
45070　82 mins　B/W　　　B, V　　　R, P
Alec Guinness, Joan Greenwood
A humble laboratory assistant in a textile mill invents a cloth that won't stain, tear, or wear-out and causes an industry-wide panic.
Universal, J Arthur Rank — *THORN EMI Home Video*

Man Inside, The　　　　1976
Drama
76640　96 mins　C　　　B, V　　　　P
James Franciscus, Stefanie Powers, Jacques Godin
An undercover agent infiltrates a powerful underworld narcotics ring and finds his honesty tested when $2 million is at stake.
CBC — *Trans World Entertainment*

Man of La Mancha　　　　1972
Musical
58839　121 mins　C　B, V, CED　　P
Peter O'Toole, Sophia Loren, James Coco, Harry Andrews, John Castle, Brian Blessed
Arrested by the Inquisition and thrown into prison, Miguel de Cervantes relates the story of Don Quixote. Based on the Broadway musical, with music by Mitch Leigh and lyrics by Joe Darion. Songs include "The Impossible Dream" and "Dulcinea."
MPAA:PG
United Artists — *CBS/Fox Video*

Man of the Frontier　　　　1936
Western
05580　60 mins　B/W　B, V, 3/4U　　P
Gene Autry, Smiley Burnette, Frances Grant
A vital irrigation project is being sabotaged, but Gene Autry exposes the culprits.
Republic — *Video Connection; Video Yesteryear*

Man on the Eiffel Tower, The　　　1948
Crime-Drama
64342　82 mins　B/W　　　B, V　　　　P
Charles Laughton, Burgess Meredith, Franchot Tone, Patricia Roc, directed by Burgess Meredith
A mysterious crazed killer defies the police to discover his identity.
A & T — *Movie Buff Video; Classic Video Cinema Collector's Club; Cable Films*

Man on the Moon　　　　1981
Space exploration
58302　80 mins　C　B, V, CED　　P
Narrated by Walter Cronkite
This program traces the birth and development of the U.S. Space Program, leading to the Apollo 11 moon landing.
CBS News — *CBS/Fox Video*

Man Who Fell to Earth, The　　　1976
Science fiction
33703　118 mins　C　　　B, V　　　　P
David Bowie
A man from another planet ventures to earth and becomes a successful businessman. His ulterior motive for this visit is to come to the aid of his family on their ailing planet, at the expense of Earth.
MPAA:R
Cinema 5 — *RCA/Columbia Pictures Home Video*

Man Who Haunted Himself, The　　　1970
Mystery/Suspense
63336　91 mins　C　　　B, V　　　R, P
Roger Moore, Hildegarde Neil, Olga Georges-Picot
A man is possessed by a mysterious force that takes control of his ideal life and turns it into a nightmare.
Associated British Productions Ltd — *THORN EMI Home Video*

Man Who Knew Too Much, The　　　1934
Mystery
08745　87 mins　B/W　　　B, V　　　　P
Leslie Banks, Edna Best, Peter Lorre, Nova Pilbeam, directed by Alfred Hitchcock

Hitchcock's first international success — a British family man on vacation in Switzerland is told about an assassination plot by a dying agent.
Gaumont — *Media Home Entertainment; Penguin Video; VCII; Blackhawk Films; Video Yesteryear; Budget Video; Video Dimensions; Sheik Video; Ampro Video Productions; Cable Films; Video Connection; Discount Video Tapes; Western Film & Video Inc; Cinema Concepts*

Man Who Loved Women, The   1983

Comedy
76030   118 mins   C   B, V   P
Burt Reynolds, Julie Andrews, Kim Basinger, Marilu Henner, Cynthia Sikes, Jennifer Edwards, directed by Blake Edwards
Burt Reynolds stars in this hilarious comedy about a Los Angeles sculptor whose reputation as a playboy leads him to a midlife crisis.
MPAA:R
Blake Edwards; Tony Adams — *RCA/Columbia Pictures Home Video*

Man Who Loved Women, The   1977

Romance
44779   119 mins   C   B, V   P
Charles Denner, Brigitte Fossey, Leslie Caron, directed by Francois Truffaut
An intelligent, sensitive bachelor worships all women. Trying to find the reasons for his obsession, he writes his memoirs and remembers all the women he has loved.
MPAA:R
Cinema 5 — *RCA/Columbia Pictures Home Video*

Man Who Shot Liberty Valance, The   1962

Western
33715   122 mins   B/W   B, V, LV   R, P
James Stewart, John Wayne, Vera Miles, Lee Marvin, Edmond O'Brien, Andy Devine, Woody Strode, directed by John Ford
Liberty Valance terrorizes a small western town and is opposed by only two men, one of whom unknowingly is given credit for killing him and eventually becomes a U.S. senator.
Paramount — *Paramount Home Video; RCA VideoDiscs*

Man Who Would Be King, The   1975

Adventure
Closed Captioned
65500   129 mins   C   B, V, CED   P
Sean Connery, Michael Caine
The two heroes are no ordinary jacks-of-trade. They have won honor fighting for the British Queen, yet found themselves adept at hustling

strangers, blackmail, forging and assorted novel ways of earning money. Now that they've done it all, what else is left but to become kings?
MPAA:PG
Lorimar — *CBS/Fox Video*

Man With a Movie Camera, The   1929

Film-Avant-garde
72493   69 mins   B/W   B, V, 3/4U   P
A classic experimental film made in 1929 by Dziga Vetou with English subtitles.
RU
VUFKU — *International Historic Films*

Man with the Golden Gun, The   1974

Adventure/Suspense
60582   125 mins   C   B, V, CED   P
Roger Moore, Christopher Lee, Richard Loo, Britt Ekland, Maude Adams, Herve Villechaize, Clifton James
Roger Moore is the debonair secret agent 007 in this ninth James Bond flick, assigned to recover a small piece of equipment which can be utilized to harness the sun's energy.
MPAA:PG
United Artists — *CBS/Fox Video; RCA VideoDiscs*

Man with Two Brains, The   1983

Comedy
69310   91 mins   C   B, V, LV, CED   R, P
Steve Martin, Kathleen Turner, David Warner, directed by Carl Reiner
A wacko brain surgeon marries a beautiful but coldhearted nymphomaniac but later falls in love with the brain of a young lady who has everything he desires—except a body.
MPAA:R
Aspen Society; William E McEuen and David Picker — *Warner Home Video*

Man, Woman and Child   1983

Drama
68248   100 mins   C   B, V   R, P
Martin Sheen, Blythe Danner, Craig T. Nelson, David Hemmings
A typical American family is shocked when the child of an affair long ago appears at their door.
MPAA:PG
Paramount Pictures Corp — *Paramount Home Video*

Mandingo   1975

Drama
44596   127 mins   C   B, V, LV   R, P
James Mason, Susan George, Perry King, Richard Ward, Ken Norton, directed by Richard Fleischer
Based on the novel by Kyle Onstott, "Mandingo" portrays the brutal nature of

slavery in the South. It deals with the tangled loves and hates of a family and their slaves. Heavyweight boxer Ken Norton makes his screen debut in the title role.
MPAA:R
Paramount, Dino De Laurentiis — *Paramount Home Video; RCA VideoDiscs*

Manhattan Merry-Go-Round   1937
Musical
54183   89 mins   B/W   B, V   P
Cab Calloway, Louis Prima, Ted Lewis, Ann Dvorak, Phil Regan, Kay Thompson, Gene Autry, Joe DiMaggio
A slightly offbeat musical with a host of guest stars, about a gangster who acquires a record company.
Republic — *Video Connection; Budget Video; Discount Video Tapes*

Manhattan Transfer in Concert   1983
Music-Performance
60571   58 mins   C   LV   P
The eclectic vocal group performs their mixture of pop, soul and jazz. Songs include "Operator," "Four Brothers," and "Gloria."
Ken Erhlich — *Pioneer Artists*

Manhunt   195?
Adventure
10035   25 mins   B/W   B, V   P, T
Kirby Grant, Gloria Winters, Ewing Mitchell
Frightened young man flees to Mexico believing he killed a classmate. Sky King seeks to tell him the truth—his classmate is alive. From the TV series "Sky King."
CBS — *Blackhawk Films*

Manhunt in the African Jungle   1954
Adventure/Serials
33952   240 mins   B/W   B, V, 3/4U   P
Rod Cameron, Joan Marsh, Duncan Renaldo
An American undercover agent battles Nazi forces in Africa. A serial in fifteen episodes.
Republic — *Video Connection*

Maniac   1981
Horror
59042   91 mins   C   B, V   P
Joe Spinell, Caroline Munro, Gail Lawrence
A psycho murderer slaughters and scalps his victims, adding the "trophies" to his collection. (This film carries a self-imposed equivalent X rating.)
Andrew Garroni — *Media Home Entertainment*

Maniac, The   1963
Suspense
62807   86 mins   B/W   B, V   P

Kerwin Mathews, Nadia Gray, Donald Houston, Liliane Brousse
An American artist living in France becomes involved with the daughter of a cafe owner, not suspecting that murder will follow.
Columbia — *RCA/Columbia Pictures Home Video*

Maniac, The   1934
Horror
08892   52 mins   B/W   B, V, 3/4U   P
Bill Woods, Horace Carpenter
A mad doctor's assistant murders his boss, then impersonates him.
Dwain Esper — *Penguin Video; Movie Buff Video; Admit One Video*

Many Adventures of Winnie the Pooh, The   1976
Cartoons
55565   74 mins   C   CED   P
Animated
This collection of stories from A.A. Milne's children's classic includes "Winnie the Pooh and the Honey Tree," "Winnie the Pooh and the Blustery Day," and "Winnie the Pooh and Tigger Too."
MPAA:G
Walt Disney — *RCA VideoDiscs*

Maps to Stars' Homes Video   1984
Television/Theater
76016   60 mins   C   B, V   P
A guided tour through Beverly Hills. See the mansions of your favorite movie and TV stars.
Shokus Video Productions — *Shokus Video*

Marathon Man   1976
Drama
38599   125 mins   C   B, V, LV   R, P
Dustin Hoffman, Laurence Olivier, Marthe Keller, Roy Scheider, directed by John Schlesinger
Nightmarish thriller in which a marathon runner (Hoffman) becomes entangled in a plot involving a murderous Nazi fugitive (Olivier). Screenplay by William Goldman, based on his novel.
MPAA:R
Paramount — *Paramount Home Video; RCA VideoDiscs*

March of Progress: The Key System   1946
Trains
68914   16 mins   B/W   B, V   P
The history of the Key System is re-capped from the turn of the century up to the opening of the Bay Bridge.
Key System — *Interurban Films*

     (For Explanation of codes, see USE GUIDE and KEY)

March of the Wooden 1934
Soldiers
Fantasy
71312   73 mins   B/W   B, V   P
Stan Laurel, Oliver Hardy
Laurel and Hardy attempt to help the people of
Toyland fight the evil Bogeymen in this
adaptation of Victor Herbert's operetta, "Babes
In Toyland."
Hal Roach — *Independent United Distributors;*
Sheik Video; Penguin Video

March with the Fuhrer 1941
(Marsch Zum Fuhrer)
Germany/Propaganda
51406   60 mins   B/W   B, V, 3/4U   P
The official film of the Hitler Youth, and the last
record of the Nurnberg Party Rally of 1938.
German with English subtitles.
GE
UFA — *Penguin Video; International Historic*
Films

Marco 1973
Adventure
75494   109 mins   C   B, V   P
Desi Arnaz Jr, Zero Mostel
This movie is a musical adventure of Marco
Polo's life.
Tomorrow Entertainment — *Prism*

Marco Polo, Jr. 1972
Cartoons/Fantasy
69806   82 mins   C   B, V   P
Animated, voice by Bobby Rydell
Marco Polo, Jr., the daring descendant of the
legendary explorer, travels the world in search
of his destiny in this song-filled, feature-length
animated fantasy.
AII and PAPI — *Family Home Entertainment*

Marco Polo's Afghanistan 197?
Middle East/Documentary
19407   60 mins   C   B, V, 3/4U,   P
                                      Q
Narrated by Lowell Thomas
A journey through Afghanistan uncovers the
struggles and hardships that travel in the area
brings, as well as showing the present way of
life among its people.
TV Sports Scene — *TV Sports Scene*

Mardi Gras Massacre 1982
Horror
63972   92 mins   C   B, V   R, P
Curt Dawson, Gwen Arment
An Aztec priest arrives in New Orleans during
Mardi Gras to revive the blood ritual of human
sacrifice to an Aztec god. A police detective
relentlessly pursues him.
J Weis — *VCII*

Marianela 197?
Drama
52793   113 mins   C   B, V   P
A disfigured peasant girl cares for a blind man,
and the two fall in love. She doesn't tell him
about her appearance until the day comes that
he regains his sight. In Spanish.
SP
Luis Sanz — *Media Home Entertainment*

Marie Osmond: Exercises 1983
for Mothers-To-Be
Pregnancy/Physical fitness
66115   60 mins   C   B, V   P
Marie Osmond demonstrates physical therapist
Elizabeth Noble's highly acclaimed toning
exercises for mothers-to-be.
3 West Prods; MGM/UA Home Entertainment
Group — *MGM/UA Home Video*

Marijuana: Devil's Weed 1936
with Roots in Hell
Drama/Exploitation
08891   58 mins   B/W   B, V, 3/4U   P
Harley Wood, Hugh McArthur, Pat Carlyle, Paul
Ellis
A dramatised investigation from the thirties into
the dangers that can result from smoking
marijuana.
Unknown — *Penguin Video*

Marijuana—The Devils' 1932
Weed
Exploitation
73555   56 mins   B/W   B, V   P
This exploitation film tells the story of two sisters
who get into a lot of trouble from smoking pot.
Independent — *Admit One Video*

Marilyn Monroe 1964
Documentary/Biographical
52770   30 mins   C   B, V   P
Narrated by Mike Wallace
Marilyn Monroe's life from birth to death is
documented. An actual television interview and
news footage are included.
Fusco Entertainment — *Karl Video*

Marina Popovich 1971
Aeronautics
72528   25 mins   B/W   B, V, 3/4U   P
A Soviet documentary about that country's first
famous test pilot.
USSR — *International Historic Films*

Marines-65 1965
Vietnam War/Armed Forces-US
53694   25 mins   C   B, V, 3/4U   P
This film highlights the Marine Corps' activities
under President Johnson on two fronts in 1965,
the Dominican Republic and Vietnam.

(For Explanation of codes, see USE GUIDE and KEY)

Unknown — *International Historic Films*

Marius   1931
Comedy
06229 125 mins B/W   B, V   P
Raimo, Pierre Fresnay, directed by Marcel
Pagnol
Marcel Pagnol wrote, produced, and directed
this trilogy about the lives, loves, joys, and
sorrows of the people of Provence, France.
Broadway play "Fanny" was adapted from this
trilogy. English subtitles.
FR
France — *Budget Video; Discount Video*
Tapes

Marjoe   1972
Documentary/Biographical
65099   88 mins   C   B, V   P
Marjoe Gortner, directed by Howard Smith and
Sarah Kernochan
This documentary follows the career of rock-
style evangelist Marjoe Gortner, who spent 25
years of his life touring the country as a
professional preacher.
Academy Awards '72: Best Documentary.
MPAA:PG
Cinema 10 — *RCA/Columbia Pictures Home*
Video

Mark of Zorro, The   1920
Adventure
13738   91 mins   B/W   B, V   P, T
Douglas Fairbanks, Marguerite De La Motte,
Noah Beery, directed by Fred Niblo
Set to Gaylord Carter's score, Zorro, the famous
Mexican Robin Hood, crusades for the rights of
oppressed Mexicans.
United Artists — *Blackhawk Films; Discount*
Video Tapes; Sheik Video; Cable Films; Penguin
Video; Video Yesteryear; Western Film & Video
Inc; Classic Video Cinema Collector's Club

Mark Twain's A   1978
Connecticut Yankee in
King Arthur's Court
Comedy-Drama/Literature-American
58734   60 mins   C   B, V   P
Richard Basehart, Roscoe Lee Brown, Paul
Rudd
A man from Connecticut falls asleep and finds
himself in King Arthur's Court.
WQED Pittsburgh — *Mastervision*

Marooned   1969
Science fiction
66011   134 mins C   B, V   P
Gregory Peck, David Janssen, Richard Crenna,
James Franciscus, Gene Hackman, Lee Grant,
directed by John Sturges
Three astronauts are stranded in space after a
retro-rocket misfires. In stereo.
MPAA:G

Columbia — *RCA/Columbia Pictures Home*
Video

Marriage and Divorce   1981
Test, The
Marriage/Divorce
57550   60 mins   C   B, V   P
Hosted by Dr. Frank Field
Viewers can test their knowledge of divorce and
marriage, and then find out the answers from
experts in the field.
NBC; Don Luftig — *Karl Video*

Martha Raye Show, The   1955
Comedy/Variety
69576   60 mins   B/W   B, V, FO   P
Martha Raye, Cesar Romero, David Burns,
Rocky Graziano, Will Jordan
This episode from Martha Raye's popular TV
series takes the form of an hour-long story
musical, with Martha being groomed for the
leading role in a new movie. Originally telecast
on December 13, 1955.
NBC — *Video Yesteryear*

Martian Chronicles, Part   1980
II-The Settlers, The
Science fiction
75463   97 mins   C   B, V   P
Rock Hudson, Bernadette Peters, Gayle
Hunnicutt
The settlers are trying to make a new life on this
strange world while the martians keep watchful
eyes on them.
King Features — *U.S.A. Home Video*

Martian Chronicles,   1980
Volume I: The
Expeditions, The
Science fiction
66618   100 mins C   B, V   P
Rock Hudson, Fritz Weaver, Roddy McDowall
The first segment of Ray Bradbury's story
collection about the first American explorers to
land on the planet Mars.
Charles Fries Productions — *U.S.A. Home*
Video

Martin   1977
Horror
65509   96 mins   C   B, V   R, P
John Amplas, Lincoln Maazel, directed by
George Romero
Martin is a charming young man, though slightly
mad. He freely admits the need to drink blood.
This contemporary vampire has found a new
abhorrent means of killing his victims.
MPAA:R
Richard Rubinstein — *THORN EMI Home*
Video

Martin Luther, His Life and Time   1924
Christianity
42958   101 mins   B/W   B, V, FO   P
This program traces the birth and youth of Luther and the great reformation within the church, examining both Luther the man and the church figure. Silent with musical score.
Lutheran Film Div — *Video Yesteryear*

Marty   1955
Drama
37526   91 mins   B/W   B, V, CED   P
Ernest Borgnine, Betsy Blair, Joe De Santis, Ester Minciotti, Jerry Paris, Karen Steele, directed by Delbert Mann
Ernest Borgnine's sensitive portrayal of Marty, a butcher from the Bronx, won him an Oscar. Marty is a painfully shy bachelor who feels trapped in a pointless life of family squabbles; when he finds love he also finds the strength to break out of what he feels is a meaningless existence.
Academy Awards '55: Best Production; Best Actor (Borgnine); Best Direction (Mann); Best Screenplay (Paddy Chayefsky).
United Artists — *CBS/Fox Video*

Marty/A Wind from the South   1953
Drama
65013   118 mins   B/W   B, V   P
Rod Steiger, Nancy Marchand, Julie Harris
Two classic original television dramas from the early 1950's are combined on this tape: Paddy Chayevsky's "Marty" with Rod Steiger as a lonely Bronx butcher; and James Costigan's "A Wind from the South," featuring Julie Harris as a romance-hungry Irish lass.
NBC; Fred Coe — *MGM/UA Home Video*

Marvelous Land of Oz, The   1982
Musical/Fantasy
47422   104 mins   C   B, V   P
The Children's Theater Company of Minneapolis
L. Frank Baum's sequel to "The Wonderful Wizard of Oz" picks up the story of the Scarecrow and Tin Woodman after Dorothy returns home to Kansas. This original musical production was taped live especially for video. VHS in stereo.
Television Theater Co — *MCA Home Video*

Marvin Mitchelson on Divorce   1984
Divorce
72902   47 mins   C   B, V   P
Marvin Mitchelson
The noted divorce lawyer discusses all aspects of divorce in a question and answer format.

Media Home Entertainment — *Media Home Entertainment*

Mary of Scotland   1936
Drama
00263   123 mins   B/W   B, V, 3/4U   P
Katharine Hepburn, Fredric March, directed by John Ford
The historical tragedy of Mary, Queen of Scots and her cousin, Queen Elizabeth I of England is enacted in this classic film.
RKO; Pandro S Berman — *Nostalgia Merchant; Blackhawk Films*

Mary Poppins   1964
Musical
54464   140 mins   C   CED   P
Julie Andrews, Dick Van Dyke, David Tomlinson, Glynis Johns, directed by Robert Stevenson
A magical English nanny arrives one day on the East Wind and takes over the household of a very proper London banker. She changes the lives of everyone, especially his two naughty children. From her they learn the wonders of life and how to make it enjoyable for themselves and others. Based on the novel by P. L. Travers.
Academy Awards '64: Best Actress (Andrews); Best Musical Score; Best Film Editing; Best Song ("Chim Chim Cher-ee").
Walt Disney — *RCA VideoDiscs*

Mary Tyler Moore Show, Vol. I, The   197?
Comedy
52604   102 mins   C   CED   P
Mary Tyler Moore, Ed Asner, Gavin McLeod, Ted Knight, Valerie Harper, Cloris Leachman
Four classic episodes from the memorable series which ran from 1970 to 1977: "Love Is All Around," the first episode, aired September 17, 1970; "The Final Show," the final episode, aired March 19, 1977; "Put on a Happy Face," aired February 24, 1973; and "Chuckles Bites the Dust," aired October 25, 1975. All four episodes won Emmys in various categories.
Emmy Awards: Outstanding Writing in a Comedy Series Single Episode '75-'76 ("Chuckles Bites the Dust"), '76-'77 ("The Final Show").
MTM Prods — *RCA VideoDiscs*

Masada   1981
Drama
50652   131 mins   C   B, V   P
Peter O'Toole, Peter Strauss, Barbara Carrera, Anthony Quayle, Giulia Pagano, David Warner, directed by Boris Sagal
Based on Ernest K. Gann's novel "The Antagonists," this dramatization recreates the first-century A.D. Roman siege of the fortress Masada, headquarters for a group of Jewish freedom fighters. This version is abridged from

the original television presentation. Musical score by Jerry Goldsmith.
MCA TV; Arnon Milchan Prods — *MCA Home Video*

M*A*S*H   1970
Comedy
08464   116 mins   C   B, V, LV   P
Donald Sutherland, Elliot Gould, Tom Skerritt, Sally Kellerman, JoAnn Pflug, Robert Duvall, directed by Robert Altman
A pair of surgeons at a Mobile Army Surgical Hospital in Korea create havoc with their late-night parties, and their practical jokes pulled on the nurses and other doctors.
MPAA:R
20th Century Fox; Aspen — *CBS/Fox Video*

M*A*S*H: Goodbye,   1983
Farewell and Amen
Comedy-Drama
64303   120 mins   C   B, V, LV,   P
                                       CED
Alan Alda, Mike Farrell, Harry Morgan, David Ogden Stiers, Loretta Swit, Jamie Farr, William Christopher
The final two-hour special episode of the TV series "M*A*S*H" follows Hawkeye, BJ, Col. Potter, Charles, Margaret, Klinger, Father Mulcahy and the rest of the men and women of the 4077th through the final days of the Korean War, the declaration of peace, the dismantling of the camp, and the fond and tearful farewells.
20th Century-Fox Television — *CBS/Fox Video*

Masked Marvel, The   1943
Adventure/Serials
07337   195 mins   B/W   B, V, 3/4U   P
William Forrest, Louise Currie, Johnny Arthur
A serial in which the Masked Marvel saves America's war industries from sabotage. In twelve episodes.
Republic — *Video Connection*

Massacre at Fort Holman   1973
Adventure
58553   92 mins   C   B, V   R, P
James Coburn, Telly Savalas, Bud Spencer
Seven condemned men are given a chance to live, if they can survive a suicide mission in the Southwest desert. Also known as "A Reason to Live, A Reason to Die."
MPAA:PG
Heritage Enterprises — *Video Gems*

Massage for Couples   1982
Massage
47365   42 mins   C   B, V   P
Elaine Hyams provides instruction in Swedish massage techniques for couples.

American Home Video Library — *American Home Video Library*

Mastectomy   1978
(Rehabilitation and
Injury)
Physical fitness
52758   30 mins   C   B, V   P
Hosted by Ann Dugan
Exercises for women who have had a mastectomy, including both specific-area and total-body movements to gradually improve muscle tone. Part of the "Rehabilitation and Injury" series.
Health 'N Action. — *RCA/Columbia Pictures Home Video*

Master Cooking Course,   1982
The
Cookery
59131   ? mins   C   LV   P
Craig Claiborne, Pierre Franey
Two of the world's greatest cooking authorities offer a step-by-step guide to the techniques of gourmet cooking. Over 100 skills essential to the art of gourmet cooking are demonstrated. A participative program. A two-sided disc.
Optical Programming Associates — *Optical Programming Associates*

Master Mind   1973
Comedy
47676   86 mins   C   B, V   P
Zero Mostel, Keiko Kishi, Brad Dillman, Herbert Berghof, Frankie Sakai
A renowned Japanese super sleuth attempts to solve the theft of a sophisticated midget android.
Malcolm Stewart — *Unicorn Video*

Master of the House   1925
Drama
42956   118 mins   B/W   B, V, FO   P
Directed by Carl Theodore Dreyer
Also known as "Thou Shalt Honour They Wife," this program is the story of a spoiled husband, a type extinct in this country but still in existence abroad. Silent with titles in English.
Unknown — *Video Yesteryear; Sheik Video*

Masters of Comedy   193?
Comedy
58719   90 mins   B/W   B, V   P
Bob Hope, Danny Kaye, W C Fields, Laurel and Hardy
Classic short subjects featuring Bob Hope ("Bob's Busy Day"), Danny Kaye ("Birth of a Star"), Laurel & Hardy ("A Day at the Studio"), and W. C. Fields ("The Barbershop," and "The Fatal Glass of Beer").
Hal Roach; Mack Sennett;
Educational — *Video Dimensions*

Masters of the World   192?
Comedy
59220   24 mins   B/W   B, V, 3/4U   P
Harry Pick
A harried cabbie picks up a mysterious fare who
seems to be eluding the police. A slapstick
silent.
Unknown — *Penguin Video*

Matilda   1978
Comedy
64356   103 mins   C   B, V, CED   P
*Elliot Gould, Robert Mitchum, Harry Guardino,
Clive Revill*
An entrepreneur decides to manage a boxing
kangaroo, which nearly succeeds in defeating
the world heavyweight champion.
MPAA:PG
American International — *Vestron Video*

Matrimaniac, The   1916
Comedy
66138   48 mins   B/W   B, V, FO   P
Douglas Fairbanks, Constance Talmadge
A man goes to great lengths to marry a woman
against her father's wishes. Silent with music
score.
Artcraft Paramount — *Video Yesteryear*

Matt the Gooseboy   1984
Cartoons/Folklore
74078   77 mins   C   B, V   P
Animated
The animated feature is based on a Hungarian
folktale about a boy who seeks vengeance on
an evil landlord who steals his goose.
Pannpnia Films — *Family Home Entertainment*

Matter of Time, A   1976
Musical/Romance
64888   97 mins   C   B, V, CED   P
*Liza Minnelli, Ingrid Bergman, Charles Boyer,
directed by Vincente Minnelli*
A young woman relives the flamboyant past of
an aging contessa.
MPAA:PG
American International Pictures — *Vestron
Video*

Mausoleum   1983
Horror
66269   96 mins   C   B, V, CED   P
Only one man can save a woman from eternal
damnation.
MPAA:R
Jerry Zimmerman; Michael
Franzese — *Embassy Home Entertainment*

Maverick Queen, The   1955
Western
74486   90 mins   C   B, V   P
Barbara Stanwyck, Barry Sullivan

This is the story of a Pinkerton detective who
infiltrates the "Wild Bunch" by becoming
involved with a woman who knows them.
Republic — *NTA Home Entertainment*

Max Dugan Returns   1983
Comedy-Drama
65329   98 mins   C   B, V, LV,   P
                                  CED
*Jason Robards, Marsha Mason, Donald
Sutherland*
An ex-con comes home from prison to visit his
daughter, carrying a suitcase full of stolen
money.
MPAA:PG
Herbert Ross — *CBS/Fox Video*

Max Roach   1981
Music-Performance
75899   19 mins   C   B, V   P
This program presents the jazz music of Max
Roach featuring the compositions "Six Bits
Blues" and "Effie."
Jazz America Ltd — *Sony Corporation of
America*

Mayerling   1937
Drama
11246   95 mins   B/W   B, V, FO   P
Charles Boyer, Danielle Darrieux
Based on the tragic and hopeless affair
between the Crown Prince Rudolph of Hapsburg
and young Baroness Marie Vetsera.
FR
Nero Films — *Video Yesteryear; Sheik Video*

Maze   1984
Music-Performance
76674   20 mins   C   B, V   P
This program presents a combination of jazz
and mellow funk.
Capitol Records Inc — *Sony Corporation of
America*

Maze Featuring Frankie   1982
Beverly
Music-Performance
47813   ? mins   C   LV   P
Maze, masters of mellow funk, perform their hits
including "Joy and Pain," "Happy Feelin's,"
"Southern Girl," and "Feel That You're Feelin'."
In stereo.
Unknown — *Pioneer Artists*

Maze Mania   1983
Games
64641   ? mins   C   LV   P
This interactive videodisc combines the action
of television with the fun of video games in a
collection of maze games requiring the player to
answer questions correctly in order to pass

through a maze of live action visuals. Four complete games are included.
Optical Programming Associates — *Optical Programming Associates*

McCabe and Mrs. Miller   1971
Western
51966   107 mins   C   B, V   R, P
Warren Beatty, Julie Christie, William Devane, Keith Carradine, Shelley Duvall, directed by Robert Altman
A gambler and a madam operate a thriving brothel and gambling house in a frontier mining town.
Warner Bros — *Warner Home Video*

McQ   1974
Crime-Drama
51961   116 mins   C   B, V   R, P
John Wayne, Eddie Albert, Diana Muldaur, Clu Gulager
After several big dope dealers kill two police officers, a lieutenant resigns to track them down.
MPAA:PG
Warner Bros — *Warner Home Video*

McVicar   1980
Drama
65604   90 mins   C   B, V   P
Roger Daltrey, Adam Faith
A brutish and realistic depiction of crime and punishment based on the life of the professional John McVicar. In stereo VHS and Beta Hi-Fi.
MPAA:R
Bill Curbishley; Roy Baird; Roger Daltrey — *Vestron Video*

Mean Johnny Barrows   1975
Crime-Drama
47671   83 mins   C   B, V   P
Fred Williamson, Roddy McDowell, Stuart Whitman, Luther Adler, Jenny Sherman, Elliot Gould
When Johnny Barrows returns to his home town after being dishonorably discharged from the Army he is offered a job as a gang hitman.
Fred Williamson — *Unicorn Video*

Mean Machine, The   1973
Adventure
66196   89 mins   C   B, V   P
Chris Mitchum, Barbara Bouchet, Arthur Kennedy
One man tries to get even with the mob.
MPAA:R
Tecisa Madrid — *Monterey Home Video*

Meatballs   1979
Comedy
44915   92 mins   C   B, V   R, P

Bill Murray, Harvey Atkin, Kate Lynch
The Activities Director at a summer camp who is supposed to organize fun for everyone prefers his own style of "fun."
MPAA:PG
Paramount — *Paramount Home Video; Vestron Video (disc only)*

Meatloaf in Concert   1977
Music-Performance
73565   60 mins   C   B, V   P
All the excitement of a Meatloaf live concert is captured here where Meatloaf performs "Bat Out of Hell" and "Dead Ringer for Love."
Robert Ellis; Mike Mansfield — *Prism*

Mechanic, The   1972
Adventure
64901   100 mins   C   B, V   P
Charles Bronson, Jan-Michael Vincent, Keenan Wynn, Jill Ireland, Linda Ridgeway
Bronson stars as Arthur Bishop, a wealthy professional killer for a powerful organization. He has innumerable ways to kill.
MPAA:PG
United Artists — *CBS/Fox Video*

Medical Aerobics for   1983
Athletic Training
Physical fitness
64337   60 mins   C   B, V, 3/4U,   P
                                  Q
Jean Rosenbaum, M.D.
Fitness researcher and instructor, Dr. Rosenbaum, conducts a medically sound, full-body aerobics workout especially beneficial for use by coaches and athletes.
Milrose Productions — *TV Sports Scene*

Medium and Long Iron   197?
Game, The
Golf
33777   60 mins   C   B, V, 3/4U   P
Golf pros Dick Lawrence, John Ferrari, Joyce Ann Jackson, and Harry Offutt give pointers on how to develop a longer, stronger, fairway shot. From the "Name of the Game Is Golf" series.
Unknown — *Sports World Cinema*

Medium Cool   1969
Drama
66036   111 mins   C   B, V   R, P
Robert Forster, Verna Bloom, Peter Bonerz, Marianna Hill, directed by Haskell Wexler
This commentary on life in the '60s focuses on a TV news cameraman and his growing apathy with the events around him.
MPAA:X
Paramount — *Paramount Home Video*

Medusa Affair, The   197?
Sports-Water
53638   27 mins   C   B, V, 3/4U,   P
                       Q
This program in the "Under Water Deep Sea
Diving" series depicts a search for the elusive
and mysterious fresh water jelly fish.
Smokey Roberts — *TV Sports Scene*

Meet Dr. Christian   1939
Drama
11765   72 mins   B/W   B, V   P
Jean Hersholt, Robert Baldwin
The good old doctor settles some problems.
RKO; William Stephens — *Discount Video
Tapes; Sheik Video; Video Yesteryear*

Meet John Doe   1941
Drama
54039   135 mins   B/W   B, V   P
*Gary Cooper, Barbara Stanwyck, Edward
Arnold, James Gleason, directed by Frank
Capra*
An unemployed, down and out man is selected
to represent the "typical American" because of
his honesty. Unfortunately, he finds that he is
being used to further the careers of corrupt
politicians.
Warner Bros, Frank Capra — *Media Home
Entertainment; Budget Video; Cinema
Concepts; VCII; Sheik Video; Ampro Video
Productions; Cable Films; Penguin Video; Video
Connection; Video Yesteryear; Discount Video
Tapes; Western Film & Video Inc; Cinema
Concepts*

Meet Marcel Marceau   1965
Mime
42974   52 mins   C   B, V, FO   P
Marcel Marceau
The most famous contemporary pantomimist,
Marcel Marceau himself does voice-over
introductions of various skits including his
popular character, "Bip," and special tributes to
Harpo Marx, Buster Keaton, and Charlie
Chaplin.
Unknown — *Video Yesteryear*

Meet Me in St. Louis   1944
Musical
44644   113 mins   C   B, V, CED   P
*Judy Garland, Margaret O'Brien, Mary Astor,
Tom Drake, June Lockhart, Harry Davenport,
directed by Vincente Minnelli*
Wonderful music sets the mood for this
charming tale of a family in St. Louis and the
1903 World's Fair. Judy Garland sings the title
song "Trolley Song," along with "The Boy Next
Door" and "Have Yourself a Merry Little
Christmas."
MGM — *MGM/UA Home Video*

Meet Mr.   196?
Washington/Meet Mr.
Lincoln
Presidency-US
58811   79 mins   C   CED   P
Two award-winning shows from the NBC series,
"Project Twenty." "Meet Mr. Washington," tells
the story of George Washington through his
own words as well as letters and diaries of
contemporaries and newspapers of the time.
"Meet Mr. Lincoln," portrays Abe Lincoln as his
contemporaries saw him.
NBC — *RCA VideoDiscs*

Meet the Navy   1946
Musical
66139   81 mins   B/W   B, V, FO   P
Joan Pratt, Margaret Hurst, Lionel Murton
A post-war musical revue about a pianist and a
dancer.
British — *Video Yesteryear*

Meet Your Animal Friends   1982
Animals
75699   52 mins   C   B, V, 3/4U,   P
                       LV, CED
Narrated by Lynn Redgrave
Young children are able to view and learn about
animals in this fun program for preschoolers.
Babyshow Productions — *Environmental
Video; Program Hunters*

Meet Your VCR   1982
Video
63997   48 mins   C   B, V   P
Joan Lunden
This program was created to help the video
consumer get the most out of his or her VCR by
providing 10 easy lessons ranging from
recording to maintenance.
3055 Corporation — *Karl Video*

Meeting at Midnight   1944
Mystery
54313   67 mins   B/W   B, V   P
*Sidney Toler, Joseph Crehan, Mantan
Moreland, Frances Chan, directed by Phil
Rosen*
Charlie Chan is invited to a seance to solve a
perplexing mystery. Chan discovers that they
use mechanical figures and from there on
solving the mystery is easy.
Monogram — *Video Connection; Video
Yesteryear*

Megaforce   1982
Science fiction
63394   99 mins   C   B, V, CED   P
*Barry Bostwick, Persis Khambutta, Edward
Mulhare, Henry Silva, Ralph Wilcox*
This futuristic thriller follows the adventures of
the military task force, Megaforce, on its mission
to save a small democratic nation from attack.

MPAA:PG
20th Century Fox — *CBS/Fox Video*

Mejore Regalo, El (The Best Gift)   197?
Comedy-Drama
73587   30 mins   C   B, V   P
Jorge Rivero, Teresa Gimpera
The wedding plans of a groom are ruined when a young boy arrives as a gift to the groom.
KNBC — *Aztec Cinevideo*

Mel Torme   1983
Music-Performance
76665   53 mins   C   B, V   P
A collection of hits from this legendary singer, composer, arranger and conductor. Includes: "New York State of Mind," "Born in the Night," "Down for Double" and many more.
One Pass Prod — *Sony Corporation of America*

Mel Torme and Della Reese in Concert   1981
Music-Performance
55562   45 mins   C   LV   P
Mel Torme, Della Reese, directed by Ron Brown
The two performers combine their talents in this concert recorded live at the Jubilee Auditorium in Edmonton, Canada. Stereo disc.
ITV — *MCA Home Video*

Melanie   1982
Drama
65362   109 mins   C   B, V   P
Glynnis O'Connor, Paul Sorvino, Burton Cummings
This gripping drama is the tale of one woman's extraordinary courage, determination, and optimism. Melanie refused to see herself as an unfit mother and emerged a winner in every way!
MPAA:PG
Richard Simpson; Peter Simpson — *Vestron Video*

Mellow Memories   1984
Music-Performance
73335   60 mins   C   B, V   P
The mellow side of the pop music spectrum is represented in this program that features performances from Neil Diamond to Helen Reddy. Available in Beta Hi-Fi and VHS stereo
USA — *U.S.A. Home Video*

Melody   1971
Drama
60445   106 mins   C   B, V, CED   P
Jack Wild, Mark Lester, Colin Barrie
A sensitive study of a special friendship which enables two adolescents to survive in a regimented and impersonal world. Features music by the Bee Gees.
MPAA:G
Levitt Pickman Films — *Embassy Home Entertainment*

Melody for Three   1941
Drama
14749   69 mins   B/W   B, V   P
Jean Hersholt, Fay Wray
Doctor Christian aids a young violinist whose lessons are being interrupted by parental bickering.
RKO — *Sheik Video; Discount Video Tapes*

Melody Master, The   1941
Musical-Drama/Biographical
46346   80 mins   B/W   B, V, FO   P
Alan Curtis, Ilona Massey, Binnie Barnes, Albert Basserman, Billy Gilbert, Sterling Holloway
A romanticized biography of composer Franz Schubert, chronicling his personal life and loves, along with performances of his compositions. Original title: New Wine.
United Artists — *Video Yesteryear; Discount Video Tapes*

Melody Ranch   1940
Musical/Western
44812   84 mins   C   B, V   P, T
Gene Autry, Jimmy Durante, George Hayes, Ann Miller
Gene returns to his home town as an honored guest.
Republic — *Blackhawk Films; Video Connection*

Melody Trail   1935
Western/Musical
44808   60 mins   B/W   B, V   P, T
Gene Autry, Smiley Burnette
Gene wins $1000 in a rodeo, loses the money to a gypsy, gets a job, falls for his employer's daughter ... and in the end captures both kidnapper and cattle rustlers.
Republic — *Blackhawk Films; Video Connection*

Melvin and Howard   1980
Comedy
55549   95 mins   C   B, V, LV   P
Paul Le Mat, Jason Robards, Mary Steenburgen, Michael J. Pollard, Dabney Coleman, Elizabeth Cheshire, directed by Jonathan Demme
The story, according to Melvin Dummar, about the man who picked up Howard Hughes in the desert and then claimed to be heir to the Hughes fortune via the disputed Mormon will.
Academy Awards '80: Best Supporting Actress (Steenburgen); Best Original Screenplay (Bo Goldman). MPAA:R

Universal; Art Linson; Don Phillips — *MCA Home Video*

Member of the Wedding, The
1983
Drama
72195   90 mins   C   B, V   R, P
While struggling through her adolescence, a twelve-year-old girl growing up in 1945 Georgia seeks solace from her family's cook.
Unknown — *VCII*

Memoirs of a Fairy Godmother
1982
Fairy tales
64952   90 mins   C   B, V   R, P
Rosemary De Camp
The Godmother, an eccentric old lady, lives in the woods with her many pets. She enjoys telling stories and the film features animated versions of the tales of Cinderella, Snow White, Sleeping Beauty and many others.
MPAA:G
Century Video — *Video Gems*

Memorandum
1965
World War II
21395   59 mins   B/W   B, V, FO   P
A Canadian Jew who survived the Holocaust in Europe returns to Germany to join a pilgrimage to the former concentration camp of Bergen-Belsen.
National Film Board of Canada — *Video Yesteryear*

Memory Lane Movies by Robert Youngson #1
195?
Documentary/Film-History
58647   62 mins   B/W   B, V, FO   P
Five shorts compiled by film historian Robert Youngson from the Pathe archives: "The World of Kids" (1951), featuring an all-kid rodeo, kid golfers, etc.; "Animals Have All the Fun" (1952), a look at animal antics highlighted by a canine fashion show; "Batter Up" (1949), scenes of Babe Ruth, Lou Gehrig, Jimmy Fox, and Joltin' Joe included; "Those Exciting Days" (1955), chronicling the years before the First World War; and "This Was Yesterday" (1954), a look at America circa 1914.
Warner Bros — *Video Yesteryear*

Memory Lane Movies by Robert Youngson #2
195?
Documentary/Film-History
58648   61 mins   B/W   B, V, FO   P
Five shorts compiled by film historian Robert Youngson from the Pathe archives: "I Never Forget a Face" (1956), including the 1920 Presidential campaign, the Scopes Monkey Trial, and other events of the day; "Horsehide Heroes" (1951), a look at the all-time greats,

from Ted Williams to Ty Cobb; "Some of the Greatest" (1955), with scenes from the 1926 classic film 'Don Juan'; "The Swim Parade" (1949), featuring bathing beauties throughout the years; and "They Were Champions" (1955), featuring the greatest boxers of all time.
Warner Bros — *Video Yesteryear*

Memory Lane Movies by Robert Youngson #3
195?
Documentary/Film-History
58649   62 mins   B/W   B, V, FO   P
Five shorts compiled by film historian Robert Youngson from the Pathe archives: "Gadgets Galore" (1955), a look at the early days of the automobile; "Faster and Faster" (1956), a potpourri of boat races; "Animals and Kids" (1956), featuring monkeys that play piano, etc; "It Happened to You" (1955), a scrapbook of World War I; and "Dare Devil Days" (1952), consisting of 'human flies' and the Like.
Warner Bros — *Video Yesteryear*

Memory Lane Movies by Robert Youngson #4
19??
Documentary/Film-History
58650   55 mins   B/W   B, V, FO   P
Five shorts compiled by film historian Robert Youngson from the Pathe archives: "Blaze Buster" (1950), with spectacular scenes of early fires; "Lighter Than Air" (1951), a look at blimps, balloons and dirigibles; "When Sports Were King" (1954), a look at sports events of the 1920's; "I Remember When" (1954), featuring scenes of 'Little Old New York,' the Wright Bros., the 'Frisco Quake,' etc; "Coming of the Auto" (1953), a look at the early days of the motor car; and "Camera Hunting" (1954), a film biography of Thomas Edison.
Warner Bros — *Video Yesteryear*

Memory Lane Movies by Robert Youngson #5
195?
Documentary/Film-History
47470   62 mins   B/W   B, V, FO   P
Six shorts compiled from Pathe newsreel footage by Robert Youngson: "This Mechanical Age" (1954), "Roaring Wheels" (1948), "Cavalcade of Girls" (1950), "They're Off!" (1949), "No Adults Allowed" (1953) and "Disaster Fighters" (1951).
Academy Awards '54: Best One-Reel Short Film ("This Mechanical Age").
Warner Bros — *Video Yesteryear*

Memory Lane Movies by Robert Youngson #6
195?
Documentary/Film-History
47471   62 mins   B/W   B, V, FO   P
Six shorts compiled by Robert Youngson from Pathe newsreel footage: "Spills and Chills" (1949), "Fire, Wind and Flood" (1955), "A-Speed on the Deep" (1950), "Head Over

Heels" (1953), "Too Much Speed" (1952) and
"Say It with Spills" (1953).
Warner Bros — *Video Yesteryear*

Memphis Belle, The   1944
Documentary/World War II
45063   43 mins   C   B, V   P
The entire final mission of the Flying Fortress,
"Memphis Belle," and its daring daylight attack
on the submarine pens at Wilhelmshaven,
Germany is seen in this newsreel footage.
Lt Col William Wyler — *Budget Video;*
International Historic Films; Western Film &
Video Inc

Men, The   1950
Drama
64545   85 mins   B/W   B, V   P
Marlon Brando, Teresa Wright, Everett Sloane,
Jack Webb, directed by Fred Zinnemann
A paraplegic World War II veteran sinks into
depression until his former girlfriend manages to
bring him out of it. Marlon Brando's first film.
United Artists; Stanley Kramer — *NTA Home*
Entertainment

Men in War   1957
War-Drama
04000   104 mins   B/W   B, V   P
Robert Ryan, Aldo Ray, Robert Keith, Philip
Pine, Vic Morrow
Grim, suspenseful war film. 1950. American
infantry platoon in Korea, surrounded by the
enemy, fight for their objective. Based on Van
Praag's novel.
UA; Security Prod — *King of Video*

Men of Destiny Volume I: 1979
World Political Figures
History-Modern/Documentary
29157   120 mins   B/W   B, V   P
Narrated by Bob Considine
Presents authentic newsreels that capture the
exact mood and drama of history. This program
records the lives and momentous achievements
of over 30 leaders in world history featuring
Winston Churchill, Herbert Hoover, Mahatma
Gandhi, Chrales De Gaulle, and many others.
Pathe News — *CBS/Fox Video*

Men of Destiny Volume II: 1979
Artists and Innovators
History-Modern/Documentary
29158   120 mins   B/W   B, V   P
Narrated by Bob Considine
Presents authentic newsreels that capture the
exact mood and drama of history. This volume
features the achievements of over thirty world-
renowned figures including Marie Curie, Thomas
Edison, Albert Einstein, Jonas Salk, the Wright
Brothers, and Charles Lindbergh.
Pathe News — *CBS/Fox Video*

Men Who Tread on the   1945
Tiger's Tail
Adventure
72472   60 mins   B/W   B, V, 3/4U   P
Directed by Akira Kurosawa
Twelfth century Japan is the setting for this
struggle of power between two brothers, one a
reigning shogun, the other on the run. English
subtitles.
JA
Toho Company Ltd; Japanese — *International*
Historic Films

Men Against   194?
Tanks/Engineers to the
Front
World War II
53380   48 mins   B/W   B, V, 3/4U   P
Two German war films: "Men Against Tanks"
(1943), which shows the drama of an
entrenched German infantry platoon repelling
an overwhelming Soviet tank attack; "Engineers
to the Front" (1940), which depicts the lightning
advance of the German army due to its
engineers who eliminate defensive barriers.
English subtitled.
GE
Germany — *International Historic Films*

Mephisto   1981
Drama
47753   140 mins   C   B, V   P
Klaus Maria Brandauer, Krystyna Janda,
directed by Istvan Szabo
The story of a provincial actor's climb to fame
before and during the Nazi period.
Academy Awards '81: Best Foreign Language
Film.
Manfred Durniok Productions — *The Video*
Station

Mercedes-Benz 300 SL   1983
Automobiles-Racing
65169   43 mins   C   B, V   P
Narrated by Ron Hughes
Several restored 300 SL's are seen, including
restored 1955, 1957 and 1958 models, both
Coupe and Roadster. Also shown is a 1956
European model in the process of restoration.
Armour Productions — *Armour Productions*

Merry Christmas Mr.   1983
Lawrence
Drama
65513   124 mins   C   B, V   P
David Bowie, Tom Conti, Ryuichi Sakamoto,
Takeshi, Jack Thompson
A taut psychological World War II drama about
clashing cultures and survival. In stereo VHS
and Beta Hi-Fi.
MPAA:R
Universal — *MCA Home Video*

Merry Christmas to You 1980
Christmas
54245 80 mins C B, V, 3/4U P
A collection of cartoons, singalongs, and Lone
Ranger and Lassie adventures that all carry a
Christmas theme.
Nostalgia Merchant — *Nostalgia Merchant*

Metalstorm 1983
Adventure/Science fiction
65514 84 mins C B, V, LV, P
CED
*Jeffrey Byron, Mike Preston, Tim Thomerson,
Kelly Preston, Richard Moll*
It's the science fiction battle of the ages with
giant cyclopses and intergalactic magicians on
the desert planet of Lemuria. In stereo VHS and
Beta Hi-Fi.
MPAA:PG
Universal — *MCA Home Video*

Meteor 1979
Science fiction
53518 107 mins C B, V R, P
*Sean Connery, Natalie Wood, Karl Malden,
Brian Keith, Martin Landau, Trevor Howard,
Henry Fonda, Joseph Campanella*
The U.S. and the Soviet Union both have an
armed satellite orbiting in space, its fire power
directed at an enemy nation. An American
scientist calculates that only their combined
weaponry can destroy the enemy.
MPAA:PG
American International — *Warner Home Video*

Metropolis 1926
Film-History
08705 120 mins B/W B, V, 3/4U P
*Brigitte Helm, Alfred Abel, Gustav Froehlich,
directed by Fritz Lang*
Portrays a city of the future. (Silent, musical
score added.)
UFA — *Penguin Video; Budget Video; Video
Yesteryear; Discount Video Tapes; International
Historic Films; Sheik Video; Cable Films; Classic
Video Cinema Collector's Club*

Michael Nesmith: 1981
Rio/Cruisin'
Music/Video
66161 11 mins C B, V P
Two songs from the "Elephant Parts" video. In
stereo.
Pacfic Arts Video — *Sony Corporation of
America*

Mick Fleetwood-The 1981
Visitor
Music-Performance
60383 106 mins C CED P
Fleetwood Mac's founder and drummer, Mick
Fleetwood, travels to Ghana, Africa in a

fascinating excursion combining rock music with
traditional African sounds.
Colin Frewin — *RCA VideoDiscs*

Mickey 1917
Comedy
11247 80 mins B/W B, V, FO P
Mabel Normand, Lew Cody, Minta Durfee
A spoof on high society which contains a scene
in which a squirrel scampers up the heroine's
leg and is retrieved by the hero. (Silent.)
Mack Sennett — *Video Yesteryear; Sheik
Video; Discount Video Tapes; Penguin Video;
Classic Video Cinema Collector's Club*

Mickey 1948
Comedy
55344 80 mins C B, V P
*Lois Butler, Bill Goodwin, Irene Hervy, Hattie
McDaniel*
A sixteen-year-old tomboy, determined to marry
her father off to the right woman, ends up falling
in love herself.
Eagle Lion — *Sheik Video*

Mickey the Great 1942
Comedy
48723 50 mins B/W B, V, 3/4U P
Mickey Rooney
Grown-up members of the Toonerville Kids get
together and reminisce about the Mickey
McGuire comedies.
Unknown — *Penguin Video*

Microwave Cooking 1982
Cookery
47361 30 mins C V P
Basic instruction in cooking in a microwave
oven is given, along with some simple recipes.
American Home Video Library — *American
Home Video Library*

Mid Channel 1920
Drama
48709 50 mins B/W B, V, 3/4U P
A woman goes out on the town every night
because her husband is never home. Silent.
Unknown — *Penguin Video*

Mid Knight Rider 1984
Drama
66491 76 mins C B, V P
Michael Christian, Keenan Wynn
A penniless actor becomes a male prostitute at
the service of bored, rich women. At an all-night
orgy, he suddenly goes on a rampage, nearly
killing one of his customers.
Trans World Entertainment — *Trans World
Entertainment*

Midnight 1934
Mystery
12809   74 mins   B/W   B, V   P
Humphrey Bogart, Sidney Fox, O.P. Hegge, Henry Hull
A jury foreman's daughter is romantically involved with a gangster who is interested in a particular case before it appears in court.
United International — *Penguin Video; Blackhawk Films; Sheik Video; Cinema Concepts*

Midnight Cowboy 1969
Drama
60564   113 mins   C   B, V   P
Dustin Hoffman, Jon Voight, Sylvia Miles, Brenda Vaccaro, John McGiver
James Leo Herlihy's novel about the relationship between a Texan and a pathetic derelict, set amidst seamy New York environs, is graphically depicted in this film.
MPAA:R
Jerome Hellman Prods; United Artists — *MGM/UA Home Video; RCA VideoDiscs*

Midnight Express 1978
Drama
35379   120 mins   C   B, V, LV   P
Brad Davis, John Hurt, Randy Quaid, directed by Alan Parker
Harrowing tale of a young American who is arrested for drug smuggling in Turkey and undergoes mental and physical torture beyond belief in a Turkish prison.
MPAA:R
Columbia — *RCA/Columbia Pictures Home Video; RCA VideoDiscs*

Midnight Girl, The 1925
Drama
48710   60 mins   B/W   B, V, 3/4U   P
Bela Lugosi, Lila Lee
A faltering opera impresario tries to get his son married into a wealthy family. Interesting glimpses of New York City jazz life are contained in the silent picture.
Chadwick Pictures — *Penguin Video*

Midsummer Night's Sex Comedy, A 1982
Comedy
63108   88 mins   C   B, V   R, P
Woody Allen, Mia Farrow, Mary Steenburgen, Tony Roberts, Julie Hagerty, directed by Woody Allen
Three turn-of-the-century couples spend an idyllic weekend in upstate New York. Music score by Felix Mendelssohn.
Orion Pictures; Robert Greenhut — *Warner Home Video*

Midway 1976
War-Drama
53394   132 mins   C   B, V   P
Charlton Heston, Henry Fonda, James Coburn, Glenn Ford, Hal Holbrook, Robert Mitchum, Cliff Robertson, Robert Wagner
The epic WWII battle of Midway, the turning point in the war, is retold through Allied and Japanese viewpoints.
MPAA:PG
Universal; Walter Mirisch — *MCA Home Video (disc only)*

Mighty Joe Young 1949
Horror
00313   94 mins   B/W   B, V, 3/4U   P
Terry Moore, Ben Johnson, Robert Armstrong
A young girl raises a giant ape in Africa, only to have it brought to New York, where it escapes. Academy Awards '49: Best Special Effects.
RKO — *Nostalgia Merchant; King of Video*

Mighty Jungle, The 1964
Adventure
66513   90 mins   C   B, V   P
Marshall Thompson, Dave DaLie
Lost in the Amazon jungle, a hunter must fight off killer iguanas, man-eating crocodiles and bloodthirsty natives who perform human sacrifices.
Rosenda Monteros; Robert Patrick — *Paragon Video Productions*

Mighty Mouse in The Great Space Chase 1983
Cartoons
69529   88 mins   C   B, V, CED   P
Animated
Mighty Mouse goes "up, up, and away" to save the day in his first full-length animated feature.
MPAA:G
Filmation Stuios — *Children's Video Library*

Mikado, The 1982
Music-Performance
66272   150 mins   C   B, V   P
Gilbert & Sullivan's comic opera, a spoof of Victorian England "disguised" as a Japanese musical drama.
Unknown — *Embassy Home Entertainment*

Mil Millones para una Rubia (The Lady Thief) 1978
Adventure
51104   90 mins   C   B, V   P
Analia Gade, J. Lopez Vazquez, Jean Sorel, Stephen Boyd
Daring thieves plan expensive jewel heists in Las Vegas, Monte Carlo, Paris, and Monaco. In Spanish.
SP
Spanish — *Budget Video*

   (For Explanation of codes, see USE GUIDE and KEY)

Mildred Pierce   1945
Drama
59343   113 mins   B/W   LV   P
Joan Crawford, Jack Carson, Zachary Scott,
Eve Arden, Ann Blyth, directed by Michael Curtiz
A dowdy housewife leaves her husband,
becomes the owner of a restaurant chain, and
survives a murder case before true love comes
her way.
Academy Awards '45: Best Actress (Crawford).
Warner Bros — *CBS/Fox Video; RCA
VideoDiscs*

Milestones of the Century   1979
Volume I: The Great Wars
History-Modern/Documentary
29155   120 mins   B/W   B, V   P
Narrated by Ed Herlihy
This volume of "Milestones of the Century I"
records over 30 momentous events in world
history and features: FDR leading the nation;
Europe ablaze—1914-1917; Hitler's Germany;
Britain's Finest Hour; and the Korean Conflict.
Pathe News — *CBS/Fox Video*

Milestones of the Century   1979
Volume II: 20th
Century—Turning Points
History-Modern/Documentary
29156   120 mins   B/W   B, V   P
Narrated by Ed Herlihy
This volume of great historic newsreels
captures the exact mood and drama of history.
Featured are: invention and industry, the era of
flight, suffragettes and prohibition, the Russian
Revolution, and the post-war world.
Pathe News — *CBS/Fox Video*

Militant Eagle   19??
Martial arts/Adventure
60512   90 mins   C   D, V   P
Choi Yue, Lu Ping, Pai Ying
A fight of good vs. evil complete with nobles,
warriors and villains who fight to the death.
Unknown — *Master Arts Video*

Milky Way, The   1936
Comedy
44972   89 mins   B/W   B, V   P
*Harold Lloyd, Adolphe Menjou, Verree
Teasdale, Helen Mack, William Gargan*
A milkman knocks out the world champion
boxer. His prize is plenty of headaches and the
women he loves.
Paramount — *Discount Video Tapes; Budget
Video*

Mill on the Floss   1937
Drama
48731   80 mins   B/W   B, V   P
James Mason, Geraldine Fitzgerald

A legal feud between two families eventually
leads to tragedy for the children of the families.
Morgan Pictures — *Movie Buff Video; Penguin
Video*

Million, Le   1930
Comedy
12448   85 mins   B/W   B, V   P
*Rene Lefebre, Annabelle, directed by Rene
Clair*
The promise of riches is the basis for the zany
series of events as a mad hunt begins for a lost
lottery ticket. French film, English subtitles.
FR
French — *Sheik Video; Video Yesteryear;
Festival Films*

Million Dollar Kid, The   1944
Drama
08859   63 mins   B/W   B, V, 3/4U   P
*Leo Gorcey, Huntz Hall, Gabriel Dell, Noah
Beery, East Side Kids*
A local crime gives the East Side Kids a bad
name. Mugs falls in love with the beautiful
daughter of a millionaire whose brother is in
trouble.
Monogram — *Penguin Video*

Milton Berle Show, The   1963
Comedy/Variety
47493   60 mins   B/W   B, V, FO   P
*Milton Berle, Janis Paige, Lena Horne, Laurence
Harvey, Jack Benny, Kirk Douglas, Charlton
Heston, Les Brown and his Orchestra*
A typical Milton Berle variety program,
highlighted by a biblical epic spoof, with
Laurence Harvey as Spartacus, Jack Benny as
Ben Hur and Milton as Cleopatra. Original
commercials included.
NBC — *Video Yesteryear*

Milton Berle Show, The   1966
Comedy/Variety
47476   59 mins   B/W   B, V, FO   P
*Milton Berle, Ben Blue, Roy Rogers, Dale
Evans, the Dan Blocker Singers*
This show, originally telecast December 2,
1966, was one of the last programs from Milton
Berle's variety series. Featured are sketches,
Vietnam and Christmas jokes and songs by Roy
Rogers and Dale Evans. Original commercials
included.
ABC — *Video Yesteryear*

Milton Berle Show, The   1956
Variety
54136   60 mins   B/W   B, V   P
*Elvis Presley, Irish "Sheena" McCalla, Debra
Paget, Barry Gordon, hosted by Milton Berle*
This is the last of Milton Berle's shows,
broadcast live in 1956. Elvis Presley, in one of
his first TV appearances, sings "Hound Dog."

NBC — *Video Dimensions*

Milton Berle Show, The 1953
Comedy
45017 120 mins B/W B, V, 3/4U P
Milton Berle, Jackie Cooper, Vic Damone, Peter Lawford, Carol Channing
Two complete (commercials included) Berle shows from 1953. Included are take-offs of "What's My Line" and "Dragnet" and Berle doing a soft-shoe routine with Lawford.
NBC — *Shokus Video*

Milton Berle Spectacular, The 1962
Variety
57289 60 mins B/W B, V P
Jack Benny, Milton Berle, Laurence Harvey, Lena Horne, Janice Page, Kirk Douglas, Charlton Heston
An all-star special featuring Jack Benny and Milton battling it out in a sketch that shows them trying to get the audience to watch their shows. Lena Horne and Janice Page provide the music, and Laurence Harvey appears in a bit about movie epics that features Milton in drag as Cleopatra. Surprise guests are Kirk Douglas and Charlton Heston.
NBC — *Video Dimensions*

Mine Own Executioner 1947
Mystery
07172 102 mins B/W B, V P
Burgess Meredith, Kieron Moore, Dulcie Gray
Ex-RAF pilot goes to psychiatrist after he crashes in Burma. Tense and well-performed British melodrama.
Alexander Korda — *Discount Video Tapes; Budget Video*

Mini Musicals 1975
Cartoons/Music
58588 75 mins C B, V R, P
Voices of Joni Mitchell, Jim Croce, Helen Reddy, Sonny and Cher
A collection of musical animated shorts, plus a special, added short—Stravinsky's "Petrouchka," conducted by the composer himself.
John Wilson — *Video Gems*

Minor Miracle, A 1983
Drama
72870 100 mins C B, V P
John Huston, Pele
This is the story of a group of people who get together to save an orphanage from the town planners.
MPAA:G
Unknown — *Embassy Home Entertainment*

Minsky's Follies 1983
Comedy
75289 60 mins C B, V P
Phyllis Diller, Rip Taylor, Stubby Kaye
This is a recreation of an old time burlesque revue complete with strippers. In VHS Dolby stereo and Beta Hi-Fi.
RKO Home Video — *RKO HomeVideo*

Miracle at City Hall 197?
Drugs
10408 24 mins C B, V, 3/4U, Q P
Al Palmquist
A special report on drugs and young people today with Al Palmquist, the preacher-cop who is respected by the youth in his area and offers answers to their problems.
TV Sports-Scene — *TV Sports Scene*

Miracle of Lake Placid: Highlights of the 1980 Winter Olympics, The 1980
Sports-Winter
39034 94 mins C CED P
Hosted by Jim McCay
A program of highlights from the 1980 Winter Olympics at Lake Placid, including excerpts of hockey games between the U.S. and Czechoslovakia, Russia, and Finland; all of Eric Heiden's five gold medal-winning speed races; the figure skating duel between Linda Fratianne and Anett Poetzch, and other events. All material was taken from ABC-TV coverage of the Games.
ABC — *RCA VideoDiscs*

Miracle of the Bells, The 1948
Drama
69315 120 mins B/W B, V P
Fred MacMurray, Alida Valli, Frank Sinatra, Lee J. Cobb
A lovely, unknown actress rises to stardom overnight and falls in love with a cynical press agent who makes all her dreams come true.
Jesse L. Lasky Productions; RKO — *NTA Home Entertainment*

Miracle on 34th Street 1947
Drama
48598 94 mins B/W B, V P
Maureen O'Hara, John Payne, Edmund Gwenn, Natalie Wood, William Frawley
Macy's hires Kris Kringle as Santa Claus for its annual Thanksgiving Day parade. The situation snowballs as a daughter and mother learn to "believe."
20th Century Fox — *CBS/Fox Video*

Miracle Rider 1935
Western/Serials
14625 195 mins B/W B, V P

(For Explanation of codes, see USE GUIDE and KEY)

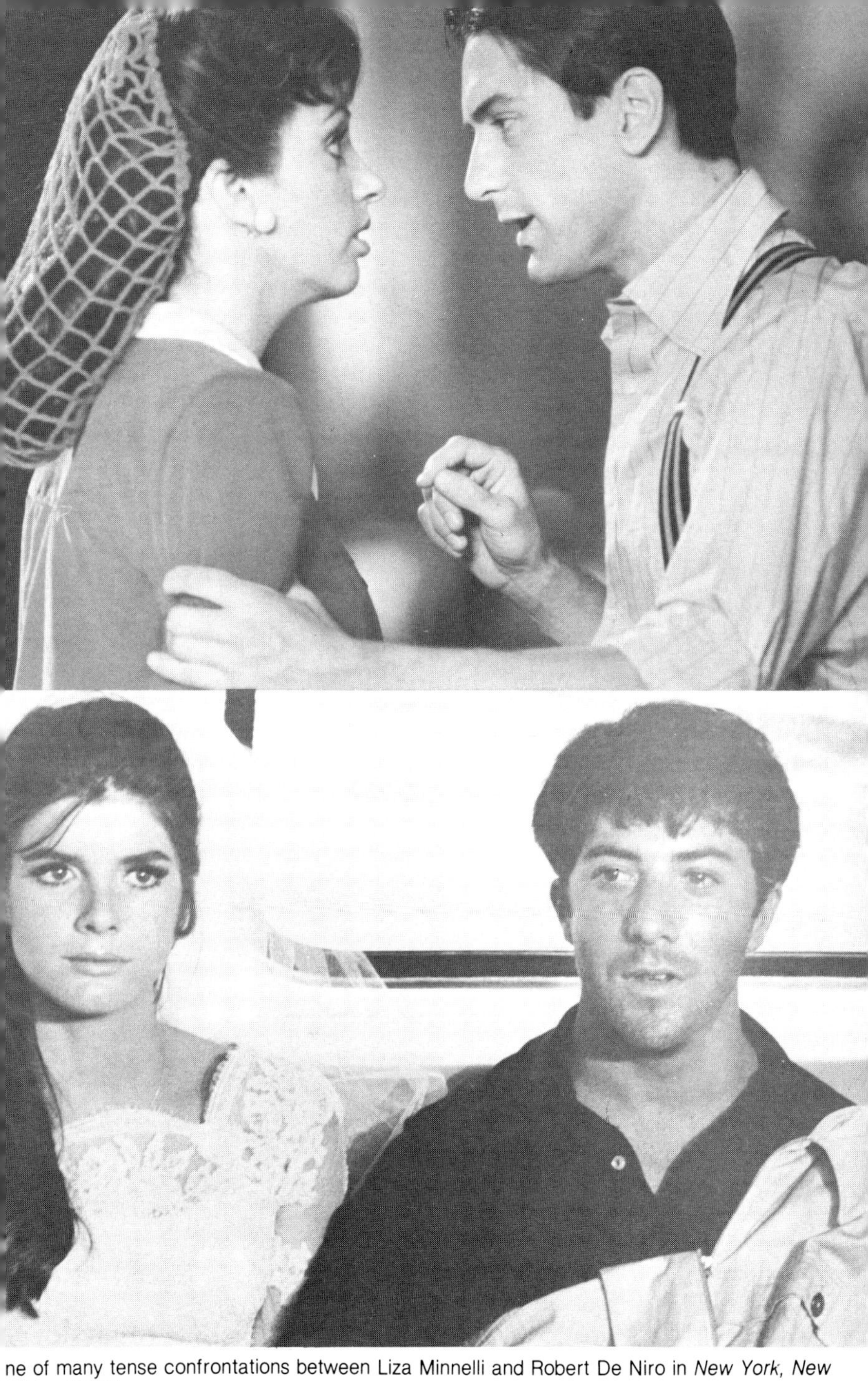

...ne of many tense confrontations between Liza Minnelli and Robert De Niro in *New York, New York*— CBS/Fox

...atherine Ross and Dustin Hoffman in the final scene from *The Graduate*—Embassy

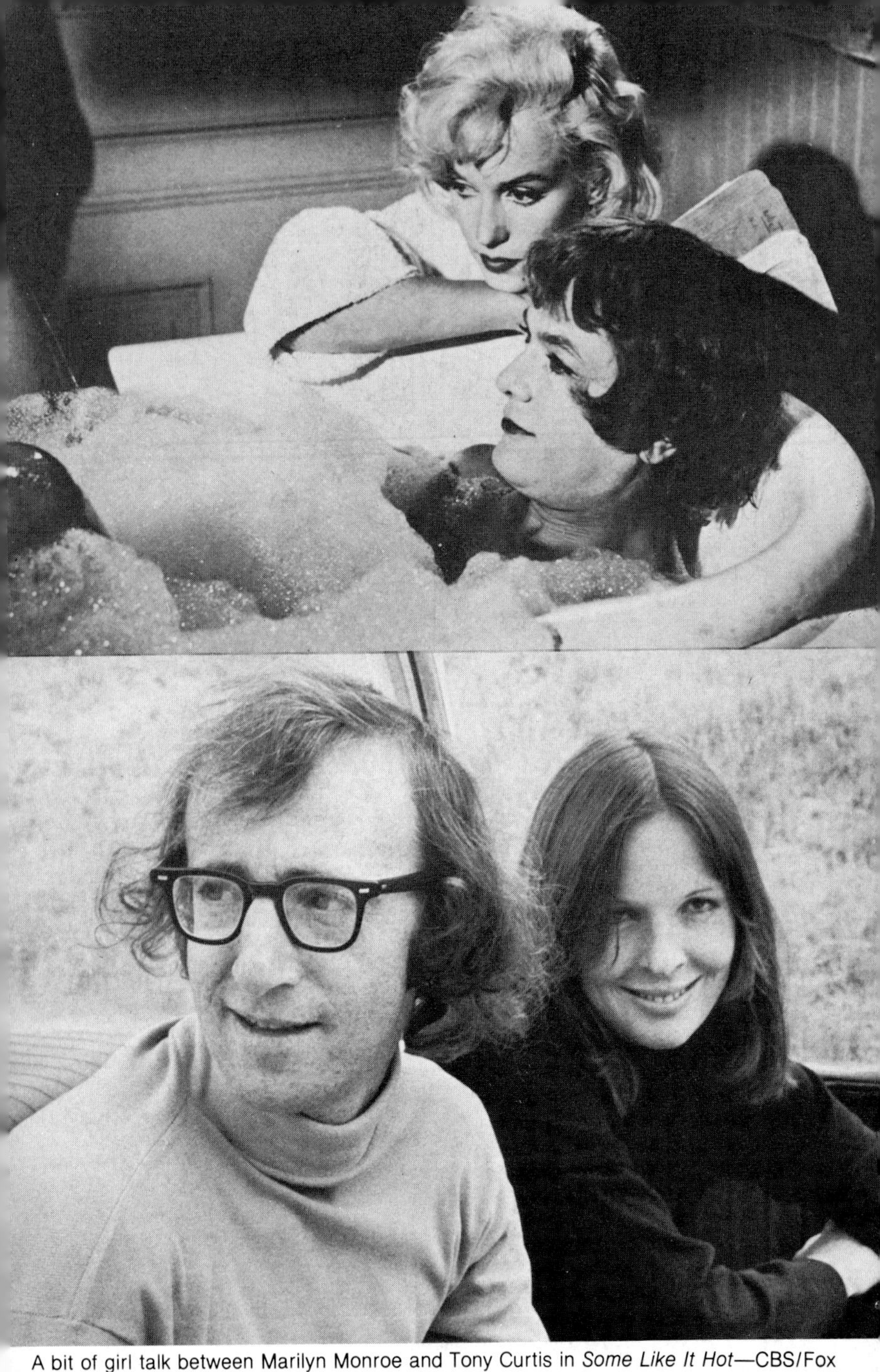

A bit of girl talk between Marilyn Monroe and Tony Curtis in *Some Like It Hot*—CBS/Fox
Woody Allen meets futuristic Diane Keaton in *Sleeper*—RCA VideoDiscs

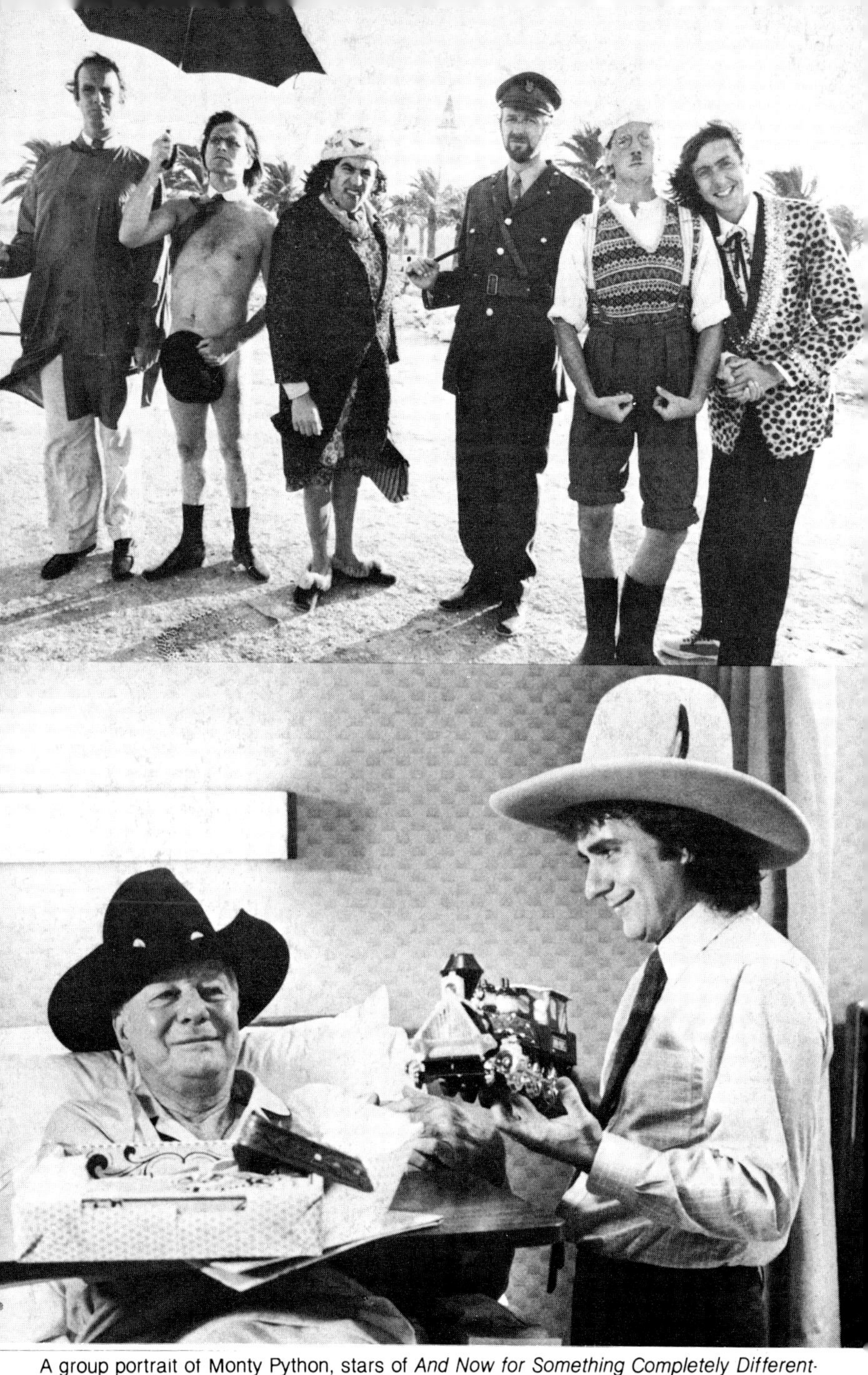

A group portrait of Monty Python, stars of *And Now for Something Completely Different*—RCA/Columbia

Sir John Gielgud is pleased by Dudley Moore's gift of a choo-choo in *Arthur*—Warner

Best Friends' Goldie Hawn and Burt Reynolds—Warner
Kurt Russell and Meryl Streep in *Silkwood*—Embassy

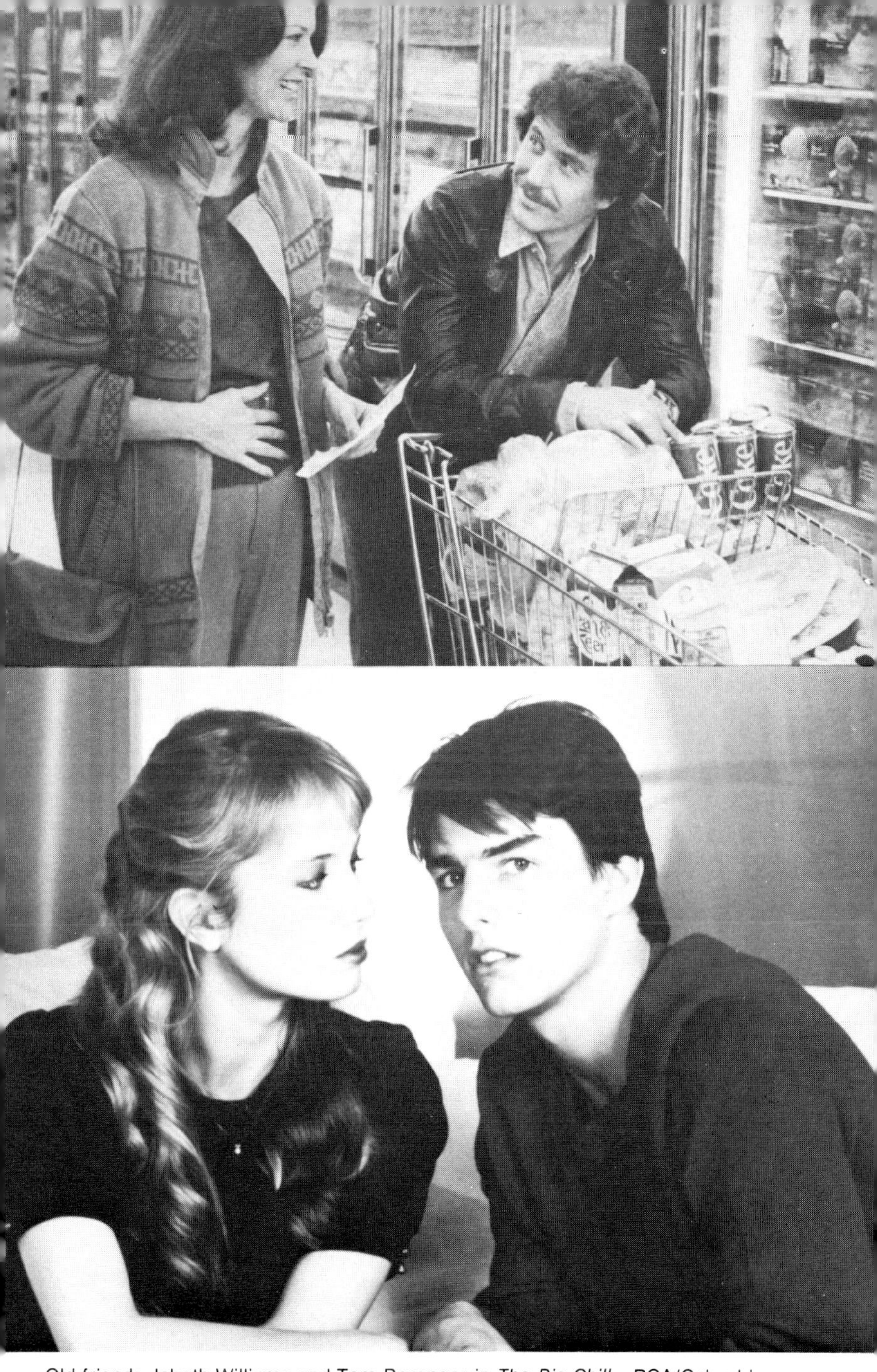

Old friends Jobeth Williams and Tom Berenger in *The Big Chill*—RCA/Columbia
New friends Rebecca DeMornay and Tom Cruise in *Risky Business*—Warner

John Wayne in *The Searchers*—Warner
Clint Eastwood in *Hang 'Em High*—CBS/Fox

Kermit the Frog on a bender in *The Muppet Movie*—CBS/Fox
An uncharacteristically pensive Bruce Lee in *The Chinese Connection*—CBS/Fox

The star of *Making Michael Jackson's Thriller*—Vestron

Flashdance's Jennifer Beals—Paramount

l Jolson, the original *Jazz Singer*—CBS/Fox

, spectacular Eleanor Powell number featured in *That's Entertainment, Part II*—MGM/UA

Sailors Gene Kelly and Frank Sinatra on leave in *Anchors Aweigh*, featured in *That's Entertainment, Part II*—MGM/UA

Marilyn Monroe in her last film, *The Misfits*—CBS/Fox

Howard Keel and Jane Powell begin a short courtship in *Seven Brides for Seven Brothers*—MGM/UA
Judy Garland in a newly restored production number from *A Star Is Born*—Warner

Giant stars Elizabeth Taylor, Rock Hudson and James Dean, featured in *James Dean: The First American Teenager*—VidAmerica

Kim Novak is tormented by James Stewart in Hitchcock's *Vertigo*—MCA

Burt Lancaster and Clark Gable in the submarine epic *Run Silent, Run Deep*—CBS/Fox
Feisty Maureen O'Hara in *The Quiet Man*—NTA

Tommy Kirk and Yeller in *Old Yeller*—Walt Disney
The aquatic Daryl Hannah with Tom Hanks in *Splash*—Touchstone

Say Goodnight, Gracie!—Video Yesteryear
Another nice mess for Stan and Ollie—Nostalgia Merchant

Forbidden Planet's menage a trois: Leslie Nielsen, Anne Francis and Robby the Robot—MGM/UA
Gelflings Jen and Kira with little Fizzgig in *The Dark Crystal*—Thorn EMI
The rabbits of *Watership Down*—Warner

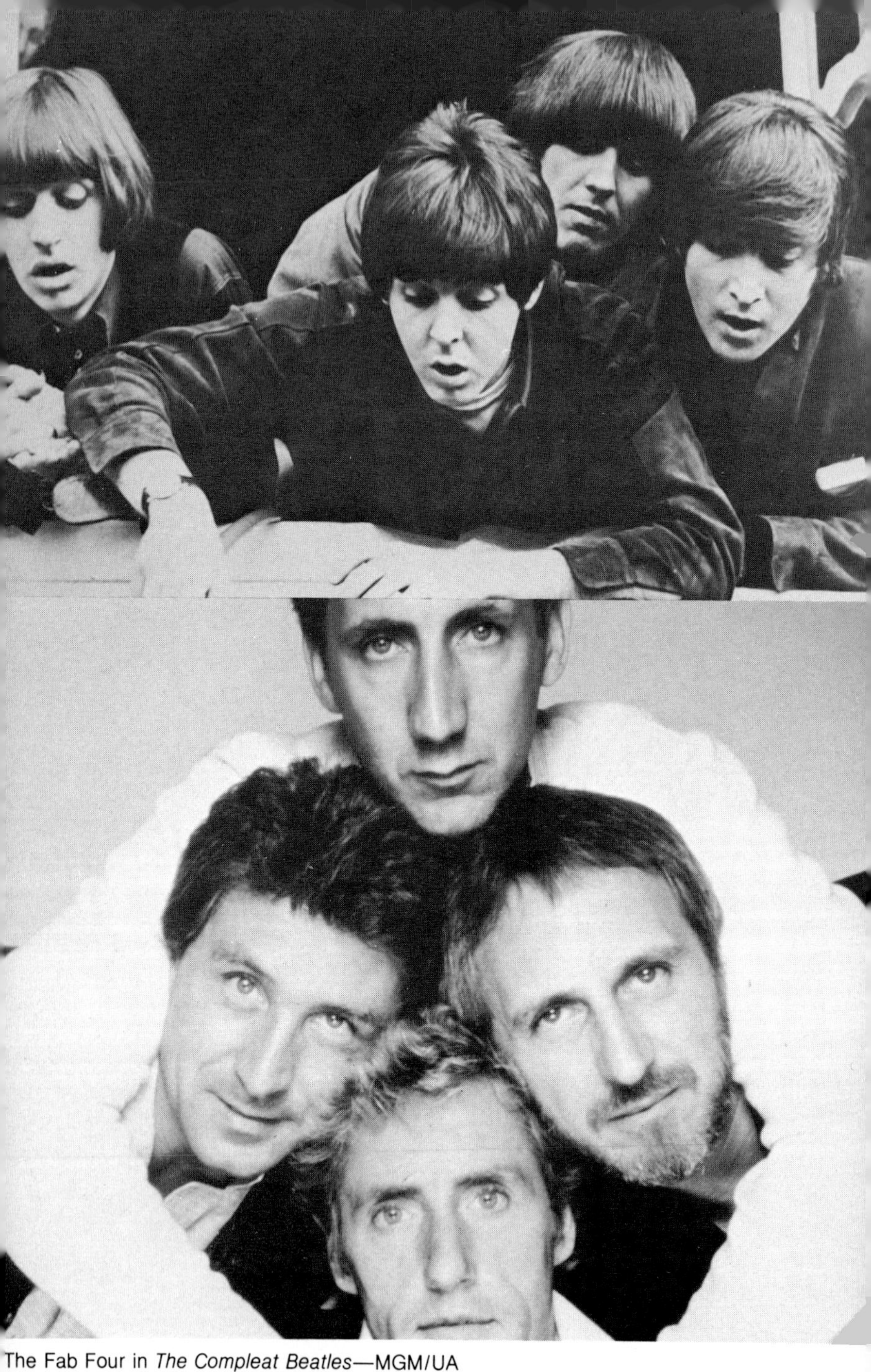

The Fab Four in *The Compleat Beatles*—MGM/UA
The Who's career is detailed in *The Kids Are Alright*—Thorn EMI

Star Trek's original TV cast—Paramount

Sean Connery and Daniela Bianchi in *From Russia with Love*—CBS/Fox

Lovebirds Anne Bancroft and Mel Brooks in the remake of *To Be or Not to Be*—CBS/Fox

Tom Mix, Joan Gale
Old West guns-and-hero tale. In fifteen chapters.
Mascot — *Video Connection; Video Yesteryear; Discount Video Tapes; Cable Films*

Miracle Worker, The 1979
Drama/Biographical
47369   98 mins   C   B, V   R, P
Patty Duke Astin, Melissa Gilbert
The story of blind, deaf and mute Helen Keller and her teacher, Annie Sullivan, whose patience and perseverance finally enables Helen to learn to communicate with the world.
Katz Gallin Productions; Halfpint Productions — *Warner Home Video*

Mirror Crack'd, The 1980
Mystery
47305   105 mins   C   B, V, CED   R, P
Elizabeth Taylor, Rock Hudson, Kim Novak, Tony Curtis
While filming a movie in the English countryside, an American actress is murdered, and Miss Marple must discover who the killer is. Based on the Agatha Christie novel.
MPAA:PG
Associated Film Dist; EMI Films Ltd — *THORN EMI Home Video*

Mirrors 1982
Mystery
72449   83 mins   C   B, V   P
The story of a women's dreams that result in horror and death in New Orleans.
John B Kelly Presentation; First American Films Release — *Monterey Home Video*

Miserables, Les 1979
Drama/Cartoons
69810   70 mins   C   B, V   P
Animated
Victor Hugo's classic novel comes to life in this beautifully animated family feature.
Toei Animation Co Ltd — *Family Home Entertainment*

Misfits, The 1961
Drama
59344   124 mins   B/W   CED   P
Clark Gable, Marilyn Monroe, Montgomery Clift, Thelma Ritter, Eli Wallach, James Barton, Estelle Winwood, directed by John Huston
Arthur Miller wrote this parable involving a disillusioned divorcee and her relationship with three cowboys in the Nevada desert.
United Artists — *CBS/Fox Video; RCA VideoDiscs*

Miss All-American Beauty 1982
Drama
75455   96 mins   C   B, V   P

Diane Lane, Cloris Leachman, Brian Kerwin
An accomplished pianist enters a beauty pageant hoping to win a scholarship so that she can return to college.
King Features — *U.S.A. Home Video*

Miss Annie Rooney 1942
Comedy-Drama
64367   86 mins   B/W   B, V, 3/4U   P
Shirley Temple, Dickie Moore, William Gargan, Guy Kibbee, Peggy Ryan
Shirley Temple received her first screen kiss in this story of a poor Irish girl who falls in love with a wealthy young man.
Edward Small — *Nostalgia Merchant*

Miss Nude America Contest, The 1980
Variety
52862   78 mins   C   B, V   P
The annual Miss Nude America Contest, presenting a group of unclad contestants being judged on physical attributes.
MPAA:R
Jim Blake; Jerry Gross Organization — *Wizard Video*

Miss Peach of the Kelly School 1980
Cartoons
59364   115 mins   C   CED   P
Animated
The students from the famed comic strip celebrate the opening of school, Thanksgiving, Valentine's Day, and the annual picnic.
Sheldon Riss — *CBS/Fox Video*

Miss Sadie Thompson 1954
Drama
44841   01 mins   C   B, V   P
Rita Hayworth, Jose Ferrer, Aldo Ray
Based on the novel "Rain" by Somerset Maugham, a promiscuous playgirl, a hypocritical minister, and a marine all clash on a Pacific island.
Columbia, Jerry Wald — *RCA/Columbia Pictures Home Video*

Missiles of October, The 1974
Drama
15388   155 mins   C   B, V   P
William Devane, Ralph Bellamy, Martin Sheen, Howard DaSilva
Story of the October 1962 Cuban Missile crisis, and how the White House dealt with the impending danger.
ABC; Herbert Brodkin; Robert Buzz Berger — *MPI Home Video*

Missing — 1982
Drama
59680   122 mins   C   B, V, LV, CED   P
Jack Lemmon, Sissy Spacek, John Shea, Melanie Mayron, directed by Costa-Gavras
At the height of a military coup in a South American country, a young American writer disappears, causing the man's wife and father to embark on a frustrating search through government bureaucracy to discover what really happened to him.
MPAA:PG
Universal — *MCA Home Video*

Mission Galactica: The Cylon Attack — 1979
Science fiction
58214   108 mins   C   B, V, LV   P
Lorne Greene, Lloyd Bridges
The Battlestar Galactica is stranded in space without fuel and open to attack from the chrome-covered Cylons. Adama (Lorne Greene) is forced to stop Commander Cain's (Lloyd Bridges) efforts to launch an attack against the Cylons, while countering the attacks of the Cylon leader.
Universal TV — *MCA Home Video*

Missionary, The — 1982
Comedy
66183   86 mins   C   B, V   R, P
Michael Palin, Maggie Smith, Trevor Howard
A missionary tries to save the souls of a group of fallen women.
MPAA:R
Columbia — *THORN EMI Home Video*

Missouri Breaks, The — 1976
Western
58953   126 mins   C   B, V, CED   P
Jack Nicholson, Marlon Brando, Randy Quaid, Kathleen Lloyd, Frederic Forrest, Harry Dean Stanton, directed by Arthur Penn
Thomas McGuane wrote the screenplay for this tale of Montana ranchers and rustlers fighting over land and livestock in the 1880's.
MPAA:PG
United Artists — *CBS/Fox Video*

Mistaken Identity — 194?
Mystery
53418   60 mins   B/W   B, V   P
Nellie Hill, George Oliver
An all-black mystery set against the background of a nightclub, and featuring a production number, " I'm a Bangi from Ubangi."
Sack Prods — *Video Connection*

Mistaken Orders — 19??
Adventure/Drama
58536   40 mins   B/W   B, V, 3/4U   P
Henry Barrows, Helen Holmes, Hal Waters, Mack Wright, Cecil Kellogg, Jack Cerrin
A railroad magnate's son gets thrown in jail, and, in order to straighten him out, the father sends him to work. Through no fault of his own, a train wreck is narrowly averted for which he is blamed. Silent.
Unknown — *Penguin Video*

Mr. & Mrs. Smith — 1941
Comedy
00287   95 mins   B/W   B, V, 3/4U   P
Carole Lombard, Robert Montgomery, directed by Alfred Hitchcock
Madcap comedy of a married couple who discover their marriage isn't legal.
RKO — *Nostalgia Merchant*

Mr. Bill Looks Back Featuring Sluggo's Greatest Hits — 1983
Comedy
64927   31 mins   C   B, V   P
Mr. Bill creator Walter Williams has filmed all new material never before televised to include with some previous footage.
Walter Williams — *Pacific Arts Video*

Mr. Bill Show, The — 1979
Comedy
16162   26 mins   C   B, V   P
Excerpts from Saturday Night Live's Mr. Bill Show. Hilarious video album of Mr. Bill's best.
Walter Williams — *Independent United Distributors*

Mr. Blandings Builds His Dream House — 1948
Comedy
00266   93 mins   B/W   B, V, 3/4U   P
Cary Grant, Myrna Loy
Domestic comedy revealing the difficulty a couple faces while trying to build their "dream house."
RKO — *Nostalgia Merchant*

Mr. Halpern and Mr. Johnson — 1983
Drama
65442   57 mins   C   B, V   P
Laurence Olivier, Jackie Gleason
The provocative and compelling story of two strangers united by the death of a woman they both loved, and their revealing and surprising confrontation.
Edie and Ely Landau — *U.S.A. Home Video*

Mr. Hulot's Holiday — 1953
Comedy
12802   86 mins   B/W   B, V, FO   P
Jacques Tati, Natalie Pascaud, Michelle Rolia

Jacques Tati's famous character Mr. Hulot, goes on vacationto a seaside resort, with slapstick results.
GDB International — *Video Yesteryear; Sheik Video; Video Dimensions; Budget Video; Discount Video Tapes; Penguin Video; Western Film & Video Inc*

Mr. Klein 1975
Drama
62815　123 mins　C　B, V　P
Alain Delon, Jeanne Moreau, directed by Joseph Losey
In France during the Nazi occupation, a Catholic man searches for a Jew who has stolen his name and identity.
Quartet Films — *RCA/Columbia Pictures Home Video*

Mr. Lucky 1943
Comedy
00286　99 mins　B/W　B, V, 3/4U　P
Cary Grant, Laraine Day, Charles Bickford
Professional gambler tries to raise a new bankroll by fleecing a wealthy young lady, but falls in love instead.
RKO — *Nostalgia Merchant*

Mr. Magoo Cartoons 196?
Comedy/Cartoons
64833　120 mins　C　CED　P
Aminated, voice of Jim Backus
Sixteen classic cartoon selections are featured, including the well-known "Trouble Indemnity."
UPA — *RCA VideoDiscs*

Mister Magoo in Sherwood Forest 1964
Cartoons/Comedy
64025　83 mins　C　B, V, LV　R, P
Animated, voice of Jim Backus
As Friar Tuck, the nearsighted Mr. Magoo involves Robin Hood and his Merry Men in a series of zany adventures.
MPAA:G
UPA Pictures — *Paramount Home Video; RCA VideoDiscs*

Mr. Magoo in the King's Service 1966
Cartoons
64939　92 mins　C　B, V　R, P
Animated, voice of Jim Backus
Mr. Magoo is off on the King's business in this wacky full-length cartoon adventure.
UPA — *Paramount Home Video*

Mister Magoo... Man of Mystery 1983
Cartoons
65619　75 mins　C　B, V　R, P
Animated, voice of Jim Backus

In this episode, Mr. Magoo plays four legendary literary and comic strip heroes: Dr. Watson, Dr. Frankenstein, the Count of Monte Cristo and Dick Tracey.
UPA Pictures — *Paramount Home Video*

Mister Magoo's Christmas Carol 1962
Cartoons/Christmas
64031　52 mins　C　B, V, LV　R, P
Animated, voice of Jim Backus
Nearsighted Mr. Magoo, as Ebenezer Scrooge, receives Christmastime visits from three ghosts in this version of Dickens' classic tale.
MPAA:G
UPA Pictures — *Paramount Home Video*

Mr. Magoo's Storybook 1964
Fairy tales/Cartoons
64507　113 mins　C　B, V　R, P
Animated, the voice of Jim Backus
Mr. Magoo acts all the parts in versions of three famous tales of literature: "Snow White and the Seven Dwarfs," "Don Quixote" and "A Midsummer Night's Dream."
UPA Pictures — *Paramount Home Video*

Mr. Mike's Mondo Video 1979
Comedy
66179　75 mins　C　B, V　P
Michael O'Donoghue, Dan Aykroyd, Jane Curtin, Carrie Fisher, Teri Garr, Joan Haskett, Deborah Harry, Margot Kidder, Bill Murray, Loraine Newman, Gilda Radner, Julius LaRosa, Paul Schaeffer?Sid Vicious
A bizarre, outrageous comedy special declared too wild for television conceived by the Saturday Night Live alumnus Mr. Mike.
Lorne Michaels — *Pacific Arts Video*

Mr. Mom 1983
Comedy
Closed Captioned
65375　92 mins　C　B, V, LV, CED　P
Michael Keaton, Teri Garr
A hard-working husband becomes a harried housewife and his wife turns into a high-powered executive.
MPAA:PG
Lynn Loring — *Vestron Video*

Mr. Moon's Magic Circus 1982
Circus
64954　90 mins　C　B, V　R, P
Marcia Lewis, John Sarantos, Chuck Quinlan, Hank Adams, Marylin Magness, Mark Ganzel
A circus of musical fantasy for children that features original music, plenty of dancing, mishaps and circus fun.
Century Video — *Video Gems*

Mr. Moto's Last Warning   1939
Mystery
07077   71 mins   B/W   B, V   P
Peter Lorre, George Sanders, Riccardo Cortez, Virginia Field
Conspirators, plotting to blow up the Suez Canal, are under the impression they have eliminated Mr. Moto.
20th Century Fox — *Discount Video Tapes; Cable Films; Video Connection; Video Yesteryear; Budget Video; Classic Video Cinema Collector's Club*

Mr. Peabody and the   1948
Mermaid
Comedy
65737   89 mins   B/W   B, V   P
William Powell, Ann Blythe
A middle-aged husband hooks a beautiful mermaid while fishing in the Caribbean and with time, falls in love with her.
Universal — *NTA Home Entertainment*

Mr. Reeder in Room 13   1938
Suspense
47651   66 mins   B/W   B, V, FO   P
Gibb McLaughlin
Based on the mystery stories created by Edgar Wallace, Mr. Reeder (a cultured English gentleman who fights crime) enlists the aid of a young man to get evidence on a gang of counterfeiters.
England — *Video Yesteryear*

Mister Roberts   1955
Comedy
38951   120 mins   C   B, V   R, P
Henry Fonda, James Cagney, Jack Lemmon, William Powell, Betsy Palmer
The comic adventures of the crew of a navy cargo freighter in the South Pacific during World War II, adapted from the long running play.
Academy Awards '55: Best Supporting Actor (Lemmon).
Warner Bros — *Warner Home Video; RCA VideoDiscs*

Mr. Robinson Crusoe   1932
Adventure
08856   76 mins   B/W   B, V   P, T
Douglas Fairbanks Sr., William Farnum, Maria Alba
Rollicking adventure in the South Seas as man makes a bet that he can live on a desert island without being left any refinements of civilization.
United Artists — *Penguin Video; Blackhawk Films; Sheik Video; Video Yesteryear; Classic Video Cinema Collector's Club*

Mister Rogers Goes to   1983
School
Education
64779   117 mins   C   CED   P
Fred Rogers explores the questions children have about school, and helps prepare them for their first day. Includes two shows, one from 1979 and the other from 1983.
Family Communications — *RCA VideoDiscs*

Mr. Rogers—Helping   1983
Children Understand
Ethics
64454   76 mins   C   CED   P
Fred Rogers
Mr. Rogers hosts four informative programs for children ages 2-7. Includes "What Is Love?," "Pretendings" and "Death of a Goldfish."
Family Communications — *RCA VideoDiscs*

Mr. Smith Goes to   1939
Washington
Drama
21292   130 mins   B/W   B, V   P
James Stewart, Jean Arthur, Edward Arnold, Claude Rains, directed by Frank Capra
An idealistic young statesman finds nothing but corruption when he takes his seat in the Senate.
Academy Awards '39: Best Original Story; N.Y. Film Critics Award '39: Best Actor (Stewart).
Columbia — *RCA/Columbia Pictures Home Video*

Mr. Super Athletic Charm   194?
Adventure
10128   56 mins   B/W   B, V   P, T
Douglas Fairbanks Sr.
Douglas Fairbanks portrays dashing swashbuckler in "Black Pirate" (1926) and "Thief of Bagdad" (1940) from the "History of Motion Picture" series.
United Artists — *Blackhawk Films*

Mr. Too Little   1979
Adventure
59071   90 mins   C   B, V   R, P
Rosanno Brazzi
The traveling adventures of a circus poodle and his Bengal tiger buddy.
GG Communications — *Video Gems*

Mr. Wise Guy   1942
Comedy
00411   70 mins   B/W   B, V, 3/4U   P
Leo Gorcey, Huntz Hall, East Side Kids
The East Side Kids break out of reform school to clear the brother of one of the Kids of a murder charge.
Prime TV — *Penguin Video; Discount Video Tapes*

Mr. Wong, Detective   1938
Mystery
05596   69 mins   B/W   B, V   P
Boris Karloff, Grant Withers

Mr. Wong traps a killer who acts guilty to throw suspicion from himself.
Monogram — *Budget Video*

Mistress Pamela 1976
Drama
53146 95 mins C B, V P
Ann Michelle, Julian Barnes
When young Pamela goes to work in the household of handsome Lord Devonish, he sets about in his wild pursuit of her virginity.
MPAA:R
Intercontinental Releasing — *Monterey Home Video*

Moby Dick 1956
Adventure
Closed Captioned
65757 116 mins C B, V, CED P
Gregory Peck, Richard Basehart, Orson Welles, Leo Genn, Friedrich Ledebur, directed by John Huston
Herman Melville's high sea saga comes to life with Captain Ahab, obsessed with desire for revenge upon the great white whale, Moby Dick.
Warner Bros — *CBS/Fox Video*

Modern Problems 1981
Comedy
59426 93 mins C B, V, CED P
Chevy Chase, Patti D'Arbanville, Mary Kay Place, Brian Doyle-Murray, Neil Carter, Dabney Coleman
A man involved in a nuclear accident discovers he has acquired telekinetic powers, which he uses to turn the tables on his professional and romantic rivals.
MPAA:PG
Twentieth Century Fox — *CBS/Fox Video*

Modern Romance 1981
Comedy
58499 102 mins C B, V P
Albert Brooks, Kathryn Harrold, Bruno Kirby, George Kennedy, Bob Einstein, directed by Albert Brooks
The romantic misadventures of a neurotic film editor who continuously breaks up with his girlfriend and then attempts to win her back.
MPAA:R
Columbia; Andrew Scheinman — *RCA/Columbia Pictures Home Video*

Modern Times 1936
Comedy
08421 89 mins B/W B, V P
Charlie Chaplin, Paulette Goddard, Henry Bergman, Chester Conklin, directed by Charlie Chaplin
In his last silent film, Chaplin plays a factory workman who goes crazy from his repetitious job on an assembly line. Chaplin wrote the musical score which incorporates the tune "Smile," and also sings a gibberish song.
United Artists — *CBS/Fox Video; RCA VideoDiscs*

Mogambo 1954
Adventure
53351 116 mins C B, V P
Clark Gable, Ava Gardner, Grace Kelly, directed by John Ford
An American showgirl and a British archaeologist and his wife team up with a White hunter in Kenya, and set off on a gorilla hunt.
Sam Zimbalist; MGM — *MGM/UA Home Video*

Molly and Lawless John 1982
Adventure/Western
72204 90 mins C B, V P
Sam Elliot, Vera Miles
The wife of a sadistic sheriff helps a prisoner escape the gallows.
Unknown — *Paragon Video Productions*

Molly (The Goldbergs) 1955
Comedy
66140 27 mins B/W B, V, FO P
Gertrude Berg, Robert Harris, Arlene McQuade, Eli Mintz, Tom Taylor
In this episode of the long-running series, Molly is being menaced by two ex-cons.
Dumont — *Video Yesteryear*

Mommie Dearest 1981
Drama
58713 129 mins C B, V, LV R, P
Faye Dunaway, Diana Scarwid, Steve Forrest, Howard DaSilva, directed by Frank Perry
Faye Dunaway portrays Joan Crawford in this film version of Christina Crawford's memoirs, describing her mother as a neurotic tyrant who abused her children while presenting a glamourous screen image to the public.
MPAA:PG
Paramount; Frank Yablans — *Paramount Home Video; RCA VideoDiscs*

Mon Oncle 1958
Comedy
57338 87 mins C B, V P
Jacques Tati, Jean-Pierre Zola, Adrienne Serrantie, Alain Bacourt, directed by Jacques Tati
Droll, gangling Mr. Hulot aids his adoring nephew in war against his parents' modernized, push-button home. Subtitled in English.
Academy Award '58: Best Foreign Language Picture. FR
Continental Dist Co — *Budget Video; Discount Video Tapes; Video Yesteryear*

Mondo Cane 1963
Documentary/Exploitation
64993   105 mins   C   B, V   P
*Narrated by Stefano Sibaldi, directed by
Gualtiero Jacopetti*
A documentary which shows all the
eccentricities of human behavior around the
world, including cannibalism, pig killing and
more.
MPAA:R
Cineriz; Times Film Corp — *VIDCREST*

Mondo Cane 2 1964
Documentary/Exploitation
64994   94 mins   C   B, V   P
Directed by Gualtiero Jacopetti
More documentary-like views of the oddities of
mankind and ethnic rituals around the world.
Also known as "Mondo Pazzo."
MPAA:R
Rizzoli Film — *VIDCREST*

Money Hunt 1984
Mystery
76394   30 mins   C   B, V   P
John Hillerman
$100,000 cash is secured in a safe deposit box;
the first person who can solve the puzzle from
the hints given in this program will claim the
prize. Magnum P.I.'s John Hillerman is the host.
Rogers & Cowan Inc — *Karl Video*

Money Madness 1979
Music
37405   92 mins   C   B, V   P
Eddie Money
Popular rock singer Eddie Money's rise to the
top of the music business is chronicled in this
program, in which he performs some of his
songs.
New Line Cinema; Michael Mason — *CBS/Fox
Video*

Money Management 1982
System: The Midas Touch
Gambling
62743   130 mins   C   B, V   P
Bruce Irwin provides step-by-step instruction of
his mathematical money management system
used for 21 years in casinos all over the world.
Casino Gaming Instruction — *Marketvisions*

Money to Burn 1983
Drama
66510   90 mins   C   B, V   P
*Jack Kruschen, Meegan King, David Wallace,
Phillip Pine*
An aging high school counselor and two senior
citizens develop a plan to steal 50 million dollars
from the Federal Reserve Bank.
Virginia L Stone; J A S McCombie — *Paragon
Video Productions*

Mongrel 1983
Horror
72203   90 mins   C   B, V   P
Aldo Ray
A man is tormented by graphically gruesome
dreams.
Unknown — *Paragon Video Productions*

Monique 1970
Drama
64967   86 mins   C   CED   P
Sibylla Kay, Joan Alcome, David Sumner
A menage a trois results when a couple hire a
pretty French girl to help with their children.
Avco-Embassy — *Embassy Home
Entertainment (disc only)*

Monsieur Verdoux 1947
Comedy
08406   123 mins   B/W   B, V   P
*Charlie Chaplin, Martha Raye, Isabella Elsom,
Mady Corell, Allison Roddan, Robert Lewis*
A prim and proper bank cashier marries and
murders rich women in order to support his real
wife.
Charles Chaplin — *CBS/Fox Video*

Monsignor 1982
Drama
60581   121 mins   C   B, V, CED   P
*Christopher Reeve, Fernando Rey, Genevieve
Bujold, Jason Miller, directed by Frank Perry*
An ambitious American priest becomes
embroiled in the high stakes game of Vatican
politics.
MPAA:R
Twentieth Century Fox — *CBS/Fox Video*

Monster from Green Hell 1958
Horror
09109   71 mins   B/W   B, V   P
*Jim Davis, Robert Griffin, Barbara Turner,
Eduardo Cianelli*
An experimental rocket containing radiation
contaminated wasps crashes in Africa making
giant killer wasps that are destroyed by a
volcano.
DCA — *Mossman Williams Productions; Video
Yesteryear; Penguin Video*

Monster Maker, The 1944
Horror
58616   65 mins   B/W   B, V, 3/4U   R, P
J. Carroll Nash, Ralph Morgan
A doctor creates monsters by his secretly
invented glandular injections.
Producers Releasing Corp — *Cable Films;
Video Connection*

Monster Walks, The 1932
Horror
12830   60 mins   B/W   B, V, FO   P

Rex Lease, Vera Reynolds, Mischa Auer
A whodunit thriller complete with stormy nights, suspicious cripples, weird servants, and a screaming gorilla.
Mayfair — *Video Yesteryear; Sheik Video; Blackhawk Films*

Monsters on the March   1960
Movie and TV trailers
42960   25 mins   B/W   B, V, FO   P
This program consists of 14 movie trailers, including frightening coming attractions for movies such as the "The Return of the Fly" with Vincent Price, "Isle of the Dead" with Boris Karloff, "I Walked with a Zombie" with Frances Dee, and other, dating as far back as 1932 and up to 1960.
20th Century Fox et al — *Video Yesteryear*

Montana Discovered   1981
States-US
47286   25 mins   C   B, V, 3/4U,   P
                                      Q
As a family travels through Montana, they discover its beauty, wilderness, and an old ghost town.
TV Sports Scene — *TV Sports Scene*

Montenegro   1981
Drama
47799   97 mins   C   B, V   R, P
Susan Anspach, Erland Josephson
The story of an American housewife living in Sweden who tires of her uncomplicated life as a wife and mother, and promptly flees her home and family in search of excitement.
Atlantic Releasing — *THORN EMI Home Video*

Monterey Historic   1981
Automobiles-Racing
53731   28 mins   C   B, V   P
Directed by Peter W. Silver
A look at the premier vintage car race in the U.S., held at the Laguna Seca Road Racing Circuit on the Monterey Peninsula of California. Former U.S. champion Phil Hill drives the star of the show, the Mercedes-Benz 300 SLR.
Peter Silver Prods — *MAS Productions*

Monty Python and the   1975
Holy Grail
Comedy
63441   90 mins   C   B, V, LV   P
John Cleese, Michael Palin, Eric Idle, Graham Chapman, Terry Jones, Terry Gilliam
The quest for the Holy Grail by King Arthur and his Knights of the Round Table is retold in the inimitable Python fashion.
MPAA:PG
Almi/Cinema V — *RCA/Columbia Pictures Home Video; RCA VideoDiscs*

Monty Python Live at the   1982
Hollywood Bowl
Comedy
64207   78 mins   C   B, V   R, P
Eric Idle, Michael Palin, John Cleese, Terry Gillian, Terry Jones, Graham Chapman
A live concert performance by the madcap comedy troupe.
George Harrison; Handmade Films — *THORN EMI Home Video; RCA VideoDiscs*

Monty Python's Life of   1979
Brian
Comedy
37424   90 mins   C   B, V   R, P
Eric Idle, Michael Palin, Graham Chapman, Terry Gilliam, John Cleese, Terry Jones
A typical Monty Python romp, this time through the Holy Land in the year 32 A.D. This is the hilarious story of Brian, a man who was born on the same night as Jesus Christ. Through a series of mishaps and misinterpretations, Brian is proclaimed the Messiah, a role he refuses to accept. Consequently, he spends most of his time running from the adoring multitudes, government officials, and several underground groups.
MPAA:R
Warner Bros — *Warner Home Video; RCA VideoDiscs*

Monty Python's The   1983
Meaning of Life
Comedy
65207   107 mins   C   B, V, LV,   P
                                      CED
John Cleese, Michael Palin, Eric Idle, Graham Chapman, Terry Jones, Terry Gilliam
No aspect of life is to sacred for the probing Python crew. Religion, birth control, sex and death all get their respective dues. This program is in stereo on all formats.
Universal — *MCA Home Video*

Moon Buggy   197?
Space exploration/USSR
52354   25 mins   C   B, V, 3/4U   P
A Russian-made documentary about the technology, theory, and experimentation behind a trip to the moon. English narration.
USSR — *International Historic Films*

Moon Is Blue, The   1953
Comedy
55467   100 mins   B/W   LV, CED   P
William Holden, David Niven, directed by Otto Preminger
A young lady, armed with utter candor and good sense, sets out to bewilder a young man about town who doesn't believe marriage is for him.
Otto Preminger — *CBS/Fox Video*

(For Explanation of codes, see USE GUIDE and KEY)

Moon of the Wolf 1972
Horror
69290 74 mins C B, V P
David Janssen, Barbara Rush, Bradford Dillman, John Beradino
A small town in bayou country is terrorized by a modern-day werewolf that rips its victims to shreds.
Filmways — *Worldvision Home Video*

Moonlight Sword and Jade Lion 197?
Martial arts
72176 94 mins C B, V P
Mao Yin, Wong Do
A Kung Fu action film taking place in ancient China.
Foreign — *Master Arts Video*

Moonlighting 1982
Drama
64795 97 mins C B, V, LV P
Jeremy Irons, Eugene Liponski, Jiri Stanislay, Eugeniusz Haczkiewicz, directed by Jerzy Skolimowski
This British/Polish film depicts four builders from Poland who travel to London to renovate a London residence. While in London, the Polish military imposes martial law, suspending the Gdansk agreement and outlawing Solidarity. Only one of the builders speaks English, and he decides not to tell the others what is happening back in Poland.
Cannes Film Festival '82: Best Screenplay.
MPAA:PG
Universal Classics — *MCA Home Video*

Moonraker 1979
Adventure
63549 126 mins C B, V P
Roger Moore, Lois Chiles, Richard Kiel, Michael Lonsdale, Corinne Clery
James Bond is aided by a female CIA agent, assaulted by a giant with jaws of steel and captured by Amazons when he sets out to protect the human race.
MPAA:PG
United Artists — *CBS/Fox Video; RCA VideoDiscs*

Moonshine County Express 1977
Adventure
51991 104 mins C B, V R, P
William Conrad, Susan Howard, Maureen McCormick, Claudia Jennings, John Saxon
Three daughters of a hillbilly moonshiner set out to avenge their father's senseless murder.
MPAA:PG
New World Pictures — *Warner Home Video*

Moonstone Gem, The 1983
Cartoons
65486 48 mins C B, V P
Animated
The Evil Baron threatens to steal the most precious gem of all—happiness—from King Gunther, Prince Jeremy and the Gunderlings.
Paul Fusco — *Media Home Entertainment*

Morals by Monsters 1980
Ethics
55042 20 mins C B, V P
Animated
Two films which communicate a potent dose of self-acceptance to enhance self worth: "Me and the Monsters," which helps small children build their self-image, and "The Bamboo Monster," which aims at social awareness.
Billy Budd Films — *Vanguard Video*

Morgan—A Suitable Case for Treatment 1966
Comedy
63324 93 mins B/W B, V R, P
Vanessa Redgrave, David Warner, Robert Stephens, Irene Handl
A schizophrenic artist refuses to recognize his wife's divorce. When she refuses to go back to him, he decides life is easier to cope with while dressed in a gorilla suit.
British Lion; Quintra — *THORN EMI Home Video*

Morning Glory 1933
Drama
29493 74 mins B/W B, V P, T
Katherine Hepburn, Douglas Fairbanks Jr., Adolphe Menjou
A small town girl takes her aspirations for a stage career very seriously.
Academy Awards '33: Best Actress (Hepburn).
RKO, Merian C Cooper — *Blackhawk Films*

Mortuary 1981
Suspense
65605 91 mins C B, V P
Christopher George, Lynda Day George
A young woman's nightmares come startlingly close to reality.
MPAA:R
Artists Releasing Corporation — *Vestron Video*

Moses 1976
Drama/Religion
63393 141 mins C B, V P
Burt Lancaster, Anthony Quayle, Ingrid Thulin, Irene Papas, William Lancaster
Lancaster portrays the plight of Moses, who struggled to free his people from tyranny.
ITC Entertainment — *CBS/Fox Video*

Most Dangerous Game, The   1932
Suspense
01677   78 mins   B/W   B, V   P
Joel McCrea, Fay Wray, Leslie Banks, Robert Armstrong
A crazed big game hunter lures guests to his secluded island so he can hunt them down like animals.
RKO — *Media Home Entertainment; Budget Video; Discount Video Tapes; Video Dimensions; Sheik Video; Cable Films; Video Yesteryear; Video Connection; Western Film & Video Inc; Cinema Concepts*

Most Memorable Games of the Decade #1   1980
Football
50091   48 mins   C   B, V, FO   R, P
Highlights from two of the longest overtime playoff games in NFL history: Miami 27, Kansas City 24, in 1971 and Oakland 37, Baltimore 31, in 1977.
NFL Films — *NFL Films Video*

Most Memorable Games of the Decade #2   1980
Football
50092   48 mins   C   B, V, FO   R, P
Last second victories in two thrilling classics from 1974: AFC Playoff, Oakland 28, Miami 26; and the 24-23 Thanksgiving Day win by Dallas over Washington led by rookie quarterback Clint Longley.
NFL Films — *NFL Films Video*

Most Memorable Games of the Decade #3   1980
Football
50093   48 mins   C   B, V, FO   R, P
Namath and Unitas combine for 872 passing yards in a 1972 regular season game: Jets 44, Colts 34. Plus, the last second victory in the 1976 AFC Playoff: Oakland 24, New England 21.
NFL Films — *NFL Films Video*

Motels, The   1984
Music-Performance
75914   14 mins   C   B, V   P
This program presents the Motels performing their latest hit songs.
Capital Records Inc — *Sony Corporation of America*

Mother   1926
Film-History
08695   70 mins   B/W   B, V, 3/4U   P
Vera Baranovskaya, Nikolai Batalov, directed by V. I. Pudovkin
A moving story of a family in the 1905 Russian uprising. Based on the novel by Maxim Gorky. Silent with English Subtitles.
Russian — *Penguin Video; International Historic Films; Sheik Video; Classic Video Cinema Collector's Club*

Mother Lode   1982
Adventure
69283   101 mins   C   B, V   P
Charlton Heston, Nick Mancuso
This action-adventure film tells of the conflict between two men, one driven by greed and the other by near madness, and the all-consuming lust for gold.
MPAA:PG
Agamemnon Films — *Vestron Video*

Mother's Day   1980
Suspense
68224   98 mins   C   B, V   P
Tiana Pierce, Nancy Hendrickson, Deborah Luee
Three former college roommates plan a reunion together in the wilderness. All was going well until they were dragged into an isolated house. The terror begins. Two boys and their mother terrorize the girls.
United Film Distributors — *Media Home Entertainment*

Mothra   1962
Horror
64915   101 mins   C   B, V   P
Yumi Ito, Emi Ito
A giant moth wreaks havoc on Tokyo.
Tomoyuki Tanaka — *RCA/Columbia Pictures Home Video*

Motion Picture Camera, The   19??
Filmmaking/Documentary
57432   32 mins   C   B, V   P, T
From the Karl Malkames collection, we see the development of the movie camera.
Unknown — *Blackhawk Films*

Motion Picture History of the Korean War, The   1958
Korean War
53684   58 mins   B/W   B, V, 3/4U   P
A film history of The Korean War, from the initial gunfire on June 25, 1950 to the armistice on July 27, 1953.
Unknown — *International Historic Films*

Motocross Professionals   1983
Motorcycles
66252   65 mins   C   B, V   P
The world's top riders show how to win during the 1978/79 GP season.

CH Wood — *Motor Cycle Video*

Mountain Family Robinson　　　　1979
Adventure
66061　　102 mins　　C　　B, V　　　　P
Robert Logan, Susan Damante Shaw, Heather Rattray, Ham Larsen
An urban family, seeking escape from the hassles of city life, moves to the Rockies.
MPAA:G
Arthur Dubs — *Media Home Entertainment*

Mountain Man　　　　1976
Drama
65725　　96 mins　　C　　B, V　　　　P
Denver Pyle, Ken Berry, Cheryl Miller
A true story of one man's lonely, dangerous and inspired fight to save a part of the vanishing wilderness west of the Mississippi, a wilderness now regarded as one of the scenic wonders of the world.
Charles E Sellier Jr — *VCI Home Video*

Mountain Men, The　　　　1980
Adventure
58210　　102 mins　　C　　B, V　　　　P
Charlton Heston, Brian Keith
A sweeping adventure drama set in the American West of the 1880's.
MPAA:R
Martin Shafer; Andrew Sheinman — *RCA/Columbia Pictures Home Video*

Mouse and His Child, The　　　　1977
Fantasy
65191　　83 mins　　C　　B, V　　　　P
Animated, voices of Peter Ustinov, Cloris Leachman, Andy Devine
A gentle fantasy adventure about a toy wind-up mouse and his child who fall into the clutches of a villainous rat when they venture into the outside world.
Sanrio Film Distribution — *RCA/Columbia Pictures Home Video*

Mouse That Roared, The　　　　1959
Satire/Comedy
64914　　83 mins　　C　　B, V　　　　P
Peter Sellers, Jean Seberg, Leo McKern
The Duchy of Grand Fenwick declares war on the United States. Peter Sellers is featured in three roles, as the Duchess, the Prime Minister, and a military leader.
Walter Shenson — *RCA/Columbia Pictures Home Video*

Movie-Mixer Featurettes　　　　1984
Movie and TV trailers
66485　　60 mins　　C　　B, V　　　　P

A number of movie promotion featurettes are packaged on this tape, showing behind the scenes activities on the sets of "The Andromeda Strain," "Romeo and Juliet," "The Way We Were," "Midnight Cowboy" and "The Fisherman."
Columbia et al — *San Francisco Rush Video*

Movie, Movie　　　　1978
Comedy
56461　　96 mins　　C　　CED　　　　P
George C. Scott, Trish Van Devere, Art Carney, Eli Wallach, Red Buttons, Barbara Harris, Ann Reinking, directed by Stanley Donen
A "double feature" movie, which simulates a typical 1930's moviegoing evening, with a newsreel, previews, a boxing drama (in black and white) and a Busby Berkeley-style musical.
MPAA:PG
Warner Bros, Lord Lew Grade — *RCA VideoDiscs*

Movie Museum I　　　　1980
Film-History
29731　600 mins　B/W　　B, V　　　　P, T
Narrated by Paul Killiam
A fascinating and entertaining review of the first 25 years of the motion picture art form. The set comes on five cassettes and totals ten hours.
Unknown — *Blackhawk Films*

Movie Museum II　　　　1980
Film-History
29732　600 mins　B/W　　B, V　　　　P, T
Narrated by Paul Killiam
A fascinating and entertaining review of the first 25 years of the motion picture art form. There are ten hours on five cassettes in the set.
Unknown — *Blackhawk Films*

Movie Struck　　　　1937
Comedy
08726　70 mins　B/W　　B, V, 3/4U　　　　P
Stan Laurel, Oliver Hardy, Jack Haley, Patsy Kelly, Rosina Lawrence
Originally released as "Pick a Star," this Hollywood behind-the scenes story features guest appearances by Laurel and Hardy.
Hal Roach — *Penguin Video; Ampro Video Productions; Cable Films; Classic Video Cinema Collector's Club*

Movie Struck/The Flying Deuces　　　　193?
Comedy
58912　140 mins　B/W　　B, V　　　　P
Stan Laurel, Oliver Hardy, Patsy Kelly, Jack Haley, Jean Parker, Reginald Gardner, Charles Middleton
A Stan and Ollie double feature: "Movie Struck" (1937), a musical comedy about a small town girl who makes it big in Hollywood; "Flying

　　　　(For Explanation of codes, see USE GUIDE and KEY)

Deuces" (1939), in which our heroes join the foreign legion.
EL, SP
RKO; Hal Roach — *Ampro Video Productions*

Moving Picture Boys in the Great War, The   1975
Film-History/Documentary
10152   51 mins   B/W   B, V   P, T
Movies had been invented and 1914-1918 found World War I being fought. Includes authentic films of the war taken from the archives of three different countries.
Blackhawk — *Blackhawk Films*

Mozart Story, The   1948
Drama
11368   91 mins   B/W   B, V, FO   P
Winnie Markus, Hans Holt
After Mozart's death, music minister to the Emperor, Antonio Solieri, reflects on how his jealousy and hatred of the musical genius held the great composer down during his brief life.
Unknown — *Video Yesteryear*

Ms. Don Juan   1980
Drama
52854   92 mins   C   B, V   P
Brigitte Bardot, Robert Hossein, Robert Walker Jr., directed by Roger Vadim
Bardot is seen at her most evil and seductive, in this tale of murder and passion.
MPAA:R
Scotia American — *Wizard Video*

Ms. 45   1981
Suspense
66198   82 mins   C   B, V   P
Zoe Tamerlis, Steve Singer, Jack Thibeau
A "psycho" type thriller.
Navaron Films — *U.S.A. Home Video*

Muerte del Che Guevara, La   197?
Drama
49748   92 mins   C   B, V   P
Che Guevara leads a group of rebels to Bolivia, where they hope to start a revolution. They meet, in a climactic battle, with the loyal forces.
SP
Unknown — *Media Home Entertainment*

Muerto, El   19??
Drama
66414   105 mins   C   B, V   P
Thelma Biral, Juan Jose Camero, Francisco Rabal
In nineteenth century Buenos Aires, a young man flees his home after killing an enemy. Arriving in Montevideo, he becomes a member of a smuggling ring. Dialogue in Spanish.
SP

Spanish — *Media Home Entertainment*

Mule Days   1984
Animals/Parades and festivals
74542   20 mins   C   B, V   P
This tape features highlights from 1983 Mules Day celebration in Bishop, California.
Mercedes Maharis Productions — *Mercedes Maharis Productions*

Muppet Movie, The   1979
Comedy
37421   94 mins   C   B, V, LV   P
The Muppets, Edgar Bergen, Milton Berle, Mel Brooks, Madeline Kahn, Steve Martin
Kermit the Frog travels to Hollywood with his Muppet pals, planning to become a movie star when he gets there.
MPAA:G
Marble Arch — *CBS/Fox Video; RCA VideoDiscs*

Muppet Musicians of Bremen, The   1972
Fairy tales/Comedy
47347   50 mins   C   B, V, LV   R, P
The Muppets
Kermit the Frog narrates this story of a group of jazz-playing animals who want to escape from their masters and seek freedom and fame.
RLP Canada/Henson Associates — *Muppet Home Video*

Murder   1930
Mystery
01746   92 mins   B/W   B, V   P
Herbert Marshall, Nora Baring, Phyllis Konstam, directed by Alfred Hitchcock
Believing in a young woman's innocence, one jurist begins to organize the pieces of her crime. Based on play "Enter Sir John," by Clemense Dane and Helen Simpson.
British Intl — *Budget Video; Sheik Video; Discount Video Tapes; Cable Films; Video Connection; Western Film & Video Inc; Classic Video Cinema Collector's Club*

Murder at Midnight   1931
Mystery
08752   69 mins   B/W   B, V, 3/4U   P
Alice White, Leslie Fenton
A game of charades leads to a case of murder and violence.
Tiffany; Phil Goldstone — *Penguin Video*

Murder at the Baskervilles   1937
Mystery
44813   67 mins   B/W   B, V   P, T
Arthur Wonter, Ian Fleming, Lyn Harding
Sherlock Holmes is invited to visit Sir Henry Baskerville at his estate, but then finds that

Baskerville's daughter's fiance is accused of stealing a race horse and murdering its keeper.
Unknown — *Blackhawk Films*

Murder by Death 1976
Comedy
44847   94 mins   C   B, V   P
Peter Falk, Alec Guiness, David Niven, Maggie Smith, Peter Sellers, Eileen Brennan, Elsa Lanchester, Nancy Walker, Estelle Winwood
An eccentric millionaire invites the world's greatest detectives to dinner and offers one million dollars to the one who can solve the evening's murder.
MPAA:PG
Columbia, Ray Stark — *RCA/Columbia Pictures Home Video; RCA VideoDiscs*

Murder by Decree 1979
Mystery
41080   120 mins   C   B, V, CED   P
Christopher Plummer, James Mason, Donald Sutherland, directed by Bob Clark
Christopher Plummer plays Sherlock Holmes as he finds his most challenging case when a group of anarchists, posing as local merchants, asks him and Dr. Watson for their help.
MPAA:PG
Avco Embassy — *Embassy Home Entertainment*

Murder By Phone 1982
Horror
65741   80 mins   C   B, V   R, P
Richard Chamberlain, John Houseman
A deranged technician has turned his phone into an instrument of electronic death.
MPAA:R
Robert Cooper — *Warner Home Video*

Murder by Television 1935
Mystery
12829   55 mins   B/W   B, V, FO   P
Bela Lugosi
A TV demonstration is the site of the murder of an electronics expert—a murder which takes place in full view of a room full of people.
Cameo — *Video Yesteryear; Discount Video Tapes*

Murder for Sale 1970
Drama
76654   90 mins   C   B, V   P
John Gavin, Margaret Lee, Curt Jurgens
Secret Agent 117 stages an elaborate scam in order to infiltrate a ring of terrorists and criminals.
Marcello Danon — *Media Home Entertainment*

Murder in Texas 1981
Drama
64867   200 mins   C   B, V   R, P

Farrah Fawcett, Katherine Ross, Andy Griffith, Sam Elliott, Craig T. Nelson, Barbara Sammeth
Based on a true story, this docu-drama looks at the strange events surrounding the death of Joan Robinson Hill, wife of Dr. John Hill and daughter of wealthy oilman Ash Robinson.
Dick Clark Production; Telepictures — *VCII*

Murder My Sweet 1944
Mystery
00264   95 mins   B/W   B, V, 3/4U   P
Dick Powell, Claire Trevor
Private detective Philip Marlowe searches for an ex-convict's missing girl friend. Based on Raymond Chandler's novel "Farewell, My Lovely."
RKO — *Nostalgia Merchant; King of Video; Blackhawk Films*

Murder on the Orient Express 1974
Mystery
38600   128 mins   C   B, V, LV   R, P
Albert Finney, Jacqueline Bisset, Ingrid Bergman, Lauren Bacall, Sean Connery, directed by Sidney Lumet
Agatha Christie's classic whodunit becomes an all-star film, with Albert Finney as Belgian master Sleuth Hercule Poirot, who eventually solves the murder puzzle aboard the famed Orient Express.
MPAA:G
Paramount — *Paramount Home Video; RCA VideoDiscs*

Murder with Music 1945
Musical-Drama
08884   60 mins   B/W   B, V, 3/4U   P
Bob Howard, Noble Sissle and Orchestra
A musical drama with an all black cast.
Century — *Penguin Video*

Murderer's Row 1966
Mystery
44842   108 mins   C   B, V   P
Dean Martin, Ann-Margret, Karl Malden, Beverly Adams
Daredevil bachelor and former counter-espionage agent Matt Helm is summoned from his life of leisure to insure the safety of an important scientist.
Columbia, Irving Allen — *RCA/Columbia Pictures Home Video*

Murderer's Wife 195?
Drama
65767   24 mins   B/W   B, V   P, T
Audrey Totter, John Howard, June Kenny, Michael Chapin
A teacher at a private school seeks to prevent one of her students from making the same mistakes she did in her youth. An episode from

the 1950's television drama series, "Fireside Theatre."
NBC — *Blackhawk Films*

Muscle Motion   1983
Physical fitness
63895   92 mins   C   B, V   P
This aerobic exercise workout is led by seven members of the Chippendales, an all-male revue cabaret for women only.
Nick De Noia; Satyr Corp — *Media Home Entertainment*

Muse Concert: No Nukes, The   1980
Music-Performance
58301   103 mins   C   B, V, CED   P
Jackson Browne, Crosby Stills and Nash, James Taylor, Bruce Springsteen, Doobie Bros, Bonnie Raitt, Carly Simon, John Hall
A concert film of performances held at New York's Madison Square Garden for the benefit of the anti-nuclear power movement.
MPAA:PG
Warner Bros; MUSE Prods — *CBS/Fox Video*

Music Box   1980
Religion
59972   30 mins   C   B, V   P
J. Neil Boyle
A gospel story in the tradition of Christ's parables and the allegorical fiction of C. S. Lewis.
White Lion Photograph Prods; James F. Robinson — *Vanguard Video*

Music of America/Our Wonderful World of Sports   1980
Parades and festivals
64009   60 mins   C   B, V   P
Highlights of the 1979 and 1980 Tournament of Roses Parades are narrated by their Grand Marshals, Frank Sinatra ('80) and Lay Leishman ('79).
Tournament Video Tapes — *Tournament Video Tapes*

Music of Melissa Manchester, The   1980
Music-Performance
59853   60 mins   C   B, V   R, P
Manchester performs her greatest hits live in concert. Songs include "Don't Cry Out Loud," "Midnight Blue," and "Come in from the Rain."
Thanksgiving Whatever Inc — *Warner Home Video*; Pioneer Artists; RCA VideoDiscs

---

Music Shoppe, The   1982
Musical
64951   93 mins   C   B, V   R, P

Gary Crosby, Nia Peeples, Benny Medina, Stephen Schwartz, David Jackson, Jesse White, Doug Kershaw, Gisele MacKenzie
Four teenagers form a rock band with the assistance of the local music store proprietor.
MPAA:G
Century Video — *Video Gems*

Music Video From "Streets of Fire"   1984
Music video
75020   30 mins   C   B, V   P
This tape features three complete stereo music videos from the movie "Streets of Fire."
MCA Home Video — *MCA Home Video*

Musical Featurettes   1984
Movie and TV trailers/Musical
66482   61 mins   C   B, V   P
This tape offers 6 short films that go behind the scenes and show the making of "Camelot," "Funny Girl," "The Boy Friend," "Oliver," "Scrooge" and "Fiddler on the Roof."
Warner Bros et al — *San Francisco Rush Video*

Musical Personalities No. 1   194?
Musical
11287   50 mins   B/W   B, V, FO   P
Aunt Jemima, Dick Powell, Shirley Temple, Al Jolson, Lena Horne, Teddy Wilson
Four segments spanning three decades of music featuring some of the musical talent of the period from 1927 to 1943.
Educational et al — *Video Yesteryear*

Musical Shorts Video Special   193?
Music/Variety
58518   60 mins   C   B, V, 3/4U   P
A color animated short on W.C. Handy featuring many of his famous tunes, followed by a collection of mini-shorts featuring many song birds of the period doing individual songs including, "Thanks for the Memory," "Mona Lisa," "Blue Velvet," "Ma, He's Making Eyes at Me," and others. (Some black and white).
Unknown — *Penguin Video*

Musicals 1: Trailers on Tape   1984
Movie and TV trailers/Musical
66478   60 mins   C   B, V   P
This tape offers original theatrical trailers for 40 musical films, including "The Wizard of Oz," "West Side Story," "Let It Be," "7 Brides for 7 Brothers," "Singing in the Rain," "The Rose" and "Funny Face." A few segments are in black-and-white.
MGM et al — *San Francisco Rush Video*

Mussolini Visits Hitler   1937
Propaganda/Germany
72475   31 mins   B/W   B, V, 3/4U   P
An original German documentary about Benito
Mussolini's state visit to Germany in 1937.
Scenes include the million-plus gathering at
Berlin's Olympic Stadium to hear the two facist
leaders' speeches, and a military tattoo
performed by musicians of the German Army.
Germany — *International Historic Films*

Mustang   197?
Drama
59551   70 mins   C   B, V   P
Filmed entirely inside an actual house of
prostitution, the Mustang Bridge Ranch, the
largest legal brothel in the U.S., this film offers a
portrait of the inner workings of a brothel.
Robert Guralnick — *Media Home
Entertainment*

Mutiny on the Bounty   1962
Drama
56754   177 mins   C   B, V   P
*Marlon Brando, Trevor Howard, Richard Harris,
directed by Lewis Milestone*
Based on the novel by Charles Nordhoff and
James Norman Hall, this account of the most
famous mutiny in history aboard the Bounty in
1789 between Fletcher Christian and Captain
Bligh is highlighted by lavish photography.
MGM, Aaron Rosenberg — *MGM/UA Home
Video*

Mutiny on the Bounty   1935
Adventure
73367   132 mins   B/W   B, V   P
*Clark Gable, Charles Laughton, directed by
Frank Lloyd*
This is the 1935 version of the story of mean
Captain Bligh, Fletcher Christian and the
problems they have aboard the HMS Bounty.
Academy Award '36: Best Picture
MGM — *MGM/UA Home Video*

**Mutiny on the Western
Front: WW I**   1981
Documentary/World War I
58576   60 mins   C   B, V   P
An untold side of World War I, filmed on the
actual locations in France and Germany, as
30,000 Anzac volunteers, suffering great
casualties, mutiny against the callous and
deluded Allied officers who lead them.
Australian — *Mastervision*

My Best Girl   1927
Comedy
59652   78 mins   B/W   B, V   P, T
*Mary Pickford, Charles "Buddy" Rogers,
directed by Sam Taylor*
Mary attempts to bring her new sweetheart
home for dinner, with disastrous results. A
gentle satire on middle-American life in the
1920's. Organ score by Gaylord Carter.
Mary Pickford — *Blackhawk Films*

My Bloody Valentine   1981
Horror
55539   91 mins   C   B, V, LV   R, P
*Paul Kelman, Lori Hallier, directed by George
Mihalka*
A deranged killer stalks a town which has not
celebrated Valentine's Day in twenty
years—ever since a grisly killing took place.
MPAA:R
Paramount; John Dunning; Andre Link; Stephen
Miller — *Paramount Home Video*

My Bodyguard   1980
Drama
55529   96 mins   C   B, V   P
*Chris Makepeace, Ruth Gordon, Matt Dillon,
John Houseman, Martin Mull, directed by Tony
Bill*
An undersized high school student fends off
attacking bullies by hiring a king-sized,
withdrawn lad as his bodyguard. Their
relationship, however, develops into true
friendship.
MPAA:PG
Twentieth Century Fox; Don
Devlin — *CBS/Fox Video*

My Brilliant Career   1980
Drama
56934   101 mins   C   B, V, CED   P
Judy Davis
Sybylla's parents despair at her refusal to resign
herself to a life of convention and drudgery, and
attempts to "civilize" her fail. Sybylla knows that
somehow she must be independent. Produced
in Australia.
MPAA:G
Analysis Film Releasing Corp — *Vestron Video*

My Champion   1984
Drama
76021   101 mins   C   B, V   P
Yoko Shimada, Chris Mitchum
A chance meeting propels Mike Gorman and
Miki Tsuwa into a relationship based on the
strong bond of love and athletic competition.
Yasuhiko Kawano — *Media Home
Entertainment*

My Dinner with Andre   1981
Comedy-Drama
60328   110 mins   C   B, V, CED   P
*Andre Gregory, Wally Shawn, directed by Louis
Malle*
Two friends who haven't seen each other for a
long time decide to catch up on each others'
lives over dinner.

George W George; Beverly Karp — *Pacific Arts Video*

My Fair Lady 1964
Musical
49829   170 mins   C   B, V, CED   P
Audrey Hepburn, Rex Harrison, Stanley Holloway, Wilfred Hyde White, Gladys Cooper, directed by George Cukor
A colorful production of Lerner and Loewe's musical version of "Pygmalion," about a Covent Garden flower girl who becomes a lady. Winner of 8 Academy Awards. Songs incude "On the Street Where You Live," "The Rain in Spain," and "I've Grown Accustomed to Her Face." Academy Awards '64: Best Picture; Best Director (Cukor); Best Actor (Harrison); Best Color Cinematography.
Warner Bros — *CBS/Fox Video*

My Favorite Brunette 1947
Comedy
12859   85 mins   B/W   B, V, FO   P
Bob Hope, Dorothy Lamour, Peter Lorre, Lon Chaney, Alan Ladd
A would-be private eye becomes involved with a murder, a spy caper, and a dangerous brunette.
Paramount — *Video Yesteryear; Budget Video; Sheik Video; Cable Films; VCII; Video Connection; Discount Video Tapes; Western Film & Video Inc; Cinema Concepts*

My Favorite Wife 1940
Comedy
64364   88 mins   B/W   B, V, 3/4U   P
Irene Dunne, Cary Grant, Randolph Scott, Gail Patrick, directed by Garson Kanin
A lady explorer returns to civilization after being shipwrecked for seven years and finds that her husband is about to remarry.
RKO — *Nostalgia Merchant*

My Favorite Year 1982
Comedy
64565   92 mins   C   B, V, CED   P
Peter O'Toole, Mark-Linn Baker, Joe Bologna, Jessica Harper, Lainie Kazan, directed by Richard Benjamin
A swashbuckling movie star who drinks too much is signed to make his television debut on a popular live variety show.
MPAA:PG
MGM/UA — *MGM/UA Home Video*

My Forbidden Past 1951
Drama
66334   81 mins   B/W   B, V, 3/4U   P
Ava Gardner, Melvyn Douglas, Robert Mitchum
A New Orleans girl inherits a fortune and vows vengeance when the doctor she loves marries another.
RKO — *Nostalgia Merchant*

My Little Chickadee 1940
Comedy
31595   91 mins   B/W   B, V   P
W.C. Fields, Mae West, directed by Edward Cline
A classic comedy starring W.C. Fields and Mae West, striking sparks with each other on a trip out West.
Universal — *MCA Home Video; RCA VideoDiscs*

My Little Margie 1954
Comedy
72518   60 mins   B/W   B, V, 3/4U   P
Gale Storm, Charles Farrell
Two funny episodes from the "My Little Margie" series: in the first, Margie wins a TV contest and gets to host her own show. In the second Margie, Freddie and Vern are involved in a murder mystery.
CBS — *International Historic Films*

My Love for Yours 1939
Comedy
10615   99 mins   B/W   B, V, 3/4U   R, P
Fred MacMurray, Madeleine Carroll
The romantic tale of a young man hoping to win the love of a beautiful girl.
Paramount — *Cable Films; Penguin Video*

My Man Godfrey 1936
Comedy
00413   95 mins   B/W   B, V   P
William Powell, Carole Lombard, Gail Patrick, directed by Gregory La Cava
A spoiled rich girl picks up a bum as part of a scavenger hunt and decides to keep him on as her butler.
Universal International; Gregory La Cava — *Media Home Entertainment; Movie Buff Video; Budget Video; Video Dimensions; Sheik Video; Cable Films; Video Connection; Video Yesteryear; Discount Video Tapes; Western Film & Video Inc*

My Pal Trigger 1946
Western
03987   79 mins   B/W   B, V   P
Roy Rogers, Gabby Hayes
Roy Rogers and Trigger head out for high adventure on the plains.
Republic — *Budget Video; Video Connection; Discount Video Tapes*

My Sister, My Love 1980
Mystery/Horror
51442   99 mins   C   B, V   P
Carol Kane, Lee Grant
The love between two sisters reaches such an obsession that they eventually are moved to murder those who enter their house.
Unknown — *Wizard Video*

My Tutor 1982
Comedy
69028   97 mins   C   B, V, LV,   P
                                   CED
Caren Kaye, Matt Lattanzi, Kevin McCarthy,
Irene Golonka
A young woman is hired to tutor a young man in
French. This film is a romantic comedy.
MPAA:R
Crown International — *MCA Home Video*

Mysterians, The 1958
Science fiction
13023   85 mins   C   B, V   P
Kenji Sahara
Race of gigantic scientific intellects attempts to
conquer Earth. Dubbed in English from
Japanese.
Exhibitor — *VCI Home Video*

Mysteries from Beyond 1976
Earth
Documentary/Speculation
55008   95 mins   C   B, V   P
The bizarre world of psychic phenomena and
the paranormal is explored in this compelling
film. Among the many areas of investigation are
UFO's, Kirlian Photography, psychic healing,
and witchcraft.
Cine Vue — *VCI Home Video*

Mysterious Doctor Satan 1940
Suspense/Serials
44793 250 mins B/W   B, V, 3/4U   P
Eduardo Ciannelli, Robert Wilcox, Ella Neal,
directed by William Witney
A mad scientist builds an army of mechanical
robots to rob and terrorize the nation. In 15
episodes.
Republic — *Video Connection*

Mysterious Island 1961
Fantasy
Closed Captioned
21293   101 mins   C   B, V   P
Herbert Lom, Michael Callan, Joan Greenwood
Some Confederate prison escapees, blown off
course in an observation balloon, find the
uncharted island of Captain Nemo. Based on
Jules Verne's novel.
Columbia — *RCA/Columbia Pictures Home*
Video

Mysterious Miniature 1983
World
Documentary/Insects
63667   90 mins   C   B, V   R, P
The earth's least visible inhabitants and its
greatest survivors, the insects, are closely
studied in this nature documentary.
Bill Burrud Productions — *Walt Disney Home*
Video

Mysterious Mr. Wong 1935
Mystery
08756   56 mins   B/W   B, V, 3/4U   P
Bela Lugosi, Arline Judge, Wallace Ford
The Thirteen Coins of Confucius put San
Francisco's Chinatown in a state of terror until
Mr. Wong came.
Monogram — *Penguin Video; Cable Films;*
Discount Video Tapes

Mystery and Espionage 195?
Mystery/Suspense
53049 100 mins B/W   B, V, 3/4U   P
James Daly, Robert Alda, Preston Foster, John
Howard
Four "camp" examples of what foreign intrigue,
suspense, mystery, and general spying was all
about on 1950's TV: "Overseas Adventure"
(1953), starring James Daly as a newspaper
correspondent in search of adventure; "Secret
File, U.S.A." (1955), starring Robert Alda as the
head of the cold war Army intelligence;
"Waterfront" (1955), starring Preston Foster as
Capt. John Herrick, commander of the tugboat
Cheryl Ann; "Dr. Hudson's Secret Journal"
(1956), starring John Howard as Center
Hospital's top neurosurgeon.
NBC et al — *Shokus Video*

Mystery Mansion 1983
Mystery
66601   95 mins   C   B, V   P
Dallas McKennon, Greg Wynne, Jane Ferguson
A fortune in gold and a hundred-year-old
mystery lead three children into an exciting
treasure hunt.
Arthur R. Dubs — *Media Home Entertainment*

Mystery Mountain 1934
Western/Serials
08877 156 mins B/W   B, V, 3/4U   P
Ken Maynard, Gene Autry, Smiley Burnette
Twelve episodes depict the villain known as the
"Rattler" attempting to stop the construction of
a railroad over Mystery Mountain.
Mascot — *Penguin Video; Video Connection;*
Cable Films; Video Yesteryear; Discount Video
Tapes

Mystery of the Hooded 1937
Horseman
Western
56604   61 mins   B/W   B, V   P
Tex Ritter
Tex finds himself pitted against a very strange
adversary.
Monogram — *Video Dimensions; Discount*
Video Tapes

Mystery of the Mary 1937
Celeste, The
Mystery
10629   64 mins   B/W   B, V   P, T

Bela Lugosi, Shirley Grey, Edmund Willard
A tale of terror based on the bizarre case of the "Marie Celeste," an American ship found adrift and derelict on the Atlantic Ocean on December 5, 1872.
Guaranteed — *Blackhawk Films; Video Yesteryear; Sheik Video; Cable Films*

Mystery of Willoughby Castle, The   1980
Religion
46831   35 mins   C   B, V, 3/4U,   P
                                    Q
The setting is a haunted house in this program that presents a Gospel message and reminds Christians of the need for self-acceptance.
Quadrus Films — *TV Sports Scene*

Mystery Plane   1939
Drama
08618   60 mins   B/W   B, V, 3/4U   P
George Trent, Jason Robards, Milburn Stone, Directed by George Waggner
"Tailspin Tommy" invents a bombing system, but before he can deliver it to the government, the gang closes in.
Monogram — *Penguin Video*

Mystery Range   1937
Western
14390   57 mins   B/W   B, V, 3/4U   P
Tom Tyler, Jerry Bergh
Cowboys get involved with fast gunplay and murdering rustlers.
Victory — *Penguin Video*

Mystery Squadron   1933
Adventure/Serials
10923   156 mins   B/W   B, V   P
Bob Steele, Guinn Williams, J. Carroll Naish
Twelve chapters, 13 minutes each. Daredevil air action in flight against the masked pilots of the Black Ace.
Mascot — *Video Connection; Discount Video Tapes; Video Dimensions; Cable Films; Video Yesteryear*

MysteryDisc #1: Murder, Anyone?   1982
Mystery/Games
63402   ? mins   C   LV   P
This interactive videodisc lets the viewer determine who murdered the millionaire. There are 16 variations with 16 possible solutions, and the viewer must hunt for clues and weigh the evidence in order to solve the mystery.
AM Available
VIDMAX — *VIDMAX; RCA VideoDiscs*

MysteryDisc #2: Many Roads to Murder   1983
Mystery/Games
64860   ? mins   C   LV   P
Set two years after "MysteryDisc #1," Detective Stew Cavanaugh assists an old college friend in solving a murder. Sixteen different plot lines and solutions are included for the viewer to investigate.
VIDMAX; Parallel Communications — *VIDMAX; RCA VideoDiscs*

N

N&WJ 611   1982
Trains
66057   114 mins   C   B, V   P
The Norfolk and Western Class J No. 611, 4-8-4 steam locomotive, on her first passenger run from Birmingham to Roanoke, is featured in this program.
JMJ Productions — *JMJ Productions*

Nadia   1984
Drama/Biographical
66612   100 mins   C   B, V   P
Carrie Snodgress, Leslie Weiner, Johanna Carlo, Joe Bennett
This is the dramatized story of Nadia Comaneci, the young Romanian gymnast who won worldwide attention as a triple gold-medal winner in the 1976 Montreal Olympics.
Tribune Entertainment; Dave Bell Productions; Jadran Film — *U.S.A. Home Video*

Naked and the Dead, The   1958
Drama
13027   131 mins   C   B, V   P
Aldo Ray, Cliff Robertson, Joey Bishop
Based on Norman Mailer's novel of WW II men in war; their feelings, hates, desires, and courage.
Warner Bros; Paul Gregory — *VCI Home Video*

Naked Civil Servant, The   1980
Drama
59704   80 mins   C   B, V   R, P
John Hurt
The biography of Quentin Crisp, the witty homosexual who grew up in the 30's and 40's and lived through years of intolerance, ostracism and violence.
British Academy Awards '80: Best Actor (Hurt).
Euston Films; Thames Video — *THORN EMI Home Video*

Naked Eyes   1983
Music-Performance
75906   14 mins   C   B, V   P

This program presents the rock group Naked Eyes performing their hits "Always Something There to Remind Me," "Promises, Promises" and "When the Lights Go Out."
EMI America Records — *Sony Corporation of America*

Naked Truth, The　　1958
Comedy
59836　92 mins　C　B, V　　P
Peter Sellers, Terry-Thomas, Shirley Eaton, Dennis Price
A greedy publisher tries to get rich quick by publishing a scandal magazine about the "lurid" lives of prominent citizens.
Mario Zampi — *Embassy Home Entertainment*

Name for Evil, A　　197?
Horror
66263　74 mins　C　B, V　　P
Robert Culp, Samantha Eggar
Having grown tired of city living, a man and his wife move to an old family estate way out in the country, near the Great Lakes. Strange sounds in the night are the first signs of the terror to come.
AEI Productions — *Paragon Video Productions*

Name of the Game Is Golf　　197?
Golf
33774　60 mins　C　B, V, 3/4U　　P
5　pgms
Established teaching golf pros give excellent tips and lessons in five phases of the game. Five one-hour lessons are included in this series. Programs are available individually.
1. Putting for the Beginner and the Pro 2. Short Iron Lessons 3. The Medium and Long Iron Game 4. Sand Lessons and Special Shots 5. Woods and Tee Shots
Sports World Cinema — *Sports World Cinema*

Nana　　1955
Drama
66388　118 mins　C　B, V　　P
Charles Boyer, Martine Carol
A French version of Emile Zola's novel about a dissolute courtesan who spends her life seducing the upper classes. English subtitles.
FR
Roitfield Productions — *Movie Buff Video*

Nanook of the North　　1921
Documentary/Eskimos
64252　55 mins　B/W　B, V　　P
Directed by Robert Flaherty
A pioneering documentary that established the form for others to come. Flaherty lived with an Eskimo family for months to produce this chronicle of their daily lives. Silent with musical score.

Revillon Freres — *Classic Video Cinema Collector's Club*

Narrow Edge　　1982
Motorcycles
66249　65 mins　C　B, V　　P
The story of a full season of Grand Prix racing (1974).
CH Wood — *Motor Cycle Video*

Nashville　　1975
Drama
38613　159 mins　C　B, V, LV　　R, P
Henry Gibson, Lily Tomlin, Ronee Blakley, Keith Carradine, directed by Robert Altman
The lives of twenty-four people during a five-day country music festival at the Grand Ole Opry are intertwined in this multi-level portrait of America at a particular time and place.
Academy Awards '75: Best Song (I'm Easy).
MPAA:R
Paramount — *Paramount Home Video; RCA VideoDiscs*

Nate and Hayes　　1983
Adventure
65616　100 mins　C　B, V, LV,　　R, P
　　　　　　　　　　CED
Tommy Lee Jones, Michael O'Keefe, Max Phipps, Jenny Seagrove
Set during the mid-1800s in the South Pacific, the notorious real-life swashbuckler Captain "Bully" Hayes and young Reverend Nate pursue a cutthroat gang which has kidnapped Nate's wife.
MPAA:PG
Lloyd Phillips; Rob Whitehouse — *Paramount Home Video*

Nation Builds Under Fire, A　　1965
Vietnam War
53698　40 mins　C　B, V, 3/4U　　P
This film tells the story of the struggle of the people of Vietnam to build a nation while war rages around them.
US Dept of Defense — *International Historic Films*

National Adultery　　19??
Comedy
65647　90 mins　C　B, V　　R, P
The eternal triangle is sketched in this comedy for adults only, starring 1981 Miss Spain.
Italian — *Video City Productions*

National Gallery: Art Awareness Collection　　19??
Artists
14178　60 mins　C　LV　　P
A look at the great works in Washington, D.C.'s National Gallery of Art. A journey into the artistic

genius of Rembrandt, Fragonard, Goya, Copley, Turner, Degas, Renoir, and a group of early American painters is included.
Unknown — *MCA Home Video*

National Gallery of Art, The　　　1984
Arts/Museums
69837　　? mins　　C　　LV　　　　P
This linear program includes the story of the museum's beginnings and development and a comprehensive, detailed tour through one of the finest art collections in the world. The collection spans seven centuries—from Byzantine painters through Leonardo da Vinci and Rembrandt to Matisse and Calder.
Videodisc Publishing; VIDMAX — *Videodisc Publishing*

National Geographic:　　　1983
Great Whales/Sharks
Fishes/Animals
64778　　120 mins　　C　　CED　　　　P
"Great Whales" (1978), an Emmy Award winning film, looks at whale anatomy, communication and migration. "Sharks" (1982) addresses man's fear and hatred of sharks while offering a look at the shark's vulnerability.
National Geographic Society — *RCA VideoDiscs*

National Geographic　　　197?
Society: The Incredible
Machine/Mysteries of the
Mind
Anatomy and physiology
64458　　87 mins　　C　　CED　　　　P
"The Incredible Machine" (1975) offers a fascinating journey inside the human body. "Mysteries of the Mind" (1980) is a documentary which uses computer graphics and a synapse sculpture to examine the brain's structures. Both are multiple award-winning films, the latter having garnered two Emmy Awards.
National Geographic Society — *RCA VideoDiscs*

National Hot Rod　　　198?
Association
Championship Drag
Racing
Automobiles-Racing
59519　　48 mins　　C　　B, V　　　　P
27　pgms
Action-packed races from tracks around the country featuring professional drivers vying for top honors in Top Fuel, Funny Car, and Pro Stock categories.
John Mullin — *Diamond P Sports*

National Lampoon's　　　1982
Class Reunion
Comedy
66101　　85 mins　　C　　B, V, LV, CED　　　　P
Shelley Smith, Gerrit Graham, Michael Lerner
A class reunion with some very wacky guests.
MPAA:R
20th Century Fox — *Vestron Video*

National Lampoon's　　　1983
Vacation
Comedy
65325　　98 mins　　C　　B, V, LV, CED　　　　P
Chevy Chase, Beverly D'Angelo, Imogene Coca, Randy Quaid, Christie Brinkley
The Clark W. Griswold family of suburban Chicago embark on a westward cross-country vacation trip to remember, earmarked by a series of hysterical misadventures.
MPAA:R
Matty Simmons — *Warner Home Video*

Naval Aviation: A　　　1960
Personal History—The
Weapon Is Tested
World War I
53655　　25 mins　　B/W　　B, V, 3/4U　　　　P
This film depicts the development of naval aviation during World War I.
US Navy — *International Historic Films*

Navy Advisor in　　　1968
Vietnam—The River
Force
Armed Forces-US/Vietnam War
72492　　55 mins　　C　　B, V, 3/4U　　　　P
A Navy training film stressing the role of the US Navy advisor working with South Vietnamese river forces.
US Navy — *International Historic Films*

Navy Flies On, The　　　194?
Armed Forces-US
68910　　20 mins　　B/W　　B, V　　　　P
The history of the U.S. Naval aviation.
US Navy — *Interurban Films*

Navy vs. the Night　　　1966
Monsters, The
Science fiction
66525　　87 mins　　C　　B, V　　　　P
Mamie Van Doren, Anthony Eisley, Pamela Mason, Bobby Van
Terrifying acid-secreting plant monsters terrorize and cremate the inhabitants of an isolated rural area.
Realart — *Paragon Video Productions*

Nazi Concentration Camps   1945
World War II
53681   59 mins   B/W   B, V, 3/4U   P
An official film record of the Nazi death camps as photographed by Allied forces advancing into Germany.
Unknown — *International Historic Films*

Nazi Propaganda Films   194?
World War II/Propaganda
48847   115 mins   B/W   B, V, 3/4U   P
An assortment of World War II German newsreels with German dialogue.
GE
Germany — *Western Film & Video Inc*

Nazi Strike   1984
World War II/Germany
76532   50 mins   B/W   B, V   P
This program, put together with actual captured film, details Germany's conquests at the beginning of WW II.
Maljack Productions Inc — *MPI Home Video*

Nazi War Crime Trials   1945
Documentary/World War II
47473   67 mins   B/W   B, V, FO   P
A collection of seven American and Russian newsreel shorts that detail the Nuremberg Trials of Nazi war criminals. Featured are Goring, Van Pappen, Hess, Schact, Streicher and others. Includes grisly scenes of hangings and firing squad executions.
RKO Pathe News et al — *Video Yesteryear; Discount Video Tapes*

Nazis, The   1984
Documentary
72861   100 mins   C   B, V   P
Rod Steiger   2   pgms
This cassette is a repackaging of two classic films.
1.Triumph of the Will 2.Night and Fog
EL, FR, GE
Leni Riefenstahl and Alain Resnais — *VIDCREST*

Nazis Strike, The /   194?
Schichlegruber Doing the Lambeth Walk
World War II/Documentary
47645   44 mins   B/W   B, V, FO   P
Directed by Frank Capra, Anatole Litvak
"Nazis Strike" is a U.S. War Department film documentary showing America's entry into the war. Includes scenes from "Triumph of the Will." "Schichlegruber Doing the Lambeth Walk" is a satirical British film combining Nazi footage with popular music. Features the "Gestapo Hep-Cats."
US War Dept — *Video Yesteryear*

Nazis Strike, The   1943
World War II/Documentary
50613   41 mins   B/W   B, V, 3/4U   P
Directed by Frank Capra
Hope for peace is abandoned when the Nazis conquer Austria and Czechoslovakia, and invade Poland. Part of the "Why We Fight" series.
US War Department — *Western Film & Video Inc; Discount Video Tapes; MPI Home Video*

NBC Comedy Hour   1956
Variety
38988   50 mins   B/W   B, V, FO   P
Jonathan Winters, Guy Mitchell, Gretchen Wyler, Shecky Greene, hosted by Alan Young
Originally telecast in June 3, 1956, this special has a variety format with a "Watching All the Girls Go By" theme. Comedy from all, and songs by Gretchen Wyler.
NBC — *Video Yesteryear*

NBC Comedy Hour   1956
Comedy/Variety
47498   60 mins   B/W   B, V, FO   P
Groucho Marx, Jonathan Winters, Stan Freberg, Gale Storm, Ben Blue, Jack Albertson
An all-star variety show, featuring numerous top comics in a succession of sketches. Originally telecast on March 4, 1956.
NBC — *Video Yesteryear*

Nea   1978
Drama
68264   101 mins   C   B, V   P
Sam Frey, Ann Zacharias, Heinz Bennent
Nea is the story of turbulent erotic passion and a young girl's striving to get away from her father's home.
MPAA:R
Andre Genoves — *RCA/Columbia Pictures Home Video*

Needlepoint with Dee   1981
Handicraft
53277   30 mins   C   B, V   P
A number of basic stitches, including the continental stitch, are shown while making a striped sampler pillow.
The Darn Yarn Shoppe — *Daya Inc*

Negro Soldier   1944
World War II/Documentary
52320   40 mins   B/W   B, V, 3/4U   P
Directed by Frank Capra
This wartime documentary focuses on the blacks' participation in World War II, and examines the important role played by the Negro in U.S. history.
US Office of War Information — *International Historic Films*

Neighbors 1981
Comedy
47431   90 mins   C   B, V, LV   P
*John Belushi, Dan Ackroyd, Kathryn Walker,
Cathy Moriarty, directed by John Avildsen*
A quiet, middle-class, suburban couple gets the
shock of their lives when two loony people
move next door.
MPAA:R
Columbia — *RCA/Columbia Pictures Home
Video; RCA VideoDiscs*

Neil Diamond: Love at the 1976
Greek
Music-Performance
65479   52 mins   C   B, V, LV,   P
                                      CED
This stereo spectacular features the Grammy
Award-winning star singing his greatest hits
"Sweet Caroline," "Play Me," "Holly Holy," "I
Am, I Said," "Song Sung Blue" and many more.
In stereo VHS and Beta Hi-Fi.
Arch Angel TV — *Vestron Video*

Neil Sedaka in Concert 1981
Music-Performance
55558   54 mins   C   B, V, LV   P
Neil Sedaka, directed by Gary Jones
From his 1960's hits ("Calendar Girl," "Oh
Carol," and "Stairway to Heaven") to his 1970's
comeback as a composer and performer of
contemporary music, Sedaka's style and music
are revealed in this concert recorded live at the
Jubilee Auditorium in Edmonton, Canada.
Doug Hutton; Doug Holtby — *MCA Home
Video*

Neil Sedaka in Concert 1984
Music-Performance
69921   60 mins   C   B, V   P
Singer/songwriter/pianist Neil Sedaka performs
his vast repertoire of hits in concert at the
Forum in Ontario, Canada. In VHS Dolby stereo
and Beta Hi-Fi.
Perry Rosemond — *RKO HomeVideo*

Nelvanamation 1980
Cartoons
54910   100 mins   C   B, V   R, P
Animated
Four cosmic fantasies are featured in this
program, including "Please Don't Eat the
Planet," "A Cosmic Christmas," "The Devil and
Daniel Mouse," and "Romie-O and Julie-8."
The latter two are also available individually.
Nelvana Ltd — *Warner Home Video*

Nelvanamation II 1981
Cartoons
47386   50 mins   C   B, V   R, P
Voices of Phil Silvers, Garrett Morris
A second anthology of fantasy cartoons for
children of all ages, featuring "Take Me Out to

the Ball Game," with music by Rick Danko, and
"The Jack Rabbit Story" with music by John
Sebastion.
Nelvana Ltd — *Warner Home Video*

Nest, The 1981
Drama
72875   109 mins   C   B, V   P
This film is about the relationship between a
widower and a young girl.
Unknown — *Embassy Home Entertainment*

Network 1976
Drama
44645   121 mins   C   B, V, LV,   P
                                      CED
*Faye Dunaway, Peter Finch, William Holden,
Robert Duvall, Wesley Addy, Ned Beatty,
Beatrice Straight, directed by Sidney Lumet*
A satire of television and the men behind the
networks.
Academy Awards '76: Best Actor (Finch); Best
Actress (Dunaway); Best Supporting Actress
(Straight); Best Screenplay Written Directly for
the Screen (Chayefsky).   MPAA:R
MGM — *MGM/UA Home Video*

Network Fall Preview 197?
Presentations
Variety
33697   110 mins   C   B, V, 3/4U   P
This program contains each of the three major
network's presentations to its affiliates,
spotlighting new shows to be seen in the
autumn season. CBS's (1966) includes, "It's
About Time," and "Run, Buddy, Run," NBC's
(1969) highlights contain "The Bill Cosby
Show," and "Then Came Bronson," and ABC's
(1974) clips preview "Happy Days," amd
"Marcus Welby, M.D." among others.
CBS et al — *Shokus Video*

Nevada City 1941
Western
54184   54 mins   B/W   B, V   P
Roy Rogers, Trigger
Roy outwits a financier who is trying to
monopolize transportation in California.
Republic — *Video Connection*

Never Cry Rape 1982
Safety education/Martial arts
64017   82 mins   C   B, V   P
This program teaches women how to recognize
a potential attack situation, offers non-violent
protection measures, and as a last resort,
provides martial arts instruction in how to fend
off an attacker.
Ng See Yuen; Roy Horan — *World Video
Enterprises*

Never Cry Wolf 1984
Drama
75927 105 mins C B, V, LV R, P
Charles Martin Smith, Brian Dennehy, Samson Jorah
The dramatic story of a young biologist's trek to the Artic region to study wolves.
Walt Disney — *Walt Disney Home Video*

Never Let Go 1960
Comedy-Drama
59837 91 mins C B, V P
Peter Sellers, Richard Todd, Elizabeth Sellars
A man unwittingly tracks down the mastermind of a gang of racketeers.
Peter de Sarigny — *Embassy Home Entertainment*

Never Say Never Again 1983
Suspense
69800 134 mins C B, V, LV, CED R, P
Sean Connery, Klaus Maria Brandauer, Max Von Sydow, Barbara Carrera
James Bond matches wits with a charming but sinister tycoon who is holding the world nuclear hostage as part of a diabolical plot by SPECTRE. In stereo on all formats.
MPAA:PG
Jack Schwartzman — *Warner Home Video*

New Adventures of Tarzan, The 1935
Adventure/Serials
08870 260 mins B/W B, V, 3/4U P
Herman Brix, Ula Holt, Frank Baker, Dale Walsh, Lewis Sargent
Twelve episodes, each 22 minutes long, depicts the adventures of Edgar Rice Burrough's tree-swinging character—Tarzan.
Burroughs and Tarzan — *Penguin Video; Budget Video; Video Connection; Video Yesteryear; Discount Video Tapes*

New Adventures of Zorro, The 1981
Cartoons/Adventure
66004 60 mins C B, V P
Animated
Daring swordplay highlights these three tales of swashbuckling adventures.
Filmation — *Family Home Entertainment*

New Centurions, The 1972
Drama
21294 109 mins C B, V P
George C. Scott, Stacy Keach, Jane Alexander
The film version of Joseph Wambaugh's novel about rookie cops on the Los Angeles Police Force.
MPAA:R

Columbia — *RCA/Columbia Pictures Home Video*

New Deal—The Thirties, The 19??
History-US/Documentary
10148 ? mins B/W B, V P, T
Covers the Depression, Mahatma Ghandi, Thomas Edison, George Gershwin, Mt. Rushmore, Al Capone, FDR, John Dillinger, the Hindenberg, Lou Gehrig, and more.
Unknown — *Blackhawk Films*

New Lion of Sonora, The 1970
Western
72891 120 mins C B, V P
Gilbert Roland, Leif Erickson
Two episodes of the "High Chaparral" TV series are herewith combined where Don Domingo (Gilbert Roland) returns to Arizona to head his family.
NBC — *NTA Home Entertainment*

New Look 1981
Variety/Filmmaking
59843 44 mins C B, V, LV, CED P
Francis Ford Coppola, Bob Rafelson
An erotic men's video magazine including a centerfold, interviews with filmmaker Francis Ford Coppola and Bob Rafelson, and a series of vignettes.
Regie Cassette Video; Blay RCV — *Embassy Home Entertainment*

New Media Bible: The Story of Joseph, The 1976
Bible
64708 90 mins C CED P
This video dramatization of the Bible presents historically accurate settings and authentic details of the biblical stories of Joseph.
Genesis Project — *RCA VideoDiscs*

New Misadventures of Ichabod Crane, The 1981
Fantasy/Holidays
47254 25 mins C B, V P
The headless horseman rides again, robbing coaches and scaring the townsfolk of Sleepy Hollow. Halloween fun begins when Ichabod comes to the rescue with his motley crew of friends.
AM Available
Coronet Films — *Embassy Home Entertainment*

New Speed Reading 1981
Education/Communication
52767 60 mins C B, V P

  (For Explanation of codes, see USE GUIDE and KEY)

This complete speed reading course is divided into video chapters and allows the viewer to refer back and review the method and progress of speed reading. An instructional booklet with study schedules is included.
AM Available
Karl Video — *Karl Video*

New Star Over Hollywood 197?
Variety
19417   60 mins   C   B, V, 3/4U, Q   P
Carol Lawrence, Tom Netherton, Susan Stafford, Debbie Boone, Ronald Reagan, Dean Jones, Pat Boone
An entertainment and variety special with a Christian format.
TV Sports Scene — *TV Sports Scene*

New Three Stooges Cartoon Show, The 1984
Cartoons
72867   60 mins   C   B, V   P
Animated
The first volume of this series features six cartoons from the series that features the voices of Moe Howard, Larry Fine and Joe de Rita.
Dick Brown, Normandy TV Three Production — *Embassy Home Entertainment*

New Thunder for the USAF 195?
Vietnam War/Armed Forces-US
53696   40 mins   C   B, V, 3/4U   P
Three aircraft promotional films, including historical footage of jet planes from the 40's and 50's.
USAF — *International Historic Films*

New Video Aerobics, The 1982
Physical fitness
63364   57 mins   C   B, V, CED   P
Leslie Lilien, Julie Lavin
This program instructs the home viewer in a complete and compact conditioning routine of aerobics. Contains a 40-minute advanced program and a 17-minute beginner's session.
Amstar Productions — *Vestron Video*

New York, New York 1977
Drama/Musical
63400   163 mins   C   B, V   P
Robert De Niro, Liza Minnelli, directed by Martin Scorsese
A tragic romance evolves between a saxaphonist and an aspiring actress in this salute to the big band era.
MPAA:PG
United Artists — *CBS/Fox Video; RCA VideoDiscs*

New Zoo Revue 1984
Children/Variety
75928   60 mins   C   B, V   P
This program presents the live children's programing package, The New Zoo Revue.
Family Home Entertainment — *Family Home Entertainment*

Newport Jazz Festival 1962
Music-Performance
55382   60 mins   B/W   B, V   P
Duke Ellington, Count Basie, Roland Kirk
Jazz greats in concert at the famed jazz festival include Count Basie, Duke Ellington, Roland Kirk, Ruby Braff, Peewee Russell, Joe Williams, Oscar Peterson Trio with Ray Brown, Lambert, Hendricks and Bavan, and others.
Unknown — *CBS/Fox Video*

News Front 1978
Drama
73663   110 mins   C   B, V   P
Bill Hunter, Wendy Hughes, John Ewart, Chris Hayward
The story of two brothers who worked in Australia's news media of the '50s and '60s is chronicled in this film. Some segments are in black and white.
David Elfick — *Embassy Home Entertainment*

NFL '81 1982
Football
47716   47 mins   C   B, V, FO   P
Highlights from the topsy-turvy 1981-82 NFL season, focusing on the great individual performances, the Playoffs, and the NFL's selections for the 1981-82 All-Pro Teams.
NFL Films — *NFL Films Video*

NFL '81 Official Season Yearbook 1982
Football
47806   120 mins   C   CED   P
Four half-hour segments: "NFL '81" - a season overview; "Superbowl XVI Highlights;" "A Very Special Team" - season highlights of the San Francisco 49'er's; "Stripes" - season highlights of the Cincy Bengals.
NFL Films — *RCA VideoDiscs*

NFL Follies Go Hollywood 1983
Football
65155   23 mins   C   B, V, FO   P
Football fumbles and goof-ups are integrated into a parody of movie genres in this entry from the "NFL Follies" series.
NFL Films — *NFL Films Video*

NFL SymFunny/Highlights of Super Bowl III   1980
Football
56792   46 mins   C   B, V   P
The antics of the NFL "ballet company" set to music by Beethoven, Bach, and "The Quarterback of Seville," plus Joe Namath's triumph against the Colts in the most incredible upset in Super Bowl history.
NFL Films — *VidAmerica*

NFL's Best Ever Coaches   1981
Football
51702   46 mins   C   B, V, FO   R, P
A profile of some of the most respected and successful coaches ever to pace the sidelines of an NFL stadium, including Paul Brown, Vince Lombardi, Don Shula, and Tom Landry.
NFL Films — *NFL Films Video*

NFL's Best Ever: The Professionals   1981
Football
51703   46 mins   C   B, V, FO   R, P
This program profiles some of the most determined, gutsy personalities ever to hit the NFL, who despite setbacks and long odds, struggled their way to success and recognition. It features Jim Plunkett, Jim Marshall, Bill Kilmer, Larry Brown, and Dick Vermeil.
NFL Films — *NFL Films Video*

NFL's Best Ever Quarterbacks   1981
Football
51704   46 mins   C   B, V, FO   R, P
The skillfully thrown passes and field leadership of former great quarterbacks Otto Graham, John Unitas, Roger Staubach, and Fran Tarkenton sparked their teams to success and provided a host of memories.
NFL Films — *NFL Films Video*

NFL's Best Ever Runners   1981
Football
51705   46 mins   C   B, V, FO   R, P
O. J. Simpson, Jim Brown, Hugh McElheny, and Walter Payton are some of the outstanding running backs who dart, slash, sweep, and fake their way through this program.
NFL Films — *NFL Films Video*

NFL's Best Ever Teams   1981
Football
51706   46 mins   C   B, V, FO   R, P
Throughout the NFL's history, there have been several teams who dominated their league for several years at a time: the Cleveland Browns of the 50's, the Green Bay Packers of the 60's, the Miami Dolphins of the early 70's, and Steelers, Cowboys, and Raiders of the middle and late 70's.

NFL Films — *NFL Films Video*

NFL's Inspirational Men and Moments, The   1980
Football
50090   48 mins   C   B, V, FO   R, P
Roger Staubach, O. J. Simpson, Fran Tarkenton, Joe Namath
A collection of short programs that reveal much about the inspirational aspects of pro football as well as the human side of a sport that's more than just a game.
NFL Films — *NFL Films Video*

Nibelungen Saga—Kriemheld's Revenge, Die   1923
Drama
72473   95 mins   B/W   B, V, 3/4U   P
Directed by Fritz Lang
To get even with her brothers, Kriemhild marries Attila the Hun only to hurry her own ruin. This film was designed to play after the showing of another, "Siegfried," but stands well on its own. Silent.
Janus Films; German — *International Historic Films*

Nicholas and Alexandra   1971
Drama
69618   183 mins   C   B, V   P
Michael Jayston, Janet Suzman, Tom Baker, Laurence Olivier, Michael Redgrave
This epic film chronicles the final years of Tsar Nicholas II and Empress Alexandra and their children from 1904 through their imprisonment and eventual execution under the new Lenin government.
MPAA:PG
Sam Spiegal — *RCA/Columbia Pictures Home Video*

Nicholas Nickleby   1947
Drama
58885   103 mins   B/W   B, V   R, P
Sir Cedric Hardwicke, Stanley Holloway, Derek Bond, Alfred Drayton, Sybil Thorndike, Sally Ann Howes
An ensemble cast is featured in this film adaptation of Charles Dickens' novel concerning an impoverished family dependent on a wealthy but villainous relative who sends young Nicholas into a series of wild adventures.
Ealing — *THORN EMI Home Video*

Night and Fog   1955
Documentary/World War II
02957   32 mins   C   B, V, FO   P
Directed by Alain Resnais
A devastating documentary showing the gruesome atrocities of Hitler's Nazi purge against almost nine million innocent people.

    (For Explanation of codes, see USE GUIDE and KEY)

Premier Prix du Concourse de la Qualite.
Argos Films — *Video Yesteryear; International Historic Films*

Night at the Opera, A   1935
Comedy
39091   96 mins   B/W   B, V   P
The Marx Brothers, Allan Jones, Kitty Carlisle, Sig Rumann, Margaret Dumont
The Marx Brothers get mixed up with grand opera in this finest of all their films. Allan Jones, as an opera singer on the rise, sings "Alone," and "Cosi Cosa."
MGM — *MGM/UA Home Video*

Night Beast   1983
Horror/Science fiction
66521   90 mins   C   B, V   P
Tom Griffith, Dick Dyszel, Jaimie Zemarel
An alien creature lands his spaceship near a small town and begins a bloody killing rampage.
Amazing Film Productions — *Paragon Video Productions*

Night Before Christmas, The   1981
Christmas
58946   30 mins   C   B, V   P
Animated, Norman Luboff Choir
A heartwarming retelling of the charming "A Visit from St. Nicholas," animated, with holiday music.
AM Available
Bill Turnball; Playhouse Pictures — *Media Home Entertainment*

Night Crossing   1981
Drama/Adventure
59809   106 mins   C   B, V   R, P
John Hurt, Jane Alexander, Glynnis O'Connor, Doug McKeon, Beau Bridges, directed by Delbert Mann
The fact-based story of two East German families who launch a daring escape to the West in a homemade hot air balloon.
MPAA:PG
Walt Disney Productions — *Walt Disney Home Video*

Night Games   1980
Drama
66051   100 mins   C   B, V, LV, CED   P
Cindy Pickett, directed by Roger Vadim
A sexually unfulfilled woman experiences a passionate fantasy life.
MPAA:R
Raymond Chow — *Embassy Home Entertainment*

Night Has Eyes, The   1942
Mystery
66389   79 mins   B/W   B, V   P
James Mason, Joyce Howard, Wilfred Lawson
A young teacher disappears on the Yorkshire moors at the same spot where her girl friend had vanished the previous year.
ABP — *Movie Buff Video*

Night in Casablanca, A   1946
Comedy
69673   85 mins   B/W   B, V   P
The Marx Brothers
Groucho, Harpo and Chico find themselves in Casablanca, where Nazis, murder, intrigue and madcap antics abound.
United Artists — *Independent United Distributors*

Night in Nevada   1939
Western
08602   60 mins   B/W   B, V, 3/4U   P
Roy Rogers, Trigger
Roy is a fine singing, two-fisted, fast-shooting hero in this Republic Pictures matinee.
Republic — *Penguin Video; Video Connection; Discount Video Tapes*

Night Is My Future, The   1947
Drama
48857   89 mins   B/W   B, V, 3/4U   P
Mai Zetterling, directed by Ingmar Bergman
A blind young man meets a girl who tries to bring him happiness.
Swedish — *Western Film & Video Inc; Video Yesteryear*

Night Mail   1936
Trains
68913   25 mins   B/W   B, V   P
A view of the operation of the L.M.S. Railway and Royal Mail System prior to World War II in England.
Basil Wright; Harry Watt — *Interurban Films*

Night Moves   1975
Suspense/Mystery
51967   100 mins   C   B, V   R, P
Gene Hackman, Susan Clark, Jennifer Warren
While tracking down a missing teenager, a Hollywood detective uncovers a bizarre smuggling ring.
MPAA:PG
Warner Bros — *Warner Home Video*

Night of Bloody Horror   1976
Horror
66264   89 mins   C   B, V   P
Gaye Yellen, Evelyn Hendricks
An eerie tale of monsters that feed off human flesh.
MPAA:R

Joy N Houck Jr — *Paragon Video Productions*

Night of the Comet   1984
Science fiction
73661   90 mins   C   B, V   R, P
Catherine Mary Stewart, Robert Beltran,
Geoffrey Lewis, Mary Woronov
The three suvivors of an exploding comet are
being chased after by two scientists who need
their blood to stay alive.
MPAA:R
Wayne Crawford; Andrew Lane — *Atlantic*
Video

Night of the Ghouls   1960
Horror
66336   75 mins   B/W   B, V, 3/4U   P
Directed by Edward D. Wood
The last in Edward Wood's celebrated series of
inept so-called horror films, begun with "Bride of
the Monster" and "Plan 9 from Outer Space."
DCA — *Nostalgia Merchant*

Night of the Iguana, The   1964
Drama
58296   125 mins   B/W   B, V   P
Richard Burton, Deborah Kerr, Ava Gardner,
Sue Lyon, directed by John Huston
A defrocked minister, acting as a guide to a
group of women on a Mexican bus trip, affects
the lives of three women. Based on Tennessee
Williams' play.
MGM; Ray Stark — *MGM/UA Home Video*

Night of the Juggler   1980
Suspense
47816   101 mins   C   B, V, 3/4U   P
James Brolin, Cliff Gorman, Richard Castellano,
Mandy Patinkin
A man encounters countless obstacles in trying
to track down his daughter's kidnapper.
MPAA:R
Columbia — *Nostalgia Merchant*

Night of the Living Dead   1968
Horror
01681   90 mins   B/W   B, V   P
Judith O'Dea, Duane Jones, Russell Streiner,
Karl Hardman
Space experiments set off high level of radiation
that makes the newly-dead return to life. They
march upon humanity devouring their flesh.
Continental; Streiner and Hardman — *Media*
Home Entertainment; Budget Video; VCII; Video
Yesteryear; Nostalgia Merchant; Video
Dimensions; Sheik Video; Cable Films; King of
Video; Penguin Video; Video Connection;
Discount Video Tapes; Western Film & Video
Inc; Vestron Video (disc only)

Night of the Strangler   1973
Horror
66294   88 mins   C   B, V   P
Mickey Dolenz, James Ralston, Susan
McCullough
A love affair between a white society girl and a
young black man starts a chain of events that
rock New Orleans with brutal murders.
Albert J Salzer — *Paragon Video Productions*

Night of the Zombies   1983
Horror
73040   101 mins   C   B, V   P
The staff of a scientific research center are
killed and then resurrected as cannibals who
prey on the living.
Motion Picture Marketing — *Vestron Video*

Night Over China   197?
China/Propaganda
52353   45 mins   B/W   B, V, 3/4U   P
A Soviet propaganda documentary, which
purports to be an "expose" of Maoism. English
narration.
USSR — *International Historic Films*

Night Porter, The   1974
Drama
59838   115 mins   C   B, V, LV,   P
                                   CED
Dirk Bogarde, Charlotte Rampling, Philippe
LeRoy, Gabriele Ferzetti
Max, a guilt-ridden ex-SS concentration camp
officer, unexpectedly meets his former lover-
victim.
Robert Gordon; Avco Embassy — *Embassy*
Home Entertainment

Night Shift   1982
Comedy
63122   106 mins   C   B, V, LV,   R, P
                                   CED
Henry Winkler, Michael Keaton, Shelley Long
Two morgue attendants decide to spice up their
late-night shift by running a call girl service on
the side.
MPAA:R
The Ladd Company — *Warner Home Video*

Night Stage to Galveston   1952
Western
65082   61 mins   B/W   B, V   P, T
Gene Autry, Pat Buttram, Virginia Huston,
Thurston Hall
Gene leads his Texas Rangers on a mission to
uncover corruption in the Texas State Police
during the turbulent post-Civil War days.
Columbia — *Blackhawk Films*

Night the Lights Went Out in Georgia, The — 1981
Drama
59335 112 mins C B, V P
Kristy McNichol, Dennis Quaid, Mark Hamill, Don Stroud
Based on the popular hit song, a brother and sister try to cash in on the country music scene in Nashville.
MPAA:PG
Elliot Geisinger; Howard Kuperman; Ronald Saland; Howard Smith — *Embassy Home Entertainment*

Night They Robbed Big Bertha's, The — 1983
Comedy
72209 83 mins C B, V P
A bungling burglar attempts to knock off Big Bertha's Massage Parlor.
Unknown — *Paragon Video Productions*

Night Visitor, The — 1970
Suspense
51115 106 mins C B, V P
Max von Sydow, Liv Ullman, Trevor Howard, Per Oscarsson
A man whose convicted insanity is actually in doubt seeks violent vengeance on his tormentors.
MPAA:PG
Mel Ferrer — *VCI Home Video*

Night Warning — 1982
Drama
69042 96 mins C B, V R, P
A portrayal of young love's perverted inner conflicts and sinister mystery.
Unknown — *THORN EMI Home Video*

Night with Lou Reed, A — 1983
Music-Performance
65698 60 mins C B, V P
This is a visual record of the legendary rock star's sold-out engagement at The Bottom Line in New York featuring many of his greatest hits, including "Sweet Jane," "Walk on the Wild Side," "I'm Waiting for My Man," and "Rock 'n' Roll." In Beta Hi-Fi.
Bill Boggs; Richard Baker; RCA Video Productions Inc — *RCA/Columbia Pictures Home Video*

Nighthawks — 1981
Suspense/Drama
55557 90 mins C B, V, LV, CED P
Sylvester Stallone, Billy Dee Williams, Rutger Hauer, Lindsay Wagner, directed by Bruce Malmuth
A New York City cop stalks Manhattan, hunting down an international terrorist on the loose, from disco, to subway, to an airborne tramway. Also available in a Spanish subtitled version.
MPAA:R
Universal; Martin Poll — *MCA Home Video*

Nightkill — 1980
Drama/Suspense
63375 104 mins C B, V P
Jaclyn Smith, Mike Connors, James Franciscus, Robert Mitchum
A bored wife plots to do away with her wealthy, powerful husband with the aid of her attractive lover.
MPAA:R
Avco Embassy — *Embassy Home Entertainment*

Nightmare Castle — 1966
Horror
01680 90 mins B/W B, V P
Barbara Steele, Paul Miller, directed by Allan Grunewald
Scientist murders his evil wife and her lover, then hides their hearts under a statue. Lovers are restored to life and avenge their murders.
Allied Artists — *Budget Video*

Nightmare in Wax — 1969
Horror
13028 95 mins C B, V P
Cameron Mitchell, Anne Helm
Famous actor, burned by wax, starts a wax museum and destroys all of his enemies.
Gold Key — *VCI Home Video*

Nightmares — 1983
Horror
66329 99 mins C B, V P
Christina Raines, Emilio Estevez, Moon Zappa, Lance Henriksen, Richard Masur, Veronica Cartwright
An anthology of four horrific tales in which common, everyday occurrences take on the ingredients of nightmare.
MPAA:PG
Universal — *MCA Home Video*

Nightwing — 1979
Suspense
68263 103 mins C B, V P
Nick Mancuso, David Warner, Kathryn Harrold
A suspense drama about three people who risk their lives to exterminate a colony of plague-carrying vampire bats.
MPAA:PG
Columbia — *RCA/Columbia Pictures Home Video*

Nine Ages of Nakedness — 197?
Drama
59548 88 mins C B, V P

(For Explanation of codes, see USE GUIDE and KEY)

The story of a man whose ancestors have been plagued by a strange problem—beautiful, naked women who create carnal chaos.
George Harrison Marks — *Media Home Entertainment*

Nine Days a Queen   1934
Drama
03819   80 mins   B/W   B, V   P
John Mills, Sir Cedric Hardwicke, directed by Robert Stevenson
Historical epic set in England. Story of young Queen executed for treason after nine-day reign.
British — *Budget Video*

984—Prisoner of the Future   1984
Drama
76646   70 mins   C   B, V   P
Don Francks, Stephen Markle and Gail Dahms
A shocking, futuristic tale of human self-destruction.
William I Macadam — *VCL Home Video*

Nine Lives of Fritz the Cat, The   1974
Comedy/Fantasy
64880   77 mins   C   CED   P
Animated
The would-be cool cat of the 60's is fed up with his establishment life in the 70's, so he takes off into his other lives on a fantasy journey.
American International Pictures — *Vestron Video (disc only)*

9 to 5   1981
Comedy
49397   111 mins   C   B, V, LV, CED   P
Jane Fonda, Lily Tomlin, Dolly Parton, Dabney Coleman
Three office secretaries rebel against their male chauvinistic boss, eventually raising office efficiency to a new all-time high.
MPAA:PG
20th Century Fox — *CBS/Fox Video*

1980 "Boomer" Team Challenge   1980
Sports-Water
59399   60 mins   C   B, V   P
A full length show of the 1980 "Boomer" Team Challenge held at Sunset Beach, Hawaii. Part of Courier Productions' Collector Series.
Courier Productions — *Courier Productions*

1981 "Boomer" Team Challenge   1981
Sports-Water
59400   60 mins   C   B, V   P

A full length show of the 1981 "Boomer" Team Challenge held at Sunset Beach, Hawaii. Part of Courier Productions' Collector Series.
Courier Productions — *Courier Productions*

1984 Winter Olympics Highlights   1984
Sports-Winter
65625   60 mins   C   B, V   P
Experience the excitement as more than 1200 of the best athletes from over 44 countries compete to bring home the gold at the XIV Winter Olympic Games held in Sarajevo, Yugoslavia.
ABC Sports; Curt Gowdy Jr — *Embassy Home Entertainment*

1981 NBA Playoffs and Championship Series: The Dynasty Renewed   1981
Basketball
53411   58 mins   C   B, V   P
While the Celtics and 76ers tear up the Eastern Conference, the Lakers try to survive through Magic Johnson's knee injury in the West. Once the long season ends, the playoffs provide plenty of upsets, drama, and classic basketball.
NBA — *CBS/Fox Video*

1983 Whitewater Rodeos   1983
Boating
69900   40 mins   C   B, V   P
This program looks at the Idaho Whitewater Triple Crown and features slalom and freestyle kayak events from the Stanley, Salmon, and Banks rodeos.
Raccoon Productions — *Gravity Sports Films*

1982-83 WWPB Championship Series   1983
Sports-Minor
59412   60 mins   C   B, V   P
10   pgms
This coverage of the women's pro bowling championship includes 10 sixty-minute shows from 10 different sites, such as Reno, Las Vegas, Seattle, San Francisco, San Diego, Los Angeles, Hawaii and others.
Courier Productions — *Courier Productions*

1980 U.S. Pro Surfing Championship   1980
Sports-Water
59397   60 mins   C   B, V   P
This program features the events of the 1980 U.S. Pro Surfing Championship held at Malibu, California. Part of Courier Productions' Collector Series.
Courier Productions — *Courier Productions*

     (For Explanation of codes, see USE GUIDE and KEY)

1981 U.S. Pro Surfing Championship
1981
Sports-Water
59398   60 mins   C   B, V   P
This program features the events of the 1981 U.S. Pro Surfing Championship held at Malibu, California. Part of Courier Productions Collector Series.
Courier Productions — *Courier Productions*

1980 USSSA Men's World Series of Slo-Pitch Softball
1980
Sports-Minor
51998   110 mins   C   B, V, 3/4U, Q   P

Feature-length coverage of the playoff game of the 1980 USSSA Men's World Series of Slo-Pitch Softball.
TV Sports Scene — *TV Sports Scene*

1980 Women's National Volleyball Championship
1980
Sports-Minor
53643   120 mins   C   B, V, 3/4U, Q   P

USC and Stanford U. compete for the national title in these two final games in the 1980 playoff.
Crowd Pleaser Sports Prods — *TV Sports Scene*

1941
1979
Comedy
42939   120 mins   C   B, V, LV   P
John Belushi, Dan Ackroyd, Ned Beatty, directed by Steven Spielberg
Spielberg has directed the most expensive comedy of all time with a budget exceeding 35 million dollars. His depiction of Los Angeles in the chaotic days after the bombing of Pearl Harbor combines elements of fantasy and black humor.
MPAA:PG
A Team Prods — *MCA Home Video*

1990: The Bronx Warriors
1983
Adventure
65368   86 mins   C   B, V   P
Vic Morrow, Christopher Connelly, Fred Williamson
The controversial film that caused big waves in the big apple. "1990: The Bronx Warriors" is a brutal, heavy-metal journey into an urban hell.
MPAA:R
Fabrizio De Angelis — *Media Home Entertainment*

1978—The New York Yankees' Miracle Year
1978
Baseball
56879   100 mins   C   CED   P
Highlights of the Yankees' 1978 season, their greatest comeback ever, including a tense game vs. the Red Sox, and memorable moments from their defeat of the Dodgers in the World Series.
Major League Baseball — *RCA VideoDiscs*

1979 U.S. National Indian Rodeo
1979
Rodeos
53642   60 mins   C   B, V, 3/4U, Q   P

The first U.S. National Rodeo comprised of all American Indians, from all over the country, competing for the national titles.
North Country Prods — *TV Sports Scene*

1979 World Series and All-Star Highlights
1979
Baseball
44845   55 mins   C   B, V   P
The Pittsburgh Pirates come back from a three games to one deficit to defeat the Baltimore Orioles in seven games in the 1979 World Series. Willie Stargell's two-run homer in Game 7 puts the Pirates ahead to stay. In the 50th All-Star Game played that July, the National League continues to dominate the American League in a 7-6 victory.
Major League Baseball — *RCA/Columbia Pictures Home Video*

1976 Summer and Winter Olympic Games
1976
Sports
33783   112 mins   C   B, V, 3/4U   P
Bruce Jenner, Leon Spinks, Sugar Ray Leonard, Olga Korbut, Nadia Comenici
The Summer Olympics segment from Montreal is 84 minutes in length and features the Spinks brothers in boxing and decathlon champ Bruce Jenner. The Winter Olympics portion from Innsbruck, Austria runs 28 minutes in length and features American speed and figure skaters, skiers, bobsledders, and hockey players.
Unknown — *Sports World Cinema*

Nixon and Ford
1977
Biographical/Presidency-US
72514   59 mins   C   B, V, 3/4U   P
The lives of former Presidents Nixon and Ford are examined in political and private contexts. Includes Nixon's "You won't have Nixon to Kick Around Anymore" and "Kitchen Debate" speeches, plus home movies of Ford.
Unknown — *International Historic Films*

No Effort: Subliminal Weight Loss Video
1984
Physical fitness
72945   20 mins   C   B, V   P

Weight loss through subliminal suggestions is featured on this self-help tape.
Dick Sutphen — *VCI Home Video*

No Man's Range   1935
Western
08800   56 mins   B/W   B, V, 3/4U   P
Bob Steele
Cowhand poses as a renegade; sets out to dynamite the barrier.
Supreme — *Penguin Video*

No Way Back   1976
Adventure
47668   92 mins   C   B, V   P
Fred Williamson, Charles Woolf, Tracy Reed, Virginia Gregg, Don Cornelius, directed by Fred Williamson
Fred Williamson portrays Jesse Crowder, a man-for-hire expert with guns, fists, and martial arts in search of a woman's missing husband.
MPAA:R
Po Boy Productions — *Unicorn Video*

No World for Men   1982
Mountaineering
69906   16 mins   C   B, V   P
This is a documentation of Nicholas Jaeger's solo attempt on Lhotse-Shar.
Telluride Mountainfilm Festival '82: Best Mountaineering Film.
Unknown — *Gravity Sports Films*

Nobody's Perfekt   1979
Comedy
58957   95 mins   C   B, V   P
Gabe Kaplan, Robert Klein, Alex Karras, Susan Clark
Three psychiatric patients decide to fight City Hall.
Mort Engelberg — *RCA/Columbia Pictures Home Video*

Nocturna   1979
Satire
55216   82 mins   C   B, V   P
Yvonne DeCarlo, John Carradine
Hard times have fallen upon the house of Dracula and to help pay the taxes on the castle it has been converted to the Hotel Transylvania. In order to increase business and the blood supply at the hotel, Nocturna books a rock group to entertain the guests.
MPAA:R
Compass International Pictures — *Media Home Entertainment*

Nomads of the North   19??
Adventure
64353   50 mins   B/W   B, V   P
Lon Chaney, Lewis Stone

A Canadian fur trapper is framed by a ruthless trader who lusts after his girl. Silent with music score.
First National; James Oliver Curwood Productions — *Classic Video Cinema Collector's Club*

None But The Lonely   1944
Heart
Drama
00265   113 mins   B/W   B, V, 3/4U   P
Cary Grant, Ethel Barrymore, Barry Fitzgerald
In the days before World War II, a Cockney drifter travels through England in search of spiritual fulfillment.
Academy Awards '44: Best Supporting Actress (Barrymore).
RKO — *Nostalgia Merchant; King of Video*

Norma Rae   1979
Drama
37411   114 mins   C   B, V, CED   P
Sally Field, Ron Leibman, Beau Bridges
Sally Field portrays a textile worker who joins forces with a New York labor organizer to unionize a Southern mill.
Academy Awards '79: Best Actress (Field); Best Song ("It Goes Like It Goes").   MPAA:PG
20th Century Fox — *CBS/Fox Video*

Norman Conquests: 1980
Table Manners, The
Comedy
59701   108 mins   C   B, V   R, P
Tom Conti, Richard Briers, Penelope Keith
Part I of playwright Alan Ayckbourn's comic trilogy of love unfulfilled.
Thames Video — *THORN EMI Home Video*

Norman Conquests: 1980
Living Together, The
Comedy
59702   93 mins   C   B, V   R, P
Tom Conti
Part II concerns the happenings in the living room during Norman's disastrous weekend of unsuccessful seduction.
Thames Video — *THORN EMI Home Video*

Norman Conquests: 1980
Round and Round the
Garden, The
Comedy
59703   106 mins   C   B, V   R, P
Tom Conti
Part III concerns Norman's furtive appearance in the garden, which suggests that the weekend is going to misfire.
Thames Video — *THORN EMI Home Video*

Norman Loves Rose 1982
Romance
79215 90 mins C B, V P
A thirteen-year-old boy has a crush on his
brother's wife.
MPAA:R
Atlantic Releasing — *Vestron Video*

Norseman, The 1978
Drama
64361 90 mins C B, V, CED P
*Lee Majors, Cornel Wilde, Mel Ferrer,
Christopher Connelly*
The leader of a band of Norsemen sets sail for
the New World in search of his missing father.
MPAA:PG
American International — *Vestron Video*

**North American Sports
Car Championship** 198?
Automobiles-Racing
59520 48 mins C B, V P
The 1980 and 1981 North American Sports Car
Championship races from Ohio are seen in this
program.
John Mullin — *Diamond P Sports*

**North Avenue Irregulars,
The** 1979
Comedy
44295 99 mins C B, V R, P
*Edward Herrmann, Barbara Harris, Susan Clark,
Karen Valentine, Cloris Leachman, Ruth Buzzi*
Playing a new minister in a small community,
Edward Herrmann tries to halt the ripping-off of
church funds by organized criminals. To do so,
he organizes some female vigilantes from the
parish, all of whom are daffy bumblers who
seem incapable for the task.
MPAA:G
Walt Disney — *Walt Disney Home Video*

North by Northwest 1959
Suspense
39088 136 mins C B, V, CED P
*Cary Grant, Eva Marie Saint, James Mason, Leo
G. Carroll, directed by Alfred Hitchcock*
Quintessential Hitchcock—the tale of a self-
assured Madison Avenue executive who
inadvertently gets mixed up with international
spies—contains the famous scene of Grant and
Miss Saint dangling from the faces on Mount
Rushmore.
MGM — *MGM/UA Home Video*

North Dallas Forty 1979
Comedy-Drama
44593 117 mins C B, V, LV R, P
*Nick Nolte, Mac Davis, Charles Durning, Bo
Svenson, directed by Ted Kotcheff*
An aging football player realizes that the game
does not hold great illusions for him anymore.
Through a woman he meets he is drawn away
from the masculine violent world he is used to.
This creates tension between him and the
team's management. He must decide whether
to submit to management or quit. Based on the
novel by former Dallas Cowboy Peter Gent.
MPAA:R
Paramount, Frank Yablans — *Paramount
Home Video; RCA VideoDiscs*

North Star, The 1943
War-Drama
07037 82 mins B/W B, V P
*Dana Andrews, Walter Huston, Anne Baxter,
Farley Granger*
Gripping war tale of Nazi over-running of
eastern Russian city, with courageous villagers
fighting back.
RKO — *Budget Video; Discount Video Tapes;
Cable Films; Video Connection; Western Film &
Video Inc; Classic Video Cinema Collector's
Club*

**Northville Cemetery
Massacre** 1976
Adventure
47631 81 mins C B, V P
David Hyry, Craig Collicott, Jan Sisk
A father goes on a rampage of revenge after his
daughter is raped.
MPAA:R
Independent — *Paragon Video Productions*

Northwest Frontier 1959
Adventure
59839 129 mins C B, V P
*Lauren Bacall, Herbert Lom, Kenneth More,
directed by J. Lee Thompson*
A turn-of-the century adventure set in India
about the courageous attempt to save the
country from rebellion, and the infant prince
from assassination.
Earl St John — *Embassy Home Entertainment*

Northwest Trail 1946
Crime-Drama
03988 75 mins C B, V P
John Litel, Bob Steele, Joan Woodbury
Mounted policeman covers the wilderness in
search of a killer.
Screen Guild; Lippert — *Budget Video; Video
Connection; Discount Video Tapes*

Nosferatu 1922
Horror
08704 63 mins B/W B, V, 3/4U P
*Max vonSchreck, Alexander Cranach, Gustav
vonWangenheim, directed by F. W. Murnau*
First film version of Bram Stoker's novel
"Dracula." (Silent, musical score added.)
Janus Films; German — *Penguin Video;
Blackhawk Films; Video Yesteryear; Sheik
Video; Discount Video Tapes; Western Film &*

Video Inc; Classic Video Cinema Collector's Club

Nostalgia World War II Video Library #1   1945
World War II/Propaganda
69573   46 mins   B, V, FO   P
These three War Department shorts were all produced during the last year of World War II and served to exhort viewers to keep up the pace of war work and not slack off. Titles are "Battle Wreckage," "The War Speeds Up" and "It Can't Last."
US War Department — *Video Yesteryear*

Nothing Personal   1980
Comedy/Romance
64887   96 mins   C   B, V, CED   P
Donald Sutherland, Suzanne Somers
A tweedy college professor engages an eager young lawyer to take up his case.
MPAA:PG
American International Pictures; Filmways — *Vestron Video*

Nothing Sacred   1937
Comedy
08582   75 mins   C   B, V, 3/4U   P
Fredric March, Carole Lombard, Walter Connolly, directed by William Wellman
A girl with a short time to live is given a gay time for two weeks, but it's all a publicity hoax. Based on James Street's novel.
David O Selznick — *Penguin Video; Video Yesteryear; Discount Video Tapes; VCII; Cable Films; Video Connection; Budget Video; Classic Video Cinema Collector's Club*

Notorious   1946
Suspense/Drama
46213   101 mins   B/W   B, V, LV, CED   P
Cary Grant, Ingrid Bergman, Claude Rains, Louis Calhern, Madame Konstantin, directed by Alfred Hitchcock.
A government agent and a girl whose father was convicted of treason undertake a dangerous mission to Brazil.
Selznick — *CBS/Fox Video*

Novio Para Dos Hermanas, Un (One Boyfriend for Two Sisters)   197?
Musical
73584   30 mins   C   B, V   P
Sara Garcia, Pili and Mili, Angel Carasa Fernando Lujan
This film tells what happens when two sisters fall in love with the same man and the conflicts that arise from it.
KNBC — *Aztec Cinevideo*

Now and Forever   1982
Drama
65118   93 mins   C   B, V, LV, CED   P
Cheryl Ladd, Robert Coleby
A young wife's life is shattered when her husband is wrongly accused and convicted of rape. After he is sent to prison, she begins drinking and taking drugs.
MPAA:R
Interplanetary Pictures — *MCA Home Video*

Now It Can Be Told/U-Boat Am Feind   1945
World War II
53665   32 mins   B/W   B, V, 3/4U   P
Two films: "Now It Can Be Told," an official US Navy film showing the German sub U-505 being boarded and captured on June 4th, 1944. "U-Boat Am Feind," an original Germany documentary about life aboard a U-Boat in the North Atlantic. (In German.)
US Navy; Germany — *International Historic Films*

Now, Voyager   1942
Drama
58836   117 mins   B/W   CED   P
Bette Davis, Gladys Cooper, Claude Rains, Paul Henreid, Bonita Granville
A lonely spinster is transformed into a vibrant young woman by her psychiatrist, and involves herself in an ill-fated affair with a suave continental.
Academy Awards '42: Best Scoring of a Comedy or Drama (Max Steiner).
Warner Bros — *RCA VideoDiscs*

Now You See It   1982
Magic/Games
59415   60 mins   C   B, V   P
Magician Paul Daniels demonstrates a number of simple tricks and explains the secret of each.
Chrysalis; Peter Wagg — *Chrysalis Visual Programming*

Nowhere to Hide   1977
Adventure
65304   74 mins   C   B, V   P
Lee Van Cleef
A United States Marshal is assigned to protect a mob hit-man scheduled to testify for the prosecution against his former chieftain.
VSC Enterprises — *U.S.A. Home Video*

Nuclear Defense At Sea   1967
Nuclear warfare/Armed Forces-US
72501   20 mins   C   B, V, 3/4U   P
A sobering study of the measures US surface ships would take to survive a nuclear attack.
US Government — *International Historic Films*

Nudie Classics   194?
Variety
57287   55 mins   B/W   B, V   P
Seven racy shorts from the 1930's and 1940's.
Includes "Why Girls Walk Home," "Dormitory
Secrets," "Uncle Si and the Sirens," "The
Follies," "Nude Frolics," "Buried Treasure,"
and "Little Annie."
Unknown — *Video Dimensions*

Nuit de Varennes, La   1983
Comedy-Drama
69617   133 mins   C   B, V   P
*Marcello Mastroianni, Harvey Keitel, Jean-Louis
Barrault, Hanna Schygulla, Jean-Claude Brialy*
This historical romp is based on an actual
chapter in French history when Louis XVI and
Marie Antoinette fled from Paris to Varennes. In
French with English subtitles.
MPAA:R
Renzo Rossellini; Opera Film; Gaumont
FR3 — *RCA/Columbia Pictures Home Video*

Number Seventeen   1932
Mystery
01747   64 mins   B/W   B, V   P
*Leon M. Lion, Anne Grey, John Stuart, directed
by Alfred Hitchcock*
Female jewel thief has change of heart and
helps detective foil an enemy gang's escape to
France.
British — *Budget Video; Cable Films; Video
Yesteryear; Western Film & Video Inc*

Nuremberg Trials, The   1946
History-Modern
08905   90 mins   B/W   B, V, 3/4U   P
The trials are shown in great detail, each
prosecutor speaking in his native tongue. Actual
newsreel footage. Narrated in English.
Russia — *Penguin Video*

Nuremberg War Trials   194?
World War II
58602   11 mins   B/W   B, V   P, T
An overview of Movietone news coverage of the
historic trials of Nazi war criminals.
Movietone — *Blackhawk Films*

Nutcracker, The   1977
Dance
63115   78 mins   C   B, V, CED   P
Mikhail Baryshnikov, Gelsey Kirkland
A lavish production of Tschaikovsky's famous
ballet, choreographed and danced by Mikhail
Baryshnikov. In stereo.
Jodav Productions; Kroyt-Brandt
Productions — *MGM/UA Home Video*

Nutcracker, The   1982
Dance
60573   79 mins   C   LV   P
*American Ballet Theatre, Gelsey Kirkland,
Alexander Minz, National Philharmonic*
Tchaikovsky's Christmas ballet under the
direction of Mikhail Baryshnikov comes alive in
this presentation. Stereo.
Herman Krawitz; Yanna Kroyt
Brandt — *Pioneer Artists*

Nutcracker Fantasy   1979
Fairy tales
65319   ? mins   C   B, V   P
*Animated, voices of Melissa Gilbert, Roddy
McDowell, narrated by Michele Lee*
An heroic mouse must rescue a beautiful
sleeping princess from wicked mice. This
delightful fairy tale is set to the music of
Tchaikovsky.
MPAA:G
Walt DeFaria; Mark L Rosen; Arthur
Tomioka — *RCA/Columbia Pictures Home
Video*

Nutcracker, The   1978
Dance
44939   86 mins   C   B, V, CED   P
*Ekaterina Maximova, Vladimir Vasiliev, Nadia
Pavlova and the Bolshoi Corps de Ballet,
directed by Elena Maceret*
Tchaikovsky's famous Christmastime ballet is
performed by the Bolshoi Ballet.
MGM — *CBS/Fox Video*

Nutty Professor, The   1963
Comedy
66411   107 mins   C   B, V   R, P
*Jerry Lewis, Stella Stevens, Howard Morris,
Kathleen Freeman, directed by Jerry Lewis*
A mild-mannered chemistry professor creates a
potion that turns him into a suave, debonair,
playboy-type with an irresistable attraction to
women.
Paramount; Jerry Lewis — *Paramount Home
Video*

Nymphing with Gary   1983
Borger
Fishing
65147   30 mins   C   B, V   P
Gary Borger
This program from the "Sportsman's Video
Collection" demonstrates the best techniques
for catching trout sub-surface.
Gary Borger — *Leisure Time Products
Project/3M*

Nyoka and the Tigerman   1942
Adventure/Serials
44792   250 mins   B/W   B, V, 3/4U   P
Kay Aldridge, Clayton Moore
The adventures of the jungle queen Nyoka and
her rival Vultura in their search for the lost
tablets of Hippocrates. In 15 episodes.

Republic — *Video Connection*

O

O Lucky Man   **1973**
Drama
68237   1/5 mins   C   B, V   R, P
A story of the rags-to-riches rise and fall of a modern-day man.
MPAA:R
Warner Bros — *Warner Home Video*

Oath of Vengeance   **1944**
Western
54185   50 mins   B/W   B, V   P
Buster Crabbe, Al "Fuzzy" St. John
Billy the Kid rides the West once more.
Producers Releasing Corp — *Video Connection*

Obsession   **1976**
Suspense
65098   98 mins   C   B, V   P
Cliff Robertson, Genevieve Bujold, John Lithgow, directed by Brian DePalma
A rich, lonely businessman meets a mysterious young girl in Italy who is the mirror image of his late wife. Music by Bernard Herrmann.
MPAA:PG
Columbia Pictures — *RCA/Columbia Pictures Home Video*

Occurrence at Owl Creek Bridge, An   **1962**
Literature/Drama
49166   27 mins   B/W   B, V   P
A man is about to be hanged when the rope snaps, and he is able to swim to safety. He entertains thoughts of his family while making his way home. Suddenly, his new-found sweetness of life comes to a halt. Based on a short story by Ambrose Bierce. Telecast on "The Twilight Zone" in 1963.
Cannes Film Festival: Blue Ribbon; American Film Festival: First Prize.
Marcel Ichac, Paul de Roubaix — *Festival Films; Sheik Video*

Ocean Waves   **1983**
Video
65545   60 mins   C   B, V   P
This program provides an hour of ocean waves—whitecaps, breakers, crashing water—to create a relaxed atmosphere.
Video Naturals — *Video Naturals*

Ocean's 11   **1960**
Comedy
63449   144 mins   C   B, V   R, P
Frank Sinatra, Dean Martin, Sammy Davis Jr., Angie Dickenson, Peter Lawford, directed by Lewis Milestone
A gang of friends make plans to rob a Las Vegas casino. Part of the "A Night at the Movies" series, this tape simulates a 1960 movie evening, with a Bugs Bunny cartoon, "Person to Bunny," a newsreel and coming attractions for "The Sundowners" and "Sunrise at Campobello."
Warner Bros — *Warner Home Video*

Octagon, The   **1980**
Martial arts/Suspense
64232   103 mins   C   B, V   P
Chuck Norris, Karen Carlson, Lee Van Cleef, Kim Lankford
A retired martial arts champion becomes involved in perilous international intrigue.
MPAA:R
American Cinema Releasing — *Media Home Entertainment*

Octopussy   **1983**
Adventure
65414   130 mins   C   B, V, LV, CED   P
Roger Moore, Maud Adams, Louis Jourdan, Kristina Wayborn, Kabir Bedi
James Bond is sent on a mission to prevent a crazed Russian general from launching a nuclear attack against NATO forces in Europe.
MPAA:PG
Albert R Broccoli — *CBS/Fox Video*

Odd Angry Shot   **1979**
War-Drama
72227   90 mins   C   B, V   P
A drama that ironically portrays the ravages of war in Australia.
Atlantic TV — *Vestron Video*

Odd Couple, The   **1968**
Comedy
38590   106 mins   C   B, V, LV   R, P
Jack Lemmon, Walter Matthau, directed by Gene Saks
Neil Simon's long-running Broadway comedy about two divorced men who live together, but can't stand each other's habits. Basis for the recent TV series.
MPAA:G
Paramount — *Paramount Home Video; RCA VideoDiscs*

Odd Job, The   **1978**
Comedy
73034   100 mins   C   B, V   P
Graham Chapman
A man unable to kill himself hires an "odd job" man to do it for him.
Atlantic Releasing — *Vestron Video*

Ode to Billy Joe — 1976
Drama/Romance
51968   106 mins   C   B, V   R, P
Robby Benson, Glynnis O'Connor, Joan Hotchkis, Sandy McPeak, James Best
The relationship of two star-crossed lovers ends in tragedy at the Tallahatchie Bridge.
MPAA:PG
Warner Bros — *Warner Home Video*

Odyssey of the Pacific — 1982
Adventure
60588   82 mins   C   B, V   P
Mickey Rooney, Monique Mercure
While on a romp through the woods, a young Cambodian refugee and his siblings help an old railroad man rejuvenate a locomotive.
Cine Pacific Inc — *MCA Home Video*

Of Cooks and Kung-Fu — 198?
Martial arts
64961   90 mins   C   B, V   P
Jacky Chen, Chia Kai, Lee Kuen
A martial arts culinary adventure.
Dragon Lady Productions — *Unicorn Video*

Of Human Bondage — 1935
Drama
11396   84 mins   B/W   B, V, FO   P
Leslie Howard, Bette Davis
The first movie version of Somerset Maugham's classic novel in which a young medical student with a club foot falls in love with a promiscuous cockney waitress.
RKO — *Video Yesteryear; King of Video; Discount Video Tapes; Sheik Video; Cable Films; Video Connection; Budget Video; Western Film & Video Inc; Cinema Concepts*

Of Unknown Origin — 1983
Horror
69801   90 mins   C   B, V   R, P
Peter Weller, Jennifer Dale, Lawrence Dane, Kenneth Welsh, Louis Del Grande, Shannon Tweed
A Manhattan brownstone is the battleground in a terror-tinged duel of survival between an upwardly mobile young executive and a destructive rodent intruder.
MPAA:R
Claude Heroux — *Warner Home Video*

Off Road Action — 1982
Motorcycles
66248   64 mins   C   B, V   P
Off-road motorcycles including European sidecar action, the world's top trials riders, and more are included on this cassette.
CH Wood — *Motor Cycle Video*

Off the Edge — 1977
Adventure/Sports
44816   77 mins   C   B, V, 3/4U   P
Mike Firth, Jeff Campbell, Blair Trenholm, directed by Mike Firth
Three men, all sharing the deep desire to be free and to be part of the natural world around them, undertake an adventurous journey into the Southern Alps to make a film capturing both the beauty and the danger of this virgin terrain. The real challenge comes from skiing and hangliding over and through these mountains while actually shooting this marvelous adventure.
Pentacle Films — *Sports World Cinema*

Office Girls — 1973
Comedy
69015   86 mins   C   B, V   P
A candid expose of the sexual activities that occur in the office.
MPAA:R
International Producers Corp — *Imperial Video Corp*

Officer and a Gentleman, An — 1982
Drama
64022   126 mins   C   B, V, LV   R, P
Richard Gere, Debra Winger, Louis Gossett Jr.
A young man enters Officer Candidate School to become a Navy pilot, and in 13 torturous weeks he learns the importance of discipline, love and friendship.
MPAA:R
Paramount; Lorimar — *Paramount Home Video; RCA VideoDiscs*

Official War Films — 1944
World War II
53680   40 mins   B/W   B, V, 3/4U   P
Includes "RAF 8th Airforce from Britain," "U.S. Marines of New Britain," "Activities on Leyte and Mendoro," and other short films.
Unknown — *International Historic Films*

Oh Alfie — 1975
Comedy-Drama
65307   99 mins   C   B, V   P
Joan Collins, Alan Price, Jill Townsend
In every man's life, there comes a time to settle down... but never when you're having as much fun as Alfie!
A D Associates Ltd — *Monterey Home Video*

Oh! Calcutta! — 1972
Musical
07863   105 mins   C   B, V   P
Bill Macy, Mark Dempsey, Raina Barrett
Nudity and nuttiness are the theme for this zany erotic musical.
Bihar Film — *VidAmerica*

Oh, God   1977
Comedy
38952   104 mins   C   B, V   R, P
George Burns, John Denver, Paul Sorvino,
directed by Carl Reiner
When God, in the person of George Burns,
appoints a young supermarket assistant
manager to spread his word, unexpected
situations develop.
MPAA:PG
Warner Bros — *Warner Home Video; RCA*
VideoDiscs

Oh God, Book II   1980
Comedy
54806   94 mins   C   B, V   R, P
George Burns, Suzanne Pleshette, David
Birney, Louanne, John Louie, Howard Duff,
directed by Gilbert Cates
God decides to enlist a child to remind people
that He is still around. The young girl sets out to
concoct a slogan which will make God a
household name. She recruits her classmates to
spread her "Think God" slogan via posters and
graffiti. This leads to her suspension from
school, and when she is seen talking to God (he
is invisible to everyone but her) the child is sent
to psychiatrists.
MPAA:PG
Warner Bros — *Warner Home Video*

O'Hara's Wife   1982
Drama
64878   87 mins   C   B, V   P
Ed Asner, Mariette Hartley, Jodie Foster
A loving wife continues to care for her family
even after her untimely death.
Davis/Panzer — *Vestron Video*

Oklahoma!   1955
Musical
56752   140 mins   C   B, V, CED   P
Gordon MacRae, Shirley Jones, Rod Steiger,
Gloria Grahame, Eddie Albert, Charlotte
Greenwood, directed by Fred Zinnemann
Based on the Rodgers and Hammerstein
Broadway hit, wherein a young cowboy's girl
goes to a dance with a hired hand, realizes she
loves the cowboy, and the hired hand threatens
to kill them both. Songs include, "Oh, What a
Beautiful Mornin," "The Surrey with the Fringe
on Top," and "Oklahoma!" Dances
choreographed by Agnes de Mille.
Academy Awards '55: Best Scoring Musical;
Best Sound Recording.
Arthur Hornblow Jr, Magna Todd
AO — *CBS/Fox Video*

Olaf Weighorst: Painter   1978
of the American West
Artists
07344   54 mins   C   B, V, 3/4U   P
Olaf Weighorst, John Wayne, Howard Hawks

Presents the life story and some of the works of
renowned western painter Olaf Weighorst.
Olaf and Roy Weighorst — *Nostalgia Merchant*

Old Barn Dance, The   1938
Western
14400   54 mins   B/W   B, V   P
Gene Autry
Autry sells horses as a sideline until competitor
puts out tractors.
Republic — *Video Connection*

Old Boyfriends   1979
Drama
37420   103 mins   C   B, V, CED   P
Talia Shire, Richard Jordan, John Belushi, Keith
Carradine
A young woman searches for her true self
through the lost loves of her past.
MPAA:R
Avco Embassy — *Embassy Home*
Entertainment

Old Corral, The   1936
Western
69572   54 mins   B/W   B, V, FO   P
Gene Autry, Roy Rogers, Smiley Burnette, The
Sons of the Pioneers
Sheriff Gene Autry romances a young woman
who has come out West to escape a vicious
Chicago mobster.
Republic — *Video Yesteryear*

Old Corral, The   1937
Western
05584   60 mins   B/W   B, V   P
Gene Autry, Smiley Burnette, Hope Manning,
Lon Chaney, Jr.
Eastern racketeers pursue a witness to a killing
to a small western town, where Gene Autry and
friends round them up.
Republic — *Sheik Video; Penguin Video*

Old Leather   1980
Football
45122   30 mins   C   B, V, FO   R, P
Narrated by John Facenda
A study of the men who gave life to pro football.
Red Grange, Johnny Blood, George Halas and
others are seen as they were in the beginning
and as they are today.
NFL Films — *NFL Films Video*

Old Rock, Champ of the   197?
Chesapeake
Fishing
33746   30 mins   C   B, V, 3/4U,   P
                                        Q
Historic Chesapeake Bay is the setting for this
story about outsmarting one of the East Coast's
best sport fish—striped bass.

TV Sports Scene — *TV Sports Scene*

Monogram; I E Chadwick — *Budget Video*

Old Soldier, The   194?
World War II
58603   11 mins   B/W   B, V   P, T
General Douglas MacArthur
This compilation of Movietone newsreel footage offers scenes from the Battle of Manila, and a mini-documentary of MacArthur's life.
Movietone — *Blackhawk Films*

Old Testament I   1980
Bible
55024   120 mins   C   B, V   P
Outstanding characters and events of the Old Testament are dramatized: Abraham: Man of Faith; Jacob: Bearer of the Promise; Joseph: the Young Man; Moses: Called by God; Joshua: the Conqueror; Gideon: the Liberator.
Family Films — *Vanguard Video*

Old Testament II   1980
Bible
55025   120 mins   C   B, V   P
Outstanding characters and events of the Old Testament are dramatized: Ruth: A Faithful Woman; Samuel: A Dedicated Man; David: A Young Hero; David: King of Israel; Solomon: A Man of Wisdom; Elijah: A Fearless Prophet.
Family Films — *Vanguard Video*

Old Yeller   1957
Drama/Adventure
53797   83 mins   C   B, V, LV   R, P
Dorothy McGuire, Fess Parker, Tommy Kirk, Kevin Corcoran, Jeff York, Beverly Washburn, Chuck Connors, directed by Robert Stevenson
A stray dog is befriended by a family of farmers in 1869 Texas. He saves the youngest boy's life, but sacrifices his in the process.
Walt Disney — *Walt Disney Home Video; RCA VideoDiscs*

Oldest Living Graduate   1982
Theater/Drama
72196   75 mins   C   B, V   R, P
Henry Fonda
In his last stage role, Henry Fonda is the oldest graduate of a Texas military school. He comes into conflict with his son when he refuses to give up a piece of land he owns for commercial purposes.
Unknown — *VCII*

Oliver Twist   1933
Drama
03821   70 mins   B/W   B, V   P
Dickie Moore, Irving Pichel, directed by William J. Cowan
Dickens' classic of ill-treated London boy involved with youthful gang.

Oliver Twist   1922
Drama
63983   77 mins   B/W   B, V   P, T
Jackie Coogan, Lon Chaney, Gladys Brockwell, George Siegmann, Esther Ralston, directed by Frank Lloyd
This version of the Dickens classic is a vehicle for young Jackie Coogan. As orphan Oliver Twist, he is subjected to many frightening incidents before finding love and someone to care for him.
Sol Lesser — *Blackhawk Films; Classic Video Cinema Collector's Club*

Oliver Twist   197?
Cartoons/Literature-English
Closed Captioned
75620   72 mins   C   B, V   P
Animated
This is an animated version of the classic tale by Charles Dickens.
WBTV Canada — *Children's Video Library*

Oliver Twist   1982
Drama/Cartoons
Closed Captioned
73044   72 mins   C   B, V   P
Based upon the Dickens classic where young Oliver Twist is left in an orphanage to defend himself until he must join a criminal gang.
Burbank Films — *Vestron Video*

Olivia   1980
Music-Performance
48540   60 mins   C   LV   P
Olivia Newton-John, Andy Gibb, ABBA
Olivia hosts this musical television special, featuring such hits as "Hopelessly Devoted to You," "Have You Ever Been Mellow," and "Please Mr. Please." Olivia, Andy, and ABBA perform a medley of classic rock songs.
Unknown — *MCA Home Video*

Olivia   1983
Drama
64868   90 mins   C   B, V   R, P
Suzanna Love, Robert Walker, Jeff Winchester, directed by Ulli Lommel
An abused housewife moonlights as a prostitute and begins killing her customers. She falls in love with an American businessman and flees to America when her husband finds out about the affair. Revenge and murder result.
Ulli Lommel — *VCII*

Olivia in Concert   1983
Music-Performance
64793   78 mins   C   B, V, LV,   P
                                 CED

Directed by Brian Grant, music produced by John Farrar
Filmed during Olivia's first live shows in five years, the concert reflects the popular singer's transformation from a sweet, romantic songstress to a strong, aggressive charmer and entertainer. In stereo.
Olivia Newton-John; Christine Smith — MCA Home Video

Olivia—Physical　　　　　　1981
Music-Performance
59034　　54 mins　　C　　B, V, LV,　　　P
　　　　　　　　　　　　　CED
Olivia Newton-John
Olivia Newton-John performs favorites, modern funk, and earthy ballads in this video album. Songs include; "Magic," "Physical," "A Little More Love," "Make a Move On Me," and "Hopelessly Devoted." In stereo on VHS and Disc.
Scott Millaney — MCA Home Video

Olvidados, Los　　　　　　　1951
Drama
57336　81 mins　B/W　　　B, V　　　　P
Alfonso Mejia, Roberto Cobo, directed by Luis Bunuel
A good boy is contaminated by young thugs in Mexico City's slums, resulting in the death of the boy and his tormentor. In Spanish with English subtitles.
SP
Mayer Kingsley; Ultramar — Budget Video; Sheik Video; Discount Video Tapes

---

Olympia: Parts I and II　　　　1936
Sports/Documentary
20417　215 mins　B/W　　　B, V　　　　P
Directed by Leni Riefenstahl
Documentary coverage of the 1936 Olympics, held in Berlin. "Olympia" is said to be the finest existing record of the Olympic Games and their athletes. Part I and II are also available individually, as are two major sequences: the Marathon sequence and the Diving sequence.
Leni Riefenstahl — Embassy Home Entertainment; Penguin Video; Video Yesteryear; International Historic Films; Sheik Video; Western Film & Video Inc

---

Omen, The　　　　　　　　1976
Horror
41079　　111 mins　　C　　B, V, LV,　　P
　　　　　　　　　　　　　CED
Gregory Peck, Lee Remick, Billie Whitelaw, David Warner, directed Richard Donner
"The Omen" is an effective horror piece on the coming of the "anti-Christ," personified in a young boy.
MPAA:R　EL, SP
20th Century Fox — CBS/Fox Video

On a Clear Day You Can　　　1970
See Forever
Romance/Musical
65618　　129 mins　　C　　B, V, LV,　　R, P
　　　　　　　　　　　　　CED
Barbra Streisand, Yves Montand, Bob Newhart, Jack Nicholson
A psychiatric hypnotist helps a girl to stop smoking, and finds that in trances she remembers previous incarnations.
Paramount Pictures — Paramount Home Video

On Any Sunday II　　　　　1981
Motorcycles
60410　　89 mins　　C　　B, V　　　　P
Bruce Penhall, Kenny Roberts, Brad Lackey, Bob Hannah
World Champion motorcycle driver Bruce Penhall is among those profiled in this motorcyclist's cinematic delight, featuring high-powered cycles giving their all.
MPAA:PG
4 Way Motorsports — Monterey Home Video

On Approval　　　　　　　1944
Comedy
00415　80 mins　B/W　　　B, V　　　　P
Clive Brooks, Beatrice Lillie
Two couples spend a holiday on a deserted isle to test their love.
Sydney Box; British — Budget Video; Sheik Video; Movie Buff Video; Classic Video Cinema Collector's Club

---

On Broadway Tonight　　　　1964
Variety
56910　52 mins　B/W　　B, V, FO　　P
Hosted by Rudy Vallee, Robert Horton
A talent show featuring professional performers looking for the big break—singers, comedians, impressionists, and musicians.
CBS — Video Yesteryear

On Golden Pond　　　　　　1981
Drama
59430　109 mins　C　B, V, LV　　　P
Henry Fonda, Jane Fonda, Katharine Hepburn, Dabney Coleman, Doug McKeon, directed by Mark Rydell
The story of three generations coming to grips with life, mortality and their own emotional distance, set at a summer home in New England.
Academy Awards '81: Best Actor (Fonda); Best Actress (Hepburn); Best Screenplay Adaptation (Ernest Thompson).　MPAA:PG
ITC; IPC Films — CBS/Fox Video; RCA VideoDiscs

On Her Majesty's Secret　　　1969
Service
Adventure
64834　　140 mins　　C　　CED　　　　P

George Lazenby, Diana Rigg, Telly Savalas
James Bond marries and he and his future wife must squelch deadly SPECTRE chief Blofeld who is about to unleash a lethal toxin.
MPAA:PG
United Artists — *RCA VideoDiscs*

On Her Majesty's Secret Service 1969
Adventure
65405   142 mins   C   B, V   P
George Lazenby, Diana Rigg, Telly Savalas
In this sixth 007 cinematic adventure, James Bond is charged with no less a task than saving the human race from a deadly plague.
United Artists — *CBS/Fox Video*

On Target 1967
Vietnam War
53703   21 mins   C   B, V, 3/4U   P
A documentary about USMC F-4's, flying a mission out of Danang, South Vietnam.
Unknown — *International Historic Films*

On the Air Live with Captain Midnight 197?
Comedy
60227   90 mins   C   B, V   P
Ziggy starts a private radio station just for the fun of it, and it becomes the hottest in Los Angeles.
Sebastian Films — *Independent United Distributors*

On the Beach 1959
Drama/Science fiction
59337   133 mins   B/W   B, V, CED   P
Gregory Peck, Anthony Perkins, Donna Anderson, Ava Gardner, Fred Astaire, directed by Stanley Kramer
Based on the novel by Nevil Shute. After most of the world has been destroyed by atomic waste, an American submarine sets out to investigate.
Stanley Kramer — *CBS/Fox Video*

On the Night Stage 1915
Western
48722   50 mins   B/W   B, V, 3/4U   P
William S. Hart, Rhea Mitchell, Robert Edeson
A gun-slinging cowboy opposes a new preacher until his dance-hall girlfriend makes him "see the light." Silent.
Unknown — *Penguin Video*

On the Night Stage/Wagon Tracks 1919
Western
64339   110 mins   B/W   B, V   P
William S. Hart

Two exciting William S. Hart western features are combined on this tape. Silent with musical score.
William S. Hart Productions — *Classic Video Cinema Collector's Club*

On the Old Spanish Trail 1947
Western
14228   56 mins   B/W   B, V   P
Roy Rogers, Jane Frazee, Andy Devine, Tito Guizar
Roy Rogers becomes a singing cowboy with a traveling tent show in order to pay off a note signed by the sons of the Pioneers.
Republic — *Video Connection*

On the Right Track 1981
Comedy
58852   98 mins   C   B, V   P
Gary Coleman, Lisa Eilbacher
A young orphan living in Chicago's Union Station has the gift of being able to pick winning race horses.
MPAA:PG
20th Century Fox — *CBS/Fox Video*

On the Road to Happiness/The Good Life 1978
Parades and festivals
64010   60 mins   C   B, V   P
Highlights of the 1977 and 1978 Tournament of Roses Parades in Pasadena are narrated by Grand Marshals Roy Rogers and Dale Evans ('77) and Gerald Ford ('78).
Tournament Video Tapes — *Tournament Video Tapes*

On the Town 1949
Musical
47055   98 mins   C   B, V, CED   P
Gene Kelly, Frank Sinatra, Vera Ellen, Ann Miller, Betty Garrett, directed by Gene Kelly and Stanley Donen
Three sailors find romance on a one-day leave in New York City. Based on the successful Broadway musical, with a score composed by Leonard Bernstein, Betty Comden, and Adolph Green. Additional songs by Roger Edens.
Academy Awards '49: Best Scoring, Musical (Roger Edens and Lennie Hayton).
MGM — *MGM/UA Home Video*

On Top of Old Smoky 1953
Western
66441   59 mins   B/W   B, V   P, T
Gene Autry, Smiley Burnette, Gail Davis, Sheila Ryan
Singing ranger Gene is mistaken for a real Texas Ranger, who is a marked man.
Columbia — *Blackhawk Films*

Once in Paris   1984
Drama
76022   100 mins   C   B, V   P
Wayne Rogers, Gayle Hunnicutt, Jean Lenoir
A bittersweet romance that is at once subtle and
believable, sophisticated and humorous about
three people who meet in Paris.
MPAA:PG
Frank D Gilroy — *Embassy Home
Entertainment*

**Once Upon a Brothers
Grimm**   1977
Fantasy
33583   102 mins   C   B, V   P
*Dean Jones, Paul Sand, Cleavon Little, Ruth
Buzzi, Chita Rivera, Teri Garr*
An original musical fantasy in which the
Brothers Grimm meet a succession of their most
famous storybook characters, including Hansel
and Gretel, the Gingerbread Lady, Little Red
Riding Hood, and Rumpelstiltskin.
Rothman-Wohl Productions; CBS — *VCI Home
Video*

Once Upon a Honeymoon   1942
Comedy
10039 115 mins B/W   B, V   P, T
Ginger Rogers, Cary Grant, Walter Slezak
American reporter predicts Hitler's movements
by trailing Gestapo agents. Reporter and agents
then attempt to outwit Germans.
RKO; Leo McCarey — *Blackhawk Films*

Once Upon a Time   1976
Cartoons/Fantasy
50962   83 mins   C   B, V   R, P
Animated
A pretty girl, her puppy, a charming prince, and a
grinch combine for a magical, wondrous
animated fantasy.
MPAA:G
N W Russo; G G Communications — *Video
Gems*

Once Upon the Wabash   1955
Trains
51436   40 mins   B/W   B, V   P
Wabash passenger service of the 1950's is
featured in this program.
Wabash Railroad — *Interurban Films*

One and Only, The   1978
Comedy
58714   98 mins   C   B, V   R, P
*Henry Winkler, Kim Darby, Gene Saks, William
Daniels, Harold Gould, Herve Villechaize,
directed by Carl Reiner*
An egotistical young man enters the world of
professional wrestling.
MPAA:PG

Paramount; First Artists — *Paramount Home
Video*

**One and Only Genuine   1968
Original Family Band, The**
Musical
55571   110 mins   C   B, V, LV   R, P
*Walter Brennan, Buddy Ebsen, Lesley Ann
Warren, John Davidson, Kurt Russell, Wally
Cox, Richard Deacon, Janet Blair*
During the 1888 presidential campaigns of
Grover Cleveland and Benjamin Harrison, old
Grandpa Bower organizes his son, daughter-in-
law, and eight grandchildren into a band, hoping
to perform at the convention.
Walt Disney — *Walt Disney Home Video*

One Armed Executioner   1983
Adventure
66296   90 mins   C   B, V   P
Franco Guerrero, Jody Kay
An Interpol agent seeks revenge on his wife's
murderers.
MPAA:R
Bobby Suarez — *Paragon Video Productions*

One Body Too Many   1944
Comedy
01701   75 mins   B/W   B, V   P
*Jack Haley Sr., Jean Parker, Bela Lugosi,
directed by Frank McDonald*
Mystery spoof with wacky insurance salesman
who's mistaken for a detective. Ends up in
comedy of errors.
Paramount; Pine Thomas — *Budget Video;
Discount Video Tapes; Video Connection*

One Dark Night   1982
Horror
65748   94 mins   C   B, V   R, P
Two high school girls plan an initiation rite for
one of their friends who is determined to shed
her "goody-goody" image.
MPAA:R
Michael Schroeder — *THORN EMI Home
Video*

One Down Two to Go   1983
Adventure
65355   84 mins   C   B, V   P
*Jim Brown, Fred Williamson, Jim Kelly, Richard
Roundtree*
When the mob is discovered to be rigging a
championship karate bout, two dynamic expert
fighters join in a climactic battle against the
hoods.
MPAA:R
Fred Williamson — *Media Home Entertainment*

One-Eyed Jacks   1961
Western
53935   141 mins   C   B, V   R, P

Marlon Brando, Karl Malden, Katy Jurado, Elisha Cook, Slim Pickens, Ben Johnson, directed by Marlon Brando
Upon completing a prison term, an outlaw goes seeking an old friend who betrayed him, and finds he has become the sheriff.
Paramount — *Paramount Home Video*

One Flew Over the Cuckoo's Nest 1975
Drama
58882   129 mins   C   B, V   R, P
Jack Nicholson, Louise Fletcher, Brad Dourif, William Redfield, Scatman Crothers, directed by Milos Forman
Ken Kesey's novel about Randall P. McMurphy, the leader of a group ofinmates of a mental ward and his war against the repressive Nurse Ratched.
Academy Awards '75: Best Picture, Best Actor (Nicholson); Best Actress (Fletcher); Best Director (Forman); Best Screenplay Adaptation (Bo Goldman, Lawrence Hauben). MPAA:R
United Artists; Fantasy Films; Saul Zaentz; Michael Douglas — *THORN EMI Home Video; RCA VideoDiscs*

One Frightened Night 1935
Mystery
66390 69 mins B/W   B, V   P
Mary Carlisle, Wallace Ford, Hedda Hopper, Charlie Grapewin
An eccentric millionaire informs his family members that he is leaving each of them one million dollars.
Mascot Pictures — *Movie Buff Video*

One from the Heart 1982
Fantasy/Musical
68259   100 mins   C   B, V   P
Teri Garr, Frederie Forrest, Natassia Kinski, Raul Julia, Laine Kazan, directed by Francis Ford Coppola
Two people somehow lost the romance in their lives and end up with other people only to realize that they miss each other. In stereo.
MPAA:R
Gray Frederickson; Fred Ross — *RCA/Columbia Pictures Home Video; RCA VideoDiscs*

100 Rifles 1969
Western
29162   110 mins   C   B, V   P
Jim Brown, Raquel Welch, Burt Reynolds, Fernando Lamas
An Indian bank robber and a black American lawman join up with a female Mexican revolutionary to help save the Mexican Indians from annihilation by a despotic military governor.
MPAA:R SP
20th Century Fox — *CBS/Fox Video*

One Man Jury 1978
Crime-Drama
59813   95 mins   C   B, V   P
Jack Palance, Christopher Mitchum, Joe Spinell, Pamela Shoop
An LAPD lieutenant, wearied by an ineffective justice system, becomes a one-man vigilante avenger.
MPAA:R
Theodor Bodnar; Steve Bono — *VCI Home Video*

One Million B. C. 1940
Science fiction
44800 80 mins B/W   B, V, 3/4U   P
Victor Mature, Carole Landis, Lon Chaney Jr., directed by Hal Roach and Hal Roach Jr.
The saga of the struggle of primitive cavemen and their battle against dinosaurs and other monsters.
United Artists, Hal Roach — *Nostalgia Merchant*

One on One 1977
Drama
51987   98 mins   C   B, V   R, P
Robby Benson, Annette O'Toole, G.D. Spradlin, Gail Strickland
A high school basketball star from the country accepts an athletic scholarship to a big city university but is unprepared for the fierce competition he must face.
MPAA:PG
Warner Bros — *Warner Home Video*

One Rainy Afternoon 1936
Comedy
11298 80 mins B/W   B, V, FO   P
Francis Lederer, Ida Lupino, Hugh Herbert, Roland Young, Donald Meek
A bit-player kisses the wrong girl in a Paris theater, causing a hilarious, massive uproar branding him as a notorious romantic "monster."
Pickford Lasky Productions — *Video Yesteryear; Sheik Video*

One Sings, the Other Doesn't 1977
Drama
64913   105 mins   C   B, V   P
Valerie Mairesse, Therese Liotard
This film follows the friendship of two young women over a period of 14 years, when each seeks to control her destiny and to find contentment. In French with English subtitles.
FR
Cine-Tamarus — *RCA/Columbia Pictures Home Video*

One Small Step for Man 1984
Space exploration
72057   60 mins   C   B, V   P

The Apollo series of lunar explorations is examined in this documentary, with an emphasis on the first manned moon landing.
NASA — *MPI Home Video*

1001 Arabian Nights　　　　　1959
Fantasy/Cartoons
69620　　76 mins　　C　　B, V　　　　　P
Animated, voices of Jim Backus, Kathryn Grant, Hans Conreid, Herschel Bernardi
In this Arabian nightmare, the nearsighted Mr. Magoo is known as "Azziz" Magoo, lamp dealer and uncle of Aladdin.
Stephen Bosustow; UPA — *RCA/Columbia Pictures Home Video*

One Touch of Venus　　　　　1948
Musical
64546　82 mins　B/W　　B, V　　　　　P
Ava Gardner, Robert Walker, Eve Arden, Dick Haymes, Olga San Juan, Tom Conway
A young man impulsively kisses a marble statue of the goddess Venus, which comes to life. Based on the Broadway musical, with songs by Kurt Weill and Ogden Nash, including "Speak Low."
Universal — *NTA Home Entertainment*

Onion Field, The　　　　　1979
Drama
44979　　126 mins　　C　　B, V, LV,　　P
　　　　　　　　　　　　　　CED
John Savage, James Woods, Ronny Cox, Franklyn Seales
This true story concerns the murder of a policeman and the slow process of justice.
MPAA:R
Avco Embassy — *Embassy Home Entertainment*

Only About Women　　　　　197?
USSR/Women
52352　45 mins　B/W　　B, V, 3/4U　　P
A Soviet documentary about the different occupations open to women in the U.S.S.R. Narrated in English.
USSR — *International Historic Films*

Only Way, The　　　　　1970
War-Drama
65159　　86 mins　　C　　B, V　　　　　P
Jane Seymour, Martin Potter, Ben Christiansen
A semi-documentary account of the plight of the Jews in Denmark during the Nazi occupation. Despite German insistence, the Danes succeeded in saving most of their Jewish population from the concentration camps.
MPAA:G
UMC Pictures; Hemisphere -- Laterna — *VCI Home Video*

Only When I Laugh　　　　　1981
Comedy
58962　100 mins　　C　　B, V　　　　　P
Marsha Mason, Kristy McNichol, James Coco, Joan Hackett, David Dukes
A poignant comedy about the relationship between a mother and her daughter, written by Neil Simon.
MPAA:R
Columbia — *RCA/Columbia Pictures Home Video*

OP 1982 IPS Pro Championships　　　　　1982
Sports-Water
59413　60 mins　　C　　B, V　　　　　P
Coverage of the surfing championships held at Huntington Beach, California.
Courier Productions — *Courier Productions*

Open City　　　　　1946
Drama
44973　103 mins　B/W　　B, V　　　　　P
Anna Magnani, Aldo Fabrizi, directed by Roberto Rossellini
A leader in the Italian underground resists Nazi control of the city. Italian dialogue with English subtitles.
Italy — *Discount Video Tapes; Video Yesteryear; Sheik Video; Budget Video; Penguin Video; Western Film & Video Inc*

Opera Cameos　　　　　1955
Opera
47490　53 mins　B/W　　B, V, FO　　P
Lucia Evangelista, Guilio Gari, Frank Valentino, Carlo Tomanelli, conducted by Giuseppe Bamboschek, hosted by John Ericson
A program from this 1950's TV series of operas, staged with full costumes and sets. Featured are highlights from Verdi's "La Traviata."
Dumont — *Video Yesteryear*

Operation Amsterdam　　　　　1960
War-Drama/Suspense
62865　103 mins　B/W　　B, V　　　　　P
Peter Finch, Eva Bartok, Tony Britton
The true story of a group of agents who went to Holland in 1940 to prevent a stock of industrial diamonds from falling into the hands of the Nazis.
20th Century Fox; Rank — *Embassy Home Entertainment*

Operation Petticoat　　　　　1959
Comedy
47995　120 mins　　C　　B, V　　　　　P
Cary Grant, Tony Curtis, Joan O'Brien, Dina Merrill, Gene Evans, Arthur O'Connell
Determined to get his sub back in action, a commander bypasses regulations and uses "enterprising" methods to procure supplies.

Universal — *NTA Home Entertainment*

Orange Box, The　　　　1983
Fantasy/Literature
66212　29 mins　C　B, V　R, P
Animated
Three stories for children - "The Story About Ping," "Harold's Fairy Tale," "The Beast of Monsieur Rancine" - are combined on one cassette.
AM Available
Weston Woods — *CC Studios*

Orca　　　　1977
Adventure
10964　92 mins　C　B, V, LV　R, P
Richard Harris, Charlotte Rampling, Bo Derek, Keenan Wynn, directed by Michael Anderson
A whale is out for revenge when a shark hunting seafarer captures and kills his pregnant mate.
MPAA:PG
Paramount; Dino De Laurentiis — *Paramount Home Video*

Ordet　　　　1955
Drama
55805　126 mins　B/W　B, V　P
Henrik Malberg, directed by Carl Theodor Dreyer
A young couple are kept apart by their families in this film which contrasts bright, happy Christianity with dark, gloomy Christianity. English subtitled.
Venice Film Festival '55: Best Film.　FR
Sweden — *Festival Films; Western Film & Video Inc; Classic Video Cinema Collector's Club*

Ordinary Guy　　　　1981
Religion
64294　70 mins　C　B, V　P
This is the story of an ordinary Christian guy who seems to have everything he wants—until he realizes that God and Christ are not part of his everyday life, and he sets out to change that.
Day Star Productions — *Vanguard Video*

Ordinary People　　　　1980
Drama
55205　125 mins　C　B, V, LV　R, P
Mary Tyler Moore, Donald Sutherland, Timothy Hutton, Judd Hirsch, Elizabeth McGovern, directed by Robert Redford
An upper-middle class, Midwestern suburban family's life disintegrates in the wake of the emotional effects of one son's accidental death and the other son's emotional trauma.
Academy Awards '80: Best Picture; Best Director (Redford); Best Supporting Actor (Hutton); Best Screenplay Adaptation (Alvin Sargeant).　MPAA:R

Wildwood Enterprises;
Paramount — *Paramount Home Video; RCA VideoDiscs*

Oregon Trail　　　　1939
Western/Serials
12547　195 mins　B/W　B, V　P
Johnny Mack Brown, Fuzzy Knight, directed by Ford Beebe
A western serial in fifteen chapters, each thirteen minutes long.
Universal — *Video Connection*

Oriental Dreams　　　　1982
Photography
47809　? mins　C　LV　P
A sensual portrait of five young women photographed with great sensitivity by Kenji Nagatomo, set to the music of Naoya Matsouka (stereo).
Unknown — *Pioneer Video Imports*

Origin of Life, The (Plus Scopes Trial Footage)　　　　1982
Biology/Science
59559　60 mins　C　B, V　P
A look at Darwinian theory and beginnings of life, plus rare Scopes Trial footage from the Rohauer Collection.
McGraw Hill — *Mastervision*

Original Amateur Hour, The　　　　1954
Variety
47478　54 mins　B/W　B, V, FO　P
Hosted by Ted Mack
Two programs from this popular series, originally telecast on May 22, 1954 and July 31, 1954. Performers include a trampoline bouncer, a Liberace imitator, the Penbrook Jug Band and New York Yankees pitcher Eddie Lopat.
NBC — *Video Yesteryear*

Original Amateur Hour, The　　　　1953
Variety
47474　54 mins　B/W　B, V, FO　P
Hosted by Ted Mack　pgms
Two programs from this long-running series, originally telecast on August 15 and August 29, 1953. Featured contestants include a girl who spins a lariat while riding a unicycle, a ventriloquist, tap dancers and a lady who plays "Yankee Doodle" on sleigh bells.
NBC — *Video Yesteryear*

Original Amateur Hour, The　　　　1954
Variety
47477　57 mins　B/W　B, V, FO　P
Hosted by Ted Mack

Two programs from this series, originally telecast on October 3, 1953 and April 24, 1954. Contestants include a Johnny Ray impersonator, a man who plays Rachmaninoff on the banjo, a female barbershop quartet and a tap-dancing lady roller skater.
NBC — *Video Yesteryear*

Orphans of the Storm 1921
Drama
44990   127 mins   B/W   B, V   P, T
Lillian Gish, Dorothy Gish, Monte Blue, Joseph Schildkraut, directed by D. W. Griffith
Two orphans marooned in Paris become separated by the turbulent maelstrom preceding the French Revolution. Silent.
United Artists — *Blackhawk Films; Classic Video Cinema Collector's Club*

Orpheus 1950
Film-Avant-garde
11398   95 mins   B/W   B, V, FO   P
Jean Marais, Francois Perier, Maria Casares, directed by Jean Cocteau
Depicts the love of a poet for a princess who travels constantly from this world to the next. A legendary tale in a modern Parisian setting.
Andre Paulve Films du Palais Royal — *Video Yesteryear; Budget Video; Sheik Video; Penguin Video; Western Film & Video Inc; Discount Video Tapes*

Oscar, The 1966
Drama
66049   119 mins   C   B, V, CED   P
Stephen Boyd, Elke Sommer, Jill St. John, Tony Bennett, Milton Berle, Eleanor Parker, Joseph Cotten, Edie Adams, Ernest Borgnine
The story of ego, greed and self-destruction in the film world of Hollywood.
MPAA:R
Joseph E Levine — *Embassy Home Entertainment*

Osterman Weekend, The 1983
Suspense
65507   102 mins   C   B, V   R, P
Burt Lancaster, Rutger Hauer, Craig Nelson, Dennis Hopper
A TV personality is looking forward to a reunion party with his closest friends. That is, until the CIA warns him that they are all Soviet agents. Suddenly, he and his family are caught in a nightmare of terror, deception, helplessness and violent death.
MPAA:R
Peter S Davis; William N Panzer — *THORN EMI Home Video*

Othello 1922
Drama
47463   81 mins   B/W   B, V, FO   P
Emil Jannings, Lya de Putti, Werner Krauss

A silent version of Shakespeare's tragedy, featuring Emil Jannings as the tragic Moor. Titles are in English; music score.
UFA — *Video Yesteryear; Discount Video Tapes; Classic Video Cinema Collector's Club*

Othello 1922
Drama
58533   60 mins   B/W   B, V, 3/4U   P
Emil Jannings
Shakespeare's drama in which Jannings portrays the tragic Moor in this silent version.
Unknown — *Penguin Video*

Other Side of Nashville, The 1984
Music-Performance/Documentary
66598   118 mins   C   B, V, LV,   P
                                    CED
Johnny Cash, Kris Kristofferson, Bob Dylan, Kenny Rogers, Willie Nelson, Hank Williams, Jr, Emmylou Harris, Carl Perkins
Live performances, interviews and backstage footage combine to form a picture of the Nashville music scene. Over 40 songs are heard in renditions by country music's biggest stars. In stereo.
Geoffrey Menin; MGM UA — *MGM/UA Home Video*

Our Daily Bread 1934
Drama
11394   74 mins   B/W   B, V, FO   P
Tom Keene, Karen Morley, Barbara Pepper, directed by King Vidor
Desperate men and women from the Depression era come together and form a subsistence farm.
United Artists — *Video Yesteryear; Cable Films; Sheik Video; Budget Video; Discount Video Tapes; Western Film & Video Inc*

Our Finest Hour 1981
Football
50647   24 mins   C   B, V, FO   R, P
Oakland Raiders
When newly acquired quarterback Dan Pastorini was lost for the 1980 season with an injury, veteran Jim Plunkett calmly stepped in and made Raider fans forget the departed Ken Stabler. Plunkett's steadiness led the well-balanced Raiders to the Super Bowl championship, amidst owner Al Davis' battle with Oakland fans and commissioner Pete Rozelle, over Davis' attempt to move his team to Los Angeles.
NFL Films — *NFL Films Video*

Our Friend Angela 197?
Civil rights/Propaganda
52351   25 mins   B/W   B, V, 3/4U   P

A Soviet-filmed report about Angela Davis and her friends Kondra and Franklin Alexander in the U.S.S.R. Narrated in English.
USSR — *International Historic Films*

Our Relations 1936
Comedy
33905   65 mins   B/W   B, V, 3/4U   P
Stan Laurel, Oliver Hardy, Alan Hale, Sidney Toler, James Finlayson, Daphne Pollard
Confusion reigns when Stan and Ollie meet their twin brothers, a pair of happy-go-lucky sailors whom the boys previously didn't know existed.
Hal Roach, MGM — *Nostalgia Merchant; Blackhawk Films*

Our Relations 1936
Comedy
63987   95 mins   B/W   B, V   P, T
Stan Laurel, Oliver Hardy, James Finlayson, Alan Hale, Daphne Pollard
Stan and Ollie's long-lost twin brothers come to town after being at sea for years, to the consternation of all concerned. This tape also includes a 1935 Charley Chase short, "Southern Exposure."
Hal Roach; MGM — *Blackhawk Films*

Our Russian Front 1941
World War II
53645   43 mins   B/W   B, V, 3/4U   P
A documentary look at the Russian people's determination and preparation for war against the advancing German army, including many scenes of civilian life and abrupt changes incurred by war.
Lewis Milestone; Joris Ivans — *International Historic Films; Discount Video Tapes*

Our Town 1940
Drama
08854   90 mins   B/W   B, V   P
Martha Scott, William Holden, Thomas Mitchell, Fay Bainter, narrated by Frank Craven
Life, love, and death in a small New England town; based on the play by Thornton Wilder.
United Artists; Sol Lesser Prods — *Movie Buff Video; Penguin Video; Budget Video; Video Yesteryear; Sheik Video; Cable Films; Video Connection; Discount Video Tapes; Western Film & Video Inc*

Our Town 1977
Drama
56891   120 mins   C   B, V   P
Ned Beatty, Sada Thompson, Ronny Cox, Glynnis O'Connor, Robby Benson, Hal Holbrook, John Houseman
This is the television version of Thornton Wilder's classic play about everyday life in Grovers Corners, a small New England town at the turn of the century.

Hartwest Productions; Saul Jaffe — *Mastervision; RCA VideoDiscs*

Out of the Blue 1982
Drama
65694   94 mins   C   B, V   P
Dennis Hopper, Linda Manz, Raymond Burr
A frustrated teenager with a father in prison and a promiscuous and weak-willed mother runs away and quickly gets into trouble with the law. Her return home and her father's release from prison is anything than happy.
MPAA:R
Leonard Yakir, Gary Jules Jouvenat — *Media Home Entertainment*

Out of the Past 1947
Suspense
00290   97 mins   B/W   B, V, 3/4U   P
Robert Mitchum, Kirk Douglas, Jane Greer
A cool and calculating private detective undermines a ruthless tycoon's empire.
RKO; Eagle Lion — *Nostalgia Merchant*

Out of the Shadow Into the Sun 1975
Mountaineering
69917   40 mins   C   B, V   R, P
This is a filmed-as-it-happened account of a successful ascent of the Eiger's north face—a blank wall of rock stretching upwards over a mile.
Leo Dickinson; HTV Wales — *Gravity Sports Films*

Out-Of-Towners, The 1970
Comedy
65733   98 mins   C   B, V   R, P
Jack Lemmon, Sandy Dennis
Incredible mishaps occur when a middle-aged Ohio couple fly to New York City for the husband's job interview.
MPAA:G
Paramount; Jalem — *Paramount Home Video*

Outland 1981
Science fiction
58242   109 mins   C   B, V, LV   R, P
Sean Connery, Peter Boyle, Frances Sternhagen, James B. Sikking, directed by Peter Hyams
On Jupiter's volcanic moon, miners are suddenly plunging into insanity—and a lone federal marshal must uncover the secret that threatens everyone's survival.
MPAA:R
Outland Prods — *Warner Home Video; RCA VideoDiscs*

Outlaw, The 1943
Western
05538   95 mins   B/W   B, V   P

Jane Russell, Jack Beutel, Walter Huston, Thomas Mitchell
A variation on the saga of Billy the Kid, wherein Billy and girlfriend Rio have a romantic interlude before the final showdown with Pat Garrett.
Howard Hughes — *Video Connection; King of Video; VCII; Discount Video Tapes; Video Yesteryear; Sheik Video; Cable Films; Classic Video Cinema Collector's Club*

Outlaw Josey Wales, The   1976
Western
58243   135 mins   C   B, V   R, P
Clint Eastwood, Chief Dan George, Sondra Locke, directed by Clint Eastwood
A farmer becomes a one-man army to avenge the slaughter of his wife and child by Civil War renegades.
MPAA:PG
Warner Bros — *Warner Home Video*

Outlaw Rule   1936
Western
54187   61 mins   B/W   B, V   P
Reb Russell
An action-packed western adventure pitting outlaws against the law of the West.
Supreme — *Video Connection*

Outlaw Tamer   1933
Western
15537   56 mins   B/W   B, V   P
Lane Chandler
Western adventure starring Lane Chandler.
Unknown — *Video Connection*

Outlaws   1982
Music-Performance
75921   81 mins   C   B, V   P
This program presents the outlaws performing some of their greatest hits.
High Tide Management Inc — *Sony Corporation of America*

Outlaws of the Range   19??
Western
57984   60 mins   B/W   B, V   P
Bill Cody
Bill Cody stars in this action western which features outlaws who terrorize the countryside.
Spectrum — *Video Connection*

Outrageous   1977
Comedy
58963   100 mins   C   B, V   P
Craig Russell, Hollis McLaren, Richard Easley, Allan Moyle
A comedy about the unlikely but touching relationship between a female impersonator and his schizophrenic girl friend.
MPAA:R

Herbert R Steinmann; Billy Baxter — *RCA/Columbia Pictures Home Video*

Outside the Law   1921
Crime-Drama
10121   77 mins   B/W   B, V   P, T
Lon Chaney, Priscilla Dean
Lon Chaney plays dual roles of the underworld hood in "Black Mike Sylva," and a Chinese servant in "Ah Wing."
Universal — *Blackhawk Films; Classic Video Cinema Collector's Club*

Outsiders, The   1983
Drama
69025   91 mins   C   B, V, CED   R, P
Matt Dillon
"The Outsiders" depicts the explosive conflict between rival gangs of poor and rich kids in the mid-1960's.
MPAA:PG
Zoetrope Studios — *Warner Home Video*

Outtakes I   197?
Outtakes and bloopers
33690   120 mins   C   B, V, 3/4U   P
A large assortment of foul-ups, goofs, and laughs featuring stars and shows such as "Abbott and Costello," "Rowan and Martin," "Garry Moore," "The Tonight Show," "Star Trek," "The Twilight Zone," and "Cannon," in scenes that never made it to the television screen. Some black and white.
NBC et al — *Shokus Video*

Outtakes II   197?
Outtakes and bloopers
35528   120 mins   C   B, V, 3/4U   P
Stars from popular TV shows including "Starsky and Hutch," "Three's Company," "The Newlywed Game" and "McHale's Navy" are seen messing up their lines and cracking up in these scenes that were edited from the finished programs. Some black and white segments are included.
ABC et al — *Shokus Video*

Outtakes III   1980
Outtakes and bloopers
45018   60 mins   C   B, V, 3/4U   P
The casts of "WKRP," "MASH," "Mary Tyler Moore," and more blow lines, miss cues, and generally mess up.
CBS et al — *Shokus Video*

Outtakes IV   1980
Outtakes and bloopers
45020   120 mins   C   B, V, 3/4U   P
The casts of "MASH," "Carol Burnett," "The Don Adams-Don Rickles Special," "Match Game," and more goof up, mess up and break

up. Included are outtakes from 1950's commercials.
CBS et al — *Shokus Video*

Outtakes VI   1982
Outtakes and bloopers
47613   60 mins   C   B, V, 3/4U   P
Boris Karloff, Bela Lugosi, The Marx Brothers, W. C. Fields, William Shatner, Leonard Nimoy, Jackie Cooper, Joe Garagiola
Another hour of flubs, goofs and breakdowns featuring favorite performers of movies and TV. There is no duplication between this program and any other Shokus "Outtake" tape. Some segments are in black and white.
NBC et al — *Shokus Video*

Outtakes VII   1983
Outtakes and bloopers
66462   60 mins   B/W   B, V, 3/4U   P
Richard Simmons, Ted Knight, Alan Alda, Redd Foxx
More goofs and blunders from popular television shows are featured in this installment of the "Outtakes" series.
CBS et al — *Shokus Video*

Outtakes V   197?
Outtakes and bloopers
53053   60 mins   C   B, V, 3/4U   P
Johnny Carson, Ed McMahon, Alan Alda, Mike Farrell, Harry Morgan, Jamie Farr, Bing Crosby, Jimmy Durante, Van Johnson
TV outtakes which also feature Sammy Davis Jr., Peter Lawford, Tony Randall, Alan Sherman, Martha Raye, Carol Burnett, Harvey Korman, Vicki Lawrence, Tim Conway, Bob Barker, Jim Lange, and others. Also included are outtakes from commercials, plus actual foreign commercials.
CBS et al — *Shokus Video*

Over the Edge   1979
Drama
52711   95 mins   C   B, V   R, P
Michael Kramer, Matt Dillon, Pamela Ludwig, directed by Jonathan Kaplan
The music of Cheap Trick, The Cars, and The Ramones highlights this realistic tale of suburban youth on the rampage.
MPAA:PG
Orion Pictures — *Warner Home Video*

Overland Mail   1941
Western
58632   225 mins   B/W   B, V   P
Lon Chaney Jr., Helen Parrish
Fifteen episodes of the vintage serial filled with western action.
Universal — *Video Connection*

Owl and the Pussycat, The   1970
Comedy
44846   96 mins   C   B, V   P
Barbra Streisand, George Segal, Robert Klein, directed by Herbert Ross
A hooker meets a bookstore clerk and, after some initial antagonism, they fall in love.
MPAA:R
Columbia, Ray Stark — *RCA/Columbia Pictures Home Video; RCA VideoDiscs*

P

P-47 Thunderbolt High Altitude Flight and Aerobatics   1943
Armed Forces-US/Aeronautics
72512   22 mins   B/W   B, V, 3/4U   P
An exciting look at the Air Force P-47 in power diving and aerobatic maneuvers set to classical music. Most of the movie contains action footage with attention paid to technical aspects of the plane.
Army Air Force in cooperation with Republic Aviation — *International Historic Films*

Pacific Challenge   1974
Boating
57194   55 mins   C   B, V   P
Twelve men from seven nations sail three balsa wood rafts from Ecuador to Australia—9,000 miles nonstop.
AM Available
Manuel Arango — *Alti Corporation*

Pack Up Your Troubles   1932
Comedy
33902   68 mins   B/W   B, V, 3/4U   P
Stan Laurel, Oliver Hardy, James Finlayson, Jacquie Lyn
World War I veterans try to find the family of an orphaned little girl with humorous results.
Hal Roach, MGM — *Nostalgia Merchant*

Padre Padrone   1977
Drama
63436   90 mins   C   B, V   P
Omero Antonutti, Saverio Marconi
This is the story of the personal rebellion of a Sardinian shepherd who was separated from the world by his father until he was 20 years old. Italian dialogue, English subtitles.
Cannes Film Festival: Golden Palm Award. IT
Almi/Cinema V; Guiliani G. de Negri — *RCA/Columbia Pictures Home Video*

Paint Your Wagon   1970
Musical
59860   164 mins   C   B, V, LV   R, P
*Lee Marvin, Clint Eastwood, Jean Seberg,
Harve Presnell, directed by Joshua Logan*
A western musical-comedy about a goldmining
boom town, complete with a classic Lerner and
Lowe score.
MPAA:PG
Paramount — *Paramount Home Video*

Painted Desert, The   1931
Western
44811   80 mins   B/W   B, V   P, T
*William Boyd, Helen Twelvetrees, George
O'Brien, Clark Gable*
Clark Gable's first film role of any consequence
came in this early sound western. Gable plays a
villain opposite "good guy" William Boyd.
RKO — *Budget Video; Discount Video Tapes;
Video Connection*

Painted Stallion, The   1937
Western/Serials
08878   215 mins   B/W   B, V, 3/4U   P
Ray 'Crash' Corrigan, Hoot Gibson
Twelve episodes, each running 18 minutes.
Republic — *Penguin Video; Video Connection;
Video Yesteryear; Nostalgia Merchant*

Paisan   1948
Film-Avant-garde
06232   90 mins   B/W   B, V   P
*Maria Michi, Gar Moore, directed by Roberto
Rossellini*
Six stories of Allied soldiers encountering Italy's
liberation during WWII. Italian film, English
subtitles.
IT
J Burstyn; Italian — *Budget Video; Sheik
Video; Cable Films; Video Yesteryear; Penguin
Video; Western Film & Video Inc; Discount
Video Tapes*

Pajama Tops   1983
Comedy
72456   120 mins   C   B, V   P
Susan George, Robert Klein, Pia Zadora
This film was adapted, from the French farce,
"Mou Mod."
Unknown — *U.S.A. Home Video*

Palm Tree Beach   1978
Video
08569   30 mins   C   B, V, 3/4U   P
A continuous picture of a calm tropical beach
viewed from under a shady palm tree to create a
relaxed background.
Nebulae Prods — *Nebulae Productions*

Palooka   1934
Comedy-Drama
12858   94 mins   B/W   B, V, FO   P
Jimmy Durante, Stuart Erwin, Lupe Velez
Based on the classic comic strip. Durante plays
a fast-talking manager Knobby Walsh and sings
his own classic, "Inka-Dinka-Doo."
Edward Small Prods — *Video Yesteryear;
Cable Films; Sheik Video; Penguin Video; Video
Connection; Discount Video Tapes; Western
Film & Video Inc*

Panama Lady   1939
Drama
70050   65 mins   B/W   B, V   P
Lucille Ball
A dance hall girl and oil prospector experience a
series of mis-adventures before finding
happiness out west.
RKO — *VidAmerica*

Panama Lady   1939
Romance
69588   65 mins   B/W   B, V   P
Lucille Ball, Evelyn Brent
Lucille Ball stars as the sexy, sultry "Panama
Lady" in this old-fashioned romance.
RKO — *VidAmerica*

Panda and the Magic Serpent   1975
Cartoons/Fantasy
53140   78 mins   C   B, V   P
Animated
An ancient Chinese legend tells of a boy who
found a white snake his parents wouldn't let him
keep. When he grows up, the snake turns into a
beautiful maiden who saves his life.
Ziv Intl — *Family Home Entertainment*

Panda's Adventures   1984
Cartoons
76031   60 mins   C   B, V   P
Animated
An animated tale of a Panda Prince, Lonlon,
who is exiled from his Kingdom when he fails a
test of courage. Through his adventures, he
learns that true heroism and real courage come
from the heart.
John Watkins; Simon
Nuchtern — *RCA/Columbia Pictures Home
Video*

Panic in Echo Park   1977
Drama
66619   77 mins   C   B, V   P
*Dorian Harewood, Catlin Adams, Robin
Gammell, Norman Barthold*
A dedicated physician fights hospital authorities
to trace the cause of an epidemic in a minority
community.

Edgar J Scherick Associates — *U.S.A. Home Video*

Panique 1940
Drama
06233 87 mins B/W B, V P
Michel Simon, Viviane Romance, directed by Julien Duvivier
Study of mob psychology in slums of Paris after war. Two lovers frame a stranger for murder. French film, English subtitles.
FR
French — *Budget Video; Cable Films; Penguin Video; Discount Video Tapes*

Paper Chase, The 1973
Drama
08469 111 mins C B, V, CED P
Timothy Bottoms, Lindsay Wagner, John Houseman, Graham Beckel
Examines the repressive cloistered world of first-year students at Harvard Law School. Academy Awards '73: Best Supporting Actor (Houseman). MPAA:PG
20th Century Fox — *CBS/Fox Video*

Paper Moon 1973
Comedy
38601 102 mins B/W B, V, LV R, P
Ryan O'Neal, Tatum O'Neal, Madeline Kahn, John Hillerman, directed by Peter Bogdanovich
Bright, winning story of a con man (Ryan O'Neal) who is left with a nine-year old orphan (Tatum O'Neal in her film debut) who proves to be a better crook. Set in depression-era Kansas, circa 1936.
Academy Awards '73: Best Supporting Actress (Tatum O'Neal). MPAA:PG
Paramount — *Paramount Home Video; RCA VideoDiscs*

Papillon 1973
Drama
59308 150 mins C B, V, CED P
Steve McQueen, Dustin Hoffman, directed by Franklin Schaffner
The story of two convicts and their harrowing experiences on Devil's Island.
MPAA:PG
Robert Dorfmann — *CBS/Fox Video*

Paradise 1982
Romance
63368 100 mins C B, V, CED P
Phoebe Cates, Willie Aames, Richard Curnock, Tuvio Tavi
A young American boy and a beautiful English girl are the sole survivors of a caravan massacre in the Middle East during the 19th century. They discover a magnificent oasis and experience their sexual awakening.
MPAA:R

Robert Lantos; Stephen J. Ross — *Embassy Home Entertainment*

Paradise Canyon 1935
Western
54188 55 mins B/W B, V P
John Wayne
One of John Wayne's early action westerns.
Monogram — *Video Connection*

Paradise, Hawaiian Style 1966
Musical
08387 91 mins C B, V P
Elvis Presley, Suzanna Leigh, James Shigeta
Out-of-work pilot returns to Hawaii, where he and a buddy start a charter service with two helicopters.
EL, SP
Paramount; Hal Wallis — *CBS/Fox Video*

Paradise in Harlem 1940
Drama
42951 83 mins B/W B, V, FO P
Frank Wilson, Mamie Smith, Edna Mae Harris
An all-black musical in which a cabaret performer witnesses a gangland murder, sees his sick wife die, and is pressured into leaving town by the mob.
Unknown — *Video Yesteryear; Sheik Video; Video Connection; Discount Video Tapes*

Parallax View, The 1974
Suspense
60331 102 mins C B, V R, P
Warren Beatty, Hume Cronyn, William Daniels, Paula Prentiss, directed by Alan J. Pakula
A reporter tries to disprove a report which stated that a presidential candidate's assassination was not a conspiracy.
MPAA:R
Paramount — *Paramount Home Video*

Paranoia 1969
Suspense
66475 94 mins C B, V P
Carroll Baker, Lou Castel, Colette Descombes
A beautiful jet-set widow is trapped in her own Italian villa by a young couple and slowly fed drugs as part of a murder plan.
MPAA:X
Commonwealth United — *NTA Home Entertainment*

Parasite 1981
Horror/Science fiction
60431 85 mins C B, V P
Demi Moore, Robert Glaudini, James Davidson
In 1992, a doctor, a victim of the atomic age, is being eaten alive from the inside out.
MPAA:R

Irwin Yablans; Charles Band — *Wizard Video; Embassy Home Entertainment (disc only)*

Pardon Mon Affaire 1977
Comedy
65427   105 mins   C   B, V   P
Jean Rochefort
The story of the complications that bedevil male-female relationships, here, there and everywhere.
MPAA:PG
First Artists — *Embassy Home Entertainment*

Pardon Us 1931
Comedy
59152   71 mins   B/W   B, V, 3/4U   P
Stan Laurel, Oliver Hardy, June Marlowe
Two bootleggers find themselves in and out of prison.
Hal Roach;MGM — *Nostalgia Merchant*

Parent Trap, The 1961
Comedy
66321   127 mins   C   B, V, LV,   R, P
                                 CED
Hayley Mills, Maureen O'Hara, Brian Keith, Charlie Ruggles, directed by David Swift
Hayley Mills plays a dual role in this heartwarming comedy as twin sisters who conspire to bring their divorced parents together again.
Buena Vista — *Walt Disney Home Video*

Paris Holiday 1957
Comedy
47664   100 mins   C   B, V   P
Bob Hope, Fernandel, Anita Ekberg, Martha Hyer, Preston Sturges
An actor heading for Paris to find a noted author; latest screenplay finds mystery and romance.
United Artists — *Unicorn Video*

Parlor, Bedroom and Bath 1931
Comedy
57288   75 mins   B/W   B, V   P
Buster Keaton, Charlotte Greenwood, Cliff Edwards
Buster Keaton stars in another one of his classic comedies from the Thirties.
Buster Keaton — *Video Dimensions; Budget Video; Discount Video Tapes; Classic Video Cinema Collector's Club*

Partners 1982
Comedy
60332   92 mins   C   B, V   R, P
Ryan O'Neal, John Hurt, Kenneth McMillan, Robyn Douglass, Jay Robinson, Rick Jason
A macho cop must go "undercover" with a gay cop to investigate the murder of a gay model.

MPAA:R
Paramount — *Paramount Home Video*

Party Games—For Adults Only 1984
Games
75019   130 mins   C   LV   P
This tape features sixty good-natured sexy party games for adult parties.
Bosustow Entertainment Productions — *MCA Home Video*

Party Girl 1933
Drama
08901   60 mins   B/W   B, V, 3/4U   P
Douglas Fairbanks Jr., Lucien Prival, Jeanette Toff
A young college student is forced to marry an enterprising young woman who leads him to believe that he had taken advantage of her while in a drunken stupor.
Unknown — *Penguin Video*

Passion of Joan of Arc 1928
Film-Avant-garde
11385   114 mins   B/W   B, V, FO   P
Maria Falconeth, Eugena Sylvain, Maurice Schutz, directed by Carl Theodore Dreyer
A classic silent masterpiece and a notable cinema treatment of Joan of Arc.
Societe Generale de Films — *Video Yesteryear; Sheik Video; Penguin Video; Western Film & Video Inc; Discount Video Tapes; Classic Video Cinema Collector's Club*

Passion of Love 1982
Drama/Romance
64355   117 mins   C   B, V, CED   P
Laura Antonelli
Laura Antonelli is featured in this passionate, historical romance from filmmaker Ettore Scola. The film has won a special award at the Cannes Film Festival.
Franco Commipteri — *Vestron Video*

Pastures of Heaven 1951
Drama
66391   90 mins   B/W   B, V   P
Buddy Ebsen, Thomas Mitchell, Lew Ayres, Tommy Rettig, John Steinbeck
A selection of dramatized stories by John Steinbeck, each introduced by the author.
Bryna Pictures — *Movie Buff Video*

Pat Benatar Hit Videos 1984
Music video
72929   60 mins   C   B, V   P
Pat Benatar
A collection of Pat's videos from "Get Nervous" and "Live from Earth," this tape also includes a documentary on the making of "Love Is a Battlefield."

Rising Star Video
Productions — *RCA/Columbia Pictures Home Video*

Pat Garrett and Billy the Kid　1973
Western
72466　106 mins　C　B, V　　　　P
Kris Kristofferson, James Coburn, Bob Dylan
The story of the famous Southwestern outlaw who was tracked and killed by a man he once rode with. Sound track music by Bob Dylan.
MGM — *MGM/UA Home Video*

Patchwork Girl of Oz, The　1914
Fantasy
59221　40 mins　B/W　B, V, 3/4U　　P
Directed by L. Frank Baum
Two hungry Munchkins journey to Oz, meeting an eccentric magician on the way. This silent film was one of several produced by "Oz" creator L. Frank Baum.
L Frank Baum — *Penguin Video*

Paternity　1981
Comedy
58715　94 mins　C　B, V, LV　　R, P
Burt Reynolds, Beverly D'Angelo, Lauren Hutton, Norman Fell, Paul Dooley, Elizabeth Ashley, directed by David Steinberg
A middle-aged man sets out to find a woman to bear his child and then leave him alone.
MPAA:PG
Paramount — *Paramount Home Video; RCA VideoDiscs*

Paths of Glory　1957
War-Drama
64905　86 mins　B/W　B, V, CED　　P
Kirk Douglas, George Macready, Ralph Meeker, Adolphe Menjou, Susanne Christian, directed by Stanley Kubrick
This adaptation of a novel by Humphrey Cobb examines the arrogance of generals and the senseless punishment of three soldiers in the French army during World War I.
United Artists — *CBS/Fox Video*

Patrick　1978
Suspense
54537　115 mins　C　B, V　　　　P
Sir Robert Helpmann, Susan Penhaligon, Rod Mullinar
A coma patient suddenly develops strange powers and has a weird effect on the people he comes in contact with.
MPAA:PG
Vanguard/Monarch
Release — *HarmonyVision*

Patton　1970
War-Drama
08428　171 mins　C　B, V, LV　　P
George C. Scott, Karl Malden, Stephen Young, directed by Franklin J. Schaffner
George C. Scott portrays the brilliant and maniacal General Patton, whose leadership produced victory after victory in North Africa and Europe during World War II.
Academy Awards '70: Best Picture; Best Actor (Scott); Best Director (Shaffner).　MPAA:PG
EL, SP
20th Century Fox — *CBS/Fox Video*

Patty Berg: Fairway to Fame　1954
Biographical/Golf
44240　15 mins　B/W　B, V　　　　P
The story of the famed woman golfer, Patty Berg. Classic newsreel footage.
Fox Movietone News — *Two Star Films*

Paul Simon in Concert　1981
Music-Performance
47376　60 mins　C　B, V　　　R, P
Paul Simon
At a live concert in Philadelphia, Paul Simon performs some of his greatest old and new hits, including "Me and Julio," "Fifty Ways to Leave Your Lover," " One-Trick Pony," and "Sounds of Silence."
Michael Tannen; Phil Ramone; Peregrine Inc — *Warner Home Video; RCA VideoDiscs; Pioneer Artists*

Paul Simon Special, The　1977
Music-Performance/Variety
66444　60 mins　C　B, V　　　　P
Paul Simon, Art Garfunkel, Chevy Chase, Lily Tomlin, Charles Grodin, The Jesse Dixon Singers
This 1977 TV special was produced by Lorne Michaels of "Saturday Night Live" and features appearances by a number of "SNL's" stars. Singer-songwriter Paul Simon performs eight of his songs, assisted on several by Art Garfunkel.
NBC; Lorne Michaels — *Pacific Arts Video*

Pavarotti　1984
Opera/Music-Performance
66611　75 mins　C　B, V　　　　P
Luciano Pavarotti, Andrea Griminelli
Operatic tenor Luciano Pavarotti stars in this live concert taped in the Superstar Center of Las Vegas' Riviera Hotel. The program includes songs and arias by Verdi, Donizetti, Puccini and di Curtis.
Tibor Rudas Productions — *Trans World Entertainment*

Pavarotti in London　1982
Music-Performance/Opera
64831　51 mins　C　B, V　　　　P

London's Royal Albert Hall was the setting for this concert which launched the Royal Philharmonic Orchestra's national fund appeal starring Pavarotti performing "Tosca," "Macbeth" and others. In stereo.
BBC; Polygram; Rodney Greenberg — *RCA/Columbia Pictures Home Video; Pioneer Artists; RCA VideoDiscs*

Pawnbroker, The　1965
Drama
64540　100 mins　B/W　B, V　P
Rod Steiger, Brock Peters, Geraldine Fitzgerald, directed by Sidney Lumet
A middle-aged Jewish pawnbroker in New York's Spanish Harlem finds that he cannot forget his terrible experiences in a Nazi concentration camp during World War II.
Commonwealth United — *NTA Home Entertainment*

Pay Less Tax Legally　1984
Personal finance
69839　46 mins　C　B, V　P
Barry Steiner, a busy CPA and a former Internal Revenue Agent, helps clients save money by answering a broad range of income tax questions. Steiner's answers are all in layman's terms with no legal jargon.
John McNaughton — *Barry Raymond Steiner*

Payday　1972
Musical-Drama
63333　98 mins　C　B, V　R, P
Rip Torn, Ahna Capri, Michael C. Gwynne, Jeff Morris
Rip Torn stars as a declining country music star on tour in this portrayal of the seamy side of show business, from groupies to grimy motels.
Saul Zaentz Company — *THORN EMI Home Video*

Peace Fund　196?
Vietnam War/Propaganda
53712　30 mins　B/W　B, V, 3/4U　P
Workers in the USSR are seen contributing to the fund which help victims of U.S. bombing raids in North Vietnam.
USSR — *International Historic Films*

Peacock Fan, The　1929
Drama
59206　50 mins　B/W　B, V, 3/4U　P
Lucian Preval
The Peacock Fan is protected by a deadly curse, with certain death to anyone who possesses it.
Chesterfield Motion Picture Corp — *Penguin Video; Video Yesteryear*

Peck's Bad Boy　1921
Comedy
60047　51 mins　B/W　B, V　P, T
Jackie Coogan, Doris Day, Raymond Hatton, Wheeler Oakman, Lillian Leighton
Jackie and his friends let a circus lion loose and Jackie's father won't allow him to see the circus. He then decides to blackmail his father. A Blackhawk orchestral score has been added to this silent film.
First National — *Blackhawk Films; Classic Video Cinema Collector's Club*

Peck's Bad Boy with the Circus　1938
Comedy
12812　67 mins　B/W　B, V, FO　P
Tommy Kelly, Ann Gillis, Spanky MacFarland, Edgar Kennedy, Billy Gilbert
A troublesome youngster and his pals nearly wreck a circus and throw an obstacle race off course.
RKO — *Video Yesteryear*

Pedestrian, The　1974
Drama
65391　97 mins　C　B, V　P
Maximillian Schell
This is the story of a powerful industrialist and his secret. A human drama builds as a newspaper's investigation probes deep into the past to reveal the memory of events that time and fortune could not erase.
MPAA:PG
Cinerama Releasing — *Embassy Home Entertainment*

Peeping Tom　1963
Horror/Drama
73552　88 mins　C　B, V　P
Moira Shearer, Karl Boehm, directed by Michael Powell
A filmmaker kills women while filming the acts with a 16 millimeter camera. This is the original uncut version of the film.
Michael Powell — *Admit One Video*

Peerce, Anderson & Segovia　1981
Music-Performance
57253　56 mins　B/W　B, V　P
Jan Peerce, Marian Anderson, Andres Segovia
Three separate short films highlight performances by guitarist Andres Segovia, tenor Jan Peerce, assisted by Nadine Connor and contralto Marian Anderson.
Kultur — *Kultur*

Pele—The Master and His Method　1980
Soccer
56453　60 mins　C　B, V　P

Soccer star Pele gives tips on improving your play, and talks about the game.
Pepsico — *CBS/Fox Video*

Penitentiary 1979
Drama
52861   99 mins   C   B, V   P
Leon Isaacs, Jamaa Fanaka
A realistic story of a black fighter in prison.
MPAA:R
Jerry Gross — *Wizard Video*

Pennies from Heaven 1981
Musical
47776   107 mins   C   B, V, CED   P
Steve Martin, Bernadette Peters, Christopher Walken, Jessica Harper, Vernel Bagneris, directed by Herbert Ross
An avante-garde reworking of 30's musicals involving a sheet music salesman accused of murder.
MPAA:R
MGM — *MGM/UA Home Video*

Penny Serenade 1936
Drama
11249 120 mins B/W   B, V   P
Cary Grant, Irene Dunne, Beulah Bondi, Edgar Buchanan
A young couple, having lost their baby, adopts a child, but their new found happiness is short-lived.
Columbia — *Video Yesteryear; NTA Home Entertainment; Budget Video; Sheik Video; Cable Films; Video Connection; Discount Video Tapes*

People Are Funny 1946
Comedy
57364   94 mins B/W   B, V, FO   P
Jack Haley, Rudy Vallee, Ozzie Nelson, Art Linkletter, Helen Walker
Battling radio producers vie to land the big sponsor with an original radio idea. Comedy ensues when one of them comes up with a great idea—stolen from a local station.
Paramount — *Video Yesteryear*

People That Time Forgot, The 1977
Science fiction
66045   90 mins   C   B, V   P
Edgar Rice Burroughs' novel about a rescue team that discovers a world of prehistoric monsters and tribes people provides the basis for this film.
MPAA:PG
John Dark — *Embassy Home Entertainment*

People Who Own the Dark, The 1979
Horror
63410   87 mins   C   B, V   P
Maria Pershing, Terry Kemper, Tom Weyland, Anita Brock, Paul Mackey
A small farming community becomes possessed by a supernatural light during an explosion. The people, who have all been blinded, become Masters of the night.
MPAA:R
Sean S. Cunningham Films Ltd — *Sun Video*

Pepe Le Moko 1937
Adventure
06235   87 mins   B/W   B, V   P
Jean Gabin, Mireille Balin, directed by Julien Duvivier
Violence, betrayal, and isolation are presented in this hide-and-seek game with police. Based on D'Ashelbe's novel. French film, English subtitles.
FR
French — *Budget Video; Cable Films; Penguin Video; Discount Video Tapes*

Pepper 1982
Adventure/Suspense
63362   88 mins   C   B, V   P
International intrigue and super spying abound in this fast-paced, sexy adventure featuring Pepper, a female secret agent in the James Bond tradition.
Amero Brothers — *Vestron Video*

Pepper and His Wacky Taxi 196?
Comedy
66110   79 mins   C   B, V   P
John Astin, Frank Sinatra Jr, Jackie Gayle, Alan Shorman
A father of four buys a '59 Cadillac and starts a cab company.
MPAA:G
Samuel S Dikel — *Unicorn Video*

Percy Faith and his Orchestra (The Best of Both Worlds) 1960
Music-Performance
12842 41 mins B/W   B, V, FO   P
Percy Faith and his Orchestra, Peter Nero
Percy Faith's 50-piece orchestra plays easy listening popular favorites.
BBC — *Video Yesteryear*

Perdicion de Mujeres 197?
Drama
63855   90 mins   B/W   B, V   P
Directed by Juan Orol

This is the story of the anguish and terror
experienced by the members of an illicit love
triangle. In Spanish.
SP
Mexican — *Budget Video*

Performance 1970
Drama
58244   105 mins   C   B, V, LV   R, P
*James Fox, Mick Jagger, Anita Pallenberg,
directed by Donald Cammell and Nicolas Roeg*
The story of a hunted murderer who takes
refuge with an outcast rock and roll star—and
sees his sense of reality vanish in an orgiastic
breakdown of barriers and roles.
MPAA:R
Warner Bros — *Warner Home Video*

Perils of Pauline, The 1947
Musical
03825   96 mins   B/W   B, V   P
*Betty Hutton, John Lund, Billy DeWolfe, directed
by George Marshall*
A musical biography of Pearl White, the original
queen of silent movie serials. Songs by Frank
Loesser include "I Wish I Didn't Love You So,"
an Academy Award nominee.
Paramount; Sol C Siegel — *Budget Video;
Video Yesteryear; Movie Buff Video; Discount
Video Tapes; Sheik Video; Cable Films; Media
Home Entertainment; VCII; Video Connection*

Perils of Penelope Pitstop, The 1984
Cartoons
66576   60 mins   C   B, V   P
Animated
This compilation of cartoons stars lovely
Penelope Pitstop, international race car driver,
who has to ward off the advances of villainous
Sylvester Sneekly while she drives.
Hanna Barbera — *Worldvision Home Video*

Perils of the Darkest Jungle 1944
Adventure/Serials
59149   180 mins   B/W   B, V, 3/4U   P
Linda Sterling, Allan Lane
A white jungle goddess battles money-mad oil
profiteers to prevent them from despoiling the
jungle. Original title: "The Tiger Woman." A
serial in twelve episodes, on two cassettes.
Republic — *Nostalgia Merchant*

Perry Como Show, The 1956
Variety
56613   60 mins   B/W   B, V   P
*Perry Como, Henry Fonda, Vera Ellen, Paul
Winchell, Jerry Mahoney, The Platters, Anne
Francis, Robbie the Robot*
Perry sings his biggest hits, Fonda does a spoof
on westerns, and Anne Francis and Robbie the
Robot (from "Forbidden Planet") perform.

NBC — *Video Dimensions*

Pershing Story, The/American Siberian Expeditionary Force 19??
World War I
53384   59 mins   B/W   B, V, 3/4U   P
General Pershing's exploits during WWI are
chronicled in "Pershing Story." "American
Siberian Expeditionary Force" shows the
activities of the expeditionary force which
journeyed into Russia following WWI.
USA — *International Historic Films*

Persona 1967
Drama
14440   83 mins   C   B, V, FO   P
*Bibi Andersson, Liv Ullmann, directed by Ingmar
Bergman*
A famous actress is stricken with
psychosomatic dumbness and is placed under a
nurse's care in an isolated house.
Svensk Filmindustri — *Video Yesteryear; Video
Dimensions; Sheik Video; Budget Video*

Personal Best 1982
Drama
59854   124 mins   C   B, V   R, P
*Mariel Hemingway, Scott Glenn, Patrice
Donnelly, directed by Robert Towne*
Two woman athletes, Olympic runners, fall in
love while competing against each other.
MPAA:R
Geffen Co; Warner Bros — *Warner Home
Video*

Peruvian Paso: For Those with Champagne Taste 1984
Animals/Horse racing
74543   25 mins   C   B, V   P
The program looks at the world's smoothest,
natural gaited breed of horse.
Equestrian Video Library — *Mercedes Maharis
Productions*

Pervertion (Perversion) 1980
Suspense
51103   90 mins   C   B, V   P
Carlos Estrada, Nadiuska
A woman begins a love affair with her boss, only
to uncover the shocking secret that he is a
horrible murderer. In Spanish.
SP
Spanish — *Budget Video*

Pete Seeger...A Song and a Stone 1972
Music
33444   85 mins   C   B, V   P
Pete Seeger, Johnny Cash, Lester Flatt

Pete Seeger and his pals strum, sing, and talk their way through various places in the U.S. in a year and a half's time.
Elfstrom — *Budget Video*

Pete Townsend 1982
Music-Performance
76675 30 mins C B, V P
This program presents Pete Townsend performing his new hit songs.
Trinifold Ltd Warner Amex Satellite Entertainment Co — *Sony Corporation of America*

Peter Allen and the Rockettes 1981
Music-Performance
58955 87 mins C B, V, CED P
Peter Allen, the Rockettes
Peter Allen — recorded live at his three-night, sell-out engagement, performing more than 20 songs, including: "Everything Old." "Flyaway," "Bicoastal," "You and Me," & "Don't Cry Out Loud" and " I Go to Rio." In Stereo.
20th Century Fox — *CBS/Fox Video; MCA Home Video (disc only)*

Peter and the Magic Egg 1983
Cartoons
66182 60 mins C B, V P
Animated, voices by Ray Bolger
The story of Mama and Papa Doppler, in danger of losing their farm to greedy Tobias Tinwhiskers.
RLR Associates — *Family Home Entertainment*

Peter Cottontail's Adventures 1978
Cartoons
53141 70 mins C B, V P
Animated
Peter loves to play practical jokes until no one wants to be his friend anymore, teaching him the importance of his Green Forest friends, Johnny and Polly Woodchuck, Jimmy Skunk, Chatterer Chipmunk, Reddy and Granny Fox, and Sammy Bluejay.
Ziv Intl — *Family Home Entertainment*

Peter Grimes 1981
Opera
59874 210 mins C LV P
Jon Vickers
The Royal Opera's production of Benjamin Britten's three-act opera set in a small English fishing town and concerning the inquest into the death of Grime's apprentice. In stereo.
Covent Garden Video — *Pioneer Artists*

Peter Lind Hayes Show, The 1957
Variety
59087 51 mins B/W B, V, FO P
Peter Lind Hayes, Mary Healy, Jack Whiting, Genevieve, the Step Brothers, Zippy the chimp, Tony Marvin
A variety show set in Central Park with Peter and Mary singing, Peter miming, and Jack imitating famous mayors of New York.
CBS — *Video Yesteryear*

Peter-No-Tail 1983
Fantasy/Cartoons
69537 82 mins C B, V, CED P
Animated, voices of Ken Berry, Dom DeLuise, Richard Kline, Tina Louise, Larry Storch, June Lockhart
A tail-less kitten wins the Cats Mastership and the heart of Molly Cream-Nose.
Stig Lasseby — *Children's Video Library*

Petrified Forest, The 1936
Drama
64330 83 mins B/W CED P
Bette Davis, Leslie Howard, Humphrey Bogart, Dick Foran, directed by Archie Mayo
Customers and employees at a diner in the Arizona desert are held captive by a group of thugs. Based on the play by Robert Sherwood.
Warner Bros — *CBS/Fox Video; RCA VideoDiscs*

Pets 1973
Drama
45058 103 mins C B, V P
Candy Rialson, Ed Bishop, Joan Blackman
Girls become helpless caged "Pets" of pleasure and pain to the man with the whip in his hand.
MPAA:R
International Producers Corp — *Imperial Video Corp*

Phantasm 1977
Horror
44980 90 mins C B, V, LV, CED P
Michael Baldwin, Bill Thornberry, Reggie Bannister, Kathy Lester
Two brothers discover the startling secret of the living dead when their friend is murdered.
MPAA:R
Avco Embassy — *Embassy Home Entertainment; RCA VideoDiscs*

Phantom Creeps 1939
Mystery/Serials
14263 156 mins B/W B, V P
Bela Lugosi, Dorothy Arnold, Robert Kent, Regis Toomey
Spine-tingling mystery by a master monster. Serial in 12 chapters, 13 minutes each.

Universal — *Video Connection; Cable Films; Discount Video Tapes*

Phantom Empire　　　　　　　　　1935
Western/Serials
38986　245 mins　B/W　　B, V, FO　　　　P
Gene Autry, Frankie Darro, Betsy King Ross, Smiley Burnette
Gene faces the futuristic "Thunder Riders" from the subterranean city of Murania, which is located 20,000 feet beneath his ranch. A complete serial in twelve episodes.
Mascot — *Video Yesteryear; Video Connection; Sheik Video; Nostalgia Merchant; Discount Video Tapes*

Phantom Empire, The　　　　　　　1984
Music video
72928　　60 mins　C　　B, V　　　　　P
Phantom Empire
The first of fifteen episodes of a rock video/cliffhanger serial inspired by the comics and pulps of the '40s.
Michael Uslan — *RCA/Columbia Pictures Home Video*

Phantom Express　　　　　　　　　1932
Mystery
08616　70 mins　B/W　　B, V, 3/4U　　　P
J. Farrell Mac Donald, Sally Blane, William Collier Jr., Hobart Bosworth
Experienced old engineer is dismissed from his job because his explanation that a mysterious train caused the wreck of his own train is not believed.
Majestic — *Penguin Video; Interurban Films; Discount Video Tapes*

Phantom of the Opera　　　　　　　1925
Horror
10628　85 mins　B/W　　B, V　　　P, T
Lon Chaney Sr., Norman Kerry, Mary Philbin
An unknown entity terrorizes a Paris opera house. Silent with two-color Technicolor "Bal Masque" sequence.
Universal — *Blackhawk Films; Penguin Video; Sheik Video; Video Yesteryear; Cable Films; Video Connection; Budget Video; Western Film & Video Inc; Discount Video Tapes; Cinema Concepts*

Phantom of the West　　　　　　　1931
Western
57366　166 mins　B/W　　B, V, FO　　　P
Tom Tyler
Ten-episode serial about a rancher who becomes "The Phantom of the West," in order to smoke out his father's killer.
Mascot — *Video Yesteryear; Video Connection*

Phantom Rancher, The　　　　　　　1939
Western
15484　61 mins　B/W　　B, V　　　　P
Ken Maynard
This roaring melodrama finds Maynard donning a mask to find the real Phantom who is causing havoc.
Nat Saland — *VCI Home Video; Video Connection*

Phantom Rider　　　　　　　　　　1937
Mystery/Serials
33953　152 mins　B/W　　B, V, 3/4U　　　P
Buck Jones, Maria Shelton
Mystery fills the old West in this serial composed of fifteen chapters.
Universal — *Video Connection*

Phantom Tollbooth, The　　　　　　1970
Adventure/Cartoons
63111　　89 mins　C　　B, V, CED　　　P
Animated, directed by Chuck Jones
A young boy drives his car into a strange and enchanting fantasy land.
MPAA:G
MGM — *MGM/UA Home Video*

Pharmacist, The　　　　　　　　　1932
Comedy
62868　19 mins　B/W　　B, V　　　P, T
W.C. Fields, Grady Sutton
A typical day of frustration for druggist Fields, with grouchy customers and a robbery stick-up to top things off.
Mack Sennett — *Blackhawk Films*

Phase IV　　　　　　　　　　　　1974
Science fiction
66033　　83 mins　C　　B, V　　　R, P
Nigel Davenport, Michael Murphy, Lynne Frederick
A tale of killer ants retaliating against the humans attempting their extermination.
MPAA:PG
Paramount — *Paramount Home Video*

Phedre　　　　　　　　　　　　　1968
Drama
63617　　93 mins　C　　B, V, FO　　　P
Marie Bell
Jean Racine's adaptation of the Greek legend involving Phedre, Theseus and Hippolyte is presented in French with English subtitles.
FR
French — *Video Yesteryear*

Phil Collins　　　　　　　　　　　1983
Music-Performance
75910　　17 mins　C　　B, V　　　　P
This program presents Phil Collins singing his hit songs "In the Air Tonight," "Through These Walls" and others.

　　　　(For Explanation of codes, see USE GUIDE and KEY)

Philip Collins; Hit and Run Music — *Sony Corporation of America*

Phil Collins Live at Perkins Palace 1984
Music-Performance
72181 60 mins C B, V R, P
The singer from Genesis performs many of the recent hits that have made him popular with audiences around the world.
DIR Broadcasting Inc — *THORN EMI Home Video*

Phil Silvers Special: Summer in New York 1960
Comedy/Variety
52457 60 mins B/W B, V, FO P
Phil Silvers, Carol Lawrence, Carol Haney, Jack Gilford
A comedy special tribute to New York City, which includes sketches, songs, and two dance numbers by Broadway star Carol Haney. The cast of Silvers' "Sgt. Bilko" series makes a cameo appearance.
CBS — *Video Yesteryear*

Philadelphia Story, The 1940
Comedy
47053 112 mins B/W B, V P
Katherine Hepburn, Cary Grant, James Stewart, Ruth Hussey, Roland Young, directed by George Cukor
A strong-willed Philadelphia girl finds the plans for her second marriage going awry when her first husband turns up. Based on the play by Philip Barry.
Academy Awards '40: Best Actor (Stewart); Best Screenplay (Donald Ogden Stewart).
MGM; Joseph L Mankiewicz — *MGM/UA Home Video*

Philco TV Playhouse: "Ernie Barger Is 50" 1953
Drama
47485 60 mins B/W B, V, FO P
Ed Begley, Carmen Matthews, Howard St. John, directed by Delbert Mann
A live TV drama written by Tad Mosel. Ernie Barger is a middle class manufacturer who discovers that life has passed him by and no one needs him anymore.
NBC — *Video Yesteryear*

Photographing the Nude 1982
Photography
59414 30 mins C B, V P
The creative aspects and techniques of nude photography are uncovered, for both the amateur and professional photographer.
Lee Kraft; Videocraft Prods — *New Age Video Inc*

Photonos 1982
Music-Performance
66244 58 mins C B, V R, P
A video album by the Emmy-winning group Emerald Web. In stereo VHS.
Bob Kat Productions — *Video City Productions*

Piaf 1981
Musical-Drama/Biographical
58703 115 mins C CED P
Jane Lapotaire
Jane Lapotaire portrays the legendary French singer Edith Piaf in this Broadway performance which won her a Tony Award for Best Actress.
MGM; CBS — *CBS/Fox Video*

Picture Music 1981
Music-Performance
65377 60 mins C B, V P
A compilation of 14 of the hottest music videos, including top-ten hits by Kim Carnes, America, Steve Miller, J. Geils Band, Billy Squier and Thomas Dolby.
EMI Music — *Vestron Video; Pioneer Video Imports*

Pieces 1983
Horror
65606 90 mins C B, V P
Christopher George
A chain-saw wielding madman roams a college campus in search of human parts for a ghastly jigsaw puzzle.
MPAA:R
Spectacular Trading — *Vestron Video*

Pieces of Eight 19??
Economics/Documentary
19409 30 mins C B, V, 3/4U, Q P
Fess Parker
Documentary which traces the origins of the monetary system and use of coins to the current modern age and minting.
TV Sports Scene — *TV Sports Scene*

Pied Piper, The/Cinderella 1981
Fairy tales
59706 70 mins C B, V R, P
Animated
A puppet animation version of the two classic fairy tales.
Mark Hall; Brian Cosgrove — *THORN EMI Home Video*

Pied Piper of Hamelin, The 1957
Fairy tales
65291 90 mins C B, V P
Van Johnson, Claude Raines, Jim Backus, Kay Starr, Lori Nelson

This is the evergreen classic of the magical piper who claims an entire village and then disappears with the village children into a mountain when the townspeople fail to keep a promise.
Hal Stanley Productions Unlimited — *Media Home Entertainment*

Pied Piper of Hamelin, The   1984
Fairy tales
Closed Captioned
73573   60 mins   C   B, V, CED   P
Eric Idle
From "Faerie Tale Theatre" comes the story of a man who had a way with a magic flute and how it charmed the rats out of Hamelin.
Gaylord Productions; Platypus Productions — *CBS/Fox Video*

Piedmont and Susquehanna Limiteds Plus, The   1980
Trains
46925   74 mins   C.   B, V   P
This program looks at the Piedmont Limited's run from Alexandria to Charlottesville, Virginia, the Susquehanna Valley Limited's run from Washington D.C. to Philadelphia and back, and the Transportation Museum in Roanoke, Virginia.
JMJ Prods — *JMJ Productions*

Pillow Talk   1959
Comedy-Drama
69032   102 mins   C   B, V   P
Rock Hudson, Doris Day, Tony Randall, Thelma Ritter
An interior decorator and a songwriter and notorious playboy share a party line telephone, but no other interests. In the process of disliking each other, they fall in love.
Universal International — *MCA Home Video*

Pilot, The   1982
Adventure/Drama
72211   90 mins   C   B, V   P
An ace pilot insists on flying whether he's drunk or sober.
Unknown — *Paragon Video Productions*

Pimpernel Smith   1942
Drama
66392   121 mins   B/W   B, V   P
Leslie Howard, Mary Morris, Francis L. Sullivan, David Tomlinson
An absent-minded archeology professor travels into war-torn Europe to rescue refugees. Also titled: "Mr. V."
British National — *Movie Buff Video; Video Yesteryear*

Pinchcliffe Grand Prix, The   1981
Comedy
59993   88 mins   C   B, V   R, P
Animated
A master inventor designs the ultimate race car.
MPAA:G
Caprino Film Centre — *Video Gems*

Pink Flamingos   1973
Satire
64844   95 mins   C   B, V   P
Divine, David Lochary, Mink Stole, Edith Massey, directed by John Waters
Divine, the dainty 300-pound transvestite, faces the biggest challenge of his/her career when he/she competes for the title of World's Filthiest Person.
MPAA:R
Saliva Films — *HarmonyVision*

Pink Floyd at Pompeii   1974
Music-Performance
59079   90 mins   C   B, V   P
Directed by Adrian Maben
The British rock group performs some of its most famous songs in this concert set at a ruined amphitheatre in Pompeii. Songs include "Echoes I & II," "Dark Side of the Moon," and "A Saucerful of Secrets." In stereo.
MPAA:G
April Fools — *HarmonyVision; RCA VideoDiscs; Vestron Video*

Pink Floyd The Wall   1982
Musical-Drama
65221   95 mins   C   B, V   P
Bob Geldof, directed by Alan Parker
Film version of Pink Floyd's 1979 LP, "The Wall." A surreal, impressionistic tour-de-force about a boy who grows up numb from society's pressures.
MPAA:R
MGM — *MGM/UA Home Video*

Pink Floyd's David Gilmour   1984
Music video
72896   101 mins   C   B, V   P
David Gilmour, Pete Townshend
This program contains the videos "After the Floyd," "Blue Light" and "All Lovers Are Deranged."
Pink Floyd — *CBS/Fox Video*

Pink Motel   1982
Comedy
69394   90 mins   C   B, V   R, P
Phyllis Diller, Slim Pickens
This is the story of several people and one hilarious night at a pink stucco motel which caters to couples.
MPAA:R

New Image; Wescom Productions — *THORN EMI Home Video*

Pink Panther, The   1964
Comedy
55587   113 mins   C   B, V, LV   P
Peter Sellers, David Niven, Robert Wagner, Claudia Cardinale
A priceless gem is sought by a wanted jewel thief whose accomplice is the wife of a French police inspector.
United Artists — *CBS/Fox Video; RCA VideoDiscs*

Pink Panther Strikes Again, The   1976
Comedy
59628   103 mins   C   B, V, LV   P
Peter Sellers, Herbert Lom, Lesley-Anne Down, Colin Blakely, Leonard Rossiter, directed by Blake Edwards
The fourth Panther film has Clouseau being hunted by Chief Inspector Dreyfus, who plans to rid the world of Clouseau once and for all.
MPAA:PG
United Artists — *CBS/Fox Video; RCA VideoDiscs*

Pinocchio   1976
Musical
06061   76 mins   C   B, V   P
Danny Kaye, Sandy Duncan
Classical story of Pinocchio in musical form.
Rothman and Wahl; Vidronics Company — *VCI Home Video*

Pinocchio   1968
Fairy tales
47675   74 mins   C   B, V   P
Collodi's classic tale of the little puppet boy and his adventures in becoming a real boy. Live action actors are combined with puppets from the Prague Marionette Theater.
Ron Merk — *Unicorn Video*

Pinocchio   1978
Fantasy
56923   90 mins   C   B, V   R, P
Animated
Another version of the classic story about a puppet who becomes a boy. This film adapted from the original 1882 manuscript.
GG Communications — *Video Gems*

Pinocchio   1984
Fairy tales
Closed Captioned
73146   60 mins   C   B, V, CED   P
Pee Wee Herman, James Coburn, Carl Reiner, Lainie Kazan
Pee Wee Herman is the puppet who wants to be a real little boy in this "Faerie Tale Theatre" adaptation of this childrens classic.
Shelley Duvall — *CBS/Fox Video*

Pinocchio in Outer Space   1964
Cartoons/Fantasy
47436   71 mins   C   B, V   P
Voices of Arnold Stang, Minerva Pious, Peter Lazer, Conrad Jameson
A new adventure featuring Pinocchio and his friends on a magical trip to Mars.
SFM Entertainment — *RCA/Columbia Pictures Home Video*

Pinwheel Songbook, The   1981
Variety
47383   57 mins   C   B, V   R, P
Dale Engle, George James, Jim Jinkins, Arline Miyazaki, Betty Rozek
Entertainment for preschoolers, featuring songs, stories and characters from the award-winning TV series, "Pinwheel."
Warner Amex Satellite Entertainment Company — *Warner Home Video*

Pioneer Cinema (1895-1905)   19??
Film-History
63851   25 mins   B/W   B, V   P
A compilation of some early film works, including a Lumiere program from 1895, Melies' "Trip to the Moon," and "El Spectro Rojo," a color short.
George Melies et al — *Budget Video*

Pioneers, The   1941
Western
06352   59 mins   B/W   B, V   P
Tex Ritter
Tex Ritter sets out to protect the frontier.
Monogram — *Video Connection*

Pippi Goes on Board   1975
Adventure
29347   83 mins   C   B, V   R, P
Inger Nilsson, directed by Olle Hellbom
Pippi's father arrives one day to take her sailing to Taka-Kuka, his island kingdom. She can't bear to leave her friends and jumps off the ship to return home. Based on the classic by Astrid Lindgren.
MPAA:G
N.W. Russo; GG Communications — *Video Gems*

Pippi in the South Seas   1974
Adventure
29236   99 mins   C   B, V   R, P
Inger Nilsson, directed by Olle Hellbom

(For Explanation of codes, see USE GUIDE and KEY)

Pippi and her two friends decide to rescue her father, who is being held captive by a band of pirates. Based on the classic by Astrid Lindgren.
MPAA:G
N.W. Russo; GG Communications — *Video Gems*

Pippi Longstocking 1973
Comedy
50961   99 mins   C   B, V   R, P
Inger Nillson
Mischievous Pippi creates havoc in her town through the antics of her pets, a monkey and a horse. Based on the children's book by Astrid Lindgren.
MPAA:G
N.W. Russo; GG Communications — *Video Gems*

Pippi on the Run 1974
Adventure
58586   99 mins   C   B, V   R, P
The further adventures of Pippi, who, among other things, is "the strongest kid alive."
MPAA:G
N W Russo; GG Communications — *Video Gems*

Pippin 1981
Musical
53134   120 mins   C   B, V   P
Ben Vereen, William Katt, Martha Raye, Chita Rivera
An original video production of Bob Fosse's Broadway smash featuring Ben Vereen recreating his original Tony-Award-winning role.
Sheehan Elkins Video Venture Ltd — *Family Home Entertainment; RCA VideoDiscs; Pioneer Artists*

Piranha 1978
Horror
64300   90 mins   C   B, V   R, P
Bradford Dillman, Heather Menzies, Kevin McCarthy, Keenan Wynn
A rural Texas resort area is plagued by attacks from ferocious man-eating fish which a scientist created to be used as a secret weapon in the Vietnam War.
MPAA:R
New World Pictures — *Warner Home Video*

Pirate, The 1948
Musical
58869   102 mins   C   B, V, CED   P
Judy Garland, Gene Kelly, Walter Slezak, Gladys Cooper, George Zucco, Reginald Owen, the Nicholas Brothers, directed by Vincente Minnelli
A lonely girl on a remote Caribbean isle dreams of her romantic hero, the legendary pirate Black Macoco. To woo her, a traveling actor masquerades as the pirate. Music by Cole

Porter, including "Be a Clown," "Mack the Black" and "You Can Do No Wrong."
MGM; Arthur Freed — *MGM/UA Home Video*

Pirate Movie, The 1982
Musical
60424   98 mins   C   B, V, CED   P
Kristy McNichol, Christopher Atkins, Ted Hamilton
Gilbert and Sullivan's "The Pirates of Penzance" is combined with new pop songs in this tale of fantasy and romance.
MPAA:PG
Twentieth Century Fox — *CBS/Fox Video*

Pirates of Capri, The 1949
Adventure
66393   94 mins   B/W   B, V   P
Louis Hayward, Binnie Barnes
Louis Hayward plays a dual role in this swashbuckler as a daring pirate and a mild-mannered clerk.
Italo English Coproductions — *Movie Buff Video*

Pirates of Penzance, The 1983
Musical/Comedy
64787   112 mins   C   B, V, LV,   P
                                       CED
Kevin Kline, Angela Lansbury, Linda Ronstadt, Rex Smith, George Rose
This Gilbert and Sullivan musical comedy is the story of a band of fun-loving pirates and their young apprentice. An adaptation of the award-winning Broadway play. In stereo VHS and laser disc.
Universal — *MCA Home Video; CBS/Fox Video*

Pit, The 1981
Science fiction/Horror
65714   96 mins   C   B, V   P
Sammy Snyders
A 12-year-old autistic boy gets his change for revenge against the people in his town who humiliate him when he stumbles on a huge hole in the forest, at the bottom of which are strange and deadly creatures.
MPAA:R
Bennett Fode — *Embassy Home Entertainment*

Pit and the Pendulum, 1961
The
Horror
53519   80 mins   C   B, V   R, P
Vincent Price, John Kerr, Barbara Steele, Luana Anders, directed by Roger Corman
A woman and her lover plan to drive her brother mad, and he responds by locking them in his torture chamber. Loosely based on the Poe story.

American International; Roger Corman — *Warner Home Video; Vestron Video (disc only)*

Pittsburgh Steelers: The Championship Years 1982
Football
63162   96 mins   C   B, V, FO   P
Pittsburgh Steelers
Highlights from the first four championship seasons of the 1970's team of the decade.
NFL Films — *NFL Films Video*

Pixote 1981
Drama
47432   127 mins   C   B, V   P
Fernando Ramos Da Silva, Marilla Pera, Jorge Juliao, directed by Hector Babenco
Pixote is a ten-year-old street kid in Sao Paolo, Brazil. When he is sent to a juvenile detention center, he and his companions become hardened to criminal life. In Portuguese with English subtitles.
PR
Embrafilms — *RCA/Columbia Pictures Home Video*

Place Called Today, A 1971
Drama
60416   105 mins   C   B, V   P
Lana Wood
A tale of big city politics where violence and fear in the streets is at the heart of the campaign.
Today Productions — *Monterey Home Video*

Place in the Sun, A 1951
Drama
55542   122 mins   B/W   B, V, LV   R, P
Montgomery Cliff, Elizabeth Taylor, Shelley Winters, directed by George Stevens
A confused, ambitious factory worker in love with a wealthy debutante is threatened with a drab future by a simple working girl. Adapted from Theodore Dreiser's "An American Tragedy."
Academy Awards '51: Best Direction (Stevens); Best Screenplay (Michael Wilson, Harry Brown); Best Scoring (Franz Waxman).
Paramount; George Stevens — *Paramount Home Video; RCA VideoDiscs*

Plan 9 from Outer Space 1956
Science fiction/Horror
09112   78 mins   B/W   B, V, 3/4U   P
Bela Lugosi, Tors Johnson, Lyle Talbot, Vampira
UFO's containing strange inhabitants from an unknown planet invade the earth. Includes previews of coming attractions from classic science fiction films.
Golden Turkey Awards for Worst Films of All Time: First Place.

DCA — *Nostalgia Merchant; Sheik Video; Video Yesteryear; Admit One Video*

Planet of the Apes 1968
Science fiction
29164   112 mins   C   B, V   P
Charlton Heston, Roddy McDowall, Kim Hunter, directed by Franklin J. Schaffner
Four American astronauts are hurtled 2,000 years through time and space and crashland in the wilderness of a strange planet. They discover this world is dominated by apes.
EL, SP
20th Century Fox — *CBS/Fox Video*

Plastic Man 1982
Cartoons
65662   56 mins   C   B, V   P
Animated
With his amazing ability to mold and stretch himself into any shape, Plastic Man stretches himself into new dimensions to play with Baby Plas.
Ruby Spears — *Worldvision Home Video*

Play It Again, Sam 1972
Comedy
38591   85 mins   C   B, V, LV   R, P
Woody Allen, Diane Keaton, Tony Roberts, directed by Herbert Ross
Woody Allen's homage to "Casablanca," in which he plays a movie critic with the recurring hallucination of Humphrey Bogart offering him tips on how to make it with women. Bogart's advice comes in handy when Woody falls in love with his best friend's wife.
MPAA:PG
Paramount — *Paramount Home Video; RCA VideoDiscs*

Play Misty for Me 1971
Mystery/Drama
55551   102 mins   C   B, V, LV   P
Clint Eastwood, Jessica Walter, Donna Mills, directed by Clint Eastwood
A disc jockey meets up with a psychotic fan and she becomes emotionally involved with him. Conflicts arise between the disc jockey's girlfriend and the obsessed fan, who becomes dangerously violent.
MPAA:R
Universal; Jennings Lang Malpaso Co — *MCA Home Video*

Play Your Best Tennis, Volume I 1983
Tennis
65263   90 mins   C   B, V   P
This program improves the competitive edge of tennis players by providing insights into all aspects of the game. Featured are the fundamentals of "Building Your Best Game,"

"The Basics of Groundstroke," and "Serve and Return of Serve."
Caravatt Communications; United States Tennis Association — *Caravatt Home Entertainment*

Play Your Best Tennis, Volume II   1983
Tennis
65264   90 mins   C   B, V   P
This continuation in the series on improving the competitive edge of tennis features the strokes and strategies of "Net Play," "Specialty Shots," "Preparation for Match Play" and "Match Play."
Caravatt Communications; United States Tennis Association — *Caravatt Home Entertainment*

Playboy of the Western World, The   1962
Comedy
63319   96 mins   C   B, V   R, P
Siobhan McKenna, Gary Raymond, directed by Brian Desmond Hurst
An innkeeper's daughter is infatuated with an upstart young playboy. Adapted from the classic play by John Millington Synge.
4 Provinces Films Ltd — *THORN EMI Home Video*

Playboy Video, Volume I   1982
Variety
63390   85 mins   C   B, V, LV, CED   P
Barbara Carrera, John and Bo Derek, Lonny Chin, Shannon Tweed
This collector's edition contains interviews with John and Bo Derek and actress Barbara Carrera. Photo sessions with Shannon Tweed, 1982 Playmate of the year and Lonny Chin, the first video centerfold, are featured. Also includes a review of Playboy's history and a look at Paris' famed Crazy Horse saloon.
Playboy Enterprises — *CBS/Fox Video*

Playboy Video, Volume II   1983
Variety
64561   81 mins   C   B, V, LV, CED   P
Dudley Moore, Sylvia Kristel, Lynda Wiesmeier, Candy Loving, Duran Duran
The second issue of this video magazine features interviews with Dudley Moore and Sylvia Kristel. Other segments include the "Playmate Playoffs," "Playmate of the Month" and "Ribald Classics," as well as a look at New Wave rock band Duran Duran.
Playboy Enterprises — *CBS/Fox Video*

Playboy Video, Volume 3   1983
Variety
64907   85 mins   C   B, V, LV, CED   P
Cheech and Chong, Marianne Gravatte, Craig Blankenhorn, Charlotte Kemp, Carol Doda

This volume features "Playboy's" 1983 Playmate of the Year, comedians Cheech Marin and Tommy Chong, "Sex in Public Places," December '82 Playmate of the Month, a Ribald Classic, the first topless dancer, and comedy capers.
Playboy Enterprises — *CBS/Fox Video*

Playboy Video, Volume 4   1983
Variety
65416   85 mins   C   B, V, LV, CED   P
Willie Nelson, Marilyn Chambers, Barbara Edwards
The fourth volume of this series features Barbara Edwards, Playboy magazine's Miss September 1983, an interview with country music legend Willie Nelson, a tribute to 1980 Playmate of the Year Dorothy Stratten and a profile of x-rated movie star Marilyn Chambers.
Playboy Enterprises — *CBS/Fox Video*

Playboy Video, Volume 5   1984
Variety
72189   75 mins   C   B, V   P
"Playboy" magazine's 30th anniversary playmate, Morgan Fairchild and the "Playboy" candid camera are featured.
Playboy Enterprises — *CBS/Fox Video*

Players   1979
Drama
44594   120 mins   C   B, V   R, P
Ali MacGraw, Dean-Paul Martin, Maximillian Schell, Pancho Gonzales, directed by Anthony Harvey
A young tennis hustler touring Mexico hooks up with a beautiful mysterious older woman. They seem to be from different worlds yet their love grows. She inspires him enough to enter Wimbledon. Several tennis pros appear, including Guillermo Vilas, John McEnroe, and Ilie Nastase.
MPAA:PG
Paramount, Robert Evans — *Paramount Home Video*

Playing Folk Guitar   1980
Music
47325   60 mins   C   B, V, 3/4U   P
Techniques of basic and complex strums, fingerpicking, and flatpicking are demonstrated. Detailed sections on blues and country and western styles are included.
AM Available
Vision Productions — *Vision Productions*

Playmate Review   1983
Variety
66072   90 mins   C   B, V, LV, CED   P

Ten playmates from Playboy magazine, including 1982 Playmate of the Year Shannon Tweed, are featured in this candid pictorial.
Playboy Enterprises — *CBS/Fox Video*

Playwrights '56: "The Battler"   1955
Drama
47486   60 mins   B/W   B, V, FO   P
Paul Newman, Dewey Martin, Phyllis Kirk, directed by Arthur Penn
An early dramatic TV appearance by Paul Newman, as a young drifter who meets an interesting cross-section of people while hitchhiking around the country. Based on a story by Ernest Hemingway.
NBC — *Video Yesteryear*

Plaza Suite   1971
Comedy
65735   114 mins   C   B, V   R, P
Walter Matthau, Maureen Stapleton, Barbara Harris, Lee Grant, Louise Sorel
Three sketches set in Suite 719 of New York City's Plaza Hotel, based on the play by Neil Simon.
MPAA:PG
Paramount — *Paramount Home Video*

Pleasure Doing Business, A   1979
Comedy
63971   86 mins   C   B, V   R, P
Conrad Bain, John Byner, Alan Oppenheimer, Misty Rowe, Phyllis Diller, Tom Smothers
Three high school buddies, now in their 40's, are reunited at a stag party, where they decide to go into business as managers in "the oldest profession."
Steve Vagnino — *VCII*

Plisetskaya Dances   1964
Documentary/Dance
69834   70 mins   B/W   B, V   P
A look at the world famous dancer, Maya Plisetskaya. This documentary chronicles a career which has been little seen in the west, offering some important insights into the Soviet dance world. Narrated in English.
Sovexportfilm USSR — *Video Arts International*

Ploesti   194?
Armed Forces-US
68911   22 mins   B/W   B, V   P
Follow the crews of the B-17s and B-24s as they fly over Yugoslavia to Ploesti.
US Army — *Interurban Films*

Plow That Broke the Plains, The/The River   1937
History-US/Documentary
52319   60 mins   B/W   B, V   P, T
Written and directed by Pare Lorentz
Two classic documentaries: "The Plow That Broke the Plains" deals with the New Deal efforts to improve the lot of Oklahoma "Dust Bowl" farmers. "The River" is a poetic history of the Mississippi River and its ecological balance.
US Information Service — *Blackhawk Films; Western Film & Video Inc; Classic Video Cinema Collector's Club*

Pocatello Kid   1931
Western
13078   60 mins   B/W   B, V   P
Ken Maynard
A Western adventure featuring Ken Maynard.
Tiffany — *Video Connection; Video Dimensions; Discount Video Tapes*

Poco   1977
Adventure
69531   88 mins   C   B, V, CED   P
Chill Wills, Michelle Asburn, John Steadman
A dog named Poco gets separated from the girl who owns her in Yosemite National Park, and Poco tries to find her way home.
MPAA:G
Cinema Shares — *Children's Video Library*

Policewomen   1974
Crime-Drama
64295   99 mins   C   B, V   P
Sondra Currie, Tony Young, Phil Hoover, Elizabeth Stuart, Jeanie Bell
A female undercover agent must stop a ring of gold smugglers.
MPAA:R
Crown International Pictures — *VCI Home Video*

Polka Film, The   1983
Music/Folklore
60454   30 mins   C   B, V, 3/4U   P
A look at the folk music form of the polka. Scenes from Pennsylvania, New York, Connecticut and Chicago show off the vigorous joy of this music-dance form.
Les Blank — *Flower Films*

Pollyanna   1960
Comedy-Drama
59062   134 mins   C   B, V, LV, CED   R, P
Hayley Mills, Jane Wyman, Richard Egan, Karl Malden, Nancy Olsen, Adolphe Menjou, Donald Crisp, Agnes Moorehead, Kevin Corcoran
A penniless American orphan comes to live with her aunt in the small town of Harrington, gradually changing the hearts of the entire community.

Academy Awards '60: Honorary Award for the most outstanding Juvenile Performance (Hayley Mills).
Walt Disney — *Walt Disney Home Video*

Pollyanna 1920
Comedy-Drama
66304   60 mins   B/W   B, V   P, T
Mary Pickford
A young orphan girl is adopted by her cold, embittered aunt and does her best to bring joy and gladness to all the new people she meets. Silent with music score.
Mary Pickford Company — *Blackhawk Films*

Poltergeist 1982
Horror
47780   114 mins   C   B, V, CED   P
Jobeth Williams, Craig T. Nelson, Beatrice Straight, Heather O'Rourke, Zelda Rubinstein, directed by Tobe Hooper
The presence of menacing spirits terrorizes a middle-class family, transporting the youngest member into a "world beyond."
MPAA:R
MGM; United Artists — *MGM/UA Home Video*

Pom-Pom Girls, The 1976
Comedy
48481   90 mins   C   B, V   P
Robert Carradine, Jennifer Ashley
High school seniors, intent on having one last fling before graduating, get involved in crazy antics, clumsy romances, and football rivalries.
MPAA:R
Crown International — *VCI Home Video*

Poor Little Rich Girl, The 1917
Comedy-Drama
66118   64 mins   B/W   B, V   P, T
Mary Pickford
Mary Pickford received raves in this film, in which she portrayed Gwendolyn, one of her most tender child performances. Organ score.
Adolph Zukor — *Blackhawk Films*

Pop Goes the Cork 1922
Comedy
59409   87 mins   B/W   B, V   P, T
Max Linder
Three films by the man Chaplin referred to as his "professor," Max Linder: "Be My Wife," "Seven Years Bad Luck," and "The Three Must-Get-Theres." Linder was the foremost film comedian in early twentieth-century France, and made these three films during a stay in America.
Max Linder Productions — *Blackhawk Films*

Popeye 1980
Comedy/Musical
55538   114 mins   C   B, V, LV   R, P
Robin Williams, Shelley Duvall, Roy Walston, Paul Dooley, directed by Robert Altman
The cartoon sailor brought to life is on a search to find his long-lost father. Along the way, he meets Olive Oyl and adopts little Sweet Pea. Script by Jules Feiffer, music by Harry Nilsson.
MPAA:PG
Paramount; Robert Evans — *Paramount Home Video; RCA VideoDiscs*

Popeye and Friends in Outer Space 19??
Cartoons
65695   60 mins   C   B, V   P
Animated
Popeye and Olive Oyl take their act into the ozone and beyond. As always, they get into big trouble with their arch enemy, Bluto. Luckily for Popeye and all concerned, cans of spinach are not as rare in outer space as Haley's Comet.
Paramount; Max Fleischer — *Media Home Entertainment*

Popeye and Friends in the Wild West 1984
Cartoons
65370   60 mins   C   B, V   P
Animated
The famous spinach eating sailor is back in ten gallon hat and spurs for uproarious western adventures. Also included in this cartoon collection are Krazy Kat, Beetle Bailey and Snuffy Smith.
Max Fleischer — *Media Home Entertainment*

Popeye Festival 193?
Cartoons
53802   60 mins   C   B, V   P
Animated
This collection of Popeye cartoons features the first two-reel technicolor Popeye productions. Included are "Popeye Meets Aladdin and His Wonderful Lamp," "Popeye Meets Ali Baba and His 40 Thieves," and "Popeye the Sailor Meets Sinbad the Sailor."
Paramount; Max Fleischer — *Budget Video*

Popeye the Sailor 193?
Cartoons
53800   54 mins   C   B, V, FO   P
Animated
This cartoon package includes "Popeye Meets Aladdin and His Wonderful Lamp," "Popeye Meets Ali Baba and His 40 Thieves," and "Popeye the Sailor Meets Sinbad the Sailor."
Paramount; Max Fleischer — *Video Yesteryear; Western Film & Video Inc*

Popeye—Travelin' On About Travel 1984
Travel
76652   60 mins   C   B, V   P
Animated

Popeye and Olive Oyl visit foreign and exotic lands in this hilarious program.
Media Home Entertainment — *Media Home Entertainment*

Poppies Are Also Flowers　　1966
Adventure
59840　　90 mins　　C　　B, V　　　　P
Senta Berger, Stephen Boyd, Yul Brynner, Angie Dickinson, Rita Hayworth, Trevor Howard, Trini Lopez, E. G. Marshall, Eli Wallach, Omar Sharif
Also known as "The Poppy Is Also a Flower," this Ian Fleming thriller about the illegal world drug trade focuses on how the poppies converted into heroin are being channeled into the U.S.
Terence Young — *Embassy Home Entertainment*

Porky's　　1982
Comedy
64908　　94 mins　　C　　B, V, LV, CED　　P
Dan Monahan, Wyatt Knight, Tony Ganios, Mark Herrier, Cyril O'Reilly, Roger Wilson
Set in south Florida in the early 1950's, this irreverent comedy follows the misadventures of six youths of Angel Beach High School. Their main interest is girls.
MPAA:R
Melvin Simon Productions; Astral Bellevue Pathe — *CBS/Fox Video*

Porky's II: The Next Day　　1983
Comedy
65492　　100 mins　　C　　B, V　　　　P
Bill Wiley, Dan Monahan, Wyatt Knight, Cyril O'Reilly, Roger Wilson, Tony Ganious, Mark Herrier, Scott Colomby
The Angel Beach gang stir up their sleepy southern Florida town when they join forces to participate in the high school project, an innocent sounding tribute to Shakespeare. What starts out as a simple school project soon explodes into a townwide controversy... until our ingenious heroes strike back with an explosively comic scheme.
MPAA:R
Astral Bellevue Pathe Inc; 20th Century Fox Films — *CBS/Fox Video*

Porsche Carrera 6, The　　1983
Automobiles-Racing
65173　　30 mins　　C　　B, V　　　　P
Narrated by Ron Hughes
Several restored Porsche Carrera 6 models are shown, including the only 906E that is presently in the U.S. Racing scenes from the 1982 Monterey Vintage Races at Laguna Seca are also included.
Armour Productions — *Armour Productions*

Porsche 917　　1983
Automobiles
76386　　44 mins　　C　　B, V　　　　P
The King of the Porsche racers in 12 cylinder form. Seen are the 917LH, 917K, 917-10, 917-10K, and 917-30 close-up.
Armour Productions — *Armour Productions*

Porsche 904 GTS Carrera, The　　1983
Automobiles-Racing
65174　　38 mins　　C　　B, V　　　　P
Both restored and unrestored Porsche Carreras are seen, most licensed for street use with certain modifications to the original specs. Also included are racing sequences at Riverside Raceway and Laguna Seca.
Armour Productions — *Armour Productions*

Porsche 930 Turbo　　1983
Automobiles-Racing
65171　　34 mins　　C　　B, V　　　　P
Narrated by Ron Hughes
1976-1979 Porsche 930 Turbos are seen, all with varying options and modifications. Also included is an interview with Dieter Inzenhofer of Andial Porsche Service, Santa Ana, California.
Armour Productions — *Armour Productions*

Porsche Parade 1983　　1983
Automobiles
76385　　45 mins　　C　　B, V　　　　P
A trip through the week-long "World Series" of Porsche events.
Armour Productions — *Armour Productions*

Porsche RSK, RS-60, 61, The　　1983
Automobiles-Racing
65175　　38 mins　　C　　B, V　　　　P
Narrated by Ron Hughes
Several Porsche racers of these models are seen, most of which have extensive European racing histories. The Porsche RS-60 Spare Parts Manual is reviewed and the tape also includes footage of RSK racing action circa 1961-62.
Armour Productions — *Armour Productions*

Port of Call　　1948
Drama/Romance
65628　　100 mins　　B/W　　B, V　　　　P
Nine-Christine Jonsson, Bengt Eklund, directed by Ingmar Bergman
A direct, almost documentary telling of the love that grows between a seaman and a girl from reform school who has lost her self-respect.
Janus Films — *Embassy Home Entertainment*

Port of New York　　1949
Crime-Drama
47466　　82 mins　　B/W　　B, V, FO　　P

Scott Brady, Yul Brynner, K. T. Stevens
A narcotics gang is smuggling large quantities of
drugs into New York. A government agent
poses as a gang member in order to infiltrate
the mob and get the goods on them.
Eagle Lion — *Video Yesteryear; Movie Buff
Video*

Portholes   1984
Boating
69684   60 mins   C   B, V, LV,   S
                                  CED
This bimonthly video magazine explores a wide
range of boating interests and includes such
subjects as seamanship, navigation, racing
(power and sail), maintenance and new
products. Each issue contains a "Letters to the
Editor" segment and some advertising.
Available by subscription only.
Nutech Video Publishing Co — *Nutech Video
Publishing Company*

Portnoy's Complaint   1972
Comedy-Drama
51969   101 mins   C   B, V   R, P
Richard Benjamin, Karen Black, Lee Grant
The screen adaptation of Philip Roth's novel
follows the frustrating experiences of a sexually
obsessed young man as he relates them to his
psychiatrist.
MPAA:R
Warner Bros — *Warner Home Video*

Portrait of a Hitman   19??
Crime-Drama
66505   85 mins   C   B, V   P
*Jack Palance, Rod Steiger, Richard Roundtree,
Bo Svenson*
An aspiring painter leads a double life as a
professional hitman.
Wildlife Productions — *Program Hunters*

Poseidon Adventure, The   1972
Adventure
09094   117 mins   C   B, V, CED   P
*Gene Hackman, Ernest Borgnine, Shelley
Winters, Red Buttons, Jack Albertson, Carol
Lynley*
The S.S. Poseidon, on her last voyage from
New York to Athens, is capsized by a tidal wave
on New Year's Eve.
Academy Awards '72: Best Song ("The Morning
After"); Special Effects. MPAA:PG EL, SP
Twentieth Century-Fox; Irwin
Allen — *CBS/Fox Video*

Postman Always Rings   1981
Twice, The
Drama
53555   122 mins   C   B, V, CED   P
*Jack Nicholson, Jessica Lange, John Colicos,
Anjelica Huston, Michael Lerner, John P. Ryan,
directed by Bob Rafelson*

A luckless drifter becomes attracted to the
unhappy wife of a middle-aged roadhouse
owner, and the two attempt to kill the husband.
Based on James M. Cain's novel.
MPAA:R
Bob Rafelson; Charles Mulvehill;
MGM — *CBS/Fox Video*

Postnatal (Rehabilitation   1978
and Injury)
Physical fitness
52756   30 mins   C   B, V   P
Hosted by Ann Dugan
Reconditioning exercises after childbirth,
including both specific-area and total-body
movements to gradually improve muscle tone.
Part of the "Rehabilitation and Injury" series.
Health 'N Action — *RCA/Columbia Pictures
Home Video*

Pot O' Gold   1941
Musical
13045   87 mins   B/W   B, V   P, T
*Paulette Goddard, James Stewart, Horace Heidt
Band*
Girl's father, who hates dance bands, schedules
Heidt on his radio quiz show.
United Artists — *Blackhawk Films; Movie Buff
Video; Video Yesteryear; Sheik Video; Video
Connection; Cable Films*

Pot Shots   1982
Documentary
66238   65 mins   C   B, V   R, P
A candid look at the home-growing of marijuana.
Unknown — *Video City Productions*

Potemkin   1925
Film-History
08699   67 mins   B/W   B, V, 3/4U   P
*Alexander Antonov, Grigory Alexandrov,
Vladimir Barsky, Mikhail Gomorov, directed by
Sergei Eisentein*
Recounts the heroic mutiny of Russian sailors in
1905.
Russian — *Penguin Video; International
Historic Films; Blackhawk Films; Sheik Video;
Video Yesteryear; Budget Video; Western Film
& Video Inc; Discount Video Tapes*

Powdersmoke Range   1935
Western
64414   71 mins   B/W   B, V, 3/4U   P
Harry Carey, Hoot Gibson, Tom Tyler
A crooked frontier politician plots to steal
valuable ranch property, until the law rides into
town.
RKO — *Nostalgia Merchant*

Power, The   1981
Football
50651   24 mins   C   B, V, FO   R, P

San Diego Chargers
The passing attack of Dan Fouts to John Jefferson, Kellen Winslow, and Charley Joiner was nearly unstoppable in 1980. Coach Don Coryell's 1980 Chargers travelled to the AFC Championship Game where they met the Oakland Raiders.
NFL Films — *NFL Films Video*

Power, The   1983
Horror
73032   87 mins   C   B, V   P
As a small Aztec idol passes down from generation to generation the power of the idol becomes stronger.
MPAA:R
Film Ventures — *Vestron Video*

Power Dive   1941
Drama
66394   69 mins   B/W   B, V   P
Richard Arlen, Jean Parker, Cliff Edwards
Test pilots from a large aviation company experience danger in the skies and romance on the ground.
Paramount — *Movie Buff Video*

Power of the Resurrection   1962
Religion
55030   60 mins   C   B, V   P
The passion of Christ, as seen through the eyes of Simon and Peter.
Family Films — *Vanguard Video*

Power Play   1978
Suspense
65012   95 mins   C   B, V, 3/4U   P
Peter O'Toole, David Hemmings, Donald Pleasance
A young army colonel of a small European country joins forces with rebels to overthrow the government. After the coup, it is discovered that one of the rebels is a traitor.
Peter Cooper; Ronald I. Cohen — *Nostalgia Merchant*

Powerforce   1983
Martial arts
75630   98 mins   C   B, V   P
A CIA agent must use martial arts in order to save the free world.
Evart Enterprises — *Independent United Distributors*

Prairie Badmen   1946
Western
13046   55 mins   B/W   B, V   P
Buster Crabbe
Another action-packed Billy the Kid western
PRC — *Video Connection*

Prairie Moon   1938
Western/Musical
44806   58 mins   B/W   B, V   P, T
Gene Autry, Smiley Burnette
Gene becomes guardian of a gangster's sons and gets involved with cattle rustlers.
Republic — *Blackhawk Films; Video Connection*

Prairie Pals   1942
Western
57975   60 mins   B/W   B, V   P
Bill Boyd, Lee Powell
A frontier Marshall blazes into action.
Producers Releasing Corp — *Video Connection*

Pre-War German Featurettes   1937
Documentary/Philosophy and ideology
52373   60 mins   B/W   B, V, 3/4U   P
This tape offers four short documentary films from the mid-1930's produced by German filmmakers. All reflect the prevailing Nazi ideology: "Yesterday and Today," "Three Years of Adolph Hitler," "Honor of Work," and "Becoming an Army." In German with English subtitles.
GE
UFA et al — *International Historic Films*

Preacherman   1983
Comedy-Drama
66515   90 mins   C   B, V   P
Amos Huxley, Marian Brown, Adam Hesse
A phony preacher travels through the South, fleecing gullible congregations wherever he goes.
MPAA:R
Albert T Viola — *Paragon Video Productions*

Predators of the Sea   1977
Documentary/Fishes
29166   93 mins   C   B, V   R, P
An underwater program that reveals the fascinating world of the creatures of the deep. Highlights include a thrilling fight between an octopus and a deadly moray eel, a look at the seagoing crocodile, and deadly sharks in action.
Bill Burrud Productions — *Walt Disney Home Video*

Pregnancy and the Newborn Child   1980
Pregnancy/Infants
47327   72 mins   C   B, V, 3/4U   P
A complete pregnancy instruction program is provided, along with demonstrations of holding, washing, and diapering a newborn baby.
Vision Productions — *Vision Productions*

Prelude to War   1942
World War II/Documentary
08907   53 mins   B/W   B, V   P
Directed by Frank Capra
A compact look at the events of 1931-39;
includes a series of contrasts between free
societies and totalitarian governments. From
the "Why We Fight" series.
Academy Awards '42: Best Documentary.
US War Department — *Penguin Video; Budget
Video; Western Film & Video Inc; Discount
Video Tapes; MPI Home Video*

Premiere of "A Star Is   1954
Born"
Film-History
42959   30 mins   B/W   B, V, FO   P
*Doris Day, Judy Garland, Edward G. Robinson,
James Dean, Elizabeth Taylor, Joan Crawford,
Debbie Reynolds, Shelley Winters, Kim Novak,
Lucille Ball, Desi Arnaz*
From the lobby of the Pantages Theater in
Hollywood, George Fisher, Jack Carson,
George Jessel, and Larry Finley interview the
brightest of Hollywood's stars of that era
including Dean Martin, Hedda Hopper, Liberace
(and his mother), Peggy Lee, Ray Bolger, and
countless others.
Unknown — *Video Yesteryear*

Premonition, The   1975
Horror
66267   94 mins   C   B, V   P
Sharon Farrel, Edward Bell, Danielle Brisebois
A parapsychologist searching for a missing child
is drawn into a frightening maze of dream
therapy and communication with the dead.
MPAA:PG
Robert Allen Schnitzer — *Embassy Home
Entertainment*

Prenatal (Rehabilitation   1978
and Injury)
Physical fitness/Pregnancy
52755   30 mins   C   B, V   P
Hosted by Ann Dugan
Conditioning exercises for pregnant women
including both specific-area and total body
movements to gradually improve muscle tone.
Part of the "Rehabilitation and Injury" series.
Health 'N Action — *RCA/Columbia Pictures
Home Video*

Presenting Johnny   196?
Mathis
Music-Performance
12822   46 mins   B/W   B, V, FO   P
Johnny Mathis
Johnny Mathis in concert performing some of
his best-known songs.
Unknown — *Video Yesteryear*

Presidential Blooper Reel   1981
Outtakes and bloopers
57339   55 mins   B/W   B, V   P
This collection of excerpts from television and
motion pictures features Ronald Reagan, Bette
Davis, Humphrey Bogard, James Cagney, Red
Skelton, James Arness, and Edward G.
Robinson.
Budget Video — *Budget Video; Discount Video
Tapes*

Pretty Baby   1978
Drama
38602   109 mins   C   B, V, LV   R, P
*Brooke Shields, Keith Carradine, Susan
Sarandon, directed by Louis Malle*
A photographer obsessed with the prostitutes in
New Orleans red-light district, circa 1917, is
bewitched by a twelve-year-old child prostitute.
A sincere, human study of a controversial
subject.
MPAA:R
Paramount — *Paramount Home Video; RCA
VideoDiscs*

Preview Tape II   1982
Trains
66059   60 mins   C   B, V   P
A sampler of JMJ Productions' railroading
programs produced from 1980-82.
JMJ Productions — *JMJ Productions*

Prey, The   1980
Horror
73025   80 mins   C   B, V   R, P
Debbie Thurseon, Steve Bond
A predator is looking for a mate in the Colorado
Rockies and kills five campers in the process.
MPAA:R
Unknown — *THORN EMI Home Video*

Pride and Prejudice   1940
Drama
59135   114 mins   B/W   B, V   P
*Greer Garson, Laurence Olivier, Edmund
Gwenn, Edna May Oliver, Mary Boland,
Maureen O'Sullivan, Ann Rutherford, Frieda
Inescort*
Jane Austen's classic novel of a proud and
spirited English girl's fight against the prejudice
of the man she loves.
MGM; Hunt Stromberg — *MGM/UA Home
Video*

Pride and the Passion,   1957
The
Drama
69382   132 mins   C   B, V, CED   P
*Cary Grant, Frank Sinatra, Sophia Loren,
directed by Stanley Kramer*
A small group of resistance fighters battling for
Spanish independence in 1810 must smuggle a

6-ton cannon across the rugged terrain of
Spain.
United Artists — *CBS/Fox Video*

Pride of Eagles Football   1980
Football
45129   24 mins   C   B, V, FO   R, P
Philadelphia Eagles
Highlights of the 1979 Philadelphia Eagles
football season.
NFL Films — *NFL Films Video*

Pride of the Bowery   1941
Comedy
58967   61 mins   B/W   B, V, 3/4U   P
*Leo Gorcey, Huntz Hall, Gabriel Dell, Billy
Halop, Bobby Jordan*
The Dead End Kids in a story about a boy of the
streets set against the outdoor life of a C.C.C.
camp in the late 1930's.
Monogram — *Cable Films; Discount Video
Tapes; Penguin Video*

Pride of the Yankees, The   1942
Biographical/Drama
65009   128 mins   B/W   B, V, LV,   P
                              CED
Gary Cooper, Teresa Wright, Babe Ruth
This is the classic story of baseball
phenomenon Lou Gehrig who was stifled at the
peak of his career by an incurable disease.
Samuel Goldwyn — *CBS/Fox Video*

Prime Cuts   1984
Music-Performance
72190   45 mins   C   B, V   P
A collection of rock videos featuring
performances by Quiet Riot, Toto, Bonnie Tyler
and other notables.
CBS Fox Video Music — *CBS/Fox Video*

Prime Suspect   1982
Mystery
75457   96 mins   C   B, V   P
Mike Farrell, Teri Garr
A man is hunted for a sex murder.
King Features — *U.S.A. Home Video*

Prime Time   1980
Comedy
60409   73 mins   C   B, V   P
Warren Oates, David Spielberg
A satirical comedy about what would happen if
the censors took a day off from American TV.
MPAA:R
Cannon Releasing — *Paragon Video
Productions; Electric Video*

Prince and the Pauper, The   1937
Drama
64933   118 mins   B/W   CED   P
*Errol Flynn, Claude Rains, Alan Hale, Billy and
Bobby Mauch*
Young Edward VI changes places with a street
urchin.
Warner Bros — *CBS/Fox Video*

Prince and the Showgirl, The   1957
Comedy
47619   127 mins   C   B, V   R, P
*Laurence Olivier, Marilyn Monroe, Sybil
Thorndike, directed by Laurence Olivier*
An American showgirl in 1910 London is wooed
by the Prince of Carpathia. Part of the "A Night
at the Movies" series, this tape simulates a
1957 movie evening, with a Sylvester the Cat
cartoon, "Greedy for Tweety," a newsreel and
coming attractions for "Spirit of St. Louis."
Warner Bros — *Warner Home Video*

Prince Charming Revue, The   1983
Music-Performance
65003   74 mins   C   B, V, CED   P
England's New Wave rock group, Adam and the
Ants, performs its hit singles in an elaborately
staged show including a hand-painted pirate
ship and castle backdrops. In stereo.
CBS — *CBS/Fox Video*

Prince of the City   1981
Drama
51994   167 mins   C   B, V, LV   R, P
*Treat Williams, Jerry Orbach, Richard Foronjy,
Don Billett, Kenny Marino, directed by Sidney
Lumet*
An undercover cop is pressured into becoming
an informant in an FBI investigation of
corruption among police officers.
MPAA:R
Orion Pictures — *Warner Home Video; RCA
VideoDiscs*

Prisoner of Second Avenue, The   1974
Comedy-Drama
52707   105 mins   C   B, V   R, P
*Jack Lemmon, Anne Bancroft, Gene Saks,
Elizabeth Wilson, directed by Melvin Frank*
A New Yorker in his late forties faces the future,
without a job or any confidence in his ability,
with the help of his understanding wife. Based
on the Broadway play by Neil Simon.
MPAA:PG
Warner Bros — *Warner Home Video*

Prisoner of Zenda, The — 1952
Adventure
47400   101 mins   C   B, V   P
Stewart Granger, Deborah Kerr, Louis Calhern, James Mason
A wanderer who closely resembles the king of a small European country becomes involved in a murder plot. Based on the novel by Anthony Hope.
MGM — *MGM/UA Home Video*

Prisoner of Zenda, The — 1979
Comedy
69033   108 mins   C   B, V   P
Peter Sellers, Jeremy Kemp, Lynne Frederick, Lionel Jeffries, Elke Sommer
Peter Sellers stars in the double role of Prince Rudolph of Ruritania and Syd, the cockney cab driver who doubles for Rudolph when the Prince is imprisoned by his jealous brother Michael.
Universal — *MCA Home Video*

Pritikin Promise, The — 1984
Physical fitness
76649   90 mins   C   B, V   P
Hosted by Lorne Greene
This program tells how the Pritikin Promise assures you that you will be on your way to a longer, healthier life in just 28 days.
Robert Katz — *Media Home Entertainment*

Pritikin Promise Home Exercise Program, The — 1984
Physical fitness
76651   60 mins   C   B, V   P
Hosted by Lorne Greene
Follow world triathalon champion Dave Scott and the Pritikin Exercise team through a series of three exercise levels.
Robert Katz — *Media Home Entertainment*

Private Benjamin — 1980
Comedy
58245   110 mins   C   B, V, LV   R, P
Goldie Hawn, Eileen Brennan, Albert Brooks, Robert Webber, Barbara Barrie, Mary Kay Place, directed by Howard Zieff
A pampered, spoiled, upper-middle-class princess rebounds from a bad marriage by joining the army.
MPAA:R
Warner Bros — *Warner Home Video; RCA VideoDiscs*

Private Buckaroo — 1942
Musical
07229   65 mins   B/W   B, V, FO   P
The Andrews Sisters, Harry James and his Orchestra, Joe E. Lewis, Dick Foran
War-time entertainment in which Harry James and his Orchestra get drafted.

Universal — *Video Yesteryear; Cable Films; Budget Video; Discount Video Tapes*

Private Eyes, The — 1980
Comedy
57231   91 mins   C   B, V, LV, CED   P
Don Knotts, Tim Conway, Trisha Noble, Bernard Fox
Two bungling sleuths are engaged to investigate two deaths and are led on a merry chase through secret passages, past exploding bombs, and finally to a meeting with a ghostly adversary.
Lang Elliot; Wanda Dell; TriStar Pictures — *Vestron Video*

Private Lessons — 1981
Comedy
59677   83 mins   C   B, V, LV, CED   P
Eric Brown, Sylvia Kristel, Howard Hesseman
A teenage boy is left alone for the summer in the care of an alluring maid and a scheming chauffer.
MPAA:R
Barry and Enright — *MCA Home Video*

Private Life of Don Juan — 1934
Adventure
11250   97 mins   B/W   B, V, FO   P
Douglas Fairbanks Sr., Merle Oberon, directed by Alexander Korda
Tired of his romantic reputation, Don Juan still finds his life complicated by an imposter using his identity.
United Artists — *Video Yesteryear; Movie Buff Video; Discount Video Tapes; Sheik Video; Cable Films; Budget Video; Western Film & Video Inc*

Private Life of Henry VIII, The — 1933
Drama
08693   97 mins   B/W   B, V, 3/4U   P
Charles Laughton, Elsa Lanchester, Robert Dunat, Merle Oberon, directed by Alexander Korda
The life and loves of infamous English King Henry VIII are lustily portrayed in this film, a tour de force for Charles Laughton.
Academy Awards '33: Best Actor (Laughton); Film Daily Poll Ten Best Pictures of the Year '33.
UA; Alexander Korda — *Penguin Video; VCII; Blackhawk Films; Sheik Video; Cable Films; Video Connection; Video Yesteryear; Budget Video; Discount Video Tapes; Western Film & Video Inc; Cinema Concepts*

Private Popsicle — 1982
Comedy
68242   111 mins   C   B, V, CED   P
Zachi Noy, Jonathan Segall, Yftach Katzur

A hilarious sex comedy starring Europe's
popular Popsicle team. Dubbed in English.
MPAA:R
Noah Films — *MGM/UA Home Video*

Private School 1983
Drama
65338　　82 mins　　C　　B, V, LV,　　P
　　　　　　　　　　　　　　　　CED
Phoebe Cates, Sylvia Kristel, Ray Walston
Two high school girls from the exclusive
Cherryvale Academy for Women compete for
the affections of a young man from nearby
Freemount Academy for Men, while
Cherryvale's headmistress is trying to raise
funds to build a new wing.
MPAA:R
Universal — *MCA Home Video*

Private Snafu Cartoon 194?
Festival
Cartoons
55340　55 mins　B/W　　B, V　　P
Animated
A collection of cartoons produced for the Armed
Forces during World War II as humorous
instructional films. The language is strictly G.I.
Titles include: "Censored," "Gas," "Goldbrick,"
"Going Home," "Rumors," and "Spies." Also
included are two more Warner Bros. World War
II cartoons, "Tokio Jokio," and "Confusions of a
Nutzy Spy."
Warner Bros — *Budget Video; Discount Video
Tapes*

Prize Fighter, The 1979
Comedy
63384　　99 mins　　C　　B, V　　P
Tim Conway, Don Knotts
Two fight managers unknowingly get involved
with a powerful gangster, who convinces one of
them to fight in a fixed championship match.
MPAA:PG
New World Pictures — *Media Home
Entertainment*

Pro-Karate 1981
**Championships (1976-
1981)**
Martial arts
59570　　60 mins　　C　　B, V　　P
Highlights of the 1981 Full Contact Matches
conducted under the auspices of the U.S.
Professional Karate Association.
Professional Karate Assn — *Mastervision*

Problems, 1950's Style 195?
Television/Interview
62692　120 mins　B/W　B, V, 3/4U　　P
Three TV panel discussion/interview programs
from the 1950's: "Stand Up and Be Counted!"
(1956), in which audience members and guests

discuss their problems; "People in Conflict,"
where guests ask advice of the panel; and "The
Verdict Is Yours," with an actual courtroom trial.
CBS et al — *Shokus Video*

Prodigal Boxer, The 1980
Adventure/Martial arts
56931　　90 mins　　C　　B, V　　R, P
The great Kung-fu masters from all over China
assemble for a championship, but anyone can
participate if willing to die if defeated. A student
of martial arts decides to risk his life for revenge.
MPAA:R
Fourseas Film Company — *Video Gems*

Producers, The 1968
Comedy
41081　　88 mins　　C　　B, V　　P
*Zero Mostel, Gene Wilder, Dick Shawn,
Kenneth Mars, Estelle Winwood, directed by
Mel Brooks*
Two conniving producers embark upon a get-
rich-quick scheme to produce a flop Broadway
show, "Springtime for Hitler."
EL, JA
Avco Embassy — *Embassy Home
Entertainment; RCA VideoDiscs*

Professional Planting 1982
(Horticulture)
Gardening/Plants
59576　　50 mins　　C　　B, V　　P
This program offers the amateur an inside look
at plant propagation from seed to tissue culture
and examines techniques used by specialists for
planting and transplanting.
Brooklyn Botanical Gardens — *Mastervision*

Professional Techniques 1982
(Horticulture)
Gardening/Plants
59577　　50 mins　　C　　B, V　　P
This program presents a variety of skillful
pruning techniques, examines the art of bonsai,
and reveals the secrets of botanists who obtain
natural dyes and colorings from plants and
trees.
Brooklyn Botanical Gardens — *Mastervision*

Professionals, The 1966
Western
13270　117 mins　　C　　B, V　　P
*Burt Lancaster, Lee Marvin, Claudia Cardinale,
Jack Palance, Robert Ryan, directed by Richard
Brooks*
Two men are hired to rescue a railroad tycoon's
daughter from her kidnapper, a Mexican
cutthroat.
MPAA:PG
Columbia; Pax Enterprises — *RCA/Columbia
Pictures Home Video*

Professor Hippie, El 1979
Drama
47859   95 mins   C   B, V   P
A history teacher befriends a group of students, taking them to a far-off part of the country where adventures befall them. In Spanish.
SP
Nicolas Carreras; Luis Repetto — *Media Home Entertainment*

Programming Your Personal Computer 1984
Electronic data processing
72970   27 mins   C   B, V   P
Programming a personal computer in a step by step manner is shown on this video cassette.
Star Merchants — *Increase Video*

Progress on the Rails 195?
Trains
68916   15 mins   B/W   B, V   P
Both passenger and freight operations are covered in this program.
Unknown — *Interurban Films*

Project: Kill! 1977
Drama
66518   94 mins   C   B, V   P
Leslie Nielsen, Gary Lockwood, Nancy Kwan
The head of a murder-for-hire squad suddenly disappears and his former assistant is hired to track him down—dead or alive.
David Shelton — *Paragon Video Productions*

Prom Night 1980
Horror
48939   91 mins   C   B, V, LV   P
Jamie Lee Curtis, Leslie Nielsen
A masked killer stalks four high school senior girls during their senior prom, as revenge for a murder which took place six years ago.
MPAA:R
Avco Embassy, Peter Simpson — *MCA Home Video*

Promises in the Dark 1979
Drama
52713   119 mins   C   B, V   R, P
Marsha Mason, Ned Beatty, Kathleen Beller, Susan Clark, Paul Clemens
This drama focuses on the complex relationship between a woman doctor and her seventeen-year-old female patient terminally ill with cancer.
MPAA:PG
Orion Pictures — *Warner Home Video*

Promises! Promises! 1963
Comedy
47311   90 mins   B/W   B, V   P
Jayne Mansfield, Marie McDonald, Tommy Noonan, Fritz Feld, Claude Stroud

Two couples go on a cruise together. Mayhem results when a fertility pill meant for one man is taken by the other and his wife becomes pregnant.
Adrian Weiss Productions — *Weiss Global Enterprises*

Propaganda Parade 195?
World War II/Propaganda
72483   55 mins   B/W   B, V, 3/4U   P
A study of American wartime propaganda films including Warner's cartoon character Private Snafu, a Red Scare film narrated by Jack Webb and a recently declassified account of the atomic bombs dropped on Japan.
Warner Bros et al — *International Historic Films*

Prophecy 1979
Horror
44595   102 mins   C   B, V   R, P
Talia Shire, Robert Foxworth, Armand Assante, Victoria Racimo, Richard Dysart, directed by John Frankenheimer
A doctor and his wife travel to Maine to research the effects of pollution caused by the lumber industry. They encounter several terrifying freaks of nature and a series of bizarre human deaths.
MPAA:PG
Paramount, Robert L. Rosen — *Paramount Home Video*

Proud Rebel, The 1958
Western/Drama
69551   99 mins   C   B, V   P
Alan Ladd, Olivia De Havilland, Dean Jagger, directed by Michael Curtiz
After his wife's death, a proud, stubborn man goes searching for a doctor who can help his mute son.
Buena Vista; Samuel Goldwyn Jr — *Embassy Home Entertainment*

Providence 1976
Drama
57230   104 mins   C   B, V   P
John Gielgud, Dirk Bogarde, Ellen Burstyn, directed by Alain Resnais
A dying novelist plans one last novel—a haunting story about the people he knows and the horrors of death he envisages.
Cinema 5; Yves Gasser; Klaus Hellwig — *RCA/Columbia Pictures Home Video*

Prowler, The 1951
Mystery
59142   92 mins   B/W   B, V   R, P
Van Heflin, Evelyn Keyes, Katherine Warren, John Maxwell
A policeman contrives to murder the husband of the woman he is in love with for his wealth.

Horizon Pictures;SP Eagle Prod — *VCII*

Prudential Family   1950
Playhouse, The
Drama
47641   53 mins B/W   B, V, FO   P
*Ruth Chatterton, Walter Abel, Cliff Hall, Eva
Marie Saint*
Sinclair Lewis' "Dodsworth," the story of a
wealthy American couple who travel from their
small American town to Europe.
CBS — *Video Yesteryear*

Prudential Family   1950
Playhouse, The
Drama
69579   53 mins B/W   B, V, FO   P
*Ruth Chatterton, Walter Abel, Cliff Hall, Eva
Marie Saint*
An early television adaptation of Sinclair Lewis'
classic novel about middle-age disaffection
between a wealthy American couple. Originally
telecast on October 24, 1950.
CBS — *Video Yesteryear*

Psycho   1960
Suspense
11598 109 mins B/W   B, V, LV   P
*Anthony Perkins, Janet Leigh, Vera Miles, John
Gavin, Martin Balsam, directed by Alfred
Hitchcock*
A young woman steals a fortune and
encounters a young peculiar man and his
mysterious mother.
Paramount Prods — *MCA Home Video; RCA
VideoDiscs*

Psycho from Texas   1983
Horror
66520   85 mins C   B, V   P
John King III, Candy Dee, Janel King
A quiet Southern town is disrupted by the
kidnapping of a wealthy oil man, followed by a
string of meaningless murders.
MPAA:R
Unknown — *Paragon Video Productions*

Psycho II   1983
Suspense
65208 113 mins C   B, V, LV,   P
                           CED
*Anthony Perkins, Vera Miles, Meg Tilly, Robert
Loggia*
After 22 years, Norman Bates is back home at
the old Bates Motel in anticipation of new
customers.
Universal Oak — *MCA Home Video*

Psychomania   1973
Mystery
01682   95 mins C   B, V   P

---

*Lee Philips, Sheppard Strudwick, Jean Hale,
directed by Richard Hilliard*
Former war hero and painter is suspected of
being demented killer stalking girls' campus.
Finally, he identifies the true killer.
Victoria Films; British — *Budget Video*

Psychomania   1973
Horror
56737   89 mins C   B, V   P
George Sanders, Beryl Reid, Nicky Henson
A drama of the supernatural, the occult, and the
violence which lies just beyond the conventions
of society for a group of motorcyclists.
MPAA:R
Del Tenney — *Media Home Entertainment;
Sheik Video*

PT 109   1963
War-Drama
63452 159 mins C   B, V   R, P
*Cliff Robertson, Ty Hardin, Robert Blake, Robert
Culp*
The World War II exploits of Lieutenant J.G.
John F. Kennedy in the South Pacific. Part of the
"A Night at the Movies" series, this tape
simulates a 1963 movie evening, with a Foghorn
Leghorn cartoon, "Banty Raids," a newsreel on
the JFK assassination and coming attractions
for "Critic's Choice" and "Four for Texas."
Warner Bros — *Warner Home Video*

Public Cowboy No. 1   1937
Western
15402   54 mins B/W   B, V   P
Gene Autry, William Farnum
Cattle thieves use a radio, airplanes, and
refrigerator trucks in their updated rustling
schemes.
Republic — *Video Connection*

Public Enemy   1931
Crime-Drama
59427   85 mins B/W   B, V   P
*James Cagney, Edward Woods, Leslie Fenton,
Joan Blondell, Mae Clarke, Jean Harlow,
directed by William Wellman*
Two slum boys begin as bootleggers, and get in
over their heads.
Warner Bros — *CBS/Fox Video; RCA
VideoDiscs*

Pump It   1983
Physical fitness
66270   55 mins C   B, V   P
Hosted by Dr. David Engel
A body-building program focusing on specific
parts of the body.
Al Eicher — *Embassy Home Entertainment*

Pumping Iron — 1977
Documentary/Physical fitness
39086   85 mins   C   B, V   P
Arnold Schwarzenegger, Mike Katz, Franco Columbu, Lou Ferrigno, directed by George Butler
A widely acclaimed documentary look at the sport of bodybuilding, following the behind-the-scenes action surrounding the competition for the Mr. Olympia title. The grueling training ritual and the constant striving for perfection are all explored.
MPAA:PG
Cinema 5 — *RCA/Columbia Pictures Home Video; RCA VideoDiscs*

Punk Rock Movie, The — 1978
Music-Performance/Documentary
63411   90 mins   C   B, V   P
The Sex Pistols, The Clash, Siouxsie and the Banshees, The Slits, Wayne County
The musical explosion known as punk rock is documented here in its early days (circa 1977) at the Roxy in England, featuring leading punk rock artists and looking at the entire counterculture that is punk.
Notting Hill Studios; Peter Clifton — *Sun Video*

Punt, a Pass and a Prayer, A — 1968
Drama
64852   76 mins   C   B, V, 3/4U   P
Hugh O'Brien, Betsy Palmer, directed by Tom Donovan
A former star football quarterback attempts a comeback after a serious head injury. His obsession causes his wife to leave him, and he is forced to make a crucial decision. Part of "George Schaefer's Showcase Theatre."
George Schaefer — *Enter-Tel Inc*

Puppet Playhouse Presents Howdy Doody — 195?
Variety
38995   60 mins   B/W   B, V, FO   P
Buffalo Bob Smith, Clarabell the Clown, Chief Thundercloud 2 pgms
Two complete programs from September 13, 1948, and August 2, 1959, featuring the Peanut Gallery and all the familiar Howdy Doody characters and routines Commercials included.
NBC — *Video Yesteryear*

Purlie Victorious — 1963
Comedy
58579   93 mins   C   B, V   P
Ossie Davis, Ruby Dee, Godfrey Cambridge, Alan Alda
The award-winning Broadway hit, a comedy which takes a look at racial integration.
Hammer Bros — *Mastervision*

Purple Box, The — 1983
Fantasy/Literature
66215   29 mins   C   B, V   R, P
Animated
Three children's stories - "The Three Robbers," "The Five Chinese Brothers," "Strega Nonna" - are combined on one cassette.
AM Available
Weston Woods — *CC Studios*

Purple Hearts — 1984
War-Drama
73014   115 mins   C   B, V   P
Cheryl Ladd, Ken Wahl, directed by Sidney Furie
Ken Wahl stars as a Navy doctor who falls in love with nurse Cheryl Ladd against the backdrop of the Vietnam war.
MPAA:R
Sidney Furie; Warner Bros — *Warner Home Video*

Purple Monster Strikes, The — 1945
Science fiction/Serials
07339 188 mins B/W   B, V, 3/4U   P
Dennis Moore, Linda Stirling, Roy Barcroft
A martian plots to conquer Earth to save his dying planet. Serial in fifteen episodes.
Republic — *Video Connection*

Purple Taxi, The — 1977
Drama
60342   93 mins   C   B, V   P
Fred Astaire, Charlotte Rampling, Peter Ustinov
A romantic drama revolving around several wealthy foreigners who have taken refuge in beautiful southern Ireland.
CPH; BLD — *RCA/Columbia Pictures Home Video*

Purple Vigilantes — 1938
Western
54191   54 mins   B/W   B, V   P
Bob Livingston, Ray Corrigan, Max Terhune
The Three Mesquiteers uncover a gang of vigilantes.
Republic — *Video Connection*

Pursuit of D. B. Cooper, The — 1981
Drama
47423   100 mins   C   B, V   P
Robert Duvall, Treat Williams, Kathryn Harrold
This film recreates an actual hijacking that took place on Thanksgiving eve, 1971, when J. R. Meade (alias D. B. Cooper) bailed out of a 727 with $200,000 of the airline's money. He was never heard from again.
MPAA:PG
Universal — *MCA Home Video*

Puss in Boots 1982
Fairy tales
63169   89 mins   C   B, V   P
*Garry Q. Lewis, Jason McLean, Carl Beck,
Nancy Wagner*
The Children's Theater Company of
Minneapolis present a jazzed-up, New Orleans-
style version of the "Puss in Boots" tale. VHS is
in stereo.
Television Theater Company — *MCA Home
Video*

**Puss 'n' Boots Travels
Around the World** 1983
Cartoons
66346   60 mins   C   B, V   P
Animated
An all-new magical cartoon featuring the hero,
Pussty, who is challenged by the villainous
Rumblehog to complete a trip around the world
in 80 days, while Rumblehog tries to thwart him
at every turn. In Beta Hi-Fi.
MPAA:G
John Watkins; Simo
Nuchtern — *RCA/Columbia Pictures Home
Video*

Puss 'n Boots 1980
Adventure
63380   80 mins   C   B, V   P
Animated
This is an animated version of the classic
children's adventure tale of a clever, brave cat.
MPAA:G
Toei Company — *Media Home Entertainment*

Puss 'N' Boots 1984
Fairy tales
Closed Captioned
73574   60 mins   C   B, V, CED   P
Ben Vereen, Gregory Hines
From "Faerie Tale Theatre" comes the story of
a cat who makes a serf a rich landowning
nobleman.
Gaylord Productions; Platypus
Productions — *CBS/Fox Video*

Putney Swope 1969
Comedy
44780   84 mins   B/W   B, V   P
*Arnold Johnson, Laura Greene, Stanley
Gottlieb, directed by Robert Downey*
A mild mannered token black is mistakenly
elected chairman of the board of the advertising
firm he works for. He turns the straight-laced
corporation into the wide open "Truth and Soul,
Inc."
MPAA:R
Cinema 5 — *RCA/Columbia Pictures Home
Video*

**Putting for the Beginner
and the Pro** 197?
Golf
33775   60 mins   C   B, V, 3/4U   P
Golf pros Toby Lyons, Carla Glasgow, Dick
Lawrence, Neal Doyle, and Linda Craft teach
the most deceptively simple shots in golf. From
the "Name of the Game Is Golf" series.
Unknown — *Sports World Cinema*

Pygmalion 1938
Romance/Comedy
58617   96 mins   B/W   B, V, 3/4U   P
*Leslie Howard, Wendy Hiller, Wilfred Lawson,
Scott Sunderland, directed by Anthony Asquith
and Leslie Howard*
George Bernard Shaw's play about a stuffy
phonetics professor who takes a cockney girl
from the streets of London and trains her to be
accepted by high society.
Gabriel Pascal — *Western Film & Video Inc*

Q

Q Ships 192?
Drama
48711   40 mins   C   B, V, 3/4U   P
A German submarine commander struggles
between his own personal morals and loyalty to
his country. Silent.
Unknown — *Penguin Video*

Q—The Winged Serpent 1983
Horror
68253   92 mins   C   B, V   P
*Michael Moriarty, Candy Clark, David Carradine,
Richard Roundtree*
Two city policemen and a petty crook are trying
to track down the perpetrator of a bizarre series
of slayings.
MPAA:R
Larco — *MCA Home Video*

QB VII 1974
Drama
47784   313 mins   C   B, V   P
*Anthony Hopkins, Ben Gazzara, Lee Remick,
Leslie Caron, Juliet Mills, John Gielgud, Anthony
Quayle*
A knighted physician brings a suit for libel
against a novelist for implicating him of war
crimes in a best-selling novel. Adapted from the
novel by Leon Uris. Available only as a three-
cassette set.
Emmy Awards '74: Best Supporting Actor,
Single Performance, Comedy or Drama Special
(Quayle); Best Supporting Actress, Single
Performance, Comedy or Drama Special (Mills);
Music Composition; Graphic Design and Title
Sequence; Film Editing; Film Sound Editing.

Douglas S Cramer — *RCA/Columbia Pictures Home Video*

Quackser Fortune Has a Cousin in the Bronx   1970
Drama/Comedy
51114   88 mins   C   B, V   P
Gene Wilder, Margot Kidder
An Irish fertilizer salesman meets an exchange student from the U.S., who finds herself attracted to this unlearned, but not unknowing, man.
MPAA:R
John H Cunningham; Mel Howard — *VCI Home Video*

Quadrophenia   1979
Musical-Drama
65066   115 mins   C   CED   P
Phil Daniels, Mark Wingett, Philip Davis, Leslie Ash, Sting
Pete Townshend's rock opera about an alienated youth circa 1963 in Britain's rock scene who suffers from a 4-way split personality. Music by the Who.
MPAA:R
World Northal — *RCA VideoDiscs*

Quadrophenia   1979
Music
65320   120 mins   C   B, V   P
Sting, Phil Daniels, Leslie Ash
This program takes a powerful, provocative look at life at a time when the gangs of Mods and Rockers terrorized seaside towns and caused havoc. In VHS stereo and Beta Hi-Fi.
MPAA:R
Curbishley Baird — *RCA/Columbia Pictures Home Video*

Quartet   1981
Drama
66125   101 mins   C   B, V   R, P
Isabelle Adjani, Alan Bates, Maggie Smith, directed by James Ivory
Jean Rhys' novel concerning a young wife drawn into the social and emotional trap of a domineering English couple is the basis of this film.
Cannes Film Festival '81: Best Actress (Adjani).
MPAA:R
New World Pictures — *Warner Home Video*

Queen—Greatest Flix   1981
Music
58724   60 mins   C   B, V   R, P
A compilation of original video promos made to accompany the hit records which propelled the rock group Queen on their way to worldwide success. Songs include "Bohemian Rhapsody," "We Will Rock You," "Another One Bites the Dust," "Flash," "Killer Queen," "We Are the Champions," "Crazy Little Thing Called Love."

EMI Music — *THORN EMI Home Video; Pioneer Artists; RCA VideoDiscs*

Queen of the Amazons   1947
Adventure
29681   60 mins   B/W   B, V   P
Robert Lowery, Patricia Morrison, J. Edward Bromberg, John Miljan
A girl searches for her fiance and finds him captive of a tribe of women who rule the jungle.
Robert L. Lippert Prods — *Sheik Video; Penguin Video*

Queen of the Stardust Ballroom   1975
Drama
52401   98 mins   C   B, V   P
Maureen Stapleton, Charles Durning
A lonely widow goes to a local dance hall, where she meets a man and begins an unconventional late love.
AM Available
Robert Christiansen, Rick Rosenberg Prods — *Prism*

Querelle   1983
Drama
65188   106 mins   C   B, V   P
Brad Davis, Jeanne Moreau, Franco Nero, directed by Rainer Werner Fassbinder
Fassbinder's last film explores the seamy underworld of the French port of Brest, where Querelle, a handsome sailor, finds himself involved in a bewildering environment of drug smuggling and homosexuality. Dubbed in English.
MPAA:R
Triumph Films — *RCA/Columbia Pictures Home Video*

Quest for Fire   1982
Adventure
62775   75 mins   C   B, V, LV, CED   P
Everett McGill, Ron Perlman, Nameer El-Kadi, Rae Dawn Chong, directed by Jean-Jacques Annaud
A group of primitive men in the distant past fight rival tribes for the possession of fire.
MPAA:R
20th Century Fox — *CBS/Fox Video*

Question of Love, A   1978
Drama
65305   90 mins   C   B, V   P
Gena Rowlands, Jane Alexander
An admitted homosexual living in a lesbian relationship struggles to retain custody of her son from her ex-husband.
Viacom Enterprises — *U.S.A. Home Video*

     (For Explanation of codes, see USE GUIDE and KEY)

Question 7 — 1963
Ethics
55029   107 mins   B/W   B, V   P
The fifteen-year-old son of a pastor who lives behind the iron curtain faces a dilemma: should he answer a political question the way his teacher wants or the way he believes?
Family Films — *Vanguard Video*

Quick Dog Training with Barbara Woodhouse — 1982
Pets
66271   90 mins   C   B, V   P
A program on how to train your dog or pup.
Pillar Prods — *Embassy Home Entertainment*

Quiet Man, The — 1952
Comedy-Drama
55511   129 mins   C   B, V   P
John Wayne, Maureen O'Hara, Barry Fitzgerald, Victor McLaglen, Ward Bond, Mildred Natwick, directed by John Ford
An archetypal John Ford comedy, an Irish village version of "Taming of the Shrew," the tamer being an ex-boxer retired to the land of his fathers and in need of a wife.
Academy Awards '52: Best Director (Ford); Best Color Cinematography (Winton Hoch, Archie Stout).
Republic; Argosy; John Ford; Merian C Cooper — *NTA Home Entertainment; RCA VideoDiscs*

Quiet One, The — 1948
Poverty/Minorities
15609   68 mins   B/W   B, V   P
Commentary by James Agee
Explores the ghetto's psychological effects on a ten-year old black child.
Venice International Film Festival: First Prize.
Film Documents — *Budget Video; Festival Films; Texture Films*

Quiz Kids — 1950
Game show
12851   30 mins   B/W   B, V, FO   P
Fran Allison
Quizmistress Fran Allison asks the questions to a panel of five youngsters ranging in age from seven to fourteen.
CBS — *Video Yesteryear*

Quo Vadis — 1974
Population
64167   3 mins   C   B, V   P
Animated
A funny comment on the problem of overpopulation, with an unexpected and shocking conclusion.
Zagreb Films — *Classic Video Cinema Collector's Club*

R

Rabid — 1977
Horror
53520   90 mins   C   B, V   R, P
Marilyn Chambers, Frank Moore, Joe Silver
A young girl undergoes a radical plastic surgery technique and develops a strange and unexplained lesion in her armpit—along with a craving for human blood.
MPAA:R
New World Pictures; Cinema Entertainment Enterprises — *Warner Home Video*

Raccoons—Let's Dance, The — 1984
Music video
66625   30 mins   C   B, V   P
Animated, songs performed by Rita Coolidge, Leo Sayer, John Schneider, Dottie West
Melissa, Ralph and Bert Raccoon perform in six of their own original music videos, designed especially for children.
Evergreen Marketing — *Embassy Home Entertainment*

Raccoons on Ice — 1982
Fantasy
63378   49 mins   C   B, V, LV   P
Animated, narrated by Rich Little, music by Leo Sayer, Rita Coolidge and Rupert Holmes
Two cartoons featuring Ralph, Melissa and Bert Raccoon are contained on this cassette. In "Raccoons on Ice," they play a hockey game against the Brutish Bears. "Christmas Raccoons" finds them fighting to protect Evergreen Forest and their "raccoondominium" home.
Kevin Gillis; Sheldon S Wiseman — *Embassy Home Entertainment*

Race for Your Life, Charlie Brown — 1977
Comedy/Cartoons
38610   76 mins   C   B, V, LV   R, P
Animated
Another in the popular series of "Peanuts" character films, featuring Charlie Brown, Snoopy, and all the gang spending an exciting summer in the American wilderness.
MPAA:G
Paramount — *Paramount Home Video; RCA VideoDiscs*

Race to the Top — 1982
Motorcycles
66250   65 mins   C   B, V   P
A racing double feature about the 1977 Dutch TT and the 1981 Race of the Year.
CH Wood — *Motor Cycle Video*

Rachel and the Stranger 1948
Drama
66333   93 mins   B/W   B, V, 3/4U   P
Loretta Young, Robert Mitchum, William Holden, Gary Gray
A God-fearing farmer declares his love for his wife when a handsome stranger nearly woos her away.
RKO — *Nostalgia Merchant*

Racing Ferraris 1983
Automobiles
76391   42 mins   C   B, V   P
This program looks at the 250 GT SWB, 206 SP, 250 LM, and 512 BBLM up close and in action.
Armour Productions — *Armour Productions*

Racket, The 1951
Crime-Drama
64366   88 mins   B/W   B, V, 3/4U   P
Robert Ryan, Robert Mitchum, Lizabeth Scott
A police captain attempts to break up the crime empire of a powerful racketeer.
RKO — *Nostalgia Merchant*

Racket Squad 1952
Crime-Drama
49061   25 mins   B/W   B, V   P
Reed Hadley
An episode from the popular TV show "Racket Squad," entitled "Flying Fish," in which a meek accountant answers an ad which promises an escape from his hum-drum lifestyle.
CBS — *Sheik Video*

Racketeers of the Range 1939
Western
64413   62 mins   B/W   B, V, 3/4U   P
George O'Brien, Marjorie Reynolds
A cattleman fights a crooked attorney who wants to sell his client's stock to a large meat packing company.
RKO — *Nostalgia Merchant*

Racquet 1979
Comedy-Drama/Tennis
63975   87 mins   C   B, V   R, P
Bert Convy, Edie Adams, Lynda Day George, Phil Silvers, Bobby Riggs, Bjorn Borg
A professional tennis instructor searches for true love and a tennis court of his own while caught up in the hedonistic lifestyle of the "beautiful people."
Creswin Release — *VCII*

Radar Men from the Moon 1952
Science fiction/Serials
07343   152 mins   B/W   B, V, 3/4U   P
George Wallace, Aline Towne
Commando Cody protects the world from invaders from the moon. Serial in twelve episodes.
Republic — *Nostalgia Merchant; Video Connection; Discount Video Tapes*

Radio Ranch 1935
Science fiction
07202   80 mins   B/W   B, V, FO   P
Gene Autry, Frankie Darro, Betsy King Ross
Gene Autry and friends are up against an underground world that is complete with robots and death rays.
Mascot Pictures — *Video Yesteryear; Sheik Video*

Rafael en Raphael 1975
Music-Performance
47722   90 mins   C   B, V   P
Rafael
The great Spanish singer/actor Rafael is seen on tour in several countries. In Spanish.
SP
Independent — *Telecine Spanish Video*

Rage 1981
Drama
73536   98 mins   C   B, V   P
David Soul, James Whitmore, Yaphet Kotto
A convicted rapist is sent to a therapy program to reform sex offenders. Available in Beta Hi-Fi and VHS stereo
Diane Silver Prods; Charles Fries Prods — *U.S.A. Home Video*

Rage of Paris, The 1938
Comedy
00419   78 mins   B/W   B, V   P
Danielle Darrieux, Douglas Fairbanks Jr., Mischa Auer
Ex-actress and head waiter pool their money to help a beautiful French girl catch a millionaire husband.
Universal; Buddy De Sylva — *Discount Video Tapes; Cable Films; King of Video; Budget Video; Movie Buff Video; Classic Video Cinema Collector's Club*

Raggedy Ann and Andy: A Musical Adventure 1977
Cartoons
59309   87 mins   C   B, V, CED   P
Animated, directed by Richard Williams
The fun-filled exploits of America's favorite fictional doll, transformed into an enchanting animated musical, with sixteen songs by Joe Raposo.
MPAA:G
Lester Osterman — *CBS/Fox Video*

Raggedy Man 1981
Drama
59035　94 mins　C　B, V, LV　　P
*Sissy Spacek, Eric Roberts, Sam Shepard,
directed by Jack Fisk*
A story of a woman raising two sons alone in a
small Texas town during World War II, and the
sailor who enters her lonely life.
MPAA:PG
Universal — *MCA Home Video*

Raging Bull 1980
Drama
53450　128 mins　B/W　B, V, LV　　P
*Robert DeNiro, Cathy Moriarty, Joe Pesci, Frank
Vincent, directed by Martin Scorcese*
The story of Jake La Motta the tough New York
street kid who slugged his way to the world
middle-weight boxing championship and then
went on to lose everything, chronicling his ups
and downs with women, his family, and the law.
Academy Awards '80: Best Actor (DeNiro); Best
Editing (Thelma Schoonmaker).　MPAA:R
Irwin Winkler; Robert Chartoff; United
Artists — *CBS/Fox Video; RCA VideoDiscs*

Raging River of 1982
Annapurna, The
Boating
69915　55 mins　C　B, V　　P
This program documents the 1980 International
Kayak Expedition down the Marsayandi River in
the Annapurna Himalayas of Nepal.
Chameleon Films — *Gravity Sports Films*

Ragtime 1981
Drama
59858　156 mins　C　B, V, LV　　R, P
*James Cagney, Brad Dourif, Moses Gunn,
Elizabeth McGovern, Ken McMillan, Pat
O'Brien, Donald O'Connor, Mary Steenburgen,
Howard E. Rollins, directed by Miles Forman*
E. L. Doctorow's epic novel interweaving the
lives and passions of a middle-class family
against the scandals and events of America in
transition circa 1906. Music composed by
Randy Newman.
MPAA:PG
Dino De Laurentis; Paramount — *Paramount
Home Video; RCA VideoDiscs*

Raid on Entebbe 1984
War-Drama
72184　113 mins　C　B, V　　R, P
Charles Bronson, Peter Finch
Dramatization of the Israeli rescue of
passengers held hostage by terrorists at
Uganda's Entebbe Airport.
MPAA:R
Edgar J Sherick Assocs; 20th Century
Fox — *THORN EMI Home Video*

Raiders of Red Gap 1943
Western
43019　56 mins　B/W　B, V, FO　　P
Al "Fuzzy" St. John, Bob Livingston
A cattle company tries running homesteaders
off their land to get control of it. The Lone Rider
saves the day.
Producers Releasing Corp — *Video
Yesteryear; Video Connection*

Raiders of the Lost Ark 1981
Adventure
Closed Captioned
69539　115 mins　C　B, V, LV,　　P
　　　　　　　　　　　　　CED
*Harrison Ford, Karen Allen, Wolf Kahler, Paul
Freeman, directed by Steven Spielberg*
An adventurer and a feisty woman search for
the Lost Ark of the Covenant, eluding Nazis,
spies and others in the process.
MPAA:PG
Lucasfilm Ltd — *Paramount Home Video*

Railroad at Work 1948
Trains
51434　35 mins　B/W　B, V　　P
This classic film shows the operation of the
Milwaukee Railroad.
Milwaukee Railroad — *Interurban Films*

Railroad Signal, The 194?
Trains
68906　18 mins　B/W　B, V　　P
An exploration of the interworkings of the New
York City Signal System.
New York City Transit — *Interurban Films*

Railroadin' 1941
Trains
60049　27 mins　C　B, V　　P, T
This story of America's railroad system begins
with foot power, then animal, then the wheel,
and finally progresses to a discussion of
railroads. Includes shots of early locomotives up
to 1941.
General Electric Company — *Blackhawk Films*

Rain 1932
Drama
08781　77 mins　B/W　B, V　　P
*Joan Crawford, Walter Huston, William Gargan,
Guy Kibbee*
Somerset Maugham's tale of Puritanical
minister's attempt to reclaim a "lost woman" on
the island of Pago Pago.
United Artists — *VCI Home Video; Discount
Video Tapes; Penguin Video; VCII; Cable Films;
Video Connection; Western Film & Video Inc*

Rain People, The   1969
Drama
69026   102 mins   C   B, V   R, P
Shirley Knight, James Caan, Robert Duvall
In an effort to escape the responsibilities of her marriage and impending motherhood, a young woman sets out on a cross country trip. On her way she becomes involved with a football player who is retarded due to a sports injury.
MPAA:R
Warner Bros — *Warner Home Video*

Rainbow   1978
Biographical/Drama
72974   100 mins   C   B, V   R, P
Andrea McArdle, Jack Carter, Don Murray
Andrea McArdle plays Judy Garland from her early years in vaudeville to her starring years at M.G.M. The film is based upon the book by Christopher Finch.
Ten Four Productions — *VCII*

Rainbow Brite in Peril in the Pits   1983
Cartoons
75611   30 mins   C   B, V   P
Rainbow Brite must bring color to the world and battle Murky Dismal who is determined to drain all color.
Hallmark Properties — *Children's Video Library*

Rainbow Goblins Story   1981
Music-Performance
47297   52 mins   C   LV   P
Masayoshi Takanaka
In a live concert at Budokan, Masayoshi Takanaka performs the music he composed to interpret a book called "Rainbow Goblins Story."
Yutaka Tanaka — *Pioneer Video Imports*

Rainbow: Live Between the Eyes   1984
Music-Performance
76032   60 mins   C   B, V   P
This music video features Rainbow's hit songs, including "Stone Cold," "Power" and "Smoke on the Water."
Aubrey Powell — *RCA/Columbia Pictures Home Video*

Rainbow Parade, The   193?
Cartoons
29484   50 mins   C   B, V   P, T
Animated
Animator/director Burt Gillette's "Rainbow Parade" contains some of the most subtly textured color work to be found in animation. Features cartoon characters "Felix," "Molly Moo Cow," and "the Toonerville Folks."
Unknown — *Blackhawk Films*

Raise the Titanic   1980
Drama/Adventure
56901   112 mins   C   B, V, LV, CED   P
Jason Robards, Richard Jordan, Anne Archer
America's defense depends on the raising of the ship, discovered seventy years after it sank. This action drama chronicles the valiant efforts to lift it from its icy grave.
MPAA:PG
William Frye — *CBS/Fox Video*

Raisin in the Sun, A   1961
Drama
60340   128 mins   B/W   B, V   P
Sidney Poitier, Claudia McNeil, Ruby Dee, directed by Daniel Petrie
A sensitive drama of a black family's escape from their frustrating life in a crowded Chicago apartment.
Columbia — *RCA/Columbia Pictures Home Video*

Ramparts of Clay   1984
Drama
72926   87 mins   C   B, V   P
A young Tunisian girl wants to liberate herself from old customs ofher people. This film is in Arabic with subtitles.
MPAA:PG AB
Almi — *RCA/Columbia Pictures Home Video*

Rancho Notorious   1952
Western
33592   89 mins   C   B, V   P
Marlene Dietrich, Arthur Kennedy, Mel Ferrer, directed by Fritz Lang
Kennedy looks for the murderer of his sweetheart, and falls in love with Dietrich in the process. Tragic consequences follow.
RKO — *VCI Home Video*

Randy Rides Alone   1934
Western
06356   53 mins   B/W   B, V   P
John Wayne
Young man single-handedly cleans up the territory.
Monogram — *Video Connection; Cable Films; Discount Video Tapes*

Range Busters   1940
Western
15407   55 mins   B/W   B, V   P
Ray Corrigan, Max Terhune
Range Busters are called in to find the identity of the phantom killer.
Monogram — *Video Connection; Penguin Video*

Rangeland Racket 1941
Western
66145 60 mins B/W B, V, FO P
George Houston, Hillary Brooke, Al St. John
The Lone Rider (Houston) has been wrongly
accused of a crime.
Unknown — *Video Yesteryear*

Rangers Take Over, The 1943
Western
51643 62 mins B/W B, V P
Dave O'Brien, James Newill
Gunlords are driven out by the Texas Rangers.
Producers Releasing Corp — *Video
Yesteryear; Discount Video Tapes*

Ransom 1984
Drama
72910 90 mins C B, V P
Oliver Reed, Deborah Raffin
A group of wealthy citizens decide to take on an
assassin who stalks a resort town.
Unknown — *Vestron Video*

**Rape! A Crime of
Violence** 1982
Rape
60515 48 mins C B, V P
Awareness, precaution and defense of rape are
exposed in this docudrama.
Bob Chaney — *Master Arts Video*

Rape of Love 1979
Drama
58500 117 mins C B, V P
*Nathalie Nell, Alain Foures, directed by Yannick
Bellon*
One of the most chilling rape scenes on film
opens this attempt at analyzing the emotional
impact of such a crime on its victim. French with
English subtitles.
FR
Films de L'Equinoxe — *RCA/Columbia
Pictures Home Video*

Rapunzel 1983
Fairy tales
Closed Captioned
69323 60 mins C B, V, LV, P
CED
Shelley Duvall, Gena Rowlands, Jeff Bridges
The classic tale of the beautiful young woman
locked in a tall tower by a witch who is saved by
the handsome prince who climbs her golden
tresses is retold in this program from "Faerie
Tale Theatre."
Shelley Duvall — *CBS/Fox Video*

Rare Breed, A 1981
Drama
65210 96 mins C B, V P
Forrest Tucker, George Kennedy

A young girl's filly is kidnapped en route to
Europe for training, sparking a treacherous race
against odds with time running out.
MPAA:PG
Carnoba Company — *U.S.A. Home Video*

Rascal Dazzle 1981
Comedy
74087 100 mins B/W B, V P
Narrated by Jerry Lewis
This is a montage-like tribute to that best-loved
group of children, the Our Gang kids. Narrated
by Jerry Lewis, this feature includes scenes with
Spanky, Alfalfa, Darla and the rest of the gang.
Michael King; Bob King — *Embassy Home
Entertainment*

Rascals, The 1981
Comedy-Drama
65392 93 mins C B, V P
This film depicts the coming of age of an
irrepressible youth at a rural Catholic boys'
school.
MPAA:R
Gilbert de Goldschmidt — *Embassy Home
Entertainment*

Rashomon 1950
Film-Avant-garde
08583 90 mins B/W B, V, 3/4U P
*Machito Kyo, Toshiro Mifune, Massayura Mori,
directed by Skira Kurosawa*
In medieval Japan four people involved in a
rape-murder recite their differing versions of the
sequence of events.
Academy Awards '51:Best Foreign Film; Venice
Film Festival '51 Grand Prize.
Japanese — *Penguin Video; Video
Dimensions; Festival Films*

Rattle of a Simple Man 1964
Comedy-Drama
63325 91 mins B/W B, V R, P
*Harry H. Corbett, Diane Cilento, Michael
Medwin, Thora Hird*
A naive bachelor in London spends the night
with a prostitute in order to win a bet.
Sydney Box — *THORN EMI Home Video*

Raven, The 1963
Horror
64886 86 mins C B, V R, P
*Vincent Price, Boris Karloff, Peter Lorre, Jack
Nicholson*
A chilling tale of black magic based on the poem
by Edgar Allan Poe.
American International Pictures — *Warner
Home Video; Vestron Video (disc only)*

Raven, The 1943
Suspense
08691 92 mins B, V, 3/4U P

Pierre Fresnay, Sylvie, directed by Henri Clouzet
A strong adult drama of suspicion and intrigue
and its effect on a French province.
France — *Penguin Video*

Raw Force   1981
Adventure/Martial arts
63385   90 mins   C   B, V   P
Cameron Mitchell, Geoff Binney, John Dresden,
John Locke, Ralph Lombardi
Three karate enthusiasts visit an island
inhabited by a sect of cannibalistic monks who
have the power to raise the dead.
MPAA:R
Ansor International Picture — *Media Home*
Entertainment

Rawhide   1938
Western
10072   60 mins   B/W   B, V   P, T
Lou Gehrig, Smith Ballew
Rancher's Protection Association forces
landowners to knuckle under. Friction results.
20th Century Fox — *Blackhawk Films*

RCA's All-Star Country   · 1982
Music Fair
Music-Performance
60388   82 mins   C   B, V   P
Charlie Pride, Razzy Bailey, Sylvia, Earl Thomas
Conley
A hoe-down recorded live at the 1982 Nashville
Fan Fair, featuring a line-up of Nashville talent.
In stereo.
RCA — *RCA/Columbia Pictures Home Video;*
RCA VideoDiscs

Reaching for the Moon   1931
Romance
28923   62 mins   B/W   B, V, 3/4U   P
Douglas Fairbanks Sr., Bebe Daniels, Bing
Crosby, Edward Everett Horton
A wizard of finance ignores the ladies until one,
Bebe Daniels, makes him fall. Music by Irving
Berlin.
United Artists — *Penguin Video; Sheik Video;*
Cable Films; Classic Video Cinema Collector's
Club

Ready Steady Go   1983
Music
65508   60 mins   B/W   B, V   R, P
The Beatles, The Rolling Stones, The Who, The
Animals, Gerry and the Pacemakers
The first in a series of classic rock video
collectibles from the 1960's. This volume
contains 16 of the '60's top hits which capture
the magic and energy of this exciting rock era.
Dave Clark Production International; Picture
Music International — *THORN EMI Home*
Video

Real Bruce Lee, The   1979
Adventure/Martial arts
35390   108 mins   C   B, V   R, P
Bruce Lee
This program contains actual early films of
Bruce Lee, once feared lost but recently
discovered in the Chinese film archives.
MPAA:R
Madison World Film Company — *Video Gems;*
Sun Video

Real Life   1979
Comedy/Satire
60212   99 mins   C   B, V   R, P
Charles Grodin, Frances Lee McCain, Albert
Brooks, directed by Albert Brooks
When a group of filmmakers moves into the
home of a typical American family, they record
an account of "real life" — Albert Brooks style.
MPAA:R
Penelope Spheers — *Paramount Home Video*

Rear Window   1954
Drama/Suspense
66587   112 mins   C   B, V, LV,   P
                                        CED
James Stewart, Grace Kelly, Thelma Ritter,
Wendell Corey, Raymond Burr, directed by
Alfred Hitchcock
A newspaper photographer with a broken leg
passes the time while recuperating by observing
his neighbors through the window. When he
sees what he believes to be a murder
committed, he decides to solve the crime
himself.
Universal Classics — *MCA Home Video*

Rebecca   1940
Drama
46214   130 mins   B/W   B, V   P
Joan Fontaine, Laurence Olivier, Judith
Anderson, George Sanders, C. Aubrey Smith,
directed by Alfred Hitchcock.
Based on Daphne du Maurier's best selling
novel about a young unsophisticated girl who
marries a prominent country gentleman who is
dominated by the memory of his first wife.
Hitchcock's first American film.
Academy Awards '40: Best Picture; Best
Cinematography.
Selznick — *CBS/Fox Video*

Rebecca of Sunnybrook   1917
Farm
Comedy-Drama
63981   77 mins   B/W   B, V   P, T
Mary Pickford, Eugene O'Brien, Marjorie Daw
The original film version of the tale about an ·
orphan who spreads sunshine and good cheer
to all those around her. Silent with organ score
by Gaylord Carter.
Artcraft Pictures — *Blackhawk Films*

Rebel 1973
Drama
47632　80 mins　C　B, V　P
Sylvester Stallone, Antony Page, Rebecca Grimes
A student radical must decide between his love for a country girl or his loyalty to an underground terrorist organization.
MPAA:PG
Independent — *Paragon Video Productions; Electric Video*

Rebel Rousers 1969
Drama
03573　81 mins　C　B, V　P
Jack Nicholson, Cameron Mitchell, Diane Ladd, Bruce Dern
A violent motorcycle gang abuses women.
Paragon International Picture — *Media Home Entertainment; King of Video*

Rebel Without a Cause 1955
Drama
38941　105 mins　C　B, V, LV　R, P
James Dean, Natalie Wood, Sal Mineo, Jim Backus, directed by Nicholas Ray
James Dean's most remembered screen appearance, as a troubled teenager trying to find himself as his family settles in a new town.
Warner Bros — *Warner Home Video; RCA VideoDiscs*

Rebelion de las Muertas, La 1972
Drama
47725　90 mins　C　B, V　P
Paul Naschey, Rommy, Mirta Miller
In "The Rebellion of the Dead," two brothers get involved in a diabolical scheme to gain immortality and seek revenge. In Spanish.
SP
Independent — *Telecine Spanish Video*

Reborn 1984
Drama
72911　91 mins　C　B, V　P
Dennnis Hopper, Michael Moriarty
A faith healer and a talent scout hire actors to be cured of fake ailments.
Unknown — *Vestron Video*

Reckless 1984
Adventure/Romance
75536　93 mins　C　B, V　P
Aidan Quinn, Daryl Hannah
The passion and rebelliousness of a teenage couple upsets the small town they are trying to escape.
MPAA:R
MGM UA Entertainment Company — *MGM/UA Home Video*

Reckon with the Wind/Kialoa to Jamaica 1976
Boating
33769　59 mins　C　B, V, 3/4U　P
Two separate programs which cover the 1976 Maui Race and the 1975 Miami Race: "Reckon with the Wind" and "Kialoa to Jamaica."
Unknown — *Sports World Cinema*

Reconnaissance Pilot 1941
Aeronautics/Armed Forces-US
74479　27 mins　B/W　B, V　P
This tape is a dramatization of the role that reconnaissance flying plays in the military.
US Office of War Information — *Interurban Films*

Red Balloon, The 1956
Fantasy
65620　34 mins　C　B, V, CED　P
Pascal Lamorisse, directed by Albert Lamorisse
This is the story of Pascal, a lonely French boy who befriends a wondrous red balloon which follows him everywhere.
Academy Awards '56: Best Original Screenplay.
FR
Films Montsouris; Lopert Films — *Embassy Home Entertainment; Video Yesteryear; Sheik Video; Western Film & Video Inc*

Red Balloon, The/An Occurrence at Owl Creek Bridge 19??
Fantasy/Drama
63845　60 mins　C　B, V　P
Two classic award-winning shorts have been combined on one tape: "The Red Balloon" (color, 1956) and "An Occurrence at Owl Creek Bridge" (black and white, 1962).
Academy Awards '56: Best Original Screenplay ("The Red Balloon"); Cannes Film Festival: Blue Ribbon and American Film Festival: First Prize ("An Occurrence at Owl Creek Bridge").
Albert Lamorisse; Marcel Ichac and Paul de Roubaix — *Budget Video*

Red Box, The 1983
Fantasy/Literature
66213　27 mins　C　B, V　R, P
Animated
The children's stories - "The Red Carpet," "Whistle for Willie," "Charlie Needs a Cloak" - are combined on one cassette.
AM Available
Weston Woods — *CC Studios*

Red House, The 1947
Suspense/Mystery
51950　100 mins　B/W　B, V　P
Edward G. Robinson, Lon McCallister, Judith Anderson, Allene Roberts, directed by Delmar Daves

What is the secret that lies hidden in the abandoned Red House and the dark paths of Oxhead Wood? Why is one man so determined to keep people away from the Red House? United Artists; Sol Lesser — *Budget Video; Discount Video Tapes; Festival Films; Classic Video Cinema Collector's Club*

Red Kimono, The   1925
Drama/Exploitation
48741   70 mins   B/W   B, V, 3/4U   P
Dorothy Davenport Reid, Priscilla Bonner, Theodore von Eltz, Tyrone Power, directed by Walter Lang
Part of a series of 1920's silent pictures about the vices and sins of the people of this world. Mrs Wallace Reid Prods — *Penguin Video; Video Yesteryear*

Red Nightmare   1953
Drama
39000   30 mins   B/W   B, V, FO   P
Jack Webb, Jack Kelly, Jeanne Cooper, Peter Brown
This anti-communist propaganda film, produced for the Department of Defense by Warner Brothers, features the cast of "Dragnet." The story dramatizes the Red Menace, with communists conspiring to take over America, and shows what would happen to life in a small American town if the Commies took over. A typical Mc Carthy-era production. Warner Bros — *Video Yesteryear*

Red Pony, The   1949
Drama
64541   89 mins   C   B, V   P
Myrna Loy, Robert Mitchum, Peter Miles, Louis Calhern, Margaret Hamilton, Beau Bridges, directed by Louis Milestone
A young boy loses faith in his father when his pet pony dies. Based on a story by John Steinbeck, with musical score by Aaron Copland. Republic — *NTA Home Entertainment*

Red River   1948
Western
31665   125 mins   B/W   CED   P
John Wayne, Montgomery Clift, Walter Brennan, Joanne Dru, directed by Howard Hawks
The story of a cattle baron and the empire he builds. United Artists — *RCA VideoDiscs*

Red River Valley   1941
Western
49063   62 mins   B/W   B, V   P
Roy Rogers, George Hayes, Gale Storm, Sally Payne
Roy returns home and resumes his childhood romance with the sheriff's daughter.

Republic — *Sheik Video*

Red Shoes, The   1948
Drama
44365   133 mins   C   CED   P
Moira Shearer, Anton Walbrook, Marius Goring, Robert Helpmann
A lovely ballerina is in a bitter struggle between career and marriage. Academy Awards '48: Best Art Director, Color; Best Scoring, Drama (Brian Easdale). Eagle Lion, J Arthur Rank — *RCA VideoDiscs*

Redd Foxx—Video in a Plain Brown Wrapper   1983
Comedy-Performance
66201   60 mins   C   B, V, LV, CED   P
Foxx tackles all of his favorite subjectssex, marriage, death, crime and more sex. Command Entertainment Marketing — *Vestron Video*

Redeemer, The   1977
Horror
35388   83 mins   C   B, V   P
Christopher Flint, T.G. Finkbinder, Damien Knight
The Son of Satan sends invitations to a class reunion. In the style of "The Omen." MPAA:R
Sheldon Tromberg — *VCI Home Video*

Redneck   1973
Drama
12041   92 mins   C   B, V   P
Telly Savalas
A psychopathic killer and his partner take a teenage boy hostage. Int'l Amusement Corp — *King of Video*

Reds   1981
Drama
63425   200 mins   C   B, V, LV   R, P
Warren Beatty, Diane Keaton, Jack Nicholson, Maureen Stapleton, directed by Warren Beatty
"Reds" is the story of John Reed, a liberal American journalist who helped found the American Communist Party, documented the Bolshevik Revolution, and ultimately became the only American ever to be buried within the walls of the Kremlin. Academy Awards '81: Best Supporting Actress (Stapleton); Best Direction; Best Cinematography. MPAA:PG
Paramount; Warren Beatty — *Paramount Home Video; RCA VideoDiscs*

Reefer Madness   1938
Exploitation
03565   67 mins   B/W   B, V   P

Considered seriously at the time of its release, this low-budget depiction of the horrors of marijuana usage has become an underground comedy favorite. Overwrought acting and the lurid script contribute to the fun.
MPAA:PG
Dwain Esper Productions — *Media Home Entertainment; Budget Video; VCII; Select-a-Tape; Video Dimensions; Discount Video Tapes; Video Yesteryear; Sheik Video; Penguin Video; Video Connection; Western Film & Video Inc; Vestron Video (disc only)*

Reet, Petite and Gone   1947
Musical
08888   75 mins   B/W   B, V, 3/4U   P
Louis Jordan and his Tympany Five, June Richmond
A story about a girl whose mother dies, leaving a will which a crooked lawyer alters.
Unknown — *Penguin Video; Video Yesteryear; Discount Video Tapes*

Reflections   1978
Video
08564   30 mins   C   B, V, 3/4U   P
A continuous picture of a pond shimmering in the afternoon hours to create a relaxed background.
Nebulae Prods — *Nebulae Productions*

Reg'lar Fellers   1941
Comedy
66395   67 mins   B/W   B, V   P
Alfalfa Switzer, Roscoe Ates, Sara Padden
The misadventures of a neighborhood gang of kids, based on the then-popular comic strip of the same name.
Producers Releasing Corporation — *Movie Buff Video*

Rehabilitation and Injury   1978
Health education
42781   30 mins   C   B, V   P
Hosted by Ann Dugan 6   pgms
This series of cassettes covers aspects of rehabilitation and preventive medical care. See individual program listings.
1.Prenatal 2.Postnatal 3.Hysterectomy 4.Mastectomy 5.Knee 6.Back
Health 'N Action — *RCA/Columbia Pictures Home Video*

Reil   1982
Western
72336   180 mins   C   B, V   P
Arthur Hill, William Shatner
The pioneer days of Canada's western frontier days serve as the backdrop for this drama.
Canadian Broadcasting Corporation — *Prism*

Rejoice   1983
Parades and festivals
64007   45 mins   C   B, V   P
Highlights of the 1983 Tournament of Roses Parade in Pasadena with Grand Marshal Merlin Olsen.
Tournament Video Tapes — *Tournament Video Tapes*

Relationship of Conformation to Lameness   19??
Veterinary medicine
69644   56 mins   C   B, V   P
This program discusses equine lameness due to plating, fractures, hoof wall wear, winging, knock knees, open knees, buck knees and other physical problems.
Colorado State U — *Mercedes Maharis Productions*

Renegade Monk   1982
Martial arts
64946   90 mins   C   B, V   R, P
Lui Chung Liang, Hwang Hsing Shaw, Ko Shou Liang, Lang Shih Chia, Hsu Chung Hsing
An invincible warrior-monk dispenses his own brand of justicewith his fists.
MPAA:R
Foreign — *Video Gems*

Renfrew of the Royal Mounted in Crashing Through   1937
Adventure
29677   58 mins   B/W   B, V   P
James Newill, Warren Hull, Jean Carmen, Dave O'Brien
Presents action in the north woods as two mounties track a stolen shipment of gold and bring the thieves to justice
Grand National — *Sheik Video*

Renfrew on the Great White Trail   1937
Western
08807   60 mins   B/W   B, V, 3/4U   P
James Newill
Western featuring James Newill.
Grand Natl — *Penguin Video*

Repo Man   1983
Comedy
75016   92 mins   C   B, V   P
Harry Dean Stanton, Emilie Estevez
This is a comedy about a young punk rocker who tries to win a '64 Chevy Malibu in a contest.
Universal — *MCA Home Video*

Report on German Morale, A　　1994?
World War II/Propaganda
53651　21 mins　B/W　B, V, 3/4U　　　P
This film purports to examine methods used by the Nazis to control morale.
US War Dept — *International Historic Films; Interurban Films*

Reproduction of Life: Sex Education　　1982
Reproduction/Sexuality
59565　53 mins　C　　B, V　　　P
The entire process from conception through prenatal development to birth itself is explained.
McGraw Hill — *Mastervision*

Repulsion　　1965
Film-Avant-garde
12047　105 mins　B/W　　B, V　　　P
Catherine Deneuve, Yvonne Furneaux, Ian Hendry, directed by Roman Polanski
A French girl is repulsed by her sister's lover. When her sister goes away on vacation she locks herself in their apartment.
Michael Klinger; Tony Tenser Prod — *Video Dimensions; Sheik Video; Video Connection*

Rescue Squad　　197?
Health education
19410　22 mins　C　B, V, 3/4U, Q　　　P
Displays actual rescue techniques and treatment of major injuries.
TV Sports Scene — *TV Sports Scene*

Restricted U.S. and British Training Films　　1944
World War II
53649　110 mins　B/W　B, V, 3/4U　　　P
Six short films from WWII: "Parachute Training in the German Army"; "Captured Japanese Weapons"; "U-Boat Identification"; "Crack That Tank"; "Time Out Hollywood"; and "Secret Weapon."
Unknown — *International Historic Films*

Resurrection of Zachary Wheeler, The　　1972
Science fiction
33595　100 mins　C　　B, V　　　P
Angie Dickinson, Bradford Dillman, Leslie Nielson
A presidential candidate who narrowly escaped death in an auto crash is brought to a mysterious clinic. A reporter sneaks into the clinic and discovers the horrors of cloning.
MPAA:G
Gold Key — *VCI Home Video*

Return, The　　1980
Science fiction
63323　90 mins　C　　B, V　　　R, P
Raymond Burr, Cybill Shepherd, Martin Landau, Jan-Michael Vincent
Two friends seek clues to the bizarre phenomena of the present in an extraterrestrial encounter they shared as children 25 years earlier.
Independent — *THORN EMI Home Video*

Return of a Man Called Horse, The　　1976
Adventure
59429　125 mins　C　B, V, CED　　　P
Richard Harris, Gail Sondergaard, Geoffrey Lewis, directed by Ervin Kershner
This sequel to "A Man Called Horse" tells the story of an English aristocrat who was captured and raised by Sioux Indians, and then returned to his native homeland.
United Artists — *CBS/Fox Video*

Return of Chandu　　1934
Science fiction/Serials
10930　156 mins　B/W　　B, V　　　P
Bela Lugosi, Maria Alba
Twelve chapters. Features Bela Lugosi, as Chandu, who exercises his powers to conquer the Black Sorcerers who inhabit the island of Lemuria.
Mascot — *Discount Video Tapes; Video Connection; Penguin Video; Video Dimensions*

Return of Chandu, The　　1934
Suspense
38979　61 mins　B/W　B, V, FO　　　P
Bela Lugosi, Clara Kimball Young
Chandu the Magician fights to save the Princess Nadji from being sacrificed by a religious sect of cat worshippers. Story by Raymond Chandler.
Mascot — *Video Yesteryear; Sheik Video; Cable Films; Video Connection*

Return of Martin Guerre, The　　1983
Mystery
65623　111 mins　C　B, V, LV　　　P
Gerard Depardieu, Natalie Baye
A true, satisfyingly ingenious and provocative story, which revolves around Martin Guerre, who had disappeared as a young husband and resumed his marriage years later.
Societe Francaise de Production Cinematographique — *Embassy Home Entertainment*

Return of the Bad Men　　1948
Western
10068　90 mins　B/W　　B, V　　　P, T
Randolph Scott, Robert Ryan, Anne Jeffreys, Gabby Hayes, Jason Robards, Jacqueline White

Man plans to stake claim in Oklahoma during land rush and finds romance.
RKO, Nat Holt — *Blackhawk Films; Nostalgia Merchant*

Return of the Daylight   1981
Trains
59172   60 mins   C   B, V   P
A look at Southern Pacific's "Daylight" special.
De Luz Video — *De Luz Video*

Return of the Dragon   1972
Adventure/Martial arts
55832   91 mins   C   B, V   P
Bruce Lee, Nora Miao, Chuck Norris, directed by Bruce Lee
Lee's last picture concerns a Chinese restaurant in Rome which is menaced by gangsters who want to buy the property. On behalf of the owners, Lee duels an American karate champ in the Roman forum.
MPAA:R
Bryanston Pictures — *CBS/Fox Video; Video Gems*

Return of the Pink Panther, The   1975
Comedy
13595   113 mins   C   B, V, LV   P
Peter Sellers, Christopher Plummer, Catherine Schell, directed by Blake Edwards
Inspector Clousseau is called upon to rescue the Pink Panther diamond stolen from a museum.
MPAA:G
United Artists; Blake Edwards — *CBS/Fox Video; RCA VideoDiscs*

Return of the Rams/NFL '83   1984
Football
75890   46 mins   C   B, V, FO   P
This program presents scenes from the Los Angeles Rams' 1983 season.
NFL Films — *NFL Films Video*

Return of the Red Tiger   1981
Martial arts/Adventure
59416   82 mins   C   B, V   P
Bruce Lee
Kung-Fu master Bruce Lee displays one of the foremost and exciting styles of kung-fu—the Tiger.
Unknown — *HarmonyVision*

Return of the Secaucus 7   1981
Comedy-Drama
60341   110 mins   C   B, V   P
Mark Arnott, Gordon Clapp, Maggie Cousineau-Arndt, directed by John Sayles

A weekend reunion of seven friends who were activists during the turbulent '60's serves as the basis for this look at a group turning 30.
Libra Specialty Films — *RCA/Columbia Pictures Home Video*

Return of the Tiger   1978
Adventure/Martial arts
50732   95 mins   C   B, V   P
Bruce Li, Paul Smith, Chaing I, Angelea Mao, directed by Jimmy Shaw
The Hovver Night Club in Bangkok is used to cover up the operations of an international narcotic group headed by an American. A rival Chinese gang tries to dominate the drug market, and conflict ensues.
Jimmy Shaw — *Media Home Entertainment*

Return to Boggy Creek   1977
Suspense
65330   87 mins   C   B, V, CED   P
Dawn Wells
In a small fishing village, the townspeople learn from a photogrpaher that a "killer" beast whom they thought had disappeared has returned and is living in Boggy Creek. Some children follow the photographer into the swamp, despite hurricane warnings.
MPAA:PG
Bayou Productions — *CBS/Fox Video*

Return to Macon County   1975
Adventure
66097   90 mins   C   B, V, CED   P
Nick Nolte, Don Johnson, Robin Mattson
A tale of three young, reckless youths on the loose.
American International Pictures — *Vestron Video*

Revenge   1972
Drama
59841   89 mins   C   B, V   P
Joan Collins, James Booth, Ray Barrett, Ken Griffith
A thriller about the drive for revenge that ultimately destroys the family of a young girl who was brutally murdered.
Peter Rogers; George H Brown — *Embassy Home Entertainment*

Revenge of the Ninja   1983
Adventure/Martial arts
65661   90 mins   C   B, V, CED   P
Sho Kosugi
A Ninja hoping to escape his bloody past in Los Angeles gets mixed up with a drug trafficker, who turns out to be an American Ninja and his archfoe. The two polish off a slew of mobsters before their own inevitable showdown.
MPAA:R
Cannon Films — *MGM/UA Home Video*

Revenge of the Pink   1978
Panther
Comedy
47804   99 mins   C   B, V, LV,   P
                        CED
Peter Sellers, Herbert Lom, Dyan Cannon,
Robert Webber, directed by Blake Edwards
Inspector Clouseau tracks down an international
drug ring which takes him around the world.
MPAA:PG
United Artists — *CBS/Fox Video; RCA*
VideoDiscs

Revenge of the Virgins,   1962
The
Western
48740   60 mins   B/W   B, V, 3/4U   P
Charles Veltman, Romona Rogers, Jan Lee,
Joanne Bowers
A motley crew of cowhands, bamboozlers, and
drunkards set out to go gold prospecting in the
heart of Indian country. They are subsequently
menaced by a horde of female Indians.
Unknown — *Penguin Video*

Revenge of TV Bloopers   196?
Outtakes and bloopers
55130   50 mins   B/W   B, V   P
Tim Conway, Bing Crosby, Jack Klugman, Don
Rickles, Ozzie Nelson, Orson Welles, Dick Van
Dyke, Three Stooges, Marx Brothers
A group of stars including Sammy Davis Jr., E.G.
Marshall, Roddy McDowall, Jack Palance,
James Coburn, Suzanne Pleshette, Eddie
Fisher, Zero Mostel, Goldie Hawn, Mamie Van
Doren, and others are caught in the act of
making goofups and blunders on the set. Also
included are rare old TV commercials featuring
Dick Van Dyke, the Marx Brothers, the Three
Stooges and others. Bloopers from such series
as "The Defenders," "Ben Casey," "McHale's
Navy," "Ozzie and Harriet," "Laugh-In," "The
Nurses," "Burke's Law," and more are shown.
Video Dimensions — *Video Dimensions*

Revolt of Job, The   1984
Drama
75541   98 mins   C   B, V   P
An elderly Jewish couple adopt an 8-year-old
Gentile boy although it is illegal and against the
beliefs of the orthodox community.
TeleCulture Inc — *MGM/UA Home Video*

Revolt of the Dragon   1975
Martial arts
63860   90 mins   C   B, V   P
A martial arts expert visits friends in his
hometown and finds himself battling a ruthless
gang that terrorizes the people.
MPAA:R
United International Pictures — *Budget Video*

Rhythm and Blues 1   1983
Music-Performance
65225   57 mins   C   B, V   P
Billy Eckstine, Ruth Brown, Billy Preston, Gloria
Lynne, Sheer Delight, Gil Askey
Gospel roots are joyously evident in this
program documenting the Rhythm and Blues
movement from the farms to the cities.
Skylark Savoy Productions Ltd — *Video Gems*

Ribald Tales of Robin   1980
Hood, The
Satire
55214   83 mins   C   B, V   P
The Robin Hood legend is satirized in this
comedy which concentrates on Prince John and
his favorite pastimes: rape, pillage and plunder.
MPAA:R
Lima Productions — *Media Home*
Entertainment

Rich and Famous   1981
Comedy-Drama
59311   117 mins   C   B, V, CED   P
Jacqueline Bisset, Candice Bergen, David
Selby, Hart Bochner, Matt Lattanzi, directed by
George Cukor
The story of the 25-year friendship of two
women, through college, marriage, and
success.
MPAA:R
MGM — *MGM/UA Home Video*

Rich Little's Great   1984
Hollywood Trivia Game
Game show
65601   60 mins   C   B, V   P
The multi-talented impressionist brings his
Hollywood repertoire together for the show biz
trivia challenge of the year.
Vestron — *Vestron Video*

Richard   197?
Nixon—Checkers, Old
Glory, Resignation
Documentary/Presidency-US
57358   45 mins   B/W   B, V, FO   P
Three historic broadcasts in the career of
Richard Nixon: the "Checkers Speech" (1952)
where Nixon defended himself against
accusations of misusing campaign funds; "Old
Glory" (1957), a short talk from New York's
Chrysler Building in honor of flag day; and
"Resignation" (1974), a kinescope of the TV
pool feed from the Oval Room of the White
House as Nixon announces he will leave office.
Unknown — *Video Yesteryear*

Richard Pryor: Here and   1983
Now
Comedy-Performance
65697   75 mins   C   B, V, CED   P

Richard Pryor
Filmed at the Saenger Theater in New Orleans, Pryor's sharp, witty commentaries are delivered with a unique piercing humor.
MPAA:R
Bob Parkinson; Andy Friendly — *RCA/Columbia Pictures Home Video*

Richard Pryor Live in Concert — 197?
Comedy-Performance
58898   78 mins   C   B, V   P
Richard Pryor
Richard Pryor demonstrates his unique brand of humor before an enthusiastic audience.
Unknown — *Vestron Video; RCA VideoDiscs*

Richard Pryor Live on the Sunset Strip — 1982
Comedy-Performance
63438   82 mins   C   B, V   P
Richard Pryor
Filmed live at the Hollywood Palladium, this program captures Richard Pryor at his funniest, including his segment about "Pryor on fire."
MPAA:R
Columbia; Richard Pryor — *RCA/Columbia Pictures Home Video; RCA VideoDiscs*

Richard's Things — 1980
Drama
69549   104 mins   C   B, V   P
Liv Ullman, Amanda Redman
A man's wife and his girlfriend find love and comfort in each other after his death.
MPAA:R
Unknown — *Embassy Home Entertainment*

Richie Rich — 1983
Cartoons
66575   60 mins   C   B, V   P
Animated
Rich kid Richie Rich is featured in this compilation of exotic and comical adventures with his adolescent pals.
Hanna Barbera — *Worldvision Home Video*

Rick Derringer — 1982
Music-Performance
75909   58 mins   C   B, V   P
This program presents Rick Derringer performing his hit songs at the Ritz in New York City.
Harrison Suggs Productions Inc — *Sony Corporation of America*

Rick Springfield Platinum Videos — 1983
Music video
66632   30 mins   C   B, V   P
This music video collection of Rick Springfield hits contains the following six songs: "Affair of the Heart," "Human Touch," "Souls," "Don't Talk to Strangers," "What Kind of Fool Am I" and "Jessie's Girl."
RCA Video Productions — *RCA/Columbia Pictures Home Video*

Riddle of the Sands — 1984
Adventure
72533   99 mins   C   B, V   P
Michael York, Jenny Agutter, Simon Mac Corkindale, directed by Tony Maylam
Two English yachtsmen in 1903 inadvertently stumble upon a German plot to invade England by sea.
Satori — *VidAmerica*

Ride 'Em Cowgirl — 1941
Western
14673   51 mins   B/W   3/4U   P
Dorothy Paige
Girl handles the riding and roping.
Grand National — *Video Connection*

Ride in the Whirlwind — 1967
Western
09005   83 mins   C   B, V   P
Jack Nicholson, Cameron Mitchell, Millie Perkins, Katherine Squire
Three cowboys are mistaken for members of a gang by a posse.
Jack Nicholson; Monte Hellman — *Media Home Entertainment; Budget Video; Sheik Video; Video Yesteryear; Discount Video Tapes; Western Film & Video Inc*

Ride on the Cumbres and Toltec Scenic Railway, A — 1979
Trains
46926   63 mins   C   B, V   P
Scenes of an ex-D and RGW Class K-36 outside frame Mikado steam loco en route from Antonito, Colorado to Chama, New Mexico, plus "Great Freight '79's" special freight run to the top of Windy Point.
JMJ Prods — *JMJ Productions*

Ride Pacific Electric San Bernardino — 1939
Trains
74480   10 mins   B/W   B, V   P
This tape features a dramatization of the historical trip of the new Pacific Electric between Los Angeles and San Bernardino.
South California Railroad Boosters — *Interurban Films*

Ride, Ranger, Ride — 1936
Western
05586   56 mins   B/W   B, V, 3/4U   P

Gene Autry, Smiley Burnette, Kaye Hughes, Max Terhune
Gene Autry joins the cavalry and foils a plot to start an Indian uprising.
Republic — *Penguin Video; Nostalgia Merchant; Video Yesteryear*

Ride the Last of the Big Red Cars 1979
Trains
51435 18 mins C B, V P
This program takes the viewer on a ride on Pacific Electric's last line from Los Angeles to Long Beach.
Bruce Frenzinger — *Interurban Films*

Ride the Man Down 1953
Western
74487 90 mins C B, V P
Rod Cameron, Ella Raines
This is the story of a murderous land war between neighboring landowners.
Republic — *NTA Home Entertainment*

Ride the Wind 1966
Western
72892 120 mins C B, V P
Lorne Greene, Dan Blocker
The "Bonanza" gang goes to the aid of the Pony Express.
NBC — *NTA Home Entertainment*

Rider on the Rain 1970
Suspense
64973 115 mins C B, V P
Marlene Jobert, Charles Bronson, Jill Ireland
A young housewife is viciously raped by an escaped sex maniac. She kills him and disposes of his body, not knowing that he is being relentlessly pursued by a tough colonel.
Avco-Embassy — *Embassy Home Entertainment*

Riders of Death Valley 1941
Western/Serials
12550 195 mins B/W B, V P
Buck Jones, Lon Chaney, Jr., Dick Foran, directed by Ford Beebe, Ray Taylor
Western action serial in fifteen episodes of thirteen minutes each.
Universal — *Video Connection*

Riders of Destiny 1933
Western
15489 59 mins B/W B, V P
John Wayne
John Wayne leads a group of Rangers on the trail of justice.
Monogram — *Video Connection; Discount Video Tapes; Video Dimensions*

Riders of the Desert 1932
Western
11371 57 mins B/W B, V, FO P
Bob Steele
Plenty of hoofbeats through desert sands.
Worldwide — *Video Yesteryear; Video Connection*

Riders of the Law 1935
Western
08815 56 mins B/W B, V, 3/4U P
Bob Steele
Western featuring Bob Steele.
Supreme — *Penguin Video*

Riders of the Rockies 1937
Western
15457 60 mins B/W B, V P
Tex Ritter, Yakima Canutt, directed by Robert N. Bradbury
An honest cowboy turns rustler in order to trap a border gang.
Grand National — *VCI Home Video; Video Connection; Discount Video Tapes*

Riders of the Sage 1939
Western
58488 40 mins B/W B, V, 3/4U P
Bob Steele, Clare Rochelle
Cattlemen, sheepherders and homesteaders turn a peaceful valley into a range war.
Aurora — *Penguin Video*

Riders of the Whistling Pines 1949
Western
64391 70 mins B/W B, V, 3/4U P
Gene Autry, Patricia White, Jimmy Lloyd
Gene solves a murder committed by a band of lumber thieves.
Gene Autry Productions; Columbia — *Nostalgia Merchant*

Riders of the Whistling Skull 1937
Western
15440 54 mins B/W B, V P
Bob Livingston, Ray Corrigan
Three Mesquiteers rescue professor of archeology captured by lost Indian tribe.
Republic — *Video Connection*

Ridin' on a Rainbow 1941
Western
54112 79 mins B/W B, V P, T
Gene Autry, Smiley Burnette
A has-been performer on a steamboat decides to rob a bank in the hopes of starting a new life for himself and his daughter. The money he robs had just been deposited by some cattlemen. One of the cattlemen joins the steamboat's

crew, wins the daughter's heart, and gets to the father.
Republic — *Blackhawk Films; Video Connection*

Ridin' the California Trail — 1947
Western
58489   40 mins   B/W   B, V, 3/4U   P
Gilbert Roland
The Cisco Kid is wanted dead or alive in several states.
Monogram — *Penguin Video*

Riding Avenger, The — 1936
Western
08785   56 mins   B/W   B, V, 3/4U   P
Hoot Gibson, Ruth Mix, Buzz Barton
To gain the love of a beautiful lady, a cowboy vows never to fight again, but is forced to break his promise when the town is terrorized.
Diversion — *Penguin Video; Video Connection*

Rififi — 1954
Mystery
44160   115 mins   B/W   B, V   P
Jean Servais, Carl Mohner, Robert Manuel, Jules Dassin, directed by Jules Dassin
A suspensful story of a successful jewel robbery in which the four thieves betray each other. French with English subtitles.
FR
UMPO; French — *Movie Buff Video; Budget Video; Discount Video Tapes; Cable Films; Western Film & Video Inc*

Right of Way — 1984
Drama
74110   102 mins   C   B, V   P
Bette Davis, James Stewart, Melinda Dillon
A touching story of true love featuring two of the biggest stars to ever grace the silver screen. Stewart plays an elderly man who makes a suicide pact when he learns of his wife's terminal illness.
George Schaefer — *VCL Home Video*

Right Stuff, The — 1983
Drama
Closed Captioned
74210   193 mins   C   B, V, LV   R, P
Charles Frank, Scott Glenn, Ed Harris, Dennis Quaid, Sam Shephard
This program is based on the best-selling book by Tom Wolfe. It is the up-close and personal story of America's space program at its conception.
Academy Awards '83: Best Music Score; Best Film Editing; Best Sound; Best Sound Effect Editing.   MPAA:PG
Irwin Winkler; Robert Chartoff — *Warner Home Video*

Right Stuff/NFL '83, The — 1984
Football
72939   46 mins   C   B, V, FO   P
Pittsburgh Steelers
Highlights from the Pittsburgh Steelers' 1983 season and "NFL 1983."
NFL Films — *NFL Films Video*

Rigoletto — 1954
Opera
56916   90 mins   C   B, V, FO   P
Aldo Silvani, Gerard Landry, Janet Vidor
Verdi's great opera concerning the intrigues in the court of the Duke of Mantua, and the clever plottings of Rigoletto—the hunchbacked court jester. Sung in Italian with dialogue dubbed in English.
Italy — *Video Yesteryear*

Rime of the Ancient Mariner — 198?
Literature
47405   60 mins   C   B, V   P
Narrated by Sir Michael Redgrave, directed by Raul De Silva
An adaptation of Samuel Taylor Coleridge's epic poem, set to images both real and animated; in two parts—Part I: The Life of Samuel Coleridge; Part II: The Rime of the Ancient Mariner. International Film and Television Festival of New York: Gold Medal.
Kultur — *Kultur*

Ringing Bell — 1983
Fairy tales
65467   ? mins   C   B, V   P
Animated
This is the story of a fluffly lamb whose mother is killed by a terrifying black wolf, leaving him alone and resolved to avenge her death. In Beta Hi-Fi.
Tsunemasa Hatano — *RCA/Columbia Pictures Home Video*

Rink, The/The Immigrant — 191?
Comedy
59368   56 mins   B/W   B, V, FO   P
Charlie Chaplin, Mack Swain, Edna Purviance
Two Chaplin shorts: 'The Rink" (1916), in which Charlie defends his girlfriend's honor at a local roller skating rink; "The Immigrant" (1917), features Charlie as a newcomer to America.
Mutual — *Video Yesteryear*

Rio Bravo — 1959
Western
58246   140 mins   C   B, V   R, P
John Wayne, Dean Martin, Angie Dickinson, Rick Nelson, Walter Brennan, directed by Howard Hawks
The sheriff of a Texas border town takes a brutal murderer into custody—and faces a

---

blockade of hired gunmen determined to keep his prisoner from being brought to justice.
Armada Productions — *Warner Home Video; RCA VideoDiscs*

Rio Grande 1950
Western
66466 105 mins B/W B, V P
John Wayne, Maureen O'Hara, Ben Jonson, Claude Jarman, Jr., directed by John Ford
A U.S. Cavalry unit on the Mexican border conducts an unsuccessful campaign against marauding Indians.
Republic — *NTA Home Entertainment*

Rio Lobo 1970
Western
54104 114 mins C B, V, CED P
John Wayne, Jorge Rivero, Jennifer O'Neill, Jack Elam, directed by Howard Hawks
After the Civil War, a Union Colonel goes to Rio Lobo to take revenge on two traitors. When he gets there he finds that one of the traitors is in a conspiracy with the town sheriff, trying to force a rancher to sign over all his land.
MPAA:G
National General Pictures, Cinema Center — *CBS/Fox Video*

Rio Rattler 1935
Western
08600 60 mins B/W B, V, 3/4U P
Tom Tyler
A vintage fast-shooting matinee western starring Tom Tyler.
Commodore — *Penguin Video; Video Connection*

Rise and Fall of the Third Reich 1968
Documentary/History-Modern
68247 120 mins C B, V P
A pictorial record which tracks Adolph Hitler's path through the years between 1920 and 1945. Some segments are in black and white.
MGM — *MGM/UA Home Video*

Risky Business 1983
Comedy
65357 99 mins C B, V, LV, CED P
Tom Cruise, Rebecca de Mornay
A straight-arrow college-bound student encounters a street-smart call girl while his parents are out of town, resulting in a funny and harrowing week-long odyssey toward maturity. In VHS Dolby stereo/Beta Hi-fi.
MPAA:R
Steve Tisch Jon Avnet Production — *Warner Home Video*

Rituals 1979
Drama
60447 100 mins C B, V P
Hal Holbrook, Laurence Dane
A group of five calm, rational men suddenly turn desperate after a chain of nightmarish events.
Lawrence Dane; Day and Date Intl — *Embassy Home Entertainment*

Rivals of the Silver Fox 1980
Martial arts
69281 80 mins C B, V P
Casanova Wong, Barry Lam, Chen Shao Peng, Lee Fat Yuen
Wang Fung seeks and finds his wife's murderer, but revenge is not easy. Mandarin dialogue, English subtitles.
CH
IFD Films & Arts — *Silverline Video*

Road Agent 1926
Western
58491 70 mins B/W B, V, 3/4U P
Al Hoxie
A crooked attorney tries to beat a young woman out of her inherited ranch.
Unknown — *Penguin Video; Discount Video Tapes*

Road Games 1981
Suspense
60448 100 mins C B, V, CED P
Stacy Keach, Jamie Lee Curtis
A trucker is drawn into a web of intrigue surrounding a series of highway murders.
MPAA:PG
Avco Embassy; Richard Franklin — *Embassy Home Entertainment*

Road to Bali 1953
Comedy
47663 91 mins C B, V P
Bob Hope, Bing Crosby, Dorothy Lamour, Mervyn Vye, Ralph Moody, Jane Russell, Jerry Lewis, Dean Martin
Two vaudervillians performing in Australia are forced to hit the high seas due to a pair of matrimony-minded females.
Paramount — *Unicorn Video*

Road to Ruin, The 1928
Drama/Exploitation
48742 50 mins B/W B, V, 3/4U P
Grant Withers
A girl's disillusionment leads to a life of prostitution and an eventual surprise meeting with her father. Silent.
Cliff Broughton Prods — *Penguin Video*

Road to Yesterday, The 1925
Fantasy
64313 87 mins B/W B, V P

William Boyd, Joseph Schildkraut, directed by Cecil B. DeMille
Following an accident, two friends are hurled back in time and transformed into different characters. Silent with musical score.
Producers Distributing Corp — *Classic Video Cinema Collector's Club*

Road to Yesterday/The Yankee Clipper 1927
Film-History
50640   56 mins   B/W   B, V   P, T
William Boyd, Elinor Fair, Joseph Schildkraut, Jetta Boudal, Vera Reynolds
Four train passengers are transported back to previous lives in "The Road to Yesterday." "The Yankee Clipper races the British Lord of the Isles from China to New England to capture the tea trade. Both of these pictures are abridged versions. Silent.
Cecil B DeMille; Rupert Julian — *Blackhawk Films*

Road Warrior, The 1982
Adventure
63453   95 mins   C   B, V, LV,   R, P
                                    CED
Mel Gibson, directed by George Miller
A sequel to 1979's "Mad Max," this film continues the futuristic adventures of Max, a lone driver who cruises through a barren, lawless country that has been destroyed by a major war. In search of precious gasoline, Max faces the marauding Humungus, who plunder the wasteland. VHS in stereo.
MPAA:R
Warner Bros; Kennedy Miller Productions — *Warner Home Video*

Road Warriors, The/NFL '82 1983
Football
66221   45 mins   C   B, V, FO   P
Highlights of the N.Y. Jets 1982-83 season, plus an overview of the whole NFL season.
NFL Films — *NFL Films Video*

Roadhouse 66 1984
Drama
73660   90 mins   C   B, V   R, P
When a preppie and a musician get stuck in an Arizona town for car repairs, the duo wind up in a drag race and fall in love. The soundtrack features music from Los Lobos, The Pretenders, and Dave Edmunds.
MPAA:R
Scott Rosenfelt; Mark Levinson — *Atlantic Video*

Roaming Wild 1936
Western
08836   60 mins   B/W   B, V, 3/4U   P

Tom Tyler
Action western with Tom Tyler.
Reliable — *Penguin Video*

Roarin' Lead 1937
Western
15437   54 mins   B/W   B, V   P
Bob Livingston, Ray Corrigan, Max Terhune
Three Mesquiteers stop gang of rustlers, thus helping orphan's and cattlemen's associations.
Republic — *Video Connection*

Roaring Fire 1982
Suspense/Martial arts
66025   95 mins   C   B, V   R, P
Sonny Chiba
A martial arts thriller set against the backdrop of exotic Japan.
Shiteru Okada — *THORN EMI Home Video*

Roaring Guns 1936
Western
13092   66 mins   B/W   B, V   P
Tim McCoy, Rex Lease
Small-time ranchers overcome a crooked cattle combine.
Puritan — *Video Connection; Penguin Video*

Roaring Six Guns 1937
Western
08831   60 mins   B/W   B, V, 3/4U   P
Kermit Maynard
James Oliver Curwood story of the Northwest's fight for its rights.
Ambassador Conn — *Penguin Video; Discount Video Tapes; Video Connection*

Roaring Twenties, The 1939
Drama
64786   106 mins   B/W   CED   P
James Cagney, Humphrey Bogart, Jeffrey Lynn, Priscilla Lane
A WWI veteran returns to New York and becomes involved in bootlegging, builds up an empire and dies in a gang war.
Warner; Hal B. Wallis — *RCA VideoDiscs*

Roaring Twenties, The 192?
History-US/Documentary
10147   ? mins   B/W   B, V   P, T
Newsreels picture Ku Klux Klan, the automobile era, the first total solar eclipse, the Charleston, Babe Ruth, Rudolph Valentino's death, Charles Lindbergh, and Black Tuesday when stock market crashed.
Unknown — *Blackhawk Films*

Rob McConnell 1983
Music-Performance
75916   25 mins   C   B, V   P

(For Explanation of codes, see USE GUIDE and KEY)

This program presents the jazz music of Rob McConnell featuring his hits "The Waltz I Blew for You" and "My Man Bill."
digit recordings — *Sony Corporation of America*

Robbers of the Sacred Mountain   1983
Adventure
75489   95 mins   C   B, V   P
Two adventurers seek meteorites in the jungles of Mexico.
Unknown — *Prism*

Robe, The   1953
Drama
08455   133 mins   C   B, V   P
Richard Burton, Jean Simmons, Victor Mature, Michael Rennie
This moving religious picture follows the career of a drunken and dissolute Roman tribune, Marcellus, after he wins the robe of Christ in a dice game.
EL, SP
20th Century Fox — *CBS/Fox Video*

Robert A. Taft: Mr. Republican   1954
Biographical/Politics and government-US
44243   15 mins   B/W   B, V   P
An account of the political career of Robert A. Taft, son of the U.S. President, who was noted as a great leader of the Republican Party. Classic newsreel footage.
Fox Movietone News — *Two Star Films*

Robert et Robert   1979
Comedy-Drama
47022   95 mins   C   B, V   P
Charles Denner, Jacques Villeret, Jean-Claude Brialy
Two "ineligible" bachelors resort to a computerized matrimonial agency to find the girls of their dreams. French with English subtitles.
FR
Quartet Films — *RCA/Columbia Pictures Home Video*

Robert Youngson Specials   19??
Variety/Documentary
29782   60 mins   C   B, V   P
6   pgms
A series of six programs that shows fads, culture, sports, famous personalities, and great moments in the first half of the twentieth century. Each show is headlined by a theatrical short done by Robert Youngson, built around laughter and action.
1. Spills and Chills 2. This Mechanical Age 3. The World of Kids 4. Blaze Busters 5. Gadgets Galore 6. I Never Forget a Face

Robert Youngson, Warner Bros — *Budget Video*

Roberto Clemente: A Touch of Royalty   1975
Baseball
33831   26 mins   C   B, V   P
Roberto Clemente
The story of the near-legendary Pittsburgh Pirate outfielder and Hall of Famer is told through action footage of Clemente, on-location shooting in his native Puerto Rico, and interview with friends and family. His tragic death occurred on a mercy mission to aid Nicaraguan Refugees.
W and W Productions — *Major League Baseball Productions*

Robin and Marian   1976
Drama
65097   106 mins   C   B, V   P
Sean Connery, Audrey Hepburn, Robert Shaw, Richard Harris, directed by Richard Lester
After a separation of twenty years, Robin Hood is reunited with Maid Marian, who is now a nun. Their dormant feelings for each other are reawakened as Robin spirits her to Sherwood Forest.
MPAA:PG
Columbia; Rastar — *RCA/Columbia Pictures Home Video*

Robinhood of Texas   1947
Western/Musical
44807   71 mins   B/W   B, V   P, T
Gene Autry, Cass County Boys
Gene and his friend help a sheriff round up a team of bank robbers and their loot while salvaging an almost defunct ranch and turning it into a fancy dude ranch.
Republic — *Blackhawk Films; Video Connection*

Robinson Crusoe   1936
Adventure
38978   34 mins   B/W   B, V, FO   P
Narrated by "Uncle Don" Carney
A real oddity—this is a British silent film that was originally made in 1927. Ten years later, the film was re-edited, music and sound effects were added, along with a narration by children's radio personality "Uncle Don" Carney, which follows the plot of the famous adventure story.
Unknown — *Video Yesteryear*

Robinson Crusoe of Clipper Island   1936
Adventure
08875   221 mins   B/W   B, V, 3/4U   P
Mala, Rex, Buck, Mamo Clark, John Ward, Tracy Lane, Robert Kortman
Fourteen episodes featuring the investigative expertise of Mala, a Polynesian in the employ of

the U.S. Intelligence Service. 16 minute
episodes.
Republic — *Penguin Video; Video Connection*

Robinson Crusoe of Mystery Island   1936
Adventure
12563   100 mins   B/W   B, V   P
Mala, Rex, Buck
Polynesian employed by U.S. Intelligence
Service investigates saboteurs on mysterious
island.
Republic — *Video Connection*

Robot Monster   1953
Science fiction
64921   58 mins   B/W   B, V   P
*George Nader, Claudia Barrett, directed by Phil
Tucker*
This ludicrous cheapie is considered to be one
of the worst films of all time. Alien invaders
(dressed in motheaten gorilla suits and diving
helmets) attack mankind with a giant soap -
bubble machine.
Astor — *Video Dimensions; Festival Films;
Admit One Video*

Rock, The   1978
Video
08574   30 mins   C   B, V, 3/4U   P
A continuous picture of a calm, shimmering
ocean inlet featuring a large rock which has
been shaped by wind and water to create a
relaxed background.
Nebulae Prods — *Nebulae Productions*

Rock Adventure   1981
Music
47298   29 mins   C   LV   P
Music by Baenzai and breathtaking visuals
combine to express a mood of wild adventure.
Masaru Ohtaki; Tokyo Eizosha
Company — *Pioneer Video Imports*

Rock and Roll Revue   1955
Music-Performance
08886   75 mins   B/W   B, V, 3/4U   P
*Duke Ellington, Nat King Cole, Joe Turner, Larry
Darnell, Lionel Hampton*
Features popular black entertainers on stage at
the Apollo Theater in Harlem.
Unknown — *Penguin Video*

Rock 'n' Roll High School   1979
Musical
64299   94 mins   C   B, V   P
P. J. Soles, Clint Howard, The Ramones
The music of the Ramones highlights this story
of a high school out to thwart the principal at
every turn.
MPAA:PG

New World Pictures — *Warner Home Video*

Rock, Rock, Rock   1956
Musical
59155   78 mins   B/W   B, V, 3/4U   P
*Chuck Berry, Fats Domino, Tuesday Weld,
Frankie Lymon and the Teeangers* ·
A young girl's father insists she earn enough
money to buy a new gown for the Senior Prom.
Classic musical numbers performed by a
number of rock'n'roll pioneers.
DCA — *Nostalgia Merchant*

Rock, You Sinners   1957
Musical
59370   59 mins   B/W   B, V, FO   P
Vintage rock 'n' roll from pre-Beatles England. A
BBC DJ forced to play rock 'n' roll records gets
the idea to put on a rock 'n' roll TV show.
England — *Video Yesteryear*

Rockabilly Glamourcize   1983
Physical fitness
66224   60 mins   C   B, V   P
Ray Campi and His Rockabilly Rebels
An aerobic exercise program set to the beat of
rockabilly-style rock'n'roll.
Ronny Weiser Productions — *Intra-Video
Properties*

Rocketship/Mars Attacks the World   193?
Science fiction
58913   141 mins   B/W   B, V   P
Buster Crabbe, Jean Rogers, Charles Middleton
A Flash Gordon double feature: "Rocket Ship"
(1936), in which Flash and friends fly to the
planet Mongo; "Mars Attacks the World"
(1938), a feature version of the serial, "Flash
Gordon's Trip to Mars."
EL, SP
Universal — *Ampro Video Productions*

Rocketship X-M—Special Edition   1950
Science fiction/Adventure
44357   77 mins   B/W   B, V, 3/4U   P
*Lloyd Bridges, Osa Massen, John Emery, Hugh
O'Brien*
A lunar mission goes awry and the crew lands
on Mars. Contains newly photographed footage,
a tinted sequence and previews of coming
attractions from classic science fiction films.
Lippert — *Nostalgia Merchant*

Rockshow   1981
Music-Performance
58884   102 mins   C   B, V   R, P
Paul McCartney and Wings
Paul and Wings perform 23 of their best songs
before an audience of 67,000 fans at the King
Dome in Seattle, Washington. Selections

---

include "Jet," "Band on the Run," "Venus and Mars," "Maybe I'm Amazed," and "Yesterday."
MPL Communications — *THORN EMI Home Video; Pioneer Artists; RCA VideoDiscs*

Rocky　　　　　　　　　　　　1976
Drama
37521　　119 mins　　C　　B, V, LV, 　　P
　　　　　　　　　　　　　　　CED
Sylvester Stallone, Talia Shire, Burgess Meredith, directed by John G. Avildsen
A young man from the slums of Philadelphia pursues his dream of becoming a boxing champion.
Academy Awards '76: Best Picture; Best Director (Avildsen); Best Achievement in Film Editing.　MPAA:PG
United Artists — *CBS/Fox Video; RCA VideoDiscs*

Rocky II　　　　　　　　　　　　1979
Drama
58810　　119 mins　　C　　B, V, LV, 　　P
　　　　　　　　　　　　　　　CED
Sylvester Stallone, Talia Shire, Burt Young, Burgess Meredith, Carl Weathers
This sequel to the box office smash finds Rocky frustrated by the commercialism which followed his match to Apollo, and soon considers a return bout.
MPAA:PG
United Artists; Irwin Winkler; Robert Chartoff — *CBS/Fox Video; RCA VideoDiscs*

Rocky III　　　　　　　　　　　　1982
Drama
63395　　100 mins　　C　　B, V, LV, 　　P
　　　　　　　　　　　　　　　CED
Sylvester Stallone, Talia Shire, Burgess Meredith, Carl Weathers
The third in the "Rocky" trilogy finds heavyweight champ Rocky Balboa training with his former opponent Apollo Creed to prepare for a rematch with Clubber Lang.
MPAA:PG
United Artists — *CBS/Fox Video; RCA VideoDiscs*

Rocky Jones, Space　　　　　　195?
Ranger
Science fiction
57285　　75 mins　　B/W　　B, V　　　P
Richard Crane, Scott Becket, Sally Mansfield, Robert Lyden
Three episodes of the early 1950's television series about Rocky Jones, chief of the Space Rangers, an organizaton established to protect the planets of a united solar system. This presentation is entitled "Forbidden Moon."
NBC — *Video Dimensions*

Rocky Jones, Space　　　　　　1953
Ranger: Blast Off
Science fiction
11280　　75 mins　　B/W　　B, V, FO　　P
Richard Crane, Scotty Beckett, Sally Mansfield, Maurice Cass
Rocky, his sidekick Winky, and Professor Newton travel through another space adventure in their ship, "The Orbit Jet."
Roland Reed — *Video Yesteryear*

Rocky Jones, Space　　　　　　1953
Ranger: Pirates of Prah
Science fiction
11279　　75 mins　　B/W　　B, V, FO　　P
Richard Crane, Scotty Beckett, Sally Mansfield, Maurice Cass
Rocky Jones, sidekick Winky, and Professor Newton confront space pirates in this episode.
Roland Reed — *Video Yesteryear*

Rocky Jones, Space　　　　　　1953
Ranger: The Cold Sun
Science fiction
11278　　75 mins　　B/W　　B, V, FO　　P
Richard Crane, Scotty Beckett, Sally Mansfield, Maurice Cass
An adventure in the series "Rocky Jones, Space Ranger," as Rocky, Winky, and Professor Newton travel through space.
Roland Reed — *Video Yesteryear*

Rocky Jones, Space　　　　　　1953
Ranger: Trial of Rocky Jones
Science fiction
11281　　75 mins　　B/W　　B, V, FO　　P
Richard Crane, Scotty Beckett, Sally Mansfield, Maurice Cass
Rocky Jones, trouble-shooter for the Office of Space Affairs, travels through the universe in his spaceship "The Orbit Jet" along with his pal Winky and Professor Newton.
Roland Reed — *Video Yesteryear*

Rocky King, Detective　　　　　1954
Crime-Drama
47482　　25 mins　　B/W　　B, V, FO　　P
Roscoe Karnes, Todd Karnes, Grace Carney, Jack Klugman
In the story "Return for Death," New York City Police detective Rocky King solves a murder in a mausoleum. An early, live cop show from TV's Golden Age.
Dumont — *Video Yesteryear*

Rocky Mountain Rails　　　　　1981
Trains
59173　　60 mins　　C　　B, V　　　　P
A ride on the nation's longest and highest narrow gauge steam railroad, the "Cumbres and

Toltec Scenic Railroad.'' Includes lots of railroad yard action.
De Luz Video — *De Luz Video*

Rocky Powder Picture Show, The 1981
Sports-Winter
69903   16 mins   C   B, V   P
This program gives an excellent picture of state-of-the-art three-pin skiing in the Wasatch Mountains.
Raccoon Productions — *Gravity Sports Films*

Rod Stewart 1983
Music-Performance
76671   16 mins   C   B, V   P
This program presents Rod Stewart performing "Do Ya Think I'm Sexy," "Passion" and "Young Turks."
Embassy Home Entertainment — *Sony Corporation of America*

Rod Stewart Live at the L.A. Forum 1980
Music-Performance
54688   60 mins   C   B, V   R, P
Rod Stewart
A look at highlights from Rod Stewart's 1979 appearance at the Forum. Songs include "Hot Legs," "Do Ya Think I'm Sexy," "Blondes Have More Fun," "Maggie May," and "You're in My Heart."
Warner Bros — *Warner Home Video; RCA VideoDiscs*

Rod Stewart: Tonight He's Yours 1982
Music-Performance
60449   90 mins   C   B, V, LV, CED   P
Rod Stewart, Tina Turner
Rod the Mod offers up 17 top hits from this concert taped at the L.A. Forum, including: "Do Ya Think I'm Sexy," "Maggie Mae" "You're in My Heart," and more.
Unknown — *Embassy Home Entertainment*

Rodan 1956
Horror
63968   74 mins   C   B, V, LV, CED   P
Kenji Sahara, Yumi Shirakawa
A gigantic prehistoric bird is disturbed from his slumber by H-bomb tests; he awakens to wreak havoc on civilization.
Toho Productions — *Vestron Video*

Roderick Wrestling Program 1980
Sports-Minor
51408   60 mins   C   B, V, 3/4U   P
Two-time NCAA wrestling champion and twice runnerup Pat Milkovich and his brother Tom demonstrate their winning techniques and style, then outline the Roderick Wrestling Program.
Michael P Milkovich — *Milkovich Enterprises*

Rogue of the Rio Grande 1930
Western
58730   60 mins   B/W   B, V   P
Myrna Loy, Jose Bohr, Raymond Hatton, Carmelita Geraghty
A "musical western" in which El Malo, a notorious robber, descends on the town of Sierra Blanca.
World Wide — *Sheik Video; Video Connection*

Roll Wagons Roll 1939
Western
53457   52 mins   B/W   B, V   P
Tex Ritter
A musical western featuring Tex Ritter.
Monogram — *Video Connection*

Rollerball 1975
Science fiction
13596   123 mins   C   B, V, CED   P
James Caan, John Houseman, Maud Adams, Moses Gunn, directed by Norman Jewison
In the year 2018 there is rollerball, a brutal sport combining the violence of all other sports.
MPAA:R
United Artists — *CBS/Fox Video*

Rolling Home 1948
Drama
58729   71 mins   B/W   B, V   P
Jean Parker, Russell Hayden, Buss Henry, Raymond Hatton
The story of an old-time rodeo performer and his grandson who owns a fine trotter.
Robert Lippert — *Sheik Video*

Rolling Plains 1938
Western
08792   60 mins   B/W   B, V, 3/4U   P
Tex Ritter
Singing cowboy tries to bring cattlemen and sheepmen together.
Grand Natl — *Penguin Video; Video Connection*

Rolling Thunder 1977
Drama
64360   99 mins   C   B, V, CED   P
William Devane, Tommy Lee Jones, Linda Haynes
A Vietnam veteran returns home after eight years as a POW. Shortly afterward, his wife and son are murdered, causing him to seek revenge.
MPAA:R
American International — *Vestron Video*

Rollover 1981
Drama
59855 118 mins C B, V R, P
Jane Fonda, Kris Kristofferson, Hume Cronyn, directed by Alan J. Pakula
A banker and board chairman get involved in the intrigue and danger of multi-million dollar world finance.
MPAA:R
Orion; Warner Bros. — *Warner Home Video*

Roman Holiday 1953
Comedy/Romance
64782 118 mins B/W B, V P
Audrey Hepburn, Gregory Peck, Eddie Albert, directed by William Wyler
A princess on an official visit to Rome slips away without notice and falls in love with a newspaperman.
Academy Awards '53: Best Actress (Hepburn); Writing (Ian McLellan Hunter); Costume Design B&W (Edith Head).
Paramount; William Wyler — *Paramount Home Video; RCA VideoDiscs*

Romance on the Range 1942
Western
05545 60 mins B/W B, V P
Roy Rogers, Gabby Hayes, Sally Payne
Roy Rogers sets out to trap a gang of fur thieves and finds romance.
Republic — *Video Connection*

Romancing the Stone 1984
Adventure/Romance
Closed Captioned
73140 106 mins C B, V, CED P
Micheal Douglas, Kathleen Turner, Danny De Vito, directed by Robert Zemeckis
Kathleen Turner stars as a writer of romance novels who gets a chance to live out her story when she receives a phone call that her sister has been kidnapped in South America.
MPAA:PG
Micheal Douglas; 20th Century Fox — *CBS/Fox Video*

Romantic Comedy 1983
Comedy
72897 102 mins C B, V P
Dudley Moore, Mary Steenburgen
A married man is in love with a single girl and when he becomes unhitched she marries another man.
MPAA:PG
Walter Mirisch; Morton Gottlieb — *CBS/Fox Video*

Romantic Englishwoman, The 1975
Romance/Comedy
49925 117 mins C B, V R, P
Glenda Jackson, Michael Caine, Helmut Berger, directed by Joseph Losey
A married couple tests fidelity to its limits.
MPAA:R
New World — *Warner Home Video*

Romeo and Juliet 1968
Drama
38603 138 mins C B, V, LV R, P
Olivia Hussey, Leonard Whiting, Michael York, directed by Franco Zeffirelli
A fresh, vital version of Shakespeare's classic romantic play, which won critical acclaim upon its release.
MPAA:PG
Paramount — *Paramount Home Video; RCA VideoDiscs*

Romeo and Juliet 1954
Drama
59902 138 mins C B, V P
Laurence Harvey, Susan Shantall, Aldo Zollo, Sebastian Cabot, John Gielgud
Shakespeare's tale of young love, shot on Italian locations.
Rank; Verona — *Embassy Home Entertainment*

Romeo and Juliet 1954
Dance
74491 95 mins C B, V P
Bolshoi Ballet
This tape is the Bolshoi Ballet's interpretation of the ever-popular Romeo and Juliet.
Sovexportfilm USSR — *Video Arts International*

Romie-O and Julie-8 1978
Musical/Fantasy
54693 25 mins C B, V R, P
Animated
This musical fantasy tells of the special love between two young robots—an interpretation of the great love story, "Romeo and Juliet." Original songs by John Sebastian.
Nelvana Productions — *Warner Home Video*

Ronald Reagan—WW II "Identification of the Japanese Zero" 1942
World War II
53389 24 mins B/W B, V, 3/4U P
Ronald Reagan
An Air Force training film in aircraft identification which focuses on the necessity of American pilots recognizing the difference between a P-40 and a Japanese Zero. Also includes three Reagan Boraxo commercials circa 1962.
USA — *International Historic Films*

Roof, The 1956
Drama/Romance
63858   98 mins   B/W   B, V   P
Gabriella Pallotti, Giorgio Listuzzi, directed by Vittorio De Sica
A young couple who married aganist their families' wished find that setting up a home of their own is more difficult than they thought. Italian dialogue, English subtitles.
IT
Vittorio De Sica — *Budget Video; Festival Films*

Room Service 1938
Comedy
00256   78 mins   B/W   B, V, 3/4U   P
The Marx Brothers, Lucille Ball, Ann Miller, Frank Albertson
A penniless theatrical producer connives to keep his hotel room until he can find a backer for his latest play.
RKO; Pandro S Berman — *Nostalgia Merchant; Blackhawk Films; VidAmerica*

Rooster Cogburn 1975
Western
58425   107 mins   C   B, V   P
John Wayne, Katharine Hepburn, Richard Jordan, Anthony Zerbe, John McIntire
A Bible-thumping schoolmarm joins up with a hard-drinking, hard-fighting marshal in order to capture a gang of incompetent outlaws who killed her father.
MPAA:PG
Universal; Hal Wallis — *MCA Home Video*

Rootin' Tootin' Rhythm 1938
Western
11262   55 mins   B/W   B, V, FO   P
Gene Autry
All's not quiet on the range, but Gene Autry comes along to sing things back to normal.
Republic — *Video Yesteryear, Discount Video Tapes*

Roots 1977
Drama
58247   90 mins   C   B, V   R, P
Ed Asner, Lloyd Bridges, LeVar Burton, Chuck Connors, Lynda Day George, Lorne Greene, Burl Ives, O. J. Simpson, Cicely Tyson, Ben Vereen, Sandy Duncan   6   pgms
The complete version of Alex Haley's saga following a black man's search for his heritage, revealing an epic panorama of America's past. Available on six 90-minute tapes.
Wolper Pictures — *Warner Home Video*

Rose, The 1979
Musical
44932   134 mins   C   B, V, LV,   P
                          CED
Bette Midler, Alan Bates
A young, multitalented, and self-destructive rock star tries to come to grips with her love affairs, professional triumphs, and lonely restlessness.
MPAA:R
20th Century Fox — *CBS/Fox Video*

Roseland 1977
Drama
64885   103 mins   C   B, V   P
Christopher Walken, Geraldine Chaplin, Joan Copeland, Teresa Wright, Lou Jacobi
Three interlocking stories, set within New York's Roseland Ballroom, tell about lonely people who live to dance.
Cinema Shares International — *Vestron Video*

Rosemary's Baby 1968
Horror
55543   137 mins   C   B, V, LV   R, P
Mia Farrrow, John Cassavettes, Ruth Gordon, Maurice Evans, Patsy Kelly, Elisha Cook, Charles Grodin, directed by Roman Polanski
After unwittingly becoming friendly with a coven of witches and warlocks, a young wife is impregnated by the Devil.
Academy Awards '68: Best Supporting Actress (Gordon).   MPAA:R
Paramount; William Castle — *Paramount Home Video; RCA VideoDiscs*

Rostropovich 1982
Music-Performance
60576   65 mins   C   LV   P
Mstislav Rostropovich, London Philharmonic Orchestra conducted by Carlo Maria Giulini
The great cellist performs Dvorak's "Cello Concerto" and Saint-Saens' "Cello Concerto No. 1." In stereo.
EMI Music Video — *Pioneer Artists*

Rough Cut 1980
Adventure
54672   111 mins   C   B, V, LV   R, P
Burt Reynolds, Lesley-Anne Down, David Niven, Timothy West, Patrick Magee, directed by Donald Siegel
An American diamond thief living in London is pursued by a Scotland Yard detective who is about to retire and wants to finish his career in a blaze of glory.
MPAA:PG
Paramount — *Paramount Home Video*

Rough Riders of Cheyenne 1945
Western
64421   54 mins   B/W   B, V, 3/4U   P
Sunset Carson, Peggy Stewart
Sunset ends the feud between the Carsons and the Sterlings.
Republic — *Nostalgia Merchant*

Rough Riders Roundup — 1938
Western
53456   60 mins   B/W   B, V   P
Roy Rogers
Roy and the gang hit the trail for more adventures.
Republic — *Sheik Video*

Rough Riding Rangers — 1935
Western
08808   57 mins   B/W   B, V   P
Rex Lease, Janet Chandler
Mysterious letter-writer plagues a western ranch family.
First Division — *Video Connection*

Roulette — 1982
Gambling
62742   50 mins   C   B, V   P
Strategies and ways to win roulette are covered in this instructional cassette.
Casino Gaming Instruction — *Marketvisions*

Round-Up Time in Texas — 1937
Western
08895   54 mins   B/W   B, V, 3/4U   P
Gene Autry, Smiley Burnette
Autry answers an urgent call for horses from South Africa's jungle-blocked diamond belt.
Republic — *Penguin Video; Video Connection; Video Yesteryear; Discount Video Tapes*

Roundhouse Show, the — 197?
Variety
33757   30 mins   C   B, V, 3/4U, Q   P

34   pgms
A sports, science, travel, safety, humor, and human involvement series aimed at the broad range of young people today. Thirty-four untitled programs.
TV Sports Scene — *TV Sports Scene*

Roustabout — 1964
Musical-Drama
08384   101 mins   C   B, V   P
Elvis Presley, Barbara Stanwyck, Joan Freeman, Leif Erickson, Sue Ann Langdon
A roving, reckless singer joins a carnival and romances the owner's daughter.
EL, SP
Paramount; Hal Wallis — *CBS/Fox Video*

Routine Dental Care of the Equine — 1978
Veterinary medicine
69658   33 mins   C   B, V   P
This program presents dental care procedures for horses.
US Government — *Mercedes Maharis Productions*

Roxy Music: The High Road — 1983
Music-Performance
65462   ? mins   C   B, V   P
This concert film was recorded during Brian Ferry and Roxy Music's 1982 World Tour and features old standards such as ''Avalon'' and ''Dance Away,'' plus many new songs. In stereo VHS and Beta Hi-Fi.
Robin Nash — *RCA/Columbia Pictures Home Video*

Roy Rogers and Dale Evans Show, The — 1962
Television/Variety
63627   55 mins   B/W   B, V, FO   P
Roy Rogers, Dale Evans, Cliff Arquette, The Sons of the Pioneers
A musical cross-country tour is provided in this show, first telecast on October 27, 1962. Original commercials for Tang and Dodge are included.
ABC — *Video Yesteryear*

Royal Bed, The — 1931
Romance
11252   74 mins   B/W   B, V, FO   P
Lowell Sherman, Nance O'Neill, Mary Astor, Anthony Bushell, Gilbert Emery, Robert Emery
King Eric VIII is beset by many problems, the foremost being his wife, the Queen.
RKO — *Video Yesteryear*

Royal Wedding — 1951
Musical
58873   100 mins   C   B, V, CED   P
Fred Astaire, Jane Powell, Peter Lawford, Keenan Wynn, directed by Stanley Donen
A brother and sister dance team goes to London at the time of the royal wedding of Princess Elizabeth.
MGM — *MGM/UA Home Video*

Royal Wedding, The — 1981
Documentary/Great Britain
58465   60 mins   C   B, V   R, P
Highlights of the Royal Wedding of Prince Charles and Princess Diana, with all of the pageantry and splendor.
Thames TV — *THORN EMI Home Video*

Rubber Rodeo — 1984
Music-Performance
76666   18 mins   C   B, V   P
This program presents the band with the unique punk-country sound. Songs included are: ''Anywhere with You,'' ''How the West Was Won,'' ''The Theme from Rubber Rodeo'' and many more.
Polygram Records Inc — *Sony Corporation of America*

Rubber Tires 192?
Comedy
48689   60 mins   B/W   B, V, 3/4U   P
Besse Love, Harrison Ford, John Patrick
A less than intelligent family leaves New York to seek their fortune in California. Silent.
Unknown — *Penguin Video*

Ruby 1977
Horror
35380   85 mins   C   B, V   P
Piper Laurie
Horrifying tale of a young woman christened in blood and raised in sin, having a love affair with the supernatural.
MPAA:R
George Edwards — *VCI Home Video*

Ruby Gentry 1952
Drama
65331   82 mins   B/W   B, V   P
Charlton Heston, Jennifer Jones, Karl Malden
A girl from the wrong side of the tracks, cast aside by the man she loves, marries a wealthy businessman and sets out to destroy all those who snubbed her
David Selznick — *CBS/Fox Video*

Ruckus 1981
Adventure
47633   91 mins   C   B, V   P
Dirk Benedict, Linda Blair, Ben Johnson
An army vet uses his training to defend himself when he runs into trouble in a small town.
MPAA:PG
International Vision — *Paragon Video Productions*

Ruddigore 19??
Opera/Comedy
65493   112 mins   C   B, V   P
Vincent Price, Keith Michell, Sandra Dugdale
The Lords of Ruddigore have been bound for centuries by a terribly inconvenient curse; they must commit a crime every day or die a horribly painful death. When the Lord of Ruddigore passes his mantle on to the new heir, the young heir loses both his good reputation and his very proper fiancee. A new version of Gilbert and Sullivan's opera.
W L Leasing Limited — *CBS/Fox Video*

Rude Boy 1980
Music-Performance
54105   60 mins   C   B, V   P
The Clash, Ray Gange, directed by Jack Hazan and David Mingay
"Rude Boy" depicts the rise of The Clash, a top British rock band. Live concert footage features The Clash performing such hits as "White Riot" and "I Fought the Law." Included are rare films of early Clash shows.
Jack Hazan, David Mingay — *CBS/Fox Video*

Ruggles, The 1951
Comedy
47642   24 mins   B/W   B, V, FO   P
Charlie Ruggles, Erin O'Brien-Moore
Vintage TV sitcom with Charlie, his wife and children. In this episode, the Ruggles are presented with a pair of rabbits.
ABC — *Video Yesteryear*

Rulers of the City 1971
Adventure/Crime-Drama
60391   91 mins   C   B, V   P
Jack Palance, Edmund Purdom, Al Cliver, Harry Baer
A young gangster avenges his father's death.
Daunia 70 — *VIDCREST*

Rules of the Game 1939
Film-Avant-garde
06237   110 mins   B/W   B, V   P
Marcel Dalio, Nora Gregor, Jean Renoir, directed by Jean Renoir
Renoir satirizes the social and sexual mores of the decadent French leisure class before WWII. French film, English subtitles.
FR
French — *Budget Video; International Historic Films; Sheik Video; Cable Films; Video Yesteryear; Penguin Video; Western Film & Video Inc; Discount Video Tapes*

Ruling Class, The 1972
Comedy/Satire
64983   154 mins   C   B, V, CED   P
Peter O'Toole, Alastair Sim, Arthur Lowe
This irreverant comedy tells the story of the unbalanced 14th Earl of Gurney, who believes that he is Jesus Christ.
MPAA:PG
Avco-Embassy — *Embassy Home Entertainment*

Rumble Fish 1983
Drama
65515   94 mins   B/W   B, V, LV, CED   P
Matt Dillon, Mickey Rourke, Dennis Hopper, Diane Lane, Vincent Spano, Nicolas Cage, directed by Francis Coppola
The story of two brothers whose relationship with themselves and their world leads to death for one and a new life for the other. In stereo VHS and Beta Hi-Fi.
MPAA:R
Universal — *MCA Home Video*

Rumble of Wheels 19??
Animals
69668   14 mins   C   B, V   P

The story of the Budweiser Clydesdales is presented in this program.
Anheiser Busch — *Mercedes Maharis Productions*

Rumpelstiltskin　　1968
Fairy tales
47674　75 mins　C　B, V　　P
A beautiful young girl is tricked into promising her firstborn to a magic elf in return for his spinning straw into gold for her.
Ron Merk — *Unicorn Video*

Rumpelstiltskin　　1984
Fairy tales
Closed Captioned
73144　60 mins　C　B, V, CED　　P
Ned Beatty, Shelley Duvall, Herve Villechaize, Paul Dooley
From "Faerie Tale Theatre" comes the story of a woman who can spin straw into gold (Shelley Duvall) and the strange man who saves her life (Herve Villechaize).
Shelley Duvall — *CBS/Fox Video*

Run, Angel, Run!　　1969
Adventure
65728　90 mins　C　B, V　　P
William Smith, Valerie Starrett
An ex-biker is on the run from his former motorcycle gang.
MPAA:R
Fanfare — *VidAmerica*

Run for Life: An Olympic Fable　　1979
Sports
72233　68 mins　C　B, V　　P
Animated
This animated feature concerns a young athlete running to restore support for his country's King in Ancient Greece.
Toei Animation — *Children's Video Library*

Run of the Arrow　　1956
Western
13096　85 mins　C　B, V　　P
Rod Steiger, Brian Keith, Charles Bronson
An ex-Confederate soldier joins the Sioux nation, which is engaged in war against the white man.
Universal; RKO; Samuel Fuller — *VCI Home Video*

Run Silent, Run Deep　　1958
War-Drama
68226　93 mins　B/W　B, V, CED　　P
Burt Lancaster, Clark Gable, Jack Warden, Don Rickles
A tense look at the realities of submarine warfare and underwater combat.

Jeffrey Productions — *CBS/Fox Video*

Runaway Barge　　1982
Adventure
75464　72 mins　C　B, V　　P
Nick Nolte, Tim Matheson, Jim Davis
An attempt is made to hijack a Mississippi River cargo.
King Features — *U.S.A. Home Video*

Runaway Truck　　195?
Adventure
10033　25 mins　B/W　B, V　　P, T
Kirby Grant
Sky King takes to the air with novice pilot. Student pilot is then forced to make crucial decision. From the TV series "Sky King."
Unknown — *Blackhawk Films*

Running Brave　　1983
Drama
66322　90 mins　C　B, V, LV, CED　　R, P
Robbie Benson, Claudia Cron, Pat Hingle, Denis Lacroix
The true story of Billy Mills, a South Dakota Sioux Indian who became the only American in Olympic history to win the Gold Medal in the 10,000 meter run at the 1964 Tokyo Olympics.
Buena Vista; Englander Productions — *Walt Disney Home Video*

Running Hot　　1983
Romance
73043　88 mins　C　B, V　　P
A hot romance develops between an escaped convict and the woman who wrote to him while he was in prison.
MPAA:R
Wescom — *Vestron Video*

Running Scared　　1979
Drama
65091　92 mins　C　B, V　　R, P
Ken Wahl
Two young men, returning from military service as stowaways aboard an Army cargo plane, are caught by a paranoid intelligence agent and are thought to be spies.
MPAA:PG
EMI Films — *THORN EMI Home Video*

Running Start, A　　19??
Horse racing
69631　28 mins　C　B, V　　P
Thirty years of California's finest moments in racing and breeding history are chronicled in this program.
Joe Burnham — *Mercedes Maharis Productions*

Rush—Exit Stage Left　　1981
Music-Performance
60384　　60 mins　　C　　B, V　　　　　P
This concert includes highlights from the group's two-hour stage show. Songs include "Limelight," "Xanadu," "The Trees," "Freewill" and "Closer to the Heart." In stereo.
Polygram Records; Moon Video Production — *RCA/Columbia Pictures Home Video; RCA VideoDiscs; Pioneer Artists*

Russian Folk Song and Dance　　1981
Music-Performance/Dance
57257　　70 mins　　C　　B, V　　　　　P
Narrated by Tony Randall
Four of Russia's great troupes perform their colorful native songs and dances: the Pyatnitsky Russian Folk and Dance Ensemble (primarily Ukranian), the Siberian-Omsk Folk Chorus (from Siberia and Northern Russia), the Uzbekistan Dance Ensemble (from Samarkand and Central Asia) and the Moldavia Folk Song and Dance Ensemble (from Southwest Russia).
Kultur — *Kultur*

Russians Are Coming, the Russians Are Coming, The　　1966
Comedy
58837　　126 mins　　C　　CED　　　　　P
Alan Arkin, Carl Reiner, Theo Bikel, Eva Marie Saint, Brian Keith, Paul Ford, Jonathan Winters, Ben Blue, Tessie O'Shea, Doro Merande
A Russian sub accidentally runs aground off the New England coast causing havoc for the residents.
United Artists — *CBS/Fox Video; RCA VideoDiscs*

Rust Never Sleeps　　1979
Music-Performance
31659　　111 mins　　C　　B, V　　　　　P
Neil Young
Neil Young performs all the songs that made him a star in this concert film. These include "I Am A Child" (Buffalo Springfield), "My, My, Hey, Hey" (Out of the Blue), "Comes a Time," "Sugar Mountain," "Cinnamon Girl," "Hurricane," "Thrasher," and many more.
LA Johnson — *Vestron Video; RCA VideoDiscs*

Rust Never Sleeps　　1981
Music-Performance
72221　　111 mins　　C　　B, V　　　　　P
Neil Young's conceptual tour is captured in full swing, complete with four foot "roadeyes."
Independent — *Vestron Video*

S

Sabotage　　1936
Suspense
13052　　81 mins　　B/W　　B, V　　　　　P
Oscar Homolka, directed by Alfred Hitchcock
Saboteur finds his world closing in on him when a bomb he made kills his young brother-in-law and his wife seeks secret revenge.
GB Prods — *Budget Video; Video Dimensions; Sheik Video; Cable Films; Video Yesteryear; Video Connection; Western Film & Video Inc; Discount Video Tapes; Classic Video Cinema Collector's Club*

Sabrina, Volume 1　　1969
Cartoons
65622　　23 mins　　C　　B, V　　　　　P
Animated
What happens when a pretty teenage girl is also a witch? If it's Sabrina, you know you're in for plenty of amazing, amusing and action-packed adventures.
Filmation — *Embassy Home Entertainment*

Sacco and Vanzetti　　1971
Drama
51116　　120 mins　　C　　B, V　　　　　P
Milo O'Shea, Gian Maria Volonte, Cyril Cusak
An account of the flagrant miscarriage of justice subjected upon two Italian immigrants caught amidst witch-hunts and judicial negligence in the 1920's.
MPAA:PG
Unidis Largo Messico 6 Rome — *VCI Home Video*

Sacketts, The　　1979
Western/Adventure
63979　　191 mins　　C　　B, V　　　　R, P
Jeff Osterhage, Tom Selleck, Sam Elliot, Glenn Ford, Ben Johnson, Mercedes McCambridge
Three boys who grew up in Tennessee migrate west after the Civil War.
Media Productions — *VCII*

Sacred Ground　　1983
Drama
Closed Captioned
65501　　100 mins　　C　　B, V, CED　　　P
Tim McIntire, Jack Elam, Mindi Miller
A trapper and his pregnant wife unknowingly build shelter on the Paiute Indian's sacred burial ground. When the wife dies in childbirth, the pioneer is forced to kidnap a Paiute woman who has just buried her own deceased infant.
MPAA:PG
Pacific International — *CBS/Fox Video*

Sacred Music of Duke Ellington   1982
Music-Performance
63114   90 mins   C   B, V, CED   P
Tony Bennett, Phyllis Hyman, The Duke Ellington Orchestra
The immortal music of Duke Ellington is featured in one of his Sacred Concerts, which is performed by an all-star cast of singers and musicians. In stereo.
Independent Film Production Associates Limited — *MGM/UA Home Video*

Safety Last   1923
Comedy
64244   60 mins   B/W   B, V   P
Harold Lloyd, Mildred David, Noah Young
A small town fellow arrives in the big city. To impress his girlfriend, he enters a skyscraper-climbing contest. Silent with musical score.
Harold Lloyd — *Classic Video Cinema Collector's Club*

Saga de los Draculas, La   1972
Horror
47719   91 mins   C   B, V   P
Narciso Ibanez Menta
In "The Saga of the Draculas," Count Dracula seeks to perpetuate himself through his soon-to-be-born grandson. In Spanish.
SP
Independent — *Telecine Spanish Video*

Saga of Death Valley   1939
Western
05533   56 mins   B/W   B, V   P
Roy Rogers, Gabby Hayes, Donald Barry, Doris Day
Roy Rogers battles a band of outlaws and discovers that their leader is his own brother.
Republic — *Video Connection; Sheik Video; Cable Films; Nostalgia Merchant*

Saga of the Skyraider   1970
Armed Forces-US
74483   11 mins   C   B, V   P
This program looks at the twenty year history of the Douglas Skyraider.
US Office of War Information — *Interurban Films*

Sagebrush Trail   1933
Western
08845   63 mins   B/W   B, V, 3/4U   P
John Wayne
Action on the plains as John Wayne rides into Indian trouble.
Monogram — *Penguin Video; Video Connection; Cable Films; Discount Video Tapes*

Sahara   1943
War-Drama
58964   97 mins   B/W   B, V   P
Humphrey Bogart, Dan Duryea, Bruce Bennett, Lloyd Bridges, Rex Ingram, J. Carrol Naish
An action story of desert battle and survival during World War II.
Columbia — *RCA/Columbia Pictures Home Video*

Sailor Who Fell from Grace with the Sea, The   1976
Drama
13663   105 mins   C   CED   P
Sarah Miles, Kris Kristofferson, Jonathan Kahn, Margo Cunningham, directed by Lewis John Carlino
A disillusioned sailor rejects the sea for the love of a young, sexually repressed widow.
MPAA:R
Avco Embassy; Martino Poll Production — *RCA VideoDiscs*

Saint Benny the Dip   1951
Comedy
57341   80 mins   B/W   B, V   P
Dick Haymes, Nina Foch, Roland Young, Lionel Stander, Freddie Bartholomew
An off-beat account of con-men posing as clergymen who predictably become reformed.
United Artists — *Budget Video; Discount Video Tapes*

St. Helen's, Killer Volcano   1982
Drama
64884   95 mins   C   B, V   P
Art Carney, David Huffman, Cassie Yates
A young man and an old man develop a deep friendship amidst the devastation, fear, greed and panic surrounding the eruption of a volcano.
Michael Murphy — *Vestron Video*

Saint in London, The   1939
Mystery
64380   72 mins   B/W   B, V, 3/4U   P
George Sanders, Sally Grey
The Saint picks up a wounded man lying at the side of a country road and becomes involved in murder and intrigue.
RKO — *Nostalgia Merchant*

Saint in New York, The   1938
Mystery
00297   71 mins   B/W   B, V   P
Louis Hayward, Kay Sutton, Jack Carson
The Saint turns Robin Hood to help Civic Committee clean up a gang of desperados.
RKO — *Nostalgia Merchant*

St. Ives   1976
Crime-Drama
72920   94 mins   C   B, V   P

Charles Bronson, Jacqueline Bissett
A former police reporter goes undercover when he gets framed for a murder.
MPAA:PG
Warner Bros — *Warner Home Video*

Saint Jack   1979
Drama
65384   112 mins   C   B, V   P
Ben Gazzara
The story of a small-time pimp with big dreams working the pleasure palaces of late-night Singapore. Directed by Peter Bogdonovich.
MPAA:R
Peter Bogdonovich Productions — *Vestron Video*

Salem's Lot: The Movie   1979
Horror
69798   112 mins   C   B, V   R, P
David Soul, James Mason, Lance Kerwin, Bonnie Bedelia, Lew Ayres, directed by Tobe Hooper
This film is based on Stephen King's novel about a sleepy New England village which is infiltrated by evil when a mysterious antiques dealer takes up residence in a forbidding hilltop house—and it becomes apparent that a vampire is on the loose.
Warner Bros — *Warner Home Video*

Sally of the Sawdust   1925
Comedy
10097   92 mins   B/W   B, V   P, T
W. C. Fields, Carol Dempster, Alfred Lunt, directed by D. W. Griffith
W. C. Fields' first silent feature film where he portrays a carnival barker who adopts a young woman. Displays his talents at juggling, conning customers, and car chasing. Musical score.
United Artists — *Blackhawk Films*

Salute John Citizen   1942
War-Drama
69560   74 mins   B/W   B, V, FO   P
Peggy Cummins, Stanley Holloway, Dinah Sheridan, Jimmy Hanley
The life of an average English family during the early days of World War II is depicted, focusing on the deprivation and horror of the Nazi blitzkrieg.
Gaumont — *Video Yesteryear*

Same Time, Next Year   1978
Drama
31598   119 mins   C   B, V   P
Ellen Burstyn, Alan Alda
A chance meeting between a traveling executive and a liberated housewife results in a sometimes sometimes tragic, always sentimental 25-year affair—but they meet only one day a year. Based on the Broadway play by Bernard Slade.

Universal — *MCA Home Video*

Sammy Bluejay   1983
Cartoons
65654   60 mins   C   B, V   P
Animated
This program features two escapades—"Brainy Bluejay" and "Sammy's Revenge"—starring Sammy Bluejay, Peter Cottontail, and Reddy the Fox.
Ziv International — *Family Home Entertainment*

Samson and Delilah   1949
Drama
55544   128 mins   C   B, V, LV   R, P
Victor Mature, Hedy Lamarr, Angela Lansbury, George Sanders, Henry Wilcoxon, Olive Deering, Fay Holden, directed by Cecil B. De Mille
The biblical story of Delilah, who after being rejected by Samson, cuts his hair and delivers him to his enemies.
Paramount; Cecil B De Mille — *Paramount Home Video*

Samson et Dalila   1981
Opera
59877   210 mins   C   LV   P
The Royal Opera performs Camille Saint-Saens' first major opera, based in the biblical story of Samson, who sucumbs to the wiles of Dalila. In stereo.
Covent Garden Video — *Pioneer Artists*

Samson vs. the Vampire Women   1961
Horror
51951   89 mins   B/W   B, V   P
Samson, Lorena Velazquez, Jaime Fernandez, Maria Duval, directed by Alfonso Corona Blake
Samson, the masked hero and athlete, battles the forces of darkness as a horde of female vampires attempt to make an unsuspecting girl their next queen.
Azteca — *Budget Video*

San Francisco Blues Festival   1983
Music-Performance
76664   60 mins   C   B, V   P
A blues celebration including "S.F. Bay Blues," "Louisiana Two Step," "What I Say" and many more.
Image Integration — *Sony Corporation of America*

Sand Lessons and Special Shots   197?
Golf
33778   60 mins   C   B, V, 3/4U   P

Golf pros Toby Lyons, Harry Offutt, Penny Zavichas, and Dick Lawrence demonstrate bunker shots, showing how the sand trap can become a nicer place for the golfer to visit. Part of the series, "The Name of the Game Is Golf." Unknown — *Sports World Cinema*

Sand Pebbles, The   1966
Drama
08459   195 mins   C   B, V   P
Steve McQueen, Richard Crenna, Richard Attenborough, Candice Bergen, Larry Gates
An American expatriate, transferred to a gunboat on the Yangtze River in 1926, falls in love with a missionary teacher.
EL, SP
20th Century Fox; Robert Wise — *CBS/Fox Video*

Sandahl Bergman's Body   1983
Physical fitness/Dance
65215   60 mins   C   B, V   P
A unique program combining fitness and the art of dance.
Cassini and Ray Productions — *Monterey Home Video*

Sanders of the River   1935
Mystery
11369   80 mins   B/W   B, V, FO   P
Paul Robeson, Leslie Banks, Robert Cochran
An officer of the river patrol causes rebellion among the natives when he tracks down those seeking to break the law.
Korda — *Video Yesteryear; Cable Films; Sheik Video; Video Connection*

Sands of Iwo Jima   1949
War-Drama
47057   109 mins   B/W   B, V   P
John Wayne, Forrest Tucker, John Agar
A tough Marine sergeant trains a squad of rebellious recruits in New Zealand, and they later are responsible for the capture of Iwo Jima from the Japanese.
Republic — *NTA Home Entertainment; RCA VideoDiscs*

Sanjuro   1962
Drama
57340   96 mins   B/W   B, V   P
Toshiro Mifune, Tatsuya Nakadai
Originally titled "Tsubaki Sanjuro." In mid-nineteenth century Japan, the chamberlain is suspected of fomenting political unrest. Subtitled in English.
JA
Toho — *Budget Video; Festival Films; Discount Video Tapes*

Santa Fe Bound   1934
Western
58490   40 mins   B/W   B, V, 3/4U   P
Tom Tyler, Jeanette Martel
Our hero is falsely accused of murder, and must set out to prove his innocence.
Reliable — *Penguin Video*

Santa Fe Trail   1940
Western
08782   110 mins   B/W   B, V, 3/4U   P
Errol Flynn, Olivia de Havilland, Ronald Reagan, Van Heflin, Raymond Massey
Pre-Civil War historical fight for "bloody Kansas" with Jeb Stuart and George Custer beginning their military careers.
Warner Bros — *Nostalgia Merchant; Penguin Video; Budget Video; VCII; Video Yesteryear; Sheik Video; Cable Films; Video Connection; Discount Video Tapes; Classic Video Cinema Collector's Club*

Santa Fe Uprising   1946
Western
64410   54 mins   B/W   B, V, 3/4U   P
Allan "Rocky" Lane, Bobby Blake
Red Ryder has to save Little Beaver from kidnappers.
Republic — *Nostalgia Merchant*

Saps at Sea   1940
Comedy
33908   57 mins   B/W   B, V, 3/4U   P
Stan Laurel, Oliver Hardy, James Finlayson, Ben Turpin, Rychard Cramer
A doctor advises Ollie to take a rest away from his job at a horn factory. He and Stan rent a boat, which they plan to keep tied to the dock until an escaped criminal happens by and uses the boys for his getaway.
Hal Roach, United Artists — *Nostalgia Merchant; Blackhawk Films*

Saps at Sea   1940
Comedy
63988   80 mins   B/W   B, V   P, T
Stan Laurel, Oliver Hardy, Jimmy Finlayson, Ben Turpin, Rychard Kramer
Stan and Ollie are cast out to sea on the same boat with an escaped criminal. This tape also includes a 1934 Charley Chase short, "The Chases of Pimple Street."
Hal Roach; MGM — *Blackhawk Films*

Sasquatch   1976
Speculation
13101   94 mins   C   B, V   P
Story of seven men who defied death in a primitive wilderness where no man had gone before. They lived to tell the tale of this legendary creature.
Gold Key — *VCI Home Video*

Satan's Satellites 1958
Science fiction
73548 70 mins B/W B, V P
Judd Holdren, John Crawford, Leonard Nimoy, Ray Boyle
A rocket lands on earth with zombies that invade the planet.
Republic Pictures — *Admit One Video*

Saturday Night Fever 1977
Drama
38958 118 mins C B, V R, P
John Travolta, Karen Gorney, Donna Pescow
A slightly edited version of the popular disco drama, with the sex-oriented scenes and some strong language toned down for PG audiences. Music by the Bee Gees.
MPAA:PG
Paramount — *Paramount Home Video*

Saturday Night Fever 1977
Drama
38614 118 mins C B, V, LV R, P
John Travolta, Karen Gorney, Donna Pescow
A Brooklyn teenager who is king of the local disco begins to question his narrow view of life. Acclaimed for its disco dance sequences, with music by the Bee Gees.
MPAA:R
Paramount — *Paramount Home Video; RCA VideoDiscs*

Saturday Night Live: 1978
Carrie Fisher
Comedy
66131 67 mins C B, V R, P
Carrie Fisher, Not Ready For Prime Time Players
Carrie Fisher joins in a spoof of her Star Wars character in the sketch "New Kid on Earth," a beach party parody.
NBC — *Warner Home Video*

Saturday Night Live: 1978
Steve Martin 2
Comedy
66132 110 mins C B, V R, P
Steve Martin, Not Ready for Prime Time Players
One of the "wild and crazy guy's" hilarious SNL appearances.
NBC — *Warner Home Video*

Saturday Night Live, Vol. 197?
II
Comedy/Variety
60376 115 mins C CED P
Steve Martin, Richard Pryor, John Belushi, Chevy Chase, Bill Murray, Gilda Radner
Two Saturday Night Live programs with the original cast; Richard Pryor is host for a show telecast on December 13, 1975 and Steve

Martin appears on an episode with an airdate of April 12, 1978.
NBC Enterprises; Lorne Michaels — *RCA VideoDiscs*

Saturday Night Live, Vol. I 1975
Comedy/Variety
53792 112 mins C CED P
George Carlin, Steve Martin, John Belushi, Chevy Chase, Jane Curtin, Gilda Radner, Laraine Newman, Dan Ackroyd
The premiere telecast of October 11, 1975, hosted by George Carlin, which featured the Weekend Update, The Bees, The Muppets, Andy Kaufman, a film by Albert Brooks, musical guest Billy Preston, and a commercial for "New Dad." The other episode is the 29th original telecast from October 23, 1976, representing Steve Martin's first appearance as host. Sketches included "Jeopardy 1999," a spoof of the Mary Tyler Moore Show, Chevy's Weekend Update and his milk commercial, and a skit about beatniks. (11 minutes have been edited from the premiere show, and 5 minutes from the Martin show, of music and film segments).
NBC Enterprises; Lorne Michaels — *RCA VideoDiscs*

Saturday Night Live with 1975
Richard Pryor
Comedy/Variety
47621 65 mins C B, V R, P
Richard Pryor, Gil Scott-Heron, John Belushi, Dan Ackroyd, Gilda Radner, Laraine Newman, Jane Curtin, Chevy Chase
Richard Pryor appears in a samurai bellhop sketch, a spoof of "The Exorcist," and undergoes a peculiar personnel interview in this "SNL" episode. Other highlights include two songs by Gil Scott-Heron and a film by Albert Brooks.
NBC Enterprises; Lorne Michaels — *Warner Home Video*

Saturday Night Live with 1978
Steve Martin
Comedy/Variety
47622 65 mins C B, V R, P
Steve Martin, John Belushi, Dan Ackroyd, Laraine Newman, Gilda Radner, Bill Murray, Garrett Morris, Jane Curtin
Highlights from this 1978 show include the Czechoslovakian brothers, Steve Martin singing "King Tut," an appearance by the Blues Brothers and Steve and Gilda dancing frenetically to "Dancing in the Dark."
NBC Enterprises; Lorne Michaels — *Warner Home Video*

Saturday Serials 195?
Adventure
53050 50 mins B/W B, V, 3/4U P
Richard Greene, Buster Crabbe, Al "Fuzzy" Knight

(For Explanation of codes, see USE GUIDE and KEY) **473**

Two classic 1950's adventure shows: "The Adventures of Robin Hood" (1955), a British-made series staring Richard Greene as a man who robbed the rich and gave to the poor; and "Captain Gallant of the Foreign Legion" (1955), starring Buster Crabbe and Al "Fuzzy" Knight.
NBC et al — *Shokus Video*

Saturn 3   1980
Science fiction
41497   88 mins   C   B, V, LV   P
Farrah Fawcett, Kirk Douglas
Two research scientists create a futuristic Garden of Eden in an isolated sector of our solar system, but love story turns to horror story when a killer robot arrives.
MPAA:R EL, SP
Associated Film Distribution Corp — *CBS/Fox Video*

Saul and David   197?
Bible
35374   120 mins   C   B, V   P
A beautifully filmed story of David's life with King Saul, the battle with Goliath, and the tragic end of Saul. From the "Bible" series.
Sunn Classic — *VCI Home Video*

Savage Abduction   1982
Horror
72200   90 mins   C   B, V   P
Two girls visiting Los Angeles are kidnapped by a bizarre man.
Wrightwood Enterprises Ltd — *Paragon Video Productions*

Savage Attraction   1984
Drama
72869   93 mins   C   B, V   P
The true story of a sixteen year old who was debauched across three continents.
MPAA:R
Unknown — *Embassy Home Entertainment*

Savage Fury   1935
Adventure
08880   80 mins   B/W   B, V, 3/4U   P
Noah Beery Jr., Dorothy Short
Depicts the life of a Tarzan-like character in this jungle thriller.
Unknown — *Penguin Video*

Savage Is Loose, The   1974
Drama
63977   114 mins   C   B, V   R, P
George C. Scott, Trish Van Devere, John David Carson
A family is caught between society-induced moral behavior and uncontrolled primal instincts, as they share 20 years of their lives on a deserted island.
MPAA:R

Campbell Devon Productions — *VCII*

Savage Weekend   1980
Horror
47624   88 mins   C   B, V   P
A killer behind a ghoulish mask stalks human prey.
MPAA:R
Independent — *Paragon Video Productions; Electric Video*

Savages   1972
Drama
63998   108 mins   C   B, V   P
Susan Blakely, Sam Waterston, Ultra Violet, Salome Jens, Martin Kove, directed by James Ivory
This film portrays the rise and fall of civilization as savages become socialites of the 1920's. The film progresses from black and white to sepia to full color, paralleling the development of the savages.
MPAA:R
Angeliks Productions — *Intra-Video Properties*

Savannah Smiles   1982
Drama
66046   104 mins   C   B, V, LV,   P
                                    CED
Bridgette Andersen, Mark Miller, Donovan Scott
A six-year old runaway befriends two escaped convicts.
MPAA:PG
Clark Paylow — *Embassy Home Entertainment*

Save the Tiger   1973
Drama
58716   100 mins   C   B, V, LV   R, P
Jack Lemmon, Jack Gilford, Laurie Heineman, Patricia Smith, Norman Burton, directed by John Avildsen
A middle-aged man, faced with a failing business, struggles with his conscience and changing American values.
Academy Awards '73: Best Actor (Lemmon).
MPAA:R
Paramount; Steve Shagan — *Paramount Home Video*

Saviors, Saints, and Sinners   1981
Football
50645   50 mins   C   B, V, FO   R, P
A summary of the 1980 NFL season, including a look at the All-Pro selections.
NFL Films — *NFL Films Video*

Say Amen, Somebody   1980
Documentary/Music
66445   100 mins   C   B, V   P
Willie May Ford Smith, Thomas A. Dorsey, Sallie Martin, Delois Barrett Cambell

A documentary look at the joyful world of gospel music. Two old-timers, Thomas A. Dorsey, the "Father of Gospel Music" and Sallie Martin, also known as Mother Smith, talk and sing about the gospel heritage as they experienced it.
UnitedArtists Classics; GTN Productions — *Pacific Arts Video*

Sayonara 1957
Drama
69379   147 mins   C   B, V, CED   P
Marlon Brando, James Garner, Ricardo Montalban, Patricia Owens, Red Buttons, Miyoshi Umeki
Based on the novel by James A. Michener, this is the story of American servicemen on leave in Japan during the Korean War, and the Japanese women that some have fallen in love with.
Academy Awards'57: Best Supporting Actor (Buttons); Best Supporting Actress (Umeki); Best Art Direction; Best Sound.
Warner Bros — *CBS/Fox Video*

Scandalous 1984
Comedy/Mystery
66606   93 mins   C   B, V, LV, CED   P
Robert Hays, John Gielgud, Jim Dale, Pamela Stephenson
A bumbling American TV reporter becomes involved with a gang of British con artists.
MPAA:PG
Orion — *Vestron Video*

Scandinavian Cooking 1982
Cookery
47353   30 mins   C   V   P
Recipes for preparing traditional Scandinavian dishes are demonstrated.
American Home Video Library — *American Home Video Library*

Scanners 1981
Horror
59339   102 mins   C   B, V, CED   P
Stephen Lack, Jennifer O'Neill, Patrick McGoohan, Lawrence Dane
"Scanners" are telepaths who can will people to explode. One scanner in particular harbors Hitlerian aspirations for his band of psychic gangsters.
MPAA:R
Filmplan International — *Embassy Home Entertainment*

Scarecrow 1973
Drama
58248   112 mins   C   B, V   R, P
Gene Hackman, Al Pacino, Ann Wedgeworth, Eileen Brennan, directed by Jerry Schatzberg

The tragicomic tale of two born losers adrift on the road.
MPAA:R
Warner Bros — *Warner Home Video*

Scared to Death 1947
Mystery
01684   70 mins   C   B, V   P, T
Bela Lugosi, George Zucco, Joyce Compton, directed by Walt Mattox
Woman dies of fright when shown death mask of man she framed.
Screen Guild; Robert L Lippert — *Mossman Williams Productions; Sheik Video; King of Video; Video Connection; Video Yesteryear; Admit One Video*

Scarface 1932
Drama
31599   94 mins   B/W   B, V   P
Paul Muni, Ann Dvorak
A small-time crook builds himself up to a hot shot ganster, who eventually is double crossed by his mob.
United Artists — *MCA Home Video*

Scarface 1932
Crime-Drama
66588   90 mins   B/W   B, V   P
Paul Muni, Ann Dvorak, George Raft, Boris Karloff, directed by Howard Hawks
The brutal story of the life and death of a Chicago gangster is portrayed in this hard-hitting movie classic.
Howard Hughes; Universal — *MCA Home Video*

Scarface 1983
Crime-Drama
66509   170 mins   C   B, V, LV, CED   P
Al Pacino, Steven Bauer, Michelle Pfeiffer, Robert Loggia, directed by Brian De Palma
A remake of the 1932 classic film, with Al Pacino as a Cuban refugee who works his way up to becoming a major figure in Miami's crime scene. In stereo.
MPAA:R
Universal — *MCA Home Video*

Scarlet Letter, The 1934
Drama
58525   98 mins   B/W   B, V, 3/4U   P
Colleen Moore, Harry B. Walthall, Alan Hale, Betty Blythe
Nathaniel Hawthorne's novel of sin and redemption in Puritan New England.
London Films; Alexander Korda — *Penguin Video; Classic Video Cinema Collector's Club*

Scarlet Pimpernel, The　　　　1935
Drama
08625　98 mins　B/W　　B, V　　　　P
Leslie Howard, Merle Oberon, Raymond
Massey, Anthony Bushell, John Gardner
"The Scarlet Pimpernel," supposed dandy of
the English court, outwits the French
Republicans during the Revolution.
United Artists; Alexander Korda;
British — *Media Home Entertainment; Budget*
Video; Blackhawk Films; Penguin Video; VCII;
Sheik Video; Cable Films; Video Connection;
Discount Video Tapes

Scarlet Street　　　　1945
Mystery
01731　103 mins　B/W　　B, V　　　　P
Edward G. Robinson, Joan Bennett, Dan
Duryea, directed by Fritz Lang
Middle-aged cashier becomes an embezzler
when he gets involved with a predatory,
manipulating woman.
Universal — *Budget Video; Sheik Video; Cable*
Films; Video Connection; Video Yesteryear;
Discount Video Tapes; Classic Video Cinema
Collector's Club

Scars of Dracula　　　　1971
Horror
63980　93 mins　C　　B, V　　　R, P
Christopher Lee, Jenny Hanley, Dennis
Waterman, Wendy Hamilton
A young couple tangles with Dracula in their
search for the man's missing brother.
MPAA:R
Hammer Productions — *THORN EMI Home*
Video

Scavenger Hunt　　　　1979
Comedy
65409　117 mins　C　　B, V　　　　P
Richard Benjamin, James Coco, Ruth Buzzi,
Cloris Leachman, Cleavon Little, Roddy
McDowall, Scatman Cruthers, Tony Randall,
Robert Morley
The action begins when a deceased
millionaire's will states that his 15 would-be
heirs must compete in a scavenger hunt, and
whoever collects all the items first wins the
entire fortune.
MPAA:PG
Melvin Simon — *CBS/Fox Video*

Scenes from a Marriage　　　　1973
Drama
39080　168 mins　C　　B, V　　　　P
Liv Ullmann, Erland Josephson, directed by
Ingmar Bergman
Originally produced for Swedish television, this
is an intimate chronicle of the disintegration of
the "perfect" marraige.
Cinema 5 — *RCA/Columbia Pictures Home*
Video

Schizo　　　　1977
Drama
06085　109 mins　C　　B, V　　　　P
Lynne Rederick, John Layton
Devious intentions abound as a middleaged
man is overcome by weird scenes and
revelations. Much violent intensity.
MPAA:R
Pete Walker — *Media Home Entertainment*

Schizoid　　　　1980
Horror
55552　91 mins　C　　B, V　　　　P
Klaus Kinski, Mariana Hill, directed by David
Paulsen
An advice-to-the-lovelorn columnist receives a
series of threatening letters causing her to
wonder whether a psychiatrist is bumping off his
own patients.
MPAA:R
Golan Globus Prod — *MCA Home Video*

Schlock　　　　1973
Horror/Comedy
59056　78 mins　C　　B, V　　　　P
Eliza Garrett, Saul Kahan, directed by John
Landis
The classic story of beauty and the beast
updated.
MPAA:PG
James C O'Rourke — *Wizard Video*

Scholastic Productions:　　　　1980
As We Grow
Children/Identity
56885　70 mins　C　　CED　　　　P
Twelve real-life episodes presenting early
experiences in the lives of children at work and
play. Produced by experts on children, this
program will help children understand
themselves and their world.
AM　Available
Scholastic Inc — *RCA VideoDiscs*

School for Scandal　　　　1965
Satire
69581　100 mins　B/W　　B, V　　　　P
Joan Plowright, Felix Aylmer
A British television adaptation of Richard
Sheridan's play of the morals and manners of
18th century England.
BBC — *Video Yesteryear*

School of Bass, A　　　　1974
Fishing
33744　30 mins　C　B, V, 3/4U,　　　P
　　　　　　　　　　　Q
The nature and habits of bass are depicted in
many interesting and educational scenes.
Proper methods and equipment for catching
bass are stressed.
TV Sports Scene — *TV Sports Scene*

Science Fiction Combo — 196?
Science fiction
33700   125 mins   C   B, V, 3/4U   P
Angela Cartwright, Billy Mumy, William Shatner, Leonard Nimoy
Three complete episodes from sci-fi TV series of the 1960's: "Lost in Space—The Reluctant Stowaway" (1965 pilot film), "The Twilight Zone—An Occurrence at Owl Creek Bridge" (1962), and "Star Trek—The Enemy Within" (1966). Only the "Star Trek" episode is in color.
CBS et al — *Shokus Video*

Scooby and Scrappy-Doo — 1979
Cartoons
47692   60 mins   C   B, V   P
Animated
Scooby and his energetic nephew pub, Scrappy-Doo, sniff out mysteries with their detective friends—Fred, Velma, Daphne and Shaggy. Three episodes.
Hanna Barbera — *Worldvision Home Video*

Scooby and Scrappy-Doo, Volume II — 19??
Cartoons
69589   60 mins   C   B, V   P
Animated
Scooby, Scrappy, Fred, Daphne, Velma and Shaggy get into more comical scrapes as they attempt to solve a mystery.
Hanna Barbera — *Worldvision Home Video*

Scooby Goes Hollywood — 197?
Cartoons/Musical
47691   48 mins   C   B, V   P
Animated
Everyone's favorite canine hits Hollywood in an attempt to be a star.
Hanna Barbera — *Worldvision Home Video*

Scoring — 1980
Comedy
59143   90 mins   C   B, V   R, P
Myra Taylor, Greg Perrie, Freya Crane, Pete Maravich
A battle between an all-girl's basketball team and a men's team ensues, combining fun, sex and athletic prowess.
Michael De Gaetano — *VCII*

Scrambled Feet — 1983
Satire
75290   100 mins   C   B, V   P
Madeline Kahn
This is an uninhibited satire of the world of show business. In Beta Hi-Fi and VHS Dolby stereo.
RKO Home Video — *RKO Home Video*

Scrambling in the 50's — 1983
Motorcycles
72857   60 mins   C   B, V   P
A trial run and five motorcycle scrambles are featured.
Motorcycle Racing on Video — *Motor Cycle Video*

Scream Bloody Murder — 197?
Suspense/Mystery
45051   90 mins   C   B, V   P
Fred Holbert, Leigh Mitchell, Robert Knox, Suzette Hamilton
A young boy grinds his father to death with a tractor but mangles his own hand trying to jump off. After receiving a steel claw and being released from a mental institution he continues his murderous ways in and around his home town.
First American Films — *VCI Home Video*

Screaming Eagles in Vietnam — 1967
Armed Forces-US/Vietnam War
72491   30 mins   C   B, V, 3/4U   P
The heroics of the 101st Airborne Division in Vietnam are seen in this documentary.
US Air Force — *International Historic Films*

Screams of a Winter Night — 1979
Horror
35382   92 mins   C   B, V   P
Ghostly tale of an evil monster from the lake and the terror he causes.
MPAA:PG
Richard H Wadsack, James L Wilson — *VCI Home Video*

Screwballs — 1983
Comedy
65742   80 mins   C   B, V   R, P
Peter Keleghan, Lynda Speciale
A freewheeling group of high school boys stirs up trouble for their snooty and virginal homecoming queen.
MPAA:R
Maurice Smith — *Warner Home Video*

Scrooge — 1935
Fantasy
11397   61 mins   B/W   B, V, FO   P
Seymour Hicks, Maurice Evans, Robert Cochran
A miser changes his ways after receiving visits from ghosts of Christmas past, present, and future. Based on the classic novel "A Christmas Carol" by Charles Dickens.
Unknown — *Video Yesteryear; Blackhawk Films; Sheik Video*

Scrooge's Rock 'n' Roll Christmas — 1983
Musical/Christmas
75900   44 mins   C   B, V   P

This program presents the Dickens story with Christmas carols sung by Three Dog Night, Rush and others.
Hitbound Records — *Sony Corporation of America*

Scruggs   1970
Music-Performance
37404   87 mins   C   B, V   P
Earl Scruggs, Bob Dylan, Joan Baez, Doc Watson, The Byrds
A tribute to banjo virtuoso Earl Scruggs, featuring Scruggs in performance, along with Dylan, Baez, and others.
WNET New York — *CBS/Fox Video*

Sea, The   197?
Video
08573   30 mins   C   B, V, 3/4U   P
A continuous picture of waves splashing past a small jetty of rocks onto a small beach to create a relaxed background.
Nebulae Prods — *Nebulae Productions*

Sea Around Us, The   1952
Documentary/Oceanography
10158   61 mins   C   B, V   P, T
Narrated by Don Forbes
Science documentary of history and life of the ocean based on Rachel Carson's study.
Academy Award '52: Best Feature Documentary.
Irwin Allen; RKO — *Blackhawk Films; Nostalgia Merchant*

Sea Lion, The   1921
Drama
48712   50 mins   B/W   B, V, FO   P
Hobart Basworth
A vicious sea captain, embittered by a past romance, becomes sadistic and intolerable, until the truth emerges. Silent.
Hobart Bosworth Prods — *Video Yesteryear*

Sea Prince and the Fire Child, The   1982
Adventure/Cartoons
64910   70 mins   C   B, V   P
Animated
This Japanese animated film follows two young lovers who set off on an adventure to escape the disapproval of their parents.

Scrubbers   1982
Drama
73024   93 mins   C   B, V   R, P
Amanda York, Chrissie Cotterill
A young girl is sentenced to prison where she's forced to survive in a cruel and brutal environment.
MPAA:R
Don Boyd — *THORN EMI Home Video*

Tsunemasa Hatano — *RCA/Columbia Pictures Home Video*

Sea Wolves, The   1981
Adventure
53557   120 mins   C   B, V, CED   P
Gregory Peck, Roger Moore, David Niven, Trevor Howard, Patrick Macnee, directed by Andrew V. McLaglen
A true WW II story about a commando-style operation undertaken by a group of middle-aged, boozing British businessmen in India in 1943.
MPAA:PG
Euan Lloyd; Lorimar — *CBS/Fox Video*

Seals and Crofts with Martin Mull Live   197?
Music-Performance
71289   30 mins   C   B, V   P
In this film Seals and Crofts perform such hits as "Hummingbird," "Summer Breeze," and "The Eighth of January." Also includes Martin Mull, who also performs.
Independent — *Media Home Entertainment*

Seance on a Wet Afternoon   1964
Suspense
08587   115 mins   B/W   B, V, 3/4U   P
Kim Stanley, Richard Attenborough, Margaret Lacey, directed by Bryan Forbes
To gain recognition of supernatural powers a medium decides to kidnap a wealthy child.
Artixo Productions — *Penguin Video; Cable Films; VidAmerica*

Search and Destroy   1978
Drama
64871   93 mins   C   B, V, CED   P
Perry King, George Kennedy, Tisa Farrow
A deadly vendetta, born in the midst of battle in a Vietnamese jungle, is kept alive.
MPAA:PG
James Margellos — *Vestron Video*

Searchers, The   1956
Western
38954   119 mins   C   B, V, LV   R, P
John Wayne, Jeffrey Hunter, Vera Miles, Natalie Wood, Ward Bond, directed by John Ford
John Wayne plays a Civil War veteran on the trail of a Comanche raiding party that kidnapped the daughter of one of his friends in this classic John Ford western.
Warner Bros — *Warner Home Video; RCA VideoDiscs*

Seasons for Assassins   1971
Suspense
65448   102 mins   C   B, V   P
Joe Dallesandro, Martin Balsam

A gang of young ruthless hoodlums bring a wave of violence and terror upon the hapless citizens of Rome.
MPAA:R
Carlo Maietto — *U.S.A. Home Video*

Second Chance   1953
Suspense/Drama
64370   82 mins   C   B, V, 3/4U   P
Robert Mitchum, Linda Darnell, Jack Palance, directed by Rudolph Mate
A former prizefighter travels to South America where he protects a gangster's moll who is targeted for murder.
RKO — *Nostalgia Merchant*

Second Chorus   1940
Musical
01617   90 mins   B/W   B, V   P
Fred Astaire, Paulette Goddard, Burgess Meredith, Artie Shaw, Directed by H.C. Potter
Rivalry of two trumpet players for a girl and a job with Artie Shaw Orchestra. Music, dance, and romance.
Paramount — *Budget Video; Penguin Video; Sheik Video; Cable Films; VCII; Video Connection; Video Yesteryear; Discount Video Tapes; Cinema Concepts; Classic Video Cinema Collector's Club*

Second City Insanity   1981
Comedy
59076   60 mins   C   B, V   P
Fred Willard, John Candy
The famed Second City improvisational troupe performs their unique brand of humor.
Toby Martin; Carol N Raskin — *Karl Video*

Second Coming of Suzanne, The   1980
Drama
50920   90 mins   C   B, V   R, P
Sondra Locke, Richard Dreyfuss, Gene Barry
A beautiful woman encounters a Manson-like, hypnotic film director. Her role—to star in a Crucifixion. Set in 1969 San Francisco. A world premiere edition, winner at two international film festivals.
Michael Barry — *Video Gems*

Second Thoughts   1983
Comedy-Drama
65090   109 mins   C   B, V   R, P
Lucie Arnaz, Craig Wasson, Ken Howard
A lady attorney becomes pregnant by one of her clients, an itinerant street musician. When she decides to get an abortion, he kidnaps her and tries to change her mind.
MPAA:PG
EMI Films; Universal — *THORN EMI Home Video*

Secret Agent   1936
Mystery
11317   83 mins   B/W   B, V, FO   P
Madeleine Carroll, Peter Lorre, Robert Young, John Gielgud, Lilli Palmer
A British Intelligence agent has orders to eliminate an enemy agent and thinks he has succeeded. He later finds out that he killed an innocent tourist in Geneva.
Gaumont — *Video Yesteryear; Budget Video; Video Dimensions; Discount Video Tapes; Video Connection; Ampro Video Productions; Cable Films; Western Film & Video Inc*

Secret Agent/The Man Who Knew Too Much   193?
Suspense
58914   162 mins   B/W   B, V   P
Peter Lorre, Robert Young, Lilli Palmer, Madeleine Carroll, Edna Best, Leslie Banks, directed by Alfred Hitchcock
A Lorre-Hitchcock double feature: "Secret Agent" (1936), Somerset Maugham's story about a British Intelligence agent ordered to eliminate an enemy agent, who kills an innocent tourist instead; "The Man Who Knew Too Much" (1934), in which a British family on holiday are told, by a dying secret agent, about an assassination plot.
NTSC, PAL
Gaumont British — *Ampro Video Productions*

Secret Fantasy   1981
Drama
63383   88 mins   C   B, V   P
Laura Antonelli
A musician overcomes his fears of inferiority as he makes his fantasies a reality by having other men admire his wife's beautiful body.
MPAA:R
Film Ventures — *Media Home Entertainment*

Secret Life of Adolph Hitler, The   1969
World War II/Documentary
08910   52 mins   B/W   B, V, 3/4U   P
Narrated by Westbrook Van Voorhis
A documentary on Adolph Hitler uses rare footage to portray the growth of the Third Reich.
Wolper — *Penguin Video; Video Yesteryear; International Historic Films; Discount Video Tapes*

Secret Lives of Waldo Kitty Volume I, The   1975
Cartoons
72886   48 mins   C   B, V   P
Animated
A cartoon where Waldo Kitty imagines himself to be a variety of heroes such as Robin Cat and the Lone Kitty.
Filmation — *Embassy Home Entertainment*

Secret of NIMH, The 1982
Fantasy
60565 83 mins C B, V, CED P
*Animated, directed by Don Bluth, voices by
Hermione Baddeley, John Carradine, Dom
DeLuise, Elizabeth Hartman, Peter Strauss,
Aldo Ray, Edie McClurg*
Based on the story by Robert O'Brien, this
animated tale produced by a staff of Disney-
trained artists concerns a newly-widowed
mouse with four wee ones to care for and
protect against a series of dangers. Stereo.
MPAA:G
Mrs Brisby Ltd; MGM — *MGM/UA Home
Video*

Secret of the Snake and 197?
Crane, The
Martial arts
72174 90 mins C B, V P
A resistance group relies on ancient fighting
techniques to battle the rule of the Ching
Dynasty in this Kung Fu action film.
Foreign — *Master Arts Video*

Secret of Yolanda, The 1982
Drama
68246 90 mins C B, V P
Aviva Ger, Asher Zarfati, Shraga Harpaz
A steamy romance about a young deaf-mute
whose guardian and riding instructor both fall for
her.
MPAA:R
Noah Films — *MGM/UA Home Video*

Secret Policeman's Other 1982
Ball, The
Music-Performance/Comedy
63117 101 mins C B, V, CED P
*John Cleese, Graham Chapman, Michael Palin,
Terry Jones, Peter Townsend, Sting*
A live concert by most of the Monty Python
troupe and guest rock artists, staged for
Amnesty International. In stereo.
MPAA:R
Amnesty International; Miramax
Films — *MGM/UA Home Video*

Secret Squirrel 196?
Cartoons
47693 53 mins C B, V P
Animated
Eight episodes of adventure with the clever
secret agent.
Hanna Barbera — *Worldvision Home Video*

Secret Valley 1936
Western
08809 63 mins B/W B, V, 3/4U P
Richard Arlen, Virginia Grey
The horse and its value in developing the West
are shown.

Sol Lesser Prods — *Penguin Video*

Secret War of Harry 1968
Frigg, The
Comedy
64559 123 mins C B, V P
*Paul Newman, Sylva Koscina, Tom Bosley,
Andrew Duggan*
Private Harry Frigg, a nonconformist World War
II G.I., is promoted to the rank of general as part
of a scheme to help five Allied generals escape
from the custody of the Germans.
MPAA:R
Universal — *MCA Home Video*

Secret World of Reptiles, 1977
The
Animals/Documentary
29170 94 mins C B, V R, P
A series that presents rare living relics of
primeval times and traces the history of the
reptile kingdom.
Bill Burrud Productions — *Walt Disney Home
Video*

Secrets of a Soul 1926
Drama/Film-Avant-garde
64311 58 mins B/W B, V P
Werner Kraus, directed by G.W. Pabst
An expressionistic melodrama about
psychoanalysis, which was the first of its kind,
using several Freudian - based dream
sequences. Silent with musical score.
UFA — *Classic Video Cinema Collector's Club*

Secrets of Women 1952
Comedy-Drama
65630 108 mins B/W B, V P
*Anita Bjork, Karl Arne Homsten, Jarl Kulle,
directed by Ingar Bergman*
Three sisters-in-law tell about their affairs and
marriages as they await their husbands at a
lakeside resort.
Janus Films — *Embassy Home Entertainment*

Seduced and Abandoned 1964
Comedy-Drama
53427 118 mins B/W B, V P
*Saro Urzi, Stefani Sandrelli, Aldo Paglisi,
directed by Pietro Germi*
The fiance of an Italian girl seduces her sister,
and when pressed to marry her, tells the father
that he won't marry an unchaste girl.
Cannes Film Festival '64: Best Actor; Italian
Academy Award: Best Director (Germi).
Italian — *Budget Video; Festival Films*

Seducers, The 1980
Drama
56930 90 mins C B, V R, P
Sondra Locke, Colleen Camp, Seymour Cassel

A wealthy, middle-aged man unsuspectingly allows two young girls to use his telephone, and once inside, a night of bizarre mayhem and brutal murder begins.
MPAA:R
Peter Traynor, Larry Spiegel — *Video Gems*

Seduction, The 1982
Drama
59676   104 mins   C   B, V   P
Morgan Fairchild, Michael Sarrazin, Vince Edwards, Andrew Stevens, Colleen Camp, Kevin Brophy
A superstar TV anchorwoman is harassed by a psychotic male admirer.
MPAA:R
Irwin Yablans; Bruce Cohn Curtis — *Media Home Entertainment; Embassy Home Entertainment (disc only)*

Seduction of Joe Tynan, The 1979
Drama
29735   107 mins   C   B, V, LV   P
Alan Alda, Meryl Streep, Melvyn Douglas, directed by Alan Alda
Alan Alda wrote, directed, and starred in this movie about a senator who is torn between his political career and his personal life.
MPAA:R
Universal, Martin Bregman — *MCA Home Video*

Seduction of Mimi, The 1974
Film-Avant-garde
37402   92 mins   C   B, V   P
Giancarlo Giannini, Mariangelo Melato, directed by Lina Wertmuller
A comic farce of politics and seduction about a Sicilian laborer's escapades with the Communists and the local Mafia.
MPAA:R
New Line Cinema — *CBS/Fox Video*

Seeds of Evil 1976
Horror
47666   80 mins   C   B, V   P
Katherine Houghton, Joe Dallesandro, Rita Gam
A strange gardener grows flowers that can kill.
Chalmer Kirkbride — *Unicorn Video*

Seems Like Old Times 1980
Comedy
51571   102 mins   C   B, V, LV   P
Goldie Hawn, Chevy Chase, Charles Grodin, Robert Guillaume, Harold Gould, directed by Jay Sandrich
A woman with a weakness for her ex-husband comes to his aid when two robbers force him to hold up a bank.
MPAA:PG

Columbia Pictures — *RCA/Columbia Pictures Home Video; RCA VideoDiscs*

Self Defense 1980
Martial arts/Safety education
47333   50 mins   C   B, V, 3/4U   P
Techniques of self defense that can be used by people of all ages in any physical condition, which are a combination of martial arts and military unarmed combat, are demonstrated.
Vision Productions — *Vision Productions*

Self-Defense for Women 1982
Martial arts
47300   60 mins   C   B, V   P
This program provides training in simple yet effective martial arts techniques designed to help women defend themselves against an attack.
Martial Arts Video — *Martial Arts Video*

Sell Out, The 1976
Adventure
76657   102 mins   C   B, V   P
Richard Widmark, Oliver Reed, Gayle Hunnicutt, Sam Wanamaker
Oscar-winning actor Richard Widmark, and a highly-acclaimed cast star in a high-stakes game of tag, but no one's sure who "it" is.
MPAA:PG
Josef Shaftel — *Media Home Entertainment*

Selling Movies on Television 197?
Movie and TV trailers
42975   55 mins   C   B, V, FO   P
Here are 67 TV commercials for some of the best and worst films ever released, featuring stars and scenes from such movies as "The Great Dictator," "The Glass Bottom Boat," and "Portnoy's Complaint."
CBS et al — *Video Yesteryear*

Semi-Tough 1977
Comedy
13313   107 mins   C   B, V, LV   P
Burt Reynolds, Kris Kristofferson, Jill Clayburgh, directed by Michael Ritchie
Social satire involving a couple of pro-football buddies and the team owner's daughter.
MPAA:R
United Artists; David Merrick — *CBS/Fox Video; RCA VideoDiscs*

Senator Was Indiscreet, The 1947
Comedy
65736   81 mins   B/W   B, V   P
William Powell, Ella Raines
A senator, seeking the Presidential nomination, tours the country making ridiculous and contradictory campaign promises.

Universal — *NTA Home Entertainment*

Sender, The 1982
Horror
64504   92 mins   C   B, V, LV   R, P
Kathryn Harrold, Zeljko Ivanek, Shirley Knight
A amnesiac young man is studied by a
psychiatrist who discovers that her patient is a
"sender," who can transmit his nightmares to
other people. In stereo.
MPAA:R
Paramount — *Paramount Home Video*

Seniors 1978
Comedy
63363   87 mins   C   B, V, CED   P
*Dennis Quaid, Priscilla Barnes, Jeffrey Byron,
Gary Imhoff*
Fast-paced antics abound in this satire of
students, sex and society.
MPAA:R
Cine Artists — *Vestron Video*

Senora Tentacion 1949
Musical-Drama
57360   82 mins   B/W   B, V, FO   P
David Silva, Susana Guizar, Ninon Sevilla
Musical melodrama about a composer who
fights to leave his mother, sister, and girlfriend in
order to flee with Hortensia, a famous singer.
SP
Mexican — *Video Yesteryear*

Sensational Sixties 1980
Football
45124   30 mins   C   B, V, FO   R, P
Narrated by John Facenda
The best players, plays, games, and moments
from pro football's golden decade are captured
in this memory-provoking program.
NFL Films — *NFL Films Video*

Sensations of 1945 1945
Musical
54128   87 mins   B/W   B, V   P
*W. C. Fields, Eleanor Powell, Sophie Tucker,
Cab Calloway, Woody Herman*
A dancer goes to extreme means to put on a
show and gain publicity. Of particular interest in
this program is the famous musical number in
which Eleanor Powell appears as a ball in a
pinball machine.
United Artists — *Video Dimensions*

Sense of Loss, A 1972
Documentary/Great Britain
76038   135 mins   B/W   B, V   P
This documentary deals with the on-going
controversy in Northern Ireland, and the impact
that it has on the day-to-day lives of the Irish.

Marcel Ophuls; Max
Palevsky — *RCA/Columbia Pictures Home
Video*

Sensual Man, The 1974
Comedy
68267   90 mins   C   B, V   P
*Giancarlo Giannini, Rossana Podesta, Lionel
Stowder*
A hot blooded Italian falls in love and gets
married only to find out that his wife cannot
consummate their marriage.
MPAA:R
Medusa Distribuzione — *RCA/Columbia
Pictures Home Video*

Sensuous Caterer, The 1982
Comedy
64845   60 mins   C   B, V   P
Marc Stevens
Stevens hosts a video Valentine's Day orgy and
invites an uninhibited crowd of erotic stars and
starlets to come and show their stuff.
A.O.E. Productions — *HarmonyVision*

Sensuous Teenager, The 1977
Drama
63412   80 mins   C   B, V   P
A teenage girl is overwhelmingly erotic and
uncontrollably seductive, and she aims to
please by releasing all the sensuality within her.
MPAA:R
Madison World Films — *Sun Video*

Sentinels of Silence 1972
Mexico/Archeology
20473   18 mins   C   B, V   P
Narrated by Orson Welles
Aerial views of seven archeological sites in
Mexico—ruins of unknown pre-Columbian
civilizations. Spanish version available, narrated
by Ricardo Montalban.
Academy Awards '71: Best Documentary Short
Subject; Best Short Subject--Live Action.
AM Available EL, SP
Manuel Arango — *Alti Corporation*

Separacion Matrimonial 197?
Drama
52794   96 mins   C   B, V   P
Jacqueline Andere, Ana Belen, Simon Andreu
A woman decides to forgive her husband and
stop divorce proceedings when his outside love
affair ends. Soon, however, he is up to his old
tricks again. In Spanish.
SP
Luis Sanz — *Media Home Entertainment*

Separate Peace, A 1973
Drama
64028   104 mins   C   B, V   R, P

            (For Explanation of codes, see USE GUIDE and KEY)

John Heyl, Parker Stevenson, William Roerick
Based on the novel by John Knowles, this is the story of how responsibility for a crippling accident brings a young man face to face with his inner nature.
MPAA:PG
Paramount — *Paramount Home Video*

Separate Tables 1958
Drama
68231 98 mins B/W B, V, CED P
Burt Lancaster, Rita Hayworth, David Niven, Deborah Kerr
This film explores the separate yet connected dreams of people staying in the same hotel.
Clifton Productions — *CBS/Fox Video*

Separate Ways 1982
Drama
62864 92 mins C B, V, LV, CED P
Karen Black, Tony LoBianco, David Naughton
A middle-class couple find they must split up for a while to gain a new perspective of themselves and their marriage.
MPAA:R
Hickmar Productions — *Vestron Video*

Sergeant Pepper's Lonely Hearts Club Band 1978
Musical
14003 113 mins C B, V, LV P
Peter Frampton, the Bee Gees, Steve Martin, Aerosmith, Earth Wind and Fire, George Burns
The Beatles' famous story-in-song album is transferred to the screen starring some of the most popular rock n' roll singer-musicians of our time.
MPAA:PG
Universal; Robert Stigwood — *MCA Home Video*

Sergeant York 1941
Drama
58950 134 mins B/W B, V, CED P
Gary Cooper, Joan Leslie, Walter Brennan, Dickie Moore, Ward Bond, directed by Howard Hawks
The story of the gentle, hillbilly farmer who becomes a hero of World War I.
Academy Awards '41: Best Actor (Cooper).
Warner Bros — *CBS/Fox Video; RCA VideoDiscs*

Serial 1980
Comedy
55540 92 mins C B, V, LV R, P
Martin Mull, Sally Kellerman, Tuesday Weld, Tom Smothers, Bill Macy, Barbara Rhoades, Christopher Lee
Cyra McFadden's novel about life in Marin County, California, spoofing open marriage, health foods, exercise, psychiatry, and cult religions comes to life in this film.
MPAA:R
Paramount; Sidney Beckerman — *Paramount Home Video*

Serial Previews #1 194?
Movie and TV trailers/Serials
64417 60 mins B/W B, V, 3/4U P
An assortment of theatrical trailers from over thirty serials. Titles featured include "The Adventures of Red Ryder," "The Fighting Devil Dogs," "Superman," "The Spy Smasher," "The Adventures of Captain Marvel" and many others.
Republic et al — *Nostalgia Merchant*

Serpico 1974
Drama
29797 130 mins C B, V, LV R, P
Al Pacino, John Randolf, Jack Kehoe, Barbara Eda-Young
The story of Frank Serpico, a New York policeman who uncovered corruption in the police department.
MPAA:R
Dino De Laurentiis — *Paramount Home Video; RCA VideoDiscs*

Servant, The 1963
Drama
36933 112 mins B/W B, V R, P
Dirk Bogarde, James Fox, Sarah Miles, Wendy Craig, directed by Joseph Losey
British class hypocrisy is starkly portrayed in this story of a spoiled young gentleman's ruin by his socially inferior but crafty and ambitious manservant.
British Film Academy: Best Actor (Bogarde); Best Photography (Black and White); Most Promising Newcomer (Fox).
Springbok Prod, Landau Unger — *THORN EMI Home Video*

Sesenta Horas en el Cielo 1946
Comedy
57359 76 mins B/W B, V, FO P
Alady y Lepe
A comedy about two air cadets who gain fame by establishing a new record for duration in the air.
SP
Spain — *Video Yesteryear*

Set Up, The 1949
Drama
44986 72 mins B/W B, V P, T
Robert Ryan, Audrey Totter
The story of an average fighter who refuses to take a dive for a group of crooked gamblers, and fights to win.

Anglo Amalgamated Film — *Blackhawk Films; Nostalgia Merchant*

Seven Arts — *Paramount Home Video*

Seven Alone   1975
Adventure
44949   85 mins   C   B, V   P
Dewey Martin, Aldo Ray, Anne Collins, Dean Smith, Stewart Peterson, directed by Earl Bellamy
Seven orphaned children, led by the oldest, a thirteen-year-old boy, undertake a treacherous 2000 mile journey from Missouri to Oregon. Based on the book "On to Oregon" by Monroe Morrow.
MPAA:G.
Doty Dayton — *Children's Video Library*

Seven-Per-Cent Solution, The   1976
Mystery
14002   113 mins   C   B, V   P
Alan Arkin, Nicol Williamson, Laurence Olivier, Robert Duvall, Venessa Redgrave, Joel Grey, Samantha Eggar, directed by Herbert Ross
Sigmund Freud joins forces with Sherlock Holmes and Dr. Watson in the search for the real Professor Moriarity.
MPAA:PG
Universal; Herbert Ross Prod — *MCA Home Video*

Seven Beauties   1976
Comedy
44774   116 mins   C   B, V   P
Giancarlo Giannini, Fernando Rey, Shirley Stoler, directed by Lina Wertmuller
The story of a dumb but likeable hood who shoots his sister's pimp to save his family's honor. He is caught and sent to an insane asylum. After volunteering for the Italian army, he finds himself in a Nazi concentration camp.
Cinema 5 — *RCA/Columbia Pictures Home Video*

Seven Samurai   1954
Adventure
29761   204 mins   B/W   B, V   P
Takashi Shimura, Toshiro Mifune, Yoshio Inaba
A small Japanese farming village is beset by marauding bandits. Powerless to prevent these ongoing raids, the villagers hire seven professional soldiers. Japanese dialogue with English subtitles.
Academy Awards '55: Honorary Award.   JA Kingsley Intl, Toho Prod — *Embassy Home Entertainment; Budget Video; International Historic Films; Sheik Video; Discount Video Tapes*

7 Blows of the Dragon   1973
Adventure/Martial arts
54810   81 mins   C   B, V   R, P
David Chiang
The Chinese novel, "All Men Are Brothers," is the basis for this spectacular martial arts epic.
MPAA:R
New World Pictures — *Warner Home Video*

765 North/4501 Steam   1980
Trains
55518   60 mins   C   B, V   P
Vivid scenes of steam locomotives in action, featuring the massive Nickel Plate Berkshire No. 765 and the Southern Railway's beautiful Mikado No. 4501.
De Luz — *De Luz Video*

Seven Brides for Seven Brothers   1954
Musical
58705   103 mins   C   B, V, CED   P
Howard Keel, Jane Powell, Russ Tamblyn, Julie Newmar, Jeff Richards, Tommy Rall, Virginia Gibson, directed by Stanley Donen
When the eldest of seven brothers in the Oregon Territory brings home a wife, the other six sneak into town looking for brides.
Academy Awards '54: Best Scoring, Musical (Adloph Deutsch, Saul Chaplin).
MGM — *MGM/UA Home Video*

Seven Year Itch, The   1955
Comedy
08467   105 mins   C   B, V   P
Marilyn Monroe, Tom Ewell, Evelyn Keyes, Sonny Tufts, Robert Strauss, Oscar Homolka
After a man sees his wife and son off to the country for the summer, he returns home to find that a lovely blonde has sublet the apartment above his.
20th Century Fox; Charles K Feldman and Billy Wilder — *CBS/Fox Video*

Seven Days in May   1964
Mystery/Drama
65617   120 mins   B/W   B, V, LV,   R, P
                            CED
Burt Lancaster, Kirk Douglas, Frederic March, Ava Gardner, John Houseman
An American general's aide discovers that his boss intends a military takeover because he considers the President's pacifism traitorous.

1776   1972
Musical
64235   141 mins   C   B, V   P
Howard da Silva, William Daniels, Ken Howard, Donald Madden, Blythe Danner
Based on the musical play, this is a light-hearted look at the signing of the Declaration of Independence. In simulated stereo.
MPAA:PG

Columbia — *RCA/Columbia Pictures Home Video*

7th Voyage of Sinbad, The   1958
Fantasy
19083   89 mins   C   B, V   P
Kerwin Matthews, Kathryn Grant
Sinbad seeks to restore his fiancee from the midget size to which an evil magician has reduced her.
Columbia — *RCA/Columbia Pictures Home Video*

Severed Arm, The   1973
Horror
58551   89 mins   C   B, V   R, P
Deborah Waller, Paul Carr, David Cannon
Trapped in a cave, five men cut off the arm of a companion in order to ward off starvation.
Heritage Enterprises — *Video Gems*

Sex and Love Test, The   1981
Sexuality
57549   60 mins   C   B, V   P
Hosted by Dr. Frank Field
Viewers can test their knowledge on sexual problems, and find out the answers from psychiatrists and sex therapists.
International Film and TV Festival of New York: Silver Medal.
NBC; Don Luftig — *Karl Video*

Sex and the Office Girl   197?
Drama
59552   76 mins   C   B, V   P
An advertising agency turns into an after hours pleasure dome of erotic complications.
Filmco — *Media Home Entertainment*

Sex in the Comics   197?
Comedy
66084   70 mins   C   B, V   P
Live actors recreate the erotic comic book characters of years ago.
MPAA:R
Swab Prods — *Best Film & Video Corporation*

Sex Machine, The   1976
Drama
47750   80 mins   C   B, V   P
Agostina Belli
Set in the year 2037, a scientist finds two of the world's greatest lovers and unites them so he can transform their reciprocating motion into electricity.
MPAA:R
, Sylvio Clementelli — *Media Home Entertainment*

Sex Madness   1937
Exploitation
05530   50 mins   B/W   B, V, FO   P
A 1930's campy melodrama about the evils of lechery, lust, and passion.
Unknown — *Video Yesteryear; Budget Video; Video Dimensions; Sheik Video; Discount Video Tapes; Penguin Video*

Sex on the Run   1978
Comedy
57228   88 mins   C   B, V, LV, CED   R, P
Tony Curtis, Marisa Berenson, Britt Ekland
The love-starved wife of an oil-rich sheik, stimulated by the idea of having Casanova, an amourous adventurer, for her lover, teases her master into delivering him, but Casanova finds peace in the arms of three convent lovelies.
MPAA:R
Franz Antel — *Wonderlust Video*

Sex Pleasuring, An Enrichment Series, Volumes 1-3   1982
Sexuality
59391   45 mins   C   B, V   P
3 pgms
This three volume series has been compiled from EDCOA films, acknowledged leaders in the sex education field. These sexually explicit programs employ Masters and Johnson techniques and are designed to enrich and enhance a couple's sexual pleasure.
New Age Video — *New Age Video Inc*

Sex Shop, Le   1973
Satire
47781   92 mins   C   B, V   P
Claude Berri, Juliet Berto
A man owns a shop where he sells exotic books and paraphernalia. When his relationship with his wife gets boring, they make use of the merchandise and adopt a swinging lifestyle.
MPAA:R
Pierre Grunstein — *RCA/Columbia Pictures Home Video*

Sex with a Smile   1976
Comedy
43072   100 mins   C   B, V   R, P
Marty Feldman, Edvice Finich, Alex Marino, Enrico Monterrano, Giovanni Ralli
Five slapstick episodes by five different directors with lots of sexual satire pointed at religion and politics in Italy.
MPAA:R
Surrogate — *Video Gems*

Sextette   1978
Musical/Comedy
59665   91 mins   C   B, V   P

Mae West, Timothy Dalton, Ringo Starr, George Hamilton, Dom DeLuise, Tony Curtis, Alice Cooper, Keith Moon, George Raft, Rona Barrett
A lavish musical about an elderly star who is constantly interrupted by former spouses and well-wishers while on a honeymoon with her sixth husband.
MPAA:PG
Daniel Briggs; Robert Sullivan — *Media Home Entertainment*

Sexton Blake and the Hooded Terror 1953
Mystery
12808   70 mins   B/W   B, V, FO   P
Tod Slaughter, Greta Gynt
A British private detective is after "The Snake," a master criminal.
Unknown — *Video Yesteryear*

Sextoons 197?
Cartoons
64846   90 mins   C   B, V   P
Animated
This offers a collection of some of the world's greatest erotic animation.
Saliva Films — *HarmonyVision*

Sexy Cat 19??
Mystery
59394   ? mins   C   B, V   P
Monika Kolpek, Maria Villa, Vidal Molina, Marques De Toro
A comic strip character comes to life to duplicate the murders committed in the strip.
SP
Paramount Films — *Telecine Spanish Video*

Shadow of Chinatown 1946
Horror
05522   70 mins   B/W   B, V   P
Bela Lugosi, Herman Brix, Joan Barclay
A mad scientist creates a wave of murder and terror in Chinatown.
Monogram — *Video Connection*

Shadow of the Eagle 1932
Mystery/Serials
12551   226 mins   B/W   B, V, FO   P
John Wayne, Dorothy Gulliver, directed by Ford Beebe
Intrigue and mystery of carnival life. Twelve chapters, 13 minutes each.
Mascot — *Video Yesteryear; Video Connection*

Shadow Strikes, The 1937
Mystery
58618   61 mins   B/W   B, V   P, T
Rod LaRocque, Lynn Anders
A "Shadow" murder mystery.

Grand National — *Video Connection; Cable Films*

Shadows 1922
Drama
64354   70 mins   B/W   B, V   P
Lon Chaney
A Chinese laundryman lives with a group of his countrymen in a New England seacoast village. All is peaceful until the local minister decides to convert the "heathen" Chinese. Silent with music score.
Preferred Pictures — *Classic Video Cinema Collector's Club*

Shadows of Death 1945
Western
13105   60 mins   B/W   B, V   P
Buster Crabbe, Al 'Fuzzy' St. John
Billy the Kid comes to the rescue again.
PRC — *Video Connection*

Shaft 1971
Crime-Drama
60566   98 mins   C   B, V, CED   P
Richard Roundtree
A black private eye finds himself at odds with a powerful racketeer.
MPAA:R
MGM — *MGM/UA Home Video*

Shaggy Dog, The 1959
Comedy
58626   101 mins   B/W   B, V, LV   R, P
Fred MacMurray, Jean Hagen, Tommy Kirk, Annette Funicello, Tim Considine, Kevin Corcoran, directed by Charles Barton
When young Wilby Daniels utters some magical words from the inscription of an ancient ring he turns into a shaggy dog causing havoc to family and neighbors.
MPAA:G
Walt Disney Productions — *Walt Disney Home Video; RCA VideoDiscs*

Shalako 1968
Western
69384   113 mins   C   B, V   P
Brigitte Bardot, Sean Connery
While on a hunting trip in New Mexico in the 1880's, a European countess is captured by an Apache, and a U.S. Army scout is sent to save her.
Cinerama Releasing — *CBS/Fox Video*

Shall We Dance 1937
Musical
10051   116 mins   B/W   B, V   P, T
Fred Astaire, Ginger Rogers, Edward Everett Horton
A famous ballet dancer marries a showgirl—or does he? The score by George and Ira

Gershwin includes such memorable songs as "They All Laughed," "Let's Call the Whole Thing Off" and "They Can't Take That Away from Me."
RKO; Pandro S Berman — *Blackhawk Films; King of Video; Nostalgia Merchant*

Shame   1969
Drama/History
49072   102 mins   B/W   B, V   P
Liv Ullman, Max von Sydow, written and directed by Ingmar Bergman
A husband and wife flee to an island to avoid the Civil War taking place on the mainland. They are subsequently drained of their individual strength and hope through the loss of spiritual foundations in the modern world. Swedish with English subtitles.
SW
Swedish — *Sheik Video*

Shame   1965
Drama
48717   90 mins   B/W   B, V, 3/4U   P
William Shatner, directed by Roger Corman
Racial prejudice and hatred emerge in a small Southern town on the verge of integration.
Unknown — *Penguin Video*

Shamus   1973
Comedy
21295   91 mins   C   B, V   P
Burt Reynolds, Dyan Cannon
A detective hired to recover some missing diamonds becomes involved with the syndicate, a beautiful woman, and an army officer smuggling government surplus.
MPAA:PG
Columbia — *RCA/Columbia Pictures Home Video*

Shane   1953
Western
38619   117 mins   C   B, V, LV   R, P
Alan Ladd, Jean Arthur, Van Heflin, Brandon de Wilde, Jack Palance, directed by George Stevens
A retired gunfighter, now drifter, comes to the assistance of a homestead family terrorized by a hired gunman. A classic of the Western film genre.
Academy Awards '53: Best Cinematography, Color.
Paramount — *Paramount Home Video; RCA VideoDiscs*

Shao Lin Kung Fu Mystagogue/Kung Fu of Eight Drunkards   197?
Martial arts/Adventure
66086   188 mins   C   B, V   P
A kung-fu double feature filled with martial arts action.

MPAA:R
Unknown — *Best Film & Video Corporation*

Shaolin Death Squad   1983
Martial arts
64564   90 mins   C   B, V   P
A ruthless Japanese premier murders a statesman as the first step in his plan to become Emperor. The murdered man's daughter swears vengeance and enlists the Shaolin Death Squad to help.
MPAA:R
Satellite Consultants — *CBS/Fox Video*

Shaolin Traitor   1982
Martial arts
64944   99 mins   C   B, V   R, P
Carter Wong, Shangkuan Ling-Feng, Lung Chun-Erh, Chang Yi, Lung Fei
Exotic weapons and dazzling martial-arts action are featured in this exciting tale of intrigue and mystery.
MPAA:R
L and T Films Corp Ltd — *Video Gems*

Shape Up   1983
Physical fitness
65610   30 mins   C   B, V   P
8 pgms
Beautiful instructors put you through a no-holds-barred exercise regimen guaranteed to make you look and feel your best. Programs available individually.
1.*Shape Up with Carrie* 2.*Shape Up with Pauline* 3.*Shape Up with Pat* 4.*Shape Up with Charlene* 5.*Shape Up with Carrie—Advanced* 6.*Shape Up with Pauline—Advanced* 7.*Shape Up with Pat—Advanced* 8.*Shape Up with Charlene—Advanced*
Anthony DiVona; Gold Stripe Video — *Gold Stripe Video*

Shark!   1968
Drama
65686   92 mins   C   B, V   P
Burt Reynolds, Barry Sullivan, Arthur Kennedy
An American gun smuggler stranded in a tiny seaport in the Middle East joins the crew of a marine biologist's boat, and soon discovers the boat's owner and his wife are trying to retrieve gold bullion that lies deep in shark-infested waters.
Excelsior — *NTA Home Entertainment*

Sharks   1984
Fishes
72963   28 mins   C   B, V   P
This program examines the history of sharks and dispells some of the myths surrounding the animal.
Star Merchants — *Increase Video*

Sharky's Machine   1981
Adventure
59856   119 mins   C   B, V   R, P
*Burt Reynolds, Rachel Ward, Vittorio Gassman,
Brian Keith, Charles Durning, Earl Holliman,
directed by Burt Reynolds*
A lively detective tale about an undercover cop
hot on the trail of a crooked czar.
MPAA:R
Orion; Warner Bros — *Warner Home Video;
RCA VideoDiscs*

Shattered   1972
Drama
65372   100 mins   C   B, V   P
Peter Finch, Shelley Winters, Colin Blakely
Finch plays Harry, a man not only blamed for a
failed marriage, but also held hostage in his
home by his own paranoia and driven bouts of
drinking. Slowly Harry's tenuous grip on sanity
slips and at any moment his fragile and
crumbling life may be shattered.
MPAA:R
Michael Klinger — *Media Home Entertainment*

Shazam   1981
Cartoons/Adventure
66007   60 mins   C   B, V   P
Animated
Young Billy Batson says "shazam" and turns
into the mighty Captain Marvel.
Filmation — *Family Home Entertainment*

Shazam!, Volume 2   1981
Cartoons/Adventure
69808   60 mins   C   B, V   P
Animated
Three more adventures feature young Billy
Batson, who transforms himself into the mighty
Captain Marvel to fight dastardly villains.
Filmation — *Family Home Entertainment*

Shazzan   1983
Cartoons
66577   60 mins   C   B, V   P
Animated
Arabian nights adventures with Shazzan the
genie are featured on this tape.
Hanna Barbera — *Worldvision Home Video*

She   1925
Adventure
47462   77 mins   B/W   B, V, FO   P
Betty Blythe, Carlyle Blackwell, Mary Odette
H. Rider Haggard's famous story about the
ageless Queen Ayesha, who renews her life
force periodically by walking through a pillar of
cold flame. Silent film with music score.
Reciprocity Films — *Video Yesteryear;
Discount Video Tapes; Classic Video Cinema
Collector's Club*

She   1925
Adventure
58537   40 mins   B/W   B, V, 3/4U   P
Betty Blythe, Carlisle Blackwell, Mary Odette
Sir Henry Rider Haggard's novel about a lost
city wherein dwells a queen who cannot die,
until she falls in love. Silent.
Reciprocity Films — *Penguin Video*

She Beast   1966
Horror
69796   73 mins   C   B, V   P
Barbara Steele, Mel Wells
Burned at the stake in 18th century
Transylvania, a witch returns in the body of a
beautiful 20th century woman and once again
wreaks death and destruction.
Europix Consolidated — *Gorgon Video*

She Couldn't Say No   1952
Comedy
10029   88 mins   B/W   B, V   P, T
*Robert Mitchum, Jean Simmons, Arthur
Hunnicutt, Edgar Buchanan, Wallace Ford,
directed by Lloyd Bacon*
A wealthy heiress with good intentions plans to
give her money away to those friends who had
helped her when she was struggling. Things
don't go quite as planned, however.
RKO — *Blackhawk Films*

She Wore a Yellow   1949
Ribbon
Western
00275   103 mins   C   B, V, 3/4U   P
John Wayne, Joanne Dru, directed by John Ford
An undermanned cavalry outpost makes a
desperate attempt to repel invading Indians.
Academy Award '49: Best Cinematography,
Color.
RKO; Argosy Pictures Corp — *Nostalgia
Merchant; VidAmerica; King of Video*

Sheena Easton   1983
Music-Performance
75907   15 mins   C   B, V   P
This program presents Sheena Easton
performing her hit songs "Morning Train,"
"Machinery" and "Telefone."
EMI America Records — *Sony Corporation of
America*

Sheena Easton: Act One   1983
Music-Performance/Variety
73563   60 mins   C   B, V   P
Sheena sings her hits "For Your Eyes Only,"
"Out Here on My Own" and "Wind Beneath My
Wings" and Al Jarreau sings "Roof Garden" in
this program that was originally broadcast on
NBC.
Smith Hemion Productions — *Prism*

          (For Explanation of codes, see USE GUIDE and KEY)

Sheena Easton—Live at the Palace, Hollywood 1982
Music-Performance
66184   60 mins   C   B, V   R, P
The Grammy Award winner sings "Modern Girl," "Morning Train," "For Your Eyes Only" and others.
Unknown — *THORN EMI Home Video; RCA VideoDiscs*

Shenandoah 1965
Drama
53396   105 mins   C   B, V   P
James Stewart, Doug McClure, Glenn Corbett, Patrick Wayne, Rosemary Forsythe, Katherine Ross
During the Civil War, a farmer tries to remain neutral but becomes involved when his only daughter becomes engaged to a Confederate soldier.
Universal — *MCA Home Video*

Sheriff Terrible, El 1963
Comedy
47723   90 mins   C   B, V   P
A comedy western about two drifters trying to make a living by cheating others out of their money. In Spanish.
SP
Independent — *Telecine Spanish Video*

Sherlock Holmes and the Baskerville Curse 1984
Mystery
65851   70 mins   C   B, V   P
Animated, voice of Peter O'Toole
This production is an animated feature film with Peter O'Toole starring as the voice of Sherlock Holmes.
Pacific Arts Video Records — *Pacific Arts Video*

Sherlock Holmes and the Secret Weapon 1942
Mystery
58893   68 mins   B/W   B, V, FO   P
Basil Rathbone, Nigel Bruce, Lionel Atwill
Based on "The Dancing Men" by Sir Arthur Conan Doyle, Holmes battles Dr. Moriarty in order to save the British war effort.
Universal — *Video Yesteryear; Movie Buff Video; Admit One Video; Ampro Video Productions; Cable Films; Video Connection; Western Film & Video Inc; Budget Video; Discount Video Tapes*

Sherlock Holmes and the Silver Blaze 1941
Mystery
14295   67 mins   B/W   B, V   P
Arthur Wontner, Ian Fleming, Lyn Harding
Sherlock Holmes mystery based on the Arthur Conan Doyle classic "The Silver Blaze."
Astor; British — *Mossman Williams Productions; Video Yesteryear*

Sherlock Holmes and the Woman in Green 1945
Mystery
42927   67 mins   B/W   B, V   P
Basil Rathbone, Nigel Bruce
Based on a character developed by Sir Arthur Conan Doyle, this mystery finds Holmes and Watson matching wits against the infamous Professor Moriarity.
Universal, Howard Benedict — *Movie Buff Video; Cable Films; Video Connection; Budget Video; Discount Video Tapes; Western Film & Video Inc*

Sherlock Holmes Double Feature 194?
Mystery
55591   147 mins   B/W   B, V   P
Basil Rathbone, Nigel Bruce
Two classic Sherlock Holmes features on one cassette: "The Adventures of Sherlock Holmes" (1939) and "Sherlock Holmes and the Voice of Terror" (1942).
Twentieth Century Fox; Universal — *CBS/Fox Video*

Sherlock Holmes Double Feature I 194?
Mystery
64582   120 mins   B/W   B, V, 3/4U   P
Basil Rathbone, Nigel Bruce
Paired in this double feature are "Sherlock Holmes and the Secret Weapon" and "The Woman in Green."
Universal — *Nostalgia Merchant*

Sherlock Holmes Double Feature II 1946
Mystery
64583   120 mins   B/W   B, V, 3/4U   P
Basil Rathbone, Nigel Bruce
This double feature contains "Dressed to Kill" and "Terror by Night."
Universal — *Nostalgia Merchant*

Sherlock Holmes I 1954
Mystery
38997   54 mins   B/W   B, V, FO   P
Ronald Howard, H. Marion Crawford   2 pgms
Two episodes from the English syndicated series bases on the exploits of master detective Sherlock Holmes: "The Case of the Impromptu Performance," and "The Case of the Exhumed Client."
British — *Video Yesteryear*

Sherlock Holmes II   1954
Mystery
38998   54 mins   B/W   B, V, FO   P
Ronald Howard, H. Marion Crawford 2 pgms
Two more episodes from the syndicated British
TV series of the 1950's: "The Case of the Baker
Street Nursemaids" and "The Case of the
Pennsylvania Gun."
British — *Video Yesteryear*

She's Dressed to Kill   1979
Suspense
66622   98 mins   C   B, V   P
*Eleanor Parker, Jessica Walter, John
Rubenstein*
A mysterious killer murders a group of fashion
models one by one, in the incongruous setting
of a secluded mountaintop resort.
Grant Case McGrath Enterprises; Barry Weitz
Productions — *U.S.A. Home Video*

Shinbone Alley   1970
Musical/Cartoons
50960   83 mins   C   B, V   R, P
*Animated, voices of Carol Channing, Eddie
Bracken, John Carradine, Alan Reed*
An animated musical about Archy, a free-verse
poet reincarnated as a cockroach, and
Mehitabel, the alley cat with a zest for life.
Based on the short stories by Don Marquis.
MPAA:G
Fine Arts Films — *Video Gems*

Shine on Harvest Moon   1938
Western
05534   60 mins   B/W   B, V, FO   P
Roy Rogers, Mary Hart, Stanley Andrews
Roy Rogers brings a band of outlaws to justice
and clears an old man suspected of being their
accomplice.
Republic — *Video Yesteryear*

Shining, The   1980
Horror
58249   143 mins   C   B, V   R, P
*Jack Nicholson, Shelley Duvall, Scatman
Crothers, Danny Lloyd, directed by Stanley
Kubrick*
Terror and violence overwhelms a family
isolated and snowbound in a huge resort hotel
with a history of violence. Based on the novel by
Stephen King.
MPAA:R
Warner Bros — *Warner Home Video; RCA
VideoDiscs*

Shipwreck Beach   1978
Video
08565   30 mins   C   B, V, 3/4U   P
A continuous picture of a long beach shot
highlighting cliff formations in the distance to
create a relaxed background.

Nebulae Prods — *Nebulae Productions*

Shock   1946
Mystery/Horror
53442   70 mins   B/W   B, V, FO   P
*Vincent Price, Lynn Bari, Frank Latimore,
Anabel Shaw*
A doctor is called upon to treat a woman and
discovers that she saw him kill his wife.
AM Available
Twentieth Century Fox — *Video Yesteryear*

Shock, The   1922
Drama
48713   50 mins   B/W   B, V, FO   P
Lon Chaney, Virginia Valli Chaney
A crippled agent is sent to keep an eye on a
blackmailed banker. Silent.
Universal — *Video Yesteryear; Penguin Video;
Classic Video Cinema Collector's Club*

Shogun   1980
Drama
54670   120 mins   C   B, V, LV   R, P
Richard Chamberlain, Toshiro Mifune
A made for television feature that depicts the
people, life-style, and traditions of Japan. A
special 2-hour length version, based on the
novel by James Clavell.
NBC — *Paramount Home Video; RCA
VideoDiscs*

Shogun Assassin   1980
Adventure
55553   89 mins   C   B, V, LV   P
Tomisaburo Wakayama
The story of a proud samurai named Lone Wolf
who served his Shogun master well as the
Official Decapitator, until the fateful day when
the aging Shogun turned against him.
MPAA:R
Toho Company; Katsu Prod — *MCA Home
Video*

Shogun's Ninja   1983
Martial arts/Suspense
64233   115 mins   C   B, V   P
Henry Sanada, Sue Shiomi, Sonny Chiba
In 16th century Japan, an age-old rivalry
between two ninja clans sparks a search for a
dagger which will lead to one clan's hidden gold.
Toei Studios; Shigeru Okada — *Media Home
Entertainment*

**Shoot It Black, Shoot It
Blue**   1974
Crime-Drama
64212   93 mins   C   B, V   R, P
Michael Moriarty
A rogue cop shoots a black purse snatcher and
thinks he has gotten away with it. Unknown to

him, however, a witness has filmed the incident
and turns the evidence over to a lawyer.
Shoot It Company — *THORN EMI Home Video*

Shoot the Moon   1982
Drama
47775   124 mins   C   B, V, CED   P
*Diane Keaton, Albert Finney, Karen Allen, Peter
Weller, Dana Hill, Viveka Davis, Tracey Gold,
Tina Yothers, directed by Alan Parker*
An affluent California family experiences
jealousy, anger and love following the breakup
of the marriage.
MPAA:R
MGM — *MGM/UA Home Video*

Shoot the Piano Player   1962
Drama
49065   84 mins   B/W   B, V   P
*Charles Aznavour, Marie Dubois, Nicole Berger,
directed by Francois Truffaut*
A former great piano player reluctantly agrees to
try a comeback at the urging of the girl he loves.
Italian — *Sheik Video; Budget Video; Western
Film & Video Inc; Cable Films*

Shoot the Sun Down   1974
Adventure
59812   102 mins   C   B, V   P
*Christopher Walken, Margot Kidder, Geoffrey
Lewis*
Four offbeat characters united in their lust for
gold soon turn against each other.
MPAA:PG
David Leeds — *VCI Home Video*

Shooting, The   1966
Western
13629   82 mins   C   B, V   P
Warren Oates, Millie Perkins, Jack Nicholson
A mysterious woman, bent on revenge,
persuades a former bounty hunter and his
partner to escort her across the desert, with
tragic results.
Monte Hellman; Jack Nicholson — *Media
Home Entertainment; Discount Video Tapes;
King of Video; Sheik Video; Budget Video;
Western Film & Video Inc*

Shootist, The   1976
Western
38620   100 mins   C   B, V, LV   R, P
*John Wayne, Lauren Bacall, James Stewart,
Ron Howard, directed by Don Siegel*
John Wayne's last film appearance as an aging
gunslinger afflicted with cancer, who seeks
peace and solace in his final days, but finds
himself involved in one final gun battle.
MPAA:PG
Paramount — *Paramount Home Video; RCA
VideoDiscs*

Short Films of D. W.   1912
Griffith, Vol. I, The
Film-History
47461   45 mins   B/W   B, V, FO   P
Blanche Sweet, Mary Pickford, Charles West
Three early shorts made by the great director
are on this tape: "The Battle," "The Female of
the Species" and "The New York Hat." Silent
with music score.
Biograph — *Video Yesteryear*

Short Iron Lessons   197?
Golf
33776   60 mins   C   B, V, 3/4U   P
Golf pros Linda Craft, Toby Lyons, Penny
Zavichas, Neal Doyle, and Harry Offutt teach
the golfer how to play short iron shots well,
which can save many agonizing strokes on the
course. From the "Name of the Game Is Golf"
series.
Unknown — *Sports World Cinema*

Shot in the Dark, A   1964
Comedy
47151   101 mins   C   B, V, CED   P
*Peter Sellers, Elke Sommer, Herbert Lom,
George Sanders, directed by Blake Edwards*
The Second in the "Inspector Clouseau-Pink
Panther" series of films. The bumbling Inspector
Clouseau investigates the case of a parlormaid
who is accused of murdering her lover.
EL, SP
United Artists; Walter Mirisch — *CBS/Fox
Video; RCA VideoDiscs*

Shout, The   1978
Horror
36189   87 mins   C   B, V   P
*Alan Bates, Susannah York, John Hurt, Tim
Curry*
A married couple becomes dominated by a
malevolent seducer with aboriginal powers.
Cannes Film Festival '78: Jury Prize.   MPAA:R
CPH; BLD — *RCA/Columbia Pictures Home
Video*

Shout at the Devil   1976
War-Drama
65378   128 mins   C   B, V   P
Lee Marvin, Roger Moore, Barbara Parkins
A story based on an actual World War I incident
involving the destruction of a German battleship
on a river in Africa in 1913. Based on the novel
by Wilbur Smith.
MPAA:PG
American International — *Vestron Video*

Show Boat   1951
Musical-Drama
47054   115 mins   C   B, V   P
*Kathryn Grayson, Howard Keel, Ava Gardner,
William Warfield, Joe E. Brown, Agnes
Moorehead*

(For Explanation of codes, see USE GUIDE and KEY)

The third movie version of Jerome Kern and Oscar Hammerstein II's 1927 musical play about the life and loves of a Mississippi riverboat theater troupe. The famous score includes "Old Man River," "Make Believe," "Can't Help Lovin' Dat Man," "Why Do I Love You," and "Bill."
MGM — *MGM/UA Home Video*

Show Business 1944
Musical
44989   92 mins   B/W   B, V   P, T
Eddie Cantor, Joan Davis
Romantic story of two show business teams: the boys are in burlesque and the girls are in vaudeville.
RKO — *Blackhawk Films*

Show Jumping World Cup 1981
Sports-Minor
59567   75 mins   C   B, V   P
The 1981 horse show-jumping competition for the Federation of Equestrians International World Cup.
Grand Prix Show Jumping — *Mastervision*

Showbiz Goes to War 1982
Documentary/World War II
66623   90 mins   C   B, V   P
Narrated by David Steinberg
The activities of Hollywood's biggest stars during World War II are the subject of this feature. Pin-up girls, USO shows, propaganda films, patriotic musicals and war bond drives are a few of the subjects seen along the way.
TAD Productions — *U.S.A. Home Video*

Showdown: Sugar Ray Leonard vs. Thomas Hearns, The 1981
Boxing
59018   62 mins   C   CED   P
The classic match between Sugar Ray Leonard and Tommy Hearns.
Main Event Prods — *RCA VideoDiscs*

Showmanship at Halter 19??
Sports-Minor
69657   16 mins   C   B, V   P
This program is designed to instruct youngsters in the correct methods for showing at halter. It covers basic rules, grooming techniques, cleanliness of tack, control of the horse and other points.
American Saddlebred Association — *Mercedes Maharis Productions*

Showtime at the Apollo 1955
Music-Performance
11276   75 mins   B/W   B, V, FO   P

Duke Ellington, Dinah Washington, Nipsey Russell, Count Basie, Big Joe Turner, Nat 'King' Cole, Lionel Hampton
The Harlem Variety Revue features blues, jazz, and rock n' roll performances from great black artists of the 1950's.
Unknown — *Video Yesteryear*

Showtime at the Apollo 1955
Music-Performance
11277   75 mins   B/W   B, V, FO   P
Lionel Hampton, Cab Calloway, Sarah Vaughn, The Four Tops, Herb Jeffries, Lulu Brown, Bill Bailey, Amos Vogel
Blues, jazz, and rock n' roll from the nostalgic 1950's; features some of the great black performers of the era.
Unknown — *Video Yesteryear*

Showtime at the Apollo 1954
Variety/Music-Performance
47643   79 mins   B/W   B, V, FO   P
Hosted by Willie Bryant, Nipsy Russell, Mantan Moreland, Duke Ellington, Sarah Vaughn, Lionel Hampton, Nat King Cole Trio, Delta Rhythm Boys, Herb Jeffries, The Larks, Martha Davis and Spouse
Three syndicated rhythm and swing shows from the Apollo in New York City's Harlem: "Harlem Merry Go Round," "All-Star Revue," and "Showtime in Harlem."
Unknown — *Video Yesteryear*

Shriek in the Night 1933
Mystery
08780   67 mins   B/W   B, V, 3/4U   P
Ginger Rogers, Lyle Talbot
The peaceful slumber of an exclusive apartment house is broken by the sound of a piercing scream.
Allied Pictures Corp — *Penguin Video*

Sidewalks of London 1940
Drama
03833   86 mins   B/W   B, V   P
Charles Laughton, Vivien Leigh, Rex Harrison, directed by Tim Whelen
Sidewalk entertainer takes in homeless waif, helps her achieve fame.
Mayfair Pictures; Gaumont; British — *Budget Video; Cable Films; Video Connection; Classic Video Cinema Collector's Club*

Sidney Sheldon's Bloodline 1979
Suspense
38929   116 mins   C   B, V   R, P
Audrey Hepburn, Ben Gazzara, James Mason, directed by Terence Young
The popular best-selling novel transferred to film, starring Audrey Hepburn as a wealthy businesswoman who finds she is marked for death by persons unknown.

          (For Explanation of codes, see USE GUIDE and KEY)

MPAA:R
Paramount — *Paramount Home Video*

Sieg im Western (Victory in the West) 1940
World War II/Documentary
52371 120 mins B/W B, V, 3/4U P
A Nazi-produced documentary which covers through front-line footage the initial Axis victories in Holland, Belgium and France in the spring of 1940. Original German language soundtrack with printed translations included.
AM Available GE
Germany — *International Historic Films*

Siegfried 1924
Drama
63993 100 mins B/W B, V P, T
Paul Richter, Margareta Schoen, directed by Fritz Lang
A massive extravaganza film, based on the legends of the Nibelungen. These same tales were also the basis of Richard Wagner's "Ring" cycle of operas. Silent with organ score.
UFA — *Blackhawk Films; Classic Video Cinema Collector's Club*

Sign Language: Exact English 1980
Deaf
47335 110 mins C B, V, 3/4U P
A vocabulary of 480 signs and practice sentences are taught in this program designed for parents whose children are learning to sign Exact English at school. Explanations are captioned for the hearing impaired.
Vision Productions — *Vision Productions*

Sign of Zorro, The 1957
Adventure
59064 89 mins C B, V R, P
Guy Williams, Henry Calvin, Gene Sheldon, Romney Brent, Britt Lomond
The adventures of the masked swordsman as he champions the cause of the oppressed in early California. A full-length version of the popular late-50's Disney TV series.
Walt Disney Productions — *Walt Disney Home Video*

Silence of the North 1981
Drama
47424 94 mins C B, V P
Ellen Burstyn, Tom Skerrit
A true story about a widow with three children struggling to survive under rugged pioneer conditions on the Canadian frontier.
MPAA:PG
Universal — *MCA Home Video*

Silent Enemy, The 1930
Indians-North American/Documentary
12853 110 mins B/W B, V, FO P
An interesting documentary which tells the Ojibway Indian's way of life before the arrival of the white man. The title is a reference to hunger.
Unknown — *Video Yesteryear; Blackhawk Films; Classic Video Cinema Collector's Club*

Silent Laugh Makers No. 1 192?
Comedy
11283 50 mins B/W B, V, FO P
Charlie Chase, Stan Laurel, Oliver Hardy, Charlie Chaplin, Ben Turpin, Arthur Lake
A collection of four hilarious short movies from the silent picture era: "One Mama Man," "Lucky Dog," "His Night Out," and "Hop-a-Long."
Hal Roach — *Video Yesteryear*

Silent Laugh Makers No. 2 192?
Comedy
11284 50 mins B/W B, V, FO P
Charlie Chase, Oliver Hardy, Billy Bevan
Four short funny films of the silent era: "Fluttering Hearts," "Long Live the King," and "A Sea Dog Tale."
Hal Roach — *Video Yesteryear*

Silent Laugh Makers #3 192?
Comedy
66141 55 mins B/W B, V, FO P
Harry Langdon, Harold Lloyd, Bebe Daniels, Snub Pollard
Four comedy shorts: "Picking Peaches" (1924), directed by Frank Capra, Langdon's first for Mack Sennett; "All Tied Up" (1925), featuring "A Ton of Fun"—four rotund comedians; "Don't Shove" (1919), featuring Harold Lloyd wooing Bebe Daniels; "Some Baby" (1922), with Snub Pollard, written by Hal Roach.
Hal Roach et al — *Video Yesteryear*

Silent Movies—In Color 19??
Film-History
56915 52 mins C B, V, FO P
Five films produced in France between 1904 and 1914 in which color tints were added one frame at a time by hand. Films include: "The Nobleman's Dog," "Bob's Electric Theatre," "A Slave's Love," "A New Way of Traveling," and "The Life of Our Savior."
French — *Video Yesteryear*

Silent Night Bloody Night 1973
Horror
66265 90 mins C B, V P
Patrick O'Neal, John Carradine, Walter Able
A tale of madness set in a gothic mansion.
Cannon Releasing; Ami Artzi — *Paragon Video Productions; Electric Video*

Silent Partner, The 1978
Drama
45068   103 mins   C   B, V, LV,   P
                              CED
Elliot Gould, Christopher Plummer, Susannah York
A bank teller foils a robbery, but keeps some of the money for himself. Trouble ensues because the robber knows it and wants the money.
EMC Film Corp — *Vestron Video*

Silent Rage 1982
Adventure/Martial arts
62811   100 mins   C   B, V   P
Chuck Norris, Ron Silver, Steven Keats, Toni Kalem, Brian Libby
The sheriff of a small Texas town must destroy a murderous killer who has been made indestructible through genetic engineering.
MPAA:R
Columbia — *RCA/Columbia Pictures Home Video; RCA VideoDiscs*

Silent Running 1971
Science fiction
53393   90 mins   C   B, V   P
Bruce Dern, Cliff Potts, Ron Rifkin
Members of a space station crew in 2001 are space gardening to replenish a nuclear-devastated earth.
MPAA:G
Universal; Michel Gruskoff; Doug Trumbull — *MCA Home Video*

Silent Scream 1980
Horror
59669   87 mins   C   B, V   P
Rebecca Balding, Cameron Mitchell, Avery Schreiber, Barbara Steele, Steve Doubet, Brad Reardon, Yvonne De Carlo
A gloomy old victorian mansion by the sea has a silent terror lurking within the walls.
MPAA:R
Jim Wheat; Ken Wheat — *Media Home Entertainment*

Silent Valley 1935
Western
14394   60 mins   B/W   B, V   P
Tom Tyler
Adventure in the Old West with American cowboy star Tom Tyler.
Commodore — *Video Connection*

Silk Stockings 1957
Musical/Comedy
52747   117 mins   C   B, V   P
Fred Astaire, Cyd Charisse, Janis Paige, Peter Lorre, George Tobias, directed by Rouben Mamoulian
A musical comedy adaptation of ''Ninotchka,'' with Astaire as a charming American movie

man, and Charisse as a Soviet official. Music and lyrics by Cole Porter highlight this film adapted from George S. Kaufman's hit Broadway play.
MGM; Arthur Freed — *MGM/UA Home Video*

Silkwood 1983
Drama
65720   131 mins   C   B, V, LV,   P
                              CED
Meryl Streep, Kurt Russell, Cher
A dramatization of the life of Karen Silkwood, the nuclear plant worker ad activist, who died in the 1974 under suspicious circumstances while investigating shoddy practices at ther plant.
MPAA:R
Mike Nichols; Michael Hausman — *Embassy Home Entertainment*

Silver Queen 1942
Western
72055   81 mins   B/W   B, V   P
Priscilla Lane, George Brent, Bruce Cabot
A woman gambles in order to pay her father's debts, only to have her boyfriend spend the money on a silver mine.
United Artists — *Independent United Distributors*

Silver Spurs 1943
Western
57981   60 mins   B/W   B, V   P
Roy Rogers, Jerome Cowan, John Carradine
Ranchers waiting to get the right-of-way through oil land run into an ambitious resort owner.
Republic — *Video Connection*

Silver Streak 1976
Comedy
41078   113 mins   C   B, V, CED   P
Gene Wilder, Jill Clayburgh, Patrick McGoohan
Gene Wilder becomes involved with murder, intrigue, and a beautiful woman aboard a transcontinental express train.
MPAA:PG EL, SP
20th Century Fox — *CBS/Fox Video*

Silver Streak 1934
Drama
54115   72 mins   B/W   B, V   P, T
Sally Blane, Charles Starett, Arthur Lake, Edgar Kennedy
A young train designer creates a super fast diesel train. The son of a rival train builder develops paralysis and his only hope of survival is to get an iron lung as quickly as possible. The diesel train is asked to the job. In spite of a murder attempt, a runaway engine, an open bridge span, and a frightened crew, the train arrives in time.
RKO — *Blackhawk Films*

Silverstone '83　　　　1983
Motorcycles
72858　　60 mins　　C　　B, V　　　　P
Highlights from the Silverstone 1983 Motorcycle race are shown.
Videovision Broadcast Production — *Motor Cycle Video*

Simon　　　　1980
Comedy
52715　　97 mins　　C　　B, V　　　　R, P
Alan Arkin, Madeline Kahn, directed by Marshall Brickman
A group of demented scientists brainwash a college professor into believing that his real mother is a Martian spaceship.
MPAA:PG
Orion Pictures — *Warner Home Video*

Simon & Garfunkel: The Concert in Central Park　　　　1982
Music-Performance
47402　　87 mins　　C　　B, V, LV, CED　　　　P
Paul Simon, Art Garfunkel
The September 1981 reunion concert by Simon and Garfunkel before 500,000 delirious fans in New York's Central Park is captured on this tape. Among the 20 selections performed are "April Come She Will," "Mrs. Robinson," "Scarborough Fair" and "The Sounds of Silence."
James Signorelli — *CBS/Fox Video*

Simon of the Desert　　　　1966
Drama
48750　　43 mins　　B/W　　B, V　　　　P
Directed by Luis Bunuel
A mocking allegory which tells of a man's fall from grace.
SP
Unknown — *Shoik Vidoo; Budgot Vidoo; Discount Video Tapes*

Simple Plumbing Repair　　　　1980
Home improvement
44275　　25 mins　　C　　V　　　　P
This program offers a practical step-by-step procedure for fixing over 80% of home plumbing problems, covering leaks, clogging, and replacement of worn parts. It saves money because parts are reasonably priced, and often aren't needed at all.
American Home Video Library — *American Home Video Library*

Simple Story, A　　　　1980
Drama
59383　　110 mins　　C　　B, V　　　　P
Romy Schneider, Bruno Cremer, Claude Brasseur, directed by Claude Sautet
A woman faces her fortieth birthday with increasing uneasiness, though her life seems perfect from the outside.
Columbia — *RCA/Columbia Pictures Home Video*

Simtameciu Godos　　　　1969
Documentary/USSR
53717　　22 mins　　B/W　　B, V, 3/4U　　　　P
An award-winning documentary about Lithuania's centenarian citizens.
USSR — *International Historic Films*

Sin of Adam and Eve, The　　　　1972
Drama
69804　　72 mins　　C　　B, V　　　　P
Candy Wilson, George Rivers
This is the story of Adam and Eve in the Garden of Eden and their fall from grace.
MPAA:R
Michael Zachary — *VCI Home Video*

Sin of Harold Diddlebock, The　　　　1947
Comedy
11312　　95 mins　　B/W　　B, V, FO　　　　P
Harold Lloyd, Raymond Walburn, Edgar Kennedy, Franklin Pangborn
Harold Lloyd's last film which folows the life of the hero of Lloyd's classic silent picture, "The Freshman," in later years.
Preston Sturges — *Video Yesteryear; Budget Video; Discount Video Tapes; Glenn Video Vistas; Sheik Video; Cable Films; King of Video; Video Connection; Western Film & Video Inc; Classic Video Cinema Collector's Club*

Sinbad and the Eye of the Tiger　　　　1977
Fantasy
21296　　113 mins　　C　　B, V, LV　　　　P
Patrick Wayne, Jane Seymour, Taryn Power
The swashbuckling adventures of Sinbad the Sailor.
Columbia — *RCA/Columbia Pictures Home Video; RCA VideoDiscs*

Sinbad the Sailor　　　　1947
Drama
00310　　117 mins　　C　　B, V, 3/4U　　　　P
Douglas Fairbanks Jr., Maureen O'Hara, Anthony Quinn
Swashbuckler seeks a treasure island in this Arabian Nights film.
RKO; Stephen Ames — *Nostalgia Merchant; VidAmerica; King of Video*

Sing Along with Little Lulu　　　　1983
Cartoons
66472　　86 mins　　C　　B, V　　　　P
Animated

Little Lulu is herewith featured in a special collection of her popular cartoons.
Famous Studios — *NTA Home Entertainment*

Sing Along with Mitch 1961
Music/Variety
52462   52 mins   B/W   B, V, FO   P
Mitch Miller and the Sing Along Gang, Leslie Uggams, Diana Trask
This episode of the popular 60's series features Leslie Uggams in her first TV appearance. Mitch and the Sing Along Gang perform "Heart of My Heart," "Sweet Rosie O'Grady," "The Sidewalks of New York," and other songs.
NBC — *Video Yesteryear*

Sing, Cowboy, Sing 1937
Western
08793   60 mins   B/W   B, V, 3/4U   P
Tex Ritter
Badmen murder to end a wagon train franchise.
Grand Natl — *Penguin Video*

Sing While You're Able 1937
Musical
08743   68 mins   B/W   B, V, 3/4U   P
Pinky Tomlin, Toby Wing
Lively musical comedy.
Ambassador; Conn — *Penguin Video*

Sing Your Worries Away 1942
Musical/Comedy
45102   71 mins   B/W   B, V   P, T
Buddy Ebsen, Bert Lahr, June Havoc
Two struggling songwriters and their girlfriends get entangled in a gaint swindle.
RKO — *Blackhawk Films*

Singer Presents Elvis (The 1968 Comeback Special) Outtakes 1968
Music-Performance/Outtakes and bloopers
47488   54 mins   C   B, V, FO   P
Elvis Presley
Scenes and songs from Elvis' famous 1968 Singer special that were cut for being too sexy, too long, or because mistakes were made.
NBC — *Video Yesteryear*

Singer Presents "Elvis" (The 1968 Comeback Special) 1968
Music-Performance
47501   52 mins   C   B, V, FO   P
Elvis Presley
The famous TV spectacular that brought Elvis back to performing in public. Songs featured include "Heartbreak Hotel," "Hound Dog" and "All Shook Up." Originally telecast on December 3, 1968.
NBC — *Video Yesteryear*

Singin' in the Rain 1952
Musical
39087   103 mins   C   B, V, CED   P
Gene Kelly, Donald O'Connor, Jean Hagen, Debbie Reynolds, Rita Moreno, Cyd Charisse, directed by Gene Kelly and Stanley Donen
One of the all-time great movie musicals—an affectionate spoof of the turmoil that afflicted the motion picture industry in the late 1920's during the changeover from silent films to sound. Songs include the title tune, "Make 'Em Laugh," "All I Do Is Dream of You," and "You Are My Lucky Star." Music and lyrics by Arthur Freed and Nacio Herb Brown.
MGM — *MGM/UA Home Video*

Sinister Urge, The 1960
Drama
73553   82 mins   B/W   B, V   P
Directed by Ed Wood
An early Ed Wood film about two policemen who are searching for the murderer of three call girls.
Edward Wood — *Admit One Video*

Sioux City Sue 1946
Western/Musical
44805   69 mins   B/W   B, V   P, T
Gene Autry, Lynne Roberts, Sterling Holloway
Talent scouts are looking for a singing cowboy, find Gene, then trick him into being the voice of a talking donkey.
Republic — *Blackhawk Films; Video Connection*

Sir Arthur Conan Doyle 1927
Literature-English/Biographical
59411   11 mins   B/W   B, V   P, T
An intimate portrait of the man who created Sherlock Holmes.
Unknown — *Blackhawk Films*

Sister Kenny 1946
Drama
10061   116 mins   B/W   B, V   P, T
Rosalind Russell, Dean Jagger, Alexander Knox
Follows story of legendary nurse crusading for her treatment of infantile paralysis. Based on Elizabeth Kenny's novel, "And They Shall Walk."
RKO; Dudley Nichols — *Blackhawk Films*

Sisters 1973
Horror
53521   93 mins   C   B, V   R, P
Margot Kidder, Charles Durning, directed by Brian DePalma
Siamese twins separated at birth are involved in a murder and the wrong one is arrested.
MPAA:R
American International; Edward R Pressman — *Warner Home Video*

Sisters of Death   1978
Suspense
48415   87 mins   C   B, V   P
Arthur Franz, Claudia Jennings
Five women who were once members of a
secret club are invited to a reunion at a remote
castle in California. There they are trapped by
an evil man on the edge of madness.
MPAA:PG
John B Kelly Presentations — *VCI Home Video*

Sisters of Satan   197?
Horror
69034   91 mins   C   B, V   P
The nuns of the infamous convent St.
Archangelo choose to survive by trading God for
the devil.
Tony Cervi — *Gorgon Video*

Sitting Ducks   1980
Comedy
66066   88 mins   C   B, V   P
*Michael Emil, Zack Norman, directed by Henry
Jaglom*
Two friends involved in a scam attempt to
outrun the moball the while swapping songs and
confessions.
MPAA:R
Meira Attia Dor — *Media Home Entertainment*

Six Gun Rhythm   1939
Western
56603   59 mins   B/W   B, V   P
Tex Fletcher
Murder and mystery in an action western.
Grand National — *Video Dimensions*

600 Days to Cocos Island   1975
Adventure
66240   93 mins   C   B, V   R, P
A story about a young couple who sell
everything and sail away to adventure.
Gene Evans — *Video City Productions*

Six Pack   1982
Adventure
63396   108 mins   C   B, V, CED   P
*Kenny Rogers, Diane Lane, Erin Gray, Barry
Corbin*
Rogers stars as Brewster Baker, who returns to
the stock car racing circuit with the help of six
larcenous orphans adept at mechanics.
MPAA:PG
Kenny Loggins Productions — *CBS/Fox Video*

Six Shootin' Sheriff   1938
Western
11374   59 mins   B/W   B, V   P
Ken Maynard
A member of a wild gang redeems himself and
turns sheriff to make up for all his evil ways.

Worldwide — *VCI Home Video; Video
Yesteryear; Video Connection; Sheik Video*

Six Weeks   1982
Comedy-Drama
68268   107 mins   C   B, V   P
*Dudley Moore, Mary Tyler Moore, Katherine
Healy*
Two opposite people are brought together by
the illness of a little girl.
MPAA:PG
Peter Guber; Jon Peters — *RCA/Columbia
Pictures Home Video; RCA VideoDiscs*

Sixteen Candles   1984
Comedy
73183   93 mins   C   B, V   P
*Molly Ringwald, Paul Dooley, Anthony Michael
Hall, directed by John Hughes*
Molly Ringwald stars as a young girl who has
just turned sweet sixteen and no one
remembers her birthday. Title song performed
by The Stray Cats.
MPAA:PG
Hilton A Green; Universal — *MCA Home Video*

6th Marine Division on   1945
Okinawa, The
World War II/Armed Forces-US
53683   56 mins   C   B, V, 3/4U   P
A film record of the bloody 1945 battle against
the Japanese.
US Navy — *International Historic Films*

$64,000 Question   195?
Game show
58636   29 mins   B/W   B, V, FO   P
Hosted by Hal March
This episode of the classic show which ushered
in the big-money quiz game features a
Philippine-American lady lawyer who decides to
keep her money, Virgil Earp (Wyatt's nephew)
winning $32,000 in the Wild West category, and
a Brooklyn woman winning $4,000 in the opera
category. Sponsored by Revlon.
CBS — *Video Yesteryear*

Skateboard Madness   198?
Sports
75584   92 mins   C   B, V   P
This program offers a tour of skating spots and
performing skateboarding celebrities.
MPAA:PG
Unknown — *Monterey Home Video*

Ski   1978
Sports-Winter
44923   30 mins   C   B, V   P
Fitness expert Ann Dugan demonstrates
exercises for skiers which show how to exert
constant muscular effort to maintain body

position, move with agility, and avoid injury.
From the "Sports Conditioning" series.
Health N Action — *RCA/Columbia Pictures Home Video*

Ski Instructors Holiday 197?
Sports-Winter
19411   30 mins   C   B, V, 3/4U,   P
                                          Q
A group of American skiers visit Chamioux, France, compare American and French teaching methods, and mix in a little entertainment.
TV Sports Scene — *TV Sports Scene*

Ski Scene 197?
Sports-Winter
48382   30 mins   C   B, V, 3/4U   P
13   pgms
Ski celebrities from around the world meet in famous ski areas to show off their talents on the slopes. Programs are available individually.
1.Steamboat 2.Steamboat Springs, Colorado 3.Vail, Colorado 4.Jackson Hole, Wyoming 5.Aspen, Colorado 6.New Hampshire 7.Utah 8.Taos, New Mexico 9.NASTAR 10.The Super Experts Ski the Limits 11.Squaw Valley, California 12.Stowe, Vermont 13.Ski Stars
TV Sports Scene — *TV Sports Scene*

Ski-Vision One 1978
Sports-Winter
33730   30 mins   C   B, V, 3/4U,   P
                                          Q
Suzy Chaffee
The program recalls the pioneer days of skiing in the 1920's, then moves on to a race between a mad motorcyclist and a skier down the 18,000 Piz Corvatsch in Switzerland, coverage of ballet skiers, and an adventure starring Suzy Chaffee, and Abominable Snowman, and a Caped Crusader on skis.
Willy Bogner, TV Sports Scene — *TV Sports Scene*

Ski-Vision Two 1978
Sports-Winter
33731   30 mins   C   B, V, 3/4U,   P
                                          Q
Suzy Chaffee, Gerald Ford, Omar Sharif, the Shah of Iran
An old-fashioned ski race in which everyone starts down the hill at the same time, is held in St. Moritz, Switzerland. The scene shifts to Vail, Colorado, and Snowbird, Utah for talks with ski celebrities Gerald Ford, Omar Sharif, and the Shah of Iran.
TV Sports Scene — *TV Sports Scene*

Ski-Vision Three 1978
Sports-Winter
33732   30 mins   C   B, V, 3/4U   P
Fuzzi Garhammer, Willy Bogner, Suzy Chaffee

Superb freestyle skiing, a comedy sketch featuring three policemen on skis trying to maintain order on a crowded mountain, and a chase between Suzy Chaffee and an Abominable Snowman are contained in this program.
Willy Bagner, TV Sports Scene — *TV Sports Scene*

Ski-Vision Four 1978
Sports-Winter
33733   30 mins   C   B, V, 3/4U,   P
                                          Q
Jean-Claude Killy, Tony Sailer, Guy Perillat, Buddy Werner
A tribute to some of the world's greatest skiers accompanied by music performed by the 48-piece London Symphony Orchestra, and the beauty of the Swiss Alps.
Willy Bagner, TV Sports Scene — *TV Sports Scene*

Skiing Lessons with Gene 1982
Heinz Landsmann 1
Sports-Winter
59168   60 mins   C   B, V, 3/4U,   R, P
                                          FO
Skiing expert Gene Heinz Landsmann guides the beginning skier from the simple straight fun and basic wedge turns through basic Christie turns and the early stages of parallel skiing.
Star Video Prods — *Star Video Productions*

Skiing Lessons with Gene 1982
Heinz Landsmann 2
Sports-Winter
59169   60 mins   C   B, V, 3/4U,   R, P
                                          FO
In this program, Landsmann discusses parallel turns, approaches to quick, short, swing turns into fall line, and skiing moguls and powder.
Star Video Prods — *Star Video Productions*

Skull and Crown 1935
Adventure
08617   60 mins   B/W   B, V, 3/4U   P
Rin-Tin-Tin, Jr., Regis Toomey, Jack Mulhall, Molly O'Day, Jack Mower
An adventure story featuring the lovable Rin-Tin-Tin, Jr. A favorite of children.
Reliance — *Penguin Video*

Sky Bandits 1940
Western
15444   56 mins   B/W   B, V   P
James Newill, Dave O'Brien, Louise Stanley
Mounties uncover mystery of disappearing plane carrying gold from Yukon mine. A Renfew picture.
Monogram; Grand Natl — *Video Connection*

Sky High 1973
Aeronautics
57195   59 mins   C   B, V   P
The Air Force Thunderbirds
This program traces the history of pylon racing,
from the first track at Theims, France, in 1909,
to the Cleveland Air Races. The program
provides aerobatics, wing walking,
barnstorming, gliding, sky diving, hang gliding,
ballooning, and just about every kind of flying
imaginable.
AM Available
Manuel Arango — *Alti Corporation*

Sky's The Limit, The 1943
Comedy
43017   89 mins   B/W   B, V, FO   P
Fred Astaire, Joan Leslie
A war hero spends his leave in New York City
dressed in civilian clothes and falls in love.
RKO; David Hempstead — *Video Yesteryear;
King of Video; Nostalgia Merchant*

Slap, The 1976
Comedy
65721   103 mins   C   CED   P
Isabelle Adjani, Lino Ventura
This program is meant to express the problems
of adults and young people when they arrive at
certain equinoxes in their lives.
MPAA:PG
Joseph Green — *Embassy Home
Entertainment (disc only)*

Slap Shot 1977
Comedy-Drama
14005   123 mins   C   B, V, LV   P
*Paul Newman, Michael Ontkean, Jennifer
Warren, Lindsay Crouse, Strother Martin,
directed by George Roy Hill*
A satire of the world of professional hockey. An
over-the-hill player-coach gathers an odd-ball
mixture of has-beens and young players and
reluctantly initiates using violence on the ice to
make his team win.
MPAA:R
Universal; Robert J Wunsch; Stephen
Friedman — *MCA Home Video*

Slaughterhouse Five 1972
Science fiction/Folklore
62728   104 mins   C   B, V   P
Michael Sacks, Ron Leibman, Valerie Perrine
A suburban optometrist comes unstuck in time
and he experiences events during World War II,
in the future on an alien planet and even his own
death.
AM Available MPAA:R
Universal — *MCA Home Video*

Slave of the Cannibal 1979
God
Adventure
59300   86 mins   C   CED   P
Stacy Keach, Ursula Andress, Claudio Cassinelli
A beautiful woman, searching for her missing
husband in the jungles of New Guinea, hires a
man bent on revenge against the human-eating
cannibals as her guide.
MPAA:R
Dania Film — *Vestron Video*

Slave Trade in the World 1964
Today
Documentary/Exploitation
64995   87 mins   C   B, V   P
Directed by Roberto Malenotti
Slavery practices in the modern world are
shown, including actual scenes of a sheik's
harem, slave auctions and the kidnapping and
selling of young women.
Continental; GESI Cinematographica-CIAS-Les
Films Agiman — *VIDCREST*

Slavers 1977
Drama
66233   102 mins   C   B, V   R, P
*Trevor Howard, Britt Ekland, Ron Ely, Cameron
Mitchell, Ray Milland*
A tale of the African slave trade a la
"Mandingo."
MPAA:R
Jurgen Goslav — *Video City Productions*

Slaves of Love 197?
Drama
59549   86 mins   C   B, V   P
Two men, stranded on a desert island, discover
it is inhabited by sex-starved females.
Dave Ackerman — *Media Home Entertainment*

Sleeper 1973
Comedy/Science fiction
64331   88 mins   C   CED   P
*Woody Allen, Diane Keaton, John Beck,
directed by Woody Allen*
A New York schnook is frozen solid after a
botched operation and revived two hundred
years in the future, where he inadvertently gets
mixed up with the political underground.
MPAA:PG
United Artists — *RCA VideoDiscs*

Sleeping Beauty 1982
Dance
76677   120 mins   C   B, V   P
*Fernando Bujones, Maryse Egasse, Berthica
Prieto, Elba Rey, the Corps de Ballet and
soloists of the Ballet del Teatro*
This made-for-video production of the
Tchaikovsky ballet was taped live at the Ballet
del Teatro Municipal in Santiago, Chile and is a
recreation of the 1939 Sadler's Wells staging.

Kultur — *Kultur*

Billie C Lange — *Billie C. Lange*

Sleeping Beauty 1983
Fairy tales
Closed Captioned
69322　　60 mins　　C　　B, V, LV, 　　　　P
　　　　　　　　　　　　　　CED
Christopher Reeve, Bernadette Peters, Beverly D'Angelo
The classic tale of Sleeping Beauty and the handsome prince who wakens her is told by combining live action and animation. Part of "Faerie Tale Theatre."
Shelley Duvall — *CBS/Fox Video*

Sleeping Dogs 1982
Drama
65729　　107 mins　　C　　B, V　　　　P
Sam Neill, Warren Oates
A man is caught between two powers: a repressive government and a violent resistance movement.
Roger Donaldson — *VidAmerica*

Sleuth 1972
Suspense/Mystery
37413　　138 mins　　C　　B, V　　　　P
Sir Laurence Olivier, Michael Caine, Margo Channing, directed by Joseph L. Mankiewicz
A mystery novelist takes his work to the limits by playing diabolical and deadly tricks on his guest.
MPAA:PG
20th Century Fox — *Media Home Entertainment*

Slightly Honorable 1939
Mystery
08720　　85 mins　　B/W　　B, V　　　　P
Pat O'Brien, Broderick Crawford, Edward Arnold, Eve Arden, directed by Tay Barnett
Crime in high society and police grafters, as a lawyer tangles with crooked politics.
United Artists; Walter Wanger — *Movie Buff Video; Penguin Video*

Slim and Trim Yoga with Billie In and Out of Pool 1980
Yoga/Physical fitness
63547　　24 mins　　C　　B, V, 3/4U　　　　P
This entertaining and instructional program presents a system of exercises and meditation on dry land and in the water.
Billie C. Lange — *Billie C. Lange*

Slim and Trim Yoga with Billie Out of Pool 1983
Yoga/Physical fitness
76404　　24 mins　　C　　B, V, 3/4U　　　　P
This entertaining and instructional program presents a system of exercises and meditation out of the pool.

Slim and Trim Yoga with Billie In Pool 1983
Yoga/Physical fitness
76403　　24 mins　　C　　B, V, 3/4U　　　　P
This entertaining and instructional program presents a system of exercises and meditation in the water.
Billie C Lange — *Billie C. Lange*

Slim Gourmet, The 1984
Cookery
72901　　90 mins　　C　　B, V　　　　P
Barbara Gibbons, narrated by McLean Stevenson
Barbara Gibbons demonstrates the preparation of gourmet dishes that are low in calories.
Media Home Entertainment — *Media Home Entertainment*

Slime People 1963
Horror
58547　　76 mins　　B/W　　B, V　　　　R, P
Robert Hutton, Les Tremayne, Robert Burton
Huge prehistoric monsters are let loose by an atomic explosion in Los Angeles.
Hansen Pictures — *Video Gems*

Slithis 1979
Science fiction
42911　　86 mins　　C　　B, V　　　　P
This science fiction thriller has nature unleashing its revenge from the pollution of nuclear waste. Slithis was the killer they could not destroy.
Dick Davis — *Media Home Entertainment*

Slumber Party '57 1976
Comedy
55745　　83 mins　　C　　B, V, LV　　　　P
At a slumber party, six girls get together and exchange stories of how they lost their virginity. Music by the Platters, Big Bopper, Jerry Lee Lewis, the Crewcuts, and Paul and Paula.
Unknown — *Vestron Video*

Small Change 1976
Comedy
54804　　104 mins　　C　　B, V　　　　R, P
Geory Desmouceaux, Philippe Goldman, Jean-Francois Stevenin, Chantal Mercier, Francis Devlaeminck, directed by Francois Truffaut
"Small Change" captures the precious feeling of what it is like to be a child. It consists of a series of anecdotes, conversations, vignettes, and reflections—all spinning around the triumphs, frustrations, and intimate longings of a group of French children.
MPAA:PG

　　　　(For Explanation of codes, see USE GUIDE and KEY)

New World Pictures; Roger Corman — *Warner Home Video*

Small Town in Texas, A   1976
Drama
64359   96 mins   C   B, V, CED   P
Timothy Bottoms, Susan George, Bo Hopkins
An ex-con returns home seeking revenge on the sheriff who framed him.
MPAA:PG
American International — *Vestron Video*

Smallmouth Bass   1981
Fishing
65151   30 mins   C   B, V   P
Homer Circle, Al Lindner, Glen Lau
Experts demonstrate the methods they use in lakes and rivers to consistently take smallmouth bass. Part of the "Sportsman's Video Collection."
Glen Lau — *Leisure Time Products Project/3M*

Smash Palace   1982
Drama
65363   100 mins   C   B, V   P
Bruno Lawrence, Anna Jemison, Greer Robson, Keith Aberdein
Smash Palace is a compelling drama of a marriage jeopardized by a man's obsession with auto racing, and a women's need for love and affection.
Roger Donaldson — *Vestron Video*

Smash-Up   1947
Drama
05481   103 mins   B/W   B, V   P
Susan Hayward, Lee Bowman, Marsha Hunt, Eddie Albert
A famous singer becomes an alcoholic, and her constant drunkenness drives her husband and child away.
United Artists — *Movie Buff Video*

Smashing of the Reich, The   1962
World War II
42962   84 mins   B/W   B, V, FO   P
This program examines the fall of the German war machine with emphasis on air power.
Unknown — *Video Yesteryear; International Historic Films; Penguin Video; Discount Video Tapes; Interurban Films*

Smokey and the Bandit   1977
Comedy
14008   96 mins   C   B, V, LV   P
Burt Reynolds, Sally Field, Jackie Gleason, Jerry Reed, Mike Henry, directed by Hal Needham
A legendary truck driver and CB radio fanatic gives a lift to a female hitchhiker and sets off a crazy chain of events climaxing in a wild car chase.
MPAA:PG
Universal; Mort Engleberg — *MCA Home Video; RCA VideoDiscs*

Smokey and the Bandit II   1980
Comedy
48637   101 mins   C   B, V, LV, CED   P
Burt Reynolds, Sally Field, Jackie Gleason, Jerry Reed, Mike Henry
The sequel to "Smokey and the Bandit." The Bandit is hired to transport a pregnant elephant from Miami to the Republican convention in Dallas. Sheriff Buford T. Justice and family are in hot pursuit.
MPAA:PG
Universal — *MCA Home Video*

Smokey and the Bandit Part 3   1983
Comedy/Adventure
66330   86 mins   C   B, V, LV, CED   P
Jackie Gleason, Paul Williams, Jerry Reed, Pat McCormick
In this third installment of the "Smokey" saga, Sheriff Buford T. Justice is ready to retire when he is given the racing challenge of his life.
MPAA:PG
Universal — *MCA Home Video*

Smokey and the Judge   1980
Adventure/Comedy
63413   90 mins   C   B, V   P
Gene Price, Wayde Preston, Juanita Curiel
A police officer has his hands full with a trio of lovely ladies.
MPAA:PG
Harry Hope — *Sun Video*

Smokey Smith   1936
Western
15510   59 mins   B/W   B, V   P
Bob Steele
Justice is brought to outlaws who murdered a man's parents on a wagon.
Artclass — *Video Connection*

Smouldering Fires   1925
Drama
65199   100 mins   B/W   B, V   P
Pauline Frederick, Laura La Plante, Tully Marshall, directed by Clarence Brown
A tough businesswoman falls in love with an ambitious young employee, who is fifteen years younger than her. After they marry, problems arise in the form of the wife's attractive younger sister.
Universal Jewel — *Video Yesteryear*

Smurfs and the Magic Flute, The 1981
Cartoons
65376   74 mins   C   B, V, LV, CED   P
Animated
The Smurfs star in this musical tale about a flute with magical powers.
MPAA:G
Hanna Barbera Sepp
International — *Children's Video Library*

Snake in the Monkey's Shadow 1982
Martial arts/Suspense
75628   85 mins   C   B, V   P
A martial arts expert demonstrates the deadliest fighting techniques.
MPAA:R
Ng See Yuen — *Trans World Entertainment*

Snow Dream 19??
Sports
19412   15 mins   C   B, V, 3/4U, Q   P
Aerial photography captures the action and excitement of snowmobiling in the great winter outdoors.
Ted Higgenbotham — *TV Sports Scene*

Snow Queen, The 1984
Fairy tales
Closed Captioned
73570   60 mins   C   B, V, CED   P
Melissa Gilbert, Lee Remick, Lance Kerwin
From "Fairy Tale Theatre" comes the adaptation of the Hans Christian Andersen tale about a boy and a girl who grow up together and are separated by evil spirits.
Gaylord Productions; Platypus Productions — *CBS/Fox Video*

Snow, The Movie 1983
Comedy
65648   83 mins   C   B, V   R, P
David Argue, Lance Curtis
Skiing, growing up, romance and good times is what it's all about in this film from 'down under.'
Snow Films Ltd — *Video City Productions*

Snow Treasure 1967
Adventure
66624   96 mins   C   B, V   P
James Franciscus, Ilona Rodgers, Paul Austad, Raoul Oyen
A group of children work to keep the Nazis from finding a cache of gold that is hidden in their Norwegian village. Filmed on location.
MPAA:PG
Sagittarius Productions — *U.S.A. Home Video*

Snow White Live at Radio City Music Hall 1980
Variety
55569   90 mins   C   B, V   R, P
Disney's film classic has been transformed into a stage show presented at New York City's Radio City Music Hall. The original music remains intact and a finale has been added.
Walt Disney — *Walt Disney Home Video*

Snowball Express 1972
Comedy
63125   120 mins   C   B, V   R, P
Dean Jones, Nancy Olson, Harry Morgan, Keenan Wynn
When a New York City accountant inherits a hotel in the Rocky Mountains, he decides to move his family there. Upon arrival, they find that the place is falling apart.
MPAA:G
Walt Disney Productions — *Walt Disney Home Video*

Snowman, The 1982
Cartoons
76673   26 mins   C   B, V   P
This program presents an animated story of a snowman who comes to life.
Snowman Enterprises LTD — *Sony Corporation of America*

So Fine 1981
Comedy
47395   91 mins   C   B, V   R, P
Ryan O'Neal, Jack Warden, Mariangela Melato, Richard Kiel, directed by Andrew Bergman
Ryan O'Neal is a pants manufacturer who invents cellophane pants. Orders pour in for the new peekaboo style and zaniness ensues.
MPAA:R
Warner Bros; Mike Lobell — *Warner Home Video*

So This is Washington 1943
Comedy
08721   mins   B/W   B, V, 3/4U   P
Lum and Abner
Lum and Abner comedy genius.
Unknown — *Penguin Video*

Soap Opera Scandals 197?
Outtakes and bloopers
56615   50 mins   C   B, V   P
Ruth Warrick
Heroes and heroines of television's daytime soap operas are seen in outtakes as lines are blown, props fall, and the dialogue turns risque.
Unknown — *Video Dimensions*

S.O.B. 1981
Comedy
53554   121 mins   C   B, V, CED   P

        (For Explanation of codes, see USE GUIDE and KEY)

Julie Andrews, William Holden, Richard Mulligan, Robert Preston, Shelley Winters, Robert Webber, Marisa Berenson, Robert Vaughn, Larry Hagman
Blake Edwards' bitter farce about Hollywood and the film industry wheelers and dealers who inhabit it. When a multi-million dollar picture bombs at the box office, the director turns suicidal, until he envisions reshooting it with a steamy, X-rated scene starring his wife, a star with a goody-two-shoes image.
MPAA:R
Blake Edwards; Tony Adams — *CBS/Fox Video*

Soccer for Everyone   197?
Soccer
33780   120 mins   C   B, V, 3/4U   P
Kyle Rote Jr., Bob Rigby, Julie Veee, Al Miller
2 pgms
Part I of this series covers skills necessary in soccer, including dribbling, attacking, defending, and goalkeeping. Part II covers such topics as fitness, starting a team, and laws and referees. Each part is available individually.
1.The Action Skills 2.Understanding the Game
Unknown — *Sports World Cinema*

Social Secretary, The   1916
Comedy
64307   45 mins   B/W   B, V   P
Norma Talmadge, Erich von Stroheim
A demure social secretary tries her best to avoid the attentions of a nosy reporter. Silent with musical score.
First National — *Classic Video Cinema Collector's Club*

Sodom and Gomorrah   1979
Drama/Bible
55012   49 mins   C   B, V   P
Ed Ames, Dorothy Malone, Peter Mark Richman, Rick Jason, David Opatoshu, Gene Barry, narrated by Victor Jory
The story of Lot and his wife and the sinful cities of Sodom and Gomorrah. Part of the "Greatest Heroes of the Bible" series.
Sunn Classics — *Vanguard Video*

Soft Cell   1983
Music-Performance
66022   55 mins   C   B, V   R, P
"Tainted Love" and "Memorabilia" are two of the hits performed by this talented new band.
EMI Music — *THORN EMI Home Video*

Soldier, The   1982
Drama
63370   90 mins   C   B, V, CED   P
Ken Wahl, Klaus Kinski
The Russians are holding the world at ransom with a pile of stolen plutonium, and a soldier finds himself in the position to carry out an unauthorized and dangerous plan to preserve the balance of world power.
MPAA:R
Embassy — *Embassy Home Entertainment*

Soldier Blue   1970
Western
13665   109 mins   C   B, V, CED   P
Candice Bergen, Peter Strauss, Donald Pleasance, Dana Elcar, directed by Ralph Nelson
A western adventure about a U.S. Calvary unit escorting gold across Cheyenne territory.
MPAA:R
Avco Embassy — *Embassy Home Entertainment*

Soldier in Love   1967
Drama
64856   76 mins   C   B, V, 3/4U   P
Jean Simmons, Claire Bloom, Keith Michell, directed by George Schaefer
This teleplay from "George Schaefer's Showcase Theatre" is based on the life of John Churchill, first Duke of Marlborough, and his wife Sarah. The ambitious young couple held the favor of Queen Anne for a time, until political intrigue brought about their downfall.
George Schaefer — *Enter-Tel Inc*

Soldier's Tale, The   1984
Cartoons/Music
73015   60 mins   C   B, V   P
Animated, voices of Max Von Sydow and Andre Gregory
Igor Stravinskys' "The Soldier's Tale" is animated by New Yorker cartoonist R.O. Bleechman with the voices provided by Max Von Sydow and Andre Gregory.
MGM UA — *MGM/UA Home Video*

Solid Gold Five Day Workout, The   1984
Physical fitness
66412   100 mins   C   B, V, LV, CED   R, P
The Solid Gold Dancers
A complete workout in five twenty-minute sessions that are designed to help develop specific and differentiated parts of the body every day. The dancers from the "Solid Gold" TV show demonstrate each exercise in an attractive setting.
Paramount Home Video — *Paramount Home Video*

Solo   1977
Romance
73039   90 mins   C   B, V   P
This is the story of a young hitchhiker who enters the lives of a fire patrol pilot and his son.
MPAA:PG

Atlantic Releasing — *Vestron Video*

Sombrero Kid   **1942**
Western
56605 54 mins B/W B, V P
Don Barry, Lynn Merrick
The Kid joins outlaws and discovers the leader is the town banker
Republic — *Video Dimensions*

Some Call It Loving   **1973**
Fantasy/Romance
72450 95 mins C B, V P
Zalman King, Richard Proyer, Tisa Farrow
James B. Harris' story is based on the classic tale of "Sleeping Beauty" brought up-to-date.
Pleasant Pastures — *Monterey Home Video*

Some Kind of Hero   **1982**
Comedy-Drama
60333 97 mins C B, V, LV R, P
Richard Pryor, Margot Kidder, Ray Sharkey, Ronny Cox, Lynne Moody, Olivia Cole
A Vietnam prisoner-of-war returns home to a changed world.
MPAA:R
Paramount — *Paramount Home Video; RCA VideoDiscs*

Some Like It Hot   **1959**
Comedy
29222 120 mins B/W B, V, LV P
Marilyn Monroe, Tony Curtis, Jack Lemmon, George Raft, Pat O'Brien, Nehemiah Persoff
Two unemployed musicians, witnesses to a Chicago murder, disguise themselves as girls and join an all-girl band headed for Miami to escape gangster's retaliation.
Academy Awards '59: Best Costume Design
EL, SP
United Artists — *CBS/Fox Video; RCA VideoDiscs*

Some Rails of Pennsylvania   **1980**
Trains
46924 77 mins C B, V P
Runbys, pacing shots, and on-board views are featured in this look at the many railroads and trains of Pennsylvania.
JMJ Prods — *JMJ Productions*

Something to Sing About   **1936**
Musical
08734 84 mins B/W B, V, 3/4U P
James Cagney, William Frawley, Evelyn Daw
Two-fisted bandleader in a musical melodrama about Hollywood studio life—the people and their problems.

Schertsinger; Meyers — *Penguin Video; VCII; Sheik Video; Ampro Video Productions; Cable Films; Video Yesteryear*

Something to Sing About/Great Guy   **1936**
Drama
58915 161 mins B/W B, V P
James Cagney, William Frawley, Evelyn Daw, Mae Clarke, Ed Brophy
A Cagney double feature: "Something to Sing About" (1936), in which Cagney plays a two-fisted bandleader in a musical melodrama of Hollywood studio life; "Great Guy" (1936), in which a food inspector wipes out graft in his town.
EL, SP
Schertsinger; Grand National — *Ampro Video Productions*

Something Wicked This Way Comes   **1983**
Fantasy
65094 94 mins C B, V, CED R, P
Jason Robards, Jonathan Pryce, Diane Ladd, Pam Grier, Richard Davalos, James Stacy, directed by Jack Clayton
Two young boys discover the evil secret of a mysterious traveling carnival that visits their town. Based on the Ray Bradbury novel.
MPAA:PG
Buena Vista — *Walt Disney Home Video*

Sometimes a Great Notion   **1971**
Drama
62876 115 mins C B, V P
Paul Newman, Henry Fonda, Lee Remick, Richard Jaeckel, Michael Sarrazin, directed by Paul Newman
Trouble in a small Oregon town is caused by an independent family of lumberjacks. Based on the novel by Ken Kesey.
MPAA:PG
Universal — *MCA Home Video*

Somewhere in Time   **1980**
Fantasy/Romance
56871 103 mins C B, V, LV P
Christopher Reeve, Jane Seymour, Christopher Plummer, Teresa Wright, directed by Jeannet Szware
A playwright falls in love with a woman in an old portrait and, through self-hypnosis, goes back in time to discover what their relationship might have been.
MPAA:PG
Rastar, Stephen Deutsch — *MCA Home Video*

Somos Novius (In Love and Engaged)   **197?**
Romance
73582 30 mins C B, V P

Angelica Maria, Armando Manzanero, Palito Ortega, Olga Zubarry, Raul Ross
A publicity agent and his friend, along with a salesclerk in a record store, find themselves at the top of the music charts.
KNBC — *Aztec Cinevideo*

Son of a Gun   1919
Western
33607 68 mins B/W B, V, 3/4U P
Broncho Billy Anderson
A loveable but ornery cowboy gets banished from the county for disturbing the peace, but he wins the favor of the townspeople when he stands up to a gang of gambling swindlers. Silent.
20th Century Fox — *Penguin Video; Discount Video Tapes*

Son of Blob   1972
Horror/Science fiction
51087 87 mins C B, V R, P
Robert Walker, Godfrey Cambridge, Carol Lynley, Shelly Berman, Larry Hagman
When a scientist unknowingly brings home a piece of frozen blob from the North Pole, his wife accidentally revives the dormant grey mass. It begins a rampage of terror by digesting nearly everyone within its reach.
MPAA:PG
Jack H Harris — *Video Gems*

Son of Flubber   1984
Comedy
72793 96 mins C B, V P
Fred MacMurray, Nancy Olson, Tommy Kirk, Leon Ames, Joanna Moore
A sequel to "The Absent Minded Professor" which finds Fred MacMurray still toying with his prodigious invention, Flubber, now in the form of Flubbergas, which causes those who inhale it to float away.
Walt Disney Productions — *Walt Disney Home Video*

Son of Football Follies, The   1980
Football
45126 30 mins C B, V, FO R, P
Narrated by Mel Blanc
An updated version of "Football Follies," with Mel Blanc using his vast array of cartoon character voices to describe the bumblings on the football field.
NFL Films — *NFL Films Video*

Son of Football Follies/Highlights of Super Bowl XIV   1980
Football
56791 46 mins C B, V P

Gridiron goofs narrated by Bugs Bunny and Daffy Duck, plus highlights of the Rams and Steelers' Super Bowl XIV.
NFL Films — *VidAmerica*

Son of Godzilla   1969
Science fiction
09003 86 mins C B, V P
Tadao Takashima, Akiro Kubo, Berbay Maeda
Godzilla engages in exciting combat to protect his infant son.
Japanese — *Budget Video; Discount Video Tapes*

Son of Hollywood Bloopers   194?
Outtakes and bloopers
54139 35 mins B/W B, V P
John Garfield, Errol Flynn, George Raft, Joan Blondell
The goofs and blunders of Hollywood stars are shown—things you would never see in the movies.
Warner Bros et al — *Video Dimensions*

Son of Kong   1933
Horror
00312 70 mins B/W B, V, 3/4U P
Robert Armstrong, Helen Mack
King Kong's descendant is discovered on an island amidst prehistoric creatures.
RKO — *Nostalgia Merchant*

Son of Monsters on the March   1977
Movie and TV trailers
42961 27 mins C B, V, FO P
A sequel package to "Monsters on the March," this compilation offers trailers to ten horror and sci-fi classics, including "The Rocky Horror Picture Show," "Planet of the Apes," "The Fearless Vampire Killers," "This Island Earth" and "I Was a Teenage Frankenstein."
20th Century Fox et al — *Video Yesteryear*

Son of Monte Cristo, The   1940
Adventure
08866 102 mins B/W B, V, 3/4U P
Louis Hayward, Joan Bennett, George Sanders, Florence Bates
A count's son meets a duchess whose country is threatened by renegades.
United Artists — *Penguin Video; Sheik Video; Cable Films; Nostalgia Merchant; Discount Video Tapes; Video Connection; Video Yesteryear; Budget Video; Western Film & Video Inc*

Son of Sinbad   1955
Adventure
15600 88 mins C B, V P

Dale Robertson, Sally Forrest, Vincent Price, Lili St. Cyr, Mari Blanchard
Sinbad, captured by Khalif of Bagdad, must bring him the secret of Greek fire to gain his freedom and free the city from the forces of mighty Tamarlane.
RKO; Howard Hughes — *VCI Home Video*

Son of the Sheik   1926
Romance
10116   62 mins   B/W   B, V   P, T
Rudolph Valentino, Vilma Banky, Agnes Ayres, directed by George Fitzmaurice
In his last film, Valentino portrays a desert sheik whoabducts an unfaithful dancing girl.
First Natl — *Blackhawk Films; Sheik Video; Video Connection; Cable Films; Classic Video Cinema Collector's Club*

Son of TV Bloopers   197?
Outtakes and bloopers
54140   35 mins   C   B, V   P
Carol Burnett, Soupy Sales, Johnny Carson
This tape features bloopers of Johnny Carson, Soupy Sales, "The Hollywood Palace," "M*A*S*H," "Gunsmoke," and "The Carol Burnett Show." Some black and white footage.
CBS et al — *Video Dimensions*

Son of Zorro   1947
Adventure/Serials
33955   164 mins   B/W   B, V, 3/4U   P
George Turner, Peggy Stewart, Roy Barcroft, Edward Cassidy
Zorro takes the law into his own hands in order to protect ranchers from bandits. A serial in thirteen chapters.
Republic Pictures — *Video Connection*

Song of Arizona   1946
Western
14376   54 mins   B/W   B, V   P
Roy Rogers, Gabby Hayes
Roy thwarts banker's plot to foreclose on orphan's home.
Republic — *Video Connection; Sheik Video*

Song of Ceylon   1934
Documentary
48848   40 mins   B/W   B, V, 3/4U   P
A pictorial documentary in four sections: "The Buddha," "The Virgin Island," "The Voices of Commerce," and "The Apparel of a God."
Ceylon Tea Board, John Grierson — *Western Film & Video Inc; Festival Films*

Song of Freedom   1938
Drama
08885   70 mins   B/W   B, V, 3/4U   P
Paul Robeson, Elizabeth Welch
The story of a black worker whose nonchalant singing is overheard by an opera impresario.

Treo — *Penguin Video; Sheik Video; Video Yesteryear; Discount Video Tapes; Cable Films*

Song of Nevada   1944
Western
03990   60 mins   B/W   B, V   P
Roy Rogers, Dale Evans
It looks like Dale Evans may marry a stuffed shirt. Does she?
Republic — *Budget Video; Discount Video Tapes; Video Connection*

Song of Texas   1943
Western
08790   54 mins   B/W   B, V, 3/4U   P
Roy Rogers, Harry Shannon, Pat Brady
Roy races Sam, once champion cowboy of the world, now drunkard.
Republic — *Penguin Video; Video Yesteryear; Video Connection; Discount Video Tapes*

Song of the Gringo   1936
Western
08604   55 mins   B/W   B, V, 3/4U   P
Tex Ritter
Tex Ritter in one of his early singing westerns with both action and a bit of romance.
Grand National — *Penguin Video; Video Connection*

Song of the Trail   1936
Western
08840   65 mins   B/W   B, V, 3/4U   P
Ken Maynard
Romance of the Old West with plenty of action.
Ambassador Conn — *Penguin Video; Video Dimensions; Video Connection; Discount Video Tapes*

Sons of Katie Elder, The   1965
Western/Drama
64024   122 mins   C   B, V   R, P
John Wayne, Dean Martin, Earl Holliman, Michael Anderson Jr., Martha Hyer
Four brothers with diverse personalities return to their home town on the day their mother is buried.
Paramount — *Paramount Home Video; RCA VideoDiscs*

Sons of the Desert   1933
Comedy
33904   69 mins   B/W   B, V, 3/4U   P
Stan Laurel, Oliver Hardy, Mae Busch, Charley Chase
The boys try to fool their wives by pretending to go to Hawaii to cure Ollie of a bad cold, when in fact they are attending a convention in Chicago.
Hal Roach, MGM — *Nostalgia Merchant; Blackhawk Films*

Sons of the Desert — 1933
Comedy
63989   84 mins   B/W   B, V   P, T
Stan Laurel, Oliver Hardy, Mae Busch, Charley Chase, Dorothy Christie
Stan and Ollie sneak away to a lodge convention in Chicago by telling their wives that they are going to Hawaii for Ollie's health. Also included on this tape is a 1935 Thelma Todd—Patsy Kelly short, "Top Flat."
Hal Roach; MGM — *Blackhawk Films*

Sophia Loren: Her Own Story — 1980
Drama/Biographical
58464   150 mins   C   B, V   R, P
Sophia Loren, Armand Assante, Ed Flanders, John Gavin
The life story of Sophia Loren, from a spindly child growing up in working-class Naples, to a world-renowned movie star and beauty queen.
EMI TV Programs; Roger Gimbel — *THORN EMI Home Video*

Sophie's Choice — 1982
Drama
66070   157 mins   C   B, V, LV
Meryl Streep, Kevin Kline, Peter MacNicol, directed by Alan J. Pakula
An Auschwitz survivor settled in America struggles to forget the past.
Academy Awards '82: Best Actress (Streep).
MPAA:R
ITC Entertainment — *CBS/Fox Video; RCA VideoDiscs*

Sorceress — 1982
Drama
65749   83 mins   C   B, V   R, P
Leigh Harris, Lynette Harris, Bob Nelson
The story of Traigon, a despotic ruler and devotee of the Black Arts, driven to become Master of the World.
MPAA:R
Jack Hill — *THORN EMI Home Video*

Sorrow and the Pity, The — 1970
World War II/Documentary
47021   265 mins   B/W   B, V   P
Pierre Mendes-France, Louis Grave, Albert Speer
A documentary about anti-Semitism and the Nazi occupation of France during the Vichy regime in World War II.
Cinema 5 — *RCA/Columbia Pictures Home Video*

S.O.S. Coastguard — 1937
Adventure/Serials
08874   ? mins   B/W   B, V, 3/4U   P
Ralph Byrd, Bela Lugosi, Maxine Doyle
Twelve episodes based on the real life duties of our famous coastguard patrol.

Republic — *Penguin Video; Video Connection*

S.O.S. Titanic — 1979
Drama
58458   98 mins   C   B, V   R, P
David Janssen, Cloris Leachman, Susan St. James, David Warner, Ian Holm, Helen Mirren
The story of the Titanic disaster, exactly as it happened. This film focuses on the courage that accompanied the tragedy and horror.
EMI — *THORN EMI Home Video*

Soul Experience, The — 1984
Music-Performance
73537   60 mins   C   B, V   P
All the greats of rhythm and blues are represented on this program from Al Green to Bill Withers performing their great hits.
USA — *U.S.A. Home Video*

Soul Patrol — 1980
Drama
63414   90 mins   C   B, V   P
Nigel Davenport, Ken Gampu, Peter Dyneley
A black newspaper reporter clashes with the all-white police department in a racist city.
MPAA:R
Martin Wragge — *Sun Video*

Sound of Music, The — 1965
Musical-Drama
08363   174 mins   C   B, V, LV, CED   P
Julie Andrews, Christopher Plummer, directed by Robert Wise
A true-life story of the Von Trapp family of Austria prior to World War II. Based on Rogers and Hammerstein play.
Academy Awards '65: Best Picture; Film Daily Poll 10 Best Pictures of Year '65.
20th Century Fox; Robert Wise — *CBS/Fox Video*

Sounder — 1972
Drama
Closed Captioned
65734   105 mins   C   B, V   R, P
Paul Winfield, Cicely Tyson, Kevin Hooks, Taj Mahal
The story of a Negro family of sharecroppers in rural Louisiana during the Depression.
MPAA:G
20th Century Fox — *Embassy Home Entertainment*

Soup for One — 1982
Comedy
47802   84 mins   C   B, V   P
Saul Rubinek, Marcia Strassman, Gerrit Graham
A hapless New Yorker searches for his "Dream Girl."
MPAA:R

(For Explanation of codes, see USE GUIDE and KEY)

Warner Bros — *Warner Home Video*

South of Monterey   1947
Western
14233   63 mins   B/W   B, V   P
Gilbert Roland
Western adventure with the Cisco kid.
Monogram — *Video Connection*

South of Pago Pago   1940
Adventure
64363   98 mins   B/W   B, V, 3/4U   P
*Victor McLaglen, Jon Hall, Frances Farmer,
Gene Lockhart*
The unsuspecting natives of a tropical isle are
exploited by a gang of pirates who are searching
for a seabed of rare pearls.
United Artists — *Nostalgia Merchant*

South of the Border   1939
Western
58605   70 mins   B/W   B, V   P, T
Gene Autry, Smiley Burnette
Gene and Frog are sent to help investigate a
threat to the Latin American country of
"Palermo," (Also known as "South of Texas").
Republic — *Blackhawk Films; Video
Connection*

South of the Rio Grande   1951
Western
72950   60 mins   B/W   B, V   P
Duncan Renaldo
The Cisco Kid rides again as he comes to the
aid of a rancher whose horses were stolen.
Eagle Lion — *VCI Home Video*

South Pacific   1958
Musical/Drama
55592   167 mins   C   B, V, CED   P
*Mitzi Gaynor, Rossano Brazzi, Ray Walston,
France Nuyen*
A young American Navy nurse and a
Frenchman fall in love in World World II Hawaii.
Based on Rodgers and Hammerstein's musical.
Academy Awards '58: Best Sound Recording.
Twentieth Century Fox — *CBS/Fox Video*

Southern Chessie 2716   1982
Trains
66058   60 mins   C   B, V   P
Ex-Chesapeake and Ohio Kanawha No. 2716 is
seen on a steam excursion from Atlanta to
Chattanooga.
JMJ Productions — *JMJ Productions*

Southern Comfort   1981
Drama
65071   106 mins   C   B, V, CED   P
*Keith Carradine, Powers Boothe, Fred Ward,
Franklyn Seales*

A nine-man National Guard patrol on routine
weekend maneuvers in Louisiana are marked
for death by Cajun natives.
MPAA:R
20th Century Fox — *Embassy Home
Entertainment*

Southern 500 Auto Race,   19??
1963 - 1979
Automobiles-Racing
15239   30 mins   C   B, V, 3/4U,   P
                              Q
17   pgms
The highlights and on-location reports of the
Southern 500 auto races from 1963 to 1979 are
presented in these seventeen individual
programs.
Custom Films — *TV Sports Scene; Custom
Films/Video*

Southern Steam   1979
Trains
55515   60 mins   C   B, V   P
A one-day excursion through Virginia on the
Royal Hudson No. 2839 and 2-8-0 No. 722,
classic trains of yesteryear, and also a look at
Southern's famous Pacific P.S. No. 1401 in the
Smithsonian.
De Luz — *De Luz Video*

Southerner, The   1945
Drama
11254   91 mins   B/W   B, V, FO   P
*Zachary Scott, Betty Field, directed by Jean
Renoir*
The story of how a poor Southern family
struggles to make a living on the farm land.
United Artists — *Video Yesteryear; Movie Buff
Video; Budget Video; VCII; Sheik Video; Video
Connection; Western Film & Video Inc; Discount
Video Tapes*

Southward Ho   1939
Western
57982   56 mins   B/W   B, V   P
Roy Rogers, Gabby Hayes
Roy Rogers stars in the action western about a
cowhand who heads south.
Republic — *Video Connection; Cable Films*

Soviet Army Chorus,   1981
Band, and Dance
Ensemble
Music-Performance
57256   70 mins   C   B, V   P
This exciting music ensemble is seen on tour at
various points in the USSR performing their
spectacular blend of singing, dancing and
acrobatics.
Kultur — *Kultur*

Soviet Army, The   196?
USSR/Propaganda
52315   60 mins   B/W   B, V, 3/4U   P
Two Soviet-made documentaries about the
Russian military forces: "The Soviet Army,"
which shows the training of a soldier, and
"Under the Soviet Flag" (in color), a featurette
about the Soviet fleet operating in the
Mediterranean Sea. Dubbed in English.
USSR — *International Historic Films*

Soviet Paradise, The   1941
Propaganda/World War II
72478   14 mins   B/W   B, V, 3/4U   P
The Nazi view of life inside the Soviet Union
after twenty years of Communist rule. English
subtitles.
GR
Germany — *International Historic Films*

Soviet People Are with   197?
Vietnam/Soviet People
Support Vietnam
Vietnam War/Propaganda
52356   32 mins   B/W   B, V, 3/4U   P
Two Soviet documentaries about the war in
Vietnam, reported by Soviet correspondents,
with the expected anti-American slant. Narrated
in English.
USSR — *International Historic Films*

Soviet Union Is Our   197?
Home, The/Rude
Awakening
USSR/Propaganda
52348   30 mins   B/W   B, V, 3/4U   P
A short propaganda documentary about the life
of Jewish people in the USSR. Also includes
"Rude Awakening," another short which tells of
Soviet Jews that had settled in Israel, but
returned to a better life in the Soviet Union.
Narrated in English.
USSR — *International Historic Films*

Soylent Green   1973
Science fiction
53940   95 mins   C   B, V, CED   P
*Charlton Heston, Leigh Taylor-Young, Chuck
Connors, Joseph Cotten, Edward G. Robinson*
In the 21st Century, a hard-boiled police
detective investigates a murder and discovers
what soylent green—the people's principal
food—is made of.
MPAA:PG
MGM — *MGM/UA Home Video*

Soyuz/Apollo Link-Up   1975
Space exploration
72495   20 mins   C   B, V, 3/4U   P
Footage of the Russian-American space
docking in June 1975. There is a rare look at
Soviet space boosters and Kosmodrome

facilities and a joint press conference in
Moscow following the mission.
USSR — *International Historic Films*

Space Angel Volume 1   1964
Science fiction/Cartoons
53150   50 mins   C   B, V   P
Animated
A futuristic animated program for children.
EL, SP
TV Comics; Ziv Intl — *Family Home
Entertainment*

Space Angel Volume 2   1964
Science fiction/Cartoons
53151   50 mins   C   B, V   P
Animated
A futuristic animated program for children.
EL, SP
TV Comics; Ziv Intl — *Family Home
Entertainment*

Space Ghost and Dino   197?
Boy
Cartoons
66281   60 mins   C   B, V   P
Animated
A ghostly cartoon character performs hilarious
hijinx.
Hanna Barbera — *Worldvision Home Video*

Space Movie, The   1980
Space exploration/Documentary
54803   78 mins   C   B, V   R, P
Directed by Tony Palmer
"The Space Movie" consists entirely of footage
from NASA and the U.S. National Archives
which tells the story of America's space effort
(specifically the Apollo 11 moon flight). The
footage, most of which has not been seen
before, is mixed with music and a little narration,
showing the beauty of space.
Virgin Films Ltd, British — *Warner Home Video*

Space Patrol   195?
Science fiction
57286   60 mins   B/W   B, V   P
Ed Kemmer, Lyn Osborn, Virginia Hewitt
Two complete episodes of the early 1950's
television series about the battle against
celestial dangers as seen through the
assignments of Buzz Corey, commander of the
Space Patrol. The episodes are entitled
"Marooned on Procyon Four" and "Double
Trouble."
ABC — *Video Dimensions*

Space Patrol   1955
Science fiction
59088   78 mins   B/W   B, V, FO   P
Ed Kemmer, Lyn Osborn

The adventures of Buzz Corey, Commander in Chief of the Space Patrol, fighting interplanetary injustice.
ABC — *Video Yesteryear*

Space Patrol   1956
Science fiction
72521   60 mins   B/W   B, V, 3/4U   P
Commander Cody and Happy blast off to the cosmos in two episodes from the 1950's TV show. In one sequence a stagehand walks in front of the space travelers, a problem that existed during the era of live TV.
ABC — *International Historic Films*

Space Patrol   1953
Science fiction
72522   60 mins   B/W   B, V, 3/4U   P
Two episodes, "Operation Rescue" and "Mysterious Ocean in Space," are featured from the popular adventure serial of the fifties. Marvin Miller ("The Millionaire") guest stars.
ABC — *International Historic Films*

Space Patrol/Twilight Zone   19??
Science fiction
17248   60 mins   B/W   B, V   P
Includes a Space Patrol television episode from the early 1950's—"Terra, the Doomed Planet." Plus an episode from the Twilight Zone from the early 1960's—"Occurrence at Owl Creek."
ABC; CBS — *Video Connection*

Space Patrol Volume 1   195?
Science fiction/Adventure
44339   120 mins   B/W   B, V, 3/4U   P
Ed Kemmer, Lyn Osborn
Buzz Corey, Commander-in-Chief of the Space Patrol, tries to maintain interplanetary peace and protect the people of Earth's neighboring planets. These episodes from the early 1950's television series includes previews of coming attractions from classic science fiction films.
ABC — *Nostalgia Merchant*

Space Patrol Volume 2   195?
Science fiction
58584   90 mins   B/W   B, V, 3/4U   P
Commander Buzz Corey maintains interplanetary peace in this early '50's TV series.
ABC — *Nostalgia Merchant*

Space Raiders   1983
Science fiction/Adventure
65743   84 mins   C   B, V   R, P
Vince Edwards, David Mendenhall
A plucky 10-year-old blasts off into a futuristic world of intergalactic desperados, crafty alien mercenaries, starship battles and cliff-hanging dangers.

MPAA:PG
Roger Corman — *Warner Home Video*

Space Sentinels Volume 1   1977
Cartoons/Science fiction
72883   44 mins   C   B, V   P
Animated
A cartoon features the Space Sentinels who are out to save the world from the evil space invaders.
Unknown — *Embassy Home Entertainment*

Spaced Out   1980
Comedy
47800   85 mins   C   B, V   R, P
A naughty sci-fi sex comedy that parodies everything from "Star Wars" to "2001."
MPAA:R
Miramax — *THORN EMI Home Video*

Spacehunter: Adventures in the Forbidden Zone   1983
Adventure
65315   90 mins   C   B, V   P
Peter Strauss, Molly Ringwald, Michael Ironside, Ernie Hudson
Peter Strauss is the galactic bounty hunter who agrees to rescue 3 maidens from a plague-ridden planet. Available in VHS stereo and Beta Hi-Fi.
MPAA:PG
Don Carmody — *RCA/Columbia Pictures Home Video; RCA VideoDiscs*

Spaceketeers   1982
Cartoons/Science fiction
63118   100 mins   C   B, V   P
Animated
An army of mutant invaders overrun a peaceful solar system. Spaceketeers to the rescue!
Toei Animation; Ginga Kikaku; Jim Terry Production Services — *Family Home Entertainment*

Spaceketeers Volume 1   1980
Science fiction/Cartoons
53163   46 mins   C   B, V   P
Animated
Princess Aurora and Jesse Dart, with the help of a scientific wizard, risk everything to save the endangered galaxy.
EL, SP
Toei Animation; Ginga Kikaku; Jim Terry Prod — *Family Home Entertainment*

Spaceketeers Volume 2   1980
Science fiction/Cartoons
53164   46 mins   C   B, V   P
Animated
Princess Aurora and Jesse Dart travel through space in search of their friend, Porkos, who is

needed to stop blood-thirsty monsters from destroying the galaxy.
EL, SP
Toei Animation; Ginga Kikaku; Jim Terry Prod — *Family Home Entertainment*

Spaceketeers Volume 3 1980
Science fiction/Cartoons
64203   46 mins   C   B, V   P
Animated
This third volume presents further adventures of Princess Aurora and her companion, Jesse Dart.
EL, SP
Toei Animation; Ginga Kikaku; Jim Jerry Prod — *Family Home Entertainment*

Sparrows 1926
Comedy-Drama
10124   75 mins   B/W   B, V   P, T
Mary Pickford, Roy Stewart, Gustov von Seyffertitz, directed by William Beaudine
Set to William Perry's score, mother cares for her nine children on impoverished farm, warding off starvation and kidnappers. (Silent).
United Artists — *Blackhawk Films; Sheik Video; Penguin Video; Discount Video Tapes; Video Yesteryear*

Spartacus 1977
Dance
69832   95 mins   C   B, V   P
Vladimir Vasiliev, The Bolshoi Ballet
A slave leads an unsuccessful revolt against the Romans.
Sovexportfilm USSR — *Video Arts International*

Spasms 1982
Horror
65511   92 mins   C   B, V   R, P
Peter Fonda, Oliver Reed
The Demon Serpent, known as N'Gana Simbu, is the deadliest snake in the world. It strikes its victims, and the result is that the victim's bodies become hideously deformed and destroyed. With uncontrollable deady fury, the monstrous snake strikes continuously causing death and destruction.
MPAA:R
John C Pozhke; Maurice Smith — *THORN EMI Home Video*

Speaking of Animals 1983
Comedy
65313   60 mins   C   B, V   P
In this hilarious film anthology, not only do the animals walk and talk like human beings, they also sing, dance and imitate the stars.
Jerry Fairbanks — *U.S.A. Home Video*

Special Day, A 1977
Drama
58501   105 mins   C   B, V   P
Sophia Loren, Marcello Mastroianni, directed by Ettore Scola
The day of a huge rally celebrating Hitler's visit to Rome in 1939 serves as the backdrop for an affair between a weary housewife and a radio announcer. Italian with English subtitles.
IT
Cinema 5; Carlo Ponti — *RCA/Columbia Pictures Home Video*

Special Olympics, The 1982
Sports
72975   60 mins   C   B, V   P
Highlights from the 1982 Special Olympics in Los Angeles, featuring interviews with the athletes and celebrities.
Courier Productions — *Courier Productions*

Special Valentine with Family Circus, A 1980
Cartoons/Holidays
75469   30 mins   C   B, V   P
Animated
Cartoonist Bil Keane animates a special valentine program.
Cullen Kasden Productions Ltd — *Family Home Entertainment*

Specialist, The 1975
Drama
64298   93 mins   C   B, V   P
Adam West, John Anderson, Ahna Capri
A lawyer is seduced by a beautiful "specialist" as part of a frame-up.
MPAA:R
Renaissance Productions — *VCI Home Video*

Spectacular Evening in Paris, A 1980
Nightclub
29238   106 mins   C   B, V   P
This videotape presents the top night club acts from the top Parisienne clubs—Moulin Rouge, Madame Arthur, Lido, and Casino de Paris.
Harlan Kleiman — *VidAmerica*

Spectreman versus Hedron 196?
Science fiction
72186   60 mins   C   B, V   P
Treacherous Dr. Gori unleashes the gas breathing Hedron on earth, while a young boy tries to revive Spectreman, the planet's last hope.
Fuji Studios — *King of Video*

Spectreman versus Zeron and Medron — 196?
Science fiction
72187   60 mins   C   B, V   P
Dr. Gori's greedy quest to conquer earth is escalated when he creates Zeron and Medron. Spectreman, having assumed the earth name, George, sets out to warn the Pollution Squad.
Fuji Studios — *King of Video*

Speed Kings? The/Love, Speed and Thrills — 1915
Comedy
64534   19 mins   B/W   B, V   R, P
Mabel Normand, Ford Sterling, Fatty Arbuckle, Mack Swain, Chester Conklin, The Keystone Cops
Two Mack Sennett comedy shorts are combined on this tape, both of which involve slapstick car chases.
Mack Sennett; Keystone — *Blackhawk Films*

Speed Learning — 1983
Education
75901   30 mins   C   B, V   P
This program shows ways to improve learning and comprehensive skills up to 300 percent.
Learn Inc — *Sony Corporation of America*

Speed Trap — 1977
Adventure
76655   101 mins   C   B, V   P
Tyne Daly, Joe Don Baker
Tyne Daly and Joe Don Baker team up to investigate a rash of mysterious car thefts in this exciting action drama.
Howard Pine; Fred Mintz — *Media Home Entertainment*

Speedway '82 World Finals Los Angeles — 1983
Motorcycles
72859   78 mins   C   B, V   P
Highlights from the big Motorcycle race in Los Angeles are shown.
Motorweek Production — *Motor Cycle Video*

Spellbound — 1945
Drama
46215   111 mins   B/W   B, V, CED   P
Ingrid Bergman, Gregory Peck, Leo G. Carroll, directed by Alfred Hitchcock
A young man suffering from amnesia and accused of murder, is helped by a female psychiatrist who loves him. One of Hitchcock's finest films of the 1940's, with a dream sequence designed by Salvador Dali.
Selznick — *CBS/Fox Video*

Spend It All — 1971
Music/Folklore
60465   41 mins   C   B, V, 3/4U   P
Balfa Brothers, Marc Savoy, Nathan Abshire
A documentary portrait of the bayou people in Cajun country in Southwest Louisiana who still retain the language, camaraderie and old world spirit, of their French - speaking Acadian ancestors. Musical artists are also featured.
Les Blank — *Flower Films*

Spetters — 1980
Drama
65424   108 mins   C   B, V   P
Rutger Hauer
The story revolves around four young people in Holland on a turbulent collision course with their dreams Tragic episodes force them to confront their strengths and weaknesses.
MPAA:R
Joop Van Der End — *Embassy Home Entertainment*

Sphinx — 1980
Suspense
58250   118 mins   C   B, V   R, P
Lesley-Anne Downe, Frank Langella, John Gielgud, directed by Franklin J. Schaffner
A young woman stumbles on a secret hidden for centuries in the tomb of an Egyptian King.
MPAA:PG
Orion Pictures — *Warner Home Video*

Spider-Woman — 1982
Cartoons/Adventure
59039   100 mins   C   B, V   P
A collection of Spider-Woman's most daring escapades.
Marvel Comics Group — *MCA Home Video*

Spiderman — 1982
Adventure
72337   90 mins   C   B, V   P
Marvel Comics' superhero fights crime in the city in this live-action feature.
Charles Frief; Daniel R Goodman — *Prism*

Spies — 1928
Adventure
11253   90 mins   B/W   B, V, FO   P
Gerda Maurus, Willy Fritsch, directed by Fritz Lang
A sly criminal poses as a famous banker to steal government information and create chaos in the world in this silent picture.
Janus Films — *Video Yesteryear; Blackhawk Films; Sheik Video; Classic Video Cinema Collector's Club*

Spinal Tap — 1983
Comedy/Musical
64980   90 mins   C   B, V, CED   P
Rob Reiner, Christopher Guest, Michael McKean, Harry Shearer

An English heavy metal rock-and-roll band attempts a comeback tour of the U.S., only to fall into a series of misadventures caused by their totally inept tour planners.
MPAA:R
Embassy Pictures — *Embassy Home Entertainment*

Spiral Ride and Standup 1980
Sports-Minor
51409 60 mins C B, V, 3/4U P
NCAA wrestling champion Pat Milkovich and his talented brother Tom demonstrate important wrestling skills with an emphasis on the spiral ride and standup.
Michael P Milkovich — *Milkovich Enterprises*

Spirit of St. Louis, The 1957
Biographical
74211 137 mins C B, V R, P
James Stewart
This is a biographical feature concerning the life of aviator Charles A. Lindbergh. Stewart stars as the pilot whose transatlantic flight made aviation history.
Leland Hayward — *Warner Home Video*

Spirit of Youth, The 1937
Adventure
08883 70 mins B/W B, V, 3/4U P
Joe Louis, Mantan Moreland
Joe Thomas supports his family with menial jobs until he shows his knack as a fighter.
Grand Natl — *Penguin Video; Video Connection*

Spitfire 1942
Drama
06205 90 mins B/W B, V P
Leslie Howard, David Niven, Rosamund John, directed by Leslie Howard
Story of Reginald Mitchell who designed "The Spitfire," which served the Allies so well during WW II.
RKO; Leslie Howard Prods — *Budget Video; Video Connection; Cable Films*

Splash 1984
Fantasy
75635 109 mins C B, V, LV, CED R, P
Tom Hanks, Daryl Hannah, Eugene Levy, John Candy, directed by Ron Howard
A mermaid ventures into New York City in search of a man she has fallen for.
Brian Grazer Production — *Touchstone Home Video*

Splendor in the Grass 1961
Drama
51970 124 mins C B, V R, P
Natalie Wood, Pat Hingle, Audrey Christie, Barbara Loden, Warren Beatty, Zohra Lampert, Sandy Dennis
A high school girl suffers an emotional collapse when the boy she loves stops seeing her. She attempts suicide, fails, and is committed to a mental institution for treatment.
Academy Awards '61: Best Original Story and Screenplay (William Inge).
Warner Bros;Elia Kazan — *Warner Home Video*

Split Enz 1982
Music-Performance
75923 54 mins C B, V P
This program presents the group Split Enz performing some of their best songs.
Enz Productions Ltd — *Sony Corporation of America*

Split Image 1982
Drama
66041 113 mins C B, V, CED P
Michael O'Keefe, Karen Allen, Peter Fonda, James Woods, directed by Ted Kotcheff
An all-American boy comes under the spell of a cult. His parents then hire a deprogrammer to bring the boy back to reality.
MPAA:R
Jeff Young — *Embassy Home Entertainment*

Spoilers, The 1914
Western
64325 90 mins B/W B, V P
William Farnum, Tom Santschi
Crooked government officials begin stealing from the richest claims during the Alaska Gold Rush. Silent with musical score.
Selig Polyscope — *Classic Video Cinema Collector's Club*

Spoilers, The 1942
Drama
65121 84 mins B/W B, V P
John Wayne, Randolph Scott, Marlene Dietrich, Margaret Lindsay
Two adventurers in the Yukon argue over land rights and the love of a saloon entertainer.
Universal — *MCA Home Video*

Spooks Run Wild 1941
Comedy
12857 64 mins B/W B, V, FO P
The Bowery Boys, Bela Lugosi
Chills and laughs combine as the eerie Lugosi almost meets his match.
Monogram — *Video Yesteryear; Sheik Video; Discount Video Tapes; Admit One Video*

Sports Conditioning 1978
Physical fitness/Sports
42780 30 mins C B, V P

Hosted by Ann Dugan 4 pgms
This series on tennis, golf, jogging, running, and skiing works toward improvement through conditioning.
1.Jog/Run 2.Golf 3.Tennis/Racquet Sports 4.Ski
Health N Action — *RCA/Columbia Pictures Home Video*

Sports Hour #2   19??
Sports-Winter
12989   59 mins   C   B, V, 3/4U   P
Franz Klammer, Rosi Mittermaier, John Clendennin, Wayne Wong
This cassette contains three programs which feature the best in exciting downhill, alpine, and freestyle skiing: "Just a Matter of Time," "Lange Connection," and "Between Chaos and Beauty."
Unknown — *Sports World Cinema*

Sports Hour #3   1982
Sports
59174   80 mins   C   B, V, 3/4U   P
Hosted by Bart Starr, Jackie Robinson, Babe Ruth, Glenn Cunningham
"Champions never quit" is the theme of this program which stresses determination in reaching your goals.
Unknown — *Sports World Cinema*

Sports Hour #4   19??
Sports
12991   60 mins   C   B, V, 3/4U   P
This cassette contains three programs on U.S. skiers and ski places ("Snowbird Sunshine," "Steamboat, There's Only One," and "Go for It"), and the final segment is about motorcycle racing ("Number One").
Unknown — *Sports World Cinema*

Sports Hour #5   19??
Sports-Winter
12992   54 mins   C   B, V, 3/4U   P
"Hot Dog Skiing," the first program on this cassette, explores the early days of freestyle skiing. In "Denali," a team of Americans attempt the summit of Mt. McKinley.
Unknown — *Sports World Cinema*

Sports Hour #6   19??
Sports-Winter
12993   58 mins   C   B, V, 3/4U   P
Three programs on skiing are featured on this cassette: "Helix," "Oh To Hell-i-copter with It," and "Good Time Skiing."
Unknown — *Sports World Cinema*

Sports Hour #7   19??
Sports
12994   60 mins   C   B, V, 3/4U   P

Skiing and championship catamaran racing are the subjects of the two programs on this cassette, "Spirit" and "Hobie Worlds."
Unknown — *Sports World Cinema*

Sports Hour #8   19??
Tennis
12995   53 mins   C   B, V, 3/4U   P
Jack Kramer
Tennis coach Jack Kramer provides instruction in "You're Playing at Wimbledon"; "U.S. Open 1975" features Manuel Orantes' miracle win over Guillermo Vilas in the semifinals.
Unknown — *Sports World Cinema*

Sports Hour #9   19??
Automobiles-Racing
12997   51 mins   C   B, V, 3/4U   P
"Fire and Rain" and "Wheels Keep Rolling" feature Gordon Johncock winning the 1973 Indianapolis "500" and Johnny Rutherford capturing the race in 1976.
Unknown — *Sports World Cinema*

Sports Hour #10   19??
Sports
12998   44 mins   C   B, V, 3/4U   P
The history of hydroplane racing in the U.S. and the world championship kite tournament are among the subjects covered in the three programs on this cassette: "Thunderboats," "Gold Times Six," and "Kitemen."
Unknown — *Sports World Cinema*

Sports Hour #11   19??
Tennis
13000   50 mins   C   B, V, 3/4U   P
Brian Gottfried, Guillermo Vilas, Jimmy Connors, Dick Stockton
The skills and talents of tennis pros are seen in the WCT match highlights featured in "Killer Instinct" and "In Pursuit of #1."
Unknown — *Sports World Cinema*

Sports Hour #12   19??
Sports-Winter
14401   55 mins   C   B, V, 3/4U   P
"Free-Style Pro-Style" and "Waitin' for the Morning Sun" thoroughly explore the grace, beauty, style, and innovative nature of freestyle skiing.
Unknown — *Sports World Cinema*

Sports Hour #13   19??
Tennis
14402   54 mins   C   B, V, 3/4U   P
Highlights of exciting tennis matches between such pros as Bjorn Borg, Jimmy Connors, Ilie Nastase, and others, are featured in the two programs on this cassette, "65,000 Miles to Dallas" and "U.S. Open 1976."
Unknown — *Sports World Cinema*

Sports Hour # 14   19??
Sports
14403   67 mins   C   B, V, 3/4U   P
Competitive and leisure bicycling are featured in "Two Wheeler" and "The Great American Bike Tour"; cross country skiing is seen in "Sunny Skiing"; and "Skateboard" takes a look at the skateboard craze.
Unknown — *Sports World Cinema*

Sports Hour # 15   19??
Aeronautics
14404   58 mins   C   B, V, 3/4U   P
Flight is the common theme in these three programs about hot air ballooning, sky sailing, and traveling air shows: "Ride the Gentle Breeze," "Sky Sails," and "North to Canada."
Unknown — *Sports World Cinema*

Sports Hour # 16   1975
Tennis
12964   52 mins   C   B, V, 3/4U   P
Peter Ustinov
A view of Wimbleton, 1975, as seen by actor Peter Ustinov. Arthur Ashe and Billie Jean King provide dramatic moments in this prestigious and exciting event.
Unknown — *Sports World Cinema*

Sports Hour # 17   1974
Tennis
12963   52 mins   C   B, V, 3/4U   P
New young champions like Jimmy Connors, Chris Evert, and Bjorn Borg begin their domination of the sport. Billie Jean King and Ken Rosewall are among the others seen in these 1974 Wimbledon matches.
Unknown — *Sports World Cinema*

Sports Hour # 18   197?
Horse racing
33772   56 mins   C   B, V, 3/4U   P
This program contains "Ruffian," a moving tribute to perhaps the greatest filly of all time, who, before her ill-fated match race with Kentucky Derby winner Foolish Pleasure in 1975, easily captured the Triple Crown for fillies. Also included is "The Big Three," featuring the great three-time Horse of the Year, Forego, 1977 Triple Crown Winner Seattle Slew, and super jockey Steve Cauthen.
Unknown — *Sports World Cinema*

Sports Hour # 19   197?
Sports-Winter
33773   55 mins   C   B, V, 3/4U   P
"Winter Wings," "Garmisch, 1978," and "Freedom" comprise this program, which features both competitive and freestyle skiing.
Unknown — *Sports World Cinema*

Sports Nutrition   1984
Nutrition
72973   30 mins   C   B, V   P
A guide to proper nutrition with an explanation of the four basic food groups is on this video cassette.
Star Merchants — *Increase Video*

Spring Break   1983
Comedy
65187   101 mins   C   B, V   P
Perry Lang, David Knell, Steve Bassett, Paul Land, Jane Modean, Corinne Alphen
Two college students go to Fort Lauderdale on their spring vacation and have a wilder time that they bargained for.
MPAA:R
Columbia — *RCA/Columbia Pictures Home Video; RCA VideoDiscs*

Spring Fever   1981
Comedy
72228   93 mins   C   B, V   P
Susan Anton
Heartaches of the junior tennis circuit are brought to the screen in this sports comedy.
Tournament Productions — *Vestron Video*

Springtime in the Rockies   1937
Western
08787   60 mins   B/W   B, V, 3/4U   P
Gene Autry, Polly Rowles, Smiley Burnette
Gene is involved with four young "scientific" gal ranchers, fresh out of Aggie School.
Republic — *Penguin Video; Video Connection*

Springtime in the Sierras   1947
Western
10709   54 mins   B/W   B, V, 3/4U   R, P
Roy Rogers, Andy Devine
Roy Rogers and Andy Devine band together to fight a gang of poachers who prey on the wildlife of a game preserve.
Republic — *Cable Films; Discount Video Tapes; Video Yesteryear*

Sprint Technique, The   1981
Track athletics
47289   25 mins   C   B, V, 3/4U,   P
        Q
Track and field coach Bill Dellinger instructs in proper techniques and training procedures for the sprint.
TV Sports Scene — *TV Sports Scene*

Sprout Wings and Fly   1981
Music/Folklore
60453   50 mins   C   B, V, 3/4U   P
A portrait of the great North Carolina fiddler Tommy Jarrel, a living, fiddling, storytelling legend who gives us a feeling for the beliefs and attitudes of the North Carolina people as well as

a grounding in fiddle-playing styles and repertoire.
Les Blank — *Flower Films*

Spunky and Tadpole   196?
Cartoons
56749   48 mins   C   B, V   P
Animated
Spunky and his faithful companion, Tadpole, get in and out of trouble and cliff-hanging adventures, spoofing some of the old classic films in the process. Available in English and Spanish versions.
EL, SP
Beverly Hills Film Corp — *Media Home Entertainment*

Spy in Black, The   1939
Adventure
11255   82 mins   B/W   B, V, FO   P
Conrad Veidt, Valerie Hobson, Sebastian Shaw
A German submarine captain returns from duty at sea and is assigned to infiltrate one of the Orkney Islands and obtain confidential British information.
Korda — *Video Yesteryear; Discount Video Tapes*

Spy of Napoleon   1936
Drama
63618   77 mins   B/W   B, V, FO   P
Richard Barthelmess, Dolly Hass, Francis I. Sullivan
During the Franco-Prussian War, Emperor Napoleon III recruits his illegitimate daughter to uncover traitors to the throne.
British — *Video Yesteryear*

Spy Smasher   1942
Mystery/Serials
33956   185 mins   B/W   B, V, 3/4U   P
Kane Richmond, Marguerite Chapman
A serial of espionage and intrigue in twelve episodes.
Republic — *Nostalgia Merchant; Video Connection; NTA Home Entertainment*

Spy Who Loved Me, The   1977
Adventure
60378   125 mins   C   B, V   P
Roger Moore, Barbara Bach
James Bond must destroy a brilliant but savage villain and his henchman Jaws, in order to prevent them from using captured American and Russian atomic submarines in a plot to destroy the world.
MPAA:PG
United Artists — *CBS/Fox Video; RCA VideoDiscs*

Spyro Gyra   1980
Music-Performance
47396   56 mins   C   B, V   R, P
Live performances of some of Spyro Gyra's well-known hits are interspersed with interviews with band members.
Hawk Productions — *Warner Home Video*

Squadron of Doom   1936
Adventure
07205   70 mins   B/W   B, V   P
John King, Jean Rogers, Noah Beery Jr.
Government troubleshooter Ace Drummond battles enemy agents out to steal a mountain of jade.
Universal — *Video Connection*

Squeeze Play   1979
Comedy
64214   92 mins   C   B, V   R, P
A group of young women start a baseball team and challenge their boyfriends' team to a game. It's a no-holds-barred competition featuring a sexy wet-T-shirt contest.
Troma Productions — *THORN EMI Home Video*

Squiddly Diddly   196?
Cartoons
69291   55 mins   C   B, V   P
Animated
This tape is a compilation of "Squiddly Diddly" cartoons, about a star-struck squid hoping to break into show business.
Hanna-Barbera — *Worldvision Home Video*

Squirm   1976
Horror
64357   92 mins   C   B, V, LV,   P
                              CED
John Scardino, Patricia Pearcy, Jean Sullivan
A storm disrupts a highly charged power cable which electrifies ordinary worms into giant monsters.
MPAA:R
American International — *Vestron Video*

SS Girls   1978
War-Drama
58468   82 mins   C   B, V   P
Gabriele Carrara, Marina Daunia, Vassilli Karis, Macha Magal, Thomas Rudy, Lucic Bogoljub Benny, Ivano Staccioli
After the attack of July 1944, Hitler does not trust the Wermacht and extends the power of the S.S. over Germany. General Berger entrusts Hans Schillemberg to recruit a specially chosen group of prostitutes who must test the fighting spirit and loyalty of the generals.
Topar Films — *Media Home Entertainment*

Stacey! 198?
Drama
64948 87 mins C B, V R, P
Anne Randall, Marjorie Bennett, Anitra Ford, Alan Landers
Anne Randall, former Playboy Playmate, stars as Stacey Hansen, a beautiful private detective who finds herself involved in something more than just a friendly job of snooping.
MPAA:R
Unknown — *Video Gems*

Stacy's Knights 1983
Drama
65608 95 mins C B, V P
Andra Millian
A seemingly shy girl happens to have an uncanny knack for Blackjack. With the odds against her and an unlikely group of "knights" to aid her, she sets up an incredible "sting" operation.
MPAA:PG
Crown — *Vestron Video*

Stage Door 1937
Comedy-Drama
10054 92 mins B/W B, V P, T
Katharine Hepburn, Ginger Rogers, Lucille Ball, Eve Arden, Andrea Leeds, directed by Gregory La Cava
Based on Edna Ferber's play, set in theatrical boarding house, film follows ambitions of young aspiring actresses.
RKO; Pandro S Berman — *Blackhawk Films; Nostalgia Merchant*

Stagedoor Canteen 1943
Musical
08667 135 mins B/W B, V, 3/4U P
Tallulah Bankhead, Merle Oberon, Katharine Hepburn, Paul Muni, Ethel Waters, Johnny Weismuller
A simple love story of a soldier who falls for a canteen hostess. Dozens of top stars and band leaders.
UA; Sol Lesser; Frank Borzage — *Movie Buff Video; Penguin Video; VCII; Sheik Video; Discount Video Tapes; Cable Films; Video Connection; Video Yesteryear*

Stage Fright 1983
Horror
72529 82 mins C B, V P
A bashful actress is transformed into a homicidal killer after a latent psychosis in her becomes active.
John Lamand; Colin Eggleston — *VidAmerica*

Stage Show with the Dorsey Brothers 1956
Variety
46345 28 mins B/W B, V, FO P
Tommy and Jimmy Dorsey and their Orchestra, Elvis Presley, Henny Youngman
A program from the Dorsey Brothers' television series featuring guest performers Elvis Presley and Henny Youngman. The original telecast date was March 17, 1956.
CBS — *Video Yesteryear*

Stagecoach 1939
Western
08599 100 mins B/W B, V P
John Wayne, Claire Trevor, Thomas Mitchell, George Bancroft, John Carradine, directed by John Ford
John Ford's western classic. Reactions of a group of people in a stagecoach under Indian attack.
Academy Awards '39: Best Supporting Actor (Thomas Mitchell); Best Scoring.
United Artists; Walter Wanger Productions — *Vestron Video; RCA VideoDiscs*

Stagecoach to Denver 1947
Western
10662 56 mins B/W B, V, 3/4U R, P
Allan Lane, Roy Barcroft, Bobby Blake
Red Ryder protects a friend's stagecoach line from outlaws.
Republic — *Cable Films; Video Connection; Discount Video Tapes; Nostalgia Merchant*

Stagestruck 1957
Drama
72946 95 mins B/W B, V P
Henry Fonda, Susan Strasberg, Christopher Plummer
A remake of 1933's "Morning Glory"; Susan Strasberg reprises the role made famous by Katharine Hepburn, as a determined, would-be actress.
RKO Radio Pictures — *VCI Home Video*

Stairway to Heaven 1947
Drama
08852 102 mins C B, V, 3/4U P
David Niven, Kim Hunter, Raymond Massey, Marius Goring
The fantasy of an RAF squadron leader who escapes death by mistake.
J Arthur Rank; UI; British — *Penguin Video*

Stalag 17 1953
Adventure
29766 120 mins B/W B, V, LV R, P
William Holden, Don Taylor, Peter Graves, Otto Preminger, directed by Billy Wilder
World War II: American G.I.'s in German prison camp, thinking cynical sharp-tongued sergeant is a spy, beat him unmercifully. Based on the play by Donald Bevan and Edmund Trzcinski.
Academy Awards '53: Best Actor (Holden).

Paramount, Billy Wilder — *Paramount Home Video; RCA VideoDiscs*

Stallions of Distinction 1983
Sports-Minor/Animals
69635   28 mins   C   B, V   P
This is a look at the 8th Annual All Arabian Horse Show presented by the Arabian Riders and Breeders Society of San Diego at the new Griffith Park Equestrian Center in Los Angeles, Easter weekend 1983.
Mercedes Maharis — *Mercedes Maharis Productions*

Stamp Day for Superman 1953
Adventure
55129   25 mins   B/W   B, V   P
George Reeves, Jack Larson, Robert Shayne
Based on the "Superman" TV series, this program was made to promote defense savings stamps for kids. A "Superman" cartoon is also included.
Dept of Defense — *Video Dimensions; Sheik Video*

Stampee Wrestling 1979
Sports-Minor
33762   60 mins   C   B, V, 3/4U, Q   P
52   pgms
No holds barred wrestling where anything goes. At times, six wrestling champions are in the ring at once. A series of fifty-two untitled programs.
TV Sports Scene — *TV Sports Scene*

Stamping Ground 1970
Music-Performance
08670   92 mins   C   B, V, 3/4U   P
Pink Floyd, Santana, the Byrds, Jefferson Airplane, Al Stewart, Canned Heat, T. Rex
This concert was filmed before an audience of 300,000 fans at the Holland Music Festival in 1970.
MPAA:R
Atlas — *Penguin Video*

Stand Easy 1952
Comedy
66396   71 mins   B/W   B, V   P
Peter Sellers, Harry Secombe, Spike Milligan, Carole Carr
A comedy of errors about a group of Army misfits who save an atomic formula from spies. Original title: "Down Among the Z Men."
EJ Fancey Productions — *Movie Buff Video*

Stand-In 1937
Comedy
66636   91 mins   B/W   B, V   P
Humphrey Bogart, Joan Blondell, Leslie Howard, Alan Mowbray, Jack Carson
An efficiency expert is sent to save a Hollywood studio from bankruptcy.
United Artists; Walter Wanger — *Monterey Home Video*

Stanley 1972
Horror
17201   108 mins   C   B, V   P
Chris Robinson, Alex Rocco, Susan Carroll
Vietnam vet uses a rattlesnake as his personal weapon of revenge against mankind.
MPAA:PG
Crown International Pictures — *VCI Home Video*

Stanley 1983
Cartoons
72866   30 mins   C   B, V   P
Animated
An animated featurette about a duckling named Stanley who's searching for his identity.
I Like Myself, Inc — *Image Magnetic Associates*

Star Bloopers 1979
Outtakes and bloopers
63334   47 mins   B/W   B, V   R, P
A collection of great movie moments that never made it to the screen, including missed cues, flubbed deliveries, malfunctioning props, and some rare Ronald Reagan footage.
Roy Self; John Gregory — *THORN EMI Home Video*

Star Chamber, The 1983
Drama
65504   109 mins   C   B, V, CED   P
Michael Douglas, Hal Holbrook
A conscientious judge who, seeing criminals freed on legal technicalities, comes to the conclusion that conventional law does not always reward the victims of crime, but often the criminals. Distressed by this, he turns to a friend and colleague for solace. His friend tells him of another type of justice that a group of judges have set up that is beyond conventional.
MPAA:R
20th Century Fox — *CBS/Fox Video*

Star Crash 1978
Science fiction/Adventure
65712   92 mins   C   B, V, LV   P
Caroline Munroe, Christopher Plummer, David Hasselhoff
A trio of adventurers square off against interstellar evil by using their wits and technological wizardry.
MPAA:PG
Nat and Patrick Wachsberger — *Embassy Home Entertainment*

Star 80   1983
Drama
65612   104 mins   C   B, V, LV,   R, P
                                  CED
Mariel Hemingway, Eric Roberts, directed by
Bob Fosse
The true show-business story of the stormy
relationship of Playboy Playmate of the Year
Dorothy Stratten and her manager-husband
Paul Snider that ended in headline-making
tragedy.
MPAA:R
Wolfgang Glattes; Kenneth Utt — *Warner*
Home Video

Star Is Born, A   1954
Musical-Drama
58251   150 mins   C   B, V   R, P
Judy Garland, James Mason, Jack Carson,
Charles Bickford, Tommy Noonan, directed by
George Cukor
A young actress achieves Hollywood success
and marries a famous leading man whose star
wanes as hers shines brighter. Songs include
"The Man That Got Away," and "Born in a
Trunk."
Warner Bros — *Warner Home Video*

Star Is Born, A   1954
Musical-Drama
66325   175 mins   C   B, V, LV,   P
                                  CED
Judy Garland, James Mason, Jack Carson,
Tommy Noonan, Charles Bickford, directed by
George Cukor
This newly restored version of the 1954 classic
reinstates over 20 minutes of long-missing
footage, including three Garland musical
numbers, "Here's What I'm Here For,"
"Shampoo Commercial" and "Lose That Long
Face." In stereo.
MPAA:PG
Warner Bros; Transcona
Enterprises — *Warner Home Video*

Star Is Born, A   1937
Drama
11217   111 mins   C   B, V, FO   P
Janet Gaynor, Fredric March, Adolphe Menjou,
May Robson, Andy Devine, directed by William
Wellman
A movie star declining in popularity marries a
shy girl and helps her become a star. Her fame
eclipses his and tragic consequences follow.
Academy Awards '37: Best Original Story;
Special Academy Award to W. Howard Greene
for color photography.
United Artists — *Video Yesteryear; Video*
Connection; VCII; Video Dimensions; Sheik
Video; Ampro Video Productions; Cable Films;
Discount Video Tapes; King of Video; Budget
Video; Western Film & Video Inc; Cinema
Concepts; Classic Video Cinema Collector's
Club

Star Is Born, A   1976
Musical
37425   140 mins   C   B, V   R, P
Barbra Streisand, Kris Kristofferson, Paul
Mazursky, Gary Busey, Oliver Clark
The tragic story of one rock star (Streisand) on
her way to the top and another (Kristofferson)
whose career is in decline. An updated version
of the 1937 and 1955 movies.
Academy Awards '76: Best Song (Evergreen).
MPAA:R
Warner Bros — *Warner Home Video; RCA*
VideoDiscs

Star Packer   1934
Western
08829   53 mins   B/W   B, V, 3/4U   P
John Wayne
"Duke" puts on a marshal's badge and cleans
out the renegades.
Monogram — *Penguin Video; Video*
Connection; Sheik Video; Cable Films; Discount
Video Tapes

Star-Spangled Cowboys   1982
Football
47710   23 mins   C   B, V, FO   P
Team highlights of the 1981 Dallas Cowboys
who recaptured the NFC Eastern Division
Championship thanks to Tony Dorsett's 1,646
yards rushing.
NFL Films — *NFL Films Video*

Star Struck   1982
Musical/Comedy
65710   95 mins   C   B, V   P
Jo Kennedy
An 18-year-old waitress dreams of becoming a
new wave singer.
MPAA:PG
David Elfick; Richard Brennan — *Embassy*
Home Entertainment

Star Trek I   1966
Science fiction
47615   100 mins   C   CED   P
William Shatner, Leonard Nimoy, Jeffrey Hunter,
Susan Oliver, DeForest Kelley
Star Trek's only two-part episode, "The
Menagerie," incorporates the original 1964 pilot
show as a flashback. Mr. Spock kidnaps the
former captain of the Enterprise and returns to
Talos IV, the scene of a mystery from years
past.
NBC — *RCA VideoDiscs*

Star Trek II   196?
Science fiction
56882   100 mins   C   CED   P
William Shatner, Leonard Nimoy, DeForest
Kelley, Joan Collins, Frank Gorshin

Two television episodes, "The City on the Edge of Forever," written by Harlan Ellison, and "Let That Be Your Last Battlefield."
NBC — *RCA VideoDiscs*

Star Trek Bloopers   1969
Outtakes and bloopers/Science fiction
64922   25 mins   C   B, V   P
William Shatner, Leonard Nimoy, DeForest Kelley, Nichelle Nichols
The TV cast of "Star Trek" appears in these flubs and goofs that were edited out of the actual episodes. The blooper reels from all three seasons are included on this tape.
Gene Roddenberry — *Video Dimensions*

Star Trek III   1967
Science fiction
59386   100 mins   C   CED   P
William Shatner, Leonard Nimoy, DeForest Kelley, Nichelle Nichols, James Doohan, Walter Koenig
A double feature of two popular "Star Trek" episodes: "The Trouble with Tribbles" and "The Tholian Web."
NBC — *RCA VideoDiscs*

Star Trek IV   1967
Science fiction
60386   100 mins   C   CED   P
William Shatner, Leonard Nimoy, DeForest Kelley, Nichelle Nichols, Ricardo Montalban
Two "Star Trek" television episodes that provided the background for the recent feature films based on the series: "Space Seed" and "The Changeling."
NBC — *RCA VideoDiscs*

Star Trek V   1967
Science fiction
64332   100 mins   C   CED   P
William Shatner, Leonard Nimoy, DeForest Kelley, Nichelle Nichols, Mark Lenard
Two more well-liked episodes from the famous television series: "Mirror Mirror" and "Balance of Terror."
NBC — *RCA VideoDiscs*

Star Trek VI   1967
Science fiction
64784   100 mins   C   CED   P
William Shatner, Leonard Nimoy, DeForest Kelley, Celia Lovsky, Mark Lenard, Jane Wyatt
Two more episodes in the popular TV series: "Amok Time" and "Journey to Babel."
NBC — *RCA VideoDiscs*

Star Trek: Space Seed   1967
Science fiction
60211   50 mins   C   B, V   R, P
William Shatner, Leonard Nimoy, DeForest Kelley, Nichelle Nichols, Ricardo Montalban

This is the classic TV episode which inspired the 1982 film "Star Trek II: The Wrath of Khan" where Khan, the leader of a race of supermen, tries to take over the Enterprise. Also included is a trailer for the feature film.
NBC — *Paramount Home Video*

Star Trek: The Motion Picture   1980
Science fiction
48512   132 mins   C   CED   P
William Shatner, Leonard Nimoy, DeForest Kelley, Stephen Collins, Persis Khambatta
The starship Enterprise must fight a mysterious alien invasion heading directly for Earth. With new equipment and a new mission, Captain Kirk orders the starship into Warp Drive to meet and conquer this destructive enemy.
MPAA:G
Gene Roddenberry — *RCA VideoDiscs*

Star Trek: The Motion Picture   1980
Science fiction
64510   144 mins   C   B, V, LV   R, P
William Shatner, Leonard Nimoy, DeForest Kelley, James Doohan, Stephen Collins, Persis Khambatta
The Enterprise fights a strange alien force that threatens Earth in this adaptation of the famous TV series. Twelve additional minutes of previously unseen footage have been added to this home video version of the theatrical feature. In stereo.
MPAA:G
Gene Roddenberry; Paramount — *Paramount Home Video*

Star Trek II: The Wrath of Khan   1982
Science fiction
62784   113 mins   C   B, V, LV   R, P
William Shatner, Leonard Nimoy, Ricardo Montalban, DeForest Kelley, directed by Nicholas Meyer
Admiral Kirk and the crew of the Enterprise are targeted for death by Khan, an old foe who blames Kirk for the death of his wife.
MPAA:PG
Paramount — *Paramount Home Video; RCA VideoDiscs*

Star Trek Volume 1   1966
Science fiction
44587   104 mins   C   B, V   R, P
William Shatner, Leonard Nimoy, DeForest Kelley, Jeffrey Hunter, Susan Oliver
"The Menagerie," a two-part episode, tells the story of what happened to the former commander of the Enterprise, Captain Christopher Pike, and why Spock almost faced court martial.
NBC — *Paramount Home Video*

Star Trek Volume 2   1967
Science fiction
44584   104 mins   C   B, V   R, P
*William Shatner, Leonard Nimoy, DeForest
Kelley, Jane Wyatt, Mark Lenard*
In "Amok Time" Kirk authorizes an unscheduled
voyage to Vulcan for Spock's marriage because
although Vulcans are normally unemotional,
when the time comes to marry they are
compelled, under penalty of madness and
death, to return to their home planet. Kirk
becomes part of this ritual wedding ceremony.
The second episode, "Journey to Babel,"
involves intrigue when the Enterprise is
assigned the task of transporting delegates
from many planets to the Babel Conference and
Kirk suspects a spy on board. Among the
delegates are Spock's parents, which presents
the opportunity for reconciliation between
Spock and his father.
NBC — *Paramount Home Video*

Star Trek Volume 3   1968
Science fiction
44583   104 mins   C   B, V   R, P
*William Shatner, Leonard Nimoy, DeForest
Kelley, Nichelle Nichols*
In the episode "Mirror, Mirror" a transporter
malfunction throws the Enterprise crew into a
parallel or mirror universe where command is
asserted by force and advancement is achieved
by assassination. The search for a missing
Federation ship, the Defiant, leads the
Enterprise into unchartered space in the
episode "The Tholian Web." The ship appears
on the viewing screen, but does not register on
the sensors. It has suffered a power loss that
also affects the Enterprise, causing weakness
and insanity among the crew. When Kirk goes
aboard the Defiant to investigate, he becomes
stranded on the empty ship.
NBC — *Paramount Home Video*

Star Trek Volume 4   196?
Science fiction
44585   104 mins   C   B, V   R, P
*William Shatner, Leonard Nimoy, DeForest
Kelley, Nichelle Nichols, James Doohan,
George Takei*
This program contains two episodes of the
popular TV series Star Trek: "The Trouble with
Tribbles ('67) and "Let That Be Your Last
Battlefield" ('69). "The Trouble with Tribbles"
speaks for itself. Tribbles—cute, fuzzy,
seemingly harmless little creatures create
problems for the crew of the Enterprise. In "Let
That Be Your Last Battlefield" an age-old battle
between two hostile alien powers engulfs the
Enterprise.
NBC — *Paramount Home Video*

Star Trek Volume 5   196?
Science fiction
44586   104 mins   C   B, V   R, P

*William Shatner, Leonard Nimoy, DeForest
Kelley, Joan Collins*
This program contains two episodes from the
popular TV series Star Trek. In "The Balance of
Terror" ('66), Captain Kirk is about to perform a
wedding for two crew members when the
Romulans attack Outpost 4. This leads the
Enterprise in pursuit of an attack ship, whose
invisibility shield ultimately causes its own
destruction. In "The City on the Edge of
Forever," McCoy accidentally beams himself
down to a strange planet, where he enters a
time vortex and drastically changes history. Kirk
and Spock must rescue him.
NBC — *Paramount Home Video*

Star Wars   1977
Science fiction/Adventure
47505   121 mins   C   B, V, LV,   P
                                CED
*Mark Hamill, Carrie Fisher, Harrison Ford, Alec
Guinness, Peter Cushing, David Prowse,
directed by George Lucas*
A long time ago in a galaxy far, far away, Rebel
forces are engaged in a life-or-death struggle
with the tyrant leaders of the Galactic Empire.
Musical score composed by John Williams.
Academy Awards '77: Best Art Decoration; Set
Decoration; Film Editing; Costume Design;
Achievement in Sound; Visual Effects; Original
Score.   MPAA:PG   EL, SP
20th Century Fox — *CBS/Fox Video*

Stars Look Down, The   1939
Drama
07263   96 mins   B/W   B, V   P
*Michael Redgrave, Margaret Lockwood, Emlyn
Williams*
A mine owner forces miners to work in an
unsafe mine in a Welsh town and disaster
strikes. Based on the A. J. Cronin novel.
MGM; Carol Reed — *Budget Video; Cable
Films; Discount Video Tapes; Video Yesteryear*

Stars of Jazz   1958
Music
21334   51 mins   B/W   B, V, FO   P
Mel Torme, Andre Previn, Shelly Manne
Two programs from this series featuring jazz
greats at their best.
ABC — *Video Yesteryear*

Stars of the Russian   1953
Ballet
Dance
69833   80 mins   C   B, V   P
Galina Vlanova, Maya Plisetskaya
This program is a compilation of excerpts from
three ballets, Swan Lake, The Fountain of
Bakhchisarai, and The Flames of Paris.
Sovexportfilm USSR — *Video Arts
International*

Stars on 45 — 1983
Music
65518   71 mins   C   B, V, LV, CED   P
An elaborate live stage revue covering the past 30 years of pop music history. Featured are nostalgia tunes by Little Richard, Chuck Berry, Elvis, and the Beatles. Woodstock, Soul and Disco tunes are all highlighted in the show. In stereo VHS and Beta Hi-Fi.
MCA Pay Television — *MCA Home Video*

Stars on Parade/Boogie Woogie Dream — 1946
Musical
11258   55 mins   B/W   B, V, FO   P
Milton Wood, Jane Cooley, Francine Everett, Bob Howard, Eddie Smith, Phil Moore, Lena Horne, Teddy Wilson
A pair of all-black musicals which shows off a host of talent from the 1940's.
All American Pictures — *Video Yesteryear*

Start to Finish the Grand Prix — 1981
Automobiles-Racing
68245   89 mins   C   B, V, CED   P
The highlights of the 1981 Grand Prix are presented in this film.
Formula One Constructors Association — *MGM/UA Home Video*

Starting a Wine Cellar — 1980
Alcoholic beverages
44276   25 mins   C   V   P
Wine expert Bill Hikok discusses how to buy and store wines, how to serve wines, and which wines to serve with which food. The program concludes with a list of the best vintage wines from the top countries in the world.
American Home Video Library — *American Home Video Library*

Starting Over — 1979
Comedy-Drama
48513   105 mins   C   B, V, LV   R, P
Burt Reynolds, Jill Clayburgh, Candice Bergen
His life racked by divorce, Phil Potter learns what it's like to be single, self-sufficient, and lonely once again. When a blind date grows into a serious affair, the romance is temporarily halted by his hang-up for his ex-wife.
MPAA:R
Alan J. Pakula — *Paramount Home Video; RCA VideoDiscs*

Starvengers — 1982
Cartoons/Science fiction
62425   105 mins   C   B, V   P
Animated
When action and excitement meet futuristic technology, the result is the high-powered super-intelligence of the robot Starvenger.
EL, SP
Toei Animation; Terry Production — *Family Home Entertainment*

State of Siege — 1973
Drama
44781   119 mins   C   B, V   P
Yves Montand, Renato Salvatori, O.E. Hasse
Unsettling American foreign policy results in the assasination of U.S. officials in South America.
Cinema 5 — *RCA/Columbia Pictures Home Video*

State of the Union — 1948
Comedy
31603   124 mins   B/W   B, V   P
Spencer Tracy, Katherine Hepburn, Angela Lansbury, Van Johnson, directed by Frank Capra
A presidential candidate, backed by a millionairess, battles for integrity with his wife.
MGM — *MCA Home Video*

Stations West — 1948
Mystery
10070   92 mins   B/W   B, V   P, T
Dick Powell, Jane Greer, Agnes Moorehead, Burl Ives, Tom Powers, Raymond Burr
Disguised Army officer is sent to uncover mystery of hijackers and murderers.
RKO — *Blackhawk Films*

Stay as You Are — 1978
Drama
47371   103 mins   C   B, V   R, P
Marcello Mastroianni, Nastassia Kinski, Francisco Rabal, Monica Randal
A sensual, psychological drama about an older man who finds himself attracted to a young girl—who may be his daughter by a long-forgotten mistress.
Giovanni Bertolucci — *Warner Home Video*

Staying Alive — 1983
Drama
Closed Captioned
65400   96 mins   C   B, V, LV, CED   R, P
John Travolta, Cynthia Rhodes, Finola Hughes
A talented young dancer struggles to obtain a role in a professional Broadway musical. Along the way, he becomes intimately involved with two attractive young women. In stereo VHS and Beta Hi-Fi.
MPAA:PG
Paramount — *Paramount Home Video*

Steam and Diesel on the   **195?**
Bessemer and Lake Erie/
The Diesels Roar on the
Pennsy
Trains
59991   24 mins   B/W   B, V   P, T
"Steam and Diesel" shows the contrast
between steam and diesel trains during the
transitional period, the twilight years of the B.
and L. E. "Diesels Roar" features the five
"Geeps" rolling east and the westbound
"Duquesne."
Fred McLeod — *Blackhawk Films*

Steam Daylight Rides   **1983**
Again, The
Ships
74474   12 mins   C   B, V   P
This tape looks at the return of a Southern
Pacific steam locomotive as a daylight
locomotive.
Bill Warrick — *Interurban Films*

Steam in the Sierras   **1978**
Trains
55514   60 mins   C   B, V   P
This program presents a nine-car train of
authentic 1920 era coaches headed by two
classic steam locomotives: the Consolidation
No. 28 and Mikado No. 34 of the Sierra Railroad
in California.
De Luz — *De Luz Video*

Steam Locomotive, The   **1941**
Trains
68903   20 mins   B/W   B, V   P
A dramatization on what a steam locomotive is,
how it performs and how it is maintained.
New York City Public Relations
Department — *Interurban Films*

Steamboat Bill, Jr.   **1928**
Comedy
10095   72 mins   B/W   B, V   P, T
Buster Keaton, Ernest Torrence, Marion Byron,
Tom Lewis
Student returns to father's Mississippi river boat.
After many misadventures, he marries daughter
of his father's rival.
United Artists; Schenk Keaton
Prod — *Blackhawk Films; Discount Video*
Tapes; Video Dimensions; Sheik Video; Video
Yesteryear; Classic Video Cinema Collector's
Club

Steel   **1980**
Drama
66608   100 mins   C   B, V, LV   P
Construction workers on a mammoth
skyscraper face insurmountable odds and
strong opposition to the completion of the
building.

MPAA:R
World Northal — *Vestron Video*

Steel Town   **1983**
Tough/Steelers 50
Seasons
Football
66218   45 mins   C   B, V, FO   P
The Pittsburgh Steelers' 1982-83 season
highlights plus a retrospective of their first 50
years.
NFL Films — *NFL Films Video*

Steinbeck's The Pearl   **1948**
Drama/Literature-American
58732   90 mins   B/W   B, V   P
Pedro Armandez, Maria Marques
John Steinbeck's classic novel concerning two
people who find a valuable pearl which disrupts
their lives. (Original screenplay by Steinbeck).
RKO — *Mastervision*

Step Lively   **1944**
Musical/Comedy
64916   88 mins   B/W   B, V   P, T
Frank Sinatra, Gloria De Haven, George
Murphy, Walter Slezak, Adolphe Menjou, Anne
Jeffreys
A young playwright tries to recover the money
he loaned to a fast-talking Broadway producer
and is forced to take the leading role in his play.
This musical remake of "Room Service" was
Frank Sinatra's first starring role.
RKO — *Blackhawk Films*

Steve Allen Plymouth   **1960**
Show, The
Comedy/Variety
69580   60 mins   B/W   B, V, FO   P
Steve Allen, Patrice Munsel, Jonathan Winters,
Phil Harris, Don Knotts, Bill Dana, Les Brown
Orchestra
This March, 1960 TV special features a large
cast of comedians and singers performing
comedy sketches, movie spoofs and musical
numbers. All original Plymouth commercials are
included.
NBC — *Video Yesteryear*

Steve Miller Band   **1983**
Music-Performance
69391   50 mins   C   B, V   R, P
This music video showcases one of America's
premier rock bands live in concert and includes
the hits "Abracadabra," "Rock 'n Me" and "Fly
Like an Eagle," among others.
EMI Music — *THORN EMI Home Video*

Stevie Nicks in Concert   **1982**
Music-Performance
60572   56 mins   C   B, V, CED   P

The song siren of Fleetwood Mac performs "Sara," "Stop Draggin' My Heart Around," "Edge of Seventeen," and more in this March 1982 solo concert featuring a back-up band comprised of Roy Bittan, Bob Glaub, Bobby Hall, Russ Kunkel, Benmont Tench, Waddy Wachtel, Sharon Celani, and Lori Perry. Stereo. Marty Callner — *CBS/Fox Video; Pioneer Artists*

Stiletto 1969
Crime-Drama
08523   101 mins   C   B, V   P
Alex Cord, Britt Ekland, Patrick O'Neal, Joseph Wiseman, Barbara McNair, Roy Scheider
A young man is rescued from a mob by a Mafia gang leader after raping a young girl. Based on a novel by Harold Robbins.
MPAA:R
Avco Embassy; Norman Rosemont — *Embassy Home Entertainment*

Still of the Night 1982
Suspense
66067   91 mins   C   B, V, CED   P
Meryl Streep, Roy Scheider, directed by Robert Benton
A Hitchcock-style thriller about a psychiatrist infatuated with a mysterious woman who may or may not be a killer.
MPAA:PG
United Artists — *CBS/Fox Video*

Still Smokin' 1983
Comedy
64937   91 mins   C   B, V   R, P
Cheech Marin, Tommy Chong
Cheech and Chong travel to Amsterdam to raise funds for a bankrupt film festival group by hosting a dope-a-thon.
MPAA:R
Paramount — *Paramount Home Video*

Stillwell Road 1947
World War II/Documentary
53647   49 mins   B/W   B, V, 3/4U   P
A documentary look at Signal Corps footage of the China-Burma front, focusing on this moment in history with American forces under the command of General Joe Stillwell.
Unknown — *International Historic Films; Penguin Video; Discount Video Tapes*

Sting, The 1973
Comedy-Drama
14009   129 mins   C   B, V, LV   P
Paul Newman, Robert Redford, Robert Shaw, Charles Durning, Eileen Brennan, directed by George Roy Hill
A pair of con-artists in Chicago of the 1930's set out to fleece a big time racketeer, pitting brain against brawn and pistol.

Academy Awards '73: Best Picture; Best Story and Screenplay; Best Art Direction; Best Set Decoration.   MPAA:PG
Universal; Richard D Zanuck — *MCA Home Video; RCA VideoDiscs*

Sting II, The 1983
Comedy
64794   102 mins   C   B, V, LV, CED   P
Jackie Gleason, Mac Davis, Teri Garr, Karl Malden, Oliver Reed, directed by Jeremy Paul Kagan
A complicated comic plot concludes with the final con game involving a fixed boxing match where the stakes top a million dollars and where the payoff could be murder. A sequel to "The Sting."
MPAA:PG
Universal — *MCA Home Video*

Sting of the West 1976
Comedy/Western
69387   90 mins   C   B, V   P
Jack Palance, Timothy Brent, Lionel Stander
A journeyman con-artist swindles his way across the Wild West.
MPAA:PG
Foreign — *Cinemagreats*

Stir Crazy 1980
Comedy
58435   104 mins   C   B, V, LV   P
Richard Pryor, Gene Wilder, Nicholas Coster, Lee Purcell, directed by Sidney Poitier
Two down-on-their luck losers find themselves convicted of a robbery they didn't commit and sentenced to 120 years behind bars with a mean assortment of inmates.
MPAA:R
Columbia; Hannah Weinstein — *RCA/Columbia Pictures Home Video; RCA VideoDiscs*

Stolen Kisses 1969
Drama
44775   90 mins   C   B, V   P
Jean-Pierre Leaud, Delphine Seyrig, directed by Francois Truffaut
A continuation of the story of Antoine Doinel (first told in the picture "The 400 Blows") and his dishonorable discharge from the army, his initially awkward, but finally successful adventures with women.
Lopert Pictures — *RCA/Columbia Pictures Home Video*

Stomach Formula 1984
Physical fitness
74076   49 mins   C   B, V   P
This is the official Richard Simmons seven-minute a day workout of abdominal fitness.

Karl Home Video — *Karl Video*

Stone Cold Dead   1980
Mystery
69306   100 mins   C   B, V   P
Richard Crenna, Paul Williams, Linda Sorensen, Belinda J. Montgomery
A sniper who selects only prostitutes as victims baits the police with photographs of the victims at the moment of their deaths.
MPAA:R
George Mendeluk; John Ryan — *Media Home Entertainment*

Stone Killer, The   1973
Drama
76039   95 mins   C   B, V   P
Charles Bronson, Martin Balsam, Norman Fell, Ralph Waite
Charles Bronson stars as a tough plainclothes cop in this action-packed drama set in the underworld of New York and Los Angeles.
MPAA:R
Michael Winner — *RCA/Columbia Pictures Home Video*

Stoner   1980
Martial arts/Adventure
59083   88 mins   C   B, V   P
A martial arts adventure featuring a showdown between special agents and a depraved crime lord.
Unknown — *HarmonyVision*

Stoney Knows How   1982
Folklore/Documentary
60456   29 mins   C   B, V, 3/4U   P
A look at the phenomenon of American tattooing, focusing on the life of a master tattoo artist.
Bruce Lane — *Flower Films*

Stooges Shorts Festival   194?
Comedy
57342   55 mins   B/W   B, V   P
This collection of shorts includes "Disorder in the Court" (1936), "Sing a Song of Six Pants" (1947), and "Malice in the Palace" (1949).
Columbia — *Budget Video*

Stop That Train   195?
Adventure
10036   25 mins   B/W   B, V   P, T
Kirby Grant, Gloria Winters, Perry Kellman, Edward Foster, William Hale
Escaped convict plants explosives aboard train with railway president on it. With ten minutes to spare, Sky King tries to make a rescue. From the TV series "Sky King."
CBS — *Blackhawk Films*

Stories and Fables—Volume 1   1984
Fairy tales
66355   40 mins   C   B, V   R, P
This first volume of children's fables contains live-action versions of "Simpleton Peter" and "The Well of the World's End."
Walt Disney — *Walt Disney Home Video*

Stories and Fables—Volume 2   1984
Fairy tales
66356   40 mins   C   B, V   R, P
The tales of "The Soldier Who Didn't Wash" and "The Five Loaves" are included in this volume of children's fables.
Walt Disney — *Walt Disney Home Video*

Stories and Fables—Volume 3   1984
Fairy tales
66357   40 mins   C   B, V   R, P
Live-action versions of "The Forbidden Door" and "Cap O'Rushes" are featured in this volume of children's tales for the whole family.
Walt Disney — *Walt Disney Home Video*

Stories and Fables, Volume 4   1984
Fantasy/Fairy tales
72788   50 mins   C   B, V   P
A tale about a lazy young man who successfully masquerades as a man of the Cloth until he has an unforeseen encounter with the King.
Walt Disney Productions — *Walt Disney Home Video*

Stories and Fables, Volume 5   1984
Fairy tales
72789   50 mins   C   B, V   P
Two amusing stories that children might learn something from.
Walt Disney Productions — *Walt Disney Home Video*

Stories and Fables, Volume 6   1984
Fairy tales
72790   50 mins   C   B, V   P
Two enchanting stories, "The Foolish Brother," and "The Twelve Months" are included; the first features an inept bandit and the latter tells the tale of a lovely young girl driven to perform incredible feats by her contempt for stepmother and sisters.
Walt Disney Productions — *Walt Disney Home Video*

Stork Club, The   1945
Musical/Comedy
66397   98 mins   B/W   B, V   P
Betty Hutton, Barry Fitzgerald, Don Defore,
Robert Benchley, Bill Goodwin
A nightclub hat-check girl saves an elderly
millionaire from drowning and he gets her a job
in a show.
Paramount — *Movie Buff Video*

Storm Over Asia   1928
Drama
53705   70 mins   B/W   B, V, 3/4U   P
Directed by V.I. Podovkin
A Mongolian trapper is discovered to be
descended from Genghis Khan and made
puppet emperor of a Soviet province. Silent.
USSR; Mezhrabpomfilm — *International*
Historic Films; Sheik Video; Festival Films

Stormy Trails   1936
Western
54193   59 mins   B/W   B, V   P
Rex Bell
The epic of a fighting Western cowpoke.
Grand National — *Video Connection*

Story in the Temple Red   197?
Lily
Martial arts
21770   88 mins   C   B, V   P
Insurrectionists capture the Prince and Princess
of the Sung Dynasty and only one man can save
them in this Kung Fu bonanza.
Foreign — *Master Arts Video*

Story of Adele H., The   1975
Drama
58252   97 mins   C   B, V   R, P
Isabelle Adjani, Bruce Robinson, directed by
Francois Truffaut
The story of Adele Hugo, daughter of Victor
Hugo, who threw her life away in self-destructive
love.
MPAA:PG
Les Films du Carosse — *Warner Home Video*

Story of Anna O, The   1980
Psychology
60452   19 mins   C   B, V, 3/4U   P
A poetic dramatization of an early
psychoanalytic case history circa 1880. The
story of 21-year-old Anna who suffers from a
bewildering set of symptoms until a pioneering
doctor with an experimental treatment provides
a cure.
Terrel Seltzer — *Flower Films*

Story of Esther, The   1979
Drama/Bible
55017   49 mins   C   B, V   P
Victoria Principal, Michael Ansara, Robert
Mandan, Eddie Mekka, Noah Beery, narrated by
Victor Jory
The story of beautiful Queen Esther of Persia
who risks her life to save her people. Part of the
"Greatest Heroes of the Bible" series.
Sunn Classics — *Vanguard Video*

Story of Lili Marlene, The   1946
World War II/Documentary
53388   22 mins   B/W   B, V, 3/4U   P
A documentary about the famous Germany WW
II song featuring excellent historical footage.
England — *International Historic Films*

Story of O, The   1975
Drama
58809   97 mins   C   B, V   P
Corinne Clery, Anthony Steel, directed by Just
Jaeckin
The story of a young woman whose love for one
man moves her to surrender herself to many
men, in order to please him. Based on the
classic novel by Pauline Reage.
MPAA:X
Allied Artists — *Independent United*
Distributors; MGM/UA Home Video (disc only)

Story of the Silent   19??
Serials, The/Girls in
Danger
Film-History
29499   54 mins   B/W   B, V   P, T
Gloria Swanson, Mae Marsh, Wallace Beery
These two selections capture the best of more
than fourteen silent serials. Featured are Gloria
Swanson tied to the railroad tracks by Wallace
Beery, Mae Marsh threatened with death (or
worse) in caveman times, and other classic
cliffhanger situations. Narration and muscial
score.
Unknown — *Blackhawk Films*

Story of Vernon and   1939
Irene Castle, The
Musical
00274   93 mins   B/W   B, V, 3/4U   P
Fred Astaire, Ginger Rogers
In this, their last film together, Astaire and
Rogers portray two internationally successful
ballroom dancers.
RKO — *Nostalgia Merchant*

Story of William S. Hart,   192?
The/The Sad Clowns
Comedy
10102   50 mins   B/W   B, V   P, T
William S. Hart, Charlie Chaplin, Buster Keaton,
Harry Langdon
Featuring William S. Hart as a cowboy in "Hell's
Hinges," and Chaplin in "Tumbleweeds,"

(1925). From "The History of the Motion Picture" series.
United Artists et al — *Blackhawk Films*

Strada, La 1954
Drama
64920 107 mins B/W B, V P
Anthony Quinn, Giulietta Masina, Richard Basehart, directed by Federico Fellini
A circus strongman adopts a simple - minded peasant girl as his assistant and treats her rudely. This film is considered a classic of Italian neo - realism.
Ponti de Laurentiis; Trans - Lux Distributing — *Video Dimensions; Festival Films*

Straight Shootin' 1917
Western
53635 53 mins B/W B, V P
Harry Carey, Hoot Gibson, Mollie Malone, directed by John Ford
The first major directorial effort of John Ford, which catapulted both Harry Carey and Hoot Gibson to national fame. Silent.
Universal — *Video Connection; Discount Video Tapes*

Straight Time 1978
Drama
58253 114 mins C B, V R, P
Dustin Hoffman, Harry Dean Stanton, Gary Busey, Theresa Russell, M. Emmet Walsh, directed by Ulu Grosbard
An ex-convict hits the streets for the first time in six years and finds he is emotionally locked into a life of crime.
MPAA:R
Sweetwall Productions; First Artists Productions; Warner Bros — *Warner Home Video*

Stralt Jacket 1964
Drama
64912 89 mins B/W B, V P
Joan Crawford, Leif Erickson, Diane Baker
After a woman is released from an insane asylum where she was sent 20 years earlier for killing her husband and his mistress, mysterious axe murders begin to occur in the neighborhood, and she is the prime suspect.
William Castle — *RCA/Columbia Pictures Home Video*

Strange Invaders 1983
Satire/Science fiction
65364 94 mins C B, V, LV P
Nancy Allen, Diana Scarwid, Louise Fletcher
The horrific and subtly humorous story of alien beings whose settlement in a small midwestern town is disturbed by a young professor determined to rescue his child from their clutches.

MPAA:PG
Walter Coblenz — *Vestron Video*

Strange Love of Martha Ivers, The 1946
Drama
66398 117 mins B/W B, V P
Barbara Stanwyck, Van Heflin, Kirk Douglas, Lisabeth Scott, Judith Anderson, directed by Lewis Milestone
An unscrupulous woman takes up with her old boyfriend, without bothering to keep the affair from her husband.
Paramount — *Movie Buff Video*

Strangeness, The 198?
Horror
75626 90 mins C B, V P
Miners release a creature while searching for golden treasures.
unknown — *Trans World Entertainment*

Stranger, The 1946
Mystery
11318 85 mins B/W B, V, FO P
Edward G. Robinson, Loretta Young, Orson Welles, Richard Long, directed by Orson Welles
A government agent is assigned to the manhunt of a Nazi from Hitler's regime who has taken the new identity of a history professor about to marry the daughter of a Supreme Court Judge.
RKO — *Video Yesteryear; Movie Buff Video; Budget Video; VCII; Discount Video Tapes; Sheik Video; Ampro Video Productions; Cable Films; Penguin Video*

Stranger from Venus 1954
Science fiction
44354 78 mins B/W B, V, 3/4U P
Patricia Neal, Helmet Dantine, Derek Bond
A frightening being from outerspace lands to warn Earth and pave the way for the arrival of a "mother ship." Includes previews of coming attractions from classic science fiction films.
Eros — *Nostalgia Merchant*

Stranger Is Watching, A 1982
Horror
59847 92 mins C B, V, CED P
Rip Torn, Kate Mulgrew
A rapist-murderer holds the victim's 10-year-old daughter hostage, along with a New York TV anchorwoman.
MPAA:R
MGM — *MGM/UA Home Video*

Stranger on the Third Floor 1940
Mystery
10065 64 mins B/W B, V P, T
Peter Lorre, John McGuire, Elisha Cook Jr.

Innocent man, released from prison, seeks his persecutors with a vengeance. Someone set him up, but who?
RKO — *Blackhawk Films; Nostalgia Merchant*

Stranger's Kiss   1983
Drama
72185   93 mins   C   B, V   R, P
The director of a 1955 Hollywood movie encourages the two leads to have an off-screen romance to bring reality to his film. Conflict arises when the leading lady's boyfriend, the films financier, gets wind of the scheme.
MPAA:R
Douglas Dilge — *THORN EMI Home Video*

Strangers on a Train   1951
Drama/Suspense
69309   101 mins   B/W   B, V   R, P
Farley Granger, Robert Walker, Ruth Roman, Leo G. Carroll, directed by Alfred Hitchcock
A demented playboy entangles a tennis star in a bizarre scheme of "exchange murders."
Warner Bros — *Warner Home Video; RCA VideoDiscs*

Strategic Air Power   1951
World War II
68896   25 mins   B/W   B, V   P
A documentary which follows the travels of planes in World War II.
US Air Force — *Interurban Films*

Straw Dogs   1972
Drama
46200   114 mins   C   B, V, LV, CED   P
Dustin Hoffman, Susan George, Peter Vaughan, T. P. McKenna, directed by Sam Peckinpah
An American mathematician, disturbed by the predominance of violence in American society, moves with his wife to an isolated Cornish village only to find a primitive savagery beneath the peaceful surface.
MPAA:R
ABC Pictures Corp. — *CBS/Fox Video*

Strawberry Shortcake and the Baby Without a Name   1984
Cartoons
73371   60 mins   C   B, V   P
Animated
Strawberry Shortcake and her friends must save a baby from the clutches of Purple Pieman and Sour Grapes.
CPG Productions — *Family Home Entertainment*

Strawberry Shortcake in Big Apple City   1982
Cartoons
60393   60 mins   C   B, V   P
Animated
Strawberry Shortcake and her friends from Strawberryland meet new friends in Big Apple City.
EL, SP
Miller Rosen Productions — *Family Home Entertainment*

Strawberry Shortcake Pets on Parade   1982
Cartoons
65656   60 mins   C   B, V   P
Animated
Strawberry Shortcake is named judge of a Pet Show and the first prize is a shiny new tricycle, and the Peculiar Purple Pieman of Porcupine Peak plots to swipe it. But Strawberry and her friends teach the Pieman a lesson he won't soon forget.
Miller Rosen Productions — *Family Home Entertainment*

Strawberry Shortcake's House-Warming Party   1983
Cartoons
69582   60 mins   C   B, V   P
Animated
Strawberry Shortcake and her friends in Strawberryland have a house-warming party.
Miller Rosen Productions — *Family Home Entertainment*

Stream Flows Home, The   1978
Video
08571   30 mins   C   B, V, 3/4U   P
A continuous picture of a small stream that finds the sea to create a relaxed background.
Nebulae Prods — *Nebulae Productions*

Stream on Dad's Birthday, The   1978
Video
08572   30 mins   C   B, V, 3/4U   P
A continuous picture of a country stream complete with a footbridge to create a relaxed background.
Nebulae Prods — *Nebulae Productions*

Streamers   1983
War-Drama
66602   118 mins   C   B, V   P
Matthew Modine, Michael Wright, Mitchell Lichenstein
Six young soldiers in a claustrophobic army barracks tensely await the orders that will send them to Vietnam. Based on the play by David Rabe.

MPAA:R
Robert Altman; Nick J. Mileti — *Media Home Entertainment*

Street Fighter, The　1975
Adventure/Martial arts
54106　85 mins　C　B, V, CED　P
Sonny Chiba
Local hoodlum engages in fast-paced marital arts action.
MPAA:R
Unknown — *CBS/Fox Video*

Street Law　1979
Crime-Drama
65727　77 mins　C　B, V　P
Franco Nero
A vivid and violent study of one man's frustrated ware on crime.
MPAA:R
Unknown — *VidAmerica*

Street Scene　1931
Drama
01735　80 mins　B/W　B, V　P
Sylvia Sydney, William Collier Jr., directed by King Vidor
Based on Elmer Rice's hit play, film depicts trials and tribulations of young love in New York tenement district.
United Artists — *Budget Video; Cable Films; Video Connection; Western Film & Video Inc; Classic Video Cinema Collector's Club*

Streetcar Named Desire, A　1951
Drama
58949　122 mins　B/W　B, V　P
Vivien Leigh, Marlon Brando, Kim Hunter, Karl Malden, directed by Elia Kazan
Powerful film version of Tennessee Williams' play about a repressed southern widow who is abused and driven mad by her brutal brother-in-law.
Academy Awards '51: Best Actress (Leigh); Best Supporting Actress (Hunter); Best Supporting Actor (Malden).
Charles K Feldman; Elia Kazan — *CBS/Fox Video; RCA VideoDiscs*

Stress Management　1982
Stress
75697　60 mins　C　B, V, 3/4U　P
This program contains subliminal messages to help the viewer better manage stress.
Environmental Video — *Environmental Video*

Strike　1924
Drama/Propaganda
72494　70 mins　B/W　B, V, 3/4U　P
Directed by Sergei Eisenstein
Eisenstein's classic film about government clashing with factory workers in 1912 Russia.
Goskino; Proletkult — *International Historic Films*

Stripes　1981
Comedy
Closed Captioned
05938　105 mins　C　B, V　P
Bill Murray, Harold Ramis, P. J. Soles, Warren Oates, John Candy, directed by Ivan Reitman
Two friends enlist in the Army to straighten out their lives.
MPAA:R
Columbia — *RCA/Columbia Pictures Home Video; RCA VideoDiscs*

Stripes　1982
Football
47709　23 mins　C　B, V, FO　P
Team highlights of the '81 Bengals, who posted a 12-4 regular season record and won their first AFC Championship.
NFL Films — *NFL Films Video*

Stroker Ace　1983
Comedy
69308　96 mins　C　B, V, CED　R, P
Burt Reynolds, Ned Beatty, Jim Nabors, Parker Stevenson, Loni Anderson
A flamboyant stock car driver tries to break an iron-clad promotional contract signed with a greedy fried-chicken magnate.
MPAA:PG
Warner Bros — *Warner Home Video*

Struggle Through Death　197?
Martial arts
72175　93 mins　C　B, V　P
Two young men escape the clutches of evil Ching Kue and attempt to free their fellow prisoners so they can overthrow the despot.
Foreign — *Master Arts Video*

Stryker　1983
Science fiction
69542　86 mins　C　B, V　P
Steve Sandor, Andria Fabio
In the future, after a devastating war, bands of marauders fight each other for the scarcest resource—water.
MPAA:R
Cirio H Santiago — *Embassy Home Entertainment*

Stud, The　1978
Drama
47801　90 mins　C　B, V　R, P
Joan Collins, Oliver Tobias
The owner of a fashionable "after hours" dance spot hires a young, handsome stud to manage the club and attend to her personal needs.

MPAA:R
Brent Walker Film Productions — *THORN EMI Home Video*

Student Bodies 1981
Satire
58717   86 mins   C   B, V, LV   R, P
Kristen Riter, Matthew Goldsby, Richard Brando, Joe Flood, directed by Mickey Rose
A spoof of high-school horror films a la "Halloween."
MPAA:R
Paramount — *Paramount Home Video*

Studio One: "The Defender" 1957
Drama
38124 104 mins B/W   B, V, FO   P
Steve McQueen, William Shatner, Ralph Bellamy, Martin Balsam
Courtroom melodrama originally televised live on the "Studio One" series in 1957.
CBS — *Video Yesteryear*

Study in Scarlet, A 1933
Mystery
48428   77 mins B/W   B, V   P
Reginald Owen, Alan Mowbray, Anna May Wong
Master sleuth Sherlock Holmes solves a series of complex murders with the aid of faithful companion Dr. Watson.
World Wide — *Budget Video; Ampro Video Productions; Cable Films; Video Yesteryear*

Study in Scarlet, A/Sherlock Holmes and the Secret Weapon 194?
Mystery
58916 145 mins B/W   B, V   P
Basil Rathbone, Nigel Bruce, Lionel Atwell, Anna May Wong, Reginald Owens
A Sherlock Holmes double feature: "A Study in Scarlet" (1933), in which Sherlock Holmes (Reginald Owen), solves a series of complex murders; "Sherlock Holmes and the Secret Weapon" (1942), in which Holmes (Basil Rathbone) enemy spies.
EL, 3P
World Wide — *Ampro Video Productions*

Stunt Man, The 1981
Drama/Satire
49398   129 mins   C   CED   P
Peter O'Toole, Steve Railsback, Barbara Hershey, directed by Richard Bush
A satire on the world of moviemaking, in which an ex-Vietnam soldier-turned-stunt-man stages a battle of wits with a power-crazed movie director.
MPAA:R
20th Century Fox — *CBS/Fox Video*

Stunt Rock 1980
Adventure
66009   90 mins   C   B, V   P
A feature film combining rock music, magic, and some of the most incredible stunts ever attempted.
MPAA:PG
Intertamar — *Monterey Home Video*

Stunts 1977
Adventure
66185   90 mins   C   B, V   R, P
Robert Forster, Fiona Lewis
A film dealing with the thrilling and often horrifying lives of professional stuntmen.
New Line Cinema — *THORN EMI Home Video*

Subliminal Persuasion Video 1983
Health education
64848   60 mins   C   B, V, 3/4U   P
3 pgms
Barrie Konicov, founder of the World Congress of Professional Hypnotists, orginated these three programs incorporating scenes from Environmental Video's surf program. The video is packaged with a audiocassette.
1.Lose Weight 2.Stop Smoking or Drinking 3.Reduce Tension
Potentials Unlimited; Environmental Video — *Environmental Video*

Submarine Alert 1942
Adventure
08614   67 mins   B/W   B, V, 3/4U   P
Richard Arlen, Wendy Barrie, Dwight Frye
An FBI agent is publicly discredited so he can become a member of a spy ring.
Paramount — *Penguin Video*

Subterfuge 1968
Drama
65685   89 mins   C   B, V   P
Joan Collins, Gene Barry, Richard Todd
When a special American security agent goes to England for a "vacation," his presence causes speculation and poses several serious questions for both British Intelligence and the underworld.
Commonwealth United TV — *NTA Home Entertainment*

Sudden Death 1977
Adventure
59041   84 mins   C   B, V   P
Robert Conrad, Felton Perry
Two professional violence merchants put themselves up for hire.
Topar Films — *Media Home Entertainment*

Sudden Impact   1983
Crime-Drama/Adventure
Closed Captioned
65613   117 mins   C   B, V, LV,   R, P
                        CED
Clint Eastwood, Sondra Locke
"Dirty Harry" Callahan tracks down a revenge-obsessed murderess at the same time that local mobsters come gunning for him.
MPAA:R
Clint Eastwood; Warner Brothers — *Warner Home Video*

Suddenly Last Summer   1959
Drama
65701   114 mins   B/W   B, V   P
Katharine Hepburn, Elizabeth Taylor, Montgomery Cliff
A psychiatrist tries to solve the mystery behind a young girl's mental breakdown. Based on the play by Tennessee Williams.
Sam Spiegel — *RCA/Columbia Pictures Home Video*

Sugar Cookies   1977
Drama
52952   89 mins   C   B, V   P
Lynn Lowry, Monique Van Vooren
An erotic horror story in which young women are the pawns as a satanic satyr and an impassioned lesbian play out a bizarre game of vengeance, love, and death.
MPAA:R
Lloyd Kaufman — *VidAmerica*

Sugar Ray Robinson—Pound for Pound   1982
Boxing
58735   120 mins   C   B, V   P
Sugar Ray Robinson, Jake LaMotta, Bobo Olsen, Randy Turpin, Carmen Basilio
The career of legendary boxer Sugar Ray Robinson is highlighted, from his earliest amateur bouts through his memorable retirement at Madison Square Garden. Some sequences are in black and white.
Big Fights Inc — *VidAmerica*

Sugarland Express, The   1974
Drama
65119   109 mins   C   B, V   P
Goldie Hawn, Ben Johnson, Michael Sacks, William Atherton, directed by Steven Spielberg
To save her son from adoption, a young woman helps her husband break out of prison. In their flight to freedom, they hijack a police car, holding the policeman hostage.
MPAA:PG
Universal — *MCA Home Video*

Summer Camp   1978
Comedy
59659   85 mins   C   B, V   P
John C. McLaughlin, Matt Michaels, Colleen O'Neil
A ten year reunion at a summer camp turns into a bizarre weekend of co-ed football, midnight panty-raids, coupling couples and a wild disco party.
MPAA:R
Mark Borde — *Media Home Entertainment*

Summer Heat   1973
Drama
55594   71 mins   C   B, V   P
Bob Garry, Nicole Avril, Pat Pascal
A no-holds-barred tour through the steamy world of the rich, the restless, and the young, when a young man spends his summer with his hypnotic aunt.
MPAA:X
World Wide Films Corp — *VidAmerica*

Summer in St. Tropez, A   1981
Drama
59698   60 mins   C   B, V   R, P
Photographer David Hamilton's erotic and lyrical study of a household of girls in their first stages of womanhood living outside of society in the south of France.
Ken Kamura — *THORN EMI Home Video*

Summer Lovers   1982
Drama
63372   98 mins   C   B, V, LV,   P
                        CED
Peter Gallagher, Daryl Hannah, Valerie Quennessen
Three young people meet on the exotic Greek island of Santorini one summer to explore life and love.
MPAA:R
Filmways — *Embassy Home Entertainment*

Summer of Fear   1978
Horror
66017   94 mins   C   B, V   R, P
Linda Blair
A happy young woman must overcome the evil forces brought on when her cousin comes to live with her.
Max A Keller; Micheline H Keller — *THORN EMI Home Video*

Summer of '42   1971
Drama
54117   102 mins   C   B, V   R, P
Jennifer O'Neill, Gary Grimes, Jerry Houser, Oliver Conant, directed by Richard Mulligan
A touching story about a 15-year-old boy's coming of sexual age during his summer vacation on an island off New England. While his two friends are fumbling with girls their own

age, he falls in love with a beautiful older woman.
Academy Award '71: Best Musical Score.
MPAA:R
Warner Bros, Mulligan Roth — *Warner Home Video; RCA VideoDiscs*

Summer Solstice   1981
Drama
59696   75 mins   C   B, V   R, P
Henry Fonda, Myrna Loy, Lindsey Crouse, Stephen Collins
An aging couple visits the beach where they first met. There they recapture many of the good and difficult times from the past.
Bruce Marson; Stephen Schlow — *THORN EMI Home Video*

Summerdog   1979
Adventure
29237   90 mins   C   B, V   R, P
James Congdon, Elizabeth Eisenman
The Norman family rescues an abandoned little dog named Hobo from a raccoon trap while they're vacationing in the mountains. In return Hobo saves them from one danger after another.
MPAA:G
GG Communications — *Video Gems*

Sunburn   1979
Comedy
38936   110 mins   C   B, V   R, P
Farrah Fawcett-Majors, Charles Grodin, Joan Collins
Action-packed comedy-mystery of an investigation into the violent death of an aging Acapulco industrialist.
MPAA:PG
Paramount — *Paramount Home Video*

Sundance and the Kid   1976
Western
66195   84 mins   C   B, V   P
John Wade, Karen Blake
Two brothers try to collect an inheritance against all odds.
MPAA:PG
Film Ventures International — *Montoroy Home Video*

Sundays and Cybele   1962
Drama
33613 110 mins B/W   B, V   P
Hardy Kruger, Nicole Courcel, directed by Serge Bourguignon
A ragged war veteran and an orphaned girl develop a strong emotional relationship, which is tragically destroyed by their townspeople.
Academy Awards '62: Best Foreign Film. FR
Romain Pines — *Budget Video; Penguin Video; Discount Video Tapes*

Sundown   1941
War-Drama
11395   91 mins   B/W   B, V, FO   P
Gene Tierney, Bruce Cabot, George Sanders, Harry Carey, Sir Cedric Hardwicke
A Eurasian girl helps the British uncover a Nazi plot in the African desert with her camel caravan.
United Artists; Walter Wanger — *Video Yesteryear; Movie Buff Video*

Sundown Fury   1942
Western
53462   56 mins   B/W   B, V   P
Don "Red" Barry
A young cowboy fights against a group of bandits to hold a telegraph office.
Republic — *Video Connection*

Sun's Gonna Shine   1968
Music
60466   10 mins   C   B, V, 3/4U   P
This program recreates the moment when, at the age of eight, bluesman Lightnin' Hopkins decided to stop chopping cotton and sing for a living. Includes a rendition of "Trouble in Mind." A companion film to "The Blues According to Lightnin' Hopkins."
Les Blank — *Flower Films*

Sunset Boulevard   1950
Drama
38605   110 mins   B/W   B, V   R, P
Gloria Swanson, William Holden, Erich von Stroheim, Nancy Olsen, directed by Billy Wilder
Famed tale of Norma Desmond, aging silent film queen, who, refusing to accept the fact that stardom has ended for her, hires a young screenwriter to help engineer her movie comeback.
Academy Awards '50: Best Story and Screenplay (Wilder, Charles Brackett, D.M. Marshman); Best Music Score (Franz Waxman).
Paramount — *Paramount Home Video; RCA VideoDiscs*

Sunset in El Dorado   194?
Western
57983   56 mins   B/W   B, V   P
Roy Rogers, Dale Evans
Roy and Dale thwart a villainous scheme to defraud farmers of their land.
Republic — *Video Connection*

Sunset Range   1935
Western
14210   59 mins   B/W   B, V   P
Hoot Gibson
Saga of the plains.
First Division — *Video Connection*

Sunset Serenade 1942
Western
05548   60 mins   B/W   B, V, 3/4U   P
Roy Rogers, Trigger, Gabby Hayes, Helen Parrish
Roy Rogers outwits a murderous duo who plans to eliminate the new heir to a ranch.
Republic — *Nostalgia Merchant*

Sunshine Boys, The 1975
Comedy
54103   109 mins   C   B, V, CED   P
George Burns, Walter Matthau, Richard Benjamin, Lee Meredith, Carol Arthur, directed by Herbert Ross
After a long separation, two veteran vaudeville partners, who have shared a hate-love relationship for decades, reunite to renew their friendship and their feud.
Academy Awards '75: Best Supporting Actor (Burns). MPAA:PG
MGM; Ray Stark — *MGM/UA Home Video*

Super Bloopers #1 197?
Outtakes and bloopers
14433   60 mins   C   B, V   P
Outtakes in this collection come from Monogram Pictures, Abbott and Costello films movies, TV shows, and the "Star Trek" series. Also featured are rare TV commercials, trailers, and other short films. Some black and white segments.
NBC et al — *Video Dimensions*

Super Bloopers #2 197?
Outtakes and bloopers
14434   60 mins   C   B, V   P
Bloopers from "Gunsmoke," CBS TV shows, the network news, the "Star Trek" series, plus a network savings bond drive with the stars of "Mission Impossible," "Mannix," and "The Odd Couple." Some black and white segments.
NBC et al — *Video Dimensions*

Super Bowl I 1980
Football
45108   30 mins   C   B, V, FO   R, P
Narrated by John Facenda, Green Bay Packers, Oakland Raiders
Vince Lombardi's mighty Packers subdue Hank Stram's Chiefs in the first meeting between AFL and NFL Champions. Veteran quarterback Bart Starr and aging receiver Max McGee spark the Packers as they pull away in the second half of the 1967 game.
NFL Films — *NFL Films Video*

Super Bowl II 1980
Football
45109   30 mins   C   B, V, FO   R, P
Narrated by John Facenda, Green Bay Packers, Oakland Raiders
The Packers romp to their second straight Super Bowl triumph, 33-14, in Vince Lombardi's last game as Packer head coach, played in 1968.
NFL Films — *NFL Films Video*

Super Bowl III 1980
Football
45110   30 mins   C   B, V, FO   R, P
Narrated by John Facenda, New York Jets, Baltimore Colts
1969: Joe Namath, the flashy young Jet's quarterback, guarantees a victory for his side and produces. Namath connects with receiver George Sauer and Don Maynard in key situations. The Jets' secondary intercepts four passes from Earl Morrow and John Unitas. Matt Snell's seven-yard touchdown run and Jim Turner's three field goals give the Jets a 16-7 victory in one of the greatest upsets in sports history.
NFL Films — *NFL Films Video*

Super Bowl Chronicles 1984
Football
75889   23 mins   C   B, V, FO   P
This program features an elaborate production of highlights from the Super Bowls of the past 18 years.
NFL Films — *NFL Films Video*

Super Bowl IV 1980
Football
45111   30 mins   C   B, V, FO   R, P
Narrated by John Facenda, Kansas City Chiefs, Minnesota Vikings
1970: Coach Hank Stram's "Offense of the 70's," led by quarterback Len Dawson and flanker Otis Taylor, confuses the Viking defense. The Chief's defensive crew stifles quarterback Joe Kapp and the Viking offense. It adds up to a 23-7 victory for Kansas City.
NFL Films — *NFL Films Video*

Super Bowl V 1980
Football
45112   30 mins   C   B, V, FO   R, P
Narrated by John Facenda, Baltimore Colts, Dallas Cowboys
1971: A game "highlighted" by bobbles, mistakes, and a questionable ruling on a Baltimore touchdown pass, is brought to a heart-stopping climax when the Colt's Jim O'Brien boots a 33-yard field goal with just six seconds to play, giving the ecstatic Baltimore team a 16-13 win.
NFL Films — *NFL Films Video*

Super Bowl VI 1980
Football
45113   30 mins   C   B, V, FO   R, P
Narrated by John Facenda, Dallas Cowboys, Miami Dolphins

(For Explanation of codes, see USE GUIDE and KEY)

1972: Dallas' "Doomsday Defense" shuts down the aerial game of Miami quarterback Bob Griese and the running of fullback Larry Csonka. Coach Tom Landry's team finally wins "the big one," 24-3. Roger Staubach and Duane Thomas lead the Cowboy attack.
NFL Films — *NFL Films Video*

Super Bowl VII 1980
Football
45114   30 mins   C   B, V, FO   R, P
Narrated by John Facenda, Miami Dolphins, Washington Redskins
1973: The Dolphins cap a perfect 17-0 season as the "No-Name Defense" holds the Redskin offense scoreless in a 14-7 triumph.
NFL Films — *NFL Films Video*

Super Bowl VIII 1980
Football
45115   30 mins   C   B, V, FO   R, P
Narrated by John Facenda, Miami Dolphins, Minnesota Vikings
The Dolphins cruise to their second straight championship as Larry Csonka runs all over the Vikings' "Purple People Eaters," and the Dolphin defense contains Vikes' quarterback Fran Tarkenton, in this 1974 game.
NFL Films — *NFL Films Video*

Super Bowl IX 1980
Football
45116   30 mins   C   B, V, FO   R, P
Narrated by John Facenda, Pittsburgh Steelers, Minnesota Vikings
The Steelers, led by Terry Bradshaw, Franco Harris, and the "Steel Curtain" defense dominate this game and the Vikings are disappointed for the third time in three Super Bowl tries (1975).
NFL Films — *NFL Films Video*

Super Bowl X 1980
Football
45117   30 mins   C   B, V, FO   R, P
Narrated by John Facenda, Pittsburgh Steelers, Dallas Cowboys
1976: Terry Bradshaw and Lynn Swan team up to lead the Steelers over the Cowboys 21-17 and capture their second consecutive Super Bowl Championship. A late rally by Roger Staubach and his Dallas mates falls short.
NFL Films — *NFL Films Video*

Super Bowl XI 1980
Football
45118   30 mins   C   B, V, FO   R, P
Narrated by John Facenda, Oakland Raiders, Minnesota Vikings
1977: Quarterback Ken Stabler leads the Raiders over the Vikings 32-14 as Minnesota once again fails to win their fourth Super Bowl effort.

NFL Films — *NFL Films Video*

Super Bowl XII 1980
Football
45119   30 mins   C   B, V, FO   R, P
Narrated by John Facenda, Dallas Cowboys, Denver Broncos
1978: The awesome Dallas pass rush forces Denver quarterback Craig Morton into numerous interceptions. The Cowboy's offense sputters at times, but capitalizes on enough breaks for a 27-13 victory.
NFL Films — *NFL Films Video*

Super Bowl XIII 1980
Football
45120   30 mins   C   B, V, FO   R, P
Narrated by John Facenda, Pittsburgh Steelers, Dallas Cowboys
In the first Super Bowl offensive explosion by both teams, the Cowboys rally from eighteen points behind with Roger Staubach at the helm. Fortunately for the Steelers, Terry Bradshaw has put enough points on the board already, and Pittsburgh has their third championship, by a 35-31 score, in the 1979 game.
NFL Films — *NFL Films Video*

Super Bowl XIV 1980
Football
45121   30 mins   C   B, V, FO   R, P
Narrated by John Facenda, Pittsburgh Steelers, Los Angeles Rams
1980: The World Champion Steelers were supposed to be too much for the supposed bunch of glamour boys from Los Angeles, who were making their first-ever Super Bowl appearance after years of frustration. The Rams proved to be more than worthy opponent however, and even outplayed the Steelers for three quarters until some late heroics by Terry Bradshaw and John Stallworth saved them from embarrassment.
NFL Films — *NFL Films Video*

Super Bowl XV 1981
Football
50646   24 mins   C   B, V, FO   R, P
Narrated by John Facenda, Oakland Raiders, Philadelphia Eagles
The Oakland Raiders, a non-playoff team the previous year, are led by quarterback Jim Plunkett and a nasty defense to a 27-10 Super Bowl victory over the NFC's best, the Philadelphia Eagles.
NFL Films — *NFL Films Video*

Super Bowl XVI 1982
Football
47717   23 mins   C   B, V, FO   P
A look at how the San Francisco 49ers fought for a 26-21 victory over the Cincy Bengals in Super Bowl XVI.

NFL Films — *NFL Films Video*

Super Bowl XVII   1983
Football
69043   23 mins   C   B, V, FO   P
This program contains the highlights of Super
Bowl XVII, played between the Washington
Redskins and the Miami Dolphins.
NFL Films — *NFL Films Video*

Super Exercises   1978
Physical fitness
42779   60 mins   C   B, V   P
Ann Dugan
This series of two 30-minute programs on one
tape is intended for those concerned with
gaining greater strength and endurance.
Health N Action — *RCA/Columbia Pictures
Home Video*

Super Fuzz   1981
Comedy
65067   97 mins   C   B, V   P
Terence Hill, Joanne Dru
A rookie policeman develops super powers after
being exposed accidentally to radiation.
Somewhat ineptly, he uses his abilities to
combat crime.
MPAA:PG
Avco Embassy — *Embassy Home
Entertainment*

Super Memories of the   1981
Super Bowls
Football
51701   46 mins   C   B, V, LV   P
This program contains highlights of the first
fifteen NFL Super Bowls. Great performances
by such memorable athletes as Bart Starr, Joe
Namath, Franco Harris and Roger Staubach are
captured.
NFL Films — *NFL Films Video*

Super Seventies, The   1980
Football
50087   48 mins   C   B, V, LV   R, P
The decade's most memorable moments of
thrilling runs and catches, exhilarating wins and
crushing defeats.
NFL Films — *NFL Films Video*

Super Weapon, The   1975
Martial arts/Documentary
63415   86 mins   C   B, V   P
*Ron Van Clief, Frank Ruiz, Pete Siringano,
Byong Hoong Park*
Masters of the martial arts demonstrate karate,
Kung fu, jui jitsu, tae kuan do, tai chi and aikido
in this documentary-format program.
MPAA:PG
Serafim Karalexis — *Sun Video*

Superbowl of Motocross,   1981
The
Sports-Minor
53730   25 mins   C   B, V   P
Directed by Peter W. Silver
Motocross racer Little Jimmy Ellis takes on
Czechoslovakian world champ Zednk Velky at
the L.A. Coliseum before 60,000 fans.
Ken Squier — *MAS Productions*

Superchick   1971
Adventure
33614   94 mins   C   B, V   P
Joyce Jillson, Louis Quinn, Thomas Reardon
An unassuming airline stewardess becomes a
sexy, leggy blonde in between flights.
MPAA:R
Unknown — *VCI Home Video*

Superfly   1972
Drama
53522   98 mins   C   B, V   R, P
*Ron O'Neal, Carl Lee, Sheila Frazier, directed
by Gordon Parks*
A Harlem dope pusher gets involved with gangs
and the police as he seeks to earn enough
money with one last deal to be able to retire.
MPAA:R
Warner Bros — *Warner Home Video*

Superfort   195?
Armed Forces-US
68912   23 mins   B/W   B, V   P
This program covers the manufacture, testing
and development of the Superfort.
US Army — *Interurban Films*

Superman   194?
Cartoons
53806   59 mins   C   B, V   P
Animated
This cartoon package features seven cartoon
shorts released between 1941 and 1943.
Included are "Superman #1," "Magnetic
Telescope," "Japoteurs," "Bulleteers," "Jungle
Drums," "Mechanical Monsters," and "The
Mummy Strikes."
Paramount; Max Fleischer — *Media Home
Entertainment*

Superman III   1983
Adventure
65358   125 mins   C   B, V, LV,   P
                                    CED
*Christopher Reeve, Richard Pryor, Jackie
Cooper, Marc McClure, Annette O'Toole, Annie
Ross, Pamela Stephenson, Robert Vaughn,
Margot Kidder*
This time the Man of Steel faces the awesome
power of a criminally insane super-computer
genius, who has been hoodwinked by a sinister
tycoon seeking global dominance. In VHS Dolby
Stereo/Beta Hi-fi.

MPAA:PG
Pierre Spengler — *Warner Home Video*

Superman Cartoons 194?
Cartoons/Adventure
59055   75 mins   C   B, V   P
A collection of rare animated Superman cartoons released from 1941 to 1943. Cartoons include: "Superman (First Episode)," "The Bulleteers," "The Magnetic Telescope," "The Japoteurs," "The Mechanical Monsters," "Volcano," "Terror on the Midway," "The Mummy Strikes," "Jungle Drums."
Max Fleischer; Paramount — *Wizard Video*

Superman Color Cartoon Festival 194?
Cartoons
53803   65 mins   C   B, V   P
Animated
This cartoon package includes "Superman" (1941), "The Mechanical Monsters" (1941), "The Bulleteers" (1942), "The Magnetic Telescope" (1942), "Terror on the Midway" (1942), "The Japoteurs" (1942), "The Mummy Strikes" (1943), and "Jungle Drums" (1943).
Paramount; Max Fleischer — *Budget Video; Western Film & Video Inc; Discount Video Tapes*

Superman Festival # 1 194?
Cartoons
57281   60 mins   C   B, V   P
Animated
This Superman cartoon package includes "Mad Scientist," "The Japoteurs," "Mechanical Monsters," "Magnetic Telescope," "Jungle Drums," "The Bulleteers," and "The Mummy Strikes."
Paramount; Max Fleischer — *Video Dimensions*

Superman Festival # 2 194?
Cartoons
57282   60 mins   B/W   B, V   P
Animated
This black and white collection of Superman cartoons includes "Eleventh Hour," "Electrical Earthquake," "Arctic Giant," "Destruction Inc," "Secret Agent," "Billion Dollar Limited," and "Volcanoe."
Paramount; Max Fleischer — *Video Dimensions*

Superman-The Cartoons 1942
Cartoons
73538   89 mins   C   B, V   P
Animated, voices of Bud Collyer and Joan Alexander
Eight of the comic book hero's adventures from 1942 are featured along with a 1953 black and white short called "Stamp Day for Superman," starring the cast of the TV show.
Fleischer Studios; Famous Studios — *Admit One Video*

Superman—The Movie 1978
Adventure
38938   144 mins   C   B, V, LV   R, P
Christopher Reeve, Margot Kidder, Marlon Brando, Gene Hackman, Glenn Ford, directed by Richard Donner
A lavish retelling of the Superman legend, from his birth and flight from his home planet Krypton, to his becoming Earth's protector from the villain, Lex Luthor.
MPAA:PG
Warner Bros — *Warner Home Video; RCA VideoDiscs*

Superman II 1980
Adventure
58254   127 mins   C   B, V, LV   R, P
Christopher Reeve, Margot Kidder, Gene Hackman, Ned Beatty, Jackie Cooper, Terence Stamp, Valerie Perrine, E. G. Marshall, directed by Richard Lester
The sequel to "the movie" about the Man of Steel. This time, he has his hands full with three super-powered villains and a love-stricken Lois Lane.
MPAA:PG
Film Export; Warner Bros — *Warner Home Video; RCA VideoDiscs*

Surface Lures and Buzz Baits 1981
Fishing
65149   30 mins   C   B, V   P
Homer Circle, Glen Lau, Al Lindner, Ricky Clunn
Experts demonstrate top water techniques for taking bass. Part of the "Sportsman's Video Collection."
Glen Lau — *Leisure Time Products Project/3M*

Surfing Beach Party 1984
Music-Performance
76644   56 mins   C   B, V   P
This program recaptures the beach-blanket fun of the '50s and '60s California rock 'n' roll. Feature songs include "Surfin' Safari," "Fun, Fun, Fun," "Barbara Anne" and many more.
Music Media — *Music Media*

Survival and Evasion in Southeast Asia 1966
Vietnam War
53702   21 mins   C   B, V, 3/4U   P
A training film for U.S. pilots on what to do if they are shot down over enemy territory.
Unknown — *International Historic Films*

Survival Anglia's World of Wildlife, Vol. I 197?
Wildlife/Documentary
47060   90 mins   C   CED   P
Narrated by Glen Campbell and David Niven
Two award-winning documentaries are featured in this package. "The Incredible Flight of the Snow Geese" follows the migration of these beautiful birds from the Canadian Arctic to the Texas plains. "Leopard of the Wild" follows the story of a man's involvement with an orphaned leopard cub.
SA Ltd — *RCA VideoDiscs*

Survival Anglia's World of Wildlife, Vol. 2 198?
Wildlife/Documentary
64455   104 mins   C   CED   P
Hosted by Peter Ustinov and David Niven
Ustinov narrates the story of the Australian kangaroo, and Niven hosts an in-depth look at the annual breeding of penguins at the Falkland Islands.
SA Ltd — *RCA VideoDiscs*

Survival Run 1980
Adventure
66287   90 mins   C   B, V   P
Peter Graves, Ray Milland, Vincent Van Patten
Six young teenagers are stranded in the desert.
MPAA:R
Lance Hool — *Media Home Entertainment*

Survivors, The 1983
Comedy
69616   102 mins   C   B, V   P
Robin Williams, Walter Matthau, Jerry Reed
Two unemployed men find themselves the target of an out-of-work hit man, whom they disarm in a robbery attempt. One of the men takes off for survivalist camp, hotly pursued by the other, and then by the hit man.
MPAA:R
Bill Sackheim; Columbia — *RCA/Columbia Pictures Home Video; RCA VideoDiscs*

Susan Slept Here 1954
Comedy
13128   98 mins   C   B, V   P
Dick Powell, Debbie Reynolds
Hollywood script writer is given protective custody of vagrant girl over Christmas vacation.
RKO — *VCI Home Video*

Susitna 1981
Boating
69904   10 mins   C   B, V   P
This program looks at the Susitna River, which flows from the slopes of Mount McKinley and which is a challenging kayaking river.
Unknown — *Gravity Sports Films*

Suspicion 1941
Suspense
00258   99 mins   B/W   B, V, 3/4U   P
Cary Grant, Joan Fontaine, Cedric Hardwicke
Alfred Hitchcock's thriller about a woman who gradually realizes she is married to a killer.
Academy Award '41: Best Actress (Fontaine); '42 Film Daily Poll Ten Best Films of Year.
RKO — *Nostalgia Merchant*

Suzanne 1980
Drama
72229   102 mins   C   B, V   P
A woman is torn between a need for adventure and a conviction for peace.
Guardian Trust Company — *Vestron Video*

Svengali 1931
Drama
54114   76 mins   B/W   B, V   P, T
John Barrymore, Marion Marsh
Maestro Svengali enchants lovely maidens by using the magical powers embodied within his evil stare. Once he has them under his powers, he uses them to advance his musical career.
Warner Bros — *Blackhawk Films; Sheik Video; Cable Films; Video Connection; Video Yesteryear; Western Film & Video Inc; Discount Video Tapes; Movie Buff Video; Classic Video Cinema Collector's Club*

Swamp Thing 1982
Mystery/Adventure
63376   91 mins   C   B, V, LV, CED   P
Adriene Barbeau, Louis Jourdan
Done in "comic-book" format, this is the story of a group of scientists performing a top secret experiment in a rural swamp and their nemesis, the lunatic Arcane.
MPAA:PG
Benjamin Melnicker; Michael Oslan — *Embassy Home Entertainment*

Swan, The 1925
Comedy/Romance
59216   50 mins   B/W   B, V, 3/4U   P
Adolphe Menjou, Ricardo Cortez, Frances Howard
A marriage arranged between a prince and princess leads to intrigue.
Paramount — *Penguin Video; Discount Video Tapes*

Swan Lake 1982
Dance
47814   ? mins   C   LV   P
Natalia Makarova, Anthony Dowell
The Royal Ballet performs "Swan Lake," recorded at the Royal Opera House Covent Garden, July 28, 1980. In stereo.
Unknown — *Pioneer Artists*

(For Explanation of codes, see USE GUIDE and KEY)

Swan Lake 1981
Dance
57254 82 mins C B, V P
*The Kirov Ballet, the Leningrad Philharmonic,
directed by Konstantin Sergeyev*
Tchaikovsky's complete "Swan Lake" ballet is
performed by the Kirov Ballet troupe featuring
Yelena Yevteyeva, John Markovsky and Valeri
Panov. This interpretation is based on the
celebrated Petipal Ivanov productions.
Kultur — *Kultur*

Swan Lake 1982
Cartoons/Adventure
59667 75 mins C B, V P
Animated
The prince searches for a future bride to be
queen when he becomes king. The swan which
bears the golden crown possesses magical
powers that hold the key.
Toei Company — *Media Home Entertainment*

Swan Lake 1957
Dance
69831 81 mins C B, V P
Maya Plisetskaya, Bolshoi Ballet
The timeless tale of redemption through love.
Sovexportfilm USSR — *Video Arts
International*

Swap, The 1980
Drama
64872 90 mins C B, V, CED P
Robert De Niro, Jennifer Warren
A man embarks on a desperate hunt for the
killer of his young brother.
Christopher Dewey — *Vestron Video*

Swarm, The 1978
Horror
53523 116 mins C B, V R, P
*Michael Caine, Katharine Ross, Richard
Widmark, Lee Grant, Richard Chamberlain,
Olivia de Havilland, Henry Fonda, Fred
MacMurray, Patty Duke Astin*
A scientist must contend with a swarm of killer
bees after the discovery of dead personnel on a
government base.
MPAA:PG
Warner Bros; Irwin Allen — *Warner Home
Video*

**Sweeney Todd—The
Demon Barber of Fleet
Street** 1984
Musical
69920 139 mins C B, V P
*Angela Lansbury, George Hearn, directed by
Harold Prince*
This is a filmed performance of the Broadway
musical by Stephen Sondheim. In VHS Dolby
stereo and Beta Hi-Fi.

Richard Barr, Charles Woodward et al — *RKO
HomeVideo*

Sweet Creek County War 1982
Western/Drama
72182 90 mins C B, V P
A story of friendship and the absurdity of war.
Unknown — *Paragon Video Productions*

Sweet 16 1981
Horror
64873 90 mins C B, V P
Susan Strasberg, Bo Hopkins
Sixteen-year-old Melissa is beautiful,
mysterious, and promiscuous, but she can't
understand why all her boyfriends end up dead.
MPAA:R
Jim Sotos; Martin Perfit — *Vestron Video*

**Sweet Sweetback's
Baadasssss Song** 1971
Drama
63416 97 mins C B, V P
Melvin Van Peebles, Simon Chuckster
A black pimp kills two policemen who had been
beating a black militant. He uses his street-wise
survival skills to elude his pursuers and escape
to Mexico.
Cinemation — *Sun Video*

Swept Away 1975
Drama
44782 116 mins C B, V P
Giancarlo Giannini
A rich and beautiful Milanese capitalist woman
is shipwrecked on a desolate island with a
swarthy Sicilian deckhand, who also happens to
be a dedicated communist.
Cinema 5 — *RCA/Columbia Pictures Home
Video; RCA VideoDiscs*

Swifty 1936
Western
14239 60 mins B/W B, V P
Hoot Gibson
A western starring Hoot Gibson.
Grand National — *Video Connection*

Swim Baby Swim 1984
Sports-Water/Infants
76393 60 mins C B, V P
Esther Williams
A step-by-step instructional guide to infant water
safety presented by Esther Williams, former
movie star, and Olympic-caliber professional
swimmer.
Rogers & Cowan Inc — *Karl Video*

Swing High, Swing Low 1937
Comedy
08666 95 mins B/W B, V, 3/4U P

Carole Lombard, Fred MacMurray, Charles Butter- worth, Dorothy Lamour, directed by Mitchell Leisen
A struggling trumpet player becomes a hit in the jazz world and marries the girl he loves.
Paramount — *Penguin Video; Budget Video; Discount Video Tapes; Video Yesteryear; Cable Films; Video Connection; Cinema Concepts*

Swing It, Sailor!   1937
Comedy
65202   61 mins   B/W   B, V   P
Wallace Ford, Ray Mayer, Isabel Jewell, Mary Treen
Two zany sailors have a series of comic adventures while on shore leave.
Grand National Films — *Video Yesteryear*

Swing Shift   1984
Comedy-Drama
73011   100 mins   C   B, V, LV   P
Goldie Hawn, Kurt Russell, Ed Harris, directed by Jonathan Demme
Goldie Hawn stars as a woman who takes a job at an aircraft plant to help make ends meet after her husband goes off to war. A loving reminiscence of the American home front during World War II.
MPAA:PG
Jerry Bick; Warner Bros — *Warner Home Video*

Swing Time   1936
Musical
00273   103 mins   B/W   B, V, 3/4U   P
Fred Astaire, Ginger Rogers, Helen Broderick, Betty Furness, Eric Blore
Fred plays a dancer who can't resist gambling, until he meets Ginger. The score by Jerome Kern and Dorothy Fields includes "Pick Yourself Up," "Never Gonna Dance," "The Waltz in Swing-time" and "A Fine Romance."
Academy Awards '36: Best Song (The Way You Look Tonight).
RKO; Pandro S Berman — *Nostalgia Merchant; RCA VideoDiscs*

Swingin' Singin' Years, The   1960
Music-Performance
21335   52 mins   B/W   B, V, FO   P
Woody Herman, Charlie Barnet, Stan Kenton, Louis Jordan, Vaughn Monroe, Jo Stafford, hosted by Ronald Reagan
Famous bands and singers appear "live" from all over the U.S. in a program designed to recapture the era of "big band remotes." Reagan acts as host and announcer for the various orchestras.
ABC — *Video Yesteryear*

Swinging Cheerleaders, The   1974
Comedy
60414   90 mins   C   B, V   P
Rainbeaux Smith, Colleen Camp, Jo Johnston
A group of amorous cheerleaders turn on the entire campus.
MPAA:PG
The Swinging Cheerleaders — *Monterey Home Video*

Swinging Ski Girls   197?
Drama
59554   85 mins   C   B, V   P
Cindy Wilton, Dick Cassidy
A group of swinging, free-loving university co-eds spend a wild weekend at a ski lodge.
Robert Marsden — *Media Home Entertainment*

Swinging Sorority Girls   197?
Drama
59553   73 mins   C   B, V   P
Susie Carlson, Anne Marlie
An intimate glimpse behind the closed doors of a sorority house during a wild homecoming weekend.
Robert Marsden — *Media Home Entertainment*

Swiss Conspiracy, The   1977
Suspense
44911   92 mins   C   B, V   P
David Janssen, Senta Berger
Against the opulent background of the world's richest financial capital and playground of the wealthy, one man battles to stop a daring and sophisticated blackmail caper.
MPAA:PG
SJ International Pictures — *VCI Home Video*

Swiss Family Robinson, The   1960
Adventure/Drama
47408   126 mins   C   B, V, LV   R, P
John Mills, Dorothy McGuire, James MacArthur, Tommy Kirk, Janet Munro, Sessue Hayakawa
A Swiss family, travelling to New Guinea, is blown off course and shipwrecked on a deserted tropical island. Forced to remain, they create a new life for themselves. Based on the novel by Johann Wyss.
Walt Disney — *Walt Disney Home Video; RCA VideoDiscs*

Swiss Miss   1938
Comedy
33907   72 mins   B/W   B, V, 3/4U   P
Stan Laurel, Oliver Hardy, Walter Woolf King, Della Lind, Eric Blore
Stan and Ollie are mousetrap salesmen who visit Switzerland and become involved with an egotistical songwriter and his wife.

Hal Roach, MGM — *Nostalgia Merchant;*
Blackhawk Films

Swiss Miss　　　　　　　　　　　**1938**
Comedy
63990　97 mins　B/W　　B, V　　　　P, T
Stan Laurel, Oliver Hardy, Della Lind, Walter
Woolf King, Eric Blore
Stan and Ollie are mousetrap salesmen on the
job in Switzerland. Also included on this tape is
a 1935 Thelma Todd-Patsy Kelly short, "Hot
Money."
Hal Roach; MGM — *Blackhawk Films*

Switchblade Sisters　　　　　　　**1975**
Adventure
63087　90 mins　C　　B, V　　　　　P
Robbie Lee, Joanne Nail
A crime gang of female ex-cons attack and kill
at the slightest provocation.
Switchblade Sisters Productions — *Monterey*
Home Video

Sword and the Dragon　　　　　**1956**
Fantasy/Folklore
51230　83 mins　B/W　B, V, 3/4U　　P
Special effects highlight this tale based on
Russian folk stories of heroes, villains, and
fantastic creatures that lived centuries ago.
Unknown — *Penguin Video*

Sword and the Sorcerer,　　　　**1982**
The
Fantasy
62780　100 mins　C　　B, V, LV　　　P
Lee Horsely, Kathleen Beller, George Maharis,
Simon MacCorkindale
A young prince finds his kingdom destroyed by
an evil usurper and a powerful magician.
MPAA:R
Group I — *MCA Home Video*

Sword of Monte Cristo　　　　　**1951**
Adventure
59140　80 mins　C　　B, V　　　R, P
George Montgomery, Paula Corday
The daring swordsman and his attractive lady
foil a villainous minister.
Edward L Alperson — *VCII*

SyberVision Cross-　　　　　　　**1983**
Country Skiing with Jeff
Nowak
Sports-Winter
69326　60 mins　C　　B, V, 3/4U　　　P
Jeff Nowak demonstrates the classic nordic
style of cross-country skiing.
AM　Available
SyberVision Systems — *SyberVision Systems*

SyberVision Golf with Al　　　　**1982**
Geiberger
Golf
47824　80 mins　C　B, V, 3/4U　　　P
Hosted by Al Geiberger
Al Geiberger completes over 1,000 perfect golf
swings in order to instill "muscle memory" in the
viewer.
AM　Available
SyberVision Systems — *SyberVision Systems*

SyberVision Skiing with　　　　**1983**
Jean Claude Killy
Sports-Winter
69327　60 mins　C　B, V, 3/4U　　　P
Jean Claude Killy and members of the American
Demonstration Ski Team demonstrate the
fundamentals of downhill skiing in intense visual
detail.
AM　Available
SyberVision Systems — *SyberVision Systems*

SyberVision Tennis with　　　　**1982**
Stan Smith
Tennis
47825　60 mins　C　B, V, 3/4U　　　P
Hosted by Stan Smith
This program allows the viewer to develop deep
"muscle memory" for the perfect tennis stroke
by watching Stan Smith's 1,000 strokes.
AM　Available
SyberVision Systems — *SyberVision Systems*

Sybil　　　　　　　　　　　　　**1976**
Drama
59363　122 mins　C　B, V, CED　　　P
Sally Field, Joanne Woodward, Brad Davis,
Martine Bartlett, Jane Hoffman, directed by
Daniel Petrie
The factually-based story of a woman who
developed 16 distinct personalities, and the
supportive psychiatrist who helped her put the
pieces of her ego together.
Emmy Awards '77: Outstanding Special
(Drama); Outstanding Lead Actress in a Drama
Special (Sally Field); Outstanding Writing in a
Special (Stewart Stern).
Lorimar — *CBS/Fox Video*

Sympathy for the Devil　　　　**1970**
Music
29175　110 mins　C　　B, V　　　　P
Mick Jagger, The Rolling Stones
A program with sequences of pop political
cartoons dealing with injustice and democracy.
In this provocative show the Rolling Stones
capture all the passionate defiance and thirst for
justice of the revolutionary 60's.
Viacom International — *CBS/Fox Video*

T

T-Men   1947
Crime-Drama
64382   96 mins   B/W   B, V, 3/4U   P
Dennis O'Keefe, June Lockhart, Wallace Ford
Two agents of the Treasury Department
infiltrate themselves into a counterfeiting gang.
Eagle-Lion; Edward Small — *Nostalgia
Merchant*

Table for Five   1983
Drama
65001   120 mins   C   B, V, CED   P
*John Voight, Millie Perkins, Richard Crenna,
Robbie Kiger, Roxana Zal, Son Hoang Bui,
Marie Christine Barrault*
A divorced father takes his children on a
Mediterranean cruise and while sailing, he
learns that his ex-wife has died. The father and
his ex-wife's husband struggle over who should
raise the children.
MPAA:PG
CBS Theatrical Films — *CBS/Fox Video*

Tag der Freiheit—Unsere   1935
Wehrmacht (Day of
Freedom—Our Armed
Forces)
World War II/Propaganda
52370   30 mins   B/W   B, V, 3/4U   P
Directed by Leni Riefenstahl
A short documentary about the role played by
generals and other officers in the Third Reich.
The tape also includes "Flieger am Feind
(Luftwaffe Against the Enemy)," a 1940
documentary designed to show German home
front audiences how a bombing raid against the
Allies was carried out. In German with English
subtitles.
GE
Unknown — *International Historic Films*

Tai Chi Chuan   1982
Yoga/Physical fitness
64019   68 mins   C   B, V   P
Master K.M. Liang demonstrates techniques of
Tai Chi Chuan, a type of yoga that is an ancient
form of Chinese slow-motion exercise.
Ng See Yuen; Roy Horan — *World Video
Enterprises*

Takanaka World   1981
Music-Performance
47296   40 mins   C   LV   P
Masayoshi Takanaka
As Masayoshi Takanaka performs his greatest
hits, vivid visuals bring alive his daydreams.
Takeshi Shimizu; Hidenori Thea — *Pioneer
Video Imports*

Take a Good Look/The   1957
Jack Benny Show
Comedy
72517   60 mins   B/W   B, V, 3/4U   P
*Ernie Kovacs, Cesar Romero, Edie Adams, Don
Wilson, Jack Benny, Eddie "Rochester"
Anderson*
Ernie Kovacs hosts "Take a Good Look," a
"What's My Line" type game show featuring
panelists Cesar Romero and Edie Adams. On
the same tape, Stingy Jack Benny welcomes
George Burns' son, Ronnie, and clowns with
regulars Don Wilson and Rochester.
ABC; CBS — *International Historic Films*

Take a Good Look with   1960
Ernie Kovacs
Game show
42965   30 mins   B/W   B, V, FO   P
*Ernie Kovacs, Cesar Romero, Edie Adams, Carl
Reiner*
Zany skits abound as panelists attempt to guess
the secret which the mystery guest is
concealing.
ABC — *Video Yesteryear*

Take It to the Limit   1980
Motorcycles
66200   90 mins   C   B, V   P
The best of motorcycle racing and champions is
shown. In stereo.
Peter Starr — *U.S.A. Home Video*

Take Me Back to   1940
Oklahoma
Western
15460   64 mins   B/W   B, V   P
Tex Ritter, directed by Al Herman
Musical western with comedy.
Monogram — *Video Connection*

Take the Money and Run   1969
Comedy
46187   85 mins   C   B, V, LV,   P
                          CED
*Woody Allen, Janet Margolin, Marcel Hillaire,
directed by Woody Allen*
A young man unsuccessfully tries to rob a bank
and from that point on is unable to stay out of jail
long enough to turn his new career into a
profitable one.
MPAA:PG
Palomar Pictures International — *CBS/Fox
Video*

Take This Job and Shove   1981
It
Comedy
58833   100 mins   C   B, V, CED   P
*Robert Hays, Art Carney, Barbara Hershey,
David Keith, Martin Mull, Eddie Albert, Penelope
Milford*

A hot-shot efficiency expert is determined to streamline the Pickett Brewing Company, a Dubuque, Iowa brewery. He upsets the lives of his closest friends in the process, before realizing that his priorities in life are scrambled. MPAA:G
Avco Embassy — *Embassy Home Entertainment*

Taking of Pelham One Two Three, The   1974
Suspense
66077   102 mins   C   B, V, CED   P
Robert Shaw, Walter Matthau, Martin Balsam, Hector Elizondo, James Broderick, directed by Joseph Sargent
A hijack team seizes a New York City subway car and holds the 17 passengers for ransom. MPAA:R
United Artists — *CBS/Fox Video*

Tale of the Frog Prince, The   1983
Fairy tales
Closed Captioned
69324   60 mins   C   B, V, LV, CED   P
Robin Williams, Teri Garr, narrated by Eric Idle
This is the story of a special friendship between a frog turned prince by a witch's spell and the self-centered princess who saves him with a kiss. From Shelley Duvall's "Faerie Tale Theatre."
Shelley Duvall — *CBS/Fox Video*

Tale of Two Cities, A   1935
Drama
58295   128 mins   B/W   B, V   P
Ronald Colman, Elizabeth Allen, Edna May Oliver, Donald Woods, Basil Rathbone, directed by Jack Conway
Dickens' classic set during the French Revolution, about two men who bear a remarkable resemblance to each other, both in love with the same girl.
Film Daily Poll Ten Best Pictures of the Year '35.
MGM; David O Selznick — *MGM/UA Home Video*

Tale of Two Cities, A   1958
Adventure
59903   117 mins   B/W   B, V   P
Dirk Bogarde, Dorothy Tutin, Christopher Lee, Donald Pleasence, Ian Bannen
Dickens' classic about a lawyer who sacrifices himself to save another man from the guillotine.
Rank — *Embassy Home Entertainment*

Tale of Two Critters, A   1977
Adventure
59065   48 mins   C   B, V   R, P
A young raccoon and a playful bear cub develop a rare friendship growing up in the wilds.

Walt Disney Productions — *Walt Disney Home Video*

Tales from Muppetland   197?
Comedy
53793   102 mins   C   CED   P
This two-sided disc contains two programs featuring the lovable Muppets: "Muppet Musicians of Bremen" (1972) and "Emmet Otter's Jug Band Christmas" (1977).
Henson Associates — *RCA VideoDiscs*

Tales from Muppetland II   1971
Comedy/Fairy tales
60382   108 mins   C   CED   P
Two enchanting Muppet variations on classic fairy tales: "Hey, Cinderella" and "The Frog Prince."
Henson Associates — *RCA VideoDiscs*

Tales of Deputy Dawg—Volumes II & III   196?
Cartoons
29176   90 mins   C   B, V   P
Animated
Two programs featuring Terrytoons' Deputy Dawg. Both available individually.
Viacom International — *CBS/Fox Video*

Tales of Hoffmann, The   1981
Opera
53400   210 mins   C   LV   P
Introduction by John Gielgud, Placido Domingo
The Royal Opera's performance of Offenbach's "Tales of Hoffmann," produced by John Schlesinger.
Covent Garden Video Prods Ltd — *Pioneer Artists; RCA VideoDiscs*

Tales of Terror   1962
Horror
53524   88 mins   C   B, V   R, P
Vincent Price, Peter Lorre, Basil Rathbone, directed by Roger Corman
Three tales of terror: "Morella," "The Black Cat," and "The Case of M. Valdemar." Based on stories by Edgar Allen Poe.
American International — *Warner Home Video*

Tales of Tomorrow Volume 1   195?
Science fiction
44338 120 mins   B/W   B, V, 3/4U   P
Lon Chaney Jr., Bruce Cabot, Leslie Nielsen, Thomas Mitchell
Four episodes from the early 1950's television series focusing on the supernatural. Includes "Frankenstein," "Dune Roller," "Appointment on Mars," and "Crystal Egg." Includes previews of coming attractions from classic science fiction films.

ABC; George F. Foley Jr. — *Nostalgia Merchant*

Tales of Tomorrow, Volume 2　　195?
Science fiction
58583　90 mins　B/W　B, V, 3/4U　　P
Boris Karloff, Walter Abel, Edmon Ryan, Rod Steiger
Four episodes from the early 1950's TV series focusing on the supernatural. "Past Tense," "A Child is Crying," "Ice from Space," and "The Window."
ABC; George F Foley Jr — *Nostalgia Merchant*

Talk of the Town　　1982
Football
47713　23 mins　C　B, V, FO　　P
Team highlights of the 1981 New York Jets, who had the top-ranked defense in the AFC, the NFL Defensive Player of the Year in Joe Klecko, and the NFL Comeback Player of the Year with Richard Todd.
NFL Films — *NFL Films Video*

Talk of the Town—Show 1　　1982
Variety
63973　60 mins　C　B, V　　R, P
J.P. Morgan, Pat Cooper, The Unknown Comic, Linda Blair, Rip Taylor, Talk of the Town Show Girls
This talk show features a panel of guest stars discussing subjects that would horrify the network televisions censors, and the Talk of the Town Show Girls model provocative lingerie and swimwear.
Michael Frydrych — *VCII*

Talk of the Town—Show II　　1984
Variety
72197　60 mins　C　B, V　　R, P
J.P. Morgan, Redd Foxx, Jack Carter
J.P. Morgan hosts an adult-oriented variety show featuring Pat Cooper and Larry Storch.
VCII — *VCII*

Talking in Your Sleep　　1984
Music/Video
65403　4 mins　C　B, V　　P
The Romantics
The video clip "Talking in Your Sleep" features The Romantics and a cast of 100 models dressed, as the song implies, in a variety of sleepwear from robes to negligees.
Bob Dyke — *CBS/Fox Video*

Tall Blond Man with One Black Shoe, The　　1973
Mystery
07139　90 mins　C　B, V　　P

Pierre Richard, Bernard Blier, Jean Rochefort, directed by Yves Robert
Decoy agent is completely unaware that he is the center of a plot by a French intelligence director to booby-trap an overly ambitious assistant. Dubbed in English.
MPAA:PG
Cinema 5 — *RCA/Columbia Pictures Home Video*

Tall in the Saddle　　1944
Western
00278　79 mins　B/W　B, V, 3/4U　　P
John Wayne, Ella Raines
Portrayal of a tough, woman-hating cowboy working for a spinster and her attractive niece.
RKO; Robert Fellows — *Nostalgia Merchant*

Taming of the Shrew, The　　1929
Drama
66354　66 mins　B/W　B, V　　P
Mary Pickford, Douglas Fairbanks, Edwin Maxwell, Joseph Cawthorn, directed by Sam Taylor
This early talkie version of Shakespeare's play is the only film that co-stars America's most popular acting couple of the 1920's. The film was re-edited in 1966, with some cleaning up of the soundtrack and a musical score added as well.
Pickford Corp; Elton Corp; United Artists — *Blackhawk Films*

Taming of the Shrew, The　　1981
Comedy
66273　152 mins　C　B, V　　P
Directed by Peter Dews
Shakespeare's comedy about Petruchio's attempt to tame his fiery, free-spirited wife.
Unknown — *Embassy Home Entertainment*

Taming of the Shrew, The　　1967
Comedy
21297　122 mins　C　B, V　　P
Elizabeth Taylor, Richard Burton, Michael York
A lavish screen version of the classic Shakespearean comedy.
Columbia — *RCA/Columbia Pictures Home Video; RCA VideoDiscs*

Tangier　　1982
Adventure
64943　95 mins　C　B, V　　P
Ronny Cox, Billie Whitelaw, Ronald Lacey, Ronald Fraser
An ex-CIA agent is blackmailed by British Intelligence to take the place of a dead gun-runner whose presence is desperately needed in Tangier.
Linked Ring Television Film Productions — *The Video Station*

Tank 1983
Drama
75017   113 mins   C   B, V, LV,   P
CED
James Garner, Shirley Jones, G.D. Spradlin
This is the unusual story of an Army officer who
takes on a small town sheriff with the aid of a
World War II Sherman tank.
MPAA:PG
Irwin Yablans — *MCA Home Video*

Tap Dancing for 1982
Beginners
Dance
47367   38 mins   C   B, V   P
Henry LeTang, choreographer of "Sophisticated
Ladies," provides elementary instruction in the
art of tap dance.
American Home Video Library — *American
Home Video Library*

Taps 1981
Drama
47398   126 mins   C   B, V, CED   P
Timothy Hutton, George C. Scott, Ronny Cox
When a military school is threatened with
closure, the students take over and start a
siege. The situation snowballs with
misunderstandings until the National Guard is
called in.
MPAA:PG
20th Century Fox — *CBS/Fox Video*

Target Eagle 1984
Adventure
72461   100 mins   C   B, V   P
Terrorists land on the Mediterranean coast and·
a mercenary and a young woman attempt to halt
them with only their wits and courage.
Unknown — *VCL Home Video*

Target for Tonight 1941
World War II/Documentary
23228   50 mins   B/W   B, V, FO   P
An English documentary about a bombing raid
on Germany during World War II.
Crown Film Unit — *Video Yesteryear;
International Historic Films*

Targets 1969
Drama
60214   90 mins   C   B, V   R, P
*Boris Karloff, James Brown, Tim O'Kelly,
directed by Peter Bogdanovich*
Bogdanovich's directorial debut concerns an
aging horror film star who confronts and disarms
a mad sniper at a drive-in movie.
MPAA:PG
Peter Bogdanovich — *Paramount Home Video*

Tarzan and the Green 1938
Goddess
Adventure
07206   72 mins   B/W   B, V   P
Herman Brix, Ula Holt, Frank Baker
Tarzan searches for a statue that could prove·
dangerous in the wrong hands.
PRI; Sol Lesser — *Budget Video; Penguin
Video*

Tarzan and the Trappers 1958
Adventure
11260   74 mins   B/W   B, V, FO   P
*Gordon Scott, Eve Brent, Ricky Sorenson,
Maurice Marsac, Cheetah*
Tarzan frees animals from trappers and
prevents them from robbing the riches of a lost
city.
RKO — *Video Yesteryear*

Tarzan of the Apes 1917
Adventure
07279   63 mins   B/W   B, V, FO   P
Elmo Lincoln, Enid Markey
The first screen version of the adventures of
Tarzan. Silent.
First National — *Video Yesteryear; Sheik
Video; Western Film & Video Inc; Cable Films*

Tarzan, the Ape Man 1932
Adventure
55209   104 mins   B/W   B, V·   P
*Johnny Weissmuller, Maureen O'Sullivan,
directed by W. S. Van Dyke*
The first Tarzan movie, featuring the characters
created by Edgar Rice Burroughs.
MGM — *MGM/UA Home Video*

Tarzan, the Ape Man 1981
Adventure
59310   112 mins   C   B, V, LV,   R
CED
*Bo Derek, Richard Harris, directed by John
Derek*
Edgar Rice Burroughs' classic remade with the
focus on Jane, as she explores the African
jungles, learning about life and love from the
Ape Man.
MPAA:R
Svengali Prods — *MGM/UA Home Video*

Tarzan the Fearless 1933
Adventure
58920   84 mins   B/W   B, V   P
Buster Crabbe, Jacqueline Wells
Tarzan helps a young girl find her missing father.
EL, SP
PRC; Sol Lesser — *Budget Video; Ampro
Video Productions; Cable Films; Video
Connection*

Tarzan's Revenge   1938
Adventure
05446   70 mins   B/W   B, V, 3/4U   R, P
Glenn Morris, Eleanor Holm, Hedda Hopper
Tarzan saves a safari of white travellers from
vicious warriors.
20th Century Fox — *Budget Video; Video
Yesteryear*

Tattoo   1981
Drama
58849   103 mins   C   B, V, CED   P
*Bruce Dern, Maud Adams, Leonard Frey, Rikke
Borge, John Getz*
A model becomes the object of obsession for a
tattoo artist who uses bodies as his canvas.
MPAA:R
20th Century Fox — *CBS/Fox Video*

Taxi Driver   1976
Drama
47785   112 mins   C   B, V   P
*Robert DeNiro, Cybill Shepherd, Peter Boyle,
Jodie Foster, directed by Martin Scorcese*
A psychotic New York City cab driver goes on a
violent rampage in an effort to rid the city of
undesirables.arR
Michael and Julia Phillips — *RCA/Columbia
Pictures Home Video; RCA VideoDiscs*

Teach Your Horse to Bow   1983
Sports-Minor
69671   25 mins   C   B, V   P
Techniques for teaching a show horse to bow
are presented in this program.
Mercedes Maharis — *Mercedes Maharis
Productions*

Team of the 80's/NFL '82   1983
Football
66222   45 mins   C   B, V, FO   P
Highlights of the San Diego Chargers' 1982-83
season along with an overview of the whole
NFL Season.
NFL Films — *NFL Films Video*

Team on a Tightrope   1980
Football
45127   24 mins   C   B, V, FO   R, P
Dallas Cowboys
Highlights of the 1979 Dallas Cowboys football
season.
NFL Films — *NFL Films Video*

**Team That Battled Back,
The**   1980
Football
50654   24 mins   C   B, V, FO   R, P
New York Jets
The 1979 New York Jets weren't given much of
a chance to be respectable. The coaching

staff's indecision over whether Matt Robinson
or Richard Todd should start at quarterback
further complicated matters. Todd gradually
settled into the role, behind an offensive line
which was chiefly responsible for New York's
leading the NFL in rushing yardage. The Jets
finished with a surprising 8-8 record.
NFL Films — *NFL Films Video*

**Team Together/NFL '83,
A**   1984
Football
72935   46 mins   C   B, V, FO   P
Denver Broncos
Highlights from the 1983 season of the Denver
Broncos plus "NFL 83."
NFL Films — *NFL Films Video*

**Teasing, Breeding and
Semen Collection in the
Horse**   19??
Veterinary medicine
69663   25 mins   C   B, V   P
Techniques for breeding horses are presented
in this program.
U of Minnesota — *Mercedes Maharis
Productions*

Teddy at the Throttle   1916
Film-History
50631   20 mins   B/W   B, V   P, T
*Bobby Vernon, Gloria Swanson, Wallace Beery,
Teddy (the Dog), directed by Clarence Badger*
Teddy the Great Dane must rescue Gloria
Swanson from a villain who has tied up her
boyfriend. Silent.
Unknown — *Blackhawk Films*

**Teddy Pendergrass Live
in London**   1982
Music-Performance
63399   75 mins   C   B, V   P
Teddy Pendergrass
Filmed at England's Hammersmith Odeon in
February 1982, this concert features the
singer's most popular tunes, including "Close
the Door," "If You Don't Know Me By Now,"
"Bad Luck," and "Wake Up Everybody."
Home Video Premiere
Productions — *CBS/Fox Video*

Teen Mothers   1980
Drama
47634   91 mins   C   B, V   P
A bittersweet story of two unwed teenagers
forced to take their child and leave home for the
tenements of New York.
MPAA:R
Independent — *Paragon Video Productions*

Teenage Drug and Alcohol Abuse 1984
Drug abuse/Adolescence
72964   28 mins   C   B, V   P
A young man, his mother and a psychologist offer their opinions on drug abuse in this program of dramatized case histories.
Star Merchants — *Increase Video*

Teenage Zombies 1960
Horror
69569   71 mins   B/W   B, V, FO   P
Don Sullivan, Katherine Victor
A lady mad scientist kidnaps teenagers and uses her secret chemical formula to turn them into zombies, as the harbinger of her plan to enslave the world.
Governor — *Video Yesteryear*

Telefon 1977
Suspense
75537   102 mins   C   B, V   P
Charles Bronson, Lee Remick
The Soviets have a secret plan to destroy key U.S. military targets. The plan is so secret that the Soviet agents don't even know they will trigger the destruction.
MPAA:PG
MGM — *MGM/UA Home Video*

Telephone Book, The 1971
Comedy
64968   88 mins   C   CED   P
Sarah Kennedy, Norman Rose, Barry Morse
A young woman falls in love with the world's greatest obscene phone caller.
Rosebud Releasing — *Embassy Home Entertainment (disc only)*

Telescope—Interview with Harry Richman 1965
Interview
46348   25 mins   B/W   B, V, FO   P
Harry Richman
Vaudeville and nightclub star Harry Richman discusses his 50-year career in this candid interview.
CBC — *Video Yesteryear*

Television's Golden Age of Comedy 195?
Comedy
11275   75 mins   B/W   B, V, FO   P
Groucho Marx, Amos and Andy, Bob Hope, Dean Martin, Jerry Lewis, Jack Benny
"You Bet Your Life," with Groucho Marx, Amos and Andy's "Rare Coin," and an episode of "The Jack Benny Show" are featured in this vintage package of television comedy.
CBS et al — *Video Yesteryear*

Tell-Tale Heart, The 1964
Horror
08589   81 mins   B/W   B, V, 3/4U   P
Laurence Payne, Adrienne Corri, Dermont Walsh, directed by Ernest Morris
Adapted from Edgar Allen Poe's story. Told in part by Poe himself while in a drug-induced fit, the story concerns a shy librarian who becomes enamored with a beautiful woman.
Britain — *Penguin Video*

Tell Them Willie Boy Is Here 1969
Western
64791   98 mins   C   B, V   P
Robert Redford, Katherine Ross, Robert Blake, Susan Clark, Barry Sullivan, directed by Abraham Polonsky
This western classic is based on the true story of a Paiute Indian, Willie Boy (Blake), and his white bride (Ross), who become the objects of the last great western manhunt after he kills her father in a "Marriage by Capture" on white man's territory. Sheriff Cooper (Redford) leads the manhunt.
MPAA:PG
Universal — *MCA Home Video*

Tempest 1928
Drama
64318   105 mins   B/W   B, V   P, T
John Barrymore, Louis Wolheim
A Russian peasant soldier rises through the ranks to become an officer, only to be undone by his love for the daughter of his commanding officer. Silent with musical score.
United Artists — *Blackhawk Films; Classic Video Cinema Collector's Club*

Tempest 1982
Drama
64573   140 mins   C   B, V   P
John Cassavetes, Gena Rowlands, Susan Sarandon, Vittorio Gassman, RaulJulia, directed by Paul Mazursky
A New York architect, fed up with city living, chucks it all and brings his daughter with him to live on a barren Greek island. VHS in stereo.
MPAA:PG
Columbia — *RCA/Columbia Pictures Home Video; RCA VideoDiscs*

Tempest, The 1963
Drama
64859   76 mins   C   B, V, 3/4U   P
Maurice Evans, Richard Burton, Roddy McDowall, Lee Remick, Tom Poston, directed by George Schaefer
Shakespeare's classic tale of the fantasy world of spirits, sorcery, monsters, maidens, and shipwreaked, scheming noblemen is brought to life in this production from "George Schaefer's Showcase Theatre."

   (For Explanation of codes, see USE GUIDE and KEY)

George Schaefer — *Enter-Tel Inc*

Tempest, The/The Eagle 1927
Film-History
50641 56 mins B/W B, V P, T
John Barrymore, Camilla Horn, Rudolph Valentino, Louise Dressler
A Russian soldier is betrayed and humiliated by the woman he loves in "The Tempest." In "The Eagle," an outcast guardsman becomes the Russian version of Robin Hood.
United Artists — *Blackhawk Films*

"10" 1979
Comedy
37423 123 mins C B, V, LV R, P
Dudley Moore, Julie Andrews, Bo Derek, directed by Blake Edwards
A successful songwriter who has everything he could want out of life somehow feels that his life is incomplete. He searches for something more—and finds it in the person of Bo Derek, the woman of his dreams, whom he rates as the ultimate on the popular girl-watching scale. He pursues her, determined to overcome any obstacles—with unpredictable results. Music by Henry Mancini; also features Ravel's "Bolero."
MPAA:R EL, SP
Orion Pictures, Warner Brothers — *Warner Home Video; RCA VideoDiscs*

Ten Brothers of Shao-lin 198?
Martial arts
64957 90 mins C B, V P
Chia Ling, Wang Tao, Chang Yi
A martial arts adventure from the days of warlords and warriors.
Dragon Lady Productions — *Unicorn Video*

Ten Commandments, The 1956
Drama
38611 219 mins C B, V, LV R, P
Charlton Heston, Yul Brynner, Anne Baxter, Yvonne DeCarlo, directed by Cecil B. DeMille
Lavish Biblical epic that tells the life story of Moses (Charlton Heston) who turned his back on a privileged life to lead his people to freedom.
Academy Awards '56: Best Special Effects.
Paramount — *Paramount Home Video; RCA VideoDiscs*

Ten Days that Shook the World 1927
Drama
08698 104 mins B/W B, V, 3/4U P
Directed by Sergei Eisenstein and Grigori Alexandrov
This Russian epic details the events which culminated in the Russian Revolution of October 1917, using the actual locations and many actual participants.

Amkino; Russian — *Penguin Video; Video Yesteryear; International Historic Films; Sheik Video; Western Film & Video Inc; Classic Video Cinema Collector's Club*

Ten from Your Show of Shows 1973
Variety
44799 92 mins B/W B, V P, T
Sid Caesar, Imogene Coca, Carl Reiner, Howard Morris
A compilation of vintage comedy routines from the famous variety series of the 50's, "Your Show of Shows." Sketches include a takeoff on "This Is Your Life," and some movie spoofs.
Walter Reade — *Sheik Video*

Ten Little Indians 1975
Mystery
64965 98 mins C B, V P
Herbert Lom, Richard Attenborough, Oliver Reed, Elke Sommer
Ten people are gathered in an isolated inn under mysterious circumstances. One by one they are murdered, each according to a verse from a children's nursery rhyme. Based on the novel and stage play by Agatha Christie.
Avco-Embassy — *Embassy Home Entertainment*

Ten Nights in a Bar Room 1913
Film-History
12501 68 mins B/W B, V P
Robert Lawrence, Marie Trado
Silent film with musical score.
Photo Drama — *Video Connection*

Ten Seconds to Go... 195?
Transportation
68902 25 mins B/W B, V P
A program used to show bus and trolley operators how important ten seconds is in a crisis situation.
Unknown — *Interurban Films*

Tenant, The 1976
Horror
68251 126 mins C B, V R, P
Roman Polanski, Isabelle Adjani, Melvyn Douglas, Jo Van Fleet, Bernard Fresson, Shelley Winters
A disturbing film about an apartment tenant whose neighbors' actions drive him to insanity.
MPAA:R
Marianne Productions — *Paramount Home Video*

Tender Mercies 1983
Drama
65087 93 mins C B, V, CED R, P
Robert Duvall, Tess Harper, Betty Buckley, directed by Bruce Beresford

---

(For Explanation of codes, see USE GUIDE and KEY) **547**

A down-and-out country-and-western singer finds his life redeemed by the love of a good woman.
MPAA:PG
Universal — *THORN EMI Home Video*

Tender Warrior, The　　　　1975
Adventure
66243　　85 mins　　C　　B, V　　　　R, P
Dan Haggerty
A beautifully photographed animal adventure.
MPAA:G
William Thompson Productions — *Video City Productions*

Tendres Cousines　　　　1983
Comedy
65602　　90 mins　　C　　B, V　　　　P
This comedy follows the exploits of two cousins coming of age in the French countryside. Along with the rest of their relatives and friends, they become entwined in a web of unrequited love and intricate relationships.
MPAA:R
Crown — *Vestron Video*

Tennessee's Partner　　　　1955
Western
52579　　87 mins　　C　　B, V　　　　P
Ronald Reagan, Rhonda Fleming, John Payne, directed by Allan Dwan
A stranger steps into the middle of an argument and becomes the friend of a gambler.
RKO — *Weiss Global Enterprises*

Tennis Lessons from Bjorn Borg　　　　1981
Tennis
53783　　60 mins　　C　　B, V, 3/4U,　　R, P
　　　　　　　　　　　　　　FO
Borg teaches all the basic strokes, the different grips and body positions, and basic strategy of the game.
Cine Video Films — *Star Video Productions*

Tennis/Racquet Sports　　　　1978
Tennis
44926　　30 mins　　C　　B, V　　　　P
Exercise specialist Ann Dugan performs exercises for tennis, squash, handball, and racquetball players to use to help mobilize the body for aggressive play. From the "Sports Conditioning" series.
Health N Action — *RCA/Columbia Pictures Home Video*

Tentacles　　　　1977
Horror
64883　　90 mins　　C　　B, V, CED　　　P
John Huston, Shelley Winters, Bo Hopkins, Henry Fonda
A giant octopus wreaks havoc and terror.
MPAA:PG
American International Pictures — *Vestron Video*

10th Victim, The　　　　1965
Drama/Science fiction
65432　　92 mins　　C　　B, V　　　　P
Ursula Andress, Marcello Mastroianni
A futuristic thriller about a society where violence is channeled into legalized murder hunts. A beautiful TV actress is the hunter and the 10th victim will bring her all the material things she desires.
Avco-Embassy — *Embassy Home Entertainment*

Terms of Endearment　　　　1983
Drama
75807　　129 mins　　C　　B, V　　　　R, P
Shirley MacLaine, Jack Nicholson, Debra Winger,　directed James L. Brooks
This story follows the relationship between a young woman and her mother, over a thirty year period.
Academy Awards '83: Best Picture; Best Actress (MacLaine); Best Supporting Actor (Nicholson); Best Director (Brooks); Best Screenplay (Brooks).　MPAA:PG
Paramount — *Paramount Home Video*

Terror　　　　1979
Horror
48502　　86 mins　　C　　B, V　　　　P
John Nolan, Carolyn Courage, James Aubrey
Supernatural forces and the shocking effect their mysterious powers have on the life of a young girl are depicted in this shocking tale.
MPAA:R
Crystal Film Production — *VCI Home Video; Video City Productions*

Terror, The　　　　1963
Horror
59664　　81 mins　　C　　B, V　　　　P
Jack Nicholson, Boris Karloff
A lieutenant in Napoleon's army finds himself trapped by a mad baron's fear of the unknown.
Roger Corman — *Media Home Entertainment; Budget Video; Discount Video Tapes; Cinema Concepts*

Terror by Night　　　　1946
Mystery
42928　　60 mins　　B/W　　B, V　　　　P
Basil Rathbone, Nigel Bruce
Based on a character developed by Sir Arthur Conan Doyle, Holmes and Watson solve two murders and thwart an attempted jewel theft on a train.
Universal, Howard Benedict — *Movie Buff Video; Video Connection; Video Yesteryear;*

Budget Video; Cable Films; Western Film & Video Inc; Discount Video Tapes

Terror by Night/Meeting at Midnight — 194?
Mystery
44856   122 mins   B/W   B, V, 3/4U   P
Basil Rathbone, Nigel Bruce, Sidney Toler
In "Terror by Night" (1946), Sherlock Holmes and Dr. Watson board a train to protect a fabulous diamond. In "Meeting at Midnight" (1944), Charlie Chan becomes involved in magic and murder.
Universal, Monogram — *Nostalgia Merchant*

Terror of Tiny Town — 1933
Western/Musical
14349   65 mins   B/W   B, V   P
Jed Buell's Midgets, directed by Sam Newfield
Terror erupts in a small midwestern town. All-midget cast.
Columbia — *Video Connection; Discount Video Tapes; Penguin Video; Budget Video; Admit One Video*

Terror on Tour — 1983
Horror
64234   90 mins   C   B, V   P
Dave Galluzzo, Richard Styles, Rick Pemberton
The Clowns, a rock group on their way up, center their stage performance around sadistic, mutilating theatrics. When real murders begin, they become prime suspects.
Rick Whitfield — *Media Home Entertainment*

Terry Bears Volume II — 196?
Cartoons
29177   90 mins   C   B, V   P
Animated
A cartoon feature with "Terry Bears."
Viacom International — *CBS/Fox Video*

Terry Fox Story, The — 1983
Drama
65349   96 mins   C   B, V, CED   P
Robert Duvall, Chris Makepiece, Eric Fryer
In the spring of 1980, a brave young man who had lost his right leg to cancer dipped his artificial limb into the Atlantic Ocean and set off on a "Marathon of Hope" across Canada. He ran 3,000 miles before he collapsed in Ontario.
Michael A Levine; Gurston Rosenfeld — *Vestron Video*

Terrytoons Salutes the Olympics — 1979
Sports/Cartoons
72234   60 mins   C   B, V   P
Animated
An animated salute to the Olympics featuring the Terrytoon all stars, including Deputy Dawg.

Viacom — *Children's Video Library*

Terrytoons, Vol. I, Featuring Mighty Mouse — 196?
Cartoons
56884   100 mins   C   CED   P
Animated
Nineteen complete cartoons featuring Mighty Mouse, Heckle and Jeckle, Deputy Dawg, Little Roquefort, and others.
Terrytoons — *RCA VideoDiscs*

Tess — 1980
Drama
52748   170 mins   C   B, V, LV   P
Nastassia Kinski, Peter Firth, Leigh Lawson, John Collin, directed by Roman Polanski
Thomas Hardy's novel "Tess of the d'Urbervilles," concerning a young woman who is a victim of both circumstance and a rigid Victorian society, tortured by guilt for the wrongs she feels she has committed, is the basis for this movie.
Academy Awards '80: Best Cinematography; Best Art Direction; Best Costume Design. MPAA:PG
Claude Beri; Renn Productions; Burrill Productions — *RCA/Columbia Pictures Home Video; RCA VideoDiscs*

Testament — 1983
Drama
Closed Captioned
65763   90 mins   C   B, V, CED   R, P
Jane Alexander, William Devane, Ross Harris, Roxana Zal
Following a massive nuclear attack, a mother and her children struggle to survive against the backdrop of death, disease and destruction.
MPAA:PG
Lynne Littman — *Paramount Home Video*

Tex — 1982
Drama
60557   103 mins   C   B, V, LV   R, P
Matt Dillon, Jim Metzler, Meg Tilly, Bill McKinney, Frances Lee McCain, Ben Johnson, Emilio Estevez
The poignant and moving story of a teenager coming of age in a small Texas town. Based on the novel by S.E. Hinton.
MPAA:PG
Walt Disney Productions — *Walt Disney Home Video*

Tex Ritter Rides With the Boy Scouts — 1937
Western
08794   60 mins   B/W   B, V, 3/4U   P
Tex Ritter
Scouts aid Tex in capturing gold bandits.
Grand Natl — *Penguin Video*

Texaco Star Theater   1951
Variety/Comedy
58264   60 mins   B/W   B, V, FO   P
Milton Berle, Danny Thomas, Fran Warren, Sid Stone, Frank Galop, Alan Roth and his Orchestra
Originally broadcast on May 29, 1951, Uncle Miltie presides over the hilarity. Guests include Carlos Ramirez and his Senoritas, novelty dancers Harold and Lola, Beatrice Kraft and her Oriental dancers, 15-year-old violinist Michael Rabin, and singer Vivian Dellachiesa. Sketches include "The Chandeliers," a comic troupe of acrobats, and "United Nations of Show Business."
NBC — *Video Yesteryear; Roll Your Own Video*

Texas Chainsaw Massacre, The   1974
Horror
59058   86 mins   C   CED, LV   P
Marilyn Burns, Paul A Partain, Edwin Neal, directed by Tobe Hooper
An idyllic summer afternoon drive becomes a nightmare for two young people pursued by a chainsaw-wielding maniac.
MPAA:R
Tobe Hooper; New Line Cinema — *Vestron Video*

Texas Hex   197?
Fishing
33747   30 mins   C   B, V, 3/4U, Q   P
The fishing magic of Texas coastal waters, from surf casting to deep sea angling, is presented.
TV Sports Scene — *TV Sports Scene*

Texas Lightning   1981
Adventure
66063   93 mins   C   B, V   P
Cameron Mitchell, Channing Mitchell, Maureen McCormick, Peter Jason
A truck driver is intent on showing his shy son the fine points of life.
MPAA:R
Jim Sotos — *Media Home Entertainment*

Texas Terror   1940
Western
29440   50 mins   B/W   B, V   P
John Wayne, Gabby Hayes
John Wayne plays a cowboy who mistakenly believes he has shot his friend. He becomes a ranch foreman and saves the ranch from horse theives, finally discovering who really shot his friend.
Monogram — *Sheik Video; Video Dimensions*

Texas to Bataan   1942
Western
11263   56 mins   B/W   B, V, FO   P

Range Busters
The Range Busters ship horses to the Philippines and encounter enemy spies.
Monogram — *Video Yesteryear*

Texas Trouble   193?
Western
15533   mins   B/W   B, V   P
Bob Steele
Western adventure starring the American cowboy Bob Steele.
Unknown — *Video Connection*

Texersize   1984
Physical fitness
65706   37 mins   C   B, V   P
Irlene Mandrell
This program exercises all major muscle groups and gives a complete cardio-vascular workout.
Panda Productions; Haghland Productions — *Embassy Home Entertainment*

Thank God It's Friday   1978
Comedy/Musical
63965   100 mins   C   B, V   P
Valerie Landsburg, Terri Nunn, Chick Vennera
A dance contest at a Hollywood disco, where the participants are caught up in the glamor and glitter of disco nightlife, is the focal point of this film. Music by Donna Summer and The Commodores.
Academy Awards '78: Best Song ("Last Dance"). MPAA:PG
Casablanca Productions; Columbia Pictures — *RCA/Columbia Pictures Home Video*

That Championship Season   1982
Drama
66116   110 mins   C   B, V, CED   P
Martin Sheen, Bruce Dern, Stacy Keach, Robert Mitchum, Paul Sorvino
Long-dormant animosities surface at the reunion of a championship basketball team.
MPAA:R
Cannon — *MGM/UA Home Video*

That Cold Day in the Park   1969
Drama
66469   91 mins   C   B, V   P
Sandy Dennis, Michael Burns, Suzanne Benton, directed by Robert Altman
A disturbed spinster entices a homeless young man into her apartment and makes him a prisoner.
MPAA:R
Commonwealth United; Robert Altman — *NTA Home Entertainment*

That Man Is Pregnant — 1980
Comedy
75631   80 mins   C   B, V   P
A NYPD detective gets the incredible news that he is pregnant.
MPAA:PG
Simon Nuchtern — *Independent United Distributors*

That Touch of Mink — 1962
Comedy/Romance
65456   99 mins   C   B, V   P
Cary Grant, Doris Day
In New York City, a young naive girl finds herself involved with a business tycoon. On a trip to Bermuda, both parties get an education as they play their game of "cat and mouse."
Universal — *NTA Home Entertainment*

That Uncertain Feeling — 1941
Comedy
05460   86 mins   B/W   B, V, FO   P
Merle Oberon, Melvyn Douglas, Burgess Meredith, Alan Mowbray, Eve Arden
A husband and wife develop marital problems when the wife gets the hiccups.
Ernst Lubitsch; United Artists — *Video Yesteryear; Discount Video Tapes; Budget Video; Classic Video Cinema Collector's Club*

That Was Rock (The TAMI/TNT Show) — 1964
Music-Performance
65481   90 mins   B/W   B, V   P
Chuck Berry, James Brown, Ray Charles, Bo Diddley, Marvin Gaye, Gerry & The Pacemakers, Lesley Gore, Jan & Dean, Smokey Robinson & the Miracles, The Ronettes, The Rolling Stones, The Supremes, Ike & Tina Turner
The TAMI/TNT shows were the greatest dance concerts ever, and now they are together in one rock and roll, rhythm and blues extravaganza. In stereo VHS and Beta Hi-Fi.
Lee Savin; Phil Spector — *Music Media*

That'll Be the Day — 1973
Musical
63320   86 mins   C   B, V   R, P
Ringo Starr, Keith Moon, David Essex, Rosemary Leach
Set in the early rock 'n' roll era of the 1950's, this is the story of a wayward young man and his aspirations to musical superstardom.
David Puttnam; Sanford Lieberson — *THORN EMI Home Video*

That's Entertainment — 1974
Musical
44646   132 mins   C   B, V, LV,   P
                                  CED
Judy Garland, Fred Astaire, Frank Sinatra, Gene Kelly, Esther Williams, Bing Crosby, directed by Jack Haley Jr.
A compilation of scenes from the classic MGM musicals beginning with "The Broadway Melody" (1929) and ending with "Gigi" (1958).
MPAA:G
MGM — *MGM/UA Home Video*

That's Entertainment, Part II — 1976
Musical
58291   133 mins   C   B, V   P
Fred Astaire, Gene Kelly, John Barrymore, Lionel Barrymore, Jack Benny, Judy Garland, Maurice Chevalier, Bing Crosby, Jimmy Durante, Clark Gable, Jean Harlow, Elizabeth Taylor, Robert Taylor
A cavalcade of great musical and comedy sequences from MGM movies of the past. Also stars Jeanette MacDonald, Nelson Eddy, the Marx Bros., Laurel and Hardy, Jack Buchanan, Ann Miller, Mickey Rooney, Louis Armstrong, Oscar Levant, Cyd Charisse.
MPAA:G
MGM — *MGM/UA Home Video*

The Howdy Doody Show (Puppet Playhouse)/Gabby Hayes Show — 1948
Comedy
72520   60 mins   B/W   B, V, 3/4U   P
Buffalo Bill, Clarabell and the peanut gallery help Howdy Doody with a nostalgic circus of fun in this popular and pioneering children's program. On the same tape Gabby Hayes sings the Quaker Oats song and tells a tale of the old west.
NBC — *International Historic Films*

Theatre of Death — 1967
Horror
13141   90 mins   C   B, V   P
Christopher Lee, Julian Glover
Paris police are baffled by a series of mysterious murders, each bearing a trace of vampirism.
Associated British Productions Ltd — *VCI Home Video*

There's a Girl in My Soup — 1970
Comedy
65316   95 mins   C   B, V   P
Peter Sellers, Goldie Hawn
Sellers is a gourmet who moonlights as a self-styled Casanova, and Goldie is the young girl who takes refuge at his London love nest when she is ejected by her boyfriend from their flat.
M J Frankovich; John Boulting — *RCA/Columbia Pictures Home Video*

(For Explanation of codes, see USE GUIDE and KEY)

There's a Meetin' Here Tonight　　1981
Music-Performance
53859　117 mins　C　　LV　　　　P
The Limelighters, Glen Yarborough, Kingston Trio
Performances by folk immortals The Limelighters, Glenn Yarborough, and the Kingston Trio.
Intl Teleview Inc; Bill Williams; Susan Shore — *Pioneer Artists*

There's Naked Bodies On My T.V.!　　197?
Satire/Comedy
59550　79 mins　C　　B, V　　　　P
A sexy spoof of TV shows, "Happy Daze," "Bernie Milner," and "Don't Come Back Kotler."
CHK Productions — *Media Home Entertainment*

There's No Business Like Show Business　　1954
Musical
37416　117 mins　C　　B, V, CED　　P
Ethel Merman, Donald O'Connor, Marilyn Monroe, Dan Dailey, Johnny Ray, Mitzi Gaynor
A top husband and wife vaudevillian act return to the stage with their three children, who are now also in the act. Includes 24 songs by Irving Berlin.
20th Century Fox — *CBS/Fox Video*

These Girls Won't Talk　　192?
Comedy
11286　50 mins　B/W　　B, V, FO　　P
Colleen Moore, Carole Lombard, Betty Compson
Three female stars of early motion pictures are featured separately in: "Her Bridal Nightmare," "Campus Carmen," and "As Luck Would Have It."
Mack Sennett et al — *Video Yesteryear*

They All Laughed　　1981
Comedy
59870　115 mins　C　　B, V, LV, CED　　P
Ben Gazzara, John Ritter, Audrey Hepburn, Colleen Camp, Patti Hansen, Dorothy Stratten, directed by Peter Bogdonovich
A madcap private eye caper involving a team of detectives who are both following and being followed by a bevy of dazzling women.
MPAA:PG
PSO; Moon Pictures — *Vestron Video*

They Call Me Bruce　　1982
Comedy/Martial arts
66091　88 mins　C　　B, V, CED　　P
Johnny Yune, Margaux Hemingway

A bumbling Bruce Lee lookalike meets a karate-chopping Mafia moll in this farce.
Elliot Hong — *Vestron Video*

They Call Me Mr. Tibbs!　　1970
Mystery
65008　108 mins　C　　B, V, CED　　P
Sidney Poitier, Barbara McNair, Martin Landau, Juano Hernandez, Anthony Zerbe, Edward Asner, Norma Crane
Lieutenant Virgil Tibbs (Poitier) must track down a murder case which involves his friend, the Reverend Logan Sharpe (Landau). He is torn between his duty as a policeman, his concern for the reverend and the threat of turmoil in the town. Sequel to "In the Heat of the Night."
MPAA:PG
United Artists — *CBS/Fox Video*

They Call Me Trinity　　1972
Western
08480　110 mins　C　　B, V, CED　　P
Terence Hill, Bud Spencer, Farley Granger, Steffen Zacharias, directed by E. B. Clucher
Lazy drifter-gunslinger and his outlaw brother join forces with Mormon farmers to rout bullying outlaws.
MPAA:G
Avco Embassy; West Film Productions — *Embassy Home Entertainment*

They Came to Cordura　　1959
Drama
64579　123 mins　C　　B, V　　　　P
Gary Cooper, Rita Hayworth, Van Heflin, Tab Hunter, directed by Robert Rossen
In Mexico circa 1916, six American heroes are recalled to their headquarters in Cordura. On the way, they encounter hardships and unexpected danger.
Columbia — *RCA/Columbia Pictures Home Video*

They Drive by Night　　1940
Drama
64934　97 mins　B/W　　CED　　　P
Humphrey Bogart, Ann Sheridan, George Raft, Ida Lupino, Alan Hale, Gale Page, Roscoe Karns
A truck driver loses his brother in an accident and subsequently gets involved in a murder.
Warner Bros — *CBS/Fox Video*

They Live by Night　　1949
Crime-Drama
59650　95 mins　B/W　　B, V　　　P
Cathy O'Donnell, Farley Granger, Howard da Silva, Jay C. Flippen, Helen Craig, directed by Nicholas Ray
A young fugitive from the law sinks deeper into a life of crime thanks to his association with two hardened criminals. His life changes when he meets a farm girl. A classic of film noir.

RKO; Dore Schary — *Budget Video*

___

They Made Me a Criminal — 1939
Drama
08762   92 mins   B/W   B, V, 3/4U   P
John Garfield, Ann Sheridan, Claude Rains, Dead End Kids
A champion prizefighter, believing he murdered a man in a drunken brawl runs away. (Remake of "The Life of Jimmy Dolan.')
Warner Bros — *Penguin Video; VCII; Video Dimensions; Sheik Video; Discount Video Tapes; Cable Films; Video Connection; Video Yesteryear; Sound Video Unlimited; Western Film & Video Inc; Cinema Concepts*

___

They Saved Hitler's Brain — 1964
Horror
13142   91 mins   B/W   B, V   P
Walter Stocker, Audrey Caire
Fanatical survivors of the Nazi holocaust give eternal life to the brain of their leader in the last hours of the war.
Crown Intl Pictures — *VCI Home Video*

___

They Went That-a-Way & That-a-Way — 1978
Comedy
69552   96 mins   C   B, V   P
Tim Conway, Richard Kiel
Two bumbling deputies pose as convicts in this madcap prison caper.
MPAA:PG
International Picture Show Company — *Embassy Home Entertainment*

___

They Won't Believe Me — 1947
Suspense
64377   95 mins   B/W   B, V, 3/4U   P
Robert Young, Susan Hayward, Rita Johnson, Jane Greer
A man plots to kill his wife, but before he does, she commits suicide. He ends up on trial for her "murder."
RKO — *Nostalgia Merchant*

___

Thief — 1981
Crime-Drama
47152   126 mins   C   B, V, CED   P
James Caan, Tuesday Weld, Willie Nelson, James Belushi, Robert Prosky
A big-time professional thief enjoys pulling off heists on his own, but is forced to work for a crime syndicate in an attempt to bring in more money for his family.
MPAA:R
United Artists — *CBS/Fox Video*

___

Thief of Bagdad, The — 1924
Adventure
13175   143 mins   B/W   B, V   P, T
Douglas Fairbanks, Anna May Wong
A fabulous Arabian Nights fantasy, with Fairbanks as a notorious thief who reforms for the love of a princess. Silent with original music score.
United Artists — *Blackhawk Films; Sheik Video; Western Film & Video Inc; Festival Films; Cable Films; Classic Video Cinema Collector's Club*

___

Thief of Baghdad, The — 1978
Fantasy
36182   101 mins   C   B, V   R, P
Peter Ustinov, Roddy McDowall, Terrence Stamp, directed by Clive Donner
A fantasy-adventure about a genie, a prince, beautiful maidens, a happy-go-lucky thief, and magic.
MPAA:G
Palm Films Ltd — *Video Gems*

___

Thighs and Whispers: The History of Lingerie — 1982
Clothing and dress
59077   45 mins   C   B, V   P
A brief history of lingerie, entertaining and informative.
Karl Video — *Karl Video*

___

Thin Thighs in 30 Day — 1983
Physical fitness
66197   60 mins   C   B, V   P
Wendy Stehling
How to have good looking legs is discussed and demonstrated.
WCP Video — *U.S.A. Home Video*

___

Thing, The — 1951
Science fiction
44002   80 mins   B/W   B, V, 3/4U   P
James Arness, Kenneth Tobey, Margaret Sheriden
Alien creature terrorizes an Arctic research team.
RKO; Howard Hawks — *Nostalgia Merchant; VidAmerica; King of Video; RCA VideoDiscs*

___

Thing, The — 1982
Science fiction/Horror
62875   127 mins   C   B, V, LV, CED   P
Kurt Russell, A. Wilford Brimely, T.K. Carter, directed by John Carpenter
A team of scientists at a remote Antarctic outpost discover a buried spaceship with an unwelcome alien survivor still alive. VHS in stereo. Also available subtitled in Spanish.
MPAA:R
Universal — *MCA Home Video*

___

(For Explanation of codes, see USE GUIDE and KEY)

Things Are Tough All Over　1982
Comedy
63433　87 mins　C　B, V　P
*Cheech Marin, Tommy Chong, Shelby Fiddis,
Rikki Marin, Evelyn Guerrero, Rip Taylor*
Cheech and Chong play dual roles as
themselves and as two rich Arab brothers who
hire Cheech and Chong to drive a car full of
money from Chicago to Las Vegas.
MPAA:R
Columbia; Howard Brown — *RCA/Columbia
Pictures Home Video; RCA VideoDiscs*

Things to Come　1936
Science fiction
12826　92 mins　B/W　B, V　P
*Raymond Massey, Ralph Richardson, Sir Cedric
Hardwicke, directed by William Cameron
Menzies*
Based on the H. G. Wells story of a war lasting
from 1940 to 2036 and how scientists aim to
rebuild the world when peace is achieved.
London Films; Alexander Korda — *Media
Home Entertainment; Movie Buff Video; Video
Yesteryear; Budget Video; Sheik Video; Cable
Films; Video Connection; Discount Video Tapes;
Cinema Concepts*

Think Dirty　1978
Comedy
64577　93 mins　C　B, V　P
Marty Feldman, Judy Cornwell, Shelley Berman
An advertising executive develops a series of
sexy commercials at the same time that his wife
is forming a "clean up TV" group.
MPAA:R
Quartet Films — *RCA/Columbia Pictures
Home Video*

Third Man, The　1949
Mystery
08595　105 mins　B/W　B, V　P
*Orson Wells, Joseph Cotton, Alida Valli,
directed by Sir Carol Reed*
An American writer arrives in Vienna to take job
with an old friend whom he finds has been
murdered. Based on Graham Greene's mystery.
Academy Awards '50: Best Cinematography.
Selznick Releasing Organization;
British — *Media Home Entertainment; Budget
Video; VCII; Video Yesteryear; Penguin Video;
Video Dimensions; Sheik Video; Ampro Video
Productions; Video Connection; Discount Video
Tapes; Cable Films; Western Film & Video Inc;
Cinema Concepts; Vestron Video (disc only)*

Third Man, The/The Stranger　194?
Drama
58917　197 mins　B/W　B, V　P
*Orson Welles, Joseph Cotton, Trevor Howard,
Loretta Young, Edward G. Robinson, Richard
Long*
An Orson Welles double feature: "The Third
Man" (1949), in which a man, searching for his
friend, Harry Lime, discovers the evil and
corruption about him; "The Stranger" (1946), a
tale about an escaped Nazi living in a quiet New
England town.
EL, SP
Selznick Releasing; RKO — *Ampro Video
Productions*

Thirsty Dead　1977
Horror
36928　90 mins　C　B, V　P
John Considine, Jennifer Billingsley
A science fiction-horror film wherein corpses
return to life.
Unknown — *King of Video*

35mm Motion Picture Projector, The　1956
Film-History
54110　30 mins　B/W　B, V　P, T
A look at a private collection of 35mm motion
picture projectors that is the largest collection in
existence anywhere.
Unknown — *Blackhawk Films*

35mm Photography　1981
Photography
59917　100 mins　C　LV　P
David Brady teaches the ten fundamentals of
35mm still-camera photography.
Inedco Productions — *INEDCO Productions*

30 Is a Dangerous Age, Cynthia　1968
Comedy
76040　85 mins　C　B, V　P
Dudley Moore, Suzy Kendall, Eddie Foy, Jr
Dudley Moore stars as a night club pianist who
has set himself a goal to get married and write a
hit musical before he reaches thirty.
Walter Shenson — *RCA/Columbia Pictures
Home Video*

39 Steps, The　1935
Mystery
48695　81 mins　B/W　B, V　P
*Robert Donat, Madeleine Carroll, Godfrey
Tearle, Lucie Mannheim, Peggy Ashcroft,
directed by Alfred Hitchcock*
A man becomes involved in a murder and an
international spy ring. Classic Hitchcock
suspense with many of his trademark directorial
touches.
Gaumont — *Embassy Home Entertainment;
VCII; Video Yesteryear; Video Dimensions;
Sheik Video; Ampro Video Productions; Cable
Films; Video Connection; Budget Video;
Western Film & Video Inc; Penguin Video;
Discount Video Tapes; RCA VideoDiscs*

Thirty-Nine Steps, The/Blackmail 193?
Suspense
58918 161 mins B/W B, V P
Robert Donat, Madeleine Carroll, John Longdon, Sarah Allgood, directed by Alfred Hitchcock
A Hitchcock double feature: ''The Thirty-Nine Steps'' (1935), in which a man involves himself in a murder and an international spy ring; ''Blackmail'' (1929), Hitch's first sound film, concerns the police investigation of a murder and a detective's attempts to keep his girlfriend from being involved.
EL, SP
Gaumont; British Intl — *Ampro Video Productions*

This Gun For Hire 1942
Western
68255 81 mins B/W B, V P
Alan Ladd, Veronica Lake, Robert Preston, Laird Cregar
Ladd plays a paid gunman working within a criminal organization who is hired by German spies, is double crossed and ends up wanting revenge.
Paramount — *MCA Home Video*

This Is a Hijack 1975
Adventure/Suspense
76661 90 mins C B, V P
Adam Roarke, Neville Brand, Jay Robinson, Lynn Borden, Dub Taylor
A story of a gambler who can't pay his debts and decides to make a deal to hijack his wealthy boss.
MPAA:PG
Fanfare Corp — *Monterey Home Video*

This Is Elvis 1981
Biographical/Musical
68238 144 mins C B, V R, P
The life of Elvis is presented in this film. There are 42 minutes of footage that has never been seen before and more than three dozen songs.
MPAA:PG
David L Wolper — *Warner Home Video*

This Is Korea/December 7th 194?
World War II
58721 85 mins C B, V P
Directed by John Ford
Two propaganda films made by John Ford for the war effort. ''This Is Korea'' was so militaristic that it has been suppressed for many years. (Some black and white).
US Army — *Video Dimensions*

This Is the Army 1943
Musical-Drama
11316 105 mins C B, V, FO P
George Murphy, Joan Leslie, Ronald Reagan, Alan Hale, Kate Smith, and the men of the Armed Services
A robust tribute to the American soldier, containing the songs, ''This is the Army, Mr. Jones,'' ''I Left My Heart at the Stage Door Canteen,'' ''Oh, How I Hate to Get Up in the Morning,'' and many more.
Academy Award '43: Best Scoring Musical. Warner Bros — *Video Yesteryear; Discount Video Tapes; Sheik Video; Cable Films; Video Connection; Budget Video; Classic Video Cinema Collector's Club*

This Is Your Life: Laurel and Hardy 1954
Interview
42972 30 mins B/W B, V, FO P
Ralph Edwards, Stan Laurel, Oliver Hardy
Stan and Ollie appear somewhat stunned as old girlfriends and assocaites from Hollywood appear, including Vivian Blaine and Leo McCarey.
NBC — *Video Yesteryear; Sheik Video*

This Island Earth 1955
Science fiction
64789 86 mins C B, V P
Jeff Morrow, Faith Domergue, Rex Reason, directed by Joseph M. Newman
The planet Metaluna is in desperate need of uranium to power their defense against enemy invaders. A nuclear scientist and a nuclear fission expert are kidnapped to help out.
Universal — *MCA Home Video*

This Nude World 193?
Sociology/Documentary
48735 60 mins B/W B, V, 3/4U P
Directed by Michael Mindlin
A documentary which attempts to bring out certain facts about nudist colonies in the 1930's. Shot in France, Germany, and the United States.
Unknown — *Penguin Video*

This Sporting Life 1963
Drama
49071 129 mins B/W B, V P
Richard Harris, Rachel Roberts, Colin Blakely
A tough, aggressive rugby player has a difficult time controlling his competitive nature off the field. His career and love life suffer for it.
Cannes Film Festival '63: Best Actor (Harris).
Continental Distributors — *Sheik Video*

Thomas Crown Affair, The 1968
Drama/Adventure
55588 102 mins C B, V P
Steve McQueen, Faye Dunaway, Jack Weston

A multi-millionaire executes a daring daylight robbery of a bank and gets away with two million in cash.
Academy Awards '68: Best Song ("Windmills of Your Mind"). EL, SP
United Artists; Mirisch Corp — *CBS/Fox Video*

Thomas Dolby 1984
Music-Performance
75913   16 mins   C   B, V   P
This program presents the new British singer Thomas Dolby performing his hit songs.
EMI Records Ltd — *Sony Corporation of America*

Thomas Dolby 1983
Music-Performance
69393   58 mins   C   B, V   R, P
This music video by the popular rock star includes such songs as "She Blinded Me with Science," "Europa" and "One of Our Submarines."
EMI Music — *THORN EMI Home Video; Pioneer Video Imports*

Thomas Edison: Let There Be Light 1954
Biographical/Inventions
44235   15 mins   B/W   B, V   P
This program contains classic newsreel footage of the inventions of Thomas Alva Edison. Included are the stock ticker, the phonograph, improvements on the telephone, a system of ship-to-shore wireless telegraphy, the radio, the fluoroscope, the first motion picture camera, and the incandescent lamp.
Fox Movietone News — *Two Star Films*

Thompson Twins Live at Liverpool, The 1983
Music-Performance
73020   60 mins   C   B, V   R, P
Tom Bailey, Joe Leeway, Alannah Currie
The Thompson Twins, recorded concert at Liverpool's Royal Court, perform "Lies and Love on Your Side".
Unknown — *THORN EMI Home Video*

Thoroughbred Heroes 19??
Horse racing
69646   55 mins   C   B, V   P
Some of the greatest thoroughbreds of the past 25 years are seen racing, including Citation, Majestic Prince and Secretariat.
Joe Burnham — *Mercedes Maharis Productions*

Thorpe's Gold 1984
Documentary/Sports
72947   75 mins   C   B, V   P

A documentary about Olympic star Jim Thorpe, multi-award winner in the 1912 Olympics. Some black-and-white segments.
VCI — *VCI Home Video*

Those Endearing Young Charms 1945
Romance
10044   82 mins   B/W   B, V   P, T
Robert Young, Laraine Day, Anne Jeffreys, Lawrence Tierney
Romance developes between young Air Corps mechanic and salesgirl. Complications arise when another man enters the scene.
RKO — *Blackhawk Films*

Those Flying Canucks 1982
Sports-Winter
59176   53 mins   C   B, V, 3/4U   P
A look at two members of the Canadian World Cup ski jumping team. The beauty of this sport is captured at speeds exceeding 70 mph.
Unknown — *Sports World Cinema*

Those Magnificent Men in Their Flying Machines 1965
Comedy
08461   138 mins   C   B, V   P
Stuart Whitman, Sarah Miles, Robert Morley, Albert Sordi, James Fox, Gert Frobe
In 1910 a wealthy British newspaper publisher is persuaded to sponsor an air race from London to Paris. Contestants from all over the world come.
EL, SP
20th Century Fox — *CBS/Fox Video*

Those Wild Bloopers 1984
Outtakes and bloopers
73549   65 mins   B/W   B, V   P
All kinds of foulups and blunders from Bogart, Abbott and Costello and Bette Davis are in this program.
Admit One — *Admit One Video*

Thoughts by the Ocean 1978
Video
08562   30 mins   C   B, V, 3/4U   P
A continuous picture of peaceful waves rolling on to the shore to create a relaxed background.
Nebulae Prods — *Nebulae Productions*

Thousand Clowns, A 1965
Comedy-Drama
58838   118 mins   B/W   CED   P
Jason Robards Jr., Barry Gordon, William Daniels, Barbara Harris, Gene Saks, Martin Balsam
A nonconformist writer resigns from his job as chief writer for an obnoxious kiddie show in order to enjoy life.

United Artists — *CBS/Fox Video*

Three Ages, The 1923
Comedy
60351   59 mins   B/W   B, V   P
Buster Keaton
Keaton's first feature film was this parody of
Griffith's "Intolerance," with Buster in
prehistoric days, ancient Rome and in modern
times. Silent with musical score.
Joseph Schenk; First National — *Video
Dimensions*

Three Broadway Girls 1932
Comedy
47774   78 mins   B/W   B, V, 3/4U   R, P
*Joan Blondell, Ina Claire, Madge Evans, David
Manners, Lowell Sherman*
Three gold-diggers go husband hunting.
United Artists — *Movie Buff Video; Cable Films*

Three Caballeros, The 1945
Cartoons
59811   70 mins   C   B, V   R, P
Animated
Donald Duck stars in this program of shorts
about South America, full of music and variety.
Stories include "Pablo the Penguin," "Little
Gauchito," and adventures with Joe Carioca.
Walt Disney — *Walt Disney Home Video*

Three Cheers for the 1983
Redskins
Football
65016   53 mins   C   B, V, FO   P
A colorful study of the Washington Redskins'
1971 season, their first with George Allen as
head coach, following the death of Vince
Lombardi.
NFL Films — *NFL Films Video*

Three Days of the 1975
Condor
Drama
38604   118 mins   C   B, V, LV   R, P
*Robert Redford, Faye Dunaway, Cliff
Robertson, Max Von Sydow, directed by
Sydney Pollack*
CIA researcher Redford finds himself on the run
from unknown killers when he is left the only
survivor of the mass murder of his office staff.
MPAA:R
Paramount — *Paramount Home Video; RCA
VideoDiscs*

Three Faces West 1940
Western
66467   79 mins   B/W   B, V   P
*John Wayne, Charles Coburn, Sigrid Gurie,
Sonny Bupp*
A dust bowl community is helped by a Viennese
doctor who left Europe to avoid Nazi capture.

Republic — *NTA Home Entertainment*

Three Husbands 1950
Drama
66399   80 mins   B/W   B, V   P
*Emlyn Williams, Eve Arden, Howard Da Silva,
Ruth Warrick, Billie Burke*
Three husbands receive letters from a dead
friend claiming that he had affairs with each of
their wives.
United Artists — *Movie Buff Video*

Three in the Attic 1968
Comedy-Drama
65069   92 mins   C   B, V   P
Christopher Jones, Yvette Mimieux, John Beck
A college student juggles three girlfriends at the
same time. When the girls find out they are
being two-timed, they lock their boyfriend in an
attic and exhaust him with forced sexual
escapades.
MPAA:R
American International Pictures — *Embassy
Home Entertainment*

Three in the Saddle 1945
Western
54194   61 mins   B/W   B, V   P
Tex Ritter
Tex Ritter and the Texas Rangers fight for law
and order.
Producers Releasing Corp — *Video
Connection*

Three Little Pigs, The 1984
Fairy tales
Closed Captioned
73571   60 mins   C   B, V, CED   P
Billy Crystal, Jeff Goldblum, Valerie Perrine
From "Faerie Tale Theatre" comes the story of
three little pigs, the houses they lived in and the
wolf that tries to do them in.
Gaylord Productions; Platypus
Productions — *CBS/Fox Video*

Three Mesquiteers 1936
Western
54195   54 mins   B/W   B, V   P
Bob Livingston, Max Terhune, Ray Corrigan
The boys run into problems with rival cattle
owners.
Republic — *Video Connection*

Three Musketeers, The 1974
Adventure
59645   107 mins   C   CED   P
*Richard Chamberlain, Raquel Welch, Michael
York, Oliver Reed, Faye Dunaway, Charlton
Heston, Christopher Lee, directed by Richard
Lester*

(For Explanation of codes, see USE GUIDE and KEY)

Sword play, romance, and slapstick comedy abound in this exuberant big-budget version of the Alexandre Dumas classic.
MPAA:PG
Alexander Salkin — *RCA VideoDiscs*

Three Musketeers, The   1973
Adventure
65440   107 mins   C   B, V   P
Richard Chamberlain, Raquel Welch, Faye Dunaway, Michael York
A tongue-in-cheek version of the Alexander Dumas classic.
MPAA:PG
Film Trust SA — *U.S.A. Home Video*

Three Musketeers, The   1976
Adventure/Cartoons
69528   74 mins   C   B, V, CED   P
Animated
D'Artagnan and the fabled Musketeers engage in swashbuckling adventures in Paris and England.
Pendennis Films — *Children's Video Library*

Three Musketeers, The   1933
Adventure/Serials
14629   156 mins   B/W   B, V   P
John Wayne, Raymond Hatton
Modern adaptation of Dumas' classic puts the three friends in fast airplanes. In twelve chapters.
Mascot — *Video Connection; Video Dimensions; Video Yesteryear; Discount Video Tapes; Classic Video Cinema Collector's Club*

Three Nuts in Search of a Bolt   1964
Comedy
47310   79 mins   C   B, V   P
Mamie Van Doren, Tommy Noonan, Ziva Rodann, Paul Gilbert, John Cronin
An unemployed actor is sent to a woman psychiatrist by his three neurotic friends. When the psychiatrist's closed circuit telecast of the actor is accidentally broadcast, chaos and comedy result.
Adrian Weiss Productions — *Weiss Global Enterprises*

Three Stooges, The   1949
Comedy
63098   60 mins   B/W   B, V   P
Moe, Larry, Curly and Shemp
Three original shorts by the comedy trio, including: "Disorder in the Court" (1936—Curly), "Sing a Song of Six Pants" (1949—Shemp) and "Malice in the Palace" (1949—Shemp).
Columbia — *Roll Your Own Video; Admit One Video*

Three Stooges Comedy Capers Volume I   194?
Comedy
60421   80 mins   B/W   B, V, 3/4U   P
Moe Howard, Larry Fine, Curly Howard, Shemp Howard
This compilation includes: "Disorder in the Court" (1936), "Malice in the Palace" (1949), "Sing a Song of Six Pants" (1947), "The Brideless Groom" (1947).
Columbia Pictures — *Nostalgia Merchant*

Three Stooges—Medium Rare, The   195?
Comedy
72952   120 mins   B/W   B, V   P
Moe Howard, Larry Fine, Shemp Howard
Moe, Larry and Shemp are featured in several rare TV appearances from the 1950's, including a guest spot on "The Ed Wynn Show" and several commercials.
NBC et al — *Budget Video*

Three Stooges Meet Hercules, The   1961
Comedy
69619   80 mins   B/W   B, V   P
The Three Stooges, Vicki Trickett, Quinn Redeker
The Three Stooges are transported back to ancient Ithaca by a time machine with a young scientist and his girlfriend. When the girl is captured, they enlist the help of Hercules to rescue her.
Norman Maurer; Columbia — *RCA/Columbia Pictures Home Video*

Three Stooges Videodisc, Vol. 1, The   194?
Comedy
60385   106 mins   B/W   CED   P
Moe Howard, Larry Fine, Curly Howard, Christine McIntyre
Four classic Three Stooges two-reelers are on this disc: "Dizzy Pilots" (1943), "A Bird in the Head" (1946), "Three Missing Links" (1938) and "Micro-Phonies" (1945).
Columbia — *RCA VideoDiscs*

Three Stooges Volume I, The   194?
Comedy
44844   60 mins   B/W   B, V   P
Moe Howard, Larry Fine, Curly Howard
Three shorts featuring Curly, Moe and Larry are included in this package: "A Bird in the Head" (1946), "Dizzy Pilots" (1943), and "Three Sappy People" (1939).
Columbia — *RCA/Columbia Pictures Home Video*

    (For Explanation of codes, see USE GUIDE and KEY)

Three Stooges Volume II, The   194?
Comedy
58540   60 mins   B/W   B, V   P
Moe Howard, Larry Fine, Curly Howard
The Three Stooges are seen in three shorts:
"Uncivil Warriors" (1935), "Three Missing
Links" (1938), and "Micro-Phonies" (1945).
Columbia — *RCA/Columbia Pictures Home
Video*

Three Stooges Volume III, The   194?
Comedy
52754   60 mins   B/W   B, V   P
Moe Howard, Larry Fine, Curly Howard
Three comedy shorts: "Pop Goes the Easel"
(1935), in which the Stooges run amuck in an art
studio; "Calling All Curs" (1939), in which a prize
pooch is stolen from the Stooges' dog hospital;
and "An Ache in Every Stake" (1941), in which
the Stooges, as icemen, are hired to prepare a
fancy birthday dinner.
Columbia — *RCA/Columbia Pictures Home
Video*

Three Stooges Volume IV, The   193?
Comedy
58958   60 mins   B/W   B, V   P
*Moe Howard, Larry Fine, Curly Howard, Charley
Chase, Walter Brennan*
Three classic "Stooges" shorts: "Woman
Haters" (1934), the story of three woman
haters, with dialogue spoken in rhyme; "Three
Little Beers" (1935), in which the boys decide to
enter a golf tournament sponsored by their
beer company; and, "Tassels in the Air" (1938),
in which the Stooges are hired as interior
decorators.
Columbia — *RCA/Columbia Pictures Home
Video*

Three Stooges Volume V, The   193?
Comedy
Closed Captioned
62813   60 mins   B/W   B, V   P
The Three Stooges
Another package of Three Stooges two-reelers,
featuring the antics of Moe, Larry and Curly. The
tape contains "Pardon My Scotch" (1935),
"Disorder in the Court" (1936) and "Healthy,
Wealthy and Dumb" (1938).
Columbia — *RCA/Columbia Pictures Home
Video*

Three Stooges Volume VI, The   193?
Comedy
64575   60 mins   B/W   B, V   P
Moe Howard, Larry Fine, Curly Howard

The Three Stooges ride again in another
package of three vintage two-reelers: "Violent Is
the Word for Curly" (1938), "Punch Drunks"
(1934) and "A-Plumbing We Will Go" (1940).
Columbia — *RCA/Columbia Pictures Home
Video*

Three Stooges Volume VII, The   194?
Comedy
65101   60 mins   B/W   B, V   P
Moe Howard, Larry Fine, Curly Howard
Those mirthful Stooges are back again in
another package of three original shorts:
"Dutiful But Dumb" (1941), "Movie Maniacs"
(1936) and "Oily to Bed, Oily to Rise" (1939).
Columbia — *RCA/Columbia Pictures Home
Video*

Three Stooges, Volume VIII, The   1984
Comedy
65702   60 mins   B/W   B, V   P
Larry Fine, Moe Howard, Curly Howard
The Three Stooges entertain in three more
short films—"Cash and Carry," "No Census, No
Feeling," and "Some More of Samoa." An
added attraction is a music video of "The Curly
Shuffle."
Columbia — *RCA/Columbia Pictures Home
Video*

Three Stooges Volume IX, The   193?
Comedy
Closed Captioned
72923   60 mins   B/W   B, V   P
Moe Howard, Larry Fine, Curly Howard
More of the classic shorts featuring Moe, Larry,
and Curly.
Columbia — *RCA/Columbia Pictures Home
Video*

Three Tales of Love & Friendship   1984
Fantasy
65722   118 mins   C   CED   P
A compilation of children's programs including
"The Red Balloon" (1956), "The Unicorn"
(1972), and "The Lone Wolf" (1983). Each story
centers on the magical powers of love and
friendship that can make dreams come true.
Films Monsouris; Carol Reed; Jadren Film
Zagreb — *Embassy Home Entertainment (disc
only)*

Three Warriors   1977
Drama
63345   100 mins   C   B, V   R, P
*Charles White Eagle, Lois Red Elk, McKee
"Kiko" Red Wing, Christopher Lloyd, Randy
Quaid*

(For Explanation of codes, see USE GUIDE and KEY)   **559**

A young Indian boy is forced to leave the city and return to the reservation, where his contempt for the traditions of his ancestors slowly turns to appreciation and love.
Saul Zaentz; Sy Gomberg — *THORN EMI Home Video*

Three Weird Sisters, The   1948
Drama
66400 100 mins B/W   B, V   P
Nova Pilbeam, Nancy Price, Mary Clare, Mary Merrall, Hugh Griffith
Three crippled sisters in a Welsh village plot to kill their wealthy half-brother and his secretary. Based on the novel by Charlotte Armstrong.
British National; Pathe — *Movie Buff Video*

Three Word Brand   1921
Western
52465 75 mins B/W   B, V, FO   P
William S. Hart, Jayne Navak, S. J. Bingham
William S. Hart plays three roles in this film, a homesteader who is killed by Indians and his twin sons, who are separated after their father's death and reunited many years later. Silent with musical score.
William S Hart Co — *Video Yesteryear; Classic Video Cinema Collector's Club*

Threepenny Opera, The   1931
Musical-Drama
52467 105 mins B/W   B, V   P
Lotte Lenya, Rudolph Forster, Carola Neher, directed by G. W. Pabst
The first film version of the Bertolt Brecht-Kurt Weill musical play about London lowlife in the 19th century. Lotte Lenya portrays her most famous character, prostitute Jenny Brown. Songs include "Mack the Knife."
UFA; Germany — *Video Dimensions; Cable Films*

Threshold   1983
Drama
65758 97 mins C   B, V   P
Donald Sutherland, Jeff Goldblum
The story of an internationally-acclaimed surgeon who is frustrated by his inability to save a dying 20-year-old woman born with a defective heart.
MPAA:PG
Jon Slan; Micheal Burns — *CBS/Fox Video*

Threshold: The Blue Angels Experience   1974
Aeronautics/Armed Forces-US
29751 89 mins C   B, V, 3/4U   P
Narrated by Leslie Nielsen
A true life adventure of six men and "a team" which they created. It is a photographic exploration of extraordinary feats accomplished by these F-14 Phantoms flyers.
MPAA:G

Paul Marlow — *Aero/Space Visuals Society*

Throne of Blood   1957
Adventure/Drama
72469 105 mins B/W   B, V, 3/4U   P
An ambitious version of "Macbeth" set in 16th century Japan. The film is filled with frantic action end fight sequences. English subtitles.
JA
Toho; Japan — *International Historic Films*

Through the Breakers   1928
Drama
48715 50 mins B/W   B, V, 3/4U   P
Holmes Herbert, Margaret Livingston
Amidst suicides and shipwrecks, South Seas passion reigns. Silent.
Gotham Prods — *Penguin Video*

Thumbelina   1984
Cartoons/Fairy tales
Closed Captioned
72924 45 mins C   B, V   P
Animated
An animated version of the Hans Christian Andersen fairy tale about a little girl who's only as tall as a thumb.
John Watkins and Simon Nuchtern — *RCA/Columbia Pictures Home Video*

Thundarr the Barbarian   1980
Cartoons
65663 57 mins C   B, V   P
In this episode, Thundarr, Princess Ariel and Ookla the Mot fight sorcery and slavery.
Ruby Spears — *Worldvision Home Video*

Thunder in the City   1937
Comedy-Drama
08865 85 mins B/W   B, V   P
Edward G. Robinson, Nigel Bruce, Ralph Richardson
An American promoter descends on London with all the modern day advertising methods.
Columbia; Alexander Esway — *Movie Buff Video; Penguin Video*

Thunder Mountain   1935
Western
58506 56 mins B/W   B, V, 3/4U   P
George O'Brien
Zane Grey's novel about two prospectors who are bushwacked on their way to file a claim.
Atherton Prods — *Penguin Video; Discount Video Tapes*

Thunder of Steam in the Blue Ridge, The   1958
Trains
47820 20 mins B/W   B, V   P, T

Photographed in the mountainous area on the Norfolk and Western's mail line between Roanoke and Bedford, Virginia, this film shows the N and W's tough locomotives pulling and pushing on the mountain grades.
Unknown — *Blackhawk Films*

Thunder Out of China   1938
World War II
53660   45 mins   B/W   B, V, 3/4U   P
A documentary that covers the Japanese-Chinese war and predicts the entry of the U.S. into the Pacific war.
Unknown — *International Historic Films*

Thunder Pass   1937
Western
55132   58 mins   B/W   B, V   P
Charles Bickford, Marsha Hunt, Gilbert Roland, Monte Blue, directed by Charles Barton
Gold and greed are the motives for murder as two brothers become separated when their wagon train is attacked and their family is slaughtered.
Amity Pictures — *Video Dimensions; Discount Video Tapes*

Thunder River Feud   1942
Western
08899   58 mins   B/W   B, V, 3/4U   P
Ray Corrigan, John King, May Terhune
The Rangebusters ride into a pack of trouble, but soon have the situation well in hand.
Monogram — *Penguin Video; Video Connection*

Thunderball   1965
Adventure
64452   125 mins   C   B, V   P
Sean Connery, Adolfo Celi, Claudine Auger
The fourth installment in Ian Fleming's James Bond series finds Bond on a mission to thwart SPECTRE, which has threatened to blow up Miami by atomic bomb if 100 million pounds of sterling ransom is not paid.
Academy Award '65: Special Visual Effects.
United Artists — *CBS/Fox Video; RCA VideoDiscs*

Thunderbirds Are Go   1966
Adventure/Puppets
68241   92 mins   C   B, V, CED   P
The world's favorite electronic puppets, the Tracy brothers, launch through the uncharted worlds of adventure.
Associated Television Limited — *MGM/UA Home Video*

Thunderbolt   1945
World War II
50642   43 mins   C   B, V, 3/4U   P
Directed by William Wyler and John Sturges

A chronicle of "Operational Strangle" in which the 57th Fighter Group destroyed vital supply routes deep behind German lines. Color cameras were mounted at several points on the P-47 Fighter-Bombers.
US Army Air Forces — *International Historic Films*

Thunderbolt and Lightfoot   1974
Drama
58847   115 mins   C   B, V, CED   P
Clint Eastwood, Jeff Bridges, George Kennedy, Geoffrey Lewis, directed by Michael Cimino
A bank robber posing as a preacher is saved by a young stranger when his former partners come gunning for him.
MPAA:R
United Artists — *CBS/Fox Video; RCA VideoDiscs*

Thundering Rails   19??
Trains
53527   17 mins   B/W   B, V   P
This classic documentary was made to promote the ventures of the American railroad system during its Golden Age. Filmed on the Pennsylvania RR, Norfolk and Western, N.Y. Central, and the C and O, with motor power, including Sharks, Elco's, PA's, N and W 4-8-4's, Pennsy Duplexes, and NYC Hudsons.
American Association of Railroads — *Interurban Films*

THX 1138   1971
Science fiction/Drama
51971   88 mins   C   B, V   R, P
Robert Duvall, Donald Pleasance, Maggie McOmie, directed by George Lucas
In the dehumanized world of the future, a computer-matched couple discover love. Since emotion is outlawed, the woman is killed for the offense, but the man escapes and tries to fight the system.
MPAA:PG
Warner Bros;American Zoetrope — *Warner Home Video*

Tiara Tahiti   1962
Adventure
59842   100 mins   C   B, V   P
James Mason, John Mills, Claude Dauphin, Rosenda Monteros
Intrigue, double-cross, romance, and violence ensue when two old army acquaintances clash in Tahiti.
Earl St John — *Embassy Home Entertainment*

Ticket to Heaven   1981
Drama
47779   109 mins   C   B, V, CED   P
Nick Mancuso, Meg Foster, Kim Cattrail

A thriller dealing with cult religions in California. A school teacher gradually falls under the influence of a quasi-religious order.
Stalker Productions — *MGM/UA Home Video*

Tiffany Sampler 1984
Movie and TV trailers
66476   30 mins   C   B, V   P
This sampler tape contains a selection of movie previews taken from each of San Francisco Rush Video's "Trailers on Tape" compilations. The 17 trailers include "Help!," "A Night at the Opera," "Sunset Boulevard" and "The Wild One." Some black-and-white segments.
MGM et al — *San Francisco Rush Video*

Tiger and Crane Shaolin Kung-Fu 1982
Martial arts
64018   55 mins   C   B, V   P
Techniques of the Hung Gar Tiger and Crane pattern of Shaolin style Kung fu are demonstrated by Master Chiu Chi Ling.
Ng See Yuen; Roy Horan — *World Video Enterprises*

Tiger Fangs 1943
War-Drama
45019   61 mins   B/W   B, V   P
Frank Buck, June Duprez
Wild tigers are used to try to stop the production of rubber in the Far East in order to halt the Allied effort.
Producers Releasing Corp — *Sheik Video*

Tiger Town 1983
Drama
65633   76 mins   C   B, V   R, P
Roy Scheider, Justin Henry, Ron McLarty, Bethany Carpenter, Noah Moazezi
A baseball player, ending an illustrious career with the Detroit Tigers, sees his hopes of winning a pennant slipping away. On the other hand, a die-hard Tigers fan is convinced that a "true believer" can make anything happen.
Susan B Landau; Thompson Street Pictures — *Walt Disney Home Video*

Tiger's Claw 197?
Martial arts/Adventure
47702   90 mins   C   B, V   P
Chin Long
Shen roves the country honing his Kung Fu technique, obsessed by his fanatical desire to challenge Kuo, the best in China.
Kwong Ming Motion Picture Co — *Master Arts Video*

Till Marriage Do Us Part 1980
Comedy
58899   97 mins   C   B, V, LV, CED   P

Laura Antonelli, Alberto Lionello, Jean Rochefort
An innocent couple discover on their wedding night that they are really brother and sister.
Pio Angeletti; Adriano de Micheli — *Vestron Video*

Till the Clouds Roll By 1946
Musical
01623   137 mins   C   B, V   P
Judy Garland, Frank Sinatra, Van Heflin, Robert Walker, Directed by Richard Whorf
A musical biography of songwriter Jerome Kern, with an all-star cast performing a cavalcade of his great tunes.
MGM; Arthur Freed — *MGM/UA Home Video; Cable Films*

Till the Clouds Roll By/A Star Is Born 194?
Musical/Drama
58919   249 mins   C   B, V   P
Judy Garland, Frank Sinatra, Robert Walker, Fredric March, Janet Gaynor, Adolph Menjou, directed by William Wellman
A double feature: "Till the Clouds Roll By" (1946), concerns the life and career of songwriter Jerome Kern; "A Star is Born" (1937), is the classic story of two lovers, one whose star is waning while the other hits the big time.
EL, SP
MGM; Selznick — *Ampro Video Productions*

Tillie's Punctured Romance 1914
Comedy
08713   73 mins   B/W   B, V, 3/4U   P
Charlie Chaplin, Marie Dressler
A silent comedy which established Chaplin and Dressler as comedians.
Paramount — *Penguin Video; Blackhawk Films; Budget Video; Sheik Video; Video Yesteryear; Discount Video Tapes; Nostalgia Merchant*

Tillie's Punctured Romance/Wild and Woolly 1917
Comedy
64309   85 mins   B/W   B, V   P
Charlie Chaplin, Marie Dressler, Mabel Normand, Douglas Fairbanks
Two uproarious silent comedy features are combined on this tape: "Tillie's Punctured Romance" (1914), with Chaplin and Dressler, and "Wild and Woolly" (1917), with Douglas Fairbanks. Musical scores have been added.
Mack Sennett; Artcraft Pictures — *Classic Video Cinema Collector's Club*

    (For Explanation of codes, see USE GUIDE and KEY)

Tilt   1979
Comedy-Drama
72172   111 mins   C   B, V   P
Brooke Shields, John Crawford, Ken Marshall,
Charles Durning
A rock musician and a pinball wizard struggle to
realize their dreams.
Warner Bros; Melvin Simon — *Continental*
Video

Tim   1979
Drama
65113   94 mins   C   B, V   P
Mel Gibson, Piper Laurie, Peter Gwynne
This Australian film tells of the evolving
relationship between a handsome, mentally
retarded young man and an attractive
businesswoman in her mid-40's.
Michael Pate; Satori Productions — *Media*
Home Entertainment

Time After Time   1979
Science fiction/Adventure
52701   112 mins   C   B, V   R, P
Malcolm McDowell, David Warner, Mary
Steenburgen, Patti D'Arbanville
H. G. Wells and Jack the Ripper leave London
circa 1893 in Wells' famous time machine and
arrive in San Francisco in 1979.
MPAA:PG
Orion Pictures; Warner Bros — *Warner Home*
Video

Time Bandits   1981
Fantasy
59389   110 mins   C   B, V, LV   R, P
John Cleese, Sean Connery, Shelley Duvall,
Katherine Helmond, Ian Holm, Michael Palin,
Ralph Richardson, David Warner, Kenny Baker,
directed by Terry Gilliam
An English youngster and a group of dwarves
pass through time holes on assignment by the
Maker to patch up part of his creation.
MPAA:PG
Handmade Films — *Paramount Home Video;*
RCA VideoDiscs

Time Capsule: The Los   1984
Angeles Olympic
Games/1932
Sports/Documentary
66613 60 mins B/W   B, V   P
Directed by Bud Greenspan
The 1932 Los Angeles Olympic Games are the
subject of this documentary which utilizes rare
and never-before-seen action footage. Among
the athletes seen participating are Mildred
''Babe'' Didrikson, Glenn Cunningham and
swimmer Eleanor Holm.
Lorimar — *U.S.A. Home Video*

Time Machine   1978
Science fiction/Adventure
45010   99 mins   C   B, V   P
John Beck, Priscilla Barnes, Andrew Duggan
Based H.G. Wells' classic novel, this movie tells
the story of a scientist who invents a machine
that enables him to travel through time and
undertakes a journey into the future, only to find
a civilization dominated by a group of hideous
people called Morlocks, the only survivors of a
devastating war.
MPAA:G
Schick Sunn Classic — *VCI Home Video*

Time Machine, The   1960
Science fiction/Adventure
63112   103 mins   C   B, V   P
Rod Taylor, Yvette Mimieux, Alan Young,
directed by George Pal
An English scientist of the year 1899 builds a
conveyance that carries him far into the future,
where he discovers the remnants of man's
civilization. Based on H.G. Well's pioneering
novel.
MGM — *MGM/UA Home Video*

Time to Die, A   1983
Adventure
65354   89 mins   C   B, V   P
Edward Albert Jr., Rex Harrison, Rod Taylor
A victim of heinous war crimes, obsessed with
revenge, stalks his prey for a final confrontation.
MPAA:R
Charles Lee — *Media Home Entertainment*

Timerider   1983
Science fiction
64581   93 mins   C   B, V, CED   P
Fred Ward, Belinda Bauer, Peter Coyote,
Richard Masur
A motorcyclist riding through the California
desert is accidentally thrown back in time to
1877, the result of a scientific experiment that
went awry.
MPAA:PG
Jensen Farley Pictures — *Pacific Arts Video*

Times Square   1980
Musical
58463   111 mins   C   B, V   R, P
Tim Curry, Trini Alvarado, Robin Johnson, Peter
Coffield, Anna Maria Horsford, directed by Alan
Moyle
A 13-year-old girl learns about life on her own
when she teams up with a defiant, anti-social
child of the streets. A New Wave rock music
score is featured.
MPAA:R
Robert Stigwood; Jacob Brackman — *THORN*
EMI Home Video

Timex All-Star Comedy Show 1962
Comedy
12849 45 mins B/W B, V, FO P
Johnny Carson, Carl Reiner, Mel Brooks, Dr. Joyce Brothers, Buddy Hackett, Kaye Stevens
Spoof on TV shows and other fun, featuring a comic cast.
ABC — *Video Yesteryear*

Timex All Star Jazz Show 1957
Music-Performance
46344 62 mins B/W B, V, FO P
Louis Armstrong, Duke Ellington and his Orchestra, Bobby Hackett, Dizzy Gillespie, George Shearing
Jackie Gleason hosts this television special which features a compendium of great performances by many jazz stars.
Unknown — *Video Yesteryear*

Tin Drum, The 1979
Drama
47370 141 mins C B, V R, P
Oskar Matzerath, a self-made dwarf, narrates this parable of modern society in violent transition. Subtitled.
Academy Awards '79: Best Foreign Language Film. GE
New World Pictures — *Warner Home Video*

Tin Man 1983
Drama
65485 95 mins C B, V P
Timothy Bottoms, Deana Jurgens, Troy Donahue
A garage mechanic born totally deaf designs and builds a computer that can both hear and speak for him. His world is complicated when a young speech therapist introduces him to a world of new and wonderful sounds, but also to a world of unscrupulous and exploitive computer salesmen. Slowly he realizes that he must make the decisions that will mold his future.
John G Thomas — *Media Home Entertainment*

Tina Turner 1982
Music-Performance
64209 55 mins C B, V R, P
Tina Turner
Tina Turner stomps and shouts her way through an exciting program of hits including "Proud Mary," "Honky-Tonk Woman," "Jumping Jack Flash" and others. In stereo.
EMI Music — *THORN EMI Home Video*

Tina Turner—Queen of Rock and Roll 1984
Music-Performance
72420 60 mins C B, V P
Tina Turner entertains at Harlem's Apollo Theatre, giving her typically enthralling performance.

Unknown — *VCL Home Video*

Tintorera...Tiger Shark 1978
Adventure
66286 91 mins C B, V P
Susan George, Fiona Lewis, Jennifer Ashley
Three shark hunters attempt to discover why swimmers are disappearing.
MPAA:R
Gerald Green — *Media Home Entertainment*

Tip Top! with Suzy Prudden—Ages 3-6 1982
Physical fitness
62887 53 mins C B, V R, P
The first home video program series designed for young children; instructor Suzy Prudden leads her viewers through warmup activities and stimulating exercises set to contemporary music.
Warner Home Video; Warner Amex — *Warner Home Video*

Tip Top! with Suzy Prudden—Age 7 and Above 1982
Physical fitness
62888 48 mins C B, V R, P
Suzy Prudden leads her video class of enthusiastic youngsters through a specially designed series of exercises for this specific age group.
Warner Home Video; Warner Amex — *Warner Home Video*

To All a Goodnight 1980
Horror
69307 90 mins C B, V P
Jennifer Runyon, Forrest Swanson, Linda Gentile, William Lover
Five young girls and their boyfriends are in for an exciting Christmas holiday until a mad Santa Claus puts a damper on things.
MPAA:R
Jay Rasumny — *Media Home Entertainment*

To Be or Not To Be 1942
Comedy
65365 102 mins B/W B, V P
Carole Lombard, Jack Benny, Robert Stack, directed by Ernst Lubitsch
Set in wartime Poland, Lombard and Benny are Maria and Josef Tura, the Barrymores of the Polish stage, who use the talents of their acting troupe against the Gestapo and manage to exit laughing.
United Artists — *Vestron Video*

To Be or Not to Be 1983
Comedy
Closed Captioned
72191 108 mins C B, V P

Mel Brooks, Anne Bancroft
Anne Bancroft and Mel Brooks are actors in Poland during WWII who plan to thwart the Nazis.
MPAA:PG
Warner Bros — *CBS/Fox Video*

To Catch a King   1984
Suspense
72338   90 mins   C   B, V   P
Robert Wagner, Teri Garr
Adaptation of Jack Higgins' novel about a Nazi plan to kidnap the Duke of Windsor.
Home Box Office — *Prism*

To Catch a Thief   1955
Mystery
53936   97 mins   C   B, V, LV   R, P
Cary Grant, Grace Kelly, Jessie Royce Landis, directed by Alfred Hitchcock
An ex-jewel thief falls for a wealthy American girl, who suspects him of his old thievery, when a similar rash of jewel thefts occur.
Paramount — *Paramount Home Video*

To Catch A Thrill   197?
Fishing
19415   60 mins   C   B, V, 3/4U,   P
                            Q
Underwater cameras capture the strange, dynamic world of fishing through fascinating techniques of fishing and glimpses of undersea life.
TV Sports Scene — *TV Sports Scene*

To Forget Venice   197?
Drama
63447   90 mins   C   B, V   P
Erland Josephson, Mariangela Melato, David Pontremoli, Eleonora Giorgi, directed by Franco Brusati
This film portrays the sensitive relationships among four people, and their shared fears of growing older. Dubbed in English.
Rizzoli Film — *RCA/Columbia Pictures Home Video; Embassy Home Entertainment (disc only)*

To Kill a Clown   1972
Drama/Suspense
66285   82 mins   C   B, V   P
Alan Alda, Blythe Danner, Heath Lamberts
A young couple who move to an isolated island find their lives filled with terror.
MPAA:R
Teddy B Sills — *Media Home Entertainment*

To Kill a Mockingbird   1962
Drama
14034   129 mins   B/W   B, V   P
Gregory Peck, Brock Peters, Phillip Afford, Mary Badham
A southern lawyer, the town's most distinguished citizen, defends a black man accused of rape. This costs him many friendships but earns him the admiration of his two motherless children.
Academy Awards '62: Best Actor (Peck).
Universal; Brentwood Prod — *MCA Home Video*

To Russia...with Elton   197?
Music-Performance
47047   75 mins   C   B, V   P
Narrated by Dudley Moore
Elton John's successful 1979 tour of the Soviet Union is captured in this concert documentary. Elton performs "Your Song," "Goodbye Yellow Brick Road," "Benny and the Jets," "Back in the USSR" and many other songs.
ITC Entertainment — *CBS/Fox Video; RCA VideoDiscs*

To See Such Fun   1981
Comedy
59929   90 mins   C   B, V   P
Peter Sellers, Marty Feldman, Benny Hill, Eric Idle, Alec Guinness, Margaret Rutherford, Dirk Bogarde, Spike Milligan
Hilarious excerpts from 80 years of the greatest British movie comedies.
Herbert Wilcox; Michael Grade — *Pacific Arts Video*

To Sir, With Love   1967
Comedy-Drama
13294   105 mins   C   B, V   P
Sidney Poitier, Lulu, Judy Geeson, Christian Roberts, Suzy Kendall, Faith Brook
Teacher in London's tough East End tosses books in the wastebasket and proceeds to teach his class about life.
Columbia; James Clavell — *RCA/Columbia Pictures Home Video*

To The Gates of Japan   194?
World War II
53668   50 mins   B/W   B, V, 3/4U   P
A U.S. Navy film explaining Japanese strategy in the Pacific war, featuring action scenes on the Solomon Islands and the Marianas.
US Navy — *International Historic Films*

Toast of New York, The   1937
Drama
57166   109 mins   B/W   B, V   P
Edward Arnold, Cary Grant, Frances Farmer, Jack Oakie, Donald Meek
Jim Fisk rises from a New England peddler to one of the first Wall Street giants of industry, in this story about the early years of the tycoon.
RKO; Edward Small — *King of Video*

Toast of the Town 1949
Comedy
12838 51 mins B/W B, V, FO P
Hosted by Ed Sullivan
Genuine vaudeville complete with dancers, a
ventriloquist, trick-shot golfers, and the "kooky"
music of Fane and Foster. Also features the Ray
Block Orchestra.
CBS — *Video Yesteryear*

Toast of the Town 1956
Variety
66459 120 mins B/W B, V, 3/4U P
*Ed Sullivan, Lucille Ball, Desi Arnaz, Vivian
Vance, William Frawley, Orson Welles, The
Ames Brothers*
Two original Ed Sullivan TV programs, both
featuring appearances by the cast of "I Love
Lucy." The program of October 3, 1954 is a full
one-hour tribute to "the Ricardos." The show of
February 5, 1956 has Lucy and Desi promoting
their latest picture, "Forever Darling," along with
other guest stars. Original commercials and
I.D.'s are included.
CBS — *Shokus Video*

Todd Rundgren 1983
Videosyncracy
Music-Performance
64928 12 mins C B, V P
Todd Rundgren performs three songs on this
Video 45: "Hideaway," "Can We Still Be
Friends" and "Time Heals."
Alchemedia Productions — *Sony Corporation
of America*

Todos los Dias, Un Dia 1979
Drama
66408 89 mins C B, V P
Julio Iglesias, Isa Lorenz, Carol Lynley
A world famous singer on an island vacation
meets and falls in love with a beautiful young girl
who is unaware of his fame.
Argentinismas — *Unicorn Video*

Tokyo Olympiad 1966
Sports/Documentary
48849 92 mins C B, V, 3/4U P
A documentary of the 1964 Summer Olympics
held in Tokyo.
Unknown — *Western Film & Video Inc;
International Historic Films*

Tol'able David 1921
Drama
33634 79 mins B/W B, V P
*Richard Barthelmess, Gladys Hulette, Ernest
Torrance, directed by Henry King*
A simple tale of mountain folk, done in the
tradition of Mark Twain stories. The youngest
son of a family yearns to be a mail driver. His
community is troubled by the presence of three
outlaws. Silent.

First National — *Festival Films; Video
Yesteryear; Blackhawk Films; Sheik Video;
Classic Video Cinema Collector's Club*

Toll Gate, The 1920
Western
15500 55 mins B/W B, V P
*William S. Hart, Anna Q. Nilsson, Jack
Richardson, Joseph Singleton, directed by
Lambert Hillyer*
An outlaw, whose hand is ever near his gun for a
quick draw, risks capture and his life to rescue a
drowning child and to warn an outlying post of
Indian uprisings. Silent classic.
Paramount — *Video Connection; Classic Video
Cinema Collector's Club*

Tom and Jerry Cartoon 195?
Festival, Vol. I
Cartoons
48860 60 mins C B, V, LV, P
CED
Animated
The cat and mouse team fight their way through
a cartoon festival including "The Flying Cat,"
"The Bodyguard," "The Little Orphan," "Jerry's
Cousin," "Dr. Jekyll and Mr. Mouse," "Mouse
Follies," "The Cat and the Mermouse," and
"The Cat Concerto."
MGM — *MGM/UA Home Video*

Tom and Jerry Cartoon 194?
Festival, Vol. II
Cartoons
59848 58 mins C B, V, CED P
A second compilation of the best of MGM's
classic Tom and Jerry cartoon shorts, including
"Mouse Trap," "Cat Napping," "Invisible
Mouse," "Saturday Evening Puss," and more.
MGM — *MGM/UA Home Video*

Tom and Jerry Cartoon 19??
Festival, Vol. 3
Cartoons
66453 59 mins C B, V, CED P
Animated
Another collection of Tom and Jerry favorites
from the 1940's and 1950's including "The
Hollywood Bowl," "Million Dollar Cat," "The
Night Before Christmas" and "Two Little
Indians."
MGM — *MGM/UA Home Video*

Tom Brown's School 1940
Days
Drama
08860 80 mins B/W B, V, 3/4U P
*Cedric Hardwicke, Jimmy Lydon, Freddie
Bartholomew*
Depicts life among the boys in an English school
during the Victorian era.

RKO — *Penguin Video; Budget Video; Sheik Video; Cable Films; Discount Video Tapes; Video Yesteryear*

Tom Corbett, Space Cadet　　1951
Science fiction
42968　　30 mins　　B/W　　B, V, FO　　　P
Frankie Thomas, Jack Grimes, Al Markhim
This popular space opera from the early days of television shows how one cadet who is the smallest in size becomes the biggest in courage and team cooperation.
ABC — *Video Yesteryear*

Tom Corbett, Space Cadet Volume 1　　195?
Science fiction/Adventure
44312　　90 mins　　B/W　　B, V, 3/4U　　P
Frankie Thomas, Jan Merlin
The adventures of Tom Corbett, a Space Cadet at the U.S. Space Academy, where men and women train to become agents to protect Earth and its neighbor planets.
ABC — *Nostalgia Merchant*

Tom Corbett, Space Cadet Volume 2　　195?
Science fiction
58585　　90 mins　　B/W　　B, V, 3/4U　　P
This early '50's TV series follows the adventures of Tom Corbett, a space cadet at the U.S. Space Academy.
ABC — *Nostalgia Merchant*

Tom, Dick, and Harry　　1941
Comedy
10038　　86 mins　　B/W　　B, V　　　P, T
Ginger Rogers, George Murphy, Burgess Meredith, Allen Marshall, Phil Silvers
Dreamy girl is engaged to three men and unable to decide which to marry. It all depends on a kiss.
RKO — *Blackhawk Films*

Tom Edison, the Boy Who Lit Up the World　　1980
Adventure/Biographical
75617　　49 mins　　C　　B, V　　　P
This is the story of Tom Edison's life and how he changed the world.
VidAmerica — *Children's Video Library*

Tom Edison: The Making of an American Legend　　19??
Biographical/Inventions
69587　　49 mins　　C　　B, V　　　P
David Huffman
This is the story of young Thomas Edison, a telegraph operator who becomes one of history's greatest inventors.

Unknown — *VidAmerica*

Tom Horn　　1980
Western
54795　　98 mins　　C　　B, V　　　R, P
Steve McQueen, Linda Evans, Richard Farnsworth, Billy Green Bush, Slim Pickens, directed by William Wiard
The true story of an Old West gunman, Tom Horn, who at the age of 40 has already been a western railroad worker, stagecoach driver, U.S. Cavalry scout, silver miner, Teddy Roosevelt Rough Rider, and a Pinkerton Detective. Now he is invited by Wyoming ranchers to stop the cattle rustlers. He does that job well, and at the same time finds romance.
MPAA:R
Warner Bros — *Warner Home Video*

Tom Jones　　1963
Comedy
52738　　129 mins　　C　　B, V, LV　　P
Albert Finney, Susannah York, Hugh Griffith, Dame Edith Evans, David Tomlinson, directed by Tony Richardson
A comedy based on Henry Fielding's novel about a rustic playboy's wild life in eighteenth-century London with brigands, beauties, and scoundrels.
Academy Awards '63: Best Picture; Best Director (Richardson); Best Screenplay (John Osborne); Best Original Score (John Addison).
EL, SP
Woodfall Prods; United Artists; Lopert Pictures — *CBS/Fox Video; RCA VideoDiscs*

Tom Jones Live in Las Vegas　　1981
Music-Performance
53137　　60 mins　　C　　B, V　　　P
Tom Jones
Superstar Tom Jones lights up a Vegas showroom performing "What's New Pussycat?," "She's a Lady," "Green Green Grass of Home," "It's Not Unusual," "Love Me Tonight," "Ladies' Night," "Working My Way Back to You," "Woman," "I'll Never Fall in Love Again," and others.
Jay Harvey Prods — *Family Home Entertainment*

Tom Thumb　　1958
Fairy tales/Fantasy
73366　　92 mins　　C　　B, V　　　P
Russ Tamblyn, Peter Sellers, Terry-Thomas, directed by George Pal
The classic Grimm Brothers fairy tale about the small boy who saves the village treasury from the bad guys is brought to life in this film.
Academy Award 1958: Best Special Effects.
Galaxy Pictures — *MGM/UA Home Video*

Tomboy 1940
Comedy
12813   70 mins   B/W   B, V, FO   P
Jackie Moran, Marcia Mae Jones
A shy country boy and a not-so-shy city girl team up to catch crooks.
Monogram — *Video Yesteryear*

Tombstone Canyon 1935
Western
08897   60 mins   B/W   B, V, 3/4U   P
Ken Maynard, Sheldon Lewis, Cecelia Parker
Death rides the range until a special agent puts a halt to it.
World Wide — *Penguin Video*

Tommy 1975
Musical
58965   108 mins   C   B, V, LV   P
Ann-Margret, Elton John, Oliver Reed, Tina Turner, Roger Daltrey, Eric Clapton, Keith Moon, directed by Ken Russell
Peter Townsend's rock-opera about the deaf, dumb, and blind boy who becomes a celebrity.
MPAA:PG
Robert Stigwood; Columbia — *RCA/Columbia Pictures Home Video; RCA VideoDiscs*

Tommy John Story, The 1979
Religion/Baseball
46825   28 mins   C   B, V, 3/4U,   P
                          Q
The inspirational story of Tommy John, a professional baseball player and a Christian, who was told in 1974 that he would never be able to pitch again.
Quadrus Films — *TV Sports Scene*

Tomorrow 1983
Drama
65455   102 mins   B/W   B, V   P
Robert Duvall
The powerful tale of the love of two lonely people of the earth, carrying them through the ordeals of pregnancy and birth and culminating in a baffling murder trial.
Gilbert Pearlman; Paul Roebling — *Monterey Home Video*

Tomorrow at Seven 1933
Mystery/Suspense
63619   62 mins   B/W   B, V, FO   P
Chester Morris, Vivienne Osborne, Frank McHugh
A mystery writer/amateur detective is determined to discover the identity of the Black Ace, a mysterious killer who always warns his intended victim, then leaves an ace of spades on the corpse as his calling card.
RKO — *Video Yesteryear*

Tomorrow's Children 1934
Drama/Exploitation
48745   60 mins   B/W   B, V, 3/4U   P
Sterling Holloway
The theme of this movie is the proposition and depiction of state-controlled sterilization.
Unknown — *Penguin Video*

Tong Man 1919
Drama
58535   40 mins   B/W   B, V, 3/4U   P
Sessue Hayakawa, Mark Robbins, Helen Jerome Eddy
Chinatown has many secret societies, and the Bo Sing Tong emerges as the most dreaded. Silent.
Haworth Pictures — *Penguin Video*

Toni Basil—Word of Mouth 1981
Music-Performance
66038   30 mins   C   B, V   P
This video is Toni Basil's debut and as a purely visual artist she presents herself as an accomplished singer, dancer and choreographer. Includes "Mickey," "My Little Red Book," "Nobody," "Time After Time," "Be Stiff," "Space Girls," and "Problem."
Radical Choice — *Chrysalis Visual Programming*

Tonight for Sure 1961
Film-Avant-garde
47644   66 mins   B/W   B, V, FO   P
Directed by Francis Ford Coppola
Coppola's first film, produced as a student at UCLA. Two men ruminate on bad experiences with naked women. Nudity. Music by Carmen Coppola.
Francis Ford Coppola — *Video Yesteryear*

Tonight Show, The 1969
Variety
42978   78 mins   C   B, V, FO   P
Jerry Lewis, Ed McMahon, Doc Severinson and his Orchestra
Appearances by George Carlin, Jim Turner and his musical saw, Charlie Callis, the Smothers Brothers, and Mason Williams highlight this zany show aired March 25, 1969. Jerry Lewis hosts.
NBC — *Video Yesteryear*

Tonio Kroger 1965
Drama
69565   92 mins   B/W   B, V, FO   P
Jean-Claude Brialy, Nadja Tiller, Gert Frobe
A young writer travels through Europe in search of intellectual and sensual relationships and a home that will suit him. German dialogue with English subtitles.
Germany — *Video Yesteryear*

Tonto Kid, The　　　　1935
Western
08820　56 mins　B/W　B, V, 3/4U　　　P
Rex Bell
Action-packed western featuring Rex Bell.
Resolute — *Penguin Video; Discount Video Tapes*

Tony Bennett Songbook, A　　　　1981
Music-Performance
60375　94 mins　C　CED　　　P
This stereo program recorded live in New York features the exciting Tony Bennett in an intimate nightclub atmosphere singing ''I Left My Heart in San Francisco,'' a Duke Ellington medley, and much more.
Dennis H. Paget — *RCA VideoDiscs*

Tony Powers　　　　1981
Music-Performance
75908　54 mins　C　B, V　　　P
This program presents Tony Powers performing his songs ''Don't Nobody Move,'' ''Midnite Trampoline'' and ''Odyssey.''
Tony Powers Music Inc — *Sony Corporation of America*

Too Hot to Handle　　　　1980
Drama
54799　88 mins　C　B, V　　R, P
Cheri Caffaro
A voluptuous lady contract killer fights against the mob with all the weapons at her disposal. Filmed on location in Manila.
New World; Roger Corman — *Warner Home Video*

Too Late the Hero　　　　1970
Drama/World War II
46205　133 mins　C　B, V　　　P
Michael Caine, Cliff Robertson, Henry Fonda, directed by Robert Aldrich
A British combat patrol whose mission is to wipe out a Japanese communication site, finds a horde of enemy planes. The Japanese chase them through the jungle relaying messages via loud speakers that their lives will be spared only if they surrender.
MPAA:PG
Cinerama Release — *CBS/Fox Video*

Toolbox Murders, The　　　　1978
Mystery
48358　93 mins　C　B, V　　　P
Cameron Mitchell, Pamelyn Ferdin
An unknown psychotic murderer brutally claims victims one at a time, leaving a town on the verge of horror, and the police mystified.
MPAA:R
Cal Am Productions — *VCI Home Video*

Tootsie　　　　1982
Comedy
66443　110 mins　C　B, V　　　P
Dustin Hoffman, Jessica Lange, Teri Garr, Dabney Coleman, Bill Murray, directed by Sydney Pollack
A desperate, unemployed actor dresses as a woman to land a starring role in a television soap opera.
MPAA:PG
Columbia Pictures — *RCA/Columbia Pictures Home Video; RCA VideoDiscs*

Top Cat　　　　196?
Cartoons
47694　50 mins　C　B, V　　　P
Animated voices of Arnold Stang, Allen Jenkins, Maurice Gosfield
Two episodes in which T.C. and his gang of street-wise cats drive Officer Dibble nuts.
Hanna Barbera — *Worldvision Home Video*

Top Cat, Volume II　　　　1983
Cartoons
66580　60 mins　C　B, V　　　P
Animated
Top Cat, the feline wise guy, leads his gang of dimwitted stooges through their usual shenanigans in this collection of early 60's TV cartoons.
Hanna Barbera — *Worldvision Home Video*

Top Hat　　　　1935
Musical
00270　97 mins　B/W　B, V, 3/4U　　　P
Fred Astaire, Ginger Rogers, Erik Rhodes, Helen Broderick, Edward Everett Horton, Eric Blore
As usual, Ginger thinks Fred is someone he isn't. It takes the whole length of the film to straighten her out. Irving Berlin's score includes, ''Top Hat,'' ''Cheek to Cheek'' and ''The Piccolino.''
RKO; Pandro S Berman — *Nostalgia Merchant; VidAmerica; King of Video*

Topkapi　　　　1964
Drama
65408　122 mins　C　B, V, CED　　　P
Melina Mercouri, Maximilian Schell, Peter Ustinov, Robert Morley
Filmed in Istanbul, the movie centers around the famed Topkapi Palace Museum, an impregnable fortress filled with wealth and splendor which seems impossible to break in to.
United Artists — *CBS/Fox Video*

Topper　　　　1937
Comedy
44797　97 mins　B/W　B, V, 3/4U　　　P
Cary Grant, Roland Young, Constance Bennett, Billie Burke, directed by Norman Z. McLeod

Based on the Thorne Smith novel this is the story of Marion and George Kirby, who after a car accident do not wish to be dead and become ghosts instead. They get involved in many ghostly escapades.
MGM, Hal Roach — *Nostalgia Merchant; Blackhawk Films*

Topper Returns 1941
Comedy
08733 87 mins B/W B, V P
Roland Young, Joan Blondell, Dennis O'Keefe, Rochester, Carole Landis
Topper finds the murderer of a girl, with the help of his ghostly friends, the Kirbys.
United Artists; Hal Roach — *Movie Buff Video; Penguin Video; Budget Video; Sheik Video; Cable Films; Video Yesteryear; Video Connection; Discount Video Tapes; Nostalgia Merchant*

Topper Takes a Trip 1939
Comedy
64371 85 mins B/W B, V, 3/4U P
Constance Bennett, Roland Young, Billie Burke, Alan Mowbray, Franklin Pangborn
Cosmo Topper takes a trip to the Riviera, with the ghostly spirit of Marion Kirby in hot pursuit.
Hal Roach — *Nostalgia Merchant*

Tora! Tora! Tora! 1970
War-Drama
08439 144 mins C B, V, LV P
Martin Balsam, Soh Yomamura, Joseph Cotten, E. G. Marshall, Jason Robards, directed by Richard Fleisher
The story of December 7, 1941 is retold from both Japanese and American viewpoints in this large-scale production.
MPAA:G
20th Century Fox; Elmo Williams — *CBS/Fox Video*

Torch, The 1950
Drama
66401 83 mins B/W B, V P
Paulette Goddard, Gilbert Roland, Pedro Armendariz
A general falls for a daughter of nobility amidst the turbulent backdrop of the Mexican Revolution.
Eagle Lion — *Movie Buff Video*

Torn Curtain 1966
Suspense
64558 125 mins C B, V P
Paul Newman, Julie Andrews, Lila Kedrova, David Opatoshu, directed by Alfred Hitchcock
An American scientist poses as a defector to East Germany in order to do some undercover work. Unfortunately, his fiancee follows him behind the Iron Curtain.

Universal — *MCA Home Video*

Toronto Rail 1980 1980
Trains
46928 102 mins C B, V P
The National Railway Historical Society's 1980 Convention is the subject in this look at a Canadian Museum, subways, commuter trains, trolleys, and historical steam locomotives.
JMJ Prods — *JMJ Productions*

Torso 1973
Horror
69389 91 mins C B, V P
Suzy Kendall, Tina Aumont, John Richardson
A crazed psychosexual killer stalks beautiful women and dismembers them.
MPAA:R
Joseph Brenner — *Cinemagreats*

Torture of Silence, The 192?
Drama
48729 50 mins B/W B, V, 3/4U P
A love triangle between a dedicated doctor, his wife, and a writer ends in attempted suicide, accidental killing, and kidnapping. Silent.
Unknown — *Penguin Video*

Torvill & Dean: Path to Perfection 1984
Skating
66572 60 mins C B, V P
Olympic ice dancing gold medalists Torvill and Dean are featured in eight of their pre-Olympic performances, including 3 World Skating Championships.
Thames Video — *THORN EMI Home Video*

Total Self-Defense 1981
Safety education
52673 45 mins C B, V P
A woman instructor shows how women can protect themselves in situations such as purse snatching, rape, or other attack. In the second part, two third degree black belts in karate demonstrate "street or full-contact karate." This tape was designed as an interactive, instructional program.
Karl Video Corp — *Karl Video*

Totally Go-Go's 1982
Music-Performance
59695 77 mins C B, V R, P
The chart-topping, all-girl rock band performs live in concert in Hollywood. Songs include "We Got the Beat," "Our Lips Are Sealed," and songs from their two hit albums.
IRS Records — *THORN EMI Home Video; RCA VideoDiscs*

Touch of Class, A — 1973
Comedy
08475   105 mins   C   B, V   P
George Segal, Glenda Jackson, Paul Sorvino, Hildegard Neil, Cec Linder
American insurance adjustor initiates a love affair with an English divorcee.
Academy Awards '73: Best Actress (Jackson).
MPAA:PG
Avco Embassy — *CBS/Fox Video*

Touch of Love: Massage, The — 1980
Massage
48635   28 mins   C   B, V, LV   P
A simple and beautiful way to experience pleasure through touch is presented.
Bruce Seth Green — *MCA Home Video*

Touch of Magic in Close-Up, A — 1982
Magic
59992   78 mins   C   B, V   R, P
Siroco
The amazing Siroco, renowned master of "close-up" magic, mystifies, and then demonstrates the secrets behind many of the illusions.
MPAA:G
Pegicorn Video Corp — *Video Gems*

Touch of Satan, A — 1974
Horror
55317   90 mins   C   B, V   P
Michael Berry, Emby Mallay, Lee Amber, Yvonne Wilson, directed by Don Henderson
Devil worshippers and evil satanic rites abound in this horror of the world beyond. (Original title "A Touch of Melissa.")
Dundee Prods — *King of Video*

Touched — 1982
Drama
65292   89 mins   C   B, V   P
Robert Hays, Kathleen Beller, Ned Beatty
Two young people struggle to cope with the outside world. They struggle against all odds to gain new confidence after being released from a psychiatric hospital. It is a story of determination, hope, and most of all, love.
MPAA:R
Barclay Lottimer; Dirk Petersmann — *Media Home Entertainment*

Tough Enough — 19??
Drama
65332   107 mins   C   B, V   P
Dennis Quaid, Charlene Watkins
A country-western singer-songwriter decides to finance his fledgling career by entering amateur boxing matches and then finds himself rising to the top of amateur boxing.
MPAA:PG
Michael Leone; Andrew D T Pfeffer — *CBS/Fox Video*

Tough Guy — 197?
Martial arts/Adventure
47701   90 mins   C   B, V   P
Chen Ying, Charlie Chiang
Two undercover policemen battle local gangsters in a bid to smash their crime ring.
Independent — *Master Arts Video*

Tourist Trap — 1979
Science fiction
42917   85 mins   C   B, V   P
Chuck Connors
While traveling through the desert, a couple's car has a flat. A woman's voice lures the man into an abandoned gas station, where he discovers that the voice belongs to a mannequin.
MPAA:PG
J. Larry Carroll — *Media Home Entertainment*

Tower of Babel — 1979
Drama/Bible
55011   49 mins   C   B, V   P
Vince Edwards, Ron Palillo, Erin Moran, Dana Elcar, Cliff Emmich, Richard Basehart, narrated by Victor Jory
The story of man's attempt to build a tower to reach God. Despite protests, Amathar begins construction, but as the building progresses, Amathar is overcome with vanity causing God to destroy the temple. Part of the "Greatest Heroes of the Bible" series.
Sunn Classics — *Vanguard Video*

Tower of Evil — 1972
Horror
48473   86 mins   C   B, V   P
Bryant Haliday, Jill Haworth
Tourists and archaeologists visit an island where ancient Phoenician treasure is buried. Most of them are haunted by terror and grisly murder.
MPAA:R
Grenadier Films Ltd — *VCI Home Video*

Towering Inferno, The — 1974
Drama
29178   165 mins   C   B, V, CED   P
Steve McQueen, Paul Newman, William Holden, Faye Dunaway, Fred Astaire
Irwin Allen's dramatic suspense story of a holocaust that engulfs the world's tallest skyscraper on the night of its glamorous and prestigious dedication ceremonies.
Academy Awards '74: Best Song ("We May Never Love Like this Again"). MPAA:PG
20th Century Fox — *CBS/Fox Video*

Town Called Hell, A　　　1972
Suspense
12025　　95 mins　　C　　B, V　　　　　P
Robert Shaw, Stella Stevens, Martin Landau,
Telly Savalas
Two men hold an entire town hostage while
looking for "Aguila," the Mexican revolutionary.
Greed, evil, and violence take over.
Philip Yordan; Official Films — *King of Video*

Town That Dreaded　　　1976
Sundown, The
Suspense
65138　　90 mins　　C　　B, V　　　R, P
Ben Johnson, Andrew Prine, Dawn Wells
A mad killer is on the loose in a small Arkansas
town. Based on a true story, this famous murder
spree remains an unsolved mystery.
MPAA:R
Charles B Pierce Productions — *Warner Home*
Video

Toy, The　　　1982
Comedy-Drama
66010　　99 mins　　C　　B, V　　　　　P
Richard Pryor, Jackie Gleason, Ned Beatty,
Wilfred Hyde-White, directed by Richard Donner
A janitor finds himself the new "toy" of the son
of a department store owner.
MPAA:PG
Columbia — *RCA/Columbia Pictures Home*
Video; RCA VideoDiscs

Tracks　　　198?
Suspense
75585　　90 mins　　C　　B, V　　　　　P
Dennis Hopper, Dean Stockwell
A disoriented soldier has paranoia and
hallucinations on a long train ride.
MPAA:R
Unknown — *Monterey Home Video*

Traction Today　　　1980
Trains/Museums
46929　　59 mins　　C　　B, V　　　　　P
The Branford Trolley Museum in East Haven,
Ct., the Connecticut Electric Railway at
Warehouse Pt., and the Seashore Trolley
Museum at Kennebunkport, Maine are seen in
this look at New England traction museums.
JMJ Prods — *JMJ Productions*

Trading Places　　　1983
Comedy
Closed Captioned
66409　　106 mins　　C　　B, V, LV,　　　R, P
　　　　　　　　　　　　　CED
Eddie Murphy, Dan Aykroyd, Jamie Lee Curtis,
Ralph Bellamy, Don Ameche, directed by John
Landis
Two elderly businessmen make a wager that
basic intelligence is more important than
heredity in creating a successful life, using their
rich nephew and an unemployed street hustler
as guinea pigs.
MPAA:R
Paramount; Aaron Russo — *Paramount Home*
Video

Tradition on　　　1982
Parade/Blood, Sweat and
Cheers
Parades and festivals/Football
64011　　60 mins　　C　　B, V　　　　　P
"Tradition on Parade" looks at the history of the
Tournament of Roses Parade from 1890;
"Blood, Sweat and Cheers" is the story of the
Rose Bowl throughout the years.
Tournament Video Tapes — *Tournament*
Video Tapes

Tragedy of King Richard　　　1982
II, The
Drama
66149　　180 mins　　C　　B, V　　　　　P
David Birney, Paul Shenar
The first of Shakespeare's 28 plays to be
released in this videocassette series is the
historical play, "Richard II."
Bard Prods — *East Texas Periodicals*

Trail Drive　　　1935
Western
10678　　63 mins　B/W　　B, V　　　　　P
Ken Maynard
Adventures of a cowboy during a big cattle
drive.
Universal — *Video Connection; Cable Films*

Trail of Terror　　　1935
Western
08816　　60 mins　B/W　　B, V, 3/4U　　　P
Bob Steele
A G-Man poses as an escaped convict to get
the goods on a gang.
Artclass — *Penguin Video; Sheik Video*

Trail of the Hawk　　　1937
Western
08603　　50 mins　B/W　　B, V, 3/4U　　　P
Yancey Lane, Betty Jordan, Dickie Jones,
directed by Edward Dymytryk
A saga of frontier justice and love on the plains.
Masterpiece — *Penguin Video; Discount Video*
Tapes

Trail of the Pink Panther　　　1982
Comedy
66074　　97 mins　　C　　B, V, CED　　　P
Peter Sellers, David Niven, Herbert Lom,
Capucine, Burt Kwuok, directed by Blake
Edwards
This sixth "Panther" vehicle concerns the
disappearance of Inspector Clouseau.
MPAA:PG

　　　(For Explanation of codes, see USE GUIDE and KEY)

United Artists — *CBS/Fox Video*

Trail of the Royal Mounted   1934
Western/Serials
54196   150 mins   B/W   B, V   P
Robert Frazer
A western adventure serial made up of ten 15-minute episodes.
Unknown — *Video Connection; Cable Films*

Trail Riders   1942
Western
11267   55 mins   B/W   B, V, FO   P
John King, David Sharpe, Max Terhune, Evelyn Finley, Forest Taylor, Charles King
The Range Busters set a trap to capture a gang of outlaws who killed the son of the town marshal during a bank robbery.
Monogram — *Video Yesteryear; Discount Video Tapes; Video Connection*

Trail Street   1947
Western
10069   84 mins   B/W   B, V   P, T
Randolph Scott, Robert Ryan, Anne Jeffreys, Gabby Hayes, Madge Meredith, Jason Robards
Traces story of men and women who began great wheat empire out of Kansas wilderness.
RKO; Nat Holt — *Blackhawk Films; Nostalgia Merchant*

Trail to Alaska   197?
Wildlife
19416   62 mins   C   B, V, 3/4U, Q   P
Many North American bird and animal species are seen in their natural habitat and in exciting hunting episodes.
TV Sports Scene — *TV Sports Scene*

Trailing Trouble   1937
Western
11266   60 mins   B/W   B, V, FO   P
Ken Maynard
A cowboy and a killer have several confrontations in between the cowboy's efforts to steer clear of the case of his own mistaken identity which marks him for treachery.
Grand National — *Video Yesteryear; Video Connection*

Trails West   194?
Western
15534   mins   B/W   B, V   P
Bob Steele
Western adventure starring Bob Steele.
Unknown — *Video Connection*

Train Robbers, The   1973
Western
74212   92 mins   C   B, V   R, P
John Wayne, Ann-Margret, Rod Taylor, Ben Johnson, Christopher George
This is the story of a widow who employs the services of three cowboys to help her recover some stolen gold.
MPAA:PG
Michael Wayne; Batjac Productions — *Warner Home Video*

Trained to Kill, U.S.A.   1983
Drama
66526   88 mins   C   B, V   P
Stephen Sander, Heidi Vaughn, Rockne Tarkington
A Vietnam veteran relives his war experiences when a gang of terrorists threaten his home town.
MPAA:R
Paul Rubey Johnson — *Paragon Video Productions*

Training Your Retriever—Advanced   1984
Hunting/Pets
74471   55 mins   C   B, V   P
This tape looks at the finishing training for a gun dog of 22 weeks and beyond.
NEO Productions — *Leisure Time Products Project/3M*

Training Your Retriever—Basic   1984
Hunting/Pets
74470   55 mins   C   B, V   P
This tape is a step by step guide to training a hunting dog from a pup to an adult.
Neo Productions — *Leisure Time Products Project/3M*

Trainwatcher I   1979
Trains
55522   60 mins   C   B, V   P
A journey on a series of classic locomotives includes Amtrak's "Starlite"; a New York Subway and a ride on the Chicago "El"; streetcars at the Orange Empire Trolley Museum in California; classics at the L.A. County Fairgrounds; and steam engines from the Union Pacific and Sierra railroads.
De Luz — *De Luz Video*

Trainwatcher II   1979
Trains
55523   60 mins   C   B, V   P
A look at the Santa Fe R.R. features a visit to the world's largest classification yard, and scenes from other great Western lines such as the Rio Grande, Burlington Northern, Union Pacific, and Southern Pacific are shown.

(For Explanation of codes, see USE GUIDE and KEY)

De Luz Video — *De Luz Video*

Trainwatcher III   1979
Trains
55524   60 mins   C   B, V   P
A ride on Washington D.C.'s "Metro" opens this look at trains, which features a ride on Southern's "Crescent" heading for New Orleans, and Union Pacific's huge Northern No. 8444 on her way to Colorado.
De Luz Video — *De Luz Video*

Trainwatcher IV   1980
Trains
55525   60 mins   C   B, V   P
A visit to the Union Pacific classification yards and a look at a diesel freight operation on the Southern Railway at Alexandria, Virginia highlight this program, which also includes the Amtrak "Starlite," two retired passenger cars of the Southern Pacific and Union Pacific, and San Francisco's BART and cable cars.
De Luz Video — *De Luz Video*

Trainwatcher V   1981
Trains
59171   60 mins   C   B, V   P
A collection of steam, diesel, and electric trains: Amtrak's Superliner, the San Francisco Zephyr, and the fabulous "Daylight" engine of the Southern Pacific. Includes a trip to the California State R.R. Museum.
De Luz Video — *De Luz Video*

Trainwatcher VI   1982
Trains
68891   60 mins   C   B, V   P
This program includes rides on steam, diesel and electric trains.
De Luz Video — *De Luz Video*

Traitor, The   1936
Western
14219   57 mins   B/W   B, V   P
Tim McCoy
Undercover man joins a gang of bandits.
Puritan — *VCI Home Video; Video Connection; Discount Video Tapes*

Tramp and A Woman, The   1915
Comedy
38966   45 mins   B/W   B, V, FO   P
Charlie Chaplin, Edna Purviance
Two shorts made for the Essanay Company in 1915 which offer the Little Tramp wooing Edna Purviance in typical Chaplin fashion. Silent with musical score.
Essanay — *Video Yesteryear*

Trango   1978
Mountaineering
69912   36 mins   C   B, V   P
This is a documentation of Joe Brown's attempt to climb the Trango Tower, a 20,000 foot vertical spire of granite in the Karakoram Himalaya of Pakistan.
Unknown — *Gravity Sports Films*

Transatlantic Tunnel   1935
Science fiction
01694   70 mins   B/W   B, V   P
Richard Dix, Leslie Banks, Madge Evans, Helen Vinson, directed by Maurice Elvey
Based on Bernard Kellerman's novel, an undersea tunnel from England to America is built despite financial trickery.
Gaumont British — *Budget Video; Video Connection; Cable Films*

Trapeze   1956
Drama
68227   105 mins   C   B, V, CED   P
Burt Lancaster, Tony Curtis, Gina Lollabrigida
The story of three people who want to perform the mid-air triple somersault, an almost impossible feat.
Susan Productions — *CBS/Fox Video*

Trapped   1949
Crime-Drama
66402   78 mins   B/W   B, V   P
Lloyd Bridges, John Hoyt, Barbara Payton
Government agents let a criminal escape their custody so he can lead them to a gang of counterfeiters.
Eagle Lion — *Movie Buff Video*

Trapped by the Mormons   1922
Drama/Exploitation
48744   80 mins   B/W   B, V, 3/4U   P
Evelyn Brent
Mormons are depicted as white slavers who lure young English girls into their harems. Silent.
Unknown — *Penguin Video*

Traviata, La   1983
Opera
65517   105 mins   C   B, V, LV,   P
                                    CED
Teresa Stratas, Placido Domingo, Cornell MacNeil, Alan Monk, Axelle Gall, Pina Cei
A film version of Giuseppe Verdi's opera classic. In stereo VHS and Beta Hi-Fi.
MPAA:G
Universal Classics; Accent Films — *MCA Home Video*

Treasure   1984
Games
72907   60 mins   C   B, V, LV   P
An actual treasure hunt is presented on this tape. Viewers are given clue questions which will lead to a jackpot of a half-million dollars

which is hidden somewhere in the United States.
Renan Productions — *Vestron Video*

Treasure Island 1934
Adventure
56756   102 mins   B/W   B, V, CED   P
Wallace Beery, Jackie Cooper, Lionel Barrymore, Nigel Bruce, directed by Victor Fleming
A stirring adaptation of Robert Louis Stevenson's pirate tale about Long John Silver and young Jim Hawkins, set in eighteenth-century England.
MGM, Hunt Stromberg — *MGM/UA Home Video*

Treasure Island 1950
Adventure
58625   87 mins   C   B, V, LV   R, P
Bobby Driscoll, Robert Newton, Basil Sydney, directed by Byron Haskin
Robert Louis Stevenson's spine-tingling tale of pirates and buried treasure, in which young cabin boy Jim Hawkins matches wits with Long John Silver.
MPAA:G
Walt Disney Productions — *Walt Disney Home Video; RCA VideoDiscs*

Treasure of Bruce Le/Big Rascal 197?
Martial arts/Adventure
66087   179 mins   C   B, V   P
Bruce Le
A kung-fu double feature filled with martial arts action.
MPAA:R
Unknown — *Best Film & Video Corporation*

Treasure of the Four Crowns 1982
Adventure/Suspense
65107   97 mins   C   B, V, CED   P
Tony Anthony
An aging history professor hires a team of tough commandos to recover four legendary crowns containing the source of mystical powers. The crowns are being held under heavy guard by a crazed cult leader. VHS in stereo.
MPAA:PG
Cannon Films — *MGM/UA Home Video*

Treasure of the Sierra Madre, The 1948
Adventure
76041   124 mins   B/W   B, V   P
Humphrey Bogart, Walter Huston
The fate that brings three soldier-of-fortune prospectors together during the days of the gold rush tempts them onward through many hardships for the sake of finding gold.

Warner Bros — *Key Video*

Treasure of the Sierra Madre, The 1948
Drama
44948   126 mins   B/W   CED   P
Humphrey Bogart, Walter Huston, Tim Holt, Bruce Bennett, directed by John Huston
Greed and suspicion surround three prospectors in their search for gold.
Academy Awards '48: Best Supporting Actor (Huston); Best Director (Huston); Best Screenplay (Huston)
Warner Bros. — *RCA VideoDiscs*

Treasure of the Yankee Zephyr 1983
Adventure
65480   97 mins   C   B, V   P
Ken Wahl, George Peppard, Lesley Ann Warren
A trio join in the quest for a plane that has been missing for 40 years... with a cargo of $50 million.
MPAA:PG
Film Ventures — *Vestron Video*

Tree of Life, The 1973
Indians-North American/Documentary
60468   20 mins   C   B, V, 3/4U   P
A documentary of the Volador ritual as performed by the Totonac Indians of Huehuetla, Pueblo, Mexico. The ritual is perhaps the oldest surviving dance in the Western Hemisphere.
Bruce Lane — *Flower Films*

Trenchcoat 1983
Comedy
66052   95 mins   C   B, V   R, P
Margot Kidder, Robert Hays
A detective spoof in which an aspiring mystery writer travels to Malta where she is drawn into a real-life conspiracy.
Jerry Leider — *Walt Disney Home Video*

Trial, The 1963
Drama
03893   118 mins   B/W   B, V   P
Orson Welles, Anthony Perkins, Jeanne Moreau
Government employee in unnamed country is arrested, harassed and examined endlessly but never told nature of his crime. Based on Franz Kafka's novel.
Gibraltar Prod; Landeau Unger — *Budget Video; Western Film & Video Inc; Discount Video Tapes; Cable Films*

Trial of the Catonsville Nine, The 1972
Drama
65190   85 mins   C   B, V   P
Ed Flanders, Douglass Watson, William Schallert, directed by Gordon Davidson

A riveting political drama that focuses on the trial of nine anti-war activists, including Father Daniel Berrigan, during the Vietnam War days of the late '60s.
MPAA:PG
Cinema 5 — *RCA/Columbia Pictures Home Video*

Tribute   1980
Drama
55744   123 mins   C   B, V, LV, CED   P
Jack Lemmon, Robby Benson, Lee Remick, directed by Bob Clark
Bernard Slade's play, brought to the screen, about Scotty Templeton, a dying man determined to achieve a reconciliation with his son. The tense conflict between father and son plays out against Scotty's fight for life, weaving moments of high comedy into the drama.
MPAA:PG
Joel B Michaels; Garth H Drabinsky — *Vestron Video*

Tribute to Billie Holiday, A   1979
Music-Performance
42923   57 mins   C   B, V   P
This tribute to Billie Holiday features the talents of Nina Simone, Maxine Weldon, Morganna King, Carmen McRae, and Esther Phillips. The orchestra was arranged and conducted by Ray Ellis with additional arranging by Tommy Newsom.
Jack Sidney III — *Media Home Entertainment*

Trigger Pals   1939
Western
57976   58 mins   B/W   B, V   P
Art Jarrett
A tale of honest men who stand together.
Grand National — *Video Connection*

Trigger Trio, The   1937
Western
15438   54 mins   B/W   B, V   P
Ray Corrigan, John King, Max Terhune
Rancher, with diseased cattle, kills a ranch inspector. Range Busters are called in on the case.
Republic — *Video Connection; Discount Video Tapes*

Trilby   1915
Drama
64312   50 mins   B/W   B, V   P
Clara Kimball Young, Wilton Lackaye, directed by Maurice Tourneur
The first film version of the classic tale. Svengali, a hypnotist, enslaves a beautiful young girl and molds her into an opera star. Silent with musical score.

Equitable Motion Pictures — *Classic Video Cinema Collector's Club*

Trilby/Svengali   193?
Drama
64340   130 mins   B/W   B, V   P
Clara Kimball Young, John Barrymore, Marian Marsh
Two versions of the same classic story on one tape: "Trilby" (1915 - silent) and "Svengali" (1931 - sound). The story concerns an opera singer who is mezmerized by a master hypnotist.
Equitable; Warner Bros — *Classic Video Cinema Collector's Club*

Trinity Is Still My Name   1975
Western
08481   117 mins   C   B, V, CED   P
Bud Spencer, Terrence Hill
Petty rustler brothers, unconcerned with danger or hopeless odds, endure mishaps and adventures as they try to right wrongs.
MPAA:G
Avco Embassy — *Embassy Home Entertainment*

Trip, The   1967
Fantasy
69288   85 mins   C   B, V   P
Peter Fonda, Dennis Hopper, Susan Strasberg, Bruce Dern
Written by Jack Nicholson, this film is a psychedelic journey to the world of inner consciousness.
American International — *Vestron Video*

Triumph of Sherlock Holmes   1935
Mystery
01760   84 mins   B/W   B, V   P
Arthur Wontner, Ian Fleming, directed by Leslie Hiscott
Sherlock Holmes' retirement is short-lived as a series of bizarre murders bring him back into action.
Unknown — *Budget Video; Cable Films; Discount Video Tapes*

Triumph of the Will   1934
Documentary/Propaganda
48850   110 mins   B/W   B, V, 3/4U   P
Directed by Leni Riefenstahl
This classic record of the Sixth Nazi Party Congress in Nuremberg retains its compelling power through impressive photography and camera movement. Dialogue in German.
GE
Leni Riefenstahl — *Western Film & Video Inc; Video Yesteryear; International Historic Films; Sheik Video; Penguin Video; Discount Video Tapes*

Triumphs of a Man Called Horse — 1982
Western
73019   91 mins   C   B, V   R, P
Richard Harris
An indian must save his people from prospectors in order to keep his title as Peace, Chief of the Yellow Hand Sioux.
MPAA:R
Cinema Center — *THORN EMI Home Video*

Trojan Women, The — 1971
Drama
65211   105 mins   C   B, V   P
Katharine Hepburn, Vanessa Redgrave
This program is strongly anti-war in its telling. All of the Trojan warriors and princes have been killed and the Conquerors must divide the only remains of the war—the Trojan women and their children.
MPAA:G
Josef Shaftel Productions — *U.S.A. Home Video*

Tron — 1982
Science fiction
63128   96 mins   C   B, V, LV, CED   R, P
Jeff Bridges, Bruce Boxleitner, David Warner, Cindy Morgan, Barnard Hughes, directed by Steven Lisberger
A video game designer is sucked into a computer and finds that he must do battle with his own creations in order to survive.
MPAA:PG
Walt Disney Productions — *Walt Disney Home Video; RCA VideoDiscs*

Tropical Birds — 1982
Birds
75696   60 mins   C   B, V, 3/4U   P
Six South American birds are studied by camera. There is no narration or music so that the viewer may enjoy the natural sound and movement of the birds.
Environmental Video — *Environmental Video*

Tropical Fish, Fireside Moments and Beautiful Birds — 1982
Fishes/Birds
75695   120 mins   C   B, V, 3/4U   P
Scenes of tropical fish and beautiful birds are shown without sound so that the viewer may add his own musical selections.
Environmental Video — *Environmental Video*

Trouble in Texas — 1937
Western
08795   65 mins   B/W   B, V, 3/4U   P
Tex Ritter, Rita Hayworth

Outlaws go to a rodeo and try to steal the prize money.
Grand Natl — *Penguin Video; Discount Video Tapes*

Trouble with Angels, The — 1966
Comedy
68266   112 mins   C   B, V   P
Hayley Mills, June Harding, Rosalind Russell, Gypsy Rose Lee, Binnie Barnes, directed by Ida Lupino
Two young girls turn a convent upside down with their endless practical jokes.
Columbia — *RCA/Columbia Pictures Home Video*

Trouble with Father — 195?
Comedy
53092   50 mins   B/W   B, V, 3/4U   P
Stu Erwin, June Erwin
Two episodes of the classic comedy series about a bumbling father whose every attempt to fix something, surprise someone, or raise his kids turned to disaster. Also titled "The Stu Erwin Show": "Yvette" (1954), in which Stu wants to surprise June with an unusual gift—a lifelike female mannequin; "What Paper Do You Read?" in which Stu enrolls in an evening class on government.
ABC — *Shokus Video*

Truck Stop Women — 1975
Adventure
64882   88 mins   C   B, V, CED   P
Claudia Jennings
Female truckers become involved in smuggling on the highway.
Mark Lester — *Vestron Video*

Truckers Woman — 1983
Drama
66527   90 mins   C   B, V   P
Michael Hawkins, Mary Cannon
A man takes a job driving an 18-wheel truck in order to find the murderers of his father.
MPAA:R
Unknown — *Paragon Video Productions*

True Confessions — 1981
Drama
59849   110 mins   C   B, V, LV, CED   P
Robert DeNiro, Robert Duvall, Ken McMillan, Charles Durning, Burgess Meredith, Louisa Moritz, directed by Ulu Grosbard
John Gregory Dunne's novel about two brothers, one a priest and the other a detective, who are pitted against each other in a tale of corruption in the Church, provides the basis for this film.
MPAA:R
United Artists — *MGM/UA Home Video*

True Game of Death, The   197?
Martial arts/Adventure
47695   90 mins   C   B, V   P
Bruce Lee, Shou Lung
A story of the circumstances behind the death of superstar Bruce Lee.
Ho Shin Motion Picture Co Ltd — *Master Arts Video*

True Glory, The   1945
World War II/Documentary
50643   85 mins   B/W   B, V, FO   P
Directed by Garson Kanin
An account of the teamwork between British and American troops in World II from the Normandy Invasion to the Allied Occupation of Germany.
Academy Award '45: Best Documentary Feature.
US War Dept; British Ministry of Information — *Video Yesteryear*

True Grit   1969
Western
38621   128 mins   C   B, V, LV   R, P
John Wayne, Glen Campbell, Kim Darby, Robert Duvall, directed by Henry Hathaway
John Wayne portrays U.S. Marshal Rooster Cogburn, who is hired by a young girl to find her father's killer, in this popular film that won Wayne his only Oscar.
Academy Awards '69: Best Actor (Wayne).
MPAA:G
Paramount — *Paramount Home Video; RCA VideoDiscs*

True Heart Susie   1919
Film-History
11389   87 mins   B/W   B, V, FO   P
Lillian Gish, Robert Harring, directed by D.W. Griffith
A simple, moving story about a girl who is in love with a man who marries a girl from the city. (Silent.)
Artcraft — *Video Yesteryear; Sheik Video; Discount Video Tapes*

Truite, La (The Trout)   1983
Drama
76033   80 mins   C   B, V   P
Isabelle Huppert, Jean-Pierre Cassel, Daniel Olbrychski, Jeanne Moreau
A young woman leaves her family's trout farm to embark on a journey around the world.
MPAA:R
Yves Rousset-Rouard — *RCA/Columbia Pictures Home Video*

Truk Lagoon   197?
Sports-Water
53636   27 mins   C   B, V, 3/4U, Q   P

This program in the "Under Water Deep Sea Diving" series portrays the story of "the graveyard under the sea," a forty mile lagoon which holds over 100 Japanese ships the Allies sank during World War II. The ghost vessels have now become exotic gardens of coral and tropical fishes.
Smokey Roberts — *TV Sports Scene*

Truman Capote's "The Glass House"   1973
Drama
52394   91 mins   C   B, V
Vic Morrow, Clu Gulager, Billy Dee Williams, Alan Alda, Kris Tabori, Dean Jagger
This program offers a look at the chilling realities of prison life and the power struggle among the inmates. Based on a story by Truman Capote.
AM Available
Tomorrow Entertainment — *Budget Video*

Trumpet Course; Beginning-Intermediate   1982
Music
47364   60 mins   C   B, V   P
Clark Terry instructs on-sight reading and basic through intermediate trumpet techniques.
American Home Video Library — *American Home Video Library*

Truth About UFO's & ET's, The   1982
Speculation/Occult sciences
66030   90 mins   C   B, V   P
Brad Steiger, the world's leading investigator of the psychic and extraterrestrial examines UFO's, ET's, impossible fossils, poltergeists and "Star People".
Atlan Productions — *VCI Home Video*

TT Tribute   1982
Motorcycles
66247   69 mins   C   B, V   P
A tribute to Mike Hailwood, spanning from his early years at the TT to his last win in 1979.
CH Wood — *Motor Cycle Video*

Tubby the Tuba   1977
Musical/Fantasy
69527   81 mins   C   B, V, CED   P
Animated voices of Dick Van Dyke, Pearl Bailey, Jack Gilford, Hermione Gingold
Tubby the Tuba searches for a melody he can call his own. In stereo.
MPAA:G
Alexander Schure Productions — *Children's Video Library*

Tubes...Live at the Greek, The — 1979
Music-Performance
65214   60 mins   C   B, V   P
Rock 'n' roll's most outrageous group appear in a night of pure musical madness. In Beta Hi-Fi and stereo VHS.
The Tubes — *Monterey Home Video*

Tubes Video, The — 1981
Music-Performance
58466   53 mins   C   B, V   R, P
This program is built around songs on the Tubes LP, "The Completion Backward Principle" but also features new numbers and a few older hits.
EMI Music — *THORN EMI Home Video; Pioneer Artists; RCA VideoDiscs*

Tulips — 1981
Comedy
60450   91 mins   C   B, V, CED   P
Gabe Kaplan, Bernadette Peters, Henry Gibson
A black comedy about a world-weary would-be suicide who secures his demise by taking a contract out on himself, and then changing his mind.
Astral Bellevue Pathe Prod — *Embassy Home Entertainment*

Tulips — 1981
Comedy/Romance
69543   91 mins   C   B, V, CED   P
Gabe Kaplan, Bernadette Peters, Henry Gibson
A would-be suicide takes a contract out on himself, and then meets a woman who makes life worth living again. Together they attempt to evade the gangland hit man.
MPAA:PG
Astral Bellevue Pathe Bennettfilms Inc — *Embassy Home Entertainment*

Tulsa — 1949
Western
03995   96 mins   C   B, V   P
Susan Hayward, Robert Preston, Chill Wills
High spirited rancher's daughter begins crusade against oil drillers when her father is killed.
Eagle Lion; Walter Wanger — *Movie Buff Video; Nostalgia Merchant; Budget Video; Discount Video Tapes; Classic Video Cinema Collector's Club*

Tumbleweed Trail — 1942
Western
57977   57 mins   B/W   B, V   P
Bill Boyd, Art Davis
An action-packed thundering western.
Producers Releasing Corp — *Video Connection*

Tumbleweeds — 1925
Western
38980   114 mins   B/W   B, V, FO   P
William S. Hart
This, William S. Hart's last western, is the story of the last great land rush in America, the opening of the Oklahoma Territory to homesteaders. The film is preceded by a sound prologue, made in 1939, in which Hart speaks for the only time on screen, to introduce the story. Silent, with musical score.
United Artists — *Video Yesteryear; Blackhawk Films*

Tumbleweeds — 1925
Western
15501   79 mins   B/W   B, V   P
William S. Hart, Lucien Littlefield, Barbara Bedford, directed by King Baggott
Story of the newly-opened Cherokee Strip. Cowboy is mistaken for a "sooner'—one who sneaks over the boundary line to stake a claim sooner than the government's official starting time. Silent classic.
United Artists — *Video Connection; Discount Video Tapes; Penguin Video; Budget Video; Western Film & Video Inc; Classic Video Cinema Collector's Club*

Tunnel, The — 1935
Drama
66403   94 mins   B/W   B, V   P
Richard Dix, Leslie Banks, Madge Evans, C. Aubrey Smith, George Arliss, Walter Huston
An American engineer battles the elements in an attempt to build an undersea transatlantic tunnel, linking the U.S. and Britain.
Gaumont British — *Movie Buff Video*

Tunnelvision — 1976
Satire
52866   75 mins   C   B, V   P
Larralne Newman, Chevy Chase
A spoof of television comprised of irreverent sketches.
MPAA:R
Worldwide Film Corp — *HarmonyVision*

Turandot — 1983
Opera
65660   138 mins   C   B, V   P
Set in Peking, Puccini's opera opens with the proclamation that Princess Turandot will become the bride of the royal suitor who can successfully answer 3 riddles. Unsuccessful suitors lose not only the hand of the princess, but their heads as well.
ORF Productions — *MGM/UA Home Video*

Turning Point, The — 1979
Drama
44933   119 mins   C   B, V, CED   P

Shirley MacLaine, Anne Bancroft, Mikhail Baryshnikov, directed by Herbert Ross
A woman who gave up ballet for motherhood must come to terms with herself as her daughter's ballet career is launched.
MPAA:PG EL, SP
20th Century Fox — *CBS/Fox Video*

Tut: The Boy King   1977
Archeology/Museums
02810   52 mins   C   B, V   R, P
Narrated by Orson Welles
Welles' narration eloquently describes some of the treasures viewed by Howard Carter when he first opened the tomb of King Tut in 1922 in this exciting artistic experience.
George Foster Peabody Award; Christopher Award.
NBC — *Warner Home Video*

Tut: The Boy King/The Louvre   197?
Museums/Archeology
47061   100 mins   C   CED   P
Narrated by Orson Welles and Charles Boyer
Two popular documentary programs are combined in this package. "Tut" presents a tour of the marvelous treasures found in Tutankhamen's tomb. "The Louvre" offers an intimate view of the art masterpieces of this most famous of museums.
NBC — *RCA VideoDiscs*

Tuttles of Tahiti, The   1942
Comedy
59648   91 mins   C   B, V   P
Charles Laughton, Jon Hall, Peggy Drake, Victor Francen, Gene Reynolds, Florence Bates, directed by Charles Vidor
Laughton stars as head of the Tuttle clan, the most dedicated group of carefree loafers in the South Pacific.
RKO — *Budget Video*

TV Bloopers   197?
Outtakes and bloopers
14445   30 mins   B/W   B, V   P
A host of TV bloopers featuring Joe Garagiola, Lee Trevino, Bill Cosby, "Hee Haw," and zany commercials. Part of the program is devoted to fun on the set of "The Mary Tyler Moore Show."
CBS et al — *Video Dimensions*

TV Variety   195?
Variety
59315   120 mins   B/W   B, V, 3/4U   P
Arthur Godfrey, Ed Sullivan, Mickey Rooney, Jaye P. Morgan, Joey Forman, Joe E. Lewis, Spike Jones
Music, comedy, and dance from TV's "Golden Age": "Arthur Godfrey's Talent Scouts" (1954), a classic live episode; "The Ed Sullivan Show" (1957), season premiere for 1957; and "The

Spike Jones Show" (1954), a musical half-hour featuring the entire City Slickers.
CBS;NBC — *Shokus Video*

TV Variety, II   195?
Variety
47614   120 mins   B/W   B, V, 3/4U   P
This tape contains three different vintage programs: "The Walter Winchell Show" (December 31, 1956), with guests Frankie Laine, Lisa Kirk, Jack Carter and Russ Tamblyn; "Texaco Star Theater" (January 18, 1949) with Milton Berle and guests Tony Martin and Carmen Miranda; "Person to Person" with Edward R. Murrow interviewing Groucho Marx (1954) and Harpo Marx (1958). All programs include original commercials and network logos.
NBC — *Shokus Video*

TV Variety III   1950
Variety/Comedy
62690   120 mins   B/W   B, V, 3/4U   P
Bob Hope, Marilyn Maxwell, Jack Carson, Hal March, Jack Gilford
Two complete kinescoped variety shows from 1950: "The Bob Hope Comedy Hour" and "4 Star Revue," hosted by Jack Carson. Original commercials and network I.D.'s are included.
NBC — *Shokus Video*

TV Variety, IV   1951
Variety
62691   60 mins   B/W   B, V, 3/4U   P
Perry Como, Faye Emerson, Fred Waring, Frankie Laine, Patti Page, Frank Fontaine, Tommy Dorsey
Two fifteen-minute programs, "The Perry Como Show" and "The Faye Emerson Show" are combined with a half-hour "Frankie Laine Show," all from 1950 kinescopes.
CBS et al — *Shokus Video*

TV Variety, V   1956
Variety
66487   115 mins   B/W   B, V   P
Four representative daytime variety shows of the mid-1950's are combined on this tape: "The Garry Moore Show," "Arthur Godfrey Time," "The Robert Q. Lewis Show" and "The Tennessee Ernie Ford Show." Original commercials and network I.D.'s are included.
CBS — *Shokus Video*

TV Variety, VI   1955
Comedy/Variety
76015   120 mins   B/W   B, V, 3/4U   P
Two tv variety shows: "Dinner with the President," with Ethel Merman, Lucy and Desi, Eddie Fisher and many more; "The Perry Como Show," with Rosemary Clooney, Nat King Cole, Rin Tin Tin, and others.
CBS; NBC — *Shokus Video*

TV's Classic Guessing Games
1956
Game show
66460   120 mins   B/W   B, V, 3/4U   P
Arlene Francis, Steve Allen, Dorothy Kilgallen, Deborah Kerr, Lucille Ball, Desi Arnaz, Bill Cullen, Fred Allen, Garry Moore
Four vintage game shows of the 1954-56 seasons are combined on this tape, including three episodes of "What's My Line" and one segment of "I've Got a Secret." Original commercials and network I.D.'s included.
CBS — *Shokus Video*

Twelve Angry Men
1957
Drama
64835   95 mins   B/W   CED   P
Henry Fonda, Martin Balsam, Lee J. Cobb, E.G. Marshall, Jack Klugman, Jack Warden, directed by Sidney Lumet
Based on a TV play by Reginald Rose, this is a classic drama of a deadlocked jury and one man who makes the others listen to reason.
United Artists — *RCA VideoDiscs*

Twelve Chairs, The
1970
Comedy
65112   94 mins   C   B, V   P
Mel Brooks, Dom DeLuise, Frank Langella, Ron Moody, directed by Mel Brooks
In 1927 Russia, a rich matron admits on her deathbed that she has hidden her jewels in the upholstery of one of twelve chairs. The chairs, however, are no longer in her home, and a madcap search begins for them.
MPAA:PG
Michael Hertzberg — *Media Home Entertainment*

Twelve O'Clock High
1949
War-Drama
29179   132 mins   B/W   B, V   P
Gregory Peck, Hugh Marlowe, Gary Merrill, Millard Mitchell, Dean Jagger
An epic drama about the heroic 8th Air Force. Peck, as a bomber-group commander, is forced to drive his men to the breaking point in the fury of battle.
Academy Awards '49: Best Supporting Actor (Jagger)
20th Century Fox — *CBS/Fox Video*

Twenty Questions
1952
Game show
58637   30 mins   B/W   B, V, FO   P
Hosted by Bill Slater
The "Mennen Mystery Voice" tells the viewing audience what secret object the panel has 20 questions to guess, in this vintage quiz show. Sponsored by Mennen.
Dumont — *Video Yesteryear*

27th Annual Academy Awards Presentations, The
1955
Variety
47495   79 mins   B/W   B, V, FO   P
Grace Kelly, Marlon Brando, Humphrey Bogart, Audrey Hepburn, Bing Crosby, William Holden, Bette Davis, hosted by Bob Hope and Thelma Ritter
Telecast on March 30, 1955, this program honored the Oscar winners of 1954 including Grace Kelly, Eva Marie Saint, Edmond O'Brien, Marlon Brando, Walt Disney, Elia Kazan and others. The nominated songs are performed by Johnny Desmond, Tony Martin, Rosemary Clooney, Peggy King and Dean Martin.
NBC — *Video Yesteryear*

20,000 Leagues Under the Sea
1954
Adventure
44303   127 mins   C   CED   P
Kirk Douglas, James Mason, Peter Lorre
From a futuristic submarine, Captain Nemo wages war against an entire fleet of battleships and has a harrowing battle with a giant squid. In the end, Nemo's atomic power plant is demolished, along with his sinister plot.
Academy Award '54: Special Effects.   MPAA:G
Walt Disney Productions — *RCA VideoDiscs*

20 Years of World Series
1958
Baseball
49553   40 mins   B/W   B, V   P
A collection of highlights from among the most exciting of the World Series played between 1938 and 1957.
Lew Fonseca — *Major League Baseball Productions*

Twilight on the Rio Grande
1941
Western
54197   54 mins   B/W   B, V   P
Gene Autry
Autry runs into a female knife thrower and some jewel smugglers.
Republic — *Video Connection*

Twilight Zone—The Movie
1983
Horror
65359   101 mins   C   B, V, LV, CED   P
Dan Aykroyd, Albert Brooks, Vic Morrow, Kathleen Quinlan, John Lithgow
Four short horrific tales are anthologized in this film as a tribute to Rod Serling and his popular TV series. Three of the episodes, "Kick the Can," "It's a Good Life" and "Nightmare at 20,000 Feet," are based on original "Twilight Zone" scripts.
MPAA:PG

Steven Spielberg; John Landis — *Warner Home Video*

Twist of Fate   1984
Music-Performance
66504   19 mins   C   B, V, LV, CED   P
Olivia Newton-John, John Travolta
Six of Olivia Newton-John's music videos are combined on this tape, including four songs from the movie "Two of a Kind;" the title tune, "Livin' in Desperate Times," "Take a Chance" and "Twist of Fate," plus "Heart Attack" and "Tied Up." Stereo in all formats.
MCA — *MCA Home Video*

Twisted Cross, The   1956
World War II/Documentary
54835   53 mins   B/W   B, V   R, P
Narrated by Alexander Scourby
The story of Adolph Hitler and the Nazi movement is recreated, tracing Hitler's lowly beginnings in 1923, to his days as conqueror of the European mainland, to his defeat and suicide.
NBC; Henry Salomon — *Warner Home Video*

Twisted Sister's Stay Hungry   1984
Music video
72876   120 mins   C   B, V   P
Twisted Sister
A conceptual version of Twisted Sisters' album "Stay Hungry" with concert footage.
Unknown — *Embassy Home Entertainment; Pioneer Artists*

Two Assassins in the Dark   198?
Martial arts
64960   90 mins   C   B, V   P
Wang Tao, Chang Yi, Lung Chun-Eng
A martial arts adventure about a pair of kung-fu killers.
Dragon Lady Productions — *Unicorn Video*

Two Best World Series Ever, The   1978
Baseball
13319   60 mins   C   B, V   P
Cincinnati Reds, Boston Red Sox, New York Yankees, Los Angeles Dodgers
Best plays from the 1975 and 1978 World Series are contained in this program. In '75 Sparky Anderson's Reds prevail in seven games over the Red Sox in one of the most exciting and dramatic series ever. The Yankees come from two games behind in '78 to win their second consecutive championship in six games over the Dodgers.
Warner Qube — *VidAmerica*

Two Graves to Kung-Fu   1982
Martial arts/Adventure
59994   95 mins   C   B, V   R, P
Liu Chia-Yung, Shek Kin, Chen Hung-Lieh
A young kung-fu student is framed for murder. When the real murderers kill his teacher, he escapes from prison to seek revenge.
MPAA:R
L and T Films Corp Ltd — *Video Gems*

Two Gun Man   1931
Western
15463   60 mins   B/W   B, V   P
Ken Maynard
Ken Maynard stars in this Western.
Tiffany — *Video Connection*

200 Motels   1971
Comedy/Musical
75538   99 mins   C   B, V   P
Frank Zappa, Ringo Starr, The Mothers of Invention
A story of what happens to a rock group that has been on the road too long.
MPAA:R
Murakami Wolf Productions Inc — *MGM/UA Home Video*

225,000 Mile Proving Ground   1953
Trains
73030   18 mins   C   B, V   P
This program shows how developmental research has provided better cargo handling, train braking and passenger comfort on the nation's railroads.
Association of American Railroads — *Interurban Films*

Two Kennedys, The   1981
Drama
69038   118 mins   C   B, V   P
This film deals extensively with the mystery surrounding the Kennedy family while making political connections with no holds barred.
Italy — *MPI Home Video*

Two Men and a Wardrobe   1958
Film-Avant-garde
72471   19 mins   B/W   B, V, 3/4U   P
Directed by Roman Polanski
A piece of absurdist cinema from Roman Polanski that deals with modern man's lack of privacy.
Roman Polanski — *International Historic Films*

Two Mules for Sister Sara   1970
Western
47425   105 mins   C   B, V   P
Clint Eastwood, Shirley MacLaine, directed by Don Siegel

An American mercenary in 19th century Mexico gets mixed up with a cigar-smoking nun. The two make plans to capture a French garrison.
MPAA:PG
Universal — *MCA Home Video*

Two of a Kind 1983
Comedy
79192   87 mins   C   B, V   P
John Travolta, Olivia Newton-John
A fantasy film riding on the premise that love can save the world.
MPAA:PG
Roger M Rothstein; Joe Wizan — *CBS/Fox Video*

Two Reelers—Comedy Classics I 1933
Comedy
38971   54 mins   B/W   B, V, FO   P
Edgar Kennedy, Harry Gribbon, Harry Sweet, Jack Norton, Maxine Jennings, Willie Best
This package includes a 1944 Edgar Kennedy short, "Feather Your Nest" (RKO), and two 1933 films, "How Comedies Are Born" and "Dog Blight."
RKO — *Video Yesteryear*

Two Reelers—Comedy Classics II 194?
Comedy
38972   53 mins   B/W   B, V, FO   P
Leon Errol, Dorothy Granger, Billy Gilbert, Edgar Kennedy
A second package of three vintage shorts: "Chicken Feed" (1939) with Billy Gilbert, "Twin Husbands" (1946) with Leon Errol, and Edgar Kennedy in "False Roomers" (1938).
RKO — *Video Yesteryear*

Two Reelers—Comedy Classics III 194?
Comedy
38973   52 mins   B/W   B, V, FO   P
Edgar Kennedy, Jed Prouty
More laughs, with two Edgar Kennedy shorts, "A Merchant of Menace" (1933), and "Social Terrors" (1946). Also, Jed Prouty is featured in "Coat Tales" (193).
RKO — *Video Yesteryear*

Two Reelers—Comedy Classics IV 1936
Comedy
38970   56 mins   B/W   B, V, FO   P
Bert Lahr, Gene Austin, June Brewster, Carol Tevis, Grady Sutton
"Bridal Bail" (1934), "No More West" (Educational-1934) with Bert Lahr singing and clowning, and "Bad Medicine" (1936) with crooner Gene Austin comprise this comedy package.

RKO — *Video Yesteryear*

Two Reelers—Comedy Classics #5 19??
Comedy
69556   55 mins   B/W   B, V, FO   P
Leon Errol, the Ritz Brothers, Charlotte Greenwood
A compilation of three vintage comedy shorts by popular stars of the 1930's: "Dear Deer" (1942) with Leon Errol, "Hotel Anchovy" (1934) with the Ritz Brothers and "Love Your Neighbor" (1930) with Charlotte Greenwood.
Educational — *Video Yesteryear*

2001: A Space Odyssey 1968
Science fiction
44639   141 mins   C   B, V, LV, CED   P
Keir Dullea, Gary Lockwood, directed by Stanley Kubrick
A space voyage to Jupiter turns into chaos when a computer, HAL 9000, takes over, killing several astronauts. This space voyage traces the context of man's history; man vs. the machinery he made.
Academy Awards '68: Best Visual Effects.
MGM — *MGM/UA Home Video*

2069: A Sex Odyssey 1978
Adventure
69020   81 mins   C   B, V   P
A team of beautiful, sensuous astronauts are sent to Earth to obtain male sperm which they must bring back to Venus.
Unknown — *Imperial Video Corp*

Two Tickets to Broadway 1951
Comedy/Musical
57167   106 mins   C   B, V   P
Tony Martin, Janet Leigh, Gloria DeHaven, Smith and Dale
A small-town singer and a crooner arrange a hoax to get themselves on Bob Crosby's TV show.
RKO; Howard Hughes — *King of Video*

Two-Way Stretch 1960
Comedy
47306   84 mins   B/W   B, V   R, P
Peter Sellers, Wilfrid Hyde-White, Liz Fraser, David Lodge
Three prison inmates in a progressive jail plan to break out, pull a diamond heist, and break back in, all in the same night.
Showcorporation; British — *THORN EMI Home Video*

Two Weeks to Live 1943
Comedy
08732   60 mins   B/W   B, V, 3/4U   P

(For Explanation of codes, see USE GUIDE and KEY)

Lum and Abner, Franklin Pangborn, Kay Linaker, directed by Mal St. Clair
Abner inherits what he thinks is a large railroad...it's actually a broken down car.
RKO — *Penguin Video*

Two Worlds of Jennie Logan, The   1981
Fantasy
75465   99 mins   C   B, V   P
Lindsay Wagner, Linda Gray, Marc Singer, John Darling
A Victorian mansion and antique dress take Jennie Logan back to the turn of the century where she finds romance, intrigue and murder.
King Features — *U.S.A. Home Video*

Tycoon   1947
Drama
29469   120 mins   C   B, V   P, T
John Wayne, Laraine Day, Sir Cedric Hardwicke
A young American railroad builder finds action and romance in Latin America.
RKO — *Blackhawk Films; Nostalgia Merchant; King of Video*

Tying Trout Flies   1983
Fishing
65142   60 mins   C   B, V   P
Gary Borger
This program illustrates techniques of tying dry flies, nymphs and streamers. Part of the "Sportsman's Video Collection."
3M — *Leisure Time Products Project/3M*

U

U2 Live at Red Rocks "Under A Blood Red Sky"   19??
Music-Performance
72933   60 mins   C   B, V   P
One of rock's hottest bands is featured, performing songs from their album "Under A Blood Red Sky," filmed in Denver, Colorado.
Steve Lilywhite — *MCA Home Video*

Ub Iwerks Cartoon Festival   193?
Cartoons
29488   57 mins   C   B, V   P, T
Animated
Seven delightful cartoons by one of the pioneering geniuses of animation. Includes: "The Brave Tin Soldier," "Happy Days," "Fiddlesticks," "Jack and the Beanstalk," "The Headless Horseman," and "The Little Red Hen."
Ub Iwerks — *Blackhawk Films*

Ub Iwerks Cartoonfest Two   193?
Cartoons
29489   46 mins   C   B, V   P, T
Animated
More cartoons from the pen of the immortal Iwerks. Six color masterpieces of such great tales as "Tom Thumb," "Jack Frost," "Aladdin and the Wonderful Lamp," "Ali Baba," "Sinbad," and "Spooks."
Ub Iwerks — *Blackhawk Films*

Ub Iwerks Cartoonfest Three   193?
Cartoons
59989   30 mins   C   B, V   P, T
Animated
A compilation of Iwerks classics: "Simple Simon" (1935), "Puss in Boots" (1934), "Dick Whittington's Cat" (1936), and "Don Quixote" (1934).
Celebrity Productions — *Blackhawk Films*

Ub Iwerks Cartoonfest Four   1935
Cartoons
62874   30 mins   C   B, V   P, T
Animated
Another collection of enjoyable cartoons from the pen of Ub Iwerks. Included are "The Valiant Tailor," "Mary's Little Lamb," "The Brementown Musicians" and "Balloonland," all from 1934-35.
Ub Iwerks — *Blackhawk Films*

UB Iwerks Cartoonfest Five   193?
Cartoons
65705   23 mins   C   B, V   P, T
Animated
Three more fabulous Cinecolor cartoons from the UB Iwerks studio are combined on this tape: "Queen of Hearts" (1934), "Old Mother Hubbard" (1935) and "Humpty Dumpty" (1935), all from the Comicolor Cartoons series.
Ub Iwerks; Celebrity Productions — *Blackhawk Films*

Ugetsu   1953
Film-Avant-garde
06241   96 mins   B/W   B, V   P
Machiko Kyo, Masayuki Mori, directed by Kenji Mizoguchi
This classic Japanese film concerns a sixteenth-century legend of of a potter and a farmer who travel in search of their dreams.
JA
Japanese — *Budget Video; Sheik Video; Western Film & Video Inc; Discount Video Tapes; Video Dimensions*

Ultimate Thrill, The　　　　　　　1974
Adventure
59069　　84 mins　　C　　B, V　　R, P
Britt Ekland, Barry Brown, Michael Blodgett
A successful man plays Russian Roulette for big stakes.
General Cinema; Centaur Films — *Video Gems*

Ultra Flash　　　　　　　　　19??
Dance
65346　　60 mins　　C　　B, V　　P
A fantasy that is performed to some of today's hottest dance music. In stereo
Niles Siegal Organization — *Vestron Video*

Ultralight Experience, The　　　　1983
Sports-Minor
69910　　8 mins　　C　　B, V　　P
Northern Utah is the setting for this look at the motorized hang-glider.
Scott Hill — *Gravity Sports Films*

Ultraman II　　　　　　　　　1984
Cartoons/Adventure
66489　　84 mins　　C　　B, V　　P
Animated
In four new adventures, superhero Ultraman battles prehistoric monsters, killer beasts, an evil tornado and a sinister, life-threatening cloud, as he fights for peace on earth.
Tsuburaya Productions — *Trans World Entertainment*

Umberto D　　　　　　　　　1955
Film-Avant-garde
07140　　89 mins　　B/W　　B, V　　P
Carlo Battista, Maria Pia Casilio, Lina Gennari, directed by Vittorio De Sica
A government pensioner, living alone with his beloved dog, struggles to keep up a semblance of dignity on his inadequate pension. Italian Film, English subtitles.
New York Film Critics Award: Best Foreign Language Film.　IT
Dear Films; Italian — *Budget Video; Discount Video Tapes; Penguin Video*

Umbrellas of Cherbourg　　　　1963
Musical-Drama
65443　　90 mins　　C　　B, V　　P
Catherine Deneuve, Nino Castelnuovo
As a universal statement of love, this tender story has become a timeless musical classic. Subtitled in English.
MPAA:G　FR
Landau Unger — *USA Home Video*

Uncanny, The　　　　　　　1978
Horror
47817　　85 mins　　C　　B, V, 3/4U　　P
Peter Cushing, Ray Milland, Samantha Eggar, Donald Pleasence
A writer theorizes that a number of mysterious deaths were caused by a secret society of fatal felines.
Astral Films — *Nostalgia Merchant*

Uncle Sam Magoo　　　　　　196?
Cartoons/History-US
66037　　60 mins　　C　　B, V　　R, P
Animated, voice of Jim Backus
Mr. Magoo provides a history lesson in his own inimitable style.
UPA — *Paramount Home Video*

Uncommon Valor　　　　　　1983
Drama
Closed Captioned
65732　　105 mins　　C　　B, V　　R, P
Gene Hackman, Fred Ward, Reb Brown, Randall "Tex" Cobb, Robert Stack
After useless appeals to the government for information on his son who is listed as "missing in action" in Vietnam, Colonel Rhodes takes matters into his own hands.
MPAA:R
John Milius; Buzz Feitshans — *Paramount Home Video*

Under California Stars　　　　1948
Western
38981　　71 mins　　C　　B, V, FO　　P
Roy Rogers, Andy Devine, Jane Frazee, the Sons of the Pioneers
A shady gang making a living rounding up wild horses decides they can make more money by capturing Roy Rogers' horse, Trigger.
Republic — *Video Yesteryear; Discount Video Tapes; VCII; Video Connection*

Under Capricorn　　　　　　1949
Mystery
07880　　117 mins　　C　　B, V　　P
Directed by Alfred Hitchcock; Ingrid Bergman, Joseph Cotten, Michael Wilding
A dark tale of love and sensitivity, frustration and terror, headed by an all-star cast.
Warner Bros — *VidAmerica*

Under Fire　　　　　　　　1983
Drama
65600　　128 mins　　C　　B, V, LV　　P
Gene Hackman, Nick Nolte, Joanna Cassidy
Three news correspondents chronicle the final days of the Samoza regime in Nicaragua.
MPAA:R
Orion Pictures — *Vestron Video*

Under Nevada Skies　　　　　1946
Western
35468　　69 mins　　B/W　　B, V　　P

Roy Rogers, Gabby Hayes, Dale Evans, Bob Nolan
Roy sets out to find his best friend's murderer. Also includes Bob Nolan and the Sons of the Pioneers.
Republic — *Sheik Video*

Under the Rainbow 1981
Comedy
51996   97 mins   C   B, V   R, P
Chevy Chase, Carrie Fisher, Eve Arden, Joseph Maher, Robert Donner, Mako, Billy Barty
Undercurrents of foreign political intrigue add to the comic situations encountered by a talent scout and a secret service agent in and around a hotel inhabited by the midgets who have been signed to play the Munchkins in "The Wizard of Oz."
MPAA:PG
Orion Pictures — *Warner Home Video*

Under the Red Robe 1936
Adventure
03896   82 mins   B/W   B, V   P
Raymond Massey, Conrad Veidt, Annabella, directed by Victor Seastrom
French swordsman, Richelieu, and his oppression of Huguenots.
RKO; Sol Lesser — *Budget Video; Western Film & Video Inc*

Under the Roofs of Paris 1929
(Sous les Toits de Paris)
Romance
12863   95 mins   B/W   B, V, FO   P
Directed by Rene Clair
A tale of young lovers in a crowded tenement. Music and imaginative technique occupy this first French sound film. French with English subtitles.
FR
Tobis — *Video Yesteryear; Sheik Video; Cable Films; Discount Video Tapes*

Under Water Deep Sea 197?
Diving with "Smokey Roberts"
Sports-Water
53644   140 mins   C   B, V, 3/4U, Q
6   pgms
This series features entertaining and beautifully photographed portraits of life under the sea and the divers who explore it for sport and recreation.
1.Truk Lagoon 2.Undersea Research 3.The Medusa Affair 4.Diving and Fishing at 11,000 Feet 5.Follow Me Down 6.Love Under the High Seas
Smokey Roberts — *TV Sports Scene*

Under Western Stars 1945
Western
29508   83 mins   B/W   B, V   P
Roy Rogers, Trigger, Smiley Burnette
Roy's first starring film, in which he finds himself pitted against an outlaw gang.
Republic — *Sheik Video; Video Connection; Cable Films; Discount Video Tapes*

Undersea Adventures of Captain Nemo Volume 1, The 1975
Cartoons
53156   60 mins   C   B, V   P
Animated
Captain Nemo and his crew of the submarine Nautilus take the viewer on a series of daring battles and rescues in this undersea adventure.
EL, SP
Rainbow Animation — *Family Home Entertainment*

Undersea Adventures of Captain Nemo Volume 2, The 1975
Cartoons
64197   60 mins   C   B, V   P
Animated
The Nautilus crew battles bloodthirsty sharks as they accidentally uncover a sunken treasure worth a fortune.
EL, SP
Rainbow Animation — *Family Home Entertainment*

Undersea Adventures of Captain Nemo Volume 3, The 1975
Cartoons
64198   60 mins   C   B, V   P
Animated
Captain Nemo's team encounters Killer Whales and a poisonous squid as it battles criminal whale poachers. Then the crew travels to the icy regions of the world to confront a ferocious polar bear and a deadly sea leopard.
EL, SP
Rainbow Animation — *Family Home Entertainment*

Undersea Kingdom 1936
Adventure/Serials
14630   136 mins   B/W   B, V   P
Ray 'Crash' Corrigan
Adventure beneath the ocean floor. In twelve chapters of thirteen minutes; the first chapter runs twenty minutes.
Republic — *Video Connection; Video Dimensions; Discount Video Tapes; Nostalgia Merchant*

Undersea Research 197?
Sports-Water
53637 27 mins C B, V, 3/4U, P
Q
This program in the "Under Water Deep Sea Diving" series depicts new underwater methods and devices for exploration.
Smokey Roberts — *TV Sports Scene*

Undersea World of 1978
Jacques Cousteau Vol. I,
The
Documentary/Adventure
47059 100 mins C CED P
Narrated by Rod Serling
Two of Cousteau's journeys on the Calypso are featured: "Sharks" and "The Singing Whale." Spectacular underwater footage is included.
Media Producers Corp — *RCA VideoDiscs*

Underwater 1955
Adventure
66332 99 mins C B, V, 3/4U P
Jane Russell, Richard Egan, Gilbert Roland
A team of skin divers face danger when they begin a search for underwater treasure.
RKO — *Nostalgia Merchant*

Unfaithfully Yours 1948
Comedy
72898 105 mins B/W B, V P
Rex Harrison, Linda Darnell
A conductor suspects his wife is cheating on him.
Preston Sturges; RKO — *CBS/Fox Video*

Unfaithfully Yours 1984
Comedy
72899 96 mins C B, V P
Dudley Moore, Nastassia Kinski, Armand Assante, Albert Brooks
A symphony conductor suspects his wife of fooling around with a musician; in retaliation, he plots an elaborate scheme to murder her. Based on the 1948 Preston Sturges film.
MPAA:PG
20th Century Fox — *CBS/Fox Video*

Unicorn, The 1983
Drama
65435 29 mins C B, V P
Diana Dors, Celia Johnson
A small boy hears the legend that if one rubs the horn of a Unicorn his wishes will come true. Mistakenly he buys a one-horned goat and sets out to fulfill his dreams.
Janus Films — *Embassy Home Entertainment*

Unicorn Tales I 1980
Fairy tales
57573 90 mins C B, V P
Four stories for children, adapted from classic fairy tales, told in a modern way, with music. "The Magic Pony Ride" (based on the Ugly Duckling) is about a lonely little girl who meets a pony considered useless, and the two of them learn how to see and believe. In "The Stowaway" (based on Pinocchio), a young boy arrives in a new city and meets a lovable old man who leads him on the path to truth. "Carnival Circus" (based on Cinderella) concerns a young girl who fails at everything until she saves the circus and realizes that everyone has a special talent for something. In "The Maltese Unicorn" (based on The Boy Who Cried Wolf), a boy discovers that if he wants to be believed he must be a man of his word.
Viacom — *CBS/Fox Video*

Unicorn Tales II 1980
Fairy tales
57574 90 mins C B, V P
Four stories for children, adapted from classic fairy tales, told in a modern way, with music. In "Big Apple Birthday" (based on Alice in Wonderland), a girl who is bored by everything visits a new city and learns that there can be joy in every moment. "The Magnificent Major" (based on The Wizard of Oz) concerns a young girl who doesn't like to read. When she is transported to a land of non-readers, she is eager to return home so she can read. In "The Magic Hat" (based on The Emperor's New Clothes), a young boy moves to a new city, finding it difficult to make friends until he wears a magic hat. The magic of friendship, however, lasts longer than the "powers" of the hat. "Alex and the Wonderful 'Doo Wah' Lamp" (based on Aladdin and the Magic Lamp) concerns a boy who conjures up three genies from an old lamp, who promise to grant his every request. After being turned into several different people, however, he realizes he is happiest as himself.
Viacom — *CBS/Fox Video*

Union City 1981
Suspense/Drama
47434 82 mins C B, V P
Deborah Harry, Everett McGill, Dennis Lipscomb, Pat Benatar, directed by Mark Reichart
Deborah Harry of Blondie stars in this "new-wave" mystery about an accidental murderer who is on the run from the law.
MPAA:R
Cantina Blues Films; Kinesis Ltd — *RCA/Columbia Pictures Home Video*

Union Pacific Steam 1978
Trains
55513 60 mins C B, V P
A chronicle of one day's excursion on the Union Pacific Railroad behind the great Northern FEF No. 8444, begun in 1944 as its last operative steam engine. Scenes from the inside show views of the train rarely seen.

De Luz — *De Luz Video*

United States Air Force in Vietnam, The — 1967
Armed Forces-US
72490   28 mins   C   B, V, 3/4U   P
The Air Force's role in Southwest Asia beginning in 1964 is examined. Includes footage of chemical, psychological and tactical warfare.
US Air Force — *International Historic Films*

Universe, The — 1982
Astronomy/Science
59558   55 mins   C   B, V   P
A comprehensive survey of what man knows today about our solar system and the seemingly infinite number of other systems and galaxies in all of universal space and time.
McGraw Hill — *Mastervision*

Unknown Powers — 1980
Drama/Occult sciences
33806   97 mins   C   B, V   R, P
Samatha Eggar, Jack Palance, Will Geer, Roscoe Lee Brown
Science and drama are combined to examine ESP and Magic. Are they gifts or curses, and how are peoples lives affected by them?
MPAA:PG
International TV Films — *Video Gems*

Unmarried Woman, An — 1978
Drama
44934   124 mins   C   B, V, CED   P
Jill Clayburgh, Alan Bates
A woman must make a new life for herself after her husband suddenly divorces her after seventeen years of marriage.
MPAA:R
20th Century Fox — *CBS/Fox Video*

Unseen, The — 1980
Horror
52951   91 mins   C   B, V   P
Barbara Bach, Sydney Lassick, Stephen Furst
Three young women from a TV station are covering a story in a remote area of California. Before nightfall, two are horribly killed, leaving the third to come face to face with the terror.
Triune Films — *VidAmerica*

Until They Get Me — 1917
Drama
59214   40 mins   B/W   B, V, 3/4U   P
Pauline Starke, directed by Frank Borzage
An extremely rare Frank Borzage feature.
Unknown — *Penguin Video*

Up from the Depths — 1979
Horror
69287   85 mins   C   B, V   P
Sam Bottoms
Something from beneath the ocean is turning the paradise of Hawaii into a nightmare.
MPAA:R
New World Pictures — *Vestron Video*

Up In Smoke — 1979
Comedy
48514   87 mins   C   B, V, LV   R, P
Cheech Marin, Tommy Chong
A pair of free-spirited burn-outs team up for a tongue-in-cheek spoof of sex, drugs, and rock and roll.
MPAA:R
Lou Adler, Lou Lombardo — *Paramount Home Video; RCA VideoDiscs*

Up Pompeii — 1971
Comedy
33642   90 mins   C   B, V   P
Frankie Howard, Patrick Cargill
A sexy, hilarious story in which a servant accidentally gains possession of a scroll containing a plot against Emperor Nero. The conspirators try every means possible to recover the scroll.
MPAA:R
Ned Sherrin — *VCI Home Video*

Up the Sandbox — 1972
Comedy-Drama
66326   98 mins   C   B, V   P
Barbra Streisand, David Selby, Jane Hoffman, Barbara Rhodes
A bored housewife fantasizes about her life in order to avoid facing her mundane existence.
MPAA:R
Warner Bros — *Warner Home Video*

Uproar in Heaven — 1977
Cartoons
73016   100 mins   C   B, V   P
Animated
The Monkey King struggles to defend truth and justice in this animated adaptation from the Chinese novel "Pilgrimage to the West."
MPAA:PG
Shanghai Animation Film Studio — *Sun Video*

Uptown New York — 1932
Romance
08776   92 mins   B/W   B, V, 3/4U   P
Jack Oakie, Shirley Grey, Alexander Carr, Raymond Hatton, Lee Moran
Romance in glamorous New York.
World Wide — *Penguin Video*

Uptown Saturday Night — 1974
Comedy
53525   104 mins   C   B, V   R, P
Sidney Poitier, Bill Cosby, Harry Belafonte, Flip Wilson, Richard Pryor, Calvin Lockhart

     (For Explanation of codes, see USE GUIDE and KEY)

Two working men attempt to recover a stolen lottery ticket from the black underworld after being ripped off at a gambling place.
MPAA:PG
Warner Bros — *Warner Home Video*

Uranium Conspiracy 1978
Adventure
47635   100 mins   C   B, V   P
Fabio Testi, Janet Agren, Assaf Dayan
A secret agent and a mercenary soldier try to stop a shipment of uranium out of Zaire from falling into enemy hands.
MPAA:PG
Noah Films — *Paragon Video Productions*

Urban Cowboy 1980
Drama
54668   135 mins   C   B, V, LV   R, P
John Travolta, Debra Winger, Scott Glenn, Madolyn Smith, Barry Corbin, directed by James Bridges
A young Texas farmer comes to Houston to work in a refinery and learns about life by hanging out at Gilley's, a roadhouse bar. Here he and his friends, dressed in their cowboy gear, drink, fight, and prove their manhood by riding a mechanical bull.
MPAA:PG
Paramount — *Paramount Home Video; RCA VideoDiscs*

Urubamba 1981
Boating
69908   45 mins   C   B, V   P
Wildwater kayaks, two-seat tourers, and a sea raft cover different stretches of the huge Urubamba, the sacred river of the Incas, in Peru.
Unknown — *Gravity Sports Films*

U.S. Army Air Force Report 1943
World War II/Armed Forces-US
53659   50 mins   B/W   B, V, 3/4U   P
The story of U.S. Army Air Force operations in Europe from 1941-43.
US Army — *International Historic Films*

U.S. Crimes in Vietnam 1977
Vietnam War
72530   30 mins   B/W   B, V, 3/4U   P
A Soviet-made film showing alleged massacres committed by the United States military during the Vietnam War.
USSR — *International Historic Films*

U. S. Men's Gymnastics Championship 1981
Gymnastics
59568   60 mins   C   B, V   P
The top male gymnasts in the U.S. compete for the 1981 titles.

CBS; Transworld Intl — *Mastervision*

U.S. Staff Reports Nos. 1-4 1944
World War II
53678   40 mins   B/W   B, V, 3/4U   P
Four U.S. Staff Reports containing from four to nine films each. Available separately. Titles include "New Jap Mines," and "General Marshall in Italy."
Unknown — *International Historic Films*

U.S. War Department Report—July 1943 1943
World War II/Documentary
52372   55 mins   B/W   B, V, 3/4U   P
This government report for war workers makes use of Nazi newsreel footage to illustrate the need for wartime industrial productivity.
US War Department — *International Historic Films*

U.S. Women's Gymnastics Championship 1981
Gymnastics/Women
59569   60 mins   C   B, V   P
The top female gymnasts in the U.S. compete for the 1981 titles.
CBS; Transworld Intl — *Mastervision*

Used Cars 1980
Comedy
51573   113 mins   C   B, V   P
Kurt Russell, Jack Warden, Deborah Harmon
A car dealer is desperate to put his jalopy shop competitors out of business. The owners go to great lengths to stay afloat.
MPAA:R
Columbia Pictures — *RCA/Columbia Pictures Home Video; RCA VideoDiscs*

Users, The 1978
Drama
75495   125 mins   C   B, V   P
Jaclyn Smith, Tony Curtis, John Forsythe, Red Buttons, George Hamilton
A small-town girl meets a faded film star and becomes involved in the movie business.
Aaron Spelling Productions — *Prism*

U.S.S. Nautilus—Operation Sunshine 1963
Documentary
53688   20 mins   C   B, V, 3/4U   P
A documentary look at the Nautilus' historic trip under the North Pole ice cap.
Unknown — *International Historic Films*

U.S.S. VD: Ship of Shame/Red Nightmare   1945
Documentary/World War II
29752   82 mins   B/W   B, V   P
A government training program produced by a major studio detailing the perils of V.D. and the consequences for the men of the ill-fated D.E. 733. WW II vintage.
Unknown — *Budget Video*

Utah   1945
Western
12593   54 mins   B/W   B, V   P
Roy Rogers, Dale Evans
Girl singer inherits a ranch and then tries to sell it.
Republic — *Video Connection; Sheik Video; Discount Video Tapes; Budget Video*

Utah Trail   1938
Western
15459   57 mins   B/W   B, V   P
Tex Ritter
Tex finds himself riding the mysterious and lonely ghost trail.
Grand Natl — *Video Connection; Discount Video Tapes*

Utopia Sampler, The   1983
Music-Performance
64929   11 mins   C   B, V   P
Utopia, featuring Todd Rundgren, performs three songs on this Video 45: "Hammer in My Heart," "You Make Me Crazy" and "Feet Don't Fail Me Now."
Neo-Utopian Laboratories — *Sony Corporation of America*

V

V-Four Victory   1983
Motorcycles
72860   60 mins   C   B, V   P
A motorcycle travels through the Isle of Man Course
C H Wood Production — *Motor Cycle Video*

V-2/German V-2 Rocket Tests   194?
World War II
53390   29 mins   B/W   B, V, 3/4U   P
"V-2" (1946), a U.S. Air Force documentary about post-war experiments with the V-2 Rocket; and "German V-2 Rockets Tests" (Germany, 1944), which includes actual color footage of V-2 tests, with a visit by Himmler.
USA; Germany — *International Historic Films*

Vagabond Lover   1929
Musical
07239   66 mins   B/W   B, V, FO   P
Rudy Vallee, Sally Blane, Marie Dressler
The amusing tale of the loves, hopes, and dreams of an aspiring saxophone player.
RKO — *Video Yesteryear*

Vagabond, The/The Floorwalker/The Rink/The Fireman   1916
Comedy
58906   80 mins   B/W   B, V   P
Charlie Chaplin
Four Chaplin shorts, in which Charlie starred, wrote and directed, between 1916 and 1917. This tape is also available combined with "Easy Street," "The Count," "Behind the Screen" and "The Immigrant."
EL, SP
Mutual — *Ampro Video Productions*

Valley Girl   1983
Comedy
69284   95 mins   C   B, V, LV, CED   P
Nicolas Cage, Deborah Foreman
A typical "valley girl" shocks her peers when she falls for a leather-jacketed freak. Contains music by Men at Work, The Clash, Culture Club and others.
MPAA:R
Wayne Crawford and Andrew Lane — *Vestron Video*

Valley of Fire   1951
Western
63995   63 mins   B/W   B, V   P, T
Gene Autry, Gail Davis, Pat Buttram
Gene is working hard cleaning up the town of Quartz Creek. He decides to import a caravan of brides for the men in town, but a local gambler kidnaps the wagon train.
Columbia — *Blackhawk Films*

Valley of Terror   1938
Western
10071   59 mins   B/W   B, V   P,.T
Kermit Maynard, Rocky the Horse
A James Oliver Curwood saga of the Old West.
Ambassador — *Blackhawk Films*

Vamping   1984
Mystery/Drama
73662   107 mins   C   B, V   R, P
Patrick Duffy, Catherine Hyland
A desperate saxophonist robs a house and winds up in a mysterious menage a trois.
MPAA:R
Howard Kling; Stratton Rawson — *Atlantic Video*

Vampire Bat, The   1932
Horror
47792   69 mins   B/W   B, V   P
Lionel Atwill, Fay Wray, Melvyn Douglas
A vampire bat and its supernatural powers
provide the basis of this suspense-horror story.
Majestic — *Movie Buff Video; Western Film &
Video Inc*

Vampyr   1932
Film-Avant-garde
08594   66 mins   B/W   B, V, 3/4U   P
*Julian West, Sybille Schmitz, Harriet Gerard,
directed by Carl H. Dreyer*
Low-key, experimental approach by Dreyer
makes for an eerie film. Music by Wolfgang
Zeller. Little dialogue.
Germany — *Penguin Video; Video Yesteryear;
Budget Video; Sheik Video; Discount Video
Tapes; Classic Video Cinema Collector's Club*

Van, The   1977
Comedy
48478   90 mins   C   B, V   P
Stuart Gertz, Deborah White
A teenage boy buys a van in hopes it will attract
girls—one in particular—to him.
MPAA:R
Crown International — *VCI Home Video*

Van Nuys Blvd.   1979
Comedy
48479   93 mins   C   B, V   P
Bill Adler, Cynthia Wood
The popular boulevard is the scene where the
cool southern California guys converge for
cruising and girl watching.
MPAA:R
Crown International — *VCI Home Video*

Vanessa   1977
Drama
55253   90 mins   C   B, V   P
The story of an innocent young girl's
introduction to the erotic pleasures of the
Orient.
MPAA:X
Intercontinental Releasing Corp — *VidAmerica*

Vanishing American   1926
Western
55815   114 mins   B/W   B, V   P
*Richard Dix, Noah Beery, directed by George B.
Seitz*
The mistreatment of the American Indian is
depicted in this sweeping Western epic. Musical
score.
Paramount — *Festival Films; Video Yesteryear*

Vanishing Legion, The   1931
Western/Serials
12554   156 mins   B/W   B, V   P
*Frankie Darro, Rin Tin Tin, Jr. Harry Carey,
directed by B. Reeves Eason*
Western serial with outdoor action and gunplay.
Twelve chapters, 13 minutes each.
Mascot — *Video Connection*

Vanishing Point   1971
Drama
08458   98 mins   C   B, V   P
*Barry Newman, Cleavon Little, Gilda Texler,
Dean Jagger*
Ex-racer and former cop sets out to deliver a
souped-up car. Taking pep pills along the way,
he eludes police, meets up with a number of
characters, and finally crashes into a roadblock.
MPAA:PG   EL, SP
20th Century Fox; Cupid
Productions — *CBS/Fox Video*

Vanity Fair   1932
Romance
29685   73 mins   B/W   B, V   P
Myrna Loy, Conway Tearle
A modern-dress version of Thackeray's famous
novel. Myrna Loy portrays Becky Sharpe, an
amoral social climber.
Hollywood — *Movie Buff Video; Sheik Video*

Vanity Fair   1911
Drama
59204   27 mins   B/W   B, V, 3/4U   P
Helen Gardner, Charles Kent, John Bunny
Thackeray's novel about the adventures of an
amoral social climber during the nineteenth
century, in an early silent version.
Unknown — *Penguin Video*

Varan the Unbelievable   1961
Horror
64296   70 mins   B/W   B, V   P
Myron Healy, Tsuruko Kobayashi
A chemical experiment near a small island in the
Japanese archipelago disturbs a prehistoric
monster beneath the water. The awakened
monster spreads terror on the island.
Jerry A. Baerwitz — *VCI Home Video*

Variety   1925
Drama
48728   104 mins   B/W   B, V, FO   P, T
*Emil Jannings, Lya de Putti, Warwick Ward,
directed by E. A. Dupont*
An aging acrobat seduces a young girl. Later, he
kills a man who is interested in the girl. Silent.
Oscar Werndorff, UFA — *Video Yesteryear;
Sheik Video; Classic Video Cinema Collector's
Club*

Vault of Horror, The   1973
Horror
54911   86 mins   C   B, V, 3/4U   P

(For Explanation of codes, see USE GUIDE and KEY)

Terry-Thomas, Curt Jurgens, Glynis Johns, Dawn Addams, Daniel Massey, Tom Baker
A collection of five terrifying tales based on original stories from the E. C. comic books of the 1950's.
MPAA:R
Cinerama Releasing — *Nostalgia Merchant*

Velnio Nuotaka (The Devil's Bride)   1975
Musical
72496   78 mins   C   B, V, 3/4U   P
A popular Lithuanian musical based on the play "Baltargio Malunas" by K. Boruta. English subtitles.
AM Available LI
Lithuanian Film Studios — *International Historic Films*

Venom   1982
Horror
64881   92 mins   C   B, V, CED   P
Sterling Hayden, Klaus Kinski, Sarah Miles
A deadly black mamba is loose in an elegant townhouse.
MPAA:R
Richard R. St. Johns — *Vestron Video*

Vera Cruz   1954
Adventure
65010   94 mins   C   B, V, CED   P
Gary Cooper, Burt Lancaster, Denise Darcel
Two soldiers of fortune become involved in the Mexican War for independence.
United Artists — *CBS/Fox Video*

Verdict, The   1982
Drama
66071   122 mins   C   B, V, LV, CED   P
Paul Newman, James Mason, Charlotte Rampling, Jack Warden, Milo O'Shea, directed by Sidney Lumet
A down-and-out lawyer takes on the system against impossible odds.
MPAA:R
20th Century Fox — *CBS/Fox Video*

Verticus Maximus   1981
Sports-Winter
69905   11 mins   C   B, V   P
This program looks at wintersticking, the newest deep powder craze in the Rockies.
Mick Worthen Productions — *Gravity Sports Films*

Vertigo   1958
Suspense
75018   126 mins   C   B, V, LV, CED   P
James Stewart, Kim Novak, Barbara Bel Geddes, Tom Helmore, directed by Alfred Hitchcock
This is the classic Hitchcock tale of obsession, fear and murder. A private detective is hired to follow a mysterious woman, whom he gradually falls in love with. Music by Bernard Herrmann.
MPAA:PG
Alfred Hitchcock; Paramount — *MCA Home Video*

Very Private Affair, A   1962
Drama
63113   95 mins   C   B, V   P
Marcello Mastroianni, Brigitte Bardot
A movie star finds that she has no privacy from the hordes of fans and newspaper people. The glare of publicity helps to destroy her relationship with a married director.
MGM — *MGM/UA Home Video*

Very Special Christmas, A/Sleeping Beauty   1982
Fairy tales/Christmas
64956   52 mins   C   B, V   P
Animated
A young boy saves Santa from trouble in "A Very Special Christmas." "Sleeping Beauty" is a new version of the classic fairy tale. Both of these animated films are combined on this tape.
Ron Merk — *Unicorn Video*

Very Special Team, A   1982
Football
47715   23 mins   C   B, V, FO   P
Team highlights of the 1981 San Francisco 49ers, who came out of nowhere to win the NFC Championship.
NFL Films — *NFL Films Video*

Vez en la Vida, Una   1949
Musical-Drama
47464   75 mins   B/W   B, V, FO   P
Libertad Lamarque, Luis Aldas, Raimundo Pastore
A young farm girl travels to the big city, where she becomes a nightclub dancer and gets involved with a shady character. Spanish dialogue.
SP
Argentina — *Video Yesteryear*

Viaje Fantastico En Groso   1984
Adventure
72961   108 mins   C   B, V   P
Let go of your imagination and launch into a thrilling adventure and fantasy in this adult-oriented drama.
SP
Foreign — *Unicorn Video*

Vic Braden's Tennis for the Future, Volume 1   1981
Tennis
63428   120 mins   C   B, V   R, P
The first volume of the series covers four tennis fundamentals: forehand, backhand, serve and volley. From Braden's successful PBS program, "Tennis for the Future."
WGBH Education Foundation — *Paramount Home Video*

Vic Braden's Tennis for the Future, Volume 2   1981
Tennis
64500   120 mins   C   B, V   R, P
This segment covers the approach shot (spin and service return), the overhead shot, lob and drop shots, and conditioning.
WGBH Education Foundation — *Paramount Home Video*

Vic Braden's Tennis for the Future, Volume 3   1981
Tennis
68250   120 mins   C   B, V   R, P
This program is rich in useful, hands-on information and demonstrations of technique.
WGBH Education Foundation — *Paramount Home Video*

Vic 'n' Sade   1957
Comedy
47491   15 mins   B/W   B, V, FO   P
Bernadine Flynn, Art Van Harvey, Eddie Gillilan
A TV adaptation of one of radio's most popular programs, featuring the original cast performing in a bare studio setting.
WNBQ Chicago — *Video Yesteryear*

Vice Squad   1982
Drama
63666   97 mins   C   B, V, LV, CED   P
Wings Hauser, Season Hubley, Gary Swanson
A violent and twisted killer-pimp goes on a murderous rampage, and a hooker helps a vice squad plainclothesman trap him.
MPAA:R
Sandy Howard; Frank Capra Jr — *Embassy Home Entertainment*

Victor/Victoria   1982
Comedy
47778   133 mins   C   B, V, CED   P
Julie Andrews, James Garner, Robert Preston, Lesley Ann Warren, Alex Karvas, directedd by Blake Edwards
A down-on-her-luck actress in Depression era Paris impersonates a man impersonating a woman in order to be a show biz success.
MPAA:PG
MGM — *MGM/UA Home Video*

Victoria Regina   1961
Drama
64851   76 mins   C   B, V, 3/4U   P
Julie Harris, James Donald, Felix Aylmer, Pamela Brown, Basil Rathbone, directed by George Schaefer
In a succession of vignettes, the life of Queen Victoria is viewed, from her ascension to the throne of England in 1837 through the celebration of her Diamond Jubilee. A presentation from "George Schaefer's Showcase Theatre."
Emmy Awards '61: Program of the Year; Outstanding Single Performance/Actress (Harris); Outstanding Performance in Supporting Role/Actress (Brown).
George Schaefer — *Enter-Tel Inc*

Victory   1981
Drama
53553   120 mins   C   B, V, CED   P
Sylvester Stallone, Michael Caine, Max von Sydow, Pele, Carole Laure, Bobby Moore, directed by John Huston
A soccer match between WW II American prisoners of war and a German team is set up so that the players can escape through the sewer tunnels of Paris.
MPAA:PG
Freddie Fields — *CBS/Fox Video*

Victory at Sea   1960
World War II/Documentary
29437   98 mins   B/W   B, V   R, P
Narrated by Alexander Scourby
This is a condensation of the classic television series which portrayed the exploits of the U.S. Navy during World War II. Its impressive musical score was composed by Richard Rodgers.
NBC — *Warner Home Video; RCA VideoDiscs*

Vida Sigue Igual, La   19??
Drama
66413   102 mins   C   B, V   P
Julio Iglesias, Jean Harrington
A famous singer turned soccer player is severely injured in an auto accident. His life and career depend on whether he will ever walk again. Dialogue in Spanish.
SP
Spanish — *Media Home Entertainment*

Vida Sigue Igual, La   197?
Drama
52796   102 mins   C   B, V   P
Jean Harrington, Charo Lopez
An up-and-coming law student and soccer player becomes paralyzed in an auto accident and must contend with a change of attitude from his friends and lover.
SP
Star Films; Filmayer Produccion — *Media Home Entertainment*

Video Aerobics — 1979
Physical fitness
59306   57 mins   C   B, V   P
Instructors Susie Murphy and Leslie Lilian demonstrate a complete conditioning routine which includes aerobic exercises for all areas of the body. Contains both a 17-minute beginners program and a challenging 40-minute advanced session.
Amstar Productions — *Vestron Video; Amstar Productions*

Video Aquarium — 1982
Video
63139   60 mins   C   B, V   P
This environmental video program consists of an hour of tropical fish swimming in an aquarium to provide a relaxed and tranquil background.
Video Naturals — *Video Naturals*

Video Astrology 1984 — 1984
Astrology
69685   90 mins   C   B, V   P
Gayle Sellers 12 pgms
Each program in this series outlines the personal year for one astrological sign and covers all areas of life experience. Programs are available individually.
1.Aquarius 2.Pisces 3.Aries 4.Taurus 5.Gemini 6.Cancer 7.Leo 8.Virgo 9.Libra 10.Scorpio 11.Sagittarius 12.Capricorn
Mark XII — *Mark XII Video*

Video Dictionary of Classical Ballet, The — 1983
Dance
76676   270 mins   C   B, V, 3/4U   P
Merrill Ashley, Denise Jackson, Kevin MacKenzie, Georgina Parkinson
An index to over 800 ballet steps. All steps are clearly written and numbered on the tape and correspondingly indicated in the accompanying booklet, enabling the viewer to find any step with ease. On four cassettes.
AM Available
Kultur — *Kultur*

Video Dictionary of Classical Ballet, The — 1984
Dance
66609   270 mins   C   B, V, 3/4U   P
Merrill Ashley, Kevin MacKenzie, Denise Jackson, Georgina Parkinson
Three of the most outstanding principal dancers of leading American ballet companies demonstrate the complete language of ballet in this program. More than 800 variations in international Russian, French and Cecchetti styles are illustrated to piano accompaniment, with many movements shown in slow motion with multiple camera angles.
AM Available

First Ballet Inc — *Kultur*

Video Fireplace — 1982
Video
63138   60 mins   C   B, V   P
A wood-burning fire ablaze in a red brick hearth is focused on for sixty minutes, providing a relaxed and tranquil background.
Video Naturals — *Video Naturals*

Video S.A.T. Review, The — 1983
Education
69695   120 mins   C   B, V   P
This interactive program helps student prepare for the SAT. The verbal section reviews the 4 types of questions found on the SAT and strategies for answering each. The math section reviews general mathematics, algebra and geometry. The final segment deals with test-taking and test anxiety.
AM Available
Dial Productions; Charlotte Dial — *Dial Productions*

Video System Test Tape, The — 1982
Video
73543   10 mins   C   B, V   P
This program shows how to test your TV and VCR systems
Admit One — *Admit One Video*

Video Wallpaper — 1978
Video/Arts
54676   30 mins   C   B, V, 3/4U   P
14 pgms
Each program in this series is a scene of a particular environment, designed to relieve stress. They contain soothing picture composition, flowing and rhythmic motion, specific color and natural sound. The programs are available individually.
1.Flowing Falls 2.Thoughts by the Ocean 3.The Gold Coast 4.Reflections 5.Shipwreck Beach 6.Clouds of Peace 7.Flowering Sea 8.Blue Sky, Blue Sea 9.Palm Tree Beach 10.Afternoon Delight 11.The Stream Flows Home 12.The Stream on Dad's Birthday 13.The Sea 14.The Rock
Nebulae Prods — *Nebulae Productions*

Video Yesterbloop — 197?
Outtakes and bloopers
57363   81 mins   C   B, V, FO   P
A few sections in black and white. A collection of bloopers from TV, including "Steve Allen Show," "All My Children," "The Price Is Right," "Happy Days," "Mork and Mindy," and "One Day at a Time." Quality is not perfect. Contains some nudity and strong language.

ABC et al — *Video Yesteryear*

Videocise (A Total Body Workout)   1982
Physical fitness
64302   24 mins   C   B, V   P
This is a total body workout for men and women of all ages. Three instructors perform eight routines beginning with a warm-up and ending with a cool-down. Background music includes pop, reggae, jazz and country. A paced workout—not too fast.
Glenda Facemire — *VideoVision Inc*

Videodrome   1983
Science fiction/Horror
64788   87 mins   C   B, V, LV   P
Deborah Harry, James Woods, directed by David Cronenberg
This film dramatizes what it would be like if television took over the world. Stars Deborah Harry, lead singer of the rock group Blondie. Special effects by Rick Baker (''An American Werewolf in London'').
Universal — *MCA Home Video*

Videotrivia, Volume I   1984
Games
75930   60 mins   C   B, V   P
This program presents the home video cassette of one of America's most popular games, wherein players' knowledge is tested on the most trivial of subjects.
Best Film and Video Co — *Best Film & Video Corporation*

Vie Continue, La   1982
Drama
64241   93 mins   C   B, V   P
Annie Giradot, Jean-Pierre Cassel, Michel Aumont, directed by Moshe Mizrahi
A woman suddenly finds herself alone after 20 years, following the death of her husband. Dubbed in English.
Cineproduction/SFPC — *RCA/Columbia Pictures Home Video*

Vietnam   1978
Vietnam War
70049   60 mins   C   B, V, 3/4U   P
A Soviet-made documentary about the reconstruction of Vietnam, particularly the reestablishment of the economy after the war.
USSR — *International Historic Films*

Vietnam: Chronicle of a War   1981
Vietnam War/Documentary
52746   88 mins   C   B, V   P
Narrated by Walter Cronkite, Dan Rather, Morley Safer, Charles Collingwood, Charles Kuralt, Mike Wallace, Eric Sevareid

Drawing upon the resources of the CBS News Archives, this CBS News Collectors Series program presents a retrospective portrait of American military involvement as witnessed by on-the-scene correspondents and camera crews. Some portions are in black-and-white.
CBS News — *CBS/Fox Video*

Vietnam Report   196?
Vietnam War/Propaganda
53711   32 mins   B/W   B, V, 3/4U   P
A report by Soviet correspondents about what effects U.S. bombing raids are having on North Vietnam.
USSR — *International Historic Films*

Vietnam: The Bombing   1969
Vietnam War/Armed Forces-US
72513   59 mins   C   B, V, 3/4U   P
The air war launched over Vietnam is examined through on-the-spot interviews with American pilots, bombadiers and navigators. Footage of fighters and bombers taking off and landing highlight the film.
US Army — *International Historic Films*

Vietnamese Cultures and Customs   1969
Vietnam War
72489   110 mins   C   B, V, 3/4U   P
An American professor discusses the politics and war strategies of the Vietnamese in a direct lecture with no accompanying footage.
US Government — *International Historic Films*

Vigilante   1983
Drama
64900   91 mins   C   B, V   P
Robert Forster
A frustrated ex-cop, tired of seeing criminals returned to the street, joins a vigilante squad dedicated to law and order.
Artists Releasing Corp — *Vestron Video*

Vigilantes Are Coming, The   19??
Adventure/Serials
12560   230 mins   B/W   B, V   P
Bob Livingston, Kay Hughes, Quinn 'Big Boy' Williams, directed by Mack V. Wright, Ray Taylor
''The Eagle'' sets out to revenge his family and upsets the plot of a would-be dictator to establish an empire in California. In twelve chapters—first is 32 minutes, each additional chapter is 18 minutes.
Republic — *Video Connection; Nostalgia Merchant*

Vigilantes of Boom Town   1946
Western
08898   54 mins   B/W   B, V, 3/4U   P
Allan 'Rocky' Lane, Bobby Blake

Senator's daughter thinks prize fighting is a disgrace.
Republic — *Penguin Video; Video Connection; Nostalgia Merchant*

Village of the Damned   1960
Science fiction
64572   78 mins   B/W   B, V, CED   P
George Sanders, Barbara Shelley, Martin Stephens, Laurence Naismith
A group of unusual children in a small English village are found to be the vanguard of an alien invasion.
MGM — *MGM/UA Home Video*

**Village that Refused to   1962
Die, The**
Documentary/Vietnam War
72488   56 mins   B/W   B, V, 3/4U   P
A group of Chinese refugees set up a village under the leadership of a Catholic priest despite continual raids by the Viet Cong.
US Government — *International Historic Films*

**Villain Still Pursued Her,   1941
The**
Comedy
08731   67 mins   B/W   B, V, 3/4U   P
Anita Louise, Alan Mowbray, Buster Keaton, Hugh Herbert
Old-fashioned melodrama; poor hero and rich villain vie for the sweet heroine.
RKO — *Movie Buff Video; Penguin Video; Video Yesteryear*

**Vincent Van Gogh: A   1983
Portrait in Two Parts**
Artists
66147   120 mins   C   LV   P
Hosted by Leonard Nimoy
Part One: A play, "Vincent," starring Leonard Nimoy; Part Two: Five overview chapters that explore the major periods of Van Gogh's life.
Guthrie Theater; ABC Video Enterprises; Magnavox Prods — *North American Philips Corporation*

Vintage Cartoon Holiday   194?
Cartoons
72524   60 mins   C   B, V, 3/4U   P
A tape of eight cartoons from the major animation studios of the 1930's and 40's that cannot be shown on TV because of extreme violence, racial slurs or ethnic stereotypes; from the Fleischer Brothers, Warners and Ub Iwerks.
Warner Bros; Fleischer Bros — *International Historic Films*

Vintage Commercials   1980
Advertising/Comedy
29733   60 mins   C   B, V, 3/4U   P

Dick Van Dyke, Mary Tyler Moore, Ernie Kovacs, Andy Griffith, Danny Thomas, Lucille Ball
A package of commercials from the 1950's and 1960's, all featuring top TV celebrities such as The Monkees, Lucille Ball and Desi Arnaz, Ozzie and Harriet, and the Flintstones, selling everything from cigarettes to orange juice. Some segments in black and white.
CBS et al — *Shokus Video*

Vintage Commercials, II   1982
Advertising/Comedy
47612   60 mins   C   B, V, 3/4U   P
Buster Keaton, The Three Stooges, Lucille Ball, Desi Arnaz, Jack Benny, Steve Allen, Jay North, Ernie Kovacs
An hour of classic television commercials from the 50's, 60's and early 70's. A number of spots featuring celebrities are included, pitching for such products as Skippy Peanut Butter, Ipana, Westinghouse, Alka Seltzer, Bosco, Quik, Seven-Up and Kool-Aid. Some segments are in black and white.
CBS et al — *Shokus Video*

Vintage Commercials, III   1983
Advertising/Documentary
66461   60 mins   B/W   B, V, 3/4U   P
Lucille Ball, Desi Arnaz, Hillary Brooke, Andy Devine, Dwayne Hickman
Another hour of classic TV commercials, mostly from the 1950's, is featured with many celebrity spokespersons. Also on this tape is a newsreel highlighting the beginnings of commercial television broadcasting at the 1939 New York World's Fair.
CBS et al — *Shokus Video*

Vintage Sitcoms   195?
Comedy
53048   100 mins   B/W   B, V, 3/4U   P
Jackie Gleason, Gale Storm, Charles Farrell, George Burns, Gracie Allen, Jackie Cooper
Four top situation comedies from the 1940's and 1950's: "The Life of Riley" (1949), starring Jackie Gleason as Chester A. Riley; "My Little Margie" (1952), starring Gale Storm and Charles Farrell as daughter and father; "The Burns and Allen Show" (1952), a classic episode involving Gracie's party plans; "The People's Choice" (1955), starring Jackie Cooper and his dog "Cleo."
NBC; CBS — *Shokus Video*

Vintage Steam   1979
Trains
55526   60 mins   C   B, V   P
This look at vintage steam engines features a Cook 4-4-0 (built in 1888) of the Sierra R.R. paired up with a Ten Wheeler No. 3, and the Shay and Heisler logging steam engines.
De Luz Video — *De Luz Video*

Violent Professionals   1982
Crime-Drama
72213   90 mins   C   B, V   P
After the police commissioner is murdered, his old friend runs into resistance inside and outside the force when he investigates.
Unknown — *Paragon Video Productions*

Violent Years, The   1952
Drama
73554   80 mins   B/W   B, V   P
An all girl gang go out and attack lonely service station attendants and couples parked in lovers' lanes.
Independent — *Admit One Video*

Viridiana   1961
Drama
57343   90 mins   B/W   B, V   P
Directed by Luis Bunuel
This ironic, biting drama portrays a young girl about to take her holy vows, but the suicide of her beloved uncle causes her to forsake the church and return to his farm with a horde of beggars and derelicts who turn her well intended charity into a nightmare. Spanish with English subtitles.
Cannes Film Festival '61: Grand Prize Co-Winner. SP
Spain; Mexico — *Budget Video; Sheik Video; Discount Video Tapes*

Virtue's Revolt   1924
Drama
48714   50 mins   B/W   B, V, 3/4U   P
Edith Thornton, Crauford Kent
A little girl with high hopes remains undaunted by the scheming managers, lecherous stage managers, and assistants surrounding her career. Silent.
William Steiner Prods — *Penguin Video*

Virus   1982
Drama/Science fiction
65369   102 mins   C   B, V   P
George Kennedy, Glenn Ford, Robert Vaughn, Chuck Connors, Olivia Hussey
"Virus" is a revealing look at both man's genius for self-destruction and his super-human determination to carry on life and hope in a destroyed world.
MPAA:PG
Haruki Kadokawa — *Media Home Entertainment*

Visions of Faith   1955
Religion/Music
59090   70 mins   B/W   B, V, FO   P
Saint Luke's Choristers
A collection of hymns with visuals showing "God's handiwork." Hymns include: "Father of Mercies," "I Wonder As I Wander," "Jesus My Lord, My God, My All," " The Hallelujah Chorus," "O Divine Redemmer," and others.
USA — *Video Yesteryear*

Visiting Hours   1982
Suspense
63392   101 mins   C   B, V, CED   P
Lee Grant, William Shatner, Linda Purl, Michael Ironside
An outspoken television journalist delivers a controversial editorial on women's rights. She is consequently brutally attacked by an angered viewer.
MPAA:R
20th Century Fox — *CBS/Fox Video*

Viva Las Vegas   1963
Musical
59137   85 mins   C   B, V, CED   P
Elvis Presley, Ann-Margret, William Demarest, Jack Carter, Cesare Danova, Nicky Blair, directed by George Sidney
A sports car enthusiast and his friend go to Las Vegas for the Grand Prix where they both fall for a swimming instructor.
MGM — *MGM/UA Home Video*

Viva Max   1969
Comedy
47994   93 mins   C   B, V   P
Peter Ustinov, Jonathan Winters, John Astin, Pamela Tiffin, Keenan Wynn, directed by Jerry Paris
A modern-day Mexican general and his men fake their way across the Alamo.
Montmorency Prods — *NTA Home Entertainment*

Vivacious Lady   1938
Comody
00289   90 mins   B/W   B, V, 3/4U   P, T
Ginger Rogers, James Stewart, James Ellison
Romantic comedy about a young college professor who marries a chorus girl.
RKO; Pandro S Berman — *Blackhawk Films; Nostalgia Merchant*

Voice from the Screen, The   1926
Film-History/Technology
58659   34 mins   B/W   B, V, FO   P
An address by Edward B. Craft, Executive Vice President of Bell Telephone Laboratories, presented before the New York Electrical Society, in which he discusses the "new Vitaphone Sound-Film system." An original demonstration of the first commercially viable method of adding sound to motion pictures.
Vitaphone — *Video Yesteryear*

Volcano 1976
Drama/Biographical
65465 ? mins C B, V P
Narrated by Donald Britlain and Richard Burton
A painful but extraordinary portrait of writer
Malcolm Lowry, author of "Under the Volcano,"
which explores his battle with alcohol and the
guilt that followed the success of this novel. In
Beta Hi-Fi.
Almi Release — *RCA/Columbia Pictures
Home Video*

Von Ryan's Express 1965
War-Drama
08426 117 mins C B, V P
*Frank Sinatra, Trevor Howard, Brad Dexter,
Edward Mulhare, directed by Mark Robson*
American Air Force Colonel leads a group of
prisoners of war in taking control of a freight
train.
EL, SP
20th Century Fox; Saul David — *CBS/Fox
Video*

Voyage en Ballon 1959
Adventure
74088 82 mins C B, V P
This is the delightful story of a young boy who
stowsaway on his grandfather's hot air balloon.
Film Sonor; Film Montsouris — *Embassy
Home Entertainment*

Voyage of the Damned 1977
Drama/World War II
46150 134 mins C B, V P
*Faye Dunaway, Max von Sydow, Oskar Werner,
Malcolm McDowell, Orson Welles, James
Mason, Lee Grant, Katherine Ross, Ben
Gazzara*
The story of one of the most tragic incidents of
World War II: the flight of 937 German-Jewish
refugees bound for Cuba aboard the Hamburg-
Amerika liner S.S. St. Louis. Based on Gordon
Thomas' and Max Morgan-Witts' novel of the
same title.
MPAA:G
Robert Fryer, Avco Embassy — *CBS/Fox
Video*

W

**Wackiest Wagon Train in
the West, The** 1977
Western/Comedy
53942 86 mins C B, V R, P
Bob Denver, Forrest Tucker, Jeannine Riley
A hapless wagon master is saddled with a
dummy assistant as they guide a party of five
characters across the West.
MPAA:G

Topar Films — *Media Home Entertainment*

Wacko 1983
Comedy
65219 84 mins C B, V P
*Stella Stevens, George Kennedy, Joe Don
Baker*
A group of nymphets and tough guys get caught
up in a wild Halloween-pumpkin-lawnmower
murder.
MPAA:PG
Michael R Starita — *Vestron Video*

Wacky and Packy 1975
Cartoons
73562 70 mins C B, V P
Animated
A caveman and his pachyderm run amok in the
modern world causing trouble wherever the pair
travel.
Filmation Studios — *Prism*

**Wacky World of Mother
Goose, The** 1967
Cartoons
08521 81 mins C B, V, CED P
Animated, voice of Margaret Rutherford
All the familiar Mother Goose characters
brought together in a delightful tale of secret
agents and sinister surprises.
Avco Embassy; Arthur Rankin, Jr. — *Embassy
Home Entertainment*

Wages of Fear 1955
Drama
06243 138 mins B/W B, V P
*Yves Montand, Charles Vanel, Peter Van Eyck,
directed by Henri-Georges Clouzot*
Realistic drama of disastrous oil well explosion
in Central America. French film, dubbed in
English.
Hal Roach Dist; DCA — *Movie Buff Video;
Budget Video; Video Yesteryear; Western Film
& Video Inc; Discount Video Tapes*

Wagon Tracks 1919
Western
64338 60 mins B/W B, V P
William S. Hart
A wagontrain guide sets off on the trail of his
brother's killer, an unscrupulous river gambler.
Silent with musical score.
William S. Hart Productions — *Classic Video
Cinema Collector's Club*

Wagon Trail 1935
Western
15504 59 mins B/W B, V P
Harry Carey
The sheriff's son is blackmailed into helping a
gang of robbers.

Ajax — *Video Connection; Penguin Video*

Wagonmaster 1950
Western
00291 85 mins B/W B, V, 3/4U P
Ben Johnson, Joanne Dru, directed by John Ford
Roving cowboys join a group of Mormons in their trek across the western frontier.
RKO — *Nostalgia Merchant*

Wait Until Dark 1967
Suspense
58255 105 mins C B, V R, P
Audrey Hepburn, Alan Arkin, Richard Crenna, Efrem Zimbalist Jr., Jack Weston
A photographer unwittingly smuggles a drug-filled doll into New York, and his blind wife, alone in their apartment, is terrorized by murderous crooks in search of it.
Warner Bros — *Warner Home Video*

Waitress 1981
Comedy
63357 85 mins C B, V R, P
Jim Harris, Carol Drake, Carol Bever
Three beautiful girls are waitresses in a crazy restaurant where the chef gets drunk, the kitchen explodes, and the customers riot.
Troma Productions — *THORN EMI Home Video*

Wake of the Red Witch, The 1948
Adventure
59091 106 mins B/W B, V P
John Wayne, Gail Russell, Gig Young
This South Sea saga pits an adventurous sea captain against a shipping magnate with a fortune of pearls and a beautiful woman at stake.
Republic — *NTA Home Entertainment*

Wake Up the Echoes 1982
Football
63165 52 mins C B, V, FO P
George Gipp, Knute Rockne, Frank Leahy, Ara Parseghian, Joe Theisman, Joe Montana, Jim Crowley
Highlights from 60 years of Notre Dame Football history are on this tape, from rare footage shot in 1913 to 1966's "Game of the Century" against Michigan State. Some sequences are in black and white.
NFL Films — *NFL Films Video*

Walt Disney Christmas, A 1982
Cartoons/Christmas
53798 45 mins C B, V R, P
Animated
Six classic cartoons with a wintry theme are combined for this program: "Pluto's Christmas Tree" (1952), "On Ice," "Donald's Snowball Fight;" two Silly Symphonies from 1932-33: "Santa's Workshop" and "The Night Before Christmas" and an excerpt from the 1948 feature "Melody Time," entitled "Once Upon a Wintertime."
Walt Disney Prods — *Walt Disney Home Video*

Waltz Across Texas 1983
Drama
65382 100 mins C B, V P
The story of a young couple whose mutual dislike for each other turns romantic as they are joined in a quest to discover oil in west Texas.
Martin Jurow — *Vestron Video*

Wanderers, The 1979
Drama
52712 113 mins C B, V R, P
Ken Wahl, John Friedrich, Karen Allen, Linda Manz, directed by Philip Kaufman
Richard Price's novel about youth gangs coming of age in the Bronx in 1963. The "Wanderers" are a non-violent gang about to graduate high school, prowling the Bronx with the feeling that something is slipping away from them.
MPAA:R
Orion Pictures — *Warner Home Video*

War and Peace 1967
Drama
47752 360 mins C B, V P
Tolstoy's classic tale of a Russian family's adventures at the time of Napoleon's invasion. On four cassettes.
Masfilm — *The Video Station; Festival Films*

War Comes to America 1945
World War II/Documentary
50617 67 mins B/W B, V, 3/4U, FO P
Directed by Frank Capra
An overview of American heritage, emphasizing the events which forced us to fight for survival. Frank Capra's philosophy paints a loving portrait of the American. Part of the "Why We Fight" series, contained on two cassettes.
US War Department — *Western Film & Video Inc; Budget Video; Discount Video Tapes*

War Department Film Communiques Nos. 1-3 1943
World War II
53679 40 mins B/W B, V, 3/4U P
Three compilations of short wartime films such as "Fifth Army in Italy" and "American Ships." Each program contains from four to nine films and are available separately.
Unknown — *International Historic Films*

War Game, The   1965
Nuclear warfare/Documentary
02964   49 mins   B/W   B, V   P
Written and directed by Peter Watkins
This powerful semi-documentary shows the
terrible aftermath of a nuclear war in Britain.
Academy Award '66: Best Documentary.
BBC; British Film Institute — *Budget Video;
International Historic Films; Festival Films;
Western Film & Video Inc.*

War Games   1983
Drama
Closed Captioned
65415   110 mins   C   B, V, LV,   P
                   CED
*Mathew Broderick, Dabney Coleman, John
Wood, Ally Sheedy*
An extremely bright young man, thinking that
he's sneaking an advance look at a new line of
video games, breaks into the country's Norod
missile-defense system and challenges it to a
game of global thermonuclear warfare.
MPAA:PG
Harold Schneider — *CBS/Fox Video; RCA
VideoDiscs*

War in the Sky   1982
World War II/Documentary
59356   90 mins   C   B, V   R, P
*Directed by William Wyler, Lloyd Bridges, James
Stewart, narrated by Peter Lawford*
Director William Wyler's account of the Army Air
Corps in action. Extraordinary footage of the
Thunderbolt, the P47 Fighter, and the B17
Bomber.
US Office of War Information — *Video Gems*

War of the Wildcats   1943
Western
59093   102 mins   B/W   B, V   P
John Wayne, Martha Scott, Albert Dekker
Western action with the Duke as a tough oil
wildcatter battling a powerful land baron.
Republic — *NTA Home Entertainment*

War of the Worlds, The   1953
Science fiction
38617   85 mins   C   B, V, LV   R, P
Gene Barry, Ann Robinson, Les Tremayne
H.G. Wells' classic novel of the invasion of
Earth by Martians, updated to 1950's California,
with spectacular special effects depicting the
destruction caused by the Martian war
machines.
Academy Awards '53: Special Effects.
Paramount — *Paramount Home Video; RCA
VideoDiscs*

War Wagon, The   1967
Western
65122   101 mins   C   B, V   P
*John Wayne, Kirk Douglas, Howard Keel,
Robert Walker Jr., Keenan Wynn, Bruce Dern,
directed by Burt Kennedy*
Two cowboys and an Indian plot to ambush the
gold-laden armored stagecoach of a ruthless
cattle baron.
Universal — *MCA Home Video*

War Years—The Forties,   194?
The
World War II/Documentary
10149   ? mins   B/W   B, V   P, T
Film covers Hitler, Stalin, Churchill, MacArthur,
the Battle of the Bulge, Nuremberg war trials,
and Harry Truman.
Unknown — *Blackhawk Films*

Warlock Moon   1975
Horror
66107   75 mins   C   B, V   P
Laurie Walters, Joe Spano
A young woman is lured to a secluded spa and
falls prey to a coven of witches.
EL, SP
Cintel Prod — *Unicorn Video*

Warlords of the 21st   1982
Century
Science fiction/Adventure
65075   91 mins   C   B, V, CED   P
*Michael Beck, Annie McEnroe, James
Wainwright*
A gang of bandits who speed around the galaxy
in an indestructible battle cruiser are challenged
by a fearless space lawman.
Lloyd Phillips; Rob Whitehouse — *Embassy
Home Entertainment*

Warner Brothers Cartoon   194?
Festival I
Cartoons
12578   55 mins   C   B, V   P
Includes "Corny Concerto," "Dover Boys,"
"Hamateur Night', "Wackiki Wabbit', "Tale of
Two Kitties', "Daffy and the Dinosaur," and
"Falling Hare."
Warner Brothers — *Budget Video; Discount
Video Tapes*

Warner Brothers Cartoon   194?
Festival II
Cartoons
12579   55 mins   C   B, V   P
Includes "Wacky Wabbit," "Daffy the
Commando," "Case of the Missing Hare,"
"Jungle Jitters," "All This and Rabbit Stew',
"Have You Got Any Castiles', "Fresh Hare,"
and "Inki and the Mina Bird."
Warner Brothers — *Budget Video; Discount
Video Tapes*

Warner Brothers Cartoon Festival III   194?
Cartoons
12580   55 mins   C   B, V   P
Includes "Robinhood Makes Good', "Flop Goes the Weasel," "Fony Fables," "Pigs in a Polka," "Fox Pop," "Fifth Column Mouse," and "Wabbit Who Came to Supper."
Warner Brothers — *Budget Video; Discount Video Tapes*

Warner Brothers Cartoon Festival IV   194?
Cartoons
53804   55 mins   C   B, V   P
Animated
Eight cartoons are included in this package, including "Presto Change-O," "Porky's Bare Facts," "Get Rich Quick, Porky," "Finn 'N Catty," "Sheepish Wolf," "Yankee Doodle Daffy," "Porky's Railroad," and "Bugs Bunny Bond Rally."
Warner Bros — *Budget Video; Discount Video Tapes*

Warner Brothers Cartoons   195?
Cartoons
53801   54 mins   C   B, V, FO   P
Animated
Included in this collection are "The Wabbit Who Came to Supper" (1942), "A Tale of Two Kitties" (1948), "Case of the Missing Hare" (1942), "Hamateur Night" (1938), "Wackiki Wabbit" (1953), "Daffy Duck and the Dinosaur" (1939), and "Fresh Hare" (1942).
Warner Bros — *Video Yesteryear*

Warning Shadows   1922
Film-History
48727   60 mins   B/W   B, V, 3/4U   P
A film which was acclaimed for its cinematic style. The post-World War I and pre-World War II attitudes of Germany are portrayed. Silent.
Unknown — *Penguin Video; Classic Video Cinema Collector's Club*

Warren Zevon   1982
Music-Performance
75924   68 mins   C   B, V   P
This program presents Warren Zevon performing his hit songs in concert.
Front Line — *Sony Corporation of America*

Warriors of the Wasteland   1983
Drama
65750   92 mins   C   B, V   R, P
Fred Williamson
In the year 2019 when the world has been devastated by a nuclear war, the few survivors try to reach a distant land which emits radio signals indicating the presence of human life but are hindered by attacks from the fierce Templars, led by a self-styled priest called One.
MPAA:R
Fabrizio De Angelis — *THORN EMI Home Video*

Warriors, The   1979
Drama
38937   94 mins   C   B, V, LV   R, P
Michael Beck, James Remer, Deborah Van Valkenburgh
A contemporary action story about a war between New York City street gangs that rages from Coney Island to the Bronx.
MPAA:R
Paramount — *Paramount Home Video*

Washington Affair, The   1977
Drama
66048   90 mins   C   B, V, CED   P
Tom Selleck, Carol Lynley, Barry Sullivan
A tale of intrigue and blackmail in the nation's capital.
MPAA:PG
Walter G O'Conner — *Embassy Home Entertainment*

Washington Square   1959
Variety
69578   59 mins   B/W   B, V, FO   P
Ray Bolger, Vera-Ellen, Jose Greco, Richard Haydn, Kay Armen
This musical variety show is set against the backdrop of New York's Greenwich village, featuring song, dance and comedy. Originally telecast in May, 1959.
NBC — *Video Yesteryear*

Wasn't That a Time!   1981
Music/Documentary
64566   78 mins   C   B, V, CED   P
Pete Seeger, Fred Hellerman, Lee Hays, Ronnie Gilbert, Don McLean, Arlo Guthrie, Holly Near, Mary Travers
A documentary about the 1980 Carnegie Hall reunion concert by the Weavers, the nationally famous folk singing group of the 1950's whose popularity was ruined by the blacklist of the McCarthy era. Songs include "Kisses Sweeter than Wine," "If I Had a Hammer" and "This Land Is Your Land."
MPAA:PG
Jim Brown Productions; UA Classics — *MGM/UA Home Video*

Watch Me When I Kill   1981
Drama/Suspense
65751   95 mins   C   B, V   R, P
Richard Stewart, Sylvia Kramer
A young nightclub dancer stops by a drugstore seconds after the owner was killed. She doesn't

see the killer's face, but his rasping voice remains to torment her.
MPAA:R
Herman Cohen — *THORN EMI Home Video*

Watch Mr. Wizard   195?
Science/Television
52461   30 mins   B/W   B, V, FO   P
Don Herbert (Mr. Wizard)
This popular children's science show of the 1950's and 60's demonstrated interesting scientific experiments for young people to do. In this episode, Mr. Wizard tells his young assistant how to make bombs.
NBC — *Video Yesteryear*

Watched   1973
Suspense
73035   95 mins   C   B, V   P
Stacy Keach
A former U.S. attorney has a nervous breakdown and kills a narcotics agent.
Palmyra Films — *Vestron Video*

Watcher in the Woods, The   1981
Suspense/Science fiction
59319   83 mins   C   B, V   P
Bette Davis, Carroll Baker, David McCallum, directed by John Hough
When a family moves to an English country house, their children encounter something frightening in the woods.
MPAA:PG
Walt Disney Prods — *Walt Disney Home Video*

Watching Birds   1983
Birds
66148   52 mins   C   B, V   P
Hosted by Roger Tory Peterson
Over 200 species are shown in natural surroundings in this video introduction to bird watching.
Houghton Mifflin; Metromedia Producers Corp — *Houghton Mifflin Company*

Water Rustlers   1939
Western
08605   55 mins   B/W   B, V, 3/4U   P
Dorothy Paige, Dave O'Brien, directed by Samuel Diege
An unscrupulous land baron builds a dam on his side of the Silver Creek with the intention of drying out the cattle pastures.
Grand National — *Penguin Video; Video Connection*

Watership Down   1978
Fantasy
53526   92 mins   C   B, V   R, P
Animated, directed by Martin Rosen

Richard Adam's allegorical novel about how a group of rabbits escape fear and overcome oppression while searching for a new and better home is the basis for this animated film.
MPAA:PG
Nepenthe Productions — *Warner Home Video; RCA VideoDiscs*

Wavelength   1983
Drama
65393   87 mins   C   B, V   P
Robert Carradine
A rock star living in the Hollywood Hills with his girlfriend stumbles on an ultrasecret government project involving aliens from outerspace recovered from a recent unidentified flying object crash site. The FBI, CIA, NASA and the Army Intelligence combine all their resources to find and destroy them.
MPAA:PG
James Rosenfield — *Embassy Home Entertainment*

Waxworks   1924
Horror
64314   93 mins   B/W   B, V   P
Conrad Veidt, Emil Jannings, Werner Kraus, directed by Paul Leni
A poet in a carnival waxwork museum dreams up three frightening tales about Haroun al Raschid, Jack the Ripper and Ivan the Terrible. Silent with musical score.
Neptun - Film — *Classic Video Cinema Collector's Club*

Way Down East   1920
Drama/Film-History
08710   119 mins   B/W   B, V   P
Lillian Gish, Richard Barthelmess, Lowell Sherman, Creighton Hale, directed by D. W. Griffith
The story of a country girl who is tricked into a fake marriage by a scheming playboy. The final sequence is in color, and this tape includes the original Griffith-approved musical score.
United Artists — *Glenn Video Vistas; Penguin Video; Sheik Video; Video Yesteryear; Western Film & Video Inc; Discount Video Tapes*

Way of the West   1935
Western
58507   52 mins   B/W   B, V, 3/4U   P
Wally Wales, William Desmond, Art Mix, Jim Sheridan
Bad guys shoot the sheriff and take it on the lam.
First Division — *Penguin Video; Discount Video Tapes*

Way Out West   1937
Comedy
33906   65 mins   B/W   B, V, 3/4U   P

     (For Explanation of codes, see USE GUIDE and KEY)

Stan Laurel, Oliver Hardy, Sharon Lynne, James Finlayson, Rosina Lawrence
The boys travel westward to deliver a mine deed to the daughter of a recently departed friend. A crooked saloonkeeper tries to swindle them.
Hal Roach, MGM — *Nostalgia Merchant; Blackhawk Films*

Way Out West   1937
Comedy
63991   87 mins   B/W   B, V   P, T
Stan Laurel, Oliver Hardy, Rosina Lawrence, Jimmy Finlayson, Sharon Lynne
The boys travel out West to deliver the deed to a gold mine to the daughter of their late prospector friend. Also included on this tape is a 1932 Thelma Todd—ZaSu Pitts short, "Red Noses."
Hal Roach; MGM — *Blackhawk Films*

Way We Were, The   1973
Drama/Romance
63963   118 mins   C   B, V   P
Barbra Streisand, Robert Redford, Bradford Dillman, Viveca Lindfors, Herb Edelman
Set during the 1940's, this is the story of the attraction of two totally opposite people, the love that binds them together, and the differences that tear them apart.
Academy Awards '73: Best Song ("The Way We Were"); Best Music Score.   MPAA:PG
Columbia Pictures; Ray Stark — *RCA/Columbia Pictures Home Video; RCA VideoDiscs*

Wayne Newton at the   1983
London Palladium
Music-Performance
66448   63 mins   C   B, V   P
Wayne Newton, The Jive Sisters, Don Vincent and his Orchestra
Wayne Newton performs a show-stopping program for his legions of fans at the London Palladium. Songs include such pop masterpieces as "Danke Schoen," "Jambalaya," "The Impossible Dream," "I Made It Through The Rain" and others. VHS in stereo.
ITC Productions — *MGM/UA Home Video*

W. C. Fields Festival   1933
Comedy
00428   60 mins   B/W   B, V   P
W.C. Fields
Included are "The Golf Specialist," "The Dentist," and "The Fatal Glass of Beer."
Mack Sennett — *Budget Video; Discount Video Tapes; Sheik Video; Sound Video Unlimited; Roll Your Own Video*

WCT Finals of 1971/1972   1971
Tennis
33781   60 mins   C   B, V, 3/4U   P

Ken Rosewall, Rod Laver, John Newcombe, Arthur Ashe
Ken Roswell meets Rod Laver in the first World Championship Tennis Finals in Dallas. The 1972 WCT Finals follows.
Unknown — *Sports World Cinema*

We All Loved Each Other   1977
So Much
Comedy
63435   124 mins   C   B, V   P
Vittorio Gassman, Nino Manfredi, Stefano Satta Flores, Stefania Sandrelli
From the end of World War II through the next 30 years, this sensitive comedy follows the lives of three friends who have all loved the same woman. Italian dialogue, English subtitles.
IT
Almi/Cinema V; Pio Angeletti and Adriano de Micheli — *RCA/Columbia Pictures Home Video*

We Dive at Dawn   1943
War-Drama
64372   98 mins   B/W   B, V, 3/4U   P
John Mills, Eric Portman, directed by Anthony Asquith
A British submarine is disabled in the Baltic sea by enemy gunfire and the crewmen desperately seek help.
J. Arthur Rank; GFD; Gainsborough — *Nostalgia Merchant*

We of the Never Never   1982
Drama
65100   136 mins   C   B, V   P
Angela Punch McGregor, Arthur Dignam, Tony Barry, directed by Igor Auzins
A city-bred Australian woman marries a cattle rancher and moves from civilized Melbourne to the barren outback of the Northern Territory.
Triumph Films — *RCA/Columbia Pictures Home Video*

Weapons of Death   1983
Martial arts
66524   90 mins   C   B, V   P
Eric Lee, Bob Ramos, Ralph Catellanos
Kung fu expert Eric Lee splatters his enemies all over San Francisco's Chintown.
Cineamerica — *Paragon Video Productions*

Weber and Fields, Al   19??
Jolson, and This Is
America
Music/Variety
57365   29 mins   B/W   B, V, FO   P
This tape contains three priceless programs. "Weber and Fields" (1930), the dynamic vaudeville duo, are seen performing their classic "Oyster" routine. "A Jolson's Screen Test" (1948) is the rarest Jolson on film. "This Is America" (1943), narrated by Dwight West, is a

---

wartime tour along the Great White Way subtitled "Broadway Dim Out."
Unknown — *Video Yesteryear*

Wedding Party, The　　　1969
Comedy
63418　90 mins　C　B, V　　　P
Jill Clayburgh, Robert DeNiro, directed by Brian DePalma
An apprehensive groom is overwhelmed by his too-eager bride and her inquisitive relatives at a prenuptial celebration.
Ajay Films — *VidAmerica*

Weekend Pass　　　1984
Comedy
73041　92 mins　C　B, V　　　P
Three rookie sailors who have just completed basic training are out on a weekend pass determined to forget everything they have learned.
MPAA:R
Marylin J Tenser Crown
International — *Vestron Video*

Weekend Rebellion　　　197?
Music
59211　85 mins　C　B, V, 3/4U　　　P
Grand Funk Railroad
Heavy-rock stars Grand Funk Railroad are featured, as thousands of young people descend on Daytona Beach for a wild weekend.
Unknown — *Penguin Video*

Weight Loss　　　1982
Physical fitness
75698　30 mins　C　B, V, 3/4U　　　P
This program contains subliminal messages to help the viewer lose weight.
Environmental Video — *Environmental Video*

Welcome to L.A.　　　1977
Drama/Satire
Closed Captioned
72193　106 mins　C　B, V　　　P
Sissy Spacek, Sally Kellerman, Keith Carradine
Robert Altman's satire of life in Southern California has become a cult favorite over the years.
MPAA:R
Lions Gate Films — *CBS/Fox Video*

Welcome to Pooh Corner,　　　1984
Volume I
Fantasy
72791　111 mins　C　B, V　　　P
A series of made-for-video episodes involving Winnie the Pooh's misadventures in the Hundred Acre Wood. The live-action series features all Pooh's cronies, Tigger, Christopher Robin and Eeyore.

Walt Disney Productions — *Walt Disney Home Video*

Well Spent Life, A　　　1971
Music
60457　44 mins　C　B, V, 3/4U　　　P
A moving portrait of the Texas bluesman Mance Lipscomb, considered by many to be one of the great guitarists of all time. The documentary captures his music and the story of his remarkable life.
Les Blank — *Flower Films*

Wendell Willkie: Of　　　1954
Perfect Loyalty
Biographical/Politics and government-US
44230　15 mins　B/W　B, V　　　P
This program tells of the political career of Wendell Willkie, who was the Republican candidate for President in 1940. He was also one of the men who planted the seed which started the United Nations. Classic newsreel footage.
Fox Movietone News — *Two Star Films*

Went the Day Well?　　　1942
War-Drama
66404　96 mins　B/W　B, V　　　P
Leslie Banks, Elizabeth Allan, Frank Lawton, Basil Sydney
English villagers fight back when a squad of German paratroopers attempt a takeover in their town.
Ealing — *Movie Buff Video*

We're No Angels　　　1955
Comedy-Drama
65401　103 mins　C　B, V　　　R, P
Humphrey Bogart, Aldo Ray, Joan Bennett, Peter Ustinov, Basil Rathbone, Leo G. Carroll
Three escapees from Devil's Island hide out with the family of a kindly French storekeeper.
Paramount — *Paramount Home Video*

Werewolf of Washington　　　1979
Horror
65308　90 mins　C　B, V　　　P
Dean Stockwell, Biff Maguire, Clifton James
As the full moon hovers over Washington, terror lies waiting in the corridors of power.
Millco Productions — *Monterey Home Video*

Werner Herzog Eats His　　　1980
Shoe
Filmmaking
60470　20 mins　C　B, V, 3/4U　　　P
A portrait of German filmmaker Werner Herzog revealing an obsessive, self-destructive, almost superhuman dimension to Herzog.
Les Blank — *Flower Films*

　(For Explanation of codes, see USE GUIDE and KEY)

Werner Herzog in Peru — 1982
Filmmaking
60455   90 mins   C   B, V, 3/4U   P
A documentary about, and interview with, German filmmaker Werner Herzog filmed during the production of "Fitzcarraldo."
Les Blank — *Flower Films*

West of Pinto Basin — 1940
Western
58508   56 mins   B/W   B, V, 3/4U   P
Ray Corrigan, Joan King
A "Rangebuster" adventure, in which stagecoach and bank robbers are plaguing Pinto Basin.
Monogram — *Penguin Video*

West of the Divide — 1934
Western
15487   60 mins   B/W   B, V   P
John Wayne
The Duke heads out west ready for action.
Monogram — *Video Connection; Discount Video Tapes; Video Dimensions; Sheik Video; Cable Films; Penguin Video*

West of the Law — 1942
Western
53463   60 mins   B/W   B, V   P
Buck Jones, Tim McCoy
A group of ranchers turn to lawmen for protection from a band of outlaws.
Monogram — *Video Connection*

West Side Story — 1961
Musical
37522   151 mins   C   B, V, LV, CED   P
Natalie Wood, Richard Beymer, Russ Tamblyn, Rita Moreno, George Chakiris, directed by Robert Wise and Jerome Robbins
Gang rivalry on New York's West Side erupts in a ground-breaking musical that won ten Academy Awards. The Jets and the Sharks fight for their own turf and Tony and Maria fight for their own love. Amid the frenetic and brilliant choreography by Jerome Robbins, who directed the original Broadway show, and the high caliber score by Leonard Bernstein and Stephin Sondheim, there is the bittersweet message that tragedy breeds friendship.
Academy Awards '61: Best Picture; Best Supporting Actor (Chakiris); Best Direction (Wise/Robbins); Best Supporting Actress (Moreno); Best Cinematography: Color; Best Scoring Musical; Best Film Editing; Best Costume Design: Color; Best Art Direction: Color; Best Sound Recording. EL, SP
United Artists; Robert Wise — *CBS/Fox Video; RCA VideoDiscs*

Western Double Feature #1 — 194?
Western
07314   120 mins   B/W   B, V, 3/4U   P
Wild Bill Elliot, Sunset Carson
Double feature; in "Calling Wild Bill Elliot" (1943), Wild Bill comes to the aid of homesteaders; in "Santa Fe Saddlemates" (1945), Sunset Carson breaks up a diamond smuggling ring.
Republic — *Nostalgia Merchant*

Western Double Feature I — 19??
Western
63849   115 mins   B/W   B, V   P
Roy Rogers, Dale Evans, Gabby Hayes, Gene Autry, Smiley Burnette
In "Utah" (1945, 55 minutes), Roy foils a land swindle and helps a lady ranch owner; in "Man from Music Mountain (1938, 60 minutes), Gene foils a worthless gold mining stock swindle.
Republic — *Budget Video*

Western Double Feature #2 — 19??
Western
07316   120 mins   B/W   B, V, 3/4U   P
John Wayne, Monte Hale
Double feature; in "Night Riders" (1939), John Wayne battles injustice; in "Home on the Range" (1946, color), Monte Hale protects a wild animal refuge.
Republic — *Nostalgia Merchant*

Western Double Feature II — 193?
Western
63848   120 mins   B/W   B, V   P
John Wayne, Gabby Hayes
John Wayne and Gabby Hayes are teamed together in two hour-long features: "Star Packer" (1934) and "West of the Divide" (1933).
Monogram — *Budget Video*

Western Double Feature #3 — 1950
Western
07318   134 mins   C   B, V, 3/4U   P
Roy Rogers, Dale Evans, Rex Allen
In "Twilight in the Sierras" (1950), Roy catches a gang of crooks. "Under Mexicali Stars" (1950), features Rex as a cowboy who uncovers a counterfeiting ring.
Republic — *Nostalgia Merchant*

Western Double Feature III — 193?
Western
63844   113 mins   B/W   B, V   P
John Wayne, Johnny Mack Brown, Marsha Hunt, Phyllis Fraser

Two John Wayne westerns are on this tape: "Helltown" (1938, 59 minutes), in which Wayne catches a cattle rustler; and "Winds of the Wasteland" (1936, 54 minutes), where he plays an out-of-work Pony Express rider.
Paramount; Republic — *Budget Video*

Western Double Feature 194?
#4
Western
07320 120 mins B/W   B, V, 3/4U   P
Roy Rogers, Dale Evans, Trigger, Gabby Hayes, Allan 'Rocky' Lane
Double feature; in "Don't Fence Me In" (1945), Roy Rogers helps out a woman reporter; in "Sheriff of Wichita" (1948), a frontier investigator solves a crime.
Republic — *Nostalgia Merchant*

Western Double Feature 193?
IV
Western
63847 112 mins B/W   B, V   P
Roy Rogers, Gene Autry, Smiley Burnette
Roy plays a dual role in a case of mistaken identity in "Billy the Kid Returns" (1938, 56 minutes); in "Round Up Time in Texas" (1937, 56 minutes), Gene is framed on a charge of diamond smuggling.
Republic — *Budget Video*

Western Double Feature 19??
#5
Western
07322 108 mins B/W   B, V, 3/4U   P
Gene Autry, Roy Rogers, Smiley Burnette, Sons of the Pioneers
"The Big Show" (1937), features songs, action, and horses. "Home in Oklahoma" (1946), has Roy tracking down a murderer.
Republic — *Nostalgia Merchant*

Western Double Feature 193?
V
Western
63846 109 mins B/W   B, V   P
John Wayne, Polly Ann Young
John Wayne stars in both halves of this double feature: in "Desert Trail" (1935, 54 minutes), he plays a rodeo star; in "Man from Utah" (1934, 55 minutes), he brings a gang of murderers to justice.
Monogram — *Budget Video*

Western Double Feature 1950
#6
Western
07324   120 mins   C   B, V, 3/4U   P
Roy Rogers, Dale Evans, Trigger, Bob Livingston, Bob Steele
Double feature; "Trigger Jr'. (1950) is the story of Trigger's colt; "Gangs of Sonora" (1941,

black and white) deals with a fight to save a small frontier newspaper.
Republic — *Nostalgia Merchant*

Western Double Feature 1945
#7
Western
07326 120 mins B/W   B, V, 3/4U   P
Wild Bill Elliott, Buster Crabbe
Double feature; "Phantom of the Plains" deals with a plan to save a woman from a gigolo; "Prairie Rustlers" tells of the problems of a man who is the identical double of Billy the Kid.
Republic; PRC — *Nostalgia Merchant*

Western Double Feature 194?
#8
Western
07328 121 mins B/W   B, V, 3/4U   P
Roy Rogers, Monte Hale, John Carradine
Ranchers waiting to get right-of-way through oil land run into an ambitious resort owner in "Silver Spurs" (1943). "Out California Way" (1946), features Monte as a young cowboy looking for work in Hollywood.
Republic — *Nostalgia Merchant*

Western Double Feature 194?
#9
Western
07330 120 mins B/W   B, V, 3/4U   P
Lash LaRue, Don 'Red' Barry, Noah Beery
Double feature; in "Cheyenne Takes Over" (1947), Lash LaRue battles outlaws; in "Tulsa Kid" (1940), a young man must face a gunfighter.
Eagle Lion; Republic — *Nostalgia Merchant*

Western Double Feature 19??
#10
Western
07332   120 mins   C   B, V, 3/4U   P
Roy Rogers, Dale Evans, Trigger
Double feature; in "Bells of Coronado" (1950), Roy Rogers must solve a murder and uranium ore theft; in "King of the Cowboys" (1943, black and white), Roy Rogers investigates a band of saboteurs.
Republic — *Nostalgia Merchant*

Western Double Feature 1950
#11
Western
33916 121 mins B/W   B, V, 3/4U   P
Roy Rogers, Penny Edwards, Gordon Jones, Riders of the Purple Sage, Gabby Hayes
Roy and Trigger act as modern day Robin Hoods to end crooked dealing in the West; Roy hides behind a a smile and a song to capture murderers of a deputy and a ranch owner.
Republic — *Nostalgia Merchant*

Western Double Feature 1944
 # 12
Western
33917   108 mins   B/W   B, V, 3/4U   P
*Bob Livingston, Wild Bill Elliot, Bobby Blake,
Duncan Renaldo*
Red Ryder learns of a plot to scare ranchers
into selling out before an oil strike is discovered;
the Three Mesquiteers are sent to the
Caribbean as U.S. envoys to sell Army horses.
Republic;Producers Releasing
Corp — *Nostalgia Merchant*

Western Double Feature 194?
 # 13
Western
33919   108 mins   B/W   B, V, 3/4U   P
Red Ryder, Three Mesquiteers, Bobby Blake
Red Ryder foils outlaws trying to swindle the
Duchess' stage line in a small isolated town in
"Wagon Wheels Westward" (1945). "Rocky
Mountain Rangers" (1940), features the Three
Mesquiteers pursuing the deadly Barton Gang.
Republic — *Nostalgia Merchant*

Western Double Feature 1952
 # 14
Western
33921   123 mins   B/W   B, V, 3/4U   P
Tim Holt, Jack Holt, Nan Leslie, Noreen Nash
Outlaws, good guys and romance on the old
frontier. Amateur Robin Hoods steal back
money wrongfully taken.
RKO — *Nostalgia Merchant*

Western Double Feature 1950
 # 15
Western
33923   122 mins   B/W   B, V, 3/4U   P
*Roy Rogers, Trigger, Penny Edwards, Don
"Red" Barry, Lynn Merrick*
Roy Rogers breaks up a cattle rustling ring; the
good guys try to bring law and order to a vast
Wyoming territory plagued by a crooked political
boss.
Republic — *Nostalgia Merchant*

Western Double Feature 1946
 # 16
Western
33925   108 mins   B/W   B, V, 3/4U   P
*Gene Autry, Smiley Burnette, Roy Rogers,
Gabby Hayes*
Autry is sent to quell a revolution in Mexico; Roy
Rogers' horse Lady and Gabby Hayes' horse
Golden Sovereign are the focal points of the
second part of this double feature.
Republic — *Nostalgia Merchant*

Western Double Feature 194?
 # 17
Western
44855   121 mins   C   B, V, 3/4U   P
Roy Rogers, Sunset Carson
This double feature stars Roy Rogers in "The
Golden Stallion" ('49). Roy battles diamond
smugglers who use wild horses to transport the
goods. The second feature, "The Cherokee
Flash" ('45), starring Sunset Carson, deals with
a respectable citizen's outlaw past catching up
to him.
Republic — *Nostalgia Merchant*

Western Double Feature 194?
 # 18
Western
33927   108 mins   B/W   B, V, 3/4U   P
Roy Rogers, Andy Devine, Dale Evans
A Roy Rogers double feature: In "Eyes of
Texas" (1948), a westerner turns his ranch into
a camp for war-orphaned boys. In "Helldorado"
(1946), Roy travels to Las Vegas.
Republic — *Nostalgia Merchant*

Western Double Feature 19??
 # 19
Western
33929   108 mins   B/W   B, V, 3/4U   P
Roy Rogers, Gene Autry
"Night Time in Nevada" (1948), has Roy
bringing a ruthless murderer to justice. "The Old
Corral" (1937), features a clash between
gangsters in limousines and deputies on
horseback.
Republic — *Nostalgia Merchant*

Western Double Feature 1945
 # 20
Western
33931   108 mins   B/W   B, V, 3/4U   P
Roy Rogers, Dale Evans, Pat Brady, Trigger
Roy helps a young woman foil a plot by crooks
to swindle her inheritance. Roy appears in his
first starring role (1938) and fights an outlaw
gang.
Republic — *Nostalgia Merchant*

Western Double Feature 194?
 # 21
Western
33933   121 mins   C   B, V, 3/4U   P
*Roy Rogers, Red Ryder, Dale Evans, Bobby
Blake*
Roy battles crooks in "Susanna Pass" (1949).
In "Sheriff of Las Vegas" (1944), Red must find
the murderer of Judge Blackwell.
Republic — *Nostalgia Merchant*

Western Double Feature #22　　194?
Western
33935　108 mins　B/W　B, V, 3/4U　　P
Roy Rogers
A Roy Rogers double feature: In "Under California Stars" (1948), Roy rounds up a gang of wild horse rustlers. In "San Fernando Valley" (1944), Roy brings law and order to the valley.
Republic, Monogram — *Nostalgia Merchant*

Western Double Feature #23　　19??
Western
59146　122 mins　B/W　B, V, 3/4U　　P
Roy Rogers, Dale Evans
In "Spoilers of the Plains" (1951), Roy finds cattle rustlers and sets out to capture the spoilers. "Lights of Old Santa Fe" (1947), features Roy as a cowboy who rescues a beautiful rodeo owner from bankruptcy.
Republic — *Nostalgia Merchant*

Western Double Feature #24　　194?
Western
59147　122 mins　C　B, V, 3/4U　　P
Roy Rogers, Dale Evans, Eddie Dean
In "Cowboy and the Senorita" (1944), Roy solves the mystery of a missing girl. "Colorado Serenade" (1946), is a musical western in Cinecolor starring Eddie Dean.
Republic;Producers Releasing Corp — *Nostalgia Merchant*

Western Double Feature #25　　19??
Western
59148　122 mins　B/W　B, V, 3/4U　　P
Roy Rogers, Dale Evans, Andy Devine, Sons of the Pioneers
In "Pals of the Golden West" (1951), Roy discovers how valuable Trigger is. "Springtime in the Sierras" (1947), features Roy raising and selling thoroughbreds.
Republic — *Nostalgia Merchant*

Western Justice　　1935
Western
08817　56 mins　B/W　B, V, 3/4U　　P
Bob Steele
Gang tries to force people to sell their land.
Commodore — *Penguin Video*

Western Maryland Shay No. 6 at Cass　　1981
Trains
59178　118 mins　C　B, V　　P
Western Maryland Shay No. 6, a 162-ton monster is seen in action. Includes a visit to the Roanoke Transportation Museum.
JMJ Prods — *JMJ Productions*

Western Steam　　1980
Trains
55517　60 mins　C　B, V　　P
A trip on the "Super Skunks" of the California Western Railway, ancient steam locomotives, and a ride on a restored Heisler steam locomotive highlight this program.
De Luz Video — *De Luz Video*

Westinghouse Studio One: Hold Back the Night　　1952
War-Drama
21332　60 mins　B/W　B, V, FO　　P
John Forsythe
A Korean war drama from one of the most famous series of early television.
CBS — *Video Yesteryear*

Westinghouse Studio One: "Little Men, Big World"　　1952
Crime-Drama
47500　60 mins　B/W　B, V, FO　　P
Jack Palance, Shepperd Strudwick, Ray Walston
An original TV drama by Reginald Rose about small town racketeers being menaced by a big city mob. Originally telecast on October 13, 1952.
CBS — *Video Yesteryear*

Westinghouse Studio One (Summer Theatre)　　1952
Drama
66144　56 mins　B/W　B, V, FO　　P
Kevin McCarthy, Frances Starr, Katharine Bard
A live TV dramatization of "Jane Eyre" by Charlotte Bronte.
CBS — *Video Yesteryear*

Westward Ho　　1935
Western
54199　55 mins　B/W　B, V　　P
John Wayne, Sheila Manners
The leader of a group of vigilantes is discovered to have an outlaw brother.
Republic — *Video Connection*

Westworld　　1973
Science fiction
59362　90 mins　C　B, V, CED　　P
Yul Brynner, Richard Benjamin, James Brolin, directed by Michael Crichton
Michael Crichton wrote this story of an adult vacation resort of the future which offers the opportunity to live in various fantasy worlds serviced by lifelike robots. When an electrical malfunction occurs, the robots begin to go berserk.
MPAA:PG
MGM — *MGM/UA Home Video*

What Ever Happened to Baby Jane? 1962
Suspense
65139   132 mins   B/W   B, V   R, P
Bette Davis, Joan Crawford, Victor Buono, Anna Lee, B.D. Merrill, directed by Robert Aldrich
Two sisters, one a demented former childhood star and the other a crippled ex-screen actress, live together in an uneasy truce until events drive one of them over the brink of madness.
Seven Arts; Warner Bros — *Warner Home Video*

What Price Hollywood 1932
Comedy
10059   88 mins   B/W   B, V   P, T
Constance Bennett, Lowel Sherman, Neil Hamilton, directed by George Cukor
Aspiring young starlet decides to crash film world by using a director.
RKO; Selznick — *Blackhawk Films*

What the Peeper Saw 1972
Horror
60349   97 mins   C   B, V   P
Britt Ekland, Mark Lester, Hardy Kruger, Lilli Palmer
A wealthy author's wife's comfortable life turns into a terrifying nightmare when her young stepson starts exhibiting strange behavior.
Joseph E Levine; Avco Embassy — *VCI Home Video*

What Would Your Mother Say? 1981
Variety
64847   83 mins   C   B, V   P
Bill Margold, Tiffany Clark, Maria Tortuga, Kevin Gibson, Tamara Webb, Mike Ranger, Monique Monge
A hidden camera takes you inside actual casting sessions with over 40 of Hollywood's erotic stars and starlets who didn't know they were being filmed.
Real Peephole Production — *HarmonyVision*

Whatever Happened to Aunt Alice? 1969
Mystery/Drama
46197   101 mins   C   B, V   P
Geraldine Page, Ruth Gordon, Rosemary Forsyth, Robert Fuller, Mildred Dunnock, directed by Lee H. Katzin
A woman murdered her husband to inherit his estate only to discover it is worthless. Meanwhile, she must continue killing for her protection until she learns that her husband's stamp collection was worth $100,000.
MPAA:PG
Robert Aldrich — *CBS/Fox Video*

What's New Pussycat? 1965
Comedy
58853   108 mins   C   B, V, CED   P
Peter Sellers, Peter O'Toole, Romy Schneider, Paula Prentiss, Woody Allen, Ursula Andress, Capucine
A young engaged man is reluctant to give up the girls who love him and seeks the aid of a married psychiatrist who turns out to have problems of his own.
United Artists — *CBS/Fox Video*

What's Up Doc? 1972
Comedy
52708   94 mins   C   B, V   R, P
Barbra Streisand, Ryan O'Neal, Kenneth Mars, Austin Pendleton, directed by Peter Bogdanovich
An eccentric woman and an equally eccentric professor become involved in a chase to recover four identical flight bags containing top secret documents, a wealthy woman's jewels, the professor's musical rocks, and the girl's clothing. Bogdanovich's homage to screwball comedies of the thirties.
MPAA:G
Warner Bros; Saticoy Productions — *Warner Home Video; RCA VideoDiscs*

What's Up Tiger Lily? 1966
Comedy
08579   90 mins   C   B, V, LV, CED   P
Woody Allen, Tatsuya Mihashi, Mie Hana
This legitimate Japanese spy movie was re-edited by Woody Allen, who also added a new dialogue track, with laughable results. Music by the Lovin' Spoonful.
Henry G Saperstein Entprs — *Vestron Video; Cable Films*

Wheel of Fortune 1942
Drama
66468   83 mins   B/W   B, V   P
John Wayne, Frances Dee, Edward Ellis
A shrewd country lawyer is forced to expose his girlfriend's father as a crooked gambler.
Republic — *NTA Home Entertainment*

Wheels-O-Rolling 1949
Transportation
74477   29 mins   C   B, V   P
This program examines the history of U.S. transportation from the stage coach to the zephyr.
Chicago Railroad Pair — *Interurban Films*

Wheels of Steel 195?
Trains
68915   15 mins   B/W   B, V   P
This documentary gives a detailed account of the preparation of the powerful GG-1

Locomotive and its train for the N.Y. to Washington D.C. run.
Unknown — *Interurban Films*

When a Stranger Calls 1979
Suspense
52753   97 mins   C   B, V, LV   P
Carol Kane, Charles Durning, Colleen Dewhurst, Rachel Roberts
A babysitter is terrorized by threatening phone calls and soon realizes that the calls are coming from within the house.
MPAA:R
Columbia; Doug Chapin; Steve Feke — *RCA/Columbia Pictures Home Video*

When Lightning Strikes 1934
Adventure
65200   51 mins   B/W   B, V   P
Francis X. Bushman, Lightning, the Wonder Dog
Lightning, the Wonder Dog prevents the owner of a rival lumber company from stealing his master's land, utilizing his talents of running, swimming, barking and smoking cigars.
Regal Productions — *Video Yesteryear*

When the North Wind Blows 1974
Adventure
45013   113 mins   C   B, V   P
Henry Brandon, Herbert Nelson, Dan Haggerty
An old, lone trapper hunts for and later befriends the majestic snow tiger of Siberia in the Alaskan wilderness.
MPAA:G
Sunn Classic Pictures — *VCI Home Video*

When the West Was Young 1933
Western
59166   48 mins   B/W   B, V   P
Randolph Scott, Sally Blaine
An outdoor adventure about rounding up horses in the Old West. Also titled, "Wild Horse Mesa."
Paramount — *Discount Video Tapes; Penguin Video*

When Worlds Collide 1951
Science fiction
55545   82 mins   C   B, V, LV   R, P
Richard Derr, Barbara Rush, Larry Keating, Peter Hanson, directed by Rudolph Mate
Another planet is found to be rushing inevitably towards earth, but before the collision a few people escape in a spaceship.
Academy Awards '51: Best Special Effects.
Paramount; George Pal — *Paramount Home Video*

When's Your Birthday? 1937
Comedy
56905   77 mins   B/W   B, V, FO   P
Joe E. Brown, Marian Marsh, Edgar Kennedy
Joe E. Brown stars in this comedy about a prize-fighter who studies the stars to secure success in the ring.
RKO — *Video Yesteryear*

Where the Boys Are 1960
Comedy
72467   99 mins   C   B, V   P
George Hamilton, Jim Hutton, Yvette Mimieux, Connie Francis, Paula Prentiss, Dolores Hart
Four college girls go to Fort Lauderdale and meet men they are conveniently compatible with during spring break.
MGM — *MGM/UA Home Video*

Where the Buffalo Roam 1980
Comedy
72932   98 mins   C   B, V   P
Bill Murray, Peter Boyle
One of Bill's early starring roles as the legendary "gonzo" journalist Dr. Hunter S. Thompson.
MPAA:R
Art Linson — *MCA Home Video*

Where Time Began 1977
Science fiction/Adventure
65716   87 mins   C   B, V   P
The discovery of a strange manuscript of a scientist's journey to the center of the earth leads to the decision to recreate the dangerous mission. Based on the Jules Verne classic novel, "Journey to the Center of the Earth."
MPAA:G
International Picture Show — *Embassy Home Entertainment*

Where's Poppa? 1970
Comedy
65334   84 mins   C   B, V   P
George Segal, Ruth Gordon, Trish Van Devere
A Jewish lawyer's aged mother constantly harms his love life, and he considers various means of getting rid of her.
United Artists — *Key Video*

Which Way Is Up? 1977
Comedy
14013   94 mins   C   B, V   P
Richard Pryor, Lonette McKee, Margaret Avery, Morgan Woodward, Marilyn Coleman, directed by Michael Schultz
The story of an orange picker who accidentally becomes a union hero. He leaves his wife and family at home while he seeks work in Los Angeles. There he finds himself a new woman, starts a new family, and sells out to the capitalists.
MPAA:R

Universal; Steve Krantz Prod — *MCA Home Video*

Whirlwind Horseman 1938
Western
08841 60 mins B/W B, V, 3/4U P
Ken Maynard
Action-adventure; bandits try for some oil land.
Grand National — *Penguin Video; Discount Video Tapes; Video Connection*

Whiskey Mountain 197?
Adventure
66080 95 mins C B, V P
Christopher George
The lure of buried treasure attracts two young motorcyclists to Whiskey Mountain. Music by Charlie Daniels.
MPAA:PG
Unknown — *Best Film & Video Corporation*

Whisky Galore 1948
Comedy
50957 81 mins B/W , B, V R, P
Basil Radford, Joan Greenwood, Gordon Jackson, James Robertson Justice
A whiskey-less Scottish island gets a lift when a ship carrying 50,000 cases of spirits becomes wrecked off their coast. A full-scale rescue operation and evasion of the British government ensues.
Ealing Studios — *THORN EMI Home Video*

Whispering Shadow 1933
Mystery/Serials
12555 156 mins B/W B, V P
Bela Lugosi, Robert Warwick, directed by Al Herman, Colbert Clark
Serial starring the master criminal known as the "faceless whisperer." Twelve chapters, 13 minutes each.
Mascot — *Video Connection; Penguin Video; Video Yesteryear*

Whistle Stop 1946
Drama
66405 84 mins B/W B, V P
George Raft, Ava Gardner, Victor McLaglen
A small-town girl divides her flirtatious attentions between an erratic playboy and a villainous night club owner.
United Artists — *Movie Buff Video*

Whistling Bullets 1936
Western
08842 58 mins B/W B, V, 3/4U P
Ken Maynard
Action galore in another James Oliver Curwood story of the West.
Ambassador — *Penguin Video*

White Dawn, The 1975
Drama
64029 110 mins C B, V R, P
Warren Oates, Timothy Bottoms, Lou Gossett
Three sailors, separated from their ship during a hunt, struggle to survive in the Arctic wasteland.
MPAA:R
Paramount — *Paramount Home Video*

White Heat 1949
Drama
29233 114 mins B/W B, V, CED P
James Cagney, Virginia Mayo, Edmond O'Brien
A ruthless gangster has a mother complex, but to all others around him, he's a heartless killer. One of Cagney's best roles.
Warner Bros — *CBS/Fox Video; RCA VideoDiscs*

White Lightning 1973
Adventure
58828 101 mins C CED P
Burt Reynolds, Ned Beatty, Bo Hopkins, Jennifer Billingsley, Louise Latham
An adventure drama of murder, revenge, and moonshine in the new South.
MPAA:PG
United Artists; Levy Gardner Lavin Productions — *CBS/Fox Video; RCA VideoDiscs*

White Line Fever 1975
Adventure
64911 89 mins C B, V P
Jan-Michael Vincent, Kay Lenz
A young trucker's search for a happy life with his childhood sweetheart is complicated by a corrupt group in control of the long-haul trucking business.
MPAA:PG
John Kemeny — *RCA/Columbia Pictures Home Video*

White Mane 1952
Drama
65621 38 mins B/W B, V P
Alain Emery, Frank Silvera
The poignant, poetic story of a proud and fierce white stallion that continually alludes attempts to be captured by ranchers, only to be "tamed" by the love of a small boy.
William Snyder — *Embassy Home Entertainment*

White Music 1981
Music
47299 35 mins C LV P
A fantasy ski adventure set in the south of France provides a visual interpretation of the background rock music composed by Talizman.
Masaru Ohtaki — *Pioneer Video Imports*

White Rose, The   1983
War-Drama
65222   108 mins   C   B, V   P
Lena Stolze, Wulf Kessler, Oliver Siebert, Ulrich Tucker, directed by Michael Verhoeven
A group of dissident students in Munich, circa 1942, put their lives in danger by distributing anti-Nazi propaganda. In German with English subtitles.
GE
TeleCulture Films — *MGM/UA Home Video*

White Tower, The   1950
Drama
59647   98 mins   C   B, V   P
Glenn Ford, Claude Rains, Sir Cedric Hardwicke, Oscar Homolka, Lloyd Bridges
The tale of five men and a woman who set out to scale the infamous White Tower in the Alps. Each person's true nature is revealed as he scales the peak, which has defied all previous attempts.
RKO — *Budget Video*

White-Water Sam   1978
Adventure
66637   87 mins   C   B, V   P
Keith Larsen
White-Water Sam and his Siberian Husky, Sybar, embark on an exciting trip through the uncharted wilds of the Great Northwest.
MPAA:G
Keith Larsen — *Monterey Home Video*

White Zombie, The   1932
Horror
08586   73 mins   B/W   B, V   P
Bela Lugosi, Madge Bellamy, John Harron, directed by Victor Halperin
Corpses return to life in this classic horror film. Zombies rob graves and take bodies to sugar mill where zombies work around the clock for mad White Zombie.
United Artists — *Mossman Williams Productions; Ampro Video Productions; Cable Films; Penguin Video; Video Connection; Video Yesteryear; Budget Video; Discount Video Tapes; Western Film & Video Inc; Admit One Video*

Whitewater   1982
Sports-Water
63134   120 mins   C   B, V   P, T
This videocassette is a compilation of five programs documenting whitewater rafting expeditions in Chile ("River of Thunder"), Africa ("The Ultimate Adventure"), Oregon, Alaska and the Grand Canyon.
International Film and TV Festival '81: Gold Medal ("River of Thunder"). AM Available
Richard Kidd Prods; Sobek Expeditions; OARS Inc — *Video Travel*

Who Has Seen the Wind?   1977
Drama
72884   102 mins   C   B, V   P
Jose Ferrer, Brian Painchaud, Charmion King
A young boy must learn how to grow up during the Depression.
Astral Films; Souris River Films — *Embassy Home Entertainment*

Who Killed Doc Robbin?   1948
Mystery
08718   50 mins   C   B, V, FO   P
Larry Olsen, Don Castle, by Bernard Carr
A group of youngsters try to clear their friend, Dan, the town handyman, when the sinister Dr. Robbins is murdered.
United Artists — *Video Yesteryear; Budget Video; Penguin Video; Sheik Video; Discount Video Tapes*

Who Killed Mary What's 'Er Name?   1971
Adventure
59352   90 mins   C   B, V   R, P
Red Buttons, Sylvia Miles, Conrad Bain, Ron Carey, Alice Playten, Sam Waterson
An ex-fighter tracks a playgirl's killer through street gangs and bizarre cults.
MPAA:PG
Heritage Enterprises — *Video Gems*

Who Rocks America—1982 American Tour, The   1983
Music-Performance
64334   118 mins   C   B, V, CED   P
The rock group's final concert of their North American tour at the Maple Leaf Gardens in Toronto, Canada on December 17, 1982 includes such songs as "Pinball Wizard," "Who's Next," and "Tommy." In stereo on VHS format.
Jack Calmes — *CBS/Fox Video*

Who'll Stop the Rain?   1978
Drama
76043   126 mins   C   B, V   P
Nick Nolte, Tuesday Weld, Michael Moriarty
Nolte plays a temperamental Vietnam veteran who is enlisted in a smuggling scheme to transport a large amount of heroin from Vietnam into California.
MPAA:R
United Artists — *Key Video*

Wholly Moses!   1980
Comedy
51572   125 mins   C   B, V, LV   P
The son of a slave in biblical times becomes convinced his mission is to lead the chosen, instead of his brother-in-law, Moses.
MPAA:PG

Columbia Pictures; Freddie
Fields — *RCA/Columbia Pictures Home Video;
RCA VideoDiscs*

Whoops Apocalypse 1983
Comedy
65336　137 mins　C　B, V　　　P
*John Cleese, John Barron, Richard Griffiths,
Peter Jones, Bruce Montague, Barry Morse*
This program is a version of the British hit
television series. It is a biting account of events
leading up to World War III, full of rapid fire wit,
one liners, and manic energy.
Humphrey Barclay — *Pacific Arts Video*

Who's Afraid of Opera? 1982
Volume I
Opera
60396　57 mins　C　B, V, CED　　　P
*Narrated by Beverly Sills, London Symphony
Orchestra*
Opera star Beverly Sills shows children that
there is nothing to fear in understanding and
enjoying opera. This volume presents "Faust"
by Gounod and "Rigoletto" by Verdi. In stereo.
Nathan Kroll — *MGM/UA Home Video*

Who's Afraid of Opera? 1982
Volume 2
Opera
60397　57 mins　C　B, V, CED　　　P
*Narrated by Beverly Sills, London Symphony
Orchestra*
Beverly Sills teaches children how to enjoy
opera. This volume features Verdi's "La
Traviata" and Donizetti's "Daughter of the
Regiment." In stereo.
Nathan Kroll — *MGM/UA Home Video*

Who's Afraid of Opera? 1982
Volume 3
Opera
60398　57 mins　C　B, V, CED　　　P
*Narrated by Beverly Sills, London Symphony
Orchestra*
This volume presents Rossini's "Barber of
Seville" and Donizetti's "Lucia di
Lammermoor." In stereo.
Nathan Kroll — *MGM/UA Home Video*

Who's Afraid of Virginia 1966
Woolf?
Drama
58256　127 mins　B/W　　B, V　　R, P
*Richard Burton, Elizabeth Taylor, George Segal,
Sandy Dennis, directed by Mike Nichols*
A night-long journey into the private hell of an
embittered, embattled marriage. Adapted from
Edward Albee's classic modern play.
Academy Awards '66: Best Actress (Taylor),
Supporting Actress (Dennis), Best

Cinematography—Black and White (Haskell
Wexler).
Warner Bros — *Warner Home Video*

Who's Out There?—A 198?
Search for
Extraterrestrial Life
Space exploration/Science fiction
72058　60 mins　C　B, V　　　P
Orson Welles narrates this informative and
entertaining film that speculates on whether life
exists beyond our solar system.
NASA — *MPI Home Video*

Whose Life Is It Anyway? 1981
Drama
59366　118 mins　C　B, V, CED　　　P
*Richard Dreyfuss, John Cassavetes, Christine
Iahti, Bob Balaban, Kenneth McMillan, Kaki
Hunter, Thomas Carter, directed by John
Badham*
A talented sculptor is paralyzed in an auto
accident and decides not to live anymore. What
follows is his struggle, both legally and morally,
to convince the hospital authorities to let him
die.
MPAA:R
MGM — *MGM/UA Home Video*

Why Do I Call You Sexy? 1983
Cosmetology
66176　90 mins　C　B, V　　　P
Famed hairstylist and makeover artist of the
Stars, Jose Eber, offers tips to women on hair
and makeup.
Karl Video — *Karl Video*

Why Shoot the Teacher 1979
Drama
65394　101 mins　C　B, V　　　P
Bud Cort, Samantha Eggar
An amusingly told story of life on the prairie at
the height of the Great Depression. It's an
account of one man's first collision with reality.
Laurence Hertzog — *Embassy Home
Entertainment*

Why Vietnam 1965
Vietnam War
53690　25 mins　B/W　B, V, 3/4U　　　P
A history of U.S. support in Southeast Asia,
including speeches by Dean Rusk, Robert
McNamara, and LBJ.
Unknown — *International Historic Films*

Why We Fight 1945
World War II/Documentary
48851　63 mins　B/W　B, V, 3/4U　　　P
Directed by Frank Capra 7　pgms
A series of feature-length documentaries
intended for Americans in the armed forces
during World War II. They later fascinated the

general public. Programs are available individually.
1.Prelude to War 2.The Nazis Strike 3.Divide and Conquer 4.The Battle of Britain 5.The Battle of Russia 6.The Battle of China 7.War Comes to America
US War Department — *Western Film & Video Inc; International Historic Films; Festival Films*

Wicker Man, The 1975
Mystery
56739 103 mins C B, V P
Edward Woodward, Britt Ekland, Diane Cilento, Ingrid Pitt, Christopher Lee
The disappearance of a young girl leads to the terrible secret of the Wicker Man.
Peter Snell — *Media Home Entertainment*

Wifemistress 1979
Drama
39031 101 mins C B, V P
Marcello Mastroianni, Laura Antonelli, directed by Marco Vicario
Set in the early 1900's, this is the story of an invalid wife who resents her neglectful husband. When he goes into hiding because of a murder he didn't commit, the wife begins to drift into a world of her fantasies. Italian dialogue, English subtitles.
MPAA:R IT
Franco Cristaldi, Quartet Films — *RCA/Columbia Pictures Home Video; CBS/Fox Video (disc only)*

Wilbur and Orville: The First to Fly 1979
Adventure/Aeronautics
75619 47 mins C B, V P
This is the story of the Wright Brothers' early unsuccessful attempts at flying.
VidAmerica — *Children's Video Library*

Wilbur Shaw: Speedway Star 1954
Biographical/Automobiles-Racing
44234 15 mins B/W B, V P
An account of the racing career of Wilbur Shaw. He won the Memorial Day Race at Indianapolis Speedway. After two additional victories his luck ran out. He crashed and was told his racing days were over. Classic newsreel footage.
Fox Movietone News — *Two Star Films*

Wild and Woolly 1917
Comedy
64308 45 mins B/W B, V P
Douglas Fairbanks
An Eastern tenderfoot fantasizes about life in the Wild West and finally gets a chance to see it in person. Silent with musical score.
Artcraft Pictures — *Classic Video Cinema Collector's Club*

Wild and Wooly 1917
Western/Comedy
69555 61 mins B/W B, V, FO P
Douglas Fairbanks Sr.
The son of a New York railroad tycoon travels out West on business expecting to find himself on the rugged frontier. Silent with musical score.
Artcraft — *Video Yesteryear*

Wild Bunch, The 1969
Western
38955 127 mins C B, V, LV R, P
William Holden, Ernest Borgnine, Robert Ryan, directed by Sam Peckinpah
A brutal, bloody western about a group of losers in the dying days of the lawless frontier, fighting and killing those in their path.
MPAA:R
Warner Bros — *Warner Home Video; RCA VideoDiscs*

Wild Geese, The 1978
Adventure
65407 132 mins C B, V, CED P
Richart Burton, Roger Moore, Richard Harris
The adventure begins when a veteran band of mercenaries land deep inside Africa to rescue the imprisoned leader of an emerging African nation. Their mission meets an unexpected turn when the soldiers are betrayed by those who helped finance their trip!
MPAA:R
Allied Artists — *CBS/Fox Video*

Wild Horse 1931
Western
43018 68 mins B/W B, V, FO P
Hoot Gibson, Stepin Fetchit
A pair of bronco busters sign up to work at a rodeo ranch and take charge when trouble strikes.
Allied — *Video Yesteryear*

Wild Horse Canyon 1925
Western
58265 68 mins B/W B, V, FO P
Yakima Canutt, Edward Cecil, Helene Rosson, Jay Talbet
Yakima Canutt, the man credited with creating the profession of stunt man, stars in this tale about a lady rancher who requires saving from her evil foreman. The climactic stampede scene gives Yakima a chance to demonstrate a high dive off a cliff and a somersault onto his horse. Silent, with musical score.
Unknown — *Video Yesteryear; Discount Video Tapes*

Wild Horses 1984
Western
75671 90 mins C B, V P

A rugged 1970's cowboy is determined to make a living by capturing and selling wild horses, but is plagued by hunters.
Satori Entertainment Corp. — *VidAmerica*

Wild in the Country   1961
Drama
64935   114 mins   C   B, V, CED   P
Elvis Presley, Hope Lange, Tuesday Weld, Millie Perkins, John Ireland, Gary Lockwood
A woman psychiatrist and a social worker rehabilitate a delinquent rural boy.
20th Century Fox — *CBS/Fox Video*

Wild Mustang   1935
Western
14348   62 mins   B/W   B, V   P
Harry Carey
Sheriff's son joins some outlaws to help father spring a trap.
William Berke — *Video Connection; Discount Video Tapes; Penguin Video*

Wild Party, The   1974
Drama
65429   90 mins   C   B, V   P
Raquel Welch, James Coco, Perry King, David Dukes
It's 1929, a year of much frivolity in Hollywood; and drinking, dancing, maneuvering and almost every sort of romance are the rule of the night at silent-film comic Jolly Grimm's sumptuous, star-studded party.
MPAA:R
United Artists — *Embassy Home Entertainment*

Wild Rapture   1950
Documentary/Africa
51231   60 mins   C   B, V, 3/4U   P
A fascinating document of the dark continent, Africa. Rare and remarkable footage of native dances, poison arrow-shooting pygmies, and spear-toting, fearless hunters.
Unknown — *Penguin Video*

Wild Ride, The   1960
Drama
38975   59 mins   B/W   B, V, FO   P
Jack Nicholson, Georgianna Carter
Jack Nicholson, in an early starring role, portrays a rebellious punk of the beat generation who hotrods his way into trouble and tragedy.
Filmgroup — *Video Yesteryear; Discount Video Tapes*

Wild Rides   1982
Documentary
66327   27 mins   C   B, V   P
Matt Dillon

Teen heartthrob Matt Dillon takes viewers on a tour of America's most exciting roller coasters. The soundtrack features music by The Who, Steely Dan, Steve Miller, The Cars and Jimi Hendrix. In stereo.
Klein & Video Programs — *Warner Home Video*

Wild Strawberries   1959
Drama
60426   90 mins   B/W   B, V   P
Victor Sjostrom, Bibi Anderson, Ingrid Thulin, Max von Sydow, Gunnar Bjornstrand, directed by Ingmar Bergman
Bergman's classic of fantasy, dreams and nightmares concerning an aging professor who must come to terms with his faults and become reconciled to the idea of approaching death.
A B Svensk; Janus Films — *CBS/Fox Video; Cable Films*

Wild Times   1979
Western
73561   200 mins   C   B, V   P
Sam Elliott, Trish Stewart, Ben Johnson, Dennis Hopper, Pat Hingle
This movie is based upon Brian Garfield's novel about Hugh Cardiff, a hero who lived his life to the hilt.
Rattlesnake Prods; Golden Circle — *Prism*

Wild, Wild World of Jayne Mansfield   1968
Documentary
52733   120 mins   C   B, V   P
The life and times of Jayne Mansfield is explored in this unique program. Jayne's world wide examination of sexual mores is traced, from prostitution, nudist colonies, and the racy strip clubs of Europe, to the transvestite and topless bars of America.
Southeastern Pictures — *Movie Buff Video*

Wildcat   1942
Adventure
08863   73 mins   B/W   B, V, 3/4U   P
Richard Arlen, Buster Crabbe, Arline Judge
A fight between rival oil prospectors to see who can bring a well in first.
Paramount; Pine Thomas Prods — *Penguin Video*

Wilderness Family Part 2   1977
Adventure
63381   104 mins   C   B, V   P
Robert Logan, Susan D. Shaw
The further adventures of the Robinson family, who left civilization for the freedom of the wilderness, are portrayed.
MPAA:G

Pacific International Enterprises — *Media Home Entertainment*

Wilderness Quest 1981
Wilderness areas
47285   24 mins   C   B, V, 3/4U,   P
                              Q
Different wilderness regions of the U.S. are explored, and methods of conservation of these diminishing areas are discussed.
TV Sports Scene — *TV Sports Scene*

Will of a People, The 1946
Spain/Documentary
12852   55 mins   C   B, V, FO   P
A well done story of the Spanish revolution and the rise to power of Generalissimo Franco, told in footage from Spanish archives.
Unknown — *Video Yesteryear; International Historic Films*

Will Rogers: Champion of the People 198?
Biographical
65726   55 mins   C   B, V   P
The true story of the young cowboy who became America's real-life folk hero.
James L Conway — *VCI Home Video*

Will Rogers: Four Two-Reelers 192?
Comedy
64251 60 mins B/W   B, V   P
Will Rogers
Will Rogers' special brand of humor is evident in these four two-reelers, which spoof politics and the movies. Silent with musical score.
Samuel Goldwyn — *Classic Video Cinema Collector's Club*

Will Rogers: The Cowboy Humorist 1954
Biographical/History-US
44260 15 mins B/W   B, V   P
The story of Will Rogers, who, during the depression, barnstormed by plane through the hard-hit Southwest, giving every cent he made to local relief. Classic newsreel footage.
Fox Movietone News — *Two Star Films*

Willie Nelson and Family In Concert 1984
Music video
72893   89 mins   C   B, V   P
Willie Nelson
Willie Nelson performs such hits as "On the Road Again" "Georgiaon My Mind."
Unknown — *CBS/Fox Video*

Win, Place, or Steal 1972
Comedy
73036   88 mins   C   B, V   P
McLean Stevenson, Alex Karras, Dean Stockwell
Three men are willing to do anything except work.
MPAA:PG
Omega — *Vestron Video*

Wind in the Willows, The 1982
Cartoons
63189   47 mins   C   B, V   R, P
Animated, narrated by Basil Rathbone, the voice of Eric Blore
"The Wind in the Willows," originally a part of the 1950 feature "Ichabod and Mr. Toad," is the tale of J. Thaddeus Toad, who has a strange mania for fast cars. Also on this tape are two Disney cartoons with similar automotive themes, "Motor Mania" with Goofy, and "Trailer Horn" with Donald Duck and Chip 'n' Dale.
Walt Disney Productions — *Walt Disney Home Video*

Wind in the Willows, The 1983
Cartoons/Literature-American
75622   97 mins   C   B, V   P
Animated
This animated film is based on Kenneth Grahame's famous tale.
Rankin Bass — *Children's Video Library*

Windom's Way 1957
Romance
75674   90 mins   B/W   B, V   P
Peter Finch, Mary Ure
Based on a novel by James Ramsey Ullman, this is a tale of abiding love.
Rank Film Distributors — *VidAmerica*

Window, The 1949
Suspense
64365   73 mins   B/W   B, V, 3/4U   P
Bobby Driscoll, Barbara Hale, Arthur Kennedy, Ruth Roman
A little boy has a reputation for telling lies, so no one believes him when he says he witnessed a murder... except the killer.
RKO — *Nostalgia Merchant*

Winds of Change 1979
Folklore/Cartoons
65102   90 mins   C   B, V   P
Animated, voice of Peter Ustinov
A magical retelling of five ancient Greek myths which features a disco-rock musical score. Written by Norman Corwin.
Sanrio Film Distribution — *RCA/Columbia Pictures Home Video*

Winds of Kitty Hawk 19??
Aeronautics/Biographical
72457   90 mins   C   B, V   P
Michael Moriarty
The struggles and ultimate triumphs of Orville
and Wilbur Wright are dramatized in this E.W.
Swackhamer film.
Lawrence Schiller — *U.S.A. Home Video*

Winds of the Wasteland 1936
Western
14398   54 mins   B/W   B, V   P
John Wayne, Phyllis Fraser
While they are out of work, Pony Express riders
win a race for a government contract.
Republic — *Video Connection; Penguin Video;
Discount Video Tapes*

Windwalker 1981
Drama
69378   108 mins   C   B, V   P
Trevor Howard
An aged Indian chief shares the extraordinary
memories of his life with his grandchildren.
Native American dialect and English subtitles
are used throughout the film.
Pacific International Pictures — *CBS/Fox
Video*

Wine Program, The 1983
Alcoholic beverages
69682   30 mins   C   V   P
An introduction to the use and enjoyment of
wine, this program covers California varietals,
proper wine service and the pairing of wine with
food in a fundamental, yet enjoyable manner.
Espresso Productions — *McKesson Corp*

Wing Chun: The Science 1982
of In-Fighting
Martial arts
64015   40 mins   C   B, V   P
Theories and techniques of the Wing Chun
Kung fu style are demonstrated by Master Wong
Shun Leung.
Ng See Yuen; Roy Horan — *World Video
Enterprises*

Wings of Steel 1941
Armed Forces-US
74476   21 mins   C   B, V   P
This program is a 1941 U.S. Army Air Corps
Cadet training film.
Warner Brothers — *Interurban Films*

Wings of the Army 1940
Armed Forces-US/Aeronautics
72480   17 mins   B/W   B, V, 3/4U   P
The relationship and overall history of American
military and civilian aviation is presented by the
U.S. Army Corps.

US Army Corps — *International Historic Films*

Wings Over the Andes 1932
Documentary/South America
58527   36 mins   B/W   B, V, 3/4U   P
Narrated by Lowell Thomas
The inner Andes of Peru, as photographed by
the Shippee-Johnson Peruvian Expedition, are
explored.
Gaumont British — *Penguin Video*

Wings Over Wyoming 1937
Western
08825   65 mins   B/W   B, V, 3/4U   P
George O'Brien
Racketeer tries to move in on the honest
cattlemen, but Hollywood film star on vacation
saves the day.
RKO — *Penguin Video*

Winners of the West 1940
Western/Serials
14266   169 mins   B/W   B, V   P
Anne Nagel, Dick Foran, James Craig
A landowner schemes to prevent a railroad from
running through his property. The railroad's
chief engineer leads the good guys in an
attempt to prevent sabotage. A serial in thirteen
chapters.
Universal — *Video Connection; Penguin Video;
Nostalgia Merchant; Video Yesteryear*

Winning 1969
Drama
64560   123 mins   C   B, V   P
*Paul Newman, Joanne Woodward, Robert
Wagner, Richard Thomas*
A race car driver will let nothing stand in the way
of his winning the Indianapolis 500, including his
wife.
MPAA:PG
Universal — *MCA Home Video*

Winning Job Interview, 1983
The
Occupations
63388   60 mins   C   B, V, 3/4U,   R, P
                              FO
John C. Crystal, Nella Barkley
Techniques and strategies for performing
successfully at a job interview are presented.
Star Video Productions — *Star Video
Productions*

Winning of the West 1953
Western
62873   57 mins   B/W   B, V   P, T
Gene Autry, Smiley Burnette
Ranger Gene vows to protect a crusading
publisher from unscrupulous crooks.
Columbia — *Blackhawk Films*

Winning Tradition: 1977 New York Yankees, A
1977
Baseball
33828   32 mins   C   B, V   P
*Thurman Munson, Ron Guidry, Graig Nettles,
Reggie Jackson, Mickey Rivers*
Highlights of the Yankees 1977 season in which
they came from behind to beat the Kansas City
Royals in the ninth inning of the fifth and final
American League Championship game, then
went on to defeat the Los Angeles Dodgers in a
six-game World Series.
Major League Baseball — *Major League
Baseball Productions*

Winslow Boy, The
1948
Drama
63326   112 mins   B/W   B, V   R, P
*Robert Donat, Cedric Hardwicke, Margaret
Leighton, Frank Lawton, directed by Anthony
Asquith*
This film fictionalizes the events of a famous
Edwardian court case, in which a cadet at the
Royal Naval College was wrongly accused of
theft and expelled. His father fought it through
the courts to a satisfactory conclusion.
British Lion — *THORN EMI Home Video;
Movie Buff Video*

Winsome Witch
196?
Cartoons
69293   55 mins.   C   B,.V   P
Animated
This tape is a compilation of "Winsome Witch"
cartoons, in which a good-natured witch helps
people in distress.
Hanna-Barbera — *Worldvision Home Video*

Winsor McCay
1979
Cartoons
54122   60 mins   B/W   B, V   P
Animated
This tribute features cartoons produced
between 1903 and 1911 such as "Little Nemo"
and "The Pet," as well as "Gertie the
Dinosaur," the first commercial animated
cartoon.
Winsor McCay — *Video Dimensions; Festival
Films*

Winter Kills
1979
Drama
37408   97 mins   C   B, V   P
Jeff Bridges, John Huston, Anthony Perkins
The investigation of the fifteen-year-old
assassination of a President results in
numerous plots and counter-plots, intrigues and
assumed identities.
MPAA:R
Avco Embassy — *CBS/Fox Video*

Winter Light
1962
Drama
65629   80 mins   B/W   B, V   P
*Max von Sydow, Gunnar Bjornstrand, Ingrid
Thulin, directed by Ingmar Bergman*
"Winter Light" examines a day in the life of a
tormented, widowed pastor who has lost his
faith in God and searches for the spiritual
guidance he is unable to give to his
congregation.
Janus Films — *Embassy Home Entertainment*

Winter of Our Dreams
1983
Drama
65444   89 mins   C   B, V   P
Judy Davis, Bryan Brown
A lonely prostitute becomes romantically
involved with a married bookshop owner. Her
love turns into a burning obsession until she is
forced to free herself from her old
dependencies and begin a new life.
Satori Entertainment Corp — *U.S.A. Home
Video*

Winter Training
1982
Aeronautics
47787   45 mins   C   B, V, 3/4U   P
This edited version of "Threshold: The Blue
Angels Experience" contains the most
spectacular highlights of the performance by the
Navy's famed precision aerobatics
demonstration team.
Paul Marlow — *Aero/Space Visuals Society*

Winterset
1937
Drama
03897   85 mins   B/W   B, V   P
*Burgess Meredith, Margo, John Carradine,
directed by Alfred Santell*
Son seeks to clear father's name of falsely
accused crime twenty years after his
electrocution.
RKO; Pandro S Berman — *Budget Video;
Cable Films; Video Connection; Classic Video
Cinema Collector's Club*

Wisdom of the Bible
1980
Religion
68748   .60 mins   C   B, V, 3/4U   P
Passages from The Bible are read with musical
accompaniment.
Vision Productions — *Vision Productions*

Witch Who Came from the Sea, The
1976
Horror
72957   98 mins   C   B, V   P
Millie Perkins, Loni Chapman, Vanessa Brown
A witch terrorizes the ships at sea in this adult
drama.
MPAA:R
Matt Cimber — *Unicorn Video*

Witchcraft Through the Ages 1922
Horror
08692 90 mins B/W B, V, 3/4U P
Maren Pedersen, Clara Pontoppidan, directed by Benjamin Christiansen.
A nightmarish world of violence and eroticism set against an historical background.
Sweden — *Penguin Video; Western Film & Video Inc; Discount Video Tapes; Classic Video Cinema Collector's Club*

Witches' Brew 1979
Comedy
64977 98 mins C B, V, CED P
Teri Garr, Richard Benjamin, Lana Turner
Three young women try to use their undeveloped skills in witchcraft and black magic to help their husbands get a prestigious position at a university, with calamitous yet hilarious results.
MPAA:PG
Merritt-White Ltd — *Embassy Home Entertainment*

Witching, The 197?
Horror
66266 90 mins C B, V P
Orson Welles, Pamela Franklin, Michael Ontkean, Lee Purcell
A story of man's continuing quest for supernatural power.
Associates Entertainment Intl — *Paragon Video Productions*

Witch's Mirror, The 1960
Horror
51952 75 mins B/W B, V P
Rosita Arenas, Armand Calvo, Isabela Corona, Dina De Marco
A sorceress plots to destroy the murderer of her goddaughter. The murderer, a surgeon, begins a project to restore the disfigured face and hands of his burned second wife, no matter who he gets the raw material from.
K Gordon Murray; Trans International — *Budget Video*

With Buffalo Bill on the U.P. Trail 1925
Western
69571 74 mins B/W B, V, FO P
Roy Stewart, Cullen Landis, Kathryn McGuire
Young Buffalo Bill Cody, wagon train scout, leads his caravan of settlers Westward through danger and uncharted land.
Independent — *Video Yesteryear*

With the Marines at Tarawa 1943
World War II/Armed Forces-US
53682 20 mins C B, V, 3/4U P

A look at the naval bombardment of this tiny Pacific island and the incredible counter-attack of Japanese fire.
Unknown — *International Historic Films*

With the Marines—Chosin Hungnam 1951
Armed Forces-US/Korean War
72485 29 mins B/W B, V, 3/4U P
During the Korean War the Marines carried out history's most successful evacuation of soldiers, civilians and war material. This film shows the evacuation and the events leading up to it.
US Government — *International Historic Films*

Without a Trace 1983
Drama
69374 119 mins C B, V, CED P
Kate Nelligan, Judd Hirsch
A mother becomes frantic when her 6-year-old son disappears, and a detective steps in to help.
MPAA:PG
Stanley Jaffe — *CBS/Fox Video*

Without Reservations 1946
Comedy
13196 101 mins B/W B, V P
Claudette Colbert, John Wayne
Hollywood-bound novelist encounters a Marine flyer and his pal aboard a train.
RKO; Mervyn LeRoy — *VCI Home Video; Video Connection*

Witness for the Prosecution 1957
Mystery/Drama
64563 114 mins B/W B, V, CED P
Charles Laughton, Tyrone Power, Marlene Dietrich, Elsa Lanchester, directed by Billy Wildor
An unemployed man is accused of murdering a wealthy widow whom he befriended. What starts out as a straightforward court case becomes increasingly complicated in this adaptation of an Agatha Christie stage play.
United Artists — *CBS/Fox Video*

Wives Under Suspicion 1938
Drama
51608 75 mins B/W B, V P
Warren William, Gail Patrick, Constance Moore, William Lundigan
While prosecuting a love-murder, a district attorney finds his home in a similar disorder.
Universal — *Discount Video Tapes; Classic Video Cinema Collector's Club*

Wiz, The 1978
Musical/Fantasy
48639 133 mins C B, V, LV P

*Diana Ross, Michael Jackson, Nipsey Russell,
Ted Ross, Mabel King, Thelma Carpenter*
A version of the long-time favorite "The Wizard
of Oz," based on the Broadway musical. It is
reset in a fantasy version of New York City,
centering on a young black woman searching
for her identity.
MPAA:G
Universal — *MCA Home Video*

Wizard of Oz, The   1982
Fantasy
65402   78 mins   C   B, V   R, P
Animated
The animated version of the classic film "The
Wizard of Oz" is ideally suited for young
children. Featured are the voices of Lorne
Greene and Aileen Quinn. In stereo VHS and
Beta Hi-Fi.
Paramount — *Paramount Home Video*

Wizard of Oz, The   1939
Musical/Fantasy
44640   101 mins   C   B, V, LV,   P
                              CED
*Judy Garland, Ray Bolger, Frank Morgan, Bert
Lahr, Jack Haley, directed by Victor Fleming*
A Kansas farm girl dreams she and her dog are
somewhere over the rainbow, in the wonderful
land of Oz. On her adventure to find the "Great
Oz" she is joined by the Scarecrow, the Tin
Man, and the Cowardly Lion. Based on the book
by Frank L. Baum.
Academy Awards '39: Best Original Music Score
(Stothart); Best Song: "Over the Rainbow"
(Harburg and Arlen).
MGM — *MGM/UA Home Video*

Wolf Call   1939
Adventure
29684   60 mins   B/W   B, V   P
John Carroll, Polly Ann Young, Movita
A playboy visits his father's radium mine and
finds a syndicate trying to take it over. Based on
Jack London's story.
Monogram — *Sheik Video*

Wolf Dog   1933
Adventure
12556   156 mins   B/W   B, V   P
*Rin Tin Tin, Jr., Frankie Darro, Boots Mallory,
directed by Harry Fraser, Colbert Clark*
A boy and his dog. Outdoor action and
adventure. Twelve chapters, 13 minutes each.
Mascot — *Video Connection*

Wolf Lake   1979
Drama
75488   90 mins   C   B, V   P
Rod Steiger, David Hoffman
A World War II veteran and a Vietnam army
deserter have a clash of personalities.

Unknown — *Prism*

Wolfen   1981
Horror
58257   115 mins   C   B, V   R, P
*Albert Finney, Gregory Hines, Tom Noonan,
directed by Michael Wadleigh*
A thriller which spins a tale of myth and menace
as creatures from the darkness live among us.
MPAA:R
Orion Pictures — *Warner Home Video*

Wolfheart's Revenge   1924
Western
08824   55 mins   B/W   B, V, 3/4U   P
Guinn 'Big Boy' Williams
Early western featuring "Big Boy" Williams.
Silent.
Aywon — *Penguin Video*

Wolfman   1982
Horror
63354   91 mins   C   B, V   R, P
Earl Owensby, Kristina Reynolds
In 1910, a young man learns that his family is
heir to the curse of the Werewolf.
UG Productions — *THORN EMI Home Video*

Woman Called Golda, A   1982
Biographical/Drama
63429   ? mins   C   B, V   R, P
Ingrid Bergman, Leonard Nimoy
Ingrid Bergman portrays the fiery Golda Meir,
one of the most powerful women and one of the
most important political figures of the 20th
century.
Emmy Awards '82: Best Actress (Bergman);
Film Editing.
Paramount TV — *Paramount Home Video*

Woman in Grey   1919
Adventure
57433   ? mins   B/W   B, V   P, T
Arline Pretty, Henry Sell
A man and a woman battle wits when they
attempt to locate and unravel the Army Code
while staying one jump ahead of J. Haviland
Hunter, a suave villain after the same fortune.
Silent.
Unknown — *Blackhawk Films*

Woman in the Dunes   1964
Drama
33443   127 mins   B/W   B, V   P
Directed by Hiroshi Teshigahara
A man and a woman are trapped in a shack at
the bottom of a sand pit among isolated dunes.
Based on the highly acclaimed novel by Kobe
Abe. In Japanese with English subtitles.
JA
Unknown — *Sheik Video; Festival Films;
Western Film & Video Inc; Budget Video*

Woman in the Moon   **1929**
Science fiction
07285   115 mins   B/W   B, V, 3/4U   P
Klaus Pohl, Willie Fritsch, Gustav von Wagenheim, Gerda Maurus, directed by Fritz Lang.
An incongruous mixture of people embark upon a trip to the moon and discover water, an area with atmosphere, and gold. (Silent with musical soundtrack).
UFA — *International Historic Films; Video Yesteryear; Festival Films*

Woman of the Town, The   **1943**
Western
66406   90 mins   B/W   B, V   P
Claire Trevor, Albert Dekker, Barry Sullivan
The story of frontier marshal Bat Masterson and Dora Hall, the dance hall girl he loved.
United Artists — *Movie Buff Video*

Woman of the Town   **1943**
Western
72056   89 mins   B/W   B, V   P
Claire Trevor, Albert Dekker
Marshall Bat Masterson has an ill-fated affair with a dance hall girl.
United Artists; Harry Sherman Productions — *Independent United Distributors*

Woman of the Year   **1942**
Comedy
58704   114 mins   B/W   B, V   P
Spencer Tracy, Katharine Hepburn, directed by George Stevens
The first of the classic Tracy/Hepburn films concerns the rocky marriage of a political columnist and a sportswriter.
Academy Awards '42: Best Original Screenplay (Ring Lardner, Jr.). Film Daily Poll '42: Ten Best of Year.
MGM — *MGM/UA Home Video*

Woman Rebels, A   **1936**
Drama
10055   88 mins   B/W   B, V   P, T
Katharine Hepburn, Herbert Marshall, Elizabeth Allan, Donald Crisp, Van Heflin
Courageous Victorian woman challenges establishment with radical positions on womens' rights.
RKO; Pandro S Berman — *Blackhawk Films*

Women in Cell Block 7   **1983**
Drama
66517   90 mins   C   B, V   P
Anita Strinberg, Eve Czemeys
The inmates of a women's prison suffer cruel and unspeakable tortures from their jailers and each other.
MPAA:R

Unknown — *Paragon Video Productions*

Women in Love   **1970**
Drama
58840   129 mins   C   B, V, CED   P
Glenda Jackson, Jennie Linden, Alan Bates, Oliver Reed, Eleanor Bron
D. H. Lawrence's novel about two girls having their first sexual encounters in the Midlands during the 1920's provides the basis for this film.
Academy Awards '70:; Best Actress (Jackson).
MPAA:R
United Artists — *CBS/Fox Video*

Women of the Prehistoric Planet   **1966**
Science fiction
66522   87 mins   C   B, V   P
Wendell Corey, Irene Tsu, Robert Ito
On a strange planet, the members of a space rescue mission face deadly perils.
Realart — *Paragon Video Productions*

Woods and Tee Shots   **197?**
Golf
33779   60 mins   C   B, V, 3/4U   P
Golf pros Neal Doyle, Joyce Ann Jackson, and Linda Craft give lessons on how to straighten and lengthen your tee shots and fairway wood shots. Part of the series, "The Name of the Game Is Golf."
Unknown — *Sports World Cinema*

Woodstock   **1970**
Musical
38957   180 mins   C   B, V   R, P
Canned Heat, Richie Havens, The Who, Joan Baez, Country Joe and the Fish, Jimi Hendrix, Santana, Crosby Stills and Nash
A chronicle of the great 1969 Woodstock rock concert, celebrating the music and lifestyle of the late sixties. Classic performances by a great number of popular rock performers and groups. Available on two tapes, labeled "Woodstock I" and "Woodstock II," each running 90 minutes.
Academy Awards '70: Best Feature Documentary. MPAA:R
Wadleigh Maurice Ltd; Bob Maurice — *Warner Home Video; RCA VideoDiscs*

Woody Woodpecker and His Friends, Volume I   **1982**
Cartoons
62781   80 mins   C   B, V, LV, CED   P
Animated
Ten favorite 1940-1955 Walter Lantz "cartunes" were chosen for this tape: "Knock Knock," "Bandmaster," "Ski for Two," "Hot Noon," "The Legend of Rockabye Point," "Wet Blanket Policy," "To Catch a Woodpecker," "Musical Moments from Chopin," "Bats in the Belfry" and "Crazy Mixed-Up Pup."

Walter Lantz — *MCA Home Video*

Woody Woodpecker and His Friends, Volume II 1983
Cartoons
65339 59 mins C B, V P
Animated
A compilation of 8 classic cartoons from 1941
through 1954 selected by Woody's creator,
Walter Lantz. Woody Woodpecker, Andy Panda
and Wally Walrus are featured.
Walter Lantz Productions; Universal — *MCA
Home Video*

Word Processor, The 1983
Electronic data processing
72968 20 mins C B, V P
How the word processor came into existence
along with an overview on the computer's
components and its functions are explained in
this program.
Star Merchants — *Increase Video*

Work/Police 1916
Comedy
58656 54 mins B/W B, V, FO P
*Charlie Chaplin, Billy Armstrong, Charles Insley,
Marta Golden, Edna Purviance, directed by
Charlie Chaplin*
Two Chaplin two-reelers: "Work (The Paper
Hanger)" (1915), in which Charlie is hired to
repaper a house; and "Police" (1916), in which
Charlie plays an ex-con who is released into the
cruel world. Silent with music score.
Essanay — *Video Yesteryear*

World According to Garp, The 1982
Comedy
63123 136 mins C B, V, CED R, P
*Robin Williams, Mary Beth Hurt, John Lithgow,
directed by George Roy Hill*
This film version of John Irving's popular novel
chronicles the life of T.S. Garp, a bizarre
everyman beset by the destructive forces of
modern society.
MPAA:R
Warner Bros — *Warner Home Video*

World at War 1943
World War II
50618 44 mins B/W B, V, 3/4U P
Directed by Samuel Spewack
The events from 1931-1941 which led to the
U.S. involvement in World War II are
documented by newsreels and enemy film
footage.
Office of War Information — *International
Historic Films*

World at War, The 1980
World War II/Documentary
59699 104 mins B/W B, V R, P
Narrated by Sir Laurence Olivier
The highly acclaimed documentary about World
War II told through newsreel footage, containing
remarkable interviews with statesmen, military
leaders, and the men and women who fought it.
Thames Video — *THORN EMI Home Video*

World at War, The 1980
World War II/Documentary
69628 52 mins B/W B, V R, P
Narrated by Sir Laurence Olivier 26 pgms
This 26-volume series depicts, through actual
film footage, all of the horror and heroism of
World War II in great historical detail. Each
program is available separately.
*1.A New Germany 1933-39 2.Distant War 1939-
40 3.France Falls—May-June 1940
4.Alone—Britain—May 1940-June 1941
5.Barbarossa—June-December 1941
6.Banzai—Japan Strikes 7.On Our
Way—America Enters the War 8.Desert—The
War in North Africa 9.Stalingrad 10.Wolfpack
11.Red Star 12.Whirlwind 13.Tough Old Gut
14.It's a Lovely Day Tomorrow 15.Home Fires
16.Inside the Reich—Germany 1940-44
17.Morning 18.Occupation 19.Pincers
20.Genocide 21.Nemesis 22.Japan 1941-45
23.The Island to Island War 24.The Bomb
25.Reckoning 26.Remember*
Jeremy Isaacs; Thames Television — *THORN
EMI Home Video*

World Gone Mad, The 1933
Drama
08749 70 mins B/W B, V, 3/4U P
Pat O'Brien, Louis Calhern, J. Carrol Naish
Crime drama set during the Prohibition Era.
Majectic Pictures — *Penguin Video; Cable
Films; Discount Video Tapes*

World of Apu, The 1959
Drama
55810 103 mins B/W B, V P
Directed by Satyajit Ray
The concluding part of Ray's highly acclaimed
"Apu Trilogy" covering Apu's manhood. In
Bengali dialogue with English subtitles.
India — *Festival Films; Budget Video; Video
Yesteryear*

World of Fashion, The 1983
Clothing and dress
69793 30 mins C B, V P
20 pgms
This series captures the essence of the fashion
world by looking at fashion models,
photographers and numerous designers.
Programs are available individually.
*1.Fashion Models 2.Fashion Photographers
3.Fashion Designers 4.The Future of Fashion
5.John Anthony 6.Bill Atkinson 7.Geoffrey*

Beene 8.Bill Blass 9.Perry Ellis 10.Mitchell Gross 11.Bill Hase 12.Halston 13.Katheryn Hipp 14.Carol Horn 15.Betsy Johnson 16.Bill Kaiserman 17.Donna Karen and Louise Del'Olio for Anne Klein 18.Ralph Lauren 19.Calvin Klein 20.Mary McFadden
Video Associates — *Gold Stripe Video*

World of Martial Arts, The   1982
Martial arts
59685   60 mins   C   B, V   P
Narrated by John Saxon, Chuck Norris, Al Thomas
This program offers a basic training in budojujutsu, a combination of techniques from seven different martial arts.
Universal — *MCA Home Video; Optical Programming Associates*

World of Polo, A   1984
Sports-Minor
74545   56 mins   C   B, V   P
This tape looks at the history and present state of the sport of polo.
Rolex — *Mercedes Maharis Productions*

World of the Vampires, The   1960
Horror
51099   75 mins   B/W   B, V   P
Mauricio Garces, Erna Martha Bauman, Silvia Fournier, Guillermo Murray
An evil count commands his vampire legions to wreak vengeance upon the family whose ancestors condemned him.
Mexican — *Budget Video*

World Series, 1943   1943
Baseball
33864   ? mins   B/W   B, V   P
New York Yankees, St. Louis Cardinals
Both teams incorporate new faces to replace stars serving in the war. The Yankees avenge their previous year's defeat by the Cardinals by winning this World Series four games to one. Spud Chandler pitches two victories for manager Joe McCarthy's Bronx Bombers.
Lou Fonseca — *Major League Baseball Productions*

World Series, 1944   1944
Baseball
33863   ? mins   B/W   B, V   P
St. Louis Cardinals, St Louis Browns
In the first and only series played between two St. Louis teams, the Cardinals prevail in six games, led by shortstop Marty Marion and pitchers Max Lanier and Ted Wilks. First baseman George McQuinn bats .438 for the Browns.
Lou Fonseca — *Major League Baseball Productions*

World Series, 1945   1945
Baseball
33862   ? mins   B/W   B, V   P
Detroit Tigers, Chicago Cubs
Tiger stars recently returned from military service, pitcher Virgil Trucks and slugger Hank Greenberg, lead the Detroit club to a four games to three victory over the Cubs.
Lou Fonseca — *Major League Baseball Productions*

World Series, 1946   1946
Baseball
33861   ? mins   B/W   B, V   P
St. Louis Cardinals, Boston Red Sox
Enos Slaughter scores all the way from first base on Harry Walker's single to score the winning run for the Cardinals in game seven. Harry Breechen recorded three victories for St. Louis against the likes of Red Sox sluggers Ted Williams, Dom DiMaggio, and Rudy York.
Lou Fonseca — *Major League Baseball Productions*

World Series, 1947   1947
Baseball
33860   ? mins   B/W   B, V   P
New York Yankees, Brooklyn Dodgers
Al Gionfriddo's leaping catch of Joe DiMaggio's long drive sends the Yankees and Dodgers into a seventh game showdown. Yankee outfielder Tommy Henrich drives in the winning run and Joe Page hurls five scoreless innings to preserve the victory.
Lou Fonseca — *Major League Baseball Productions*

World Series, 1948   1948
Baseball
33859   ? mins   B/W   B, V   P
Cleveland Indians, Boston Braves
Behind the pitching of Bob Lemon and Gene Bearden and the solid fielding of Ken Keltner, Joe Gordon, and Lou Boudreau, the Indians outlast Warren Spahn, Johnny Sain and the rest of the Braves, who were headed for Milwaukee in a few years, in six games.
Lou Fonseca — *Major League Baseball Productions*

World Series, 1949   1949
Baseball
33858   ? mins   B/W   B, V   P
New York Yankees, Brooklyn Dodgers
Allie Reynolds and Preacher Roe trade 1-0 victories in the first two games, then the Yankees win the next three with Joe Page, Gerry Coleman, and Johnny Mize in starring roles.
Lou Fonseca — *Major League Baseball Productions*

World Series, 1950   1950
Baseball
33848   ? mins   B/W   B, V   P
New York Yankees, Philadelphia Phillies
The "Whiz Kids" of Philadelphia surprise the
National League in winning the pennant, but the
Yankees, in the midst of five consecutive World
Championship seasons, make easy picking of
the Phillies in four straight games.
Lou Fonseca — *Major League Baseball
Productions*

World Series, 1951   1951
Baseball
33852   ? mins   B/W   B, V   P
New York Yankees, New York Giants
The Giants enter the series coming off their
emotional playoff victory over the Dodgers
which featured Bobby Thompson's "Shot Heard
'Round the World" in the ninth inning of the final
game. They run out of miracles against the
Yankees however, as Eddie Lopat and Allie
Reynolds lead a solid pitching staff to a six-
game victory for the Yankees in Joe DiMaggio's
final season and Mickey Mantle's first.
Lou Fonseca — *Major League Baseball
Productions*

World Series, 1952   1952
Baseball
33857   ? mins   B/W   B, V   P
New York Yankees, Brooklyn Dodgers
Vic Raschi and Allie Reynolds win two games
apiece for the Yankees and Billy Martin makes a
diving catch of Jackie Robinson's pop-up to
save the seventh and deciding game for the
New Yorkers. Pee Wee Reese and Duke Snider
each batted .345 to lead the Dodger effort.
Lou Fonseca — *Major League Baseball
Productions*

World Series, 1953   1953
Baseball
33856   ? mins   B/W   B, V   P
New York Yankees, Brooklyn Dodgers
Yankee second baseman Billy Martin bats .500
and drives in the winning run in the final game
as the Yankees defeat the Dodgers four games
to two, capturing their unprecedented fifth
consecutive World Series title.
Lou Fonseca — *Major League Baseball
Productions*

World Series, 1954   1954
Baseball
33849   ? mins   B/W   B, V   P
New York Giants, Cleveland Indians
The Indians won a record 111 games during the
regular season, but did not win their next game
until the following year. The Giants, sparked by
Willie Mays' famous catch of Vic Wertz deep
line drive, went on to defeat player-manager Lou
Boudreau's Cleveland team in four straight
games.

Lou Fonseca — *Major League Baseball
Productions*

World Series, 1955   1955
Baseball
33850   ? mins   B/W   B, V   P
Brooklyn Dodgers, New York Yankees
It's a dream come true for the bums from
Brooklyn. For the first time in six tries the
Dodgers beat their cross-town rivals, the hated
Yankees, in the World series. Johnny Padres
notches three of the Brooklyn wins, including a
2-0 masterpiece in game seven at Yankee
Stadium. Sandy Amoros' catch of Yogi Berra's
long fly ball thwarted an important Yankee rally
and was the key defensive play of the series.
Lou Fonseca — *Major League Baseball
Productions*

World Series, 1956   1956
Baseball
33855   ? mins   B/W   B, V   P
New York Yankees, Brooklyn Dodgers
The Dodgers came from behind to win each of
the first two games, but the Yankees captured
the next three contests, including Don Larsen's
perfect game in game five at Yankee Stadium.
Jackie Robinson's tenth inning hit gave the
Dodgers a 1-0 victory in game six to tie the
series. The Yankees won easily in the seventh
game to give manager Casey Stengel his sixth
world championship.
Lou Fonseca — *Major League Baseball
Productions*

World Series, 1957   1957
Baseball
33851   ? mins   B/W   B, V   P
Milwaukee Braves, New York Yankees
The Braves, led by the hitting of Hank Aaron,
Eddie Mathews, and Joe Adcock, surprise
Casey Stengel's World Champion Yankees in
seven games. Righthander Lew Burdette is the
hero, pitching three of the Braves' victories.
Lou Fonseca — *Major League Baseball
Productions*

World Series, 1958   1958
Baseball
48143   ? mins   C   B, V   P
New York Yankees, Milwaukee Braves
The Yankees avenge their previous year's
defeat by the Braves by rallying from a three
games to one deficit to defeat Eddie Mathews,
Hank Aaron and the hard-hitting Braves in
seven games. Mickey Mantle and Whitey Ford
spark the Yankee comeback.
Lou Fonseca — *Major League Baseball
Productions*

World Series, 1959   1959
Baseball
33854   ? mins   B/W   B, V   P

Los Angeles Dodgers, Chicago White Sox
After the White Sox captured the opening game 11-0; the Dodgers, with fine relief pitching by Larry Sherry and steady hitting by Gil Hodges, beat Chicago in six games. Their old Brooklyn fans saw a collection of familiar faces and few new kids playing on a team that now belonged to the West Coast.
Lou Fonseca — *Major League Baseball Productions*

World Series, 1960   1960
Baseball
33826   ? mins   B/W   B, V   P
New York Yankees, Pittsburgh Pirates
Bill Mazeroski's leadoff home run off Ralph Terry in the bottom of the ninth in game seven at Forbes Field gives the Pirates a 10-9 victory and wins the World Series over the Yankees, four games to three.
Lou Fonseca — *Major League Baseball Productions*

World Series, 1961   1961
Baseball
33853   ? mins   B/W   B, V   P
New York Yankees, Cincinnati Reds
This was the year Roger Maris and Mickey Mantle combined for 115 home runs. Although neither had a very good World Series, Elston Howard, Bobby Richardson, and several reserve players led the Yankees to a four games to one victory over Fred Hutchinson's Reds. Whitey Ford's two pitching victories gave him four straight series wins.
Lou Fonseca — *Major League Baseball Productions*

World Series, 1962   1962
Baseball
33824   ? mins   C   B, V   P
New York Yankees, San Francisco Giants
In a series frequently interrupted by rain delays, the Yankees outlast the Giants four games to three. With the Yankees leading by a run with two out in the bottom of the ninth in game seven, the Giants load the bases and big Willie McCovey steps to the plate. His scorching line drive is driven right into the glove of Yankee second baseman Bobby Richardson, for the final out.
Lou Fonseca — *Major League Baseball Productions*

World Series, 1963   1963
Baseball
33823   ? mins   C   B, V   P
Los Angeles Dodgers, New York Yankees
Sandy Koufax breaks Carl Erskine's World Series strikeout record, fanning fifteen while the Dodgers are en route to a four game sweep over the defending champion Yankees.

Lou Fonseca — *Major League Baseball Productions*

World Series, 1964   1964
Baseball
33822   ? mins   C   B, V   P
St. Louis Cardinals, New York Yankees
Young Yankee pitchers Jim Bouton and Mel Stottlemyre are impressive, but Bob Gibson is even better for the Cardinals. A grand slam home run by Ken Boyer is the big hit in this series, won by the Cardinals four games to three. The great Mickey Mantle, in what is to be his last World Series, adds to his record status for the October Classic.
Lou Fonseca — *Major League Baseball Productions*

World Series, 1965   1965
Baseball
33821   ? mins   C   B, V   P
Los Angeles Dodgers, Minnesota Twins
Sandy Koufax and Don Drysdale stymie the big Minnesota bats of Harmon Killebrew and Bob Allison long enough for the Dodgers to squeak by the Twins in seven games. "Sweet" Lou Johnson swings a hot bat for the Dodgers.
Lou Fonseca — *Major League Baseball Productions*

World Series, 1966   1966
Baseball
33820   ? mins   C   B, V   P
Baltimore Orioles, Los Angeles Dodgers
Dave McNally, Jim Palmer, Steve Barber, and Wally Bunker, with relief help from Moe Drabowsky, send the Dodgers down in four straight. Sandy Koufax and Don Drysdale pitch well for the Dodgers, but the Robinsons, Frank and Brooks, provide timely hitting for the Orioles.
Lou Fonseca — *Major League Baseball Productions*

World Series, 1967   1967
Baseball
33819   ? mins   C   B, V   P
St. Louis Cardinals, Boston Red Sox
The Red Sox, ninth place finishers the previous year, are led to the series by Carl Yastrzemski, Tony Conigliaro, and Ken Harrelson. Boston ace Jim Lonborg flirts with a no-hitter in one game, but the St. Louis bats finally quell the Sox in seven games, led by Lou Brock, Orlando Cepeda, and Tim McCarver, and the pitching of Bob Gibson.
Lou Fonseca — *Major League Baseball Productions*

World Series, 1968   19??
Baseball
33818   ? mins   C   B, V   P
Detroit Tigers, St. Louis Cardinals

(For Explanation of codes, see USE GUIDE and KEY)

The Tigers stage a comeback to beat the Cardinals in seven games after falling behind three games to one. Mickey Lolich tosses three of the Tiger victories and Mickey Stanley, normally a centerfielder, stars at shortstop. Bob Gibson wins two games for the Cardinals, setting a series game strikeout record in the process.
Lou Fonseca — *Major League Baseball Productions*

World Series, 1969   1969
Baseball
33817   40 mins   C   B, V   P
New York Mets, Baltimore Orioles
The Miracle Mets stun the world by taking four straight from the mighty Orioles after losing the opening game. Outstanding defensive plays by Tommie Agee and Ron Swoboda stymie Baltimore rallies. Jerry Koosman wins two games, and MVP Donn Clendenon and utility infielder Al Weis pace the Mets' hitting attack.
W and W Prods — *Major League Baseball Productions*

World Series, 1970   1970
Baseball
33816   40 mins   C   B, V   P
Baltimore Orioles, Cincinnati Reds
Brooks Robinson's incredible fielding and .429 batting average help the Orioles to a four games to one victory over the Reds. Baltimore's pitching staff silences the Big Red Machine sluggers like Johnny Bench and Lee May.
W and W Prods — *Major League Baseball Productions*

World Series, 1971   1971
Baseball
33815   40 mins   C   B, V   P
Pittsburgh Pirates, Baltimore Orioles
The sensational hitting of Roberto Clemente and two clutch pitching wins by Steve Blass lead the Pirates to a seven-game triumph over the defending champion Orioles. This series featured the first night game in World Series history.
W and W Productions — *Major League Baseball Productions*

World Series, 1972   1972
Baseball
33814   40 mins   C   B, V   P
Oakland A's, Cincinnati Reds
The A's win a seven-game thriller without their star outfielder Reggie Jackson, who is lost to an injury. Gene Tenace provides the home run heroics, and MVP left fielder Joe Rudi makes a remarkable catch that many consider as the turning point of the series.
W and W Prods — *Major League Baseball Productions*

World Series, 1973   1973
Baseball
33813   40 mins   C   B, V   P
Oakland A's, New York Mets
The Oakland A's win their second consecutive title, in seven games. The talented Mets pitching staff holds the powerful A's in check, but Bert Campaneris and Reggie Jackson belt home runs in the final game to finally subdue the gallant New Yorkers.
W and W Prods — *Major League Baseball Productions*

World Series, 1974   1974
Baseball
33812   26 mins   C   B, V   P
Oakland A's, Los Angeles Dodgers
The A's win their third straight world championship in a tightly contested, five game series in which four games were decided by 3-2 scores. The fielding of second baseman Dick Green and relief pitching of series MVP Rollie Fingers makes the difference for the A's.
W and W Prods — *Major League Baseball Productions*

World Series, 1975   1975
Baseball
33811   35 mins   C   B, V   P
Cincinnati Reds, Boston Red Sox
In one of the most memorable and exciting World Series ever played, the Reds take a three games to two lead after five games. Carlton Fisk's dramatic 12th inning homer evens the series in game six. The Red Sox take an early lead in the final game, but series MVP Pete Rose and Joe Morgan lead a Cincinnati comeback to give the Reds their first World Championship in 35 years.
Major League Baseball — *Major League Baseball Productions*

World Series, 1976   1976
Baseball
33810   30 mins   C   B, V   P
Cincinnati Reds, New York Yankees
The Reds demolish the Yankees in four straight, led by MVP catcher Johnny Bench. Yankee catcher Thurman Munson performs gallantly, batting .529 for the series. Reds' manager Sparky Anderson is "miked" throughout, giving the viewer a rare glimpse at a manager's feelings during pressure-filled games.
Major League Baseball — *Major League Baseball Productions*

World Series, 1977   1977
Baseball
33809   30 mins   C   B, V   P
New York Yankees, Los Angles Dodgers
Yankee slugger Reggie Jackson grabs the spotlight by belting five homers in the series, won by New York 4 games to 2. Jackson's heroics include three consecutive home runs in

the final game. Yankee pitcher Mike Torrez goes undefeated in his two starts. This program also captures the antics of Dodger manager Tom Lasorda and sets the mannerisms of baseball players to ballet music.
Major League Baseball — *Major League Baseball Productions*

World Series, 1978   1978
Baseball
33808   31 mins   C   B, V   P
New York Yankees, Los Angeles Dodgers
The Yankees beat the Dodgers in six games for the second year in a row. Yankee shortstop Bucky Dent wins the series MVP award while Graig Nettles, Reggie Jackson, Thurman Munson, and rookie Brian Doyle lead the champs at bat and on the field. Ron Cey and Davey Lopes excel for the Dodgers. The victory caps a memorable season for New York, one in which they came from 14 games out of first place in July to eventually win a one-game playoff with the Boston Red Sox for the American League East Championship.
Major League Baseball — *Major League Baseball Productions*

World Series, 1979   1979
Baseball
33847   31 mins   C   B, V   P
Pittsburgh Pirates, Baltimore Orioles
Oriole Manager Earl Weaver is hailed as a genius after expertly maneuvering his Birds to a 3-1 lead after four games. Baltimore never won another game in the series though, as MVP Willie "Pops" Stargell and the Pirate relief pitchers rose to the occasion and dominated the remainder of the series. Stargell's two-run homer off Scott McGregor in game seven moved the Pirate ahead to stay.
Major League Baseball — *Major League Baseball Productions*

World Series, 1980   1980
Baseball
49548   30 mins   C   B, V   P
Philadelphia Phillies, Kansas City Royals
The clutch hitting of Mike Schmidt and Pete Rose, and the heart-stopping relief provided by Tug McGraw leads the Phillies to a six-game victory over the Royals. George Brett, Willie Aikens, and Amos Otis try to carry the Royals back after falling behind two games to none, but their impressive efforts are not enough to overcome the Phillies.
MAJ — *Major League Baseball Productions; RCA VideoDiscs*

World Series, 1981   1981
Baseball
59377   30 mins   C   B, V   P
New York Yankees, Los Angeles Dodgers
The Yankees fall apart after winning the first two games. The series begins to turn in Los Angeles when rookie pitchers Fernando Valenzuela and Dave Righetti meet, with the Dodgers' Valenzuela emerging victorious. Timely hitting by Ron Cey, Steve Yeager, Jay Johnstone and Pedro Guerrero carries the Dodgers to a six-game victory over the faltering Yankees.
Major League Baseball Productions — *Major League Baseball Productions*

World Series, 1982   1982
Baseball
64659   45 mins   C   B, V   P
St. Louis Cardinels, Milwaukee Brewers
Willie McGee, Bruce Sutter, and MVP Darrell Porter lead the NL champion Cardinals to victories in games 6 and 7 as the Redbirds defeat the Milwaukee Brewers 4 games to 3. The big bats of Milwaukee's Robin Yount and Cecil Cooper could not overcome the loss of their injured ballpen ace, Rollie Fingers.
Major League Baseball — *Major League Baseball Productions*

World War II: The European Theatre   194?
World War II/Documentary
44984   55 mins   B/W   B, V   P, T
In this footage from the Fox/Movietone newsreel vaults, six separate subjects are covered: "Battle of the Atlantic," "Battle of Britain," "War in the Desert," "Liberation of Paris," "Fall of Hitler's Nazis," and "1945: Year of Triumph."
Movietone — *Blackhawk Films*

World War II: The Pacific Theatre   194?
World War II/Documentary
29471   55 mins   B/W   B, V   P, T
A compilation taken from actual newsreel footage of World War II. The show begins with the authentic scenes of Pearl Harbor and closes with a final surrender of Japan in 1945.
Movietone — *Blackhawk Films*

World War II Video Series—Attack: The Battle of New Britain   1945
World War II/Documentary
66361   50 mins   B/W   B, V, 3/4U   P
A filmed record of the invasion of New Britain in the South Pacific theater of war.
Office of War Information — *Nostalgia Merchant*

World War II Video Series—Something for Our Boys   1945
World War II/Documentary
66362   50 mins   B/W   B, V, 3/4U   P
Judy Garland, Bob Hope, Carmen Miranda and others

A selection of shorts featuring many Hollywood and radio stars performing overseas for the pleasure of Allied troops during 1943-1945.
Office of War Information — *Nostalgia Merchant*

World War II Video Series—The Stillwell Road   1945
Documentary/World War II
66337   50 mins   B/W   B, V, 3/4U   P
The story of the China-Burma-India campaign during World War II, with authentic documentary footage of jungle battles and aerial combat.
US Army — *Nostalgia Merchant*

World War II Video Series—Tried by Fire!   19??
World War II/Documentary
66360   50 mins   B/W   B, V, 3/4U   P
The combat history of World War II's 84th Infantry Division, from its activities early in the war through the Battle of the Bulge, is chronicled.
Office of War Information — *Nostalgia Merchant*

World's Greatest Photography Course, The   1983
Photography
66000   90 mins   C   B, V   P
A step-by-step course designed for people who want to learn how to take great 35mm pictures.
Video Corporation of America — *VidAmerica*

Worth the Wait!   1981
Baseball
55597   59 mins   C   B, V   P
Highlights of the 1980 World Series between the Kansas City Royals and the Philadelphia Phillies, and the 1980 All-Star Game in which the National League stars defeated the American League stars in the Summer Classic.
Major League Baseball — *VidAmerica*

Wrestling Women vs. the Aztec Mummy, The   1965
Horror
51100   75 mins   B/W   B, V   P
Lorena Velasquez, Armando Silvestre, Elizabeth Campbell, Chucho Salinas
The Black Dragon is out to get hidden Aztec treasure from an ancient pyramid. His chief opposition comes from two formidable lady wrestlers.
Mexican — *Budget Video; Festival Films*

Wright Brothers: Masters of the Sky, The   19??
Biographical/Aeronautics
69586   47 mins   C   B, V   P

Two young daredevils defy traditional thought, fix their eyes and hopes on the sky, and overcome a steady stream of failures to provide man with the means to fly.
Unknown — *VidAmerica*

Wright Brothers: Wings Over Kitty Hawk   1954
Biographical/Aeronautics
44268   15 mins   B/W   B, V   P
An account of the Wright Brothers' first historic flight in December, 1903 and a pictorial review of aviation's progress and development during the next 50 years. Classic newsreel footage.
Fox Movietone News — *Two Star Films*

Wrong Is Right   1982
Adventure/Comedy
60339   117 mins   C   B, V   P
Sean Connery, Katherine Ross, Robert Conrad, George Grizzard, Henry Silva, directed by Richard Brooks
A black comedy revolving around international terrorism, news reporting and the CIA.
MPAA:R
Columbia — *RCA/Columbia Pictures Home Video*

Wrong Man, The   1956
Suspense
47618   126 mins   B/W   B, V   R, P
Henry Fonda, Vera Miles, Anthony Quayle, directed by Alfred Hitchcock
A musician is accused of a robbery that he did not commit. Part of the "A Night at the Movies" series, this tape simulates a 1956 movie evening, with a color Bugs Bunny cartoon, "A Star Is Bored," a newsreel and coming attractions for "Toward the Unknown."
Warner Bros — *Warner Home Video*

X

X -- The Man with X-Ray Eyes   1963
Science fiction
65140   79 mins   C   B, V   R, P
Ray Milland, Diana Van Der Vlis, Harold J. Stone, directed by Roger Corman
A scientist uses himself as a guinea pig to test a new serum on his eyes that will enable him to see through things. Though a success, the effect continues to strengthen, driving the scientist to the brink of madness.
American International — *Warner Home Video*

Xanadu   1980
Musical/Fantasy
48640   96 mins   C   B, V, LV   P

Olivia Newton-John, Michael Beck, Gene Kelly
A beautiful muse comes down to earth and meets an artist and a nightclub owner. She helps the two of them fulfill their dreams, as they collaborate on a roller-disco venture.
MPAA:PG
Universal — *MCA Home Video*

X-Tro   1983
Science fiction/Horror
65088   80 mins   C   B, V, CED   R, P
Philip Sayer, Bernice Stegers, Danny Brainin, Simon Nash, Maryam D'Abo
A man who was mysteriously kidnapped by aliens returns to his family three years later. Infected by alien spores, he transmits the ghastly sickness by biting his wife and son.
MPAA:R
New Line Cinema — *THORN EMI Home Video*

Y

Yanco   1964
Drama
48856   95 mins   B/W   B, V, 3/4U   P
Ricardo Ancona, Jesus Medina, Maria Bustamante
A young boy makes visits to an island where he plays his homemade violin. No one can understand or tolerate his love for music. No dialogue.
Producciones Yanco — *Western Film & Video Inc; Festival Films*

Yankee Clipper   1927
Adventure
10118   51 mins   B/W   B, V   P, T
William Boyd, Elinor Fair, directed by Rupert Julian.
Deceit, treachery, and romance are combined in this depiction of fierce race from China to New England between the Yankee Clipper, and the English ship, Lord of the Isles.
PDC — *Blackhawk Films*

Yankee Doodle Dandy   1942
Musical-Drama
13317   126 mins   B/W   B, V, LV   P
James Cagney, Joan Leslie, Walter Huston, Richard Whorf, directed by Michael Curtiz
Nostalgic view of the Golden Era of show business and the man who made it glitter—George M. Cohan. His early days, triumphs, songs, musicals, and romances. Academy Awards '42: Best Actor (Cagney); Best Sound Recording; Best Musical Scores.
Warner Bros — *CBS/Fox Video; RCA VideoDiscs*

Yankee Doodle in Berlin   1919
Comedy
64305   60 mins   B/W   B, V   P, T
Ford Sterling, Ben Turpin, Marie Prevost, Bothwell Browne
A spoof of World War I dramas with the hero dressing up as a woman and seducing the Kaiser into giving up his war plans. Typical Sennett slapstick with a music and effects score added to the silent film.
Mack Sennett — *Blackhawk Films*

Year of Living Dangerously, The   1982
Adventure
Closed Captioned
64940   114 mins   C   B, V, CED   P
Mel Gibson, Sigourney Weaver, Linda Hunt, directed by Peter Weir
An Australian journalist covering a political story in Indonesia, circa 1965, becomes involved with a British attache at the height of the bloody fighting and rioting in Jakarta during the coup against President Sukarno.
MPAA:PG
MGM/UA — *MGM/UA Home Video*

Yellow Box, The   1983
Fantasy/Literature
66211   25 mins   C   B, V   R, P
Animated
Three children's stories - "Rosie's Walk," "Mike Mulligan and His Steam Shovel," "The Foolish Frog" - are combined on one cassette.
AM Available
Weston Woods — *CC Studios*

Yellow Rose of Texas, The   1944
Western
10684   55 mins   B/W   B, V   P
Roy Rogers, Dale Evans
Roy Rogers works as an undercover insurance agent to clear the name of an old man falsely accused of a stagecoach robbery.
Republic — *Video Connection; Penguin Video; Sheik Video; Cable Films; Video Yesteryear; Discount Video Tapes*

Yellowbeard   1983
Comedy
65348   97 mins   C   B, V, LV   P
Marty Feldman, Cheech and Chong, Madeline Kahn, Peter Boyle, James Mason, Graham Chapman, John Cleese
This is the saga of the infamous priate, whose 15 years in prison have done little to squelch his appetitie for larceny, lechery and lunacy.
MPAA:PG
Carter De Haven — *Vestron Video*

Yellowstone   1936
Mystery
66407   65 mins   B/W   B, V   P
Andy Devine, Ralph Morgan, Judith Barrett
An ex-con is murdered at Yellowstone National
Park, at the site of a hidden cache of money.
Universal — *Movie Buff Video*

Yeomen of the Guard,   19??
The
Opera/Comedy
65494   112 mins   C   B, V   P
*Joel Grey, Elizabeth Gale, David Hillman, Claire
Powell, Alfred Marks*
A colonel, condemned to death in the Tower of
London on false charges of sorcery, is helped to
escape by a family loyal to him. In order to save
his own life, he masks his true identity and takes
his place among the yeomen of the guard,
beginning the series of misadventures—some
humorous, some tragic—that make "Yeomen of
the Guard" one of Gilbert and Sullivan's most
beloved musicals.
Moving Pictures Company Ltd — *CBS/Fox
Video*

Yes, Giorgio   1982
Musical/Comedy
60399   111 mins   C   B, V, CED   P
Luciano Pavarotti, Kathryn Harrold
An opera star falls in love with his female doctor.
Songs include "If We Were in Love," "I Left My
Heart in San Francisco," and arias by Verdi,
Donizetti and Puccini. VHS in stereo.
MPAA:PG
MGM — *MGM/UA Home Video*

Yesterday Machine   196?
Science fiction
66239   85 mins   B/W   B, V   R, P
Tim Holt
A "camp" sci-fi film combining Nazis and rock
'n' roll.
Russ Marker — *Video City Productions*

Yodelin' Kid From Pine   1937
Ridge
Western
15543   59 mins   B/W   B, V   P
*Gene Autry, Smiley Burnett, Betty Bronson, the
Tennessee Ramblers*
Gene Autry tries to stop a war between
cattlemen and woodsmen in Florida.
Republic — *Video Connection; Penguin Video*

Yoga Moves with Alan   1983
Finger
Yoga/Physical fitness
65311   60 mins   C   B, V, LV,   P
                CED
This is a complete introductory program to more
than 26 yoga positions which help to tone and
strengthen the body and to develop flexibility.

Lynda Guber — *MCA Home Video*

Yogi's First Christmas   1980
Cartoons
69590   100 mins   C   B, V   P
Animated
Yogi Bear joins his friends for a musical
celebration of Christmas at the Jellystone
Lodge.
Hanna Barbera — *Worldvision Home Video*

Yojimbo   1962
Film-Avant-garde
06244   138 mins   B/W   B, V   P
*Toshiro Mifuen, Eijiro Tono, Suuzu Yamda,
directed by Akira Kurosawa*
19th century town is scene for political
uprisings. Professional killer comes, and battling
political sides bid for his services. Japanese
film, English subtitles.
JA
Japan — *Budget Video; International Historic
Films; Sheik Video; Cable Films; Video
Yesteryear; Penguin Video; Discount Video
Tapes*

Yol   1982
Drama
66348   111 mins   C   B, V   P
Tarik Akan, Serif Sezer, directed by Serif Goren
Five Turkish prisoners are granted temporary
leave to visit their families in this bittersweet
Turkish-made feature.
Cannes Film Festival '82: Palme d'Or for Best
Picture. MPAA:PG
Triumph Films; Edi
Hubschmid — *RCA/Columbia Pictures Home
Video*

Yor, the Hunter from the   1983
Future
Fantasy/Adventure
69615   88 mins   C   B, V   P
Reb Brown
Lost in a time warp where the past and the
future mysteriously collide, Yor sets out on a
search for his real identity, with his only clue a
golden medallion around his neck.
MPAA:PG
Michele Marsala — *RCA/Columbia Pictures
Home Video; RCA VideoDiscs*

You and Me, Kid Volume I   1983
Family/Parents
72798   111 mins   C   B, V   P
Four complete half-hour programs encourage
parents and children to participate in the viewing
of "You and Me, Kid" together.
Walt Disney Productions — *Walt Disney Home
Video*

     (For Explanation of codes, see USE GUIDE and KEY)

You Bet Your Life — 195?
Game show
33694 120 mins B/W B, V, 3/4U P
Four top episodes from the hit quiz show starring Groucho Marx and his flunkie, George Fenneman. Guest stars Harry Ruby and William Peter Blatty appear in two of the shows.
NBC — *Shokus Video*

You Bet Your Life — 1955
Comedy
72519 60 mins B/W B, V, 3/4U P
Groucho Marx, George Fenneman
The classic game show is revived in this program as two episodes featuring wisecracking Groucho Marx are featured. Groucho welcomes a variety of contestants including a 94-year-old woman and a worm salesman. George Fenneman is on hand to play Groucho's straightman.
NBC — *International Historic Films*

You Light Up My Life — 1977
Drama
21298 90 mins C B, V P
Didi Conn, Michael Zaslow, Melanie Mayron
The story of a young girl trying to break into the music business and establish herself.
Academy Awards '79: Best Song ("You Light Up My Life").
Columbia — *RCA/Columbia Pictures Home Video*

You Only Live Once — 1937
Drama
66638 86 mins B/W B, V P
Sylvia Sidney, Henry Fonda
An escaped convict and his girlfriend attempt to cross the border into Canada while remaining one step ahead of the police.
Walter Wanger — *Monterey Home Video*

You Only Live Twice — 1967
Adventure
59639 115 mins C B, V, CED P
Sean Connery, Donald Pleasence, Karin Dor, directed by Lewis Gilbert
Agent 007 battles Blofeld, the despicable head of Spectre, in this thriller set in Japan.
United Artists; Albert Broccoli — *CBS/Fox Video; RCA VideoDiscs*

You'll Find Out — 1940
Comedy/Musical
59646 97 mins B/W B, V P
Peter Lorre, Kay Kyser, Boris Karloff, Bela Lugosi, Dennis O'Keefe, Helen Parrish
A comedy spoof complete with lady in distress, sinister seances, secret passages and skullduggery.
RKO; David Butler — *Budget Video*

You'll Never Get Rich — 1941
Musical
64580 88 mins B/W B, V P
Fred Astaire, Rita Hayworth, Robert Benchley
A Broadway dance director is drafted into the Army, where his romantic troubles cause him to wind up in the guardhouse more than once. Songs by Cole Porter include "Since I Kissed My Baby Goodnight" and "The Astairable Rag."
Columbia — *RCA/Columbia Pictures Home Video*

Young and Free — 1978
Drama
65453 87 mins C B, V P
Erik Larsen
Following the death of his parents, a young boy must learn to face the perils of an unchartered wilderness alone, and ultimately must choose between returning to civilization, or remain with his beloved wife and life in the wild.
Keith Larson — *Monterey Home Video*

Young and Innocent — 1937
Mystery
01752 80 mins B/W B, V P
Derrick De Marney, Nova Pilbeam, Percy Marmont, directed by Alfred Hitchcock
Based on Josephine Tey's novel, Chief Constable's daughter helps fugitive prove he didn't strangle film star.
Gaumont; British — *Budget Video; Video Dimensions; Sheik Video; Cable Films; Video Connection; Video Yesteryear; Western Film & Video Inc*

Young and Willing — 1942
Comedy
66639 84 mins B/W B, V P
William Holden, Susan Hayward, Eddie Bracken, Robert Benchley, Martha O'Driscoll
A group of struggling actors get hold of a terrific play and try various schemes to get it produced.
United Artists — *Monterey Home Video*

Young Aphrodities — 1966
Drama
72873 87 mins B/W B, V P
A tale of two teenagers who find each other's passions in an underdeveloped country.
Unknown — *Embassy Home Entertainment*

Young at Heart — 1954
Musical-Drama
47993 117 mins C B, V P
Frank Sinatra, Doris Day, Gig Young, Ethel Barrymore, Dorothy Malone, Robert Keith, Elizabeth Fraser, Alan Hale Sr
Fanny Hurst's lighthearted tale of a cynical hard-luck musician who finds happiness when he falls for a small-town girl. A remake of the 1938 "Four Daughters." Songs include the title

tune, "You, My Love" and "Just One of Those Things."
Warner Bros — *NTA Home Entertainment*

Young Bing Crosby   193?
Musical
12824   39 mins   B/W   B, V, FO   P
Bing Crosby
Bing Crosby stars in short, delightful musical comedies by Mack Sennett made before Crosby entered feature-length musical comedy: "Crooner's Holiday," "Blue of the Night," and "Bing, Bing, Bing."
Mack Sennett — *Video Yesteryear*

Young Caruso, The   1951
Musical-Drama/Biographical
52464   78 mins   B/W   B, V, FO   P
Gina Lollobrigida, Ermanno Randi, the voice of Mario Del Monaco
A dramatic biography of legendary tenor Enrico Caruso following his life from childhood poverty in Naples to the beginning of his rise to fame. Dubbed in English.
Italian Films Export — *Video Yesteryear*

Young Doctors in Love   1982
Comedy
63420   95 mins   C   B, V, LV,   P
                              CED
Dabney Coleman, Sean Young, Michael McKean
This spoof of medical soap operas features a chaotic scenario at City Hospital, where the young men and women on the staff have better things to do than attend to their patients.
MPAA:R
ABC Motion Pictures — *Vestron Video*

Young Dragon, The   1977
Martial arts
63417   90 mins   C   B, V   P
Yang Sze, Lo Lai, Yung Man Chi, Wong Ching, Nora Miao
The Young Dragon's girlfriend is kidnapped by the underworld society, and he sets out to rescue her single-handedly.
MPAA:R
Pancosmic Films; Joseph Kong — *Sun Video*

Young Eagles   1934
Adventure/Serials
12557   156 mins   B/W   B, V   P
Bobby Cox, Jim Vance, Carter Dixon
Serial with 12 chapters, 13 minutes each.
First Division — *Video Connection*

Young Frankenstein   1974
Comedy
55576   108 mins   B/W   B, V, LV,   P
                                    CED
Peter Boyle, Gene Wilder, Marty Feldman, Madeleine Kahn, Cloris Leachman, Gene Hackman, directed by Mel Brooks
Young Frederic Frankenstein, a brain surgeon, goes back to Transylvania and learns the secrets of his grandfather's notebooks.
MPAA:PG
Twentieth Century Fox — *CBS/Fox Video*

Young Philadelphians, The   1959
Drama
63448   150 mins   B/W   B, V   R, P
Paul Newman, Barbara Rush, Alexis Smith, Billie Burke, Brian Keith
An ambitious young lawyer works hard at making an impression on the snobbish Philadelphia upper crust. Part of the "A Night at the Movies" series, this tape simulates a 1959 movie evening, with a Bugs Bunny Cartoon, "People Are Bunny," a newsreel and coming attractions for "The Nun's Story" and "The Hanging Tree."
Warner Bros — *Warner Home Video*

Young, the Old, and the Bold, Try and Catch the Wind, The   1980
Football
50094   48 mins   C   B, V, FO   R, P
A fascinating feature on sling-shot armed quarterbacks and sticky-fingered receivers of the 1960's including John Brodie, Roman Gabriel, Sonny Jurgenson, Charlie Taylor, Bob Hayes, and Paul Warfield in their prime.
NFL Films — *NFL Films Video*

Young Tiger, The   1980
Adventure/Martial arts
56921   102 mins   C   B, V   R, P
Jackie Chan
A ninety-minute movie never before seen in the U.S. featuring an expert in martial arts who is accused of murder. Also included is a twelve-minute documentary featuring Jackie Chan, kung-fu sensation, demonstrating his skills.
MPAA:R
Fourseas Film Company — *Video Gems*

Your Air Force in Action   1983
Armed Forces-US
74475   13 mins   B/W   B, V   P
This program looks at the involvement of the U.S. Air Force in the Korean War.
Warner Brothers — *Interurban Films*

Your Financial Survival   1983
Finance
73557   58 mins   C   B, V   P
This program advises you on various aspects of finance such as borrowing money and savings plans.

Admit One — *Admit One Video*

Your Hit Parade   1957
Television/Music
57362   30 mins   B/W   B, V, FO   P
Snooky Lanson, Gisele MacKenzie, Russell Arms, Dorothy Collins, Raymond Scott, Andre Baruch
Broadcast on March 2, 1957, this long-running series performed the top songs of the week, chronicling the taste of Americans in popular music from 1950 to 1959.
NBC — *Video Yesteryear*

Your Hit Parade   1952
Variety
66142   23 mins   B/W   B, V, FO   P
Dorothy Collins, Eileen Wilson, Snooky Lanson, Russell Arms, Andre Baruch
For the week of June 14, 1952, Snooky sings the No. 1 tune, "Kiss of Fire." Also, "Extras" by the Hit Parade singers and dancers and other hits of the day.
NBC — *Video Yesteryear*

Your Show of Shows   1950
Variety
11272   25 mins   B/W   B, V, FO   P
Hosted by Marsha Hunt, Sid Caesar, Imogene Coca, Marguerite Piazza, Bill Hayes, Jack Russell
A vintage edition of the legendary variety program.
NBC — *Video Yesteryear*

Your Show of Shows   1950
Variety
11273   25 mins   B/W   B, V, FO   P
Hosted by Melvyn Douglas, Sid Caesar, Imogene Coca, Marguerite Piazza, Jack Russell, Billy Williams Quartet
Comedy, song, and some technical difficulties highlight this entry in the famous series.
NBC — *Video Yesteryear*

Your Ticket Is No Longer Valid   1984
Drama
72912   96 mins   C   B, V   P
Richard Harris, George Peppard
When Richard Harris becomes impotent, he hires a hit woman to kill him.
MPAA:R
Unknown — *Vestron Video*

You're a Big Boy Now   1966
Comedy
69027   96 mins   C   B, V   R, P
Elizabeth Hartman, Geraldine Page, Peter Kastner, Julie Harris, Rip Torn, Michael Dunn, Tony Bill, Karen Black
Virginal young man working in New York Public Library, is told by his father to move out of his house and grow up. Moving out, he soon becomes involved with a man-hating actress and a discotheque dancer.
Warner Bros — *Warner Home Video*

You're the Greatest, Charlie Brown!   1979
Cartoons
75608   30 mins   C   B, V   P
Animated
Peppermint Patty coaches Charlie Brown in the decathalon event for the school's track team.
Lee Mendelson Bill Melendez Productions — *Snoopy's Home Video Library*

Yukon Flight   1937
Western
57990   57 mins   B/W   B, V   P
James Newill, Dave O'Brien
A Renfrew of the Mounties adventure.
Grand National — *Video Connection*

Yum-Yum Girls   1978
Adventure
55554   89 mins   C   B, V, LV   P
Judy Landers, Tanya Roberts, Barbara Tully, Michelle Daw
Naive and innocent Melody Pearson comes to New York to fulfill her dreams of a modeling career and soon learns the nitty-gritty of the modeling world.
MPAA:R
Canon Releasing — *MCA Home Video*

Z

Z   1969
Suspense
44783   128 mins   C   B, V   P
Yves Montand, Irene Papas
A man known as "Z" leads the growing opposition party. He is struck down by a speeding truck before hundreds of onlookers. A trial follows, but seven witnesses vanish. Academy Award '69: Best Foreign Film.
Cinema 5 — *RCA/Columbia Pictures Home Video; RCA VideoDiscs*

Zabriskie Point   1970
Drama
72468   111 mins   C   B, V   P
Two loners epitomize the counter-culture as they wander the ominous desert terrain.
MPAA:R
Metro Goldwyn Mayer — *MGM/UA Home Video*

(For Explanation of codes, see USE GUIDE and KEY)

Zapped   1982
Comedy
63373   98 mins   C   B, V, LV,   P
                                  CED
*Scott Baio, Willie Aames, Felice Schachter,
Heather Thomas, Scatman Crothers*
One of the more unassuming boys in a group of
teenagers possesses special magical powers.
MPAA:R   EL, JA
Embassy Pictures — *Embassy Home
Entertainment*

Zebra Force   1976
Crime-Drama
76656   81 mins   C   B, V   P
*Mike Lane, Richard X. Slattery, Rockne
Tarkington, Glenn Wilder, Anthony Caruso*
A group of army veterans embark on a personal
battle against organized crime, utilizing their
military training with deadly precision.
MPAA:R
Joe Tronatore; Larry Price — *Media Home
Entertainment*

Zelig   1983
Comedy
65614   79 mins   B/W   B, V, LV,   R, P
                                  CED
*Woody Allen, Mia Farrow, Susan Sontag, Saul
Bellow, Bricktop, Irving Howe, directed by
Woody Allen*
Woody Allen's spoof of documentary films stars
him as Leonard Zelig, the famous "Chameleon
Man" of the 1920's, whose personalisty was so
vague that he would take on the characteristics
of whomever he was in contact with. Filmed in
black-and-white, the movie simulates the "look"
of vintage newsreels, complete with stentorian
narration.
MPAA:PG
Robert Greenhut — *Warner Home Video*

Zero for Conduct   1933
Comedy
12856   49 mins   B/W   B, V, FO   P
Directed by Jean Vigo
A fantasy-filled rebellion against authority set in
a boys' school. French with English subtitles.
FR
Gaumont, Franco Film — *Video Yesteryear;
Sheik Video; Budget Video; Penguin Video;
Western Film & Video Inc; Discount Video
Tapes*

Zero to Sixty   1978
Comedy-Drama
65073   96 mins   C   B, V, CED   P
Darren McGavin, Sylvia Miles, Denise Nickerson
A newly divorced man finds that his car has
been repossessed for nonpayment. Seeking out
the manager of the finance company, he gets a
job as a repossession agent of high-priced,
unpaid-for cars.
MPAA:PG

Katherine Browne — *Embassy Home
Entertainment*

Ziegfeld Follies   1946
Musical
64571   109 mins   C   B, V, CED   P
*Fred Astaire, Judy Garland, Gene Kelly, Red
Skelton, Fannie Brice, Lena Horne, Lucille Ball,
Esther Williams, directed by Vincente Minelli*
A lavish revue of musical numbers and comedy
sketches featuring many MGM stars of the
World War II era. Highlights include Fred Astaire
and Gene Kelly's only duet, "The Babbitt and
the Bromide," Lena Horne singing "Love," Judy
Garland as "Madame Cremation" and a Fred
Astaire-Lucille Bremer ballet set to "Limehouse
Blues."
MGM — *MGM/UA Home Video*

Zig Zag Triumph of   197?
Stream
Documentary
50634   24 mins   C   B, V   P, T
Narrated by Jack Kelso
A tribute to the more than 120 years of history of
the steam engine in Australia.
Unknown — *Blackhawk Films*

Zis Boom Bah   1942
Musical/Comedy
66143   61 mins   B/W   B, V, FO   P
*Peter Lind Hayes, Mary Healey, Grace Hayes,
Huntz Hall, Benny Rubin*
A college throws a variety show to save itself.
Monogram — *Video Yesteryear*

Zoltan... Hound of   1977
Dracula
Horror
66024   85 mins   C   B, V   R, P
Michael Pataki, Reggie Nalder, Jose Ferrer
The vampire's canine companion carries on the
Dracula family reputation.
Albert Band; Frank Perilli — *THORN EMI
Home Video*

Zombie   1980
Horror
52860   93 mins   C   B, V   P
Tisa Farrow, Ian McCulloch
A reporter and a missing scientist's daughter go
to the island of Matool to find the scientist, and
encounter a mysterious doctor and hundreds of
man-eating zombies.
MPAA:R   EL, SP
Jerry Gross; Ugo Tucci — *Wizard Video;
Vestron Video (disc only)*

Zombies of the   1952
Stratosphere
Science fiction/Serials
33949   152 mins   B/W   B, V, 3/4U   P

          (For Explanation of codes, see USE GUIDE and KEY)

Judd Holdren, Aline Towne, Leonard Nimoy
A serial in twelve chapters in which a cosmic policeman fights Zombies attempting to blow the Earth out of orbit.
Republic — *Video Connection*

Zorba, the Greek   1964
Drama
55527 142 mins B/W   B, V   P
Anthony Quinn, Alan Bates, Irene Papas, Lila Kedrova
A British writer and a Greek opportunist on Crete take lodgings with an aging courtesan. The writer is attracted to a woman who is stoned by the villagers when they find he has spent the night with her. Based on a novel by Nicolai Kazantzakis.
Academy Awards '64: Best Supporting Actress (Kedrova); Best Cinematography; Best Art Direction.
Twentieth Century Fox — *CBS/Fox Video*

Zorro Rides Again   1937
Adventure/Serials
12559 217 mins B/W   B, V   P
John Carroll, Helen Christian, Noah Beery, directed by William Witney, John English
Zorro risks his life to outwit enemy agents endeavoring to secure ancestor's property. In twelve chapters, the first runs 30 minutes, the rest 17.
Republic — *Video Connection; Nostalgia Merchant*

Zorro, the Gay Blade   1981
Comedy
58850 96 mins C   B, V, CED   P
George Hamilton, Lauren Hutton, Brenda Vaccaro, Ron Leibman

Hamilton portrays the swashbuckling crusader and his long-lost brother, Bunny Wigglesworth, in this spoof of the Zorro legend.
MPAA:PG
20th Century Fox — *CBS/Fox Video*

Zorro's Black Whip   1944
Western/Serials
07342 168 mins B/W   B, V   P
Linda Stirling, George Lewis
A young girl dons the mask of her murdered brother to fight outlaws in the old West. Serial in twelve episodes.
Republic — *Nostalgia Merchant; Video Connection; Budget Video; Discount Video Tapes; Video Yesteryear*

Zorro's Fighting Legion   1939
Adventure/Serials
12558 215 mins B/W   B, V   P
Reed Hadley, Sheila Darcy, directed by William Witney, John English
Zorro forms a legion to help the president of Mexico fight a band of outlaws endeavoring to steal gold shipments. A serial in 12 chapters.
Republic — *Video Connection; Penguin Video; Video Dimensions; Cable Films; Nostalgia Merchant; Budget Video; Discount Video Tapes*

Zydrasis Horizontas   1957
Adventure
72499 70 mins B/W   B, V, 3/4U   P
This children's story was the first Lithuanian film made without Soviet technical assistance.
Lithuania Film — *International Historic Films*

(For Explanation of codes, see USE GUIDE and KEY)

SUBJECT CATEGORY INDEX

Adolescence

Am I Normal?
Dear Diary
Teenage Drug and Alcohol Abuse

Adventure

Abductors, The
Abdulla the Great
Across the Great Divide
Adventure 1: Trailers on Tape
Adventures of Black Beauty Vol. I, The
Adventures of Black Beauty Vol. 2, The
Adventures of Black Beauty Vol. 3, The
Adventures of Captain Marvel
Adventures of Frontier Fremont, The
Adventures of Grizzly Adams at Beaver Dam, The
Adventures of Huckleberry Finn, The
Adventures of Huckleberry Finn, The
Adventures of Red Ryder
Adventures of Rex and Rinty
Adventures of Robin Hood, The
Adventures of Robin Hood—The Inquisitor
Adventures of Sinbad the Sailor, The
Adventures of Sir Lancelot—Sheppard's War
Adventures of Tartu, The
Adventures of Tarzan, The
Adventures of the Wilderness Family, The
Adventures of Tom Sawyer, The
Adventures of Ultraman, The
African Queen, The
Aladdin and the Wonderful Lamp
Alaska Wilderness Adventure, The
Amateur, The
Amazing Dobermans, The
Amazing Spider-Man, The
Amazing Spider-Man, The
Americano, The/Variety
Amsterdam Connection
Amsterdam Kill, The
Andy's Gang—Ramar of the Jungle
Angel
Angel of H.E.A.T.
Around the World in 80 Days
Assault on Agathon
Assignment Skybolt
At Sword's Point
Ator the Fighting Eagle
Attack Force Z
Avengers, The
Baltimore Bullet, The
Bandolero
Bank Dick, The
Barbed Wire Dolls
Bears and I, The

Beastmaster, The
Bedford Incident, The
Belstone Fox, The
Beneath the Twelve Mile Reef
Big Blue Marble
Big Bus, The
Big Steal, The
Billy Boy
Black Beauty/Courage of Black Beauty
Black Coin, The
Black Magic
Black Pirate, The
Black Stallion Returns, The
Black Stallion, The
Black Widow, The
Blackstar
Blackstar, Volume 2
Blind Fist of Bruce
Blood on the Sun
Bloody Fight, The
Bloody Fist
Blue Thunder
Bobby Jo and the Outlaw
Bodyguard, The
Bold Caballero, The
Bolo
Born Free
Boy of Two Worlds
Bronson Lee, Champion
Bruce & Shao Lin Kung Fu with Fierce Boxer
Bruce Le's Greatest Revenge
Bruce Li in New Guinea
Bruce the Super Hero with Eighteen Weapons of Kung Fu
Bruce vs. Bill
Burn 'Em Up Barnes
Bushido Blade, The
Butch Cassidy and the Sundance Kid
California Gold Rush
Call of the Wild
Candleshoe
Cannonball
Cantonen Iron Kung Fu
Captain America
Captain Blood
Captain Caution
Captain Harlock
Captain Kidd
Castaway Cowboy, The
Challenge, The
Challenge, The
Challenge to Be Free
Chandu on the Magic Island
Charlie and the Talking Buzzard
Chinese Connection, The
Chinese Web, The

Circle of Iron
Clash of the Titans
Clones of Bruce Lee, The
Conan the Barbarian
Conqueror, The
Convoy
Corsican Brothers, The
Count of Monte Cristo, The
Count of Monte Cristo, The
Countryman
Crack Shadow Boxers
Crimson Ghost, The
Cross Creek
Crossfire
Cry of the Innocent
Cuchillo ("Knife")
Dangerous Holiday
Daniel Boone
Daredevils of the Red Circle
Dark Crystal, The
Dark Mountain
Davy Crockett and the River Pirates
Day It Came to Earth, The
Day of the Dolphin, The
Deadly and the Beautiful, The
Deadly Strangers
Deadly Strike/Young Hero
Death Dimension
Death Hunt
Death Journey
Death Promise
Death Sport
Death Stalk
Death Wish II
Desert of the Tartars, The
Desperate Target
Destination Saturn/Tarzan the Fearless
Devil Horse
Diamonds Are Forever
Dick Deadeye
Dick Tracy Double Feature #2
Disaster—Adventure Featurettes
Divine Nymph, The
Dr. No
Dogs of War, The
Don Q., Son of Zorro
Don Winslow of the Coast Guard
Don Winslow of the Navy
Double McGuffin, The
Dragnet
Dragonslayer
Drums of Fu Manchu
Duncan's World
El Cid
Encounter with the Unknown
Enigma
Enter the Dragon
Enter the Ninja
Escape from Death Row
Escape from New York
Escape to Athena

Escape to the Sun
Every Which Way But Loose
Exit the Dragon, Enter the Tiger
Eye for an Eye, An
Fables of the Green Forest
Fantastic Balloon Voyage, The
Fast Company
Female Bunch, The
Ferry to Hong Kong
Fiction Makers, The
Fighting Black Kings
Fighting Devil Dogs
Fighting Life
Fire and Ice
Firebird 2015 A.D.
Firecracker
Firefox
Fish Hawk
Fist
Fist of Fear—Touch of Death
Fist of Vengeance
Fists of Fury
Fists of Fury II
Five Mile Creek, Volume 1
Five Mile Creek Volume 2
Flash and Firecat
Flood of Fury
Florida Connection, The
Flying Fool, The
For Your Eyes Only
Force: Five
Force of One, A
Forced Vengeance
Foreign Legionnaire—Court Martial
Four Feathers, The
Four Musketeers, The
Four Musketeers, The
Freedom Force, The
Funeral for an Assassin
Fury on Wheels
Fuzz
Game of Death
Gator
Gauntlet, The
General Della Rovere
Getaway, The
Ginger
Girls Are for Loving
Glove, The
Golden Lady
Golden Voyage of Sinbad, The
Goldfinger
Good Guys Wear Black
Goodbye Pork Pie
Gorilla
Grand Theft Auto
Great Adventure, The
Great Locomotive Chase, The
Great Movie Stunts and The Making of Raiders
    of the Lost Ark
Great Shikar, The

Great Smokey Roadblock, The
Great Waldo Pepper, The
Gulliver's Travels
Gunga Din
Guns of Navarone, The
Hangar 18
Hatari
Hawk of the Wilderness
He-Man and the Masters of the Universe, Vol. 5
He-Man and the Masters of the Universe, Volume VI
Hells Angels Forever
Hell's Angels '69
Hercules
Hercules
Hercules Unchained
Herculoids, The
High Ballin'
High Risk
High Risk
High Road to China
High Velocity
High Voltage
Hills Have Eyes, The
Hindenburg, The
Holt of the Secret Service
Horse Soldiers, The
Huckleberry Finn
Huckleberry Finn
Hunter, The
Hurricane Express
Hurricane Express
Hurricane Express/Angel and the Badman
Image of Bruce Lee, The
In Hot Pursuit
In Search of the Castaways
Incredible Hulk, The
Incredible Journey, The
Incredible Rocky Mountain Race, The
Invincible, The
Iron Mask, The
Island, The
Island at the Top of the World, The
Island of Adventure
Ivanhoe
Jacare
Jack London Story
Jacob Two—Two Meets the Hooded Fang
James Bond 007—Coming Attractions
Jaws of Death
Jaws of the Dragon
Jeremiah Johnson
Jericho
Jig Saw
Johnny Tremain and the Sons of Liberty
Journey
Jungle Book, The
Jungle Heat
Junior G-Men
Junior G-Men of the Air
Junkman, The

Kagemusha
Kashmiri Run
Kavik the Wolf Dog
Kentuckian, The
Kentucky Blue Streak
Kid and the Killers, The
Kid Vengeance
Kidnapped
Kidnapped
Kill or Be Killed
Kill Squad
Killer Force
King Arthur, the Young Warlord
King Boxers, The
King of the Kongo
King of the Mountain
King of the Rocketmen
King of the Texas Rangers
King Solomon's Mines
Knightriders
Krull
Kung-Fu Commandos
Lassie's Rescue Rangers
Lassie's Rescue Rangers, Volume 2
Last Challenge of the Dragon, The
Last Chase, The
Last Days of Pompeii, The
Last Flight of Noah's Ark, The
Last of the Mohicans
Last of the Mohicans
Last of the Mohicans, The
Law of the Wild
Law of the Wolf
Legend of Sleepy Hollow, The
Legend of the Northwest
Life and Times of Grizzly Adams, The
Light at the Edge of the World, The
Lion Man
Little Laura and Big John
Littlest Warrior, The
Live and Let Die
Live and Let Die
Living Head, The
Local Hero
Lookin' to Get Out
Loophole
Lost City, The
Lost Patrol, The
Lost Squadron
Macon County Line
Mad Max
Magic Pony, The
Magic Sword, The
Magnificent Kick, The
Major Dundee
Man Against Crime Volume I
Man Called Horse, A
Man from Beyond
Man from Button Willow, The
Man from Snowy River, The
Man in the Iron Mask, The

Man Who Would Be King, The
Man with the Golden Gun, The
Manhunt
Manhunt in the African Jungle
Marco
Mark of Zorro, The
Masked Marvel, The
Massacre at Fort Holman
Mean Machine, The
Mechanic, The
Men Who Tread on the Tiger's Tail
Metalstorm
Mighty Jungle, The
Mil Millones para una Rubia (The Lady Thief)
Militant Eagle
Mistaken Orders
Mr. Robinson Crusoe
Mr. Super Athletic Charm
Mr. Too Little
Moby Dick
Mogambo
Molly and Lawless John
Moonraker
Moonshine County Express
Mother Lode
Mountain Family Robinson
Mountain Men, The
Mutiny on the Bounty
Mystery Squadron
Nate and Hayes
New Adventures of Tarzan, The
New Adventures of Zorro, The
Night Crossing
1990: The Bronx Warriors
No Way Back
Nomads of the North
Northville Cemetery Massacre
Northwest Frontier
Nowhere to Hide
Nyoka and the Tigerman
Octopussy
Odyssey of the Pacific
Off the Edge
Old Yeller
On Her Majesty's Secret Service
On Her Majesty's Secret Service
One Armed Executioner
One Down Two to Go
Orca
Pepe Le Moko
Pepper
Perils of the Darkest Jungle
Phantom Tollbooth, The
Pilot, The
Pippi Goes on Board
Pippi in the South Seas
Pippi on the Run
Pirates of Capri, The
Poco
Poppies Are Also Flowers
Poseidon Adventure, The

Prisoner of Zenda, The
Private Life of Don Juan
Prodigal Boxer, The
Puss 'n Boots
Queen of the Amazons
Quest for Fire
Raiders of the Lost Ark
Raise the Titanic
Raw Force
Real Bruce Lee, The
Reckless
Renfrew of the Royal Mounted in Crashing
    Through
Return of a Man Called Horse, The
Return of the Dragon
Return of the Red Tiger
Return of the Tiger
Return to Macon County
Revenge of the Ninja
Riddle of the Sands
Road Warrior, The
Robbers of the Sacred Mountain
Robinson Crusoe
Robinson Crusoe of Clipper Island
Robinson Crusoe of Mystery Island
Rocketship X-M—Special Edition
Romancing the Stone
Rough Cut
Ruckus
Rulers of the City
Run, Angel, Run!
Runaway Barge
Runaway Truck
Sacketts, The
Saturday Serials
Savage Fury
Sea Prince and the Fire Child, The
Sea Wolves, The
Sell Out, The
Seven Alone
7 Blows of the Dragon
Seven Samurai
Shao Lin Kung Fu Mystagogue/Kung Fu of Eight
    Drunkards
Sharky's Machine
Shazam
Shazam!, Volume 2
She
She
Shogun Assassin
Shoot the Sun Down
Sign of Zorro, The
Silent Rage
600 Days to Cocos Island
Six Pack
Skull and Crown
Slave of the Cannibal God
Smokey and the Bandit Part 3
Smokey and the Judge
Snow Treasure
Son of Monte Cristo, The

Son of Sinbad
Son of Zorro
S.O.S. Coastguard
South of Pago Pago
Space Patrol Volume 1
Space Raiders
Spacehunter: Adventures in the Forbidden Zone
Speed Trap
Spider-Woman
Spiderman
Spies
Spirit of Youth, The
Spy in Black, The
Spy Who Loved Me, The
Squadron of Doom
Stalag 17
Stamp Day for Superman
Star Crash
Star Wars
Stoner
Stop That Train
Street Fighter, The
Stunt Rock
Stunts
Submarine Alert
Sudden Death
Sudden Impact
Summerdog
Superchick
Superman III
Superman Cartoons
Superman—The Movie
Superman II
Survival Run
Swamp Thing
Swan Lake
Swiss Family Robinson, The
Switchblade Sisters
Sword of Monte Cristo
Tale of Two Cities, A
Tale of Two Critters, A
Tangier
Target Eagle
Tarzan and the Green Goddess
Tarzan and the Trappers
Tarzan of the Apes
Tarzan, the Ape Man
Tarzan, the Ape Man
Tarzan the Fearless
Tarzan's Revenge
Tender Warrior, The
Texas Lightning
Thief of Bagdad, The
This Is a Hijack
Thomas Crown Affair, The
Three Musketeers, The
Three Musketeers, The
Three Musketeers, The
Three Musketeers, The
Throne of Blood
Thunderball

Thunderbirds Are Go
Tiara Tahiti
Tiger's Claw
Time After Time
Time Machine
Time Machine, The
Time to Die, A
Tintorera...Tiger Shark
Tom Corbett, Space Cadet Volume 1
Tom Edison, the Boy Who Lit Up the World
Tough Guy
Treasure Island
Treasure Island
Treasure of Bruce Le/Big Rascal
Treasure of the Four Crowns
Treasure of the Sierra Madre, The
Treasure of the Yankee Zephyr
Truck Stop Women
True Game of Death, The
20,000 Leagues Under the Sea
Two Graves to Kung-Fu
2069: A Sex Odyssey
Ultimate Thrill, The
Ultraman II
Under the Red Robe
Undersea Kingdom
Undersea World of Jacques Cousteau Vol. I, The
Underwater
Uranium Conspiracy
Vera Cruz
Viaje Fantastico En Groso
Vigilantes Are Coming, The
Voyage en Ballon
Wake of the Red Witch, The
Warlords of the 21st Century
When Lightning Strikes
When the North Wind Blows
Where Time Began
Whiskey Mountain
White Lightning
White Line Fever
White-Water Sam
Who Killed Mary What's 'Er Name?
Wilbur and Orville: The First to Fly
Wild Geese, The
Wildcat
Wilderness Family Part 2
Wolf Call
Wolf Dog
Woman in Grey
Wrong Is Right
Yankee Clipper
Year of Living Dangerously, The
Yor, the Hunter from the Future
You Only Live Twice
Young Eagles
Young Tiger, The
Yum-Yum Girls
Zorro Rides Again
Zorro's Fighting Legion
Zydrasis Horizontas

Advertising

Vintage Commercials
Vintage Commercials, II
Vintage Commercials, III

Aeronautics

Admiral Rosendahl: The Sky Giant
Airborne, The
Aircraft Recognition
Aviation Volume I
Flak
Flight That Became a Legend
History of Aviation, The
Hughes Flying Boat, The
Lockheed L-1011 Tristar
Marina Popovich
P-47 Thunderbolt High Altitude Flight and
   Aerobatics
Reconnaissance Pilot
Sky High
Sports Hour #15
Threshold: The Blue Angels Experience
Wilbur and Orville: The First to Fly
Winds of Kitty Hawk
Wings of the Army
Winter Training
Wright Brothers: Masters of the Sky, The
Wright Brothers: Wings Over Kitty Hawk

Africa

Africa Speaks
Belafonte Presents Fincho
Borneo
Bride of the Beast
Wild Rapture

Agriculture

Chicken Real

Alcoholic beverages

Home Bartending
Starting a Wine Cellar
Wine Program, The

Alcoholism

American Alcoholic, The/Reading, Writing and
   Reefer
Emotions of Life, The

Anatomy and physiology

National Geographic Society: The Incredible
   Machine/Mysteries of the Mind

Animals

Amazing Apes, The
Animal Quiz #1
Animal Quiz #2
Animal Quiz #3
Animal Quiz #4
Animal Quiz #5
Animal Quiz #6
Any Family
Arabian, Palomino and Saddlebred
Australia: Pace and A Race of Horses
Ballad of the Irish Horse, The
Benji Takes a Dive at Marineland/Benji at Work
Birth of a Foal: Red Wing and Rain Drop, The
Carnivores, The
Corrective Shoeing for Conformational Defects
Draft Horse Pulling
Exercises for Travel
For the Love of Benji
Fundamentals of Normal and Corrective
   Horseshoeing
Give a Horse a Home!
Horse Sense
Horseshoeing
Incredible Journey, The
Kellogg Dream, The
Loading and Transporting the Horse and Knots
   for Restraint
Maintenance and Show Grooming
Meet Your Animal Friends
Mule Days
National Geographic: Great Whales/Sharks
Peruvian Paso: For Those with Champagne
   Taste
Rumble of Wheels
Secret World of Reptiles, The
Stallions of Distinction

Anthropology

Goona Goona

Archeology

Sentinels of Silence
Tut: The Boy King
Tut: The Boy King/The Louvre

Armed Forces-US

Air Force Story, The
Air Force Story: The Beginning, The
Air Pattern Pacific
American Navy in Vietnam, The
Army on Wheels
Basic Marksmanship—45 Caliber Pistol
Bombers Over North Africa
Carrier Action off Korea
China Crisis
Demonstrations of Ordance Material, Aberdeen
   Proving Ground, Maryland

Face of War, A
40mm Twin Anti-Aircraft Gun
High Altitude Ship Recognition
Last Bomb, The
Marines-65
Navy Advisor in Vietnam—The River Force
Navy Flies On, The
New Thunder for the USAF
Nuclear Defense At Sea
Ploesti
P-47 Thunderbolt High Altitude Flight and Aerobatics
Reconnaissance Pilot
Saga of the Skyraider
Screaming Eagles in Vietnam
6th Marine Division on Okinawa, The
Superfort
Threshold: The Blue Angels Experience
United States Air Force in Vietnam, The
U.S. Army Air Force Report
Vietnam: The Bombing
Wings of Steel
Wings of the Army
With the Marines at Tarawa
With the Marines—Chosin Hungnam
Your Air Force in Action

Artists

National Gallery: Art Awareness Collection
Olaf Weighorst: Painter of the American West
Vincent Van Gogh: A Portrait in Two Parts

Arts

Art of the Baltic States
Basic Pottery
Degas, Erte and Chagall
National Gallery of Art, The
Video Wallpaper

Asia

Beyond Bengal

Astrology

Video Astrology 1984

Astronomy

Universe, The

Automobiles

Auto Tuneup
Basic Automobile Maintenance
Cobra 289-427
Competition Corvettes
Early Birds, The
Ferrari Daytona
Henry Ford: The Mark of a Man

Henry Ford's America
How the Automobile Works
Lambos, The
Porsche 917
Porsche Parade 1983
Racing Ferraris

Automobiles-Racing

American Nitro
Daytona 500—1971, The
Ferrari 275GTB, The
Ford GT-40
Malcolm Campbell: Man Against Time
Mercedes-Benz 300 SL
Monterey Historic
National Hot Rod Association Championship Drag Racing
North American Sports Car Championship
Porsche Carrera 6, The
Porsche 904 GTS Carrera, The
Porsche 930 Turbo
Porsche RSK, RS-60, 61, The
Southern 500 Auto Race, 1963 - 1979
Sports Hour #9
Start to Finish the Grand Prix
Wilbur Shaw: Speedway Star

Baseball

All-Star Batting Tips
All-Star Catching and Base Stealing Tips
All-Star Game, 1967
All-Star Game, 1970: What Makes an All-Star
All-Star Game, 1971: Home Run Heroes
All-Star Game, 1972: Years of Tradition, Night of Pride
All-Star Game, 1973: A New Generation of Stars
All-Star Game, 1974: Mid-Summer Magic
All-Star Game, 1975: All-Star Fever
All-Star Game, 1976: Champions of Pride
All-Star Game, 1977: The Man Behind the Mask
All-Star Game, 1978: What Makes an All-Star
All-Star Game, 1979: Inches and Jinxes
All-Star Game, 1980: Heroes to Remember
All-Star Game, 1981
All-Star Game, 1982
All-Star Pitching Tips
Babe Ruth: The Fence Buster
Baseball: Fun and Games
Baseball Miracles
Baseball: The Now Career
Baseball's Hall of Fame
Batty World of Baseball, The
Boys of Summer, The
Bullpen
Connie Mack: Mr. Baseball
50 Years of Baseball Memories
Golden Moments
Great Moments in Baseball
Greatest Comeback Ever, The

Hall of Famers
It Don't Come Easy: 1978 New York Yankees
King of the Hill
Legendary Greats
Lou Gehrig: King of Diamonds
1978—The New York Yankees' Miracle Year
1979 World Series and All-Star Highlights
Roberto Clemente: A Touch of Royalty
Tommy John Story, The
20 Years of World Series
Two Best World Series Ever, The
Winning Tradition: 1977 New York Yankees, A
World Series, 1943
World Series, 1944
World Series, 1945
World Series, 1946
World Series, 1947
World Series, 1948
World Series, 1949
World Series, 1950
World Series, 1951
World Series, 1952
World Series, 1953
World Series, 1954
World Series, 1955
World Series, 1956
World Series, 1957
World Series, 1958
World Series, 1959
World Series, 1960
World Series, 1961
World Series, 1962
World Series, 1963
World Series, 1964
World Series, 1965
World Series, 1966
World Series, 1967
World Series, 1968
World Series, 1969
World Series, 1970
World Series, 1971
World Series, 1972
World Series, 1973
World Series, 1974
World Series, 1975
World Series, 1976
World Series, 1977
World Series, 1978
World Series, 1979
World Series, 1980
World Series, 1981
World Series, 1982
Worth the Wait!

Basketball

Basketball with Gail Goodrich
George Mikan: Mr. Basketball
Greatest Legends of Basketball
1981 NBA Playoffs and Championship Series:
　The Dynasty Renewed

Bible

Abraham's Sacrifice
Daniel and Nebuchadnezzar
Daniel in the Lion's Den
David and Goliath
Deluge, The
Great Leaders
Heritage of the Bible, The
In Search of Noah's Ark
Jacob: The Man Who Fought with God
Jacob's Challenge
Joseph and His Brothers
Judgement of Solomon, The
Life of Christ I
Life of Christ II
Life of Christ III
New Media Bible: The Story of Joseph, The
Old Testament I
Old Testament II
Saul and David
Sodom and Gomorrah
Story of Esther, The
Tower of Babel

Biographical

Abe Lincoln: Freedom Fighter
Admiral Byrd: To the Ends of the Earth
Admiral Nimitz: Freedom's Admiral
Admiral Rosendahl: The Sky Giant
Alfred E. Smith: The Happy Warrior
Amazing Howard Hughes, The
Amin: The Rise and Fall
Babe Ruth: The Fence Buster
Ben Jones: Monarch of the Turf
Bernard Baruch: The Trouble Shooter
Bobby Jones: Old Man Par
Clarence Darrow
Connie Mack: Mr. Baseball
Cordell Hull: The Good Neighbor
Cross Creek
Danton
Dionne Quintuplets
Eddie Rickenbacker: Ace of Aces
Evel Knievel
Evening with Quentin Crisp, An
Father Hubbard: The Glacier Priest
Fiorello La Guardia: The Crusader
Flights and Flyers
Flights and Flyers: Amelia Earhart
Florence Chadwick: The Challenge
Franklin D. Roosevelt: F.D.R.
Gar Wood: The Silver Fox
General Doolittle: Wild Blue Yonder
General Douglas MacArthur: I Shall Return
General Marshall: Soldier of Peace
General Montgomery: The Black Beret
General Patton: The Fighting Man
General Pershing: The Iron Commander
George Mikan: Mr. Basketball

Give 'Em Hell, Harry!
Goodyear TV Playhouse: "The Gene Austin Story"
Grover Whalen: Mr. New York
Helen Wills: Miss Poker Face
Henry Ford: The Mark of a Man
I Am a Dancer
Igor Sikorsky: Explorer of the Sky
Iron Duke, The
James Dean Story, The
James Dean: The First American Teenager
Jesus of Nazareth
Joe Louis Story, The
King Edward VIII: For Love of a Woman
Knute Rockne: The Rock of Notre Dame
Kurt Carlsen: Man Against the Sea
Legend of Valentino, The
Lou Gehrig: King of Diamonds
Malcolm Campbell: Man Against Time
Marilyn Monroe
Marjoe
Melody Master, The
Miracle Worker, The
Nadia
Nixon and Ford
Patty Berg: Fairway to Fame
Piaf
Pride of the Yankees, The
Rainbow
Robert A. Taft: Mr. Republican
Sir Arthur Conan Doyle
Sophia Loren: Her Own Story
Spirit of St. Louis, The
This Is Elvis
Thomas Edison: Let There Be Light
Tom Edison, the Boy Who Lit Up the World
Tom Edison: The Making of an American Legend
Volcano
Wendell Willkie: Of Perfect Loyalty
Wilbur Shaw: Speedway Star
Will Rogers: Champion of the People
Will Rogers: The Cowboy Humorist
Winds of Kitty Hawk
Woman Called Golda, A
Wright Brothers: Masters of the Sky, The
Wright Brothers: Wings Over Kitty Hawk
Young Caruso, The

Biology

Building Blocks of Life, The
Expansion of Life, The
Origin of Life, The (Plus Scopes Trial Footage)

Birds

Tropical Birds
Tropical Fish, Fireside Moments and Beautiful Birds
Watching Birds

Boating

America's Cup 1977/Heavy Weather Slalom/Big Boats
Arctic Canoe Race, The
Best Defense, The
Boating and Boat Safety
Coaster Adventure of the John F. Leavitt
Fast and Clean
Gar Wood: The Silver Fox
Kiel Olympiad
Liquid Madness
Little Dory Story
1983 Whitewater Rodeos
Pacific Challenge
Portholes
Raging River of Annapurna, The
Reckon with the Wind/Kialoa to Jamaica
Susitna
Urubamba

Boxing

Ali: Skill, Brains and Guts
Baer vs. Louis/Louis vs. Schmeling
Big Fights, Vol. 1—Muhammad Ali's Greatest Fights, The
Big Fights, Vol. 2—Heavyweight Champions' Greatest Fights, The
Big Fights, Vol. 3—Sugar Ray Robinson's Greatest Fights, The
Boxing's Greatest Champions
Greatest Fights of the 70's
Grudge Fights
Showdown: Sugar Ray Leonard vs. Thomas Hearns, The
Sugar Ray Robinson—Pound for Pound

Camps and camping

Back-Packer

Canada

City of Gold/Drylanders

Cartoons

Abbott and Costello Cartoon Carnival #1
Adventures of Black Beauty Vol. I, The
Adventures of Black Beauty Vol. 2, The
Adventures of Black Beauty Vol. 3, The
Adventures of Buster the Bear, The
Adventures of Captain Future Volume 1, The
Adventures of Captain Future Volume 2, The
Adventures of Felix the Cat, The
Adventures of Little Lulu and Tubby Volume 1, The
Adventures of Little Lulu and Tubby Volume 2, The
Adventures of Mighty Mouse-Volumes IV & V, The

Adventures of Reddy the Fox, The
Adventures of Sinbad the Sailor, The
Adventures of Superman, The
Adventures of Ultraman, The
Aesop and His Friends
Aladdin and the Wonderful Lamp
Alice in Wonderland
All Star Cartoon Parade
Amazing Spider-Man, The
Angel
Animalympics
Animation in the 1930's
Animation Wonderland
Archie
Archie, Volume 2
Atom Ant
Banana Splits & Friends, The
Beany & Cecil, Volume III
Beany and Cecil, Volume Four
Beany & Cecil, Volumes 1 & 2
Berenstain Bears' Comic Valentine, The
Berenstain Bears' Easter Surprise, The
Berenstein Bears' Play Ball, The
Best of Betty Boop, Volume I, The
Best of Betty Boop Volume II
Best of George Pal, The
Best of Heckle and Jeckle and Friends, The
Best of Heckle and Jeckle—Volumes IV & V, The
Best of Little Lulu
Best of Marvel Comics, The
Best of Popeye, The
Best of Terrytoons, The
Best of Warner Brothers (Vol. 1)
Betty Boop #1
Betty Boop Cartoon Festival
Betty Boop Classics
Betty Boop Festival #1
Betty Boop Festival #2
Betty Boop Festival #3
Betty Boop Special Collectors Edition
Birdman & Galaxy Trio
Black Beauty
Black Planet, The
Blackstar
Blackstar Volume III
Blackstar, Volume 2
Blaxploitation Cartoons
Bon Voyage, Charlie Brown
Bozo the Clown Volume I
Bozo the Clown Volume 2
Bozo the Clown Volume 3
Bozo the Clown Volume 4
Bugs Bunny/Road Runner Movie, The
Bugs Bunny's 3rd Movie: 1,001 Rabbit Tales
Bullwinkle & Rocky and Friends, Volume I
Canadian Capers... Cartoons Volume I
Canadian Capers... Cartoons Volume II
Candy-Candy
Cantinflas
Captain Future in Space
Captain Harlock

Captain Harlock
Care Bears in the Land Without Feeling, The
Cartoon Carnival #1
Cartoon Carnival #2
Cartoon Carnival Volume I
Cartoon Carnival Volume II
Cartoon Classics Limited Gold Edition: Daisy
Cartoon Classics Limited Gold Edition: Disney's
　　Best: The Fabulous 50's
Cartoon Classics Limited Gold Edition: Donald
Cartoon Classics Limited Gold Edition: Mickey
Cartoon Classics Limited Gold Edition: Minnie
Cartoon Classics Limited Gold Edition: Pluto
Cartoon Classics Limited Gold Edition: Silly
　　Symphonies
Cartoon Classics of the 1930's
Cartoon Classics Volume One: Chip 'n' Dale
　　Featuring Donald Duck
Cartoon Classics Volume Two: Pluto
Cartoon Classics Volume Three: Disney's Scary
　　Tales
Cartoon Classics Volume Four: Sport Goofy
Cartoon Classics Volume 5: Disney's Best of
　　1931-1948
Cartoon Classics Volume 7: More of Disney's
　　Best: 1932-1946
Cartoon Classics Volume 8: Sport Goofy's
　　Vacation
Cartoon Classics Volume 9: Donald Duck's First
　　50 Years
Cartoon Classics Volume 10: Mickey's Crazy
　　Careers
Cartoon Collection I
Cartoon Collection II: Warner Brothers Cartoons
Cartoon Collection III: Vintage Warner Bros.
　　Cartoons
Cartoon Collection IV: Early Animation
Cartoon Magic
Cartoon Parade No. 1
Cartoon Parade No. 2
Cartoon Parade No. 3
Cartoon Parade No. 4
Cartoon Supershow #1
Casper and the Angels
Casper and the Angels II
Charlie Brown Festival, A
Charlie Brown Festival Vol. II, A
Charlie Brown Festival Vol. III, A
Charlie Brown Festival Vol. IV, A
Charlie Brown's All Stars
Charlotte's Web
Chatterer the Squirrel
Children's Heroes of the Bible—David and
　　Moses
Color Adventures of Superman, The
Color Cartoon Program A
Color Cartoon Program B
Color Cartoon Program C
Color Cartoon Program D
Color Cartoon Program I
Color Cartoon Program II

Color Cartoon Program III
Color Cartoon Program IV
Columbia Pictures Cartoons Volume I: Mr. Magoo
Columbia Pictures Cartoons Volume II: Mr. Magoo
Columbia Pictures Cartoons Volume III: Gerald McBoing-Boing
Columbia Pictures Cartoons Volume IV: UPA Classics
Columbia Pictures Cartoons Volume V: Mr. Magoo
Columbia Pictures Cartoons, Volume VI
Cuckoo Clock That Wouldn't Cuckoo, The
Curious George
Daffy Duck's Movie: Fantastic Island
Danguard Ace
Dastardly & Muttley
Disney Cartoon Parade, Vol. 1
Disney Cartoon Parade, Vol. 2
Disney Cartoon Parade, Vol. 3
Disney Cartoon Parade, Vol. 4
Disney Cartoon Parade, Vol. 5
Disney's American Heroes
Disney's Storybook Classics
Dr. Seuss Video Festival
Doonesbury Special, A
Dorothy in the Land of Oz
Dot and the Bunny
Dumbo
Early Warner Brothers
Fables of the Green Forest
Fabulous Funnies
Fairy Tales, Volume Two
Fairy Tales, Volume I
Family Circus Christmas, A
Family Circus Easter, A
Fangface
Fantastic Animation Festival
Fat Albert and the Cosby Kids
Fat Albert, Volume 2
Favorite Black Exploitation Cartoons
Favorite Celebrity Cartoons
Favorite Racists Cartoons
Felix's Magic Bag of Tricks
Flower Angel, The
Four for Thrills
Fraidy Cat
Freedom Force, The
Gaiking
Galaxy Express
Goofy Over Sports
Grandizer
Great Bear Scare, The
Great Expectations
Gulliver's Travels
Gumby Adventure, A
Gumby Adventure Volume 1, A
Gumby Adventure Volume 2, A
Gumby Adventure Volume 3, A
Gumby Adventure Volume 4, A
Gumby Adventure Volume 5, A
He-Man and the Masters of the Universe
He-Man and the Masters of the Universe, Vol. 5
He-Man and the Masters of the Universe: The Greatest Adventures of All
Heathcliff and Marmaduke
Heckle y Jeckle
Heidi's Song
Herculoids, The
Hero High Volume 1
Hoppity Goes to Town
Houndcats, The
How the Animals Discovered Christmas
Hugo the Hippo
Inspector Gaget, Volume 1
It's Magic, Charlie Brown!
Jack and the Beanstalk
Johnny Woodchuck's Adventures
Josie and the Pussycats in Outer Space
Journey Back to Oz
Katy Caterpillar
King Arthur & the Knights of the Round Table Vol. 1
King Arthur & the Knights of the Round Table Vol. 2
Koko the Clown
Lassie's Rescue Rangers
Lassie's Rescue Rangers, Volume 2
Last Unicorn, The
Laurel and Hardy Volume 1
Laurel and Hardy Volume 2
Laurel and Hardy Volume 3
Laurel and Hardy Volume 4
Legend of Hiawatha, The
Legend of Sleepy Hollow, The
Life Is a Circus, Charlie Brown!
Little Brown Burro, The
Little Lulu
Little Mermaid, The
Little Women
Littlest Warrior, The
Lone Ranger, The
Looney Looney Looney Bugs Bunny Movie, The
Looney Tunes and Merrie Melodies I
Looney Tunes and Merrie Melodies II
Looney Tunes and Merrie Melodies #3
Looney Tunes Video Show #1, The
Looney Tunes Video Show #2, The
Looney Tunes Video Show #3, The
Looney Tunes Video Show #4, The
Looney Tunes Video Show #5, The
Looney Tunes Video Show #6, The
Looney Tunes Video Show #7, The
Lucky Luke: Daisy Town
Lucky Luke: The Ballad of the Daltons
Magic Horse, The
Many Adventures of Winnie the Pooh, The
Marco Polo, Jr.
Matt the Gooseboy
Mighty Mouse in The Great Space Chase
Mini Musicals

Miserables, Les
Miss Peach of the Kelly School
Mr. Magoo Cartoons
Mister Magoo in Sherwood Forest
Mr. Magoo in the King's Service
Mister Magoo... Man of Mystery
Mister Magoo's Christmas Carol
Mr. Magoo's Storybook
Moonstone Gem, The
Nelvanamation
Nelvanamation II
New Adventures of Zorro, The
New Three Stooges Cartoon Show, The
Oliver Twist
Oliver Twist
Once Upon a Time
1001 Arabian Nights
Panda and the Magic Serpent
Panda's Adventures
Perils of Penelope Pitstop, The
Peter and the Magic Egg
Peter Cottontail's Adventures
Peter-No-Tail
Phantom Tollbooth, The
Pinocchio in Outer Space
Plastic Man
Popeye and Friends in Outer Space
Popeye and Friends in the Wild West
Popeye Festival
Popeye the Sailor
Private Snafu Cartoon Festival
Puss 'n' Boots Travels Around the World
Race for Your Life, Charlie Brown
Raggedy Ann and Andy: A Musical Adventure
Rainbow Brite in Peril in the Pits
Rainbow Parade, The
Richie Rich
Sabrina, Volume 1
Sammy Bluejay
Scooby and Scrappy-Doo
Scooby and Scrappy-Doo, Volume II
Scooby Goes Hollywood
Sea Prince and the Fire Child, The
Secret Lives of Waldo Kitty Volume I, The
Secret Squirrel
Sextoons
Shazam
Shazam!, Volume 2
Shazzan
Shinbone Alley
Sing Along with Little Lulu
Smurfs and the Magic Flute, The
Snowman, The
Soldier's Tale, The
Space Angel Volume 1
Space Angel Volume 2
Space Ghost and Dino Boy
Space Sentinels Volume 1
Spaceketeers
Spaceketeers Volume 1
Spaceketeers Volume 2

Spaceketeers Volume 3
Special Valentine with Family Circus, A
Spider-Woman
Spunky and Tadpole
Squiddly Diddly
Stanley
Starvengers
Strawberry Shortcake and the Baby Without a Name
Strawberry Shortcake in Big Apple City
Strawberry Shortcake Pets on Parade
Strawberry Shortcake's House-Warming Party
Superman
Superman Cartoons
Superman Color Cartoon Festival
Superman Festival #1
Superman Festival #2
Superman-The Cartoons
Swan Lake
Tales of Deputy Dawg—Volumes II & III
Terry Bears Volume II
Terrytoons Salutes the Olympics
Terrytoons, Vol. I, Featuring Mighty Mouse
Three Caballeros, The
Three Musketeers, The
Thumbelina
Thundarr the Barbarian
Tom and Jerry Cartoon Festival, Vol. I
Tom and Jerry Cartoon Festival, Vol. II
Tom and Jerry Cartoon Festival, Vol. 3
Top Cat
Top Cat, Volume II
Ub Iwerks Cartoon Festival
Ub Iwerks Cartoonfest Two
Ub Iwerks Cartoonfest Three
Ub Iwerks Cartoonfest Four
UB Iwerks Cartoonfest Five
Ultraman II
Uncle Sam Magoo
Undersea Adventures of Captain Nemo Volume 1, The
Undersea Adventures of Captain Nemo Volume 2, The
Undersea Adventures of Captain Nemo Volume 3, The
Uproar in Heaven
Vintage Cartoon Holiday
Wacky and Packy
Wacky World of Mother Goose, The
Walt Disney Christmas, A
Warner Brothers Cartoon Festival I
Warner Brothers Cartoon Festival II
Warner Brothers Cartoon Festival III
Warner Brothers Cartoon Festival IV
Warner Brothers Cartoons
Wind in the Willows, The
Wind in the Willows, The
Winds of Change
Winsome Witch
Winsor McCay
Woody Woodpecker and His Friends, Volume I

Woody Woodpecker and His Friends, Volume II
Yogi's First Christmas
You're the Greatest, Charlie Brown!

Chemistry

Forces of Life, The

Childbirth

Lamaze Method: Techniques for Childbirth
   Preparation, The

Children

Always a New Beginning
Free to Be... You and Me
New Zoo Revue
Scholastic Productions: As We Grow

China

Chinese Gods
Night Over China

Christianity

Church Collection, The
Early Church Collection, The
Holy Land and Holy City
Martin Luther, His Life and Time

Christmas

Bear Who Slept Through Christmas, The
Benji's Very Own Christmas Story
Canadian Capers... Cartoons Volume I
Christmas Collection, The
Christmas on Grandfather's Farm
Cricket on the Hearth, The
Currier & Ives Christmas, A
Family Circus Christmas, A
First Christmas, The
How the Animals Discovered Christmas
Little Brown Burro, The
Little Rascals Christmas Special, The
Merry Christmas to You
Mister Magoo's Christmas Carol
Night Before Christmas, The
Scrooge's Rock 'n' Roll Christmas
Very Special Christmas, A/Sleeping Beauty
Walt Disney Christmas, A

Circus

Emmett Kelly Circus, The
High Grass Circus
Mr. Moon's Magic Circus

Cities and towns

Great Cities: London, Rome, Dublin, Athens

Civil rights

Our Friend Angela

Clothing and dress

Frederick's of Hollywood Presents...
Thighs and Whispers: The History of Lingerie
World of Fashion, The

Comedy

A Mi Las Mujeres Ni Fu, Ni
Abbott and Costello in Hollywood
Abbott and Costello Meet Captain Kidd
Abbott and Costello Meet Dr. Jekyll and Mr.
   Hyde
Abbott and Costello Meet Frankenstein
Absent-Minded Professor, The
Abuelo Made in Spain
Act, The
Adam's Rib
Admiral Was a Lady, The
Adventures of Curley and His Gang, The
Adventures of Ozzie and Harriet, The
Adventures of Ozzie and Harriet, The
Adventures of Ozzie and Harriet I, The
Adventures of Ozzie and Harriet, The
Adventures of Ozzie and Harriet V
Adventures of Ozzie and Harriet II, The
Adventures of Ozzie and Harriet III, The
Adventures of Ozzie and Harriet IV, The
Adventures of Sherlock Holmes' Smarter
   Brother, The
Affairs of Annabel
Africa Screams
After the Fox
Ahi Madre (Oh Mother)
Airplane!
Airplane II: The Sequel
Aldrich Family, The
Alice Doesn't Live Here Anymore
Alice Goodbody
Alice's Adventures in Wonderland
Alice's Restaurant
All Night Long
All the Marbles
All You Need Is Cash
Amarcord
American Graffiti
American Hot Wax
Amorous Adventures of Don Quixote & Sancho
   Panza, The
Amos n' Andy
Amos 'n' Andy Show, The
Amos 'n' Andy Show II, The
Amos 'n' Andy Show III, The
Amos 'n' Andy Show IV, The
Amos 'n' Andy Show V, The
Amos 'n' Andy Show VI, The
Amos ''n'' Andy Show VII, The
Amos 'n' Andy—Vol 1 thru 23

And Now for Something Completely Different
Animal Crackers
Animal House
Annie Hall
Any Which Way You Can
Apple Dumpling Gang, The
Apple Dumpling Gang Rides Again, The
Arsenic and Old Lace
Arthur
As You Like It
Asi No Hay Cama Que Aguante
At the Circus
At War with the Army
Atoll K
Attack of the Killer Tomatoes
Attack of the Robots
Audience with Mel Brooks, An
Auditions
Auntie Mame
Author! Author!
Bachelor and the Bobby Soxer, The
Bachelor Bait
Bachelor Mother
Bad News Bears, The
Bad News Bears in Breaking Training, The
Bakery, The/The Grocery Clerk
Balloonatic, The/One Week
Bananas
Bank Dick, The
Barber Shop, The
Barefoot in the Park
Battling Bunyan/Home Stretch The
Beach Girls, The
Beach House
Beach Party
Beatles—Comedy Featurettes
Bedazzled
Bedtime for Bonzo
Being There
Bela Lugosi Meets a Brooklyn Gorilla
Bell, Book and Candle
Belles of St. Trinian's, The
Bells Are Ringing
Ben Turpin Rides Again
Best Friends
Best Little Whorehouse in Texas, The
Best of Amos 'n Andy Vol. 1, The
Best of Benny Hill, The
Best of the Benny Hill Show, Vol. II, The
Best of the Benny Hill Show, Vol. III, The
Best of the Kenny Everett Video Show, The
Between the Lines
Beulah Show, The
Beyond Tomorrow
Big Bus, The
Big Time, The
Billion Dollar Hobo, The
Bingo Long Traveling All-Stars & Motor Kings, The
Bizarre Bizarre
Black Bird, The
Blackbeard's Ghost
Blacksmith, The/Cops
Blacksmith, The/The Balloonatic
Blame It on Rio
Blazing Saddles
Blockheads
Blockheads
Bloodsucking Freaks
Blue Country
Blue Skies Again
Blues Brothers, The
Blume in Love
Boarding School
Boatniks, The
Bob & Carol & Ted & Alice
Bob & Ray, Jane, Laraine & Gilda
Bob Hope Chevy Show I, The
Bob Hope Chevy Show II, The
Bobo, The
Bohemian Girl, The
Bon Voyage, Charlie Brown
Born Yesterday
Boum, La
Bourgeois Gentilhomme, Le
Bowery Blitzkrieg
Boys from Brooklyn, The
Breakfast at Tiffany's
Breakfast in Hollywood
Breaking Away
Britannia Hospital
Bronco Billy
Buck Privates
Buddy Buddy
Bugs Bunny/Road Runner Movie, The
Buick-Berle Show, The
Bundle of Joy
Bus Stop
Buster Keaton: Four Short Films
Buster Keaton Rides Again/The Railrodder
Buster Keaton: The Great Stone Face
Bustin' Loose
Butler's Dilemma, The
By Design
Cactus Flower
Caddyshack
Caesar's Hour
Caesar's Hour
Cage aux Folles, La
Cage Aux Folles II, La
California Suite
Can I Do It...Till I Need Glasses?
Candid Candid Camera
Candleshoe
Cannon Ball, The/The Eyes Have It
Cannonball Run, The
Captain's Paradise, The
Car Wash
Carbon Copy
Carol Burnett Show: Bloopers and Outtakes, The
Carry On Behind
Carry On Cleo

Carry On Nurse
Carson's Cellar
Carson's Cellar/The Jack Paar Show
Casa Flora
Cat from Outer Space, The
Catherine and Co.
Cavaleur, Le (Practice Makes Perfect)
Caveman
Cesar
Champagne for Caesar
Change of Habit
Change of Seasons, A
Chaplin: A Character Is Born/Keaton: The Great Stone Face
Chaplin at Essanay #1
Chaplin at Essanay #2
Chaplin at Keystone #1
Chaplin at Keystone #2
Chaplin Cavalcade
Chaplin Mutuals #1
Chaplin Mutuals #2
Chaplin Mutuals #3
Chaplin Mutuals, Volume I
Chaplin Mutuals, Volume II
Chaplin Mutuals, Volume III
Chaplin Mutuals, Volume IV
Chaplin Revue, The
Charade
Charge of the Model T's
Charley Chase Festival (Vol. 1)
Charlie Chan and the Curse of the Dragon Queen
Charlie Chaplin Carnival
Charlie Chaplin Cavalcade
Charlie Chaplin Festival, The
Charlie Chaplin: The Funniest Man in the World
Charlie Chaplin's Keystone Comedies
Chatterbox
Check and Double Check
Cheech and Chong's Next Movie
Cheech & Chong's Nice Dreams
Cheerleaders, The
Cheerleader's Beach Party
Cherry Hill High
Chesty Anderson U.S. Navy
Chimpo's Wild Animal Safari
Chu Chu and the Philly Flash
Chump at Oxford, A
Chump at Oxford, A
City Lights
Class
Coach
Cockeyed Cavaliers
Colgate Comedy Hour, The
Colgate Comedy Hour, The
College
Columbia Pictures Cartoons Volume I: Mr. Magoo
Columbia Pictures Cartoons Volume II: Mr. Magoo

Columbia Pictures Cartoons Volume V: Mr. Magoo
Columbia Pictures Cartoons, Volume VII
Comedy 1: Trailers on Tape
Comedy and Kid Stuff I
Comedy and Kid Stuff II
Comedy Festival #1
Comedy Festival #2
Comedy Festival #3
Comedy Festival #4
Comedy Special I
Comedy Special II
Committee, The
Condorman
Continental Divide
Copacabana
Count, The/The Adventurer
Country Gentlemen
Court Jester, The
Cousin, Cousine
Crackers
Cracking Up
Curley
Curley and His Gang in the Haunted Mansion
Curse of the Pink Panther, The
Daffy Duck's Movie: Fantastic Island
Danger Ahead!
Day at the Races, A
Day the Bookies Wept, The
D.C. Cab
Dead Men Don't Wear Plaid
Deal of the Century
Demi-Paradise, The
Dentist, The
Derek and Clive Get the Horn
Devil and Max Devlin, The
Devil and Miss Jones, The
Die Laughing
Diplomaniacs
Dirty Mind of Young Sally, The
Dirty Tricks
Dixiana
Dixie Jamboree
Dr. Detroit
Dr. Heckyl and Mr. Hype
Dr. Strangelove
Dona Flor and Her Two Husbands
Donovan's Reef
Don's Party
Don't Raise the Bridge, Lower the River
Don't Shove/Two Gun Gussie
Double Bunk
Double McGuffin, The
Doughnuts and Society
Dreaming Out Loud
Duchess and the Dirtwater Fox, The
Duck Soup
Early Days
East Side Kids, The
Easy Money

Easy Street/The Count/Behind the Screen/The Immigrant
Eating Raoul
Ed Wynn: Double Feature #1
Ed Wynn: Double Feature #2
Ed Wynn: Double Feature #3
Ed Wynn: Double Feature #4
Ed Wynn Show, The
Ed Wynn Show, The
Edgar Kennedy Slow Burn Festival, The
Elephant Parts
Emmet Otter's Jug-Band Christmas
End, The
Ensign Pulver
Ernie Kovacs: Television's Original Genius
Erotic Three, The
Eternally Yours
Evening with Sir William Martin, An
Every Which Way But Loose
Everything You Always Wanted to Know About Sex But (Were Afraid to Ask)
Ex-Mrs. Bradford, The
Experience Preferred... But Not Essential
Expertos en Pinchazos
Extra Girl, The
Fabulous Joe, The
Falling in Love Again
Fanny
Farmer's Daughter, The
Fast Break
Fast Times at Ridgemont High
Fatal Glass of Beer, The
Father Goose
Fatty and Mabel
Fatty and Mabel Adrift/Mabel, Fatty and the Law
Fatty's Tin-Type Tangle/Our Congressman
Favorite Celebrity Cartoons
Fiendish Plot of Dr. Fu Manchu, The
Fiesta
Fire Over England/As You Like It
Firemen's Ball
Firesign Theatre Presents Nick Danger in The Case of the Missing Yolk, The
First Family
First Monday in October
First Nudie Musical, The
First Time, The
Five Mack Sennett Shorts
Flask of Fields, A
Flirting with Fate
Flying Deuces, The
Follow a Star
Follow Me, Boys!
Follow That Camel
Foolin' Around
For Love of Ivy
For Pete's Sake
For the Love of It
Foreplay
Fortune's Fool
Forty Carats
48 Hrs.
Foul Play
Four Musketeers, The
Four Seasons, The
Fowl Play
Freaky Friday
French Line
Frisco Kid, The
Fritz the Cat
Frolics on Ice
Front Page, The
Fun and Fancy Free
Fun Factory/Clown Princes of Hollywood
Fun with Dick and Jane
Funnier Side of Eastern Canada with Steve Martin, The
Funny Farm, The
Funny Guys and Gals of the Talkies
Funny Thing Happened on the Way to the Forum, A
Funstuff
Galaxina
Gas
Gas Pump Girls
General, The
Genevieve
Gentlemen Prefer Blondes
George Burns and Gracie Allen Show, The
George Burns Show, The
Get Crazy
Get Happy
Get Out Your Handkerchiefs
Getting It On
Getting Mama Married
Getting Wasted
Ghosts of Berkeley Square, The
Gilda Live
Girl in Every Port, A
Girl Most Likely, The
Go West
Going Apo!
Going in Style
Going Steady
Gold Rush, The
Gold Rush, The/Payday
Golden Age of Comedy, The
Gondoliers, The
Goodbye Columbus
Goodbye Girl, The
Goon Movie (Stand Easy), The
Gorilla, The
Grass Is Greener, The
Greaser's Palace
Great Dictator, The
Great McGonagall, The
Great Muppet Caper, The
Great Race, The
Great St. Trinian's Train Robbery, The
Great Scout and Cathouse Thursday, The
Great Texas Dynamite Chase, The
Groucho/Howdy Doody Show

Group Marriage
Guess What We Learned in School
Gumby for President Volume 9
Gus
Hal Roach Comedy Classics Volume I
Half-Shot at Sunrise
Hanky Panky
Happy Hooker, The
Happy Hooker Goes Hollywood, The
Happy Hooker Goes to Washington, The
Harold and Maude
Harold Lloyd's Comedy Classics
Harold Lloyd's Short Films
Harper Valley P.T.A.
Harry and Walter Go to New York
Hash House Fraud, A/The Sultan's Wife
Hawmps!
Headless Horseman, The/Will Rogers
Heartaches
Heartbeeps
Heartbreak Kid, The
Heavens Above
Heavy Petting
Heavy Traffic
Herbie Rides Again
Hercules Goes Bananas
Here Comes Trouble
Here We Go Again!
Hey Abbott!
Hey Cinderella!
High Anxiety
High Voltage
Hijazo De Mi Vidaza (Son of My Life)
Hips, Hips, Hooray
His Girl Friday
His Royal Slyness/Haunted Spooks
History of the World: Part I
Hobson's Choice
Hold 'Em Jail
Hold That Ghost
Hold That Woman
Hollywood Boulevard
Honky Tonk Freeway
Hooper
Hopscotch
Hot Bubblegum
Hot Rock, The
Hot Stuff
Hot Summer in Barefoot County
Hot T-Shirts
Hot Wire
Hothead (Coup de Tete)
House Calls
How Funny Can Sex Be?
How to Beat the High Cost of Living
How to Marry a Millionaire
How to Stuff a Wild Bikini
Howdy Doody
Hysterical
I Hate Blondes
I Love You, Alice B. Toklas

I Married Joan
I Married Joan
I Married Joan/The Burns and Allen Show
I Ought to Be in Pictures
Ice Pirates, The
I'm All Right Jack
I'm on My Way/The Non-Stop Kid
Improper Channels
In-Laws, The
In Love With An Older Woman
In Praise of Older Women
Incoming Freshmen
Incredible Rocky Mountain Race, The
Incredible Shrinking Woman, The
Indiscreet
Indiscreet
Inspector General, The
Irma La Douce
It Should Happen to You
It's a Joke Son
It's a Mad, Mad, Mad, Mad World
It's in the Bag
Jabberwalk
Jabberwocky
Jack and the Beanstalk
Jack Benny, II
Jack Benny Program, The
Jack Benny Program, The
Jack Benny Show, The
Jack Benny Show, The
JD and the Salt Flat Kid
Jekyll and Hyde...Together Again
Jerk, The
Jimmy the Kid
Jinxed
Johnny Carson
Jonathan Winters Show, The
Joy Sticks
Juke Joint
Just Tell Me What You Want
Kentucky Fried Movie
Kid, The and The Idle Class
Kid Dynamite
Kid 'n' Hollywood & Polly Tix in Washington
Kid Sister, The
Kid with the Broken Halo, The
Kid's Auto Race/Mabel's Married Life
Kind Hearts and Coronets
Kings, Queens, Jokers
Kiss Me Goodbye
Kitty and the Bagman
Knockout, The/Dough and Dynamite
Kovacs on the Corner
Lady Takes a Chance
Ladykillers, The
Last American Virgin, The
Last Married Couple in America, The
Last of the Red Hot Lovers
Late Show, The
Laughfest
Laurel and Hardy Comedy Classics Volume I

Laurel and Hardy Comedy Classics Volume II
Laurel and Hardy Comedy Classics Volume III
Laurel and Hardy Comedy Classics Volume IV
Laurel and Hardy Comedy Classics Volume V
Laurel and Hardy Comedy Classics Volume VI
Laurel and Hardy Comedy Classics Volume VII
Laurel and Hardy Comedy Classics Volume VIII
Laurel and Hardy Comedy Classics Volume IX
Lavender Hill Mob, The
Let's Do It Again
Let's Do It
Let's Get Tough
Life with Father
Little Darlings
Little Miss Marker
Little Rascals, Book I, The
Little Rascals, Book II, The
Little Rascals, Book III, The
Little Rascals, Book IV, The
Little Rascals, Book V, The
Little Rascals, Book VI, The
Little Rascals, Book VII, The
Little Rascals Book VIII, The
Little Rascals Book IX, The
Little Rascals, Book X, The
Little Rascals, Book XI, The
Little Rascals, Book XII, The
Little Rascals, Book XIII, The
Little Rascals, Book XIV, The
Little Rascals, Book XV, The
Little Rascals, Book XVI, The
Little Rascals Comedy Classics 1
Little Sex, A
Lonely Guy, The
Lonely Hearts
Lonely Wives
Longest Yard, The
Lookin' to Get Out
Looney Tunes and Merrie Melodies I
Looney Tunes and Merrie Melodies II
Losin' It
Lost and Found
Love and Death
Love at First Bite
Love Bug, The
Love Happy
Love Laughs at Andy Hardy
Lovers and Liars
Lovesick
Loving Couples
Lucky Jim
Lum and Abner
Lunatics and Lovers
Lunch Wagon
Luv
Mad About Money
Mad Monster Party
Magic Christian, The
Magic Garden, The
Magic Show, The
Main Event, The

Make a Million
Make Mine Mink
Making the Grade
Malibu Beach
Mama (I Remember Mama)
Mama (I Remember Mama)
Man, a Woman, and a Bank, A
Man from Clover Grove, The
Man in the White Suit, The
Man Who Loved Women, The
Man with Two Brains, The
Marius
Martha Raye Show, The
Mary Tyler Moore Show, Vol. I, The
M*A*S*H
Master Mind
Masters of Comedy
Masters of the World
Matilda
Matrimaniac, The
Meatballs
Melvin and Howard
Mickey
Mickey
Mickey the Great
Midsummer Night's Sex Comedy, A
Milky Way, The
Million, Le
Milton Berle Show, The
Milton Berle Show, The
Milton Berle Show, The
Minsky's Follies
Missionary, The
Mr. & Mrs. Smith
Mr. Bill Looks Back Featuring Sluggo's Greatest
   Hits
Mr. Bill Show, The
Mr. Blandings Builds His Dream House
Mr. Hulot's Holiday
Mr. Lucky
Mr. Magoo Cartoons
Mister Magoo in Sherwood Forest
Mr. Mike's Mondo Video
Mr. Mom
Mr. Peabody and the Mermaid
Mister Roberts
Mr. Wise Guy
Modern Problems
Modern Romance
Modern Times
Molly (The Goldbergs)
Mon Oncle
Monsieur Verdoux
Monty Python and the Holy Grail
Monty Python Live at the Hollywood Bowl
Monty Python's Life of Brian
Monty Python's The Meaning of Life
Moon Is Blue, The
Morgan—A Suitable Case for Treatment
Mouse That Roared, The
Movie, Movie

Movie Struck
Movie Struck/The Flying Deuces
Muppet Movie, The
Muppet Musicians of Bremen, The
Murder by Death
My Best Girl
My Favorite Brunette
My Favorite Wife
My Favorite Year
My Little Chickadee
My Little Margie
My Love for Yours
My Man Godfrey
My Tutor
Naked Truth, The
National Adultery
National Lampoon's Class Reunion
National Lampoon's Vacation
NBC Comedy Hour
Neighbors
Night at the Opera, A
Night in Casablanca, A
Night Shift
Night They Robbed Big Bertha's, The
Nine Lives of Fritz the Cat, The
9 to 5
1941
Nobody's Perfekt
Norman Conquests: Table Manners, The
Norman Conquests: Living Together, The
Norman Conquests: Round and Round the Garden, The
North Avenue Irregulars, The
Nothing Personal
Nothing Sacred
Nutty Professor, The
Ocean's 11
Odd Couple, The
Odd Job, The
Office Girls
Oh, God
Oh God, Book II
On Approval
On the Air Live with Captain Midnight
On the Right Track
Once Upon a Honeymoon
One and Only, The
One Body Too Many
One Rainy Afternoon
Only When I Laugh
Operation Petticoat
Our Relations
Our Relations
Out-Of-Towners, The
Outrageous
Owl and the Pussycat, The
Pack Up Your Troubles
Pajama Tops
Paper Moon
Pardon Mon Affaire
Pardon Us

Parent Trap, The
Paris Holiday
Parlor, Bedroom and Bath
Partners
Paternity
Peck's Bad Boy
Peck's Bad Boy with the Circus
People Are Funny
Pepper and His Wacky Taxi
Pharmacist, The
Phil Silvers Special: Summer in New York
Philadelphia Story, The
Pinchcliffe Grand Prix, The
Pink Motel
Pink Panther, The
Pink Panther Strikes Again, The
Pippi Longstocking
Pirates of Penzance, The
Play It Again, Sam
Playboy of the Western World, The
Plaza Suite
Pleasure Doing Business, A
Pom-Pom Girls, The
Pop Goes the Cork
Popeye
Porky's
Porky's II: The Next Day
Pride of the Bowery
Prime Time
Prince and the Showgirl, The
Prisoner of Zenda, The
Private Benjamin
Private Eyes, The
Private Lessons
Private Popsicle
Prize Fighter, The
Producers, The
Promises! Promises!
Purlie Victorious
Putney Swope
Pygmalion
Quackser Fortune Has a Cousin in the Bronx
Race for Your Life, Charlie Brown
Rage of Paris, The
Rascal Dazzle
Real Life
Reg'lar Fellers
Repo Man
Return of the Pink Panther, The
Revenge of the Pink Panther
Rink, The/The Immigrant
Risky Business
Road to Bali
Roman Holiday
Romantic Comedy
Romantic Englishwoman, The
Room Service
Rubber Tires
Ruddigore
Ruggles, The
Ruling Class, The

Russians Are Coming, the Russians Are Coming,
   The
Safety Last
Saint Benny the Dip
Sally of the Sawdust
Saps at Sea
Saps at Sea
Saturday Night Live: Carrie Fisher
Saturday Night Live: Steve Martin 2
Saturday Night Live, Vol. II
Saturday Night Live, Vol. I
Saturday Night Live with Richard Pryor
Saturday Night Live with Steve Martin
Scandalous
Scavenger Hunt
Schlock
Scoring
Screwballs
Second City Insanity
Secret Policeman's Other Ball, The
Secret War of Harry Frigg, The
Seems Like Old Times
Semi-Tough
Senator Was Indiscreet, The
Seniors
Sensual Man, The
Sensuous Caterer, The
Serial
Sesenta Horas en el Cielo
Seven Beauties
Seven Year Itch, The
Sex in the Comics
Sex on the Run
Sex with a Smile
Sextette
Shaggy Dog, The
Shamus
She Couldn't Say No
Sheriff Terrible, El
Shot in the Dark, A
Silent Laugh Makers No. 1
Silent Laugh Makers No. 2
Silent Laugh Makers #3
Silk Stockings
Silver Streak
Simon
Sin of Harold Diddlebock, The
Sing Your Worries Away
Sitting Ducks
Sixteen Candles
Sky's The Limit, The
Slap, The
Sleeper
Slumber Party '57
Small Change
Smokey and the Bandit
Smokey and the Bandit II
Smokey and the Bandit Part 3
Smokey and the Judge
Snow, The Movie
Snowball Express

So Fine
So This is Washington
S.O.B.
Social Secretary, The
Some Like It Hot
Son of Flubber
Sons of the Desert
Sons of the Desert
Soup for One
Spaced Out
Speaking of Animals
Speed Kings? The/Love, Speed and Thrills
Spinal Tap
Spooks Run Wild
Spring Break
Spring Fever
Squeeze Play
Stand Easy
Stand-In
Star Struck
State of the Union
Steamboat Bill, Jr.
Step Lively
Steve Allen Plymouth Show, The
Still Smokin'
Sting II, The
Sting of the West
Stir Crazy
Stooges Shorts Festival
Stork Club, The
Story of William S. Hart, The/The Sad Clowns
Stripes
Stroker Ace
Summer Camp
Sunburn
Sunshine Boys, The
Super Fuzz
Survivors, The
Susan Slept Here
Swan, The
Swing High, Swing Low
Swing It, Sailor!
Swinging Cheerleaders, The
Swiss Miss
Swiss Miss
Take a Good Look/The Jack Benny Show
Take the Money and Run
Take This Job and Shove It
Tales from Muppetland
Tales from Muppetland II
Taming of the Shrew, The
Taming of the Shrew, The
Telephone Book, The
Television's Golden Age of Comedy
"10"
Tendres Cousines
Texaco Star Theater
Thank God It's Friday
That Man Is Pregnant
That Touch of Mink
That Uncertain Feeling

The Howdy Doody Show (Puppet Playhouse)/Gabby Hayes Show
There's a Girl in My Soup
There's Naked Bodies On My T.V.!
These Girls Won't Talk
They All Laughed
They Call Me Bruce
They Went That-a-Way & That-a-Way
Things Are Tough All Over
Think Dirty
30 Is a Dangerous Age, Cynthia
Those Magnificent Men in Their Flying Machines
Three Ages, The
Three Broadway Girls
Three Nuts in Search of a Bolt
Three Stooges, The
Three Stooges Comedy Capers Volume I
Three Stooges—Medium Rare, The
Three Stooges Meet Hercules, The
Three Stooges Videodisc, Vol. 1, The
Three Stooges Volume I, The
Three Stooges Volume II, The
Three Stooges Volume III, The
Three Stooges Volume IV, The
Three Stooges Volume V, The
Three Stooges Volume VI, The
Three Stooges Volume VII, The
Three Stooges, Volume VIII, The
Three Stooges Volume IX, The
Till Marriage Do Us Part
Tillie's Punctured Romance
Tillie's Punctured Romance/Wild and Woolly
Timex All-Star Comedy Show
To Be or Not To Be
To Be or Not to Be
To See Such Fun
Toast of the Town
Tom, Dick, and Harry
Tom Jones
Tomboy
Tootsie
Topper
Topper Returns
Topper Takes a Trip
Touch of Class, A
Trading Places
Trail of the Pink Panther
Tramp and A Woman, The
Trenchcoat
Trouble with Angels, The
Trouble with Father
Tulips
Tulips
Tuttles of Tahiti, The
TV Variety III
TV Variety, VI
Twelve Chairs, The
200 Motels
Two of a Kind
Two Reelers—Comedy Classics I
Two Reelers—Comedy Classics II
Two Reelers—Comedy Classics III
Two Reelers—Comedy Classics IV
Two Reelers—Comedy Classics #5
Two Tickets to Broadway
Two-Way Stretch
Two Weeks to Live
Under the Rainbow
Unfaithfully Yours
Unfaithfully Yours
Up In Smoke
Up Pompeii
Uptown Saturday Night
Used Cars
Vagabond, The/The Floorwalker/The Rink/The Fireman
Valley Girl
Van, The
Van Nuys Blvd.
Vic 'n' Sade
Victor/Victoria
Villain Still Pursued Her, The
Vintage Commercials
Vintage Commercials, II
Vintage Sitcoms
Viva Max
Vivacious Lady
Wackiest Wagon Train in the West, The
Wacko
Waitress
Way Out West
Way Out West
W. C. Fields Festival
We All Loved Each Other So Much
Wedding Party, The
Weekend Pass
What Price Hollywood
What's New Pussycat?
What's Up Doc?
What's Up Tiger Lily?
When's Your Birthday?
Where the Boys Are
Where the Buffalo Roam
Where's Poppa?
Which Way Is Up?
Whisky Galore
Wholly Moses!
Whoops Apocalypse
Wild and Woolly
Wild and Wooly
Will Rogers: Four Two-Reelers
Win, Place, or Steal
Witches' Brew
Without Reservations
Woman of the Year
Work/Police
World According to Garp, The
Wrong Is Right
Yankee Doodle in Berlin
Yellowbeard
Yeomen of the Guard, The
Yes, Giorgio

You Bet Your Life
You'll Find Out
Young and Willing
Young Doctors in Love
Young Frankenstein
You're a Big Boy Now
Zapped
Zelig
Zero for Conduct
Zis Boom Bah
Zorro, the Gay Blade

Comedy-Drama

Apartment, The
Apprenticeship of Duddy Kravitz, The
Back Roads
Barney Oldfield's Race for a Life/Super-Hooper-
    Dyne Lizzies
Baron Muenchhausen
Benji
Big Chill, The
Billy Liar
Breach of Promise
Buck and the Preacher
Butterflies Are Free
Cafe Express
Can She Bake a Cherry Pie?
Cannery Row
Casey's Shadow
Cheaper to Keep Her
Clown, The
Coast to Coast
Cristo Del Oceano (Christ from the Ocean)
Dangerous Relations
Danny Boy
Devil's Eye
Diary of a Mad Housewife
Diner
Dog Day Afternoon
Eyes Right
Fireside Theatre: Sergeant Sullivan Speaking
For the Love of Benji
Four Friends
Fuzz
Gin Game, The
Good Sam
Goodbye People, The
Graduate, The
Grandes Amigos (Great Friends)
Heat
Hotel New Hampshire, The
If You Could See What I Hear
It's My Turn
Joe
Judge Priest
King of Comedy, The
Last Detail, The
Last Word, The
Little Lord Fauntleroy
Magic Town

Magician, The
Mama (I Remember Mama)
Mark Twain's A Connecticut Yankee in King
    Arthur's Court
M*A*S*H: Goodbye, Farewell and Amen
Max Dugan Returns
Mejore Regalo, El (The Best Gift)
Miss Annie Rooney
My Dinner with Andre
Never Let Go
North Dallas Forty
Nuit de Varennes, La
Oh Alfie
Palooka
Pillow Talk
Pollyanna
Pollyanna
Poor Little Rich Girl, The
Portnoy's Complaint
Preacherman
Prisoner of Second Avenue, The
Quiet Man, The
Racquet
Rascals, The
Rattle of a Simple Man
Rebecca of Sunnybrook Farm
Return of the Secaucus 7
Rich and Famous
Robert et Robert
Second Thoughts
Secrets of Women
Seduced and Abandoned
Six Weeks
Slap Shot
Some Kind of Hero
Sparrows
Stage Door
Starting Over
Sting, The
Swing Shift
Thousand Clowns, A
Three in the Attic
Thunder in the City
Tilt
To Sir, With Love
Toy, The
Up the Sandbox
We're No Angels
Zero to Sixty

Comedy-Performance

Best of the Big Laff-Off, The
Billy Connolly—Bites Yer Bum
Buddy Hackett: Live and Uncensored
Carlin at Carnegie
Carrott Gets Rowdie
Comedy Tonight
Evening with Robin Williams, An
Franken and Davis Special, The
Hungry i Reunion

Joe Piscopo
Lenny Bruce
Lenny Bruce Performance Film, The
Redd Foxx—Video in a Plain Brown Wrapper
Richard Pryor: Here and Now
Richard Pryor Live in Concert
Richard Pryor Live on the Sunset Strip

Communication

Behind the Scenes of Telstar
Ham MasterTapes
New Speed Reading

Cookery

Anne Byrd's Cookery
Baking Pastry
Cake Decorating
Cooking a French Meal
Cooking a Japanese Meal
Cooking a Mexican Meal
Cooking an Italian Meal
Cooking Chinese Food
Cuisine Pratique, La
Flavors of China
Food Processing
Indian Cooking
Julia Child—The French Chef, Vol. I
Master Cooking Course, The
Microwave Cooking
Scandinavian Cooking
Slim Gourmet, The

Cosmetology

Beauty Bible
Why Do I Call You Sexy?

Crime-Drama

Adventures of Ellery Queen, The
Black Marble, The
Blade
Brannigan
Con Artists, The
Corrupt
Cross Country
Dear Detective
Detour
Dick Tracy
Dick Tracy
Dick Tracy
Dick Tracy Double Feature #1
Dick Tracy Meets Gruesome
Dick Tracy Returns
Dick Tracy Returns
Dick Tracy vs. Crime Inc.
Dick Tracy vs. Crime Inc.
Dick Tracy's G-Men
Dick Tracy's G-Men
Dillinger

Enforcer, The
Family, The
French Connection, The
Gangs, Inc.
Gangster Wars, The
Gangsters
Gauntlet, The
High Crime
Hit Men, The
House on Garibaldi Street, The
Justice
Last Mile, The
Laura
Let 'Em Have It
Little Caesar
Long Good Friday, The
Magnum Force
Man Against Crime Volume II
Man on the Eiffel Tower, The
McQ
Mean Johnny Barrows
Northwest Trail
One Man Jury
Outside the Law
Policewomen
Port of New York
Portrait of a Hitman
Public Enemy
Racket, The
Racket Squad
Rocky King, Detective
Rulers of the City
St. Ives
Scarface
Scarface
Shaft
Shoot It Black, Shoot It Blue
Stiletto
Street Law
Sudden Impact
T-Men
They Live by Night
Thief
Trapped
Violent Professionals
Westinghouse Studio One: "Little Men, Big World"
Zebra Force

Dance

Aerobic Dancing
Aerobic Dancing—Encore
All the Best from Russia
Anna Karenina
Backstage at the Kirov
Ballerina: Karen Kain
Ballerina: Lynn Seymour
Ballet Class for Beginners, A
Belly Dancing—You Can Do It!
Bellydancing

Bolshoi Ballet
Carmen
Dance and Body Movement for Children
Dance Masters
Dazzledancin
Evening with the Royal Ballet, An
Coppelia with Fernando Bujones
Fille Mal Gardee, La
Giselle
I Am a Dancer
John Curry's Ice Dancing
Kids from Fame, The
La Sylphide
Learn to Dance: Disco/Hustle
Learn to Dance: Fox Trot/Cha Cha
Let's Break
Let's Break: A Visual Guide to Break Dancing
Let's Dance with Arthur Murray
Let's Jazzercise
Lietuviskos Dainos Suente
Little Humpbacked Horse, The
Nutcracker, The
Nutcracker, The
Nutcracker, The
Plisetskaya Dances
Romeo and Juliet
Russian Folk Song and Dance
Sandahl Bergman's Body
Sleeping Beauty
Spartacus
Stars of the Russian Ballet
Swan Lake
Swan Lake
Swan Lake
Tap Dancing for Beginners
Ultra Flash
Video Dictionary of Classical Ballet, The
Video Dictionary of Classical Ballet, The

Deaf

Sign Language: Exact English

Death

Beyond Death's Door
Faces of Death
Jill

Disasters

Encounter with Disaster
Filming the Big Thrills/Filming the Fantastic

Divorce

Marriage and Divorce Test, The
Marvin Mitchelson on Divorce

Documentary

Africa, Blood and Guts

Africa Speaks
After Mein Kampf (The Story of Adolf Hitler)
Air Force Story, The
Amazing Apes, The
America at the Movies
America Between the Great Wars
Animals Are Beautiful People
Atomic Cafe, The
Barricade
Battle for the Falklands
Battle of Britain, The
Battle of China, The
Battle of Russia, The
Battle of San Pietro, The
Behind Your Radio Dial
Belafonte Presents Fincho
Bermuda Triangle, The
Beyond and Back
Beyond Bengal
Borneo
Bride of the Beast
Brother, Can You Spare a Dime?
Buster Keaton Rides Again/The Railrodder
Buster Keaton: The Great Stone Face
Carnivores, The
Century of Progress Exposition, The/New York
     World's Fair 1939-40
Chariots of the Gods
Charlie Chaplin: The Funniest Man in the World
Chicken Ranch
Chicken Real
City of Gold/Drylanders
Coaster Adventure of the John F. Leavitt
Cool Cats: 25 Years of Rock 'n' Roll Style
Cool World, The
Cousteau—The Nile
Divide and Conquer
Dream Called Walt Disney World, A
D.W. Griffith: An American Genius
Eisenstein
Elvis on Tour
Endless Summer, The
Eruption: St. Helens Explodes
Fabulous Fifties, The
Faces of Death
Fight for the Sky
Filming the Big Thrills/Filming the Fantastic
Flights and Flyers
Flights and Flyers: Amelia Earhart
Garlic Is as Good as Ten Mothers
Germany Awake
Girl Groups: The Story of a Sound
Gizmo!
Go! Go! Go! World
God Respects Us When We Work But Loves Us
     When We Dance
Good Old Days
Goona Goona
Gorilla
Gotta Dance, Gotta Sing
Grateful Dead in Concert, The

Great Battle of the Volga
Great Figures in History: John F. Kennedy
Greatest Adventure, The
Gypsies
Harlan County, U.S.A.
Hearts and Minds
Hellstrom Chronicle, The
Historical Yesterdays
History of Pro Football, The
Hitler—February 10th, 1933
Hollywood Goes to War
Hughes Flying Boat, The
I Crave the Waves
Icarus Mania
In Search of Noah's Ark
It Came from Hollywood
J.F.K.
Kellogg Dream, The
Killing of President Kennedy, The
Killing of President Kennedy: New Revelations
    Twenty Years Later, The
Klaipedos Atvadavimas
Land Without Bread
Land Without Bread
Lash of the Penitentes
Leben von Adolf Hitler, Das (The Life of Adolf
    Hitler)
Legend of Valentino, The
Let There Be Light
Lincoln Conspiracy, The
Loch Ness Monster, The
Lonely Boy/Satan's Choice
Love Goddesses, The
Mahalia Jackson and Elizabeth Cotten: Two
    Remarkable Ladies
Marco Polo's Afghanistan
Marilyn Monroe
Marjoe
Memory Lane Movies by Robert Youngson #1
Memory Lane Movies by Robert Youngson #2
Memory Lane Movies by Robert Youngson #3
Memory Lane Movies by Robert Youngson #4
Memory Lane Movies by Robert Youngson #5
Memory Lane Movies by Robert Youngson #6
Memphis Belle, The
Men of Destiny Volume I: World Political Figures
Men of Destiny Volume II: Artists and Innovators
Milestones of the Century Volume I: The Great
    Wars
Milestones of the Century Volume II: 20th
    Century—Turning Points
Mondo Cane
Mondo Cane 2
Motion Picture Camera, The
Moving Picture Boys in the Great War, The
Mutiny on the Western Front: WW I
Mysteries from Beyond Earth
Mysterious Miniature World
Nanook of the North
Nazi War Crime Trials
Nazis, The

Nazis Strike, The / Schichlegruber Doing the
    Lambeth Walk
Nazis Strike, The
Negro Soldier
New Deal—The Thirties, The
Night and Fog
Olympia: Parts I and II
Other Side of Nashville, The
Pieces of Eight
Plisetskaya Dances
Plow That Broke the Plains, The/The River
Pot Shots
Pre-War German Featurettes
Predators of the Sea
Prelude to War
Pumping Iron
Punk Rock Movie, The
Richard   Nixon—Checkers,   Old   Glory,
    Resignation
Rise and Fall of the Third Reich
Roaring Twenties, The
Robert Youngson Specials
Royal Wedding, The
Say Amen, Somebody
Sea Around Us, The
Secret Life of Adolph Hitler, The
Secret World of Reptiles, The
Sense of Loss, A
Showbiz Goes to War
Sieg im Western (Victory in the West)
Silent Enemy, The
Simtameciu Godos
Slave Trade in the World Today
Song of Ceylon
Sorrow and the Pity, The
Space Movie, The
Stillwell Road
Stoney Knows How
Story of Lili Marlene, The
Super Weapon, The
Survival Anglia's World of Wildlife, Vol. I
Survival Anglia's World of Wildlife, Vol. 2
Target for Tonight
This Nude World
Thorpe's Gold
Time Capsule: The Los Angeles Olympic
    Games/1932
Tokyo Olympiad
Tree of Life, The
Triumph of the Will
True Glory, The
Twisted Cross, The
Undersea World of Jacques Cousteau Vol. I, The
U.S. War Department Report—July 1943
U.S.S. Nautilus—Operation Sunshine
U.S.S. VD: Ship of Shame/Red Nightmare
Victory at Sea
Vietnam: Chronicle of a War
Village that Refused to Die, The
Vintage Commercials, III
War Comes to America

War Game, The
War in the Sky
War Years—The Forties, The
Wasn't That a Time!
Why We Fight
Wild Rapture
Wild Rides
Wild, Wild World of Jayne Mansfield
Will of a People, The
Wings Over the Andes
World at War, The
World at War, The
World War II: The European Theatre
World War II: The Pacific Theatre
World War II Video Series—Attack: The Battle of
    New Britain
World War II Video Series—Something for Our
    Boys
World War II Video Series—The Stillwell Road
World War II Video Series—Tried by Fire!
Zig Zag Triumph of Stream

Drama

Abduction
Abe Lincoln: Freedom Fighter
Abe Lincoln in Illinois
Abraham Lincoln
Abraham's Sacrifice
Absence of Malice
Accident
Ace Drummond
Acting Out
Adam Had Four Sons
Adomas Nori Buti Zmogumi (Adam Wants to Be
    a Man)
Affair
Agency
Airport
Albino
Alexander Nevsky
Algiers
Alice Adams
Alice Doesn't Live Here Anymore
Alice's Restaurant
All About Eve
All Mine to Give
All Quiet on the Western Front
All Quiet on the Western Front
All the President's Men
All the Right Moves
Alpha Incident, The
Alphabet City
Altered States
Amante, La
Amante Para Dos
Amazing Howard Hughes, The
American Friend
American Gigolo
American Nightmare
Americana
Amin: The Rise and Fall
Amy
And God Created Woman
...And Justice for All
Angel
Angela
Angelo My Love
Angels Die Hard
Angels with Dirty Faces
Anna to the Infinite Power
Annie Oakley
Aphrodite
Apocalypse Now
Arch of Triumph
Assassin of Youth
Assault
At Gunpoint
Atlantic City
Atrocities of the Orient
Autobiography of Miss Jane Pittman, The
Autumn Born
Ay Jalisco No Te Rajes!
Baby, the Rain Must Fall
Babylon Story from "Intolerance," The
Back from Eternity
Bad Boys
Badlands
Baffled
Ballad of a Soldier
Ballad of Gregorio Cortez, The
Bandits of Orogosolo, The
Bang the Drum Slowly
Barabbas
Barefoot Contessa, The
Barefoot in Athens
Barry Lyndon
Battle at Elderbush Gulch, The/The Musketeers
    of Pig Alley
Battle of Neretva
Battling Bunyan/Home Stretch The
Beachcomber, The
Beau Revel
Becket
Bed and Sofa
Bees, The
Behold a Pale Horse
Bell Jar, The
Bells, The
Bells of St. Mary's, The
Below the Belt
Below the Surface
Ben Hur
Berlin Alexanderplatz
Best of Broadway, "The Philadelphia Story,"
    The
Betrayal
Betsy, The
Between Friends
Beyond Reasonable Doubt
Beyond the Limit
Beyond the Valley of the Dolls

Bible, The
Big Bad Mama
Big Bird Cage
Big Chance, The
Big Heat, The
Big Jake
Big Red
Big Trees, The
Bilitis
Bill
Billy Jack
Birdman of Alcatraz, The
Bitch, The
Black Emanuelle
Black Jack
Black Like Me
Black Narcissus
Black Orpheus
Black Stallion Returns, The
Black Sunday
Blake of Scotland Yard
Blind Husbands
Blood and Sand
Blood Feud
Bloodbrothers
Bloody Brood, The
Bloody Mama
Blow-Up
Blue Angels
Blue Collar
Blue Fire Lady
Blue Lagoon, The
Blue Max, The
Bluebeard
Bluebeard
Blume in Love
Bob Le Flambeur
Bobby Deerfield
Bobby Jo and the Outlaw
Body and Soul
Body and Soul
Body Heat
Bolero
Bonnie and Clyde
Bonnie's Kids
Border, The
Borderline
Born Innocent
Born Losers
Boss' Son, The
Boxcar Bertha
Boy with the Green Hair, The
Boys from Brazil, The
Boys in the Band, The
Brainwash
Breaker, Breaker!
Breaker Morant
Breakout
Breathless
Breathless
Brian's Song

Bride and the Beast, The
Bridge on the River Kwai, The
Brimstone and Treacle
Brink of Life
Broken Blossoms
Broken Strings
Bronson's Revenge
Brood, The
Brother Sun, Sister Moon
Brubaker
Brute Man, The
Buddy System, The
Bullitt
Burn!
Bury Me an Angel
Bus Is Coming, The
Butterfly
Butterfly Affair, The
Bye Bye Brazil
Cabo Blanco
Caddie
Caged Women
Caligula
Caligula
Captains Courageous
Carnal Knowledge
Carnival Story
Carny
Carola de Dia, Carola de Noche
Cas du Dr. Laurent, Le
Casablanca
Case of Libel, A
Cat in the Cage
Cat on a Hot Tin Roof
Catherine The Great
Catholics
Chained for Life
Chained Heat
Challenge, The
Champ, The
Champion
Champions, The
Champions
Chanel Solitaire
Change of Habit
Chapayev
Charge of the Light Brigade, The
Chariots of Fire
Charley Varrick
Chase, The
Cheers for Miss Bishop
Child Bride
Children of Sanchez
China Syndrome, The
Chosen, The
Christmas Carol, A
Christmas Tree, The
Cincinnati Kid, The
Circle of Two
Circus World
Citizen Kane

Clarence Darrow
Clash by Night
Class of 1984
Cleopatra
Clodhopper, The
Closely Watched Trains
Cloud Dancer
Clowns, The
Coal Miner's Daughter
Coast Patrol, The
Cocaine Cowboys
Cocaine Fiends
Cockfighter
Cold River
Collector, The
Come Back to the 5 and Dime Jimmy Dean,
    Jimmy Dean
Comeback
Coming Home
Coming Out Alive
Competition, The
Concrete Jungle, The
Confessions of a Blue Movie Star
Confessions of a Young American Housewife
Conformist, The
Contempt
Conversation, The
Coogan's Bluff
Cool Hand Luke
Cool World, The
Count of Monte Cristo, The
Country Girl, The
Country Girl, The
Countryman
Courageous Dr. Christian, The
Cousin, Cousine
Covergirl
Coward, The
Cranes Are Flying, The
Crash of Flight 401, The
Crazy Mama
Cricket on the Hearth, The
Cries and Whispers
Crossfire
Crowded Paradise
Cruising
Cuando Tu No Estas
Cutter's Way
Cyrano de Bergerac
Damaged Lives
Damned, The
Danger Lights
Danger on Wheels
Daniel
Daniel and Nebuchadnezzar
Daniel in the Lion's Den
Dark Victory
Darling
David and Goliath
Day After, The
Day for Night

Day in the Country, A
Day of the Locust
Days of Heaven
Days of Wine and Roses
Days of Wine and Roses, The
Deadly Game, The
Deadly Thief
Death in Venice
Death of a Centerfold
Death Race 2000
Death Valley
Death Watch
Death Wish
Decameron Nights
Deep in the Heart
Deer Hunter, The
Deerslayer, The
Defiance
Defiant Ones, The
Delinquent Daughters
Deliverance
Delta Fox
Deluge, The
Delusion
Desde el Abismo
Despair
Devi
Devil at 4 O'Clock, The
Devils, The
Diary of Anne Frank, The
Dinner at the Ritz
Dirty Gertie From Harlem U.S.A.
Dirty Harry
Dr. Kildare's Strange Case
Dr. Syn
Doctor Zhivago
Dogs of War, The
Dolce Vita, La
Doll's House, A
Doll's House, A
Doll's House, A
Dominique Is Dead
Domino Principle, The
Donner Pass—The Road to Survival
Don't Change My World
Don't Cry, It's Only Thunder
Don't Look Now
Dos Chicas de Revista
Double Life, A
Downhill Racer
Drama—Romance: Trailers on Tape
Dream Street
Dreaming Lips
Duellists, The
Dybbuk, The
Eagle, The
Early Days
Earth
Earthling, The
Earthquake
East End Chant

East of Borneo
East of Eden
East of Eden
East of Elephants Rock
Easy Rider
Eat My Dust
Ecstasy
Eddie and the Cruisers
Eddie Macon's Run
Edie in Ciao! Manhattan
Edward and Mrs. Simpson
8 1/2
Electric Horseman, The
Elephant Man, The
Elizabeth of Ladymead
Elizabeth the Queen
Elmer Gantry
Elusive Corporal, The
Emanuelle Around the World
Emanuelle in America
Emanuelle in Bangkok
Emanuelle on Taboo Island
Emanuelle the Queen
Emilienne
Emily
Emmanuelle
Emmanuelle, the Joys of a Woman
Emperor Jones, The
Enchanted Island
Endangered Species
Endless Love
Enigma
Entertaining Mr. Sloane
Escape from Alcatraz
Esposa y Amante
Europeans, The
Evel Knievel
Every Man for Himself and God Against All
Evil Mind, The
Executive Action
Exodus
Fabulous Dorseys, The
Fail Safe
Fall of the House of Usher, The
Fall of the Roman Empire, The
Fallen Idol
Fame Is the Spur
Family Life
Fangs of Hate
Fanny
Fanny and Alexander
Fanny Hill: Memoirs of a Woman of Pleasure
Fantasy in Blue
Farewell to Arms, A
Farewell to Arms, A /Meet John Doe
Father
Fear
55 Days at Peking
Fighter, The
Final Countdown, The
Final Extra, The

Fiona
Fire Over England
Fire Over England/As You Like It
Firepower
Fires on the Plain
First Blood
First Deadly Sin, The
First Love
F.I.S.T.
Fitzcarraldo
Flaming Star
Flesh and Blood
Flight from Vienna
Flying Blind
Foolish Wives
Foolish Wives
For Ladies Only
For Love of Ivy
For Your Love Only
Forced Landing
Ford Startime
Forever Emmanuelle
Formula, The
Fort Apache, The Bronx
Frances
Frantic
French Lieutenant's Woman, The
French Quarter
French Woman, The
Front, The
Fugitive: The Final Episode, The
Full Hearts and Empty Pockets
Futz
Fyre
Gallipoli
Gambler, The
Gambling with Souls
Gandhi
Garden of the Finzi-Continis, The
Gator Bait
General Line, The
Gentleman Jim
George Schaefer's Showcase Theatre
Gervaise
Getting of Wisdom, The
Gideon's Trumpet
Gift for Heidi, A
Gift, The (Le Cadeau)
Gilda
Girlfriends
Give 'Em Hell, Harry!
Give Us Barabbas!
Glass House, The
Glen or Glenda
Gloria
Godfather 1902-1959—The Complete Epic, The
Godfather, The
Godfather Part II, The
God's Little Acre
Goin' All the Way
Going Places

Golden Boy
Golden Seal, The
Goldengirl
Good Earth, The
Goodbye Columbus
Goodbye Emmanuelle
Goodbye Norma Jean
Goodyear TV Playhouse: "Marty"
Gorgo
Gospel According to St. Matthew, The
Grapes of Wrath, The
Grazuole
Greased Lightning
Great Escape, The
Great Expectations
Great Gabbo, The
Great Gatsby, The
Great Gundown, The
Great Guy
Great Santini, The
Great White Trail, The
Greatest Show on Earth, The
Greatest Story Ever Told, The
Greek Tycoon, The
Green Eyes
Green Promise, The
Green Room, The
Grey Fox, The
Grit of the Girl Telegrapher, The/In the Switch Tower
Gun in the House, A
Guns and Fury
Guyana Tragedy: The Story of Jim Jones
Hallmark Theater (Sometimes She's Sunday)
Hamlet
Hanna K
Hanover Street
Hardcore
Hard Country
Hard Times
Harder They Fall, The
Harrad Experiment, The
Harrad Summer, The
Harry and Son
Harry Tracy
Hawaii
Hazel's People
Heart Like a Wheel
Heartbeat
Heartland
Hearts of Humanity
Heat and Dust
Heatwave
Heidi
Heidi
Hell on Frisco Bay
Hell's House
Henry V
Her Silent Sacrifice
Hideaways, The
High Ballin'

High Command
High Country, The
High Gear
High Ice
High School Confidential
High Sierra
His Kind of Woman
Hit and Run
Hitchhikers, The
Hitler: The Last Ten Days
Hitler's Children
Hollywood Man
Holocaust
Holy Terror, The
Hombres sin Alma
Home Sweet Home
Homework
Honey
Honkytonk Man
Honor Thy Father
Horse Soldiers, The
Hospital, The
Hostage Tower, The
Hot Times
House Across the Bay, The
House on Chelouche Street, The
Hud
Hughie
Human Gorilla, The
Hunchback of Notre Dame, The
Hunchback of Notre Dame, The
Hunter, The
Hurricane
Hussy
Hustling
I Accuse My Parents
I Am a Fugitive from a Chain Gang
I Cover the Waterfront
I Heard the Owl Call My Name
I Never Promised You a Rose Garden
I Remember Mama
I Sent a Letter to My Love
I Will Fight No More Forever
Ice Castles
Iceman
If...
I'm Dancing as Fast as I Can
Impact
In Cold Blood
In Name Only
In the Heat of the Night
Independence Day
Infierno de los Pobres, El
Informer, The
Inherit the Wind
Inheritance, The
Inn of the Sixth Happiness, The
Innocent, The
Inside Moves
Inside the Lines
Intermezzo

International Velvet
Intimate Moments
Invincible Mr. Disraeli, The
Invitation au Voyage
Invitation to a Gunfighter
Iphigenia
Irishman, The
Iron Duke, The
Isabel's Choice
Isla Encantada, La (Enchanted Island)
Island, The
Islands in the Stream
It
It's a Wonderful Life
Ivan the Terrible—Part I
Ivan the Terrible—Part II
Jack the Ripper
Jackson County Jail
Jacob's Challenge
Jailbait
Jamaica Inn
James Dean Story, The
Jeremiah Johnson
Jesse Owens Story, The
Jessi's Girls
Jesus
Jesus of Nazareth
Jezebel
Joan of Arc
Joe Louis Story, The
Johnny Belinda
Johnny Got His Gun
Johnny Tremain and the Sons of Liberty
Joseph and His Brethren
Joseph and His Brothers
Joseph Andrews
Josepha
Jour Se Leve, Le
Joyless Street
Jubilee
Judex
Judgement of Solomon, The
Judgment at Nuremburg
Juggernaut
Julia
Julia
Justin Morgan Had a Horse
Kameradschaft
Key Largo
Kid from Not-So-Big, The
Kidnapping of the President, The
Kill and Kill Again
Kill Castro
Killers, The
Killing of Angel Street, The
King of the Gypsies
King, Queen, Knave
Kipperbang
Kipps
Kitty Foyle
Klute

Knock on Any Door
Kol Nevelu (Before It's Too Late)
Kraft Television Theater
Kramer vs. Kramer
Kriemhilde's Revenge
Lady Chatterley's Lover
Lady Cocoa
Lady for a Night
Lady from Louisiana, The
Lady Ice
Lady in Red
Lady of the House
Lady on the Bus
Lady Refuses, The
Lamp at Midnight
Las Vegas Story, The
Lassiter
Last Flight of Noah's Ark, The
Last Laugh, The
Last of Sheila, The
Last Tango in Paris
Last Wave, The
Laura
Lawrence of Arabia
Lazarus Syndrome, The
LCA Presents Family Entertainment Playhouse
Legend of Sleepy Hollow, The
Legend of Young Robin Hood, The
Leonor
Leopard in the Snow
Let the Balloon Go
Letter of Introduction
Liana
Liar's Moon
Life of Oharu
Limelight
Lion in Winter, The
Lion of the Desert
Lipstick
Listen to Your Heart
Little Annie Roonie
Little Girl...Big Tease
Little House on the Prairie
Little Lord Fauntleroy
Little Men
Little Orphan Annie
Little Princess, The
Little Romance, A
Little Tough Guys
Little Women
Live Television
Lolita
Lone Wolf, The
Loneliness of the Long Distance Runner
Lonely Lady, The
Long Ago Tomorrow
Long Dark Hall, The
Long Day's Journey Into Night
Long Shot
Look Back in Anger
Looking for Mr. Goodbar

Lord Jim
Lords of Discipline, The
Lost Honeymoon
Lost Honor of Katharina Blum, The
Lost World, The
Lottery Bride, The
Love and Anarchy
Love Child
Love in the City
Love Is a Many-Splendored Thing
Love of Jeanne Ney, The
Love of Three Queens, The
Love on the Run
Love Story
Loveless, The
Macao
Macbeth
Macon County Line
Madame Bovary
Madame Rosa
Made for Each Other
Magic
Magician, The
Magnavox Theater (The Three Musketeers)
Magnificent Ambersons, The
Magnificent Matador
Mahogany
Maid in Sweden
Make a Wish
Making Love
Malibu High
Malibu Hot Summer
Malicious
Mama (I Remember Mama)
Man for All Seasons, A
Man from Beyond
Man Inside, The
Man, Woman and Child
Mandingo
Marathon Man
Marianela
Marijuana: Devil's Weed with Roots in Hell
Marty
Marty/A Wind from the South
Mary of Scotland
Masada
Master of the House
Mayerling
McVicar
Medium Cool
Meet Dr. Christian
Meet John Doe
Melanie
Melody
Melody for Three
Member of the Wedding, The
Men, The
Mephisto
Merry Christmas Mr. Lawrence
Mid Channel
Mid Knight Rider

Midnight Cowboy
Midnight Express
Midnight Girl, The
Mildred Pierce
Mill on the Floss
Million Dollar Kid, The
Minor Miracle, A
Miracle of the Bells, The
Miracle on 34th Street
Miracle Worker, The
Miserables, Les
Misfits, The
Miss All-American Beauty
Miss Sadie Thompson
Missiles of October, The
Missing
Mistaken Orders
Mr. Halpern and Mr. Johnson
Mr. Klein
Mr. Smith Goes to Washington
Mistress Pamela
Mommie Dearest
Money to Burn
Monique
Monsignor
Montenegro
Moonlighting
Morning Glory
Moses
Mountain Man
Mozart Story, The
Ms. Don Juan
Muerte del Che Guevara, La
Muerto, El
Murder for Sale
Murder in Texas
Murderer's Wife
Mustang
Mutiny on the Bounty
My Bodyguard
My Brilliant Career
My Champion
My Forbidden Past
Mystery Plane
Nadia
Naked and the Dead, The
Naked Civil Servant, The
Nana
Nashville
Nea
Nest, The
Network
Never Cry Wolf
New Centurions, The
New York, New York
News Front
Nibelungen Saga—Kriemheld's Revenge, Die
Nicholas and Alexandra
Nicholas Nickleby
Night Crossing
Night Games

Night Is My Future, The
Night of the Iguana, The
Night Porter, The
Night the Lights Went Out in Georgia, The
Night Warning
Nighthawks
Nightkill
Nine Ages of Nakedness
Nine Days a Queen
984—Prisoner of the Future
None But The Lonely Heart
Norma Rae
Norseman, The
Notorious
Now and Forever
Now, Voyager
O Lucky Man
Occurrence at Owl Creek Bridge, An
Ode to Billy Joe
Of Human Bondage
Officer and a Gentleman, An
O'Hara's Wife
Old Boyfriends
Old Yeller
Oldest Living Graduate
Oliver Twist
Oliver Twist
Oliver Twist
Olivia
Olvidados, Los
On Golden Pond
On the Beach
Once in Paris
One Flew Over the Cuckoo's Nest
One on One
One Sings, the Other Doesn't
Onion Field, The
Open City
Ordet
Ordinary People
Orphans of the Storm
Oscar, The
Othello
Othello
Our Daily Bread
Our Town
Our Town
Out of the Blue
Outsiders, The
Over the Edge
Padre Padrone
Panama Lady
Panic in Echo Park
Panique
Paper Chase, The
Papillon
Paradise in Harlem
Party Girl
Passion of Love
Pastures of Heaven
Pawnbroker, The

Peacock Fan, The
Pedestrian, The
Peeping Tom
Penitentiary
Penny Serenade
Perdicion de Mujeres
Performance
Persona
Personal Best
Petrified Forest, The
Pets
Phedre
Philco TV Playhouse: "Ernie Barger Is 50"
Pilot, The
Pimpernel Smith
Pixote
Place Called Today, A
Place in the Sun, A
Play Misty for Me
Players
Playwrights '56: "The Battler"
Port of Call
Postman Always Rings Twice, The
Power Dive
Pretty Baby
Pride and Prejudice
Pride and the Passion, The
Pride of the Yankees, The
Prince and the Pauper, The
Prince of the City
Private Life of Henry VIII, The
Private School
Professor Hippie, El
Project: Kill!
Promises in the Dark
Proud Rebel, The
Providence
Prudential Family Playhouse, The
Prudential Family Playhouse, The
Punt, a Pass and a Prayer, A
Purple Taxi, The
Pursuit of D. B. Cooper, The
Q Ships
QB VII
Quackser Fortune Has a Cousin in the Bronx
Quartet
Queen of the Stardust Ballroom
Querelle
Question of Love, A
Rachel and the Stranger
Rage
Raggedy Man
Raging Bull
Ragtime
Rain
Rain People, The
Rainbow
Raise the Titanic
Raisin in the Sun, A
Ramparts of Clay
Ransom

Rape of Love
Rare Breed, A
Rear Window
Rebecca
Rebel
Rebel Rousers
Rebel Without a Cause
Rebelion de las Muertas, La
Reborn
Red Balloon, The/An Occurrence at Owl Creek
    Bridge
Red Kimono, The
Red Nightmare
Red Pony, The
Red Shoes, The
Redneck
Reds
Revenge
Revolt of Job, The
Richard's Things
Right of Way
Right Stuff, The
Rituals
Road to Ruin, The
Roadhouse 66
Roaring Twenties, The
Robe, The
Robin and Marian
Rocky
Rocky II
Rocky III
Rolling Home
Rolling Thunder
Rollover
Romeo and Juliet
Romeo and Juliet
Roof, The
Roots
Roseland
Ruby Gentry
Rumble Fish
Running Brave
Running Scared
Sacco and Vanzetti
Sacred Ground
Sailor Who Fell from Grace with the Sea, The
St. Helen's, Killer Volcano
Saint Jack
Same Time, Next Year
Samson and Delilah
Sand Pebbles, The
Sanjuro
Saturday Night Fever
Saturday Night Fever
Savage Attraction
Savage Is Loose, The
Savages
Savannah Smiles
Save the Tiger
Sayonara
Scarecrow

Scarface
Scarlet Letter, The
Scarlet Pimpernel, The
Scenes from a Marriage
Schizo
Scrubbers
Sea Lion, The
Search and Destroy
Second Chance
Second Coming of Suzanne, The
Secret Fantasy
Secret of Yolanda, The
Secrets of a Soul
Seducers, The
Seduction, The
Seduction of Joe Tynan, The
Sensuous Teenager, The
Separacion Matrimonial
Separate Peace, A
Separate Tables
Separate Ways
Sergeant York
Serpico
Servant, The
Set Up, The
Seven Days in May
Sex and the Office Girl
Sex Machine, The
Shadows
Shame
Shame
Shark!
Shattered
Shenandoah
Shock, The
Shogun
Shoot the Moon
Shoot the Piano Player
Sidewalks of London
Siegfried
Silence of the North
Silent Partner, The
Silkwood
Silver Streak
Simon of the Desert
Simple Story, A
Sin of Adam and Eve, The
Sinbad the Sailor
Sinister Urge, The
Sister Kenny
Slavers
Slaves of Love
Sleeping Dogs
Small Town in Texas, A
Smash Palace
Smash-Up
Smouldering Fires
Sodom and Gomorrah
Soldier, The
Soldier in Love
Something to Sing About/Great Guy

Sometimes a Great Notion
Song of Freedom
Sons of Katie Elder, The
Sophia Loren: Her Own Story
Sophie's Choice
Sorceress
S.O.S. Titanic
Soul Patrol
Sounder
South Pacific
Southern Comfort
Southerner, The
Special Day, A
Specialist, The
Spellbound
Spetters
Spitfire
Splendor in the Grass
Split Image
Spoilers, The
Spy of Napoleon
Stacey!
Stacy's Knights
Stagestruck
Stairway to Heaven
Star Chamber, The
Star 80
Star Is Born, A
Stars Look Down, The
State of Siege
Stay as You Are
Staying Alive
Steel
Steinbeck's The Pearl
Stolen Kisses
Stone Killer, The
Storm Over Asia
Story of Adele H., The
Story of Esther, The
Story of O, The
Strada, La
Straight Time
Strait Jacket
Strange Love of Martha Ivers, The
Stranger's Kiss
Strangers on a Train
Straw Dogs
Street Scene
Streetcar Named Desire, A
Strike
Stud, The
Studio One: "The Defender"
Stunt Man, The
Subterfuge
Suddenly Last Summer
Sugar Cookies
Sugarland Express, The
Summer Heat
Summer in St. Tropez, A
Summer Lovers
Summer of '42

Summer Solstice
Sundays and Cybele
Sunset Boulevard
Superfly
Suzanne
Svengali
Swap, The
Sweet Creek County War
Sweet Sweetback's Baadasssss Song
Swept Away
Swinging Ski Girls
Swinging Sorority Girls
Swiss Family Robinson, The
Sybil
Table for Five
Tale of Two Cities, A
Taming of the Shrew, The
Tank
Taps
Targets
Tattoo
Taxi Driver
Teen Mothers
Tempest
Tempest
Tempest, The
Ten Commandments, The
Ten Days that Shook the World
Tender Mercies
10th Victim, The
Terms of Endearment
Terry Fox Story, The
Tess
Testament
Tex
That Championship Season
That Cold Day in the Park
They Came to Cordura
They Drive by Night
They Made Me a Criminal
Third Man, The/The Stranger
This Sporting Life
Thomas Crown Affair, The
Three Days of the Condor
Three Husbands
Three Warriors
Three Weird Sisters, The
Threshold
Throne of Blood
Through the Breakers
Thunderbolt and Lightfoot
THX 1138
Ticket to Heaven
Tiger Town
Till the Clouds Roll By/A Star Is Born
Tim
Tin Drum, The
Tin Man
To Forget Venice
To Kill a Clown
To Kill a Mockingbird

Toast of New York, The
Todos los Dias, Un Dia
Tol'able David
Tom Brown's School Days
Tomorrow
Tomorrow's Children
Tong Man
Tonio Kroger
Too Hot to Handle
Too Late the Hero
Topkapi
Torch, The
Torture of Silence, The
Touched
Tough Enough
Tower of Babel
Towering Inferno, The
Tragedy of King Richard II, The
Trained to Kill, U.S.A.
Trapeze
Trapped by the Mormons
Treasure of the Sierra Madre, The
Trial, The
Trial of the Catonsville Nine, The
Tribute
Trilby
Trilby/Svengali
Trojan Women, The
Truckers Woman
True Confessions
Truite, La (The Trout)
Truman Capote's "The Glass House"
Tunnel, The
Turning Point, The
Twelve Angry Men
Two Kennedys, The
Tycoon
Uncommon Valor
Under Fire
Unicorn, The
Union City
Unknown Powers
Unmarried Woman, An
Until They Get Me
Urban Cowboy
Users, The
Vamping
Vanessa
Vanishing Point
Vanity Fair
Variety
Verdict, The
Very Private Affair, A
Vice Squad
Victoria Regina
Victory
Vida Sigue Igual, La
Vida Sigue Igual, La
Vie Continue, La
Vigilante
Violent Years, The

Viridiana
Virtue's Revolt
Virus
Volcano
Voyage of the Damned
Wages of Fear
Waltz Across Texas
Wanderers, The
War and Peace
War Games
Warriors of the Wasteland
Warriors, The
Washington Affair, The
Watch Me When I Kill
Wavelength
Way Down East
Way We Were, The
We of the Never Never
Welcome to L.A.
Westinghouse Studio One (Summer Theatre)
Whatever Happened to Aunt Alice?
Wheel of Fortune
Whistle Stop
White Dawn, The
White Heat
White Mane
White Tower, The
Who Has Seen the Wind?
Who'll Stop the Rain?
Who's Afraid of Virginia Woolf?
Whose Life Is It Anyway?
Why Shoot the Teacher
Wifemistress
Wild in the Country
Wild Party, The
Wild Ride, The
Wild Strawberries
Windwalker
Winning
Winslow Boy, The
Winter Kills
Winter Light
Winter of Our Dreams
Winterset
Without a Trace
Witness for the Prosecution
Wives Under Suspicion
Wolf Lake
Woman Called Golda, A
Woman in the Dunes
Woman Rebels, A
Women in Cell Block 7
Women in Love
World Gone Mad, The
World of Apu, The
Yanco
Yol
You Light Up My Life
You Only Live Once
Young and Free
Young Aphrodities

Young Philadelphians, The
Your Ticket Is No Longer Valid
Zabriskie Point
Zorba, the Greek

Drawing

Jon Gnagy Learn to Draw I & II
Journey into Art, A

Drug abuse

American Alcoholic, The/Reading, Writing and
   Reefer
Teenage Drug and Alcohol Abuse

Drugs

Miracle at City Hall

Ecology and environment

Acid Rain: The Choice Is Ours
Farmer and the Sportsman, The
God's Wonders

Economics

Pieces of Eight

Education

Mister Rogers Goes to School
New Speed Reading
Speed Learning
Video S.A.T. Review, The

Electricity

Basic Home Electric Repairs

Electronic data processing

Career Possibilities: Computer Programming
Computability
Introduction to Computers
Introduction to Computers for Children
Programming Your Personal Computer
Word Processor, The

Emergencies

Emergency First Aid

Energy

Alternative Energy Sources

Eskimos

Nanook of the North

Ethics

Adventures in Life
Human Values
Mr. Rogers—Helping Children Understand
Morals by Monsters
Question 7

Etiquette

Etiquette/Entertaining

Europe

Great Cities: London, Rome, Dublin, Athens

Exploitation

Assassin of Youth
Chained for Life
Child Bride
Cocaine Fiends
Damaged Lives
Gambling with Souls
Glen or Glenda
I Accuse My Parents
Lash of the Penitentes
Marijuana: Devil's Weed with Roots in Hell
Marijuana—The Devils' Weed
Mondo Cane
Mondo Cane 2
Red Kimono, The
Reefer Madness
Road to Ruin, The
Sex Madness
Slave Trade in the World Today
Tomorrow's Children
Trapped by the Mormons

Explorers

Admiral Byrd: To the Ends of the Earth

Fairy tales

Aesop and His Friends
Boy Who Left Home to Find Out About the
   Shivers, The
Cinderella
Cuckoo Clock That Wouldn't Cuckoo, The
Daydreamer, The
Emperor's New Clothes, The
Faerie Tale Theatre
Fairy Tale Classics
Fairy Tale Classics: Volume II
Fairy Tales, Volume Two
Frog Prince, The
Geppetto's Music Shop
Goldilocks and the Three Bears
Hansel and Gretel
Hansel and Gretel
Hey Cinderella!

Jack and the Beanstalk
Jack and the Beanstalk
Jack and the Beanstalk
Last Unicorn, The
Little Match Girl, The
Little Mermaid, The
Little Mermaid, The
Little Red Riding Hood
Memoirs of a Fairy Godmother
Mr. Magoo's Storybook
Muppet Musicians of Bremen, The
Nutcracker Fantasy
Pied Piper, The/Cinderella
Pied Piper of Hamelin, The
Pied Piper of Hamelin, The
Pinocchio
Pinocchio
Puss in Boots
Puss 'N' Boots
Rapunzel
Ringing Bell
Rumpelstiltskin
Rumpelstiltskin
Sleeping Beauty
Snow Queen, The
Stories and Fables—Volume 1
Stories and Fables—Volume 2
Stories and Fables—Volume 3
Stories and Fables, Volume 4
Stories and Fables, Volume 5
Stories and Fables, Volume 6
Tale of the Frog Prince, The
Tales from Muppetland II
Three Little Pigs, The
Thumbelina
Tom Thumb
Unicorn Tales I
Unicorn Tales II
Very Special Christmas, A/Sleeping Beauty

Family

Any Family
Joy of Family
You and Me, Kid Volume I

Fantasy

Alice in Wonderland
Alice in Wonderland
Alice's Adventures in Wonderland
Angel on My Shoulder
Angel on My Shoulder
Ator the Fighting Eagle
Barbarella
Beauty and the Beast
Benji's Very Own Christmas Story
Best of Marvel Comics, The
Bill and Coo
Blue Box, The
Care Bears Battle the Freeze Machine, The
Chitty Chitty Bang Bang
Comic Book Kids, The
Curse of the Cat People
Daddy Long Legs
Darby O'Gill and the Little People
Dark Crystal, The
Daydreamer, The
Devil and Daniel Mouse, The
Devil and Max Devlin, The
Dorothy in the Land of Oz
Dot and Santa Claus
Dot and the Kangaroo
Dragonslayer
Dunderklumpen
Escape to Witch Mountain
Excalibur
Fantastic Animation Festival
Final Programme, The
Fire and Ice
Flight of Dragons
Fraggle Songs, Volume One
Freaky Friday
Galaxy Express
Golden Voyage of Sinbad, The
Green Box, The
Grendel, Grendel, Grendel
Gulliver's Travels
Gumby Summer, A
Gumby's Incredible Journey
Heaven Can Wait
Here Comes Mr. Jordan
Hobbit, The
Hoppity Goes to Town
Island of Nevawuz, The
Jason and the Argonauts
Jonathan Livingston Seagull
Journey Back to Oz
Journey Back to Oz
Kiss Me Goodbye
Lisztomania
Little Mermaid, The
Lord of the Rings
Magic Horse, The
Magic Pony, The
March of the Wooden Soldiers
Marco Polo, Jr.
Marvelous Land of Oz, The
Mouse and His Child, The
Mysterious Island
New Misadventures of Ichabod Crane, The
Nine Lives of Fritz the Cat, The
Once Upon a Brothers Grimm
Once Upon a Time
One from the Heart
1001 Arabian Nights
Orange Box, The
Panda and the Magic Serpent
Patchwork Girl of Oz, The
Peter-No-Tail
Pinocchio
Pinocchio in Outer Space

Purple Box, The
Raccoons on Ice
Red Balloon, The
Red Balloon, The/An Occurrence at Owl Creek
    Bridge
Red Box, The
Road to Yesterday, The
Romie-O and Julie-8
Scrooge
Secret of NIMH, The
7th Voyage of Sinbad, The
Sinbad and the Eye of the Tiger
Some Call It Loving
Something Wicked This Way Comes
Somewhere in Time
Splash
Stories and Fables, Volume 4
Sword and the Dragon
Sword and the Sorcerer, The
Thief of Baghdad, The
Three Tales of Love & Friendship
Time Bandits
Tom Thumb
Trip, The
Tubby the Tuba
Two Worlds of Jennie Logan, The
Watership Down
Welcome to Pooh Corner, Volume I
Wiz, The
Wizard of Oz, The
Wizard of Oz, The
Xanadu
Yellow Box, The
Yor, the Hunter from the Future

Film

Best of the New York Erotic Film Festival Parts I
    & II

Film-Avant-garde

All Screwed Up
Atalante, L'
Avant Garde and Experimental Film Program No.
    1
Avant-Garde #2
Berlin—Symphony of a Great City
Bete Humaine, La
Blood of a Poet
Blue Angel, The
Cabinet of Dr. Caligari
Chien Andalou, Un/The Dove
Chien Andalou, Un
Destiny
Electric Light Voyage
Eraserhead
Experimental Avant-Garde Video Special
Experimental Program #1
Experimental Program #2
Forbidden Zone

Grand Illusion
Hiroshima, Mon Amour
Knife in the Water
Koyaanisqatsi
M
Man With a Movie Camera, The
Orpheus
Paisan
Passion of Joan of Arc
Rashomon
Repulsion
Rules of the Game
Secrets of a Soul
Seduction of Mimi, The
Tonight for Sure
Two Men and a Wardrobe
Ugetsu
Umberto D
Vampyr
Yojimbo

Film-History

America at the Movies
America/The Fall of Babylon
Arsenal
Avenging Conscience, The
Battle at Elderbush Gulch, The/The Musketeers
    of Pig Alley
Battle of Elderbush Gulch, The
Birth of a Nation, The
Birth of a Nation
Birth of a Nation, The
Blood and Sand/Son of the Sheik
Broken Blossoms
Camp Classics #1
Chapayev
Chaplin: A Character Is Born/Keaton: The Great
    Stone Face
Civilization
Color in the Movies
Count of Monte Cristo, The
Custer's Last Fight
D'Artagnan
Dr. Mabuse: The Fatal Passion
Dracula/The Garden of Eden
D.W. Griffith: An American Genius
D.W. Griffith: The Completion of the
    Apprenticeship
D.W. Griffith: The Invention of Film Grammer
Early Films #1
Earth
Eisenstein
Enchanted Studio, The/More from the
    Enchanted Studio
End of St. Petersburg, The
Father Sergius
Faust
Favorite Black Exploitation Cartoons
Favorite Racists Cartoons
Film Firsts

From Broadway to Hollywood
General Line, The
General, The/Slapstick
George Melies, Cinema Magician
Golem, The
Good Old Days
Haunted Castle, The (Schloss Vogelod)
Hey Abbott!
Hollywood at War
Hollywood Goes to War
Hollywood My Hometown
Hollywood Outtakes and Rare Footage
Hollywood Without Makeup
Hoodoo Ann
Intolerance
James Dean: The First American Teenager
Judith of Bethulia
Kameradschaft
Keaton Special/Valentino Mystique
Kriemhilde's Revenge
Legendary Personalities
Light of Faith
Lumiere Program
Memory Lane Movies by Robert Youngson #1
Memory Lane Movies by Robert Youngson #2
Memory Lane Movies by Robert Youngson #3
Memory Lane Movies by Robert Youngson #4
Memory Lane Movies by Robert Youngson #5
Memory Lane Movies by Robert Youngson #6
Metropolis
Mother
Movie Museum I
Movie Museum II
Moving Picture Boys in the Great War, The
Pioneer Cinema (1895-1905)
Potemkin
Premiere of "A Star Is Born"
Road to Yesterday/The Yankee Clipper
Short Films of D. W. Griffith, Vol. I, The
Silent Movies—In Color
Story of the Silent Serials, The/Girls in Danger
Teddy at the Throttle
Tempest, The/The Eagle
Ten Nights in a Bar Room
35mm Motion Picture Projector, The
True Heart Susie
Voice from the Screen, The
Warning Shadows
Way Down East

Filmmaking

Eye Hears, the Ear Sees, The
Great Movie Stunts and The Making of Raiders
    of the Lost Ark
Hollywood Boulevard
Making of Star Wars, The/S.P.F.X. — The
    Empire Strikes Back
Making of Superman, The
Making of Superman—The Movie and
    Superman II, The
Making of Superman II, The
Motion Picture Camera, The
New Look
Werner Herzog Eats His Shoe
Werner Herzog in Peru

Finance

Joy of Stocks: The Forbes Guide to the Stock
    Market, The
Your Financial Survival

First aid

CPR for Infants and Children
Emergency First Aid
First Aid
First Aid: The Video Kit
First Aid Video Book, The

Fishes

National Geographic: Great Whales/Sharks
Predators of the Sea
Sharks
Tropical Fish, Fireside Moments and Beautiful
    Birds

Fishing

Anybody Can Catch Fish
Bass Fishing: Top to Bottom
Bass in Heavy Cover
Bigmouth
Cousin Smallmouth Bass
Feeding Habits of Bass
Fishing/Hunting/Snowmobiling
Fishing in the Land of the Sky Blue Waters
Fishing the Dry Fly
Fishing the Last Frontier
Fishing U.S.A.
Fly Fishing for Trout
Fly Fishing Secrets I: The Dry Fly
Fly Fishing Secrets II: The Wet Fly and Nymph
Hal Janssen's Fly Fishing Secrets -- The Dry Fly
Hal Janssen's Fly Fishing Secrets -- The Wet Fly
Holiday in Mazatland
Nymphing with Gary Borger
Old Rock, Champ of the Chesapeake
School of Bass, A
Smallmouth Bass
Surface Lures and Buzz Baits
Texas Hex
To Catch A Thrill
Tying Trout Flies

Folklore

Chinese Gods
Chulas Fronteras
Del Mero Corazon
Disney's American Heroes

Dry Wood
Garlic Is as Good as Ten Mothers
Hot Pepper
Matt the Gooseboy
Polka Film, The
Slaughterhouse Five
Spend It All
Sprout Wings and Fly
Stoney Knows How
Sword and the Dragon
Winds of Change

Football

America's Team: The Dallas Cowboys 1975-79
Back Among the Best/NFL '83
Beat Goes On, The
Better Team, A
Big Game America
Black Sunday: Highlights of Super Bowl XVII
Champions of the AFC East
Cinderella Seahawks/NFL '83, The
Cliffhangers, Comebacks, and Character
Color Them Tough
Come Back Champions/NFL '83
Coming of Age: The Story of the Dallas Cowboys
    1970-74
Commitment to Excellence/NFL '82
Cut Above, A
Cut Above/NFL '83, A
Day of Frustration—Season of Triumph
Day of the Dolphins/NFL '82
Defenders, The
Detour
Festival of Funnies, A
Football Follies
Football Follies/Highlights of Super Bowl V
From Worst to First
Giant Step, A
Go Bears! A Look to the 80's
Great Expectations/The Man with the Funny Hat
Great Teams/Great Years Volume One
History of Pro Football, The
How to Watch Pro Football
Joe Gibbs' Washington Redskins: Two Years to
    the Title
Just Win, Baby/NFL 83
Kardiac Kids...Again
Knute Rockne: The Rock of Notre Dame
Like a Mighty River...
Lombardi
Luv-Ya Blue!
Most Memorable Games of the Decade #1
Most Memorable Games of the Decade #2
Most Memorable Games of the Decade #3
NFL '81
NFL '81 Official Season Yearbook
NFL Follies Go Hollywood
NFL SymFunny/Highlights of Super Bowl III
NFL's Best Ever Coaches
NFL's Best Ever: The Professionals

NFL's Best Ever Quarterbacks
NFL's Best Ever Runners
NFL's Best Ever Teams
NFL's Inspirational Men and Moments, The
Old Leather
Our Finest Hour
Pittsburgh Steelers: The Championship Years
Power, The
Pride of Eagles Football
Return of the Rams/NFL '83
Right Stuff/NFL '83, The
Road Warriors, The/NFL '82
Saviors, Saints, and Sinners
Sensational Sixties
Son of Football Follies, The
Son of Football Follies/Highlights of Super Bowl
    XIV
Star-Spangled Cowboys
Steel Town Tough/Steelers 50 Seasons
Stripes
Super Bowl I
Super Bowl II
Super Bowl III
Super Bowl Chronicles
Super Bowl IV
Super Bowl V
Super Bowl VI
Super Bowl VII
Super Bowl VIII
Super Bowl IX
Super Bowl X
Super Bowl XI
Super Bowl XII
Super Bowl XIII
Super Bowl XIV
Super Bowl XV
Super Bowl XVI
Super Bowl XVII
Super Memories of the Super Bowls
Super Seventies, The
Talk of the Town
Team of the 80's/NFL '82
Team on a Tightrope
Team That Battled Back, The
Team Together/NFL '83, A
Three Cheers for the Redskins
Tradition on Parade/Blood, Sweat and Cheers
Very Special Team, A
Wake Up the Echoes
Young, the Old, and the Bold, Try and Catch the
    Wind, The

France

Invitation to Paris

Gambling

Blackjack
Casino Gambling
Craps

Introduction to Casino Gaming
Money Management System: The Midas Touch
Roulette

Game show

Bank on the Stars
Big Surprise, The
Dr. I. Q.
Game Show Program
Game Show Program II
Game Show Program III
Quiz Kids
Rich Little's Great Hollywood Trivia Game
$64,000 Question
Take a Good Look with Ernie Kovacs
TV's Classic Guessing Games
Twenty Questions
You Bet Your Life

Games

Basic Card Magic
Bridge Lessons from Shelly de Satnick
Fun and Games
How to Avoid Being Cheated at Cards
How to Beat Home Video Games Volume I
How to Beat Home Video Games Volume II
How to Beat Home Video Games Volume III
How to Win in Blackjack
Maze Mania
MysteryDisc #1: Murder, Anyone?
MysteryDisc #2: Many Roads to Murder
Now You See It
Party Games—For Adults Only
Treasure
Videotrivia, Volume I

Gardening

Gardening at Home
Gardening in the City: I
Gardening in the City: II
Growing Indoor Plants
Professional Planting (Horticulture)
Professional Techniques (Horticulture)

Germany

Berlin—Symphony of a Great City
Germany Celebrates Hitler's Birthday
Hitler—February 10th, 1933
Hitler's Newsreels, Part 2
Hitler's Newsreels, Part 3
March with the Fuhrer (Marsch Zum Fuhrer)
Mussolini Visits Hitler
Nazi Strike

Golf

Basic Golf 1
Basic Golf 2

Bobby Jones: Old Man Par
Golf
Golf Lessons from Sam Snead
Golf My Way
Golf My Way with Jack Nicklaus
How to Play Your Best Golf, Volume 1
How to Play Your Best Golf, Volume 2
Jack Nicklaus Sports Clinic
Medium and Long Iron Game, The
Name of the Game Is Golf
Patty Berg: Fairway to Fame
Putting for the Beginner and the Pro
Sand Lessons and Special Shots
Short Iron Lessons
SyberVision Golf with Al Geiberger
Woods and Tee Shots

Great Britain

Battle for the Falklands
King Edward VIII: For Love of a Woman
Royal Wedding, The
Sense of Loss, A

Gymnastics

U. S. Men's Gymnastics Championship
U.S. Women's Gymnastics Championship

Handicapped

Crossbar
Helen Keller: Separate Views

Handicraft

Basic Crocheting—Needlepoint
Basic Pottery
Ceramics and Pottery
Crocheting with Dee
Dried Flower Arranging and Silk Flower Making
Knitting with Dee I
Knitting with Dee II
Making Stained Glass
Needlepoint with Dee

Health education

Rehabilitation and Injury
Rescue Squad
Subliminal Persuasion Video

History

Shame

History-Modern

Best of 60 Minutes, The
Dionne Quintuplets
History Disquiz, The
Men of Destiny Volume I: World Political Figures

History-Modern

Men of Destiny Volume II: Artists and Innovators
Milestones of the Century Volume I: The Great Wars
Milestones of the Century Volume II: 20th Century—Turning Points
Nuremberg Trials, The
Rise and Fall of the Third Reich

History-US

Admiral Nimitz: Freedom's Admiral
America Between the Great Wars
American History: America Grows Up (1850-1900's)
American History: Americans Courageous (1600-Today)
American History: Colonial America (1500's-1600's)
American History: Gathering Strength (1840-1914)
American History: Opening the West (1860-1900)
American History: Roots of Democracy (1700's)
American History: The Game of Monopoly (1870-1914)
American History: Two Great Crusades (1930-1945)
American History: War Between the States (1800's)
American History: Warring and Roaring (1914-1929)
Bernard Baruch: The Trouble Shooter
Brother, Can You Spare a Dime?
Cordell Hull: The Good Neighbor
Eddie Rickenbacker: Ace of Aces
Fabulous Fifties, The
Freedom's Finest Hour
General Doolittle: Wild Blue Yonder
General Douglas MacArthur: I Shall Return
General Marshall: Soldier of Peace
General Pershing: The Iron Commander
Grover Whalen: Mr. New York
Historical Yesterdays
Kurt Carlsen: Man Against the Sea
New Deal—The Thirties, The
Plow That Broke the Plains, The/The River
Roaring Twenties, The
Uncle Sam Magoo
Will Rogers: The Cowboy Humorist

Holidays

Children's Easter Collection
Easter Bunny Is Coming to Town, The
Easter Collection, The
Family Circus Easter, A
Gumby's Holiday Special
New Misadventures of Ichabod Crane, The
Special Valentine with Family Circus, A

Home improvement

Basic Home Electric Repairs
Basic Home Painting
Basic Home Wallpapering
Furniture Refinishing
Simple Plumbing Repair

Horror

Abbott and Costello Meet Dr. Jekyll and Mr. Hyde
Abominable Dr. Phibes, The
Alien Contamination
Alison's Birthday
Alone in the Dark
Alone in the Dark
American Werewolf in London, An
Amityville Horror, The
Amityville 3D
Amityville II: The Possession
And Now the Screaming Starts
Andy Warhol's Dracula
Andy Warhol's Frankenstein
Ape Man, The
Assault on Precinct 13
Astro Zombies, The
Asylum
Atom Age Vampire
Audrey Rose
Autopsy
Awakening, The
Basket Case
Beast in the Cellar, The
Beast Must Die, The
Beast Within, The
Bedlam
Being, The
Bela Lugosi Meets a Brooklyn Gorilla
Beyond Evil
Beyond the Door
Beyond the Door II
Billy the Kid Versus Dracula
Birds, The
Black Cat, The/The Raven
Blackenstein
Blind Man's Bluff
Blood Beach
Blood Legacy
Blood of Dracula's Castle
Blood on Satan's Claw
Blood Spattered Bride, The
Bloodsucking Freaks
Blue Sunshine
Boardinghouse
Body Snatcher, The
Boogey Man, The
Boogeyman II
Brain That Wouldn't Die, The
Braniac, The
Bride of the Monster

Brood, The
Bug
Burning, The
Captain Kronos: Vampire Hunter
Carrie
Cat People
Cat People
Chamber of Horrors
Changeling, The
Children of the Corn
Children Shouldn't Play with Dead Things
Color Me Blood Red
Crater Lake Monster, The
Crawling Eye, The
Crawling Hand, The
Creeping Flesh, The
Creeping Terror
Creepshow
Crocodile
Crucible of Terror
Cujo
Curse of the Crying Woman, The
Curse of the Mummy, The/The Robot vs. the
   Aztec Mummy
Curtains
Daddy's Deadly Darling
Dagora, the Space Monster
Damien—Omen II
Dark, The
Dark Places
Daughter of Horror
Dawn of the Dead
Dawn of the Mummy
Day of the Animals
Day of Wrath
Dead and Buried
Deadline
Deadly Blessing
Deadly Eyes
Deadly Games
Deathdream
Deep Red: Hatchet Murders
Delirium
Demented
Dementia 13
Demon, The
Demon, The
Demon Lover, The
Demon Rage
Demon Seed
Demonoid
Devil Bat, The
Devil Doll
Devil Times Five
Devil's Daughter, The
Devil's Rain
Devonsville Terror, The
Dr. Black, Mr. Hyde
Doctor Butcher M.D.
Dr. Jekyll and Mr. Hyde
Doctor of Doom

Doin What the Crowd Does
Don't Answer the Phone
Don't Go in the House
Don't Go in the Woods
Don't Look in the Basement
Dorian Gray
Dorm That Dripped Blood, The
Dracula
Dracula
Dracula and Son
Dracula's Dog
Dracula's Last Rites
Dunwich Horror, The
Eaten Alive
Echoes
Entity, The
Equinox
Evictors, The
Evil Dead, The
Evilspeak
Exorcist II: The Heretic
Eyes of a Stranger
Fade to Black
Fall of the House of Usher, The
Fear in the Night
Fear No Evil
Final Conflict, The
Final Exam
Fog, The
Forbidden World
Frankenstein
Frankenstein '80
Freakmaker, The
Friday the 13th
Friday the 13th, Part 2
Friday the 13th, Part 3
Frightmare
Frogs
Funeral Home
Funhouse, The
Fury, The
Galaxy of Terror
Gates of Hell, The
Ghost Dance
Godsend, The
Godzilla
Godzilla vs. Monster Zero
Godzilla vs. Mothra
Graduation Day
Great Alligator, The
Grizzly
Halloween
Halloween II
Halloween III: The Season of the Witch
Hallucination
Hand, The
Happy Birthday to Me
Haunted, The
Haunted Strangler, The
Haunting of Julia, The
He Knows You're Alone

Hearse, The
Hell Night
Hideous Sun Demon
Hillbillys in a Haunted House
Horrible Double Feature
Horror Express
Horror Hospital
Horror Hotel
Horror of Frankenstein
Horror Planet
Hospital Massacre
House of Exorcism, The
House of Seven Corpses, The
House of Shadows
House on Sorority Row, The
House That Vanished, The
Howling, The
Human Experiments
Human Monster, The
Humanoids from the Deep
Humongous
Hunger, The
I Married a Monster from Outer Space
I Spit on Your Grave
I Walked with a Zombie
Incubus, The
Invasion of the Body Snatchers
Invisible Ghost, The
Invisible Ghost, The/The Human Monster
Just Before Dawn
Keep, The
Keep My Grave Open
Keeper, The
Kill and Go Hide
Killer Bats (Devil Bat)
Killer Bats/White Zombie
King Kong
King Kong
King of Kong Island
King of the Zombies
Kingdom of the Spiders
Kiss of the Tarantula
Kiss of the Tarantula
Kwaidan
Land of the Minotaur
Last Horror Film, The
Last House on Dead End Street
Legend of the Wolfwoman
Leopard Man, The
Little Shop of Horrors
Living Dead, The
Looking Glass War, The
Love Butcher, The
Lust for a Vampire
Macabre Moments from The Phantom of the
  Opera
Mad Monster
Madhouse
Madman
Maniac
Maniac, The

Mardi Gras Massacre
Martin
Mausoleum
Mighty Joe Young
Mongrel
Monster from Green Hell
Monster Maker, The
Monster Walks, The
Moon of the Wolf
Mothra
Murder By Phone
My Bloody Valentine
My Sister, My Love
Name for Evil, A
Night Beast
Night of Bloody Horror
Night of the Ghouls
Night of the Living Dead
Night of the Strangler
Night of the Zombies
Nightmare Castle
Nightmare in Wax
Nightmares
Nosferatu
Of Unknown Origin
Omen, The
One Dark Night
Parasite
Peeping Tom
People Who Own the Dark, The
Phantasm
Phantom of the Opera
Pieces
Piranha
Pit, The
Pit and the Pendulum, The
Plan 9 from Outer Space
Poltergeist
Power, The
Premonition, The
Prey, The
Prom Night
Prophecy
Psycho from Texas
Psychomania
Q—The Winged Serpent
Rabid
Raven, The
Redeemer, The
Rodan
Rosemary's Baby
Ruby
Saga de los Draculas, La
Salem's Lot: The Movie
Samson vs. the Vampire Women
Savage Abduction
Savage Weekend
Scanners
Scars of Dracula
Schizoid
Schlock

Screams of a Winter Night
Seeds of Evil
Sender, The
Severed Arm, The
Shadow of Chinatown
She Beast
Shining, The
Shock
Shout, The
Silent Night Bloody Night
Silent Scream
Sisters
Sisters of Satan
Slime People
Son of Blob
Son of Kong
Spasms
Squirm
Stage Fright
Stanley
Strangeness, The
Stranger Is Watching, A
Summer of Fear
Swarm, The
Sweet 16
Tales of Terror
Teenage Zombies
Tell-Tale Heart, The
Tenant, The
Tentacles
Terror
Terror, The
Terror on Tour
Texas Chainsaw Massacre, The
Theatre of Death
They Saved Hitler's Brain
Thing, The
Thirsty Dead
To All a Goodnight
Torso
Touch of Satan, A
Tower of Evil
Twilight Zone—The Movie
Uncanny, The
Unseen, The
Up from the Depths
Vampire Bat, The
Varan the Unbelievable
Vault of Horror, The
Venom
Videodrome
Warlock Moon
Waxworks
Werewolf of Washington
What the Peeper Saw
White Zombie, The
Witch Who Came from the Sea, The
Witchcraft Through the Ages
Witching, The
Witch's Mirror, The
Wolfen

Wolfman
World of the Vampires, The
Wrestling Women vs. the Aztec Mummy, The
X-Tro
Zoltan... Hound of Dracula
Zombie

Horse racing

Australia: Pace and A Race of Horses
Backstretch, The
Ballad of the Irish Horse, The
Ben Jones: Monarch of the Turf
Exercises for Travel
Invitation to the Japan Cup
Keeneland
King of Sports
Locomotion of the Horse
Peruvian Paso: For Those with Champagne
　　Taste
Running Start, A
Sports Hour #18
Thoroughbred Heroes

Human relations

Ballad of Billie Blue, The

Hunting

Duck and Goose Hunting
Duck Hunting Time
Farmer and the Sportsman, The
Training Your Retriever—Advanced
Training Your Retriever—Basic

Identity

Circle of Life I
Circle of Life II
Free to Be... You and Me
Inner Circle I
Inner Circle II
Inner Circle II
Late Liz, The
Letter to Nancy, A
Scholastic Productions: As We Grow

Indians-North American

Silent Enemy, The
Tree of Life, The

Infants

Baby Care
Caring for Your Newborn with Dr. Benjamin
　　Spock
Pregnancy and the Newborn Child
Swim Baby Swim

Insects

Hellstrom Chronicle, The
Mysterious Miniature World

Interview

John Lennon: Interview with a Legend
Problems, 1950's Style
Telescope—Interview with Harry Richman
This Is Your Life: Laurel and Hardy

Inventions

Gizmo!
Igor Sikorsky: Explorer of the Sky
Thomas Edison: Let There Be Light

Islam

Holy Koran, The

Judaism

Kitty: A Return to Auschwitz

Korean War

Carrier Action off Korea
Motion Picture History of the Korean War, The
Tom Edison: The Making of an American Legend
With the Marines—Chosin Hungnam

Language arts

Language in Life

Languages-Instruction

Basic English Grammar by Video
Basic French by Video
Basic Italian by Video
Basic Spanish by Video

Literature

Blue Box, The
Family Entertainment Playhouse, Vol. 2
Gielgud's Chekhov 1
Gielgud's Chekhov 2
Gielgud's Chekhov 3
Green Box, The
Little Engine That Could, The
Little Women
Occurrence at Owl Creek Bridge, An
Orange Box, The
Purple Box, The
Red Box, The
Rime of the Ancient Mariner
Yellow Box, The

Literature-American

Ambrose Bierce: The Man and the Snake/The
  Return
Four for Thrills
Mark Twain's A Connecticut Yankee in King
  Arthur's Court
Steinbeck's The Pearl
Wind in the Willows, The

Literature-English

Great Expectations
Lady Chatterley's Lover
Oliver Twist
Sir Arthur Conan Doyle

Magic

Basic Card Magic
Dick Cavett's Hocus Pocus, It's Magic
Magic Show, The
Now You See It
Touch of Magic in Close-Up, A

Marriage

Marriage and Divorce Test, The

Martial arts

Aerobic Self-Defense
Alley Cat
Amsterdam Connection
Art of High-Impact Kicking, The
Assassin, The
Basic Karate and Self-Defense
Black Belt
Black Belt Karate I
Black Belt Karate II
Black Belt Karate III
Black Dragon, The
Black Dragon's Revenge, The
Blind Fist of Bruce
Blind Rage
Blood on the Sun
Bloody Fight, The
Bloody Fist
Bodyguard, The
Bolo
Breaker, Breaker!
Bronson Lee, Champion
Bruce & Shao Lin Kung Fu with Fierce Boxer
Bruce Lee Fights Back from the Grave
Bruce Le's Greatest Revenge
Bruce Li in New Guinea
Bruce the Super Hero with Eighteen Weapons of
  Kung Fu
Bruce vs. Bill
Cantonen Iron Kung Fu
Chinese Connection, The
Chinese Connection II

Clones of Bruce Lee, The
Crack Shadow Boxers
Deadly Strike/Young Hero
Death Duel of Mantis
Death Machines
Dragon Lives Again, The
Dragon Princess
Dragon Strikes Back, The
Dragon the Hero, The
Duel of the Iron Fist
Empire of the Dragon
Enter the Dragon
Enter the Ninja
Enter Three Dragons
Exit the Dragon, Enter the Tiger
Fast Fists, The
Fight for Survival
Fighting Black Kings
Fighting Life
Firecracker
Fist
Fist of Vengeance
Fists of Fury
Fists of Fury II
Force of One, A
Forced Vengeance
From China with Death
Fundamentals of Karate
Game of Death
Gang Wars
Golden Exterminator
Heroes in the Ming Dynasty
Image of Bruce Lee, The
Incredible Master Beggars
Invincible from Hell, The
Invincible, The
Japanese Connection
Jaws of the Dragon
Karate Killer
Karate Warriors
Kill and Kill Again
Kill or Be Killed
Kill Squad
Kill the Golden Goose
King Boxers, The
King of Kung-Fu
Kung-Fu Commandos
Last Challenge of the Dragon, The
Last Challenge of the Dragon
Lone Wolf McQuade
Magnificent, The
Magnificent Kick, The
Militant Eagle
Moonlight Sword and Jade Lion
Never Cry Rape
Octagon, The
Of Cooks and Kung-Fu
Powerforce
Pro-Karate Championships (1976-1981)
Prodigal Boxer, The

Raw Force
Real Bruce Lee, The
Renegade Monk
Return of the Dragon
Return of the Red Tiger
Return of the Tiger
Revenge of the Ninja
Revolt of the Dragon
Rivals of the Silver Fox
Roaring Fire
Secret of the Snake and Crane, The
Self Defense
Self-Defense for Women
7 Blows of the Dragon
Shao Lin Kung Fu Mystagogue/Kung Fu of Eight
    Drunkards
Shaolin Death Squad
Shaolin Traitor
Shogun's Ninja
Silent Rage
Snake in the Monkey's Shadow
Stoner
Story in the Temple Red Lily
Street Fighter, The
Struggle Through Death
Super Weapon, The
Ten Brothers of Shao-lin
They Call Me Bruce
Tiger and Crane Shaolin Kung-Fu
Tiger's Claw
Tough Guy
Treasure of Bruce Le/Big Rascal
True Game of Death, The
Two Assassins in the Dark
Two Graves to Kung-Fu
Weapons of Death
Wing Chun: The Science of In-Fighting
World of Martial Arts, The
Young Dragon, The
Young Tiger, The

Mass media

Behind Your Radio Dial
Ham MasterTapes

Massage

Acupressure Massage (Shiatsu)
Complete Body Massage
Massage for Couples
Touch of Love: Massage, The

Medical care

Hospice

Mexico

Sentinels of Silence

Middle East

Beyond a Mirage
Hear O Israel
Holy Koran, The
Israel—The Pressure Cooker
Marco Polo's Afghanistan

Mime

Meet Marcel Marceau

Miners and mining

Harlan County, U.S.A.

Minorities

Black Panthers: Huey Newton/Black Panther
　　Newsreel
Gypsies
Quiet One, The

Motorcycles

Against the Odds
American Challenge
Austrian Enduro
Daytona '83/1 Superbike/Supercross
Daytona '83/2 200 Classic
Donnington '82
Enduro International
Honda—The Technology
Island Highlights
Island, The
Italian Finale
Motocross Professionals
Narrow Edge
Off Road Action
On Any Sunday II
Race to the Top
Scrambling in the 50's
Silverstone '83
Speedway '82 World Finals Los Angeles
Take It to the Limit
TT Tribute
V-Four Victory

Mountaineering

Bat, The
Everest in Winter
Everest the Hard Way
K2—The Savage Mountain
Kongur
No World for Men
Out of the Shadow Into the Sun
Trango

Movie and TV trailers

Adventure 1: Trailers on Tape
Beatles—Comedy Featurettes
Best of Sex and Violence, The
Comedy 1: Trailers on Tape
Coming Attractions #1—The Super Stars
Coming Next Week: Those Great Movie Trailers
Coming Soon
Cowboy Previews #1
Disaster—Adventure Featurettes
Drama—Romance: Trailers on Tape
Hollywood's Greatest Trailers
Horror—Sci-Fi: Trailers on Tape
Monsters on the March
Movie-Mixer Featurettes
Musical Featurettes
Musicals 1: Trailers on Tape
Selling Movies on Television
Serial Previews #1
Son of Monsters on the March
Tiffany Sampler

Museums

National Gallery of Art, The
Traction Today
Tut: The Boy King
Tut: The Boy King/The Louvre

Music

Alice Cooper: Welcome to My Nightmare
All You Need Is Cash
Always for Pleasure
Argentinisima I
Best of the Big Bands, The
Blues Accordin' to Lightnin' Hopkins, The
Caledonian Dreams
Christopher Tree
Chulas Fronteras
Comeback
Compleat Beatles, The
Cool Cats: 25 Years of Rock 'n' Roll Style
Del Mero Corazon
Dizzy Gillespie
Drum Course for Beginners
Dry Wood
Duke Ellington Story, The
Duran Duran: Girls on Film/Hungry Like the Wolf
Elementary Guitar Practice and Theory Parts 1
　　and 2
Elephant Parts
Ella Fitzgerald In Concert
Flower Out of Place, A
Four Seasons, The
Fraggle Songs, Volume One
Girl Groups: The Story of a Sound
Hot Pepper
Humans: Happy Hour, The
Jazz and Jive
Jesse Rae: Rusha/D.E.S.I.R.E.
John Lennon: Interview with a Legend
Judy, Judy, Judy

Kraft Music Hall, The
Lawrence Welk Show, The
Lonely Boy/Satan's Choice
Mahalia Jackson and Elizabeth Cotten: Two Remarkable Ladies
Michael Nesmith: Rio/Cruisin'
Mini Musicals
Money Madness
Musical Shorts Video Special
Pete Seeger...A Song and a Stone
Playing Folk Guitar
Polka Film, The
Quadrophenia
Queen—Greatest Flix
Ready Steady Go
Rock Adventure
Say Amen, Somebody
Sing Along with Mitch
Soldier's Tale, The
Spend It All
Sprout Wings and Fly
Stars of Jazz
Stars on 45
Sun's Gonna Shine
Sympathy for the Devil
Talking in Your Sleep
Trumpet Course; Beginning-Intermediate
Visions of Faith
Wasn't That a Time!
Weber and Fields, Al Jolson, and This Is America
Weekend Rebellion
Well Spent Life, A
White Music
Your Hit Parade

Music video

Beast of I.R.S. Volume I, The
Blondie Live
Blues Alive
Music Video From "Streets of Fire"
Pat Benatar Hit Videos
Phantom Empire, The
Pink Floyd's David Gilmour
Raccoons—Let's Dance, The
Rick Springfield Platinum Videos
Twisted Sister's Stay Hungry
Willie Nelson and Family In Concert

Music-Performance

Abba
Abba
Abba in Concert
ABC—Mantrap
Air Supply Live in Hawaii
Alice Cooper and Friends
America Live in Central Park
April Wine
A.R.M.S. Concert, The
Artur Rubinstein

Ashford and Simpson
Ashford and Simpson
Asia in Asia
Barry Manilow Live at the Greek
Basin Street Revue
Beatlemania—The Movie
Bernadette Peters in Concert
Best of Blondie, The
Bette Midler Show, The
Big Country Live
Bill Watrous
Bill Wyman
Billy Joel: Live from Long Island
Billy Squier
Black Music Video Special
Black Sabbath Live
Blondie—Eat to the Beat
Blues Alive
Blues 1
Bob Marley and the Wailers Live from the Santa Barbara Bowl
Bob Welch and Friends
Bobby Vinton
Boxcar Willie in Concert
Canned Heat Boogie Assault
Carole King: One to One
Celebration, A
Charlie Daniels Band: The Saratoga Concert, The
Cheryl Ladd—Fascinated
Chick Corea/Gary Burton Live in Tokyo
Christine McVie Concert, The
Chuck Berry Live at The Roxy
Claude Bolling: Concerto for Classic Guitar and Jazz Piano
Concert For Bangladesh, The
Country-Western All-Stars
Crosby, Stills & Nash: Daylight Again
Crystal Gayle in Concert
Culture Club: Kiss Across the Ocean
Danspak II
Daryl Hall & John Oates—Rock 'n Soul Live
Dave Mason Live at Perkins Palace
David Bowie
David Bowie—Serious Moonlight
Devo
Devo: The Men Who Make the Music
Diana Ross in Concert
Dionne Warwick in Concert
Dire Straits
Dirt Band Tonight, The
Divine Madness
Dizzy Gillespie
Dizzy Gillespie's Dream Band
Dolly in London
Don Kirshner's Rock Concert, Vol. 1
Doobie Brothers Live, The
Doors: A Tribute to Jim Morrison, The
Doozer Music
Duran Duran
Duran Duran

Dvorak's Slavic Dance
Early Elvis
Earth, Wind & Fire in Concert
Earth, Wind and Fire
Electric Light Orchestra Live at Wembly
Elton John
Elton John Live in Central Park
Elton John: Visions
Elvis...Aloha from Hawaii
Elvis—His 1968 Comeback Special
Elvis...1968 Comeback Special
Elvis on Tour
Elvis: The Early Years
Erick Friedman Plays Fritz Kreisler
Eurythmics—Sweet Dreams (The Video Album)
Eve, The
Evening with Liza Minnelli, An
Evening with Ray Charles, An
Evening with Sister Sledge, An
Evening with Utopia, An
Everly Brothers Reunion Concert
Evolutionary Spiral
Favorita, La
First Barry Manilow Special, The
Fleetwood Mac, Documentary and Live Concert
Fleetwood Mac in Concert—Mirage Tour 1982
Flock of Seagulls, A
Ford Star Jubilee: "Together with Music"
Frankie Valli: Twentieth Anniversary Concert
Freddie Hubbard
From the New World
Gary Numan—The Touring Principal '79
Genesis/Three Sides Live
Gerry Mulligan
Gimme Shelter
Gino Vannelli
Gladys Knight & the Pips and Ray Charles in
   Concert
Gladys Knight & The Pips and Ray Charles
Goodyear Jazz Concert with Bobby Hackett
Goodyear Jazz Concert with Duke Ellington
Goodyear Jazz Concert with Eddie Condon
Goodyear Jazz Concert with Louis Armstrong
Gospel
Grace Jones—One Man Show
Graham Parker
Grateful Dead — Dead Ahead, The
Grateful Dead in Concert, The
Grover Washington, Jr. in Concert
Guess Who Reunion, The
Harry Chapin:The Final Concert
Heifetz and Piatigorsky
Herbie Hancock and the Rockit Band
Horowitz in London
Horowitz in London
Hot Summer Night.. With Donna, A
Huberman Festival, The
Hullabaloo
Hullabaloo
Hungry i Reunion
Hymn of the Nations

In Person: Noel Paul Stookey
Iron Maiden
Itzhak Perlman
J. Geils Band
James Brown Live in Concert
James Taylor in Concert
Jazz in America
Jazz in America
Jefferson Starship
Jesse Rae
Jethro Tull—Slipstream
Jimi Hendrix at Rainbow Bridge
Jimi Plays Berkeley
Jimi Plays Berkeley
Jivin' in Bebop
Johnny Mathis' Twenty-Fifth Anniversary
   Concert
Johnny Winter Live
Joni Mitchell: Shadows and Light
Journey—Frontier and Beyond
Journey—Frontiers and Beyond
Jubilee U.S.A.
Judy and Her Guests
Judy Garland Show, The
Kajagoogoo
Kansas
Kate Bush, Live at Hammersmith
Kenny Loggins Alive
Kids Are Alright, The
Kids from Fame, The
Kim Carnes
Kinks: One for the Road, The
Knack—Live at Carnegie Hall, The
Kool and the Gang in Concert
Last Waltz, The
Last Waltz, The
Lena Horne: The Lady and Her Music
Let's Spend the Night Together
Liberace in Las Vegas
Lietuviskos Dainos Suente
Lietuvos Dainu Svente (Lithuanian Song
   Festival)
Linda Ronstadt—Nelson Riddle "What's New"
Lionel Hampton
Lionel Hampton's One Night Stand
Lithuanian Ethnographic Ensemble, The
Little River Band
Live Infidelity: REO Speedwagon in Concert
Liza in Concert
Loretta
Ma Vlast (My Fatherland)
Making Michael Jackson's Thriller
Manhattan Transfer in Concert
Max Roach
Maze
Maze Featuring Frankie Beverly
Meatloaf in Concert
Mel Torme
Mel Torme and Della Reese in Concert
Mellow Memories
Mick Fleetwood-The Visitor

Mikado, The
Motels, The
Muse Concert: No Nukes, The
Music of Melissa Manchester, The
Naked Eyes
Neil Diamond: Love at the Greek
Neil Sedaka in Concert
Neil Sedaka in Concert
Newport Jazz Festival
Night with Lou Reed, A
Olivia
Olivia in Concert
Olivia—Physical
Other Side of Nashville, The
Outlaws
Paul Simon in Concert
Paul Simon Special, The
Pavarotti
Pavarotti in London
Peerce, Anderson & Segovia
Percy Faith and his Orchestra (The Best of Both
    Worlds)
Pete Townsend
Peter Allen and the Rockettes
Phil Collins
Phil Collins Live at Perkins Palace
Photonos
Picture Music
Pink Floyd at Pompeii
Presenting Johnny Mathis
Prime Cuts
Prince Charming Revue, The
Punk Rock Movie, The
Rafael en Raphael
Rainbow Goblins Story
Rainbow: Live Between the Eyes
RCA's All-Star Country Music Fair
Rhythm and Blues 1
Rick Derringer
Rob McConnell
Rock and Roll Revue
Rockshow
Rod Stewart
Rod Stewart Live at the L.A. Forum
Rod Stewart: Tonight He's Yours
Rostropovich
Roxy Music: The High Road
Rubber Rodeo
Rude Boy
Rush—Exit Stage Left
Russian Folk Song and Dance
Rust Never Sleeps
Rust Never Sleeps
Sacred Music of Duke Ellington
San Francisco Blues Festival
Scruggs
Seals and Crofts with Martin Mull Live
Secret Policeman's Other Ball, The
Sheena Easton
Sheena Easton: Act One
Sheena Easton—Live at the Palace, Hollywood

Showtime at the Apollo
Showtime at the Apollo
Showtime at the Apollo
Simon & Garfunkel: The Concert in Central Park
Singer Presents Elvis (The 1968 Comeback
    Special) Outtakes
Singer Presents "Elvis" (The 1968 Comeback
    Special)
Soft Cell
Soul Experience, The
Soviet Army Chorus, Band, and Dance
    Ensemble
Split Enz
Spyro Gyra
Stamping Ground
Steve Miller Band
Stevie Nicks in Concert
Surfing Beach Party
Swingin' Singin' Years, The
Takanaka World
Teddy Pendergrass Live in London
That Was Rock (The TAMI/TNT Show)
There's a Meetin' Here Tonight
Thomas Dolby
Thomas Dolby
Thompson Twins Live at Liverpool, The
Timex All Star Jazz Show
Tina Turner
Tina Turner—Queen of Rock and Roll
To Russia...with Elton
Todd Rundgren Videosyncracy
Tom Jones Live in Las Vegas
Toni Basil—Word of Mouth
Tony Bennett Songbook, A
Tony Powers
Totally Go-Go's
Tribute to Billie Holiday, A
Tubes...Live at the Greek, The
Tubes Video, The
Twist of Fate
U2 Live at Red Rocks "Under A Blood Red Sky"
Utopia Sampler, The
Warren Zevon
Wayne Newton at the London Palladium
Who Rocks America—1982 American Tour, The

Musical

Acompaname (Accompany Me)
Adventure Called Menudo, An
Alice in Wonderland
American in Paris, An
Annie
Apple, The
Babes in Toyland
Bal, Le
Band Wagon, The
Beach Party
Bells Are Ringing
Best Little Whorehouse in Texas, The
Bikini Beach

Bing Crosby Festival
Black and Tan/St. Louis Blues
Blue Hawaii
Blues Brothers, The
Bohemian Girl, The
Breaking Glass
Breaking the Ice
Brigadoon
Bugsy Malone
Bye, Bye, Birdie
Camelot
Cancion de Juventud (The Song of Youth)
Can't Stop the Music
Carefree
Charlotte's Web
Charm of La Boheme, The
Chitty Chitty Bang Bang
Colgate Comedy Hour: "Let's Face It," The
Comic Book Kids, The
Como Dos Gotas de Agua (Like Two Drops of
    Water)
Copacabana
Damn Yankees
Damsel in Distress, A
Dixie Jamboree
Doctor Doolittle
Doll Face
Dos Gallos Y Dos Gallinas (Two Roosters For
    Two Hens)
Doug Stevens Special Delivery
Duke Is Tops, The
Dynamite Chicken
Easy Come, Easy Go
Eubie!
Eubie!
Evergreen
Everything is Rhythm
Fabulous Dorseys, The
Fashions (Fashions of 1934)
Femmes de Paris
Fiddler on the Roof
Fiesta
Finian's Rainbow
Flying Down To Rio
Follow the Fleet
42nd Street
Fun and Fancy Free
Fun in Acapulco
Gaiety
Gangway
Gay Divorcee, The
George White's Scandals
Get Crazy
G. I. Blues
Girls, Girls, Girls
Glorifying the American Girl
Gold Diggers of 1933
Gotta Dance, Gotta Sing
Grease
Grease 2
Great Caruso, The

Greek Street
Guys and Dolls
Gypsy
Hair
Hallelujah, I'm a "Tramp"
Happiest Millionaire, The
Hard Day's Night, A
Harlem Rides the Range
Harmony Lane
Heidi's Song
Hello, Dolly!
Hi-Di-Ho
Higher and Higher
Hillbillys in a Haunted House
Hips, Hips, Hooray
Holiday Inn
I Do! I Do!
I Dream Too Much
If You Knew Susie
Invitation to the Dance
It's Love Again
Jack and the Beanstalk
Jive Junction
Jubilee
Killer Diller
King and I, The
King of Jazz, The
Kismet
Lady Sings the Blues
Let It Be
Liberace Show Volumes 1 & 2, The
Li'l Abner
Lili
Little Johnny Jones
Little Kid's Dynamite All-Star Band, The
Little Match Girl, The
Little Night Music, A
Little Prince, The
Loving You
Magical Mystery Tour
Mame
Man of La Mancha
Manhattan Merry-Go-Round
Marvelous Land of Oz, The
Mary Poppins
Matter of Time, A
Meet Me in St. Louis
Meet the Navy
Melody Ranch
Melody Trail
Music Shoppe, The
Musical Featurettes
Musical Personalities No. 1
Musicals 1: Trailers on Tape
My Fair Lady
New York, New York
Novio Para Dos Hermanas, Un (One Boyfriend
    for Two Sisters)
Oh! Calcutta!
Oklahoma!
On a Clear Day You Can See Forever

On the Town
One and Only Genuine Original Family. Band, The
One from the Heart
One Touch of Venus
Paint Your Wagon
Paradise, Hawaiian Style
Pennies from Heaven
Perils of Pauline, The
Pinocchio
Pippin
Pirate, The
Pirate Movie, The
Pirates of Penzance, The
Popeye
Pot O' Gold
Prairie Moon
Private Buckaroo
Reet, Petite and Gone
Robinhood of Texas
Rock 'n' Roll High School
Rock, Rock, Rock
Rock, You Sinners
Romie-O and Julie-8
Rose, The
Royal Wedding
Scooby Goes Hollywood
Scrooge's Rock 'n' Roll Christmas
Second Chorus
Sensations of 1945
Sergeant Pepper's Lonely Hearts Club Band
Seven Brides for Seven Brothers
1776
Sextette
Shall We Dance
Shinbone Alley
Show Business
Silk Stockings
Sing While You're Able
Sing Your Worries Away
Singin' in the Rain
Sioux City Sue
Something to Sing About
South Pacific
Spinal Tap
Stagedoor Canteen
Star Is Born, A
Star Struck
Stars on Parade/Boogie Woogie Dream
Step Lively
Stork Club, The
Story of Vernon and Irene Castle, The
Sweeney Todd—The Demon Barber of Fleet Street
Swing Time
Terror of Tiny Town
Thank God It's Friday
That'll Be the Day
That's Entertainment
That's Entertainment, Part II
There's No Business Like Show Business

This Is Elvis
Till the Clouds Roll By
Till the Clouds Roll By/A Star Is Born
Times Square
Tommy
Top Hat
Tubby the Tuba
200 Motels
Two Tickets to Broadway
Vagabond Lover
Velnio Nuotaka (The Devil's Bride)
Viva Las Vegas
West Side Story
Wiz, The
Wizard of Oz, The
Woodstock
Xanadu
Yes, Giorgio
You'll Find Out
You'll Never Get Rich
Young Bing Crosby
Ziegfeld Follies
Zis Boom Bah

Musical-Drama

All That Jazz
Bittersweet
Cabaret
Carnival Rock
Cucaracha, La
Fame
Flashdance
Footloose
Frankie and Johnnie
Funny Girl
Going My Way
Goodyear TV Playhouse: "The Gene Austin Story"
Hard to Hold
Harder They Come, The
Heart's Desire
Honeysuckle Rose
It Happened in New Orleans
Jailhouse Rock
Jazz Singer, The
Jazz Singer, The
Jesus Christ Superstar
King Creole
Love Me Tender
Melody Master, The
Murder with Music
Payday
Piaf
Pink Floyd The Wall
Quadrophenia
Roustabout
Senora Tentacion
Show Boat
Sound of Music, The
Star Is Born, A

Star Is Born, A
This Is the Army
Threepenny Opera, The
Umbrellas of Cherbourg
Vez en la Vida, Una
Yankee Doodle Dandy
Young at Heart
Young Caruso, The

Mystery

Adventures of Ellery Queen, The
Agatha
Albino
All in a Night's Work
Ambrose Bierce: The Man and the Snake/The Return
And Then There Were None
Arsenic and Old Lace
Beyond Reasonable Doubt
Bird with the Crystal Plumage, The
Blackmail
Born to Kill
Bowery at Midnight
Bulldog Drummond Comes Back
Bulldog Drummond Double Feature
Bulldog Drummond Escapes
Carnival Lady
Case of the Mukkinese Battle Horn, The
Cat and Mouse
Cat and the Canary, The
Cat and the Canary, The
Chandu on the Magic Island
Charade
Children, The
Chinatown
Clutching Hand, The
Collectors Item: The Left Fist of David
Condemned to Live
Corpse Vanishes, The
Curley and His Gang in the Haunted Mansion
Cutter's Way
Dain Curse, The
Dangerous Mission
Daughter of the Tong
Dead Easy
Death Kiss, The
Death on the Nile
Detective, The
Diabolique
Dick Tracy Double Feature #2
Doomed to Die
Door with Seven Locks
Dressed to Kill
Drowning Pool, The
Early Frost
Easy Virtue
Endless Night
Evil Under the Sun
Ex-Mrs. Bradford, The
Eyes of Laura Mars

Falcon in Mexico, The
Falcon's Brother, The
Farewell, My Lovely
Fifth Floor, The
Frankenstein Island
French Intrigue
Gangbusters
Ghosts on the Loose
Gorky Park
Green Archer, The
Hammett
Harper
He Walked by Night
Hound of the Baskervilles, The
House That Vanished, The
Human Monster, The
Hustle
Infamous Crimes
International Crime
Johnny Angel
Juggernaut
Kennel Murder Case
Lady Ice
Lady of Burlesque
Lady Vanishes, The
Late Show, The
Laura
LCA Presents Family Entertainment Playhouse
Lost Jungle, The
Lying Lips
Maltese Falcon, The
Man Betrayed, A
Man Who Haunted Himself, The
Man Who Knew Too Much, The
Meeting at Midnight
Midnight
Mine Own Executioner
Mirror Crack'd, The
Mirrors
Mistaken Identity
Mr. Moto's Last Warning
Mr. Wong, Detective
Money Hunt
Murder
Murder at Midnight
Murder at the Baskervilles
Murder by Decree
Murder by Television
Murder My Sweet
Murder on the Orient Express
Murderer's Row
My Sister, My Love
Mysterious Mr. Wong
Mystery and Espionage
Mystery Mansion
Mystery of the Mary Celeste, The
MysteryDisc #1: Murder, Anyone?
MysteryDisc #2: Many Roads to Murder
Night Has Eyes, The
Night Moves
Number Seventeen

One Frightened Night
Phantom Creeps
Phantom Express
Phantom Rider
Play Misty for Me
Prime Suspect
Prowler, The
Psychomania
Red House, The
Return of Martin Guerre, The
Rififi
Saint in London, The
Saint in New York, The
Sanders of the River
Scandalous
Scared to Death
Scarlet Street
Scream Bloody Murder
Secret Agent
Seven Days in May
Seven-Per-Cent Solution, The
Sexton Blake and the Hooded Terror
Sexy Cat
Shadow of the Eagle
Shadow Strikes, The
Sherlock Holmes and the Baskerville Curse
Sherlock Holmes and the Secret Weapon
Sherlock Holmes and the Silver Blaze
Sherlock Holmes and the Woman in Green
Sherlock Holmes Double Feature
Sherlock Holmes Double Feature I
Sherlock Holmes Double Feature II
Sherlock Holmes I
Sherlock Holmes II
Shock
Shriek in the Night
Sleuth
Slightly Honorable
Spy Smasher
Stations West
Stone Cold Dead
Stranger, The
Stranger on the Third Floor
Study in Scarlet, A
Study in Scarlet, A/Sherlock Holmes and the
   Secret Weapon
Swamp Thing
Tall Blond Man with One Black Shoe, The
Ten Little Indians
Terror by Night
Terror by Night/Meeting at Midnight
They Call Me Mr. Tibbs!
Third Man, The
39 Steps, The
To Catch a Thief
Tomorrow at Seven
Toolbox Murders, The
Triumph of Sherlock Holmes
Under Capricorn
Vamping
Whatever Happened to Aunt Alice?

Whispering Shadow
Who Killed Doc Robbin?
Wicker Man, The
Witness for the Prosecution
Yellowstone
Young and Innocent

Natural resources

Aqua Follies

Nightclub

Broadway Highlights
Ladies Night Out
Spectacular Evening in Paris, A

Nuclear warfare

Day After, The
Nuclear Defense At Sea
War Game, The

Nutrition

Great American Diet and Nutrition Test, The
Sports Nutrition

Occult sciences

Amazing World of Psychic Phenomena, The
Force Beyond, The
Truth About UFO's & ET's, The
Unknown Powers

Occupations

Career Possibilities: Computer Programming
Winning Job Interview, The

Oceanography

Cousteau—Diving for Roman Plunder
Sea Around Us, The

Opera

Aida
Boheme, La
Falstaff
Gentlemen of Titpu
Gondoliers, The
H.M.S. Pinafore
I Dream Too Much
Opera Cameos
Pavarotti
Pavarotti in London
Peter Grimes
Rigoletto
Ruddigore
Samson et Dalila
Tales of Hoffmann, The

Traviata, La
Turandot
Who's Afraid of Opera? Volume I
Who's Afraid of Opera? Volume 2
Who's Afraid of Opera? Volume 3
Yeomen of the Guard, The

Outtakes and bloopers

Big Breakdowns—Hollywood Bloopers of the
    1930's, The
Bloopers #1
Bloopers from Star Trek and Laugh-In
Carol Burnett Show: Bloopers and Outtakes, The
Hollywood Bloopers
Hollywood Outtakes and Rare Footage
Outtakes I
Outtakes II
Outtakes III
Outtakes IV
Outtakes VI
Outtakes VII
Outtakes V
Presidential Blooper Reel
Revenge of TV Bloopers
Singer Presents Elvis (The 1968 Comeback
    Special) Outtakes
Soap Opera Scandals
Son of Hollywood Bloopers
Son of TV Bloopers
Star Bloopers
Star Trek Bloopers
Super Bloopers #1
Super Bloopers #2
Those Wild Bloopers
TV Bloopers
Video Yesterbloop

Painting

Degas, Erte and Chagall

Parades and festivals

Always for Pleasure
Draft Horse Pulling
Friends and Neighbors/The Great Outdoors
Mule Days
Music of America/Our Wonderful World of
    Sports
On the Road to Happiness/The Good Life
Rejoice
Tradition on Parade/Blood, Sweat and Cheers

Parents

You and Me, Kid Volume I

Personal finance

Developing Your Financial Strategy
IRA

Pay Less Tax Legally

Personality

Confessions of Tom Harris

Pets

CBS/Fox Guide to Complete Dog Care, The
Dog Training with the Grossmans
Grooming Pets
Quick Dog Training with Barbara Woodhouse
Training Your Retriever—Advanced
Training Your Retriever—Basic

Philosophy and ideology

Pre-War German Featurettes

Photography

Basic Photography
Caledonian Dreams
Centerfold
Color in the Movies
Creative Camera, The
Famous Photographer Series Volume I, The
Famous Photographer Series Volume II: Robert
    Farber
Kanako
Oriental Dreams
Photographing the Nude
35mm Photography
World's Greatest Photography Course, The

Physical fitness

Aerobic Dancing
Aerobic Dancing
Aerobic Dancing—Encore
Aerobic Self-Defense
Aerobicise: The Beautiful Workout
Aerobicise: The Beginning Workout
Aerobicise: The Ultimate Workout
Aerobics
Armed Forces Workout
Arnold Schwarzenegger: Mr. Olympia (The
    Comeback)
Back (Rehabilitation and Injury)
Belly Dance for Fitness and Fun
Body Beautiful
Cats' Cradle
Eroticise
Everyday with Richard Simmons: Family Fitness
Exercise
Exercise at Home
Exercise Now!
Fundamentals of Karate
Get Fit, Stay Fit
Health 'n Action Exercise Programs
Home Exercise for All Ages
Hypnovision Weight Loss Video Programming

Hysterectomy (Rehabilitation and Injury)
Jane Fonda Challenge
Jane Fonda's Workout
Jane Fonda's Workout for Pregnancy, Birth and
    Recovery
Jazzercise
Jazzercise
Joy of Relaxation, The
Knee (Rehabilitation and Injury)
Let's Jazzercise
Love Your Body
Marie Osmond: Exercises for Mothers-To-Be
Mastectomy (Rehabilitation and Injury)
Medical Aerobics for Athletic Training
Muscle Motion
New Video Aerobics, The
No Effort: Subliminal Weight Loss Video
Postnatal (Rehabilitation and Injury)
Prenatal (Rehabilitation and Injury)
Pritikin Promise Home Exercise Program, The
Pritikin Promise, The
Pumping Iron
Pump It
Rockabilly Glamourcize
Sandahl Bergman's Body
Shape Up
Slim and Trim Yoga with Billie In and Out of Pool
Slim and Trim Yoga with Billie In Pool
Slim and Trim Yoga with Billie Out of Pool
Solid Gold Five Day Workout, The
Sports Conditioning
Stomach Formula
Super Exercises
Tai Chi Chuan
Texersize
Thin Thighs in 30 Day
Tip Top! with Suzy Prudden—Ages 3-6
Tip Top! with Suzy Prudden—Age 7 and Above
Video Aerobics
Videocise (A Total Body Workout)
Weight Loss
Yoga Moves with Alan Finger

Physics

Forces of Life, The

Plants

All About Houseplants
Gardening in the City: I
Gardening in the City: II
Growing Indoor Plants
Professional Planting (Horticulture)
Professional Techniques (Horticulture)

Politics and government-US

Alfred E. Smith: The Happy Warrior
Fiorello La Guardia: The Crusader
John F. Kennedy: Pursuit of Happiness
Robert A. Taft: Mr. Republican
Wendell Willkie: Of Perfect Loyalty

Population

Quo Vadis

Poverty

Quiet One, The

Pregnancy

Jane Fonda's Workout for Pregnancy, Birth and
    Recovery
Marie Osmond: Exercises for Mothers-To-Be
Pregnancy and the Newborn Child
Prenatal (Rehabilitation and Injury)

Presidency-US

Franklin D. Roosevelt, Declaration of War
Franklin D. Roosevelt: F.D.R.
Great Figures in History: John F. Kennedy
J.F.K.
John F. Kennedy: Pursuit of Happiness
Killing of President Kennedy, The
Meet Mr. Washington/Meet Mr. Lincoln
Nixon and Ford
Richard Nixon—Checkers, Old Glory,
    Resignation

Prisons

Domino Principle, The

Propaganda

After Mein Kampf
Anarchy, U.S.A.
Arsenal
Assorted U.S. Government War Films Program
    No. 1
Assorted U.S. Government War Films Program
    No. 2
Deutsche Wochen-Schau, Die (Nazi Newsreel)
Frontschau, Die (The Front Shows)
German Propaganda Video Special
Germany Awake
Germany Celebrates Hitler's Birthday
Hitler's Newsreels
Lion Has Wings, The
March with the Fuhrer (Marsch Zum Fuhrer)
Mussolini Visits Hitler
Nazi Propaganda Films
Night Over China
Nostalgia World War II Video Library #1
Our Friend Angela
Peace Fund
Propaganda Parade
Report on German Morale, A
Soviet Army, The

Soviet Paradise, The
Soviet People Are with Vietnam/Soviet People
   Support Vietnam
Soviet Union Is Our Home, The/Rude
   Awakening
Strike
Tag der Freiheit—Unsere Wehrmacht (Day of
   Freedom—Our Armed Forces)
Triumph of the Will
Vietnam Report

Psychology

Circle of Life I
Circle of Life II
Emotions of Life, The
Inner Circle I
Story of Anna O, The

Puppets

Have I Got a Story For You
Thunderbirds Are Go

Rape

Rape! A Crime of Violence

Religion

Christmas Collection, The
Confessions of Tom Harris
Crossfire
Declarations of Faith
Easter Collection, The
God Has No Grandchildren
God's Wonders
Great Banana Pie Caper, The
Greatest Heroes of the Bible
Hear O Israel
High Adventure
Holocaust: Susan Sontag
Holy Land and Holy City
If I Perish
In Person: Noel Paul Stookey
In Search of Historic Jesus
Jesus
Jill
Letter to Nancy, A
Life Is Worth Living
Lost Years of Jesus, The
Moses
Music Box
Mystery of Willoughby Castle, The
Ordinary Guy
Power of the Resurrection
Tommy John Story, The
Visions of Faith
Wisdom of the Bible

Reproduction

Reproduction of Life: Sex Education

Rodeos

1979 U.S. National Indian Rodeo

Romance

Acompaname (Accompany Me)
Al Ponerse el Sol
Bird of Paradise
Blood and Sand
Bus Is Coming, The
Change of Seasons, A
Chapter Two
Circle of Two
Continental Divide
Day the Loving Stopped, The
Diva
Donovan's Reef
Dreams of Desire
Dubarry
East of Borneo
Elvira Madigan
Falling in Love Again
First Love
Five Days One Summer
Foolin' Around
Heartbeat
In Love With An Older Woman
Indiscretion of an American Wife
Intermezzo
Isabel's Choice
Italian Straw Hat, The
Jules et Jim
Kipperbang
Lady Takes a Chance
Laura
Legon
Little Night Music, A
Lonely Hearts
Love in the City
Lovers and Liars
Madame Bovary
Magnificent Matador
Man in Grey, The
Man Who Loved Women, The
Matter of Time, A
Norman Loves Rose
Nothing Personal
Ode to Billy Joe
On a Clear Day You Can See Forever
Panama Lady
Paradise
Passion of Love
Port of Call
Pygmalion
Reaching for the Moon
Reckless
Roman Holiday

Romancing the Stone
Romantic Englishwoman, The
Roof, The
Royal Bed, The
Running Hot
Solo
Some Call It Loving
Somewhere in Time
Somos Novius (In Love and Engaged)
Son of the Sheik
Swan, The
That Touch of Mink
Those Endearing Young Charms
Tulips
Under the Roofs of Paris (Sous les Toits de Paris)
Uptown New York
Vanity Fair
Way We Were, The
Windom's Way

Running

Frank Shorter's Run
Jim Fixx on Running
Jog/Run

Safety education

Dangerous Playground
Never Cry Rape
Self Defense
Total Self-Defense

Satire

A Nous La Liberte
Alice in Wonderland
Animal Farm
Atomic Cafe, The
Candidate, The
Carry On Cleo
Catch-22
Charlie Chan and the Curse of the Dragon Queen
Committee, The
Creature from the Haunted Sea
Doonesbury Special, A
Dracula and Son
Dracula Sucks
Eraserhead
Fairytales
Flesh Gordon
Going Berserk
Great Dictator, The
Groove Tube, The
Hail
Hardware Wars and Other Film Farces
Hey Good Lookin'
Horror of Frankenstein
I Love You

King in New York, A
King of Hearts
Mouse That Roared, The
Nocturna
Pink Flamingos
Real Life
Ribald Tales of Robin Hood, The
Ruling Class, The
School for Scandal
Scrambled Feet
Sex Shop, Le
Strange Invaders
Student Bodies
Stunt Man, The
There's Naked Bodies On My T.V.!
Tunnelvision
Welcome to L.A.

Science

Building Blocks of Life, The
Expansion of Life, The
Language in Life
Origin of Life, The (Plus Scopes Trial Footage)
Universe, The
Watch Mr. Wizard

Science fiction

Adventures of Captain Future Volume 1, The
Adventures of Captain Future Volume 2, The
Alien
Alien Contamination
Alien Factor, The
Aliens from Spaceship Earth
Alpha Incident, The
Altered States
Android
Andromeda Strain, The
At the Earth's Core
Battle Beneath the Earth
Battle Beyond the Stars
Battlestar Galactica
Black Hole, The
Blade Runner
Blob, The
Boy and His Dog, A
Brain From Planet Arous, The
Brain Machine
Brain That Wouldn't Die, The
Brainwaves
Brainstorm
Buck Rogers Conquers the Universe
Buck Rogers in the 25th Century
Buck Rogers: Planet Outlaws
Bug
Capricorn One
Captain Future in Space
Captain Harlock
Captain Kronos: Vampire Hunter
Cat Women of the Moon

Chud
Clockwork Orange, A
Close Encounters of the Third Kind (The Special
    Edition)
Cosmos—War of the Planets
Countdown
Crawling Eye, The
Crawling Hand, The
Dagora, the Space Monster
Danguard Ace
Dark Star
Dark Star—The Special Edition
Day It Came to Earth, The
Day of the Triffids
Day the Earth Caught Fire, The
Day the Earth Stood Still, The
Day Time Ended, The
Demon Seed
Destination Moon
Destination Moonbase Alpha
Destination Saturn
Devil Girl from Mars
Embryo
End of the World
Escape from New York
Escape 2000
Fantastic Planet
Fantastic Voyage
Fiend Without a Face
Fighting Marines, The
Final Programme, The
Firebird 2015 A.D.
First Spaceship on Venus, The
Flash Gordon
Flash Gordon
Flash Gordon Conquers the Universe
Flash Gordon: Mars Attacks the World
Flash Gordon: Rocketship
Flight to Mars
Forbidden Planet
Forbidden World
Forbidden Zone
From the Earth to the Moon
Futureworld
Galactica III: Conquest of the Earth
Galaxina
Galaxy of Terror
George Melies, Cinema Magician
Ghidrah the Three Headed Monster
Godzilla vs. Monster Zero
Godzilla vs. the Sea Monster
Grandizer
Hangar 18
Hardware Wars and Other Film Farces
He-Man and the Masters of the Universe
Heartbeeps
Horror Planet
Horror—Sci-Fi: Trailers on Tape
I Married a Monster from Outer Space
Ice Pirates, The
Incredible Hulk, The

Invaders from Mars
Invasion of the Body Snatchers
Invasion of the Body Snatchers
Invasion of the Body Stealers
Island of Dr. Moreau, The
It Came from Hollywood
Johnny Jupiter
Kamikaze '89
Kiss of the Tarantula
Kronos
Land That Time Forgot, The
Laserblast
Last Days of Man on Earth
Liquid Sky
Logan's Run
Looker
Lost in Space
Making of Star Wars, The/S.P.F.X. — The
    Empire Strikes Back
Making of Superman—The Movie and
    Superman II, The
Man from Atlantis
Man Who Fell to Earth, The
Marooned
Martian Chronicles, Part II-The Settlers, The
Martian Chronicles, Volume I: The Expeditions,
    The
Megaforce
Metalstorm
Meteor
Mission Galactica: The Cylon Attack
Mysterians, The
Navy vs. the Night Monsters, The
Night Beast
Night of the Comet
On the Beach
One Million B. C.
Outland
Parasite
People That Time Forgot, The
Phase IV
Pit, The
Plan 9 from Outer Space
Planet of the Apes
Purple Monster Strikes, The
Radar Men from the Moon
Radio Ranch
Resurrection of Zachary Wheeler, The
Return, The
Return of Chandu
Robot Monster
Rocketship/Mars Attacks the World
Rocketship X-M—Special Edition
Rocky Jones, Space Ranger
Rocky Jones, Space Ranger: Blast Off
Rocky Jones, Space Ranger: Pirates of Prah
Rocky Jones, Space Ranger: The Cold Sun
Rocky Jones, Space Ranger: Trial of Rocky
    Jones
Rollerball
Satan's Satellites

Saturn 3
Science Fiction Combo
Silent Running
Slaughterhouse Five
Sleeper
Slithis
Son of Blob
Son of Godzilla
Soylent Green
Space Angel Volume 1
Space Angel Volume 2
Space Patrol
Space Patrol
Space Patrol
Space Patrol
Space Patrol/Twilight Zone
Space Patrol Volume 1
Space Patrol Volume 2
Space Raiders
Space Sentinels Volume 1
Spaceketeers
Spaceketeers Volume 1
Spaceketeers Volume 2
Spaceketeers Volume 3
Spectreman versus Hedron
Spectreman versus Zeron and Medron
Star Crash
Star Trek I
Star Trek II
Star Trek Bloopers
Star Trek III
Star Trek IV
Star Trek V
Star Trek VI
Star Trek: Space Seed
Star Trek: The Motion Picture
Star Trek: The Motion Picture
Star Trek II: The Wrath of Khan
Star Trek Volume 1
Star Trek Volume 2
Star Trek Volume 3
Star Trek Volume 4
Star Trek Volume 5
Star Wars
Starvengers
Strange Invaders
Stranger from Venus
Stryker
Tales of Tomorrow Volume 1
Tales of Tomorrow, Volume 2
10th Victim, The
Thing, The
Thing, The
Things to Come
This Island Earth
THX 1138
Time After Time
Time Machine
Time Machine, The
Timerider
Tom Corbett, Space Cadet

Tom Corbett, Space Cadet Volume 1
Tom Corbett, Space Cadet Volume 2
Tourist Trap
Transatlantic Tunnel
Tron
2001: A Space Odyssey
Videodrome
Village of the Damned
Virus
War of the Worlds, The
Warlords of the 21st Century
Watcher in the Woods, The
Westworld
When Worlds Collide
Where Time Began
Who's Out There?—A Search for Extraterrestrial
  Life
Woman in the Moon
Women of the Prehistoric Planet
X -- The Man with X-Ray Eyes
X-Tro
Yesterday Machine
Zombies of the Stratosphere

Scientists

Father Hubbard: The Glacier Priest

Serials

Ace Drummond
Adventures of Captain Marvel
Adventures of Red Ryder
Adventures of Rex and Rinty
Adventures of Tarzan, The
Battling with Buffalo Bill
Black Widow, The
Blake of Scotland Yard
Burn 'Em Up Barnes
Captain America
Clutching Hand, The
Crimson Ghost, The
Daredevils of the Red Circle
Dick Tracy
Dick Tracy Returns
Dick Tracy vs. Crime Inc.
Dick Tracy's G-Men
Don Daredevil Rides Again
Don Winslow of the Coast Guard
Don Winslow of the Navy
Drums of Fu Manchu
Fighting Devil Dogs
Fighting Marines, The
Fighting with Kit Carson
Flaming Frontiers
Flash Gordon Conquers the Universe
Gangbusters
Hawk of the Wilderness
Heroes of the West
Holt of the Secret Service
Hurricane Express

Junior G-Men
Junior G-Men of the Air
King of the Kongo
King of the Rocketmen
King of the Texas Rangers
Last Frontier, The
Last of the Mohicans
Lightning Warrior
Lone Ranger, The
Lost Jungle, The
Manhunt in the African Jungle
Masked Marvel, The
Miracle Rider
Mysterious Doctor Satan
Mystery Mountain
Mystery Squadron
New Adventures of Tarzan, The
Nyoka and the Tigerman
Oregon Trail
Painted Stallion, The
Perils of the Darkest Jungle
Phantom Creeps
Phantom Empire
Phantom Rider
Purple Monster Strikes, The
Radar Men from the Moon
Return of Chandu
Riders of Death Valley
Serial Previews #1
Shadow of the Eagle
Son of Zorro
S.O.S. Coastguard
Spy Smasher
Three Musketeers, The
Trail of the Royal Mounted
Undersea Kingdom
Vanishing Legion, The
Vigilantes Are Coming, The
Whispering Shadow
Winners of the West
Young Eagles
Zombies of the Stratosphere
Zorro Rides Again
Zorro's Black Whip
Zorro's Fighting Legion

Sexuality

Am I Normal?
Amour, L'
Dear Diary
Guide to Making Love, A
Reproduction of Life: Sex Education
Sex and Love Test, The
Sex Pleasuring, An Enrichment Series, Volumes
   1-3

Ships

Fighting Lady, The
Great Steamers of the Great Lakes

Steam Daylight Rides Again, The

Skating

Torvill & Dean: path to Perfection

Smoking

Hypnovision Stop Smoking Video Programming

Soccer

Cosmos: The Championship Years 1977-1980
Pele—The Master and His Method
Soccer for Everyone

Sociology

God Respects Us When We Work But Loves Us
   When We Dance
This Nude World

South America

Wings Over the Andes

Space exploration

Behind the Scenes of Telstar
Greatest Adventure, The
Man on the Moon
Moon Buggy
One Small Step for Man
Soyuz/Apollo Link-Up
Space Movie, The
Who's Out There?—A Search for Extraterrestrial
   Life

Spain

Land Without Bread
Land Without Bread
Will of a People, The

Speculation

Bermuda Triangle, The
Beyond and Back
Beyond Death's Door
Chariots of the Gods
Force Beyond, The
In Search of Historic Jesus
Jupiter Menace, The
Lost Years of Jesus, The
Mysteries from Beyond Earth
Sasquatch
Truth About UFO's & ET's, The

Sports

Dreams of Gold
Filming the Impossible

Go for It
GSF Hilites, a Visual Catalog
1976 Summer and Winter Olympic Games
Off the Edge
Olympia: Parts I and II
Run for Life: An Olympic Fable
Skateboard Madness
Snow Dream
Special Olympics, The
Sports Conditioning
Sports Hour #3
Sports Hour #4
Sports Hour #7
Sports Hour #10
Sports Hour #14
Terrytoons Salutes the Olympics
Thorpe's Gold
Time Capsule: The Los Angeles Olympic
    Games/1932
Tokyo Olympiad

Sports-Minor

Arnold Schwarzenegger: Mr. Olympia (The
    Comeback)
Basic Bowling
Basic Pool
Basic Racquetball
Cal-Poly University's 17th Annual Horsemanship
    Seminar
Cal-Poly University's 17th Annual Horsemanship
    Seminar
Cal-Poly University's 17th Annual Horsemanship
    Seminar
Icarus Mania
Let's Bowl
1982-83 WWPB Championship Series
1980 USSSA Men's World Series of Slo-Pitch
    Softball
1980 Women's National Volleyball
    Championship
Roderick Wrestling Program
Show Jumping World Cup
Showmanship at Halter
Spiral Ride and Standup
Stallions of Distinction
Stampee Wrestling
Superbowl of Motocross, The
Teach Your Horse to Bow
Ultralight Experience, The
World of Polo, A

Sports-Water

California's Nude Beaches
Diving and Fishing at 11,000 Feet
Endless Summer, The
Florence Chadwick: The Challenge
Follow Me Down
I Crave the Waves
Island Magic

Love Under the High Seas
Medusa Affair, The
1980 "Boomer" Team Challenge
1981 "Boomer" Team Challenge
1980 U.S. Pro Surfing Championship
1981 U.S. Pro Surfing Championship
OP 1982 IPS Pro Championships
Swim Baby Swim
Truk Lagoon
Under Water Deep Sea Diving with "Smokey
    Roberts"
Undersea Research
Whitewater

Sports-Winter

Alpine Ski School, The
American Ski Scene with Billy Kidd, The
Benjamin
Dream Never Dies, The
Fishing/Hunting/Snowmobiling
500 Miles Below Zero
Four Days to St. Paul
Freshness of Skiing, The
John Jay's Wonderful World of Skiing
Miracle of Lake Placid: Highlights of the 1980
    Winter Olympics, The
1984 Winter Olympics Highlights
Rocky Powder Picture Show, The
Ski
Ski Instructors Holiday
Ski Scene
Ski-Vision One
Ski-Vision Two
Ski-Vision Three
Ski-Vision Four
Skiing Lessons with Gene Heinz Landsmann 1
Skiing Lessons with Gene Heinz Landsmann 2
Sports Hour #2
Sports Hour #5
Sports Hour #6
Sports Hour #12
Sports Hour #19
SyberVision Cross-Country Skiing with Jeff
    Nowak
SyberVision Skiing with Jean Claude Killy
Those Flying Canucks
Verticus Maximus

States-US

Montana Discovered

Stress

Stress Management

Suspense

Alice Sweet Alice
Anderson Tapes, The
Are You in the House Alone?

Assignment Skybolt
Avalanche
Baby, The
Baffled
Barcelona Kill, The
Big Sleep, The
Birgitt Haas Must Be Killed
Blood on the Sun
Bloodrage
Blow Out
Body Heat
Boston Strangler, The
Brannigan
Bushido Blade, The
Centerfold Girls, The
Children, The
Christine
Coma
Crimes of Dr. Mabuse
Cross Country
Crucible of Horror
Cruise Missile
Cuatro Budas de Kriminal, Los
Custodio de Senoras
Dain Curse, The
Dangerous Summer, A
Day of the Jackal, The
Dead Easy
Dead of Night
Dead Zone, The
Deadly Force
Deadly Game, The
Death Games
Death Machines
Death Rage
Deathtrap
Deep, The
Deep Red: Hatchet Murders
Devil's Undead, The
Dial "M" for Murder
Dias de Ilusion
Disappearance, The
Dishonored Lady
Diva
D.O.A.
Don't Go in the Woods
Double Agents
Double Exposure
Dressed to Kill
Driver's Seat, The
Duel
Eiger Sanction, The
Enigma
Escape to the Sun
Exorcist, The
Exposed
Exterminator, The
Eye of the Needle
Eyewitness
Fade to Black
Family Plot

Fan, The
Fatal Games
Fear in the Night
Fiction Makers, The
Fifth Floor, The
Firepower
Fog Island
Forced Entry
French Detective, The
French Intrigue
Frenzy
From Russia with Love
Ghost Story
Golden Rendezvous
Guest in the House
Hide in Plain Sight
Hindenburg, The
House on Garibaldi Street, The
I, the Jury
Inheritance, The
Jaws 3
Jaws
Jaws II
Journey Into Fear
Kelly's Heroes
Kill the Golden Goose
Killer Bait
Killers, The
Kiss Me, Kill Me
Kwaidan
Last of Sheila, The
Last Wave, The
Little Girl Who Lives Down the Lane, The
Lodger, The
Mad Bomber
Magnum Force
Man Who Haunted Himself, The
Man with the Golden Gun, The
Maniac, The
Mr. Reeder in Room 13
Mortuary
Most Dangerous Game, The
Mother's Day
Ms. 45
Mysterious Doctor Satan
Mystery and Espionage
Never Say Never Again
Night Moves
Night of the Juggler
Night Visitor, The
Nighthawks
Nightkill
Nightwing
North by Northwest
Notorious
Obsession
Octagon, The
Operation Amsterdam
Osterman Weekend, The
Out of the Past
Parallax View, The

Paranoia
Patrick
Pepper
Pervertion (Perversion)
Power Play
Psycho
Psycho II
Raven, The
Rear Window
Red House, The
Return of Chandu, The
Return to Boggy Creek
Rider on the Rain
Road Games
Roaring Fire
Sabotage
Scream Bloody Murder
Seance on a Wet Afternoon
Seasons for Assassins
Second Chance
Secret Agent/The Man Who Knew Too Much
She's Dressed to Kill
Shogun's Ninja
Sidney Sheldon's Bloodline
Sisters of Death
Sleuth
Snake in the Monkey's Shadow
Sphinx
Still of the Night
Strangers on a Train
Suspicion
Swiss Conspiracy, The
Taking of Pelham One-Two Three, The
Telefon
They Won't Believe Me
Thirty-Nine Steps, The/Blackmail
This Is a Hijack
To Catch a King
To Kill a Clown
Tomorrow at Seven
Torn Curtain
Town Called Hell, A
Town That Dreaded Sundown, The
Tracks
Treasure of the Four Crowns
Union City
Vertigo
Visiting Hours
Wait Until Dark
Watch Me When I Kill
Watched
Watcher in the Woods, The
What Ever Happened to Baby Jane?
When a Stranger Calls
Window, The
Wrong Man, The
Z

Technology

Voice from the Screen, The

Television

Adventures of Ozzie and Harriet, The
Best of 60 Minutes, The
Caesar's Hour
Ernie Kovacs: Television's Original Genius
Help Yourself to Better Color TV
Lawrence Welk Show, The
Lum and Abner
Maps to Stars' Homes Video
Problems, 1950's Style
Roy Rogers and Dale Evans Show, The
Watch Mr. Wizard
Your Hit Parade

Tennis

Basic Tennis
Complete Tennis from the Pros
Helen Wills: Miss Poker Face
John McEnroe Story: The Rites of Passage, The
Play Your Best Tennis, Volume I
Play Your Best Tennis, Volume II
Racquet
Sports Hour #8
Sports Hour #11
Sports Hour #13
Sports Hour #16
Sports Hour #17
SyberVision Tennis with Stan Smith
Tennis Lessons from Bjorn Borg
Tennis/Racquet Sports
Vic Braden's Tennis for the Future, Volume 1
Vic Braden's Tennis for the Future, Volume 2
Vic Braden's Tennis for the Future, Volume 3
WCT Finals of 1971/1972

Theater

Birth of a Legend, The
Evening with Quentin Crisp, An
Maps to Stars' Homes Video
Oldest Living Graduate

Therapeutic cults

Accupressure for Common Ailments

Track athletics

Sprint Technique, The

Trains

Aboard the Santa Fe Chief
American Steam
American Steam Vol. 2
Berkshires and Hudsons of the Boston & Albany/Railroading in the Northeast
Best of Steam I
Best of Steam II
Big Trains A—Rolling

Boston and Maine—Its Fitchburg Division and Hoosac Tunnel in Steam Days
Cass Scenic Railroad 1980 Special
Challenger Special, The
Chessie in Florida
Clear Track Ahead
Colorado Rails
Cumbres and Toltec Revisited
Dangerous Playground
Day on the Silverton, A
Daylighting the Padre Trail
Double Heading on the Sierra
Durango and Silverton Narrow Gauge Railroad
Empire on Parade
Farewell to Santa Fe Steam
Fast Freight
Flight of the Century
Freight Yard, The
Getting Around
Great Age of Steam, The
Green Mountain Railroading on the Rutland & When Steam Was King
Illinois Steam Freight
Iron Horses at Promontory
It's a Big Job
Mainline U.S.A.
March of Progress: The Key System
N&WJ 611
Night Mail
Once Upon the Wabash
Piedmont and Susquehanna Limiteds Plus, The
Preview Tape II
Progress on the Rails
Railroad at Work
Railroad Signal, The
Railroadin'
Return of the Daylight
Ride on the Cumbres and Toltec Scenic Railway, A
Ride Pacific Electric San Bernardino
Ride the Last of the Big Red Cars
Rocky Mountain Rails
765 North/4501 Steam
Some Rails of Pennsylvania
Southern Chessie 2716
Southern Steam
Steam and Diesel on the Bessemer and Lake Erie/ The Diesels Roar on the Pennsy
Steam in the Sierras
Steam Locomotive, The
Thunder of Steam in the Blue Ridge, The
Thundering Rails
Toronto Rail 1980
Traction Today
Trainwatcher I
Trainwatcher II
Trainwatcher III
Trainwatcher IV
Trainwatcher V
Trainwatcher VI
225,000 Mile Proving Ground

Union Pacific Steam
Vintage Steam
Western Maryland Shay No. 6 at Cass
Western Steam
Wheels of Steel

Transportation

Carriage Restoration; Coaching in America
Ten Seconds to Go...
Wheels-O-Rolling

Travel

Cousteau—The Nile
Day at Disneyland, A
Funnier Side of Eastern Canada with Steve Martin, The
Let's Go Catalina
Popeye—Travelin' On About Travel

USSR

Battle of Stalingrad, The
Inside Russia with an American Cameraman
Moon Buggy
Only About Women
Simtameciu Godos
Soviet Army, The
Soviet Union Is Our Home, The/Rude Awakening

Variety

All the Best from Russia
Arthur Godfrey Show, The
Bing Crosby Show, The
Bob Hope Chevy Show
Bob Hope Chevy Show I, The
Bob Hope Chevy Show II, The
Bobby Darin and Friends
Bottoms Up '81
Caesar's Hour
Cavalcade of Stars
Chevy Show, The
Chuck's Choice Cuts
Coke Time with Eddie Fisher and The Perry Como Show
Colgate Comedy Hour
Colgate Comedy Hour, The
Colgate Comedy Hour, The
Colgate Comedy Hour, The
Colgate Comedy Hour (The Eddie Cantor Show)
Colgate Comedy Hour (The Tony Martin Show)
Colgate Comedy Hour with Martin and Lewis, The
Country Style USA and Community Jamboree
Country-Western All-Stars
Dean Martin and Jerry Lewis Television Party for Muscular Dystrophy
Dinah Shore Show, The
Ed Sullivan Show, The

Ed Wynn: Double Feature #1
Ed Wynn: Double Feature #2
Ed Wynn: Double Feature #3
Ed Wynn: Double Feature #4
Ed Wynn Show, The
Ed Wynn Show, The
Fabulous Fred Astaire, The
Famous T and A
First National Kidisc, The
Ford Show, The
Frankie Laine Show with Connie Haines
Great British Striptease
Great Space Coaster Supershow, The
Here It Is, Burlesque
Hollywood on Parade
Hollywood Palace
Hollywood Palace, The
Hollywood Palace Farewell Show, The
Invitation to Paris
Jack Benny
Jerry Lewis Show, The
Jerry Lewis Show, The
Jonathan Winters Show, The
Judy Garland Christmas Show
Kraft Music Hall
Kraft Music Hall Presents "Alan King Stops the
   Press"
Kraft Music Hall, The
Liberace Show Volumes 1 & 2, The
Martha Raye Show, The
Milton Berle Show, The
Milton Berle Show, The
Milton Berle Show, The
Milton Berle Spectacular, The
Miss Nude America Contest, The
Musical Shorts Video Special
NBC Comedy Hour
NBC Comedy Hour
Network Fall Preview Presentations
New Look
New Star Over Hollywood
New Zoo Revue
Nudie Classics
On Broadway Tonight
Original Amateur Hour, The
Original Amateur Hour, The
Original Amateur Hour, The
Paul Simon Special, The
Perry Como Show, The
Peter Lind Hayes Show, The
Phil Silvers Special: Summer in New York
Pinwheel Songbook, The
Playboy Video, Volume I
Playboy Video, Volume II
Playboy Video, Volume 3
Playboy Video, Volume 4
Playboy Video, Volume 5
Playmate Review
Puppet Playhouse Presents Howdy Doody
Robert Youngson Specials
Roundhouse Show, the

Roy Rogers and Dale Evans Show, The
Saturday Night Live, Vol. II
Saturday Night Live, Vol. I
Saturday Night Live with Richard Pryor
Saturday Night Live with Steve Martin
Sheena Easton: Act One
Showtime at the Apollo
Sing Along with Mitch
Snow White Live at Radio City Music Hall
Stage Show with the Dorsey Brothers
Steve Allen Plymouth Show, The
Talk of the Town—Show 1
Talk of the Town—Show II
Ten from Your Show of Shows
Texaco Star Theater
Toast of the Town
Tonight Show, The
TV Variety
TV Variety, II
TV Variety III
TV Variety, IV
TV Variety, V
TV Variety, VI
27th Annual Academy Awards Presentations,
   The
Washington Square
Weber and Fields, Al Jolson, and This Is America
What Would Your Mother Say?
Your Hit Parade
Your Show of Shows
Your Show of Shows

Veterinary medicine

African Horse Sickness
Breeding by Artificial Insemination
Diagnosis of Forelimb Lameness
Diagnosis of Hindlimb Lameness
Diseases of the Hoof
Equine Infectious Anemia
Essential Care: First Aid for Horses
Lameness of Both Fore and Hindlimbs
Lameness of the Forelimb, Part 1
Lameness of the Forelimb, Part 2
Lameness of the Forelimb, Part 3
Lameness of the Forelimb, Part 4
Lameness of the Forelimb, Part 5
Lameness of the Hindlimb, Part 1
Lameness of the Hindlimb, Part 2
Lameness of the Hindlimb, Part 3
Relationship of Conformation to Lameness
Routine Dental Care of the Equine
Teasing, Breeding and Semen Collection in the
   Horse

Video

Afternoon Delight
Ask Video Dave, Vol. I
Beautiful Birds/Tropical Fish/Fireside Moments
Blue Sky, Blue Sea

CBS/FOX Guide to Home Videography, The
Clouds of Peace
Duran Duran: Girls on Film/Hungry Like the Wolf
Electric Light Voyage
Environmental Video
Evolutionary Spiral
Experimental Avant-Garde Video Special
Flowing Falls
Flowing Sea
Gold Coast, The
Hawaii Experience
How to Beat Home Video Games Volume I
How to Beat Home Video Games Volume II
How to Beat Home Video Games Volume III
Jesse Rae: Rusha/D.E.S.I.R.E.
Lumia Lights
Meet Your VCR
Michael Nesmith: Rio/Cruisin'
Ocean Waves
Palm Tree Beach
Reflections
Rock, The
Sea, The
Shipwreck Beach
Stream Flows Home, The
Stream on Dad's Birthday, The
Talking in Your Sleep
Thoughts by the Ocean
Video Aquarium
Video Fireplace
Video System Test Tape, The
Video Wallpaper

Vietnam War

American Navy in Vietnam, The
Big Picture—The Fight for Vietnam
Eye of the Dragon/Vietnamese Junk Navy
Face of War, A
Gentle Hand, The
Hearts and Minds
Know Your Enemy—The Viet Cong
Marines-65
Nation Builds Under Fire, A
Navy Advisor in Vietnam—The River Force
New Thunder for the USAF
On Target
Peace Fund
Screaming Eagles in Vietnam
Soviet People Are with Vietnam/Soviet People
   Support Vietnam
Survival and Evasion in Southeast Asia
U.S. Crimes in Vietnam
Vietnam
Vietnam: Chronicle of a War
Vietnam Report
Vietnam: The Bombing
Vietnamese Cultures and Customs
Village that Refused to Die, The
Why Vietnam

Volcanoes

Eruption: St. Helens Explodes

War-Drama

Adventures of the Flying Cadets
Air Force
Airborne
Back to Bataan
Battle Cry
Battle of El Alamein, The
Battle of the Bulge, The
Beguiled, The
Berlin Express
Big Red One, The
Birth of a Nation, The
Black Dragons
Boat, The
Boys in Company C, The
Brady's Escape
Breakthrough
Bridge Too Far, A
Burmese Harp, The
Civilization
Colditz Story, The
Commandos
Cross of Iron
Cruel Sea, The
Dam Busters, The
Deep Six, The
Desert Fox, The
Dirty Dozen, The
Double Agents
Eagle Has Landed, The
Fighting Marines, The
Fighting Seabees, The
Flying Leathernecks
Force 10 from Navarone
Glory at Sea
Go Tell the Spartans
Green Berets, The
Gung Ho
Heart of Humanity, The
Hell River
Hellcats of the Navy
Hell's Brigade: The Final Assault
Hustler Squad
Ill Met by Moonlight
Immortal Battalion
In Which We Serve
King Rat
Legion of Missing Men, The
Longest Day, The
MacArthur
Malta Story
Men in War
Midway
North Star, The
Odd Angry Shot
Only Way, The

Operation Amsterdam
Paths of Glory
Patton
PT 109
Purple Hearts
Raid on Entebbe
Run Silent, Run Deep
Sahara
Salute John Citizen
Sands of Iwo Jima
Shout at the Devil
SS Girls
Streamers
Sundown
Tiger Fangs
Tora! Tora! Tora!
Twelve O'Clock High
Von Ryan's Express
We Dive at Dawn
Went the Day Well?
Westinghouse Studio One: Hold Back the Night
White Rose, The

Western

Abilene Town
Adventures of Gallant Bess, The
Alamo, The
Allegheny Uprising
Along the Sundown Trail
Alvarez Kelly
American Empire
American Empire
Angel and the Badman
Apache
Apache Rose
Apple Dumpling Gang Rides Again, The
Arizona Bound
Arizona Days
Arizona Raiders
Arizona Stagecoach
Arizona Terror
Bad Man's River
Badmen of Nevada
Bandits, The
Barbarosa
Bargain, The
Battling Marshal
Battling Outlaws
Battling with Buffalo Bill
Bells of Rosarita
Between Men
Big Cat, The
Big Show
Billy the Kid in Texas
Billy the Kid Returns
Billy the Kid Versus Dracula
Bite the Bullet
Black Lash
Black Market Rustlers
Blood on the Moon

Blue Blazes Rawden
Blue Canadian Rockies
Blue Steel
Boiling Point
Boots and Saddles
Border Romance
Brand of the Devil
Brandy Sheriff
Breakheart Pass
Broadway to Cheyenne
Bronze Buckaroo/Harlem Rides the Range
Brothers of the West
Buck and the Preacher
Buckskin Frontier
Buffalo Bill and the Indians
Buffalo Stampede
Bulldog Courage
Cahill: United States Marshal
California Gold Rush
California in '49
Call of the Canyon
Captain Apache
Carson City Kid
Cat Ballou
Cattle Queen of Montana
Cavalcade of the West
Chance
Cheyenne Kid
Cheyenne Rides Again
Chino
Chisum
Circle of Death
Clearing the Range
Colorado
Comancheros, The
Come On, Cowboys
Come On Tarzan
Comes a Horseman
Cow Town
Cowboy Millionaire
Cowboy Previews #1
Cowboys, The
Cowboys from Texas
Coyote Trail
Custer's Last Stand
Dakota
Dakota Incident
Daniel Boone
Dark Command
Dawn on the Great Divide
Dead or Alive
Death Rides the Plains
Death Rides the Range
Desert Trail
Disciple, The
Disciple, The/Hell's Hinges
Dodge City
Down Texas Way
Drifter, The
Drum Beat
Drum Taps

Duchess and the Dirtwater Fox, The
Dude Bandit, The
Dude Ranger, The
Durango Valley Raiders
Dynamite Pass
El Diablo Rides
El Dorado
El Paso Stampede
Enemy of the Law
Every Man's Law
Eyes of Texas
Fargo Express
Fast Bullets
Feud of the West
Feud on the Range
$50,000 Reward
Fighting Caravans
Fighting Renegade
Fighting Trooper, The
Fighting with Kit Carson
Fistful of Dollars, A
Flaming Frontiers
Flying Lariats, The
For a Few Dollars More
Forbidden Trail
Fort Apache
Four Rode Out
Frontier Justice
Frontier Pony Express
Frontier Scout
Frontier Vengeance
Fuerte Perdido (Fort Lost)
Fugitive, The (The Taking of Luke McVane)
Galloping Dynamite
Gambling Terror, The
Gay Ranchero, The
Ghost Patrol
Ghost Town Law
Git Along Little Dogies
God's Gun
Goin' South
Good, the Bad and the Ugly, The
Grand Canyon Trail
Greaser's Palace
Great Gundown, The
Great Scout and Cathouse Thursday, The
Grey Fox, The
Guerrillera de Villa, La (The Warrior of Villa)
Gun Ranger
Gun Riders
Gunfight at the O.K. Corral
Gunman From Bodie
Gunners and Guns
Gunplay
Guns in the Dark
Guns of Fury
Hang 'Em High
Hard Hombre
Harlem Rides the Range
Harmony Trail
Haunted Ranch

Heart of Texas Ryan, The
Heart of the Golden West
Heart of the Rio Grande
Heart of the Rockies
Heaven's Gate
Hell Fire Austin
Helldorado
Hell's Hinges
Helltown
Heroes of the Hills
Heroes of the West
Hidden Gold
High Noon
High Noon, Part II: The Return of Will Kane
High Plains Drifter
Hills of Utah, The
His Fighting Blood
Hit the Saddle
Hombre
Homesteaders of Paradise Valley
Horse Soldiers, The
Hurricane Express/Angel and the Badman
Idaho
In Old Caliente
In Old California
In Old Cheyenne
In Old New Mexico
In Old Santa Fe
In the Days of the Thundering Herd
Iron Horse, The
Jesse James at Bay
Joe Kidd
Johnny Guitar
Justice Rides Again
Kansan, The
Keep Rollin'
Kentuckian, The
Kid Vengeance
King of the Bullwhip
King of the Cowboys
Kit Carson
Knights of the Range
Laramie Kid, The
Last Frontier, The
Last of the Pony Riders
Last Outlaw, The
Law of the Lash
Law of the Saddle
Law Rides, The
Law West of Tombstone
Lawless Frontier
Lawmen
Legend of the Lone Ranger, The
Legion of the Lawless
Ley del Revolver, La (The Law of the Gun)
Life and Times of Judge Roy Bean, The
Lightning Strikes West
Lightning Warrior
Lights of Old Santa Fe
Loaded Pistols
Lone Avenger, The

Lone Bandit, The
Lone Ranger, The
Lone Ranger, The
Lone Wolf McQuade
Louisiana Gal
Lucky Terror
Lucky Texan
Lusty Men, The
Magnificent Seven, The
Man Alone, A
Man From Cheyenne
Man from Music Mountain, The
Man from Utah, The
Man of the Frontier
Man Who Shot Liberty Valance, The
Maverick Queen, The
McCabe and Mrs. Miller
Melody Ranch
Melody Trail
Miracle Rider
Missouri Breaks, The
Molly and Lawless John
My Pal Trigger
Mystery Mountain
Mystery of the Hooded Horseman
Mystery Range
Nevada City
New Lion of Sonora, The
Night in Nevada
Night Stage to Galveston
No Man's Range
Oath of Vengeance
Old Barn Dance, The
Old Corral, The
Old Corral, The
On the Night Stage
On the Night Stage/Wagon Tracks
On the Old Spanish Trail
On Top of Old Smoky
One-Eyed Jacks
100 Rifles
Oregon Trail
Outlaw, The
Outlaw Josey Wales, The
Outlaw Rule
Outlaw Tamer
Outlaws of the Range
Overland Mail
Painted Desert, The
Painted Stallion, The
Paradise Canyon
Pat Garrett and Billy the Kid
Phantom Empire
Phantom of the West
Phantom Rancher, The
Pioneers, The
Pocatello Kid
Powdersmoke Range
Prairie Badmen
Prairie Moon
Prairie Pals

Professionals, The
Proud Rebel, The
Public Cowboy No. 1
Purple Vigilantes
Racketeers of the Range
Raiders of Red Gap
Rancho Notorious
Randy Rides Alone
Range Busters
Rangeland Racket
Rangers Take Over, The
Rawhide
Red River
Red River Valley
Reil
Renfrew on the Great White Trail
Return of the Bad Men
Revenge of the Virgins, The
Ride 'Em Cowgirl
Ride in the Whirlwind
Ride, Ranger, Ride
Ride the Man Down
Ride the Wind
Riders of Death Valley
Riders of Destiny
Riders of the Desert
Riders of the Law
Riders of the Rockies
Riders of the Sage
Riders of the Whistling Pines
Riders of the Whistling Skull
Ridin' on a Rainbow
Ridin' the California Trail
Riding Avenger, The
Rio Bravo
Rio Grande
Rio Lobo
Rio Rattler
Road Agent
Roaming Wild
Roarin' Lead
Roaring Guns
Roaring Six Guns
Robinhood of Texas
Rogue of the Rio Grande
Roll Wagons Roll
Rolling Plains
Romance on the Range
Rooster Cogburn
Rootin' Tootin' Rhythm
Rough Riders of Cheyenne
Rough Riders Roundup
Rough Riding Rangers
Round-Up Time in Texas
Run of the Arrow
Sacketts, The
Saga of Death Valley
Sagebrush Trail
Santa Fe Bound
Santa Fe Trail
Santa Fe Uprising

Searchers, The
Secret Valley
Shadows of Death
Shalako
Shane
She Wore a Yellow Ribbon
Shine on Harvest Moon
Shooting, The
Shootist, The
Silent Valley
Silver Queen
Silver Spurs
Sing, Cowboy, Sing
Sioux City Sue
Six Gun Rhythm
Six Shootin' Sheriff
Sky Bandits
Smokey Smith
Soldier Blue
Sombrero Kid
Son of a Gun
Song of Arizona
Song of Nevada
Song of Texas
Song of the Gringo
Song of the Trail
Sons of Katie Elder, The
South of Monterey
South of the Border
South of the Rio Grande
Southward Ho
Spoilers, The
Springtime in the Rockies
Springtime in the Sierras
Stagecoach
Stagecoach to Denver
Star Packer
Sting of the West
Stormy Trails
Straight Shootin'
Sundance and the Kid
Sundown Fury
Sunset in El Dorado
Sunset Range
Sunset Serenade
Sweet Creek County War
Swifty
Take Me Back to Oklahoma
Tall in the Saddle
Tell Them Willie Boy Is Here
Tennessee's Partner
Terror of Tiny Town
Tex Ritter Rides With the Boy Scouts
Texas Terror
Texas to Bataan
Texas Trouble
They Call Me Trinity
This Gun For Hire
Three Faces West
Three in the Saddle
Three Mesquiteers

Three Word Brand
Thunder Mountain
Thunder Pass
Thunder River Feud
Toll Gate, The
Tom Horn
Tombstone Canyon
Tonto Kid, The
Trail Drive
Trail of Terror
Trail of the Hawk
Trail of the Royal Mounted
Trail Riders
Trail Street
Trailing Trouble
Trails West
Train Robbers, The
Traitor, The
Trigger Pals
Trigger Trio, The
Trinity Is Still My Name
Triumphs of a Man Called Horse
Trouble in Texas
True Grit
Tulsa
Tumbleweed Trail
Tumbleweeds
Tumbleweeds
Twilight on the Rio Grande
Two Gun Man
Two Mules for Sister Sara
Under California Stars
Under Nevada Skies
Under Western Stars
Utah
Utah Trail
Valley of Fire
Valley of Terror
Vanishing American
Vanishing Legion, The
Vigilantes of Boom Town
Wackiest Wagon Train in the West, The
Wagon Tracks
Wagon Trail
Wagonmaster
War of the Wildcats
War Wagon, The
Water Rustlers
Way of the West
West of Pinto Basin
West of the Divide
West of the Law
Western Double Feature #1
Western Double Feature I
Western Double Feature #2
Western Double Feature II
Western Double Feature #3
Western Double Feature III
Western Double Feature #4
Western Double Feature IV
Western Double Feature #5

Western Double Feature V
Western Double Feature #6
Western Double Feature #7
Western Double Feature #8
Western Double Feature #9
Western Double Feature #10
Western Double Feature #11
Western Double Feature #12
Western Double Feature #13
Western Double Feature #14
Western Double Feature #15
Western Double Feature #16
Western Double Feature #17
Western Double Feature #18
Western Double Feature #19
Western Double Feature #20
Western Double Feature #21
Western Double Feature #22
Western Double Feature #23
Western Double Feature #24
Western Double Feature #25
Western Justice
Westward Ho
When the West Was Young
Whirlwind Horseman
Whistling Bullets
Wild and Wooly
Wild Bunch, The
Wild Horse
Wild Horse Canyon
Wild Horses
Wild Mustang
Wild Times
Winds of the Wasteland
Wings Over Wyoming
Winners of the West
Winning of the West
With Buffalo Bill on the U.P. Trail
Wolfheart's Revenge
Woman of the Town, The
Woman of the Town
Yellow Rose of Texas, The
Yodelin' Kid From Pine Ridge
Yukon Flight
Zorro's Black Whip

Wilderness areas

Wilderness Quest

Wildlife

Animals Are Beautiful People
Survival Anglia's World of Wildlife, Vol. I
Survival Anglia's World of Wildlife, Vol. 2
Trail to Alaska

Women

Helen Keller: Separate Views
Late Liz, The
Love Goddesses, The
Only About Women
U.S. Women's Gymnastics Championship

Woodwork

Basic Carpentry

World War I

American History: Warring and Roaring (1914-1929)
Guns of August
Mutiny on the Western Front: WW I
Naval Aviation: A Personal History—The Weapon Is Tested
Pershing Story, The/American Siberian Expeditionary Force

World War II

Abandon Ship
After Mein Kampf
After Mein Kampf (The Story of Adolf Hitler)
American History: Two Great Crusades (1930-1945)
Assorted U.S. Government War Films Program No. 1
Assorted U.S. Government War Films Program No. 2
Attack!—The Battle of New Britain
Baltic Tragedy, The
Battle of Britain, The
Battle of China, The
Battle of Midway, The
Battle of Russia, The
Battle of San Pietro, The
Battle of Stalingrad, The
Camouflage
China Crisis
Combat Bulletin
Combat Bulletins Nos. 1-14
Countdown to World War II
Demonstrations of Ordance Material, Aberdeen Proving Ground, Maryland
Desert Victory
Deutsche Wochen-Schau, Die (Nazi Newsreel)
Divide and Conquer
European Operations
Fall of Berlin, The
Fight for the Sky
Fight for the Sky, The/Mission Accomplished
Fighting Lady, The
Flak
Forty Ninth Parallel, The
Franklin D. Roosevelt, Declaration of War
Frontschau, Die (The Front Shows)
General Montgomery: The Black Beret
General Patton: The Fighting Man
German Invasion of Poland
Great Battle of the Volga

Guilty Men
High Altitude Ship Recognition
Hitler's Newsreels
Hitler's Newsreels, Part 2
Hitler's Newsreels, Part 3
Holocaust: Susan Sontag
Kamikaze
Kamikaze
Katyn Forest Massacre
Kitty: A Return to Auschwitz
Know Your Enemy—Japan
Kriegsmarine, Die
Leben von Adolf Hitler, Das (The Life of Adolf Hitler)
Lion Has Wings, The
Memorandum
Memphis Belle, The
Men Against Tanks/Engineers to the Front
Nazi Concentration Camps
Nazi Propaganda Films
Nazi Strike
Nazi War Crime Trials
Nazis Strike, The / Schichlegruber Doing the Lambeth Walk
Nazis Strike, The
Negro Soldier
Night and Fog
Nostalgia World War II Video Library # 1
Now It Can Be Told/U-Boat Am Feind
Nuremberg War Trials
Official War Films
Old Soldier, The
Our Russian Front
Prelude to War
Propaganda Parade
Report on German Morale, A
Restricted U.S. and British Training Films
Ronald Reagan—WW II "Identification of the Japanese Zero"
Secret Life of Adolph Hitler, The
Showbiz Goes to War
Sieg im Western (Victory in the West)
6th Marine Division on Okinawa, The
Smashing of the Reich, The
Sorrow and the Pity, The
Soviet Paradise, The

Stillwell Road
Story of Lili Marlene, The
Strategic Air Power
Tag der Freiheit—Unsere Wehrmacht (Day of Freedom—Our Armed Forces)
Target for Tonight
This Is Korea/December 7th
Thunder Out of China
Thunderbolt
To The Gates of Japan
Too Late the Hero
True Glory, The
Twisted Cross, The
U.S. Army Air Force Report
U.S. Staff Reports Nos. 1-4
U.S. War Department Report—July 1943
U.S.S. VD: Ship of Shame/Red Nightmare
V-2/German V-2 Rocket Tests
Victory at Sea
Voyage of the Damned
War Comes to America
War Department Film Communiques Nos. 1-3
War in the Sky
War Years—The Forties, The
Why We Fight
With the Marines at Tarawa
World at War
World at War, The
World at War, The
World War II: The European Theatre
World War II: The Pacific Theatre
World War II Video Series—Attack: The Battle of New Britain
World War II Video Series—Something for Our Boys
World War II Video Series—The Stillwell Road
World War II Video Series—Tried by Fire!

Yoga

Slim and Trim Yoga with Billie In and Out of Pool
Slim and Trim Yoga with Billie In Pool
Slim and Trim Yoga with Billie Out of Pool
Tai Chi Chuan
Yoga Moves with Alan Finger

Cast Index

Complete videographies for more than 275 actors, actresses, directors and other screen personalities will be found in this index.

Cameo appearances, soundtrack narrations and other special situations have been included in the listings, where known, to provide as thorough a reference as possible.

Many interesting bits of trivia may be noted herein; for example, the small parts played by current superstars Richard Dreyfuss *(The Graduate)* and Sylvester Stallone (*Bananas*) early in their careers. Also, if you wonder why Charles Laughton is listed as appearing in, of all things, *Early Elvis*, that's because he was the substitute host of "The Ed Sullivan Show" when Elvis made his first appearance; not Ed himself, as history would have it.

In compiling this index we have been guided by the desire to list most of the performers that readers are likely to look for, while also striving to keep the section down to manageable length. Should any of your favorites be omitted, you are welcome to write and let us know. However, remember that many worthwhile films have not yet seen the light of video and a classic star like Greta Garbo, for example, is totally unrepresented on video at press time.

—D.J.W.

ABBOTT AND COSTELLO
Abbott and Costello in Hollywood
Abbott and Costello Meet Captain Kidd
Abbott and Costello Meet Dr. Jekyll and Mr. Hyde
Abbott and Costello Meet Frankenstein
Abbott and Costello Show, The
Africa Screams
Buck Privates
Comedy and Kid Stuff
Hey Abbott!
Hold That Ghost
Hollywood Goes to War
Jack and the Beanstalk
Outtakes I
Super Bloopers I

ALAN ALDA
California Suite
Four Seasons, The
Free to Be . . . You and Me

Glass House, The
M*A*S*H:
  Goodbye,
  Farewell
  and Amen
Outtakes IV, V, VII
Purlie Victorious
Same Time, Next
  Year
Seduction of Joe
  Tynan, The
To Kill a Clown

WOODY ALLEN
Annie Hall
Bananas
Everything You
  Always Wanted
  to Know About
  Sex
Front, The
Love and Death
Midsummer
  Night's Sex
  Comedy, A
Play It Again, Sam
Sleeper
Take the Money
  and Run
What's New
  Pussycat?
What's Up Tiger
  Lily?
Zelig

JULIE ANDREWS
Hawaii
Little Miss Marker
Man Who Loved
  Women, The
Mary Poppins
Outtakes IV
S.O.B.
Sound of Music,
  The
"10"
Torn Curtain
Victor/Victoria

GENE AUTRY
Blue Canadian
  Rockies
Boots and Saddles
Call of the Canyon
Cow Town
Git Along, Little
  Dogies
Heart of the Rio
  Grande
Hills of Utah, The
Last of the Pony
  Riders
Man from Music
  Mountain, The
Man of the
  Frontier
Manhattan
  Merry-Go-Round
Melody Ranch
Melody Trail
Mystery Mountain
Night Stage to
  Galveston
Old Corral, The
On Top of Old
  Smoky
Phantom Empire
Prairie Moon
Radio Ranch
Ridin' on a
  Rainbow
Robinhood of
  Texas
Rootin' Tootin'
  Rhythm
Sioux City Sue
South of the
  Border
Valley of Fire
Western Double
  Feature #5, 16
Winning of the
  West

LAUREN BACALL
Big Sleep, The
Fan, The

How to Marry a
  Millionaire
Key Largo
Murder on the
  Orient Express
Northwest Frontier
Premiere of "A
  Star Is Born"
Shootist, The

LUCILLE BALL
Abbott and
  Costello in
  Hollywood
Affairs of Annabel,
  The
Bob Hope Chevy
  Show, The
Comedy and Kid
  Stuff
Follow the Fleet
Great
  Gildersleeve,
  The
I Dream Too Much
Mame
Panama Lady
Premiere of "A
  Star Is Born"
Room Service
Stage Door
Toast of the Town
Top Hat
TV's Classic
  Guessing
  Games
Vintage
  Commercials
  I-III

ANN-MARGRET
Bye Bye Birdie
Carnal Knowledge
Cincinnati Kid, The
I Ought to Be in
  Pictures
Joseph Andrews
Lookin' to Get Out

Magic
Murderer's Row
Tommy
Train Robbers, The
Viva Las Vegas

**LAURA
ANTONELLI**
How Funny Can
    Sex Be?
Innocent, The
Passion of Love
Secret Fantasy

**LOUIS
ARMSTRONG**
Best of Louis
    Armstrong, The
Goodyear Jazz
    Concert with
    Louis Armstrong
Hello, Dolly!
That's
    Entertainment,
    Part II
Timex All Star
    Jazz Show

JEAN ARTHUR
Devil and Miss
    Jones, The
Lady Takes a
    Chance, The
Mr. Smith Goes to
    Washington

FRED ASTAIRE
Amazing
    Dobermans, The
Band Wagon, The
Carefree
Damsel in Distress
Easter Bunny Is
    Coming to
    Town, The
Finian's Rainbow
Flying Down to Rio

Follow the Fleet
Gay Divorcee, The
Ghost Story
Gotta Dance,
    Gotta Sing
Holiday Inn
Hollywood Palace,
    The
On the Beach
Purple Taxi, The
Royal Wedding
Second Chorus
Shall We Dance
Silk Stockings
Sky's the Limit,
    The
Story of Vernon
    and Irene
    Castle, The
Swing Time
That's
    Entertainment
That's
    Entertainment,
    Part II
Top Hat
Towering Inferno,
    The
You'll Never Get
    Rich
Ziegfeld Follies

ANNE BANCROFT
Audience with Mel
    Brooks, An
Bell Jar, The
Graduate, The
Hindenberg, The
Jesus of Nazareth
Lipstick
Prisoner of Second
    Avenue, The
To Be or Not to Be
Turning Point, The

BRIGITTE BARDOT
Contempt

Doctor at Sea
Famous T and A
Shalako
Very Private Affair,
    A

**JOHN
BARRYMORE**
Bulldog
    Drummond
    Double Feature
Dr. Jekyll and
    Mr. Hyde
Horrible Double
    Feature
Svengali
Tempest, The/The
    Eagle
That's
    Entertainment,
    Part II

**LIONEL
BARRYMORE**
America
Bells, The
Captains
    Courageous
Dr. Kildare's
    Strange Case
It's a Wonderful
    Life
Key Largo
That's
    Entertainment,
    Part II
Treasure Island

ALAN BATES
King of Hearts
Quartet
Rose, The
Shout, The
Unmarried Woman,
    An
Women in Love
Zorba the Greek

WARREN BEATTY
Bonnie and Clyde
Heaven Can Wait
McCabe and Mrs.
   Miller
Parallax View, The
Reds
Splendor in the
   Grass

JOHN BELUSHI
All You Need Is
   Cash
Animal House
Blues Brothers,
   The
Continental Divide
Goin' South
Neighbors
1941
Saturday Night
   Live Vol. I-II
Saturday Night
   Live with
   Richard Pryor
Saturday Night
   Live with Steve
   Martin

**RICHARD
BENJAMIN**
Catch-22
Diary of a Mad
   Housewife
First Family
Goodbye
   Columbus
House Calls
How to Beat the
   High Cost of
   Living
Last Married
   Couple in
   America, The
Last of Sheila, The
Love at First Bite

Portnoy's
   Complaint
Scavenger Hunt
Sunshine Boys,
   The
Westworld
Witches' Brew

JACK BENNY
Big Time, The
Hollywood Palace,
   The
It's a Mad, Mad,
   Mad, Mad World
It's in the Bag
Jack Benny
Jack Benny II
Jack Benny
   Program, The
Jack Benny
   Show, The
Jack Benny Visits
   Walt Disney
Milton Berle
   Spectacular, The
Take a Good
   Look/The Jack
   Benny Show
That's
   Entertainment,
   Part II
To Be or Not to Be
Vintage
   Commercials II

ROBBY BENSON
Chosen, The
Die Laughing
End, The
Harry and Son
Ice Castles
Ode to Billy Joe
One on One
Our Town
Running Brave
Tribute

**CANDICE
BERGEN**
Bite the Bullet
Carnal Knowledge
Domino Principle,
   The
Gandhi
Rich and Famous
Sand Pebbles, The
Starting Over

**INGMAR
BERGMAN**
Brink of Life
Cries and
   Whispers
Devil's Eye
Fanny and
   Alexander
Magician, The
Night Is My
   Future, The
Persona
Port of Call
Scenes from a
   Marriage
Secrets of Women
Wild Strawberries
Winter Light

INGRID BERGMAN
Adam Had Four
   Sons
Arch of Triumph
Bells of St. Mary's,
   The
Cactus Flower
Casablanca
Fear
Hideaways, The
Indiscreet
Inn of the Sixth
   Happiness, The
Intermezzo
Joan of Arc
Matter of Time, A
Murder on the

Orient Express
Notorious
Spellbound
Under Capricorn
Woman Called
  Golda, A

MILTON BERLE
Bloopers from
  "Star Trek" and
  "Laugh-In"
Broadway
  Highlights
Cracking Up
Hey Abbott!
It's a Mad, Mad,
  Mad, Mad World
Journey Back to
  Oz
Kraft Music Hall,
  The
Milton Berle Hour,
  The
Milton Berle Show,
  The
Muppet Movie, The
Oscar, The
Texaco Star
  Theatre
TV Variety, II

**JACQUELINE
BISSET**
Airport
Bullitt
Class
Day for Night
Deep, The
Detective, The
Famous T and A
Greek Tycoon, The
Magnifique, Le
Murder on the
  Orient Express
Rich and Famous
Secrets
St. Ives

KAREN BLACK
Can She Bake a
  Cherry Pie?
Capricorn One
Chanel Solitaire
Come Back to the 5
  and Dime Jimmy
  Dean, Jimmy
  Dean
Day of the Locust
Easy Rider
Family Plot
Great Gatsby, The
In Praise of Older
  Women
Last Word, The
Little Laura and
  Big John
Nashville
Portnoy's
  Complaint
Separate Ways
You're a Big Boy
  Now

**HUMPHREY
BOGART**
African Queen,
  The
Angels with Dirty
  Faces
Barefoot
  Contessa, The
Big Breakdowns,
  The
Big Sleep, The
Casablanca
Coming
  Attractions
Dark Victory
Harder They Fall,
  The
High Sierra
Hollywood
  Outtakes and
  Rare Footage
Jack Benny, II
Key Largo

Knock on Any
  Door
Maltese Falcon,
  The
Midnight
Petrified Forest,
  The
Presidential
  Blooper Reel
Roaring Twenties,
  The
Sahara
Stand-In
They Drive by
  Night
Treasure of the
  Sierra Madre,
  The
27th Annual
  Academy
  Awards
We're No Angels

MARLON BRANDO
Apocalypse Now
Burn!
Formula, The
Godfather, The
Godfather: The
  Complete Epic,
  The
Guys and Dolls
Last Tango in
  Paris
Men, The
Missouri Breaks,
  The
Mutiny on the
  Bounty
One-Eyed Jacks
Sayonara
Streetcar Named
  Desire, A
Superman—The
  Movie
27th Annual
  Academy
  Awards

BEAU BRIDGES
For Love of Ivy
Four Feathers
Greased Lightning
Heart Like a Wheel
Honky Tonk
   Freeway
Hotel New
   Hampshire, The
Love Child
Night Crossing
Norma Rae
Red Pony, The

JEFF BRIDGES
Cutter's Way
Heaven's Gate
Kiss Me Goodbye
King Kong
Last Unicorn, The
Rapunzel
Thunderbolt and
   Lightfoot
Tron
Winter Kills

LLOYD BRIDGES
Abilene Town
Airplane!
Airplane II: The
   Sequel
Crash of Flight
   401, The
East of Eden
High Noon
Mission Galactica:
   The Cylon
   Attack
Roots
Sahara
Trapped
War in the Sky
White Tower, The

**CHARLES
BRONSON**
Borderline
Breakheart Pass

Breakout
Cabo Blanco
Chino
Death Hunt
Death Wish
Death Wish II
Dirty Dozen, The
Drum Beat
Family, The
Great Escape, The
Hard Times
Magnificent Seven,
   The
Mechanic, The
Raid on Entebbe
Rider on the Rain
Run of the Arrow
St. Ives
Stone Killer, The
Telefon

MEL BROOKS
Audience with Mel
   Brooks, An
Blazing Saddles
Free to Be. . .
   You and Me
High Anxiety
History of the
   World: Part I,
   The
Muppet Movie, The
New Faces
Producers, The
Timex All Star
   Comedy Show
To Be or Not to Be
Twelve Chairs, The
Young
   Frankenstein

**GENEVIEVE
BUJOLD**
Caesar and
   Cleopatra
Coma
Earthquake
Journey

King of Hearts
Last Flight of
   Noah's Ark, The
Monsignor
Murder by Decree
Obsession

CAROL BURNETT
Annie
Between Friends
Carol Burnett
   Show: Bloopers
   and Outtakes,
   The
Chu Chu and the
   Philly Flash
Four Seasons, The
Son of TV
   Bloopers

GEORGE BURNS
Big Time, The
Broadway
   Highlights
Comedy and Kid
   Stuff
Damsel in Distress
George Burns and
   Gracie Allen
   Show, The
George Burns
   Show, The
Going in Style
Hollywood Palace,
   The
I Married Joan/The
   Burns and Allen
   Show
Jack Benny
Jack Benny Show,
   The
Oh, God!
Oh, God! Book II
Sgt. Pepper's
   Lonely Hearts
   Club Band
Sunshine Boys,
   The

Vintage Sitcoms

ELLEN BURSTYN
Alice Doesn't Live
   Here Anymore
Exorcist, The
Providence
Same Time, Next
   Year
Silence of the
   North

**RICHARD
   BURTON**
Becket
Bluebeard
Breakthrough
Circle of Two
Cleopatra
Exorcist II: The
   Heretic
Longest Day, The
Look Back in
   Anger
Night of the
   Iguana, The
Robe, The
Taming of the
   Shrew, The
Tempest, The
Who's Afraid of
   Virginia Woolf?
Wild Geese, The

GARY BUSEY
Barbarosa
Carny
D.C. Cab
Foolin' Around
Star Is Born, A
Straight Time

JAMES CAAN
Bolero
Brian's Song
Bridge Too Far, A
Chapter Two
Comes a

Horseman
Coming
   Attractions
Countdown
El Dorado
Gambler, The
Godfather, The
Godfather: The
   Complete Epic,
   The
Harry and Walter
   Go to New York
Hide in Plain Sight
Kiss Me Goodbye
Rain People, The
Rollerball
Thief

SID CAESAR
Caesar's Hour
Dorothy in the
   Land of Oz
Fiendish Plot of
   Dr. Fu Manchu,
   The
Grease II
History of the
   World: Part I,
   The
Hollywood Palace,
   The
It's a Mad, Mad,
   Mad, Mad World
Your Show of
   Shows

JAMES CAGNEY
Angels with Dirty
   Faces
Big Breakdowns,
   The
Blood on the Sun
Bob Hope Chevy
   Show, The
Coming
   Attractions
Great Guy
Mister Roberts

Presidential
   Blooper Reel
Public Enemy, The
Ragtime
Roaring Twenties,
   The
Something to Sing
   About
White Heat
Yankee Doodle
   Dandy

MICHAEL CAINE
Beyond the Limit
Blame It on Rio
Bridge Too Far, A
California Suite
Deathtrap
Dressed to Kill
Eagle Has Landed,
   The
Hand, The
Harry and Walter
   Go to New York
Island, The
Man Who Would
   Be King, The
Romantic English-
   woman, The
Sleuth
Swarm, The
Too Late the Hero
Victory

DYAN CANNON
Author! Author!
Bob & Carol & Ted
   & Alice
Coast to Coast
Deathtrap
Heaven Can Wait
Honeysuckle Rose
Lady of the House
Last of Sheila, The
Shamus

EDDIE CANTOR
Big Time, The

Colgate Comedy
  Hour, The
Hollywood Goes to
  War
If You Knew Susie
Show Business

FRANK CAPRA
Arsenic and Old
  Lace
Attack!—The
  Battle of New
  Britain
It's a Wonderful
  Life
Meet John Doe
Mr. Smith Goes to
  Washington
Prelude to War
Silent Laugh
  Makers #3
State of the Union
Under Nazi
  Guns/On to
  Tokyo

ART CARNEY
Cavalcade of Stars
Defiance
Emperor's New
  Clothes, The
Going in Style
House Calls
Late Show, The
Movie Movie
St. Helens, Killer
  Volcano
Sunburn

LESLIE CARON
American in Paris,
  An
Fanny
Father Goose
Gigi
Lili
Man Who Loved
  Women, The

That's
  Entertainment

**JOHN
CARRADINE**
Bees, The
Best of Sex and
  Violence, The
Billy the Kid
  Versus Dracula
Black Cat, The/The
  Raven
Blood Legacy
Blood of Dracula's
  Castle
Bogey Man, The
Captain Kidd
Captains
  Courageous
Daniel Boone
Demon Rage
Everything You
  Always Wanted
  to Know About
  Sex
Frankenstein's
  Island
Golden
  Rendezvous
Grapes of Wrath,
  The
Greatest Heroes of
  the Bible
Gun Riders
House of Seven
  Corpses
Howling, The
Judgement of
  Solomon, The
Secret of NIMH,
  The
Shootist, The
Silent Night,
  Bloody Night
Silver Spurs
Stagecoach
Ten
  Commandments,

The

LON CHANEY
Horrible Double
  Feature
Hunchback of
  Notre Dame, The
Macabre Moments
  from The
  Phantom of the
  Opera
Outside the Law
Phantom of the
  Opera, The

**CHARLIE
CHAPLIN**
America Between
  the Great Wars
Chaplin: Keystone
  Beginnings
Chaplin Mutuals,
  Vol. I-IV
Chaplin Revue,
  The
Charlie Chaplin
  Carnival
Charlie Chaplin
  Cavalcade
Charlie Chaplin
  Festival
Charlie Chaplin's
  Keystone
  Comedies
City Lights
Flicker Flashbacks
Fun Factory/Clown
  Princes of
  Hollywood
Gold Rush, The
Great Dictator, The
Kid's Auto
  Race/Mabel's
  Married Life
King in New York,
  A
Knockout,
  The/Dough

and Dynamite
Laughfest
Limelight
Modern Times
Monsieur Verdoux
Rink, The/The
  Immigrant
Tillie's Punctured
  Romance
Work/Police

CYD CHARISSE
Band Wagon, The
Brigadoon
Silk Stockings
Singin' in the Rain
That's
  Entertainment
That's
  Entertainment,
  Part II
Ziegfeld Follies

CHEVY CHASE
Caddyshack
Deal of the
  Century
Ernie Kovacs:
  Television's
  Original Genius
Foul Play
Groove Tube, The
Modern Problems
Saturday Night
  Live, Vol. I-II
Saturday Night
  Live with
  Richard Pryor
Seems Like Old
  Times
Under the Rainbow

**MAURICE
CHEVALIER**
Fanny
Gigi
In Search of the
  Castaways

Invitation to Paris
That's
  Entertainment

JULIE CHRISTIE
Billy Liar
Darling
Doctor Zhivago
Don't Look Now
Heat and Dust
Heaven Can Wait
McCabe and Mrs.
  Miller

JILL CLAYBURGH
First Monday in
  October
Griffin and
  Phoenix
Hanna K.
Hustling
I'm Dancing as
  Fast as I Can
It's My Turn
Silver Streak
Starting Over
Unmarried Woman,
  An
Wedding Party,
  The

**MONTGOMERY
CLIFT**
Indiscretion of an
  American Wife
Judgment at
  Nuremburg
Misfits, The
Place in the Sun, A
Red River
Suddenly, Last
  Summer

JOAN COLLINS
Big Sleep, The
Bitch, The
Dark Places
Decameron Nights

Great Adventure,
  The
Hansel and Gretel
Homework
Oh Alfie
Star Trek II
Star Trek
  Volume 5
Stud, The
Subterfuge
Sunburn

SEAN CONNERY
Anderson Tapes,
  The
Bridge Too Far, A
Darby O'Gill and
  the
  Little People
Diamonds Are
  Forever
Dr. No
Five Days One
  Summer
From Russia with
  Love
Goldfinger
James Bond 007—
  Coming
  Attractions
Longest Day, The
Man Who Would
  Be King, The
Meteor
Murder on the
  Orient Express
Never Say Never
  Again
Outland
Robin and Marian
Shalako
Thunderball
Wrong Is Right
You Only Live
  Twice

GARY COOPER
Farewell to Arms, A

Fighting Caravans
Good Sam
High Noon
It
Meet John Doe
Pride of the
Yankees
Sergeant York
They Came to
Cordura
Vera Cruz

**FRANCIS FORD
COPPOLA**
Apocalypse Now
Conversation, The
Dementia 13
Godfather, The
Godfather, Part II,
The
Godfather: The
Complete Epic,
The
New Look
One from the
Heart
Rain People, The
Tonight for Sure
You're a Big Boy
Now

JOAN CRAWFORD
Hollywood
Outtakes
and Rare
Footage
Johnny Guitar
Mildred Pierce
Premiere of "A
Star Is Born"
Rain
Strait Jacket
What Ever
Happened to
Baby Jane?

BING CROSBY
Bells of St. Mary's,

The
Bing Crosby
Festival
Bing Crosby Show,
The
Country Girl, The
Going My Way
Holiday Inn
Hollywood Goes to
War
Hollywood Palace,
The
Jack Benny
King of Jazz, The
Legend of Sleepy
Hollow, The
Outtakes III, V
Road to Bali, The
That's
Entertainment
That's
Entertainment,
Part II
Young Bing
Crosby

TONY CURTIS
Boston Strangler,
The
Brainwaves
Count of Monte
Cristo, The
Defiant Ones, The
Great Race, The
Little Miss Marker
Mirror Crack'd, The
Operation
Petticoat
Premiere of "A
Star Is Born"
Sex on the Run
Sextette
Some Like It Hot
Trapeze
Users, The

BETTE DAVIS
All About Eve

Big Breakdowns,
The
Dark Victory
Death on the Nile
Fashions of 1934
Hell House
Hollywood
Outtakes and
Rare Footage
Hollywood Palace,
The
Jezebel
Now Voyager
Of Human
Bondage
Petrified Forest,
The
Presidential
Blooper Reel
Right of Way
27th Annual
Academy
Awards
Watcher in the
Woods, The
What Ever
Happened to
Baby Jane?

DORIS DAY
Pillow Talk
That Touch of
Mink
Young at Heart

JAMES DEAN
America at the
Movies
East of Eden
Hollywood
Outtakes and
Rare Footage
James Dean: The
First American
Teenager
Premiere of "A
Star Is Born"
Rebel Without a

Cause

**OLIVIA DE
HAVILLAND**
Adventures of
   Robin Hood, The
Captain Blood
Charge of the
   Light Brigade,
   The
Dodge City
Proud Rebel, The
Santa Fe Trail
Swarm, The

DOM DELUISE
Best Little
   Whorehouse in
   Texas, The
Cannonball Run,
   The
End, The
History of the
   World: Part I,
   The
Hot Stuff
Last Married
   Couple in
   America,The
Muppet Movie, the
Peter-No-Tail
Secret of NIMH,
   The
Twelve Chairs, The
Wholly Moses!

ROBERT DE NIRO
America at the
   Movies
Bang the Drum
   Slowly
Bloody Mama
Deer Hunter, The
Godfather Part II,
   The
Godfather: The
   Complete Epic,
   The

King of Comedy
New York, New
   York
Obsession
Raging Bull
Scarface
Swap, The
Taxi Driver
True Confessions
Wedding Party,
   The

BRIAN DE PALMA
Blow Out
Carrie
Dressed to Kill
Fury, The
Sisters
Wedding Party,
   The

BO DEREK
Change of
   Seasons, A
Orca
Playboy Video,
   Volume 1
Tarzan, the Ape
   Man
"10"

BRUCE DERN
Black Sunday
Bloody Mama
Coming Home
Cowboys
Family Plot
Great Gatsby, The
Harry Tracy
Rebel Rousers
Silet Running
Tattoo
That
   Championship
   Season
Trip, The
War Wagon, The

**MARLENE
DIETRICH**
Around the World
   in 80 Days
Black Fox
Blue Angel, The
Judgment at
   Nuremburg
Love Goddesses,
   The
Piaf, the Woman
Rancho Notorious
Spoilers, The
Witness for the
   Prosecution

KIRK DOUGLAS
Champion
Eddie Macon's
   Run
Final Countdown,
   The
Fury, The
Gunfight at the
   O.K. Corral
Hollywood
   Bloopers
Jack Benny, II
Light at the Edge
   of the World,
   The
Man from Snowy
   River, The
Milton Berle
   Spectacular, The
My Dear Secretary
Out of the Past
Paths of Glory
Saturn 3
Seven Days in May
Strange Love of
   Martha Ivers,
   The
20,000 Leagues
   Under the Sea
War Wagon, The

MELVYN DOUGLAS
Annie Oakley
Being There
Candidate, The
Captains
    Courageous
Ghost Story
Hud
I Never Sang for
    My Father
Lamp at Midnight
Mr. Blandings
    Builds His
    Dream
    House
My Forbidden Past
Seduction of Joe
    Tynan, The
Tenant, The
That Uncertain
    Feeling
Your Show of
    Shows

MICHAEL DOUGLAS
China Syndrome,
    The
Coma
It's My Turn
Romancing the
    Stone
Star Chamber, The

RICHARD DREYFUSS
American Graffiti
Apprenticeship of
    Duddy Kravitz,
    The
Buddy System,
    The
Close Encounters
    of the Third Kind
Competition, The
Dillinger
Goodbye Girl, The

Graduate, The
Jaws
Second Coming of
    Suzanne, The

FAYE DUNAWAY
Bonnie and Clyde
Champ, the
Chinatown
Country Girl, The
Eyes of Laura
    Mars
First Deadly Sin,
    The
Four Musketeers,
    The
Mommie Dearest
Network
Thomas Crown
    Affair, The
Three Days of the
    Condor
Three Musketeers,
    The
Towering Inferno,
    The
Voyage of the
    Damned

IRENE DUNNE
I Remember Mama
Life with Father
Penny Serenade

JIMMY DURANTE
Broadway
    Highlights
Hollywood Goes to
    War
Hollywood Palace,
    The
It's a Mad, Mad,
    Mad, Mad World
Melody Ranch
Outtakes V
Palooka
That's
    Entertainment

That's
    Entertainment,
    Part II

CHARLES DURNING
Best Little
    Whorehouse in
    Texas, The
Breakheart Pass
Die Laughing
Dog Day Afternoon
Final Countdown,
    The
Fury, The
Greek Tycoon, The
Harry and Walter
    Go to New York
North Dallas Forty
Sharky's Machine
Sisters
Starting Over
Sting, The
Tilt
True Confessions
When a Stranger
    Calls

ROBERT DUVALL
Apocalypse Now
Betsy, The
Breakout
Bullitt
Conversation, The
Countdown
Eagle Has Landed,
    The
Godfather, The
Godfather Part II
Godfather:
    The Complete
    Epic, The
Great Santini, The
Joe Kidd
Lady Ice
M*A*S*H
Pursuit of D.B.
    Cooper, The

Rain People, The
Seven-Per-Cent
 Solution, The
Tender Mercies
Terry Fox Story,
 The
THX 1138
Tomorrow
True Confessions
True Grit

SHELLEY DUVALL
Annie Hall
Faerie Tale
 Theatre
McCabe and Mrs.
 Miller
Nashville
Popeye
Rapunzel
Rumpelstiltskin
Shining, The

CLINT EASTWOOD
Any Which Way
 You Can
Beguiled, The
Bronco Billy
Coogan's Bluff
Dirty Harry
Eiger Sanction,
 The
Enforcer, The
Escape from
 Alcatraz
Every Which Way
 But Loose
Firefox
Fistful of Dollars,
 A
For a Few Dollars
 More
Gauntlet, The
Good, the Bad and
 the Ugly, The
Hang 'Em High
High Plains Drifter
Honkytonk Man

Joe Kidd
Kelly's Heroes
Magnum Force
Outlaw Josey
 Wales,
 The
Paint Your Wagon
Play Misty for Me
Sudden Impact
Thunderbolt and
 Lightfoot

**SAMANTHA
EGGAR**
Collector, The
Curtains
Demonoid
Doctor Doolittle
Exterminator, The
Light at the Edge
 of the World,
 The
Seven-Per-Cent
 Solution, The
Unknown Powers
Why Shoot the
 Teacher?

DUKE ELLINGTON
Black and Tan
Check and Double
 Check
Duke Ellington
 Story, The
Ella Fitzgerald in
 Concert
Goodyear Jazz
 Concert with
 Duke Ellington
Jazz and Jive
Sacred Music of
 Duke Ellington,
 The
Showtime at the
 Apollo
Timex All Star
 Jazz Show

**DOUGLAS
FAIRBANKS SR.**
Americano, The
Birth of a Legend
Black Pirate, The
Don Q., Son of
 Zorro
Iron Mask, The
Mark of Zorro, The
Matrimaniac, The
Mr. Robinson
 Crusoe
Mr. Super Athletic
 Charm
Private Life of Don
 Juan, The
Taming of the
 Shrew, The
Thief of Bagdad,
 The
Wild and Woolly

MIA FARROW
Avalanche
Death on the Nile
Great Gatsby, The
Hurricane
Haunting of Julia,
 The
Last Unicorn, The
Midsummer
 Night's Sex
 Comedy, A
Rosemary's Baby
Zelig

**FARRAH
FAWCETT**
Cannonball Run,
 The
Logan's Run
Murder in Texas
Saturn 3
Sunburn

SALLY FIELD
Absence of Malice
Back Roads

End, The
Hooper
Kiss Me Goodbye
Norma Rae
Smokey and the
  Bandit
Smokey and the
  Bandit II
Sybil

W.C. FIELDS
Bank Dick, The
Barber Shop, The
Dentist, The
Fatal Glass of
  Beer,
  The
Funny Guys and
  Gals of the
  Talkies
My Little
  Chickadee
Outtakes VI
Pharmacist, The
Sally of the
  Sawdust
W.C. Fields
  Festival

ALBERT FINNEY
Annie
Duellists, The
Looker
Loophole
Murder on the
  Orient Express
Shoot the Moon
Tom Jones
Wolfen

CARRIE FISHER
Making of Star
  Wars,
  The/S.P.F.X.
  —The Empire
  Strikes Back
Mr. Mike's Mondo
  Video

Saturday Night
  Live: Carrie
  Fisher
Star Wars
Under the Rainbow

ERROL FLYNN
Adventures of
  Robin Hood, The
Big Breakdowns,
  The
Big Surprise, The
Captain Blood
Charge of the
  Light Brigade,
  The
Dodge City
Gentleman Jim
Prince and the
  Pauper, The
Sante Fe Trail
Son of Hollywood
  Bloopers

HENRY FONDA
Battle of the
  Bulge, The
Boston Strangler,
  The
Fail Safe
Fort Apache
Gideon's Trumpet
Grapes of Wrath,
  The
Great Smokey
  Roadblock, The
I Dream Too Much
Jezebel
Longest Day, The
Meteor
Midway
Mister Roberts
Oldest Living
  Graduate, The
On Golden Pond
Perry Como Show,
  The

Sometimes a
  Great Notion
Stagestruck
Summer Solstice
Swarm, The
Tentacles
Too Late the Hero
Twelve Angry Men
Wings of the
  Morning
You Only Live
  Once

JANE FONDA
Barbarella
Barefoot in the
  Park
California Suite
Cat Ballou
China Syndrome,
  The
Comes a
  Horseman
Coming Home
Doll's House, A
Electric Horseman,
  The
Fun with Dick and
  Jane
Jane Fonda's
  Workout
Jane Fonda's
  Workout for
  Pregnancy, Birth
  and Recovery
Julia
Klute
9 to 5
On Golden Pond
Rollover

PETER FONDA
Cannonball Run,
  The
Easy Rider
Futureworld
High Ballin'
Hostage Tower,

The
Jungle Heat
Killer Force
Spasms
Split Image
Trip, The

JOAN FONTAINE
Damsel in Distress
Decameron Nights
Gunga Din
Ivanhoe
Rebecca
Suspicion

GLENN FORD
Big Heat, The
Gilda
Happy Birthday to
  Me
Midway
Sacketts, The
Superman—The
  Movie
White Tower, The

HARRISON FORD
American Graffiti
Apocalypse Now
Blade Runner
Conversation, The
Force 10 from
  Navarone
Frisco Kid, The
Great Movie Stunts
  and The Making
  of Raiders of the
  Lost Ark
Hanover Street
Making of Star
  Wars, The/
  S.P.F.X.—
  The Empire
  Strikes Back
Raiders of the
  Lost Ark
Star Wars

JOHN FORD
Fort Apache
Grapes of Wrath,
  The
Horse Soldiers,
  The
Informer, The
Man Who Shot
  Liberty Valance,
  The
Mary of Scotland
Mister Roberts
Mogambo
Quiet Man, The
Searchers, The
She Wore a Yellow
  Ribbon
Stagecoach
Straight Shootin'
This Is Korea/
  December 7th
Wagonmaster

JODIE FOSTER
Alice Doesn't Live
  Here Anymore
Candleshoe
Carny
Freaky Friday
Hotel New
  Hampshire, The
Little Girl Who
  Lives Down the
  Lane,
  The
O'Hara's Wife
Taxi Driver

CLARK GABLE
Misfits, The
Mogambo
Mutiny on the
  Bounty
Painted Desert,
  The
Premiere of "A
  Star Is Born"

Run Silent, Run
  Deep
That's
  Entertainment
That's
  Entertainment,
  Part II

AVA GARDNER
Barefoot
  Contessa,
  The
Bible, The
Cassandra
  Crossing, The
Earthquake
55 Days at Peking
Ghosts on the
  Loose
Mogambo
My Forbidden Past
Night of the
  Iguana, The
On the Beach
One Touch of
  Venus
Seven Days in May
Show Boat
That's
  Entertainment
Whistle Stop

JUDY GARLAND
Coming
  Attractions
Hollywood
  Outtakes and
  Rare Footage
Hollywood Palace,
  The
Judgment at
  Nuremburg
Judy and Her
  Guests
Judy Garland
  Christmas Show
Judy Garland
  Show, The

Judy, Judy, Judy
Meet Me in St.
   Louis
Pirate, The
Premiere of "A
   Star Is Born"
That's
   Entertainment
That's
   Entertainment,
   Part II
Till the Clouds
   Roll By
Wizard of Oz, The
World War II Video
   Series—
   Something for
   the Boys
Ziegfeld Follies

JAMES GARNER
Castaway Cowboy
Great Escape, The
Fan, The
Sayonara
Victor/Victoria

TERI GARR
Black Stallion
   Returns, The
Do It Debbie's Way
Mr. Mom
Prime Suspect
Tale of the Frog
   Prince, The
Tootsie
Young
   Frankenstein

RICHARD GERE
American Gigolo
Beyond the Limit
Bloodbrothers
Breathless
Days of Heaven
Looking for Mr.
   Goodbar
Officer and a

Gentleman, An

MEL GIBSON
Attack Force Z
Gallipoli
Mad Max
Road Warrior, The
Tim
Year of Living
   Dangerously,
   The

LILLIAN GISH
Battle of
   Elderbush
   Gulch, The
Birth of a Nation
Broken Blossoms
Follow Me, Boys!
Home Sweet
   Home
Intolerance
Orphans of the
   Storm
True Heart Susie
Way Down East

JACKIE GLEASON
Cavalcade of Stars
Mr. Halpern and
   Mr. Johnson
Smokey and the
   Bandit I–III
Sting II, The
Toy, The
Vintage Sitcoms

RUTH GORDON
Abe Lincoln in
   Illinois
Any Which Way
   You Can
Every Which Way
   But Loose
Harold and Maude
Jimmy the Kid
My Bodyguard
Rosemary's Baby

Where's Poppa?

ELLIOT GOULD
Bob & Carol & Ted
   & Alice
Bridge Too Far, A
Capricorn One
Devil and Max
   Devlin, The
Dirty Tricks
Escape to Athena
Falling in Love
   Again
Harry and Walter
   Go to New York
Jack and the
   Beanstalk
Last Flight of
   Noah's Ark, The
M*A*S*H
Matilda
Mean Johnny
   Barrows
Muppet Movie, The

BETTY GRABLE
Bob Hope Chevy
   Show II, The
Day the Bookies
   Wept, The
Follow the Fleet
Gay Divorcee, The
Gotta Dance,
   Gotta Sing
Hollywood Goes to
   War
How to Marry a
   Millionaire
Love Goddesses,
   The

CARY GRANT
Arsenic and Old
   Lace
Bachelor and the
   Bobby Soxer,
   The
Charade

Father Goose
Grass Is Greener,
  The
Gunga Din
His Girl Friday
In Name Only
Indiscreet
Mr. Blandings
  Builds His
  Dream House
Mr. Lucky
My Favorite Wife
None But the
  Lonely Heart
North by
  Northwest
Notorious
Once Upon a
  Honeymoon
Operation
  Petticoat
Penny Serenade
Philadelphia Story,
  The
Pride and the
  Passion, The
Suspicion
That Touch of
  Mink
To Catch a Thief
Toast of New York
Topper

D.W. GRIFFITH
Abraham Lincoln
Avenging
  Conscience, The
Babylon Story from
  "Intolerance,"
  The
Battle of
  Elderbush
  Gulch, The
Birth of a Nation
Broken Blossoms
Dream Street
D.W. Griffith: An
  American
Genius
Film Firsts
Home Sweet
  Home
Intolerance
Movies' Story, The
Orphans of the
  Storm
Short Films of
  D.W. Griffith,
  Vol. I, The
True Heart Susie
Way Down East

**CHARLES
GRODIN**
All Night Long
Great Muppet
  Caper, The
Heartbreak Kid,
  The
Heaven Can Wait
It's My Turn
King Kong
Paul Simon
  Special, The
Rosemary's Baby
Seems Like Old
  Times
Sunburn

ALEC GUINNESS
Bridge on the
  River Kwai, The
Brother Sun, Sister
  Moon
Captain's
  Paradise, The
Fall of the Roman
  Empire, The
Kind Hearts and
  Coronets
Ladykillers, The
Lavender Hill Mob,
  The
Lawrence of
  Arabia
Little Lord
Fauntleroy
Lovesick
Making of Star
  Wars, The
Malta Story, The
Man in the White
  Suit, The
Murder by Death
Star Wars
To See Such Fun

GENE HACKMAN
All Night Long
America at the
  Movies
Bite the Bullet
Bonnie and Clyde
Bridge Too Far, A
Conversation, The
Domino Principle,
  The
Downhill Racer
French
  Connection, The
Hawaii
Marooned
Night Moves
Poseidon
  Adventure, The
Scarecrow
Superman—The
  Movie
Superman II
Uncommon Valor
Under Fire

**GEORGE
HAMILTON**
Evel Knievel
Happy Hooker
  Goes to
  Washington, The
Love at First Bite
Once Is Not
  Enough
Zorro, the Gay
  Blade

JEAN HARLOW
Love Goddesses,
The
That's
Entertainment

RICHARD HARRIS
Camelot
Golden
Rendezvous
Hawaii
Last Word, The
Major Dundee
Mutiny on the
Bounty
Return of a Man
Called Horse,
The
Robin and Marian
Tarzan, the Ape
Man
Triumphs of a Man
Called Horse
Wild Geese, The
Your Ticket Is No
Longer Valid

GOLDIE HAWN
Best Friends
Bloopers from
"Star Trek" and
"Laugh-In"
Cactus Flower
Duchess and the
Dirtwater Fox,
The
Foul Play
Lovers and Liars
Outtakes I
Private Benjamin
Seems Like Old
Times
Sugarland
Express,
The
Swing Shift
There's a Girl in
My Soup

HELEN HAYES
Airport
Candleshoe
Farewell to Arms,
A
Herbie Rides
Again
Stagedoor
Canteen

RITA HAYWORTH
Circus World
Gilda
Love Goddesses,
The
Miss Sadie
Thompson
Poppies Are Also
Flowers
Separate Tables
They Came to
Cordura
Trouble in Texas
You'll Never Get
Rich

**AUDREY
HEPBURN**
Breakfast at
Tiffany's
Charade
Lavender Hill Mob,
The
My Fair Lady
Robin and Marian
Roman Holiday
Sidney Sheldon's
Bloodline
They All Laughed
27th Annual
Academy
Awards
Wait Until Dark

**KATHARINE
HEPBURN**
Adam's Rib
African Queen, The

Alice Adams
Lion in Winter, The
Little Women
Long Day's
Journey Into
Night
Mary of Scotland
Morning Glory
On Golden Pond
Philadelphia Story,
The
Rooster Cogburn
Stage Door
Stagedoor
Canteen
State of the Union
Suddenly, Last
Summer
Trojan Woman,
The
Woman of the
Year
Woman Rebels, A

**CHARLTON
HESTON**
Awakening, The
Ben Hur
Call of the Wild
Earthquake
El Cid
Elizabeth the
Queen
55 Days at Peking
Four Musketeers,
The
Greatest Show on
Earth, The
Greatest Story
Ever Told, The
Major Dundee
Midway
Mother Lode
Mountain Men,
The
Planet of the Apes
Ruby Gentry
Son of Monsters

on the March
Soylent Green
Ten
 Commandments,
 The
Three Musketeers,
 The

**ALFRED
HITCHCOCK**
Birds, The
Blackmail
Family Plot
Frenzy
Lady Vanishes,
 The
Lodger, The
Man Who Knew
 Too Much, The
Mr. and Mrs. Smith
Murder
North by
 Northwest
Notorious
Number Seventeen
Psycho
Rear Window
Rebecca
Sabotage
Secret Agent
Spellbound
Strangers on a
 Train
Suspicion
Thirty-Nine Steps,
 The
To Catch a Thief
Torn Curtain
Under Capricorn
Vertigo
Wrong Man, The
Young and
 Innocent

**DUSTIN
HOFFMAN**
Agatha

All the President's
 Men
Graduate, The
Kramer vs. Kramer
Marathon Man
Midnight Cowboy
Papillon
Straight Time
Straw Dogs

WILLIAM HOLDEN
Alvarez Kelly
Born Yesterday
Bridge on the
 River Kwai, The
Christmas Tree,
 The
Country Girl, The
Damien—Omen II
Earthling, The
Golden Boy
Horse Soldiers,
 The
Moon Is Blue, The
Network
Our Town
Rachel and the
 Stranger
S.O.B.
Stalag 17
Sunset Boulevard
Towering Inferno,
 The
27th Annual
 Academy
 Awards
Wild Bunch, The
Young and Willing

JUDY HOLLIDAY
Adam's Rib
Bells Are Ringing
Born Yesterday
It Should Happen
 to You

BOB HOPE
Big Crosby Show,

The
Bloopers from
 "Star Trek" and
 "Laugh-In"
Bob Hope Chevy
 Show
Bob Hope Chevy
 Show I-II, The
Bobby Darin and
 Friends
Hollywood at War
Hollywood Goes to
 War
Jack Benny
Jack Benny Show,
 The
Jack Benny Visits
 Walt Disney
Muppet Movie, The
My Favorite
 Brunette
Paris Holiday
Road to Bali, The
Television's
 Golden Age of
 Comedy
27th Annual
 Academy
 Awards
World War II Video
 Series—
 Something for
 Our Boys

LESLIE HOWARD
Big Breakdowns,
 The
Forty-Ninth
 Parallel, The
Intermezzo
Of Human
 Bondage
Petrified Forest,
 The
Pimpernel Smith
Scarlet Pimpernel,
 The
Spitfire

Stand-In

WILLIAM HURT
Altered States
Big Chill, The
Body Heat
Eyewitness
Gorky Park

JOHN HUSTON
African Queen,
    The
Angela
Annie
Bible, The
Breakout
Chinatown
Great Cities:
    London, Rome,
    Dublin, Athens
Hobbit, The
Let There Be Light
Lovesick
Maltese Falcon,
    The
Minor Miracle, A
Misfits, The
Moby Dick
Tentacles
Treasure of the
    Sierra Madre, The
Winter Kills

LAUREN HUTTON
American Gigolo
Gambler, The
Gator
Lassiter
Zorro, the Gay
    Blade

TIMOTHY HUTTON
Ordinary People
Taps

AMY IRVING
Carrie
Competition, The

Fury, The
Honeysuckle Rose

AL JOLSON
Coming
    Attractions
Jazz Singer, The
Musical
    Personalities
    No. 1
Weber and Fields,
    Al Jolson and
    This Is America

JENNIFER JONES
Dick Tracy's
    G-Men
Indiscretion of an
    American Wife
Madame Bovary
Towering Inferno,
    The

**TOMMY LEE
JONES**
Amazing Howard
    Hughes, The
Back Roads
Betsy, The
Coal Miner's
    Daughter
Eyes of Laura
    Mars
Jackson County
    Jail
Nate and Hayes
Rolling Thunder

MADELINE KAHN
At Long Last Love
Blazing Saddles
First Family
Hideaways, The
High Anxiety
History of the
    World: Part I,
    The
Muppet Movie, The

Paper Moon
Scrambled Feet
Simon
Slapstick of
    Another Kind
What's Up Doc?
Wholly Moses!
Yellowbeard
Young
    Frankenstein

BORIS KARLOFF
Abbott and
    Costello Meet
    Dr. Jekyll and
    Mr. Hyde
Bedlam
Bells, The
Big Breakdowns,
    The
Black Cat, The/The
    Raven
Blind Man's Bluff
Body Snatcher,
    The
Daydreamer, The
Frankenstein
Haunted Strangler,
    The
Juggernaut
Lost Patrol, The
Mr. Wong,
    Detective
Monsters on the
    March
Outtakes VI
Raven, The
Scarface
Tales of Tomorrow
Terror, The
You'll Find Out

BUSTER KEATON
Balloonatic,
    The/One Week
Blacksmith, The
Buster Keaton
    Rides

Again/The
Railrodder
College
Ed Wynn Show,
The
Fun Factory/Clown
Princes of
Hollywood
Funny Thing
Happened on
the Way to the
Forum, A
General, The
Hollywood Palace,
The
How to Stuff a
Wild Bikini
It's a Mad, Mad,
Mad, Mad World
Keaton Special/
Valentino
Mystique
L'il Abner
Limelight
Parlour, Bedroom
and Bath
Silent Laugh
Makers
Steamboat Bill, Jr.
Sunset Boulevard

DIANE KEATON
Annie Hall
Godfather, The
Godfather Part
II, The
Godfather: The
Complete Epic,
The
Harry and Walter
Go to New York
Looking for Mr.
Goodbar
Love and Death
Lovers and Other
Strangers
Play It Again, Sam
Reds

Shoot the Moon
Sleeper

GENE KELLY
American in Paris,
An
Brigadoon
Forty Carats
Hello, Dolly!
Hollywood Palace,
The
Inherit the Wind
Invitation to the
Dance
Jack and the
Beanstalk
On the Town
Pirate, The
Singin' in the Rain
That's
Entertainment
That's
Entertainment,
Part II
Xanadu
Ziegfeld Follies

GRACE KELLY
Country Girl, The
Dial M for Murder
Fabulous Fifties,
The
High Noon
Mogambo
Rear Window
To Catch a Thief
27th Annual
Academy
Awards

DEBORAH KERR
America at the
Movies
Grass Is Greener,
The
King and I, The
Night of the
Iguana, The

Prisoner of Zenda,
The
Separate Tables
TV's Classic
Guessing
Games

MARGOT KIDDER
Amityville Horror,
The
Heartaches
Making of
Superman I and
II, The
Mr. Mike's Mondo
Video
Quackser Fortune
Has a Cousin in
the Bronx
Shoot the Sun
Down
Sisters
Some Kind of Hero
Superman—The
Movie
Superman II
Superman III
Trenchcoat

**NASTASSIA
KINSKI**
Boarding School
Exposed
For Your Love
Only
Hotel New
Hampshire, The
Tess
Unfaithfully Yours

ERNIE KOVACS
Bell, Book and
Candle
Ernie Kovacs:
Television's
Original Genius
Game Show
Program II

Kovacs on the
  Corner
Take a Good Look/
  The Jack Benny
  Show
Take a Good Look
  with Ernie
  Kovacs
Vintage
  Commercials, II

**KRIS
KRISTOFFERSON**
Alice Doesn't Live
  Here Anymore
Blume in Love
Celebration, A
Convoy
Heaven's Gate
Other Side of
  Nashville, The
Pat Garrett and
  Billy the Kid
Rollover
Sailor Who Fell
  from Grace
  with the Sea,
  The
Semi-Tough
Star Is Born, A

**STANLEY
KUBRICK**
Clockwork Orange,
  A
Dr. Strangelove
Lolita
Paths of Glory
Shining, The
2001: A Space
  Odyssey

ALAN LADD
Boy on a Dolphin
Captain Caution
Deep Six, The
Drum Beat
Hell on Frisco Bay

Joan of Paris
My Favorite
  Brunette
Premiere of "A
  Star Is Born"
Proud Rebel, The
Shane
This Gun for Hire

BURT LANCASTER
Airport
America at the
  Movies
Apache
Atlantic City
Bird Man of
  Alcatraz, The
Elmer Gantry
Executive Action
Go Tell the
  Spartans
Gunfight at the
  O.K. Corral
Island of Dr.
  Moreau, The
Judgment at
  Nuremburg
Kentuckian, The
Moses
Osterman
  Weekend, The
Professionals, The
Run Silent, Run
  Deep
Separate Tables
Seven Days in May
Trapeze
Vera Cruz

JESSICA LANGE
All that Jazz
Frances
How to Beat the
  High Cost of
  Living
King Kong

**CHARLES
LAUGHTON**
Abbott and
  Costello
  Meet Captain
  Kidd
Arch of Triumph
Beachcomber, The
Captain Kidd
Early Elvis
Hobson's Choice
Hunchback of
  Notre Dame, The
Mutiny on the
  Bounty
Private Life of
  Henry VIII, The
Sidewalks of
  London
Tuttles of Tahiti,
  The
Witness for the
  Prosecution

**LAUREL AND
HARDY**
Atoll K (Utopia)
Blockheads
Bohemian Girl,
  The
Chump at Oxford,
  A
Flying Deuces, The
Fun Factory/Clown
  Princes of
  Hollywood
Hal Roach
  Comedy
  Classics
Laurel and Hardy
  Comedy
  Classics
  Volumes I–IX
Live Television
Movie Struck
Our Relations
Pack Up Your
  Troubles

Pardon Us
Saps at Sea
Silent Laugh
  Makers
Sons of the Desert
Swiss Miss
That's
  Entertainment,
  Part II
This Is Your Life:
  Laurel and
  Hardy
Way Out West

BRUCE LEE
Chinese
  Connection,
  The
Enter the Dragon
Fist of Fear, Touch
  of Death
Fists of Fury
Game of Death,
  The
Real Bruce Lee,
  The
Return of the
  Dragon
True Game of
  Death, The

**CHRISTOPHER
LEE**
Albino
Boy Who Left
  Home to Find
  Out About the
  Shivers, The
Circle of Iron
Dark Places
Devil's Undead,
  The
Dracula and Son
End of the World
Eye for an Eye, An
Horror Express
Horror Hotel
Keeper, The

Last Unicorn, The
Longest Day, The
Man with the
  Golden Gun, The
Meatcleaver
  Massacre
1941
Scars of Dracula
Serial
Son of Monsters
  on the March
Tale of Two Cities,
  A
Theatre of Death
Three Musketeers,
  The
Wicker Man, The

JANET LEIGH
Bye Bye Birdie
Premiere of "A
  Star Is Born"
Psycho
Two Tickets to
  Broadway

VIVIEN LEIGH
Fire Over England
Hollywood
Outtakes and Rare
  Footage
Sidewalks of
  London
Streetcar Named
  Desire, A

JACK LEMMON
Apartment, The
Bell, Book and
  Candle
Buddy Buddy
China Syndrome,
  The
Days of Wine and
  Roses, The
Ernie Kovacs:
  Television's
  Original Genius

Great Race, the
Irma La Douce
It Should Happen
  to You
Kotch
Luv
Missing
Mister Roberts
Odd Couple, The
Out-of-Towners,
  The
Prisoner of Second
  Avenue, The
Save the Tiger
Some Like It Hot
Tribute

JERRY LEWIS
At War with the
  Army
Colgate Comedy
  Hour, The
Cracking Up
Dean Martin and
  Jerry Lewis
  Television Party
Don't Raise the
  Bridge, Lower
  the River
It's a Mad, Mad,
  Mad, Mad World
Jack Benny
Jack Benny Show,
  The
Jerry Lewis Show,
  The
King of Comedy
Nutty Professor,
  The
Rascal Dazzle
Road to Bali, The
Slapstick of
  Another Kind
Television's
  Golden Age of
  Comedy
Tonight Show, The
  27th Annual

Academy
Awards

HAROLD LLOYD
Don't Shove/Two
Gun Gussie
Fun Factory/Clown
Princes of
Hollywood
Funstuff
Harold Lloyd's
Comedy
Classics
His Royal Slyness/
Haunted Spooks
Kings, Queens,
Jokers
Silent Laugh
Makers #3
Sin of Harold
Diddlebock, The
This Is Your Life

**CAROLE
LOMBARD**
Hollywood
Outtakes and
Rare Footage
In Name Only
Made for Each
Other
My Man Godfrey
Mr. and Mrs. Smith
Nothing Sacred
Racketeer
Swing High, Swing
Low
These Girls Won't
Talk
To Be or Not to Be

SOPHIA LOREN
Aida
Angela
Blood Feud
Chase, The
El Cid
Fall of the Roman

Empire, The
Favorita, La
Firepower
Man of La Mancha
Pride and the
Passion, The
Sophia Loren: Her
Own Story
Special Day, A

PETER LORRE
Algiers
Arsenic and Old
Lace
Casablanca
Collectors Item:
The Left Fist
of David
Coming
Attractions
M
Maltese Falcon,
The
Man Who Knew
Too Much, The
Mr. Moto's Last
Warning
Raven, The
Secret Agent
Silk Stockings
Stranger on the
Third Floor
Tales of Terror
20,000 Leagues
Under the Sea
You'll Find Out

MYRNA LOY
Bachelor and the
Bobby Soxer,
The
End, The
Just Tell Me What
You Want
Mr. Blandings
Builds His
Dream House
Red Pony, The

Summer Solstice

BELA LUGOSI
Bela Lugosi Meets
a Brooklyn
Gorilla
Black Cat, The/The
Raven
Body Snatcher,
The
Bowery at
Midnight
Bride of the
Monster
Chandu on the
Magic Island
Devil Bat, The
Dracula
Ghosts on the
Loose
Glen or Glenda
Hollywood on
Parade
Human Monster,
The
Invisible Ghost
Killer Bats
Monsters on the
March
Murder by
Television
Mystery of the
Mary Celeste,
The
One Body Too
Many
Outtakes VI
Plan Nine from
Outer Space
Scared to Death
S.O.S. Coastguard
Spooks Run Wild
White Zombie
You'll Find Out

**MALCOLM
MCDOWELL**
Blue Thunder

Britannia Hospital
Caligula
Cat People
Clockwork Orange,
  A
If...
Get Crazy
Little Red Riding
  Hood
Long Ago
  Tomorrow
Time After Time
Voyage of the
  Damned

ALI MACGRAW
Convoy
Getaway, The
Goodbye
  Columbus
Just Tell Me What
  You Want
Love Story
Players

**SHIRLEY
MACLAINE**
All in a Night's
  Work
Apartment, The
Around the World
  in 80 Days
Being There
Change of
  Seasons, A
Irma La Douce
Loving Couples
Terms of
  Endearment
Turning Point, The

**KRISTY
MCNICHOL**
End, The
Little Darlings
Only When I Laugh
Pirate Movie, The

STEVE MCQUEEN
Baby, the Rain
  Must Fall
Blob, The
Bullitt
Cincinnati Kid, The
Getaway, The
Great Escape, The
Hunter, The
Magnificent Seven,
  The
Papillon
Sand Pebbles, The
Thomas Crown
  Affair, The
Tom Horn
Towering Inferno,
  The

DEAN MARTIN
Airport
All in a Night's
  Work
At War with the
  Army
Bandolero
Bells Are Ringing
Cannonball Run,
  The
Colgate Comedy
  Hour, The
Dean Martin and
  Jerry Lewis
  Television Party
Hollywood Palace,
  The
Jack Benny Show,
  The
Murderer's Row
Ocean's 11
Premiere of "A
  Star Is Born"
Rio Bravo
Road to Bali, The
Sons of Katie
  Elder, The
Television's
  Golden Age of

Comedy

STEVE MARTIN
Dead Men Don't
  Wear Plaid
Funnier Side of
  Eastern Canada,
  The
Jerk, The
Kids Are Alright,
  The
Lonely Guy, The
Man with Two
  Brains, The
Pennies from
  Heaven
Saturday Night
  Live, Vol. II
Saturday Night
  Live: Steve
  Martin 2
Saturday Night
  Live with Steve
  Martin
Sgt. Pepper's
  Lonely Hearts
  Club Band

LEE MARVIN
Big Red One, The
Big Sleep, The
Cat Ballou
Death Hunt
Dirty Dozen, The
Donovan's Reef
Gorky Park
Great Scout and
  Cathouse
  Thursday, The
Killers, The
Man Who Shot
  Liberty Valance,
  The
Paint Your Wagon
Professionals, The
Shout at the Devil

THE MARX BROTHERS/ GROUCHO MARX
Animal Crackers
At the Circus
Copacabana
Day at the Races, A
Duck Soup
Funny Guys and Gals of the Talkies
Game Show Program
Girl in Every Port, A
Go West
Hollywood Goes to War
Hollywood Palace, The
Love Happy
NBC Comedy Hour
Night at the Opera, A
Night in Casablanca, A
Outtakes VI
Room Service
Stagedoor Canteen
Television's Golden Age of Comedy
That's Entertainment, Part II
TV Variety, II
Vintage Commercials
You Bet Your Life

JAMES MASON
Blue Max, The
Cross of Iron
Boys from Brazil, The
Dangerous

Summer, A
Desert Fox, The
Evil Under the Sun
Fall of the House of Usher, The
Fall of the Roman Empire, The
Fire Over England
Heaven Can Wait
High Command
Jesus of Nazareth
Last of Sheila, The
Lolita
Madame Bovary
Man in Grey, The
Mandingo
Night Has Eyes, The
North by Northwest
Prisoner of Zenda, The
Salem's Lot: The Movie
Sidney Sheldon's Bloodline
Star Is Born, A
Tiara Tahiti
20,000 Leagues Under the Sea
Verdict, The
Voyage of the Damned
Yellowbeard

MARSHA MASON
Audrey Rose
Blume in Love
Chapter Two
Goodbye Girl, The
Max Dugan Returns
Only When I Laugh
Promises in the Dark

WALTER MATTHAU

Bad News Bears, The
Buddy Buddy
Cactus Flower
California Suite
Casey's Shadow
Charade
Charley Varrick
Ensign Pulver
Fail Safe
First Monday in October
Hello, Dolly!
Hopscotch
House Calls
I Ought to Be in Pictures
Kentuckian, The
King Creole
Kotch
Little Miss Marker
Odd Couple, The
Plaza Suite
Sunburn
Sunshine Boys, The
Survivors, The
Taking of Pelham One Two Three, The

RAY MILLAND
Escape to Witch Mountain
Lost Weekend, The
Love Story
Man Alone, A
Slavers
X—The Man with X-Ray Eyes

ANN MILLER
Melody Ranch
On the Town
Room Service
Stage Door
That's Entertainment

That's
Entertainment,
Part II

HAYLEY MILLS
Deadly Strangers
In Search of the
Castaways
Parent Trap, The
Pollyanna

LIZA MINNELLI
Arthur
Cabaret
Evening with Liza
Minnelli, An
Journey Back to
Oz
Liza in Concert
Matter of Time, A
New York, New
York
That's
Entertainment

**VINCENTE
MINNELLI**
American in Paris,
An
Band Wagon, The
Bells Are Ringimg
Brigadoon
Gigi
Kismet
Madame Bovary
Matter of Time, A
Meet Me in St.
Louis
Pirate, The
Ziegfeld Follies

**ROBERT
MITCHUM**
Amsterdam Kill,
The
Big Sleep, The
Blood on the Moon
Breakthrough

Crossfire
El Dorado
Farewell, My
Lovely
Grass Is Greener,
The
Gung Ho
His Kind of
Woman
Locket, The
Longest Day, The
Lusty Men, The
Macao
Matilda
Midway
My Forbidden Past
Nightkill
Out of the Past
Rachel and the
Stranger
Racket, The
Red Pony, The
Second Chance
She Couldn't Say
No
That
Championship
Season

**MARILYN
MONROE**
All About Eve
Bus Stop
Clash by Night
Gentlemen Prefer
Blondes
Hollywood
Outtakes and
Rare Footage
How to Marry a
Millionaire
Love Goddesses,
The
Love Happy
Marilyn Monroe
Misfits, The
Seven Year Itch,
The

Some Like It Hot
There's No
Business Like
Show Business

MONTY PYTHON
All You Need Is
Cash *(Idle)*
And Now for
Something
Completely
Different
Great Muppet
Caper,
The *(Cleese)*
Jabberwocky
(Palin)
Missionary, The
(Palin)
Monty Python and
the Holy Grail
Monty Python's
Life of Brian
Monty Python's
The Meaning of
Life
Odd Job, The
(Chapman)
Pied Piper of
Hamelin,
The *(Idle)*
Secret
Policeman's
Other Ball, The
*(Cleese,
Chapman, Palin,
Jones)*
Tale of the Frog
Prince, The *(Idle)*
Time Bandits
*(Cleese, Palin,
Gilliam)*
To See Such Fun
(Idle)
Whoops
Apocalypse
(Cleese)
Yellowbeard

(Chapman,
Cleese)

DUDLEY MOORE
Alice's Adventures
in Wonderland
Arthur
Bedazzled
Derek and Clive
Get the Horn
Foul Play
Lovesick
Playboy Video,
Volume II
Romantic Comedy
Six Weeks
"10"
30 Is a Dangerous
Age, Cynthia
Unfaithfully Yours
Wholly Moses!

**MARY TYLER
MOORE**
Change of Habit
Mary Tyler Moore
Show, Vol. I, The
Ordinary People
Outtakes III
Six Weeks
Vintage
Commercials

ROGER MOORE
Cannonball Run,
The
Escape to Athena
Fiction Makers,
The
For Your Eyes
Only
James Bond 007—
Coming
Attractions
Live and Let Die
Man Who Haunted
Himself, The
Man with the

Golden Gun, The
Octopussy
Sea Wolves, The
Shout at the Devil
Wild Geese, The

ZERO MOSTEL
Foreplay
Front, The
Funny Thing
Happened on
the Way to the
Forum, A
Hot Rock, The
Marco
Producers, The

BILL MURRAY
Caddyshack
Meatballs
Mr. Mike's Mondo
Video
Saturday Night
Live, Vol. II
Saturday Night
Live with Steve
Martin
Stripes
Where the Buffalo
Roam

PAUL NEWMAN
Absence of Malice
Buffalo Bill and
the Indians
Butch Cassidy and
the Sundance
Kid
Cat on a Hot Tin
Roof
Cool Hand Luke
Drowning Pool,
The
Exodus
Fort Apache, The
Bronx
Harper
Harry and Son

Hombre
Hud
Life and Times of
Judge Roy Bean,
The
Playwrights '56:
"The Battler"
Secret War of
Harry Frigg, The
Slapshot
Sometimes a
Great Notion
Sting, The
Torn Curtain
Towering Inferno,
The
Verdict, The
Winning
Young
Philadelphians,
The

JACK NICHOLSON
Black Cat, The/The
Raven
Border, The
Carnal Knowledge
Chinatown
Easy Rider
Goin' South
Last Detail, The
Little Shop of
Horrors, The
Missouri Breaks,
The
On a Clear Day
You Can See
Forever
One Flew Over the
Cuckoo's Nest
Postman Always
Rings Twice,
The
Raven, The
Rebel Rousers
Reds
Ride in the
Whirlwind

Shining, The
Shooting, The
Terms of
    Endearment
Terror, The
Wild Ride, The

DAVID NIVEN
Around the World
    in 80 Days
Bachelor Mother
Candleshoe
Charge of the
    Light Brigade,
    The
Curse of the Pink
    Panther, The
Death on the Nile
Dinner at the Ritz
Escape to Athena
Eternally Yours
55 Days at Peking
Guns of Navarone,
    The
Immortal Battalion
King, Queen,
    Knave
Moon Is Blue, The
Murder by Death
Pink Panther, The
Rough Cut
Sea Wolves
Separate Tables
Spitfire
Stairway to
    Heaven
Survival Anglia's
    World of
    Wildlife, Vol. 2
Trail of the Pink
    Panther, The

NICK NOLTE
Cannery Row
Deep, The
48 Hrs.
Heartbeat
North Dallas Forty

Return to Macon
    County
Runaway Barge
Under Fire
Who'll Stop the
    Rain

KIM NOVAK
Bell, Book and
    Candle
Mirror Crack'd, The
Premiere of "A
    Star Is Born"
Vertigo

**MAUREEN
O'HARA**
At Sword's Point
Big Jake
Hunchback of
    Notre Dame, The
Magnificent
    Matador
Miracle on 34th
    Steet
Parent Trap, The
Quiet Man, The
Rio Grande
Sinbad the Sailor

**LAURENCE
OLIVIER**
As You Like It
Betsy, The
Boys from Brazil,
    The
Bridge Too Far, A
Clash of the Titans
Dracula
Fire Over England
Forty-Ninth
    Parallel, The
Hamlet
Henry V
I Stand
    Condemned
Jesus of Nazareth
Little Romance, A

Marathon Man
Mr. Halpern and
    Mr. Johnson
Nicholas and
    Alexandra
Pride and
    Prejudice
Rebecca
Romeo and Juliet
Seven-Per-Cent
    Solution, The
Sleuth
World at War, The

RYAN O'NEAL
Barry Lyndon
Bridge Too Far, A
Love Story
Main Event, The
Paper Moon
Partners
So Fine
What's Up Doc?

TATUM O'NEAL
Bad News Bears,
    The
Circle of Two
Goldilocks and the
    Three Bears
International
    Velvet
Little Darlings
Paper Moon

PETER O'TOOLE
Becket
Bible, The
Caligula
Kidnapped
Lawrence of
    Arabia
Lion in Winter, The
Man of La Mancha
Masada
My Favorite Year
Power Play
Ruling Class, The

Sherlock Holmes
  and the
  Baskerville
  Curse
Stunt Man, The
What's New
  Pussycat?

AL PACINO
America at the
  Movies. . .
And
  Justice for All
Author! Author!
Bobby Deerfield
Cruising
Dog Day Afternoon
Godfather, The
Godfather Part II,
Godfather: The
  Complete Epic,
  The
Scarecrow
Scarface
Serpico

DOLLY PARTON
Best Little
  Whorehouse in
  Texas, The
Dolly in London
9 to 5

GREGORY PECK
Behold a Pale
  Horse
Boys from Brazil,
  The
Guns of Navarone,
  The
MacArthur
Marooned
Moby Dick
Omen, The
On the Beach
Roman Holiday
Sea Wolves
Spellbound

740

Twelve O'Clock
  High

**ANTHONY
PERKINS**
Black Hole, The
Catch-22
Mahogany
Murder on the
  Orient Express
On the Beach
Psycho
Psycho II
Trail, The
Winter Kills

**BERNADETTE
PETERS**
Annie
Heartbeeps
Jerk, The
Martian
  Chronicles,
  Part II
Pennies from
  Heaven
Sleeping Beauty
Tulips

MARY PICKFORD
Birth of a Legend,
  The
Hollywood on
  Parade
Little Annie
  Rooney
My Best Girl
Pollyanna
Poor Little Rich
  Girl
Rebecca of
  Sunnybrook
  Farm
Short Films of
  D.W. Griffith,
  The
Sparrows
Taming of the

Shrew, The

SIDNEY POITIER
Bedford Incident,
  The
Buck and the
  Preacher
Defiant Ones, The
For Love of Ivy
Greatest Story
  Ever Told, The
In the Heat of the
  Night
Let's Do It Again
Raisin in the Sun,
  A
Stir Crazy
They Call Me Mr.
  Tibbs!
To Sir, with Love
Uptown Saturday
  Night

DICK POWELL
Big Breakdowns,
  The
Coming
  Attractions
Conqueror, The
42nd Street
Gold Diggers of
  1933
Jack Benny, II
Murder My Sweet
Musical
  Personalities
  No. 1
Susan Slept Here

TYRONE POWER
Witness for the
  Prosecution

ELVIS PRESLEY
Blue Hawaii
Change of Habit
Coming
  Attractions

Early Elvis
Easy Come, Easy
    Go
Elvis Comeback
    Special
Elvis in Concert in
    Hawaii
Elvis in Concert
    in 1968
Elvis Live in '56
Elvis on Television
Elvis on Tour
Flaming Star
Fun in Acapulco
G.I. Blues
Girls, Girls, Girls
Jailhouse Rock
King Creole
Love Me Tender
Loving You
Paradise Hawaiian
    Style
Roustabout
Singer Presents
    "Elvis"
Stage Show
Viva Las Vegas
Wild in the
    Country

VINCENT PRICE
Abbott and
    Costello Meet
    Frankenstein
Abominable Dr.
    Phibes, The
Alice Cooper:
    Welcome to My
    Nightmare
Black Cat, The/The
    Raven
Boy Who Left
    Home to Find
    Out About the
    Shivers, The
Champagne for
    Caesar
Fall of the House

of Usher, The
Laura
Pit and the
    Pendulum, The
Raven, The
Ruddigore
Shock
Son of Sinbad
Tales of Terror
Ten
    Commandments,
    The

RICHARD PRYOR
Bingo Long
    Traveling
    All-Stars &
    Motor Kings,
    The
Blue Collar
Bustin' Loose
California Suite
Car Wash
Greased Lightning
Lady Sings the
    Blues
Muppet Movie, The
Outtakes II
Richard Pryor:
    Here and Now
Richard Pryor Live
    in Concert
Richard Pryor Live
    on the Sunset
    Strip
Saturday Night
    Live, Vol. II
Saturday Night
    Live with
    Richard Pryor
Silver Streak
Some Call It
    Loving
Some Kind of Hero
Stir Crazy
Superman III
Toy, The
Uptown Saturday

Night
Which Way Is Up?
Wholly Moses!
Wiz, The

BASIL RATHBONE
Adventures of
    Robin Hood, The
Captain Blood
Court Jester, The
Dressed to Kill
Last Days of
    Pompeii, The
Magic Sword, The
Make a Wish
Sherlock Holmes
    and the Secret
    Weapon
Sherlock Holmes
    Double Features
Tale of Two Cities,
    A
Tales of Terror
Terror by Night/
    Meeting at
    Midnight
Victoria Regina
We're No Angels
Wind in the
    Willows, The
Woman in Green,
    The

RONALD REAGAN
Bedtime for Bonzo
Dark Victory
Fight for the Sky,
    The
Hellcats of the
    Navy
Hollywood
    Outtakes and
    Rare Footage
Jack Benny, II
Killers, The
Outtakes II
Presidential
    Blooper Reel

Santa Fe Trail
Star Bloopers
Swingin' Singin'
  Years, The
Take 1: Rescued
  from the
  Editor's Floor
This Is the Army

**ROBERT
REDFORD**
All the President's
  Men
Barefoot in the
  Park
Bridge Too Far, A
Brubaker
Butch Cassidy and
  the Sundance
Candidate, The
Downhill Racer
Electric Horseman,
  The
Great Gatsby, The
Great Waldo
  Pepper, The
Hot Rock, The
Jeremiah Johnson
Ordinary People
Sting, The
Tell Them Willie
  Boy Is Here
Three Days of the
  Condor
Way We Were, The

**SIR MICHAEL
REDGRAVE**
Dam Busters, The
Dead of Night
Fame Is the Spur
Kipps
Lady Vanishes,
  The
Nicholas and
  Alexandra
Rime of the
  Ancient

Mariner
Stars Look Down,
  The

**VANESSA
REDGRAVE**
Agatha
Blow Up
Camelot
Julia
Man for All
  Seasons, A
Morgan—A
  Suitable Case
  for Treatment
Murder on the
  Orient Express
Trojan Woman,
  The

**CHRISTOPHER
REEVE**
Deathtrap
Making of
  Superman
  I and II
Monsignor
Sleeping Beauty
Somewhere in
  Time
Superman—The
  Movie
Superman II
Superman III

CARL REINER
Caesar's Hour
Dead Men Don't
  Wear Plaid
End, The
It's a Mad, Mad,
  Mad, Mad World
Jerk, The
Man with Two
  Brains, The
Oh, God!
Oh, God! Book II

Pinocchio
Russians Are
  Coming, The
Take a Good Look
  with Ernie
  Kovacs
Timex All-Star
  Comedy Show,
  The

BURT REYNOLDS
At Long Last Love
Best Friends
Best Little
  Whorehouse in
  Texas, The
Cannonball Run,
  The
Deliverance
End, The
Everything You
  Always Wanted
  to Know About
  Sex
Fuzz
Gator
Hooper
Hustle
Longest Yard, The
Man Who Loved
  Women, The
100 Rifles
Outtakes III
Paternity
Rough Cut
Semi-Tough
Shamus
Shark!
Sharkey's Machine
Smokey and the
  Bandit
Smokey and the
  Bandit II
Starting Over
Stroker Ace
White Lightning

EDWARD G. ROBINSON
Big Breakdowns,
    The
Breakdowns of
    1936 and 1937
Cincinnati Kid, The
Hell on Frisco Bay
Key Largo
Little Caesar
Premiere of "A
    Star Is Born"
Presidential
    Blooper Reel
Red House, The
Scarlet Street
Soylent Green
Stranger, The
Ten
    Commandments

GINGER ROGERS
Bachelor Mother
Carefree
Flying Down to Rio
Follow the Fleet
42nd Street
Gay Divorcee, The
Gold Diggers of
    1933
Gotta Dance,
    Gotta Sing
Hollywood on
    Parade
Kitty Foyle
Once Upon a
    Honeymoon
Shall We Dance
Stage Door
Story of Vernon
    and Irene
    Castle, The
Swing Time
That's
    Entertainment
Tom, Dick and
    Harry
Top Hat

Vivacious Lady

ROY ROGERS
Billy the Kid
    Returns
Colorado
Dark Command
Disney's American
    Heroes
Frontier Pony
    Express
Grand Canyon
    Trail
Heart of the
    Golden West
Jesse James at
    Bay
Milton Berle Show,
    The
My Pal Trigger
Old Corral, The
Roy Rogers and
    Dale Evans
    Show, The
Saga of Death
    Valley
Shine on
    Harvest Moon
Song of Nevada
Song of Texas
Sunset Serenade
Under California
    Stars
Western Double
    Feature #3, 4, 6,
    8, 10, 11, 15,
    17-25
Yellow Rose of
    Texas

MICKEY ROONEY
Adventures of
    Huckleberry
    Finn, The
Bill
Black Stallion, The
Breakfast at
    Tiffany's

Captains
    Courageous
Domino Principle,
    The
How to Stuff a
    Wild Bikini
It's a Mad, Mad,
    Mad, Mad World
Journey Back to
    Oz
Little Lord
    Fauntleroy
Love Laughs at
    Andy Hardy
Milton Berle Hour,
    The
Odyssey of the
    Pacific
Outtakes II, III
That's
    Entertainment
That's
    Entertainment,
    Part II
TV Variety

DIANA ROSS
Diana Ross in
    Concert
Free to Be . . . You
    and Me
Lady Sings the
    Blues
Mahogany
Wiz, The

KATHERINE ROSS
Betsy, The
Butch Cassidy and
    the Sundance
    Kid
Daddy's Deadly
    Darling
Final Countdown,
    The
Graduate, The
Murder in Texas
Shenandoah

Swarm, The
Tell Them Willie
    Boy Is Here
Voyage of the
    Damned
Wrong Is Right

JANE RUSSELL
French Line, The
Gentlemen Prefer
    Blondes
His Kind of
    Woman
Las Vegas Story,
    The
Macao
Outlaw, The
Road to Bali, The
Underwater

**SUSAN
SARANDON**
Atlantic City
Buddy System,
    The
Great Smokey
    Roadblock, The
Great Waldo
    Pepper, The
Hunger, The
Joe
King of the
    Gypsies
Pretty Baby
Tempest

JOHN SAVAGE
Deer Hunter, The
Inside Moves
Onion Field, The

ROY SCHEIDER
All That Jazz
Blue Thunder
French
    Connection, The
Jaws
Jaws II

Klute
Marathon Man
Still of the Night
Tiger Town

**MARTIN
SCORSESE**
Alice Doesn't Live
    Here Anymore
Boxcar Bertha
King of Comedy
Last Waltz, The
New York, New
    York
Raging Bull

**GEORGE C.
SCOTT**
Bible, The
Changeling, The
Dr. Strangelove
Formula, The
Hardcore
Hindenberg, The
Hospital, The
Islands in the
    Stream
Movie Movie
New Centurions,
    The
Patton
Savage Is Loose,
    The
Taps

**RANDOLPH
SCOTT**
Abilene Town
Captain Kidd
Follow the Fleet
Gung Ho
My Favorite Wife
Return of the Bad
    Men
Spoilers, The
Trail Street

GEORGE SEGAL
Black Bird, The
Blume in Love
Carbon Copy
Deadly Game, The
Duchess and the
    Dirtwater Fox,
    The
Fun with Dick and
    Jane
Hot Rock, The
Invitation to a
    Gunfighter
King Rat
Last Married
    Couple in
    America, The
Lost and Found
Owl and the
    Pussycat
Touch of Class, A
Where's Poppa?
Who's Afraid of
    Virginia Woolf?

PETER SELLERS
After the Fox
Alice's Adventures
    in Wonderland
America at the
    Movies
Battle of the
    Sexes, The
Being There
Bobo, The
Dr. Strangelove
Fiendish Plot of
    Dr. Fu Manchu,
    The
Great McGonagall,
    The
Heavens Above
I Love You, Alice
    B. Toklas
I'm All Right Jack
Ladykillers, The
Lolita

Magic Christian, The
Mouse That
    Roared, The
Murder by Death
Naked Truth, The
Never Let Go
Pink Panther, The
Pink Panther
    Strikes Again,
    The
Prisoner of Zenda,
    The
Return of the Pink
    Panther, The
Shot in the Dark, A
Stand Easy
There's a Girl in
    My Soup
To See Such Fun
Tom Thumb
Trail of the Pink
    Panther, The
Two-Way Stretch
What's New
    Pussycat?
Woman Times
    Seven

MARTIN SHEEN
Apocalypse Now
Badlands
Cassandra
    Crossing, The
Catch-22
Catholics
Dead Zone, The
Enigma
Final Countdown,
    The
Little Girl Who
    Lives Down the
    Lane, The
Loophole
Missiles of
    October, The
That
    Championship
    Season

BROOKE SHIELDS
Alice Sweet Alice
Blue Lagoon, The
Endless Love
King of the
    Gypsies
Pretty Baby
Tilt

TALIA SHIRE
Godfather, The
Godfather Part II,
    The
Godfather: The
    Complete Epic,
    The
Old Boyfriends
Prophecy
Rocky
Rocky II
Rocky III

FRANK SINATRA
Around the World
    in 80 Days
Bob Hope Chevy
    Show, II
Colgate Comedy
    Hour, The
Devil at 4 O'Clock,
    The
First Deadly Sin,
    The
Guys and Dolls
Higher and Higher
Hollywood Goes to
    War
Miracle of the
    Bells, The
Ocean's 11
On the Town
Pride and the
    Passion, The
Step Lively
That's
    Entertainment
That's
    Entertainment,

Part II
Till the Clouds
    Roll By
Von Ryan's
    Express
Young at Heart

SISSY SPACEK
Badlands
Carrie
Coal Miner's
    Daughter
Heartbeat
Missing
Raggedy Man
Welcome to L.A.

**STEVEN
SPIELBERG**
Close Encounters
    of the Third Kind
Duel
Jaws
1941
Poltergeist
Raiders of the
    Lost Ark
Sugarland
    Express, The

**SYLVESTER
STALLONE**
Bananas
Death Race 2000
First Blood
F.I.S.T.
Nighthawks
Rebel
Rocky
Rocky II
Rocky III
Victory

**BARBARA
STANWYCK**
Annie Oakley
Golden Boy
Lady of Burlesque

Maverick Queen,
    The
Meet John Doe
Roustabout
Strange Love of
    Martha Ivers,
    The

**MARY
STEENBURGEN**
Cross Creek
Goin' South
Little Red Riding
    Hood
Melvin and
    Howard
Midsummer
    Night's Sex
    Comedy, A
Old Boyfriends
Ragtime
Romantic Comedy
Time After Time

ROD STEIGER
Amityville Horror,
    The
Back from Eternity
Breakthrough
Chosen, The
Dr. Zhivago
F.I.S.T.
Goodyear TV
    Playhouse:
    "Marty"
Harder They Fall,
    The
In the Heat of the
    Night
Jesus of Nazareth
Lion of the Desert
Longest Day, The
Marty
Nazis, The
Oklahoma!
Pawnbroker, The
Run of the Arrow
Tales of Tomorrow

27th Annual
    Academy
    Awards
Wolf Lake

JAMES STEWART
Bandolero
Bell, Book and
    Candle
Big Sleep, The
Greatest Show on
    Earth, The
It's a Wonderful
    Life
Made for Each
    Other
Magic Town
Man Who Shot
    Liberty Valance,
    The
Mr. Smith Goes to
    Washington
Philadelphia Story,
    The
Pot O'Gold
Rear Window
Right of Way
Shenandoah
Shootist, The
Spirit of St. Louis,
    The
That's
    Entertainment
Vertigo
Vivacious Lady
War in the Sky

MERYL STREEP
Deer Hunter, The
French
    Lieutenant's
    Woman, The
Holocaust
Kramer vs. Kramer
Seduction of Joe
    Tynan, The
Silkwood
Sophie's Choice

Still of the Night

**BARBRA
STREISAND**
All Night Long
Coming
    Attractions
For Pete's Sake
Funny Girl
Hello, Dolly!
Main Event, The
On a Clear Day
    You Can See
    Forever
Owl and the
    Pussycat, The
Star Is Born, A
Up the Sandbox
Way We Were, The
What's Up Doc?

**DONALD
SUTHERLAND**
Animal House
Crackers
Day of the Locust
Disappearance,
    The
Don't Look Now
Eagle Has Landed,
    The
Eye of the Needle
Gas
Invasion of the
    Body Snatchers
Johnny Got His
    Gun
Kelly's Heroes
Kentucky Fried
    Movie
Klute
Lady Ice
M*A*S*H
Max Dugan
    Returns
Nothing Personal
Ordinary People
Threshold

**GLORIA
SWANSON**
Hash House
  Fraud, A/The
  Sultan's Wife
Hollywood Palace,
  The
Love Goddesses,
  The
Sunset Boulevard
Teddy at the
  Throttle

**ELIZABETH
TAYLOR**
Between Friends
Cat on a Hot
  Tin Roof
Cleopatra
Driver's Seat, The
Ivanhoe
James Dean: The
  First American
  Teenager
Life with Father
Little Night Music,
  A
Love Goddesses,
  The
Mirror Crack'd, The
Place in the Sun, A
Premiere of "A
  Star Is Born"
Suddenly, Last
  Summer
Taming of the
  Shrew, The
That's
  Entertainment
That's
  Entertainment,
  Part II
Who's Afraid of
  Virginia Woolf?
Winter Kills

SHIRLEY TEMPLE
Bachelor and the

Bobby Soxer,
  The
Comedy Festival
  #3
From Broadway to
  Hollywood
Funny Guys and
  Gals of the
  Talkies
Funstuff
Get Happy
Good Old Days
Gotta Dance,
  Gotta Sing
Heidi
Kid 'n' Hollywood
  & Polly Tix
  in Washington
Little Princess,
  The
Miss Annie
  Rooney
Musical
  Personalities,
  No. 1

**THE THREE
STOOGES**
Comedy Festival
  #1
It's a Mad, Mad,
  Mad, Mad World
Stooges Shorts
  Festival
Three Stooges,
  The
Three Stooges
  Festival, The
Three Stooges
  Meet Hercules,
  The
Three Stooges
  Videodisc, Vol. I,
  The
Three Stooges
  Vols. I-IX
Vintage
  Commercials II

GENE TIERNEY
Laura
Sundown

LILY TOMLIN
Incredible
  Shrinking
  Woman, The
Late Show, The
Nashville
9 to 5
Paul Simon
  Special, The

SPENCER TRACY
Adam's Rib
Captains
  Courageous
Devil at 4 O'Clock,
  The
Inherit the Wind
It's a Mad, Mad,
  Mad, Mad
  World
Judgment at
  Nuremburg
State of the Union
Woman of the
  Year

JOHN TRAVOLTA
Blow Out
Carrie
Grease
Saturday Night
  Fever
Staying Alive
Twist of Fate
Two of a Kind
Urban Cowboy

LIV ULLMAN
Bridge Too Far, A
Cries and
  Whispers
Forty Carats
Leonor
Persona

Richard's Things
Scenes from a
    Marriage

**RUDOLPH
VALENTINO**
Blood and Sand
Eagle, The
Keaton Special/
    Valentino
    Mystique
Roaring Twenties,
    The
Son of the Sheik
Tempest, The/The
    Eagle

DICK VAN DYKE
Bye Bye Birdie
Chitty Chitty Bang
    Bang
Country Girl, The
Mary Poppins
Outtakes I
Tubby the Tuba
Vintage
    Commercials

JON VOIGHT
Catch-22
Champ, The
Coming Home
Deliverance
Lookin' to Get Out
Midnight Cowboy
Table for Five

**ERIC VON
STROHEIM**
Blind Husbands
Foolish Wives
Grand Illusion
Great Gabbo, The
Lost Squadron
Sunset Boulevard

MAX VON SYDOW
Conan the

Barbarian
Death Watch
Exorcist, The
Exorcist II: The
    Heretic
Greatest Story
    Ever Told, The
Hawaii
Hurricane
Magician, The
Never Say Never
    Again
Night Visitor, The
Shame
Soldier's Tale, The
Three Days of the
    Condor
Wild Strawberries
Winter Light

**CHRISTOPHER
WALKEN**
Annie Hall
Brainstorm
Dead Zone, The
Deer Hunter, The
Heaven's Gate
Pennies from
    Heaven

JOHN WAYNE
Allegheny Uprising
America at the
    Movies
Angel and the
    Badman
Back to Bataan
Big Jake
Brannigan
Cahill: United
    States Marshal
Chisum
Circus World
Comancheros, The
Conqueror, The
Cowboys, The
Dark Command
Donovan's Reef

El Dorado
Fighting Seabees,
    The
Flying
    Leathernecks
Fort Apache
Green Berets, The
Hatari
Horse Soldiers,
    The
In Old California
John Wayne
    Double
    Features I-II
Lady for a Night
Lady from
    Louisiana, The
Lady Takes a
    Chance, The
Longest Day, The
Lucky Texan
Man from Utah,
    The
Man Who Shot
    Liberty Valance,
    The
McQ
Quiet Man, The
Red River
Rio Bravo
Rio Grande
Rio Lobo
Rooster Cogburn
Sands of Iwo Jima
Searchers, The
Shadow of the
    Eagle
She Wore a Yellow
    Ribbon
Shootist, The
Sons of Katie
    Elder, The
Spoilers, The
Stagecoach
Tall in the Saddle
Three Faces West
Three Musketeers,
    The

Train Robbers, The
True Grit
Tycoon
Wake of the Red
   Witch, The
War of the
   Wildcats
War Wagon, The
Western Double
   Feature #2
Wheel of Fortune

RAQUEL WELCH
Bandolero
Bedazzled
Bluebeard
Fantastic Voyage
Four Musketeers,
   The
Fuzz
Last of Sheila, The
Magic Christian,
   The
100 Rifles
Son of Monsters
   on the March
Three Musketeers,
   The
Wild Party, The

TUESDAY WELD
Author! Author!
Cincinnati Kid, The
Looking for Mr.
   Goodbar
Rock, Rock, Rock
Serial
Thief
Who'll Stop the
   Rain
Wild in the
   Country

ORSON WELLES
America at the
   Movies
Battle of Neretva
Black Magic

Bloopers from
   "Star Trek" and
   "Laugh-In"
Butterfly
Catch-22
Citizen Kane
Ferry to Hong
   Kong
Finest Hours, The
Greatest
   Adventure, The
Journey Into Fear
King's Story, A
Macbeth
Man for All
   Seasons, A
Moby Dick
Muppet Movie, The
Stranger, The
Third Man, The
Toast of the Town
Trial, The
Tut: The Boy King
Voyage of the
   Damned
Who's Out There?
Witching, The

MAE WEST
Love Goddesses,
   The
My Little
   Chickadee
Sextette

BILLY WILDER
Apartment, The
Irma La Douce
Lost Weekend, The
Seven Year Itch,
   The
Some Like It Hot
Stalag 17
Sunset Boulevard
Witness for the
   Prosecution

GENE WILDER
Blazing Saddles
Bonnie and Clyde
Everything You
   Always Wanted
   to Know About
   Sex
Frisco Kid, The
Hanky Panky
Little Prince, The
Producers, The
Quackser Fortune
   Has a Cousin in
   the Bronx
Silver Streak
Stir Crazy
Young
   Frankenstein

ROBIN WILLIAMS
Can I Do It . . . Till
   I Need Glasses?
Comedy Tonight
Evening with
   Robin Williams,
   An
Popeye
Survivors, The
Tale of the Frog
   Prince, The
World According
   to Garp, The

**SHELLEY
WINTERS**
Bloody Mama
Blume in Love
Diary of Anne
   Frank, The
Double Life, A
Elvis
King of the
   Gypsies
Lolita
Place in the Sun, A
Poseidon
   Adventure, The

Premiere of "A
    Star Is Born"
Shattered
S.O.B.
Tenant, The
Tentacles

NATALIE WOOD
Bob & Carol & Ted
    & Alice
Bob Hope Chevy
    Show II, The
Brainstorm
Candidate, The
Great Race, The
Gypsy
I'm a Stranger
    Here Myself

James Dean: The
    First American
    Teenager
Last Married
    Couple in
    America, The
Meteor
Miracle on 34th
    Street
Rebel Without a
    Cause
Searchers, The
Splendor in the
    Grass
West Side Story

MICHAEL YORK
Accident

Brother Sun Sister
    Moon
Cabaret
Four Musketeers,
    The
Island of Dr.
    Moreau, The
Logan's Run
Murder on the
    Orient Express
Riddle of the
    Sands
Romeo and Juliet
Taming of the
    Shrew, The
Three Musketeers,
    The

Video Program Sources Index

Following is an alphabetical index of companies whose video programs are included in *The Video Tape & Disc Guide to Home Entertainment*. The corporate name, address and phone number(s) are listed for each. Most companies' programs may be purchased at a local retail or video specialty store. However, a consumer may have to contact the company directly when the program cannot be rented or purchased at a nearby store. Comments concerning videodisc availability are indicated where appropriate.

**A M
PRODUCTIONS**
46 South DeLacey
   Avenue
Suite 15
Pasadena, CA 91105
213-449-0638

ADMIT ONE VIDEO
311 Adelaide Street
   East
Toronto, Ontario
Canada M5A IN2
416-863-9316

**AERO/SPACE
VISUALS SOCIETY**
2500 Seattle Tower
Seattle, WA 98101
206-624-9090

**ALTI
CORPORATION**
3333 North
   Torrey Pines Court
Suite 320
La Jolla, CA 92037
619-452-7703

**AMERICAN
HOME VIDEO
LIBRARY**
PO Box 669
Old Chelsea Station
New York, NY 10113
212-254-1482

**AMPRO VIDEO
PRODUCTIONS INC**
234 Fifth Avenue
New York, NY 10016
212-243-7726

**AMSTAR
PRODUCTIONS**
2020 Avenue of the
Stars
Suite 240
Century City, CA
   90067
213-556-1325

**ARMOUR
PRODUCTIONS**
1030-B N. Grove
   Street
Anaheim, CA 92806
714-630-3042

**ATLANTIC FILM
GROUP I**
Box 102 Harbour
Road
Kittery Point, ME
   03905
207-439-3739

ATLANTIC VIDEO
1211 Avenue of the
   Americas
New York, NY 10036
212-355-5049

AZTEC CINEVIDEO
620 East Yosemite
   Avenue
Madera,CA 93638
209-673-4734

**BARRY
RAYMOND
STEINER**
1211 West Farwell
   Avenue
Chicago, IL 60626
312-274-1053

**BEST FILM & VIDEO
CORPORATION**
98 Cutter Mill Road
Great Neck, NY
   11021
516-487-4515

BILLIE C. LANGE
PO Box 386
Cullman, AL 35055
205-734-2993

BLACKHAWK FILMS
1235 West Fifth
Box 3990
Davenport, IA
   52808
319-323-9736

BUDGET VIDEO
1534 North Highland
   Avenue# 108
Hollywood, CA 90028
213-466-2431

CABLE FILMS
Country Club Station
Box 7171
Kansas City, MO 64113
913-362-2804

**CARAVATT
HOME
ENTERTAINMENT**
551 Fifth Avenue
New York, NY 10017
212-986-2005

CBS/FOX VIDEO
1211 Avenue of the
   Americas
New York, NY 10036
212-819-3200
*(Some programs
available on LV and
CED)*

CC STUDIOS INC
Weston, CT 06883
203-226-4666

**CHILDREN'S VIDEO
LIBRARY**
1011 High Ridge
   Road
PO Box 4995
Stamford, CT 06907
203-968-0100

**CHRYSALIS VISUAL
PROGRAMMING INC**
645 Madison Avenue
15th Floor
New York, NY 10022
212-758-3555

**CINEMA CONCEPTS
INC**
2461 Berlin Turnpike
Newington, CT 06111
203-667-1251

CINEMAGREATS
15825 Rob Roy Drive
Oak Forest, IL
   60452
312-687-7881

**CLASSIC VIDEO
CINEMA
COLLECTOR'S CLUB**
17420 East Goldwin
Southfield, MI 48075
313-552-1055

**CONTINENTAL
VIDEO**
2320 Cotner
Los Angeles, CA
   90064
213-477-8055

**COURIER
PRODUCTIONS**
4121 Wilshire
   Boulevard
Suite 207
Los Angeles, CA
   90010
213-382-3009

**CUSTOM FILMS/
VIDEO INC**
11 Cob Drive
Westport, CT 06880
203-226-0300

DAYA INC
132 North Avenue
Westport, CT 06880
203-226-1964

DE LUZ VIDEO
PO Box 23892
Pleasant Hill, CA
   94523
415-930-6379

DIAL PRODUCTIONS
12077 Wilshire
   Boulevard
Los Angeles, CA
   90025
213-456-6980

**DIAMOND P SPORTS
INC**
7715 Sunset
   Boulevard
Hollywood, CA
   90046
213-874-1512

**DISCOUNT VIDEO
TAPES INC**
1117 North
   Hollywood Way
PO Box 7122
Burbank, CA 91510
213-843-3366

**EAST TEXAS
PERIODICALS**
PO Box 20285
Houston, TX 77225
713-748-8120
800-231-6648
800-392-4437 *(Texas)*

**ELECTRIC VIDEO
INC**
1116 Edgewater
 Avenue
Ridgefield, NJ 07657
201-941-4404
800-645-7186

**EMBASSY HOME
ENTERTAINMENT**
1901 Avenue of the
 Stars
Los Angeles, CA
 90067
213-553-3600
*(Some programs
available on LV and
CED)*

ENTER-TEL INC
25200 Chagrin
 Boulevard
Beachwood, OH
 44122
216-831-6940

**ENVIRONMENTAL
VIDEO INC**
1731 N. Sepulveda
 Boulevard
Manhattan Beach,
 CA 90266
800-492-3548

ESSEX VIDEO
8841 Wilbur Avenue
Northridge, CA 91324
213-993-5322
800-421-4150

**FAMILY HOME
ENTERTAINMENT**
A Division of
International Video
Entertainment
7920 Alabama
 Avenue
Canoga Park, CA
 91304-4991
818-888-3040
800-423-5558
*(Programs are
distributed by MGM/
UA Home Video)*

FESTIVAL FILMS
2841 Irving Avenue
 South
Minneapolis, MN
 55408
612-870-4744

FLOWER FILMS
10341 San Pablo
 Avenue
El Cerrito, CA 94530
415-525-0942

**4 POINT
ENTERTAINMENT**
4401 Sunset
 Boulevard
Los Angeles, CA
 90027
213-667-9400

**GLENN VIDEO
VISTAS LTD**
6924 Canby Avenue
Suite 103
Reseda, CA 91335
213-981-5506

**GOLD STRIPE
VIDEO**
PO Box 180
Nesconset, NY 11767
516-724-4119

GORGON VIDEO
15825 Rob Roy Drive
Oak Forest, IL 60452
312-687-7881

**GRAVITY SPORTS
FILMS, INC**
1591 South 11th East
Salt Lake City, UT
 84105
801-485-3702

**HAM MASTER
TAPES**
136 East 31st Street
New York, NY 10016
212-685-7844
212-673-0680

HARMONYVISION
116 North Robertson
 Boulevard
Suite 610
Los Angeles, CA
 90048
213-652-8844
*(HarmonyVision
titles are distributed
by Vestron Video.)*

**HOUGHTON
MIFFLIN
COMPANY**
Special Sales
2 Park Street
Boston, MA 02108
617-725-5000

**IMAGE MAGNETIC
ASSOCIATES**
5514 Satsuma
 Avenue
North Hollywood, CA
 91601
818-762-3993

**IMPERIAL VIDEO
CORPORATION**
106A Benkert Street
Bethpage, NY 11714
516-935-5050
800-645-5060 *(outside
New York)*

INCREASE VIDEO
8265 Sunset
 Boulevard
Suite 105
Hollywood, CA
 90046
213-654-8808

**INDEPENDENT
UNITED
DISTRIBUTORS**
430 West 54th Street
New York, NY 10019
212-582-6405
800-223-4057

INEDCO PRODUCTIONS
3334 Founders Road
Indianapolis, IN
   46268
317-875-6806
(Programs available on LV)

INTERNATIONAL HISTORIC FILMS
PO Box 29035
Chicago, IL 60629
312-436-8051

INTERURBAN FILMS
PO Box 60
Seal Beach, CA
   90740
213-431-1473

INTRA-VIDEO PROPERTIES
14640 Burbank
   Boulevard
Suite 205
Van Nuys, CA 91411
213-760-1310

IRS VIDEO
633 North La Brea
Los Angeles, CA
   90036
213-931-9119

JMJ PRODUCTIONS
PO Box 4449
Hollywood, FL 33083
305-652-3952

KARL HOME VIDEO
899 West 16th Street
Newport Beach, CA
   92663
714-645-7053

KEY VIDEO
1298 Prospect
   Avenue
La Jolla, CA 92037
213-697-0544

KING OF VIDEO
3529 South
   Valley View
   Boulevard
Las Vegas, NV 89103
702-362-2520
800-634-6143

KULTUR
1340 Ocean Avenue
Sea Bright, NJ 07760
201-842-6693

LEISURE TIME PRODUCTS PROJECT/3M
3M Center
St. Paul, MN 55144
612-733-4751

MAJOR LEAGUE BASEBALL PRODUCTIONS
1212 Avenue of the
   Americas
New York, NY 10036
212-921-8100

MARK XII VIDEO
1111 North Loop
   West
Houston, TX 77008
713-861-5410

MARKETVISIONS
405 West Fourth
   Street
PO Box 3473
Williamsport, PA
   17701
717-326-4200
800-233-8488

MARTIAL ARTS VIDEO
1614 Hesiod Street
PO Box 9545
Metairie, LA 70005
504-833-4399
504-521-8888 *(orders only)*

MAS PRODUCTIONS
18434 Bermuda
   Street
Northridge, CA 91326
213-360-0371

MASTER ARTS VIDEO
11549 Amigo Avenue
Northridge, CA 91326
213-368-9220

MASTERVISION INC
969 Park Avenue
New York, NY 10028
212-879-0448

MCKESSON CORPORATION
One Post Road
San Francisco, CA
   94104
415-983-8300

MCA HOME VIDEO
70 Universal City
   Plaza
Universal City, CA
   91608
818-508-4000
(Some programs available on LV or CED)

MEDIA HOME ENTERTAINMENT INC
116 North Robertson
   Boulevard
Suite 909
Los Angeles, CA
   90048
213-855-1611
800-421-4509
(Some programs available on LV)

MERCEDES MAHARIS PRODUCTIONS
712 Wilshire
    Boulevard
Santa Monica, CA
    90401
213-393-5800

MGM/UA HOME VIDEO
1350 Avenue of the
    Americas
New York, NY 10019
212-408-0600
(Some programs
available on LV and
CED)

MILKOVICH ENTERPRISES INC
4505 West 78th
    Street
Prairie Village, KS
    66208
913-341-1421

MONTEREY HOME VIDEO
A division of
International Video
Entertainment
7920 Alabama
    Avenue
Canoga Park, CA
    91304-4991
818-888-3040
800-423-5558

MOSSMAN WILLIAMS PRODUCTIONS
Box 7135
Kansas City, MO
    64113
816-363-4352

MOTORCYCLE VIDEO
PO Box 0550
Lakeland, FL 33802
813-686-9380

MOVIE BUFF VIDEO
c/o Manhattan
    Movietime
250 West 95 Street
New York, NY 10025
212-666-0331

MPI HOME VIDEO
15825 Rob Roy Drive
Oak Forest, IL 60452
312-687-7881
(Some programs
available on LV or
CED)

MUPPET HOME VIDEO
500 South Buena
    Vista Street
Burbank, CA 91521
818-840-1859
(Muppet Home Video
titles are distributed
by Walt Disney.)

MUPPET MUSIC HOME VIDEO
500 South Buena
    Vista Street
Burbank, CA 91521
818-840-1859
(Muppet Music Home
Video titles are
distributed by Walt
Disney.)

MUSIC MEDIA
116 North Robertson
    Boulevard
Suite 909
Los Angeles, CA
    90048
213-855-1611
800-421-4509
(Music Media titles
are distributed by
Media Home
Entertainment Inc.)

NEBULAE PRODUCTIONS
31-90 140th Street
Flushing, NY 11354
212-886-6242

NEW AGE VIDEO INC
PO Box 669
Old Chelsea Station
New York, NY 10113
212-254-1484

NFL FILMS VIDEO
330 Fellowship Road
Mt. Laurel, NJ 08054
609-778-1600
(Some programs
available on LV)

NORTH AMERICAN PHILIPS CORPORATION
100 East 42nd Street
New York, NY 10017
212-697-3600
(Programs available
on LV)

NOSTALGIA MERCHANT
6255 Sunset
    Boulevard
Suite 1019
Hollywood, CA 90028
213-464-1406
800-421-4495
(Nostalgia Merchant
titles are distributed
by Media Home
Entertainment Inc.)

NTA HOME ENTERTAINMENT
12636 Beatrice Street
Los Angeles, CA
    90066
213-306-4040

NUTECH VIDEO PUBLISHING COMPANY
21405 Colina Drive
Topanga, CA 90290
213-455-1587

**OPTICAL
PROGRAMMING
ASSOCIATES**
c/o MCA Home Video
70 Universal City
   Plaza
Universal City, CA
   91608
213-508-4315
800-257-5209
*(consumer orders
only)*
*(Programs available
on LV)*

**PACIFIC ARTS
VIDEO RECORDS**
PO Box 22770
Carmel, CA 93922
408-624-4704
800-538-5856
*(Some programs
available on CED)*

**PARAGON VIDEO
PRODUCTIONS**
3529 South Valley
   View Boulevard
Las Vegas, NV 89103
702-362-2520
800-634-6143

**PARAMOUNT HOME
VIDEO**
5555 Melrose Avenue
Los Angeles, CA
   90038
213-468-5000
*(Some programs
available on LV and
CED)*

**PENGUIN VIDEO
PRODUCTIONS**
3500 Verdugo Road
Box 65157
Los Angeles, CA
   90065
213-222-2707

**PIONEER ARTISTIS
INC**
200 West Grand
   Avenue
Montvale, NJ 07645
201-573-1122
*(Programs available
on LV)*

**PIONEER VIDEO
IMPORTS**
200 West Grand
   Avenue
Montvale, NJ 07645
201-573-1122
*(Programs available
on LV)*

PRISM
1875 Century Park
   East
Suite 1010
Los Angeles, CA
   90067
213-277-3270

**PROGRAM
HUNTERS, INC**
11669 Santa Monica
   Boulevard
Suite 106
Los Angeles, CA
   90025
213-477-3088

**RCA/COLUMBIA
PICTURES HOME
VIDEO**
2901 W. Alameda
   Avenue
Burbank, CA 91505
818-954-4905
*(Some programs
available on LV or
CED)*

RCA VIDEODISCS
1133 Avenue of the
   Americas
New York, NY 10036
212-930-4700
*(Programs available
on CED)*

RKO HOMEVIDEO
15840 Ventura
   Boulevard
Suite 303
Encino, CA 91436
818-906-1722

**ROLL YOUR OWN
VIDEO**
4971 Via Piccoli
Santa Barbara, CA
   93111
805-964-2490

**SAN
FRANCISCO RUSH
VIDEO**
156 Tiffany Street
San Francisco, CA
   94110
415-824-2543

SELECT-A-TAPE
8750 Holloway Drive
Los Angeles, CA
   90069
213-652-6552
800-421-4465

**SELF IMPROVEMENT
VIDEO, INC**
77 Ives Street
Suite 282
Providence, RI 02906
401-246-0810

**SHEIK VIDEO
CORPORATION**
1823-25 Airline
   Highway
Metairie, LA 70001
504-833-9458
800-535-6005

**SHERWOOD VIDEO
PRODUCTION
COMPANY**
676 North St. Clair
   Street
Suite 1716
Chicago, IL 60611
312-275-9191

SHOKUS VIDEO
PO Box 8434
Van Nuys, CA 91409
818-704-0400

SILVERLINE VIDEO
PO Box 247
Clayton, CA 94517
415-672-5011

**SNOOPY'S HOME
VIDEO LIBRARY**
116 North Robertson
  Boulevard
Los Angeles, CA
  90048
213-855-1611
800-421-4509
*(Snoopy's Home
Video Library titles
are distributed by
Media Home
Entertainment.)*

**SONY
CORPORATION OF
AMERICA**
Video Software
  Operations
9 West 57 Street
New York, NY 10019
212-371-5800

**SOUND VIDEO
UNLIMITED**
7000 North Austin
  Avenue
Niles, IL 60648
312-561-2500
800-323-4243

**SPORTS WORLD
CINEMA**
PO Box 17022
Salt Lake City, UT
  84117
801-486-3925

**STAR VIDEO
PRODUCTIONS**
6161 N. Memorial
  Highway
Suite 1612
Tampa, FL 33615
813-885-6854
800-237-7010

SUN VIDEO
170 Washington
  Avenue
Dumont, NJ 07628
201-387-8410

**SYBERVISION
SYSTEMS INC**
2450 Washington
  Avenue
Suite 270
San Leandro, CA
  94577
415-352-3526

**TELECINE SPANISH
VIDEO**
2151 Belmont Avenue
New York, NY 10457
212-798-7028

THOMAS PAGE
2008 Deerpark
Fullerton, CA 92631
714-993-2336

**THOMAS
PRODUCTIONS**
3495 La Sombra
  Drive
Hollywood, CA 90068

**THORN EMI VIDEO
PROGRAMMING
ENTERPRISES**
1370 Avenue of the
  Americas
New York, NY 10019
212-977-8990
*(Some programs
available on CED)*

**TOUCHSTONE
HOME
VIDEO**
500 South Buena
  Vista Street
Burbank, CA 91521
818-840-6056

**TOURNAMENT
VIDEO TAPES**
1615 West Burbank
  Boulevard
Burbank, CA 91506
213-843-0373

**TRANS WORLD
ENTERTAINMENT**
6430 Sunset
  Boulevard
Suite 501
Hollywood, CA 90028
213-461-0467
800-521-0107

**TV SPORTS SCENE
INC (TVSS INC)**
5804 Ayrshire
  Boulevard
Minneapolis, MN
  55436
612-925-9661

**TWO STAR FILMS
INC**
Box 495
Saint James, NY
  11780
516-584-7285

UNICORN VIDEO INC
PO Box 1084
Reseda, CA 91335
818-343-2992

USA HOME VIDEO
A Division of
International Video
Entertainment
7920 Alabama
  Avenue
Canoga Park, CA
  91304-4991
818-888-3040
800-423-5558

**VANDAM
PRODUCTIONS**
1350 Avenue of the
  Americas
New York, NY 10019
212-408-0624
*(Programs are
distributed by MGM/UA.)*

VANGUARD VIDEO
6535 East Skelly
   Drive
Tulsa, OK 74145
918-622-6500

VCI HOME VIDEO
6535 East Skelly
   Drive
Tulsa, OK 74145
918-622-6460
800-331-4077
*(VCI titles are
distributed by Media
Home Entertainment.)*

VCII INC
7313 Varna Avenue
North Hollywood, CA
   91605
213-764-0319
800-423-2587

VCL HOME VIDEO
3660 San Vicente
   Boulevard
Suite 301
Los Angeles, CA
   90048
213-933-5893
*(VCL Home Video
titles are distributed
by Media Home
Entertainment)*

VESTRON VIDEO
1011 High Ridge
   Road
PO Box 4000
Stamford, CT 06907
203-968-0000
*(Some programs
available on LV and
CED)*

VIDAMERICA INC
231 East 55th Street
New York, NY 10022
212-355-1600
*(VidAmerica titles
are distributed by
Vestron Video; some
programs available
on CED)*

VIDCREST
PO Box 69642
Los Angeles, CA
   90069
213-768-0903
213-466-7127

**VIDEO ARTS
INTERNATIONAL
INC**
PO Box 153
Ansonia Station
New York, NY 10023
212-799-7798

**VIDEO CITY
PRODUCTIONS**
4266 Broadway
Oakland, CA 94611
415-428-0202

VIDEO CONNECTION
3123 Sylvania Avenue
Toledo, OH 43163
419-472-7727

VIDEO DIMENSIONS
100 East 23rd Street
Suite 603
New York, NY 10010
212-533-5999

VIDEO GEMS
731 North La Brea
   Avenue
PO Box 38188
Los Angeles, CA
   90038
213-938-2385
800-421-3252

**THE VIDEO KIT
MANUFACTURING
COMPANY**
PO Box 8571
Rowland Heights, CA
   91748
213-965-6740

VIDEO NATURALS
2590 Glen Green
Los Angeles, CA
   90068
213-469-0019

THE VIDEO STATION
1740 Stanford Street
Santa Monica, CA
   90404
213-453-5535

**VIDEO TRAVEL
INC**
PO Box 1572
Williamsport, PA
   17701
717-326-6525

VIDEO YESTERYEAR
Box C
Sandy Hook, CT
   06482
203-426-2574
800-243-0987

VIDEOBRARY
3518 Cahuenga West
Suite 301
Hollywood, CA 90068
213-851-5811

**VIDEODISC
PUBLISHING INC**
381 Park Avenue
   South
Suite 1601
New York, NY 10016
212-685-5522
*(Programs available
on LV)*

**VIDEOVISION
INC**
232 Lawrenceville
Norcross, GA 30071
404-448-3181

VIDMAX
36 East 4th Street
Suite 734
Cincinnati, OH 45202
513-421-3999
*(Programs available
on LV)*

**VISION
PRODUCTIONS
LTD**
PO Box 8778
Moscow, ID 83843
208-883-0105

**WALT DISNEY HOME
VIDEO**
500 South Buena
  Vista Street
Burbank, CA 91521
818-840-1859
800-423-2259
*(Some programs
available on LV and
CED)*

**WARNER HOME
VIDEO INC**
4000 Warner
  Boulevard
Burbank, CA 91522
213-954-6000
*(Some programs
available on LV and
CED)*

**WEISS GLOBAL
ENTERPRISES**
2055 Saviers Road
Suite 12
Oxnard, CA 93030
805-486-4495

**WESTERN FILM &
VIDEO INC**
30941 Agoura Road
Suite 302
Westlake Village, CA
  91361
213-889-7350

WIZARD VIDEO INC
948 North Fairfax
  Avenue
Los Angeles, CA
  90046
213-859-0034
*(Wizard Video
distributed by
Spectrum Video
Distributors. Discs
distributed by
Vestron Video.)*

**WONDERLUST
VIDEO**
c/o Vestron Video
1011 High Ridge
  Road
PO Box 4000
Stamford, CT 06907
203-968-0000
*(Some programs
available on LV or
CED)*

**WORLD VIDEO
ENTERPRISES
INC**
6736 Laurelgrove
  Avenue
No. 106
North Hollywood, CA
  91060
818-764-1194

**WORLDVISION
HOME VIDEO INC**
660 Madison Avenue
New York, NY 10021
212-832-3838

XEROX PUBLISHING
1 Pickwick Plaza
PO Box 6710
Greenwich, CT
  06836
203-625-5600
*(Programs available
on LV)*

Photo Copyrights

Photo section pictures courtesy of:

BLACKHAWK FILMS
The Little Rascals, © Hal Roach Studios
CBS/FOX VIDEO
The Chinese Connection, © 1973 National General Pictures
From Russia with Love, © 1963 United Artists Corporation
Hang 'Em High, © 1967 United Artists Corporation
Al Jolson, © Warner Bros. Pictures
*M*A*S*H*, ©CBS Television
The Misfits, © 1961 Seven Arts Productions
The Muppet Movie, © 1979 Associated Film Distribution
New York, New York, © 1977 United Artists Corporation
Run Silent, Run Deep, © 1958 United Artists Corporation
Some Like It Hot, © 1959 Ashton Productions
To Be or Not to Be, © 1983 Brooksfilm Productions
EMBASSY HOME ENTERTAINMENT
The Graduate, © 1967 Embassy Pictures
Silkwood, © 1983 ABC Motion Pictures
MCA HOME VIDEO
Vertigo, © 1958 Alfred Hitchcock Productions
MGM/UA HOME VIDEO
Adam's Rib, © 1949 Loew's Inc., renewed 1976
The Compleat Beatles, © 1982 Delilah Films
Forbidden Planet, © 1956 Loew's Inc.
Seven Brides for Seven Brothers, © 1954 Loew's Inc.
That's Entertainment, Part II, © 1976 MGM
THE NOSTALGIA MERCHANT
Laurel and Hardy (Hog Wild), © 1930 Hal Roach Studios, renewed 1958
Suspicion, © 1941 RKO Radio Pictures, renewed 1969
NTA HOME ENTERTAINMENT
Quiet Man, © 1952 Republic Pictures
PARAMOUNT HOME VIDEO
Flashdance, © 1983 Paramount Pictures Corporation
Star Trek, © Paramount Pictures Corporation

RCA/COLUMBIA PICTURES HOME VIDEO
And Now for Something Completely Different, © 1971 Python
(Monty) Pictures Ltd.
The Big Chill, © 1983 Columbia Pictures
Golden Boy, © 1939 Columbia Pictures Corp., renewed 1967
The Three Stooges, © Columbia Pictures Corp.
The Way We Were, © 1973 Columbia Pictures
RCA VIDEODISCS
Sleeper, © 1973 United Artists Corporation
THORN EMI VIDEO PROGRAMMING ENTERPRISES
The Dark Crystal, © 1982 ITC Entertainment
The Kids Are Alright, © 1979 Who Films Ltd.
TOUCHSTONE HOME VIDEO
Splash, © 1984 Buena Vista Distribution Company
VESTRON VIDEO
Michael Jackson, © Epic Records
VIDAMERICA
Giant, © 1956 Giant Productions
VIDEO YESTERYEAR
Burns and Allen, © CBS Television
WALT DISNEY HOME VIDEO
Mickey Mouse and Pluto, © Walt Disney Productions
Old Yeller, © 1957 Walt Disney Productions
WARNER HOME VIDEO
Arthur, © 1981 Orion Pictures
Best Friends, © 1982 Warner Bros.
Bugs Bunny, © Vitaphone Corp.
Risky Business, © 1983 Warner Bros.
The Searchers, © 1956 C.V. Whitney Pictures
A Star Is Born, © 1954 Warner Bros. Pictures
Watership Down, © 1978 Nepenthe Productions Ltd.

David J. Welner, Photo Editor

Printed in Canada